Physics for the IB Diploma

Fifth edition

K. A. Tsokos

CAMBRIDGE UNIVERSITY PRESS
Cambridge, New York, Melbourne, Madrid, Cape Town,
Singapore, São Paulo, Delhi, Mexico City

Cambridge University Press
The Edinburgh Building, Cambridge CB2 8RU, UK

www.cambridge.org
Information on this title: www.cambridge.org/9780521138215

First published by K. A. Tsokos 1998
Second edition 1999
Third edition 2001
Fourth edition published by Cambridge University Press 2005
Fifth edition 2008
Fifth edition (full colour version) 2010
5th printing 2012

Printed in the United Kingdom by Latimer Trend

A catalogue record for this publication is available from the British Library

ISBN 978-0-521-13821-5 Paperback

ACKNOWLEDGEMENTS
We are grateful to the following for permission to reproduce photographs:
76, 526(t), 644 Science Photo Library; 89 Harold Edgerton/Science Photo Library; 255, Bettmann/CORBIS; 256 Reuters; 276 Sheila Terry/Science Photo Library; 315 Richard Megna/Science Photo Library; 400 (Francis Simon), 403 (Segre Collection), 526(b), 725 (Physics Today Collection) American Institute of Physics/Science Photo Library; 464(l) Robert Gendler/Science Photo Library; 464(r) John Walsh/Science Photo Library; 492, 535c Anglo-Australian Observatory/David Malin Images; 535a, b NOAO/Science Photo Library; 733 Stanford Linear Accelerator Center/Science Photo Library; 737a CERN PHOTO/ Frédéric Pitchal/Sygma/CORBIS; 737b David Parker/Science Photo Library; 741 Goronwy Tudor Jones/University of Birmingham/Science Photo Library; 742 CERN/Science Photo Library; 747 Klaus Guldbranden/Science Photo Library: cover image Michael Dunning/Science Photo Library

Contents

The content of Options A–D (except Option A1) is identical to that in the appropriate chapter in the Core and AHL material, to which the reader is referred (details are given in the text).

For Alexios and Alkeos

Preface

Physics is a fundamental science, and those who study it will gain an understanding of the basic laws that govern everything from the very small subatomic to the very large cosmic scale. The study of physics provides us with an unparalleled power of analysis that is useful in the study of the other sciences, engineering and mathematics, as well as in daily life.

This fifth edition of *Physics for the IB Diploma* follows the previous edition, but contains material for the new syllabus that will be examined for the first time in May 2009. It covers the entire International Baccalaureate (IB) syllabus, including all options at both standard level (SL) and higher level (HL). It includes a chapter on the role of physics in the theory of knowledge (TOK), along with many discussion questions for TOK. Each chapter opens with a list of objectives, which include the important formulae that will be covered in that chapter. The questions at the end of each chapter have been increased, and there are answers at the end of the book for all those involving calculation (and for some others too).

Part I of the book covers the core material and the additional higher level (AHL) material. The title and running heads of each chapter clearly indicate whether the chapter is part of the core or AHL. Part II covers the optional subjects. There are now four options that are available to SL students only (Option A, Sight and wave phenomena; Option B, Quantum physics; Option C, Digital technology; and Option D, Relativity and particle physics). The material for these is the same as the corresponding AHL material, and so these four SL options are neither repeated nor presented separately (except for one chapter, Option A1, The eye and sight, which is not part of the AHL core). Three options (Option E, Astrophysics; Option F, Communications; and Option G, Electromagnetic waves) are available to both SL and HL students. Finally, there are three options (Option H, Special and general relativity; Option I, Biomedical physics; and Option J, Particle physics) that are available to HL students only.

The division of this book into chapters and sections usually follows quite closely the syllabus published by the International Baccalaureate Organization (IBO). This does not mean, however, that this particular order should be followed in teaching. Within reason, the sections are fairly independent of each other, and so alternative teaching sequences may be used. It must also be stressed that this book is not an official guide to the IB syllabus, nor is this book connected with the IBO in any way.

The book contains many example questions and answers that are meant to make the student more comfortable with solving problems. Some are more involved than others. There are also questions at the end of each chapter, which the student should attempt to answer to test his or her understanding. Even though the IB does not require calculus for physics, I have used calculus, on occasion, in the text and in the questions for the benefit of those students taking both physics and mathematics at higher level. They can apply what they are learning in mathematics in a concrete and well-defined context. However, calculus is not essential for following the book. It is assumed that a student starting a physics course at this level knows the basics of trigonometry and is comfortable with simple algebraic manipulations.

In many questions and examples I have not resisted the temptation to use 10 m s^{-2} as the numerical value of the acceleration due to gravity. I have also followed the conventions of symbols used by the IBO in their *Physics Data Booklet*, with one major exception. The *Data Booklet* uses the symbol *s* for displacement. Almost universally, the symbol *s* is reserved for distance, and so *s* stands for distance in this book, not displacement. Also, I have chosen to call initial velocities, speeds, etc. by v_0 rather than the IBO's u.

I wish to thank my wife, Ellie Tragakes, for her great help and support. I am indebted to fellow teacher Wim Reimert for his careful reading of the book and his extensive comments that have improved the book – I thank him sincerely. I would like to thank Geoff Amor, who has edited the new material for the fifth edition, implemented my changes, and made many suggestions for its improvement.

K. A. Tsokos
Athens
May 2007

A note to the reader

The main text of each chapter contains a number of different features, which are clearly identified by the use of headings or by other typographical means, as outlined below.

Learning outcomes/objectives

These are provided as bullet lists at the beginning of each chapter, and indicate what you will have learned or be able to do when you have finished studying the chapter.

Important results, laws, definitions and significant formulae

Particularly important material, such as important results, laws, definitions and significant formulae, appear in a shaded box.

Example questions

These occur in nearly all of the chapters. They are indicated by the heading 'Example question(s)' and all have a full answer. It is a good idea to attempt to solve these problems before reading the answers. There are over 500 such example questions in this book.

Material for higher level students

This material is highlighted in a shaded box that is labelled 'HL only'.

Material that is outside the IB syllabus

Some material is included that is outside the IB syllabus and will not be examined in the IB exams. It is included here for two reasons. The first is that I believe that it clarifies syllabus material and in some cases it does so in essential ways. The second is that it gives the interested student a more rounded view of the subject that is not bounded by the rigid syllabus content. Such material is highlighted in a shaded box that is labelled 'Supplementary material'. There is also a small amount of other similar material with different labels.

Questions

Each chapter ends with a set of numbered questions. Answers to all those that involve calculation are given at the end of the book. Answers are also provided for some other questions where it is useful for students to be able to check their answers.

Part I
Core and AHL

The realm of physics

Physics is an experimental science in which measurements made must be expressed in units. In the International System of units used throughout this book, the SI system, there are seven fundamental units, which are defined in this chapter. All quantities are expressed in terms of these units directly or as a combination of them.

Objectives

By the end of this chapter you should be able to:

- appreciate the order of magnitude of various quantities;
- perform simple order-of-magnitude calculations *mentally*;
- state the *fundamental units* of the SI system.

Orders of magnitude and units

How many molecules are there in the sun? This may sound like a very difficult question with which to start a physics textbook, but very basic physics can give us the answer. Before we try to work out the answer, guess what you think the answer is by giving a power of 10. The number of molecules in the sun is 10 to the power . . . ?

To answer the question we must first have an idea of the mass of the sun. You may know this, or you can easily look it up (to save you doing this for this example, we can tell you that it is about 10^{30} kg). Next, you will need to know what the chemical composition of the sun is. It is made up of 75% hydrogen and 25% helium, but as we are only making a rough estimate, we may assume that it is made out of hydrogen entirely. The molar mass of hydrogen is 2 g mol^{-1} and so the sun contains $10^{33}/2$ mol $= 5 \times 10^{32}$ mol. The number of molecules in one mole of any substance is given by the Avogadro constant, which is about 6×10^{23}, so the sun has around $5 \times 10^{32} \times 6 \times 10^{23} = 3 \times 10^{56}$ molecules. How close was your guess?

The point of this exercise is that, first, we need units to express the magnitude of physical quantities. We must have a consistent set of units we all agree upon. One such set is the International System (SI system), which has seven basic or fundamental units. The units of all other physical quantities are *combinations* of these seven. These units are presented later in this section. The second point is that we have been able to answer a fairly complicated sounding question without too much detailed knowledge – a few simplifying assumptions and general knowledge have been enough. The third point you may already have experienced. How close was your guess for the number of molecules in the sun? By how much did your exponent differ from 56? Many of you will have guessed a number around 10^{1000} and that is way off. The number 10^{1000} is a huge number – you cannot find anything real to associate with such a number. The mass of the universe is about 10^{53} kg and so repeating the calculation above we find that the number of hydrogen molecules in the entire universe (assuming it is all hydrogen) is about 10^{79} – a big number to be sure but nowhere near 10^{1000}. Part of learning physics is to appreciate the magnitude of things – whether they are masses, times, distances, forces or just pure numbers such as the number of hydrogen molecules in the universe. Hopefully, you will be able to do that after finishing this course.

The SI system

The seven basic SI units are:

1 The *metre* (m). This is the unit of distance. It is the distance travelled by light in a vacuum in a time of 1/299 792 458 seconds.

2 The *kilogram* (kg). This is the unit of mass. It is the mass of a certain quantity of a platinum–iridium alloy kept at the Bureau International des Poids et Mesures in France.

3 The *second* (s). This is the unit of time. A second is the duration of 9 192 631 770 full oscillations of the electromagnetic radiation emitted in a transition between the two hyperfine energy levels in the ground state of a caesium-133 atom.

4 The *ampere* (A). This is the unit of electric current. It is defined as that current which, when flowing in two parallel conductors 1 m apart, produces a force of 2×10^{-7} N on a length of 1 m of the conductors.

5 The *kelvin* (K). This is the unit of temperature. It is $\frac{1}{273.16}$ of the thermodynamic temperature of the triple point of water.

6 The *mole* (mol). One mole of a substance contains as many molecules as there are atoms in 12 g of carbon-12. This special number of molecules is called Avogadro's number and is approximately 6.02×10^{23}.

7 The *candela* (cd). This is a unit of luminous intensity. It is the intensity of a source of frequency 5.40×10^{14} Hz emitting $\frac{1}{683}$ W per steradian.

The details of these definitions should not be memorized.

In this book we will use all of the basic units except the last one. Some of these definitions probably do not make sense right now – but eventually they will.

Physical quantities other than those above have units that are combinations of the seven fundamental units. They have *derived* units. For example, speed has units of distance over time, metres per second (i.e. m/s or, preferably, m s^{-1}). Acceleration has units of metres per second squared (i.e. m/s^2, which we write as m s^{-2}). In other words, we treat the symbols for units as algebraic quantities. Similarly, the unit of force is the newton (N). It equals the combination kg m s^{-2}. Energy, a very important quantity in physics, has the joule (J) as its unit. The joule is the combination N m and so equals (kg m s^{-2} m), or kg m^2 s^{-2}. The quantity power has units of energy per unit of time and so is measured in J s^{-1}. This combination is called a watt. Thus,

$$1 \text{ W} = (1 \text{ N m s}^{-1}) = (1 \text{ kg m s}^{-2} \text{ m s}^{-1}) = 1 \text{ kg m}^2 \text{ s}^{-3}.$$

Occasionally, small or large quantities can be expressed in terms of units that are related to the basic ones by powers of 10. Thus, a nanometre (symbol nm) is 10^{-9} m, a microgram (μg) is 10^{-6} g $= 10^{-9}$ kg, a gigaelectron volt (GeV) equals 10^9 eV, etc. The most common prefixes are given in Table 1.1.

Power	Prefix	Symbol	Power	Prefix	Symbol
10^{-18}	atto-	a	10^1	deka-	da*
10^{-15}	femto-	f	10^2	hecto-	h*
10^{-12}	pico-	p	10^3	kilo-	k
10^{-9}	nano-	n	10^6	mega-	M
10^{-6}	micro-	μ	10^9	giga-	G
10^{-3}	milli-	m	10^{12}	tera-	T
10^{-2}	centi-	c	10^{15}	peta-	P*
10^{-1}	deci-	d	10^{18}	exa-	E*

*Rarely used.

Table 1.1 Common prefixes.

When we write an equation in physics, we have to make sure that the units of the quantity on the left-hand side of the equation are the same as the units on the right-hand side. If the units do not match, the equation cannot be right. For example, the period T (a quantity with units of time) of a pendulum is related to the length of the pendulum l (a quantity with units of length) and the acceleration due to gravity g (units of acceleration) through

$$T = 2\pi\sqrt{\frac{l}{g}}$$

The units on the right-hand side must reduce to units of time. Indeed, the right-hand side units are

$$\sqrt{\frac{\mathrm{m}}{\mathrm{m\,s^{-2}}}} = \sqrt{\mathrm{s}^2} = \mathrm{s}$$

as required (note that 2π is a dimensionless constant). The fact that the units on both sides of an equation must match actually offers a powerful method for guessing equations.

For example, the velocity of a wave on a string is related to the length l and mass m of the string, and the tension force F the string is subjected to. How exactly does the velocity depend on these three variables? One guess is to write

$$v = cF^x l^y m^z$$

where c is a numerical constant (a pure number without units) and x, y and z are numbers to be determined. There could be some confusion here because m stands for mass but we also use the symbol m for the metre. To avoid this we will use the notation $[M]$ to stand for the unit of mass, $[L]$ for the unit of length, $[T]$ for the unit of time, etc. Then, looking at the units of the last equation we have that

$$\frac{[L]}{[T]} = ([M][L][T]^{-2})^x[L]^y[M]^z$$

$$[L][T]^{-1} = [M]^{x+z}[L]^{x+y}[T]^{-2x}$$

The two equations match if the exponents of $[L]$, $[M]$ and $[T]$ match – that is, if

$$x + z = 0$$
$$x + y = 1$$
$$-2x = -1$$

These equations imply that

$$x = \frac{1}{2}, \quad y = \frac{1}{2} \quad \text{and} \quad z = -\frac{1}{2}$$

In other words, the original formula becomes

$$v = cF^{1/2}l^{1/2}m^{-1/2} = c\sqrt{\frac{Fl}{m}}$$

Obviously this method cannot give the value of the dimensionless constant c. To do that we have to learn some physics!

Tables 1.2–1.4 give approximate values for some interesting sizes, masses and time intervals.

Expressing a quantity as a plain power of 10 gives what is called the 'order of magnitude' of that quantity. Thus, the mass of the universe

	Length/m
Distance to edge of observable universe	10^{26}
Distance to the Andromeda galaxy	10^{22}
Diameter of the Milky Way galaxy	10^{21}
Distance to nearest star	10^{16}
Diameter of solar system	10^{13}
Distance to sun	10^{11}
Radius of the earth	10^{7}
Size of a cell	10^{-5}
Size of a hydrogen atom	10^{-10}
Size of a nucleus	10^{-15}
Size of a proton	10^{-15}
Planck length	10^{-35}

Table 1.2 Some interesting sizes.

	Mass/kg
The universe	10^{53}
The Milky Way galaxy	10^{41}
The sun	10^{30}
The earth	10^{24}
Boeing 747 (empty)	10^{5}
An apple	0.25
A raindrop	10^{-6}
A bacterium	10^{-15}
Smallest virus	10^{-21}
A hydrogen atom	10^{-27}
An electron	10^{-30}

Table 1.3 Some interesting masses.

	Time/s
Age of the universe	10^{17}
Age of the earth	10^{17}
Time of travel by light to nearby star	10^{8}
One year	10^{7}
One day	10^{5}
Period of a heartbeat	1
Period of red light	10^{-15}
Time of passage of light across a nucleus	10^{-24}
Planck time	10^{-43}

Table 1.4 Some interesting time intervals.

has an order of magnitude of 10^{53} kg and the mass of the Milky Way galaxy has an order of magnitude of 10^{41} kg. The ratio of the two masses is then simply 10^{12}.

Fundamental interactions

There are four basic or fundamental interactions in physics. However, in 1972, the electromagnetic and weak interactions were unified into one – the electroweak interaction. In this sense, then, we may speak of just three fundamental interactions (see Figure 1.1).

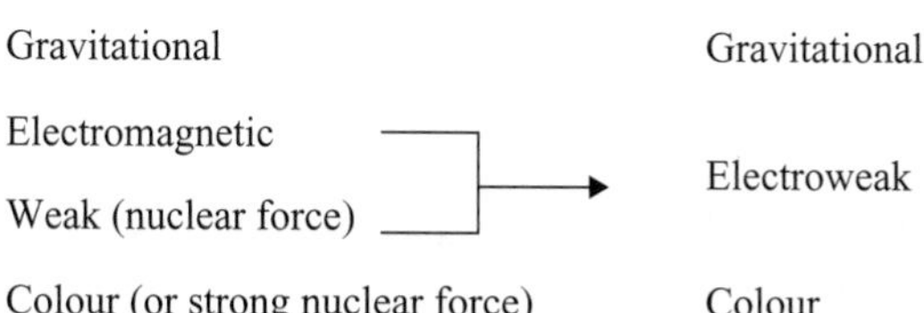

Figure 1.1 The fundamental interactions of physics. Since 1972, the electromagnetic and weak interactions have been shown to be part of a generalized interaction called the electroweak interaction.

Example questions

Let us close this chapter with a few problems similar to the one we started with. These problems are sometimes known as Fermi problems, after the great physicist Enrico Fermi, who was a master in this kind of estimation.

Q1

How many grains of sand are required to fill the earth? (This is a classic problem that goes back to Aristotle.)

Answer

The radius of the earth is about 6400 km, which we may approximate to 10 000 km. The volume of the earth is thus approximately $8 \times (10 \times 10^6)^3\ \text{m}^3 \approx 8 \times 10^{21}\ \text{m}^3$. We are assuming a cubical earth of side equal to twice the radius. This is a simplifying assumption. The true volume is $\frac{4}{3}\pi R^3 = 1.1 \times 10^{21}\ \text{m}^3$, which agrees with our estimate (we are only interested in the power of 10 not the number in front). The diameter of a grain of sand varies of course but we will take 1 mm as a fair estimate. Then the number of grains of sand required to fill the earth is

$$\frac{8 \times 10^{21}\ \text{m}^3}{(1 \times 10^{-3})^3\ \text{m}^3} = 8 \times 10^{30} \approx 10^{31}$$

Q2

Estimate the speed with which human hair grows.

Answer

I cut my hair every 2 months and the barber cuts a length of about 2 cm. The speed is thus

$$\frac{2 \times 10^{-2}}{2 \times 30 \times 24 \times 60 \times 60}\ \text{m s}^{-1} \approx \frac{10^{-2}}{3 \times 2 \times 36 \times 10^4} \approx \frac{10^{-6}}{6 \times 40} = \frac{10^{-6}}{240} \approx 4 \times 10^{-9}\ \text{m s}^{-1}$$

Q3

If all the people on earth were to hold hands in a straight line, how long would the line be? How many times would it wrap around the earth?

Answer

Assume that each person has his or her hands stretched out to a distance of 1.5 m and that the population of earth is 6×10^9 people. Then the length would be $6 \times 10^9 \times 1.5\ \text{m} = 9 \times 10^9\ \text{m}$. The circumference of the earth is $2\pi R \approx 6 \times 6 \times 10^6\ \text{m} \approx 4 \times 10^7\ \text{m}$ and so the line would wrap $\frac{9 \times 10^9}{4 \times 10^7} \approx 200$ times around the equator.

Q4

How many revolutions do the wheels of a car make before it is junked?

Answer

We assume that the car runs 250 000 km before it is junked and that the wheels have a radius of 30 cm. Then the number of revolutions is

$$\frac{2.5 \times 10^8}{2\pi \times 0.3} \approx \frac{2.5}{2 \times 1} 10^8 \approx 10^8$$

Q5

What depth of car tyre wears off with each turn? (This is another classic problem.)

Answer

We assume that a depth of 5 mm wears off every 60 000 km. (These numbers are 'standard' for people who own cars.) Then, for a wheel of radius 30 cm the number of revolutions is (see previous problem) $\frac{6 \times 10^7}{2\pi \times 0.3} \approx \frac{6}{2 \times 1} 10^7 \approx 3 \times 10^7$ and so the wear per revolution is $\frac{5}{3 \times 10^7}$ mm/rev $\approx$ 10^{-7} mm/rev.

? QUESTIONS

Have a look through these questions and answer any that you can. However, don't worry about any you can't answer; leave them for now and come back to them when you reach the end of the course.

1 How long does light take to travel across a proton?

2 How many hydrogen atoms does it take to make up the mass of the earth?

3 What is the age of the universe expressed in units of the Planck time?

4 What is the radius of the earth (6380 km) expressed in units of the Planck length?

5 How many heartbeats are there in the lifetime of a person (75 years)?

6 What is the mass of our galaxy in terms of a solar mass?

7 What is the diameter of our galaxy in terms of the astronomical unit, i.e. the distance between the earth and the sun?

8 The molar mass of water is 18 g mol^{-1}. How many molecules of water are there in a glass of water (of volume 0.3 L)?

9 Assuming that the mass of a person is made up entirely of water, how many molecules are there in a human body (of mass 60 kg)?

10 Assuming the entire universe to be made up of hydrogen gas, how many molecules of hydrogen are there?

11 Give an order-of-magnitude estimate of the density of a proton.

12 How long does light from the sun take to arrive on earth?

13 How many apples do you need to make up the mass of an average elephant?

14 How many bricks are used to build an average two-storey family house?

15 (a) How many metres are there in 5.356 nm?
(b) How many in 1.2 fm?
(c) How many in 3.4 mm?

16 (a) How many joules of energy are there in 4.834 MJ?
(b) How many in 2.23 pJ?
(c) How many in 364 GJ?

17 (a) How many seconds are there in 4.76 ns?
(b) How many in 24.0 ms?
(c) How many in 8.5 as?

18 What is the velocity of an electron that covers a distance of 15.68 mm in 87.50 ns?

19 An electron volt (eV) is a unit of energy equal to 1.6×10^{-19} J. An electron has a kinetic energy of 2.5 eV.
(a) How many joules is that?
(b) What is the energy in eV of an electron that has an energy of 8.6×10^{-18} J?

20 What is the volume in cubic metres of a cube of side 2.8 cm?

21 What is the side in metres of a cube that has a volume of 588 cubic millimetres?

22 One inch is 2.54 cm and one foot has 12 inches. The acceleration due to gravity is about 9.8 m s^{-2}. What is it in feet per square second?

23 One fluid ounce is a volume of about 2.96×10^{-5} m^3. What is the side, in inches, of a cube whose volume is 125 fluid ounces? (One inch is 2.54 cm.)

24 A horsepower (hp) is a unit of power equal to about 746 W. What is the power in hp of a 224 kW car engine?

25 Give an order-of-magnitude estimate for the mass of:

(a) an apple;

(b) this physics book;

(c) a soccer ball.

26 Give an order-of-magnitude estimate for the time taken by light to travel across the diameter of the Milky Way galaxy.

27 A white dwarf star has a mass about that of the sun and a radius about that of the earth. Give an order-of-magnitude estimate of the density of a white dwarf.

28 A sports car accelerates from rest to 100 km per hour in 4.0 s. What fraction of the acceleration due to gravity is the car's acceleration?

29 Give an order-of-magnitude estimate for the number of electrons in your body.

30 Give an order-of-magnitude estimate for the gravitational force of attraction between two people 1 m apart.

31 Give an order-of-magnitude estimate for the ratio of the electric force between two electrons 1 m apart to the gravitational force between the electrons.

32 The frequency f of oscillation (a quantity with units of inverse seconds) of a mass m attached to a spring of spring constant k (a quantity with units of force per length) is related to m and k. By writing $f = cm^x k^y$ and matching units on both sides show that $f = c\sqrt{\frac{k}{m}}$, where c is a dimensionless constant.

33 Without using a calculator *estimate* the value of the following expressions and then compare with the exact value using a calculator:

(a) $\frac{243}{43}$;

(b) 2.80×1.90;

(c) $\frac{312 \times 480}{160}$;

(d) $\frac{8.99 \times 10^{9} \times 7 \times 10^{-6} \times 7 \times 10^{-6}}{(8 \times 10^{2})^2}$;

(e) $\frac{6.6 \times 10^{-11} \times 6 \times 10^{24}}{(6.4 \times 10^{6})^2}$.

Uncertainties and errors

This chapter introduces the basic methods of dealing with experimental error and uncertainty in measured physical quantities. Physics is an experimental science and often the experimenter will perform an experiment to test the prediction of a given theory. No measurement will ever be completely accurate, however, and so the result of the experiment will be presented with an experimental error. Thus, in comparing the results of an experiment with the prediction of the theory being tested, the experimenter will have to decide if the disagreement between theory and experiment is due to failure of the theory or whether the disagreement falls within the bounds of experimental error and so can be tolerated.

Objectives

By the end of this chapter you should be able to:

- state the *various types of errors* that may arise in the measurement of a physical quantity;
- state the difference between *accuracy* and *precision*;
- draw a *line of best fit*;
- appreciate the importance of *significant digits*.

Errors of measurement

There are two *main* types of error of measurement or observation. They can be grouped into *random* and *systematic* even though in many cases it is not possible to sharply distinguish between the two. We may say that random errors are almost always the fault of the observer whereas systematic errors are due to both the observer and the instrument being used. In practice, all errors are a combination of the two.

A random error is characterized by the fact that it is revealed by repeated measurements (the measurements *fluctuate* about some value – they are sometimes larger and sometimes smaller) whereas a systematic error is not. Random errors can be reduced by averaging over repeated measurements, whereas errors that are systematic cannot.

We may also consider a third class of errors called *reading errors*. This is a familiar type of error that has to do with the fact that it is often difficult to read the instrument being used with absolute precision. This type of reading error is inherent in the instrument being used and *cannot be improved upon by repeated measurements*. If a length is measured using a ruler whose smallest division is a millimetre and the end of the object to be measured falls in between two divisions on the ruler, it is easy to determine that the length is, say, between 14.5 cm and 14.6 cm, but there is some guesswork involved in stating that the length is 14.54 cm. It is standard practice to assume that the reading error is half the smallest division interval on the instrument. For the ruler, this interval is 1 mm, and half of this is 0.5 mm or 0.05 cm. We may state the position of the right end of the object we are measuring as (14.54 ± 0.05) cm. In practice, though, to measure the length means also finding the position of the left end of the object, and there is a similar uncertainty in that measurement. Suppose that the left end is recorded at (1.00 ± 0.05) cm. The length is then the difference of the measurements for the positions of the right and left ends of the object, and this is 13.54 cm. As we will see later, the subtraction of the two measurements implies that the uncertainties will *add*, so that we end up with a length measurement that is uncertain by ± 0.1 cm. In that case it does not make sense to quote the answer for the length to more than one decimal place, and we may quote the length as (13.5 ± 0.1) cm.

For digital instruments we may take the reading error to be the smallest division that the instrument can read. So a stopwatch that reads time to two decimal places, e.g. 25.38 s, will have a reading error of ± 0.01 s, and a weighing scale that records a mass as 184.5 g will have a reading error of ± 0.1 g. The typical reading errors for some common instruments are listed in Table 2.1.

Instrument	Reading error
Ruler	±0.5 mm
Vernier calipers	±0.05 mm
Micrometer	±0.005 mm
Volumetric (measuring) cylinder	±0.5 mL
Electronic weighing scale	±0.1 g
Stopwatch	±0.01 s

Table 2.1 Reading errors for some common instruments.

Random errors

If a measurement is repeated many times, it can be expected that the measurement will be too large as often as it will be too small. So, if an average of these measurements is taken, the error will tend to cancel. The experimental result of the measurement of a given quantity x will thus be the average of the individual measurements, i.e.

$$\bar{x} = \frac{x_1 + x_2 + \cdots + x_N}{N}$$

where N is the total number of measurements. We then define the deviation of each individual measurement from the average by $\Delta x_i = x_i - \bar{x}$. If the absolute magnitudes of all these deviations are smaller than the reading error, then we can quote the experimental result as

$$\bar{x} \pm \text{reading error}$$

However, if the deviations from the mean are larger in magnitude than the reading error, the experimental error in the quantity x will have to include random errors as well. To estimate the random error we calculate the quantity

$$e = \sqrt{\frac{(\Delta x_1)^2 + (\Delta x_2)^2 + \cdots + (\Delta x_N)^2}{N - 1}}$$

which is called the unbiased estimate of the standard deviation of the N measurements x_i. (With graphic calculators this can be done quite easily and quickly.) The result of the experiment is then expressed as

$$\bar{x} \pm e$$

To illustrate these points consider the measurement of a length using a ruler. The reading error according to one observer is ± 0.1 cm. The experimenter produces a table of results and, after computing the average of the measurements, the deviation and its square are also inserted in the table – see Table 2.2.

Length/cm (±0.1 cm)	Deviation Δx/cm	$(\Delta x)^2$/cm^2
14.88	0.09	0.0081
14.84	0.05	0.0025
15.02	0.23	0.0529
14.57	−0.22	0.0484
14.76	−0.03	0.0009
14.66	−0.13	0.0169

Table 2.2 A table of results.

The average is 14.79 cm and the standard deviation of these measurements is 0.1611 cm. The random error is larger than the reading error and so it must be included in the result. The result of the measurement is thus expressed as 14.8 ± 0.2 cm. This is much more realistic than simply quoting the average and the reading error, 14.79 ± 0.1 cm. Note that it does not make sense to quote the average to more than one decimal point as the error makes even the first decimal point uncertain. Note also that once a large number of measurements are accumulated, further measurements do not appreciably change the estimate of the error. Thus, it is of little use to take, say, 50 measurements of the length of the object in the example above.

Note also, finally, that even the calculation of a standard deviation is not all that necessary. The largest deviation from the mean in Table 2.2 is 0.23 cm, which we may round to 0.2 cm and accept that as a rough estimate of the error.

Systematic errors

The most common source of a systematic error is an incorrectly *calibrated* instrument. For example, consider a digital force sensor. When the sensor is to be used for the first time, it must be calibrated. This means that we must apply a force whose value we are confident we know, say 5.0 N, and then adjust the sensor so that it too reads 5.0 N. If we apply the 5.0 N force and then adjust the instrument to read 4.9 N, the instrument will be incorrectly calibrated. It will also be incorrectly calibrated if the sensor is adjusted to read 5.0 N when the 'known' force that we apply is not really 5.0 N. If we use this sensor to verify Newton's second law, we would expect to get a straight-line graph through the origin if we plot the net force on the body versus its acceleration. Since all measurements of the force will be off by the same amount, the straight line will not pass through the origin. The systematic error in the force would then be the vertical intercept (see Figure 2.1a).

A systematic error will also arise if we use an instrument that has a *zero error*. For example, if an ammeter shows a current of 0.1 A even before it is connected to a circuit, it has a zero error. It must be adjusted to read zero. If the adjustment is not done, every measurement of current made with this ammeter will be larger than the true value of the current by 0.1 A. Thus, if this ammeter is used to investigate the voltage–current characteristic of an ohmic resistor, we will not get the expected straight line through the origin but a straight line that misses the origin. The systematic error in the current would then be the horizontal intercept (see Figure 2.1b).

Systematic errors are not always easy to estimate but sometimes the direction of the error is. Thus, suppose that an experimenter assumes that no friction is present in an experiment on an air track, where the velocity of an object sliding on it is measured after having travelled a certain distance. A small amount of friction will slow down the object and so the velocity measurements will be consistently lower than their true values. It is difficult though to estimate by how much.

A systematic error will also arise if the experimenter makes the same error for all the measurements she takes. For example, consider measuring a length with a ruler. The ruler is aligned with the object to be measured and the experimenter must then position her eye directly above the ruler. If, however, the experimenter consistently stands to the side, as shown in Figure 2.2, the measured value will always be larger than the true length. If she stands on the other side, the

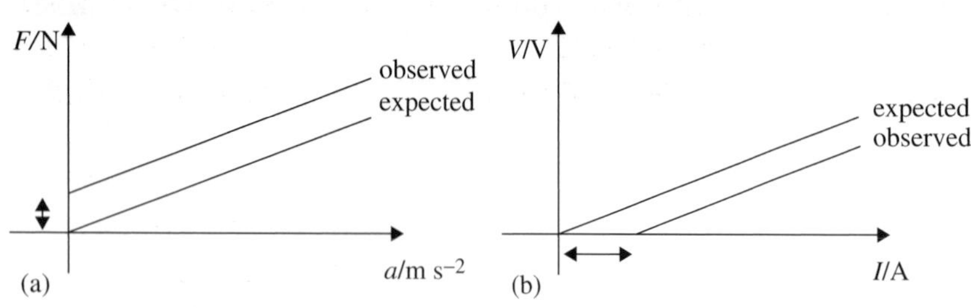

Figure 2.1 The types of systematic error that arise from incorrectly calibrated instruments and instruments that have a zero error.

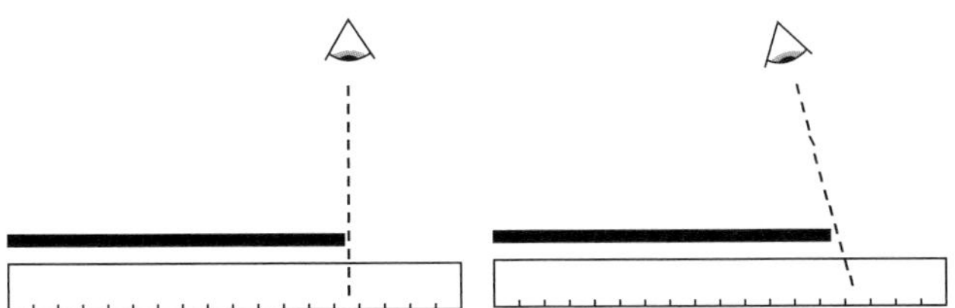

Figure 2.2 An example of a systematic error that is due to the observer.

measured value will always be smaller than the true length.

A similar systematic error would occur in measuring the volume of a liquid inside a graduated tube if the tube is not exactly vertical. The measured values would always be *larger* than the true value.

Accuracy and precision

In everyday language, the words 'accuracy' and 'precision' are usually taken to mean the same thing, but this is not the case in physics.

▶ Measurements are *accurate* if the systematic error is small. They are *precise* if the random error is small (see Figure 2.3).

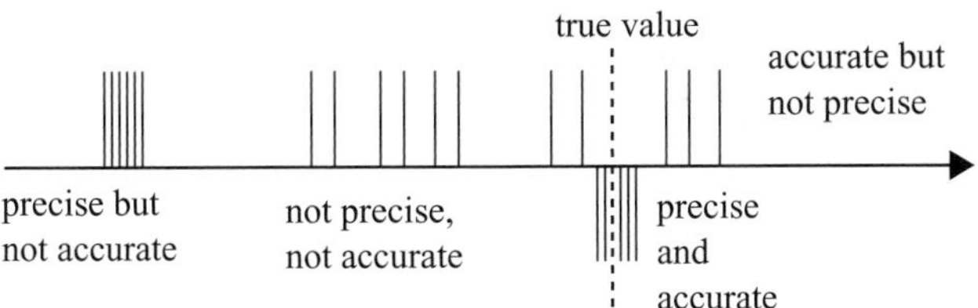

Figure 2.3 The meaning of accurate and precise measurements. Four different sets of six measurements each are shown.

Measurements of a physical quantity can be accurate but not precise, or precise but not accurate. Consider, for example, measurements of voltage taken with a high-quality digital voltmeter that suffers from a systematic error. The voltmeter allows us to record the voltage to many significant figures and repeated measurements of the same voltage give essentially the same reading. These measurements are very precise but they are not accurate, since the systematic error in the readings means that they are not representative of the true voltage. Similarly, readings can be accurate in that their average gives the correct reading, but if individual readings differ wildly from each other, they are not precise.

Significant digits

Let us multiply the numbers 24 and 328. The answer is 7872. However, if these numbers are the result of a measurement, then at the very least we would expect that the last digit of each is uncertain. In other words, the first number could be anything from 23 to 25 and the other from 327 to 329. The product could thus range from 7251 to 8225. Thus, it makes no sense to retain so many digits in our answer for the product of 7872. The first number has been given to two significant digits, the second to three. Thus, the answer for the product must be given to no more than two significant digits – that is, as 7900 or 7.9×10^3. Keeping only two significant digits in the answer for the product ensures that the process of multiplication does not introduce, incorrectly, additional significant figures.

The rules for significant figures are as follows.

The leftmost non-zero digit is significant and is in fact the most significant digit in the number. If the number has no decimal point, the rightmost non-zero digit is significant and is in fact the least significant. If the number does have a decimal point, the least significant digit is the rightmost digit (which may be zero). The number of significant digits of a number is the number of digits from the most to the least significant. Thus, 0.345 has 3 as the most significant digit and 5 as the least. The number thus has three significant digits. In the number 0.000 0006 the most and least significant digit is 6 and so we have one significant digit. The number 5460 has three significant digits (no decimal point hence the last zero does not count), 54 has two and 300 000 has one. Similarly, 3.450 has four significant digits, 54.0 has three and 0.000 500 has three.

▶ In multiplication or division (or raising a number to a power or taking a root) the result must have as many significant digits as those of the number with the least significant digits entering the operation.

Line of best fit

If we have reason to suspect that the data points we have plotted fall on a straight line, we must draw the best straight line through the points. This means using a ruler and choosing that line which goes through as many data points as possible in such a way that the distances between the line and the points on one side of it are, on average, the same as the distances between the line and points on the other side of it.

Thus, suppose that in an experiment to verify Hooke's law, data for the tension and extension of a spring are collected and plotted as shown in Figure 2.4. The experimenter has included vertical uncertainty bars representing an uncertainty of ± 10 N in the values of the tension (the length of the vertical bar is thus 20 N). Uncertainties in the extension could also be shown by placing horizontal bars at the positions of the data points, but we will not do this here.

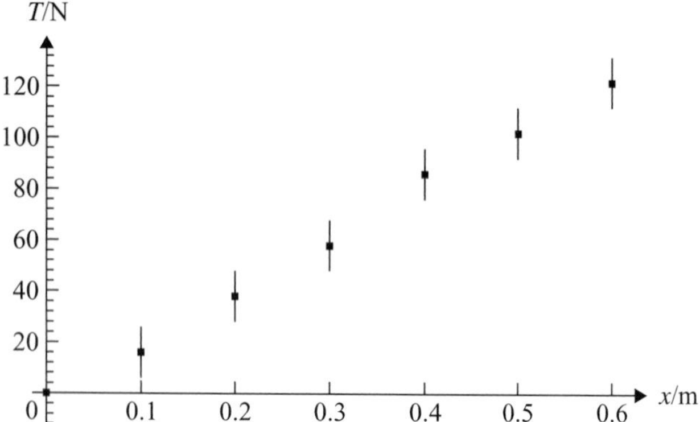

Figure 2.4 Data points plotted together with uncertainties in the values for the tension.

The experimenter then draws the line of best fit through the data points and obtains a straight line in the graph shown in Figure 2.5. The line of best fit will ideally pass through the error bars of all the data points. *Note that we never join points by straight-line segments.* The slope of this line is 200 N m^{-1} and this represents the spring constant.

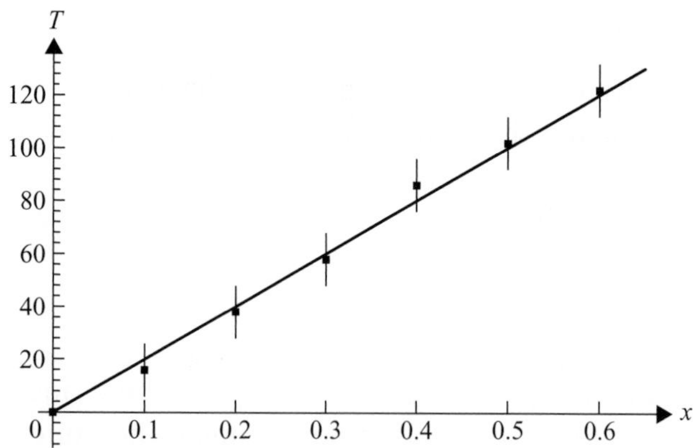

Figure 2.5 The line of best fit through the data points.

In many experiments it will be necessary to obtain the slope (gradient) of the graph. Here the slope of this line is 200 N m^{-1} and represents the spring constant. To find the slope one must use the line of best fit and not data points (see Figure 2.6). We must take two points on the line of best fit, which must be chosen to be as far apart as possible and then apply the formula

$$\text{slope} = \frac{\Delta y}{\Delta x}$$

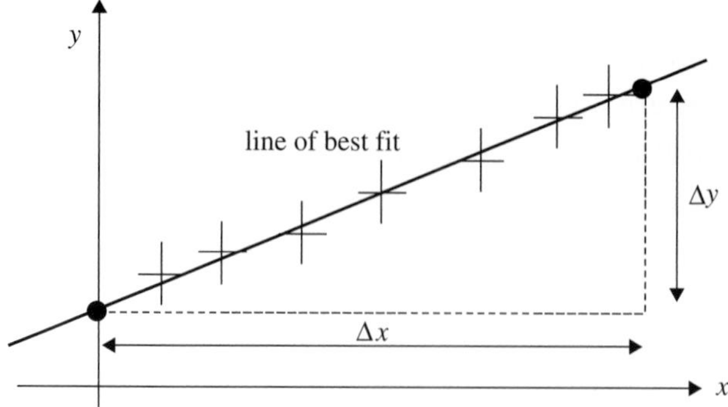

Figure 2.6 Finding the slope of a straight line uses the line of best fit and two widely separated points on the line of best fit.

QUESTIONS

1 A student measured a given quantity many times and got the results shown in Figure 2.7. The true value of the quantity is indicated by the dotted line. Should she continue accumulating more data in the hope of getting a result that agrees with the true value?

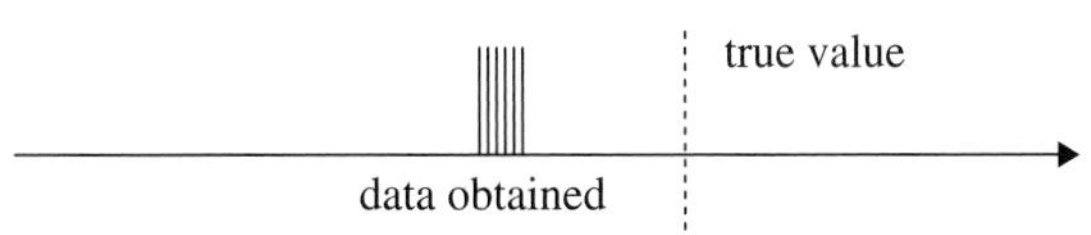

Figure 2.7 For question 1.

2 In the data of question 1, is the source of error systematic or random?

3 In an experiment to measure current and voltage across a device, the following data was collected: $(V, I) = \{(0.1, 26), (0.2, 48), (0.3, 65), (0.4, 90)\}$. The current was measured in mA and the voltage in mV. The uncertainty in the current was ± 4 mA. Plot the *current versus the voltage* and draw the line of best fit through the points. Does the line pass through the origin?

4 In a similar experiment, the following data was collected for current and voltage: $(V, I) = \{(0.1, 27), (0.2, 44), (0.3, 60), (0.4, 78)\}$ with an uncertainty of ± 4 mA in the current. Plot the *current versus the voltage* and draw the line of best fit. Can it be claimed that the line passes through the origin?

5 In yet another experiment, the following data was collected for current and voltage: $(V, I) = \{(0.1, 29), (0.2, 46), (0.3, 62), (0.4, 80)\}$, with uncertainty of ± 4 mA in the current. Plot the *current versus the voltage* and draw the line of best fit. Can it be claimed that the line passes through the origin? The experimenter is convinced that the straight line fitting the data should go through the origin. What can allow for this?

6 The velocity of an object after a distance x is given by $v^2 = 2ax$ where a is the constant acceleration. Figure 2.8 shows the results of an experiment in which velocity and distance travelled were measured. Draw a smooth curve through the points. Estimate the acceleration, and the velocity of the object after a distance of 2.0 m.

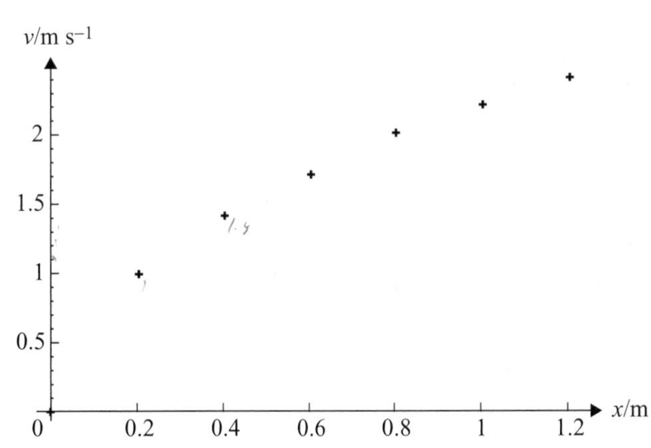

Figure 2.8 For question 6.

Mathematical and graphical techniques

This chapter is an introduction to the basic techniques of graphical analysis in physics, in particular how to graph variables in order to obtain straight-line graphs.

Objectives

By the end of this chapter you should be able to:

- find the *change in a variable* given the changes in other variables related to it;
- *transform the variables of an equation* so that a *linear* relationship and graph are obtained;
- extract relevant information from a graph;
- understand the need for *assumptions* in simplifying various situations.

Multiplicative changes

Given an equation that relates one variable, say y, to one or more other variables, it is essential that we learn how the value of y changes when one (or more) of the other variables change multiplicatively. Consider as a simple first example the equation

$$y = cx$$

where c is a constant. How does the value of y change if x is tripled? Obviously, the value of y is also tripled since y and x are directly proportional to each other. More formally, let us call y' the new value of y; then $y' = c(3x) = 3(cx) = 3y$. That is, the value of y is tripled as expected. The answer in this case is simple since the direct proportionality of the variables is clear. When the variables are not so simply related, the answer can still be easily found.

Suppose that we are given the variation with tension T of frequency f

$$f = \frac{1}{2L}\sqrt{\frac{T}{\mu}}$$

(the other variables in this equation are constants). How does the frequency change if the tension is tripled? Again we call the new value of the frequency f' and then

$$\begin{aligned} f' &= \frac{1}{2L}\sqrt{\frac{3T}{\mu}} \\ &= \sqrt{3}\left(\frac{1}{2L}\sqrt{\frac{T}{\mu}}\right) \\ &= \sqrt{3}f \end{aligned}$$

that is, the value of the frequency is increased by a factor of root 3. Equivalently we could have written

$$\frac{f'}{f} = \frac{\frac{1}{2L}\sqrt{\frac{3T}{\mu}}}{\frac{1}{2L}\sqrt{\frac{T}{\mu}}}$$
$$= \sqrt{3}$$

since all the common variables cancel out.

Similarly, the average kinetic energy of the molecules of a gas depends on absolute temperature through

$$\tfrac{1}{2}mc^2 = \tfrac{3}{2}kT$$

If the temperature is doubled what happens to the speed c? Taking ratios

$$\frac{\frac{1}{2}m(c')^2}{\frac{1}{2}mc^2} = \frac{\frac{3}{2}k(2T)}{\frac{3}{2}kT} = 2$$
$$\Rightarrow \frac{(c')^2}{c^2} = 2$$
$$\Rightarrow c' = \sqrt{2}c$$

The speed increases by $\sqrt{2}$.

The pressure, volume, temperature and number of molecules of an ideal gas are related by

$$pV = NkT$$

where k is a constant. If the pressure of a gas is doubled while the temperature is halved and the number of molecules is left unchanged, what will be the new volume of the gas?

In this case the ratio method gives

$$\frac{(2p)V'}{pV} = \frac{Nk\left(\frac{T}{2}\right)}{NkT} = \frac{1}{2}$$
$$\Rightarrow \frac{2V'}{V} = \frac{1}{2}$$
$$\Rightarrow V' = \frac{V}{4}$$

Straight-line graphs

The easiest graph to deal with is that of the straight line: $y = mx + c$. In this form, the constant m represents the slope (also known as the gradient) of the straight line and c the intercept on the y (vertical) axis. Figures 3.1–3.3 show three examples of straight-line graphs. Figure 3.1 represents a force F (plotted on the vertical axis and measured in newtons, N) as a function of distance x (measured in metres, m). We can read off the intercept on the F axis as 1.2 N. The gradient can be measured to be 0.4 N m^{-1}. Note that the units for the gradient must be given. Thus, the equation of this line is $F = 0.4(\text{N m}^{-1})\,x + 1.2$ N. It is usually convenient not to mention units in the equation of the line so that we can write the simpler $F = 0.4x + 1.2$, but it is then crucial to note that x must be expressed in metres so that F ends up being expressed in newtons.

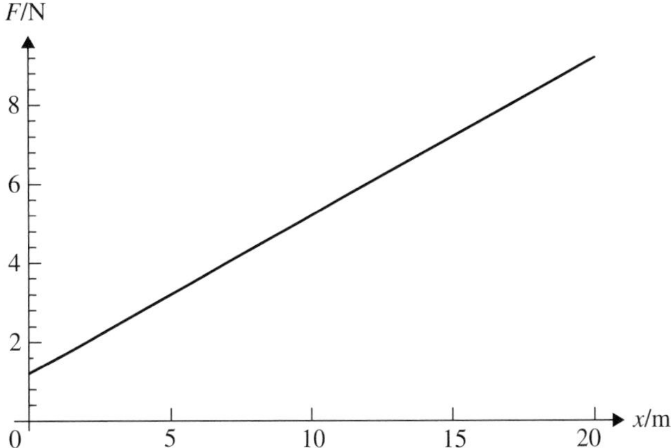

Figure 3.1 The straight-line graph of tension versus extension.

Figure 3.2 shows distance x on the vertical axis (measured in metres) plotted as a function of time t (measured in seconds). The intercept on the vertical axis is -1.6 m and the gradient is 0.6 m s^{-1}. Thus, the equation of this line is $x = 0.6(\text{m s}^{-1})\,t - 1.6$ m, or simply $x = 0.6t - 1.6$.

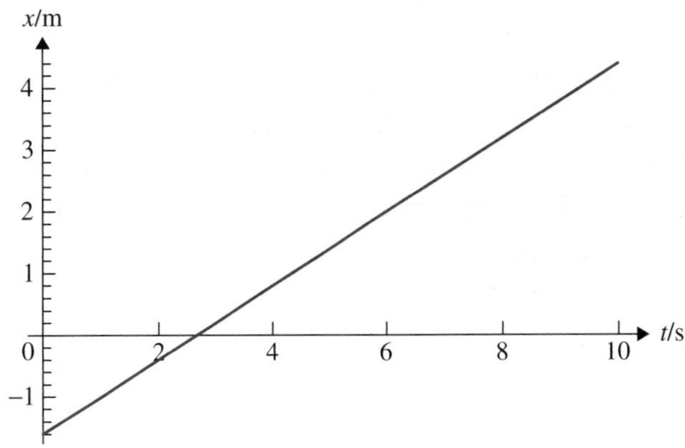

Figure 3.2 Graph of distance versus time.

The third example (Figure 3.3) is a graph of velocity v (measured in metres per second) versus time t (measured in seconds). The intercept on the vertical axis is 2 m s^{-1} and the gradient is -0.2 m s^{-2}. Thus $v = -0.2(\text{m s}^{-2})\,t + 2(\text{m s}^{-1})$, or just $v = -0.2t + 2$.

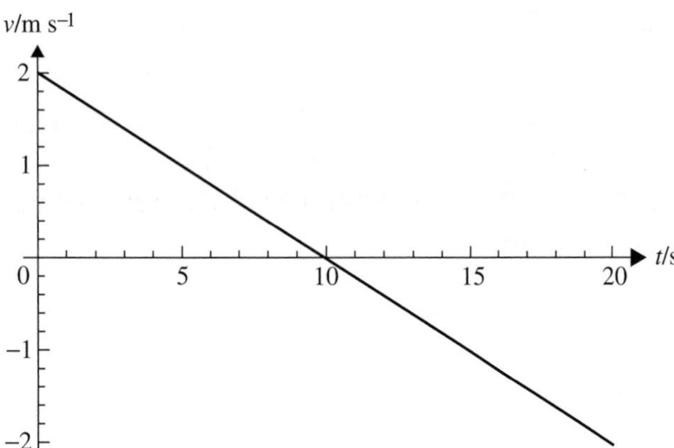

Figure 3.3 Graph of velocity versus time.

As we will see in our study of motion in mechanics, the area under a velocity–time graph represents the displacement *change* of the moving object.

Suppose that initially the object is at a displacement of 20 m from the origin. To find the displacement of the object 5 s after the start we need to find the area that is bounded by the graph and the time axis from $t = 0$ s to $t = 5$ s. This shape is a trapezoid and its area is $\left(\frac{2+1}{2}\right) \times 5 = 7.5$ m. Note that the units of the area in this graph are units of distance, since we multiply a velocity (m s^{-1}) by time (s). (If the vertical axis represented a force measured in newtons and the horizontal axis distance measured in metres, the area in that case would have units of N × m, i.e. joules.) This means that the displacement at $t = 5$ s is 20 m + 7.5 m = 27.5 m. The displacement at $t = 10$ s is found by calculating the area bounded by the graph and the time axis from $t = 0$ to $t = 10$ s. This area has the shape of a triangle and so the area is $\left(\frac{2\times10}{2}\right) = 10$ m. The displacement at $t = 10$ s is thus 20 m + 10 m = 30 m. After $t = 10$ s, the graph goes below the time axis. This means that areas will now be counted as negative. Thus, to find the displacement at $t = 15$ s we proceed as follows: first find the area from $t = 0$ to $t = 10$ s, which is 10 m. Then find the area from $t = 10$ s to $t = 15$ s. It is -7.5 m. The area from $t = 0$ to $t = 15$ s is thus 10 m − 7.5 m = 2.5 m. The displacement at $t = 15$ s is thus 20 m + 2.5 m = 22.5 m.

Getting a linear graph

In an experiment it is more than likely that when a measured quantity y is plotted against another measured quantity x on which it depends, a straight-line graph will not result. Thus, suppose that the expected theoretical relationship between the variables is $y = ax^2 + b$, as in Figure 3.4.

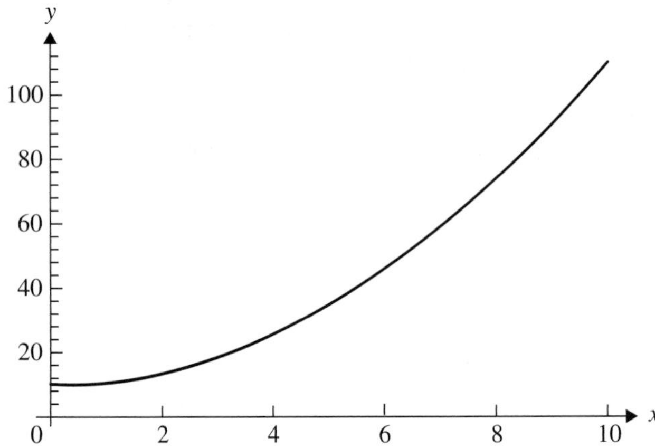

Figure 3.4 Graph of the parabola $y = ax^2 + b$.

Then if we call the variable $x^2 = w$, the expected relationship becomes $y = aw + b$, which is the equation of a standard straight line with gradient a and intercept b. Hence, we must plot y versus w (i.e. x^2) to get a straight line (see Figure 3.5).

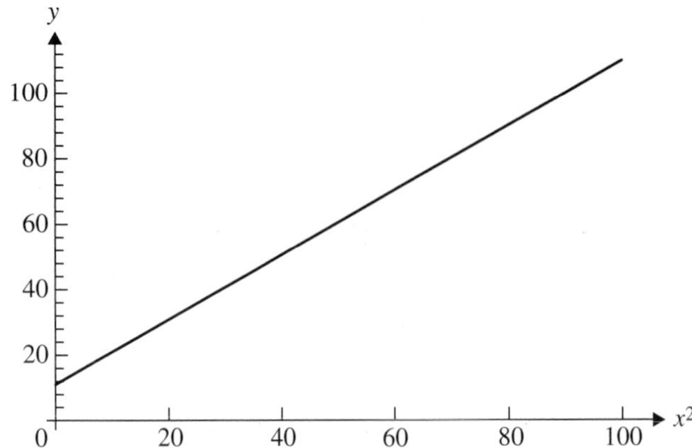

Figure 3.5 By graphing against the variable x^2 we get a straight line.

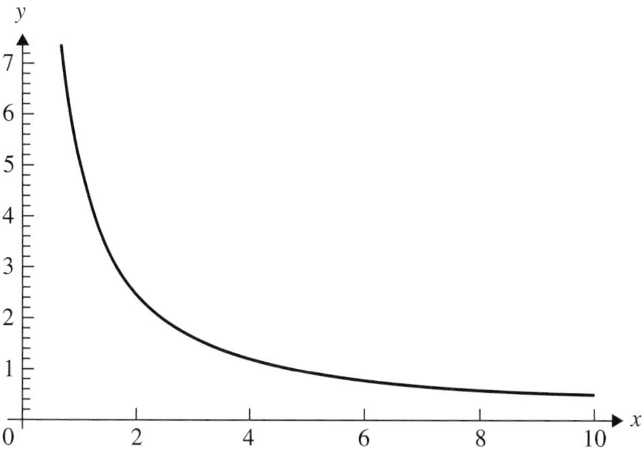

Figure 3.6 Graph of the hyperbola $xy = c$.

Similarly if the expected relationship is $xy = c$ (Figure 3.6), we call $\frac{1}{x} = w$ in which case the expected relationship is $y = \frac{c}{x} = cw$, which again is a straight line going through the origin with gradient c. Thus we must plot y versus $\frac{1}{x}$ to get a straight line (Figure 3.7).

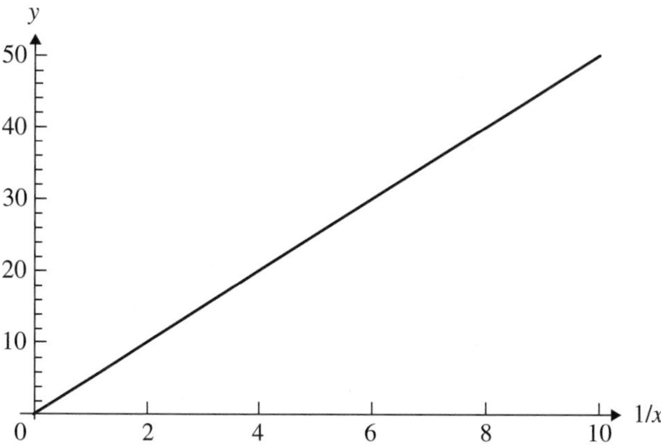

Figure 3.7 We get a straight line by plotting against the variable $\frac{1}{x}$.

If y and x are related by $y = ae^x + b$, a straight line is obtained by plotting y versus e^x. The gradient is then a and the intercept b. If the relationship is $y = \frac{a}{x^2+b}$, we rewrite it as $\frac{1}{y} = \frac{x^2+b}{a}$ so that a graph of $\frac{1}{y}$ versus x^2 is a straight line. Finally, a relationship such as $y^2 = cx^3$ yields a straight line when y^2 is plotted against x^3.

Interpreting graphs

Given a graph, we should be able to extract information from it and use that information to give a description of what is going on. In Figure 3.8 the velocity is decreasing uniformly from an initial value of 20 m s^{-1}. The velocity becomes zero at 2 s and then becomes negative. The graph could represent the motion of an object thrown vertically up with an initial velocity of 20 m s^{-1}. The time of 2 s then represents the time when the object reaches its highest point.

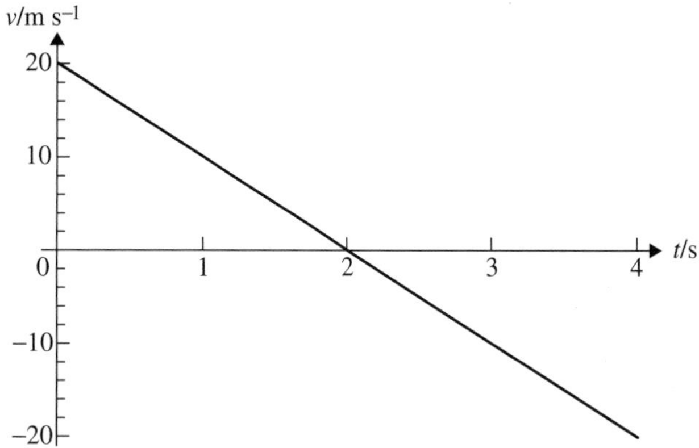

Figure 3.8 The velocity is decreasing uniformly and becomes zero at 2 s. The object then changes its direction of motion.

In Figure 3.9, displacement is graphed against time for a given motion. The object is at displacement zero at time zero and becomes a maximum at 2 s. The object returns to its initial position after 4 s.

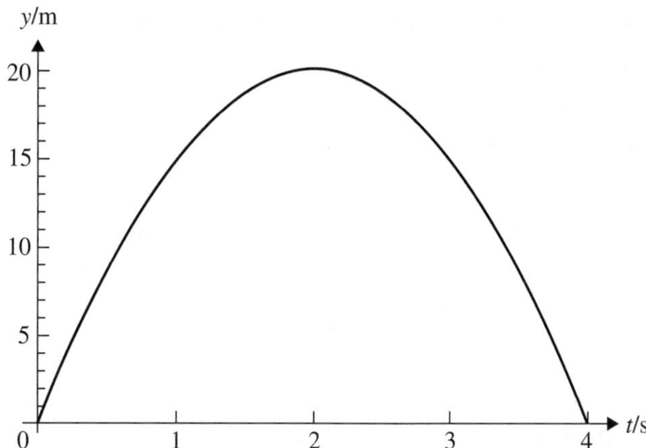

Figure 3.9 The displacement reaches a maximum at 2 s and becomes zero at 4 s.

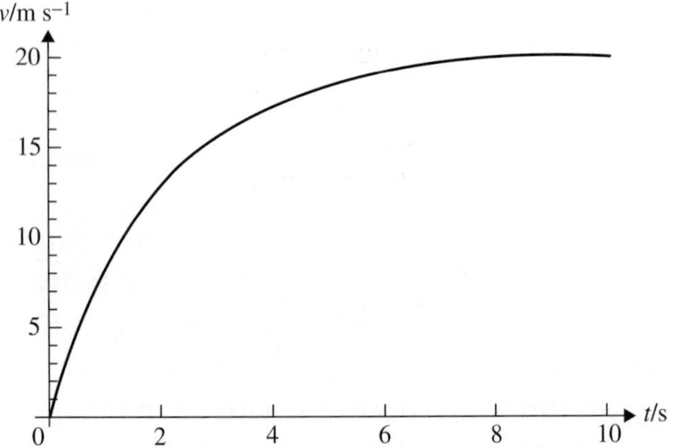

Figure 3.10 The velocity is becoming constant and so the acceleration becomes zero.

In Figure 3.10, the velocity appears to be approaching a constant value of about 20 m s^{-1}. The acceleration of the object thus approaches zero.

Sine curves

When describing waves, as well as in many other parts of physics, we deal with quantities that depend on other variables through a sine function, $y = C\sin(ax + b)$, with C, a and b being constants. For example, the disturbance of a harmonic wave at a distance x at a specific instant of time can be shown to be

$$y = A\sin\left[2\pi\frac{x}{\lambda}\right]$$

where the constants A and λ are known as the amplitude and wavelength of the wave. The amplitude is thus the largest possible disturbance (i.e. y value) and for the graph in Figure 3.11 this can be read as 1.5 m. The wavelength of the wave is extracted from the graph by measuring the distance between two consecutive peaks. In Figure 3.11 we thus find a wavelength of 2 m.

Similarly, the disturbance of a harmonic wave looked at as a function of time is given by

$$y = A\sin\left[2\pi\frac{t}{T}\right]$$

where A is again the amplitude (in Figure 3.12 it has a value of 0.4 m) and T is the period of the wave. The period is found by taking the time separation of two consecutive peaks; in Figure 3.12, $T = 0.5$ s.

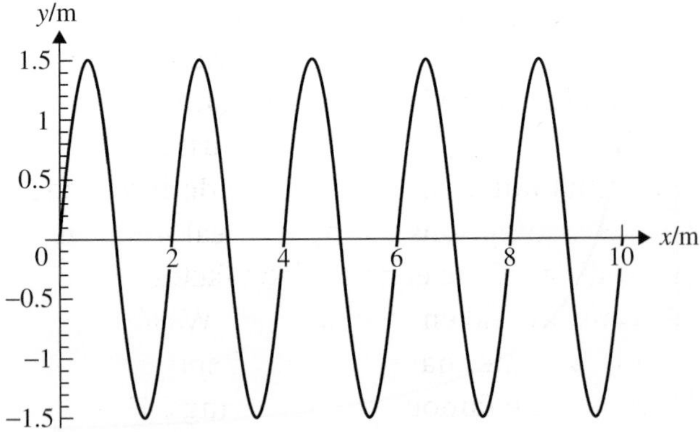

Figure 3.11 Graph of a harmonic wave as a function of position. The wavelength of the wave can be determined from this graph.

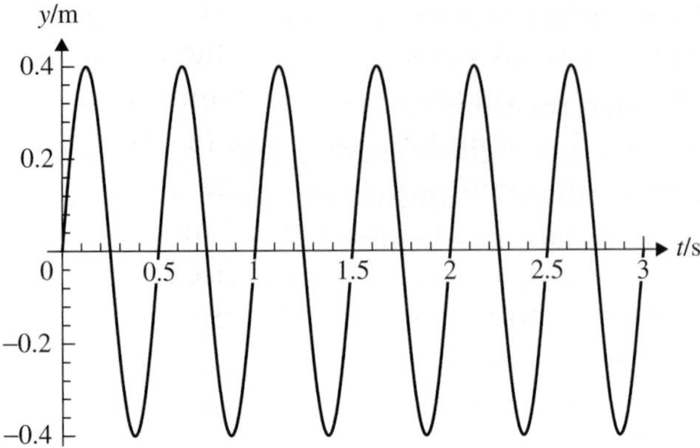

Figure 3.12 Graph of a harmonic wave as a function of time. The period of the wave can be determined from this graph.

Making assumptions

When we solve a physics problem, we always make assumptions that simplify the problem. Sometimes we are careful to list our assumptions and sometimes not.

For example, in most of the chapters on mechanics we will be solving problems involving 'bodies' in motion acted upon by forces. The 'bodies' can be anything from human beings to leaves, bricks, cars or planets. However, we will always be treating them as *point particles*, because this simplifies the problem. We will mostly ignore frictional forces unless told otherwise, because again this simplifies the problem. But we must always be aware that our solution has been derived under various assumptions and so the real solution might differ if the effects of the factors we neglected are taken into account. We also, usually, assume that strings (and springs) have no mass – the famous physics strings. This makes life easier and the assumption is good provided the other bodies in the problem really have masses much larger than that of the string.

When studying thermal physics we usually don't take into account the fact that thermal energy is always lost to the surroundings no matter how careful we have been to prevent that. If you were asked to calculate the number of atoms in your body, you would have to make a simplifying assumption otherwise the problem is hopelessly difficult – pretending that all your mass is made of out of water is such a simplifying assumption. You must then justify why it is a good simplifying assumption. In dealing with gases we assume that the gas is ideal. This is a good assumption for the air in a football but not a very good one for the material of a star that is about to become a white dwarf!

In the chapters on electricity you will learn about Coulomb's law, which allows us to find the force between two spherical charges. We cannot use this law to find the force between two plane sheets of charge though. Using Coulomb's law will only be an estimate of the force, not a precise calculation of it. Under certain conditions (which we must identify) this estimate may be a very good approximation to the real answer. In other cases it might not be. In electric circuits we usually assume that connecting wires and ammeters have no resistance. If a device used in the circuit has a resistance of a few tens of ohms, this assumption is good. But if the device has a very low resistance, comparable to that of the connecting wires and the ammeter, the assumption is not good. Similarly, voltmeters are assumed to have an infinite resistance. This means, in practice, a resistance much larger than the rest of the resistors in the circuit. If the largest resistor in the circuit is 100 ohms and the voltmeter has a resistance of 100 000 ohms the assumption is good. But if you are dealing with 100 000 ohm resistors the assumption of an infinite voltmeter resistance breaks down.

So, part of learning physics involves identifying assumptions in a problem and being able to explain whether the assumptions are justified or not.

? QUESTIONS

1 The pressure of an ideal gas is 4 atm. If the only change is to increase the temperature by a factor of 4, what will the new pressure of the gas be? (Use $pV = NkT$.)

2 The kinetic energy of a mass m is given by $\frac{1}{2}mv^2$. If the speed v is doubled, by what factor does the energy change?

3 The kinetic energy ($E_k = \frac{1}{2}mv^2$) of a body doubles. By what factor did the speed increase?

4 A constant force F brings a body of mass m and initial speed v to rest over a distance d. If the initial speed doubles, over what distance will the same force stop the same body? (Use $v^2 = \frac{2Fd}{m}$.)

5 The electric force between two charges Q_1 and Q_2 a distance r apart is given by $F = k\frac{Q_1 Q_2}{r^2}$, where k is a constant.
  (a) If both charges double, by what factor does the force between them increase?
  (b) If both charges double but the force between them stays the same, by what factor did their separation change?

6 The frequency of a standing wave on a string of fixed length L kept under tension T is given by $f = \frac{\sqrt{cT}}{2L}$, where c is a constant. By what factor should the tension be changed so that the frequency triples?

7 The period of a pendulum of length L is given by $T = 2\pi\sqrt{\frac{L}{g}}$, where g is a constant. If the

period doubles, by what factor did the length change?

8 The frequency of oscillation of a mass m attached to a spring is given by $f = \frac{1}{2\pi}\sqrt{\frac{k}{m}}$, where k is a constant. If the frequency increases by a factor of 4, by what factor did the mass change?

9 The power radiated by a body kept at a temperature T is given by $P = kT^4$, where k is a constant. If the temperature is doubled, by what factor does the power increase?

10 The period of a planet around the sun is given by $T^2 = kR^3$, where k is a constant and R is the mean distance of the planet from the sun. A planet orbits the sun at a distance from the sun that is twice the distance of earth from the sun. What is the period of this planet. (The earth's period is one year.)

11 When a strong wind creates waves on a pond, a piece of cork floating in the water oscillates so that its distance from the bottom of the pond is given by the graph in Figure 3.13.

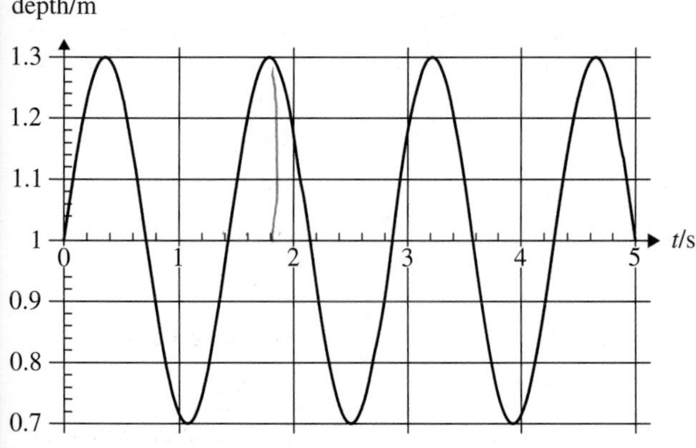

Figure 3.13 For question 11.

(a) What is the depth of the pond?
(b) What is the frequency of the wave travelling on the pond?
(c) What is the amplitude of the wave?

12 The image of an object a distance a from a lens is formed at a distance b from the lens, where a and b are related through the equation $\frac{1}{a} + \frac{1}{b} = \frac{1}{f}$ and f is the (constant) focal length of the lens.

(a) If a set of data for a and b is collected, how should it be plotted in order to give a straight line?
(b) How can the focal length of the lens be measured from the graph?

13 The pressure of a fixed quantity of gas at constant volume is related to temperature in kelvin by

$$\frac{P}{T} = \text{constant}$$

(a) What form does a graph of pressure versus temperature take?
(b) If the temperature is expressed in degrees Celsius ($T(\text{K}) = T(°\text{C}) + 273$) what does a graph of pressure versus temperature give?

14 The period of a planet around the sun is related to the mean distance of the planet from the sun through Kepler's third law

$$T^2 = \text{constant} \times R^3$$

If a student plots the period T on the vertical axis, what must be plotted on the horizontal axis in order that the resulting graph is a straight line?

15 The kinetic energy of a mass m moving in a straight line with speed v is given by $E_k = \frac{1}{2}mv^2$, where the speed is related to acceleration a (assumed constant) and distance travelled d through $v^2 = 2ad$. What would a graph of E_k versus d give?

16 In the photoelectric effect, light of frequency f falling on a metallic surface causes the emission of electrons of kinetic energy E_k. Einstein's formula relates these through

$$E_k = hf - \phi$$

where ϕ and h are constants. ϕ depends on the surface used whereas h is a universal constant. A graph of E_k versus f gives a straight line.

(a) How can ϕ be measured from the graph?
(b) How can h be measured?
(c) In a second experiment with a different surface, a second straight line is obtained. What do the two lines have in common?

Vectors and scalars

Quantities in physics are either scalars (i.e. they just have magnitude) or vectors (i.e. they have magnitude and direction). The tools for dealing with vectors are presented in this chapter.

Objectives

By the end of this chapter you should be able to:

- describe the difference between *vector* and *scalar quantities* and give examples of each;
- *add* and *subtract vectors* by a *graphical technique*, such as the parallelogram rule;
- find the *components of a vector* along a given set of axes;
- reconstruct the *magnitude* and *direction* of a vector from its given components;
- solve problems with vectors.

Vectors

Some quantities in physics, such as time, distance, mass, speed, temperature, etc., just need one number to specify them. These are called *scalar* quantities. For example, it is sufficient to say that the mass of a body is 10 kg or that the temperature today is 18°C. On the other hand, many quantities are fully specified only if, in addition to a number, a direction is given. Examples are velocity, acceleration, force, etc. These are called *vector* quantities. For example, when describing the velocity of an object, it is necessary to specify both the magnitude of velocity (speed) and the direction in which the object is moving. Table 4.1 lists some examples of vectors and scalars.

Vectors	Scalars
Displacement	Distance
Velocity	Speed
Acceleration	Mass
Force	Time
Weight	Density
Electric field	Electric potential
Magnetic field	Energy
Gravitational field	Gravitational potential
Torque	Temperature
Area	Volume
Momentum	Electric charge
Angular velocity	Work

Table 4.1 Examples of vectors and scalars.

A vector is represented by a straight line with an arrow at one end, as shown in Figure 4.1a. The direction of the arrow represents the direction of the vector and the length of the line represents the magnitude of the vector. To say that two vectors are the same means that both magnitude and direction are the same. Two vectors with the same direction are not necessarily along the same line. As long as they are parallel to each other and have the same

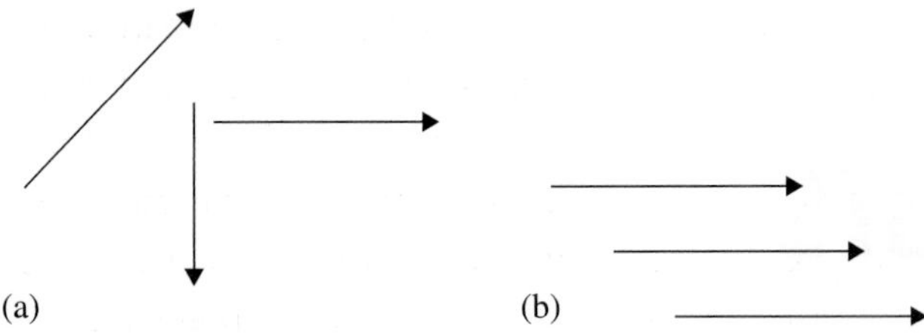

Figure 4.1 (a) Representation of vectors by arrows. (b) These three vectors are equal to each other.

magnitude, they are the same. Thus, the vectors in Figure 4.1b are all equal to each other. This ability to shift a vector around parallel to itself (called parallel transport) is very important in what follows.

Vectors are represented symbolically either with an arrow on top of the symbol for the vector or in bold type. Thus, both $\vec{a}$ and **a** represent a vector, and its magnitude is denoted by $|\vec{a}|$, $|\mathbf{a}|$ or just a.

Two vectors that have the same magnitude but are opposite to each other in direction are the negatives of one another (see Figure 4.2).

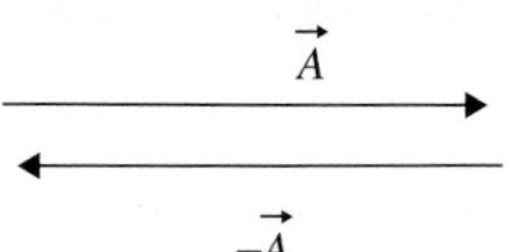

Figure 4.2 Two opposite vectors that are equal in magnitude.

Multiplication of a vector by a scalar

A vector can be multiplied by a scalar (i.e. a number) in a simple way. If the vector $\vec{a}$ is multiplied by the number k, then the resulting vector $k\vec{a}$ has the same direction as $\vec{a}$ if $k > 0$ and opposite to $\vec{a}$ if $k < 0$. The magnitude of the vector $k\vec{a}$ is simply $k\,|\vec{a}|$. Thus, if the vector $\vec{a}$ has a magnitude of 10 units, multiplying $\vec{a}$ by the number -0.5 results in a vector of magnitude 5 units in the opposite direction to $\vec{a}$. (See Figure 4.3.)

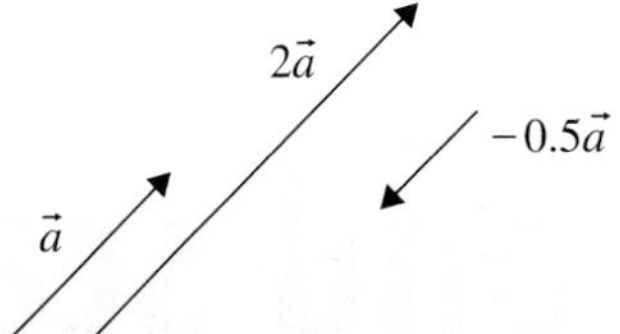

Figure 4.3 Multiplication of vectors by a scalar.

Addition of vectors

Figure 4.4 shows vectors $\vec{a}$ and $\vec{b}$. We want to find the vector that equals $\vec{a}+\vec{b}$. Adding two or more vectors together gives the vector sum, which is the combined effect of the vectors acting on a body. Thus, if two forces act on a mass, their vector sum is the one force whose effect on the mass is the same as the effects of the two forces together. For this reason, the sum of a number of vectors is called the net vector or the resultant vector.

There are two equivalent graphical methods for adding two vectors. The first is the parallelogram method (see Figure 4.4):

1. Shift $\vec{b}$ parallel to itself so that its beginning point coincides with the beginning point of $\vec{a}$.
2. Complete the parallelogram whose two sides are $\vec{a}$ and $\vec{b}$.
3. Draw the diagonal of the parallelogram which starts at the beginning of $\vec{a}$ and $\vec{b}$. This diagonal is $\vec{a}+\vec{b}$.

The second method is the head-to-tail method (see Figure 4.5):

1. Shift $\vec{b}$ parallel to itself so that its beginning point touches the end point of $\vec{a}$.
2. Join the beginning point of $\vec{a}$ to the end point of $\vec{b}$. This is vector $\vec{a}+\vec{b}$.

You might ask if we would have obtained a different answer if, instead, we had shifted $\vec{a}$ to

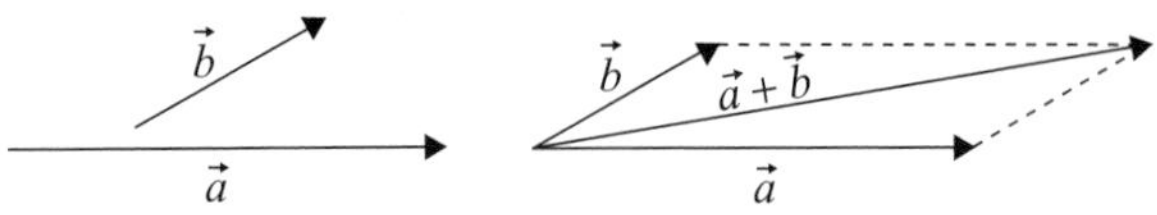

Figure 4.4 Adding two vectors involves shifting one of them parallel to itself so as to form a parallelogram with the two vectors as the two sides. The diagonal represents the sum.

Figure 4.5 One of the vectors is shifted parallel to itself until its beginning point coincides with the end of the other vector. The sum is then the arrow that joins the only beginning point to the only end point.

the end of $\vec{b}$ and then joined the beginning of $\vec{b}$ to the end of $\vec{a}$. Check that you get the same answer if you do this. This is a way of seeing that $\vec{a}+\vec{b}=\vec{b}+\vec{a}$.

Example questions

Q1

Add together two vectors: the first has a magnitude of 100 units and is directed east, the other has a magnitude of 50 units directed at 45° to the first.

Answer

See Figure 4.6. First we make a scale representing 10 units of the vector magnitude with 1 cm on paper. Measuring the diagonal we find a length of 13.85 cm, implying a sum of 138.5 units. Using a protractor we find that $\theta = 14.2°$.

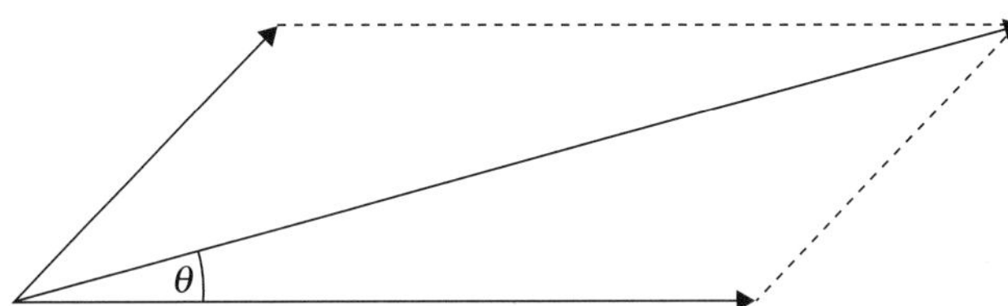

Figure 4.6 (Not to scale).

Q2

A velocity vector of magnitude $1.2\,\mathrm{m\,s^{-1}}$ is horizontal. A second velocity vector of magnitude $2\,\mathrm{m\,s^{-1}}$ must be added to the first so that the sum is vertical in direction. What is the direction of the second vector and what is the magnitude of the sum?

Answer

See Figure 4.7. Again we need a scale. Representing $1\,\mathrm{m\,s^{-1}}$ by 2 cm, we see that the $1.2\,\mathrm{m\,s^{-1}}$ corresponds to 2.4 cm and $2\,\mathrm{m\,s^{-1}}$ to 4 cm. First draw the horizontal vector; mark the vertical direction and using a compass (or a ruler) mark a distance of 4 cm from A. It intersects the vertical line at B. AB must be one of the sides of the parallelogram we are looking for. Thus, measure a distance of 2.4 cm horizontally from B to C and join O to C. This is the direction in which the second velocity vector must be pointing. Measuring the diagonal (i.e. the vector representing the sum) we find 3.2 cm, which represents $1.6\,\mathrm{m\,s^{-1}}$. Using a protractor we find that the $2\,\mathrm{m\,s^{-1}}$ velocity vector makes an angle of about 37° with the vertical.

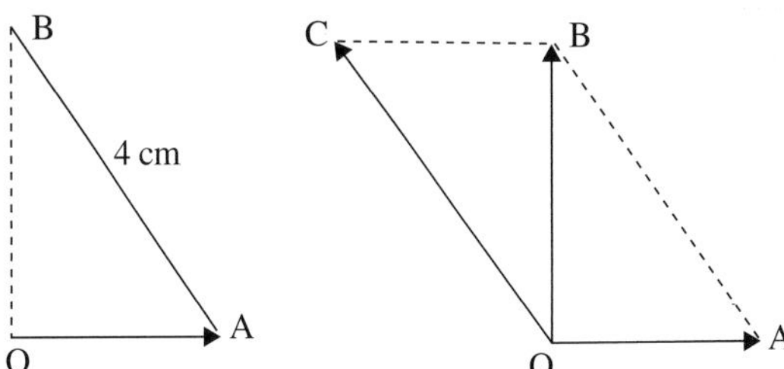

Figure 4.7 (Not to scale).

Q3

A person walks 5 km east, followed by 3 km north and then another 4 km east. Where does he end up?

Answer

The walk consists of three steps and we may represent each one by a vector (see Figure 4.8). The first step is a vector of magnitude 5 km directed east. The second is a vector of magnitude 3 km directed north and the last step is represented by a vector of 4 km directed east. The person will end up at a place that is given by the vector sum of these three vectors, that is **OA** + **AB** + **BC**, which equals the vector **OC**. By measurement or by simple geometry, the distance from O to C is 9.5 km and the angle to the horizontal is 18.4°.

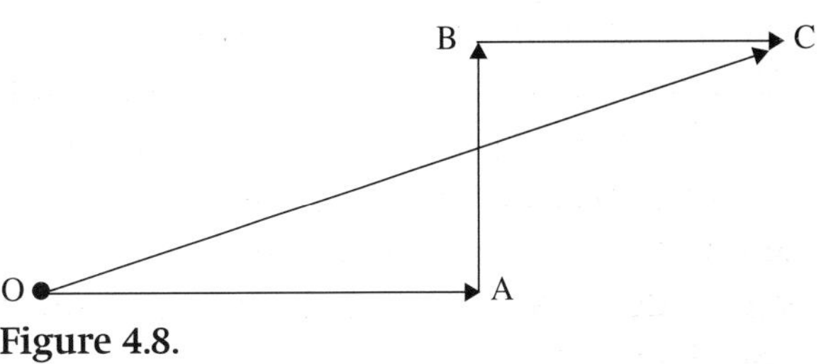

Figure 4.8.

Subtraction of vectors

We are given two vectors $\vec{a}$ and $\vec{b}$. We want to find $\vec{a} - \vec{b}$. Since $\vec{a} - \vec{b}$ is the same as $\vec{a} + (-\vec{b})$, all we have to do is find the vector $-\vec{b}$ and add that to $\vec{a}$ (see Figure 4.9).

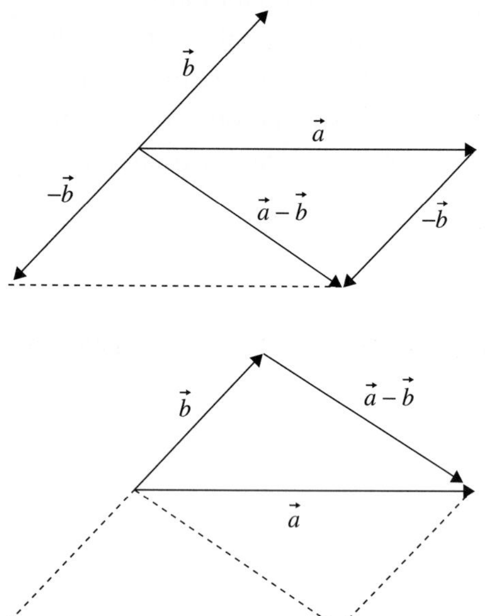

Figure 4.9 Subtraction of vectors.

We have the important result that:

► The vector $\vec{a} - \vec{b}$ is the vector from the tip of vector $\vec{b}$ to the tip of vector $\vec{a}$.

This is very useful because in physics we are often interested in finding the *change* in a vector. For example, consider a body whose velocity changes from $\vec{v}_1$ to $\vec{v}_2$. The vector representing the change in the velocity is the vector $\overrightarrow{\Delta v} = \vec{v}_2 - \vec{v}_1$, which is the vector joining the tip of $\vec{v}_1$ to the tip of $\vec{v}_2$ (see Figure 4.10).

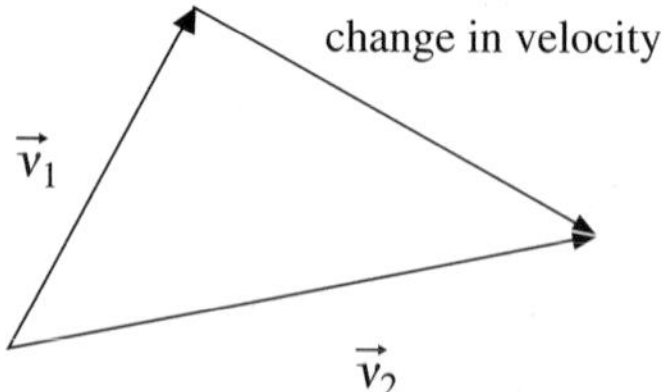

Figure 4.10 The vector representing the change in velocity, $\vec{v}_2 - \vec{v}_1$.

Example question

Q4

A body moves in a circle of radius 3 m with a constant speed of 6.0 m s^{-1}. The velocity vector is at all times tangent to the circle. The body starts at A and proceeds to B and then C. Find the change in the velocity vector between A and B and between B and C. (See Figure 4.11.)

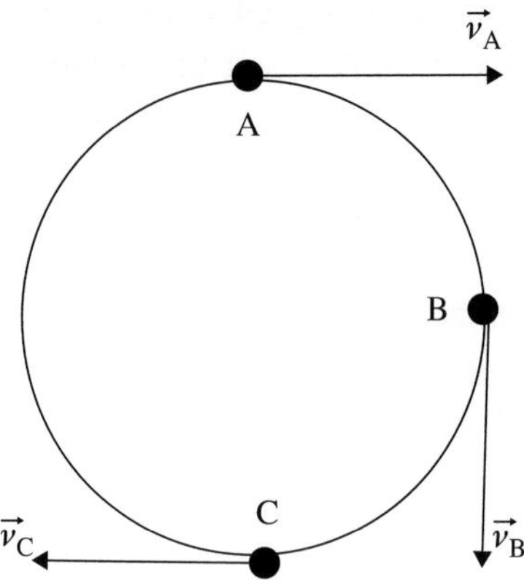

Figure 4.11.

Answer

From A to B we have to find the difference $\vec{v}_B - \vec{v}_A$. The vectors are shown in Figure 4.12.

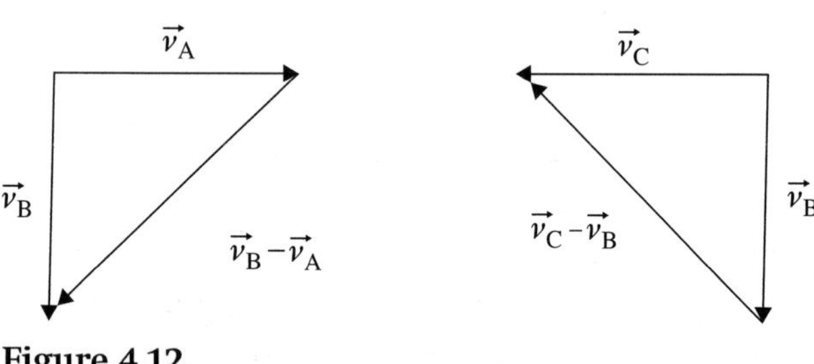

Figure 4.12.

The vector $\vec{v}_B - \vec{v}_A$ is directed south-west and its magnitude is (by the Pythagorean theorem)

$$\sqrt{v_A^2 + v_B^2} = \sqrt{6^2 + 6^2}$$
$$= \sqrt{72}$$
$$= 8.49 \text{ m s}^{-1}$$

The vector $\vec{v}_C - \vec{v}_B$ has the same magnitude as $\vec{v}_B - \vec{v}_A$ but is directed north-west.

Components of a vector

Suppose that we use perpendicular axes x and y and draw vectors on this x–y plane. We take the origin of the axes as the starting point of the vector. (Other vectors whose beginning points are not at the origin can be shifted parallel to themselves until they, too, begin at the origin.) Given a vector $\vec{a}$ we define its *components along the axes* as follows. From the tip of the vector draw lines parallel to the axes and mark the point on each axis where the lines intersect the axes (Figure 4.13).

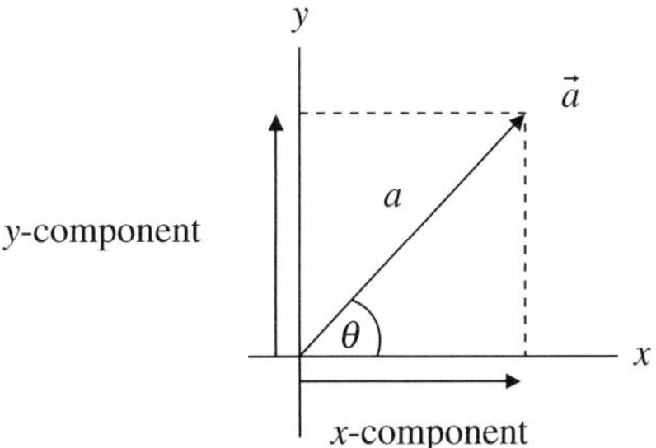

Figure 4.13 The components of a vector.

The x and y components of $\vec{a}$ are called a_x and a_y. They are given by

$$a_x = a\cos\theta$$
$$a_y = a\sin\theta$$

where a is the magnitude of the vector $\vec{a}$ and θ is the angle between the vector and the positive x-axis. Some care must be taken in identifying the correct angle that goes in these formulae. The angle is properly measured from the positive x-axis to the vector, in the counter-clockwise direction (see Figure 4.14).

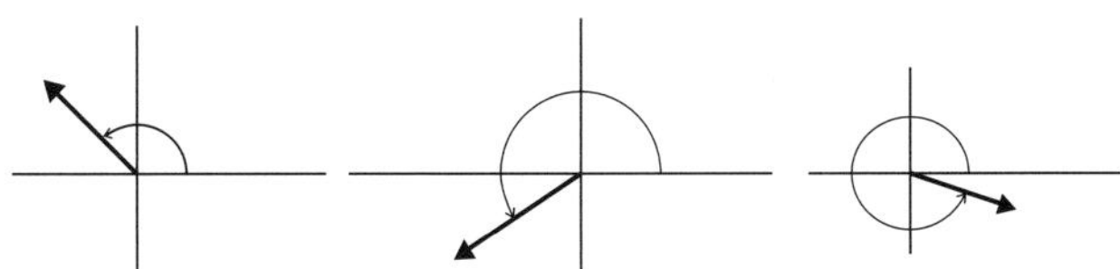

Figure 4.14 The angle of a vector is measured from the positive x-axis to the vector, in the counter-clockwise direction.

Example question

Q5

Find the components of the vectors in Figure 4.15. The magnitude of $\vec{a}$ is 10 units and that of $\vec{b}$ is 20 units.

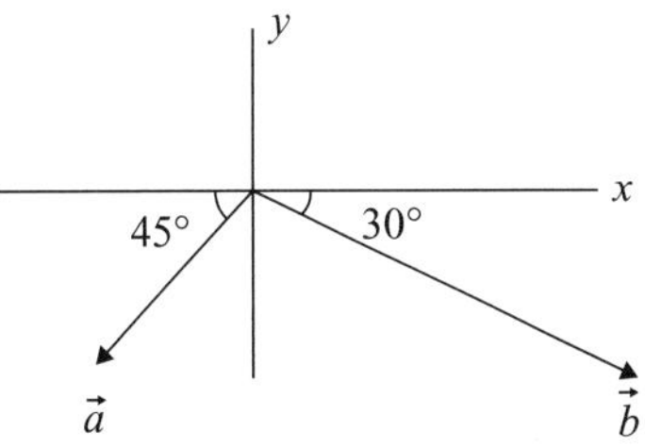

Figure 4.15.

Answer

The relevant angle for $\vec{a}$ is $180° + 45° = 225°$ and that for $\vec{b}$ is $330°$. Thus

$$\begin{aligned} a_x &= 10.0\cos 225° \\ &= -7.07 \\ a_y &= 10.0\sin 225° \\ &= -7.07 \\ b_x &= 20.0\cos 330° \\ &= 17.3 \\ b_y &= 20.0\sin 330° \\ &= -10.0 \end{aligned}$$

As we see, the components of a vector can be negative as well as positive. It is somewhat less precise, but in practice more convenient, not to have to deal with negative components. Consider the vector shown in Figure 4.16.

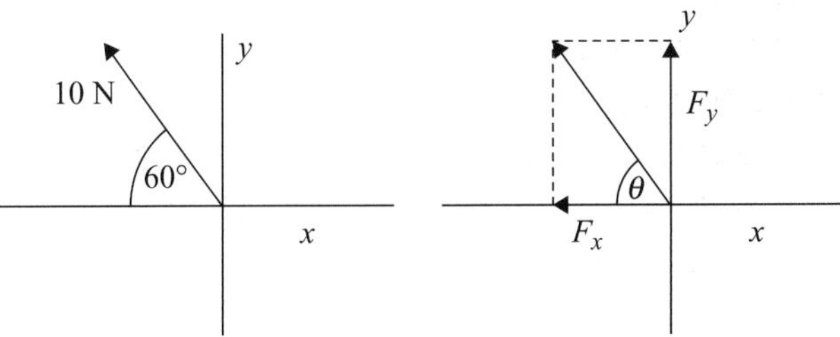

Figure 4.16 Any angle can be used to find the magnitude of the components.

Its x component is clearly negative, $F_x = 10\cos 120° = -5$ N. We could state, however, that the x component of the vector is 5 N in the negative x direction. This is equivalent to stating that $F_x = -5$ N. It has the advantage that by using trigonometry, we can find the numerical value of the component by choosing the most convenient angle in the problem (here the angle of 60°). We do not have to deal with the awkward 'the counter-clockwise angle from the positive x-axis' (here the angle of 120°). In any case treating the components as positive or negative is a question of convenience and up to you, provided you are clear about what are you are doing.

Example question

Q6

Find the components of the vector $\vec{W}$ along the axes shown in Figure 4.17.

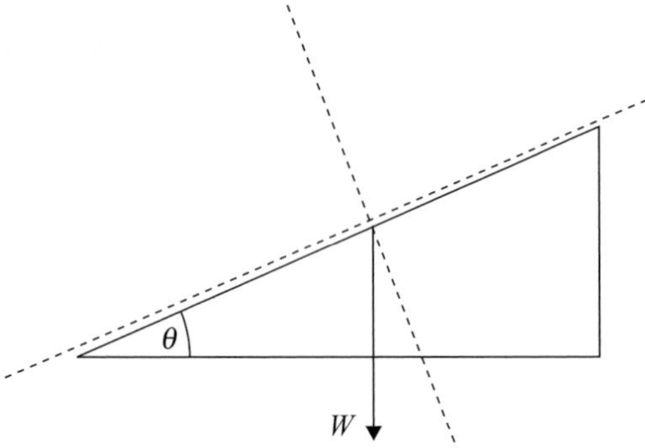

Figure 4.17.

Answer

See Figure 4.18. Notice that the angle between the vector $\vec{W}$ and the y-axis is θ.

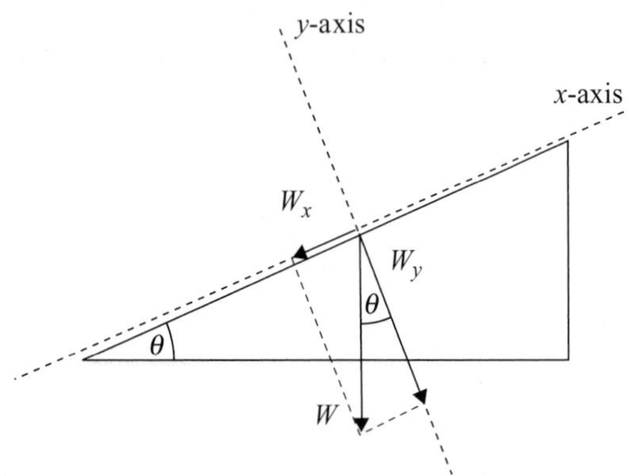

Figure 4.18.

Then by simple trigonometry

$W_x = W \sin\theta$ (W_x is opposite the angle θ so the sine is used)

$W_y = W \cos\theta$ (W_y is adjacent to the angle θ so the cosine is used)

An additional notation for vectors is to give the x and y components as an ordered pair so that, for example, $\vec{a} = (2, 1)$ denotes a vector with x component equal to 2 and y component equal to 1.

Reconstructing the vector from its components

Knowing the components of a vector allows us to reconstruct it (i.e. to find the magnitude and direction of the vector). Suppose that we are given that the x and y components of a vector are F_x and F_y. We need to find the magnitude of the vector $\vec{F}$ and the angle (θ) it makes with the x-axis (see Figure 4.19). The magnitude is found by using the Pythagorean theorem and the angle by using the definition of tangent.

$$F = \sqrt{F_x{}^2 + F_y{}^2}, \qquad \theta = \arctan\frac{F_y}{F_x}$$

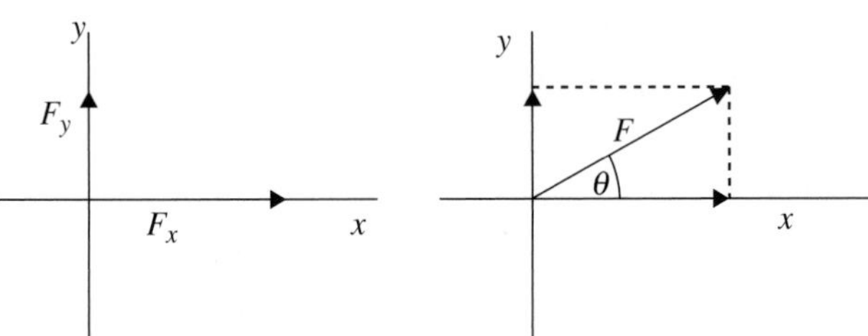

Figure 4.19 Given the components of a vector we can find its magnitude and direction.

As an example, consider the vector whose components are $F_x = 4.0$ and $F_y = 3.0$. Then the magnitude is simply

$$F = \sqrt{F_x{}^2 + F_y{}^2} = \sqrt{4^2 + 3^2} = \sqrt{25} = 5.0$$

and the direction is found from

$$\theta = \arctan\frac{F_y}{F_x} = \arctan\frac{3}{4} = 36.87° \approx 37°$$

Here is another example. We need to find the magnitude and direction of the vector with components $F_x = -2.0$ and $F_y = -4.0$. From Figure 4.20, it follows that the vector lies in the third quadrant.

The magnitude is

$$F = \sqrt{F_x{}^2 + F_y{}^2} = \sqrt{(-2)^2 + (-4)^2}$$
$$= \sqrt{20} = 4.47 \approx 4.5$$

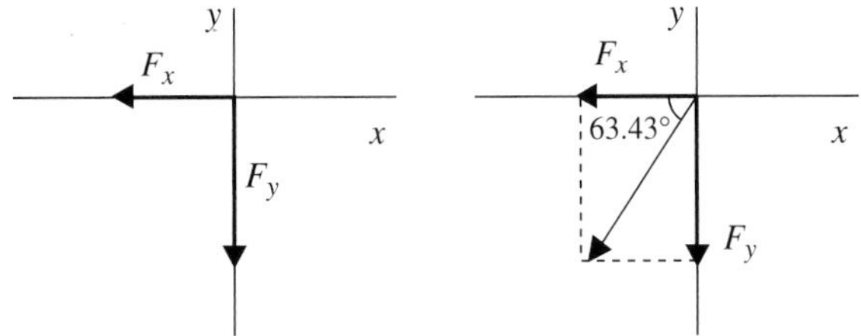

Figure 4.20 The vector is in the third quadrant. We expect the angle it makes with the positive x-axis to be between 180 and 270 degrees.

The direction is found from

$$\theta = \arctan \frac{F_y}{F_x} = \arctan \frac{-4}{-2} = \arctan 2$$

The calculator gives $\theta = \tan^{-1} 2 = 63°$. Here we must be careful. Our vector is in the third quadrant, so the angle it makes with the positive x-axis must be between 180° and 270°. We now realize that there is another angle whose tangent is 2. It is the angle $180° + 63° = 243°$ and this is what we want. Thus, in finding the direction, first make a diagram to see what quadrant your vector lies in so that you know what angles to expect. Never blindly take what the calculator gives. Of course if you denote the angle as in Figure 4.20, you still give a complete description of the vector and that is fine.

As a final example consider the vector with $F_x = 5.0$ and $F_y = -4.0$. It lies in the fourth quadrant. Its magnitude is $F = \sqrt{5^2 + (-4)^2} = 6.4$ and its direction is $\theta = \arctan\frac{-4}{5} = -39°$. The calculator gives the angle from the x-axis to the vector in the clockwise direction. We are expecting an angle between 270 and 360 degrees. The angle is $360° - 39° = 321°$.

Adding vectors by components

Adding vectors whose components are given is straightforward. If $\vec{a} = (a_x, a_y)$ and $\vec{b} = (b_x, b_y)$, then $\vec{c} = \vec{a} + \vec{b}$ implies that $\vec{c}$ has components

$$c_x = a_x + b_x, \quad c_y = a_y + b_y$$

For example, if $\vec{a} = (1, 1)$ and $\vec{b} = (-3, 2)$ then $\vec{a} + \vec{b} = (1 - 3, 1 + 2) = (-2, 3)$; that is, the x component of the sum is the sum of the x components of the individual vectors and so on. Similarly if $\vec{d} = \vec{a} - \vec{b}$, then

$$d_x = a_x - b_x = 4, \quad d_y = a_y - b_y = -1$$

Example questions

Q7

$\vec{a} = (1, 1)$, $\vec{b} = (1, -1)$. Find the magnitude of $\vec{a}$ and $\vec{b}$ and the magnitude of $\vec{a} + \vec{b}$.

Answer

$a = \sqrt{2}$
$b = \sqrt{2}$
$\vec{a} + \vec{b} = (2, 0)$

so the magnitude is 2.

Q8

$\vec{a} = (1, 3)$, $\vec{b} = (2, -2)$. Find the vector $\vec{c}$ such that $\vec{a} + \vec{b} + \vec{c} = 0$.

Answer

$$\vec{c} = -(\vec{a} + \vec{b}) = -(3, 1) = (-3, -1).$$

If the components are not given, then we have to find them.

Figure 4.21 shows two vectors $\vec{F}_1$ and $\vec{F}_2$ of magnitude 10 and 14, respectively. Vector $\vec{F}_1$ makes an angle of 60° with the x-axis and vector $\vec{F}_2$ an angle of 30°. We want to find the magnitude and direction of the vector $\vec{F}_1 + \vec{F}_2$.

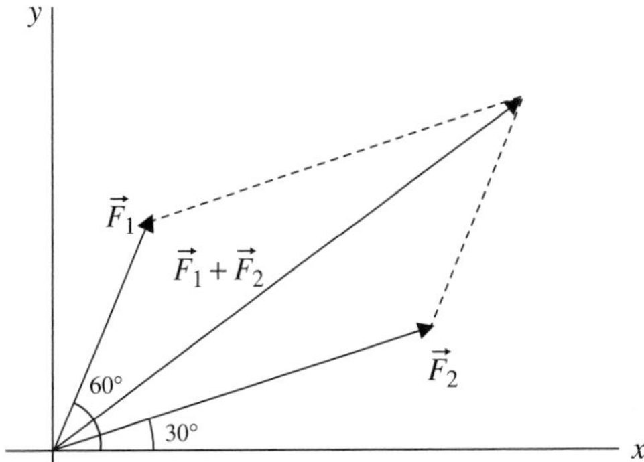

Figure 4.21 Finding the sum of two vectors using components. (Not to scale.)

The components of the vectors are

$$F_{1x} = F_1 \cos 60° = 5.0$$

$$F_{1y} = F_1 \sin 60^\circ$$
$$= 8.660$$
$$F_{2x} = F_2 \cos 30^\circ$$
$$= 12.124$$
$$F_{2y} = F_2 \sin 30^\circ$$
$$= 7.0$$

Hence the components of the vector $\vec{F} = \vec{F}_1 + \vec{F}_2$ are

$$F_x = F_{1x} + F_{2x}$$
$$= 17.124$$
$$F_y = F_{1y} + F_{2y}$$
$$= 15.660$$

The vector $\vec{F} = \vec{F}_1 + \vec{F}_2$ thus has magnitude

$$F = \sqrt{F_x{}^2 + F_y{}^2}$$
$$= \sqrt{17.124^2 + 15.660^2}$$
$$= 23.2 \approx 23$$

The direction of $\vec{F} = \vec{F}_1 + \vec{F}_2$ is given by

$$\tan\theta = \frac{F_y}{F_x}$$
$$= \frac{15.660}{17.124}$$
$$= 0.9145$$

so that

$$\theta = \arctan 0.9145$$
$$= 42.4^\circ \approx 42^\circ$$

Example question

Q9

Find the sum of the vectors shown in Figure 4.22. $\vec{F}_1$ has magnitude 8.0 units and $\vec{F}_2$ magnitude 12 units. Their directions are as indicated.

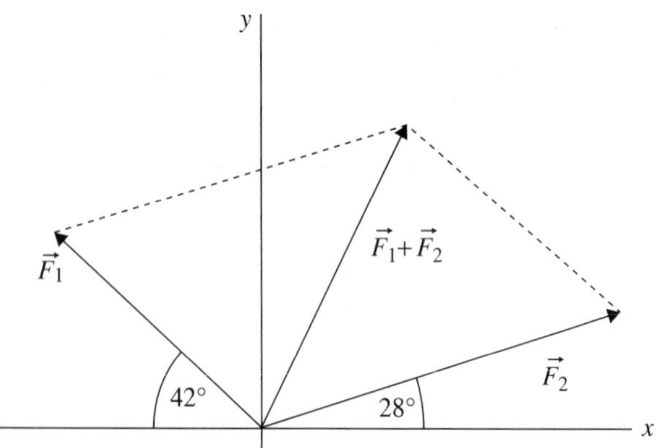

Figure 4.22 (Not to scale).

Answer

$$F_{1x} = -F_1 \cos 42^\circ$$
$$= -5.945$$
$$F_{1y} = F_1 \sin 42^\circ$$
$$= 5.353$$
$$F_{2x} = F_2 \cos 28^\circ$$
$$= 10.595$$
$$F_{2y} = F_2 \sin 28^\circ$$
$$= 5.634$$

The sum $\vec{F} = \vec{F}_1 + \vec{F}_2$ then has components

$$F_x = F_{1x} + F_{2x}$$
$$= 4.650$$
$$F_y = F_{1y} + F_{2y}$$
$$= 10.987$$

Thus, the magnitude of the sum is

$$F = \sqrt{4.650^2 + 10.987^2}$$
$$= 11.9 \approx 12$$

and its direction is

$$\theta = \arctan\frac{10.987}{4.65}$$
$$= 67.1^\circ \approx 67^\circ$$

? QUESTIONS

1 A body is acted upon by the two forces shown in Figure 4.23. In each case draw the one force whose effect on the body is the same as the two together.

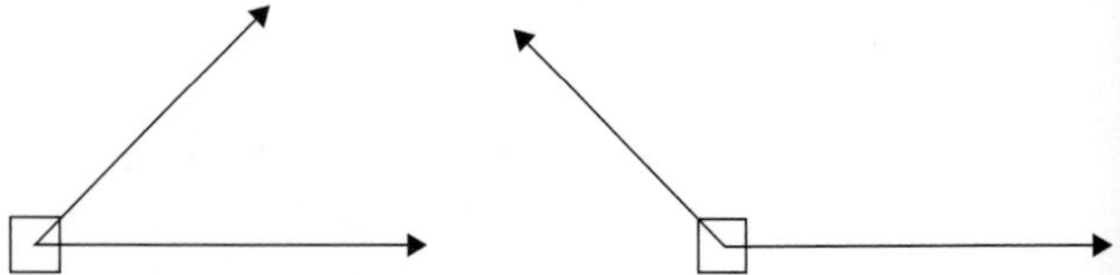

Figure 4.23 For question 1.

2 Vector A has a magnitude of 12.0 units and makes an angle of 30° with the positive x-axis. Vector B has a magnitude of 8.00 units and makes an angle of 80° with the positive x-axis. Using a graphical method, find the magnitude and direction of the vectors

(a) $\vec{A} + \vec{B}$

(b) $\vec{A} - \vec{B}$

(c) $\vec{A} - 2\vec{B}$.

3 Repeat the previous problem, this time using components.

4 A person walks 5.0 km due east, then 3.0 km due north and finally stops after walking an additional 2.0 km due north-east. How far and in what direction relative to her starting point is she?

5 Find the magnitude and direction of the vectors with components:
(a) $A_x = -4.0\,\text{cm}, \quad A_y = -4.0\,\text{cm}$
(b) $A_x = 124\,\text{km}, \quad A_y = -158\,\text{km}$
(c) $A_x = 0, \quad A_y = -5.0\,\text{m}$
(d) $A_x = 8.0\,\text{N}, \quad A_y = 0$.

6 The components of vectors $\vec{A}$ and $\vec{B}$ are as follows: $(A_x = 2.00, A_y = 3.00)$, $(B_x = -2.00, B_y = 5.00)$. Find the magnitude and direction of the vectors:
(a) $\vec{A}$;
(b) $\vec{B}$;
(c) $\vec{A} + \vec{B}$;
(d) $\vec{A} - \vec{B}$;
(e) $2\vec{A} - \vec{B}$.

7 Vectors $\vec{A}$ and $\vec{B}$ have components $(A_x = 3.00, A_y = 4.00)$, $(B_x = -1.00, B_y = 5.00)$. Find the magnitude and direction of the vector $\vec{C}$ such that $\vec{A} - \vec{B} + \vec{C} = 0$.

8 The displacement vector of a moving object has components $(r_x = 2, r_y = 2)$ initially. After a certain time the displacement vector has components $(r_x = 4, r_y = 8)$. What vector represents the change in the displacement vector?

9 Figure 4.24 shows the velocity vector of a particle moving in a circle with speed $10\,\text{m s}^{-1}$ at two separate points. The velocity vector is tangential to the circle. Find the vector representing the *change* in the velocity vector.

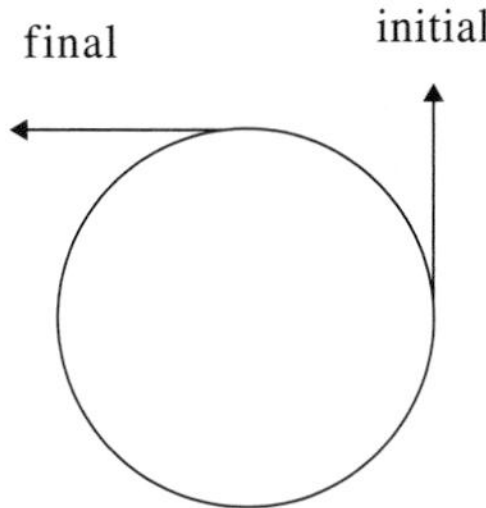

Figure 4.24 For question 9.

10 In a certain collision, the momentum vector of a particle changes direction but not magnitude. Let $\vec{p}$ be the momentum vector of a particle suffering an elastic collision and changing direction by 30°. Find, in terms of $p\,(=|\vec{p}|)$, the magnitude of the vector representing the change in the momentum vector.

11 Points P and Q have coordinates $P = (x_1, y_1)$, $Q = (x_2, y_2)$.
(a) Find the components of the vector from P to Q.
(b) What are the components of the vector from Q to P?
(c) What is the magnitude of the vector from the origin to P?

12 The velocity vector of an object moving on a circular path has a direction that is tangent to the path (see Figure 4.25). If the speed (magnitude of velocity) is constant at $4.0\,\text{m s}^{-1}$ find the change in the velocity vector as the object moves (a) from A to B and (b) from B to C. (c) What is the change in the velocity vector from A to C? How is this related to your answers to (a) and (b)?

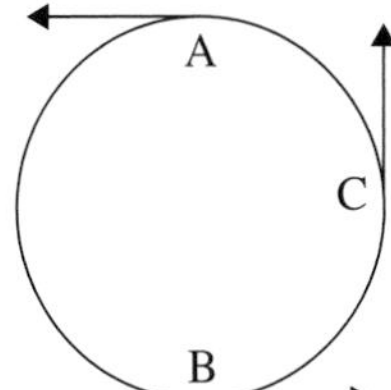

Figure 4.25 For question 12.

13 A molecule with a velocity of $352\,\text{m s}^{-1}$ collides with a wall as shown in Figure 4.26 and bounces back with the same speed.
(a) What is the change in the molecule's velocity?
(b) What is the change in the speed?

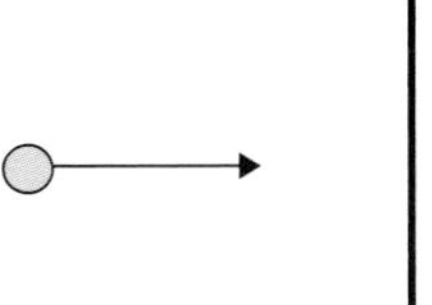

Figure 4.26 For question 9.

14 Find the components of the vectors shown along the axes indicated by a + in Figure 4.27. Take the magnitude of each vector to be 10.0 units.

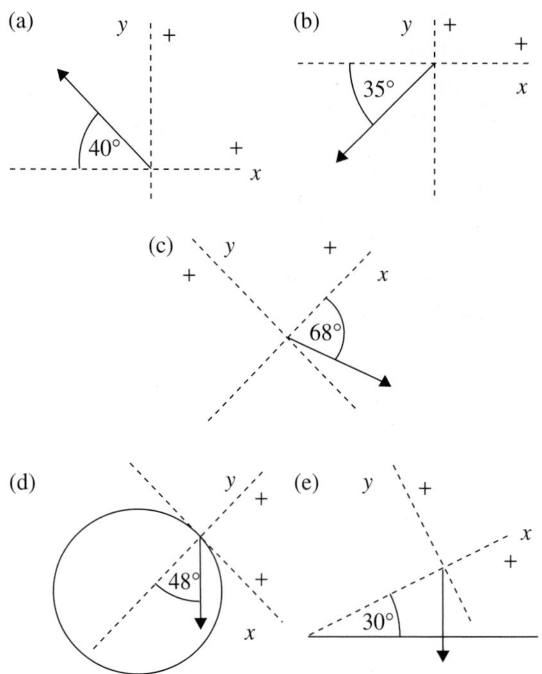

Figure 4.27 For question 14.

15 Vector A has a magnitude of 6.00 units and is directed at 60° to the positive x-axis. Vector B has a magnitude of 6.00 units and is directed at 120° to the positive x-axis. Find the magnitude and direction of vector C such that $\vec{A} + \vec{B} + \vec{C} = 0$. Place the three vectors so that one begins where the previous ends. What do you observe?

16 Plot the following pairs of vectors on a set of x- and y-axes. The angles given are measured counter-clockwise from the positive x-axis. Then, using the algebraic component method, find their sum in magnitude and direction:

(a) 12.0 N at 20° and 14.0 N at 50°

(b) 15.0 N at 15° and 18.0 N at 105°

(c) 20.0 N at 40° and 15.0 N at 310° (i.e. −50°).

Graphical analysis and uncertainties

This chapter introduces the basic methods of dealing with logarithmic and exponential functions in physics. It also introduces the basic methods for calculating the uncertainty in a quantity, which is a function of other measured quantities. The uncertainty in measured quantities will produce an uncertainty in a number obtained using the measured quantities.

Objectives

By the end of this chapter you should be able to:

- deal with logarithmic functions, semi-logarithmic and logarithmic plots;
- find the *error* in a calculated quantity in terms of the errors of the dependent quantities;
- find the error in the *slope* and *intercept* of a straight-line graph.

Logarithmic functions

Semi-logarithmic plots

The exponential function $y = e^x$ plays a significant role in many areas of physics. The activity (number of decays per unit time) as a function of time for a radioactive element behaves as $A = A_0e^{-\lambda t}$, where λ is known as the decay constant. The current through a diode varies with applied voltage as $I = I_0e^{kV/T}$, where T is the temperature in kelvin and k is a constant. When the exponential is negative, we speak of a decay problem, whereas positive exponentials represent growth problems.

Let us concentrate on the radioactive decay problem. Consider the data in Table 5.1, which was collected in an experiment.

Time, t/min	Activity/Bq
0	120
1	93
2	73
3	57
4	44
5	35
6	27
7	21
8	16
9	13
10	10

Table 5.1 Experimental data.

The graph of activity versus time is an exponential decay curve as expected. This is shown in Figure 5.1.

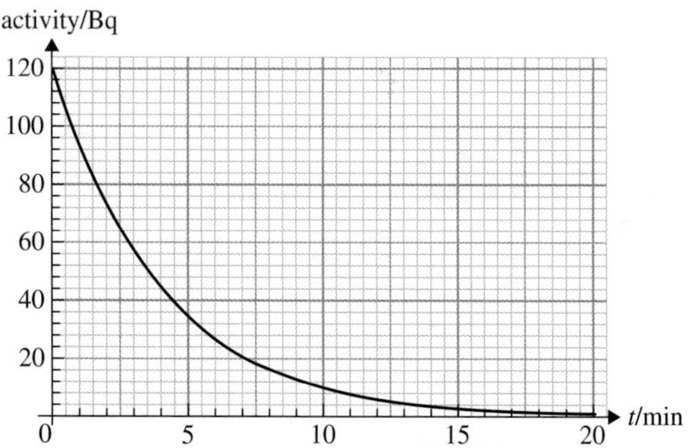

Figure 5.1 The exponential decay curve.

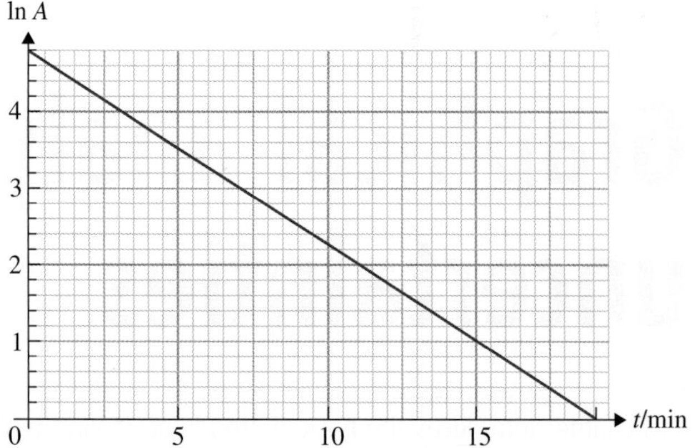

Figure 5.2 The exponential decay curve becomes linear if we plot the logarithm of activity versus time.

The half-life can be determined from this graph by finding the time at which the activity is 60 decays per minute (i.e. half its original value). From the graph, this is found to be about 2.8 minutes. It is more convenient, however, to plot a different graph so that a straight line is obtained.

▶ Since $A = A_0 e^{-\lambda t}$, it follows by taking natural logarithms that

$$\ln A = \ln A_0 - \lambda t$$

and thus a graph of ln A versus time is a straight line with slope equal to the negative decay constant, and the vertical intercept is the logarithm of the initial activity. This is called a semi-logarithmic plot as it involves the logarithm of only one of the variables.

Such a graph can be made by using a calculator to compute the natural logarithm of each activity value and plotting the logarithm against time, as in Figure 5.2.

Finding the slope of this straight line as usual, we obtain:

$$\text{slope} = -\frac{4.8}{19} \approx -0.25\ \text{min}^{-1}$$

Thus, the decay constant is 0.25 min^{-1}. Using the known relationship between the decay constant and the half-life

$$\lambda T_{1/2} = \ln 2$$

it follows that the half-life is

$$T_{1/2} = \frac{\ln 2}{\lambda} = \frac{0.693}{0.25} = 2.8\ \text{min}$$

The vertical intercept is about 4.8 and equals $\ln A_0$. Hence, the initial activity is found to be

$$4.8 = \ln A_0 \Rightarrow A_0 = e^{4.8} \approx 120\ \text{Bq}$$

Logarithmic plots

Consider now a variable that depends on another through a power.

If $y = kx^n$, then $\ln y = \ln k + n \ln x$, which means that a graph of $\ln y$ versus $\ln x$ gives a straight line with slope n and vertical intercept equal to $\ln k$.

Thus, consider the following data for the maximum current I that can flow in a wire of diameter D (see Table 5.2 and Figure 5.3).

This is a curve of unknown equation. Suspecting a power relationship between the

I/A	D/mm
0	0
1	2.2
2	3.5
3	4.6
4	5.57
5	6.47
6	7.31
7	8.1
8	8.86
9	9.59
10	10.29

Table 5.2 The maximum current that can flow in a particular wire.

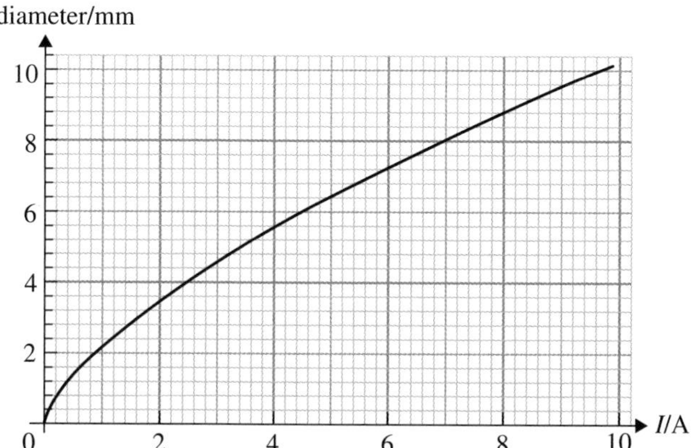

Figure 5.3 A plot of diameter versus current gives a curve of unknown equation.

diameter D and the current I, we take natural logarithms of both variables and plot ln D versus ln I (Figure 5.4). (Note that the zero on the vertical axis has been suppressed.)

We find the slope in the usual way:

$$\text{slope} = \frac{2-1}{1.8-0.3} = 0.67$$

Thus, $D = kI^{0.67}$. The constant k can also be determined by finding the intercept of the line with the vertical axis. The intercept is 0.8 and so $\ln k = 0.80 \Rightarrow k = e^{0.80} \approx 2.2$. Finally, $D = 2.2I^{0.67}$, where the current is in amps and the diameter in mm.

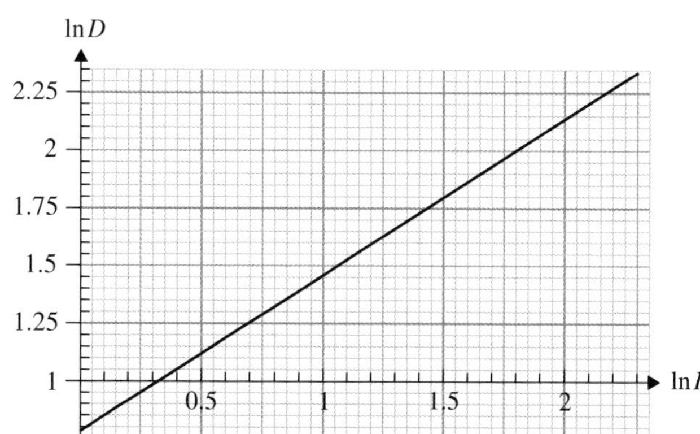

Figure 5.4 A plot of ln D versus ln I gives a straight line.

Propagation of errors

Suppose that in an experiment quantities a, b, c, etc., are measured, each with an error Δa, Δb, Δc, etc. That is $a = a_0 \pm \Delta a$, $b = b_0 \pm \Delta b$, $c = c_0 \pm \Delta c$, etc., where the subscript zero indicates the mean value of the quantity. Thus, if a mass is measured to be 4.5 kg ± 0.1 kg, $m_0 = 4.5$ kg, and $\Delta m = 0.1$ kg.

▶ If $a = a_0 \pm \Delta a$, the quantity Δa is called the *absolute uncertainty* or error in the measurement of the quantity a and the ratio $\frac{\Delta a}{a_0}$ is the *fractional* or *relative uncertainty* or error. The quantity $\frac{\Delta a}{a_0} \times 100\%$ gives the percentage error in the quantity a.

Thus, in the measurement of mass, the absolute error is 0.1 kg and the fractional or relative error is $0.1/4.5 = 0.02$ or 2%.

If we wish to calculate a quantity Q in terms of a, b, c, etc., an error in Q will arise as a result of the individual errors in a, b and c. That is, the errors in a, b and c propagate to Q. How do we find the error in Q given the errors in a, b, c, etc.?

There are two cases to consider and we will give the results without proof.

Addition and subtraction

The first case involves the operations of addition and/or subtraction. For example, we might have $Q = a + b$ or $Q = a - b$ or $Q = a + b - c$. Then, in all cases the absolute uncertainty in Q is the *sum* of the *absolute* uncertainties in a, b and c.

$$Q = a + b \quad \Rightarrow \quad \Delta Q = \Delta a + \Delta b$$
$$Q = a - b \quad \Rightarrow \quad \Delta Q = \Delta a + \Delta b$$
$$Q = a + b - c \quad \Rightarrow \quad \Delta Q = \Delta a + \Delta b + \Delta c$$

Example question

Q1

The side a of a square is measured to be 12.4 cm ± 0.1 cm. Find the error in a calculation of the perimeter S of the square.

Answer

Here we have addition and so the error in S is

$$\Delta S = \Delta a + \Delta a + \Delta a + \Delta a$$
$$= 4\Delta a$$
$$= 0.4 \text{ cm}$$

Thus

$S = 49.6$ cm ± 0.4 cm

Considerable errors result if the small difference of two large numbers is taken. If $Q = a - b$, and $a = 538.7 \pm 0.4$ and $b = 537.3 \pm 0.4$, then $Q = 1.4 \pm 0.8$. The fractional error in this case is 0.57 or 57%. The error in the quantities a and b is small compared with the mean values of a and b but huge compared with the difference.

Multiplication, division, powers and roots

Suppose now that the quantity to be calculated involves a multiplication such as in $Q = ab$, a division as in $Q = \frac{a}{b}$ or $Q = \frac{ab}{c}$, or a power $Q = a^n$, or a root $Q = \sqrt[n]{a}$. In all these cases the fractional uncertainty in Q is the *sum* of the *fractional* uncertainties of a, b and c.

$$Q = ab \quad \Rightarrow \quad \frac{\Delta Q}{Q_0} = \frac{\Delta a}{a_0} + \frac{\Delta b}{b_0}$$

$$Q = \frac{a}{b} \quad \Rightarrow \quad \frac{\Delta Q}{Q_0} = \frac{\Delta a}{a_0} + \frac{\Delta b}{b_0}$$

$$Q = \frac{ab}{c} \quad \Rightarrow \quad \frac{\Delta Q}{Q_0} = \frac{\Delta a}{a_0} + \frac{\Delta b}{b_0} + \frac{\Delta c}{c_0}$$

$$Q = a^n \quad \Rightarrow \quad \frac{\Delta Q}{Q_0} = |n|\frac{\Delta a}{a_0}$$

$$Q = \sqrt[n]{a} \quad \Rightarrow \quad \frac{\Delta Q}{Q_0} = \frac{1}{n}\frac{\Delta a}{a_0}$$

Example questions

Q2

The sides of a rectangle are measured to be $a = 2.5$ cm ± 0.1 cm and $b = 5.0$ cm ± 0.1 cm. Find the area A of the rectangle.

Answer

The fractional uncertainty in a is

$$\frac{\Delta a}{a} = \frac{0.1}{2.5}$$
$$= 0.04$$

or 4%

That in b is

$$\frac{\Delta b}{b} = \frac{0.1}{5.0}$$
$$= 0.02$$

or 2%

Thus, the fractional uncertainty in the area is

$0.04 + 0.02 = 0.06$ or 6%

Since

$$A_0 = 2.5 \times 5.0$$
$$= 12.5 \text{ cm}^2$$

and

$$\frac{\Delta A}{A_0} = 0.06$$
$$\Rightarrow \Delta A = 0.06 \times 12.5$$
$$= 0.75 \text{ cm}^2$$

Hence

$A = 12.5 \text{ cm}^2 \pm 0.8 \text{ cm}^2$

Q3

A mass is measured to be $m = 4.4 \pm 0.2$ kg and its speed $18 \pm 2 \text{ m s}^{-1}$. Find the kinetic energy of the mass.

Answer

The kinetic energy is $E_k = \frac{1}{2}mv^2$ (i.e. $E_{k0} = 713$ J) and from

$$\frac{\Delta E_k}{E_{k0}} = \frac{\Delta m}{m_0} + 2\frac{\Delta v}{v_0}$$

it follows that $\Delta E_k = 191$ J; that is $E_k = 713 \pm 191$ J or just $E_k = 700 \pm 200$ J.

Q4

The length of a simple pendulum is increased by 4%. What is the fractional increase in the pendulum's period?

Answer

The period is related to the length through $T = 2\pi\sqrt{\frac{L}{g}}$. Thus $\frac{\Delta T}{T_0} = \frac{1}{2}\frac{\Delta L}{L_0}$ and since $\frac{\Delta L}{L_0} = 4\%$ we have $\frac{\Delta T}{T_0} = \frac{1}{2} \times 4\% = 2\%$.

Q5

A body radiates according to the black-body law $P = cT^4$, where T is the temperature and c is a constant. If the temperature of the body is increased by 3%, how does the radiated power change?

Answer

$$\frac{\Delta P}{P} = 4\frac{\Delta T}{T} = 4 \times 3\% = 12\%.$$

Other functions

Suppose, finally, that the calculated quantity Q depends on a variable a through a sine, $Q = \sin a$. If a is measured to be $58° \pm 2°$ what is the error in Q? Using calculus (and being very careful to change from degrees to radians before we differentiate) we can show that, approximately,

$$\begin{aligned}\Delta Q &= \cos a \,\Delta a \\ &= \cos 58° \times 2° \times \frac{\pi}{180°} \\ &= 0.0185 \\ &\approx 0.02\end{aligned}$$

It is easier in practice, however, to find the largest and smallest values of Q through

$$\begin{aligned}Q_{max} &= \sin(58° + 2°) \\ &= 0.8660 \\ Q_{min} &= \sin(58° - 2°) \\ &= 0.8290\end{aligned}$$

so we can deduce that the error is half of the difference

$$\begin{aligned}\Delta Q &= \tfrac{1}{2}(0.8660 - 0.8290) \\ &= 0.0175 \\ &\approx 0.02\end{aligned}$$

The mean value of Q is

$$\begin{aligned}Q_{mean} &= \sin 58° \\ &= 0.8480 \\ &\approx 0.85\end{aligned}$$

and so

$$Q = 0.85 \pm 0.02$$

This method can be applied to any other functional form relating Q to a.

Uncertainties in the slope and intercept

Having decided the line of best fit for a given set of data that are expected to fall on a straight line, it is usually necessary to calculate the slope and intercept of that straight line. However, since the data points are the result of measurements in an experiment, they are subject to experimental uncertainties. Thus, let us return to the example of Chapter 1.2. In an experiment to verify Hooke's law, data for the tension and extension of a spring are collected and plotted as shown in Figure 5.5. The experimenter has included vertical uncertainty bars representing an uncertainty of ±10 N in the values of the tension in Figure 5.5 (the length of the vertical bar is thus 20 N).

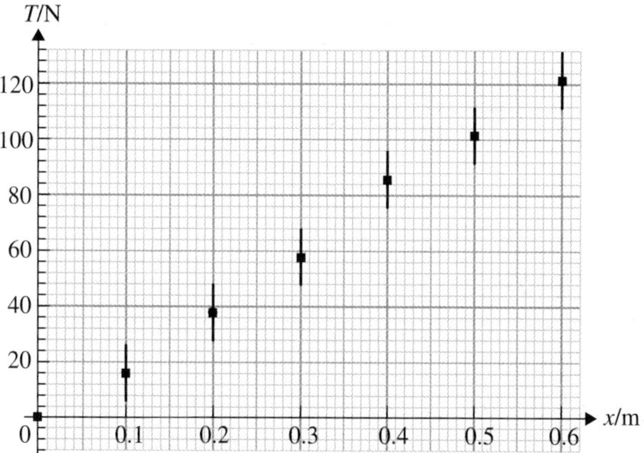

Figure 5.5 Data points plotted together with uncertainties in the values for the tension.

The experimenter then draws the line of best fit through the data points and obtains a straight line, as shown in Figure 5.6. The slope of this line is 200 N m^{-1} and this represents the spring constant. What is the uncertainty in the slope and intercept?

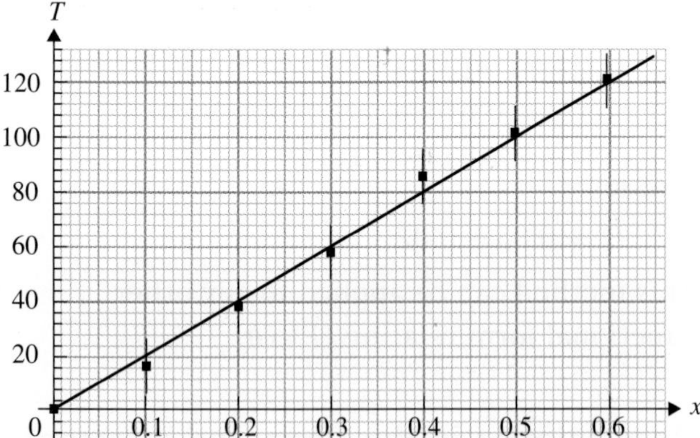

Figure 5.6 The line of best fit through the data points.

A simple way to estimate these uncertainties is by drawing two extreme straight lines as in Figure 5.7 and finding the slope of each. Both straight lines are made to pass through a point that is halfway in the range of the x values: in this case the point with $x = 0.3$ m. The first line is then drawn so as to have the largest slope and still fit the data (this means it will pass at the extremes of the vertical error bars). The second line is made to have the least slope and still fit the data. The two slopes are then measured.

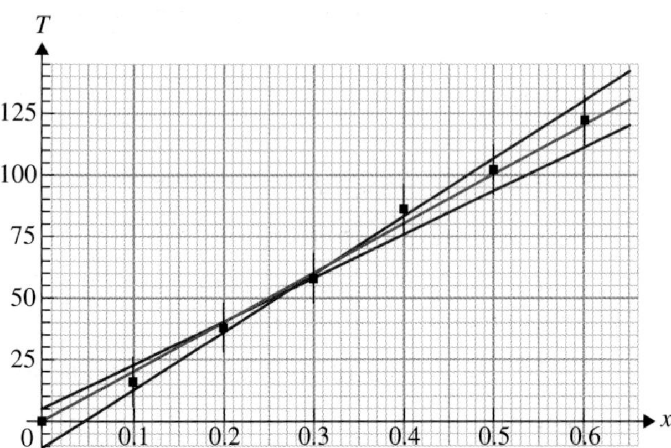

Figure 5.7 The uncertainty in the slope can be estimated by drawing two extreme additional graphs through the centre point.

Measurement of the two slopes gives 235 N m^{-1} and 177 N m^{-1}; that is, errors of +35 N m^{-1} and −23 N m^{-1}. Taking the *average* of these two errors gives 29 N m^{-1}, so we may state that the spring constant is 200 ± 30 N m^{-1}. The same procedure allows an estimate of the vertical intercept. The line of best fit gives an intercept of zero. The line with the largest slope has an intercept of −11 N and the line of least slope has an intercept of +5 N. The *average* of the *absolute* values of these errors is $(11 + 5)/2 = 8$ and so the intercept is calculated to be 0 ± 8 N.

? QUESTIONS

1 A circle and a square have the same perimeter. Which shape has the largest area?

2 A sphere and a cube have the same surface area. Which shape has the largest volume?

3 What is the approximate value of $1 - \cos x$ when x is small?

4 The natural logarithm of the voltage across a capacitor of capacitance $C = 5\ \mu\text{F}$ as a function of time is shown in Figure 5.8. The voltage is given by the equation $V = V_0 e^{-t/RC}$, where R is the resistance of the circuit. Find
(a) the initial voltage;
(b) the time for the voltage to be reduced to half its initial value;
(c) the resistance of the circuit.

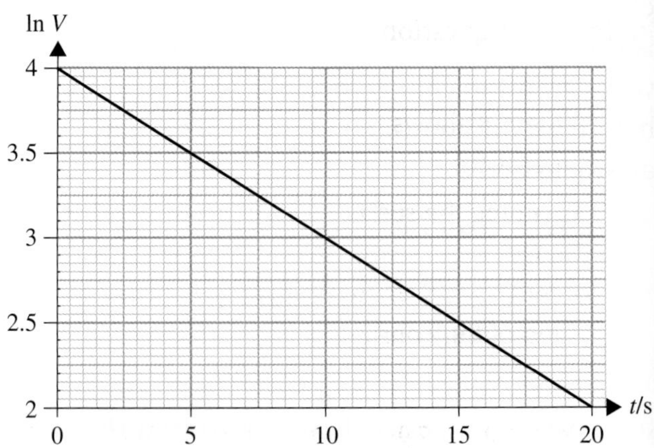

Figure 5.8 For question 4.

5 Figure 5.9 shows how the velocity of a steel ball depends on time as it falls through a viscous medium. Find the equation that gives the velocity as a function of time.

6 Table 5.3 shows the mass M of several stars and their corresponding luminosity L (power emitted). By plotting the luminosity versus the mass on logarithmic paper, find the

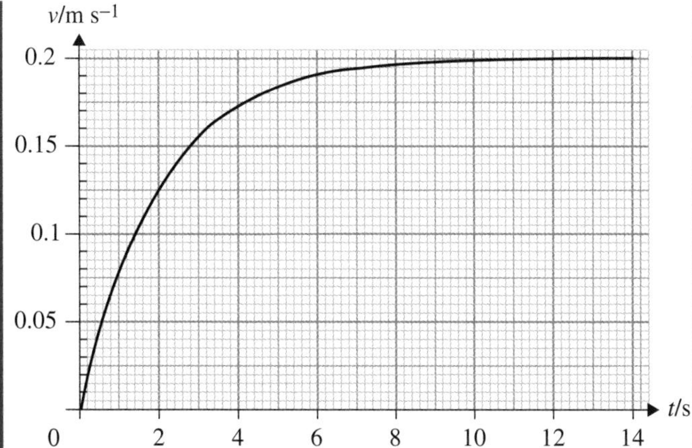

Figure 5.9 For question 5.

relationship between these quantities, assuming a power law of the kind $L = kM^{\alpha}$, giving the numerical value of the parameter α.

Mass M (in solar masses)	Luminosity L (in terms of the sun's luminosity)
1	1
3	42
5	238
12	4700
20	26500

Table 5.3 For question 6.

7 Table 5.4 shows the data collected in an experiment.

Assuming the suspected relationship between the variables is $y = cx^{2.5}$, plot the data in order to get a straight line and then find the value of the constant c.

x	1.0	2.0	3.0	4.0	5.0	6.0
y	2.0	11.3	31.2	64.0	111.8	176.4

Table 5.4 For question 7.

8 The variable y depends on x through $y = ke^{x^2}$. How should these two variables be plotted in order to get a straight-line graph?

9 Two forces are measured to be 120 ± 5 N and 60 ± 3 N. Find the sum and difference of the two forces, giving the uncertainty in each case.

10 The quantity Q depends on the measured values a and b in the following ways:

(a) $Q = a/b$, $a = 20 \pm 1$, $b = 10 \pm 1$;

(b) $Q = 2a + 3b$, $a = 20 \pm 2$, $b = 15 \pm 3$;

(c) $Q = a - 2b$, $a = 50 \pm 1$, $b = 24 \pm 0.5$;

(d) $Q = a^2$, $a = 10.0 \pm 0.3$;

(e) $Q = a^2/b^2$, $a = 100 \pm 5$, $b = 20 \pm 2$.

In each case find the value of Q and its uncertainty.

11 The centripetal force is given by $F = \frac{mv^2}{r}$. If the mass is measured to be 2.8 ± 0.1 kg, the velocity 14 ± 2 m s^{-1} and the radius 8.0 ± 0.2 m, find the force on the mass, including the uncertainty.

12 The mass of a rectangular block is measured to be 2.2 kg with an uncertainty of 0.2 kg. The sides are measured as 60 ± 3 mm, 50 ± 1 mm and 40 ± 2 mm. Find the density of the cube in kilograms per cubic metre, giving the uncertainty in the result.

13 The radius r of a circle is measured to be 2.4 cm $\pm$ 0.1 cm.

(a) What is the error in the area of the circle?

(b) What is the error in the circumference?

14 The radius r of a sphere is measured to be 22.7 cm $\pm$ 0.2 cm.

(a) What is the error in the surface area of the sphere?

(b) What is the error in the volume?

15 The sides of a rectangle are measured as 4.4 ± 0.2 cm and 8.5 ± 0.3 cm. Find the area and perimeter of the rectangle.

16 The period of a simple pendulum depends on length through $T = 2\pi\sqrt{\frac{L}{g}}$. If the length is increased by a factor of 2, by what factor does the period change?

17 In the previous question, if the length of the pendulum is increased by 2%, what is the fractional increase in the period?

18 If the length of a pendulum is measured with a fractional uncertainty of 0.5% and the period with a fractional uncertainty of 0.6%, what is the fractional uncertainty in the measured value of the acceleration due to gravity?

Kinematic concepts

Motion is a fundamental part of physics and this chapter introduces the basic quantities used in the description of motion. Even the simplest of motions, such as a leaf falling from a tree, can be a fairly complicated thing to analyse. To learn how to do that requires that we sharpen our definitions of everyday concepts such as speed, distance and time. As we will see, once we master motion in a straight line, more complicated types of motion such as circular and parabolic motion will follow easily.

Objectives

By the end of this chapter you should be able to:

- describe the difference between *distance* and *displacement*;
- state the definitions of *velocity, average velocity, speed* and *average speed*;
- solve problems of *motion in a straight line with constant velocity*, $x = x_0 + vt$;
- appreciate that different observers belonging to different *frames of reference* can give differing but equally valid descriptions of motion;
- use graphs in describing motion;
- understand that the slope of a displacement–time graph is the velocity and that the area under a velocity–time graph is the change in displacement.

Displacement and velocity

Consider the motion of a point particle that is constrained to move in a straight line, such as the one in Figure 1.1. Our first task is to choose a point on this line from which to measure distances. This point can be chosen arbitrarily and we denote it by O.

When we say that the distance of a point P from O is 3 m, we mean that the point in question could be 3 m to the left or right of O. To distinguish the two points we introduce the concept of *displacement*. The displacement of a point from O will be a quantity whose numerical value will be the distance and its sign will tell us if the point is to the right or left of O. Thus a displacement of −4 m means the point is at a distance of 4 m to the left of O, whereas a displacement of 5 m means a distance of 5 m to the right of O. Displacement is a vector; for the case of motion in a straight line, the displacement vector is very simple. It can be determined just by giving its magnitude and its sign. We will use the convention that positive displacements correspond to the right of O, negative to the left. (This is entirely arbitrary and we may choose any side of the origin as the positive displacement; this takes care of cases where it is not obvious what

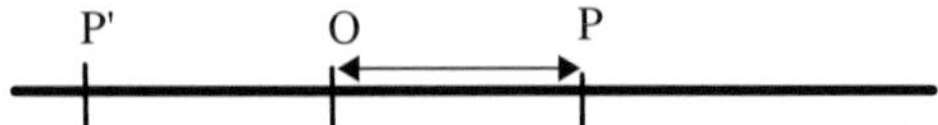

Figure 1.1 To measure distance we need an origin to measure distances from.

'right' means.) We will use the symbol x for displacement in a straight line (we reserve the symbol $\vec{r}$ for displacements in more than one dimension) and s for distance (from the Latin *spatium*). Displacement, being a vector, is represented graphically by an arrow that begins at O and ends at the point of interest. (See Figure 1.2.)

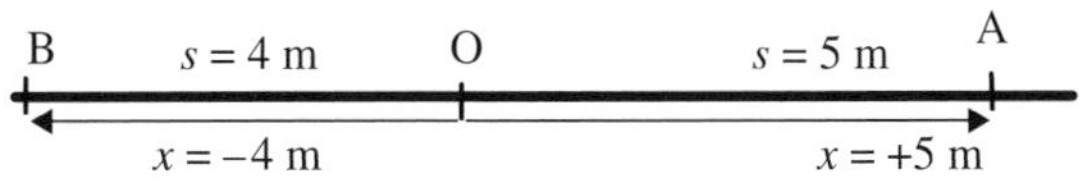

B $s = 4$ m O $s = 5$ m A

$x = -4$ m $x = +5$ m

Figure 1.2 Displacement can be positive (point A) or negative (point B).

We will use the capital letter S to stand for the total distance travelled, and Δx for the change in displacement. The change in displacement is defined by

$$\Delta x = \text{final displacement} - \text{initial displacement}$$

If the motion consists of many parts, then the change in displacement is the sum of the displacements in each part of the motion. Thus, if an object starts at the origin, say, and changes its displacement first by 12 m, then by −4 m and then by 3 m, the change in displacement is $12 - 4 + 3 = 11$ m. The final displacement is thus $11 + 0 = 11$ m.

Example questions

Q1

A mass initially at O moves 10 m to the right and then 2 m to the left. What is the final displacement of the mass?

Answer

$\Delta x = +10 \text{ m} - 2 \text{ m} = 8$ m. Hence the final displacement is $0 \text{ m} + 8 \text{ m} = 8$ m.

Q2

A mass initially at O, first moves 5 m to the right and then 12 m to the left. What is the total distance covered by the mass and what is its change in displacement?

Answer

The total distance is $5 \text{ m} + 12 \text{ m} = 17$ m. The change in displacement is $+5 \text{ m} - 12 \text{ m} = -7$ m. The mass now finds itself at a distance of 7 m to the left of the starting point.

Q3

An object has a displacement of −5 m. It moves a distance to the right equal to 15 m and then a distance of 10 m to the left. What is the total distance travelled and final displacement of the object? What is the change in displacement of the object?

Answer

The distance travelled is $15 \text{ m} + 10 \text{ m} = 25$ m. The object now finds itself at a distance of 0 m from O and thus its displacement is zero. The original displacement was $x = -5$ m and thus the change in displacement is $\Delta x = 0 \text{ m} - (-5 \text{ m}) = +5$ m.

Speed

If an object covers a total distance S in a total time T, the average speed of the object is defined by

$$\bar{v} = \frac{S}{T}$$

Suppose that you drive your car for a given amount of time, say 50 minutes. The odometer of the car shows that in those 50 minutes a distance of 30 km was covered. The average speed for this motion is

$$\bar{v} = \frac{30\,\text{km}}{50\,\text{min}} = 0.60\,\frac{\text{km}}{\text{min}}$$
$$= 0.60\,\frac{1000\,\text{m}}{60\,\text{s}} = 10\,\text{m}\,\text{s}^{-1}$$

Using the concept of the average speed is only a crude way of describing motion. In the example above, the car could, at various times, have gone faster or slower than the average speed of 10 m s^{-1}. Cars are equipped with an instrument called a speedometer, which shows the speed of the car at a particular instant in time. We call the speedometer reading the instantaneous speed or just speed. Speed is defined by measuring the distance the car (or whatever it is that is moving) covers in a very short interval of time (see Figure 1.3). If this distance is δs and the time interval δt then the *instantaneous speed* is

$$v = \frac{\delta s}{\delta t}$$

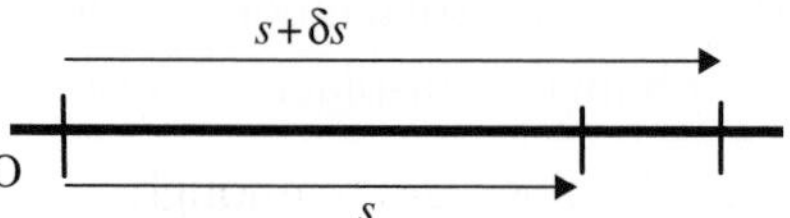

Figure 1.3 Speed at a given time t is defined in terms of the small distance δs travelled in a small interval of time δt right after t.

Note that, by definition, speed is always a positive number.

A word on notation

If Q is any physical quantity, we will use ΔQ to denote the change in Q:

$$\Delta Q = Q_{\text{final}} - Q_{\text{initial}}$$

The symbol Δ will thus represent a *finite* change in a quantity. The symbol δQ represents an *infinitesimal* change in Q. Thus, δQ plays roughly the same role as the calculus quantity $\mathrm{d}Q$. So the definition of instantaneous speed $\frac{\delta s}{\delta t}$ is to be understood as the *calculus quantity* $\frac{\mathrm{d}s}{\mathrm{d}t}$: that is, the derivative of distance with respect to time. Equivalently, we may understand it as

$$\frac{\delta s}{\delta t} = \lim_{\Delta t \to 0} \frac{\Delta s}{\Delta t}$$

If a quantity Q depends on, say, time in a linear way, then the graph showing the variation of Q with t will be a straight line. In that case (and only in that case)

$$\frac{\delta Q}{\delta t} = \frac{\Delta Q}{\Delta t}$$

and each of these quantities represent the (constant) gradient of the graph.

In order to avoid a proliferation of deltas, we will mostly use the capital delta; when infinitesimal quantities are involved, we will simply state it explicitly.

Example question

Q4

A car of length 4.2 m travelling in a straight line takes 0.56 s to go past a mark on the road. What is the speed of the car?

Answer

From $v = \frac{\Delta s}{\Delta t}$, we find $v = 7.5\ \text{m s}^{-1}$. This is taken as the speed of the car the instant the middle point of the car goes past the mark on the road.

Velocity

Average speed and instantaneous speed are positive quantities that do not take into account the direction in which the object moves. To do that we introduce the concept of velocity. The average velocity for a motion is defined as the change in displacement of the object divided by the total time taken. (Recall that the change in displacement, Δx, means final minus initial displacement.)

$$\bar{v} = \frac{\Delta x}{\Delta t}$$

Similarly, the **instantaneous velocity** at some time t, or just velocity, is defined by the ratio of the change in displacement, δx, divided by the time taken, δt.

$$v = \frac{\delta x}{\delta t}$$

(See Figure 1.4.)

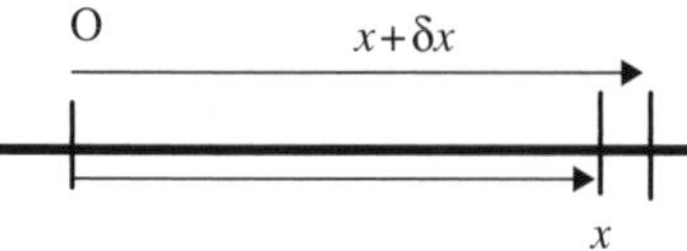

Figure 1.4 The definition of velocity at time t involves the small displacement change δx in the small time interval δt right after t.

We are using the same symbol for speed and velocity. It will always be clear which of the two we are talking about.

Unlike speed, which is always a positive number, velocity can be positive or negative. Positive velocity means the object is *increasing its displacement* – that is, it moves toward the 'right' by our convention. Negative velocity signifies motion in which the displacement is *decreasing* – that is, toward the 'left'. Thus, it is important to realize that the quantity δx can be positive or negative. (It is worthwhile to note that the magnitude of velocity is speed but the magnitude of average velocity is not related to average speed.)

Example questions

Q5

A car starts out from O in a straight line and moves a distance of 20 km towards the right, and then returns to its starting position 1 h later. What is the average speed and the average velocity for this trip?

Answer

The total distance covered is 40 km. Thus, the average speed is 40 km h^{-1}. The change in displacement for this trip is 0 m because

$$\begin{aligned}\text{displacement} &= \text{final} - \text{initial}\\ &= 0\text{ m} - 0\text{ m}\\ &= 0\text{ m}\end{aligned}$$

So the average velocity is zero.

Q6

A car moves in exactly the same way as in example question 5, but this time it starts out not at O but a point 100 km to the right of O. What is the average speed and the average velocity for this trip?

Answer

The distance travelled is still 40 km and hence the average speed is the same, 40 km h^{-1}. The change in displacement is given by

$$\begin{aligned}\text{displacement} &= \text{final} - \text{initial}\\ &= 100\text{ km} - 100\text{ km}\\ &= 0\text{ km}\end{aligned}$$

Hence the average velocity is zero as before. This example shows that the starting point is irrelevant. We have the freedom to choose the origin so that it is always at the point where the motion starts.

Q7

A car 4.0 m long is moving to the left. It is observed that it takes 0.10 s for the car to pass a given point on the road. What is the speed and velocity of the car at this instant of time?

Answer

We can safely take 0.10 s as a small enough interval of time. We are told that in this interval of time the distance travelled is 4.0 m and so the speed is 40 m s^{-1}. The velocity is simply -40 m s^{-1}, since the car is moving to the left.

Motion with uniform velocity (or just *uniform motion*) means motion in which the velocity is constant. This implies that the displacement changes by equal amounts in equal intervals of time (no matter how small or large). Let us take the interval of time from $t = 0$ to time t.

▶ If the displacement at $t = 0$ is x_0 and the displacement at time t is x, then it follows that

$$\begin{aligned}v &= \frac{\Delta x}{\Delta t}\\ &= \frac{x - x_0}{t - 0}\\ &\Rightarrow x = x_0 + vt\end{aligned}$$

This formula gives the displacement x at time t in terms of the constant velocity v and the initial displacement x_0. Note that t in this formula stands for the time for which the object has been moving.

Example questions

Q8

The initial displacement of a body moving with a constant velocity 5 m s^{-1} is -10 m. When does the body reach the point with displacement 10 m? What distance does the body cover in this time?

Answer

From

$x = x_0 + vt$
$\Rightarrow 10 = -10 + 5t$
$\Rightarrow t = 4\ \text{s}$

So the distance travelled is 20 m.

Q9

Bicyclist A starts with initial displacement zero and moves with velocity 3 m s^{-1}. At the same time, bicyclist B starts from a point with displacement 200 m and moves with velocity -2 m s^{-1}. When does A meet B and where are they when this happens?

Answer

The formula giving the displacement of A is

$x_A = 0 + 3t$

and that for B is

$x_B = 200 + (-2)t$
$= 200 - 2t$

When they meet they have the same displacement, so

$x_A = x_B$
$\Rightarrow 3t = 200 - 2t$
$\Rightarrow 5t = 200$
$\Rightarrow t = 40\ \text{s}$

Their common displacement is then 120 m.

Q10

Object A starts from the origin with velocity 3 m s^{-1} and object B starts from the same place with velocity 5 m s^{-1}, 6 seconds later. When will B catch up with A?

Answer

We take object A to start its motion when the clock shows zero. The displacement of A is then given by

$x_A = 3t$

and that of B by

$x_B = 5(t - 6)$

The formula for B is understood as follows. When the clock shows that t seconds have gone by, object B has only been moving for $(t - 6)$ seconds. When B catches up with A, they will have the same displacement and so

$3t = 5(t - 6)$
$\Rightarrow 2t = 30$
$\Rightarrow t = 15\ \text{s}$

The displacement then is 45 m.

Frames of reference

We are used to measuring velocities with respect to observers who are 'at rest'. Thus, velocities of cars, aeroplanes, clouds and falling leaves are all measured by observers who are at rest on the surface of the earth. However, other observers are also entitled to observe and record a given motion and they may reach different results from the observer fixed on the surface of the earth. These other observers, who may themselves be moving with respect to the fixed observer on earth, are just as entitled to claim that they are 'at rest'. There is in fact no absolute meaning to the statement 'being at rest' – a fact that is the starting point of Einstein's theory of special relativity. No experiment can be performed the result of which will be to let observers know that they are moving with constant velocity and that they are not at rest. Consider two observers: observer A is fixed on the earth; observer B moves past A in a box without windows. B cannot, by performing experiments within his box (he cannot look outside) determine that he is moving, let alone determine his velocity with respect to A.

An observer who uses measuring tapes and stopwatches to observe and record motion is called a *frame of reference*. Consider the following three frames of reference: the first consists of observer A on the ground; the second consists of observer B, who is a passenger in a train sitting in her seat; the third consists of observer C, a passenger on the train who walks in the direction of the motion of the train at 2 m s^{-1}, as measured by the passenger sitting in her seat. The train moves in a straight line with constant velocity of 10 m s^{-1}, as measured by the observer on the ground. The three observers describe their situation as follows: A says he is at rest, that B moves forward at 10 m s^{-1} and that C moves forward at 12 m s^{-1}. This is because in 1 s the train moves forward a distance of 10 m but, in this same second, C has walked an additional distance of 2 m making him 12 m away from A. Thus A measures a velocity of 12 m s^{-1} for C. Observer B says that she is at rest. As far as B is concerned, A is moving backwards (the station is being left behind) with a velocity of −10 m s^{-1}, and C is moving forward at a velocity of 2 m s^{-1}. Observer C claims he is at rest. As far as he is concerned, A is moving backwards at −12 m s^{-1} and B at −2 m s^{-1}.

Example question

Q11

A cart moves in a straight line with constant speed. A toy cannon on the cart is pointed vertically up and fires a ball. Ignoring air resistance, where will the ball land?

Answer

The ball will land back into the cannon. For an observer moving along with the cannon, this is obvious. This observer considers herself to be at rest; so the ball will move vertically up and then fall vertically down into the cannon. As far as an observer on the ground is concerned, the cart moves forward with a certain velocity but so does the ball. The horizontal component of velocity of the cannon is the same as that of the ball, which means that the ball is at all times vertically over the cannon.

This introduces the concept of relative velocity. Let two observers P and Q have velocities $\vec{v}_P$ and $\vec{v}_Q$ as measured by the *same* frame of reference. Then the relative velocity of P with respect to Q, denoted by $\vec{v}_{PQ}$, is simply $\vec{v}_{PQ} = \vec{v}_P - \vec{v}_Q$.

(Note that we are subtracting vectors here.) This definition makes use of the fact that by subtracting the vector velocity $\vec{v}_Q$ it is as if we make Q be at rest, so that we can refer to the velocity of P. In the example of the cannon above, the relative velocity in the horizontal direction between the cannon and the ball is zero. This is why it falls back into the cannon.

Example questions

Q12

A car (A) moves to the left with speed 40 km h^{-1} (with respect to the road). Another car (B) moves to the right with speed 60 km h^{-1} (also with respect to the road). Find the relative velocity of B with respect to A.

Answer

The relative velocity of B with respect to A is given by the difference

60 km h^{-1} − (−40 km h^{-1}) = 100 km h^{-1}.

Note that we must put in the negative sign for the velocity of A.

Q13

Rain comes vertically down and the water has a velocity vector given in Figure 1.5a (as measured by an observer fixed on the surface of the earth). A girl runs towards the right with a velocity vector as shown. (Again as measured by the observer fixed on the earth.) Find the velocity of the rain relative to the running girl.

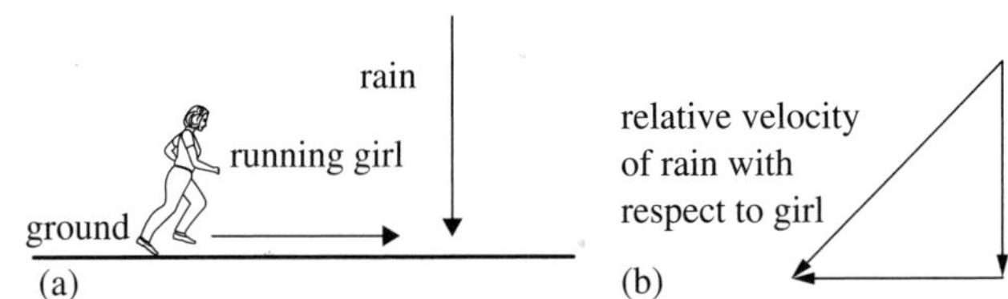

Figure 1.5.

Answer

We are asked to find the difference in the vector velocities of rain minus girl and this vector is given by Figure 1.5b. The rain thus hits the girl from the front.

Q14

This is the same as example question 9, which we did in the last section. We will do it again using the concept of relative velocity. Bicyclist A starts with initial displacement zero and moves with velocity 3 m s^{-1}. At the same time, bicyclist B starts from a point with displacement 200 m and moves with velocity −2 m s^{-1}. When does A meet B and where are they when this happens?

Answer

The velocity of B relative to A is

$$\begin{aligned} v_{BA} &= v_B - v_A \\ &= -3 - 2 \\ &= -5 \text{ m s}^{-1} \end{aligned}$$

When B meets A, the displacement of B becomes zero, since A thinks of herself sitting at the origin. Thus

$$0 = 200 - 5t$$
$$\Rightarrow t = 40\text{s}$$

Graphs for uniform motion

In uniform motion, if we make a graph of velocity versus time we must get a horizontal straight line. Figure 1.6 shows the v–t graph for motion with constant velocity v.

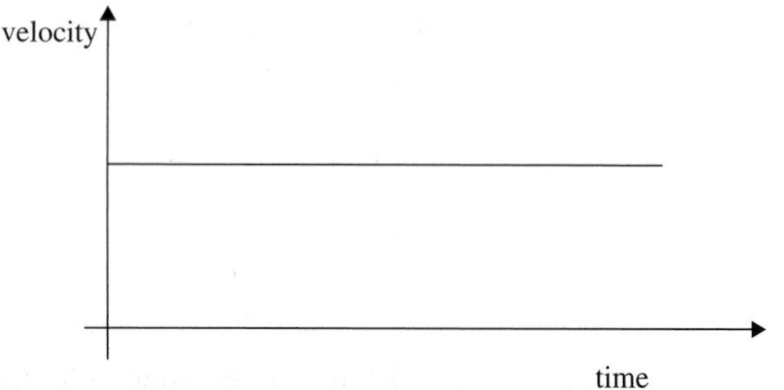

Figure 1.6 Uniform velocity means that the velocity–time graph is a horizontal straight line.

If we wanted to find the displacement from $t = 0$ to time t, the answer would be given by the formula $x = x_0 + vt$. The same answer can, however, also be obtained directly from the graph: vt is simply the area under the graph, as shown in Figure 1.7.

This means that the area under the graph gives the change in displacement. This area added to the initial displacement of the mass gives the final displacement at time t.

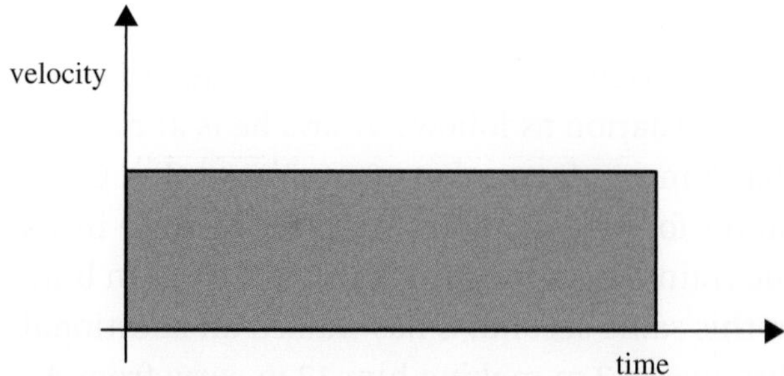

Figure 1.7 The area under the curve in a velocity–time graph gives the displacement change.

A graph of displacement versus time for *uniform motion* also gives a straight line (Figure 1.8).

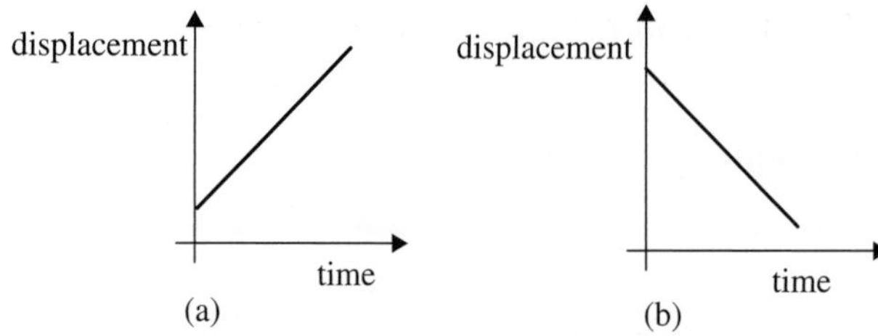

Figure 1.8 The displacement–time graph for uniform motion is a straight line: (a) motion to the right, (b) motion to the left.

This is the graph of the equation $x = x_0 + vt$. Comparing this with the standard equation of a straight line, $y = mx + c$, we see that the slope of this graph gives the velocity. We can also deduce this from the definition of velocity, $\frac{\Delta x}{\Delta t}$. But $\frac{\Delta x}{\Delta t}$ is also the definition of the slope of the straight-line x–t graph, hence the slope is the velocity. In Figure 1.8a the slope is positive, which means, therefore, that the velocity is positive, and the mass is moving to the right. In Figure 1.8b the mass is moving at constant velocity to the left.

▶ The slope of a displacement–time graph gives the velocity.

The time when the graph intersects the time axis is the time the moving object goes past point O, the point from which distances and displacements are measured.

The corresponding velocity–time graph for negative velocity is shown in Figure 1.9.

Figure 1.9 The velocity–time graph for uniform motion towards the left.

The area 'under' the curve is below the time axis and is counted as negative. This is consistent with the fact that negative velocity takes the moving object towards the left and thus towards negative displacements.

Consider now the graph of displacement versus time in Figure 1.10. We may extract the following information from it. The initial displacement is −10 m. The object moves with a positive velocity of 2 m s^{-1} for the first 10 s of the motion and with a negative velocity of 2 m s^{-1} in the next 5 s. The object is at the origin at 5 s and 15 s. The change in displacement is +10 m and the total distance travelled is 30 m. The average speed is thus 2 m s^{-1} and the average velocity is 0.67 m s^{-1}. Make sure you can verify these statements.

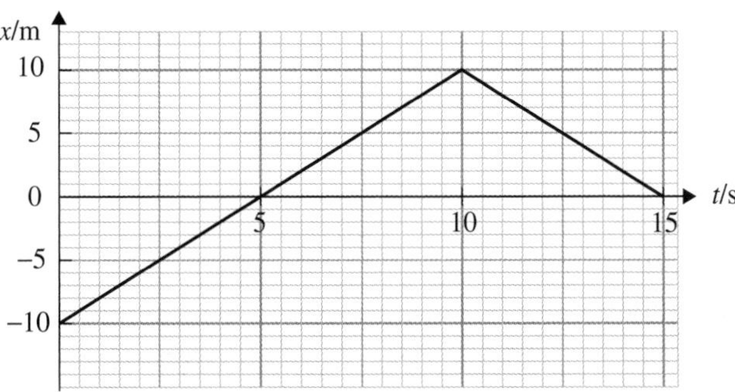

Figure 1.10.

▶ We can thus summarize our findings for uniform motion in a straight line: The graph of displacement versus time is a straight line whose slope is the velocity. The graph of velocity versus time is a horizontal straight line and the area under the graph gives the change in displacement. The displacement after time t is given by the formula $x = x_0 + vt$.

Example question

Q15

A mass starts out from O with velocity 10 m s^{-1} and continues moving at this velocity for 5 s. The velocity is then abruptly reversed to −5 m s^{-1} and the object moves at this velocity for 10 s. For this motion find:

(a) the change in displacement;
(b) the total distance travelled;
(c) the average speed;
(d) the average velocity.

Answer

The problem is best solved through the velocity–time graph, which is shown in Figure 1.11.

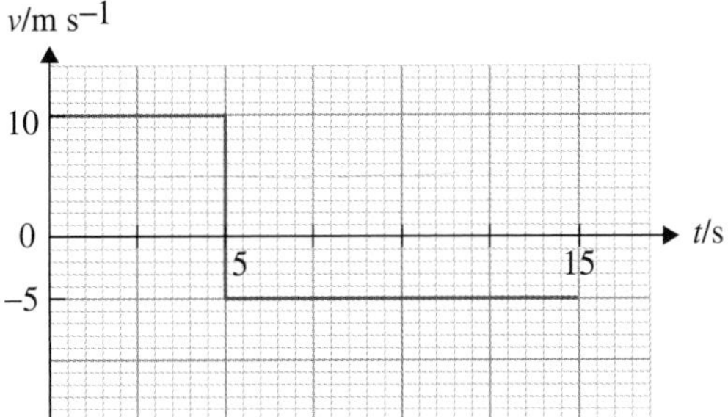

Figure 1.11.

The initial displacement is zero. Thus, after 5 s the displacement is 10 × 5 m = 50 m (area under first part of the curve). In the next 10 s the displacement changes by −5 × 10 = −50 m. The change in displacement is thus 0 m. The object moved toward the right, stopped and returned to its starting position. The distance travelled was 50 m in moving to the right and 50 m coming back giving a total of 100 m. The average velocity is zero, since the change in displacement is zero. The average speed is 100 m/15 s = 6.7 m s^{-1}.

? QUESTIONS

1 A plane flies 3000.0 km in 5.00 h. What is its average speed in metres per second?

2 A car must be driven a distance of 120.0 km in 2.5 h. During the first 1.5 h the average speed was 70 km h^{-1}. What must the average speed for the remainder of the journey be?

3 A person walks a distance of 3.0 km due south and then a distance of 2.0 km due east. If the walk lasts for 3.0 h find

(a) the average speed for the motion;
(b) the average velocity.

4 Find the displacement–time graph for an object moving in a straight line whose velocity–time graph is given in Figure 1.12. The displacement is zero initially. You do not have to put any numbers on the axes.

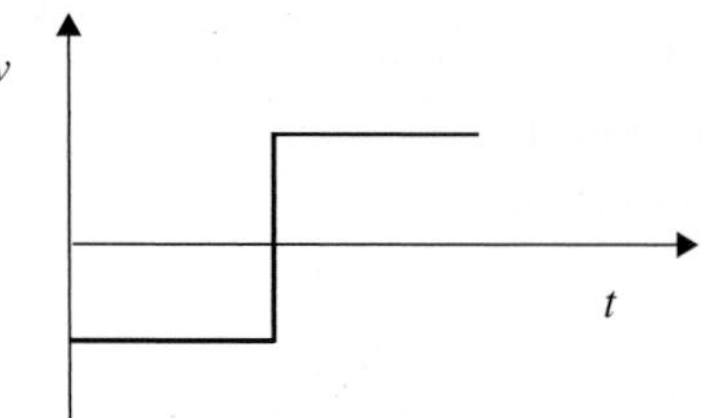

Figure 1.12 For question 4.

5 An object moving in a straight line according to the velocity–time graph shown in Figure 1.13 has an initial displacement of 8.00 m.
(a) What is the displacement after 8.00 s?
(b) What is the displacement after 12.0 s?
(c) What is the average speed and average velocity for this motion?

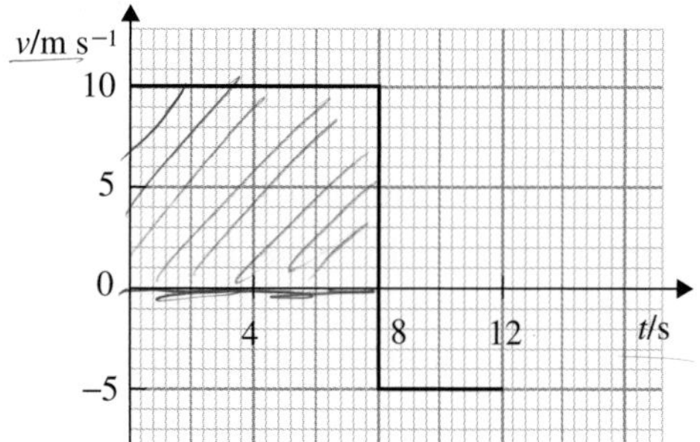

Figure 1.13 For question 5.

6 Two cyclists, A and B, have displacements 0 km and 70 km, respectively. At $t = 0$ they begin to cycle towards each other with velocities 15 km h^{-1} and 20 km h^{-1}, respectively. At the same time, a fly that was sitting on A starts flying towards B with a velocity of 30 km h^{-1}. As soon as the fly reaches B it immediately turns around and flies towards A, and so on until A and B meet.
(a) What will the displacement of the two cyclists and the fly be when all three meet?
(b) What will be the distance travelled by the fly?

HL only

7 A particle of dust is bombarded by air molecules and follows a zigzag path at constant speed v.
(a) Assuming each step has a length d, find the distance travelled by the dust particle in time t.
(b) What is the length of the displacement vector after N steps where N is large? Assume that each step is taken in a random direction on the plane. (This problem assumes you are familiar with the scalar product of two vectors.)

8 Two cars are moving on the same straight-line road. Car A moves to the right at velocity 80 km h^{-1} and car B moves at 50 km h^{-1} to the left. Both velocities are measured by an observer at rest on the road.
(a) Find the relative velocity of car B with respect to car A.
(b) Find the relative velocity of car A with respect to car B.

9 A cyclist A moves with speed 3.0 m s^{-1} to the left (with respect to the road). A second cyclist, B, moves on the same straight-line path as A with a relative velocity of 1.0 m s^{-1} with respect to A.
(a) What is the velocity of B with respect to the road?
(b) A third cyclist has a relative velocity with respect to A of -2.0 m s^{-1}. What is the velocity of C with respect to the road?

10 Two objects A and B move at a constant speed of 4 m s^{-1} along a circular path. What is the relative velocity of B (magnitude and direction) with respect to A when the objects are in the positions shown in Figure 1.14?

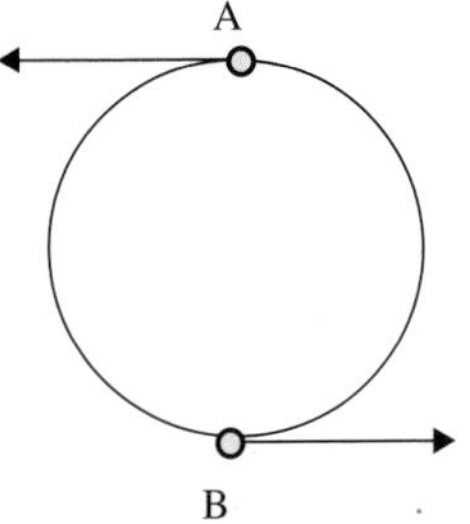

Figure 1.14 For question 10.

11 Find the velocity of the two objects whose displacement–time graphs are shown in Figure 1.15.

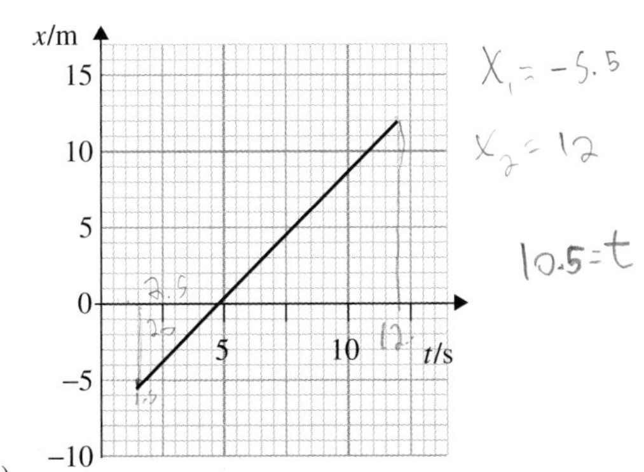

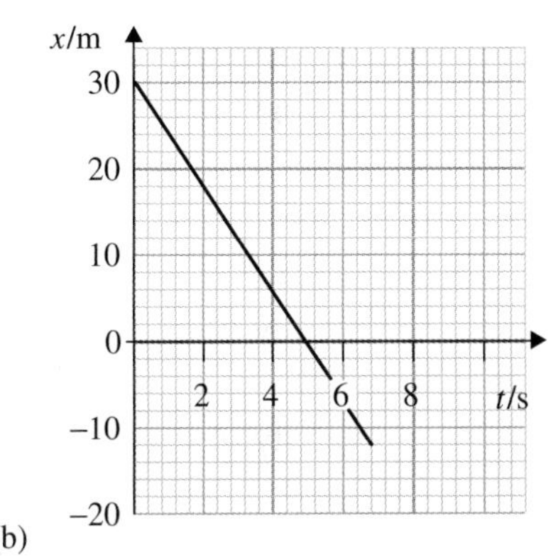

Figure 1.15 For question 11.

12 An object moving in a straight line has a displacement–time graph as shown in Figure 1.16.

(a) Find the average speed for the trip.

(b) Find the average velocity for the trip.

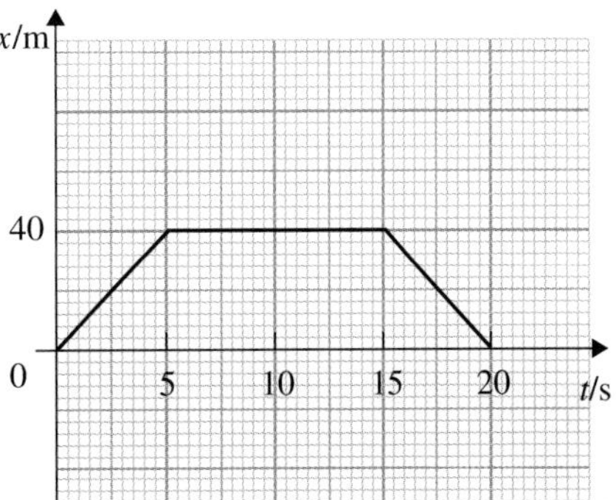

Figure 1.16 For question 12.

Motion with constant acceleration

To complete our description of motion we need the concept of acceleration. This concept and its use are introduced here.

Objectives

By the end of this chapter you should be able to:

- recognize situations of accelerated motion and to define *acceleration* as $a = \frac{\Delta v}{\Delta t}$;
- *describe a motion given a graph for that motion;*
- understand that the *slope of a displacement–time graph is the velocity;*
- understand that the *slope of a velocity–time graph is the acceleration* and the *area under a velocity–time graph is the change in displacement;*
- understand that the *area under an acceleration–time graph is the change in velocity;*
- analyse motion from *ticker tape, stroboscopic* pictures and *photogate* data;
- solve problems of kinematics for motion in a straight line with constant acceleration using

$$v = v_0 + at$$
$$x = x_0 + v_0 t + \tfrac{1}{2}at^2$$
$$x = x_0 + \left(\frac{v + v_0}{2}\right)t$$
$$v^2 = v_0^2 + 2ax$$

(It must be emphasized that these formulae *only* apply in the case of motion in a straight line with constant acceleration.)

Acceleration

To treat situations in which velocity is not constant we need to define acceleration a. If the velocity changes by Δv in a very short interval of time Δt then

$$a = \frac{\Delta v}{\Delta t}$$

is the definition of the **instantaneous acceleration**. We will mostly be interested in situations where the acceleration is constant, in which case the instantaneous acceleration and the average acceleration are the same thing. Such a motion is called *uniformly accelerated motion*. In this case the intervals Δv and Δt do not have to be infinitesimally small. Then

$$a = \frac{\Delta v}{\Delta t} = \frac{v - v_0}{t - 0}$$

where t is the total time taken for the trip, v the final velocity and v_0 the initial velocity.

▶ In this case, by rewriting the last equation we find

$$v = v_0 + at$$

This is the formula that gives the velocity at a time of t seconds after the start of the motion in terms of the (constant) acceleration a and the initial velocity.

If we put $a = 0$ in this formula, we find that $v = v_0$ at all times. The velocity does not change since there is no acceleration.

Example question

Q1

An object starting with an initial velocity of 2.0 m s^{-1} undergoes constant acceleration. After 5.0 s its velocity is found to be 12.0 m s^{-1}. What is the acceleration?

Answer

From $v = v_0 + at$ we find

$12 = 2 + a \times 5$

$\Rightarrow a = 2.0$ m s^{-2}

▶ For motion in a straight line, *positive* acceleration means that the velocity is *increasing* whereas negative acceleration implies a decreasing velocity.

In solving problems it is sometimes confusing to decide whether the acceleration is positive or negative. The only criterion is whether the acceleration increases or decreases the *velocity* (and not speed). In the top part of Figure 2.1 the velocity is increasing and so the acceleration is positive. (The direction of positive velocities is taken to be toward the right.) In the bottom part the velocity is decreasing and thus the acceleration is negative.

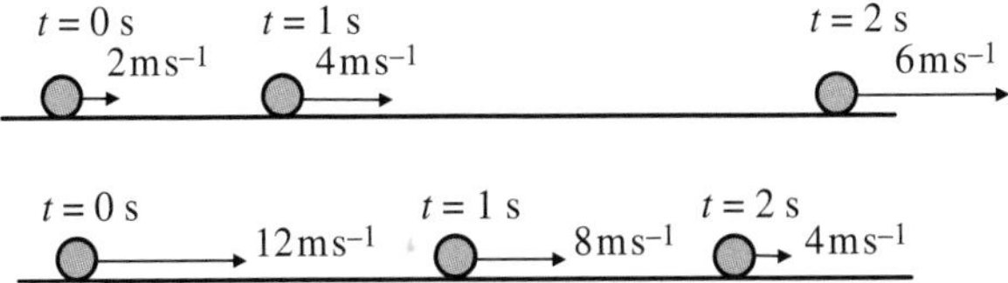

Figure 2.1 In the top part the acceleration is positive. In the bottom part the acceleration is negative.

Similarly, in the top part of Figure 2.2 the velocity is increasing (-15 m s^{-1} is larger than -20 m s^{-1}) and so the acceleration is positive. In the bottom part the velocity is decreasing (-8 m s^{-1} is less than -5 m s^{-1}) and so the acceleration is negative. In the second case note that the *speed* (i.e. the magnitude of velocity) is increasing even though the acceleration is negative.

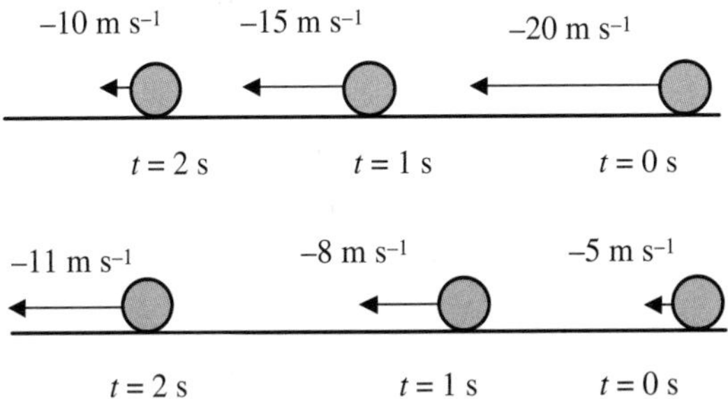

Figure 2.2 In the top diagram the acceleration is positive. In the bottom it is negative.

Acceleration due to gravity

We encounter a very special acceleration when an object is dropped or thrown. This is an acceleration that acts on all objects and has the same magnitude for all bodies independently of their mass. This assumes conditions of free fall – that is, only gravity is acting on the body. Air resistance, friction and other forces are assumed absent. Under these conditions (as will be discussed in detail in later chapters) all objects experience the same acceleration. On earth the magnitude of this acceleration is about 9.8 m s^{-2}, a number we will often approximate to 10 m s^{-2} for convenience. We always use the symbol g for the *magnitude* of the acceleration due to gravity. Consider a body falling freely under gravity. We take, as is customary, the upward direction to be the direction of positive velocities. On the way up the velocity is decreasing, hence we state that the acceleration due to gravity is negative. On the way down the velocity is still decreasing (-12.0 m s^{-1} is less than -2 m s^{-1}) and so the acceleration due to gravity is negative on the way down as well as on the way up (see Figure 2.3). (On the way down the *speed* is increasing.)

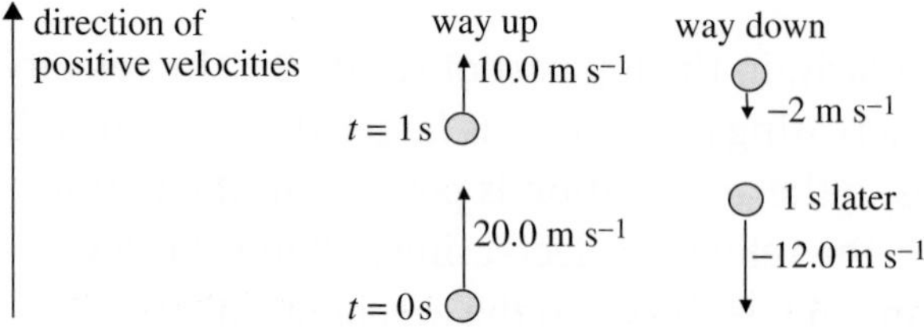

Figure 2.3 Motion in a vertical straight line under gravity. If the upward direction is the positive direction for velocity, then the acceleration due to gravity is negative for both the way up as well as the way down.

If we had decided, instead, to take the *downward* direction as the direction of positive velocities, then the acceleration due to gravity would have been positive for both the way up and the way down. Can you verify yourself that this is the case?

Example question

Q2

An object initially at $x = 12$ m has initial velocity of -8 m s^{-1} and experiences a constant acceleration of 2 m s^{-2}. Find the velocity at $t = 1$ s, 2 s, 3 s, 4 s, 5 s, 6 s and 10 s.

Answer

Applying the equation $v = v_0 + at$ we get the results shown in Table 2.1.

Time/s	1	2	3	4	5	6	10
Velocity/m s^{-1}	−6	−4	−2	0	2	4	12

Table 2.1.

This means that the body stops instantaneously at $t = 4$ s and then continues moving. We do not need to know the initial position of the body to solve this problem. Note also that the acceleration is positive and hence the velocity must be increasing. This is indeed the case as shown in Table 2.1 (e.g. -4 m s^{-1} is larger than -6 m s^{-1}). However, the speed decreases from $t = 0$ s to $t = 4$ s and increases from $t = 4$ s onwards.

In motion with constant positive acceleration the graph showing the variation of velocity with time is one of the three in Figure 2.4.

This represents a mass moving towards the right with increasing velocity. This is the graph of the equation $v = v_0 + at$.

The first graph of Figure 2.5 represents a mass that starts moving to the right (velocity is

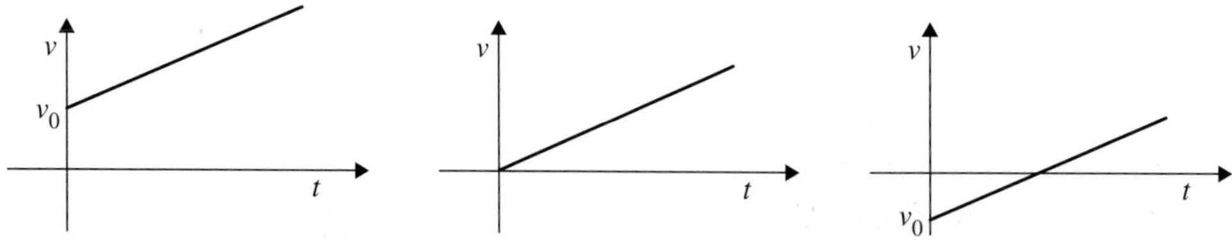

Figure 2.4 Graphs showing the variation of velocity with time when the acceleration is constant and positive. In the graphs above, the only difference is that the initial velocity v_0 is positive, zero and negative, respectively.

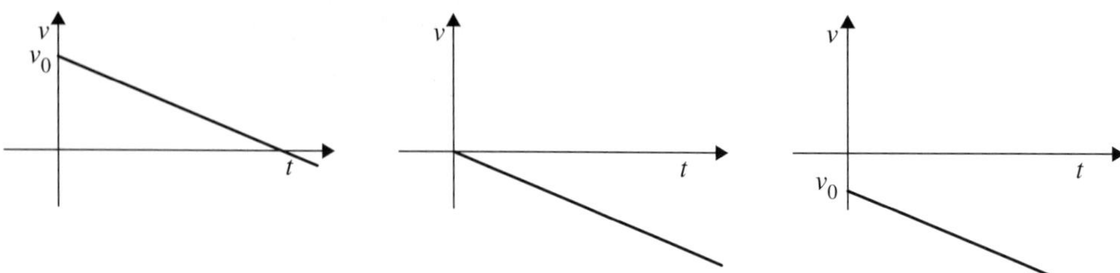

Figure 2.5 Graphs showing the variation of velocity with time when the acceleration is constant and negative. In the graphs above, the only difference is that the initial velocity v_0 is positive, zero and negative, respectively.

positive) but is decelerating (negative acceleration). At a specific time the mass stops instantaneously and begins moving again towards the left (negative velocity).

▶ The acceleration can be found from the velocity–time graph by taking the slope of the graph. We see this directly by comparing $v = v_0 + at$ and the standard equation for a straight line, $y = c + mx$.

If the acceleration is not uniform, the velocity–time graph will not be a straight line. The acceleration at a given point is found by first drawing a tangent to the curve at the point of interest. The slope of the tangent is the acceleration at that point.

In the case of uniform motion (no acceleration) the area under a velocity–time graph gave the change in displacement. We would like to know if a similar result holds in the case of accelerated motion as well.

To do this we will make use of what we learned in uniform motion together with a little trick. Consider the velocity–time graph of an accelerated motion in Figure 2.6. The trick consists of approximating this motion with another motion in four steps. We will assume that during each of the steps the velocity is constant. The velocity then changes abruptly to a new constant value in the next step. The approximation is shown in the figure. Clearly, this is a very crude approximation of the actual motion.

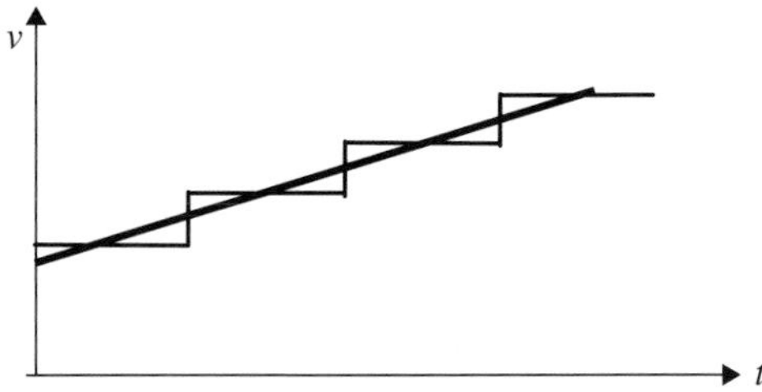

Figure 2.6 The velocity is assumed to increase abruptly and then remain constant for a period of time.

We can improve the approximation tremendously by taking more and thinner steps, as shown in Figure 2.7.

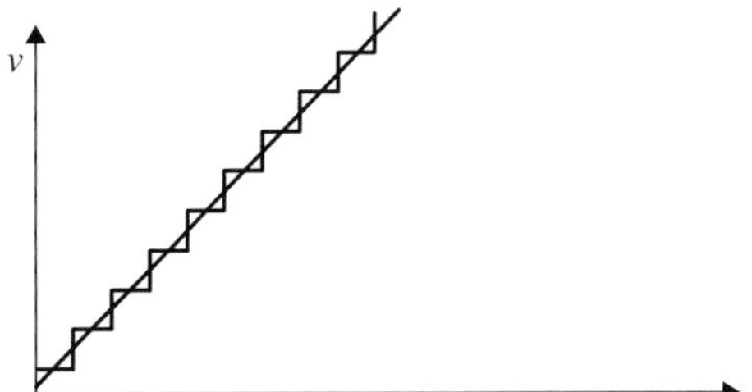

Figure 2.7 The approximation is made better by considering more steps.

Clearly, the approximation can be made as accurate as we like by choosing more and more (and thus thinner and thinner) steps.

The point of the approximation is that during each step the velocity is constant. In each step, the displacement increases by the area under the step, as we showed in the case of uniform motion. To find the total change in displacement for the entire trip we must thus add up the areas under all steps. But this gives the area under the original straight line! So we have managed to show that:

▶ Even in the case of accelerated motion, the change in displacement is the area under the velocity–time graph, just as in uniform motion. (See Figure 2.8.)

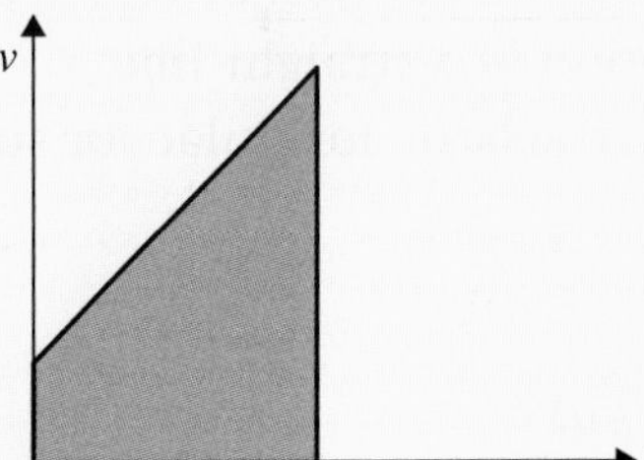

Figure 2.8 The area under the graph is the change in displacement.

Using this result we can now find a formula for the displacement after time t. We are given a velocity–time graph with constant acceleration (a straight-line graph in a v–t diagram).

We want to find the area under the line from $t = 0$ to a time of t s. Since the area we have is the shape of a trapezoid, the area is the sum of two parallel bases times height divided by two:

$$\text{area} = \left(\frac{v + v_0}{2}\right)t$$

This actually gives a useful formula for displacement for motion with constant acceleration. If x_0 is the initial displacement

$$x = x_0 \left(\frac{v + v_0}{2}\right)t$$

This is useful when we know the initial and final velocities but not the acceleration.

However, we do know that $v = v_0 + at$ and so the area (i.e. the change in displacement after time t) is

$$\text{area} = \frac{v_0 + at + v_0}{2} \times t$$
$$= v_0 t + \tfrac{1}{2}at^2$$

Thus, the displacement after time t is this area added to the initial displacement, that is

$$x = x_0 + v_0 t + \tfrac{1}{2}at^2$$

(We see that when the acceleration is zero, this formula becomes identical to the one we derived earlier for constant velocity, namely $x = x_0 + v_0 t$.) Note that this formula says that when $t = 0, x = x_0$ as it should.

In the previous section an analysis of velocity–time graphs for motion in a straight line allowed us to derive the basic formulae for such motion:

$$v = v_0 + at$$
$$x = x_0 + v_0 t + \tfrac{1}{2}at^2$$

or

$$x = \left(\frac{v + v_0}{2}\right)t$$

All of these involve time. In some cases, it is useful to have a formula that involves velocity and displacement without any reference to time. This can be done by solving the first equation for time

$$t = \frac{v - v_0}{a}$$

and using this value of time in the second equation:

$$x = x_0 + v_0 \frac{v - v_0}{a} + \frac{1}{2}a \frac{(v - v_0)^2}{a^2}$$

$$2a(x - x_0) = 2v_0 v - 2v_0^2 + v^2 + v_0^2 - 2vv_0$$

i.e.

$$v^2 = v_0^2 + 2a(x - x_0)$$

If the initial displacement is zero, then this reduces to the simpler

$$v^2 = v_0^2 + 2ax$$

Example questions

Q3

A mass has an initial velocity of 10.0 m s^{-1}. It moves with acceleration -2.00 m s^{-2}. When will it have zero velocity?

Answer

We start with

$v = v_0 + at$

$v = 0$ and so

$0 = v_0 + at$

Putting in the numbers we get

$0 = 10 + (-2.00)t$

so $t = 5.00$ s.

Q4

What is the displacement after 10.0 s of a mass whose initial velocity is 2.00 m s^{-1} and moves with acceleration $a = 4.00$ m s^{-2}?

Answer

We assume that the initial displacement is zero so that $x_0 = 0$.

$x = x_0 + v_0 t + \frac{1}{2}at^2$

so

$x = 0 + 2 \times 10 + \frac{1}{2} \times 4 \times 10^2$
$= 220$ m

Q5

A car has an initial velocity of $v_0 = 5.0\ \text{m s}^{-1}$. When its displacement increases by 20.0 m, its velocity becomes $7.0\ \text{m s}^{-1}$. What is the acceleration?

Answer

Again take $x_0 = 0$ so that

$$v^2 = v_0^2 + 2ax$$

So $7^2 = 5^2 + 2a \times 20$
therefore
$a = 0.60\ \text{m s}^{-2}$

Q6

A body has initial velocity $v_0 = 4.0\,\text{m s}^{-1}$ and a velocity of $v = 12\,\text{m s}^{-1}$ after 6.0 s. What displacement did the body cover in the 6.0 s?

Answer

We may use

$$x = \left(\frac{v + v_0}{2}\right) t$$

to get

$$x = \left(\frac{12 + 4}{2}\right) 6$$
$$= 48\ \text{m}$$

This is faster than using $v = v_0 + at$ in order to find the acceleration as

$$12 = 4 + 6a$$
$$\Rightarrow a = 1.333\ \text{m s}^{-2}$$

and then

$$x = v_0 t + \tfrac{1}{2}at$$
$$= 4 \times 6 + \tfrac{1}{2} \times 1.333 \times 36$$
$$= 48\ \text{m}$$

The two examples that follow involve motions that start at different times.

Q7

Two balls start out moving to the right with constant velocities of $5\ \text{m s}^{-1}$ and $4\ \text{m s}^{-1}$. The slow ball starts first and the other 4 s later. How far from the starting position are they when they meet?

Answer

See Figure 2.9.

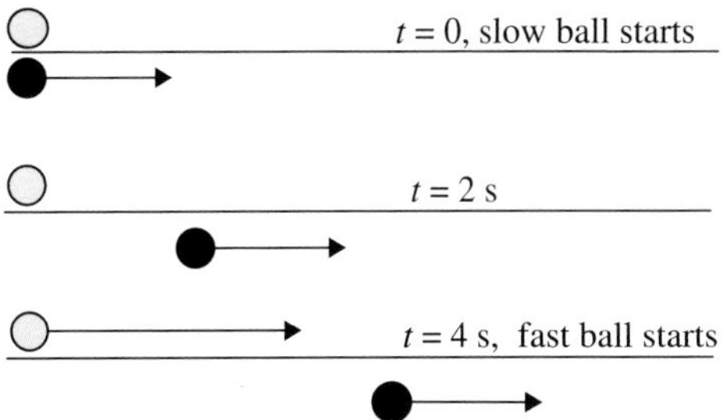

Figure 2.9.

Let the two balls meet t s after the first ball starts moving. The displacement of the slow ball is $x = 4t$ m and that travelled by the fast ball $5(t - 4)$ m. The factor $t - 4$ is there since after t s the fast ball has actually been moving for only $t - 4$ s. These two displacements are equal when the two balls meet and thus $4t = 5t - 20$, or $t = 20$ s. The common displacement is thus 80 m.

Q8

A mass is thrown upwards with an initial velocity of $30\ \text{m s}^{-1}$. A second mass is dropped from directly above, a height of 60 m from the first mass, 0.5 s later. When do the masses meet and how high is the point where they meet?

Answer

See Figure 2.10. We choose the upward direction to be positive for velocities and displacements. The masses experience an acceleration of $-10\ \text{m s}^{-2}$, the acceleration due to gravity. Since the motion is along a *vertical* straight line, we use the symbol y for displacement rather than x.

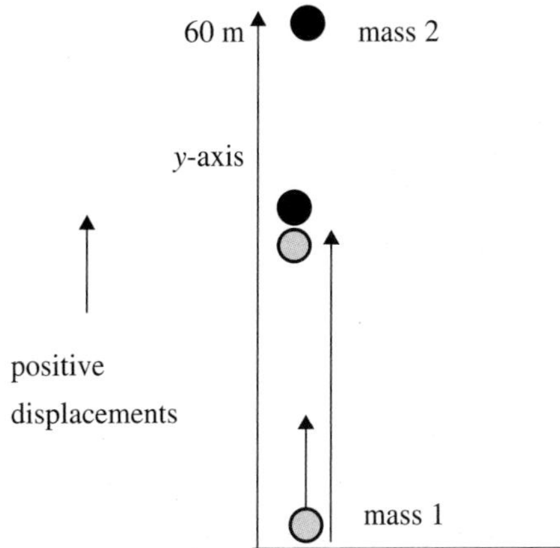

Figure 2.10.

The first mass moves to a displacement given by $y_1 = 30t - 5t^2$. The second moves to a displacement of $y_2 = 60 - 5(t - 0.5)^2$. The displacements are the same when the masses meet. Thus

$$30t - 5t^2 = 60 - 5(t - 0.5)^2$$

$$\Rightarrow t = 2.35 \text{ s}$$

The common displacement at this time is 42.9 m.

Graphs of acceleration versus time

In a graph of acceleration versus time the area under the graph gives the change in velocity. In Figure 2.11 the area from time zero to 4 s is 12 m s^{-1} and thus the velocity after 4 s is 12 m s^{-1} plus whatever initial velocity the object had.

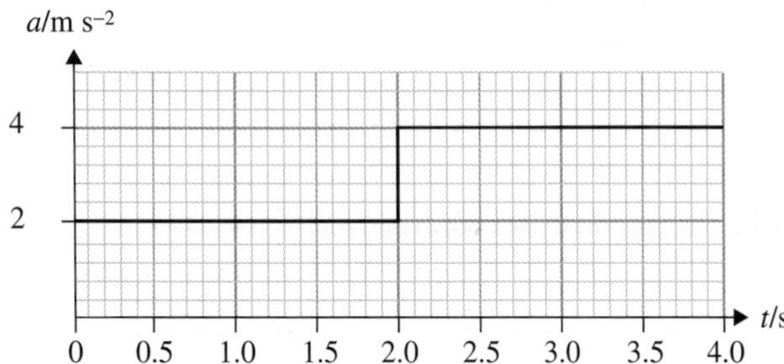

Figure 2.11 The area under an acceleration–time graph is the change in velocity.

Graphs of displacement versus time

In motion with constant acceleration, a graph of displacement versus time is a parabola. Consider a ball that is dropped from rest from a height of 20 m. The graph of displacement versus time is shown in Figure 2.12.

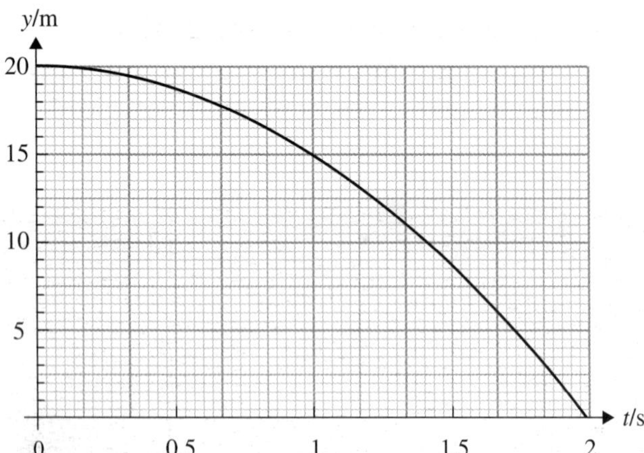

Figure 2.12 Graph of displacement versus time. The object hits the floor at 2 s.

Example question

Q9

An object with initial velocity 20 m s^{-1} and initial displacement of -75 m experiences an acceleration of -2 m s^{-2}. Draw the displacement–time graph for this motion for the first 20 s.

Answer

The displacement is given by $x = -75 + 20t - t^2$ and this is the function we must graph. The result is shown in Figure 2.13.

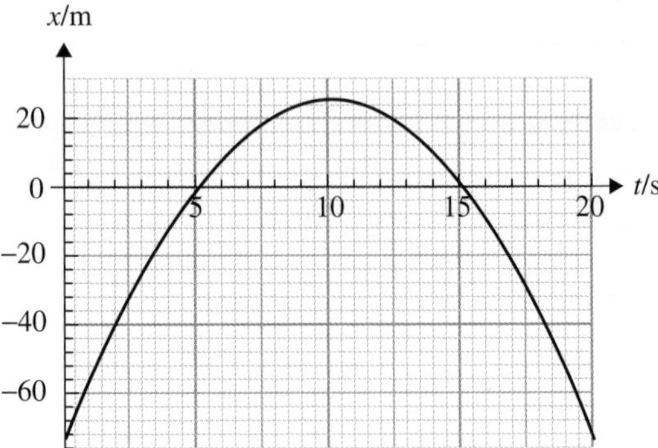

Figure 2.13.

At 5 s the object reaches the origin and overshoots it. It returns to the origin 10 s later ($t = 15$ s). The furthest it gets from the origin on the right side is 25 m. The velocity at 5 s is 10 m s^{-1} and at 15 s it is -10 m s^{-1}. At 10 s the velocity is zero.

In general, if the velocity is not constant, the graph of displacement with time will be a curve. Drawing the tangent at a point on the curve and finding the slope of the tangent gives the velocity at that point.

Measuring speed and acceleration

The speed of an object is determined experimentally by measuring the distance travelled by the object in an interval of time. Dividing the distance by the time taken gives the average speed. To get as close an approximation to the instantaneous speed as possible, we must make the time interval as small as possible. We can measure speed electronically by attaching a piece of cardboard of known length to the object so that a single photogate will record the time taken for that known length to go through the photogate, as in Figure 2.14. The ratio of the cardboard length to time taken is the speed of the object when it is halfway through the photogate.

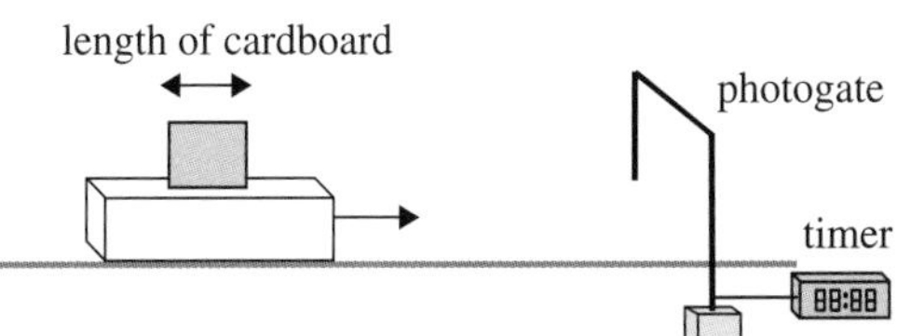

Figure 2.14 Measuring speed with a photogate.

Speed can also be measured with a tickertape, an instrument that makes marks on a paper tape at regular intervals of time (usually 50 marks per second). If one end of the tape is attached to the moving object and the other end goes through the marker, then to find the speed at a particular point we would measure the distance between two consecutive marks (distance travelled by the object) and divide by the time taken (1/50 s). In Figure 2.15 the dotted lines are supposed to be 0.5 cm apart. Then the top tape represents uniform motion with speed

$$v = \frac{0.5}{1/50}\ \text{cm s}^{-1}$$
$$= 25\ \text{cm s}^{-1}$$
$$= 0.25\ \text{m s}^{-1}$$

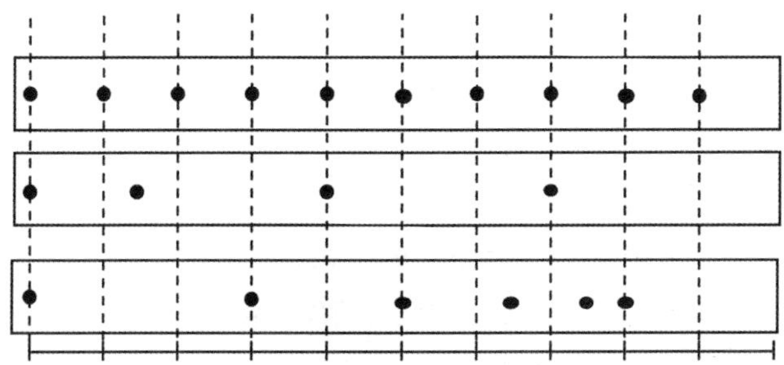

Figure 2.15 Measuring speed with a tickertape.

In the second tape the moving object is accelerating. The distance between the first two dots is about 0.75 cm so the average speed between those two dots is

$$v = \frac{0.75}{1/50}\ \text{cm s}^{-1}$$
$$= 0.375\ \text{m s}^{-1}$$

The distance between dots 2 and 3 is 1.25 cm and so the average speed between those dots is

$$v = \frac{1.25}{1/50}\ \text{cm s}^{-1}$$
$$= 0.625\ \text{m s}^{-1}$$

Between dots 3 and 4 the distance is 1.5 cm and so

$$v = \frac{1.5}{1/50}\ \text{cm s}^{-1}$$
$$= 0.750\ \text{m s}^{-1}$$

We may thus take the average speed between $t = 0$ s and $t = 1/50$ s to be 0.375 m s^{-1}, between $t = 1/50$ s and $t = 2/50$ s to be 0.625 m s^{-1} and between $t = 2/50$ s and $t = 3/50$ s to be 0.750 m s^{-1}. Thus the average acceleration in the first 1/50 s is 12.5 m s^{-2} and in the next 1/50 s it is 6.25 m s^{-2}. The acceleration is thus not constant for this motion.

The third tape shows decelerated motion.

Related to the tickertape method is that of a stroboscopic picture (see Figure 2.16). Here the moving body is photographed in rapid succession with a constant, known interval of time between pictures. The images are then developed on the same photograph, giving a multiple exposure picture of the motion. Measuring the distances covered in the known time interval allows a measurement of speed.

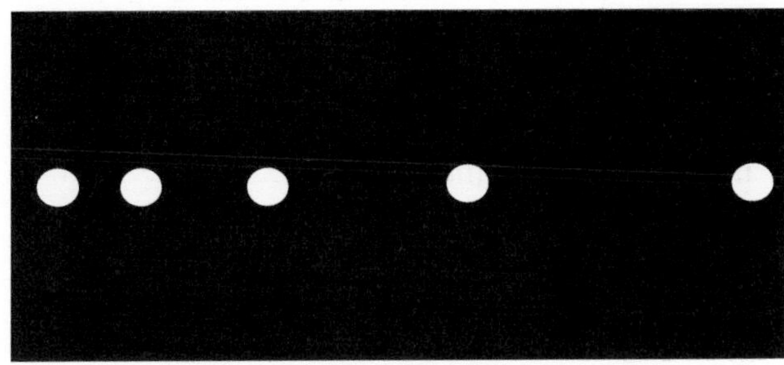

Figure 2.16 Measuring speed with a stroboscope.

Once measurement of speed is possible, acceleration can also be determined. To measure the acceleration at a specific time, t, one must first measure the velocity a short interval of time before t, say $t - T/2$ and again a short time after t, $t + T/2$ (see Figure 2.17). If the values of velocity found are respectively u and v, then

$$a = \frac{v - u}{T}$$

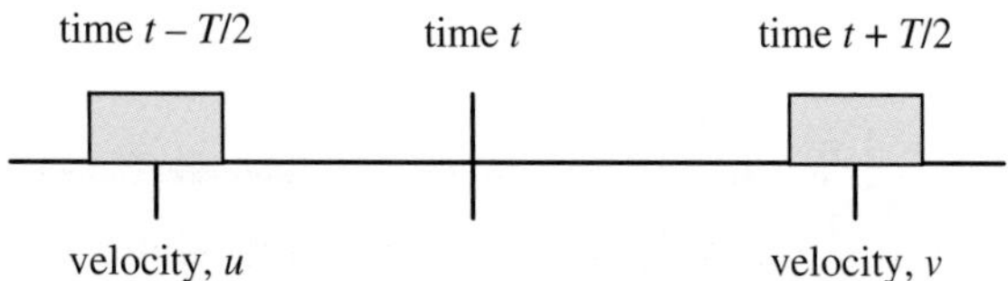

Figure 2.17 Measuring acceleration requires knowing the velocity at two separate points in time.

More on graphs

In kinematics the most useful graph is that of velocity versus time (v–t). The slope of such a graph gives the acceleration and the area under the graph gives the change in displacement. Let's examine this in detail. Consider the following problem, which is hard to solve with equations but is quite easy using a v–t graph. Two masses, A and B, are to follow the paths shown in Figure 2.18. The paths are the same length, but one involves a hill and the other a valley.

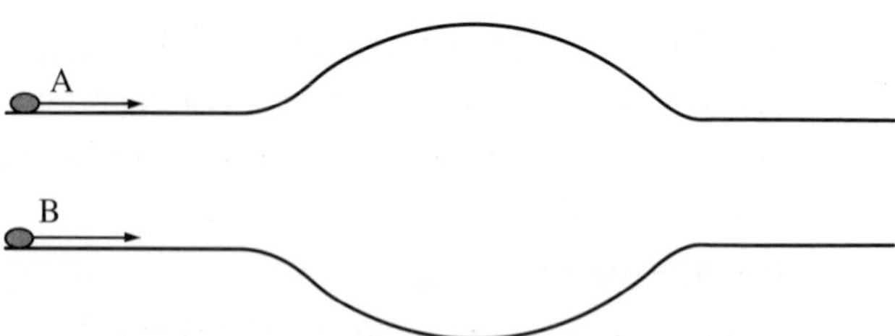

Figure 2.18 Which mass gets to the end first? They both travel the same distance.

Which mass will get to the end first? (Remember, the distance travelled is the same.) We know that the first mass will slow down as it climbs the hill and then speed up on the way down until it reaches its original speed on the level part. The second mass will first speed up on the way down the hill and slow down to its original speed when it reaches the level part. Let us make the v–t graph for each mass. The graphs for A and B must look like Figure 2.19.

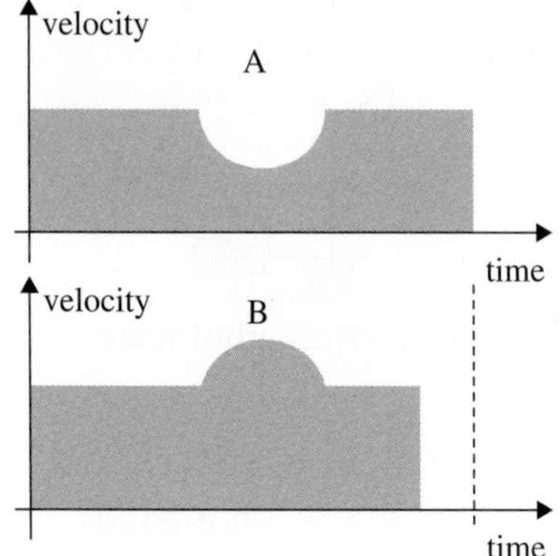

Figure 2.19.

It is then obvious that since the areas under the two curves must be the same (same displacement) the graph for B must stop earlier: that is, B gets to the end first. The same conclusion is reached more quickly if we notice that the average speed in case B is higher and so the time taken is less since the distance is the same.

Consider the following question. The graph of velocity versus time for two objects is given in Figure 2.20. Both have the same initial and final velocity. Which object has the largest average velocity?

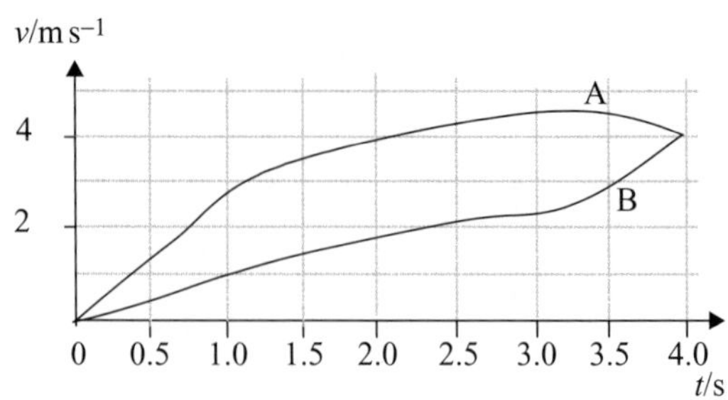

Figure 2.20 Graph showing the variation of velocity with time for two motions that have the same initial and final velocity.

Average velocity is the ratio of total displacement divided by time taken. Clearly, object A has a larger displacement (larger area under curve). Thus, it has a larger average velocity. The point is that you *cannot* say that average velocity is half of the sum of initial and final velocities. (Why? Under what circumstances *can* you say it?)

Consider finally the graph in Figure 2.21, which shows the variation of the displacement of an object with time. We would like to obtain the graph showing the variation of the velocity with time.

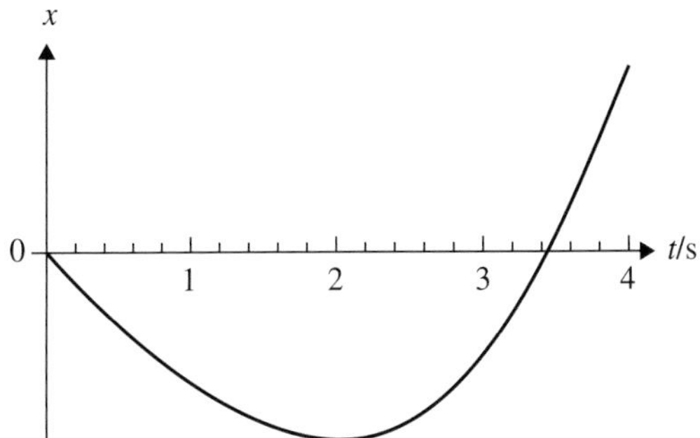

Figure 2.21 Graph showing the variation of displacement with time.

Our starting point is that *velocity is the slope of the displacement–time graph*. We see that initially the slope is negative, it becomes less negative and at $t = 2$ s it is zero. From then on the slope becomes increasingly positive. This leads to the velocity–time graph in Figure 2.22.

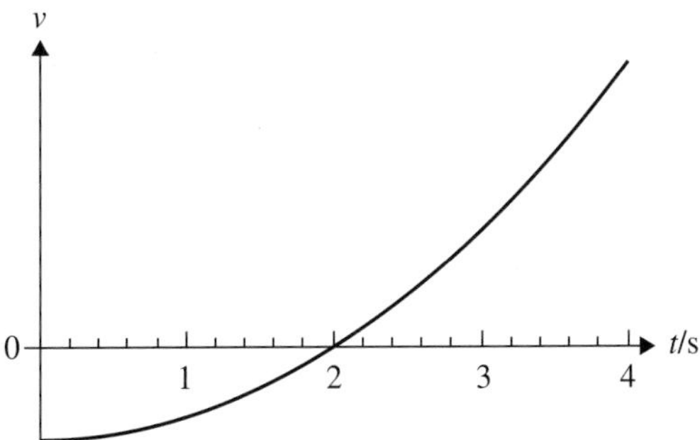

Figure 2.22 Graph showing the variation of velocity with time for the motion in Figure 2.21.

The *slope of the velocity–time graph is acceleration* and from the graph we see that the slope is initially zero but then becomes more and more positive. Hence, the acceleration–time graph must be something like Figure 2.23.

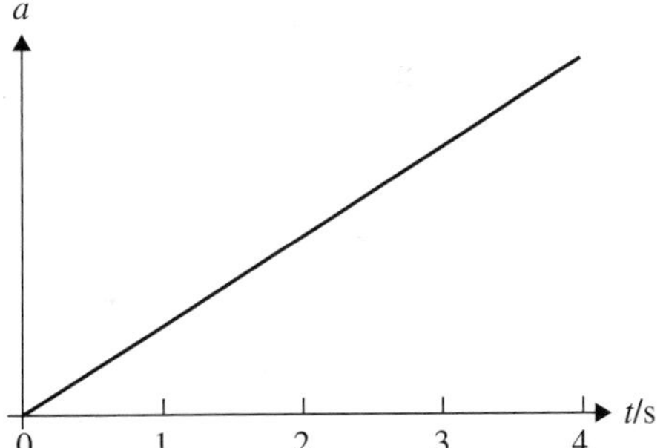

Figure 2.23 Graph showing the variation of acceleration with time for the motion in Figure 2.21.

? QUESTIONS

In the graphs in this section, the point where the axes cross is the origin unless otherwise indicated.

1. The initial velocity of a car moving on a straight road is 2.0 m s^{-1} and becomes 8.0 m s^{-1} after travelling for 2.0 s under constant acceleration. What is the acceleration?
2. A plane starting from rest takes 15.0 s to take off after speeding over a distance of 450.0 m on the runway with constant acceleration. With what velocity does it take off?
3. The acceleration of a car is assumed constant at 1.5 m s^{-2}. How long will it take the car to accelerate from 5.0 m s^{-1} to 11 m s^{-1}?
4. A car accelerates from rest to 28 m s^{-1} in 9.0 s. What distance does it travel?
5. A body has an initial velocity of 12 m s^{-1} and is brought to rest over a distance of 45 m. What is the acceleration of the body?
6. A body at the origin has an initial velocity of −6.0 m s^{-1} and moves with an acceleration of 2.0 m s^{-2}. When will its displacement become 16 m?
7. A body has an initial velocity of 3.0 m s^{-1} and after travelling 24 m the velocity becomes 13 m s^{-1}. How long did this take?
8. What deceleration does a passenger of a car experience if his car, which is moving at 100.0 km h^{-1}, hits a wall and is brought to rest in 0.100 s? Express the answer in m s^{-2}.

9 A car is travelling at 40.0 m s^{-1}. The driver sees an emergency ahead and 0.50 s later slams on the brakes. The acceleration of the car is −4 m s^{-2}.

(a) What distance will the car travel before it stops?

(b) If the driver was able to apply the brakes instantaneously without a reaction time, over what distance would the car stop?

(c) Calculate the difference in your answers to (a) and (b).

(d) Assume now that the car was travelling at 30.0 m s^{-1} instead. Without performing any calculations, would the answer to (c) now be less than, equal to or larger than before? Explain your answer.

10 A ball is thrown upwards with a speed of 24.0 m s^{-1}.

(a) When is the velocity of the ball 12.0 m s^{-1}?

(b) When is the velocity of the ball −12.0 m s^{-1}?

(c) What is the displacement of the ball at those times?

(d) What is the velocity of the ball 1.50 s after launch?

(e) What is the maximum height reached by the ball?

(Take the acceleration due to gravity to be 10.0 m s^{-2}.)

11 A stone is thrown vertically upwards with an initial speed of 10.0 m s^{-1} from a cliff that is 50.0 m high.

(a) When does it reach the bottom of the cliff?

(b) What speed does it have just before hitting the ground?

(c) What is the total distance travelled by the stone?

(Take the acceleration due to gravity to be 10.0 m s^{-2}.)

12 A rock is thrown vertically down from the roof of a 25.0 m high building with a speed of 5.0 m s^{-1}.

(a) When does the rock hit the ground?

(b) With what speed does it hit the ground?

(Take the acceleration due to gravity to be 10.0 m s^{-2}.)

13 A window is 1.50 m high. A stone falling from above passes the top of the window with a speed of 3.00 m s^{-1}. When will it pass the bottom of the window? (Take the acceleration due to gravity to be 10.0 m s^{-2}.)

14 A ball is dropped from rest from a height of 20.0 m. One second later a second ball is thrown vertically downwards. If the two balls arrive on the ground at the same time, what must have been the initial velocity of the second ball?

15 A ball is dropped from rest from the top of a 40.0 m building. A second ball is thrown downward 1.0 s later.

(a) If they hit the ground at the same time, find the speed with which the second ball was thrown.

(b) What is the ratio of the speed of the thrown ball to the speed of the other as they hit the ground?

(Take the acceleration due to gravity to be 10.0 m s^{-2}.)

16 Two balls are dropped from rest from the same height. One of the balls is dropped 1.00 s after the other. What distance separates the two balls 2.00 s after the second ball is dropped?

17 An object moves in a straight line with an acceleration that varies with time as shown in Figure 22.4. Initially the velocity of the object is 2.00 m s^{-1}.

(a) Find the maximum velocity reached in the first 6.00 s of this motion.

(b) Draw a graph of the velocity versus time.

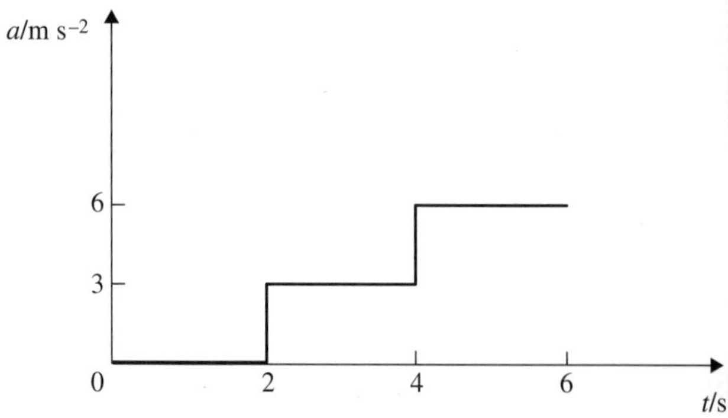

Figure 2.24 For question 17.

18 Figure 2.25 shows the variation of velocity with time of an object. Find the acceleration at 2.0 s.

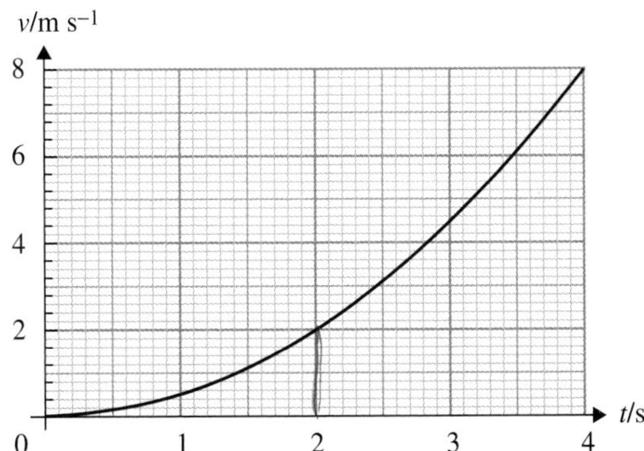

Figure 2.25 For question 18.

19 Figure 2.26 shows the variation of the displacement of a moving object with time. Draw the graph showing the variation of the velocity of the object with time.

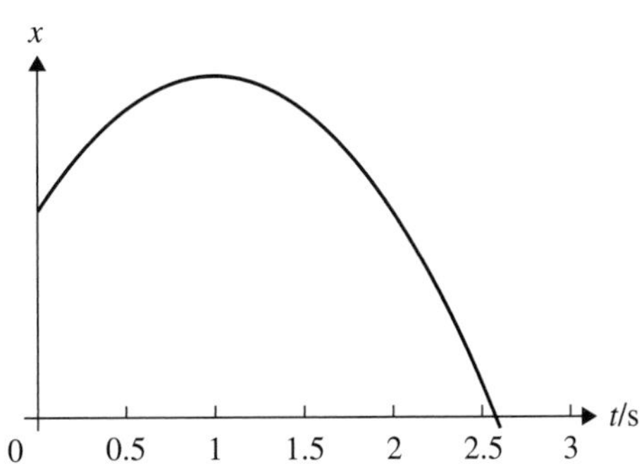

Figure 2.26 For question 19.

20 Figure 2.27 shows the variation of the displacement of a moving object with time. Draw the graph showing the variation of the velocity of the object with time.

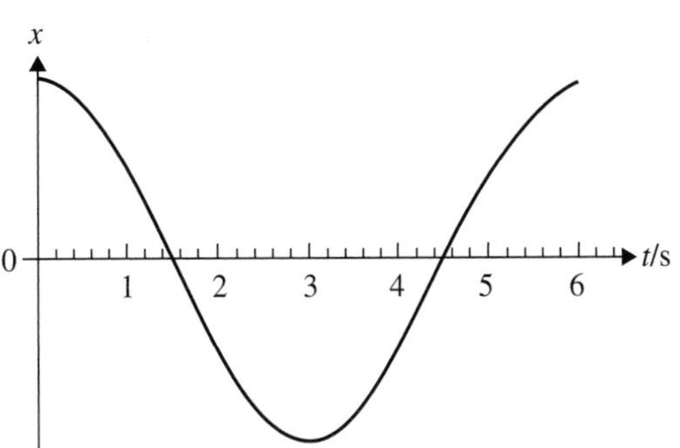

Figure 2.27 For question 20.

21 Figure 2.28 shows the variation of the displacement of a moving object with time. Draw the graph showing the variation of the velocity of the object with time.

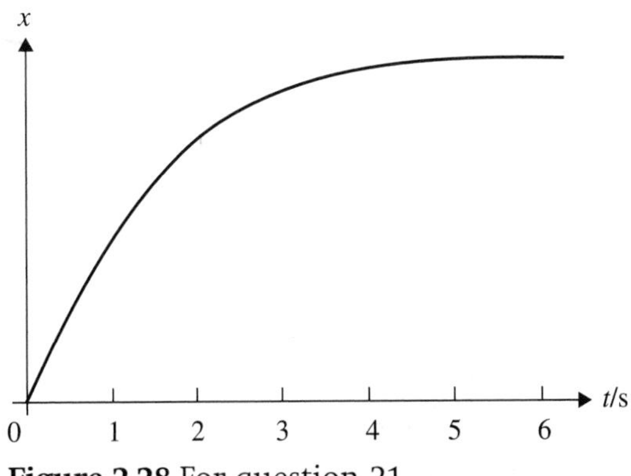

Figure 2.28 For question 21.

22 Figure 2.29 shows the variation of the displacement of a moving object with time. Draw the graph showing the variation of the velocity of the object with time.

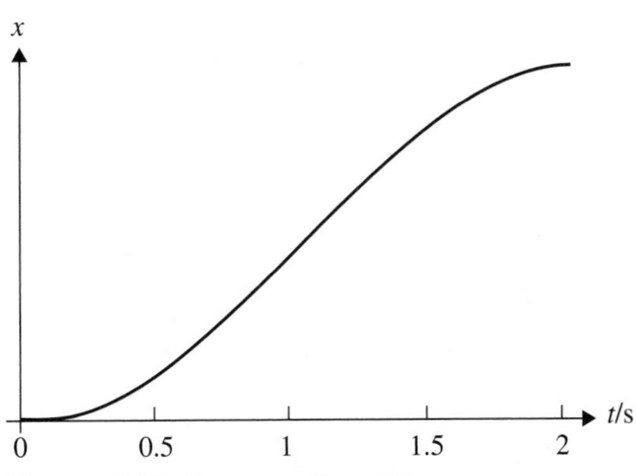

Figure 2.29 For question 22.

23 Figure 2.30 shows the variation of the displacement of a moving object with time. Draw the graph showing the variation of the velocity of the object with time.

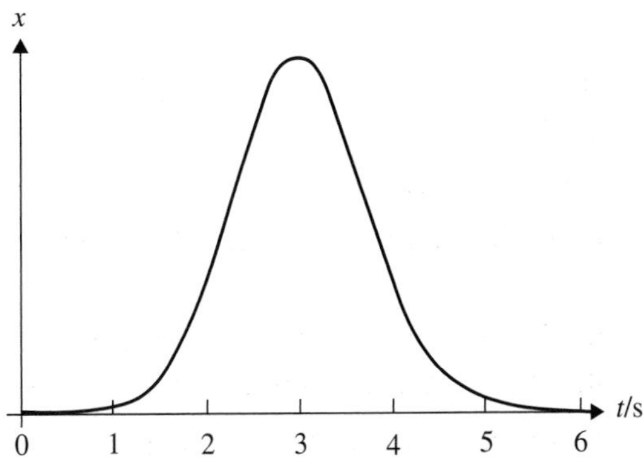

Figure 2.30 For question 23.

24 Figure 2.31 shows the variation of the velocity of a moving object with time. Draw the graph showing the variation of the displacement of the object with time.

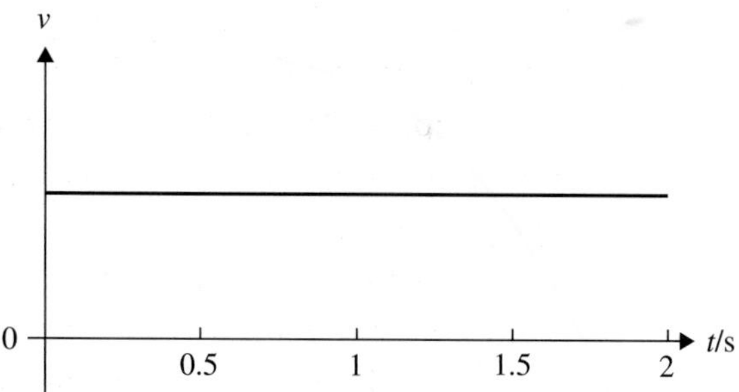

Figure 2.31 For question 24.

25 Figure 2.32 shows the variation of the velocity of a moving object with time. Draw the graph showing the variation of the displacement of the object with time.

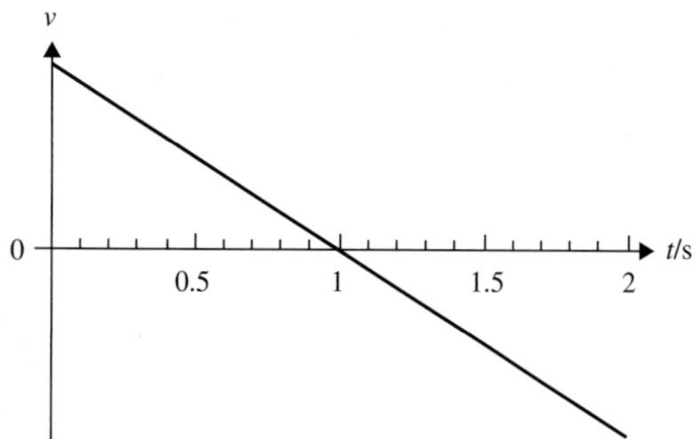

Figure 2.32 For question 25.

26 Figure 2.33 shows the variation of the velocity of a moving object with time. Draw the graph showing the variation of the displacement of the object with time (assuming a zero initial displacement).

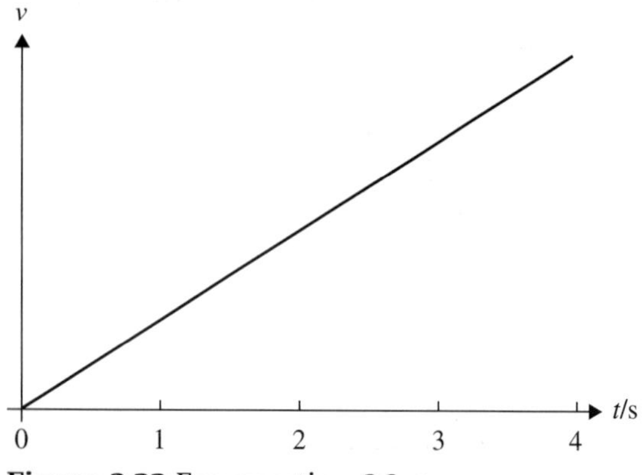

Figure 2.33 For question 26.

27 Figure 2.34 shows the variation of the velocity of a moving object with time. Draw the graph showing the variation of the displacement of the object with time (assuming a zero initial displacement).

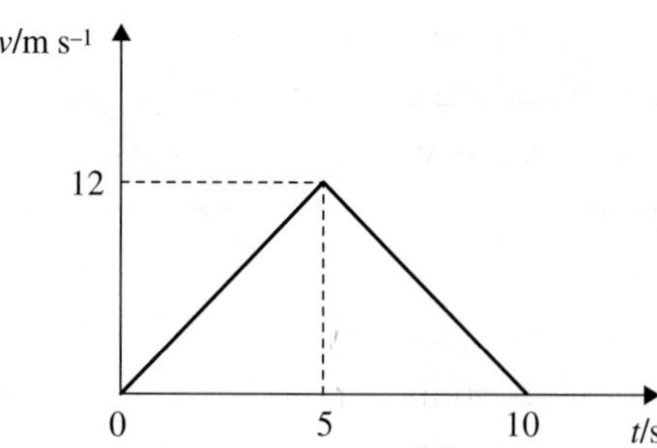

Figure 2.34 For question 27.

28 Figure 2.35 shows the variation of the velocity of a moving object with time. Draw the graph showing the variation of the acceleration of the object with time.

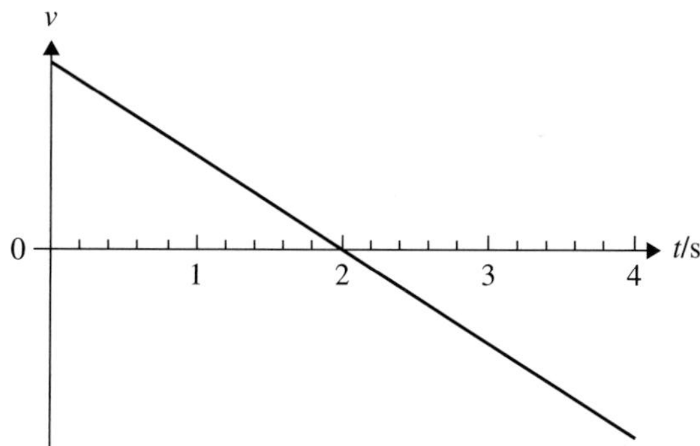

Figure 2.35 For question 28.

29 Figure 2.36 shows the variation of the velocity of a moving object with time. Draw the graph showing the variation of the acceleration of the object with time.

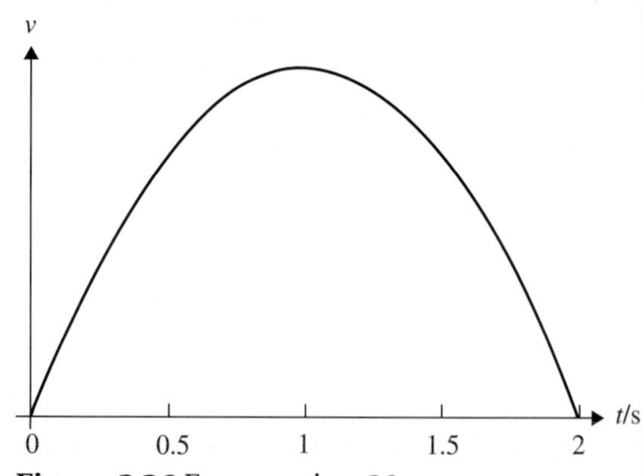

Figure 2.36 For question 29.

30 Your brand new convertible Ferrari is parked 15 m from its garage when it begins to rain. You do not have time to get the keys so you begin to push the car towards the garage. If the maximum acceleration you can give the car is 2.0 m s^{-2} by pushing and 3.0 m s^{-2} by pulling back on the car, find the least time it takes to put the car in the garage. (Assume that the car, as well as the garage, are point objects.)

31 Figure 2.37 shows the displacement versus time of an object moving in a straight line. Four points on this graph have been selected.

(a) Is the velocity between A and B positive, zero or negative?

(b) What can you say about the velocity between B and C?

(c) Is the acceleration between A and B positive, zero or negative?

(d) Is the acceleration between C and D positive, zero or negative?

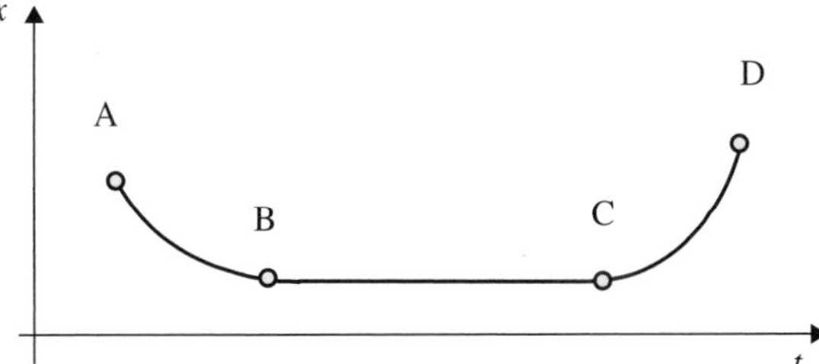

Figure 2.37 For question 31.

32 A hiker starts climbing a mountain at 08:00 in the morning and reaches the top at 12:00 (noon). He spends the night on the mountain and the next day at 08:00 starts on the way down following exactly the same path. He reaches the bottom of the mountain at 12:00. Prove that there must be a time between 08:00 and 12:00 when the hiker was at the same spot along the route on the way up and on the way down.

33 Make velocity–time sketches (no numbers are necessary on the axes) for the following motions.

(a) A ball is dropped from a certain height and bounces off a hard floor. The speed just before each impact with the floor is the same as the speed just after impact. Assume that the time of contact with the floor is negligibly small.

(b) A cart slides with negligible friction along a horizontal air track. When the cart hits the ends of the air track it reverses direction with the same speed it had right before impact. Assume the time of contact of the cart and the ends of the air track is negligibly small.

(c) A person jumps from a hovering helicopter. After a few seconds she opens a parachute. Eventually she will reach a terminal speed and will then land.

34 A cart with a sail on it is given an initial velocity and moves toward the right where, from some distance away, a fan blows air at the sail (see Figure 2.38). The fan is powerful enough to stop the cart before the cart reaches the position of the fan. Make a graph of the velocity of the cart as a function of time that best represents the motion just described. List any assumptions you made in drawing your graph.

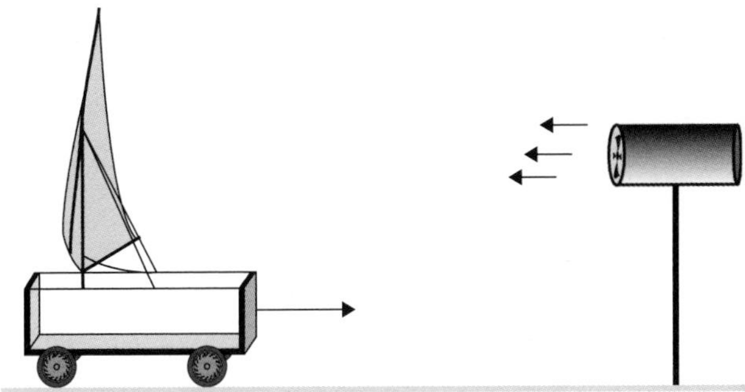

Figure 2.38 For question 34.

35 A stone is thrown vertically up from the edge of a cliff 35.0 m from the ground. The initial velocity of the stone is 8.00 m s^{-1}. (See Figure 2.39.)

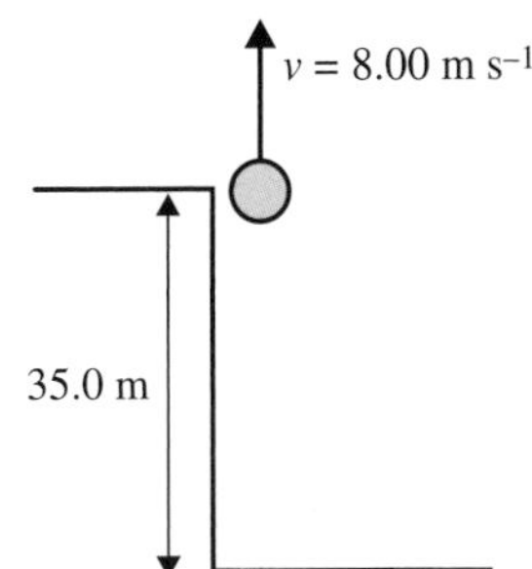

Figure 2.39 For question 35.

(a) How high will the stone get?
(b) When will it hit the ground?
(c) What velocity will it have just before hitting the ground?
(d) What distance will the stone have covered?
(e) What is the average speed and average velocity for this motion?
(f) Make a graph to show the variation of velocity with time.
(g) Make a graph to show the variation of displacement with time.

(Take the acceleration due to gravity to be $10.0\ \text{m s}^{-2}$.)

36 A ball is thrown upward from the edge of a cliff with velocity $20.0\ \text{m s}^{-1}$. It reaches the bottom of the cliff 6.0 s later.
(a) How high is the cliff?
(b) With what speed does the ball hit the ground?

37 A rocket accelerates vertically upwards from rest with a constant acceleration of $4.00\ \text{m s}^{-2}$. The fuel lasts for 5.00 s.
(a) What is the maximum height achieved by this rocket?
(b) When does the rocket reach the ground again?
(c) Sketch a graph to show the variation of the velocity of the rocket with time from the time of launch to the time it falls to the ground.

(Take the acceleration due to gravity to be $10.0\ \text{m s}^{-2}$.)

38 A hot air balloon is rising vertically at constant speed $5.0\ \text{m s}^{-1}$. A sandbag is released and it hits the ground 12.0 s later.
(a) With what speed does the sandbag hit the ground?
(b) How high was the balloon when the sandbag was released?
(c) What is the relative velocity of the sandbag with respect to the balloon 6.0 s after it was dropped?

(Assume that the balloon's velocity increased to $5.5\ \text{m s}^{-1}$ after releasing the sandbag. Take the acceleration due to gravity to be $10.0\ \text{m s}^{-2}$.)

The concept of force

Two basic ingredients of mechanics are the concepts of mass and force. A force can deform, stretch, rotate or compress a body and is intimately connected to the acceleration it can produce on a body (the relation between acceleration and force will be the detailed subject of a later chapter). Mass is a measure of the amount of material in a body, measured in kilograms; in classical mechanics the mass of an object is a constant. There are different kinds of forces in nature; the most common force of everyday life is the force of gravitation – the force with which the earth pulls us towards the centre of the earth. We give this force a special name: the weight of a body. We don't fall to the centre of the earth because the ground on which we stand exerts another force on us, upwards – a force due to the contact between ourselves and the ground. The origin of this force is electromagnetic. This is also the force that keeps us alive (atoms exist and bind into molecules because of this force), and prevents the chair on which you are sitting from collapsing, and so on. These are the only forces that affect our daily lives. It turns out that the electromagnetic force is just one very special aspect of a more general force, called the electroweak force. The other aspect of this force (the weak nuclear force) is responsible for decay processes inside atomic nuclei. Finally, the colour force, or strong nuclear force, keeps the quarks bound inside protons and neutrons. Physicists hope that the electroweak force and the nuclear force will one day be shown to be different aspects of one more general force (the 'unified force') but this has not yet been accomplished. An even more speculative expectation is that the gravitational force, too, will be shown to be part of an even more unified force, whose different aspects we see as the three different forces today. But none of these attempts for a complete unification has been achieved yet. Apart from the gravitational, electroweak and colour force, no other forces, or interactions, are known at the present time.

Objectives

By the end of this chapter you should be able to:

- state the difference between *mass* and *weight*;
- define gravitational field strength and give its units (N kg^{-1} or m s^{-2});
- draw vectors representing forces acting on a given body;
- identify situations in which frictional forces develop and draw those frictional forces;
- use Hooke's law correctly, $T = kx$.

Forces and their direction

A force is a vector quantity. Its direction is very important and it is crucial to be able to identify the direction of a given force. What follows is a list of the forces we will be dealing with in this and later chapters, as well as a discussion of their properties and direction. The unit of force is the newton; this will be properly defined when we discuss the second law of mechanics.

Weight

This force is the result of the gravitational attraction between the mass in question and the mass of the earth. (If the body finds itself on a different planet then its weight is defined as the gravitational attraction between its mass and that planet's mass.) The **weight** of a body is the gravitational force experienced by that body, which on earth is given by the formula

$$W = mg$$

where

- m is the mass of the body measured in kilograms
- g is the gravitational field strength of the earth, which is a property of the gravitational field of the earth (see Chapter 2.10). Its units are newton per kilogram, N kg^{-1}. The gravitational field strength is also known as 'the acceleration due to gravity'. The units of g are thus also m s^{-2}.

If m is in kg and g in N kg^{-1} or m s^{-2} then W is in newtons, N. On the *surface* of the earth, $g = 9.81$ N kg^{-1} – a number that we will often approximate by the more convenient 10 N kg^{-1}. This force is always directed vertically downward, as shown in Figure 3.1.

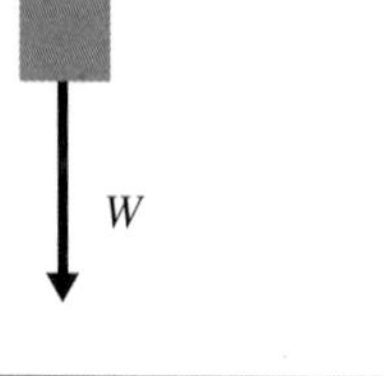

Figure 3.1 The weight of an object is always directed vertically downward.

The mass of an object is the same everywhere in the universe, but its weight depends on the *location* of the body. For example, a mass of 70 kg has a weight of 687 N on the surface of the earth ($g = 9.81$ N kg^{-1}) and a weight of 635 N at a height of 250 km from the earth's surface (where $g = 9.07$ N kg^{-1}). However, on the surface of Venus, where the gravitational field strength is only 8.9 N kg^{-1}, the weight is 623 N.

Tension

A string that is taut is said to be under tension. The force that arises in any body when it is stretched is called **tension**. This force is the result of electromagnetic interactions between the molecules of the material making up the string. A tension force in a string is created when two forces are applied in opposite directions at the ends of the string (see Figure 3.2).

Figure 3.2 A tension force in a string.

To say that there is tension in a string means that an arbitrary point on the string is acted upon by two forces (the tension T) as shown in Figure 3.3. If the string hangs from a ceiling and a mass m is tied at the other end, tension develops in the string. At the point of support at the ceiling, the tension force pulls down *on the ceiling* and at the point where the mass is tied the tension acts upwards *on the mass*.

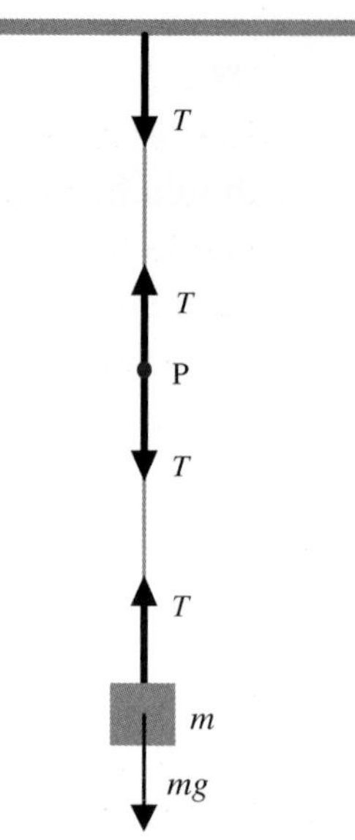

Figure 3.3 The tension is directed along the string.

In most cases we will idealize the string by assuming it is massless. This does not mean that the string *really* is massless, but rather that its mass is so small compared with any other masses in the problem that we can neglect it. In that case, the tension T is the same at all points on the string. The direction of the tension force is along the string. Further examples of tension forces in a string are given in Figure 3.4. A string or rope that is not taut has zero tension in it.

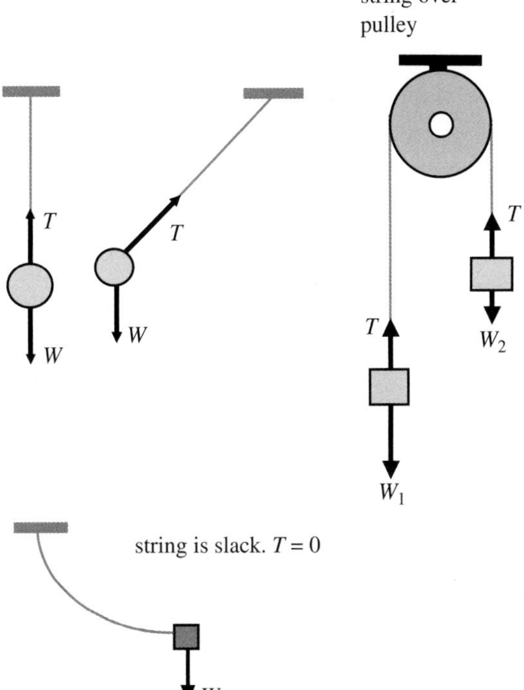

Figure 3.4 More examples of tension forces.

Normal reaction (contact) forces

If a body touches another body, there is a *force of reaction* or *contact force* between the two bodies. This force is perpendicular to the body exerting the force. Like tension, the origin of this force is also electromagnetic. In Figure 3.5 we show the reaction force on several bodies.

Drag forces

Drag forces are forces that oppose the motion of a body through a fluid (a gas or a liquid). Typical examples are the air resistance force experienced by a car (see Figure 3.6) or plane, or the resistance force experienced by a steel marble dropped into a jar of honey. Drag forces

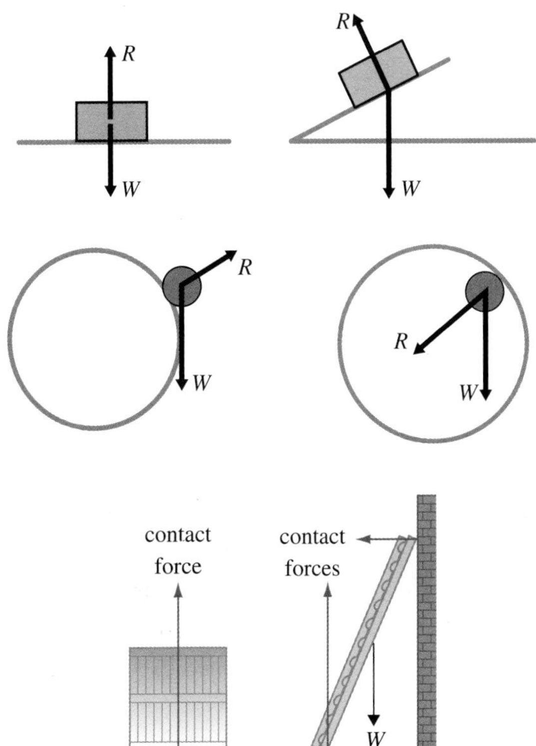

Figure 3.5 Examples of reaction forces, R.

are directed opposite to the velocity of the body and in general depend on the speed of the body. The higher the speed, the higher the drag force.

Figure 3.6 The drag force on a moving car.

Upthrust

Any object placed in a fluid experiences an upward force called upthrust (see Figure 3.7). If the upthrust force equals the weight of the body, the body will float in the fluid. If the

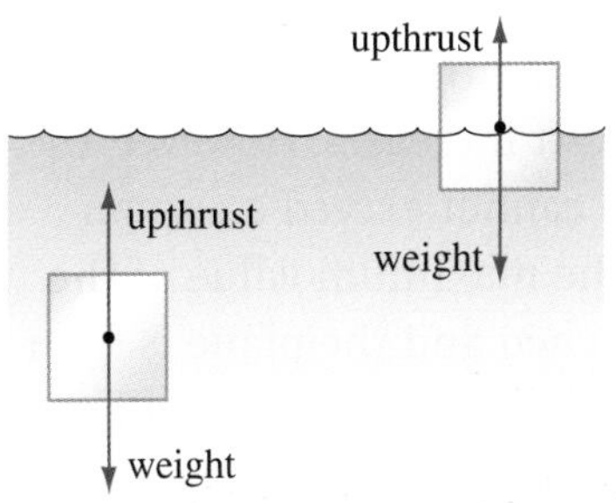

Figure 3.7 Upthrust.

upthrust is less than the weight, the body will sink. Upthrust is caused by the pressure that the fluid exerts on the body.

Frictional forces

Frictional forces oppose the motion of a body. They are also electromagnetic in origin. (See Figure 3.8.)

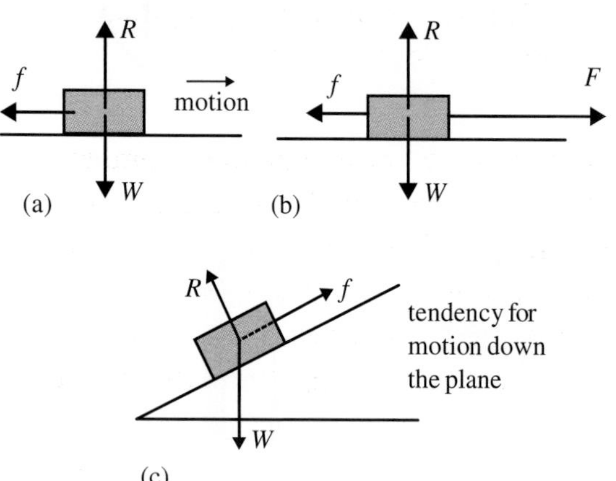

Figure 3.8 Examples of frictional forces, *f*. In (a) and (b) the motion to the right is opposed by a frictional force to the left. In (c) the body does not move but has a tendency to move down the plane. A frictional force directed up the plane opposes this tendency.

Friction arises whenever one body slides over another. In this case we speak of sliding or kinetic friction. Friction also arises whenever there is just a tendency for motion, not necessarily motion itself, such as when a block rests on an inclined plane or if a block on a level road is pulled by a small force that does not result in motion. In this case, we speak of static friction. Suppose that the plane on which the block rests is slowly elevated (Figure 3.8c). The block will tend to move to the left. This motion will be opposed by a frictional force. As the plane is elevated even more, the frictional force needed to keep the block at rest increases. However, the static frictional force cannot exceed a certain maximum value. If the maximum value of the frictional force is reached and the plane is then elevated a bit more, the frictional force will not be able to keep the body in equilibrium and the block will slide down. As soon as the body begins to slide, the frictional force opposing the motion becomes the kinetic friction force. The kinetic friction force is always less than the maximum value of the static friction force. This is a well-known phenomenon of everyday life. It takes a lot of force to get a heavy piece of furniture to start moving (you must exceed the maximum value of the static friction force), but once you get it moving, pushing it along becomes easier (you are now opposed by the smaller kinetic friction force).

Example question

Q1

A brick of weight 50 N rests on a horizontal surface. The maximum frictional force that can develop between the brick and the surface is 30 N. When the brick slides on the surface, the frictional force is 10 N. A horizontal force F is applied to the brick, its magnitude increasing slowly from zero. Find the frictional force on the brick for various values of F.

Answer

The maximum frictional force is 30 N. This means that as long as F is less than 30 N, the frictional force equals F and the brick stays where it is. If F becomes slightly more than 30 N, the frictional force cannot match it and thus the brick will move. But as soon as the brick moves, the frictional force will drop to the kinetic value 10 N, for all values of $F > 30$ N. We can summarize these results as shown in Table 3.1.

F	0 N	12 N	28 N	29 N	30 N	30.01 N	40 N
f	0 N	12 N	28 N	29 N	30 N	10 N	10 N
	no motion	no motion	no motion	no motion	no motion	motion	motion

Table 3.1.

Frictional forces between the road and the tyres are what allow a car to take a turn. Although, generally, frictional forces oppose the motion of a body, in some cases frictional forces are responsible for motion. A typical example is the wheels of a car. The engine forces the wheels to turn. The wheels exert a force on the ground and so the ground exerts an equal and opposite force on the wheels, making them move forward. This will become clearer when we look at Newton's third law in a later chapter.

Free-body diagrams

A free-body diagram is a diagram showing the magnitude and direction of all the forces acting on a chosen body. The body is shown on its own, free of its surroundings and of any other bodies it may be in contact with. In Figure 3.9 we show three situations in which forces are acting; below each is the corresponding free-body diagram for the shaded bodies.

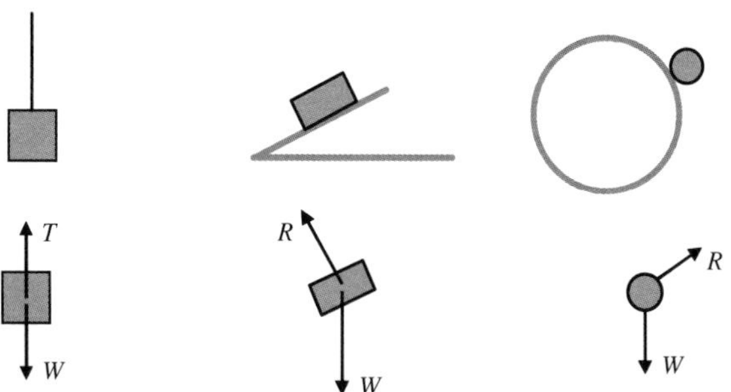

Figure 3.9 Free-body diagrams for the bodies in dark grey.

In any mechanics problem, it is important to be able to draw correctly the free-body diagrams for all the bodies of interest. It is also important that the length of the arrow representing a given force is proportional to the magnitude of the force.

Hooke's law

If we try to extend a spring, a force pulls the spring back to its original length; if we try to compress a spring, again a force tries to pull the spring back to its original length (see Figure 3.10). The force in the spring, the tension, has a simple relationship to the amount by which the spring is extended or compressed.

If this amount is x, then the tension T is proportional to x (see Figure 3.11). This statement is known as Hooke's law. This means

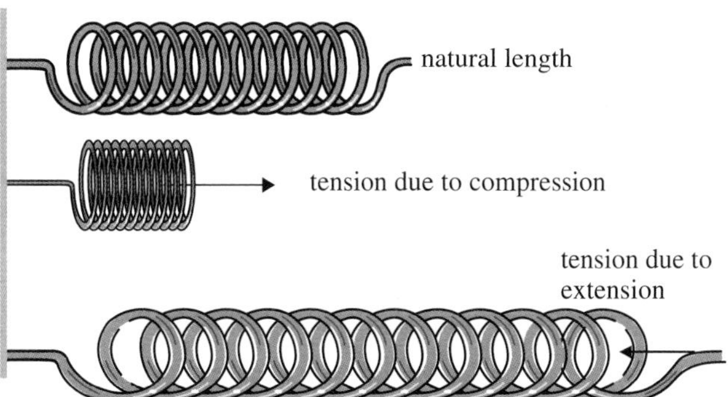

Figure 3.10 The tension in a spring is proportional and opposite to the extension.

that the more we want to extend or compress the spring, the bigger the force required to pull or push it with. In equation form it says that $T = kx$, where k is the constant of proportionality known as the spring constant. It varies from spring to spring. Its units are those of force over extension: N m^{-1}.

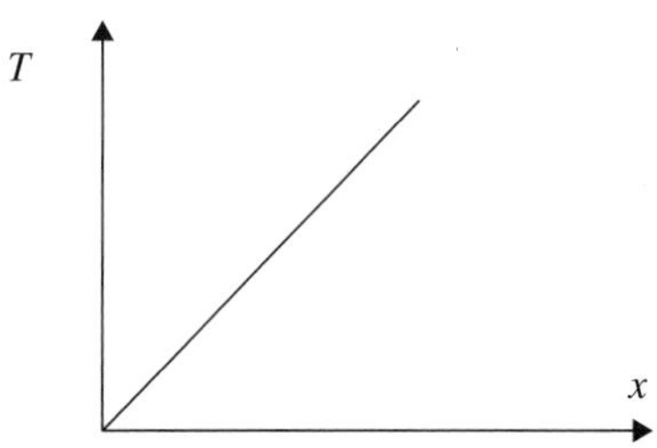

Figure 3.11 The tension in the spring is linearly proportional to the extension.

The extension or compression of the spring must not be too large, otherwise Hooke's law isn't applicable. The range of extensions (or compressions) for which Hooke's law is satisfied is known as the elastic limit; beyond the elastic limit the relationship between tension and extension is more complicated.

? QUESTIONS

1 A mass swings at the end of a string like a pendulum. Draw the forces on the mass at:
(a) its lowest position;
(b) its highest position.

2 A mass rests on a rough table and is connected by a string that goes over a pulley

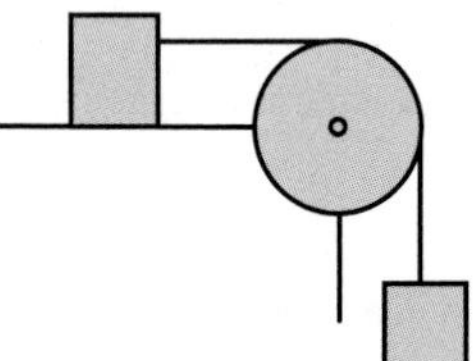

Figure 3.12 For question 2.

to a second hanging mass, as shown in Figure 3.12. Draw the forces on each mass.

3 A mass is tied to a string and rotates in a vertical circle, as shown in Figure 3.13. Draw the forces on the mass when the string is horizontal.

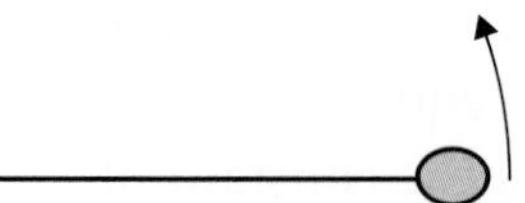

Figure 3.13 For question 3.

4 A bead rolls on the surface of a sphere, having started from the top, as shown in Figure 3.14. Draw the forces on the bead:
(a) at the top;
(b) at the point where it is about to leave the surface of the sphere.

Figure 3.14 For question 4.

5 A mass hangs at the end of a vertical spring which is attached to the ceiling. Draw the forces on:
(a) the hanging mass;
(b) the ceiling.

6 Look at Figure 3.15. In which case is the tension in the string largest?

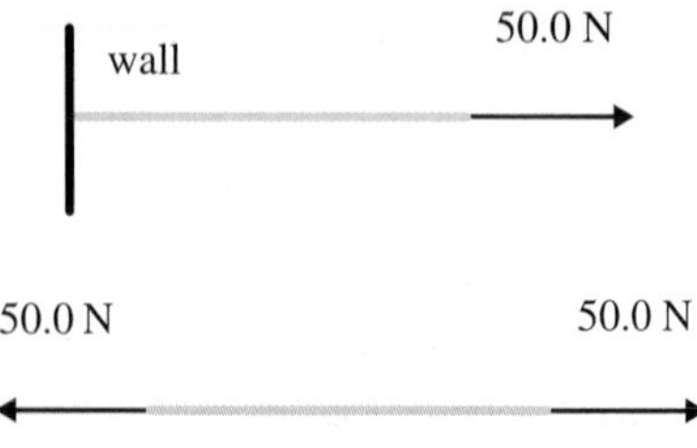

Figure 3.15 For question 6.

7 A force of 125 N is required to extend a spring by 2.8 cm. What force is required to stretch the same spring by 3.2 cm?

8 A mass hangs attached to three strings, as shown in Figure 3.16. Draw the forces on:
(a) the hanging mass;
(b) the point where the strings join.

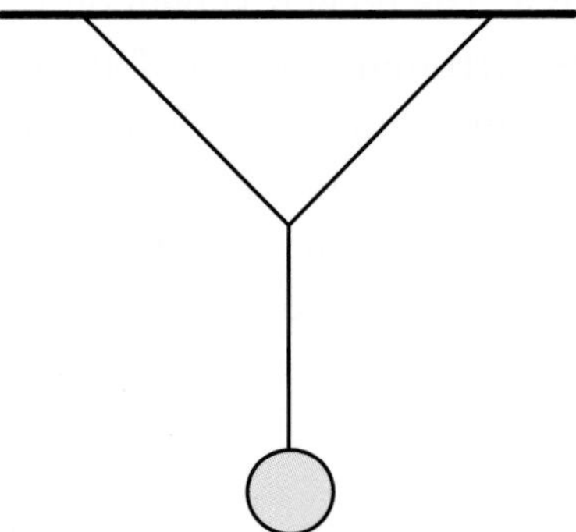

Figure 3.16 For question 8.

9 A spring is compressed by a certain distance and a mass is attached to its right end, as shown in Figure 3.17. The mass rests on a rough table. What are the forces acting on the mass?

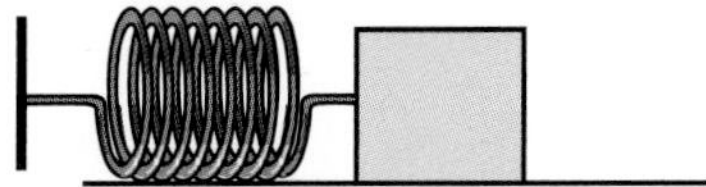

Figure 3.17 For question 9.

10 A block rests on an elevator floor as shown, as shown in Figure 3.18. The elevator is held in place by a cable attached to the ceiling. Draw the forces on:
(a) the block;
(b) the elevator.

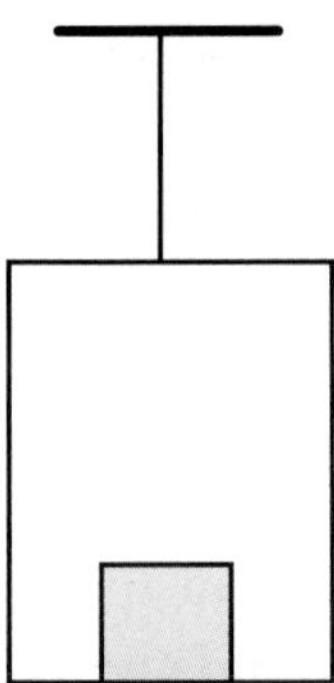

Figure 3.18 For question 10.

Newton's first law

Mechanics rests on Newton's three laws. The first law is discussed in this chapter. The first law leads to a study of systems in equilibrium, which is a state in which the net force on the system is zero.

Objectives

By the end of this chapter you should be able to:

- relate situations in which the acceleration is zero to equilibrium situations in which the net force is zero;
- find the net force on a body using the methods of vector addition;
- solve problems of equilibrium.

Newton's first law

In ancient times, Aristotle had maintained that a force is what is required in order to keep a body in motion. The higher the speed, the larger the force needed. Aristotle's idea of force is not unreasonable and is in fact in accordance with experience from everyday life: it does require a force to push a piece of furniture from one corner of a room to another. What Aristotle failed to appreciate is that everyday life is plagued by friction. An object in motion comes to rest because of friction and thus a force is required if it is to keep moving. This force is needed in order to cancel the force of friction that opposes the motion. In an idealized world with no friction, a body that is set into motion does not require a force to keep it moving. Galileo, 2000 years after Aristotle, was the first to realize that the state of no motion and the state of motion with constant speed in a straight line are indistinguishable from each other. Since no force is present in the case of no motion, no forces are required in the case of motion in a straight line with constant speed either. Force is related, as you will see, to changes in velocity (i.e. accelerations).

Newton's first law (generalizing statements of Galileo) states the following:

▶ When no forces act on a body, that body will either remain at rest or continue to move along a straight line with constant speed.

A body that moves with acceleration (i.e. changing speed or changing direction of motion) must have a force acting on it. An ice hockey puck slides on ice with practically no friction and will thus move with constant speed in a straight line. A spacecraft leaving the solar system with its engines off has no force acting on it and will continue to move in a straight line at constant speed (until it encounters another body that will attract or hit it). Using the first law, it is easy to see if a force is acting on a body. For example, the earth rotates around the sun and thus we know at once that a force must be acting on the earth.

Newton's first law is also called the law of *inertia*. Inertia is the reluctance of a body to change its state of motion. Inertia keeps the body in the same state of motion when no forces act on the body. When a car accelerates forward, the passengers are thrown back into their seats. If a car brakes abruptly, the passengers are thrown forward. This implies that a mass tends to stay in the state of motion it was in before the force acted on it. The reaction of a body to a change in its state of motion (acceleration) is inertia.

A well-known example of inertia is that of a magician who very suddenly pulls the tablecloth off a table leaving all the plates, glasses, etc., behind on the table. The inertia of these objects makes them 'want' to stay on the table where they are. Similarly, if you pull very suddenly on a roll of kitchen paper you will tear off a sheet. But if you pull gently you will only succeed in making the paper roll rotate.

Inertial frames of reference

A system on which no forces act is called an inertial frame of reference. Inertial reference frames played a crucial role in the history of physics: observers belonging to different inertial frames will come up with the same laws of physics. For example, an observer at rest on the surface of the earth is an (approximate) inertial reference frame. (We say approximate, since the earth rotates about its axis as well as around the sun – but these motions produce small accelerations and over a short interval of time we can ignore them.) A passenger on a train that moves with constant velocity relative to an observer on the earth is also an inertial reference frame. The two observers will discover the same laws of physics by performing experiments in their respective frames. There is no experiment that the observer on the train can perform whose result will be to determine that the train is moving. Nor will he ever discover laws of physics that are different from the ones discovered by the observer on the ground.

Equilibrium

When the net force on a body is zero, the body is said to be in **equilibrium**. If a body is displaced slightly from its equilibrium position, the net force on the body may or may not be zero. If it is still zero, the position of equilibrium is called a neutral equilibrium position. An example is a mass resting on a horizontal table, as in Figure 4.1.

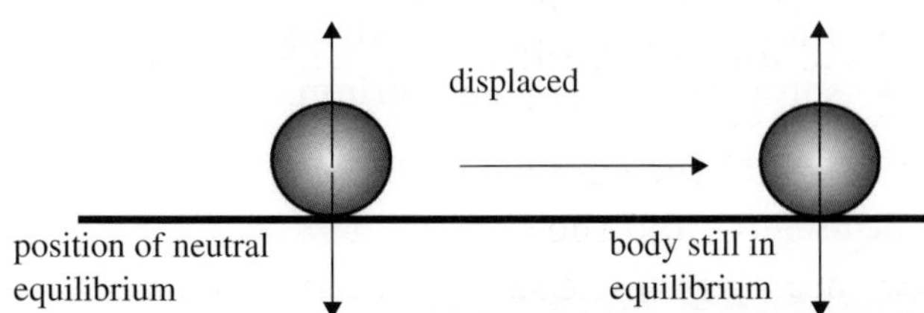

Figure 4.1 In a position of neutral equilibrium the net force on a body is zero. A displacement results in another equilibrium position.

On the other hand, if after displacing the body from its equilibrium position the net force is no longer zero, then we distinguish two kinds of equilibrium in the original position. If the net force in the displaced position tends to move the body back towards the initial equilibrium position, then we speak of stable equilibrium. If, on the other hand, the force on the body tends to make it move even further from the initial position, we speak of unstable equilibrium (see Figure 4.2).

Figure 4.2 In unstable equilibrium the net force on the body is zero, but a small displacement results in motion away from the equilibrium position. In stable equilibrium, the motion is back towards the equilibrium position.

Note that an equilibrium position can be both stable and unstable at the same time. For example, a mass on a surface that resembles a saddle is in equilibrium if placed at the centre of the saddle. The equilibrium is stable or unstable depending on the direction in which the mass is then displaced.

Equilibrium of a point particle means that the net force on the point is zero. To find the net force we must use the methods of vector addition, and here we will exclusively use the component method. We choose a set of axes whose origin is the point body in question and find the components of all the forces on the body. As promised in Chapter 1.4, we will use only positive components. Then the sum of the x components to the 'right' must equal the sum of the x components to the 'left', and the sum of the y components 'up' must equal the sum of the y components 'down'. Let us look at a simple example. A block of weight 10.0 N rests on a horizontal table. What is the normal reaction on the block from the table? Figure 4.3 shows the forces on the block, which is assumed to be a point object. The dotted lines represent the axes along which we will take components. There are no forces with horizontal components. In the vertical direction the component of R is simply R in the 'up' direction. The 10.0 N force has a component of 10.0 N in the 'down' direction. Equating the up with the down components we find $R = 10.0$ N.

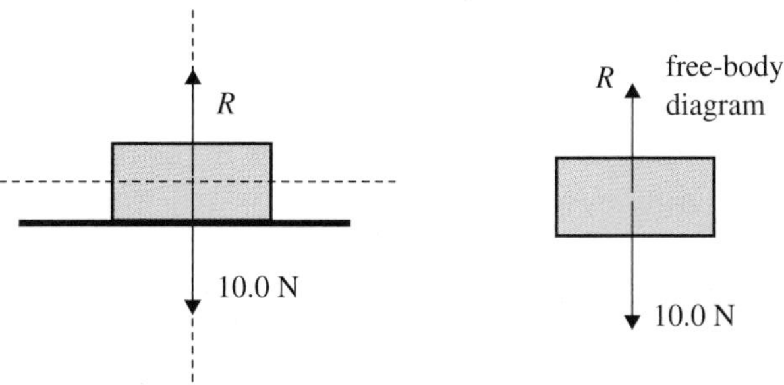

Figure 4.3 The forces acting on a block resting on a table.

Let us look at a slightly less trivial example. A 20.0 N weight hangs from strings as shown in Figure 4.4. We want to find the tension in each string.

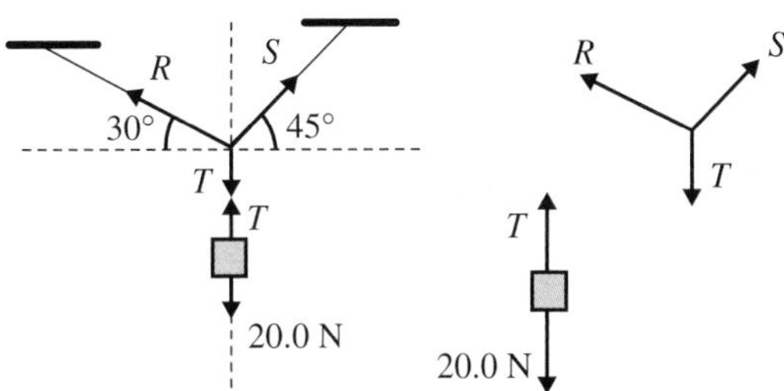

Figure 4.4 Free-body diagrams for joining point and hanging mass.

We call the tensions in the three strings T, R and S. The point where the strings meet is in equilibrium and so the net force from these three tensions is zero. Getting components along the horizontal and vertical directions we have:

$$\begin{aligned}
T_x &= 0 \\
T_y &= T \text{ 'down'} \\
R_x &= R\cos 30^\circ \\
&= 0.866R \text{ 'left'} \\
R_y &= R\sin 30^\circ \\
&= 0.500R \text{ 'up'} \\
S_x &= S\cos 45^\circ \\
&= 0.707S \text{ 'right'} \\
S_y &= S\sin 45^\circ \\
&= 0.707S \text{ 'up'}
\end{aligned}$$

We thus have

$$\begin{aligned}
0.866R &= 0.707S \\
0.707S + 0.500R &= T
\end{aligned}$$

Equilibrium of the hanging mass demands, however, that $T = 20.0$ N. Thus we can find $R = 14.6$ N and $S = 17.9$ N.

Example questions

Q1

A mass $m = 10.0$ kg hangs from two strings which are attached to the ceiling as shown in Figure 4.5. What is the tension in each string?

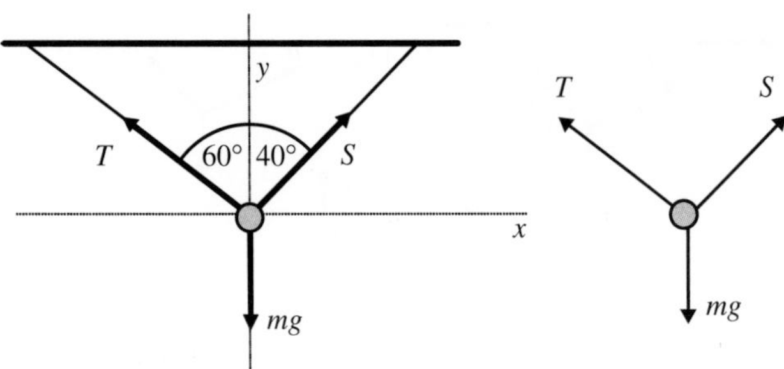

Figure 4.5.

Answer

The three forces acting on m are as shown, with T and S being the tensions in the two strings. Taking components about horizontal and vertical axes through m we find (here we will make use of only positive components) $T_x = T\cos 30° = 0.87T$ to the left, $T_y = T\sin 30° = 0.50T$ up, $S_x = S\cos 50° = 0.64S$ to the right, $S_y = S\sin 50° = 0.77S$ up. The weight mg is already along one of the axes: it has a component $mg = 100$ N down. Equilibrium thus demands (net force has zero x and y components)

$$0.87\,T = 0.64\,S$$
$$0.50\,T + 0.77\,S = 100$$

from which we find $T = 65.3$ N and $S = 87.9$ N.

Q2

A block of weight 50.0 N rests on a rough horizontal table and is attached by strings to a hanging mass of weight 12.0 N, as shown in Figure 4.6. Find the force of friction between the block and the table if the block on the table is in equilibrium.

Answer

The diagram shows the forces acting on the block and the mass as well as the tensions at the point where the three strings join. Since that point is in equilibrium, the net force on it is zero. Taking components of the forces R, S and 12.0 N along horizontal and vertical axes we find:

$$R_x = R \text{ 'left'}$$
$$R_y = 0$$

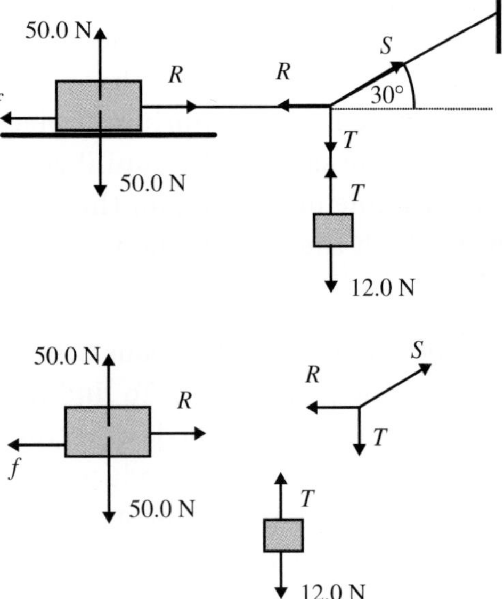

Figure 4.6.

$$S_x = S\cos 30°$$
$$= 0.866\,S \text{ 'right'}$$
$$S_y = S\sin 30°$$
$$= 0.500\,S \text{ 'up'}$$

Equilibrium then demands that

$$R = 0.866\,S$$
$$0.500\,S = T$$
$$= 12.0$$

since $T = 12.0$ N by the equilibrium of the hanging mass. We can thus find $S = 24.0$ N and so $R = 20.8$ N. Demanding now equilibrium for the block on the table, we see that the frictional force must equal R, i.e. 20.8 N.

Q3

A mass of 125 g is attached to a spring of spring constant $k = 58$ N m^{-1} that is hanging vertically.

(a) Find the extension of the spring.

(b) If the mass and the spring are placed on the moon, will there be any change in the extension of the spring?

Answer

(a) The forces on the hanging mass are its weight and the tension of the spring. Since we have equilibrium, the two forces are equal in magnitude. Therefore

$$kx = mg$$

$$x = \frac{mg}{k}$$

$$= \frac{0.125 \times 10}{58}$$

$$= 2.2 \text{ cm}$$

(b) The extension will be less, since the acceleration of gravity is less.

? QUESTIONS

1 What is the net force on each of the bodies shown in the diagrams in Figure 4.7? The only forces acting are the ones shown. Indicate direction by 'right', 'left', 'up' and 'down'.

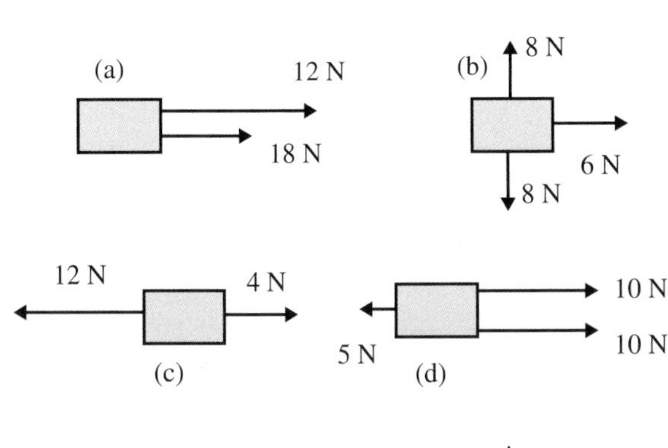

Figure 4.7 For question 1.

2 Find the magnitude and direction of the net force in Figure 4.8.

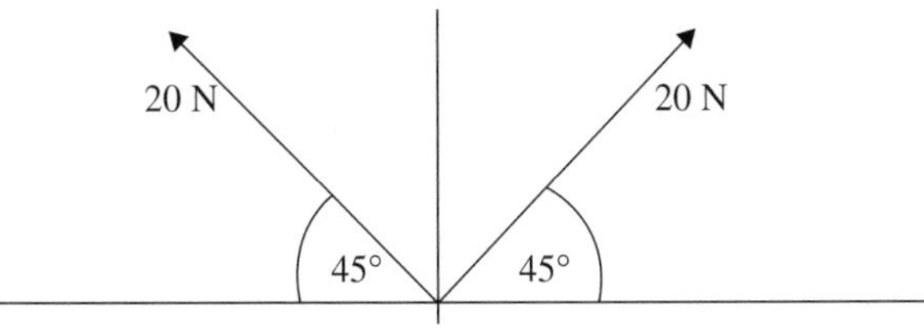

Figure 4.8 For question 2.

3 In Figure 4.9, what must F and θ be such that the three forces give a net force of zero?

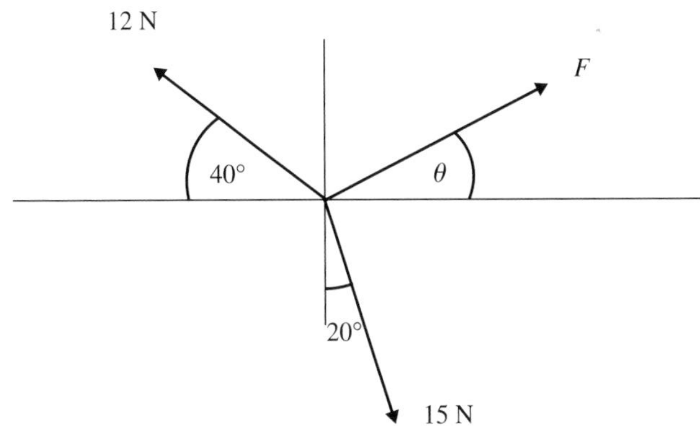

Figure 4.9 For question 3.

4 Why is it impossible for a mass to hang attached to two horizontal strings as shown in Figure 4.10?

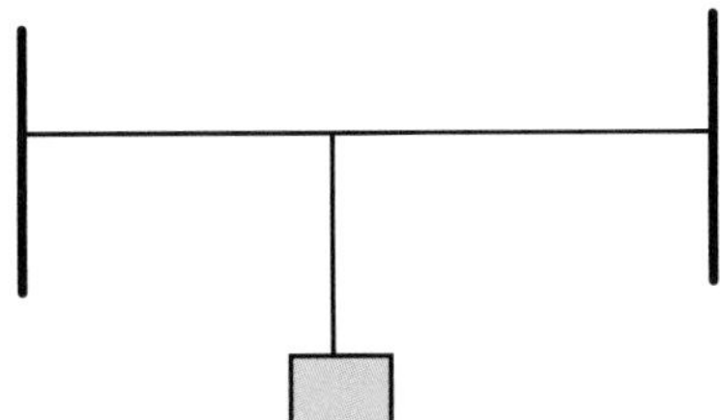

Figure 4.10 For question 4.

5 A mass is hanging from a string that is attached to the ceiling. A second piece of string (identical to the first) hangs from the lower end of the mass. (See Figure 4.11.)

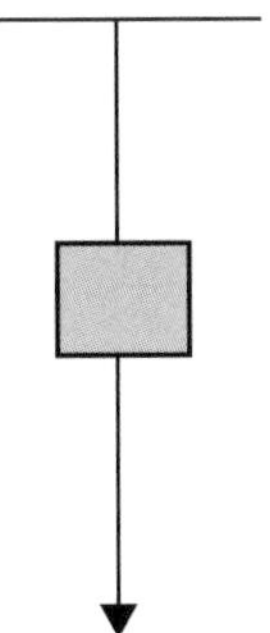

Figure 4.11 For question 5.

Which string will break if:

(a) the bottom string is slowly pulled with ever increasing force;

(b) the bottom string is very abruptly pulled down?

6 A force of 10.0 N is acting along the negative *x*-axis and a force of 5.00 N at an angle of 20° with the positive *x*-axis. Find the net force.

7 A force has components 2.45 N and 4.23 N along two perpendicular axes. What is the magnitude of the force?

8 A weight of mass 12.5 kg hangs from very light, smooth pulleys as shown in Figure 4.12. What force must be applied to the rope so that the mass stays at rest?

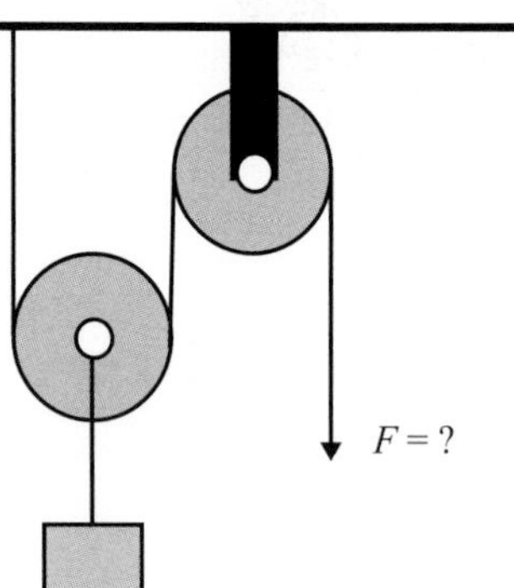

Figure 4.12 For question 8.

9 A mass of 2.00 kg rests on a rough horizontal table. The maximum frictional force between the mass and the table is 12 N. The block is attached to a hanging mass by a string that goes over a smooth pulley. What is the largest mass that can hang in this way without forcing the block to slide? (See Figure 4.13.)

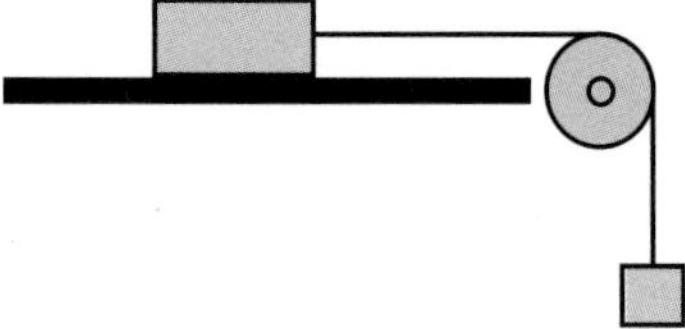

Figure 4.13 For question 9.

10 A mass of 5.00 kg hangs attached to three strings as shown in Figure 4.14. Find the tension in each string. (Hint: Consider the equilibrium of the point where the strings join.)

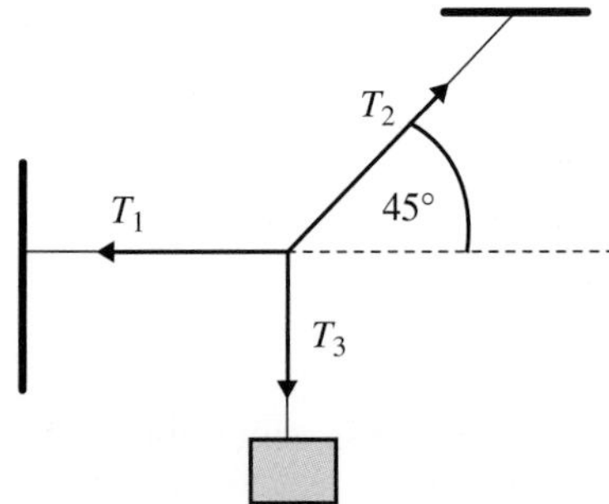

Figure 4.14 For question 10.

11 A rod of mass 5.00 kg is first pulled and then pushed at constant velocity by a force at 45° to the horizontal as shown in Figure 4.15. Assuming that in both cases the frictional force is horizontal and equal to 0.4 times the normal reaction force on the rod, find the force *F* in each case. What does this imply?

Figure 4.15 For question 11.

12 A 455 kg crate is being pulled at constant velocity by a force directed at 30° to the horizontal as shown in Figure 4.16. The frictional force on the crate is 1163 N. What is the magnitude of the pulling force?

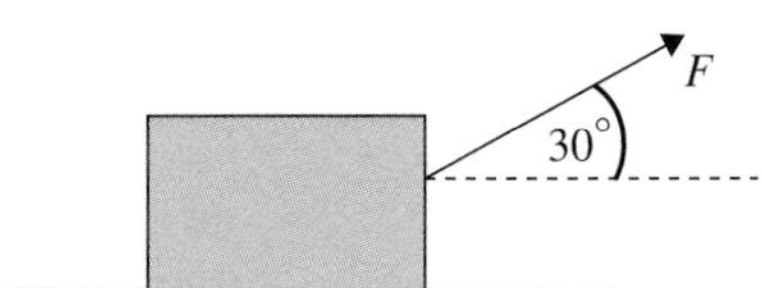

Figure 4.16 For question 12.

13 (a) A 2598 kg aeroplane is moving horizontally in a straight line at constant velocity. What is the upward force on the aeroplane?

(b) The plane is now diving (again at constant velocity) making an angle of 10° to the horizontal. Find the lift force on the plane assuming that it is normal to the velocity of the plane.

14 A mass M is connected with a string to a smaller mass m. The mass M is resting on an inclined plane and the string goes over a pulley at the top of the plane so that the mass m is hanging vertically, as shown in Figure 4.17. What must the angle of the plane be in order to have equilibrium?

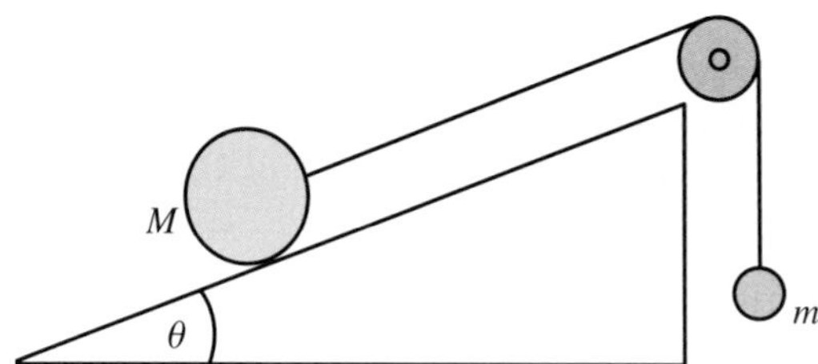

Figure 4.17 For question 14.

15 A mass m is attached to two identical springs of spring constant k. The other end of each spring is attached to the ceiling so that each makes an angle θ with the vertical, as shown in Figure 4.18. If the mass is in equilibrium, what is the extension of each spring?

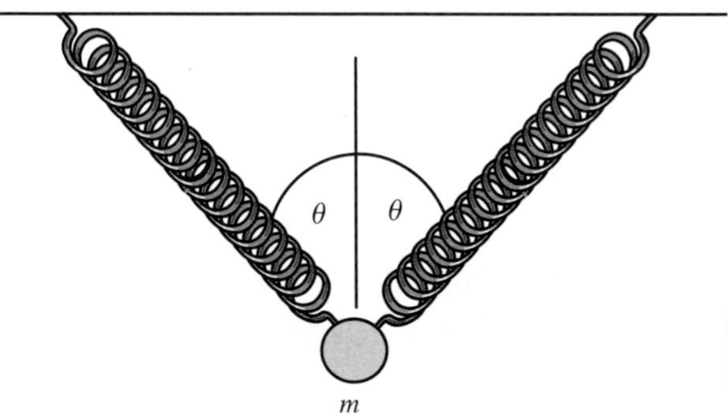

Figure 4.18 For question 15.

Newton's second and third laws

These laws are the cornerstone of what is called classical physics. They imply that, once the forces that act on a system are specified and the motion of the system is known at some point in time, then the motion of the system can be predicted at all future times. This predictability is characteristic of classical systems as opposed to quantum ones, where the uncertainty principle introduces a probabilistic interpretation on the future evolution of the system. Lately, this sharp definition of predictability has been eroded somewhat even for classical systems: chaotic behaviour can imply a loss of predictability in some cases.

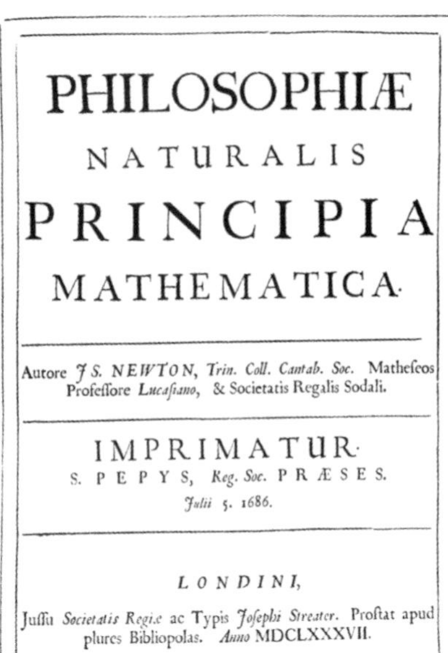

PHILOSOPHIÆ
NATURALIS
PRINCIPIA
MATHEMATICA.

Autore *J S. NEWTON*, *Trin. Coll. Cantab. Soc.* Matheſeos Profeſſore *Lucaſiano*, & Societatis Regalis Sodali.

IMPRIMATUR.
S. PEPYS, *Reg. Soc.* PRÆSES.
Julii 5. 1686.

LONDINI,
Juſſu *Societatis Regiæ* ac Typis *Joſephi Streater*. Proſtat apud plures Bibliopolas. *Anno* MDCLXXXVII.

This is the front page from Newton's book called *Principia* (Principles) in which he outlined his theories of the laws that governed the motion of objects.

Objectives

By the end of this chapter you should be able to:

- recognize situations of equilibrium, i.e. situations where *the net force and hence the acceleration are zero*;
- draw the forces on the body of interest and apply Newton's second law on that body, $F = ma$;
- recognize that the net force on a body is in the *same direction as the acceleration* of that body;
- identify pairs of forces that come from Newton's third law.

Newton's second law

This fundamental law asserts that:

▶ The net force on a body is proportional to that body's acceleration and is in the same direction as the acceleration. Mathematically

$$\vec{F} = m\vec{a}$$

where the constant of proportionality, m, is the *mass* of the body.

Figure 5.1 shows the net force on a freely falling body, which happens to be its weight, $W = mg$. By Newton's second law, the net force equals the mass times the acceleration, and so

$$mg = ma$$
$$\Rightarrow a = g$$

that is, the acceleration of the freely falling body is exactly g. Experiments going back to Galileo show us that indeed all bodies fall in a vacuum with the same acceleration (the acceleration due to gravity) irrespective of their density, their mass, their shape and the material from which they are made.

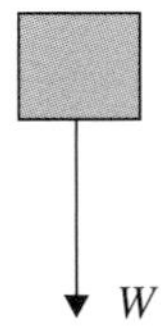

Figure 5.1 A mass falling to the ground acted upon by gravity.

▶ The equation $F = ma$ defines the unit of force, the newton (symbol N). One newton is the force required to accelerate a mass of 1 kg by 1 m s^{-2} in the direction of the force.

It is important to realize that the second law speaks of the net force on the body. Thus, if a number of individual forces act on a body, we must first find the net force by vector addition.

A simple everyday example of the second law is that when you jump from some height you bend your knees on landing. This is because by bending your knees you stretch out the time it takes to reduce your speed to zero, and thus your acceleration (deceleration) is least. This means that the force from the ground on to you is least.

Example questions

Q1

A man of mass $m = 70$ kg stands on the floor of an elevator. Find the force of reaction he experiences from the elevator floor when:

(a) the elevator is standing still;

(b) the elevator moves up at constant speed 3 m s^{-1};

(c) the elevator moves up with acceleration 4 m s^{-2};

(d) the elevator moves down with acceleration 4 m s^{-2}.

Answer

Two forces act on the man: his weight mg vertically down and the reaction force R from the floor vertically up.

(a) There is no acceleration and so by Newton's second law the net force on the man must be zero. Hence

$$R = mg$$
$$= 700 \text{ N}$$

(b) There is no acceleration and so again

$$R = mg$$
$$= 700 \text{ N}$$

(c) There is acceleration upwards. Hence

$$R - mg = ma$$

so

$$R = mg + ma$$
$$= 700 \text{ N} + 280 \text{ N}$$
$$= 980 \text{ N}$$

(d) We again have acceleration, but this time in the downward direction. Hence

$mg - R = ma$

so

$$R = mg - ma$$
$$= 700\ \text{N} - 280\ \text{N}$$
$$= 420\ \text{N}$$

Note: In (c) the acceleration is up, so we find the net force in the upward direction. In (d) the acceleration is down, so we find the net force in the downward direction. Newton's law in all cases involves accelerations and forces in the same direction.

Q2

A man of mass 70 kg is moving *upward* in an elevator at a constant speed of 3 m s^{-1}. The elevator comes to rest in a time of 2 s. What is the reaction force on the man from the elevator floor during the period of deceleration?

Answer

The acceleration experienced by the man is -1.5 m s^{-2}. So

$$R - mg = ma$$
$$\Rightarrow R = mg + ma$$
$$= 700 + (-105) = 595\ \text{N}$$

If, instead, the man was moving *downward* and then decelerated to rest, we would have

$$mg - R = ma$$
$$\Rightarrow R = mg - ma$$
$$= 700 - (-105) = 805\ \text{N}$$

Both cases are easily experienced in daily life. When the elevator goes up and then stops we feel 'lighter' during the deceleration period. When going down and about to stop, we feel 'heavier' during the deceleration period. The feeling of 'lightness' or 'heaviness' has to do with what reaction force we feel from the floor.

Q3

A hot air balloon of mass 150 kg is tied to the ground with a rope (of negligible mass). When the rope is cut, the balloon rises with an acceleration of 2 m s^{-2}. What was the tension in the rope?

Answer

The forces on the balloon originally are its weight, the upthrust and the tension (see Figure 5.2).

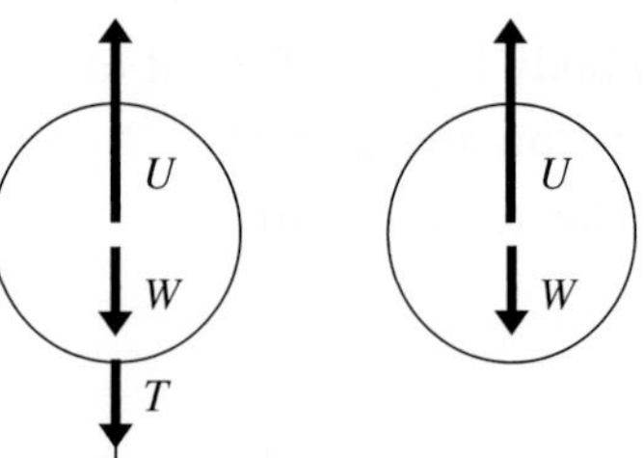

Figure 5.2.

Initially we have equilibrium and so $U = W + T$. After the rope is cut the net force is $U - W$ and so

$$U - W = ma$$
$$= 150 \times 2$$
$$= 300\ \text{N}$$

From the first equation

$T = U - W = 300$ N

The next examples show how Newton's second law is applied when more than one mass is present.

Q4

Two blocks of mass 4.0 and 6.0 kg are joined by a string and rest on a frictionless horizontal table (see Figure 5.3). If a force of 100 N is applied horizontally on one of the blocks, find the acceleration of each block.

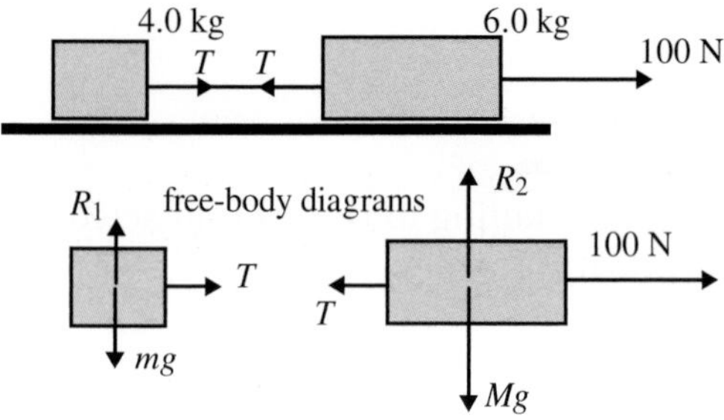

Figure 5.3.

Answer

Method 1: The net force on the 6.0 kg mass is $100 - T$ and on the 4.0 kg mass just T. Thus, applying Newton's second law separately on *each* mass

$$100 - T = 6a$$
$$T = 4a$$

Solving for a (by adding the two equations side by side) gives $a = 10\ \text{m s}^{-2}$ and the tension is thus

$$T = 4.0 \times 10$$
$$= 40\ \text{N}$$

Note: The free-body diagram makes it clear that the 100 N force acts *only* on the body to the right. It is a common mistake to say that the body to the left is also acted upon by the 100 N force.

Method 2: We may consider the two bodies as one of mass 10 kg. This is denoted by the dotted line in Figure 5.4. The net force on the body is 100 N. Note that the tensions are irrelevant now since they cancel out. (They did not in Method 1 as they acted on *different* bodies. Now they act on the *same* body. They are now *internal* forces and these are irrelevant.)

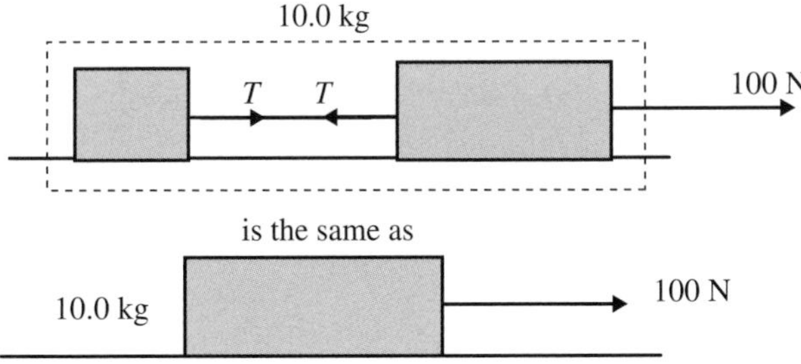

Figure 5.4.

Applying Newton's second law on the single body we have

$$100 = 10a$$
$$\Rightarrow a = 10\ \text{m s}^{-2}.$$

But to find the tension we must break up the combined body into the original two bodies. Newton's second law on the 4.0 kg body gives

$$T = 4a = 40\ \text{N}$$

(the tension on this block is the net force on the block). If we used the other block, we would see that the net force on it is $100 - T$ and so

$$100 - T = 6 \times 10$$
$$= 60$$

giving $T = 40$ N as before.

Q5

(Atwood's machine) Two masses of $m = 4.0$ kg and $M = 6.0$ kg are joined together by a string that passes over a pulley. The masses are held stationary and suddenly released. What is the acceleration of each mass?

Answer

Intuition tells us that the larger mass will start moving downward and the small mass will go up. So if we say that the larger mass's acceleration is a, then the other mass's acceleration will also be a in magnitude but, of course, in the opposite direction. The two accelerations are the same because the string cannot be extended.

Method 1: The forces on each mass are weight mg and tension T on m and weight Mg and tension T on M (see Figure 5.5).

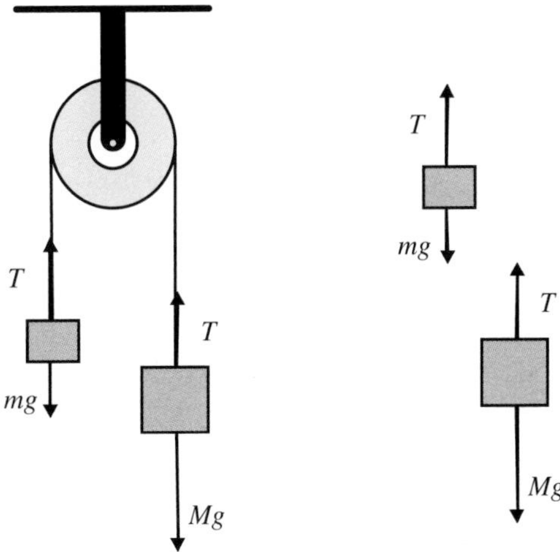

Figure 5.5.

Newton's second law applied to each mass states

$$T - mg = ma \quad (1)$$
$$Mg - T = Ma \quad (2)$$

Note these equations carefully. Each says that the net force on the mass in question is equal to that mass times that mass's acceleration. In the first equation we find the net force in the upward direction, because that is the direction of acceleration. In the second we find the net force downward, since that is the direction of acceleration in that case. We want to find the acceleration, so we simply add up these two equations side by side to find

$$Mg - mg = (m + M)a$$

hence

$$a = \frac{M - m}{M + m}g$$

(Note that if $M \gg m$, the acceleration tends to g (why?).) This shows clearly that if the two masses are equal then there is no acceleration. This is a convenient method for measuring g: Atwood's machine effectively 'slows down' g so the falling mass has a much smaller acceleration from which g can then be determined. Putting in the numbers for our example we find $a = 2.0\ \text{m s}^{-2}$. Having found the acceleration we may, if we wish, also find the tension in the string, T. Putting the value for a in formula (1) we find

$$T = m\frac{M - m}{M + m}g + mg$$
$$= 2\frac{Mm}{M + m}g$$
$$= 48\ \text{N}$$

(If $M \gg m$, the tension tends to $2mg$ (why?).)

Method 2: We treat the two masses as one body and apply Newton's second law on this body (but this is trickier than in the previous example) – see Figure 5.6.

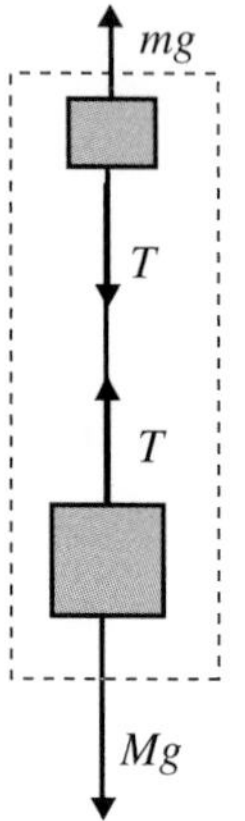

Figure 5.6.

In this case the net force is $Mg - mg$ and, since this force acts on a body of mass $M + m$, the acceleration is found as before from $F = \text{mass} \times \text{acceleration}$. Note that the tension T does not appear in this case, being now an internal force.

Q6

In Figure 5.7, a block of mass M is connected to a smaller mass m through a string that goes over a pulley. Ignoring friction, find the acceleration of each mass and the tension in the string.

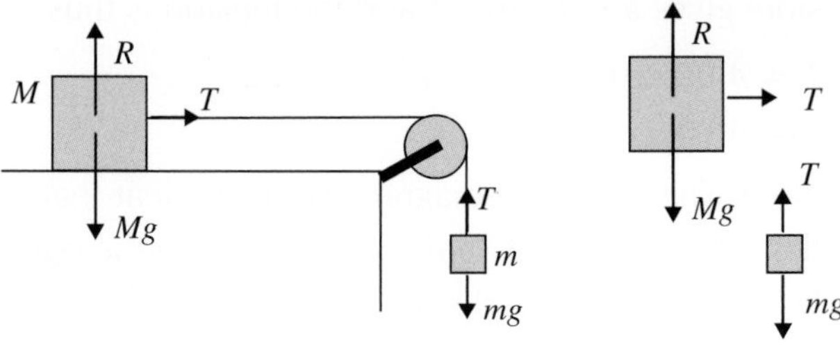

Figure 5.7.

Answer

Method 1: The forces are shown in Figure 5.7. Thus

$$mg - T = ma$$
$$T = Ma$$

from which (adding the two equations side by side)

$$a = \frac{mg}{m + M}$$

(If $M \gg m$ the acceleration tends to zero (why?).) If $M = 8.0$ kg and $m = 2.0$ kg, this gives $a = 2.0\ \text{m s}^{-2}$. Hence

$$T = \frac{Mmg}{m + M}$$
$$= 16\ \text{N}$$

Method 2: Treating the two bodies as one results in the situation shown in Figure 5.8.

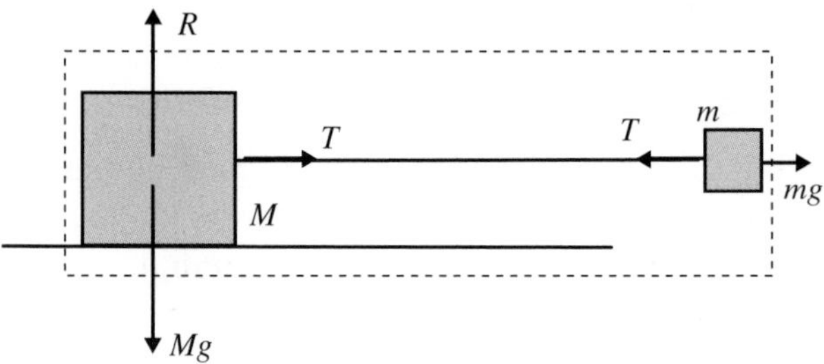

Figure 5.8.

The net force on the mass $M + m$ is mg. Hence

$$mg = (M + m)a$$
$$\Rightarrow a = \frac{mg}{m + M}$$

The tension can then be found as before.

Q7

Consider finally 100 blocks each of mass $m = 1.0$ kg that are placed next to each other in a straight line, as shown in Figure 5.9.

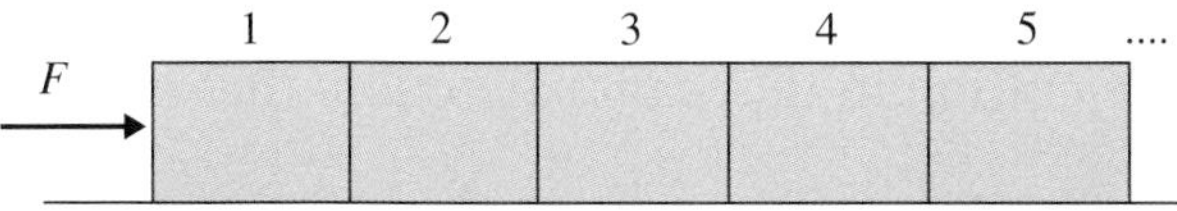

Figure 5.9.

A force $F = 100$ N is applied to the block at the left. What force does the 60th block exert on the 61st (see Figure 5.10)?

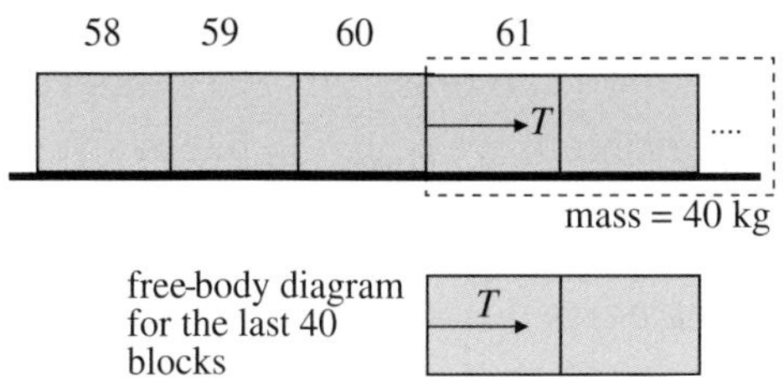

Figure 5.10.

Answer

To answer the question, we treat the 100 blocks as one body, in which case the net force on the system is 100 N. Since the mass is 100 kg, the acceleration of each block is 1 m s^{-2}.

Let T be the required force. It is the net force on the body inside the dotted line of mass 40 kg. Since this force accelerates a mass of 40 kg by 1 m s^{-2}, $T = ma = 40$ N.

Terminal velocity

When a body moves through a fluid (a gas or liquid), it experiences an opposing force that depends on the speed of the body. If the speed is small, the opposing force is proportional to the speed, whereas for larger speeds the force becomes proportional to the square of the speed. Consider, for example, a body falling through air. The forces on the body are its weight, mg, and the opposing force, which we assume is proportional to the speed, $F = kv$. Initially the speed is small, so the body falls with an acceleration that is essentially that due to gravity. As the speed increases, so does the opposing force and hence, after a while, it will become equal to the weight. In that case the acceleration becomes zero and the body continues to fall with a *constant* velocity, called *terminal velocity*. Figure 5.11 shows a body falling from rest and acquiring a terminal velocity of 50 m s^{-1} after about 25 s. The acceleration of the body is initially that due to gravity but becomes zero after about 25 s.

$$mg = kv_T \Rightarrow v_T = \frac{mg}{k}$$

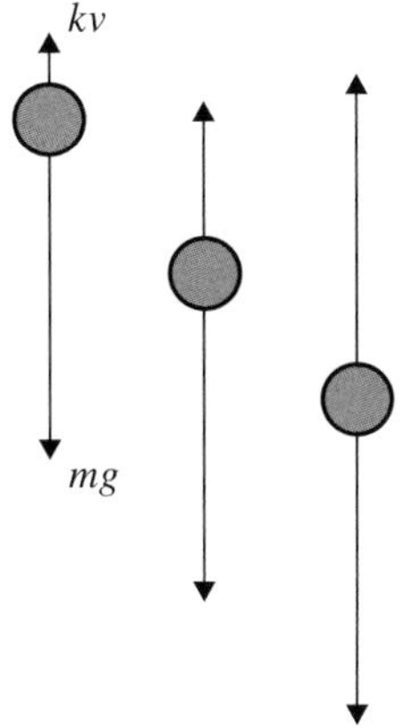

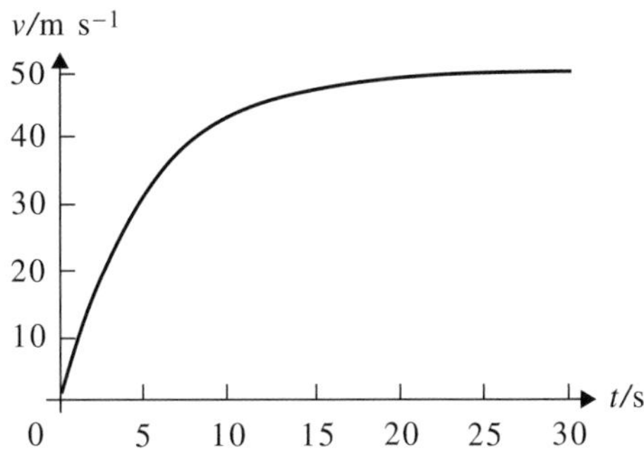

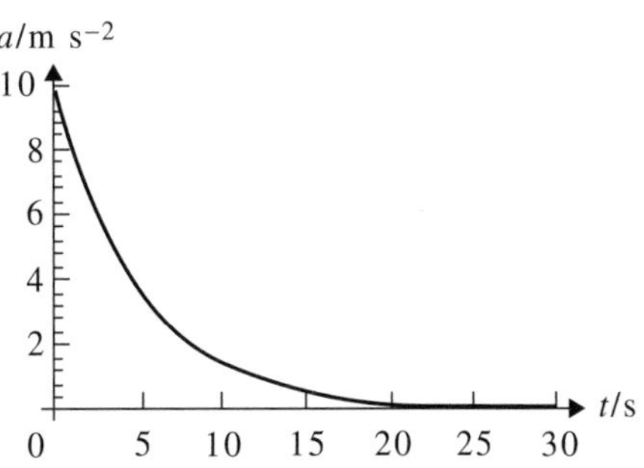

Figure 5.11 The opposing force grows as the speed increases and eventually becomes equal to the weight. From that point on, the acceleration is zero and the body has achieved its terminal velocity.

The inclined plane

The motion of a body along a straight line that is kept at an angle to the horizontal (inclined plane) is an important application of Newton's laws. The following is an example. A mass of $m = 2.0$ kg is held on a frictionless inclined plane of $30°$. What is the acceleration of the mass if it is released?

There are two forces acting on the mass (see Figure 5.12).

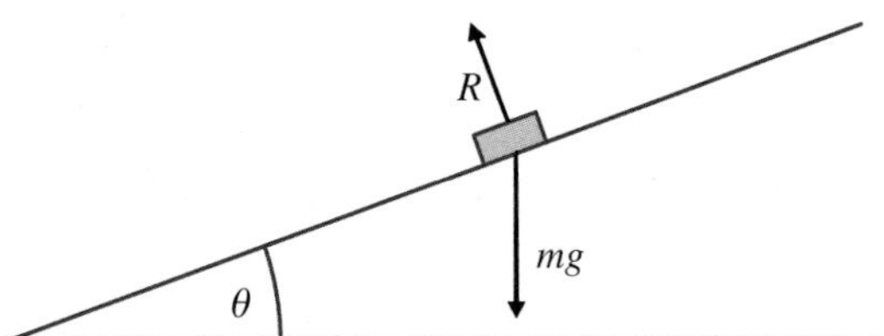

Figure 5.12 A mass on an inclined plane.

The two forces are: its weight vertically down of magnitude mg, and the reaction from the plane, which is perpendicular to the plane, of magnitude R. We can find the components of these two forces along two mutually perpendicular axes, one being along the plane (see Figure 5.13). The force R is already along one of the axes so we don't bother with that. But mg is not.

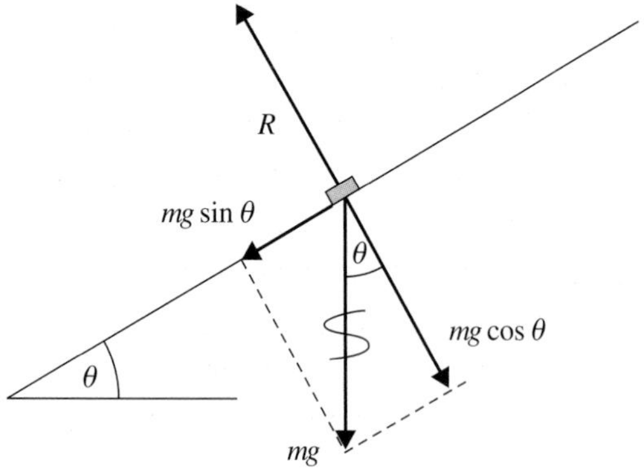

Figure 5.13 We take components along axes that lie along the plane and normally to the plane.

The magnitude of the component of mg along the plane is $mg \sin\theta$, where $\theta = 30°$ is the angle of the incline. This component lies down the plane. The other component is $mg \cos\theta$, in the direction perpendicular to the plane. In that direction there is no acceleration, hence the net force there is zero: that is, $R - mg \cos\theta = 0$. This tells us that $R = mg \cos\theta$. In the direction along the plane, there is a single unbalanced force, namely $mg \sin\theta$, and therefore by Newton's second law, this force will equal mass times acceleration in that same direction: that is

$$mg \sin\theta = ma$$

where a is the unknown acceleration. Hence, we find

$$a = g \sin\theta$$

This is an important result and we will make use of it many times. Note that the acceleration does not depend on the mass. For the numerical values of this problem we find $a = 5.0 \text{ m s}^{-2}$.

You may wonder why we took as our axes the ones along and perpendicular to the inclined plane. The answer is that we did not have to choose these axes. Any other set would have done. This choice, however, is the most convenient, because it exploits the fact that the acceleration will take place along the plane, so we choose that direction as one of our axes. If we had chosen another set of axes, say a horizontal and a vertical one, then we would find acceleration along both of these axes. Acceleration, of course, is a vector and if we combined these two accelerations, we would find the same acceleration (in magnitude and direction) as above. Try to work out the details.

An accelerometer

Consider a mass that is hanging from a string of length L, which is attached to the ceiling of a train. What will be the angle the string makes with the vertical if (a) the train moves forward with a constant speed of 3 m s^{-1}, or (b) moves forward with an acceleration of 4 m s^{-2}? If the train moves with constant speed in the horizontal direction, the acceleration in this direction is zero. Hence the net force in the horizontal direction must also be zero. The only forces on the mass are its weight vertically down, and the tension T of the string along the string. So, to produce zero force in the horizontal direction the string must be vertical. In case (b) there is acceleration in the horizontal direction and hence there must also be a net force in this direction. The string will therefore make an angle θ with the vertical (see Figure 5.14).

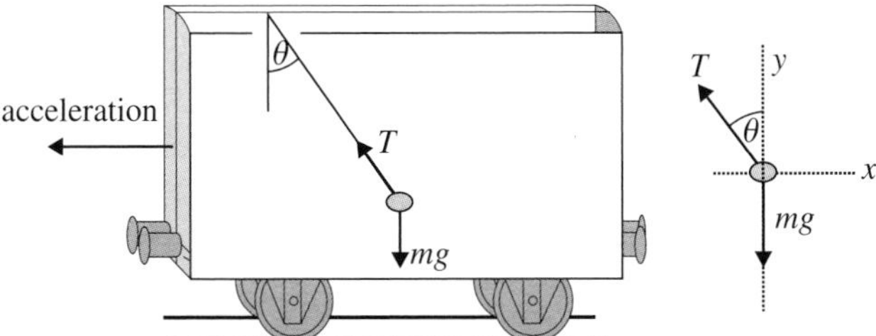

Figure 5.14 When the forces are not in the direction of acceleration, we must take components.

In this case we take components of the forces on the mass along the horizontal and vertical directions. In the horizontal direction we have only the component of T, which is $T\sin\theta$, and in the vertical direction we have $T\cos\theta$ upward and mg downward. Therefore

$$T\sin\theta = ma \quad \text{and} \quad T\cos\theta = mg$$

Hence, $a = g\tan\theta$. Note that the mass does not enter into the expression for a. This is actually a crude device that can be used to measure acceleration – an accelerometer.

Newton's third law

Newton's third law states that:

▶ If body A exerts a force F on body B, then body B exerts an equal but opposite force on body A. (See Figure 5.15.)

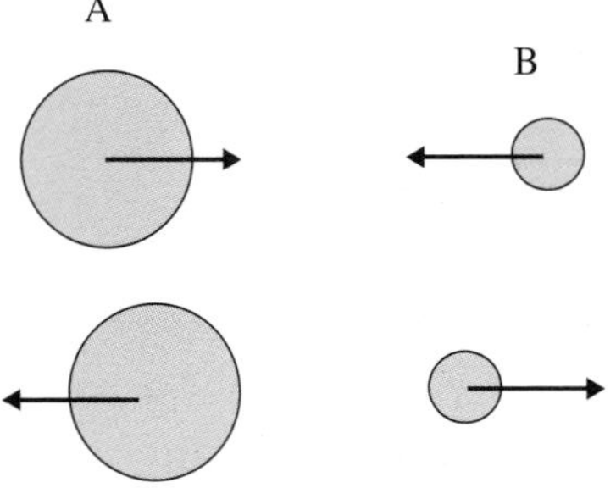

Figure 5.15 The two bodies exert equal and opposite forces on each other.

Make sure you understand that these equal and opposite forces act on *different* bodies. Thus, you cannot use this law to claim that it is impossible to ever have a net force on a body because for every force on it there is also an equal and opposite force. Here are a few examples of this law:

- You stand on roller-skates facing a wall. You push on the wall and you move away from it. This is because you exerted a force on the wall and in turn the wall exerted an equal and opposite force on you, making you accelerate away.
- You are about to step off a boat onto the dock. Your foot exerts a force on the dock, and in turn the dock exerts a force on you (your foot) in the opposite direction making you (and the boat) move away from the dock. (You probably fall in the water!)
- A helicopter hovers in air. Its rotors exert a force downward on the air. Thus, the air exerts the upward force on the helicopter that keeps it from falling.
- A book of mass 2 kg is allowed to fall feely. The earth exerts a force on the book, namely the weight of the book of about 20 N. Thus, the book exerts an equal and opposite force on the earth – a force upward equal to 20 N.

Be careful with situations where two forces are equal and opposite but have nothing to do with the third law. For example, a block of mass 3 kg resting on a horizontal table has two forces acting on it. Its weight of 30 N and the reaction from the table that is also 30 N. These two forces are equal and opposite, but they are acting on the same body and so have nothing to do with Newton's third law. (We have seen in the last bullet point above the force that pairs with the weight of the block. The one that pairs with the reaction force is a downward force on the table.)

Newton's third law also applies to cases where the force between two bodies acts at a distance: that is, the two bodies are separated by a certain distance. For example, two electric charges will exert an electric force on each other and any two masses will attract each other with the gravitational force. These forces must be equal and opposite. (See Figure 5.16.)

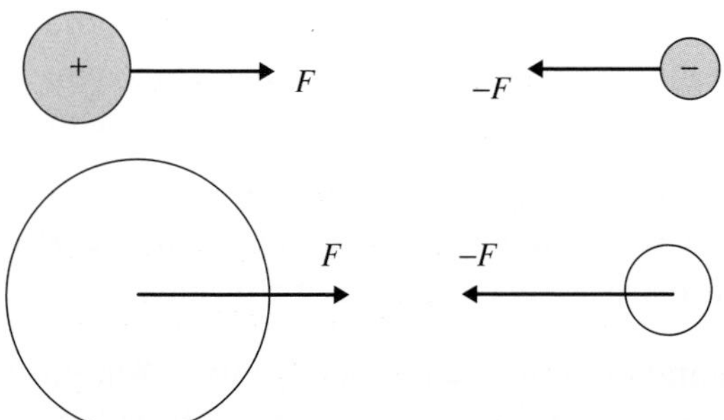

Figure 5.16 The two charges and the two masses are different but the forces are equal and opposite.

QUESTIONS

1 (a) Under what circumstances would a constant force result in an increasing acceleration on a body?
(b) Under what circumstances would a constant force result in zero acceleration on a body?

2 A car of mass 1354 kg finds itself on a muddy road. If the force from the engine pushing the car forward exceeds 575 N, the wheels slip (i.e. they rotate without rolling). What is the maximum acceleration that the car can move with on this road?

3 The net force on a mass of 1.00 kg initially at rest is 1.00 N and acts for 1.00 s. What will the velocity of the mass be at the end of the 1.00 s interval of time?

4 A mass of 2.00 kg is acted upon by two forces of 4.00 N and 10.0 N. What is the smallest and largest acceleration these two forces can produce on the mass?

5 A man of mass m stands in an elevator. Find the reaction force from the elevator floor on the man when:
(a) the elevator is standing still;
(b) the elevator moves up at constant speed v;
(c) the elevator accelerates down with acceleration a;
(d) the elevator accelerates down with acceleration $a = g$.
(e) What happens when $a > g$?

6 A bird is in a glass cage that hangs from a spring scale. Compare the readings of the scale in the following cases.
(a) The bird is sitting in the cage.
(b) The bird is hovering in the cage.
(c) The bird is moving upward with acceleration.
(d) The bird is accelerating downward.
(e) The bird is moving upward with constant velocity.

7 Get in an elevator and stretch out your arm holding your heavy physics book. Press the button to go up. What do you observe happening to your stretched arm? What happens as the elevator comes to a stop at the top floor? What happens when you press the button to go down and what happens when the elevator again stops? Explain your observations carefully using the second law of mechanics.

8 A block of mass 2.0 kg rests on top of another block of mass 10.0 kg that itself rests on a frictionless table (see Figure 5.17). The largest frictional force that can develop between the two blocks is 16 N. Calculate the largest force with which the bottom block can be pulled so that both blocks move together without sliding on each other.

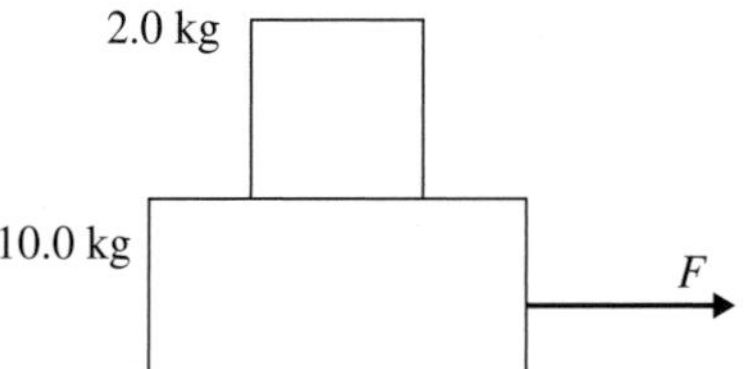

Figure 5.17 For question 8.

9 Figure 5.18 shows a person in an elevator pulling on a rope that goes over a pulley and is attached to the top of the elevator. Identify all the forces shown and for each find the reaction force (according to Newton's third law). On what body does each reaction force act?

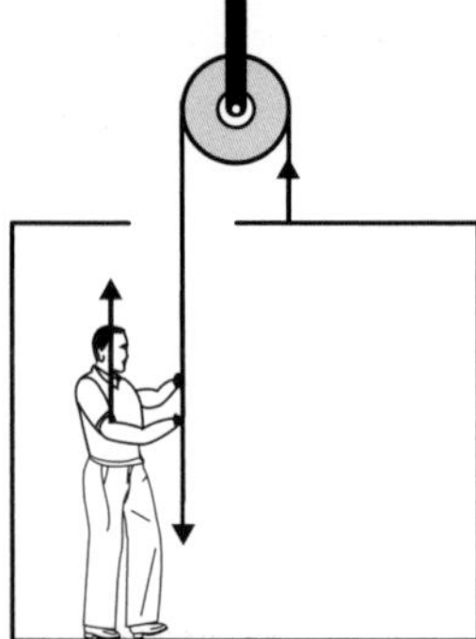

Figure 5.18 For questions 9 and 10.

10 Take the mass of the elevator shown in Figure 5.18 to be 30.0 kg and that of the person to be 70.0 kg. If the elevator accelerates upwards at 0.500 m s^{-2}, find the reaction force on the person from the elevator floor.

11 A small passenger car and a fully loaded truck collide head-on. Which vehicle experiences the greater force?

12 What force does a man of mass 80.0 kg exert on the earth as he falls freely after jumping from a table 1 m high from the surface of the earth?

13 Three blocks rest on a horizontal frictionless surface, as shown in Figure 5.19. A force of 20.0 N is applied horizontally to the right on the block of mass 2.0 kg. Find the individual forces acting on each mass. Identify action–reaction pairs.

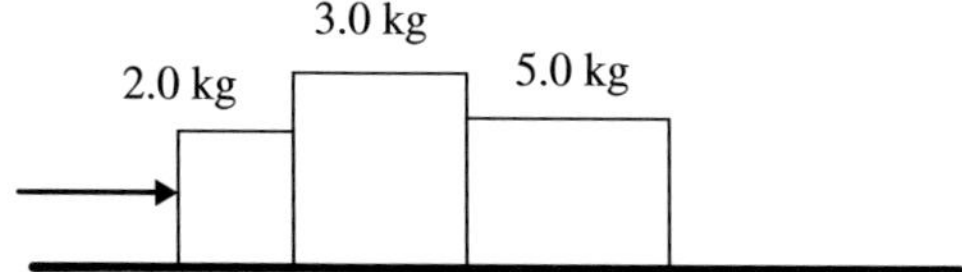

Figure 5.19 For question 13.

14 A (massless) string hangs vertically from a support in the ceiling. A mass of 10.0 kg is attached to the other end of the string. What is the force the string exerts on the support?

15 A block of mass 15.0 kg rests on a horizontal table. A force of 50.0 N is applied vertically downward on the block. Calculate the force that the block exerts on the table.

16 A block of mass 10.0 kg rests on top of a bigger block of mass 20.0 kg, which in turn rests on a horizontal table (see Figure 5.20). Find the individual forces acting on each block. Identify action–reaction pairs according to Newton's third law.

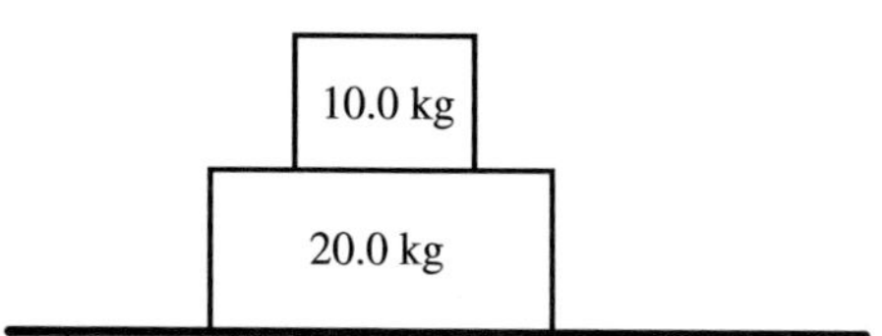

Figure 5.20 For question 16.

17 If a vertical downward force of 50.0 N acts on the top block in Figure 5.20, what are the forces on each block now.

18 A massless string has the same tension throughout its length. Can you explain why?

19 Look back at Figure 5.18. The person has a mass of 70.0 kg and the elevator a mass of 30.0 kg. If the force the person exerts on the elevator floor is 300.0 N, find the acceleration of the elevator ($g = 10$ m s^{-2}).

20 (a) Calculate the tension in the string joining the two masses in Figure 5.21.

(b) If the position of the masses is interchanged, will the tension change?

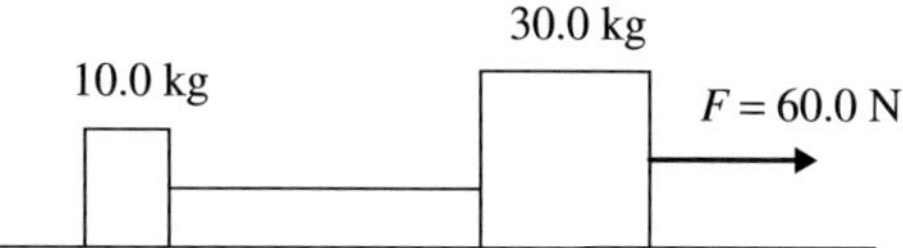

Figure 5.21 For question 20.

21 One hundred equal masses $m = 1.0$ kg are joined by strings as shown in Figure 5.22. The first mass is acted upon by a force $F = 100$ N. What is the tension in the string joining the 60th mass to the 61st?

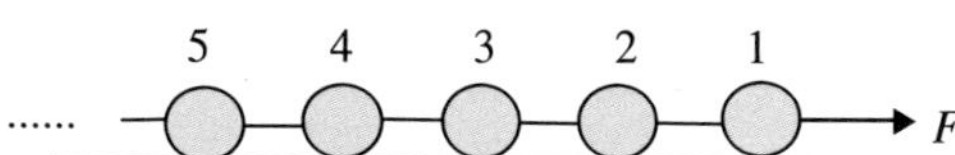

Figure 5.22 For question 21.

22 A mass of 3.0 kg is acted upon by three forces of 4.0 N, 6.0 N and 9.0 N and is in equilibrium. Convince yourself that these forces can indeed be in equilibrium. If the 9.0 N force is suddenly removed, what will the acceleration of the mass be?

23 What is the tension in the string joining the two masses in Figure 5.23? What is the acceleration of each mass?

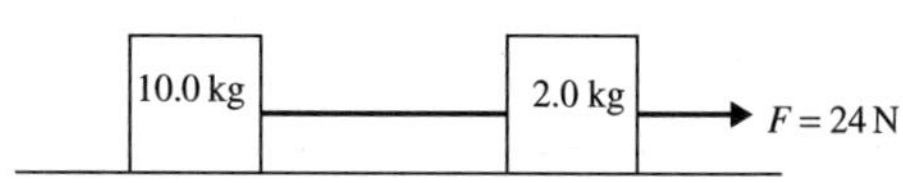

Figure 5.23.

24 Two bodies are joined by a string and are pulled up an inclined plane that makes an angle of 30° to the horizontal, as shown in Figure 5.24. Calculate the tension in the string when:

(a) the bodies move with constant speed;

(b) the bodies move up the plane with an acceleration of 2.0 m s^{-2}.

(c) What is the value of *F* in each case?

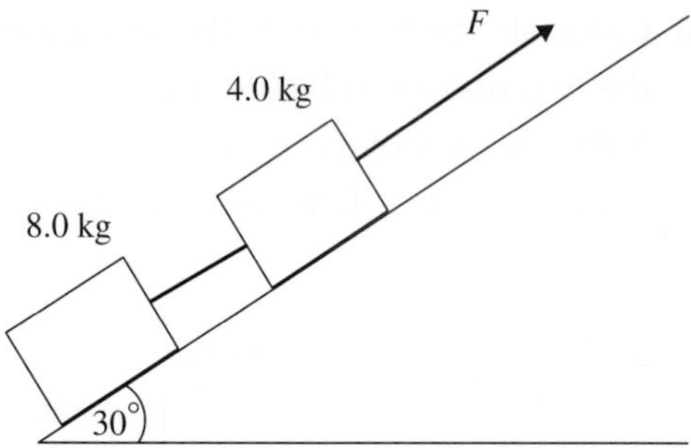

Figure 5.24 For question 24.

25 The velocity–time graph in Figure 5.25 is a student's graph for the vertical motion of a person who jumps from a helicopter and a few seconds later opens a parachute.

(a) Using the laws of mechanics *carefully* explain the shape of the curve. (When does the parachute open? When does the air resistance force reach its maximum value? Is the air resistance force constant?)

(b) How would you improve on the student's graph?

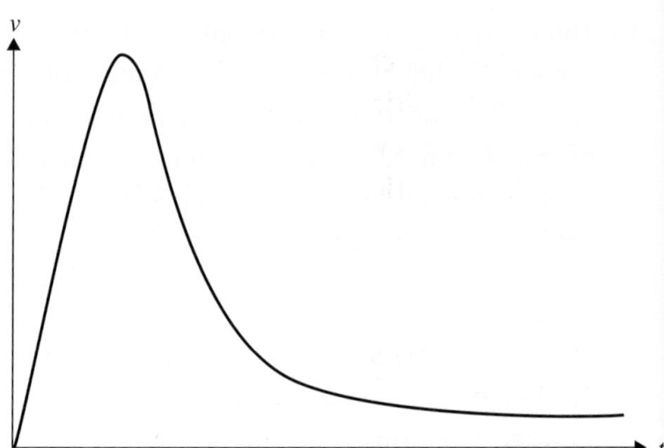

Figure 5.25 For question 25.

Linear momentum

This chapter introduces the concept of momentum and, by using Newton's second and third laws, the law of momentum conservation is derived. This law is the basis for analysing collisions.

Objectives

By the end of this chapter you should be able to:

- state the definition of *momentum* ($\vec{p} = m\vec{v}$) and appreciate that momentum is a *vector* quantity;
- state the definition of *average net force* in terms of momentum, $\vec{F}_{\text{net}} = \frac{\Delta p}{\Delta t}$;
- state the definition of *impulse* as the change in momentum and understand that the *area under a force–time graph* is the impulse of the force;
- derive the *law of conservation of momentum* using Newton's second and third laws;
- identify situations in which *momentum is conserved* and solve related problems.

The concept of momentum

Momentum is a very important and useful concept in mechanics.

▶ The momentum of a body of mass m and velocity $\vec{v}$ is defined to be

$$\vec{p} = m\vec{v}$$

Momentum is a vector quantity whose direction is the same as that of the velocity of the body. The unit of momentum is kg m s^{-1} or, equivalently, N s.

In terms of momentum, Newton's second law of mechanics can be stated as

$$\vec{F}_{\text{net}} = \frac{\Delta\vec{p}}{\Delta t}$$

that is, the (average) net force on a body equals the *rate of change* of the body's momentum.

If the mass of the body is *constant*, this reduces to the familiar $\vec{F}_{\text{net}} = m\vec{a}$. This is because in that case

$$\begin{aligned}\vec{F}_{\text{net}} &= \frac{\Delta\vec{p}}{\Delta t}\\ &= \frac{m\vec{v}_{\text{f}} - m\vec{v}_{\text{i}}}{\Delta t}\\ &= m\frac{\vec{v}_{\text{f}} - \vec{v}_{\text{i}}}{\Delta t}\\ &= m\frac{\Delta\vec{v}}{\Delta t}\\ &= m\vec{a}\end{aligned}$$

The advantage of the formulation of Newton's second law in terms of momentum is that it can be used also in cases where the mass of the body is *changing* (such as, for example, in the motion of a rocket).

Example questions

Q1

A 0.100 kg ball moving at 5 m s^{-1} bounces off a vertical wall without a change in its speed (see Figure 6.1). If the collision with the wall lasted for 0.1 s, what force was exerted on the wall?

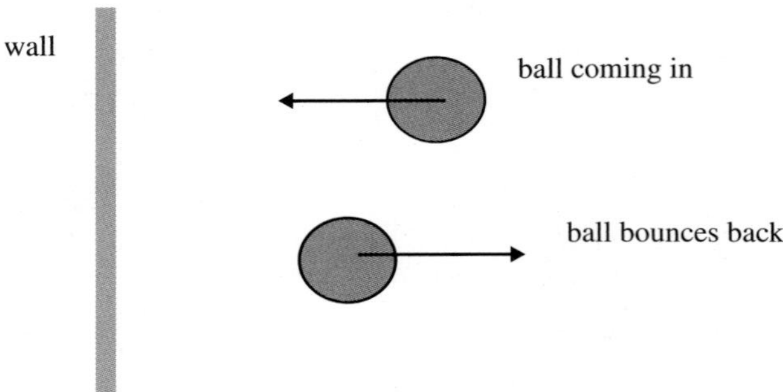

Figure 6.1.

Answer

The momentum of the ball changed from -0.5 N s to 0.5 N s in 0.1 s (note the signs: momentum is a vector). The magnitude of the average force on the ball is thus

$$|\vec{F}_{\text{net}}| = \left|\frac{\Delta\vec{p}}{\Delta t}\right|$$
$$= \frac{0.5 - (-0.5)\text{ N s}}{0.1\text{ s}} = 10\text{ N}$$

This is also the force exerted by the ball on the wall by Newton's third law.

Q2

A 0.50 kg ball bounces vertically off a hard surface. A graph of velocity versus time is shown in Figure 6.2. Find the magnitude of the momentum change of the ball during the bounce. The ball stayed in contact with floor for 0.15 s. What average force did the ball exert on the floor?

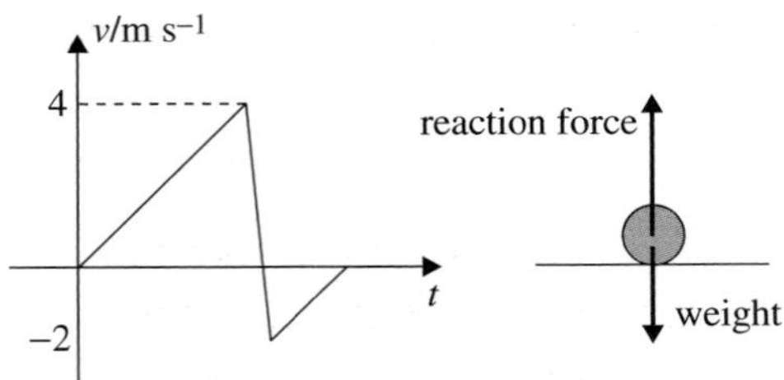

Figure 6.2.

Answer

The initial momentum is $0.50 \times 4 = 2$ N s. The final is $0.50 \times (-2) = -1$ N s. The magnitude of the change is therefore 3 N s. The forces on the ball during contact are its weight and the reaction from the floor. Thus

$$|\vec{F}_{\text{net}}| = R - mg$$
$$= \left|\frac{\Delta\vec{p}}{\Delta t}\right|$$
$$= \frac{3.0\text{ N s}}{0.15\text{ s}}$$
$$= 20\text{ N}$$

so

$$R = 20 + 5$$
$$= 25\text{ N}$$

Q3

Bullets of mass 30 g are being fired from a gun with a speed of 300 m s^{-1} at a rate of 20 per second. What force is being exerted on the gun?

Answer

Using the definition of force involving rate of change of momentum as above, we see that the momentum of one bullet changes from zero before it is fired to mv after it has been fired. If there are ΔN bullets being fired in time Δt, then the magnitude of the momentum change per second is

$$\frac{\Delta p}{\Delta t} = \frac{\Delta N}{\Delta t} mv$$
$$= 20\text{ s}^{-1} \times 0.030\text{ kg} \times 300\text{ m s}^{-1}$$
$$= 180\text{ N}$$

Q4

Mass falls at a rate of μ kg s^{-1} onto a conveyor belt which moves at constant speed v (see Figure 6.3). What force must be exerted on the belt to make it turn at constant speed?

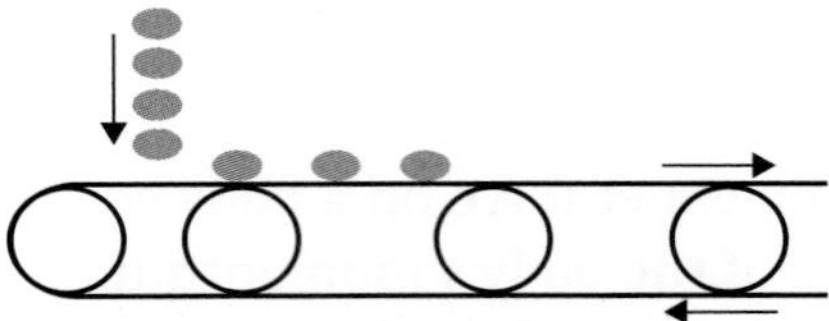

Figure 6.3.

Answer

The horizontal momentum of the falling mass increases from zero when it first hits the belt to mv. The rate of increase of momentum is thus μv and this is the force on the belt, $F = \mu v$.

Q5

A helicopter rotor whose length is $R = 5.0$ m pushes air downwards with a speed v. Assuming that the density of air is constant at $\rho = 1.20$ kg m^{-3} and the mass of the helicopter is 1200 kg, find v. You may assume that the rotor forces the air in a circle of radius R (spanned by the rotor) to move with the downward speed v.

Answer

The momentum of the air under the rotor is mv, where m is the mass of air in a circle of radius 5.0 m. In time Δt the mass is enclosed in a cylinder of radius R and height $v\Delta t$. Thus, the momentum of this mass is $\rho\pi R^2 v^2 \Delta t$ and its rate of change is $\rho\pi R^2 v^2$. This is the upward force on the helicopter, which must equal the helicopter's weight of 12 000 N. So

$$\rho\pi R^2 v^2 = Mg$$

$$\Rightarrow v = \sqrt{\frac{Mg}{\rho\pi R^2}}$$

Thus, $v = 11$ m s^{-1}.

Impulse

Newton's second law, in terms of momentum change, states that the *average* net force on a body (here we use magnitudes of forces and momenta) is given by

$$\bar{F}_{\text{net}} = \frac{\Delta p}{\Delta t}$$

If Δt is infinitesimally small, this gives the instantaneous force on the body. If not, it gives the *average* force on the body, $\bar{F}$. We may then write

$$\Delta p = \bar{F}\Delta t$$

Figure 6.4 shows a ball in contact with a tennis racket. The magnitude of the impulse delivered to the ball is Δp and equals the product of the magnitude of the average force on the ball times the interval of time for which the contact lasts.

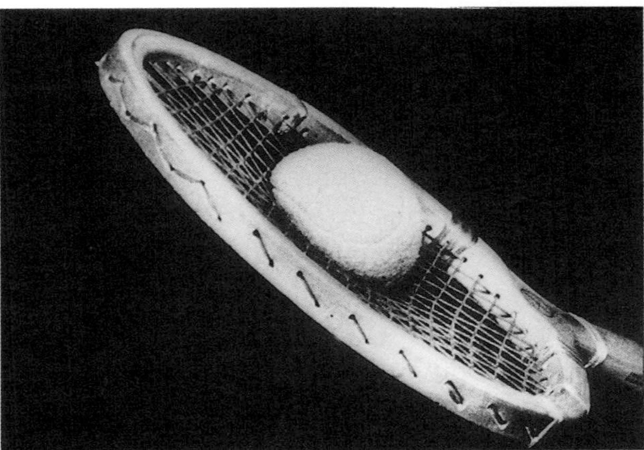

Figure 6.4 The momentum of the ball changes as a result of the collision with the tennis racket. This means there is a force on the ball while it is in contact with the racket.

The quantity $\Delta p = \bar{F}\Delta t$ is called the *impulse* of the force and has the following interpretation in terms of a graph that shows the variation of the force with time (see Figure 6.5).

▶ Impulse is the area under the curve of a force–time graph and equals the *total* momentum change of the mass.

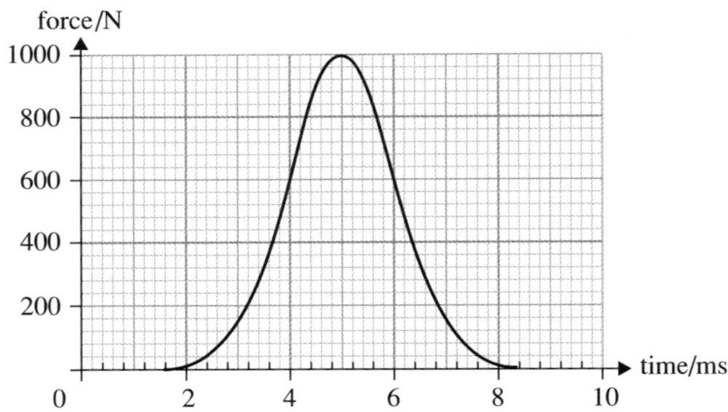

Figure 6.5 The area under the force–time graph gives the total momentum change of the body the force acts upon.

In the graph of Figure 6.5 the area is about 2.5 N s (can you verify this?) and the force acts for about 6.0 ms. This means that during the 6.0 ms the momentum of the body changed by

2.5 N s. The maximum force that acted on the body was 1000 N and the average force

$$\begin{aligned}\bar{F} &= \frac{\Delta p}{\Delta t} \\ &= \frac{2.5}{6.0 \times 10^{-3}}\ \text{N} \\ &\approx 470\ \text{N}\end{aligned}$$

Consider, then, a body of mass m that moves with velocity v and is brought to rest by a non-constant force F. The change in the momentum of the body is $\Delta p = 0 - mv = -mv$. (We may ignore the sign if we are interested only in the magnitude of the momentum change.) Let us examine two possibilities. In the first case, the force brings the body to rest over a longer period of time compared with the second. The graphs of force versus time might be as shown in Figure 6.6. The thick curve represents the force that brings the body to rest over a short time. This force is larger, on average, than the force that brings the body to rest over a longer time interval. The areas under the curves are the same since they both represent the change in the momentum of the body, which is mv in both cases.

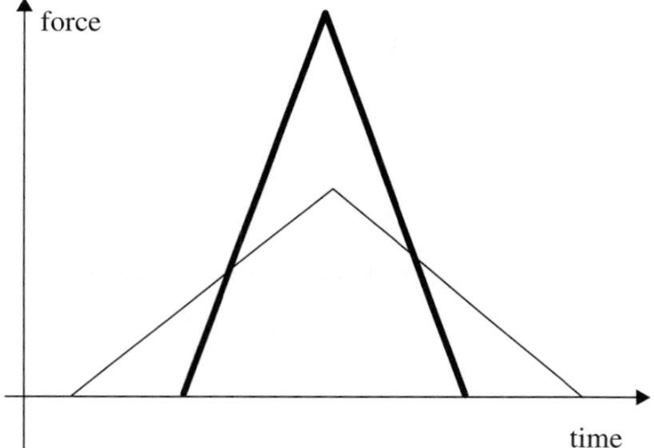

Figure 6.6 The areas under the two curves are the same so the force acting for a shorter time must be larger on average.

These graphs can be thought of as idealizations of the forces experienced by a driver of a car that is brought suddenly to rest in a crash. (What are more realistic graphs?) A driver not wearing a safety belt will quickly come to rest after hitting the steering wheel or the windscreen and will experience a large force. A driver wearing a safety belt in a car with an air-bag, however, will come to rest over a longer period of time since the belt and the air-bag start bringing him to rest earlier and allow him to move forward a bit while coming to rest. The force he experiences is thus correspondingly smaller.

Example questions

Q6

A ball of mass 0.250 kg moves on a frictionless horizontal floor and hits a vertical wall with speed 5.0 m s^{-1}. The ball rebounds with speed 4.0 m s^{-1}. If the ball was in contact with the wall for 0.150 s, find the average force that acted on the ball.

Answer

The magnitude of the change in the ball's momentum is (remember that momentum is a vector)

$$\begin{aligned}\Delta p &= p_f - p_i \\ &= 0.250 \times 4.0 - (-0.250 \times 5.0) \\ &= 1.0 - (-1.25) \\ &= 2.25\ \text{N s}\end{aligned}$$

Hence

$$\begin{aligned}\bar{F} &= \frac{\Delta p}{\Delta t} \\ &= \frac{2.25\ \text{N s}}{0.150\ \text{s}} \\ &= 15\ \text{N}\end{aligned}$$

Q7

The force in example question 6 is assumed to vary with time as shown in Figure 6.7. Deduce the *maximum* force that acted on the ball.

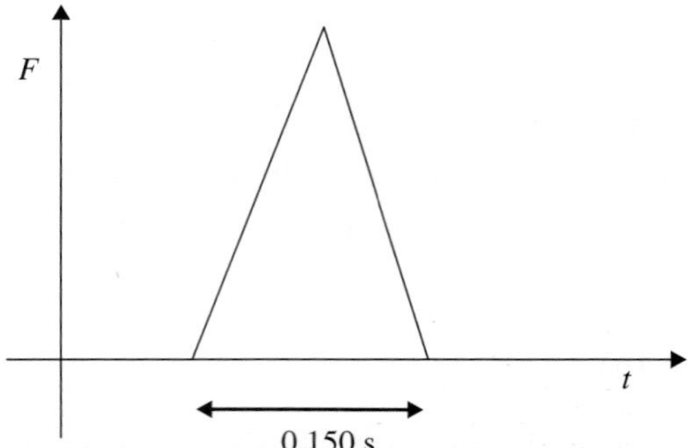

Figure 6.7.

A second, harder, ball of identical mass to the first also bounces off the wall with the same initial and final speed, but since it is harder it stays in contact with the wall for only 0.125 s. What is the maximum force exerted by the wall on this ball?

Answer

The area under the curve is the total change in the ball's momentum, which we found to be $\Delta p = 2.25$ N s. The area is a triangle and so

$\frac{1}{2} \times F_{max} \times 0.150 = 2.25$

$\Rightarrow F_{max} = 30$ N

The area under the force–time graph in the case of the harder ball will be the same. Thus

$\frac{1}{2} \times F_{max} \times 0.125 = 2.25$

$\Rightarrow F_{max} = 36$ N

Q8

A force of 1000.0 N acts on a body of 40.0 kg initially at rest for a time interval of 0.0500 s. What is the velocity of the mass?

Answer

The impulse is

$$F\Delta t = 1000 \times 0.05 \text{ N s}$$
$$= 50.0 \text{ N s}$$

and this equals the amount by which the body's momentum increases. The velocity is thus

$$\frac{50}{40} \text{ m s}^{-1} = 1.25 \text{ m s}^{-1}$$

Q9

A force F varies with time according to $F = 4 + 12t$, where F is in newtons and t in seconds. The force acts on a block of mass $m = 2.00$ kg, which is initially at rest on a frictionless horizontal surface. F makes an angle of 30° with the horizontal (see Figure 6.8). When will the force lift the body from the table? What will the velocity of the body be at that instant?

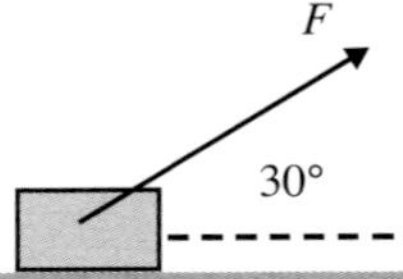

Figure 6.8.

Answer

The block will leave the table when the normal reaction force R becomes zero.

$R + F \sin 30° = mg$

so

$F = 40$ N when $R = 0$.

This happens when $t = 3.0$ s. The horizontal component of F is

$(4 + 12t) \cos 30° = 3.64 + 10.39t$

The change in the body's momentum in the horizontal direction is the area under the F_x versus t graph from $t = 0$ to $t = 3.0$ s. This area is 57.7 N s. Thus, the horizontal component of velocity is 28.8 m s^{-1}. The vertical component is zero.

The law of conservation of momentum

Given a system of two masses say m_1 and m_2 with velocities $\vec{v}_1$ and $\vec{v}_2$, the total momentum of the system is defined as the vector sum of the individual momenta

$$P_{total} = m_1\vec{v}_1 + m_2\vec{v}_2$$

Example questions

Q10

Two masses of 2.0 kg and 3.0 kg move to the right with speeds of 4.0 m s^{-1} and 5.0 m s^{-1}, respectively. What is the total momentum of the system?

Answer

$$P = (2 \times 4 + 3 \times 5) \text{ N s}$$
$$= 23 \text{ N s}$$

Q11

A mass of 2.0 kg moves to the right with a speed of 10.0 m s^{-1} and a mass of 4.0 kg moves to the left with a speed of 8.0 m s^{-1}. What is the total momentum of the system?

Answer

$P = (2 \times 10 - 4 \times 8)$ N s

$= -12$ N s

The minus sign means that the direction of this total momentum is to the left.

Consider now two bodies A and B of masses m_A and m_B on a horizontal frictionless table. The forces on each mass are the weight and the normal reaction force from the table, which equals the weight. Thus, the net force on each mass is zero. If these masses have some initial velocity, then by Newton's first law they continue moving with that same velocity until a force acts on them. If the bodies move in such a way that they will collide at some point in time, then at the point of collision a force will be exerted on each body. As a result of this force, each mass will change its velocity and thus its momentum. If we consider the two bodies together as a system, then the net force on the system is zero. As we mentioned already, the weight of each mass is cancelled by the reaction force and the only force that remains is the force during the collision. However, from Newton's third law, the force that body A experiences must be equal and opposite to that which B experiences. Thus, even though there is a net force acting on each mass for the duration of the collision, the net force on the *system* of the two masses is zero. We see that at all times the net external force on the *system* is zero. (See Figure 6.9.)

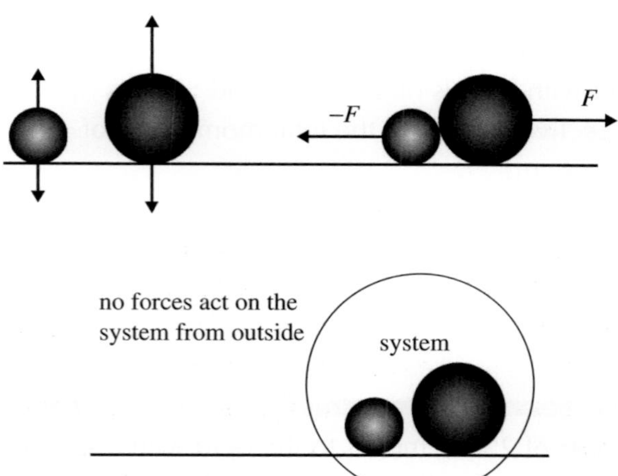

Figure 6.9 The total momentum of an isolated system is conserved.

A system in which no external forces act is called an *isolated* system. Isolated systems have the property that the total momentum stays the same at all times. If the system consists of a number of bodies (in our example, two) then the total momentum is defined as the sum of the individual momenta of the bodies in the system. If, before the collision, the bodies A and B had velocity vectors $\vec{v}_A$ and $\vec{v}_B$, then the total momentum of the system is

$$\vec{P}_{\text{total}} = m_A\vec{v}_A + m_B\vec{v}_B$$

We should remind ourselves that momentum is a vector and thus when we say that the total momentum is the sum of the individual momenta we mean the *vector sum*.

If, as a result of the collision, the two bodies now have velocity vectors $\vec{u}_A$ and $\vec{u}_B$, then the total momentum is now

$$\vec{P}_{\text{total}} = m_A\vec{u}_A + m_B\vec{u}_B$$

and equals the total momentum before the collision. The individual momenta have changed as a result of the collision but their vector sum is the same. This is the law of conservation of linear momentum.

▶ When no external forces act on a system, the total momentum of the system stays the same.

Example questions

Q12

Let a mass of 3.0 kg be standing still and a second mass of 5.0 kg come along and hit it with velocity 4.0 m s^{-1}. Suppose that the smaller mass moves off with a speed of 3.0 m s^{-1}. What happens to the larger mass? (See Figure 6.10.)

Answer

The system of the two masses is an isolated system as we discussed above. Thus, momentum will be conserved. Before the collision the total momentum of the system was $(3.0 \times 0 + 5.0 \times 4.0)$ N s = 20 N s. This must also be the total momentum after the collision. But after the collision the total

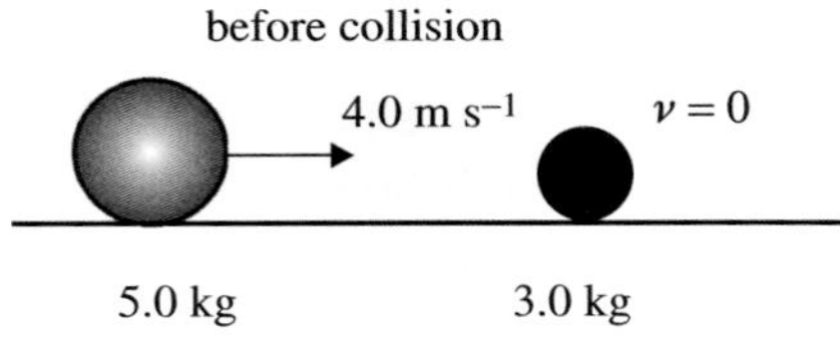

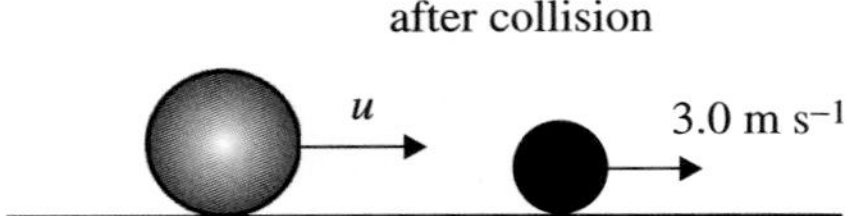

Figure 6.10.

momentum is $(3.0 \times 3.0 + 5.0 \times u)$ N s where u is the unknown speed of the larger mass. Thus $20 = 9.0 + 5.0u$ and so $u = 2.2$ m s^{-1}.

Q13

Two masses of 2.0 kg and 4.0 kg are held with a compressed spring between them. If the masses are released, the spring will push them away from each other. If the smaller mass moves off with a speed of 6.0 m s^{-1}, what is the speed of the other mass? (See Figure 6.11.)

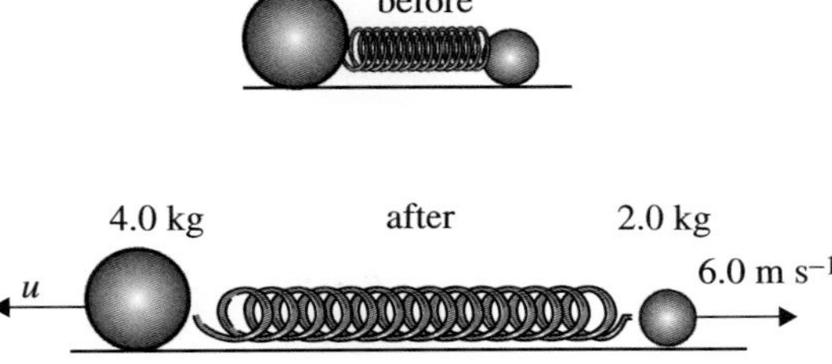

Figure 6.11.

Answer

Here our system consists of the two masses and the spring. There are no external forces here, since gravity is cancelled by the upward reaction forces from the table where the masses rest. The only force is the elastic force of the spring with which it pushes the masses away. But this is not an external force so total momentum will stay the same. The spring exerts equal and opposite forces on each mass. Before the masses start moving apart, the total momentum is zero, since nothing moves. After the masses move away, the total momentum is $(2 \times 6 - 4 \times u)$ N s, where u is the unknown speed of the heavy mass. Note the minus sign. The masses are moving in opposite directions, so one of the velocities (and also one of the momenta) is negative. Thus, $12 - 4u = 0$ and so $u = 3.0$ m s^{-1}.

Q14

A ball is released from some height above the earth's surface. Treat the ball as the entire system under consideration. As the ball falls, is the momentum of the system conserved?

Answer

No, because there is an external force acting on the ball, namely its weight.

Q15

A ball is released from some height above the earth's surface. Treat the ball and the earth as the entire system under consideration. As the ball falls, is the momentum of the system conserved?

Answer

Yes, because there are no external forces on the system. The earth exerts a force on the ball but the ball exerts an equal and opposite force on the earth. Hence the net force on the earth–ball system is zero.

(This means that as the ball falls, the earth moves up a bit!)

Proof of momentum conservation

We will now prove the law of momentum conservation for an isolated system consisting of two bodies A and B. It is easy to generalize to systems with more than two bodies. Let the two bodies have masses m_a and m_b with velocities before the collision $\vec{v}_a$ and $\vec{v}_b$. As a result of the collision the two bodies change their velocities to $\vec{u}_a$ and $\vec{u}_b$. Let $\vec{F}$ stand for the force that A experiences during the collision, which lasted a time Δt. (See Figure 6.12.)

before collision

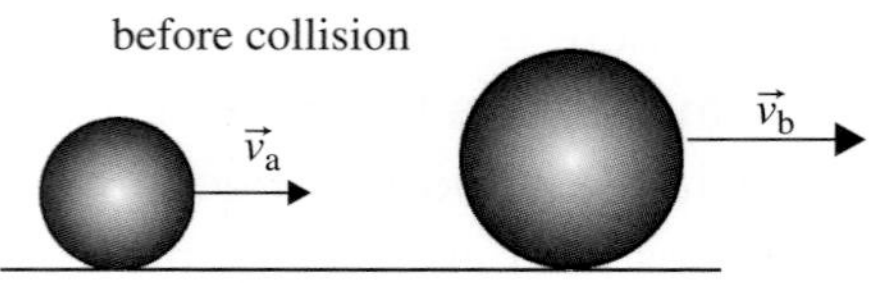

after collision

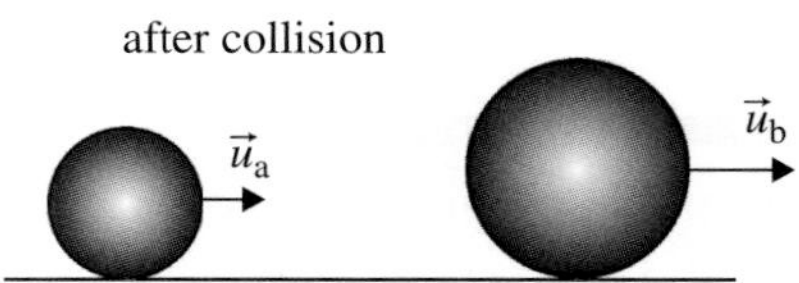

Figure 6.12 Diagram used for proof of the law of conservation of momentum.

Then, by Newton's second law

$$\vec{F} = \frac{\Delta \vec{p}_a}{\Delta t} = \frac{m_a\vec{u}_a - m_a\vec{v}_a}{\Delta t}$$

The force experienced by B is $-\vec{F}$ (Newton's third law) and so

$$-\vec{F} = \frac{\Delta \vec{p}_b}{\Delta t} = \frac{m_b\vec{u}_b - m_b\vec{v}_b}{\Delta t}$$

Thus

$$m_a\vec{u}_a - m_a\vec{v}_a = -(m_b\vec{u}_b - m_b\vec{v}_b)$$
$$\Rightarrow m_a\vec{v}_a + m_b\vec{v}_b = m_a\vec{u}_a + m_b\vec{u}_b$$

which states precisely that the total momentum before and after the collision is the same.

Example questions

Q16

(a) A man of mass m stands on a cart of mass M that rests on a horizontal frictionless surface. If the man begins to walk with velocity v *with respect to the cart*, how will the cart move? See Figure 6.13.

(b) What happens when the man gets to the edge of the cart and stops walking?

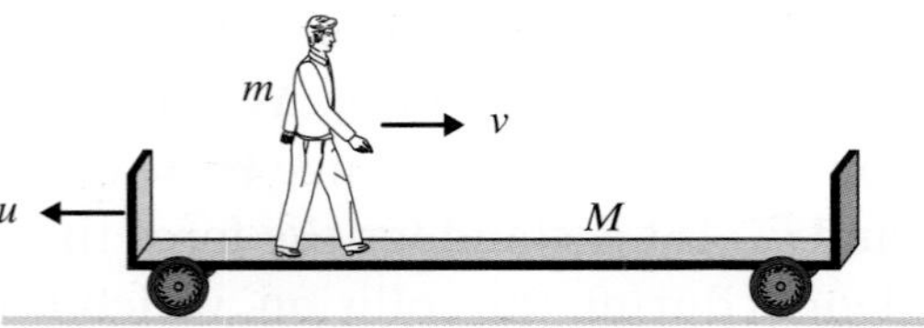

Figure 6.13.

Answer

(a) Let us look at things from the point of view of an observer at rest on the ground. The initial momentum of the man–cart system is zero. The cart will move to the left with speed u, so the man will move with velocity $v - u$ *with respect to the ground*. Hence, by momentum conservation

$$0 = m(v - u) - Mu$$
$$\Rightarrow u = \frac{mv}{M + m}$$

(b) When the man stops, the cart will stop as well, so the total momentum of the man–cart system remains zero.

Q17

A cart of mass M moves with constant velocity v on a frictionless road (see Figure 6.14). Rain is falling vertically on to the road and begins to fill the cart at a steady rate of μ kg per second. Find the velocity of the cart t seconds later.

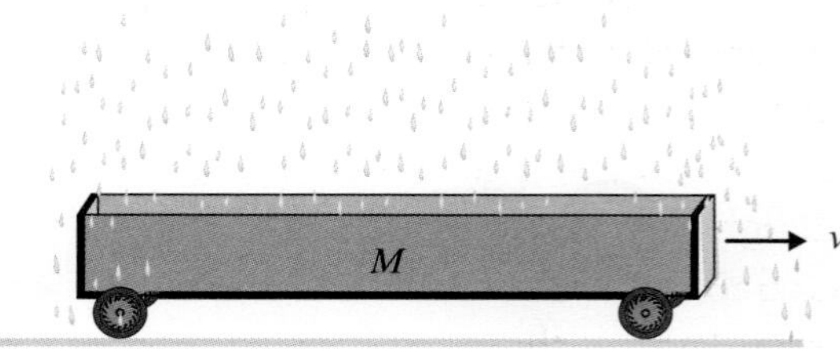

Figure 6.14.

Answer

We look at things from the point of view of an observer on the ground. After a time of t s the mass of the cart is $M + \mu t$. Momentum is conserved as there are no external forces. So if u is the velocity after time t, we must have

$$Mv = (M + \mu t)u$$
$$\Rightarrow u = \frac{M}{M + \mu t}v$$

HL only

Q18

A cart of mass M is filled with water and moves with velocity v on a frictionless road. Water begins to leak from a small hole in the base of the cart and falls out at a rate of μ kg per second. (See Figure 6.15.) What happens to the velocity of the cart?

Figure 6.15.

Answer

We look at things from the point of view of *an observer on the ground* and take as our system the cart plus *all* the water (including that which is falling out). The falling water still moves with the same velocity to the right as far as the ground observer is concerned, and since there are no external forces, momentum is conserved and there can be no change of velocity.

We can also get the same answer if we take as our system the cart and the water *inside* the cart. As far as the ground observer is concerned, the water leaves the cart with a horizontal velocity v to the right. Thus, there is a force on the cart directed to the *left* of magnitude μv. Hence, the observer deduces that, since net force = rate of change of momentum,

$$-\mu v = \frac{\delta M}{\delta t} v + M\frac{\delta v}{\delta t}$$
$$= -\mu v + M\frac{\delta v}{\delta t}$$
$$\Rightarrow \delta v = 0$$

Two-dimensional collisions

Consider a stationary body of mass 12 kg that is hit by a 4.0 kg mass moving at 12 m s^{-1}. The collision is not head-on, and the bodies move at an angle to the original direction of motion of the 4.0 kg body as shown in Figure 6.16 (the view is from the top). How can we find the speeds of the two bodies after the collision?

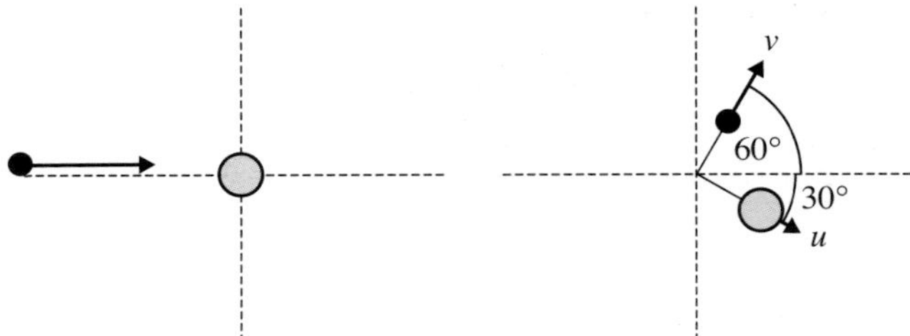

Figure 6.16.

Momentum is a vector and is conserved. This means that

x-component of total momentum before = x-component of total momentum after

y-component of total momentum before = y-component of total momentum after

Thus

$$4 \times 12 = 4 \times v \cos 60° + 12 \times u \cos 30°$$
$$0 = 4 \times v \sin 60° - 12 \times u \sin 30°$$

and so

$$2 \times v + 10.392 \times u = 48$$
$$3.464 \times v - 6 \times u = 0$$

Solving simultaneously gives

$$v = 6.0 \text{ m s}^{-1}$$
$$u = 3.5 \text{ m s}^{-1}.$$

? QUESTIONS

1 The momentum of a ball increased by 12.0 N s as a result of a force that acted on the ball for 2.00 s. What was the average force on the ball?

2 A 0.150 kg ball moving horizontally at 3.00 m s^{-1} collides normally with a vertical wall and bounces back with the same speed.
(a) What is the impulse delivered to the ball?
(b) If the ball was in contact with the wall for 0.125 s, find the average force exerted by the ball on the wall.

3 The bodies in Figure 6.17 suffer a head-on collision and stick to each other afterwards. Find their common velocity.

Figure 6.17 For question 3.

4 Two masses of 2.00 kg and 4.00 kg are kept on a frictionless horizontal table with a compressed spring between them. If the masses are released, the larger mass moves away with velocity 3.50 m s^{-1}. What is the velocity of the other mass?

5 A 70.0 kg person stands at the back of a 200.0 kg boat of length 4.00 m that floats on stationary water. She begins to walk toward the front of the boat. When she gets to the front, how far back will the boat have moved? (Neglect the resistance of the water.)

6 A ball of mass 250 g rolling on a horizontal floor with a speed 4.00 m s^{-1} hits a wall and bounces with the same speed, as shown in Figure 6.18.

(a) What is the magnitude and direction of the momentum *change* of the ball?

(b) Is momentum conserved here? Why or why not?

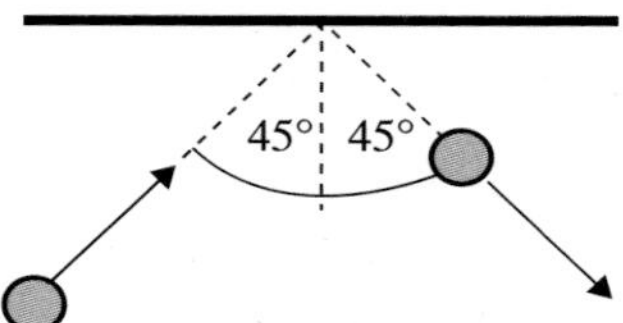

Figure 6.18 For question 6.

7 A mass of 0.500 kg moving at 6.00 m s^{-1} strikes a wall normally and bounces back with a speed of 4.00 m s^{-1}. If the mass was in contact with the wall for 0.200 s find:

(a) the change of momentum of the mass;

(b) the average force the wall exerted on the mass.

8 A person holds a book stationary in his hand and then releases it.

(a) As the book falls, is its momentum conserved?

(b) What does the law of conservation of momentum say for this example?

9 A binary star system consists of two stars that are orbiting a common centre, as shown in Figure 6.19. The only force acting on the stars is the gravitational force of attraction in a direction along the line joining the stars.

(a) Explain carefully why the total momentum of the binary star is constant.

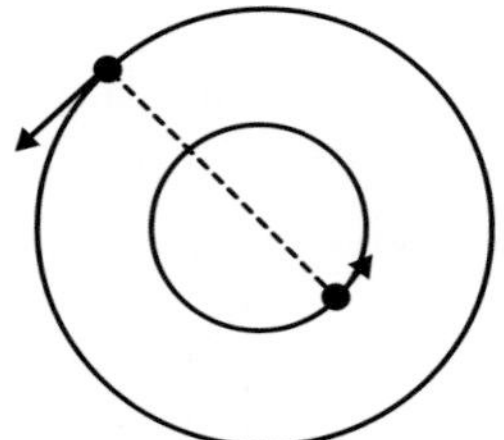

Figure 6.19 For question 9.

(b) Explain why the two stars are always in diametrically opposite positions.

(c) Hence explain why the two stars have a common period of rotation and why the inner star is the more massive of the two.

10 (a) A fan on a floating barge blows air at high speed toward the right, as shown in Figure 6.20a. Will the barge move? Explain your answer.

(b) A sail is now put up on the barge so that the fan blows air toward the sail, as shown in Figure 6.20b. Will the barge move? Explain your answer.

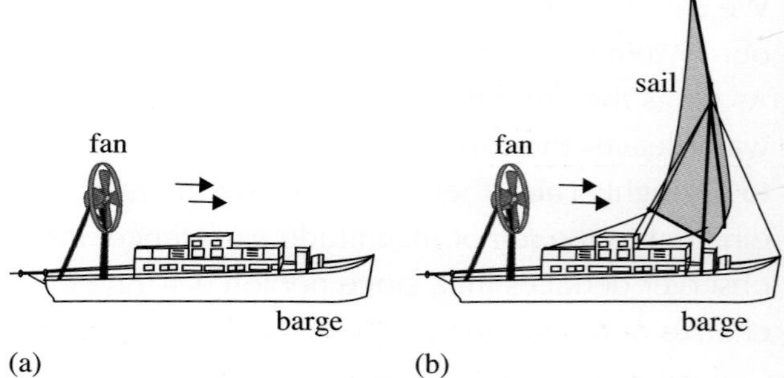

Figure 6.20 For question 10.

11 If you jump from a height of 1.0 m from the surface of the earth, the earth actually moves up a bit as you fall.

(a) Explain why.

(b) *Estimate* the distance the earth moves, listing any assumptions you make.

(c) Would the earth move more, less or the same if a heavier person jumps?

12 A time-varying force whose graph versus time is shown in Figure 6.21 acts on a body of mass 3.00 kg.

(a) Find the impulse of the force.

(b) Find the velocity of the mass at 17 s, assuming the initial velocity was zero.

(c) What should the initial velocity be if the mass had to stop at 17 s?

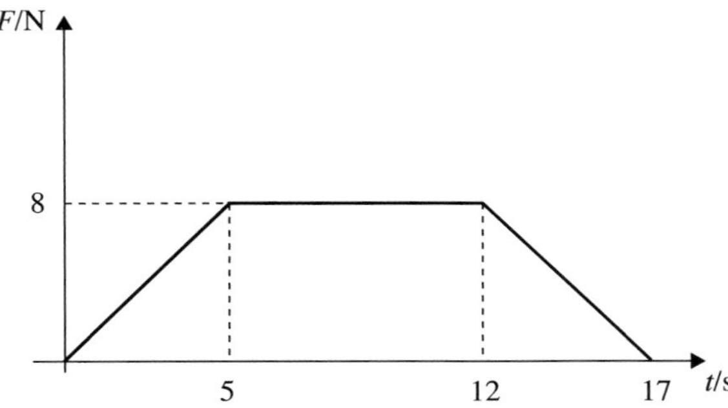

Figure 6.21 For question 12.

13 A rocket in space where gravity is negligible has a mass (including fuel) of 5000 kg. If it is desired to give the rocket an average acceleration of 15.0 m s^{-2} during the first second of firing the engine and the gases leave the rocket at a speed of 1500 m s^{-1} (relative to the rocket), how much fuel must be burned in that second?

14 Two masses moving in a straight line towards each other collide as shown in Figure 6.22. Find the velocity (magnitude and direction) of the larger mass after the collision.

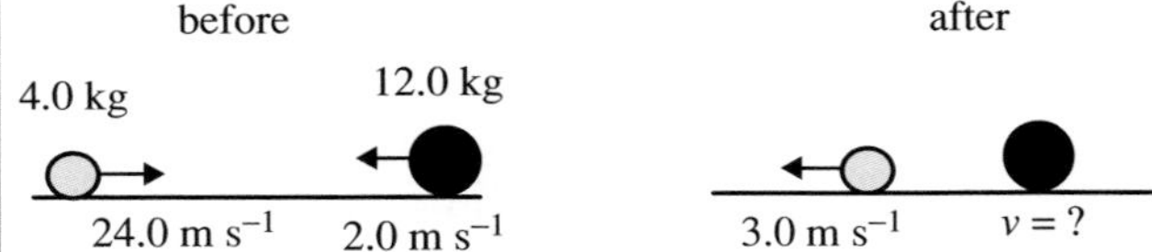

Figure 6.22 For question 14.

15 Two cars of masses 1200 kg and 1400 kg collide head-on and stick to each other. The cars are coming at each other from opposite directions with speeds of 8.0 m s^{-1} and 6 m s^{-1}, respectively. With what velocity does the wreck move away from the scene of the accident?

16 A 0.350 kg mass is approaching a moving rod with speed 8.00 m s^{-1}. The ball leaves the rod at right angles with a speed of 12.0 m s^{-1} as shown in Figure 6.23. What impulse has been imparted to the ball?

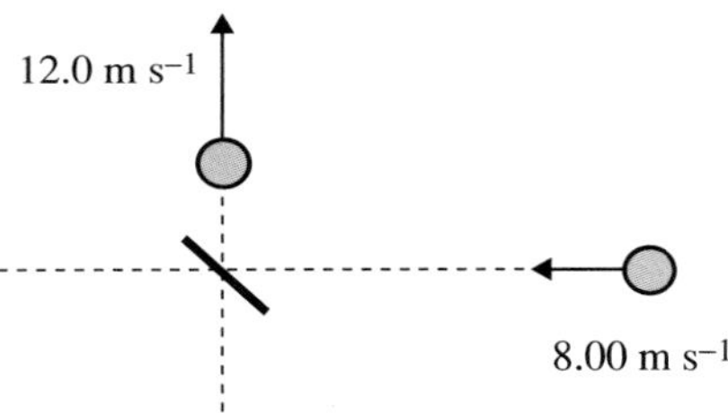

Figure 6.23 For question 16.

17 Two cars A and B of mass 1200 kg and 1300 kg, respectively, collide at an intersection and stick to each other as a result of the collision as shown in Figure 6.24. Find the speeds of A and B before the collision.

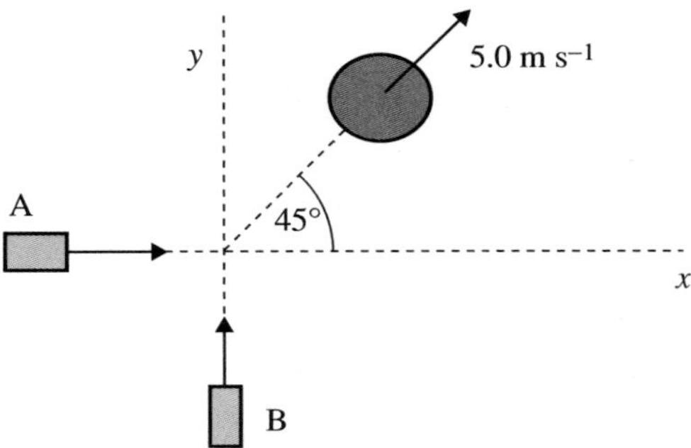

Figure 6.24 For question 17.

18 A boy rides on a scooter pushing on the road with one foot with a horizontal force that depends on time, as shown in the graph in Figure 6.25. While the scooter rolls, a constant force of 25 N opposes the motion. The combined mass of the boy and scooter is 25 kg.

(a) Find the speed of the boy after 4.0 s, assuming he started from rest.

(b) Draw a graph to represent the variation of the boy's speed with time.

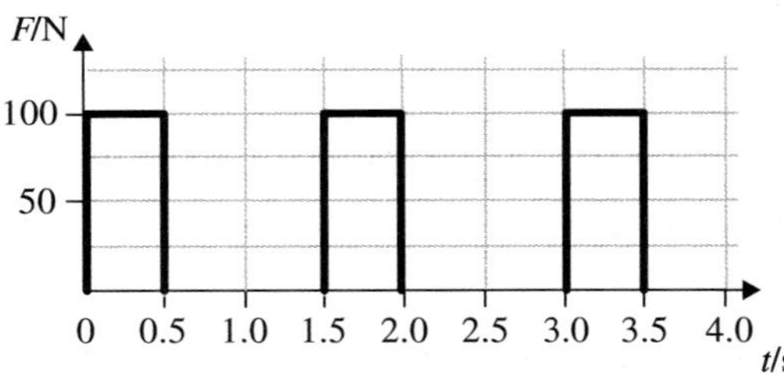

Figure 6.25 For question 18.

HL only

19 A student stands on a plate that is connected to a force sensor that measures the force exerted by the student on the plate. The student then jumps straight up. Figure 6.26 is an idealized version of the reading of the sensor as a function of time. Using this graph find the following:

(a) the mass of the student;
(b) the acceleration of the student at 0.6 s;
(c) the time the student leaves the plate;
(d) the maximum height the student jumps to.
(e) What would be a more *realistic* graph of force versus time?

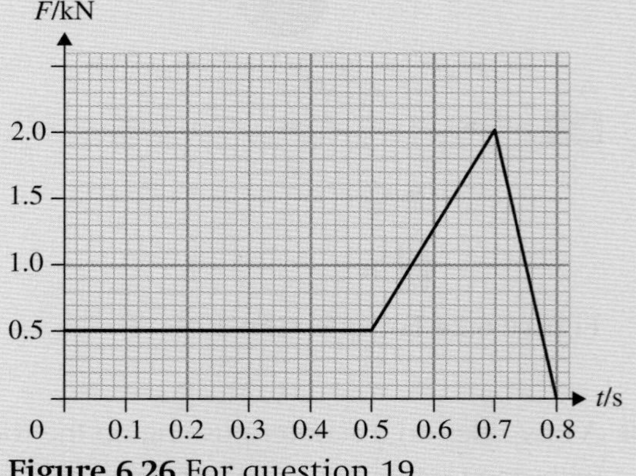

Figure 6.26 For question 19.

20 A ball of mass m is dropped from a height of h_1 and rebounds to a height of h_2. The ball is in contact with the floor for a time interval of τ.

(a) Show that the average net force on the ball is given by

$$F = m\frac{\sqrt{2gh_1} + \sqrt{2gh_2}}{\tau}$$

(b) If $h_1 = 8.0$ m, $h_2 = 6.0$ m, $\tau = 0.125$ s, $m = 0.250$ kg, calculate the average force exerted by the ball on the floor.

21 A ball of mass m hits a horizontal floor normally with speed v_1 and rebounds with speed v_2. The ball stayed in contact with the floor for a time of τ s. Show that the average force on the ball from the floor during the collision is given by $\frac{m(v_1+v_2)}{\tau} + mg$. Find an expression for the average *net* force on the ball.

22 Figure 6.27 shows the variation with time of the force exerted on a body of mass 4.0 kg that is initially at rest. Find:

(a) the acceleration of the mass at 4 s;
(b) the velocity of the mass at 5 s;
(c) the acceleration of the mass at 8 s;
(d) the velocity of the mass at 10 s.

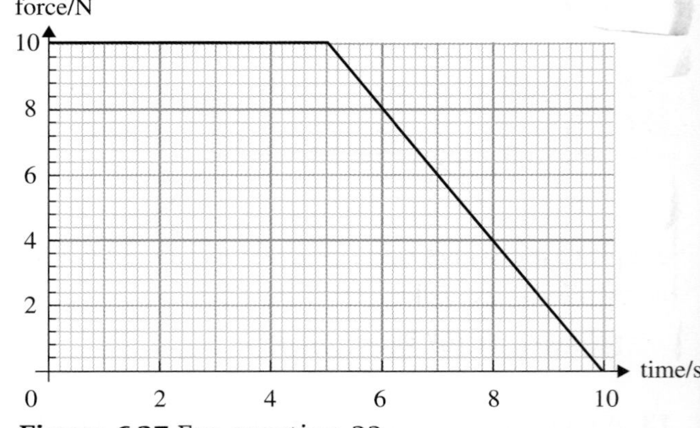

Figure 6.27 For question 22.

HL only

23 You have a mass of 60.0 kg and are floating weightless in space. You are carrying 100 coins each of mass 0.10 kg.

(a) If you throw all the coins at once with a speed of 5.0 m s^{-1} in the same direction, with what velocity will you recoil?
(b) If instead you throw the coins one at a time with a speed of 5.0 m s^{-1} *with respect to you,* discuss whether your final speed will be different from before. (Use your graphics display calculator to calculate the speed in this case.)

24 Figure 6.28 shows the variation with time of the force exerted on a ball as the ball came into contact with a spring.

(a) For how long was the spring in contact with the ball?
(b) *Estimate* the magnitude of the change in momentum of the ball.
(c) What was the *average* force that was exerted on the ball?

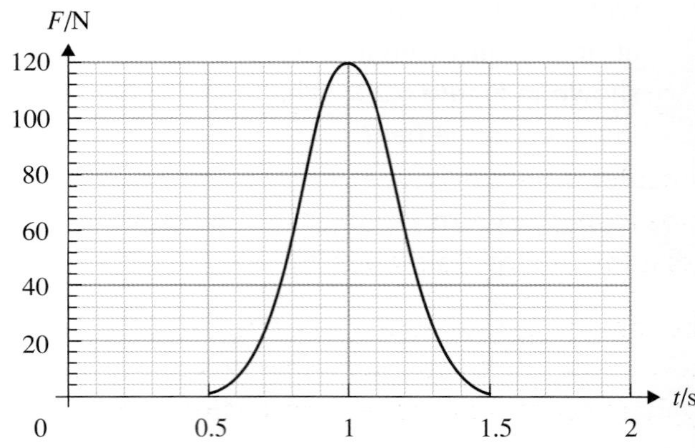

Figure 6.28 For question 24.

Work, energy and power

The topic of mechanics continues in this chapter with the fundamental concept of work done by a force, as well as the concepts of energy and power. Applications of the law of conservation of energy are discussed.

Objectives

By the end of this chapter you should be able to:

- state the definition of *work done by a force*, $W = Fs\cos\theta$, appreciate the significance of the angle appearing in the formula and understand that this formula can only be used when the force is *constant*;
- understand that the *work done by a varying* force is given by the *area under the graph* of force versus displacement;
- state the definitions of *kinetic energy*, $E_k = \frac{1}{2}mv^2$ (also $E_k = \frac{p^2}{2m}$), *gravitational potential energy*, $E_p = mgh$, and *elastic potential energy*, $E_e = \frac{1}{2}kx^2$.
- appreciate that gravitational potential energy can be calculated by measuring heights from an *arbitrary* level;
- understand that, when frictional forces are absent, the total energy $E = E_k + E_p + E_e = \frac{1}{2}mv^2 + mgh + \frac{1}{2}kx^2$ is conserved;
- use the work–kinetic energy relation that states that the work done by the net force is the *change in kinetic energy*;
- understand that, in the presence of *external forces*, the work done is the change in the mechanical energy, $W = \Delta E$;
- state the definition of *power*, $P = \frac{\Delta W}{\Delta t}$, and its very useful form in mechanics, $P = Fv$;
- calculate the *efficiency* of simple machines;
- understand that in all collisions *momentum is always conserved*, but that *kinetic energy* is only conserved in *elastic* collisions.

Work done by a force

Consider a *constant* force $\vec{F}$ acting on a body of mass m as shown in Figure 7.1. The body moves a distance s along a straight line.

The force is always acting upon the body as it moves. Note that the force moves its point of application by a distance s. We define a quantity called the **work** *done by the force* $\vec{F}$ by

$$W = Fs\cos\theta$$

where θ is the angle between the force and the direction along which the mass moves. (The cosine here can be positive, negative or zero; thus work can be positive, negative or zero. We will see what that means shortly.)

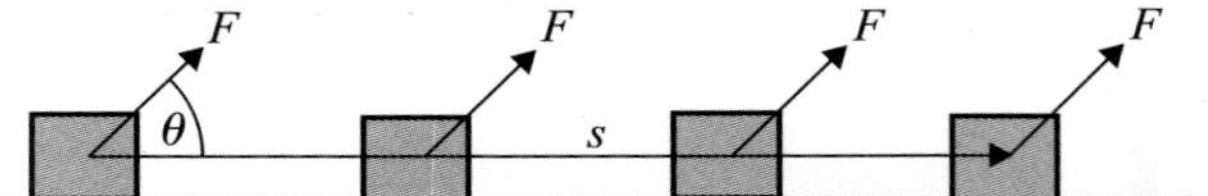

Figure 7.1 A force moving its point of application performs work.

▶ **The work done by a force is the product of the force times the distance moved by the object in the direction of the force.**

The unit of work is the joule. One joule is the work done by a force of 1 N when it moves a body a distance of 1 m in the direction of the force. 1 J = 1 N m.

Example question

Q1

A mass is being pulled along a level road by a rope attached to it in such a way that the rope makes an angle of 40.0° with the horizontal. The force in the rope is 20.0 N. What is the work done by this force in moving the mass a distance of 8.00 m along the level road?

Answer

Applying the definition of work done, we have

$W = Fs \cos\theta$

where $F = 20.0$ N, $s = 8.00$ m and $\theta = 40°$. Thus

$W = 20 \times 8 \times \cos 40°$

$= 123$ J

If the force is not constant or the motion does not take place in a straight line, or both, we must be careful. First consider the case of a force of constant magnitude when the motion is not along a straight line.

Example questions

Q2

Find the work done by the tension in a string, as a mass attached to the end of the string performs circular motion (see Figure 7.2).

Answer

This is a case where the force, although constant in magnitude, changes in direction. However, the

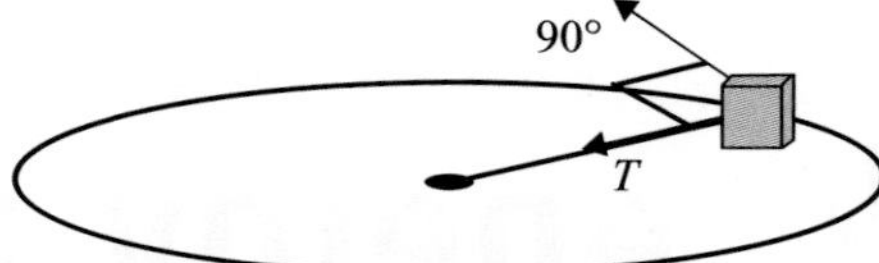

Figure 7.2.

angle between the force and *any small* displacement of the mass as it revolves around the circle is 90° and since $\cos 90° = 0$, the work done is zero.

Q3

A force of constant magnitude 25 N acts on a body that moves along a curved path. The direction of the force is along the velocity vector of the body, i.e. it is *tangential to the path*. Find the work after the mass moves a distance of 50 m along the curved path.

Answer

The diagram on the left of Figure 7.3 shows the path of the body. The diagram on the right is an enlargement of part of the path. We see that the work done when the body travels a *small distance* Δs is

$F\Delta s \cos 0° = F\Delta s$

Breaking up the entire path into small bits in this way, and adding the work done along each bit, we find that the *total* work done is $W = Fs$, where s is the distance travelled along the curved path.

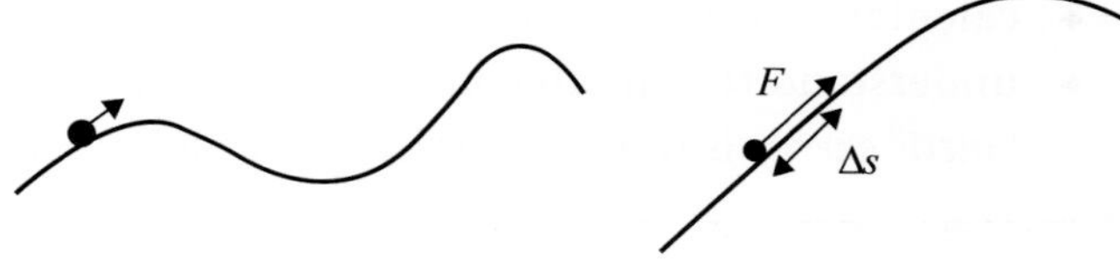

Figure 7.3.

If the force is not constant in magnitude, we must be supplied with the graph that shows the variation of the magnitude of the force with distance travelled. Then we have the following important result:

▶ **The area under the graph that shows the variation of the magnitude of the force with distance travelled is the work done.**

We can apply this result to the case of the tension in the spring. Since $T = kx$, where k is the spring constant and x the extension (or compression) of the string, the graph of force versus position is as shown in Figure 7.4.

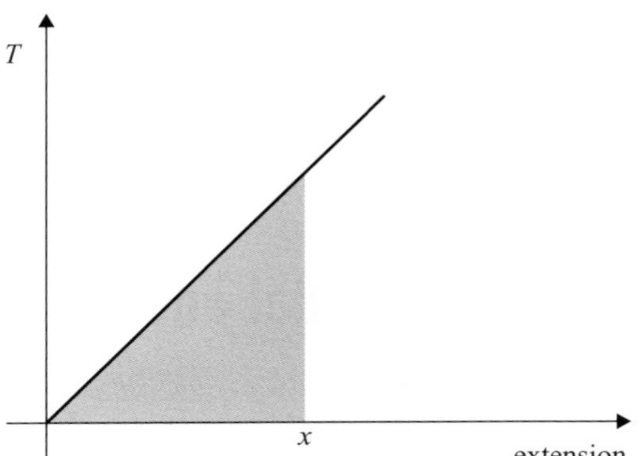

Figure 7.4 The area under a force–distance graph gives the total work performed by the non-constant force.

To find the work done in extending the spring from its natural length ($x = 0$) to extension x, we need to calculate the area of the triangle whose base is x and height is $T = kx$. Thus

$$\begin{aligned} \text{area} &= \tfrac{1}{2}kx \times x \\ &= \tfrac{1}{2}kx^2 \end{aligned}$$

The work to extend a spring from its natural length by an amount x is thus

$$W = \tfrac{1}{2}kx^2$$

It follows that the work done when extending a spring from an extension x_1 to an extension x_2 (so $x_2 > x_1$) is

$$W = \tfrac{1}{2}k\left(x_2^2 - x_1^2\right)$$

Work done by gravity

We will now concentrate on the work done by a very special force, namely the weight of a mass. Remember that weight is mass times acceleration due to gravity and is directed vertically down. Thus, if a mass is displaced horizontally, the work done by mg is zero, since in this case the angle is 90°: $W = mgd \cos 90° = 0$. (See Figure 7.5.)

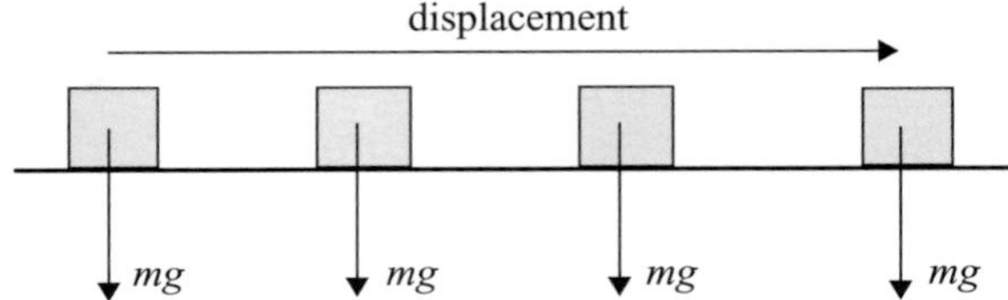

Figure 7.5 The force of gravity is normal to this horizontal displacement so no work is being done.

Note that we are not implying that it is the weight that is forcing the mass to move along the table. We are calculating the work done by a particular force (the weight) if the mass (somehow) moves in a particular way.

If the body falls a vertical distance h, then the work done by W is $+mgh$. The force of gravity is parallel to the displacement, as in Figure 7.6a.

If the mass is thrown vertically upwards to a height h from the launch point, then the work done by W is $-mgh$ since now the angle between direction of force (vertically down) and displacement (vertically up) is 180°. The force of gravity is parallel to the displacement but opposite in direction, as in Figure 7.6b.

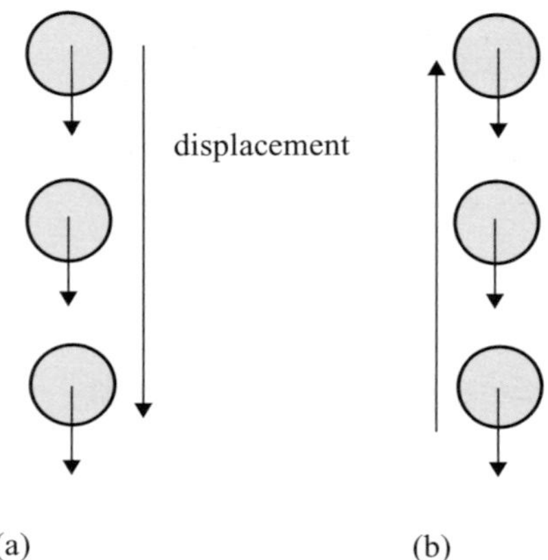

Figure 7.6 The force of gravity is parallel to the displacement in (a) and anti-parallel (i.e. parallel but opposite in direction) in (b).

Consider now the case where a mass moves along some arbitrary path, as shown in Figure 7.7.

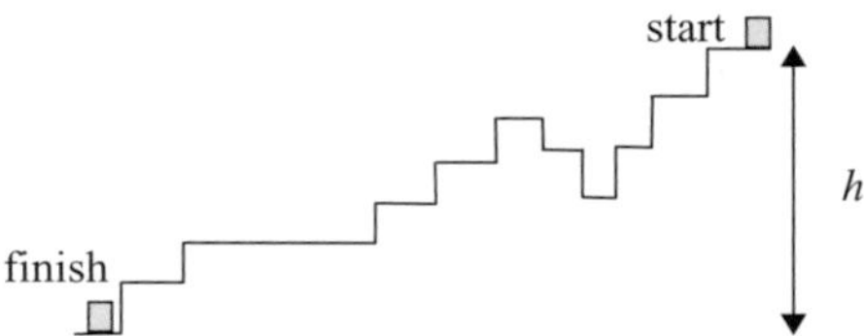

Figure 7.7 The work done by gravity is independent of the path followed.

The path consists of horizontal and vertical segments. We now ask about the work done by the weight of the mass. The work done by mg will be equal to the sum of the work done along each horizontal and vertical step. But mg does no work along the horizontal steps since the angle between the force and the displacement in that case will be $90°$ and $\cos 90° = 0$. We are thus left with the vertical steps only. The work done along each step will be $\pm mg\,\Delta h$, where Δh is the step height. The plus sign is used when we go down a step and the minus sign when we go up a step. (In Figure 7.7 the mass will be forced to go up twice and down eight times.) Thus, what counts is the net number of steps going down (six in our figure). But, this adds up to the vertical distance separating the initial and final position. Hence, the work done by mg is mgh.

If the start and finish positions are joined by an arbitrary smooth curve rather than a 'staircase', the result is still the same. This is because we can always approximate a smooth curve by a series of horizontal and vertical steps; the quality of the approximation depends on how small we take the steps to be. This means that:

▶ The work done by gravity is independent of the path followed and depends only on the vertical distance separating the initial and final positions. The independence of the work done on the path followed is a property of a class of forces (of which weight is a prominent member) called *conservative forces*.

Work done in holding something still

If you try to hold up a heavy object, such as a chair, you will soon get tired. However, the force with which you are holding the chair does zero work since there is no displacement. This is somewhat unexpected. We normally associate getting tired with doing work. Indeed, the forces inside the muscles of the arm and hand holding the chair do work. This is because the muscles stretch and compress and that requires work, just as stretching and compressing a spring does.

Gravitational potential energy

As we just saw, the weight mg of a mass m a height h from the ground will perform work mgh if this mass moves from its position down to the ground. The ability to do this work is there because the mass just happens to be at a height h from the ground. The ability to do work is called energy. When the force in question is the weight (which depends on gravity), we call this energy *gravitational* **potential energy**:

$$E_p = mgh$$

Any mass has gravitational potential energy by virtue of its position. But what determines h? Obviously, we have to choose a reference level from which we will measure heights. But we can choose any level we like. A mass $m = 2$ kg sitting on a table 1 m from the floor will have $E_p = 2 \times 10 \times 1 = 20$ J if the reference level is the floor, but will have $E_p = 0$ if the reference level is the table. If the reference level is chosen to be the ceiling, 2 m above the table, then $E_p = -2 \times 10 \times 2 = -40$ J. (See Figure 7.8.)

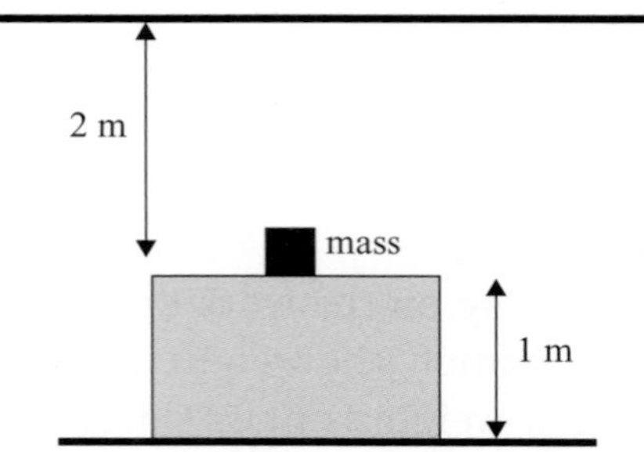

Figure 7.8 The mass has different potential energies depending on the reference level chosen.

So, the same mass will have different gravitational potential energy depending on what reference level we choose. This might seem to make E_p a useless quantity. But if you are patient, you will see that this is not the case.

Potential energy can be understood in the following way. Consider a mass resting on a horizontal floor. If an external force equal to mg is applied to the mass vertically up and the mass moves without acceleration to a position h metres higher than the floor, the work done *by the external force* is mgh. What has become of this work? This work has gone into gravitational potential energy of the mass. This energy is stored as potential energy in the new position of the mass. Similarly, if a spring is initially unstretched and an external force stretches it by an amount x, then the work done by this external force is $\frac{1}{2}kx^2$. This work is stored as elastic potential energy in the (now stretched) spring.

▶ This is a general result for all kinds of potential energies: when an *external* force changes the state of a system without acceleration and does work W in the process, the work so performed is stored as potential energy in the new state of the system.

Example question

Q4

A mass of 10 kg rests on top of a vertical spring whose base is attached to the floor. The spring compresses by 5 cm. What is the spring constant of the spring? How much energy is stored in the spring?

Answer

The mass is at equilibrium so

$$mg = kx$$

$$\Rightarrow k = \frac{mg}{x} = \frac{100}{0.05} = 2000\ \text{N m}^{-1}$$

The stored energy is

$$E_e = \frac{1}{2}kx^2 = \frac{1}{2} \times 2000(0.05)^2 = 2.5\ \text{J}$$

The work–kinetic energy relation

What effect does the work done have on a body? When a body of mass m is acted upon by a *net* force F, then this body experiences an acceleration $a = \frac{F}{m}$ in the direction of F. Suppose that this body had speed v_0 when the force was first applied to it and that the speed after moving a distance x (in the direction of the net force) becomes v_f, as shown in Figure 7.9.

Figure 7.9 A force accelerates a mass, increasing its kinetic energy.

We know from kinematics that

$$v_f^2 = v_0^2 + 2ax$$

so replacing the acceleration by F/m we find

$$v_f^2 = v_0^2 + 2\frac{F}{m}x$$

$$\Rightarrow Fx = \frac{1}{2}mv_f^2 - \frac{1}{2}mv_0^2$$

But Fx is the work done on the mass. This work equals the change in the quantity $E_k = \frac{1}{2}mv^2$, a quantity called the **kinetic energy** of the mass. We thus see that the net work done on a mass results in a change of the kinetic energy of the object. This is a very useful result with applications in many areas of physics.

▶ The work done by the *net* force on a body is equal to the change in the kinetic energy of the body

work done by net force $= \Delta E_k$

Example questions

Q5

A mass of 5.00 kg moving with an initial velocity of 12.0 m s^{-1} is brought to rest by a horizontal force over a distance of 12.0 m. What is the force?

Answer

The change in the kinetic energy of the mass is (final minus initial)

$$0 - \frac{1}{2}mv^2 = -\frac{1}{2} \times 5.00 \times 144$$
$$= -360 \text{ J}$$

The work done by the force f is

$$-fs = -12f$$

Hence

$$-12f = -360$$
$$\Rightarrow f = 30.0 \text{ N}$$

(There is a minus sign in the work done by f because the force is acting in a direction opposite to the motion and $\cos 180° = -1$.)

Q6

An electron is acted upon by an electric force that accelerates it from rest to a kinetic energy of 5.0×10^{-19} J. If this is done over a distance of 3.0 cm, find the electric force.

Answer

The work done by the electric force is the change in kinetic energy (the electric force is the only force acting and so it is the net force) and equals the product of force times distance. Hence

$$F \times 0.03 = 5.0 \times 10^{-19}$$
$$\Rightarrow F = 1.7 \times 10^{-17} \text{ N}$$

Q7

A mass m hangs from two strings attached to the ceiling such that they make the same angle with the vertical (as shown in Figure 7.10). The strings are shortened very slowly so that the mass is raised a distance h above its original position. What is the work done by the tension in each string as the mass is so raised?

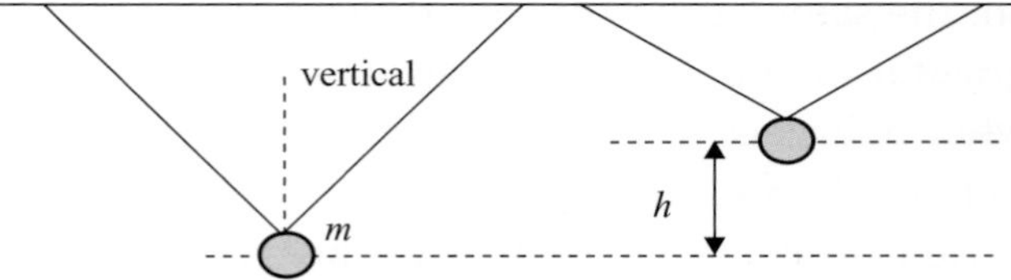

Figure 7.10.

Answer

The net work done is zero since the net force on the mass is zero. The work done by gravity is $-mgh$ and thus the work done by the two equal tension forces is $+mgh$. The work done by each is thus $mgh/2$.

Q8

A mass m hangs vertically at the end of a string of length L. A force F is applied to the mass horizontally so that it slowly moves to a position a distance h higher, as shown in Figure 7.11. What is the work done by the force F? (Note: F is not constant.)

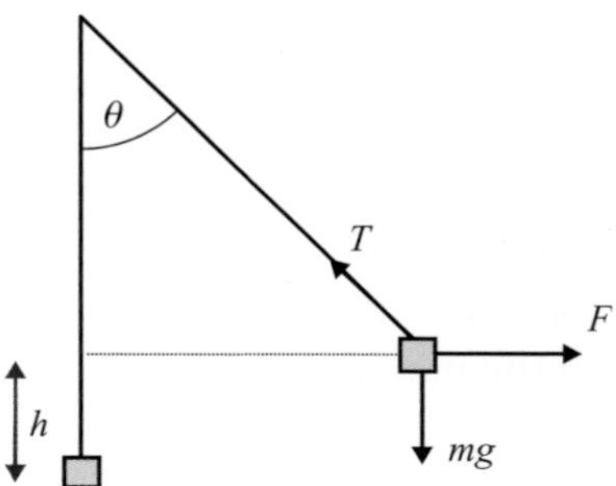

Figure 7.11.

Answer

The answer is obtained at once by noting that since the mass is in equilibrium at all times the net force is zero and hence the work done by the net force is zero. But T does zero work since it is always normal to the direction in which the mass moves (along the arc of a circle). The weight does work $-mgh$ and thus the work done by F must be $+mgh$.

Conservation of energy

We have already seen that, when a net force F performs work W on a body, then the kinetic energy of the body changes by W (here the subscripts 'i' and 'f' stand for 'initial' and 'final')

$$W = \Delta E_k$$
$$= \tfrac{1}{2}mv_f^2 - \tfrac{1}{2}mv_i^2$$

Consider now the case where the only force that does work on a body is gravity. This corresponds to motions in which the body is either in free fall (gravity is the only force acting) or the body is sliding on a frictionless surface (we now have the normal reaction force acting here as well as gravity but this force does zero work since it is normal to the direction of motion). Suppose that the vertical height of the body when the velocity is v_i is H, and the velocity becomes v_f at a height of h from the reference level (see Figure 7.12).

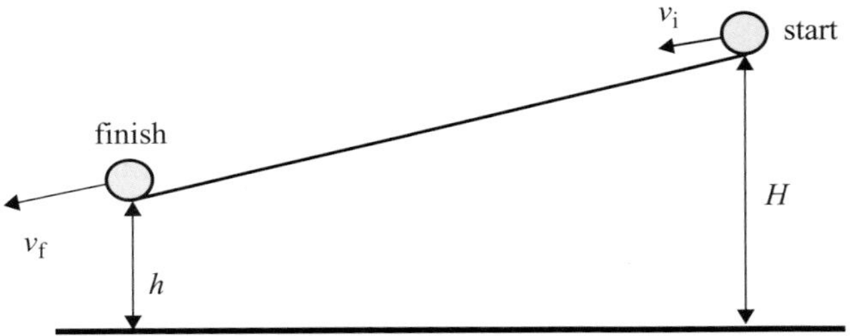

Figure 7.12 The total energy at the top and bottom (and at any point in between) of the incline is the same.

The work done by gravity is simply $mg(H-h)$ and so

$$mg(H-h) = \tfrac{1}{2}mv_f^2 - \tfrac{1}{2}mv_i^2$$

This can be rearranged as

$$mgh + \tfrac{1}{2}mv_f^2 = mgH + \tfrac{1}{2}mv_i^2$$

which shows that in the motion of this body the sum of the kinetic and potential energies of the mass stays the same. Calling the quantity $mgh + \frac{1}{2}mv^2$ the total energy of the mass, then the result we derived states that the total energy E of the mass stays the same at all times, i.e. the total energy is conserved,

$$E_i = E_f$$

As the mass comes down the plane, its potential energy decreases but its kinetic energy increases in such a way that the sum stays the same. We have proven this result in the case in which gravity is the only force doing work in our problem. Consider now the following example questions.

Example questions

Q9

Find the speed of the mass at the end of a pendulum of length 1.00 m that starts from rest at an angle of 10° with the vertical.

Answer

Let us take as the reference level the lowest point of the pendulum (Figure 7.13). Then the total energy at that point is just kinetic, $E_k = \frac{1}{2}mv^2$, where v is the unknown speed. At the initial point the total energy is just potential, $E_p = mgh$, where

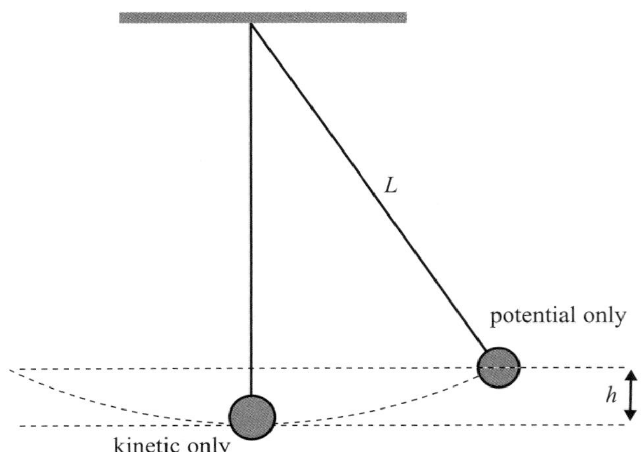

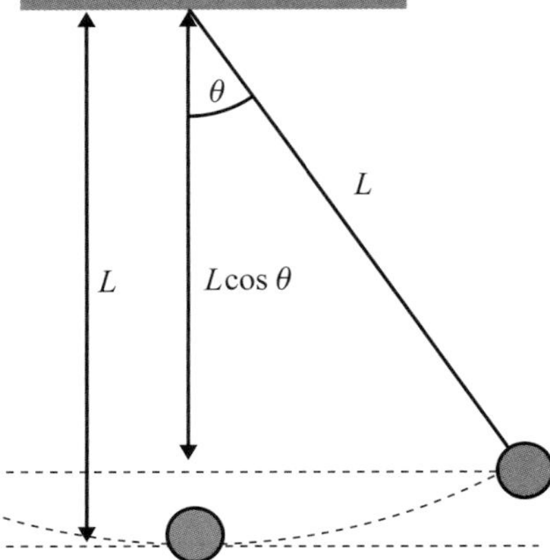

Figure 7.13.

h is the vertical difference in height between the two positions, that is

$$h = 1.00 - 1.00\cos 10^\circ$$
$$= 0.015 \text{ m}$$

(see Figure 7.13)

Thus

$$\tfrac{1}{2}mv^2 = mgh$$
$$v = \sqrt{2gh}$$
$$= 0.55 \text{ m s}^{-1}$$

Note how the mass has dropped out of the problem. (At positions other than the two shown, the mass has both kinetic and potential energy.)

Q10

A mass rolls up an incline of angle 28° with an initial speed of 3.0 m s^{-1}. How far up the incline will the mass get?

Answer

Let the furthest the mass will get be a height h from the floor, as shown in Figure 7.14. At this point the kinetic energy must be zero since otherwise the mass would have climbed higher. Then the total energy at this point is just $E = mgh$. The total energy at the initial position is

$$E = \tfrac{1}{2}mv^2$$

and so

$$h = \frac{v^2}{2g}$$

giving $h = 0.45$ m. The distance moved along the plane is thus

$$\frac{0.45}{\sin 28^\circ} = 0.96 \text{ m}.$$

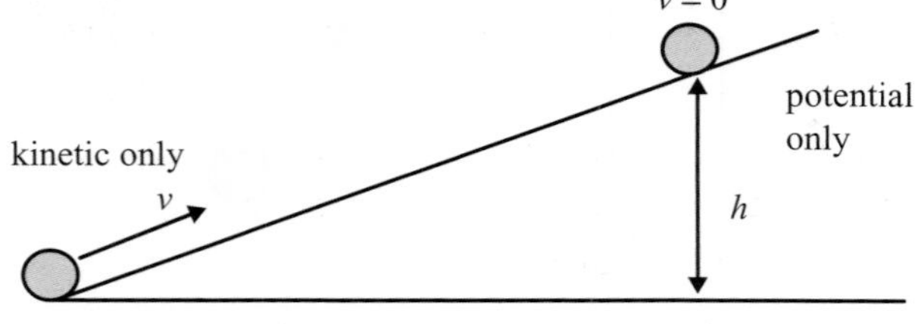

Figure 7.14.

Q11

What must the minimum speed of the mass in Figure 7.15 be at the initial point such that the mass makes it over the barrier of height h?

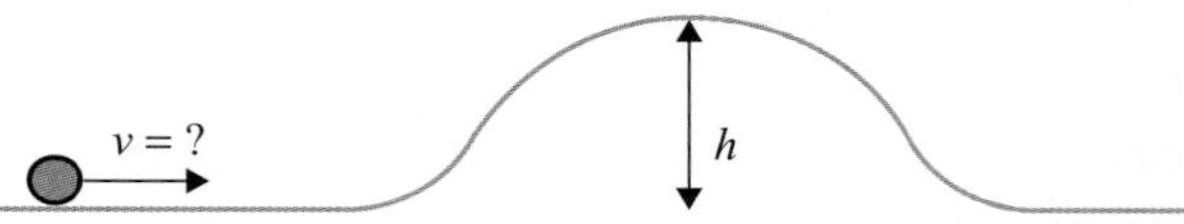

Figure 7.15.

Answer

To make it over the barrier the mass must be able to reach the highest point. Any speed it has there will then make it roll over. Thus, at the very least, we must be able to get the ball to the highest point with zero speed. Then the total energy would be just $E = mgh$ and the total energy at the starting position is $E = \tfrac{1}{2}mv^2$. Thus, the speed must be bigger than $v = \sqrt{2gh}$. Note that if the initial speed u of the mass is larger than $v = \sqrt{2gh}$, then when the mass makes it to the other side of the barrier its speed will be the same as the starting speed u.

Q12

A mass rolls off a 1.0 m high table with a speed of 4.0 m s^{-1}, as shown in Figure 7.16. With what speed does it strike the floor?

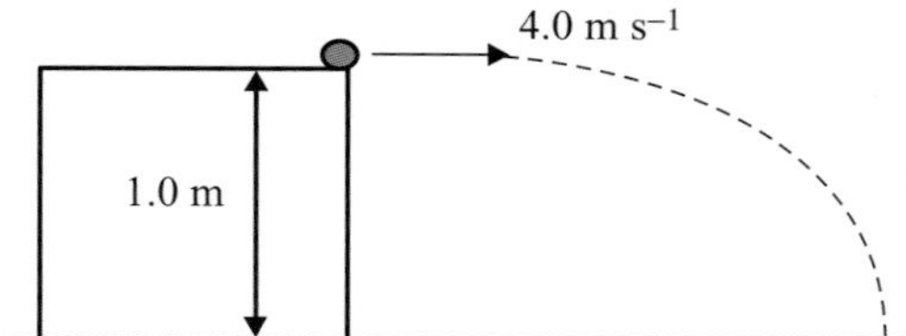

Figure 7.16.

Answer

The total energy of the mass is conserved. As it leaves the table it has total energy given by $E = \tfrac{1}{2}mv^2 + mgh$ and as it lands the total energy is $E = \tfrac{1}{2}mu^2$ (u is the speed we are looking for). Equating the two energies gives

$$\tfrac{1}{2}mu^2 = \tfrac{1}{2}mv^2 + mgh$$
$$\Rightarrow u^2 = v^2 + 2gh$$
$$= 16 + 20 = 36$$
$$\Rightarrow u = 6.0 \text{ m s}^{-1}$$

Q13

A ball is thrown vertically upward with a speed of 4.0 m s^{-1} from a height of 1.0 m from the floor, as shown in Figure 7.17. With what speed does the ball strike the floor?

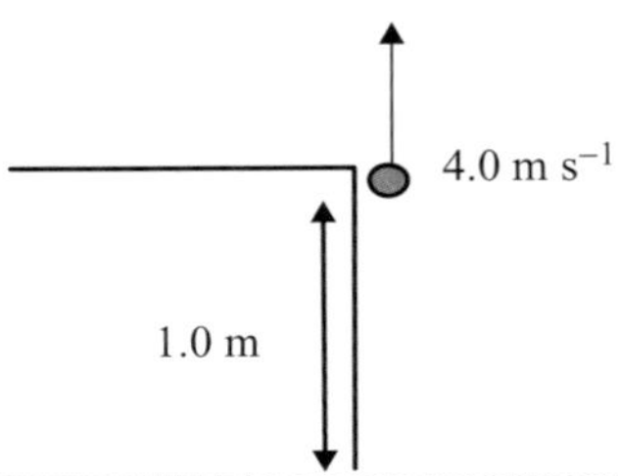

Figure 7.17.

Answer

Working in precisely the same way as in the previous example we find

$$\frac{1}{2}mu^2 = \frac{1}{2}mv^2 + mgh$$
$$\Rightarrow u^2 = v^2 + 2gh$$
$$= 16 + 20$$
$$= 36$$
$$\Rightarrow u = 6.0 \text{ m s}^{-1}$$

(The answer is the same as that for example question 12 – why?)

If, in addition to the weight, there are spring tension forces acting in our system, then the previous discussion generalizes to again lead to

$$E_i = E_f$$

where now the total mechanical energy includes elastic potential energy as well, that is

$$E = \frac{1}{2}mv^2 + mgh + \frac{1}{2}kx^2$$

Example question

Q14

A body of mass 0.40 kg is held next to a compressed spring as shown in Figure 7.18. The spring constant is $k = 250 \text{ N m}^{-1}$ and the compression of the spring is 12 cm. The mass is then released. Find the speed of the body when it is at a height of 20 cm from the horizontal.

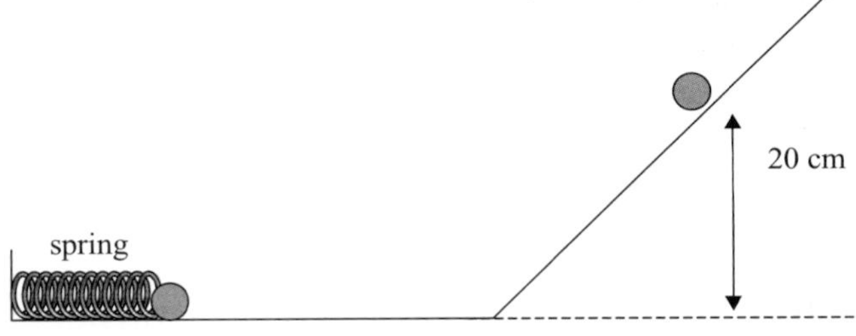

Figure 7.18.

Answer

Initially the total mechanical energy of the system is only the elastic potential energy of the spring

$$E = \frac{1}{2}kx^2$$
$$= \frac{1}{2} \times 250 \times 0.12^2$$
$$= 1.8 \text{ J}$$

At a height of 20 cm from the floor, the total mechanical energy consists of kinetic and gravitational energies only. The spring has decompressed and so has no elastic potential energy. Then

$$E = \frac{1}{2}mv^2 + mgh$$
$$= \frac{1}{2}(0.4)v^2 + (0.4)(10)(0.20)$$
$$= 0.2v^2 + 0.8$$

Thus

$$0.2v^2 + 0.8 = 1.8$$
$$\Rightarrow 0.2v^2 = 1.0$$
$$\Rightarrow v^2 = 5$$
$$\Rightarrow v = 2.2 \text{ m s}^{-1}$$

Frictional forces

In the presence of friction and other resistance forces, the *mechanical energy* of a system (i.e. the sum of kinetic, gravitational potential and elastic potential energies) will not be conserved. These forces will, in general, decrease the total mechanical energy of the system. Similarly, external forces, such as forces due to engines, may increase the mechanical energy of a system. In these cases we may write

$$W = \Delta E$$

where W stands for the total work done by the *external forces* and ΔE is the change in the mechanical energy of the system. By external forces we mean forces *other* than weight and spring tension forces.

This equation is easily understood in the following way. If there are no external forces, then $W = 0$, $\Delta E = 0$ and the total mechanical energy stays the same: it is conserved.

If, on the other hand, external forces do act on the system, then the work they do goes into changing the mechanical energy. If the work done is negative (resistance forces), the mechanical energy decreases. If the work done is positive (pulling forces), the mechanical energy increases.

Example question

Q15

A body of mass 2.0 kg (initially at rest) slides down a curved path of total length 16 m as shown in Figure 7.19. When it reaches the bottom, its speed is measured and found to equal 6.0 m s^{-1}. Show that there is a force resisting the motion. Assuming the force to have constant magnitude, determine what that magnitude is.

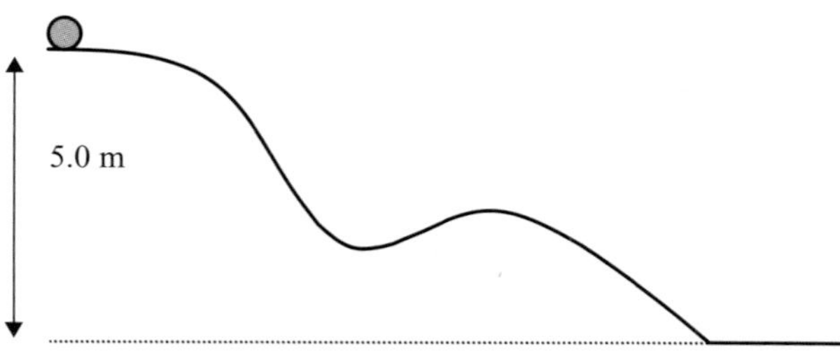

Figure 7.19.

Answer

Without any resistance forces, the speed at the bottom is expected to be

$$\begin{aligned} v &= \sqrt{2gh} \\ &= \sqrt{2 \times 10 \times 5.0} \\ &= 10 \text{ m s}^{-1} \end{aligned}$$

The measured speed is less than this and so there is a resistance force. The total mechanical energy at the top is

$$\begin{aligned} E_{\text{top}} &= mgh \\ &= 2.0 \times 10 \times 5.0 \\ &= 100 \text{ J} \end{aligned}$$

At the bottom it is

$$\begin{aligned} E_{\text{bottom}} &= \tfrac{1}{2}mv^2 \\ &= \tfrac{1}{2} \times 2.0 \times (6.0)^2 \\ &= 36 \text{ J} \end{aligned}$$

The total energy decreased by 64 J – this must be the work done by the resistance force. Thus

$$\begin{aligned} fs &= 64 \text{ J} \\ \Rightarrow f &= \frac{64}{16} \\ &= 4.0 \text{ N} \end{aligned}$$

We have seen that in the presence of external forces the total mechanical energy of a system is not conserved. The change in the total energy is the work done by the external forces. Another way of looking at this is to say the change in the mechanical energy has gone into other forms of energy *not included* in the mechanical energy, such as thermal energy ('heat') and sound. In this way *total energy* (which now includes the other forms as well as the mechanical energy) *is* conserved. This is the general form of the law of conservation of energy, one of the most important principles of physics.

▶ The total energy cannot be created or destroyed but can only be transformed from one form into another.

Power

When a machine performs work, it is important to know not only how much work is being done but also how much work is performed within a given time interval. A cyclist performs a lot of work in a lifetime of cycling, but the same work is performed by a powerful car engine in a much shorter time. **Power** is the rate at which work is being performed.

▶ When a quantity of work ΔW is performed within a time interval Δt the ratio

$$P = \frac{\Delta W}{\Delta t}$$

is called the power developed. Its unit is joule per second and this is given the name watt (W): $1\ \text{W} = 1\ \text{J s}^{-1}$.

Another common unit for power when it comes to machines and car engines is the horsepower, hp, a non-SI unit that equals 746 W.

Consider a constant force F, which acts on a body of mass m. The force does an amount of work $F\,\Delta x$ in moving the body a small distance Δx along its direction. If this work is performed in time Δt, then

$$\begin{aligned} P &= \frac{\Delta W}{\Delta t} \\ &= F\frac{\Delta x}{\Delta t} \\ &= Fv \end{aligned}$$

where v is the instantaneous speed of the mass. This is the power produced in making the body move at speed v. As the speed increases, the power necessary increases as well. Consider an aeroplane moving at constant speed on a straight-line path. If the power produced by its engines is P, and the force pushing it forward is F, then P, F and v are related by the equation above. But since the plane moves with no acceleration, the total force of air resistance must equal F. Hence the force of air resistance can be found simply from the power of the plane's engines and the constant speed with which it coasts.

Example questions

Q16

What is the minimum power required to lift a mass of 50.0 kg up a vertical distance of 12 m in 5.0 s?

Answer

The work performed to lift the mass is

$$\begin{aligned} mgh &= 50.0 \times 10 \times 12 \\ &= 6.0 \times 10^3\ \text{J} \end{aligned}$$

The power is thus

$$\frac{6.0 \times 10^3}{5.0} = 1200\ \text{W}$$

This is only the minimum power required. In practice, the mass has to be accelerated from rest, which will require additional work and hence more power.

Q17

A helicopter rotor whose length is R pushes air downwards with a speed v. Assuming that the density of air is constant and equals ρ and the mass of the helicopter is M, find v. You may assume that the rotor forces the air in a circle of radius R (spanned by the rotor) to move with the downward speed v. Hence find the power developed by the engine. How does this power depend on the linear size of the helicopter?

Answer

The momentum of the air under the rotor is mv, where m is the mass of air in a circle of radius R. In time Δt the mass is enclosed in a cylinder of radius R and height $v\Delta t$. Thus, the momentum of this mass is $\rho\pi R^2 v^2 \Delta t$ and its rate of change is $\rho\pi R^2 v^2$. This is the force on the helicopter upwards, which must equal the helicopter's weight of Mg. Thus

$$Mg = \rho\pi R^2 v^2$$

$$\Rightarrow v = \sqrt{\frac{Mg}{\rho\pi R^2}}$$

The power required from the helicopter engine is thus

$$\begin{aligned} P &= Fv \\ &= Mg\sqrt{\frac{Mg}{\rho\pi R^2}} \end{aligned}$$

To find the dependence on a typical linear size L of the helicopter, note that the weight depends on L as L^3 and so

$$P \propto L^3\sqrt{\frac{L^3}{L^2}} \propto L^{7/2}$$

This implies that if the length of a helicopter is 16 times that of a model helicopter, its required power will be $16^{7/2} \approx 16\,000$ times larger than that for the model.

Efficiency

Suppose that a mass is being pulled up along a rough inclined plane with *constant* speed. Let the mass be 15 kg and the angle of the incline 45°. The constant frictional force opposing the motion is 42 N.

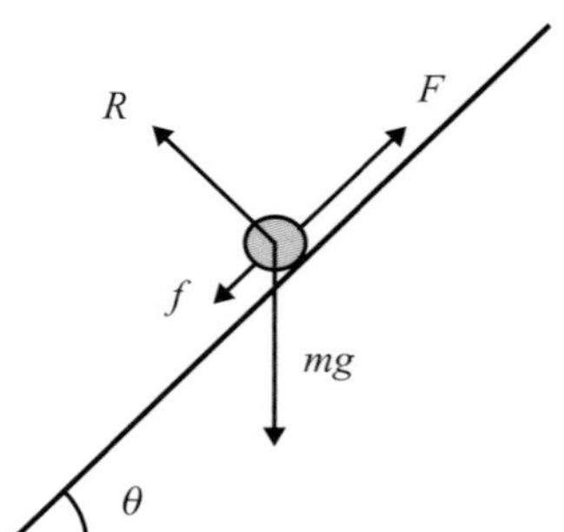

Figure 7.20.

The forces on the mass are shown in Figure 7.20 and we know that

$$\begin{aligned} R &= mg\cos\theta \\ &= 106.1\ \text{N} \end{aligned}$$

$$\begin{aligned} F &= mg\sin\theta + f \\ &= 106.1 + 42 \\ &= 148.1\ \text{N} \approx 150\ \text{N} \end{aligned}$$

since the mass has no acceleration. Let the force raise the mass a distance of 20 m along the plane. The work done by the force F is

$$\begin{aligned} W &= 148.1 \times 20 \\ &= 2960\ \text{J} \approx 3.0 \times 10^3\ \text{J} \end{aligned}$$

The force effectively raised the 15 kg a vertical height of 14.1 m and so increased the potential energy of the mass by $mgh = 2121$ J. The efficiency with which the force raised the mass is thus

$$\begin{aligned} \eta &= \frac{\text{useful work}}{\text{actual work}} \\ &= \frac{2121}{2960} \\ &= 0.72 \end{aligned}$$

Example question

Q18

A 0.50 kg battery-operated toy train moves with constant velocity 0.30 m s^{-1} along a level track. The power of the motor in the train is 2.0 W and the total force opposing the motion of the train is 5.0 N.

(a) What is the efficiency of the train's motor?

(b) Assuming the efficiency and the opposing force stay the same, calculate the speed of the train as it climbs an incline of 10.0° to the horizontal.

Answer

(a) The power delivered by the motor is 2.0 W. Since the speed is constant, the force developed by the motor is also 5.0 N. The power used in moving the train is $Fv = 5.0 \times 0.30 = 1.5$ W. Hence the efficiency is

$$\begin{aligned} \eta &= \frac{1.5\ \text{W}}{2.0\ \text{W}} \\ &= 0.75 \end{aligned}$$

(b) The net force pushing the train up the incline is

$$\begin{aligned} F &= mg\sin\theta + 5.0 \\ &= 0.50 \times 10 \times \sin 10^\circ + 5.0 \\ &= 5.89\ \text{N} \approx 5.9\ \text{N} \end{aligned}$$

Thus

$$\begin{aligned} \eta &= \frac{5.89 \times v}{2.0\ \text{W}} \\ &= 0.75 \end{aligned}$$

$$\begin{aligned} \Rightarrow v &= \frac{2.0 \times 0.75}{5.89} \\ &= 0.26\ \text{m s}^{-1} \end{aligned}$$

Kinetic energy and momentum

We have seen in Chapter 2.6 on momentum that, in a collision or explosion where no external forces are present, the total momentum of the system is conserved. You can easily convince yourself that in the three collisions illustrated in Figure 7.21 momentum is conserved. The incoming body has mass 8.0 kg and the other a mass of 12 kg.

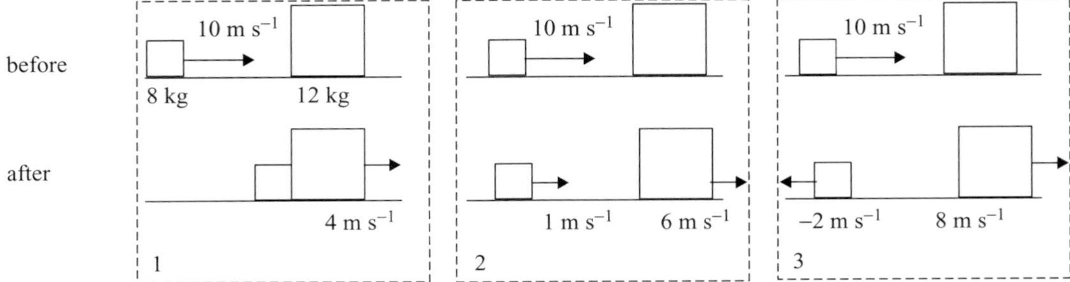

Figure 7.21 Momentum is conserved in these three collisions.

In the first collision the bodies have stuck together and move as one. In the second the incoming body has slowed down as a result of the collision and the heavy body moves faster. In the third the incoming body has bounced back.

Let us examine these collisions from the point of view of energy.

In all cases the total kinetic energy before the collision is

$$E_\mathrm{k} = \tfrac{1}{2} \times 8 \times 10^2 = 400\,\mathrm{J}$$

The total kinetic energy after the collision in each case is:

case 1 $E_\mathrm{k} = \tfrac{1}{2} \times 20 \times 4^2 = 160\,\mathrm{J}$

case 2 $E_\mathrm{k} = \tfrac{1}{2} \times 8 \times 1^2 + \tfrac{1}{2} \times 12 \times 6^2 = 220\,\mathrm{J}$

case 3 $E_\mathrm{k} = \tfrac{1}{2} \times 8 \times 2^2 + \tfrac{1}{2} \times 12 \times 8^2 = 400\,\mathrm{J}$

We thus observe that *whereas momentum is conserved in all cases,* kinetic energy is not. When kinetic energy is conserved (case 3), the collision is said to be *elastic.* When it is not (cases 1 and 2), the collision is *inelastic.* In an inelastic collision, kinetic energy is lost. When the bodies stick together after a collision (case 1), the collision is said to be *totally inelastic* and in this case the maximum possible kinetic energy is lost.

The lost kinetic energy gets transformed into other forms of energy, such as thermal energy, deformation energy (if the bodies are permanently deformed as a result of the collision) and sound energy.

Example questions

Q19

A moving body of mass m collides with a stationary body of double the mass and sticks to it. What fraction of the original kinetic energy is lost?

Answer

The original kinetic energy is $\tfrac{1}{2}mv^2$, where v is the speed of the incoming mass. After the collision the two bodies move as one with speed u that can be found from momentum conservation:

$$mv = (m + 2m)u$$

$$\Rightarrow u = \frac{v}{3}$$

The total kinetic energy after the collision is therefore

$$\frac{1}{2}(3m)\left(\frac{v}{3}\right)^2 = \frac{mv^2}{6}$$

and so the lost kinetic energy is

$$\frac{mv^2}{2} - \frac{mv^2}{6} = \frac{mv^2}{3}$$

The fraction of the original energy that is lost is thus

$$\frac{mv^2/3}{mv^2/2} = \frac{2}{3}$$

Q20

A body at rest of mass M explodes into two pieces of masses $M/4$ and $3M/4$. Calculate the ratio of the kinetic energies of the two fragments.

Answer

Here it pays to derive a very useful expression for kinetic energy in terms of momentum. Since

$$E_k = \frac{mv^2}{2}$$

it follows that

$$\begin{aligned} E_k &= \frac{mv^2}{2} \times \frac{m}{m} \\ &= \frac{m^2v^2}{2m} \\ &= \frac{p^2}{2m} \end{aligned}$$

The total momentum before the explosion is zero, so it is zero after as well. Thus, the two fragments must have *equal and opposite momenta.* Hence

$$\begin{aligned} \frac{E_{\text{light}}}{E_{\text{heavy}}} &= \frac{p^2/(2M_{\text{light}})}{p^2/(2M_{\text{heavy}})} \\ &= \frac{M_{\text{heavy}}}{M_{\text{light}}} \\ &= \frac{3M/4}{M/4} \\ &= 3 \end{aligned}$$

The problem of least time

In Figure 7.22 a number of paths join the starting position A to the final position B.

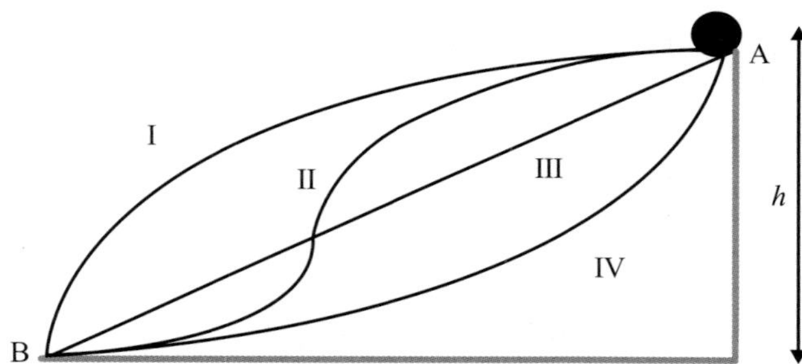

Figure 7.22.

A mass m at A will start with a tiny speed and move down to B. As we saw, the speed at B will be the same no matter what path the mass follows. The speed will equal $\sqrt{2gh}$ in all cases. This does not mean, however, that the time taken is the same for all paths. Finding the path joining A to B such that a mass takes the least time is a famous problem in physics and requires the development of a branch of calculus called the calculus of variations. It is called the brachistochrone (least time) problem. The answer is that the curve joining A to B must be a cycloid. This is the curve traced out by a point on the rim of a wheel as the wheel rolls. In Figure 7.22, curve IV resembles a cycloid most. This problem was posed to both Newton and Leibniz (the inventors of calculus) by the Swiss mathematician Bernoulli. When Bernoulli saw the solutions given by the two men, he is supposed to have said of Newton 'one can always tell a lion by its claws'.

? QUESTIONS

1 A horizontal force of 24 N pulls a body a distance of 5.0 m along its direction. Calculate the work done by the force.

2 A block slides along a rough table and is brought to rest after travelling a distance of 2.4 m. The frictional force is assumed constant at 3.2 N. Calculate the work done by the frictional force.

3 A block is pulled as shown in Figure 7.23 by a force making an angle of 20° to the horizontal. Find the work done by the pulling force when its point of application has moved 15 m.

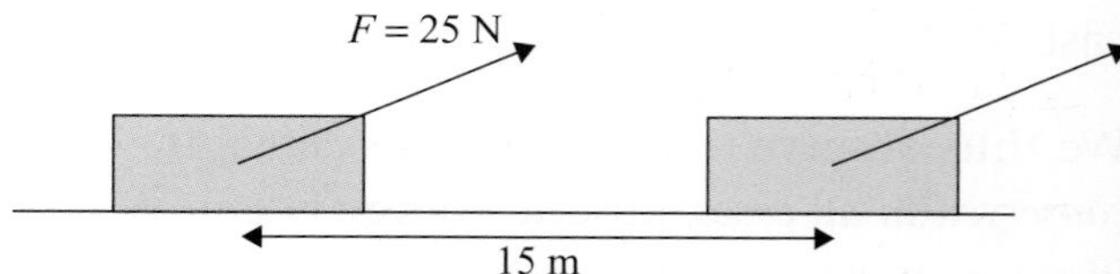

Figure 7.23 For question 3.

4 A block of mass 4.0 kg is pushed to the right by a force $F = 20.0$ N. A frictional force of 14.0 N is acting on the block while it is moved a distance of 12.0 m along a horizontal floor. The forces acting on the mass are shown in Figure 7.24.

(a) Calculate the work done by each of the four forces acting on the mass.

(b) Hence find the net work done.

(c) By how much does the kinetic energy of the mass change?

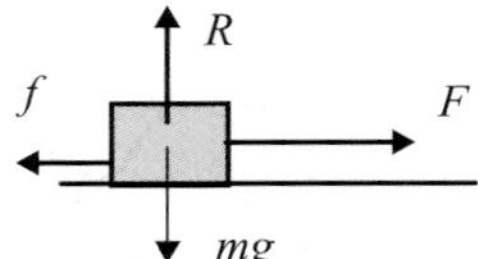

Figure 7.24 For question 4.

5 A weight lifter slowly lifts a 100 kg mass from the floor up a vertical distance of 1.90 m and then slowly lets it down to the floor again.

(a) Find the work done by the weight of the mass on the way up.

(b) Find the work done by the force exerted by the weight lifter when lifting the weight up.

(c) What is the total work done by the weight on the way up and the way down?

6 A block of mass 2.0 kg and an initial speed of 5.4 m s^{-1} slides on a rough horizontal surface and is eventually brought to rest after travelling a distance of 4.0 m. Calculate the frictional force between the block and the surface.

7 A spring of spring constant $k = 200$ N m^{-1} is slowly extended from an extension of 3.0 cm to an extension of 5.0 cm. How much work is done by the extending force?

8 A spring of spring constant $k = 150$ N m^{-1} is compressed by 4.0 cm. The spring is horizontal and a mass of 1.0 kg is held to the right end of the spring. If the mass is released, with what speed will it move away?

9 Look at Figure 7.25.

(a) What is the minimum speed v the mass must have in order to make it to position B? What speed will the mass have at B?

(b) If $v = 12.0$ m s^{-1}, what will the speed be at A and B?

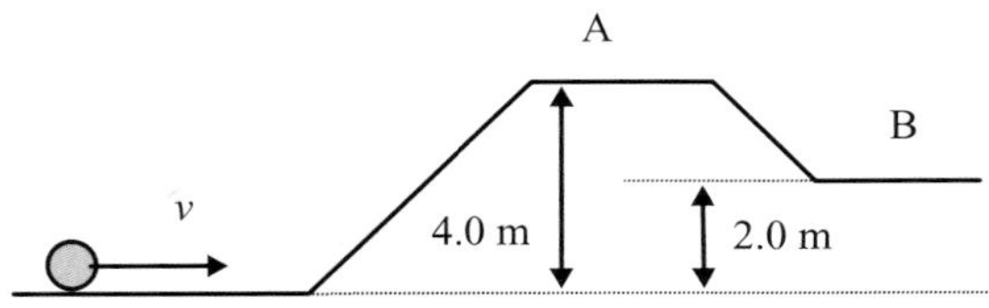

Figure 7.25 For question 9.

10 A mass is released from rest from the position shown in Figure 7.26. What will its speed be as it goes past positions A and B?

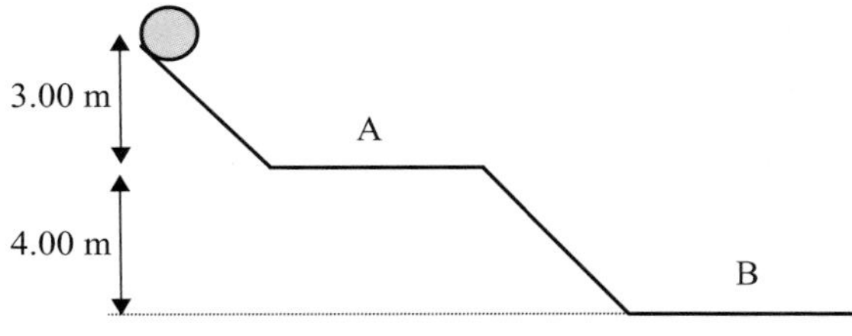

Figure 7.26 For question 10.

11 The speed of the 8.0 kg mass in position A in Figure 7.27 is 6.0 m s^{-1}. By the time it gets to B the speed is measured to be 12.0 m s^{-1}.

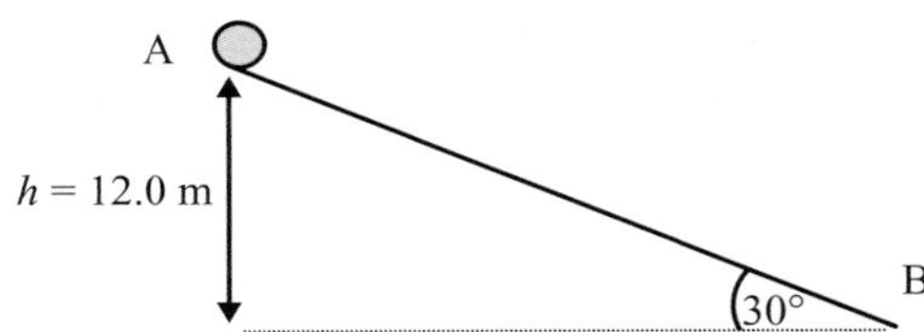

Figure 7.27 For question 11.

What is the frictional force opposing the motion? (The frictional force is acting along the plane.)

12 A toy gun shoots a 20.0 g ball when a spring of spring constant 12.0 N m^{-1} decompresses. The amount of compression is 10.0 cm (see Figure 7.28). With what speed does the ball exit the gun, assuming that there is no friction between the ball and the gun? If, instead, there is a frictional force of 0.05 N opposing the motion of the ball, what will the exit speed be in this case?

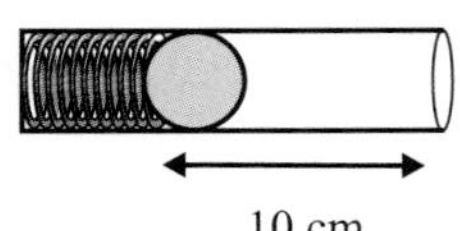

Figure 7.28 For question 12.

13 A variable force F acts on a body of mass $m = 2.0$ kg initially at rest, moving it along a straight horizontal surface. For the first 2.0 m the force is constant at 4.0 N. In the next 2.0 m it is constant at 8.0 N. In the next 2.0 m it drops from 8.0 N to 2.0 N uniformly. It then increases uniformly from 2.0 N to 6.0 N in the

next 2.0 m. It then remains constant at 6.0 N for the next 4.0 m.
(a) Draw a graph of the force versus distance.
(b) Find the work done by this force.
(c) What is the final speed of the mass?

14 A body of mass 12.0 kg is dropped vertically from rest from a height of 80.0 m. Ignoring any resistance forces during the motion of this body, draw graphs to represent the variation with distance fallen of
(a) the potential energy;
(b) the kinetic energy.
For the same motion draw graphs to represent the variation with time of
(c) the potential energy;
(d) the kinetic energy.
(e) Describe qualitatively the effect of a constant resistance force on each of the four graphs you drew.

15 A 25.0 kg block is very slowly raised up a vertical distance of 10.0 m by a rope attached to an electric motor in a time of 8.2 s. What is the power developed in the motor?

16 The engine of a car is developing a power of 90.0 kW when it is moving on a horizontal road at a constant speed of 100.0 km h^{-1}. What is the total horizontal force opposing the motion of the car?

17 The motor of an elevator develops power at a rate of 2500 W.
(a) At what speed can a 1200 kg load be raised?
(b) In practice it is found that the load is lifted more slowly than indicated by your answer to (a). Suggest reasons why this is so.

18 A load of 50.0 kg is raised a vertical distance of 15 m in 125 s by a motor.
(a) What is the power necessary for this?
(b) The power supplied by the motor is in fact 80 W. Calculate the efficiency of the motor.
(c) If the same motor is now used to raise a load of 100.0 kg and the efficiency remains the same, how long would that take?

19 For cars having the same shape but different size engines it is true that the power developed by the car's engine is proportional to the third power of the car's maximum speed. What does this imply about the speed dependence of the wind resistance force?

20 The top speed of a car whose engine is delivering 250 kW of power is 240 km h^{-1}. Calculate the value of the resistance force on the car when it is travelling at its top speed on a level road.

21 Describe the energy transformations taking place when a body of mass 5.0 kg:
(a) falls from a height of 50 m without air resistance;
(b) falls from a height of 50 m with constant speed;
(c) is being pushed up an incline of 30° to the horizontal with constant speed.

22 An elevator starts on the ground floor and stops on the 10th floor of a high-rise building. The elevator picks up a constant speed by the time it reaches the 1st floor and decelerates to rest between the 9th and 10th floors. Describe the energy transformations taking place between the 1st and 9th floors.

23 A car of mass 1200 kg starts from rest, accelerates uniformly to a speed of 4.0 m s^{-1} in 2.0 s and continues moving at this constant speed in a horizontal straight line for an additional 10 s. The brakes are then applied and the car is brought to rest in 4.0 s. A constant resistance force of 500 N is acting on the car during its entire motion.
(a) Calculate the force accelerating the car in the first 2.0 s of the motion.
(b) Calculate the average power developed by the engine in the first 2.0 s of the motion.
(c) Calculate the force pushing the car forward in the next 10 s.
(d) Calculate the power developed by the engine in those 10 s.
(e) Calculate the braking force in the last 4.0 s of the motion.
(f) Describe the energy transformations that have taken place in the 16 s of the motion of this car.

24 A mass of 6.0 kg moving at 4.0 m s^{-1} collides with a mass of 8.0 kg at rest on a frictionless surface and sticks to it. How much kinetic energy was lost in the collision?

25 Two masses of 2.0 kg and 4.0 kg are held in place, compressing a spring between them. When they are released, the 2.0 kg moves away with a speed of 3.0 m s^{-1}. What was the energy stored in the spring?

26 A block of mass 0.400 kg is kept in place so it compresses a spring of spring constant 120 N m^{-1} by 15 cm (see Figure 7.29). The block rests on a rough surface and the frictional force between the block and the surface when the block begins to slide is 1.2 N.

Figure 7.29 For question 26.

(a) What speed will the block have when the spring returns to its natural length?
(b) What percentage is this of the speed the mass would have had in the absence of friction?

27 Two bodies are connected by a string that goes over a pulley, as shown in Figure 7.30. The lighter body is resting on the floor and the other is being held in place a distance of 5.0 m from the floor. The heavier body is then released. Calculate the speeds of the two bodies as the heavy mass is about to hit the floor.

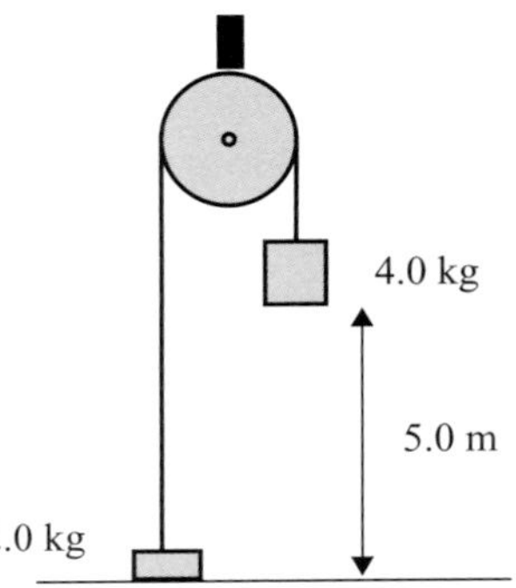

Figure 7.30 For question 27.

28 A mass m of 4.0 kg slides down a frictionless incline of $\theta = 30°$ to the horizontal. The mass starts from rest from a height of 20 m.
(a) Plot a graph of the kinetic and potential energies of the mass as a function of time.
(b) Plot a graph of the kinetic and potential energies of the mass as a function of distance travelled along the incline.
(c) On each graph, plot the sum of the potential and kinetic energies.

29 Show that an alternative formula for kinetic energy is $E_k = \frac{p^2}{2m}$, where p is the momentum of the mass m. This is very useful when dealing with collisions.

30 A body of mass M, initially at rest, explodes and splits into two pieces of mass $M/3$ and $2M/3$, respectively. Find the ratio of the kinetic energies of the two pieces. (Use the formula from the previous problem.)

31 A mass m is being pulled up an inclined plane of angle θ by a rope along the plane.
(a) What is the tension in the rope if the mass moves up at constant speed v?
(b) What is the work done by the tension when the mass moves up a distance of d m along the plane?
(c) What is the work done by the weight of the mass?
(d) What is the work done by the normal reaction force on the mass?
(e) What is the net work done on the mass?

HL only

32 A mass $m = 2.0$ kg is attached to the end of a string of length $L = 4.5$ m. The other end of the string is attached to the ceiling. The string is displaced from the vertical by an angle $\theta_0 = 50°$ and then released. What is the tension in the string when the string makes an angle $\theta = 20°$ with the vertical?

33 A car of mass 1200 kg is moving on a horizontal road with constant speed 30 m s^{-1}. The engine is then turned off and the car will eventually stop under the action of an air resistance force. Figure 7.31 shows the variation of the car's speed with time after the engine has been turned off.

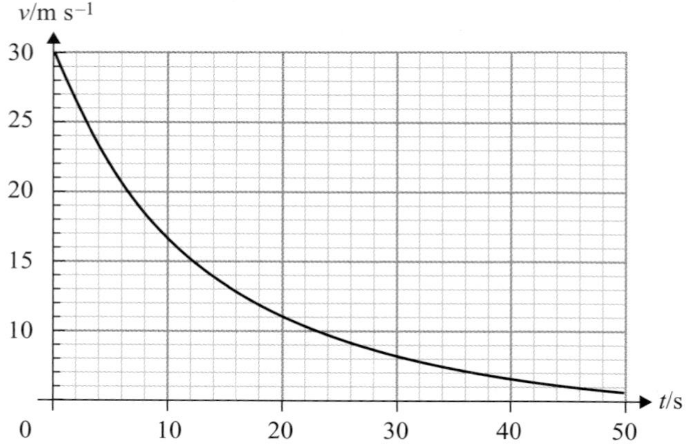

Figure 7.31 For question 33.

(a) Calculate the average acceleration of the car in the first and second 10 s intervals.
(b) Explain why it takes longer to reduce the speed from 20.0 m s^{-1} to 10.0 m s^{-1} compared with from 30.0 m s^{-1} to 20.0 m s^{-1}.
(c) The average speed in the first 10 s interval is 21.8 m s^{-1} and in the second it is 13.5 m s^{-1}. Use this information and your answer in (a) to deduce that the air resistance force is proportional to the square of the speed.
(d) Calculate the distance travelled by the car in the first and second 10 s intervals.
(e) Calculate the work done by the resistance force in the first and second 10 s intervals.

34 A bungee jumper of mass 60 kg jumps from a bridge 24 m above the surface of the water. The rope is 12 m long and is assumed to obey Hooke's law.
(a) What should the spring constant of the rope be if the woman is to just reach the water?
(b) The same rope is used by a man whose mass is more than 60 kg. Explain why the man will not stop before reaching the water. (Treat the jumper as a point and ignore any resistance to motion.)

35 For the bungee jumper of mass 60 kg in question 34, calculate:
(a) the speed of the jumper when she has fallen by 12 m;
(b) the maximum speed attained by the jumper during her fall.
(c) Explain why the maximum speed is reached after falling more than a distance of 12 m (the unstretched length of the rope).

HL only

(d) Sketch a graph to show the variation of the speed of the jumper with distance fallen.

36 A carriage of mass 800 kg moving at 5.0 m s^{-1} collides with another carriage of mass 1200 kg that is initially at rest. Both carriages are equipped with buffers. The graph in Figure 7.32 shows the velocities of the two carriages before, during and after the collision.

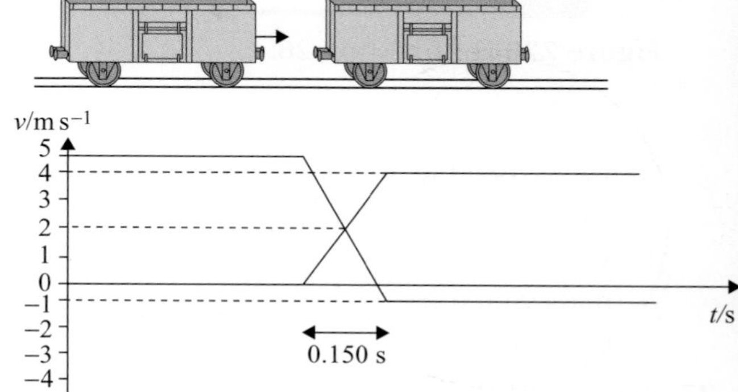

Figure 7.32 For question 36.

Use the graph to:
(a) show that the collision has been elastic;
(b) calculate the average force on each carriage during the collision;
(c) calculate the impulse given to the heavy carriage.
(d) If the buffers on the two carriages had been stiffer, the time of contact would have been less but the final velocities would be unchanged. How would your answers to (b) and (c) change?
(e) Calculate the kinetic energy of the two carriages at the time during the collision when both have the same velocity and compare your answer with the final kinetic energy of the carriages. How do you account for the difference?

HL only

37 Show that in an elastic, head-on collision of a particle of mass m with a stationary particle of mass M the fraction of the original kinetic energy transferred to M is

$$\frac{4Mm}{(m+M)^2}$$

38 Two masses of 3.0 kg and 8.0 kg collide head-on elastically. Before the collision the 8.0 kg mass is at rest and the 3.0 kg moves at speed 10.0 m s^{-1}. Find the velocities after the collision.

39 Two masses of 6.0 kg and 4.0 kg are constrained to move on a frictionless horizontal ring as shown in Figure 7.33.

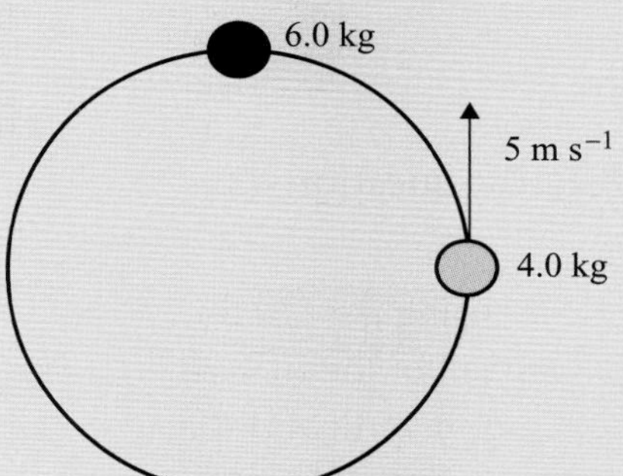

Figure 7.33 For question 39.

Initially the heavy mass is at rest and the other moves in a counter-clockwise direction with speed 5.0 m s^{-1}. At $t = 0$ s the two masses collide elastically. With what velocities do the masses move after the collision? At what points on the circle do subsequent collisions take place?

40 A mass m moves with a speed v on a horizontal table towards a wedge of mass M, as shown in Figure 7.34. How high on the wedge will m get if:

(a) the wedge is firmly fixed on the table;

(b) the wedge is free to move on the table without friction?

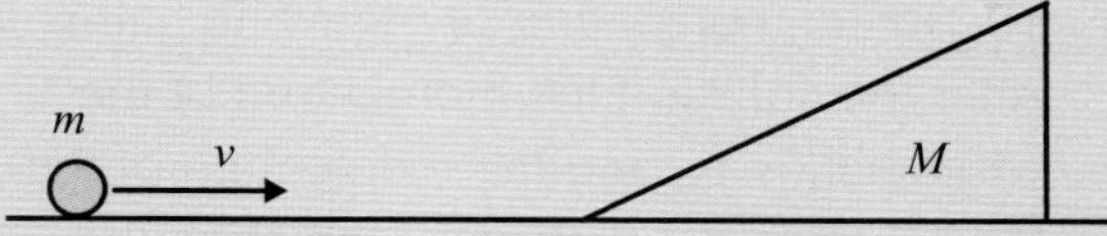

Figure 7.34 For question 40.

41 A battery toy car of mass 0.250 kg is made to move up an inclined plane which makes an angle of 30° with the horizontal. The car starts from rest and its motor provides a constant acceleration of 4.0 m s^{-2} for 5.0 s. The motor is then turned off.

(a) Find the distance travelled in the first 5 s.

(b) Find the furthest the car gets on the inclined plane.

(c) When does the car return to its starting place?

(d) Make a graph of the velocity as a function of time.

(e) On the same axes, make a graph of the kinetic energy and potential energy of the car as a function of the distance travelled.

(f) In which periods in the car's motion is its mechanical energy conserved?

(g) What is the average power developed by the car's motor?

(h) What is the maximum power developed by the motor?

42 A white billiard ball collides with a black billiard ball that is initially at rest. After the collision, the balls move off with an angle θ between them, as shown in Figure 7.35.

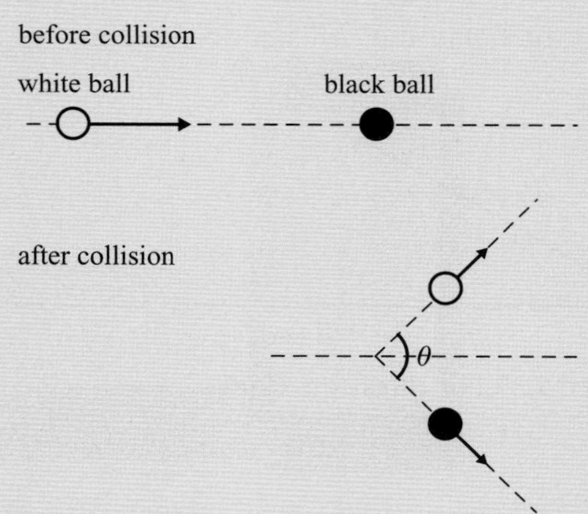

Figure 7.35 For question 42.

The initial momentum of the white ball is $\vec{p}$. After the collision the momentum of the white ball is $\vec{p}_w$ and the momentum of the black ball is $\vec{p}_b$. Arrows representing the momentum of the white ball before and after the collision are shown in Figure 7.36.

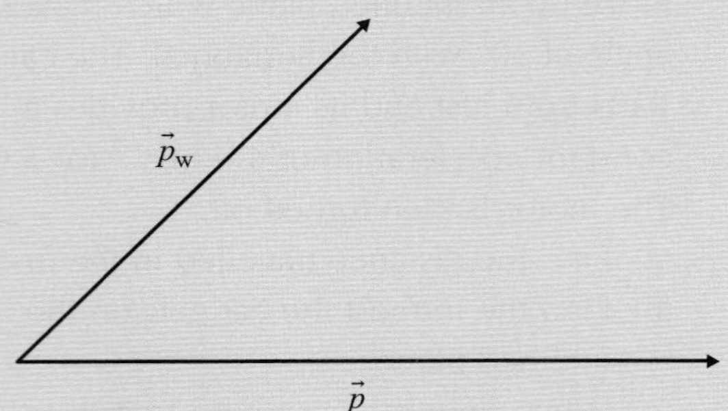

Figure 7.36 For question 42(a).

(a) Copy the diagram. On it, draw an arrow to represent the momentum of the black ball after the collision.
(b) Explain the arrow you have drawn in (a).
(c) On your copy of the diagram, label the angle θ.
(d) The collision is an *elastic* collision, and the two balls have identical masses. Deduce that the angle θ between the balls after the collision is 90°.
(e) In the case of an *inelastic* collision between the two balls, Figure 7.36 is replaced by Figure 7.37. Copy this diagram. On it, draw an arrow to represent the momentum of the black ball after the collision in this case.

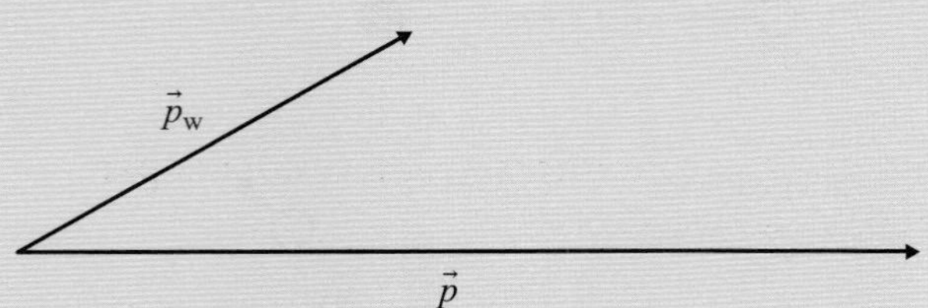

Figure 7.37 For question 42(e).

43 A spring of natural length 0.150 m and spring constant 4.00 N m^{-1} is attached at point P, as shown in Figure 5.26. The other end of the spring is attached to a ring that goes over a frictionless vertical pole. The mass of the ring is 0.100 kg. The spring may be assumed to be massless. Initially the ring is held horizontal so that the length PA is 0.300 m. The ring is then allowed to drop.

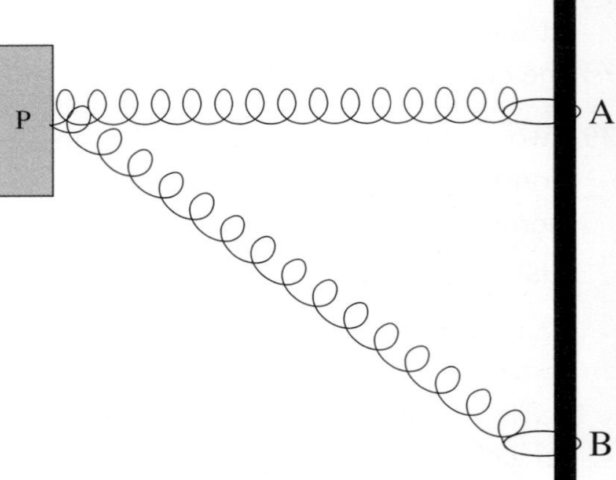

Figure 5.26 For question 43.

(a) Calculate (using $g = 10.0\ \text{m s}^{-2}$):
   (i) the speed of the ring when it reaches point B, a vertical distance of 0.400 m from point A;
   (ii) the magnitude of the force exerted on the ring by the pole at point B;
   (iii) the acceleration (magnitude and direction) of the ring at B;
   (iv) the largest distance below A to which the ring falls (use your graphical calculator);
   (v) the maximum speed of the ring during its fall and the distance fallen when this happens (use your graphical calculator).
(b) Using your graphical calculator, plot the speed of the ring as a function of distance fallen from A.
(c) The ring will start moving upwards after reaching its lowest point. Discuss whether the ring will move higher than point A or whether it will stop at A.

Circular motion

Our discussion of motion so far has been restricted to motion in a straight line. In this chapter, we examine the more complicated motion of an object along a circular path.

Objectives

By the end of this chapter you should be able to:

- understand that acceleration is present when the *magnitude of the velocity*, or its *direction*, or *both change*;
- understand that in motion on a circle with constant speed there is *centripetal acceleration* of constant magnitude, $a_c = \frac{v^2}{r}$, directed at the centre of the circle;
- recognize situations in which a force is acting in a direction *toward the centre of a circle*;
- solve problems involving applications of Newton's second law to motion on a circle, $F_{net} = ma_c = \frac{mv^2}{r}$.

Circular motion and centripetal acceleration

We now examine the case of motion on a circle. Consider the object in Figure 8.1, which rotates on a circle of radius R in the counter-clockwise direction, with constant speed v.

Let T be the time taken to complete one full revolution. We call T the *period* of the motion. Since the speed is constant and the object covers a distance of $2\pi R$ in a time of T s, it follows that

$$v = \frac{2\pi R}{T}$$

We may also note that the object sweeps out an angle of 2π radians in a time equal to the period, so we define the angular speed of the object by

$$\text{angular speed} = \frac{\text{angle swept}}{\text{time taken}}$$

that is

$$\omega = \frac{2\pi}{T}$$

The units of angular speed are radians per second or just s^{-1}.

It is important to note right away that the speed may be constant but the velocity is not. It keeps changing direction. (The velocity vector is at a tangent to the circle – see Figure 8.2.) Since the velocity changes, we have acceleration.

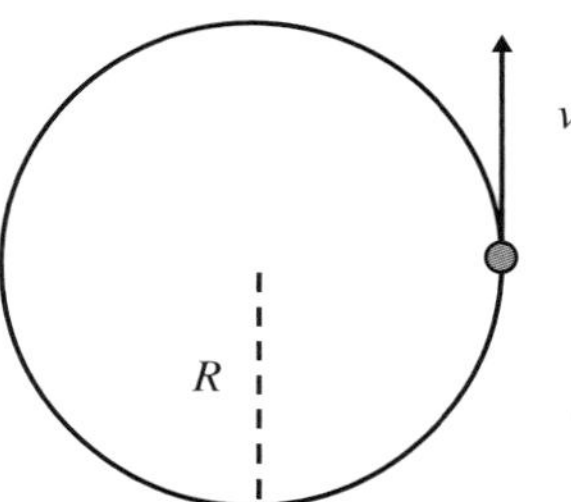

Figure 8.1 An object moving on a circle of radius R.

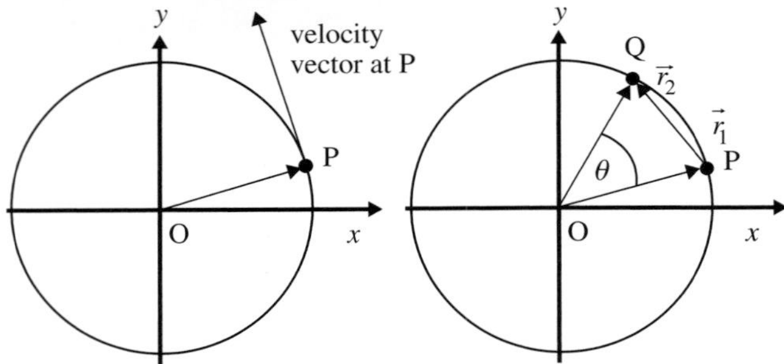

Figure 8.2 The velocity vector is tangent to the circular path.

What follows is a *derivation* of the expression for acceleration in circular motion. You may want to skip it and go directly to the result just before the end of this section (p. 120).

The position vector at time t_1 is given by $\vec{r}_1$ and at a later time t_2 by the vector $\vec{r}_2$. Note that since we chose the origin of our coordinate axes to be at the centre of the circle, the displacement vector of the moving object always has the same magnitude, equal to the radius of the circle. Thus, what changes as the object moves is the direction of the displacement vector, not its magnitude. The velocity of the object is defined as

$$\vec{v} = \frac{\Delta\vec{r}}{\Delta t}$$

where $\Delta\vec{r}$ is a vector representing the difference $\vec{r}_2 - \vec{r}_1$, and the time difference $\Delta t = t_2 - t_1$ is assumed to be as small as possible. It is clear that the vector $\Delta\vec{r}$ is the vector from P to Q. Similarly, the speed of the object is the distance travelled, which is the length of the arc Δs divided by Δt. But remember that the time interval $\Delta t = t_2 - t_1$ must be taken to be as small as possible. As this time difference becomes infinitesimal, $\Delta\vec{r}$ becomes tangential to the circle at point P.

▶ This means that the direction of the velocity for motion on a circle has a direction that is at a tangent to the circle. This is a general result. The direction of velocity is always at a tangent to the path (see Figure 8.3).

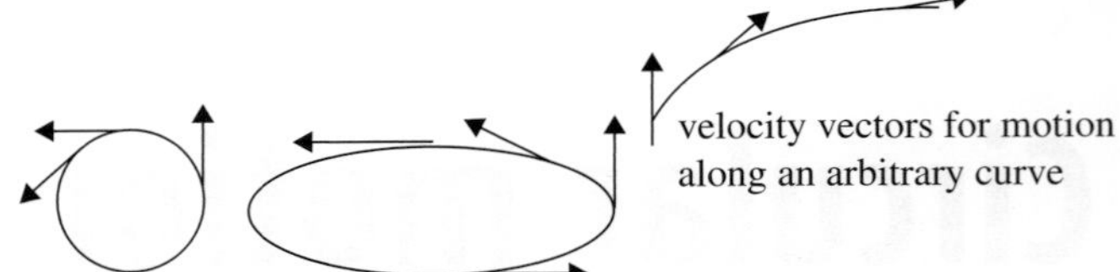

Figure 8.3 The velocity vector is tangential to the path.

The magnitude of the velocity is the magnitude of $\Delta\vec{r}$ divided by Δt. The speed, on the other hand, is the ratio of Δs, the distance travelled, to Δt. Thus, the magnitudes of velocity and speed appear to be different. But recall again that Δt must be infinitesimal, which implies that the difference in the length of Δs and that of $\Delta\vec{r}$ becomes negligible. Thus, the magnitude of velocity is the speed.

▶ Similarly, for acceleration

$$\vec{a} = \frac{\Delta\vec{v}}{\Delta t}$$

where $\Delta\vec{v}$ is a vector. Thus, we have acceleration every time the velocity *vector* changes. This vector will change if:

- its magnitude changes;
- the direction changes;
- both magnitude and direction change.

For motion in a circle with constant *speed*, it is the direction of the velocity vector that changes. We must thus find the difference $\vec{v}_Q - \vec{v}_P$. (Note that the magnitude of the velocity vectors at P and Q are the same – they equal the constant speed v of the moving object.)

In Figure 8.4 the velocity vector at Q has been moved parallel to itself so that it starts at the same point as the velocity vector at P. The difference is thus as shown. The magnitude of this vector can be found from simple trigonometry. From the sine rule

$$\frac{\Delta v}{\sin\theta} = \frac{v}{\sin\left(\frac{\pi}{2} - \frac{\theta}{2}\right)}$$

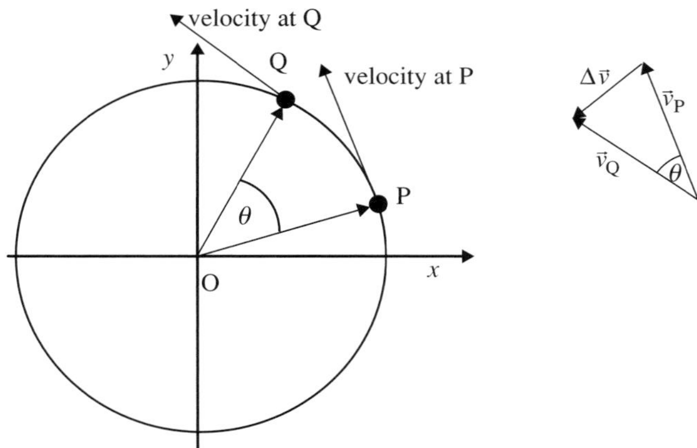

Figure 8.4 The velocity vector changes direction in circular motion, hence we have acceleration.

Recall now that the points P and Q are separated only infinitesimally from each other and so the angle θ is very small. Thus, $\sin\theta \approx \theta$ and $\sin(\frac{\pi}{2} - \frac{\theta}{2}) \approx 1$ (the angle must be expressed in radians). Further, $\theta = \frac{\Delta s}{R}$ and $\Delta s = v\Delta t$. Substituting, we find

$$\Delta v = \frac{vv\Delta t}{R}$$
$$\Rightarrow a_c = \frac{v^2}{R}$$

This gives us the magnitude of the acceleration vector for motion around a circle of radius R with constant speed v. As we see, the magnitude of the acceleration vector is constant, if v is constant. But what about its direction? As Δt gets smaller and smaller, the angle θ gets smaller and smaller, which means that the vector $\Delta\vec{v}$, which is in the direction of acceleration, becomes perpendicular to $\vec{v}$. This means that the acceleration vector is normal to the circle and directed towards the centre of the circle. It is a **centripetal acceleration**.

▶ A body moving along a circle of radius R with speed v experiences centripetal acceleration that has magnitude given by $a_c = \frac{v^2}{R}$ and is directed toward the centre of the circle. (See Figure 8.5.)

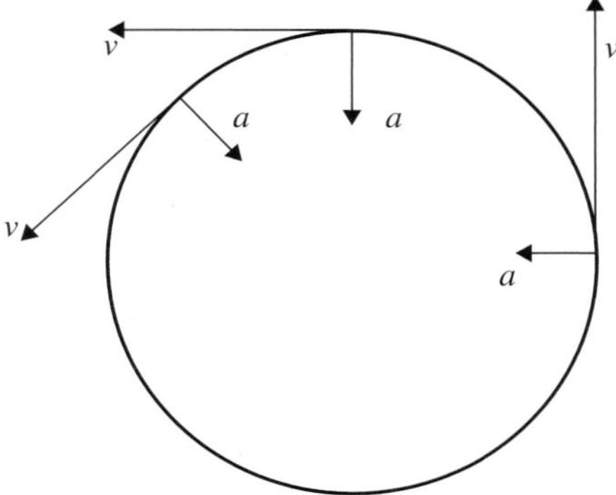

Figure 8.5 The centripetal acceleration vector is normal to the velocity vector.

If the magnitude of the velocity changes, we have **tangential acceleration.** This is a vector directed along the velocity vector if the speed is increasing and opposite to the velocity vector if the speed is decreasing. The magnitude of the tangential acceleration is given by

$$a_t = \frac{\Delta v}{\Delta t}$$

where v is the speed and Δt is infinitesimally small.

When the velocity direction and magnitude are changing, we have both centripetal acceleration and tangential acceleration. The total acceleration is then the vector sum of the vectors representing these accelerations.

Example questions

Q1

A mass moves along a circle of radius 2.0 m with constant speed. It makes one full revolution in 3.0 s. What is the acceleration of the mass?

Answer

The acceleration is v^2/R so we need to know v. But since the mass covers a distance of $2\pi R$ in a time $T = 3.0$ s, we must have

$$v = \frac{2\pi R}{T}$$
$$= \frac{2 \times 3.14 \times 2.0}{3.0\ \mathrm{m\,s^{-1}}}$$
$$= 4.2\ \mathrm{m\,s^{-1}}$$

Hence $a = 8.8\ \mathrm{m\,s^{-2}}$.

Q2

The radius of the earth is $R = 6.4 \times 10^6$ m. What is the centripetal acceleration experienced by someone on the equator?

Answer

A mass on the equator covers a distance of $2\pi R$ in a time $T = 1$ day. Thus

$v = 4.6 \times 10^2 \text{ m s}^{-1}$

and so

$a = 3.4 \times 10^{-2} \text{ m s}^{-2}$

This is quite small compared with the acceleration due to gravity.

Q3

A mass moves in a circle with constant speed in a counter-clockwise direction, as in Figure 8.6a. What is the direction of the velocity change when the mass moves from A to B?

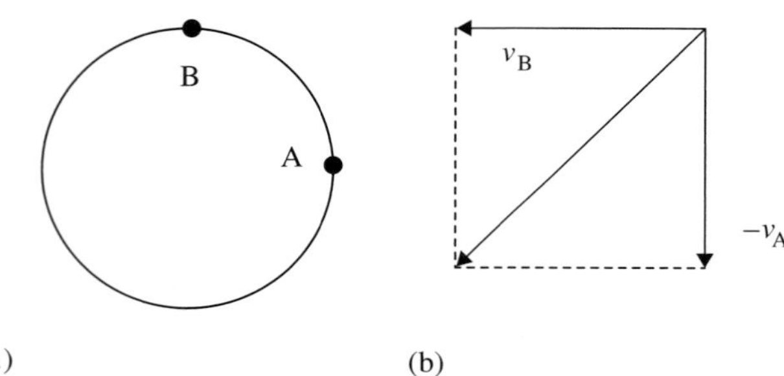

Figure 8.6.

Answer

The velocity at A is vertical and at B it points to the left. The change in the velocity vector is $\vec{v}_B - \vec{v}_A$ and this difference of vectors is directed as shown in Figure 8.6b.

Centripetal forces

If we know that a body moves in a circle, then we know at once that a net force must be acting on the body, since it moves with acceleration. If the speed is constant, the direction of the acceleration is towards the centre of the circle and therefore that is also the direction of the net force. It is a **centripetal force**. Consider a car that moves on a circular level road of radius r with constant speed v. Friction between the wheels and the road provides the necessary force directed towards the centre of the circle that enables the car to take the turn. (See Figure 8.7.)

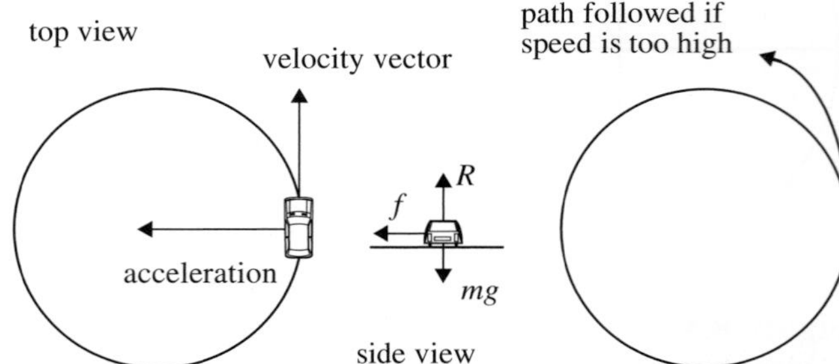

Figure 8.7 A car will skid outwards (i.e. will cover a circle of larger radius) if the friction force is not large enough.

Example questions

Q4

A mass is tied to a string and moves with constant speed in a horizontal circle. The string is tied to the ceiling, at a point higher than the mass. Draw the forces on the mass.

Answer

The common mistake here is to put a horizontal force pointing toward the centre and call it the centripetal force. When you are asked to find forces on a body, the list of forces that are available include the weight, reaction forces (if the body touches another body), friction (if there is friction), tension (if there are strings or springs), resistance forces (if the body moves in air or a fluid), electric forces (if electric charges are involved), etc. Nowhere in this list is there an entry for a centripetal force.

Think of the word centripetal as simply an adjective that *describes* forces already acting on the body, *not* as a new force. In this example, the only forces on the mass are the weight and the tension. If we decompose the tension into horizontal and vertical components, we see that the weight is equal and opposite to the vertical component of the tension. This means that the only force left on the body is the horizontal component of the tension. We may now call this force the centripetal force. But this is not a new force. It is simply the component of a force that is already acting on the body. (See Figure 8.8.)

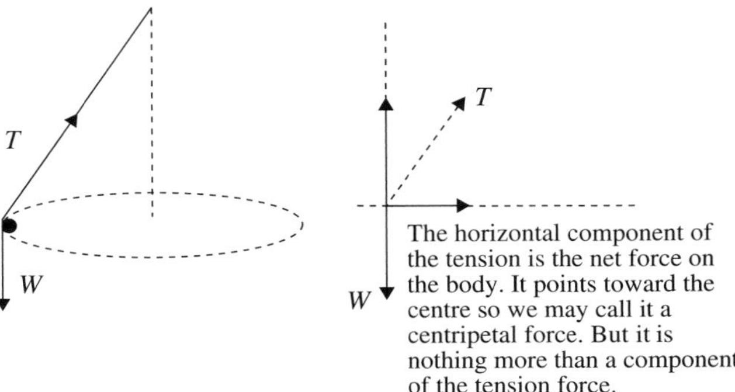

Figure 8.8.

Q5

A mass m is tied to a string and *made* to move in a vertical circle of radius R with constant speed v. Find the tension in the string at the lowest and highest points.

Answer

The forces are as shown in Figure 8.9. At the lowest point, the net force is $T_1 - mg$ and so

$$T_1 - mg = m\frac{v^2}{r}$$

giving

$$T_1 = mg + m\frac{v^2}{r}$$

At the highest point, the net force is $mg + T_2$ and so

$$T_2 = m\frac{v^2}{r} - mg$$

This shows that the string goes slack unless $v^2 > gr$.

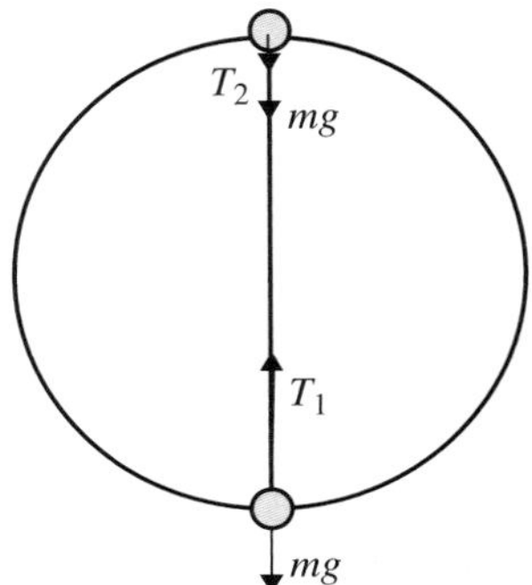

Figure 8.9 The tension in the string is different at different positions of the mass.

It is important to note that, since a centripetal force is at right angles to the direction of motion, the work done by the force is zero. (Recall that $W = Fs\cos\theta$, and here the angle is a right angle.)

It is a common mistake in circular motion problems to include a force pushing the body *away* from the centre of the circle: a **centrifugal force**. It is important to stress that no such force exists. A body in circular motion cannot be in equilibrium and so no force pushing away from the centre is required.

Supplementary material

Angular momentum

Consider a point mass m which rotates about some axis with speed v as shown in Figure 8.10.

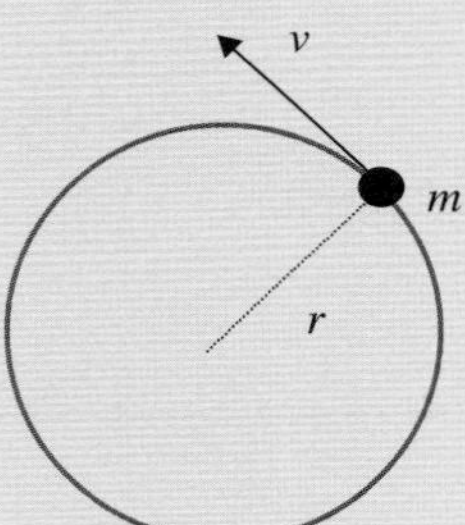

Figure 8.10 A mass rotating counter-clockwise in a circle has an angular momentum pointing out of the page.

We define the magnitude of the angular momentum of the mass m by

$$L = mvr$$

(Angular momentum is a vector but we will not make use of its vector nature here.) If the mass moves along a path other than a circle, then the angular momentum is given by

$$L = mvb$$

where b is the *perpendicular* distance of the axis from the direction of velocity. In Figure 8.11 the axis goes into the page through P. Since $b = r\sin\theta$ it follows that $L = mvr\sin\theta$, where θ is the angle between the velocity vector and the vector from the axis to the position of the mass. The units of angular momentum are J s.

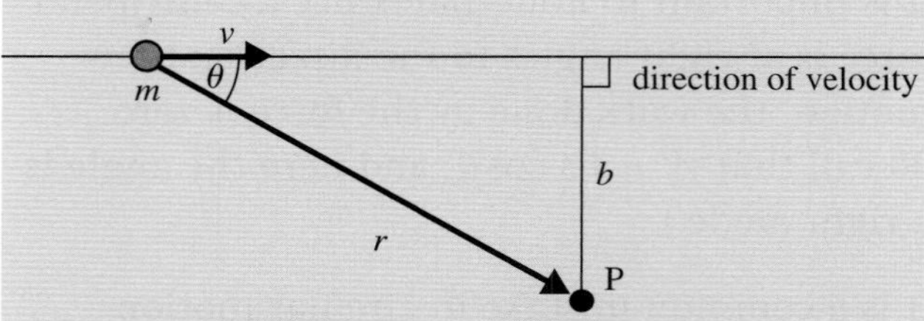

Figure 8.11 A mass has angular momentum about an axis through P.

Example question

Q6

Find the angular momentum of two masses, each of 2.0 kg, that are separated by 5.0 m and rotate about an axis along the perpendicular bisector of the line joining them with speed $v = 7.5\ \text{m s}^{-1}$ (see Figure 8.12).

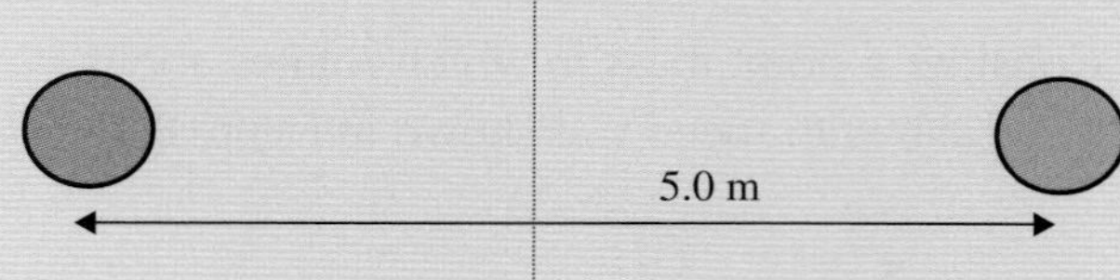

Figure 8.12.

Answer

$L = 2mvr = 75$ J s.

? QUESTIONS

1 A mass moves on a circular path of radius 2.0 m at constant speed $4.0\ \text{m s}^{-1}$ (see Figure 8.13).
   (a) What is the magnitude and direction of the *average* acceleration during a quarter of a revolution (from A to B)?
   (b) What is the centripetal acceleration of the mass?

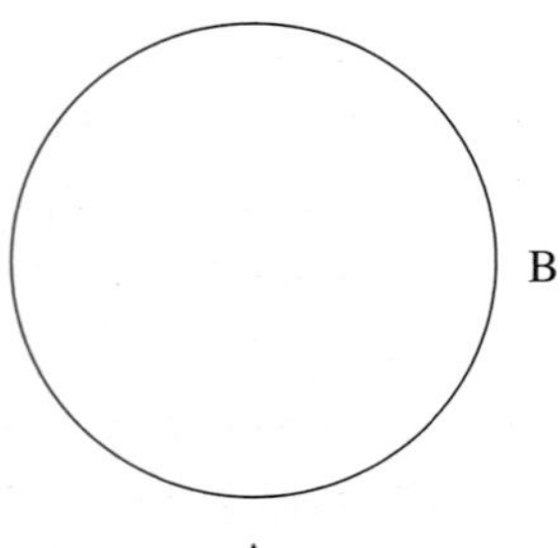

Figure 8.13 For question 1.

2 A body of mass 1.00 kg is tied to a string and rotates on a horizontal, frictionless table.
   (a) If the length of the string is 40.0 cm and the speed of revolution is $2.0\ \text{m s}^{-1}$, find the tension in the string.
   (b) If the string breaks when the tension exceeds 20.0 N, what is the largest speed the mass can rotate at?
   (c) If the breaking tension of the string is 20.0 N but you want the mass to rotate at $4.00\ \text{m s}^{-1}$, what is the shortest length string that can be used?

3 An astronaut rotates at the end of a test machine whose arm has a length of 10.0 m, as shown in Figure 8.14. If the acceleration she experiences must not exceed $5g$ ($g = 10\ \text{m s}^{-2}$), what is the maximum number of revolutions per minute of the arm?

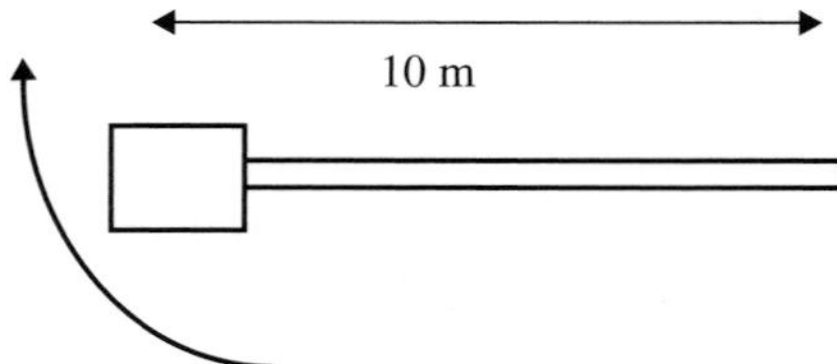

Figure 8.14 For question 3.

4 A wheel of radius R rotates making f revolutions per second. The quantity f is known as the frequency of the motion. Show that $1/f$ is the time to complete one revolution, called the period T of the motion. Show that the centripetal acceleration of a point at the rim of the wheel is

$$a = 4\pi^2 R f^2$$

5 The earth (mass $= 5.98 \times 10^{24}$ kg) rotates around the sun in an orbit that is approximately circular, with a radius of 1.5×10^{11} m.
   (a) Find the orbital speed of the earth around the sun.
   (b) Find the centripetal acceleration experienced by the earth.
   (c) Find the magnitude of the gravitational force exerted on the earth by the sun.

6 (a) What is the angular speed of a mass that completes a 3.5 m radius circle in 1.24 s?
   (b) What is the frequency of the motion?

7 What is the centripetal acceleration of a mass that moves in a circle of radius 2.45 m making 3.5 revolutions per second?

8 What would be the length of the day if the centripetal acceleration at the equator were equal to the acceleration due to gravity? ($g = 9.8\ \text{m s}^{-2}$.)

9 A loop-the-loop machine has radius R of 18 m (see Figure 8.15).
(a) What is the minimum speed at which a cart must travel so that it will safely loop the loop?
(b) What will the speed at the top be in this case?

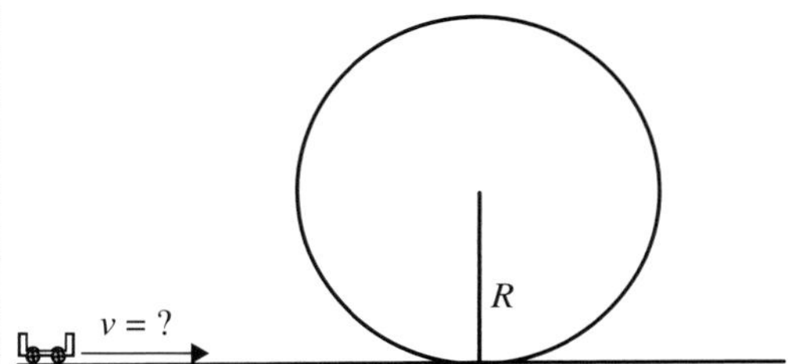

Figure 8.15 For question 9.

10 Calculate the centripetal force on the earth as it rotates around the sun. The mass of the earth is about 6.0×10^{24} kg. The earth orbits the sun in a circular orbit of radius 1.5×10^{11} m in one year.

11 What is the centripetal acceleration of a point on the earth at 50° latitude as a result of the earth's rotation about its axis? Express the answer as a fraction of g, the acceleration due to gravity. What angle to the true vertical would a mass hanging at the end of a string make? Take g to be exactly $9.8\ \text{m s}^{-2}$.

12 A horizontal disc has a hole through its centre. A string passes through the hole and connects a mass m on top of the disc to a bigger mass M that hangs below the disc. Initially the smaller mass is rotating on the disc in a circle of radius r. What must the speed of m be such that the big mass stands still? (See Figure 8.16.)

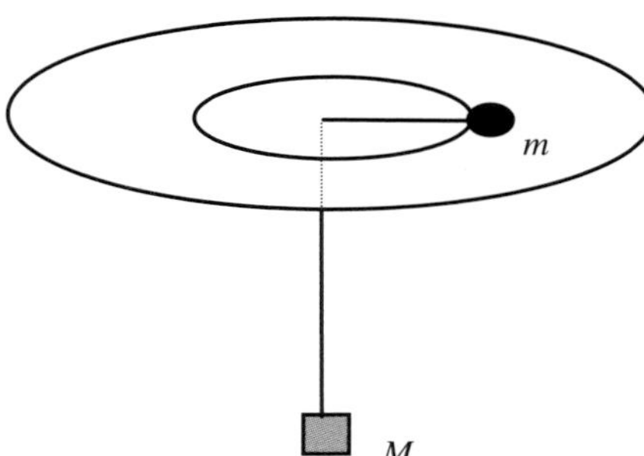

Figure 8.16 For question 12.

13 A mass of 5.00 kg is tied to two strings of equal length, which are attached to a vertical pole at points 2.0 m apart. As the pole rotates about its axis, the strings make a right angle with each other, as shown in Figure 8.17.

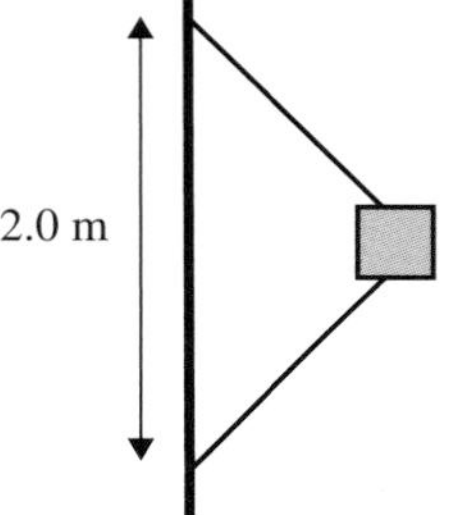

Figure 8.17 For question 13.

If the mass makes 2 revolutions per second, find:
(a) the tension in each string;
(b) the speed of revolution that makes the lower string go slack.
(c) If the mass now rotates at half the speed you found in part (b), find the angle the top string makes with the vertical.

14 A mass moves counter-clockwise along a vertical circle of radius 4.00 m. At positions A and B, where the radii make an angle of 45° with the horizontal (see Figure 8.18), the mass has speed $4.0\ \text{m s}^{-1}$. At A the speed of the mass is increasing at a rate of $3.0\ \text{m s}^{-2}$ whereas at B the speed is decreasing at a rate of $3.0\ \text{m s}^{-2}$. Thus, the acceleration of the mass in each position consists of the centripetal acceleration (which is directed toward the centre) and a tangential acceleration whose magnitude is the rate of change of speed. Find the magnitude and direction of the acceleration vector of the mass at positions A and B.

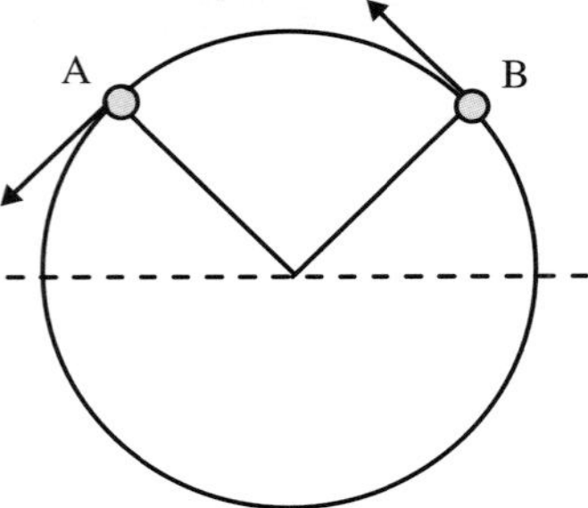

Figure 8.18 For question 14.

15 In an amusement park ride a cart of mass 300 kg and carrying four passengers each of mass 60 kg is dropped from a vertical height of 120 m along a frictionless path that leads into a loop-the-loop machine of radius 30 m. The cart then enters a straight stretch from A to C where friction brings it to rest after a distance of 40 m. (See Figure 8.19.)

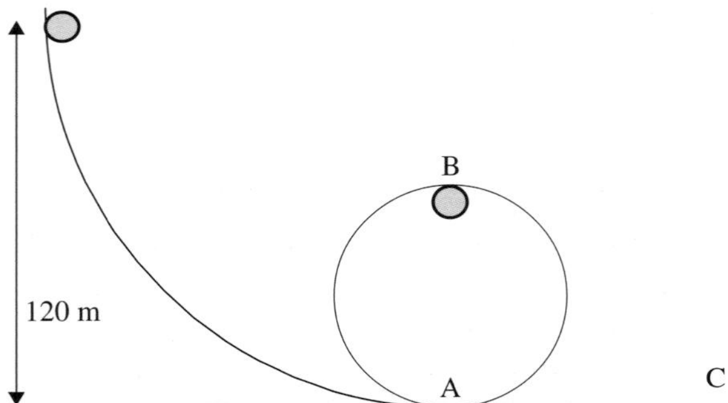

Figure 8.19 For question 15.

(a) Find the velocity of the cart at A.
(b) Find the reaction force from the seat of the cart onto a passenger at B.
(c) What is the acceleration experienced by the cart from A to C (assumed constant)?

16 A mass of 5.0 kg is attached to a string of length 2.0 m which is initially horizontal. The mass is then released. Figure 8.20 shows the mass when the string is in a vertical position.
(a) Find the speed of the mass when the string is in the vertical position.
(b) Find the acceleration of the mass.
(c) Draw the forces on the mass.
(d) Find the tension in the string.

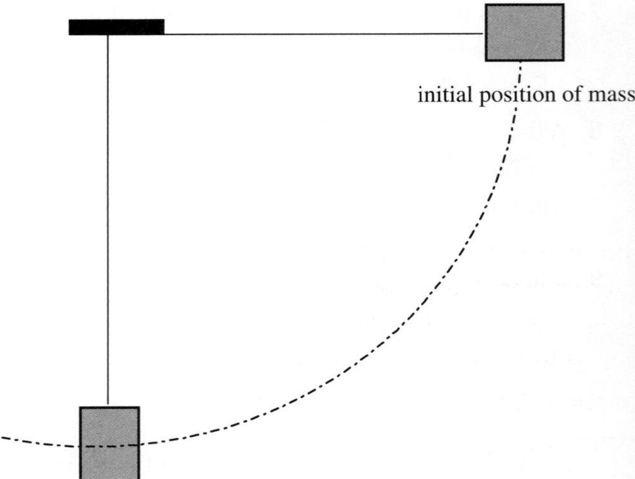

Figure 8.20 For question 16.

17 A neutron star has a radius of 50.0 km and completes one revolution every 25 ms. Calculate the centripetal acceleration experienced at the equator of the star.

18 In an amusement park a box is attached to a rod of length 25 m and rotates in a vertical circle. The park claims that the centripetal acceleration felt by the occupants sitting firmly in the box is $4g$. How many revolutions per minute does the machine make?

19 A marble rolls from the top of a big sphere as shown in Figure 8.21. What is the angle θ when the marble is about to leave the sphere? Assume a zero speed at the top.

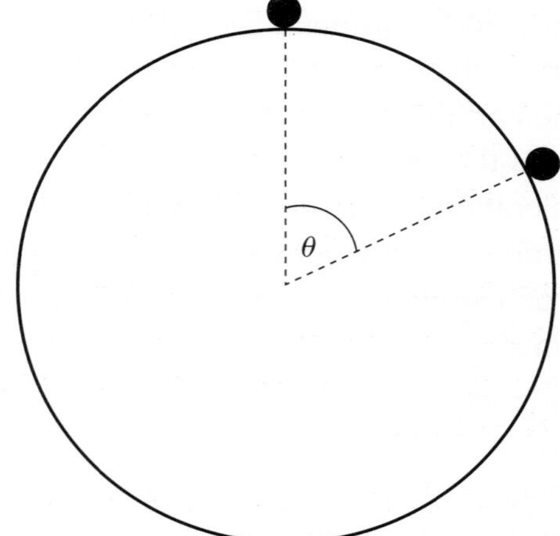

Figure 8.21 For question 19.

The law of gravitation

This chapter will introduce you to one of the fundamental laws of physics: Newton's law of gravitation. The law of gravitation makes it possible to calculate the orbits of the planets around the sun, and predicts the motion of comets, satellites and entire galaxies. Newton's law of gravitation was published in his monumental *Philosophiae Naturalis Principia Mathematica*, on 5 July 1686. Newton's law of gravitation has had great success in dealing with planetary motion.

Objectives

By the end of this chapter you should be able to:

- appreciate that there is an attractive force between any two point masses that is directed along the line joining the two masses, $F = G\frac{M_1 M_2}{r^2}$;
- state the definition of *gravitational field strength*, $g = G\frac{M}{r^2}$.

Newton's law of gravitation

We have seen that Newton's second law implies that, whenever a mass moves with acceleration, a force must be acting on it. An object falling freely under gravity is accelerating at 9.8 m s^{-2} and thus experiences a net force in the direction of the acceleration. This force is, as we know, the weight of the mass. Similarly, a planet that revolves around the sun also experiences acceleration and thus a force is acting on it. Newton hypothesized that the force responsible for the falling apple is the same as the force acting on a planet as it revolves around the sun. The conventional weight of a body is nothing more than the gravitational force of attraction between that body and the earth.

▶ Newton proposed that the attractive force of gravitation between two *point* masses is given by the formula

$$F = G\frac{M_1 M_2}{r^2}$$

where M_1 and M_2 are the masses of the attracting bodies, r the separation between them and G a new constant of physics called Newton's constant of universal gravitation. It has the value $G = 6.667 \times 10^{-11}$ N m^2 kg^{-2}. The direction of the force is along the line joining the two masses.

This formula applies to point masses, that is to say masses which are very small (in comparison with their separation). In the case of objects such as the sun, the earth, and so on, the formula still applies since the separation of, say, the sun and a planet is enormous compared with the radii of the sun and the planet. In addition, Newton proved that for bodies which are *spherical* and of uniform density one can assume that the entire mass of the body is concentrated at the centre – as if the body *is* a point mass.

Figure 9.1 shows the gravitational force between two masses. The gravitational force is always attractive.

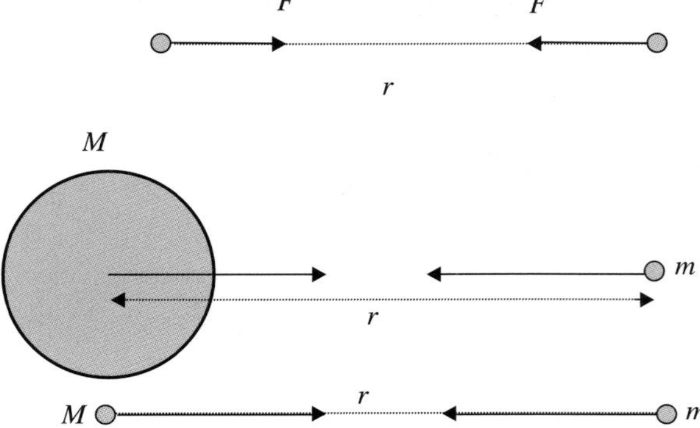

Figure 9.1 The mass of the spherical body to the left can be thought to be concentrated at the centre.

The force on each mass is the same. This follows both from the formula as well as from Newton's third law.

Example questions

Q1

Find the force between the sun and the earth.

Answer

The average distance between the earth and the sun is $R = 1.5 \times 10^{11}$ m. The mass of the earth is 5.98×10^{24} kg and that of the sun 1.99×10^{30} kg. Thus

$F = 3.5 \times 10^{22}$ N

Q2

If the distance between two bodies is doubled, what happens to the gravitational force between them?

Answer

Since the force is inversely proportional to the square of the separation, doubling the separation reduces the force by a factor of 4.

We said that the force we ordinarily call the weight of a mass (i.e. mg) is actually the force of gravitational attraction between the earth of mass M_e and the mass of the body in question. The mass of the earth is assumed to be concentrated at its centre and thus the distance that goes in Newton's formula is the radius of the earth, R_e (see Figure 9.2).

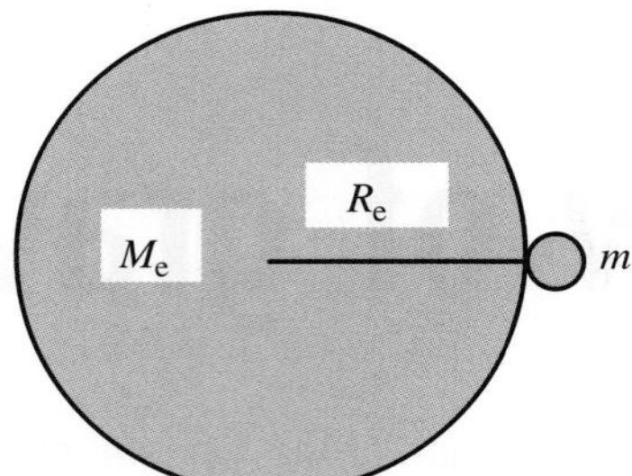

Figure 9.2 The gravitational force due to a spherical uniform mass is the same as that due to an equal point mass concentrated at the centre.

Therefore, we must have that

$$G\frac{M_e m}{R_e^2} = mg$$

$$\Rightarrow g = \frac{GM_e}{R_e^2}$$

This is an extraordinary result. It relates the acceleration of gravity to the mass and radius of the earth. Thus, the acceleration due to gravity on the surface of Jupiter is

$$g = \frac{GM_J}{R_J^2}$$

Example questions

Q3

Find the acceleration due to gravity (the gravitational field strength) on a planet 10 times as massive as the earth and with radius 20 times as large.

Answer

From

$$g = \frac{GM}{R^2}$$

we find

$$g = \frac{G(10M_e)}{(20R_e)^2} = \frac{10GM_e}{400R_e^2} = \frac{1}{40}\frac{GM_e}{R_e^2} = \frac{1}{40}g_e$$

Thus $g = 0.25$ m s^{-2}.

Q4

Find the acceleration due to gravity at a height of 300 km from the surface of the earth.

Answer

$$g = \frac{GM_e}{(R_e + h)^2}$$

where $R_e = 6.38 \times 10^6$ m is the radius of the earth and h the height from the surface. We can now put the numbers in our calculator to find $g = 8.94 \text{ m s}^{-2}$.

The order-of-magnitude arithmetic without a calculator is as follows:

$$\begin{aligned} g &= \frac{GM_e}{(R_e + h)^2} \\ &= \frac{6.67 \times 10^{-11} \times 5.98 \times 10^{24}}{(6.68 \times 10^6)^2} \\ &\approx \frac{7 \times 6}{50} \times 10 \\ &\approx \frac{42}{5} \\ &\approx 8 \text{ m s}^{-2} \end{aligned}$$

Gravitational field strength

Physicists (and philosophers) since the time of Newton, including Newton himself, wondered how a mass 'knows' about the presence of another mass nearby that will attract it. By the nineteenth century, physicists had developed the idea of a 'field', which was to provide the answer to the question. A mass M is said to create a *gravitational field* in the space around it. This means that when another mass is placed at some point near M, it 'feels' the gravitational field in the form of a gravitational force. (Similarly, an electric charge will create around it an electric field and another charge will react to this field by having an electric force on it.)

We define **gravitational field strength** as follows.

▶ The gravitational field strength at a certain point is the force per unit mass experienced by a small point mass m at that point. The force experienced by a small point mass m placed at distance r from a mass M is

$$F = G\frac{Mm}{r^2}$$

So the gravitational field strength (F/m) of the mass M is

$$g = G\frac{M}{r^2}$$

The units of gravitational field strength are N kg^{-1}.

If M stands for the mass of the earth, then the gravitational field strength is nothing more than the acceleration due to gravity at distance r from the centre of the earth.

The usefulness of the definition of the gravitational field strength is that it tells us something about the gravitational effects of a given mass without actually having to put a second mass somewhere and find the force on it.

The gravitational field strength is a vector quantity whose direction is given by the direction of the force a point mass would experience if placed at the point of interest. The gravitational field strength around a single point mass M is radial, which means that it is the same for all points equidistant from the mass and is directed towards the mass. The same is true outside a uniform spherical mass. This is illustrated in Figure 9.3.

This is to be contrasted to the assumption of a constant gravitational field strength, which would result in the situation illustrated in Figure 9.4. The assumption of constant acceleration of gravity (as, for example, when we treated projectile motion) corresponds to this case.

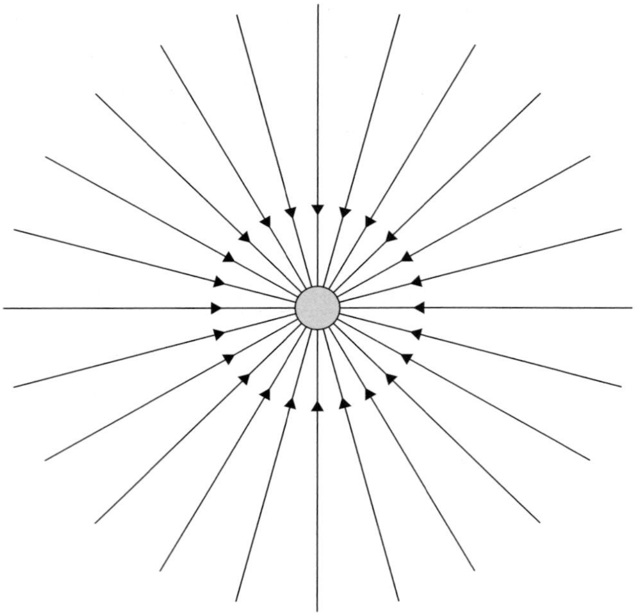

Figure 9.3 The gravitational field around a point (or spherical) mass is radial.

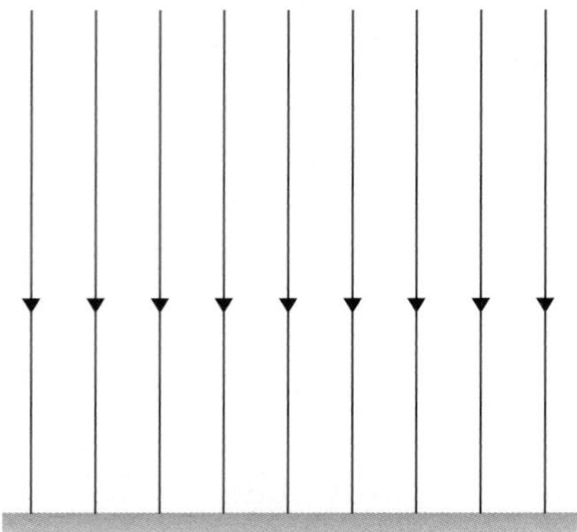

Figure 9.4 The gravitational field above a flat mass is uniform.

Example questions

Q5

Two stars have the same density but star A has double the radius of star B. Determine the ratio of the gravitational field strength at the surface of each star.

Answer

The volume of star A is 8 times that of star B since the radius of A is double. Hence the mass of A is 8 times that of B. Thus

$$\frac{g_A}{g_B} = \frac{GM_A/R_A^2}{GM_B/R_B^2}$$

$$= \frac{M_A}{M_B}\frac{R_B^2}{R_A^2}$$

$$= 8 \times \frac{1}{4}$$

$$= 2$$

Q6

Show that the gravitational field strength at the surface of a planet of density ρ has a magnitude given by $g = \frac{4G\pi\rho R}{3}$.

Answer

We have

$$g = \frac{GM}{R^2}$$

Since

$$M = \rho\frac{4\pi R^3}{3}$$

it follows that

$$g = \frac{G4\pi\rho R^3}{3R^2}$$

$$= \frac{4G\pi\rho R}{3}$$

? QUESTIONS

1 What is the gravitational force between:
(a) the earth and the moon;
(b) the sun and Jupiter;
(c) a proton and an electron separated by 10^{-10} m?
(Use the data in Appendices 1 and 3.)

2 A mass m is placed at the centre of a thin, hollow, spherical shell of mass M and radius R (see Figure 9.5a).
(a) What gravitational force does the mass m experience?
(b) What gravitational force does m exert on M?
(c) A second mass m is now placed a distance of $2R$ from the centre of the shell (see Figure 9.5b). What gravitational force does the mass inside the shell experience?
(d) What is the gravitational force experienced by the mass outside the shell?

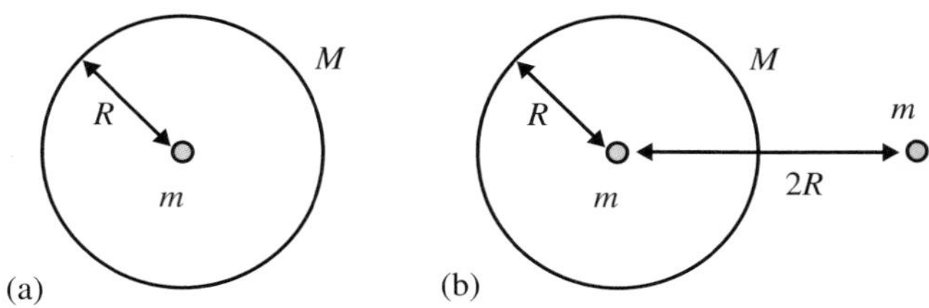

Figure 9.5 For question 2.

3 Stars A and B have the same mass and the radius of star A is 9 times larger than the radius of star B. Calculate the ratio of the gravitational field strength on star A to that on star B.

4 Planet A has a mass that is twice as large as the mass of planet B and a radius that is twice as large as the radius of planet B. Calculate the ratio of the gravitational field strength on planet A to that on planet B.

5 Stars A and B have the same density and star A is 27 times more massive than star B. Calculate the ratio of the gravitational field strength on star A to that on star B.

6 A star explodes and loses half its mass. Its radius becomes half as large. Find the new gravitational field strength on the surface of the star in terms of the original one.

7 The mass of the moon is about 81 times less than that of the earth. At what fraction of the distance from the earth to the moon is the gravitational field strength zero? (Take into account the earth and the moon only.)

8 Point P is halfway between the centres of two equal spherical masses that are separated by a distance of 2×10^9 m (see Figure 9.6). What is the gravitational field strength at:
(a) point P;
(b) point Q?

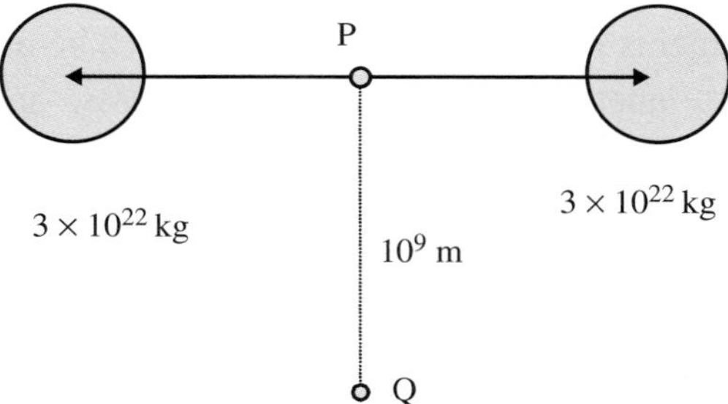

Figure 9.6 For question 8.

HL only

9 Consider two masses. There is a point somewhere on the line joining the masses where the gravitational field strength is zero, as shown in Figure 9.7. Therefore, if a third mass is placed at that point, the net force on the mass will be zero. If the mass is slightly displaced away from the equilibrium position to the left, will the net force on the mass be directed to the left or the right?

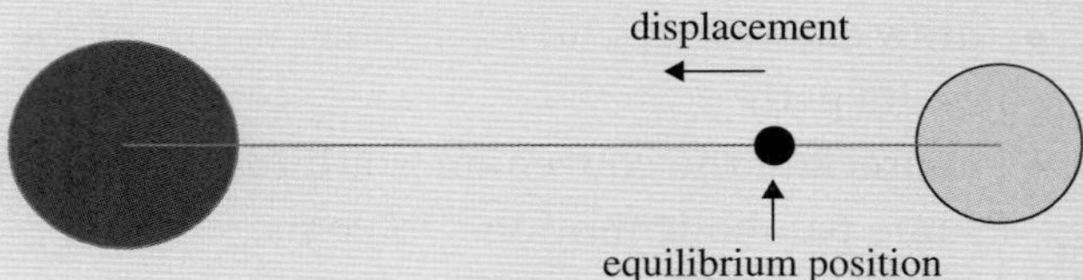

Figure 9.7 For question 9.

Projectile motion

Galileo is credited with the discovery of the secrets of parabolic motion. He did experiments with falling bodies, from which he deduced the acceleration due to gravity and its independence of the body's mass, and discovered that projectiles follow parabolic paths. Examples of parabolic motion include the paths of a stone thrown into the air at an angle, a bullet shot from a gun and water sprayed from a hose. The basic fact here is that every object that falls freely under the action of the earth's gravity experiences an acceleration g directed vertically down. In what follows, it is assumed that the earth is flat. This means that we only consider a small part of the earth's surface so that it is approximately flat, in which case the acceleration due to gravity is pointing normally to the horizontal ground.

Objectives

By the end of this chapter you should be able to:

- understand parabolic motion as a *combination of two simultaneous straight-line motions*, one horizontal and one vertical;
- understand that in parabolic motion there is an *acceleration in the vertical direction* (due to gravity) but none in the horizontal direction;
- derive expressions for maximum height (by setting $v_y = 0$) and maximum range ($y = 0$) reached by imposing appropriate conditions on the equations;
- solve problems of *parabolic motion*;
- draw the *velocity* and *acceleration vectors* of the projectile at various points on its path;
- appreciate the convenience afforded by the *law of conservation of energy* in some parabolic motion problems.

Parabolic motion

Let us begin by looking at what happens when an object is thrown horizontally from some height h above the ground with some initial velocity. Experience tells us that the object will follow a curved path and will eventually fall to the ground. What we want to know is how far the object travels, how long it takes to fall to the ground, the precise shape of the curved path, etc.

Figure 10.1 shows the positions of two objects every 0.2 s: the first was simply allowed to drop from rest, the other was launched horizontally with no vertical component of velocity. We see that the displacements in the y (i.e. vertical) direction are covered *in the same time.*

How do we understand this fact? A simple way is to make use of the concept of relative velocity. Consider two bodies, one dropped from rest and the other launched horizontally with velocity v. From the point of view of a stationary observer on the ground, body B falls vertically whereas body A follows a parabolic path. Consider now the description of the same situation from the

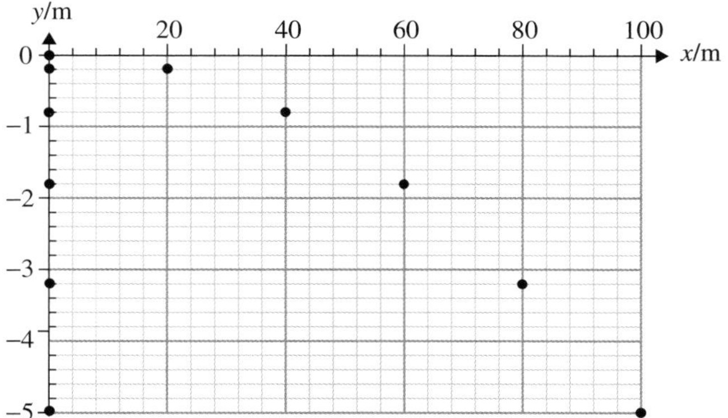

Figure 10.1 A body dropped from rest and one launched horizontally cover the same vertical displacement in the same time.

point of view of another observer on the ground who moves with velocity $v/2$ with respect to the ground. From the point of view of this observer, body A has velocity $v/2$ and body B has velocity $-v/2$. The motions of the two bodies are therefore *identical* (except for direction). So this observer will determine that the two bodies reach the ground at the *same time*. Since time is absolute in Newtonian physics, the two bodies must reach the ground at the same time as far as any other observer is concerned as well. (See Figure 10.2.)

This means that the motion of the body launched horizontally can be analysed quite simply because we can separate the vertical motion from the horizontal motion. Let v_0 be the initial velocity of the object in the horizontal direction. Since there is no acceleration in this direction, the horizontal velocity component at all times will be equal to v_0

$$v_x = v_0$$

and the displacement in the horizontal direction will be given by

$$x = v_0 t$$

In the vertical direction, the object experiences an acceleration g in the vertically down direction. Thus, the velocity in the vertical direction will be given by

$$v_y = -gt$$

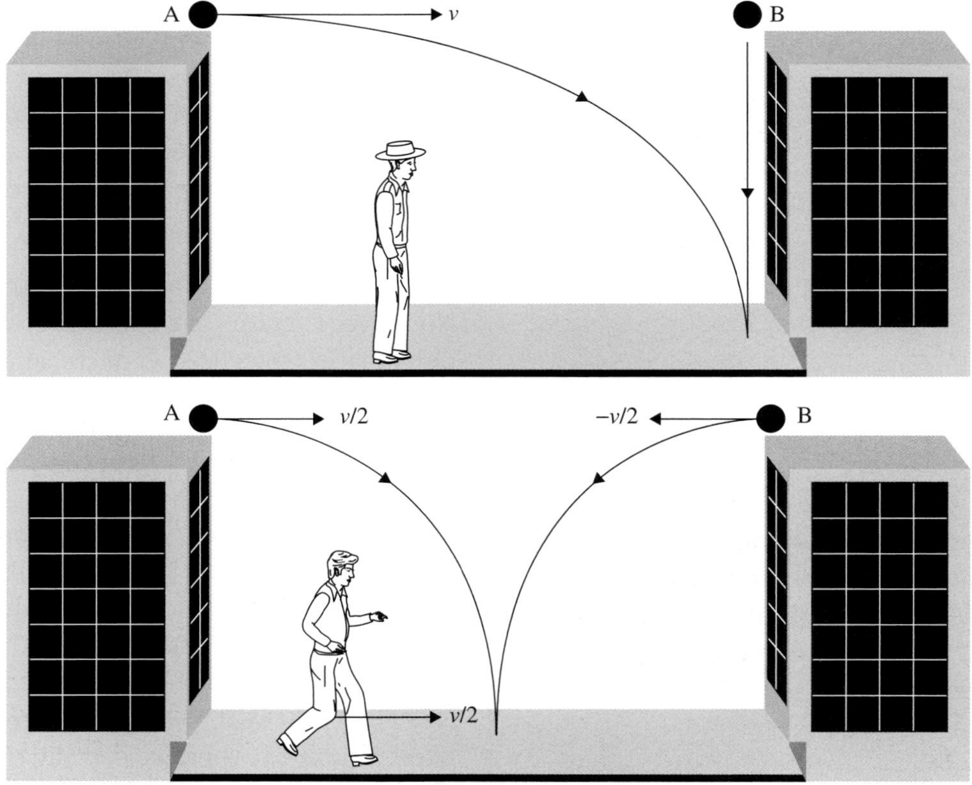

Figure 10.2 The motions of the ball projected horizontally and the ball dropped vertically from rest are identical from the point of view of the moving observer. The two balls will thus reach the ground at the same time.

(we are assuming that positive velocity means the body moves upward; the acceleration due to gravity is then negative, or $-g$) and the displacement is given by

$$y = -\tfrac{1}{2}gt^2$$

The point of launch is assumed to be the origin, as in Figure 10.3, so that the initial displacement is zero, $x = 0, y = 0$.

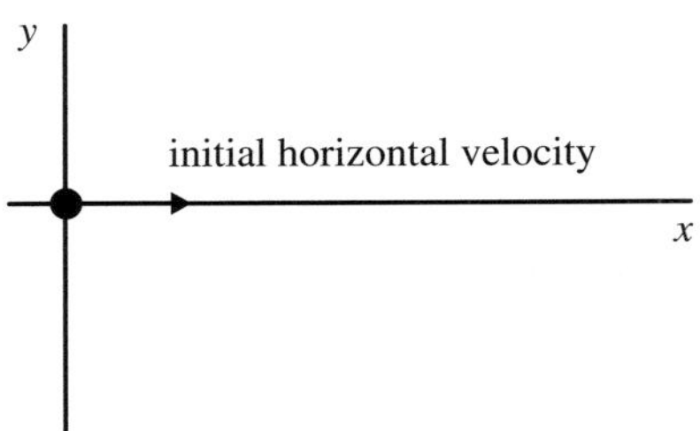

Figure 10.3.

Example questions

Q1

An object is launched horizontally from a height of 20.0 m above the ground, as shown in Figure 10.4. When will it hit the ground?

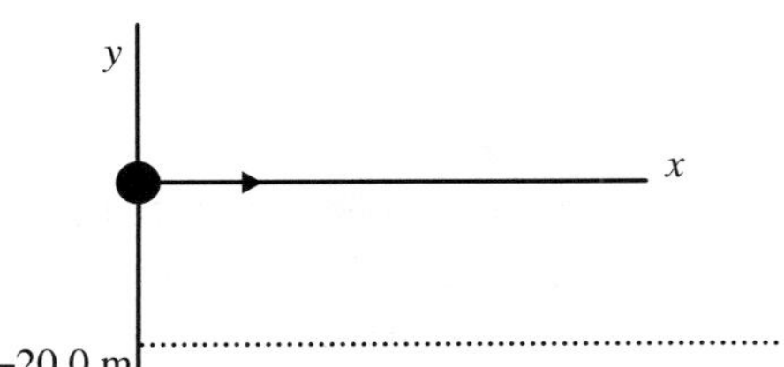

Figure 10.4.

Answer

The object will hit the ground when $y = -20.0$ m, and thus from $y = -\frac{1}{2}gt^2$ we find $-20 = -5t^2$, giving $t = 2.0$ s. Note that we do not need to know the actual velocity of launch.

Q2

An object is launched horizontally with a velocity of 12 m s^{-1}. What is the vertical component of velocity after 2.0 s? What are the coordinates of the object after 4.0 s?

Answer

The horizontal component of velocity is 12 m s^{-1} at all times. From $v_y = -gt$, the vertical component is $v_y = -20$ m s^{-1}. The coordinates after time t are

$$\begin{aligned} x &= v_0 t \\ &= 12.0 \times 4.0 \\ &= 48 \text{ m} \end{aligned}$$

and

$$\begin{aligned} y &= -\tfrac{1}{2}gt^2 \\ &= -5 \times 16 \\ &= -80 \text{ m} \end{aligned}$$

Knowing the x and y coordinates as a function of time allows us to find the shape of the curved path followed by an object launched horizontally: from $x = v_0 t$ we solve for time $t = \frac{x}{v_0}$ and substituting in $y = -\frac{1}{2}gt^2$ we find

$$y = -\frac{1}{2}g\left(\frac{x}{v_0}\right)^2$$

which is the equation of a parabola.

Launch at an arbitrary angle

In the previous section we studied the horizontal launch of a projectile. In this section we will study the more general case of launch at an arbitrary angle. Figure 10.5 shows an object thrown at an angle of $\theta = 30^\circ$ to the horizontal with initial velocity vector $\vec{v}_0$, whose magnitude is 20 m s^{-1}, and the path it follows through the air.

The position of the object is shown every 0.2 s. Note how the dots get closer together as the object rises (the speed is decreasing) and how they move apart on the way down (the speed is increasing). It reaches a maximum height of 5.1 m and travels a horizontal distance of 35 m.

As before, the easiest way to analyse what is going on is to realize that the object is actually undergoing two motions simultaneously – one in the vertical direction and another in the horizontal. Thus, if the object begins at point O (see Figure 10.6) at $t = 0$ and subsequently finds itself at point P, then we can say that during this time the object actually moved a horizontal displacement OX and a vertical displacement OY. Note that the time taken to cover the

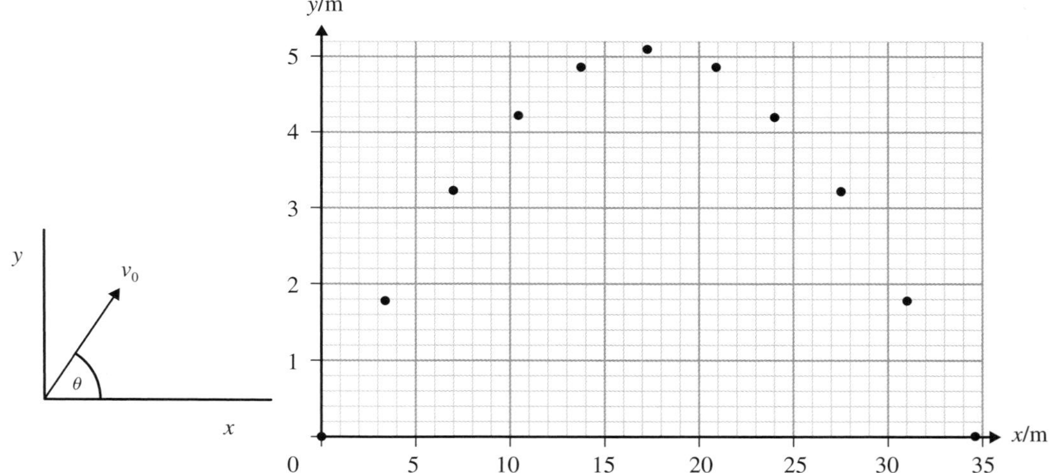

Figure 10.5 An object is launched at an arbitrary angle to the horizontal. The path followed is parabolic.

displacement OX is the same as the time taken to cover OY. OX and OY are just the components of the displacement vector of the mass at P.

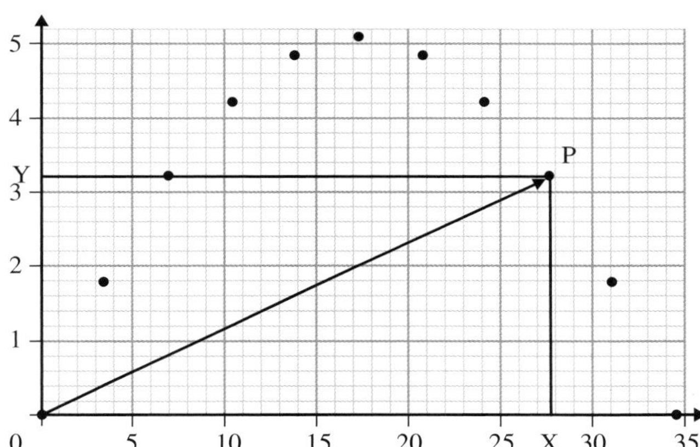

Figure 10.6 The position vector of a point P as an object executes parabolic motion.

The point of doing things this way is that we have succeeded in reducing the motion in the plane into two motions taking place at the same time on straight lines. Since we know all about straight-line motion, it means we also know all about motion in a plane.

Let us then throw an object into the air with velocity vector $\vec{v}_0$ (of magnitude v_0) at an angle θ to the horizontal. The suffix zero in $\vec{v}_0$ is to remind us that this is the initial velocity of the object. The component of initial velocity in the horizontal direction is simply $v_0 \cos\theta$.

- At any future time, the horizontal velocity component will be the same, that is

$$v_x = v_0 \cos\theta$$

since there is no acceleration horizontally. If we call the displacement in the horizontal direction x, then after a time of t s goes by

$$x = v_0 t \cos\theta$$

On the other hand, in the vertical direction there is acceleration, namely the acceleration due to gravity, g. (In our formulae, the acceleration will be taken to be negative. A positive velocity means that the mass is moving up. On the way up, the velocity decreases and so the acceleration is negative. On the way down, the velocity is getting more and more negative and so the acceleration must again be taken to be negative.)

- The initial velocity in the vertical direction is $v_0 \sin\theta$, so the vertical velocity component at any time t after launch is given by

$$v_y = v_0 \sin\theta - gt$$

The displacement in the vertical direction, y, after time t seconds is given by

$$y = v_0 t \sin\theta - \tfrac{1}{2}gt^2$$

Note that we are dealing with displacements here and not distances. The distance travelled is the length of the arc of the parabola from O to wherever the mass finds itself after time t. Setting $\theta = 0$ in these formulae gives the formulae for a horizontal launch, as in the previous section.

Unlike the velocity in the horizontal direction, which stays the same, the vertical velocity is changing. It begins with the value $v_0 \sin\theta$ at time zero, starts decreasing, becomes zero, and then keeps decreasing, becoming more and more negative. At what point in time does the vertical velocity component become zero? Setting $v_y = 0$ we find

$$0 = v_0 \sin\theta - gt$$
$$\Rightarrow t = \frac{v_0 \sin\theta}{g}$$

The time when the vertical velocity becomes zero is, of course, the time when the mass attains its maximum height. What is this height? Going back to the equation for the vertical component of displacement we find that when

$$t = \frac{v_0 \sin\theta}{g}$$

y is given by

$$y_{\text{max}} = v_0 \frac{v_0 \sin\theta}{g} \sin\theta - \frac{1}{2} g \left(\frac{v_0 \sin\theta}{g}\right)^2$$
$$= \frac{v_0^2 \sin^2\theta}{2g}$$

This is the formula for the maximum height attained by the mass. You should not remember it by heart but rather you should be able to derive it.

What about the maximum displacement in the horizontal direction (sometimes called the range)? At this point the vertical component of displacement is zero. Setting $y = 0$ in the formula for y gives

$$0 = v_0 t \sin\theta - \tfrac{1}{2} g t^2$$
$$= t(v_0 \sin\theta - \tfrac{1}{2} g t)$$

and so $t = 0$ and

$$t = \frac{2v_0 \sin\theta}{g}$$

The first time $t = 0$ is, of course, when the mass first starts out. The second time is what we want – the time in which the range is covered. Therefore the range is

$$x = \frac{2v_0^2 \sin\theta \cos\theta}{g}$$
$$= \frac{v_0^2 \sin 2\theta}{g}$$

Note, incidentally, that the time it takes to cover the range is twice the time needed to reach the maximum height. This suggests that the motion is symmetric about the highest point.

The maximum value of $\sin 2\theta$ is 1 and this happens when $2\theta = 90°$ (i.e. $\theta = 45°$); in other words, we obtain the maximum range with a launch angle of 45°. This equation also says that there are two different angles of launch that give the same range for the same initial speed. These two angles add up to a right angle (can you see why?).

Example questions

Q3

A mass is launched with a speed of 10 m s^{-1} at
(a) 30° to the horizontal;
(b) 0° to the horizontal;
(c) 90° to the horizontal.
Find the x- and y-components of the initial velocity in each case.

Answer

(a) $v_x = v_0 \cos\theta$
$= 10 \times \cos 30°$
$= 8.66 \text{ m s}^{-1}$
$v_y = v_0 \sin\theta$
$= 10 \times \sin 30°$
$= 5 \text{ m s}^{-1}$

(b) $v_x = 10 \text{ m s}^{-1}$
$v_y = 0 \text{ m s}^{-1}$

(c) $v_x = 0$
$v_y = 10 \text{ m s}^{-1}$

Q4

Sketch graphs to show the variation with time of the horizontal and vertical components of velocity of the projectile of example question 3(a).

Answer

See Figure 10.7.

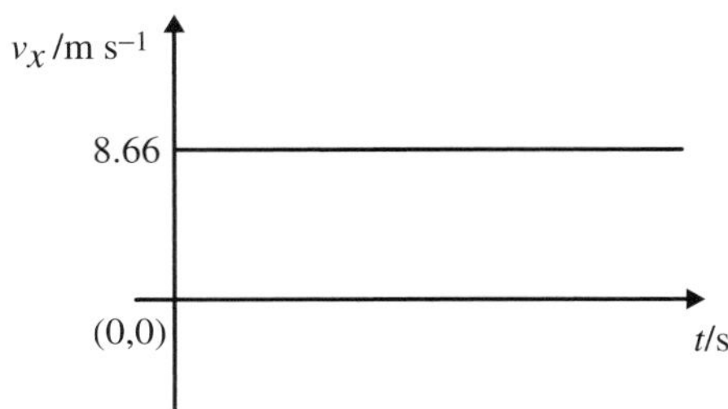

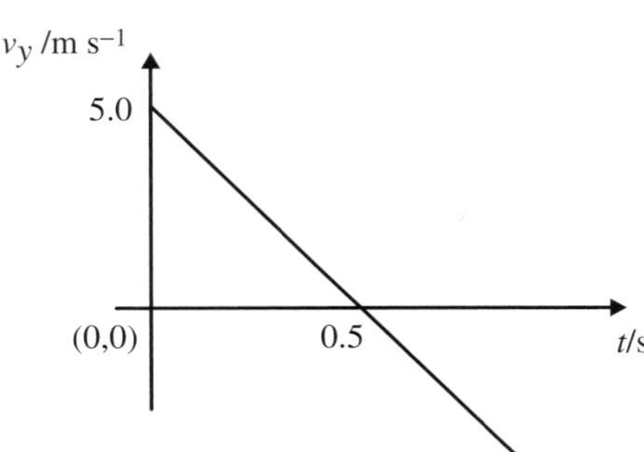

Figure 10.7.

Q5

A mass is launched at 30° to the horizontal with initial speed 25.0 m s^{-1}. What is the maximum height obtained?

Answer

The vertical velocity is given by

$$v_y = v_0 \sin\theta - gt$$

and becomes zero at the highest point. Thus

$$t = \frac{v_0 \sin\theta}{g} = 1.25 \text{ s}$$

and so maximum height = 7.82 m by substituting in the formula for y.

Q6

After what time does the mass in the previous example question move a horizontal distance of 3.0 m?

Answer

$$x = v_0 t \cos\theta$$

and so

$$t = \frac{3.0}{25.0 \times \cos 30°} = 0.14 \text{ s}$$

Q7

For the same mass as in example questions 5 and 6, when is the height of the mass 4.0 m?

Answer

From

$$y = v_0 t \sin\theta - \tfrac{1}{2}gt^2$$

we find

$$4.0 = 25t \times 0.5 - 5t^2$$

and so $y = 4.00$ m when $t = 0.38$ s and $t = 2.1$ s. There are two solutions here since the mass attains the height of 4 m twice: on its way up and on its way down.

Q8

A projectile is launched horizontally from a height of 45 m above the ground. As it hits the ground, the velocity makes an angle of 60° to the horizontal. Find the initial velocity of launch.

Answer

The time it takes to hit the ground is found from $y = -\frac{1}{2}gt^2$ (here $\theta = 0$ since the launch is horizontal) and so

$$-45 = -5t^2$$
$$\Rightarrow t = 3 \text{ s}$$

Thus, when the projectile hits the ground

$$v_y = 0 - 10 \times 3 = -30 \text{ m s}^{-1}$$

Hence

$$\tan 60° = \left|\frac{v_y}{v_x}\right|$$
$$\Rightarrow v_x = \frac{30}{\tan 60°} = 17 \text{ m s}^{-1}$$

The shape of the path

(The proof is not required for examination purposes.) The last thing that remains to be done here is to figure out the shape of the path the object follows in the air. We can do this very easily by concentrating on the formulae for displacement in the x and y directions:

$$x = v_0 t \cos\theta$$
$$y = v_0 t \sin\theta - \tfrac{1}{2}gt^2$$

Using the first equation we solve for time to find $t = \frac{x}{v_0 \cos\theta}$ and substituting in the expression for y we find

$$y = v_0 \sin\theta \left(\frac{x}{v_0 \cos\theta}\right) - \frac{1}{2}g\left(\frac{x}{v_0 \cos\theta}\right)^2$$
$$y = x \tan\theta - \frac{g}{2v_0^2 \cos^2\theta}x^2$$

which is the equation of a parabola.

Use of energy conservation

In some problems we are asked to find the speed of a projectile at some point along its path. If speed is all that is being asked for, a very simple method using the law of conservation of energy can be used. Consider the following example. A ball is launched at 12 m s^{-1} at an angle of 60° to the horizontal. It lands on the roof of a building 5 m high (see Figure 10.8). What is the speed of the ball on landing?

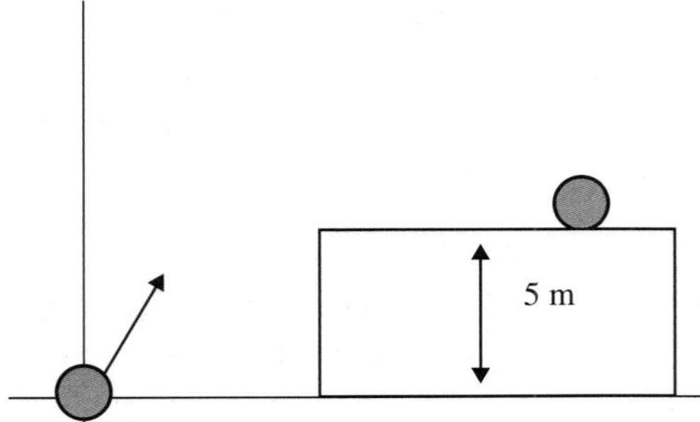

Figure 10.8 A ball is launched at ground level and lands on the roof of a building.

Let us use conservation of energy first. At launch, the total energy of the mass is $E = \frac{1}{2}mv^2$ and on landing it is $E = \frac{1}{2}mu^2 + mgh$. Equating the two results in

$$\tfrac{1}{2}mu^2 + mgh = \tfrac{1}{2}mv^2$$
$$\Rightarrow u^2 = v^2 - 2gh$$

This gives

$$u^2 = 144 - 2 \times 10 \times 5$$
$$= 44$$
$$\Rightarrow u = 6.63 \text{ m s}^{-1}$$

Another method of solution uses the equations of projectile motion and is much more complicated. We must find the vertical component of velocity when the vertical displacement of the ball is 5 m: we use $y = v_0 t \sin\theta - \frac{1}{2}gt^2$ to find the time when the vertical displacement becomes 5 m. The result is found from:

$$5 = 12t \sin 60^\circ - 5t^2$$
$$\Rightarrow 5t^2 - 10.392t + 5 = 0$$

The roots are 0.756 s and 1.322 s. At these times, the vertical velocity component is

$$v_y = v_0 \sin\theta - gt$$
$$= 12 \sin 60^\circ - 10t$$
$$= \pm 2.83 \text{ m s}^{-1}$$

The speed on landing is thus given by

$$u = \sqrt{v_y^2 + v_x^2}$$
$$= \sqrt{2.83^2 + 6^2}$$
$$= 6.63 \text{ m s}^{-1}$$

The advantage of the energy conservation method is clear.

Effect of air resistance forces

Figure 10.9 shows the effect of air resistance on the path of a projectile launched with speed 200 m s^{-1} at 60° to the horizontal. The path in black dots corresponds to the case of zero air resistance. (The position is shown every 0.8 s.) A similar projectile launched with the same velocity but with an air resistance force follows the path in open circles. Shown here is the case of a resistance force of magnitude proportional to the speed and directed opposite to the velocity. We see that with air resistance:

- the path is no longer parabolic;
- the maximum height and range are less than without air resistance;
- the angle at which the projectile impacts the ground is steeper.

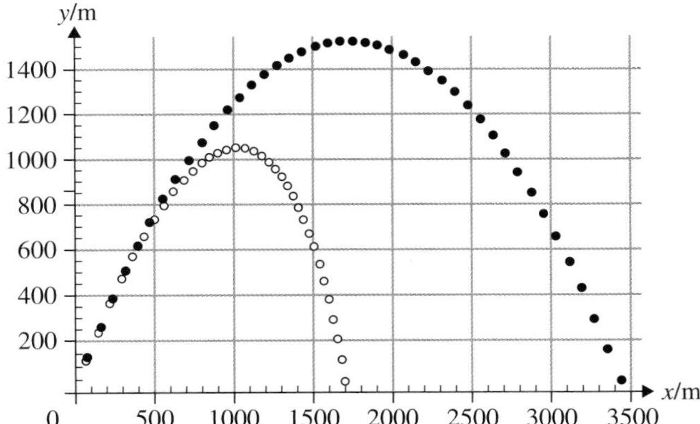

Figure 10.9 The motion of a projectile without air resistance (black dots), and with a resistance force directed opposite to the velocity and of magnitude proportional to the speed (open circles).

QUESTIONS

1 An arrow is shot horizontally towards point O, which is at a distance of 20.0 m. It hits point P 0.10 s later. (See Figure 10.10.)
(a) What is the distance OP?
(b) What was the arrow's initial velocity?

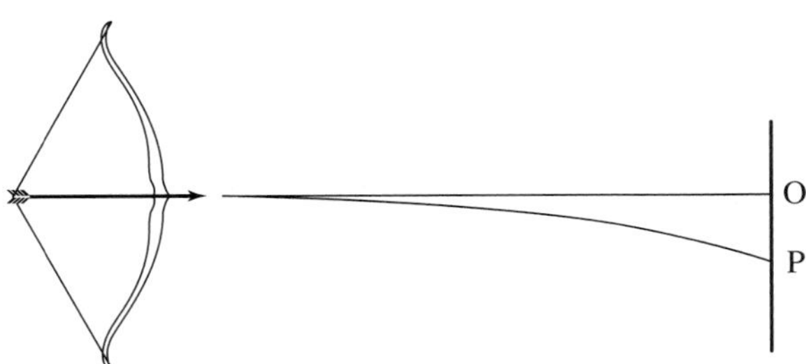

Figure 10.10 For question 1.

2 A ball rolls off a table with a horizontal speed 2.0 m s^{-1}. If the table is 1.3 m high, how far from the table will the ball land?

3 A ball is kicked horizontally with a speed of 5.0 m s^{-1} from the roof of a house 3 m high.
(a) When will the ball hit the ground?
(b) What will the speed of the ball be just before hitting the ground?

4 An object is launched horizontally with a speed of 8.0 m s^{-1} from a point 20 m from the ground.
(a) How long will it take the object to land on the ground?
(b) What is the speed of the object 1 s after launch?
(c) What angle does the velocity make with the horizontal 1 s after launch?
(d) With what velocity does the object hit the ground?

5 Two objects are thrown horizontally with the same speed (4.0 m s^{-1}) from heights of 4.0 m and 8.0 m, as shown in Figure 10.11. What distance will separate the two objects when both land on the ground?

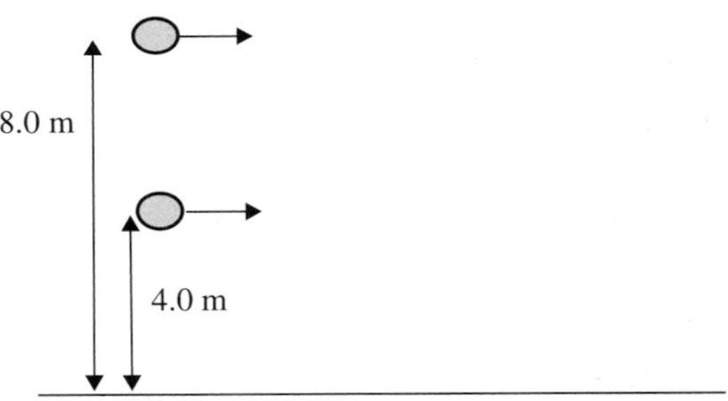

Figure 10.11 For question 5.

6 With what speed should the object at 4.0 m height in Figure 10.11 be launched if it is to land at the same point as the object launched from 8.0 m at 4.0 m s^{-1}?

7 A plane flying at a constant speed of 50.0 m s^{-1} and a constant height of 200 m drops a package of emergency supplies to a group of hikers. If the package is released just as the plane flies over a huge fir tree, find at what distance from the tree the package will land.

8 The longest distance an athlete can throw the discus is L. How high would the same athlete be able to throw the discus vertically? (Assume, unrealistically, that the speed of

throwing is the same in both cases and ignore air resistance.)

9 In a loop-the-loop cart, as shown in Figure 10.12, a passenger drops their keys when at the highest point. The cart is moving at 6 m s^{-1} and is 8 m from the ground. Where will the keys land?

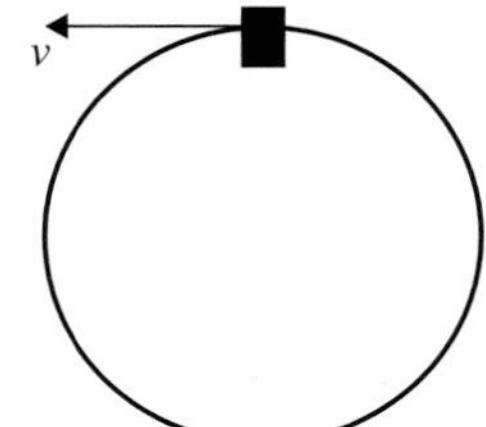

Figure 10.12 For question 9.

10 For an object thrown at an angle of 40° to the horizontal at a speed of 20 m s^{-1}, draw graphs of:
(a) horizontal velocity against time;
(b) vertical velocity against time;
(c) acceleration against time.

11 What is the highest point reached by an object thrown with speed 4.0 m s^{-1} at 40° to the horizontal?

12 A stone is thrown with initial speed 6.0 m s^{-1} at 35° to the horizontal. What is the direction of the velocity vector 1 s later?

13 An object is thrown with speed 20.0 m s^{-1} at an angle of 50° to the horizontal. Draw graphs to show the variation with time of:
(a) the horizontal displacement;
(b) the vertical displacement.

14 An object of mass 4.0 kg is thrown with speed 20.0 m s^{-1} at an angle of 30° to the horizontal. Draw graphs to show the variation with time of:
(a) the gravitational potential energy of the body;
(b) the kinetic energy of the body.

15 A cruel hunter takes aim horizontally at a monkey that is hanging from the branch of a tree, as shown in Figure 10.13. The monkey lets go of the branch as soon as the hunter pulls the trigger. Treating the monkey and the bullet as point particles, determine if the bullet will hit the monkey.

Figure 10.13 For question 15.

16 A ball is launched horizontally from a height of 20 m above ground on earth and follows the path shown in Figure 10.14. Air resistance and other frictional forces are neglected. The position of the ball is shown every 0.20 s.
(a) Determine the horizontal component of velocity of the ball.
(b) Draw the net force on the ball at $t = 1$ s.
(c) The ball is now launched under identical conditions on the surface of a planet where the acceleration due to gravity is 20 m s^{-2}. Draw the position of the ball on Figure 10.14 at time intervals of 0.20 s.

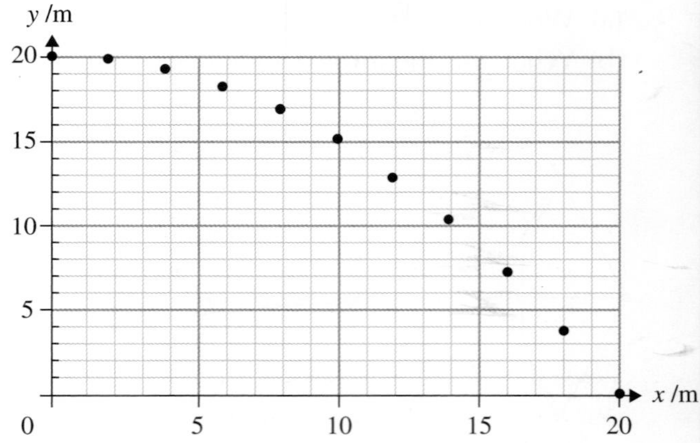

Figure 10.14 For question 16.

17 A ball is launched from the surface of a planet. Air resistance and other frictional forces are neglected. The position of the ball is shown every 0.20 s in Figure 10.15. Use this diagram to determine:

(a) the components of the initial velocity of the ball;

(b) the angle to the horizontal the ball was launched at;

(c) the acceleration due to gravity on this planet.

(d) Draw two arrows on Figure 10.15 to represent the velocity and acceleration vectors of the ball at $t = 1$ s.

(e) The ball is now launched under identical conditions from the surface of a *different* planet where the acceleration due to gravity is twice as large. Draw the path of the ball on Figure 10.15.

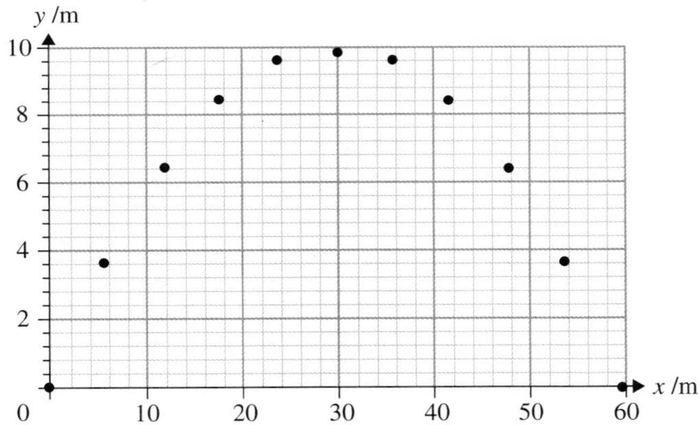

Figure 10.15 For question 16.

18 A soccer ball is kicked so that it has a range of 30 m and reaches a maximum height of 12 m. What velocity (magnitude and direction) did the ball have as it left the footballer's foot?

19 A stone is thrown with a speed of 20.0 m s^{-1} at an angle of 48° to the horizontal from the edge of a cliff 60.0 m above the surface of the sea.

(a) Calculate the velocity with which the stone hits the sea.

(b) Discuss qualitatively the effect of air resistance on your answers to (a).

20 A projectile is launched with speed v_0 at the foot of an inclined plane at an angle of θ to the horizontal, as shown in Figure 10.16. The inclined plane makes a smaller angle ϕ with the horizontal. Show that the projectile will land a distance d up the plane given by

$$d = \frac{2v_0^2 \cos\theta \, \sin(\theta - \phi)}{g \cos^2\phi}$$

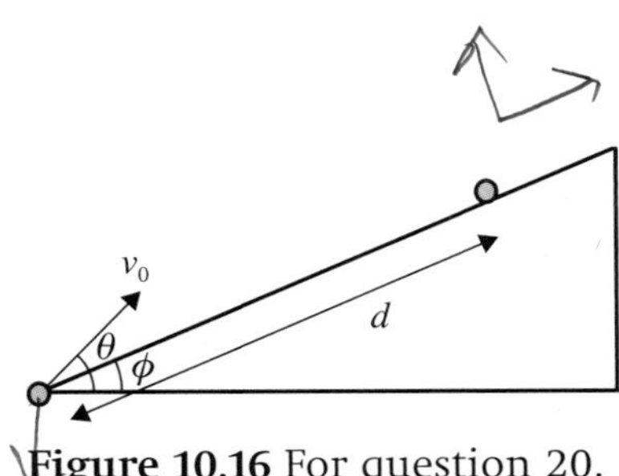

Figure 10.16 For question 20.

21 A ball is kicked with a velocity of 5.0 m s^{-1} up an inclined plane that makes an angle of 30° to the horizontal. The ball's velocity makes an angle of 25° to the base of the incline. (See Figure 10.17.) What is the shape of its path? Explain. Find how high on the incline the ball will get.

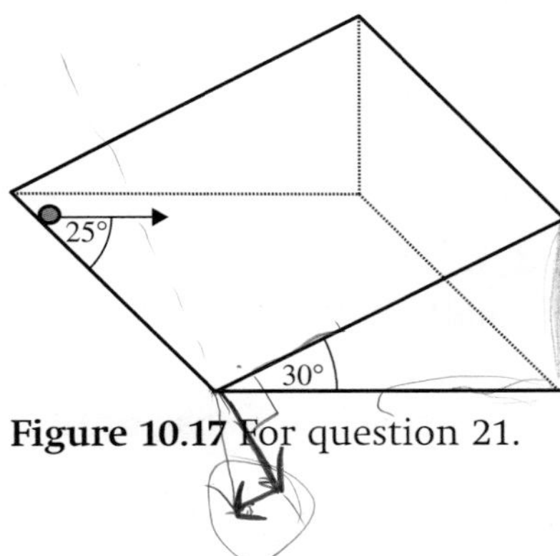

Figure 10.17 For question 21.

22 The maximum height reached by a projectile is 20 m. The direction of the velocity 1.0 s after launch is 20°; find the speed of launch.

Motion in a gravitational field

Newton's law of gravitation makes it possible to calculate the orbits of planets, comets, satellites and entire galaxies. The details of the motion of the planets were discovered by observation by Kepler, whose three laws can be seen to be a direct consequence of the gravitational law of attraction and Newton's laws of mechanics. Kepler's laws were published in 1619 in a book called the *Harmony of the World*, nearly 70 years before Newton published his work. In ancient times, Ptolemy constructed an involved system in which the sun and the planets orbited the earth in perfectly circular paths. When observations did not agree with the assumed circular paths, Ptolemy and his successors asserted that planets move along additional smaller circular paths at the same time that they complete the orbit. This elaborate theory of epicycles has no foundation in physical principles and is a good example of attempts to explain physical phenomena without an understanding of the underlying principles. The Ptolemaic world view prevailed for centuries until Copernicus, early in the sixteenth century, asserted that the sun was at the centre of the motion of the planets in the solar system. Newton's law of gravitation has had great success in dealing with planetary motion but cannot account for some small irregularities, such as the precession of the orbit of Mercury and the bending of light near very massive bodies. In 1915, Einstein introduced the general theory of relativity, which replaced Newton's theory of gravity and resolved the difficulties of the Newtonian theory.

Objectives

By the end of this chapter you should be able to:

- state the definitions of *gravitational potential energy*, $E_p = -G\frac{M_1 M_2}{r}$, *and gravitational potential*, $V = -G\frac{M}{r}$;
- understand that the work done as a mass m is moved across two points with *gravitational potential difference* ΔV is $W = m\Delta V$;
- understand the meaning of *escape velocity*, and solve related problems using the equation for escape speed from a body of mass M and radius R: $v_{esc} = \sqrt{\frac{2GM}{R}}$;
- solve problems of *orbital motion* using the equation for orbital speed at a distance r from a body of mass M: $v = \sqrt{\frac{GM}{r}}$;
- understand the term *weightlessness*.

Gravitational potential energy

Consider a mass M placed somewhere in space, and a second mass m that is a distance R from M. The two masses have gravitational potential energy, which is stored in their gravitational field. This energy is there because work had to be done in order to move one of the masses, say m, from a position very far away (infinity) to the position near the other mass. (See Figure 11.1.) The work that was done by the agent moving the mass went into potential energy.

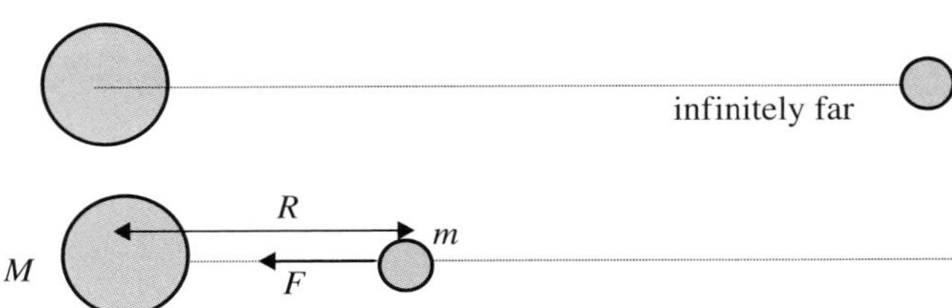

Figure 11.1 Work is being done in bringing the small mass from infinity to a given position away from the big mass. This work is stored as potential energy.

Supplementary material

The gravitational force is not constant but decreases as the separation of the masses increases, so we cannot straightforwardly compute the work done. Using calculus, the total work done in moving the mass from infinity to R is

$$W = \int_{\infty}^{R} \frac{GMm}{r^2} dr$$

$$W = -\frac{GMm}{r}\bigg|_{\infty}^{R}$$

$$W = -\frac{GMm}{R}$$

▶ This work is energy that is stored in the gravitational field of the two masses and is called the gravitational potential energy of the two masses when they are separated by a distance R:

$$E_p = -\frac{GMm}{R}$$

A satellite's total energy as it orbits the earth is the sum of its kinetic and gravitational potential energies:

$$E = \tfrac{1}{2}mv^2 - \frac{GMm}{r}$$

This expression simplifies if we use Newton's law of gravitation and the second law of mechanics

$$G\frac{Mm}{r^2} = m\frac{v^2}{r}$$

$$\Rightarrow v^2 = \frac{GM}{r}$$

$$\Rightarrow E_k = \frac{GMm}{2r}$$

so that

$$E = -\frac{GMm}{2r}$$

or

$$E = -\tfrac{1}{2}mv^2$$

Figure 11.2 shows the kinetic energy $E_k = \frac{GMm}{2r}$, potential energy $E_p = -\frac{GMm}{r}$ and total energy $E = -\frac{GMm}{2r}$ of a mass of 1 kg in orbit around the earth, as a function of distance from the earth's centre. This distance is measured in terms of the earth's radius R.

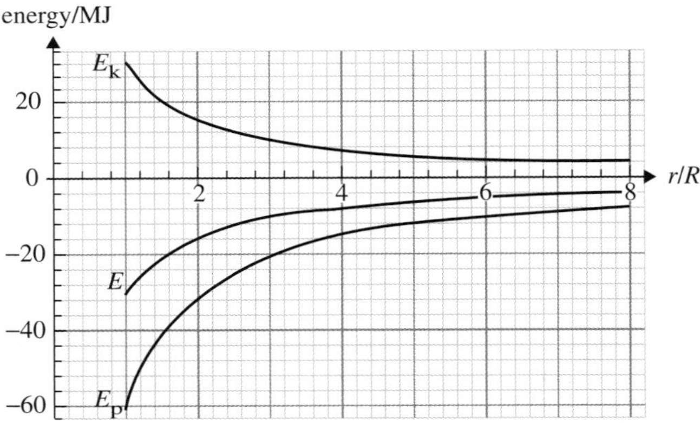

Figure 11.2 Graphs of the kinetic, potential and total energy of a mass of 1 kg in circular orbit around the earth.

Related to the concept of gravitational potential energy is that of **gravitational potential**, V. The gravitational potential is a field, because it is defined at every point in space, but unlike the gravitational field strength, it is a *scalar* quantity.

▶ The gravitational potential at a point P in the gravitational field is the work done per unit mass in bringing a small point mass m from infinity to point P. If the work done is W, then the gravitational potential is the ratio of the work done to the mass m, that is

$$V = \frac{W}{m}$$

The gravitational potential due to a *single* mass M a distance r from the centre of M is

$$V = -\frac{GM}{r}$$

The units of gravitational potential are J kg^{-1}.

If we know that a mass, or an arrangement of masses, produces a gravitational potential V at some point in space, then putting a mass m at that point means that the gravitational potential energy of the mass will be $E_p = mV$.

If a mass m is positioned at a point in a gravitational field where the gravitational potential is V_1 and is then moved to another point where the gravitational potential is V_2, then the work that is done on the mass is

$$\begin{aligned} W &= m(V_2 - V_1) \\ &= m\Delta V \end{aligned}$$

Example questions

Q1

The graph in Figure 11.3 shows the variation of the gravitational potential due to a planet with distance r. Using the graph, estimate:

(a) the gravitational potential energy of an 800 kg spacecraft that is at rest on the surface of the planet;

(b) the work done to move this spacecraft from the surface of the planet to a distance of four planet radii from the surface of the planet.

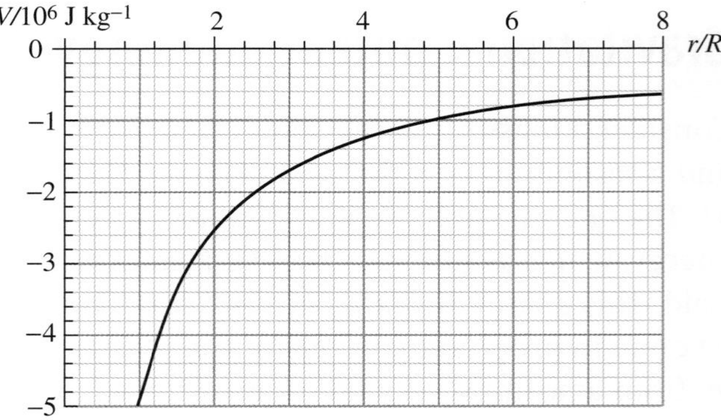

Figure 11.3.

Answer

(a) On the surface of the planet $r = R$, or $r/R = 1$, and from the graph $V = -5 \times 10^6 \text{ J kg}^{-1}$. Hence

$$\begin{aligned} E_p &= mV \\ &= 800 \times (-5 \times 10^6) \\ &= -4 \times 10^9 \text{ J} \end{aligned}$$

(b) When the distance from the *surface* is four planet radii, $r/R = 5$ and the potential there is $V = -1 \times 10^6 \text{ J kg}^{-1}$. Hence

$$\begin{aligned} W &= m\Delta V \\ &= 800 \times (-1 \times 10^6 + 5 \times 10^6) \\ &= 3.2 \times 10^9 \text{ J} \end{aligned}$$

Q2

Figure 11.4 shows the variation of the gravitational potential due to a planet and its moon with distance r from the centre of the planet. The centre-to-centre distance between the planet and the moon is d. The planet's centre is at $r = 0$ and the centre of the moon is at $r = d$.

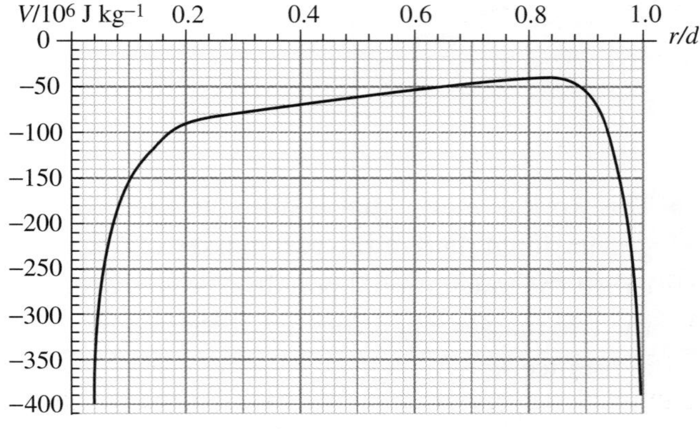

Figure 11.4.

What is the minimum energy required so that a 500 kg probe at rest on the planet's surface will arrive on the moon?

Answer

The probe will arrive at the moon provided it has enough energy to get to the peak of the curve. Once there, the moon will pull it in. On the surface of the planet $V = -390 \times 10^6\ \text{J kg}^{-1}$. At the peak the potential is $V = -40 \times 10^6\ \text{J kg}^{-1}$. Hence

$$\begin{aligned} W &= m\Delta V \\ &= 500 \times (-40 \times 10^6 + 390 \times 10^6). \\ &= 1.75 \times 10^{11}\ \text{J} \end{aligned}$$

Escape velocity

The total energy of a mass m moving near a large, stationary mass M is

$$E = \tfrac{1}{2}mv^2 - \frac{GMm}{r}$$

where v is the speed of the mass when at a distance r from M. (If M is also free to move, then the total energy would have to include a term $\frac{1}{2}Mu^2$, where u is be the speed of M. This complicates things so we assume that M is held fixed.) The only force acting on m is the gravitational force of attraction between M and m. Suppose that the mass m is launched with a speed v_0 away from M. Will m escape from the pull of M and move very far away from it? To move very far away means that the distance between M and m is so large that it is practically infinite. Then the law of energy conservation states that

$$\tfrac{1}{2}mv_0^2 - \frac{GMm}{R} = \tfrac{1}{2}mv_\infty^2$$

The left-hand side of this equation represents the total energy E (kinetic plus potential) of the mass m at the point of launch, a distance R from the centre of M, and the right-hand side is the total energy of the mass at infinity, where the potential energy is zero. Thus, if the mass m is to escape from the pull of M, it must have a total energy that is either zero or positive. If $E = 0$, then the mass m makes it to infinity and just about stops there, $v_\infty = 0$. If $E > 0$, then m not only gets to infinity but is also moving there with speed v_∞, given by the expression above. If, on the other hand, $E < 0$, then the mass cannot make it to infinity; it is forever trapped by the pull of M. So

- $E > 0$: mass escapes and never returns;
- $E < 0$: mass moves out a certain distance but returns – mass is trapped;
- $E = 0$: the critical case separating the other two – mass just barely escapes.

This is a general result: whenever the total energy of a mass is negative, that mass is trapped by the attraction of whatever is causing the total energy to be negative. Here it is gravity that is responsible. Later on we will see that the total energy of the electron in its orbit around the atomic nucleus is also negative. There it is the electrical force that is responsible for $E < 0$. The quarks inside protons also have $E < 0$. The strong nuclear force is the reason for that.

Back to gravitation again. What must the smallest launch velocity be for a mass to escape the pull of the earth?

▶ From the expression above we find that the smallest v is that for which $v_\infty = 0$ (i.e. $E = 0$). In this case

$$\tfrac{1}{2}mv^2 - \frac{GMm}{R} = 0$$

$$\Rightarrow v = \sqrt{\frac{2GM}{R}}$$

This is the minimum velocity that a mass launched from the surface of the earth must have in order to reach infinity and stop there. This is called the escape velocity, v_{esc}, from the earth. Note that the escape velocity is independent of the mass of the body escaping.

Using the fact that $g = \frac{GM_e}{R_e^2}$ we see that the escape velocity can be rewritten as

$$v_{esc} = \sqrt{2gR_e}$$

where g is the acceleration due to gravity at the surface of the earth. The numerical value of this escape velocity is about 11.2 km s^{-1}.

The order-of-magnitude arithmetic without a calculator is as follows:

$$\begin{aligned} v &= \sqrt{\frac{2GM}{R}} \\ &= \sqrt{\frac{2 \times 6.67 \times 10^{-11} \times 5.98 \times 10^{24}}{6.38 \times 10^6}} \\ &\approx \sqrt{\frac{2 \times 7 \times 6 \times 10^7}{6}} \\ &= \sqrt{2 \times 7 \times 10^7} \\ &= \sqrt{140 \times 10^6} \\ &\approx 12 \times 10^3 \text{ m s}^{-1} \end{aligned}$$

In practice, in order to escape, a mass must overcome not only the pull of the earth but also the pull of the sun and the big planets. This means that the escape velocity from the earth is somewhat larger than 11.2 km s^{-1}. This discussion does not apply to powered objects such as rockets; it applies only to objects launched from the earth like cannon balls. In other words, it applies to *ballistic* motion.

Example questions

Q3

The inevitable example! What must the radius of a star of mass M be such that the escape velocity from the star is equal to the speed of light, c?

Answer

Using

$$v = \sqrt{\frac{2GM}{R}}$$

with $v = c$, we find

$$R = \frac{2GM}{c^2}$$

Since nothing can exceed the speed of light, the result above states that if the radius of the star is equal to or less than the value above, nothing can escape from the star. It is a black hole. The interesting thing about this formula is that it correctly gives the radius of the black hole even though Newton's law of gravitation, which we used, does not apply! When dealing with very massive objects, Newton's law has to be replaced by Einstein's law of gravitation. Surprisingly, though, the answer is the same. This radius is called the Schwarzschild radius of the star.

Q4

Compute the Schwarzschild radius of the earth and the sun.

Answer

For the sun

$$\begin{aligned} R &= \frac{2GM}{c^2} \\ &= \frac{2 \times 6.67 \times 10^{-11} \times 2 \times 10^{30}}{(3 \times 10^8)^2} \text{ m} \\ &\approx 3 \times 10^3 \text{ m} \end{aligned}$$

Similarly, for the earth $R_e = 8.86$ mm. This shows that both the earth and the sun are far from being black holes!

Orbital motion

The law of gravitation combined with Newton's second law of mechanics allows an understanding of the motion of planets around the sun as well as the motion of satellites around the earth. The motion of an object that is attracted and bound to a much heavier mass is, according to the law of gravitation, necessarily an ellipse or a circle. This follows because the law of gravitation is an inverse square law: $F = \frac{GMm}{r^2}$. No other form of the law of gravitation (except for a Hooke's law type force, $F = kr$) would lead to closed orbits as observed for the planets. Elliptical orbits with the sun at the focus of the ellipse is what Kepler deduced (Kepler's first law) by analysing the observations made by Tycho Brahe. Newton's law of gravitation and his second law of mechanics provide a theoretical understanding of Kepler's conclusions.

Orbital speed

Consider a planet of mass m in a circular orbit of radius r around the sun, as shown in Figure 11.5. The force on the planet is the gravitational force between the mass of the sun and the mass of the planet, that is

$$F = \frac{GMm}{r^2}$$

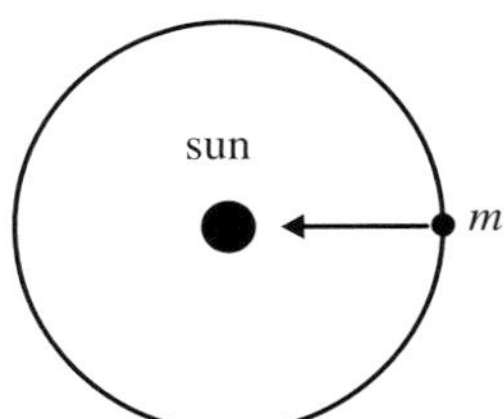

Figure 11.5.

Equating the force with the product of mass times acceleration (the acceleration here is centripetal) we get

$$\frac{GMm}{r^2} = m\frac{v^2}{r}$$

$$\Rightarrow v^2 = \frac{GM}{r}$$

This formula gives the velocity of the planet when it is in an orbit of radius r. For satellites, M stands for the mass of the earth, and this formula shows that the closer the satellite is to the earth, the larger its speed has to be (Figure 11.6 shows this relationship as a graph).

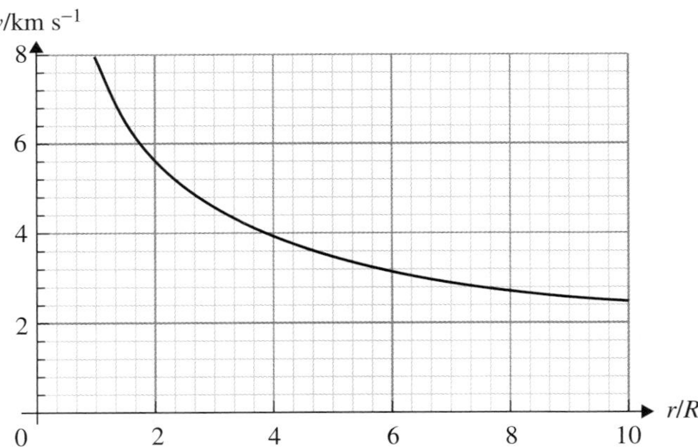

Figure 11.6 The speed of a satellite in circular orbit around the earth. The distances are from the earth's centre in terms of the earth's radius.

Note that the speed does not depend on the satellite's mass.

Example questions

Q5

Evaluate the speed of a satellite in orbit at a height of 500 km from the earth's surface and a satellite that just grazes the surface of the earth. (Take the radius of the earth to be 6.38×10^6 m.)

Answer

The speed is given by

$$v^2 = \frac{GM}{r}$$

$$= \frac{6.67 \times 10^{-11} \times 5.98 \times 10^{24}}{6.88 \times 10^6}$$

$$\Rightarrow v = 7.6 \times 10^3 \text{ m s}^{-1}$$

For a grazing orbit, using the same method

$v = 7.9 \times 10^3 \text{ m s}^{-1}$

Q6

This problem is known as the 'satellite paradox'. A satellite in a low orbit will experience a small frictional force (due to the atmosphere) in a direction opposite to the satellite's velocity.

(a) Explain why the satellite will move into a lower orbit closer to the earth's surface.

(b) Deduce that the speed of the satellite will increase.

(c) Explain how a *resistance* force actually *increases* the speed of the satellite (this is the origin of the 'paradox').

Answer

(a) Since there is a frictional force acting, the satellite's total energy will be reduced. The total energy of a satellite of mass m in a circular orbit of radius r around the earth of mass M is

$$E = -\frac{GMm}{2r}$$

A reduced total energy thus means a smaller radius, i.e. the satellite comes closer to the earth by spiralling inwards.

(b) The speed of the satellite in a circular orbit is given by

$$v = \sqrt{\frac{GM}{r}}$$

So we see that, as the satellite comes closer to earth, its speed increases.

(c) The resolution of the 'paradox' rests on the fact that, as the satellite begins to spiral towards the earth, its velocity is no longer at right angles to the force of gravity (which is directed towards the centre of the earth). Therefore the forces on the satellite in the direction of the velocity are not just the frictional force (opposite to the velocity) but also the component of the gravitational force (see Figure 11.7). Thus,

$$F \sin\theta = \frac{GMm}{r^2} \sin\theta$$

A detailed analysis shows that the magnitude of this component is approximately double that of the frictional force. Hence, the satellite increases its speed even though a frictional force opposes the motion because the tangential net force on the satellite is, in fact, in the direction of the velocity.

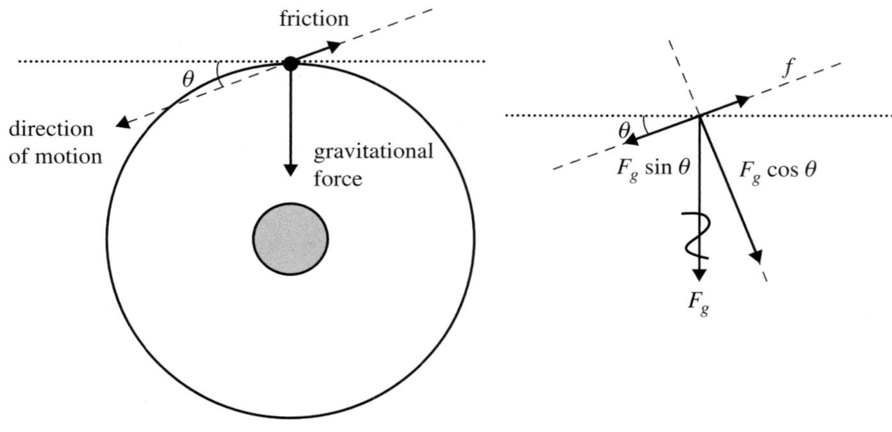

Figure 11.7.

Period of motion

If the time taken for one revolution of the satellite or planet is T, then we must have $v = \frac{2\pi r}{T}$. So, substituting in the formula for speed we find

$$\left(\frac{2\pi r}{T}\right)^2 = \frac{GM}{r}$$

$$\Rightarrow T^2 = \frac{4\pi^2}{GM} r^3$$

▶ Applied to planets (now M stands for the mass of the sun), this law states that the period of a planet around the sun is proportional to the 3/2 power of the orbit radius: this is simply Kepler's third law of planetary motion.

For elliptical orbits, r should be replaced by the semi-major axis of the ellipse or (approximately) by the average distance of the planet from the sun.

Supplementary material

Kepler's second law states that planets sweep out equal areas in equal times. This law also follows from Newton's law of gravitation and Newton's laws of mechanics.

Weightlessness

Consider an astronaut of mass m in a spacecraft *in orbit* around the earth a distance r from the earth's centre (see Figure 11.8).

The forces on the astronaut are the reaction force N from the floor and his weight W (i.e. the gravitational force from the earth). The net force on the astronaut is

$$G\frac{Mm}{r^2} - N$$

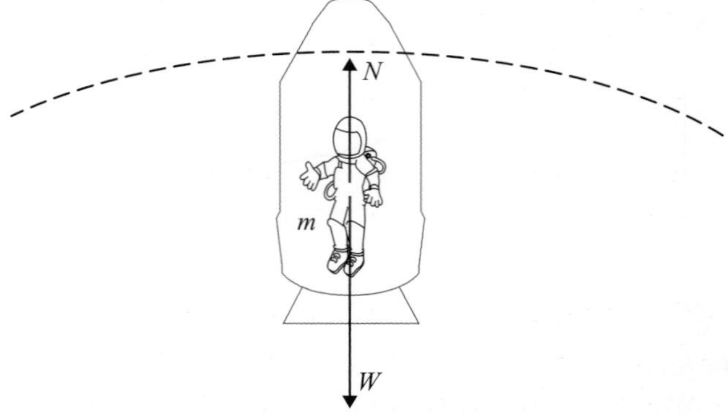

Figure 11.8.

and so

$$G\frac{Mm}{r^2} - N = m\frac{v^2}{r}$$
$$\Rightarrow N = G\frac{Mm}{r^2} - m\frac{v^2}{r}$$
$$= \frac{m}{r}\left(G\frac{M}{r} - v^2\right)$$

But the speed of the astronaut is given by $v^2 = \frac{GM}{r}$, which implies that $N = 0$. Thus, the astronaut experiences no reaction forces from the floor and so 'feels' weightless.

Looked at in a simpler way, the astronaut is falling freely but *so is the spacecraft*, hence there are no reaction forces. At a distance of 300 km from the earth's surface, gravity is not negligible. There is a force of gravity on the astronaut but no reaction force from the spacecraft floor.

Equipotential surfaces

As we have seen, the gravitational potential at a distance r from the centre of a spherical uniform mass M is given by

$$V = -\frac{GM}{r}$$

We may therefore consider all the points in space that have the same potential.

From the formula above, it follows that those points are all at the same distance from the centre of the mass, and so lie on a sphere whose centre is the same as that of the spherical mass. A two-dimensional representation of these surfaces of constant potential is given in Figure 11.9. They are called **equipotential surfaces**.

> An *equipotential surface* consists of those points that have the same potential.

Similarly, we may construct the equipotential surfaces due to more than one mass. Figure 11.10 shows the equipotential surfaces due to two equal masses centred at the points with coordinates $(-0.5, 0)$ and $(+0.5, 0)$. The shape of the surfaces is no longer spherical. (Very far from both masses, the equipotential surfaces tend to become spherical because, from far away, it looks as if we have one body of mass equal to twice the individual masses.)

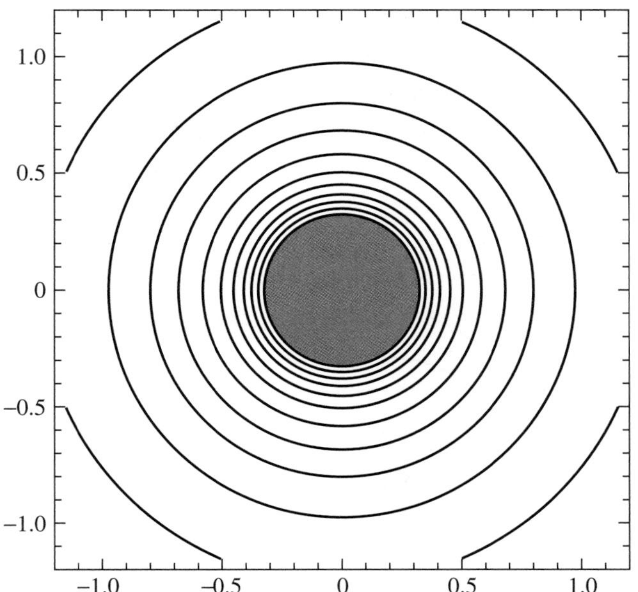

Figure 11.9 Equipotential surfaces due to one spherical mass at the origin of the axes. The difference in potential between any two adjacent surfaces is the same.

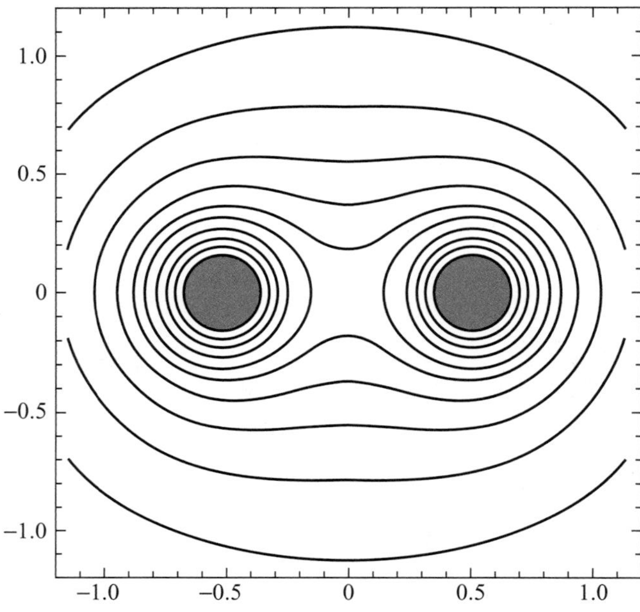

Figure 11.10 The equipotential surfaces due to two equal masses.

Figure 11.11 shows the equipotential surfaces for two unequal masses (the mass on the right is double the other).

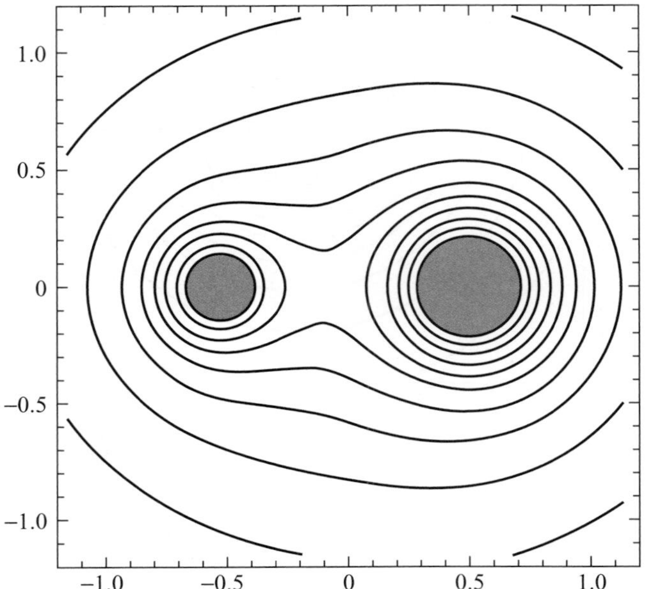

Figure 11.11 The equipotential surfaces due to two unequal masses.

There is a connection between the gravitational potential and the gravitational field, which is explained in the following paragraphs. This mathematical connection also translates to a relation between equipotential surfaces and gravitational field lines as we will soon see.

Consider two equipotential surfaces a distance Δr apart. Let ΔV be the potential difference between the two surfaces. The situation is shown in Figure 11.12. We want to move the point mass m from one equipotential surface to the other.

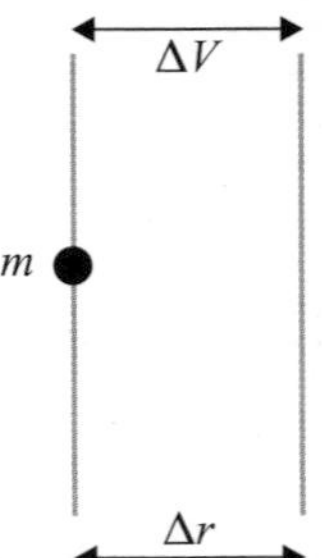

Figure 11.12 A point mass m is to be moved from one equipotential surface to the other.

We know that this requires an amount of work W given by

$$W = m\Delta V$$

But we may also calculate the work from $W =$ force $\times$ distance. The force on the point mass is the gravitational force $F = mg$, where g is the magnitude of the gravitational field strength at the position of the mass m. Assuming that the two surfaces are very close to each other means that g will not change by much as we move from one surface to the other, and so we may take g to be constant. Then the work done is also given by

$$W = (mg)\Delta r$$

Equating the two expressions for work done gives

$$g = \frac{\Delta V}{\Delta r}$$

This gives the *magnitude* of the gravitational field as the rate of change with distance of the gravitational potential.

A more careful treatment, based on calculus, gives the more precise result:

$$g = -\frac{dV}{dr}$$

This means that the gravitational field is the negative derivative of the gravitational potential with respect to distance. The minus sign is not important for our purposes here.

Consider again Figure 11.9. Recall that adjacent equipotential surfaces have the same potential difference, and notice that as we move away from the mass the surfaces are further apart. Using

$$g = \frac{\Delta V}{\Delta r}$$

implies that the magnitude of the gravitational field strength is decreasing (since ΔV is the same and Δr is getting larger). The following is also true.

▶ If we have a graph showing the variation with distance of the gravitational potential, the slope (gradient) of the graph is the magnitude of the gravitational field strength.

Another implication of this relation is that equipotential surfaces and gravitational field lines are normal (perpendicular) to each other. We already know this for the case of a single mass: the field lines are radial lines and the equipotential surfaces are spheres centred at the mass. The two are normal to each other, as shown in Figure 11.13.

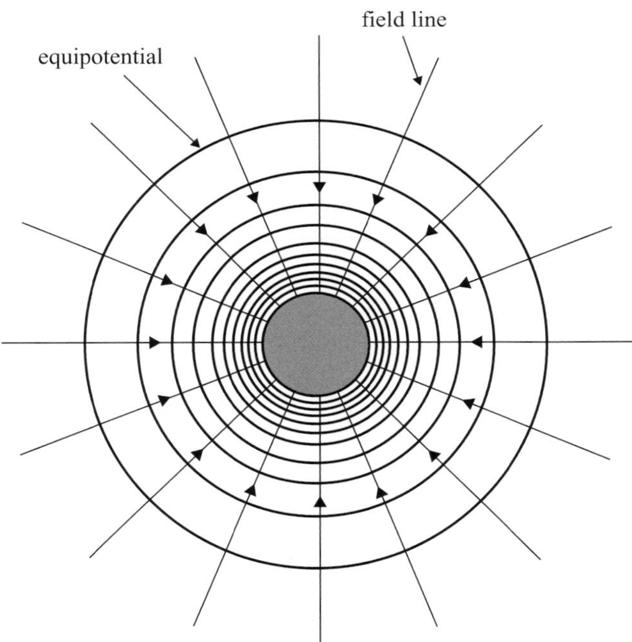

Figure 11.13 Equipotential surfaces and field lines are at right angles to each other.

The point, though, is that this is generally true for all shapes of field lines and equipotential surfaces. This means that knowing one set of lines or surfaces, we can find the other.

Supplementary material

The binary star system

(This section is not required for examination purposes but will be useful to those who study the astrophysics option.)

Two stars can orbit around each other in what is called a binary star system. The orbit of each star can be an ellipse but we will consider here the much simpler case of circular orbits. Consider two stars of mass M_1 and M_2. They attract each other with the gravitational force

$$F = G\frac{M_1 M_2}{d^2}$$

where d is the separation of their centres of mass (see Figure 11.14).

Figure 11.14 The two stars in the binary star system attract each other.

The centre of mass of the two stars is not acted upon by any external forces and is thus moving in a straight line with constant speed. Without loss of generality, we may consider the speed to be zero, in which case it follows that the two masses orbit the common centre of mass. Taking the orbits to be circular, the orbit radii (i.e. the distances of each mass from the centre of mass) are given by

$$R_1 = \frac{M_2 d}{M_1 + M_2}$$

$$R_2 = \frac{M_1 d}{M_1 + M_2}$$

See Figures 11.15 and 11.16.

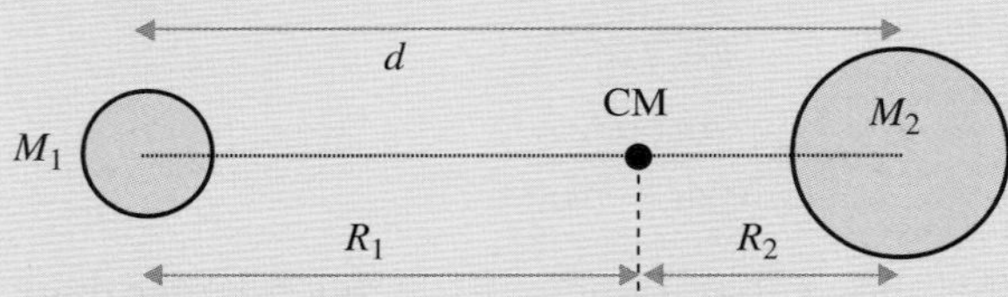

Figure 11.15 The two stars orbit their centre of mass.

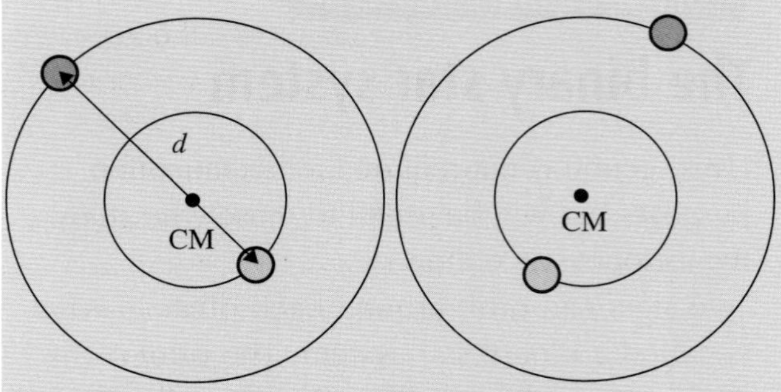

Figure 11.16 The orbits of the two stars.

The speeds of rotation can be found from

$$G\frac{M_1 M_2}{d^2} = M_1 \frac{v_1^2}{R_1}$$
$$\Rightarrow v_1^2 = G\frac{M_2 R_1}{d^2}$$
$$G\frac{M_1 M_2}{d^2} = M_2 \frac{v_2^2}{R_2}$$
$$\Rightarrow v_2^2 = G\frac{M_1 R_2}{d^2}$$

and thus

$$v_1^2 = G\frac{M_2}{d^2}\frac{M_2 d}{M_1 + M_2} = \frac{GM_2^2}{d(M_1 + M_2)}$$
$$v_2^2 = G\frac{M_1}{d^2}\frac{M_1 d}{M_1 + M_2} = \frac{GM_1^2}{d(M_1 + M_2)}$$

The common period of rotation is therefore found from

$$T^2 = \left(\frac{2\pi R_1}{v_1}\right)^2 = \frac{4\pi^2 \frac{M_2^2 d^2}{(M_1+M_2)^2}}{\frac{GM_2^2}{d(M_1+M_2)}} = \frac{4\pi^2 d^3}{G(M_1 + M_2)}$$

This shows that if one mass is much larger than the other, then the formula for T reduces to the familiar one from Kepler's third law.

The total energy of the binary star system is given by

$$E = \frac{1}{2}M_1 v_1^2 + \frac{1}{2}M_2 v_2^2 - G\frac{M_1 M_2}{d}$$
$$= \frac{1}{2}M_1 \frac{GM_2^2}{d(M_1 + M_2)} + \frac{1}{2}M_2 \frac{GM_1^2}{d(M_1 + M_2)} - G\frac{M_1 M_2}{d}$$
$$= \frac{1}{2}\frac{GM_1 M_2}{d}\left(\frac{M_2}{(M_1 + M_2)} + \frac{M_1}{(M_1 + M_2)} - 2\right)$$

that is

$$E = -\frac{1}{2}\frac{GM_1 M_2}{d}$$

If the binary star system loses energy, for example because of gravitational radiation, then the energy decreases and thus the separation of the two stars, d, decreases as well. This means that each star now moves faster and the rotational period decreases. This decrease in the rotational period of a binary star system has been observed and is indirect evidence for the existence of gravity waves.

? QUESTIONS

1 Show by applying Newton's law of gravitation and the second law of mechanics that a satellite (or planet) in a circular orbit of radius R around the earth (or the sun) has a period (i.e. time to complete one revolution) given by

$$T^2 = \frac{4\pi^2 R^3}{GM}$$

where M is the mass of the attracting body (earth or sun). This is Kepler's third law.

2 Show that a satellite orbiting the earth (mass M) in a circular orbit of radius r and angular velocity ω satisfies

$$r^3 = \frac{GM}{\omega^2}$$

3 What is the speed of a satellite that orbits the earth at a height of 500 km? How long does it take to go around the earth once?

4 A satellite that *always* looks down at the same spot on the earth's surface is called a geosynchronous satellite. Find the distance of this satellite from the surface of the earth. Could the satellite be looking down at any point on the surface of the earth?

5 (a) What is the gravitational potential energy stored in the gravitational field between the earth and the moon?
(b) What is the earth's gravitational potential at the position of the moon?
(c) Find the speed with which the moon orbits the earth. (Use the data in Appendix 3.)

6 A spacecraft of mass 30 000 kg leaves the earth on its way to the moon. Plot the spacecraft's potential energy as a function of its distance from the earth's centre.

7 (a) What is the gravitational potential at a distance from the earth's centre equal to 5 earth radii?
(b) What is the gravitational potential energy of a 500 kg satellite placed at a distance from the earth's centre equal to 5 earth radii?

8 Figure 11.17 shows cross-sections of two satellite orbits around the earth. (To be in orbit means that only gravity is acting on the satellite.) Discuss whether either of these orbits is possible.

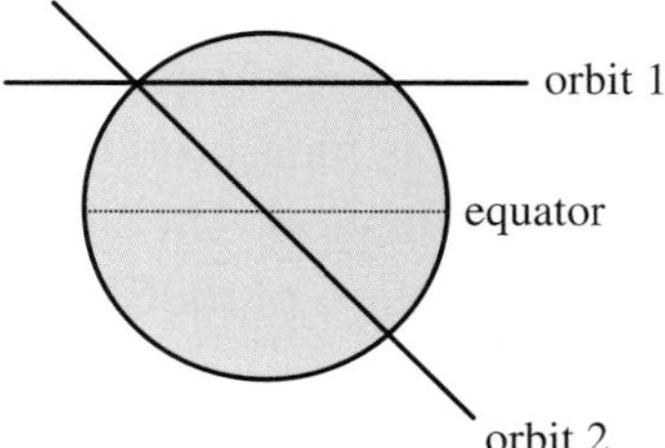

Figure 11.17 For question 8.

9 In the text it was calculated that the acceleration due to gravity at a height of 300 km above the earth's surface is far from negligible, yet astronauts orbiting in the space shuttle at such a height feel weightless. Explain why.

10 Earlier in the topic of mechanics we used the expression *mgh* for the gravitational potential energy of a mass *m*. This expression is only approximate. Show, by using $U = -\frac{GMm}{r}$, which is the correct expression, that the difference in gravitational potential energy of a mass on the surface of the earth and at a height *h* from the earth's surface is indeed *mgh* provided *h* is small compared with the radius of the earth. (Use the binomial expansion.)

11 Figure 11.18 shows the variation of the gravitational force with distance. What does the shaded area represent?

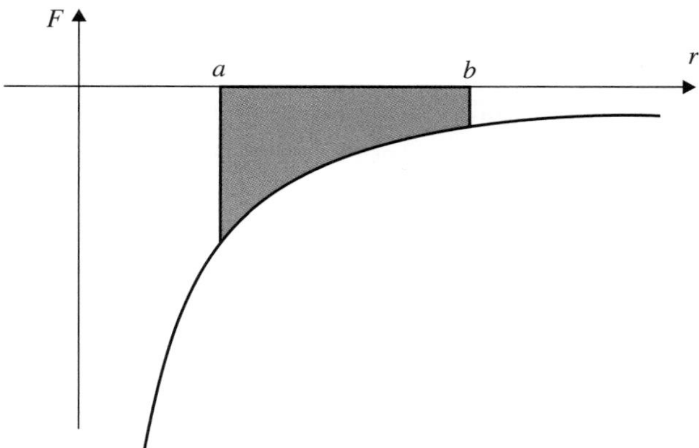

Figure 11.18 For question 11.

12 Figure 11.19 shows the variation with distance of the gravitational potential (in terajoules per kilogram) due to a planet whose radius is 2.0×10^5 m.
(a) Calculate the mass of the planet.
(b) Show that the escape speed from the surface of the planet is $v_{esc} = \sqrt{-2V}$, where V is the gravitational potential on the planet's surface.
(c) Use the graph to determine the escape speed from this planet.
(d) How much energy is required to move a rocket of mass 1500 kg from the surface of the planet to a distance of 1.0×10^6 m from the centre?
(e) A probe is released from rest at a distance from the planet's centre of 0.50×10^6 m

and allowed to crash onto the planet's surface. With what speed will the probe hit the surface?

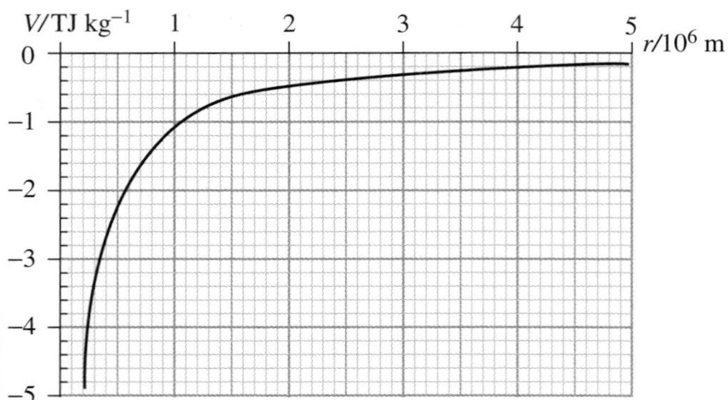

Figure 11.19 For question 12.

13 Figure 11.20 shows the variation with distance from the centre of the planet of the gravitational potential due to the planet and its moon. The planet's centre is at $r = 0$ and the centre of the moon is at $r = 1$. The units of separation are arbitrary. At the point where $r = 0.75$ the gravitational field is zero.

(a) Determine the ratio of the mass of the planet to that of the moon.

(b) With what speed must a probe be launched from the surface of the planet in order to arrive on the surface of the moon?

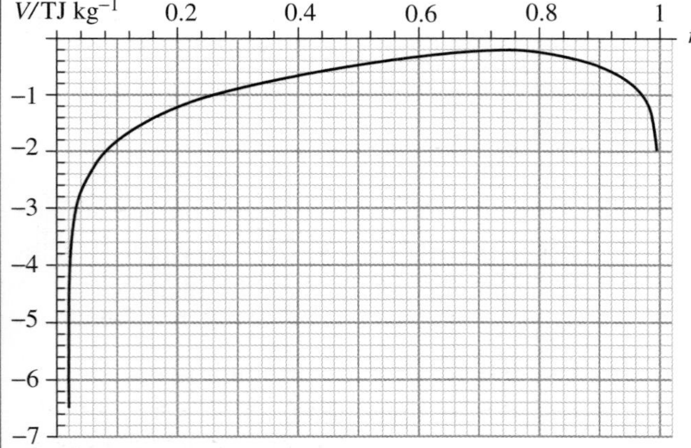

Figure 11.20 For question 13.

14 Prove that the total energy of the earth (mass m) as it orbits the sun (mass M) is $E = -\frac{1}{2}mv^2$ or $E = -\frac{GMm}{2r}$, where r is the radius of the earth's circular orbit. Calculate this energy numerically.

15 Figure 11.21 shows two identical satellites in circular orbits. Which satellite has the larger:

(a) kinetic energy;

(b) potential energy;

(c) total energy?

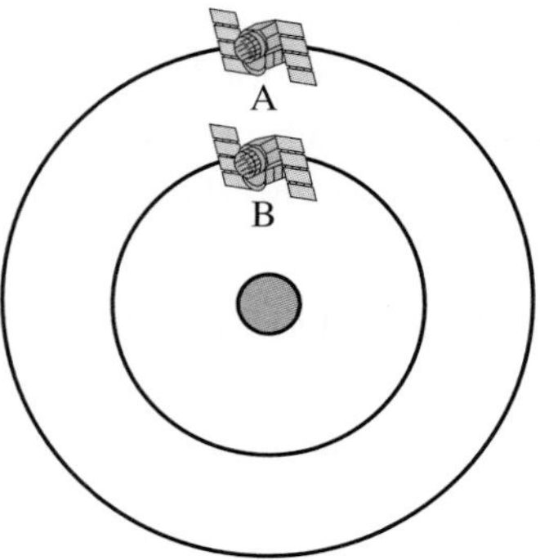

Figure 11.21 For question 15.

16 Show that the total energy of a satellite of mass m in orbit around the earth (mass M) at a distance from the Earth's centre of 5 earth radii is given by $E = -\frac{GMm}{10R}$.

17 The total energy of a satellite during launch from the earth's surface is $E = -\frac{GMm}{5R}$, where R is the radius of the earth. It eventually settles into a circular orbit; calculate the radius of that orbit.

18 What is the escape velocity from the earth if the launch takes place not on the surface of the earth but from a space station orbiting the earth at a height equal to R_e? You must find the velocity of launch as measured by an observer on the space station. The launch takes place in the direction of motion of the space station.

19 A satellite is in a circular orbit around the earth. The satellite turns on its engines so that a small force is exerted on the satellite in the direction of the velocity. The engines are on for a very short time and the satellite now finds itself in a new circular orbit.

(a) State and explain whether the new orbit is closer to or further away from the earth.

(b) Hence explain why the speed of the satellite will decrease.

(c) It appears that a force, acting in the direction of the velocity, has actually *reduced* the speed. How do you explain this observation?

20 Figure 11.22 shows a planet orbiting the sun counter-clockwise, at two positions – A and B. Also shown is the gravitational force acting on the planet at each position. By decomposing the force into components normal and tangential to the path (dotted lines), explain why it is only the tangential component that does work. Hence explain why the planet will accelerate from A to P but will slow down from P to B.

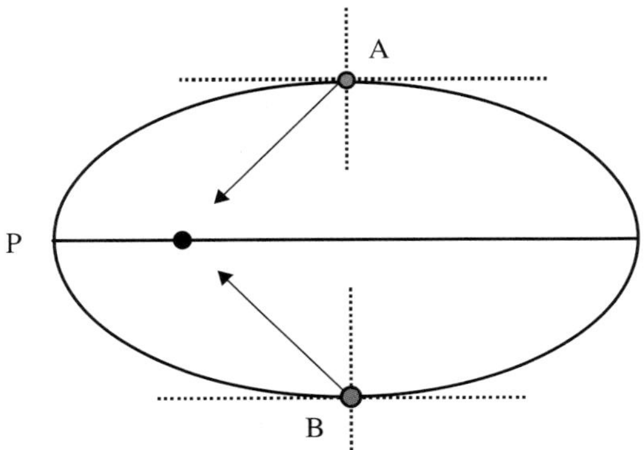

Figure 11.22 For question 20.

21 Figure 11.23 shows a planet orbiting the sun. Explain why at points A and P of the orbit the potential energy of the planet assumes its minimum and maximum values, and determine which is which. Hence determine at what point in the orbit the planet has the highest speed.

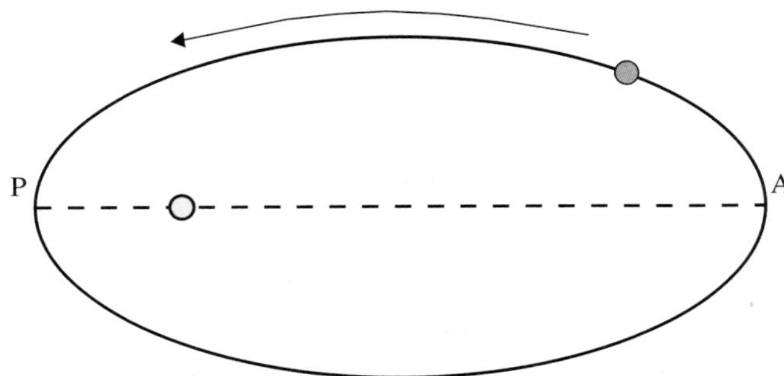

Figure 11.23 For question 21.

22 The diagrams in Figure 11.24 are not drawn to scale and show, separately, the earth and the moon, and the earth and the sun. A point mass m is placed at point A and then at point B. The force experienced by the mass at A due to the moon is F^{A}_{moon} and at B it is F^{B}_{moon}. Similarly the forces at A and B due to the sun are F^{A}_{sun} and F^{B}_{sun}.

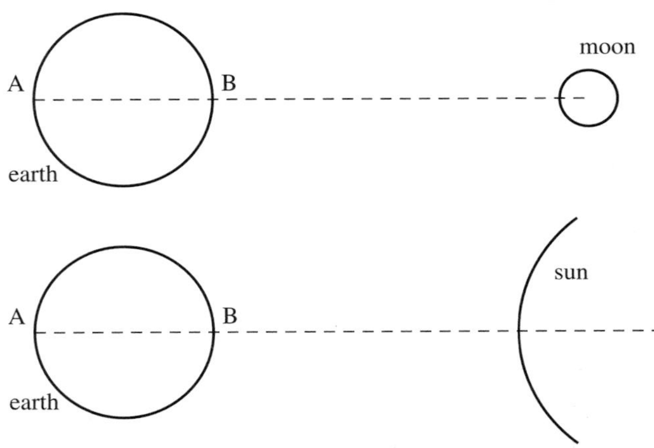

Figure 11.24 For question 22.

(a) Using data from Appendix 3, calculate the ratio $\frac{F^{B}_{moon}-F^{A}_{moon}}{F^{B}_{sun}-F^{A}_{sun}}$.

(b) The tides on the earth have to do with the difference between the forces on opposite sides of the earth. Using your answer in (a), suggest whether the sun or the moon has the dominant role for tides on earth.

23 Show that the escape speed from the surface of a planet of radius R can be written as $v_{esc} = \sqrt{2gR}$, where g is the gravitational field strength on the planet's surface.

24 Consider two particles of mass m and $16m$ separated by a distance d.

(a) Deduce that at point P, a distance $\frac{d}{5}$ from the particle with mass m, the gravitational field strength is zero.

(b) Determine the value of the gravitational potential at P.

25 (a) Deduce that a satellite orbiting a planet of mass M in a circular orbit of radius r has a period of revolution given by $T = \sqrt{\frac{4\pi^2 r^3}{GM}}$.

(b) A grazing orbit is one in which the orbit radius is approximately equal to the radius R of the planet. Deduce that the period of revolution in a grazing orbit is given by $T = \sqrt{\frac{3\pi}{G\rho}}$, where ρ is the density of the planet.

(c) The period of a grazing orbit around the earth is 85 minutes and around the planet Jupiter it is 169 minutes. Deduce the ratio $\frac{\rho_{Earth}}{\rho_{Jupiter}}$.

26 (a) The acceleration of free fall at the surface of a planet is g and the radius of the planet is R. Deduce that the period of a satellite in a very low orbit is given by $T = 2\pi\sqrt{\frac{R}{g}}$.

(b) Given that $g = 4.5\,\text{m s}^{-2}$ and $R = 3.4 \times 10^6\,\text{m}$, deduce that the orbital period of the low orbit is about 91 minutes.

(c) A spacecraft in orbit around this planet has a period of 140 minutes. Deduce the height of the spacecraft from the surface of the planet.

27 Two stars of equal mass M orbit a common centre as shown in Figure 11.25. The radius of the orbit of each star is R. Assume that each of the stars has a mass equal to 1.5 solar masses (solar mass $= 2 \times 10^{30}\,\text{kg}$) and that the initial separation of the stars is 2.0×10^9 m.

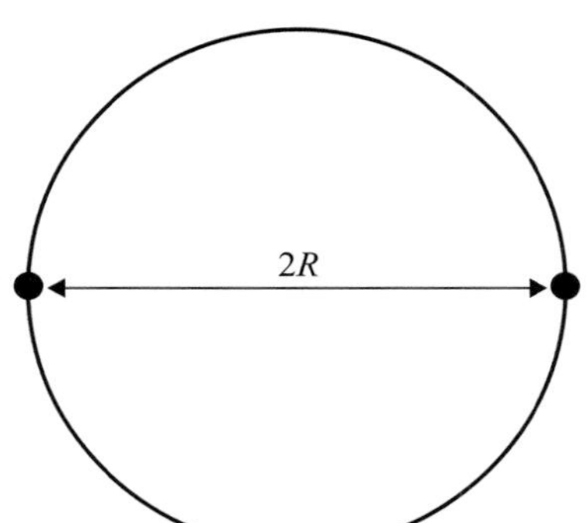

Figure 11.25 For question 27.

(a) State the magnitude of the force on each star in terms of M, R and G.

(b) Deduce that the period of revolution of each star is given by the expression

$$T^2 = \frac{16\pi^2 R^3}{GM}.$$

(c) Evaluate the period numerically.

(d) Calculate that the total energy of the two stars is given by

$$E = -\frac{GM^2}{4R}.$$

(e) The two-star system loses energy as a result of emitting gravitational radiation. Deduce that the stars will move closer to each other.

(f) (i) Explain why the fractional loss of energy per unit time may be calculated from the expression

$$\frac{\Delta E/E}{\Delta t} = \frac{3}{2}\frac{\Delta T/T}{\Delta t}$$

where $\frac{\Delta T/T}{\Delta t}$ is the fractional decrease in period per unit time.

(ii) The orbital period decreases at a rate of $\Delta T/\Delta t = 72\,\mu\text{s yr}^{-1}$. Estimate the fractional energy loss per year.

(g) The two stars will collapse into each other when $\Delta E \approx E$. Estimate the lifetime, in years, of this binary star system.

28 Figure 11.26 shows equipotential surfaces due to two spherical masses.

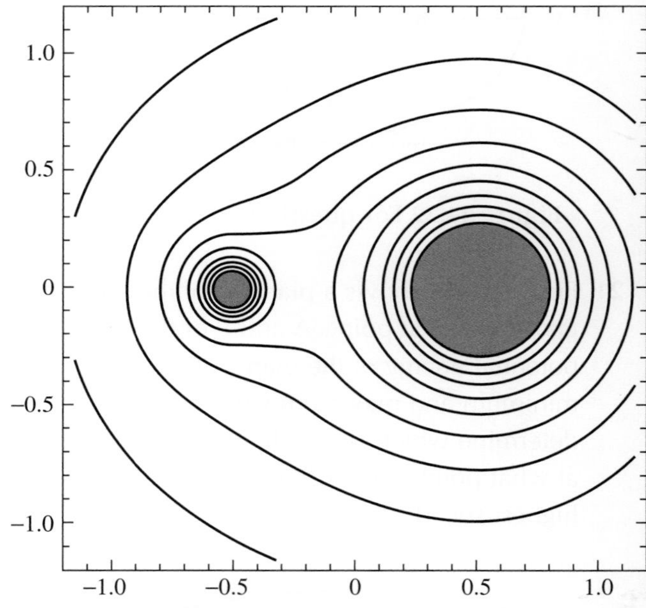

Figure 11.26 For question 28.

(a) Using the diagram, explain how it can be deduced that the masses are unequal.

(b) Copy the diagram and draw in the gravitational field lines due to the two masses.

(c) Explain why the equipotential surfaces are spherical very far from the two masses.

29 Figure 11.27 shows the variation with distance r from the centre of a planet of the combined gravitational potential due to the planet (of mass M) and its moon (of mass m) along the line joining the planet and the moon. The horizontal axis is labelled $\frac{r}{d}$, where d is the centre-to-centre separation of the planet and the moon.

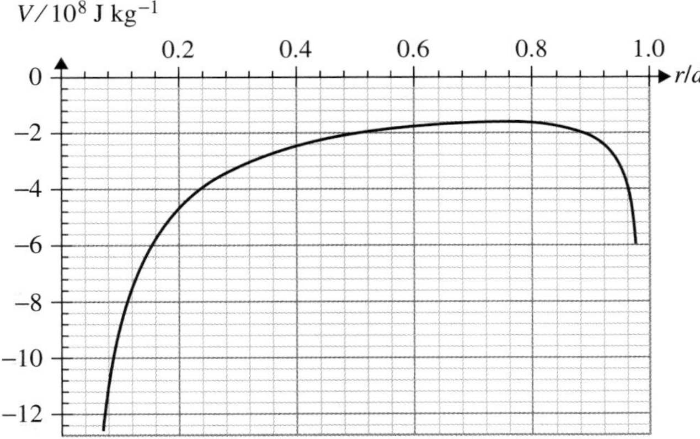

Figure 11.27 For question 29.

(a) The distance d is equal to 4.8×10^8 m. Use the graph to calculate the magnitude of the gravitational field strength at the point where $\frac{r}{d} = 0.20$.

(b) Explain the physical significance of the point where $\frac{r}{d} = 0.75$.

(c) Using the graph, calculate the ratio $\frac{M}{m}$.

Thermal concepts

This chapter is an introduction to thermal physics. It introduces the concepts of temperature, heat, internal energy and thermal equilibrium.

Objectives

By the end of this chapter you should be able to:

- understand how a *temperature scale* is constructed;
- appreciate that heat is *energy* that is exchanged between systems at *different* temperatures;
- appreciate that *internal energy* is the total kinetic energy of the molecules of a system plus the potential energy associated with the intermolecular forces;
- understand that the absolute temperature of a gas is a measure of the *average kinetic energy* of its molecules;
- state the meaning of the *mole* and the *Avogadro constant* and do calculations using them.

Temperature

Temperature is the intuitive concept of 'hotness' or 'coldness' of a substance. To measure the temperature of a body we need to find *a property of the body that changes as the 'hotness' changes*. Consider a thin tube filled with mercury – as it becomes hotter, the *length* of mercury increases (see Figure 1.1). The length of the mercury column then becomes a measure of the temperature of the mercury in the tube. (Other properties such as electrical resistance, voltage and pressure may be used, depending on the kind of thermometer to be constructed.)

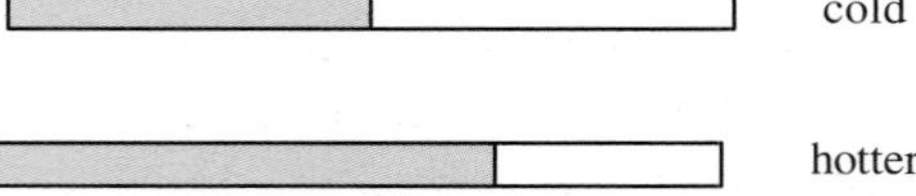

Figure 1.1 As the mercury column gets hotter, its length increases. This can be used to define a temperature scale on a thermometer.

In 1742, Andreas Celsius created the temperature scale that is commonly used today and is known by his name. In the Celsius scale a value of zero degrees is assigned to the freezing point of water and a value of one hundred degrees is assigned to the boiling point of water. A *thermometer* employing the Celsius scale can be made by first placing a glass tube containing mercury in a mixture of ice and water and labelling the length of the mercury as 0, then placing it in boiling water and labelling the new length as 100. Finally, the range from zero to one hundred degrees is subdivided into equal intervals. The degree of the Celsius scale is denoted by °C. (It is a curious historical note that Celsius himself actually assigned 0 °C to the boiling point of water and 100 °C to the freezing point.)

A thermometer like the one just described actually measures the temperature of the mercury it contains. To measure the temperature of another body we must bring the thermometer into *thermal contact* with the body of interest. If a thermometer originally at room temperature is placed in a hot cup of coffee, the length of the mercury column (i.e. the reading of the thermometer) will go up and eventually will settle to a constant value. Similarly, if the thermometer is placed in a cup containing ice water, the reading will start going down until, eventually, a constant reading is obtained. While the thermometer reading is changing, there is a *thermal interaction* between the two bodies (the thermometer and the coffee, say). When the reading settles at a constant value, the two bodies (thermometer and coffee) are in *thermal equilibrium*. When thermal equilibrium is reached, the temperature of the two bodies is the same. Thus, the reading on the thermometer is also the temperature of the body.

Thermal equilibrium can exist between more than two bodies. Consider three bodies, A, B and C. Suppose that C is in thermal equilibrium with both A and B. This implies that A and B have the same temperature as C. They therefore also have the *same* temperature as one another and hence are in thermal equilibrium with one another (see Figure 1.2).

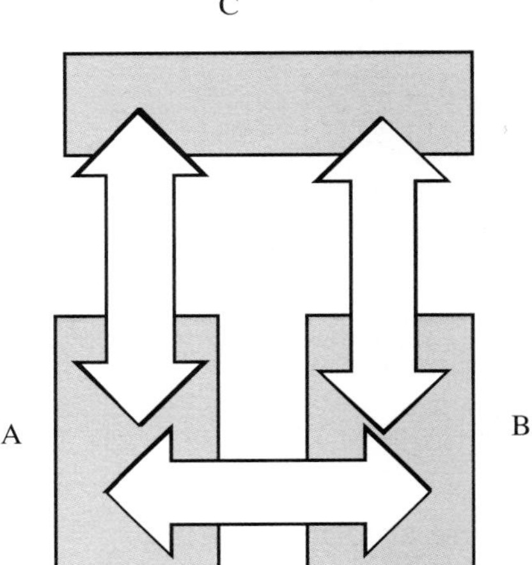

Figure 1.2 Body A and body B are each in thermal equilibrium with body C. Therefore they are in thermal equilibrium with each other and hence have the same temperature.

The **absolute temperature** scale (to be discussed in more detail in later chapters) is defined in terms of the conventional Celsius scale through

$$T\,(\text{in kelvin}) = T\,(\text{in degrees Celsius}) + 273$$

The lowest possible temperature on the absolute scale is zero kelvin, 0 K. It is not possible to achieve a lower temperature. On the Celsius scale the lowest possible temperature is, therefore, $-273\,°\text{C}$.

Heat as energy

It was not until the nineteenth century that 'heat' was recognized as a form of energy. Up to then it was regarded as a kind of fluid that moved from place to place. A historic experiment by Joule demonstrated the equivalence of heat and energy.

In the previous section, we mentioned that two bodies that are in thermal contact and have different temperatures will have a thermal interaction. This interaction involves *heat*.

▶ Heat is energy that is transferred from one body and into another as a result of a difference in temperature.

Thus, when a hot object is brought in contact with a colder body, heat will be transferred to the colder body and increase its temperature. We say that the colder body has been 'heated'.

Now, all substances consist of molecules and, whether in the solid, liquid or gas phase, the molecules are in constant motion. They therefore have kinetic energy. In a gas the molecules move randomly throughout the entire volume of the gas. In a solid the motion of the molecules is on a very much smaller scale – the molecules simply vibrate about their equilibrium positions. This requires kinetic energy as well. In addition, there are forces between molecules (intermolecular forces, which are electrical in nature). For gases these forces are very small (under reasonable conditions they are almost negligible). But they are substantial for solids. Increasing the average separation of two molecules of a solid requires work to be done. This work goes into potential energy associated with intermolecular forces. (The case of liquids is intermediate between gases and solids.)

We thus define the **internal energy** of a substance as follows:

▶ Internal energy is the total kinetic energy of the molecules of a substance, plus any potential energy associated with forces between the molecules.

Thus, the heat that is transferred from a hot to a cold body increases the internal energy of the cold body (and decreases the internal energy of the hot body by the same amount). So the term 'heat' refers to energy associated with the thermal interaction of two or more systems due to a difference of temperature.

Similarly, if we place a large number of lead pellets in a box and shake the box vigorously, the temperature of the lead pellets will go up. The lead pellets will be 'heated' and their internal energy increases. But there is no heat exchanged here. The internal energy of the pellets increases because of the *work* that we perform in shaking the box.

So the internal energy of a system can change as a result of heat added or taken out and as a result of work performed. Internal energy, heat and work are thus three different concepts. What they have in common is that they are all measured in joules. Temperature is yet another different concept. One of the big discoveries of nineteenth-century physics was the relation between temperature and kinetic energy of molecules.

▶ The absolute temperature is a measure of the average kinetic energy of the molecules of a substance. The average kinetic energy of the molecules is directly proportional to the absolute temperature in kelvin.

We therefore have a relationship between a *microscopic* concept (the average kinetic energy of molecules) and a *macroscopic* concept (temperature).

Note that the terms 'thermal energy' and 'heat' are sometimes used interchangeably. In this book, the term thermal energy will from now on be used in place of heat.

The atomic model of matter

Ordinary matter can be found in three forms or phases: solid, liquid and gaseous. The solid phase is characterized by high density and the molecules are at fixed positions. In the liquid phase, the density is lower and the molecules are further apart. Unlike the solid phase, molecules are free to move about, thus the distance between them is not fixed. In the gas phase, the molecules experience little resistance to motion and move freely about – the average distance between molecules is large. This is illustrated in Figure 1.3.

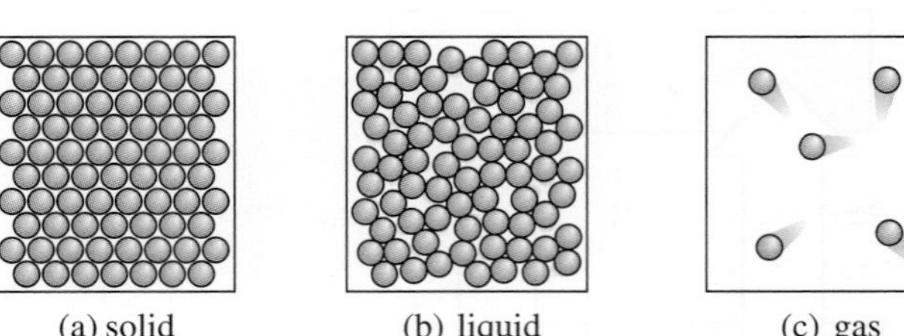

Figure 1.3 Typical arrangements of molecules in a solid, a liquid and a gas.

In all three cases there are forces acting between the molecules of the substance. These intermolecular forces are strongest in the solid phase and weakest (almost negligible) in the gas phase. In the solid phase they are responsible for keeping the molecules in their fixed positions (solids have fixed shapes) and are the reason why large forces are needed to compress or stretch solids.

If we consider a solid at low temperature, the kinetic energy of each molecule is quite small compared with the energy required to move any two molecules a large distance apart. The average distance between molecules does not change and so the solid stays a solid. As the temperature is increased, the average kinetic energy of the molecules increases and becomes comparable to the energy required for separation. When this happens, the molecules abandon their fixed positions and move apart. The solid begins to melt – it turns into a liquid. This phenomenon is called a *phase transition*. If the temperature is increased further, the molecules may have enough energy to move so far apart from each other that the intermolecular forces are no longer significant. The liquid turns into a gas.

The Avogadro constant

One mole of any substance is that quantity of the substance whose mass in grams is numerically equal to the substance's molar mass, μ. The mole is the SI unit for quantity. The molar mass of hydrogen gas (H_2) is $2\ \text{g mol}^{-1}$ and so one mole of hydrogen has a mass of 2 g; one mole of oxygen (O_2, molar mass $32\ \text{g mol}^{-1}$) has a mass of 32 g, and so on.

▶ One mole of any substance contains the same number of molecules as in 12 grams of carbon-12. This number is known as the Avogadro constant and its numerical value is

$$N_A = 6.02 \times 10^{23}\ \text{molecules mol}^{-1}$$

It follows, therefore, that the number of moles of a substance can be found by dividing the total number of molecules in the substance by the Avogadro constant

$$n = \frac{N}{N_A}$$

Equivalently, the mass m, in grams, of a substance can be expressed in terms of the number of moles n, as

$$m = n\mu$$

Example question

Q1

How many grams are there in a quantity of oxygen gas containing 1.20×10^{25} molecules?

Answer

The number of moles is

$$\frac{1.20 \times 10^{25}}{6.02 \times 10^{23}} = 19.93\ \text{mol}$$

Since the molar mass is $32\ \text{g mol}^{-1}$ the mass is

$$19.93 \times 32 = 638\ \text{g} = 0.638\ \text{kg}$$

? QUESTIONS

1 Give definitions of:
(a) temperature;
(b) heat;
(c) internal energy.

2 A hot body is brought into contact with a colder body until their temperatures are the same. Assume that no other bodies are around. Is the heat lost by one body equal to the heat gained by the other? Is the temperature drop of one body equal to the temperature increase of the other?

3 A body at a given uniform temperature of 300 K and internal energy 8×10^6 J is split into two equal halves.
(a) Has any heat been exchanged?
(b) What is the temperature of each half?
(c) What is the internal energy of each half?

4 The volume of 1 mol of hydrogen gas (molar mass $2\ \text{g mol}^{-1}$) at stp (standard temperature and pressure) is 22.4 L.

(a) Find out how much volume corresponds to each molecule of hydrogen.
(b) Consider now 1 mol of lead (molar mass 207 g mol^{-1}, density 11.3×10^3 kg m^{-3}). How much volume corresponds to each molecule of lead?
(c) Find the ratio of these volumes (hydrogen to lead).
(d) Hence determine that the order of magnitude of the ratio

$$\frac{\text{separation of hydrogen molecules}}{\text{separation of lead atoms}}$$

is 10.

5 The density of aluminium is 2.7 g cm^{-3} and its molar mass is 27 g mol^{-1}.
(a) Find the mass of an atom of aluminium.
(b) Find the number of aluminium atoms per cubic metre.

6 The density of copper is 8.96 g cm^{-3} and its molar mass is 64 g mol^{-1}.
(a) Find the mass of an atom of copper.
(b) Find the number of copper atoms per cubic metre.

Thermal properties

This chapter is an introduction to the basic principles of calorimetry and to experimental methods used in measuring specific heat capacities and latent heats.

Objectives

By the end of this chapter you should be able to:

- state the basic definitions of calorimetry, such as *specific heat capacity* and *specific latent heats of fusion* and *vaporization*;
- understand why temperature stays constant during a phase change;
- outline methods for determining specific and latent heats experimentally;
- solve *calorimetry problems* using $Q = mc\Delta T$ and $Q = mL$;
- state the factors that affect the rate of *evaporation* and distinguish evaporation from boiling;
- appreciate *Boltzmann's equation*, the fundamental relationship between the absolute temperature and the average kinetic energy of the molecules.

Specific heat capacity

When thermal energy is provided to a body, the temperature of the body will, in general, increase.

▶ The amount of thermal energy needed to raise the temperature of a mass of one kilogram of a substance by one kelvin is called the *specific heat capacity*, c, of the material. To raise the temperature of a mass m by ΔT kelvins, the amount of thermal energy required is therefore

$$Q = mc\,\Delta T$$

(assuming that c is temperature independent). The units of specific heat capacity are $\text{J kg}^{-1}\text{ K}^{-1}$.

As Table 2.1 shows, different substances have different values of **specific heat capacity**.

Consider, for example, iron and silver. The thermal energy required to raise the temperature of 1 kg of iron by 1 K is 470 J, whereas the energy required to raise the temperature of 1 kg of silver by 1 K is only 234 J, which is about half. On the other hand, it is known that the thermal energy required to raise the temperature of 1 mol of iron and 1 mol of silver by 1 K is about the same. This can

Substance	$c/\text{J kg}^{-1}\text{ K}^{-1}$
Aluminium	910
Lead	130
Iron	470
Copper	390
Silver	234
Water	4200
Ethanol	2430
Ice	2200
Marble	880

Table 2.1 Specific heat capacities.

be understood in terms of the molecular picture of matter as follows.

A given amount of thermal energy provided to 1 mol of any substance will be divided among the same number of molecules (since 1 mol has Avogadro's number of molecules) and so, on average, the kinetic energy of each molecule will increase by the same amount. This shows up macroscopically as the same increase in temperature. The reason that different materials show different temperature increases when the same amount of thermal energy is provided to 1 kg of each material (i.e. they have different specific heat capacities) is that 1 kg of each material contains a different number of molecules.

The product of mass times specific heat capacity defines the **heat capacity** of a body, C:

$$C = mc$$

Heat capacity is the amount of thermal energy required to change the temperature of a body by one kelvin. The concept of heat capacity is useful when a body consists of a number of parts of different specific heat capacities, such as, for example, a metal tank containing water. If the tank has mass M and specific heat capacity c and the water has mass m and specific heat capacity c', then the heat capacity of the water tank is

$$C = Mc + mc'$$

Knowing the heat capacity of the water tank allows us to say that, if a quantity of thermal energy Q is given to the water tank, then the rise in temperature ΔT will be found from

$$Q = C\Delta T$$

Unlike specific heat capacity, which depends on the substance, heat capacity only depends on the particular body in question.

Example question

Q1

When a car brakes, an amount of thermal energy equal to 112 500 J is generated in the brake drums. If the mass of the brake drums is 28 kg and their specific heat capacity is 460.5 J kg^{-1} K^{-1}, what is the change in their temperature?

Answer

From $Q = mc\Delta T$ we find

$$\Delta T = \frac{Q}{mc}$$
$$= \frac{112500}{28 \times 460.5}$$
$$= 8.7\,°\text{C}$$

Thermal equilibrium

It is everyday experience that thermal energy flows from hot bodies into cold bodies (see Figure 2.1). When a cold and a hot body are placed in contact, thermal energy will flow until the temperature of both bodies is the same. (In fact, temperature can be defined as that property which is common to the two bodies in this case.) This state of affairs is called thermal equilibrium. The amount of thermal energy lost by the hot body is equal to the amount of thermal energy gained by the cold body.

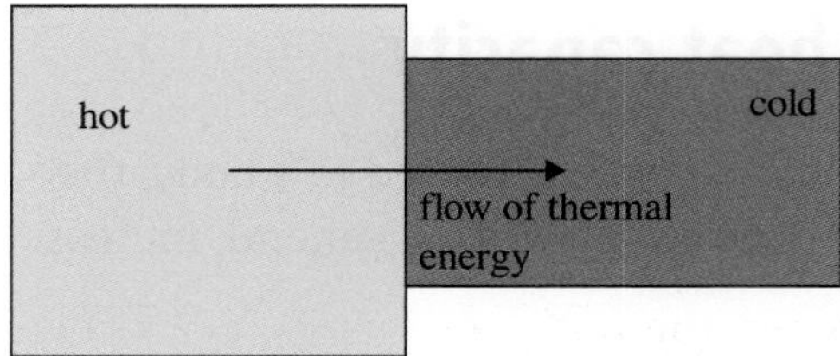

Figure 2.1 In an isolated system thermal energy always flows from the hotter body to the colder.

Example question

Q2

A piece of iron of mass 200 g and temperature 300 °C is dropped into 1.00 kg of water of temperature 20 °C. What will be the eventual temperature of the water? (Take c for iron as 470 J kg^{-1} K^{-1} and for water as 4200 J kg^{-1} K^{-1}.)

Answer

Let T be the final unknown temperature. The iron will also be at this temperature, so

amount of thermal energy lost by the iron

$$= m_{\text{iron}} c_{\text{iron}} (300 - T)$$

and

amount of thermal energy gained by water
$= m_{water} c_{water} (T - 20)$

Conservation of energy demands that
thermal energy lost = thermal energy gained, so
$m_{iron} c_{iron} (300 - T) = m_{water} c_{water} (T - 20)$
$\Rightarrow T = 26.1\ °C \approx 26\ °C$

Note how the large specific heat capacity of water results in a small increase in the temperature of water compared with the huge drop in the temperature of the iron.

Change of state

Ordinary matter can exist as a solid, a liquid or a gas. These three are called states of matter. Heating can turn ice into water and water into steam. Ice will turn into water if the temperature of the ice is its melting temperature: 0 °C. Similarly, to turn water into steam the temperature must be 100 °C. This means that if we are given a piece of ice at a temperature of, say, −10 °C, to melt it we must first raise its temperature from −10 °C to zero.

▶ Once at the melting point, any additional thermal energy supplied does not increase the temperature. Rather, this thermal energy is used to overcome the forces between the water molecules in the ice: that is, to provide the work necessary to separate the molecules and bring the solid to the liquid phase at the same temperature.

After all of the ice has turned into water, we have water at a temperature of 0 °C. Any additional thermal energy supplied will increase the temperature of the water. When the temperature reaches 100 °C, any additional thermal energy supplied is used to turn water into steam at the same temperature of 100 °C. That is, the thermal energy is used to do the work necessary to move the molecules further apart. After all of the water has turned into steam, the temperature begins to increase again. We thus see that when the state of matter is changing, the temperature does not change.

▶ The thermal energy required to melt a unit mass of material at its melting point is called the *specific latent heat of fusion*, L_f, and the thermal energy required to vaporize a unit mass at its boiling point is called the *specific latent heat of vaporization*, L_v. Thus to melt or vaporize a quantity of mass m, we require a quantity of thermal energy

$$Q = mL_f \quad \text{and} \quad Q = mL_v$$

respectively. The specific latent heats have units of J kg^{-1}.

Table 2.2 shows values of the **specific latent heats** of fusion and vaporization for various substances.

The term latent heat (without the 'specific' in front) is used to denote the thermal energy necessary to change the phase of a substance irrespective of mass.

Substance	Specific latent heat of fusion/kJ kg^{-1}	Melting temperature/°C	Specific latent heat of vaporization/kJ kg^{-1}	Boiling temperature/°C
Water	334.4	0	2257	100
Ethanol	108.9	−114	840	78.3
Aluminium	395	660	10548	2467
Lead	23	327	849.7	1740
Copper	205	1078	2567	5190
Iron	275	1540	6285	2800

Table 2.2 Latent heats of fusion and vaporization together with the melting and boiling temperatures.

Figure 2.2 shows how the temperature of 0.5 kg of a hypothetical substance changes as thermal energy is provided to it.

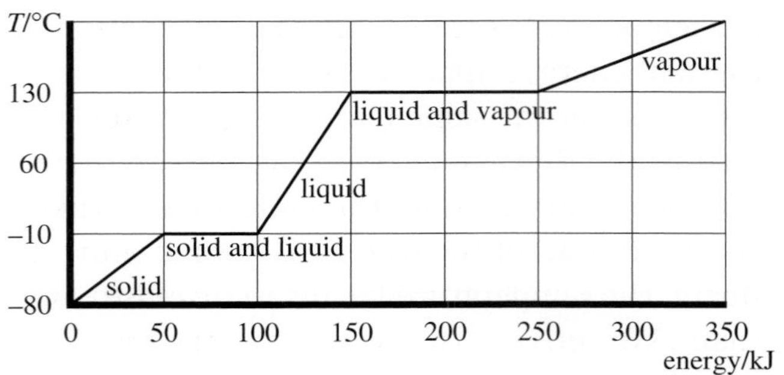

Figure 2.2 When thermal energy is provided to a solid substance, the temperature increases, except when the phase is changing.

We may deduce the following from Figure 2.2. First, that the melting and boiling points are, respectively, −10 °C and 130 °C. The specific latent heat of fusion is found from

$$Q = mL_f$$
$$\Rightarrow L_f = \frac{Q}{m}$$
$$= \frac{50\text{ kJ}}{0.5\text{ kg}}$$
$$= 100\text{ kJ kg}^{-1}$$

and the specific latent heat of vaporization is found from

$$Q = mL_v$$
$$\Rightarrow L_v = \frac{Q}{m}$$
$$= \frac{100\text{ kJ}}{0.5\text{ kg}} = 200\text{ kJ kg}^{-1}$$

The specific heat capacity in the solid phase is found from

$$Q = mc\Delta T$$
$$\Rightarrow c = \frac{Q}{m\Delta T}$$
$$= \frac{50\text{ kJ}}{0.5\text{ kg} \times 70\text{ K}}$$
$$= 1.43\text{ kJ kg}^{-1}\text{ K}^{-1}$$

In the liquid it is $c = 0.71$ kJ kg^{-1} K^{-1} and in the vapour it is $c = 2.86$ kJ kg^{-1} K^{-1}.

If thermal energy is supplied at a *constant* rate to a given mass of a solid, then its temperature as a function of time might be as shown in Figure 2.3.

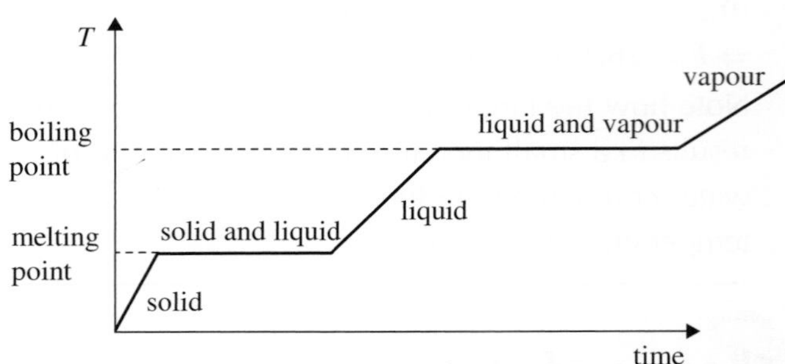

Figure 2.3 Graph of temperature as a function of time when a substance is heated at a constant rate.

The temperatures corresponding to the horizontal parts are the melting and boiling temperatures.

Knowledge of the rate of thermal energy supply and the actual time over which melting and boiling take place enables us to determine the specific latent heats. (See Example questions 4 and 5 below.)

Example questions

Q3

An ice cube of mass 25.0 g and temperature −10.0 °C is dropped into a glass of water of mass 300.0 g and temperature 20.0 °C. What is the temperature eventually? (Specific heat capacity of ice = 2200 J kg^{-1} K^{-1}; latent heat of fusion of ice = 334 kJ kg^{-1}.)

Answer

Let this final temperature be T. Ignoring thermal energy lost by the glass itself, water will cool down by losing thermal energy. This thermal energy will be taken up by the ice to:

(a) increase its temperature from −10 °C to 0 °C, the thermal energy required being $25 \times 10^{-3} \times 2200 \times 10$;

(b) melt the ice cube into water at 0 °C, the thermal energy required being $25 \times 10^{-3} \times 334 \times 10^3$;

(c) increase the temperature of the former ice cube from 0 °C to the final temperature T.

Thus

$$0.3 \times 4200 \times (20 - T) = (25 \times 10^{-3} \times 2200 \times 10) + (25 \times 10^{-3} \times 334 \times 10^{3}) + (25 \times 10^{-3} \times 4200) \times T$$

Solving for T gives $T = 11.9\ °\text{C}$.

Q4

Thermal energy is provided at a constant rate of $833\ \text{J s}^{-1}$ to 1 kg of copper at the melting temperature. If it takes 4 minutes to completely melt the copper, find the latent heat of fusion of copper.

Answer

The thermal energy needed to melt 1 kg of copper is L, the specific latent heat of fusion. In 4 minutes the heat supplied is $833 \times 60 \times 4 = 200\ \text{kJ}$, so $L_f = 200\ \text{kJ kg}^{-1}$.

Q5

Look back at Figure 2.3 and determine the relative sizes of the specific latent heats and specific heat capacities. Recall that thermal energy is provided at a constant rate.

Answer

To compare the specific heats in the solid, liquid and vapour phases remember that $\Delta Q = mc\,\Delta T$ and so

$$\frac{\Delta Q}{\Delta t} = mc\frac{\Delta T}{\Delta t}$$

$$\Rightarrow c = \frac{(\Delta Q/\Delta t)}{m(\Delta T/\Delta t)}$$

Since the rate of thermal energy supplied is constant, it follows that the phase in which the rate of increase of temperature is the largest has the *smallest* specific heat capacity. Clearly, the transition that lasts the longest also has the largest specific latent heat.

Measuring specific heats

The *specific heat capacity* of a solid or liquid can be measured using an electrical method that directly measures the amount of thermal energy flow into a body. The liquid or solid is placed inside a calorimeter of known heat capacity, C, and its mass and initial temperature recorded. The calorimeter is insulated and an electrical heating element is inserted through a small opening at the top into the liquid or into a hole drilled in the solid (see Figure 2.4). The heating element is connected to a source of potential difference and the voltage across it is recorded, as is the current through the element. A thermometer is also inserted into a hole drilled in the solid. If the material to be measured is liquid, then a similar arrangement can be used, stirring the liquid every time a temperature measurement is made.

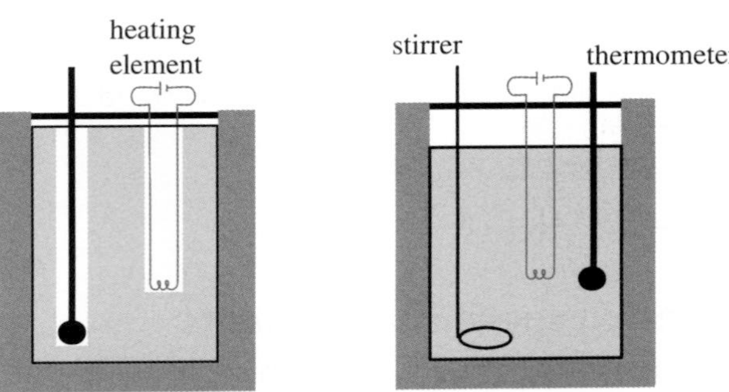

Figure 2.4 Apparatus for measuring the specific heat capacity of a solid (left) and a liquid (right).

The current is switched on at $t = 0$ and allowed to run until the temperature is increased by 40 to 50 °C. The temperature is recorded at regular intervals of about a minute. If the maximum temperature reached after time t is T_{max}, then the energy supplied by the battery to the liquid is

$$\text{energy supplied} = VIt$$

where I is the current in the heater and V the voltage across it. The thermal energy absorbed by the liquid and the calorimeter is

$$\text{energy absorbed} = mc(T_{max} - T) + C(T_{max} - T)$$

Equating the two quantities of energy allows us to determine c.

Another method, the method of mixtures, measures the specific heat capacity as follows. A hot solid of known initial temperature is put in an insulated calorimeter, of known heat capacity and initial temperature, which contains a liquid such as water. The final temperature of the water is recorded after thermal equilibrium has been reached. Thus, consider a mass of 0.400 kg of a solid at 80 °C that is put in a 100 g copper calorimeter containing 800 g of water at 20 °C. The final temperature of the water is measured to be 22 °C. From these values, we may deduce the specific heat capacity of the solid as follows.

Amount of thermal energy lost by the solid:

$$0.400 \times c \times (80 - 22) = 23.2c \text{ J}$$

Amount of thermal energy gained by the calorimeter and the water:

$$0.100 \times 390 \times (22 - 20) + 0.800 \times 4200 \times (22 - 20) = 6798 \text{ J}$$

Equating the two we find

$$c = 293 \text{ J kg}^{-1}\text{K}^{-1}$$

Measuring specific latent heats

To measure the specific latent heat of fusion of ice, a simple method (the method of mixtures) is to put a quantity of ice at 0 °C (the ice is in a mixture with water at 0 °C) into a calorimeter containing water at a few degrees above room temperature. (The ice is blotted dry before being thrown into the calorimeter. Its mass can be determined by weighing the calorimeter at the end of the experiment.) Thus, suppose that 25 g of ice at 0 °C is placed in an aluminium calorimeter of mass 250 g containing 300 g of water at 24 °C. The temperature of the water is measured at regular intervals of time until the temperature reaches a minimum value. Suppose that this temperature is 17 °C. The calorimeter and water lost thermal energy, which the ice received. So

Thermal energy lost by calorimeter and water:

$$0.250 \times 910 \times (24 - 17) + 0.300 \times 4198 \times (24 - 17) = 10408 \text{ J}$$

Thermal energy received by ice:

$$0.025 \times L + 0.025 \times 4198 \times 17 = 0.025 \times L + 1784$$

Equating the two gives

$$1784 + 0.025 \times L = 10408$$
$$\Rightarrow L \approx 340 \text{ kJ kg}^{-1}$$

To measure the specific latent heat of vaporization of water we can use an electrical method. Water is heated in a double container (as shown in Figure 2.5) with an electric heater.

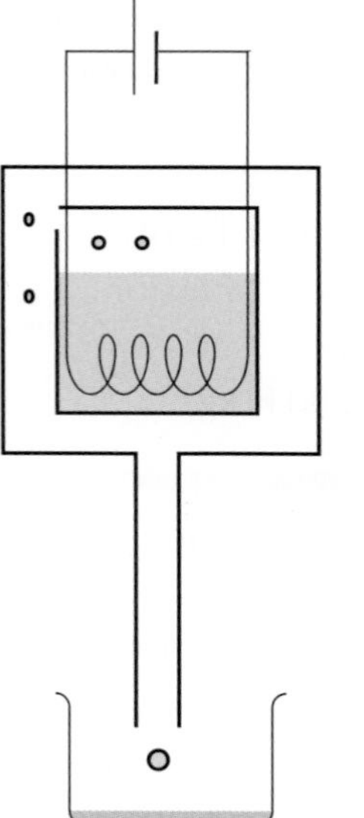

Figure 2.5 Steam condenses in the outer container and the water is collected in a beaker.

Steam can leave the inner container through a small hole and collects in the outer container, where it condenses into water. This water can be allowed to drip into a beaker, which can then be weighed to determine the mass of water that has been boiled away. If the experiment lasted for time t and the voltage and current in the heater were measured as V and I, respectively, the energy supplied was VIt. If m is the mass of water that boiled away, the thermal energy it received was mL_v. Equating the two expressions allows us to determine the specific latent heat of vaporization.

Evaporation

The molecules of a gas move about with a distribution of speeds. The same is true for the molecules of a liquid. The *faster* molecules are the *most energetic* and if they find themselves at the surface of the liquid they may escape from the liquid. This phenomenon is known as *evaporation*. Note that unlike boiling (where molecules from anywhere within the volume occupied by the liquid can escape) only surface molecules participate in evaporation. This means that the average kinetic energy of the molecules that stay behind is *reduced*, which in turn means that the temperature of the liquid is *reduced*, since temperature is a measure of the average kinetic energy of the molecules of the substance.

The rate of evaporation (that is, the number of molecules escaping the liquid per second) increases as the surface area and temperature of the liquid are increased. If the liquid is placed in an enclosed volume, then the molecules that escape collect over the liquid and their pressure is called vapour pressure. The vapour pressure increases as more molecules escape and equilibrium is reached when as many molecules escape as fall back into the liquid. Thus, if a stream of air is directed at the vapour over the liquid, hence pushing away the evaporated molecules, the rate of evaporation will increase.

The kinetic theory of gases

The properties of gases can be understood in terms of a simple but effective mechanical model. The gas consists of a very large number of molecules moving randomly about with a range of speeds and colliding with each other and the container walls. We can make a model of this by making certain assumptions and seeing what these lead to. The basic assumptions of the kinetic theory of gases are:

1 A gas consists of a large number of molecules.
2 Molecules move with a range of speeds.
3 The volume of the molecules is negligible compared with the volume of the gas itself.
4 The collisions of the molecules with each other and the container walls are elastic.
5 Molecules exert no forces on each other or the container except when in contact.
6 The duration of collisions is very small compared with the time between collisions.
7 The molecules obey Newton's laws of mechanics.

Some of these assumptions are illustrated in Figure 2.6.

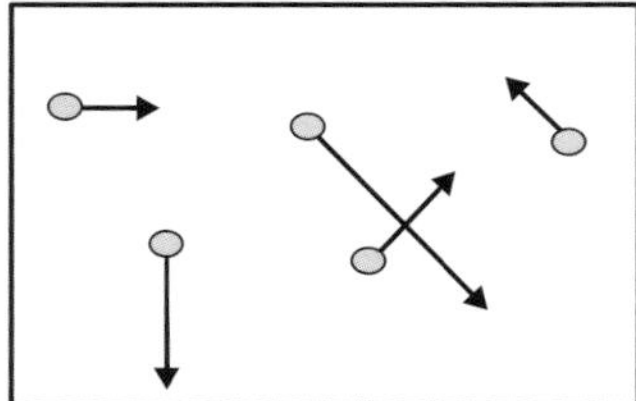

Figure 2.6 The molecules move randomly in the volume of the container with a range of speeds.

Using these assumptions together with the laws of mechanics and the equation of state allows the derivation of one of the most important formulae in physics, namely the Boltzmann equation

$$\frac{1}{2}m\overline{v^2} = \frac{3}{2}kT$$

Here the speed v is defined by

$$\overline{v^2} = \frac{(v_1^2 + v_2^2 + \cdots + v_N^2)}{N}$$

So v is the square root of the *average of the squares of the speeds of the molecules of the gas* (the average of the velocity vectors of all the molecules is zero since they move randomly in all directions). We call v the root mean square speed or rms speed. (It must be realized that v is not the average speed of the molecules – but it is numerically close to the average, so we are usually excused for calling v the average molecular speed even if it is not technically correct.)

Appearing in this equation is a new constant of physics, the Boltzmann constant k, the value of which is $k = 1.38 \times 10^{-23}$ J K^{-1} (it is the ratio of the gas constant R to the Avogadro constant).

▶ The meaning of this important relation is that

average kinetic energy of molecules
$\propto$ absolute temperature

that is, the absolute temperature is a measure of the average kinetic energy of the molecules of a substance.

Example questions

Q6

Four molecules have speeds of 300 m s^{-1}, 350 m s^{-1}, 380 m s^{-1} and 500 m s^{-1}. Find the average speed and the root mean square speed.

Answer

$$\text{average speed} = \frac{300 + 350 + 380 + 500}{4}\ \text{m s}^{-1}$$
$$= 382.5\ \text{m s}^{-1}$$

$$\sqrt{\overline{v^2}} = \sqrt{\frac{300^2 + 350^2 + 380^2 + 500^2}{4}}\ \text{m s}^{-1} = 389.5\ \text{m s}^{-1}$$

Q7

If the root mean square molecular speed is doubled, what is the new temperature?

Answer

From the Boltzmann equation it follows at once that the temperature is four times as big.

Molecular explanation of pressure

The pressure of a gas originates from the collisions of the molecules with the walls of its container. At every collision, each molecule has its momentum changed and so a force acts from the wall onto the molecule. By Newton's third law, the molecule exerts an equal and opposite force on the wall. The total force due to all the colliding molecules divided by the area over which the force acts gives the pressure of the gas.

▶ Pressure is the normal force per unit area. The pressure in a gas results from the collisions of the gas molecules with the walls of its container (and *not* from collisions between molecules).

From the molecular point of view, we may identify two factors that affect the pressure of the gas. The first is the average molecular speed (the higher the speed, the larger the change in momentum of the molecules and so the higher the force – see Figure 2.7).

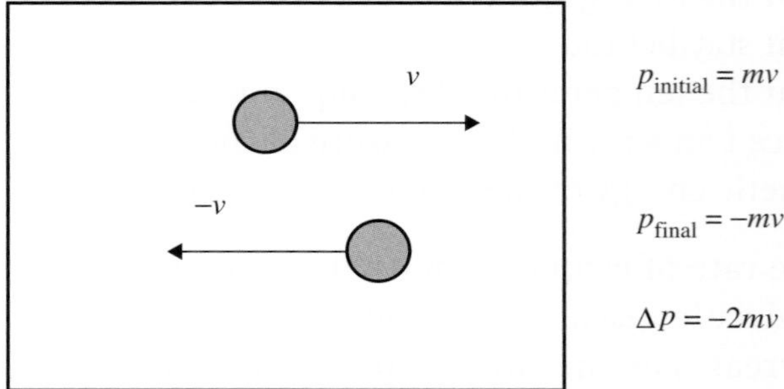

Figure 2.7 A molecule exerts a force on the container wall because its momentum p changes with every collision.

The second factor is the frequency of collisions. The more frequent the collisions, the higher the pressure. Thus, in providing molecular explanations for pressure it is sufficient to remember that roughly

$$P \propto \text{speed} \times \text{frequency of collisions}$$

As an application of this, consider a gas that has been heated under constant volume. The molecules are moving faster on average (increased temperature) and the frequency with which the collisions take place also increases (the time between collisions is reduced since molecules are moving faster). For *both* reasons (speed and frequency) the pressure then goes up.

By contrast, if a gas is compressed isothermally, the average speed stays the same. But the distance molecules have to travel between collisions with the walls is reduced (since the volume is reduced) and so the frequency of collisions increases. Hence the pressure increases (because of frequency only).

Example questions

Q8

A gas is compressed *slowly* by a piston. Explain why the temperature of the gas will stay the same.

Answer

If a gas is compressed slowly, the speed with which the molecules rebound off the piston is the same as that before the collision with the piston. Hence, the average kinetic energy of the molecules stays the same. Since the average kinetic energy is proportional to the absolute temperature of the gas, the temperature will stay the same.

Q9

A gas is compressed *rapidly* by a piston (see Figure 2.8). Explain why the temperature of the gas will increase.

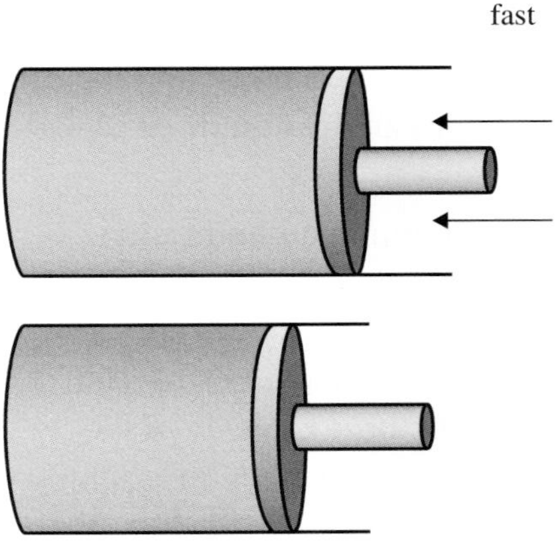

Figure 2.8.

Answer

The rapid movement of the piston means that molecules will rebound off the piston with an *increased* speed. Hence the average kinetic energy of the molecules will increase, and since the average kinetic energy is proportional to the absolute temperature of the gas, the temperature will increase as well.

Q10

A gas expands isothermally. Explain from a molecular point of view why the pressure decreases.

Answer

The volume of the gas expands, which means that, on average, molecules have a larger distance to travel between successive collisions with the walls. Thus, the collisions are less frequent than before and so the pressure decreases.

Q11

A gas is heated at constant pressure. Explain why the volume must increase as well.

Answer

The temperature increases and so the molecules move faster, on average. From $P \propto$ speed $\times$ frequency, we deduce that the frequency of collisions must decrease if the pressure is to stay the same. This can happen if the volume of the gas increases so that molecules have a longer distance to travel in between collisions.

QUESTIONS

In the questions that follow, you may need to use the specific heat capacities shown in Table 2.1 on page 163 and the latent heats shown in Table 2.2 on page 165.

1 Define what is meant by specific heat capacity of a substance. Consider two metals that have different specific heat capacities. The thermal energy required to increase the temperature of 1 mol of aluminium and 1 mol of copper by the same amount are about the same. Yet the specific heat capacities of the two metals are very different. Suggest a reason for this.

2 A body of mass 0.150 kg has its temperature increased by 5.00 °C when 385 J of thermal energy is provided to it. What is the body's specific heat capacity?

3 A radiator made out of iron has a mass of 45.0 kg and is filled with 23.0 kg of water.
- (a) What is the heat capacity of the water-filled radiator?
- (b) If thermal energy is provided to the radiator at the rate of 450 W, how long will it take for the temperature to increase by 20.0 °C?

4 A car of mass 1360 kg descends from a hill of height 86 m at a constant speed of 20 km h^{-1}. Assuming that all the potential energy of the car goes into heating the brakes, find the rise in the temperature of the brakes. (Take the heat capacity of the brakes to be 16 kJ K^{-1} and ignore any thermal energy losses to the surroundings.)

5 The water in an iron pipe has frozen to ice at −4.8 °C. The heat capacity of the pipe is 7.1 kJ K^{-1}. The volume of ice in the pipe is 12.3 L. What is the combined heat capacity of the pipe and ice? To melt the ice, a heater of power output 4.99 kW is connected to the pipe. How long will it take for the ice to melt? (Density of ice = 0.929 kg L^{-1}; specific heat capacity of ice = 2.20 kJ kg^{-1} K^{-1}; latent heat of fusion of ice = 334 kJ kg^{-1}.)

6 How much ice at −10 °C must be dropped into a cup containing 300 g of water at 20 °C in order for the temperature of the water to be reduced to 10 °C? The cup itself has a mass of 150 g and is made out of aluminium. Assume that no thermal energy is lost to the surroundings.

7 The surface of a pond of area 20 m^2 is covered by ice of uniform thickness 6 cm. The temperature of the ice is −5 °C. How much thermal energy is required to melt this amount of ice into water at 0 °C? (Take the density of ice to be 900 kg m^{-3}.)

8 A frozen pond, of surface area 50.0 m^2, is covered by a sheet of ice of thickness 15 cm. If the pond receives solar radiation of intensity 342 W m^{-2}, find out what fraction of the ice will be turned into water in 6.0 h. (Take the ice temperature to be 0.0 °C and the latent heat of fusion of ice as 334 kJ kg^{-1}. Take the density of ice to be 900 kg m^{-3}.)

9 Radiation from the sun falls on the frozen surface of a pond at a rate of 600 W m^{-2}. If the ice temperature is 0 °C, find how long it will take to melt a 1.0 cm thick layer of ice. (Take the density of ice to be 900 kg m^{-3}.) What assumption have you made in reaching your answer?

10 (a) How much thermal energy is required to warm 1.0 kg ice initially at −10 °C to ice at 0 °C?

(b) How much thermal energy is required to melt the ice at 0 °C.

(c) How much thermal energy is required to further increase the temperature of the water from 0 °C to 10 °C.

(d) In which stage (warming the ice, melting the ice, warming the water) is the thermal energy requirement largest?

11 Ice at 0 °C is added to 1 L of water at 20 °C, cooling it down to 10 °C. How much ice was added?

12 A quantity of 100 g of ice at 0 °C and 50 g steam at 100 °C are added to a container that has 150 g water at 30 °C. What is the final temperature in the container? Ignore the container itself in your calculations.

13 A calorimeter of mass 90 g and specific heat capacity 400.0 J kg^{-1} K^{-1} contains 300.0 g of a liquid at 15.0 °C. An electric heater rated at 20.0 W warms the liquid to 19.0 °C in 3.0 min. Assuming there are no thermal energy losses to the surroundings, find the specific heat capacity of the liquid.

14 A calorimeter of heat capacity 25 J K^{-1} contains 140 g of a liquid; an immersion heater is used to provide thermal energy at a rate of 40 W for a total time of 4.0 min. The temperature of the liquid increases by 15.8 °C. Calculate the specific heat capacity of the liquid. State an assumption made in reaching this result.

15 A hair dryer consists of a coil that warms air and a fan that blows the warm air out. The coil generates thermal energy at a rate of 600 W. Take the density of air to be 1.25 kg m^{-3} and its specific heat capacity to be 990 J kg^{-1} K^{-1}. The dryer takes air from a room at 20 °C and delivers it at a temperature of 60 °C.

(a) What mass of air flows through the dryer per second?

(b) What volume of air flows per second?

16 An auditorium of size 40 m × 20 m × 8 m has 600 people in it. The temperature of the air is initially 27 °C. It takes 29 J of thermal energy to raise the temperature of 1 mol of air by 1 K and the molar mass of air is about 29 g mol^{-1}. Take the density of air to be constant at 1.25 kg m^{-3}.

(a) How many moles of air are there in the auditorium?

(b) Assuming that each person gives off thermal energy at a rate of 80 W, calculate how fast the temperature in the auditorium is rising. Assume that the auditorium is closed so that cooler air does not enter.

17 (a) Discuss the factors that affect the evaporation rate of a liquid.
(b) Explain, in terms of molecular behaviour, why cooling takes place as a result of evaporation.
(c) Give one practical application of the cooling effect of evaporation.

18 A container of fixed volume is filled with an ideal gas at 0.00 °C. The total kinetic energy of the molecules in the container is E. An identical container has twice the mass of gas in it and the total kinetic energy of those molecules is $2E$. Find the temperature of the second container.

19 A container is filled with a mixture of nitrogen and oxygen. What is the ratio of the rms speed of oxygen molecules to that of nitrogen molecules? (Molar mass of oxygen = 32 g mol^{-1}; molar mass of nitrogen = 28 g mol^{-1}.)

20 By what factor does the rms speed of neon molecules increase if their temperature increases by a factor of 4?

Ideal gases

A gas is a collection of a very large number of molecules. We call the gas ideal if the molecules do not exert any forces on each other. Many real gases show behaviour that is a very close approximation of ideal gas behaviour. As a result of collisions between the molecules and the walls of the container of the gas, pressure develops. The pressure, volume, temperature and the number of moles in the gas are related through the ideal gas law. Application of the laws of mechanics to the motion of the molecules leads to the connection between the average kinetic energy of molecules and the absolute temperature of the gas.

Objectives

By the end of this chapter you should be able to:

- state the definition of *pressure*: $P = \frac{F}{A}$;
- understand that an ideal gas is a gas in which the molecules *do not exert forces on each other* except when colliding; an ideal gas obeys the law $PV = nRT$ at *all* pressures, temperatures and volumes;
- understand the *ideal gas law* and solve problems using it: $\frac{P_1V_1}{n_1T_1} = \frac{P_2V_2}{n_2T_2}$;
- appreciate that pressure in a gas develops as a result of *collisions* between the molecules and the walls of the container in which the *momentum* of molecules changes.

Pressure

Pressure is defined as the normal force to an area per unit area. The pressure on the small circular area A in Figure 3.1 is thus given by the expression

$$P = \frac{F\cos\theta}{A}$$

The unit of pressure is newton per square metre, N m^{-2}, also known as pascal, Pa. Another commonly used non-SI unit is the atmosphere, atm, which equals 1.013×10^5 Pa.

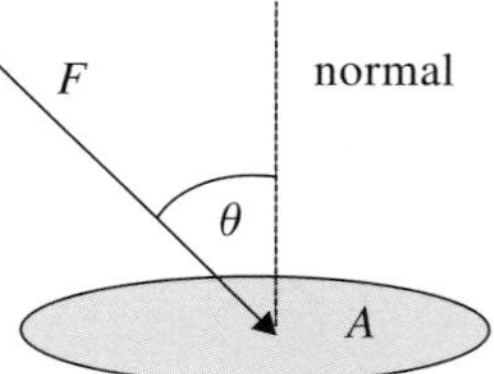

Figure 3.1 Pressure is the force normal to an area divided by that area.

Example question

Q1

Two hollow cubes of side 0.25 cm with one face missing are placed together at the missing face (see Figure 3.2). The air inside the solid formed is pumped out. What force is necessary to separate the cubes?

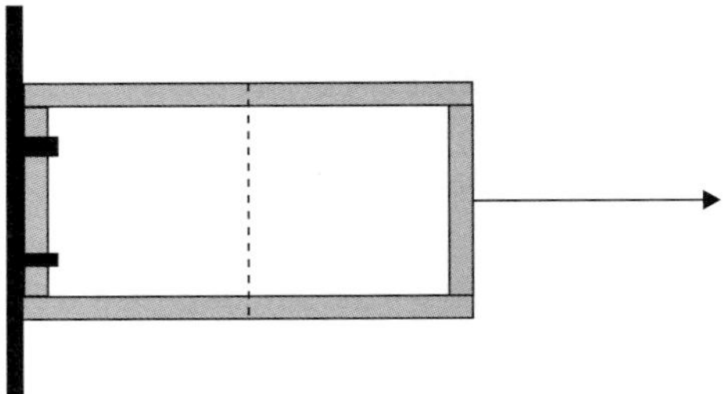

Figure 3.2 What force is necessary to separate the cubes?

Answer

The pressure inside the solid is zero and outside it equals atmospheric pressure, 1.013×10^5 Pa. Thus, the force is

$$F = PA$$
$$= 1.013 \times 10^5 \times (0.25)^2$$
$$= 6.33 \times 10^3 \text{ N}$$

Gases

It is convenient to use the number of moles, n, of the gas rather than the mass itself to specify the quantity of a gas. Recall that 1 mol of any substance contains the same number of molecules, the Avogadro constant

$$N_A = 6.02 \times 10^{23} \text{ molecules mol}^{-1}$$

and that the number of moles of a gas can be found by dividing the total number of molecules by the Avogadro constant

$$n = \frac{N}{N_A}$$

The size of molecules varies from substance to substance, but the typical order of magnitude of molecular size is in the range from 10^{-8} m to 10^{-10} m.

The parameters P, V, T and n are related to each other. The equation relating them is called the equation of state. Our objective is to discover the equation of state for a gas. To do this a number of simple experiments can be performed as described in the following sections.

Example questions

Q2

How many molecules are there in 6 g of hydrogen gas?

Answer

A quantity of 6 g of hydrogen gas corresponds to 3 mol, since the molar mass of hydrogen gas is 2 g mol^{-1}. Thus, there are $3 \times N_A$ molecules or 1.81×10^{24}.

Q3

Make a rough estimate of the number of water molecules in an ordinary glass of water.

Answer

A glass contains about 0.3 L of water, which has a mass of about 300 g. Since the molar mass of water is 18 g mol^{-1}, it follows that the glass contains

$$\frac{300}{18} \approx 17 \text{ mol}$$

or 10^{25} molecules.

The Boyle–Mariotte law

The equipment shown in Figure 3.3 can be used to investigate the relationship between pressure and volume of a fixed quantity of gas that is kept at constant temperature.

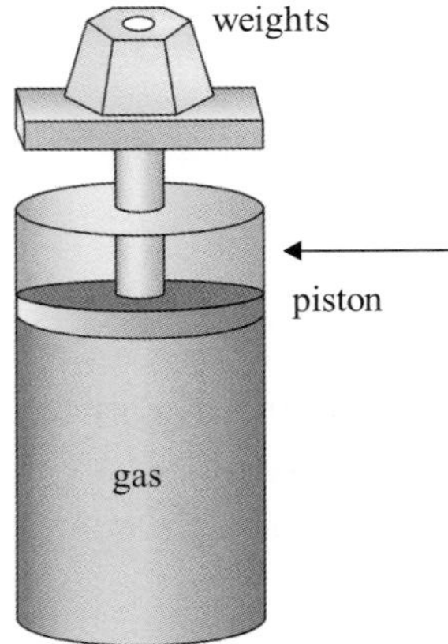

Figure 3.3 Apparatus for verifying the Boyle–Mariotte law.

It consists of a syringe inside which a quantity of air is trapped. The pressure inside the syringe (i.e. the pressure of the air) can be increased by adding weights to the piston as shown. By varying the weights on the piston and recording the changes in the volume of the gas, the pressure–volume relationship can be established.

The results of a typical experiment are shown in Figure 3.4.

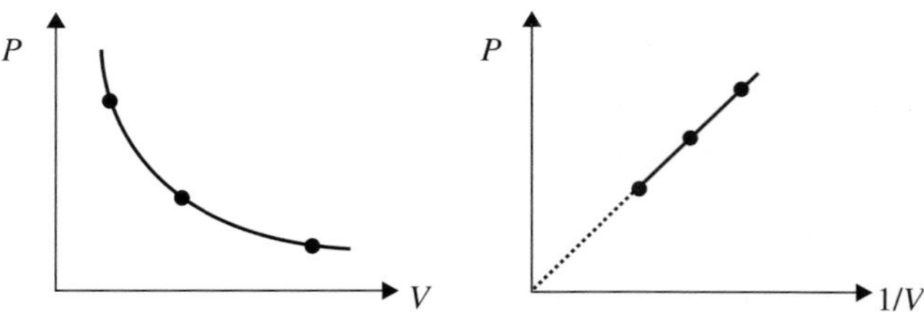

Figure 3.4 The relationship between pressure and volume at constant temperature. The points on the curves have the same temperature.

▶ We can deduce that at constant temperature and with a constant quantity of gas, pressure is inversely proportional to volume, that is

$$PV = \text{constant}$$

as illustrated in Figure 3.5. This is called the Boyle–Mariotte law. (The plot of pressure versus volume is a hyperbola, as in Figure 3.4.)

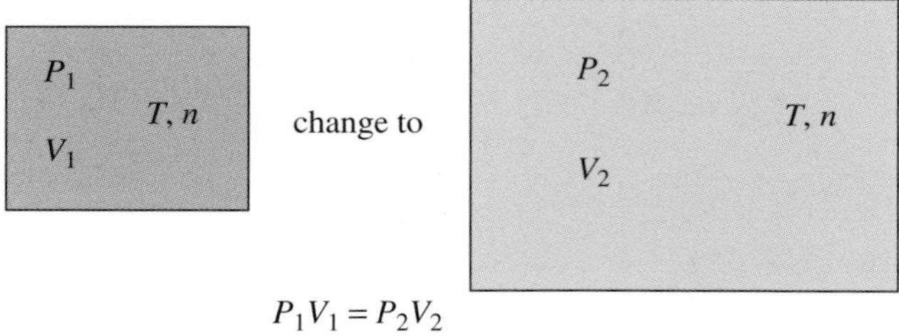

Figure 3.5 The Boyle–Mariotte law.

The hyperbola in the pressure–volume diagram is also known as an isothermal curve or isotherm: the temperature at any point on the curve is constant.

Example question

Q4

The pressure of a gas is 2 atm and its volume 0.9 L. If the pressure is increased to 6 atm at constant temperature, what is the new volume?

Answer

From $P_1V_1 = P_2V_2$ we have $2 \times 0.9 = 6 \times V$ from which $V = 0.3$ L.

The volume–temperature law

The dependence of volume on temperature of a fixed quantity of gas kept at constant pressure can be investigated with the apparatus shown in Figure 3.6. This was how it was first done by Charles and Gay-Lussac. The gas is surrounded by water that is heated from below. As it expands, the pressure is kept constant by adjusting the amount of mercury in the tube so that h stays the same. The constant gas pressure is thus the sum of atmospheric pressure plus the amount ρgh.

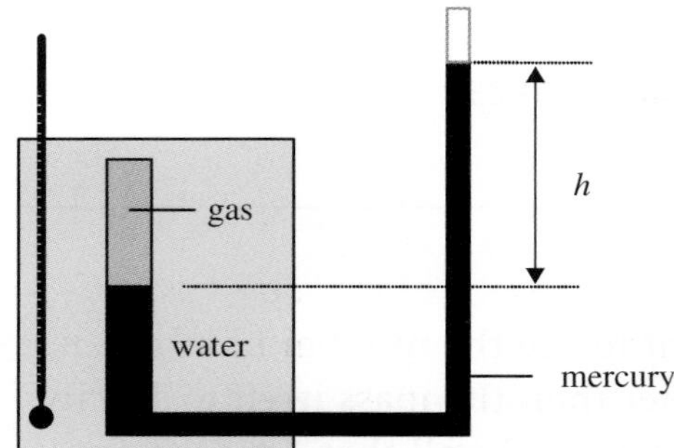

Figure 3.6 Apparatus for verifying the volume–temperature law.

It is found that the volume increases uniformly with temperature. If this same experiment is repeated with a different quantity of gas, or a gas at a different constant pressure, the result is the same. In each case, the straight-line graph of volume versus temperature is different. But the striking fact is that when each straight line is extended backwards it always crosses the temperature axis at −273.15 °C, as in Figure 3.7.

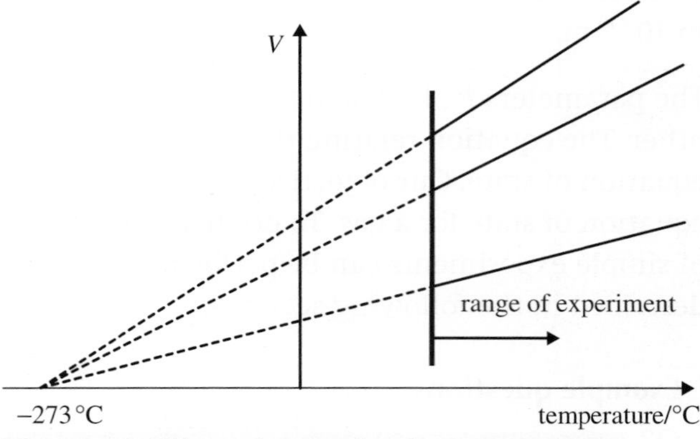

Figure 3.7 When the graph of volume versus temperature is extended backwards, all the lines intersect the temperature axis at the same point.

This suggests that there exists a minimum possible temperature, namely −273.15 °C. Thus, we can devise a new temperature scale, in which the minimum possible temperature occurs at zero. This scale is called the Kelvin scale, and the relationship between the Celsius and Kelvin scales is

$$T\text{ (in kelvin)} = T\text{ (in degrees Celsius)} + 273.15$$

(We usually approximate 273.15 to 273.)

▶ When the temperature is expressed in kelvin, this experiment implies that at constant pressure

$$\frac{V}{T} = \text{constant}$$

When the temperature in a graph of volume versus temperature is expressed in kelvin, the straight line passes through the origin, as in Figure 3.8.

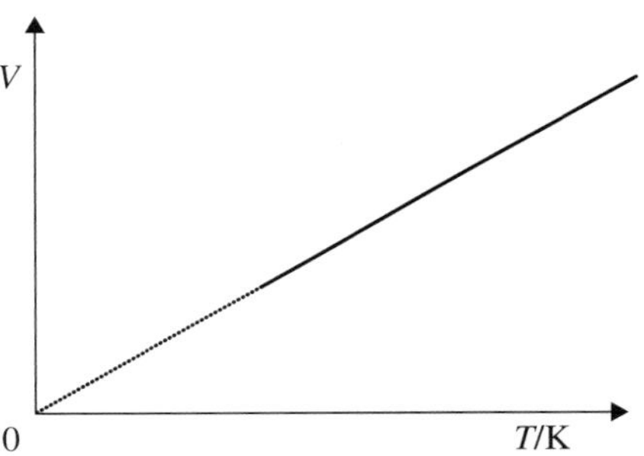

Figure 3.8 If temperature is expressed in kelvin, the graph goes through the origin.

The volume–temperature law is illustrated in Figure 3.9.

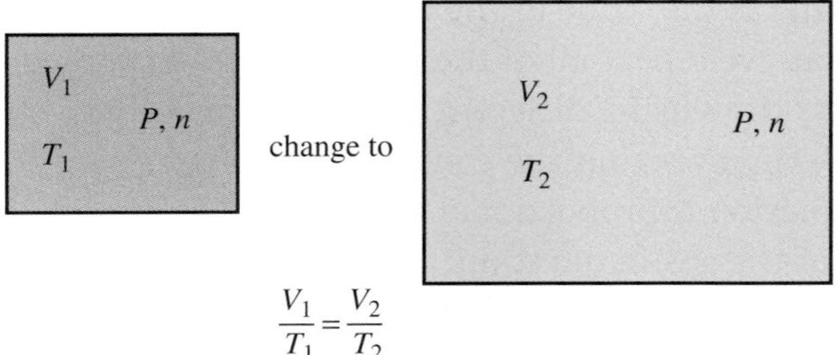

Figure 3.9 The volume–temperature law.

Example question

Q5

A gas expands at constant pressure from an original volume of 2 L at 22 °C to a volume of 4 L. What is the new temperature?

Answer

From

$$\frac{V}{T} = \text{constant}$$

it follows that

$$\frac{2}{295} = \frac{4}{T}$$

and so

$$T = 590\text{ K or } 317\text{ °C}$$

Note that we converted the original temperature into kelvin.

The pressure–temperature law

What remains now is to investigate the dependence of pressure on temperature of a fixed quantity of gas in a fixed volume. This can be done with the apparatus shown in Figure 3.10.

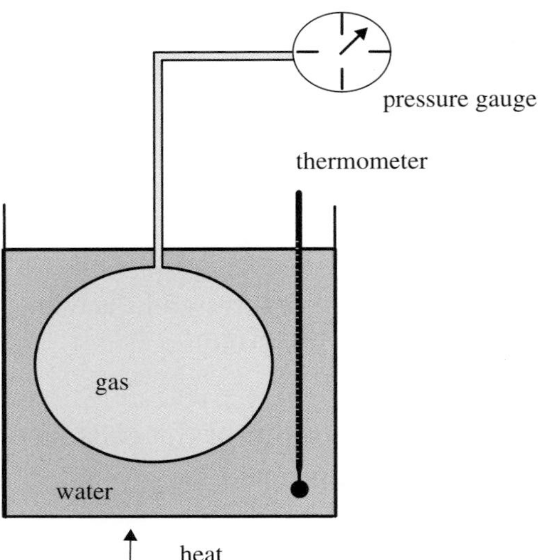

Figure 3.10 Apparatus for verifying the relationship between pressure and temperature.

The gas container is surrounded by water whose temperature can be changed and a pressure gauge measures the pressure of the gas. We find that pressure increases uniformly with increasing temperature. The graph of pressure versus temperature is a straight line that, when extended backwards, again intersects the temperature axis at −273.15 °C, as in Figure 3.11.

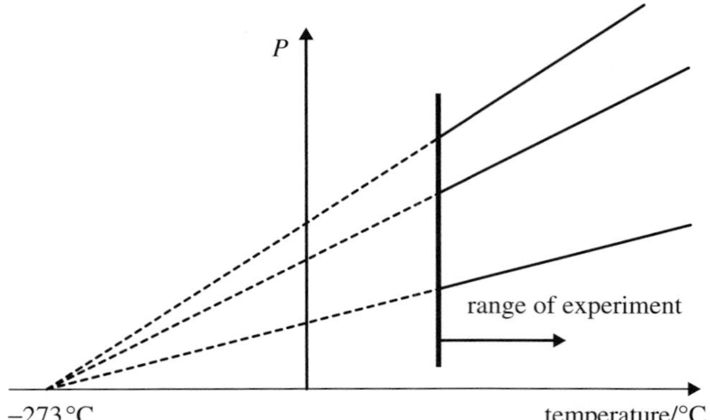

Figure 3.11 The graphs of pressure versus temperature when extended backwards intersect the temperature axis at the same point.

When the temperature in a graph of pressure versus temperature is expressed in kelvin, the straight line passes through the origin, as in Figure 3.12.

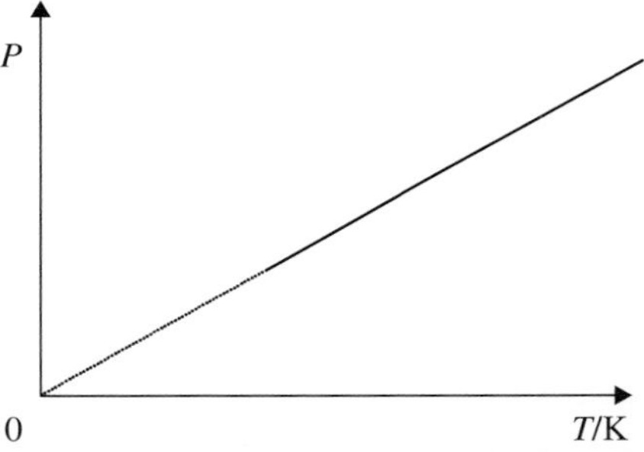

Figure 3.12 If temperature is expressed in kelvin, the graph goes through the origin.

This is more evidence in favour of the existence of an absolute temperature scale.

▶ This experiment implies that at constant volume

$$\frac{P}{T} = \text{constant}$$

The pressure–temperature law is illustrated in Figure 3.13.

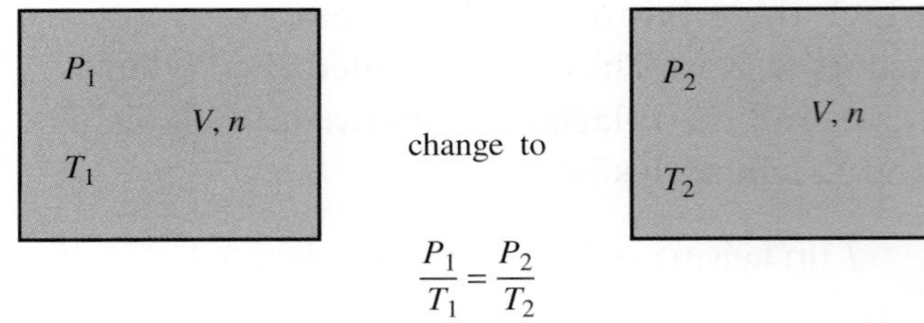

Figure 3.13 The pressure–temperature law.

Example question

Q6

A gas in a container of fixed volume is heated from a temperature of 20 °C and pressure 3 atm to a temperature of 85 °C. What is the new pressure?

Answer

From

$$\frac{P}{T} = \text{constant}$$

we have

$$\frac{3}{293} = \frac{P}{358}$$

and so

$P = 3.67$ atm

The equation of state

If we combine the results of the three preceding experiments, we see that what we have discovered is that

$$\frac{PV}{T} = \text{constant}$$

What is the value of the constant? To determine that, we repeat all of the preceding experiments, this time using different quantities of the gas. We discover that the constant in the last equation is proportional to the number of moles n of the gas in question:

$$\frac{PV}{T} = n \times \text{constant}$$

We can now measure the pressure, temperature, volume and number of moles for a large number of *different* gases and calculate the value of $\frac{PV}{nT}$. We find that this constant has the same value for all gases – it is a universal constant. We call this the gas constant R. It has the numerical value

$$R = 8.31\ \text{J K}^{-1}\ \text{mol}^{-1}$$

▶ Thus, finally, the equation of state is

$$PV = RnT$$

(Remember that temperature must always be in kelvin.)

A gas that obeys this law at all temperatures, pressures and volumes is said to be an **ideal gas**. Real gases obey this law only for a range of temperatures, pressures and volumes. The equation of state can be illustrated as in Figure 3.14.

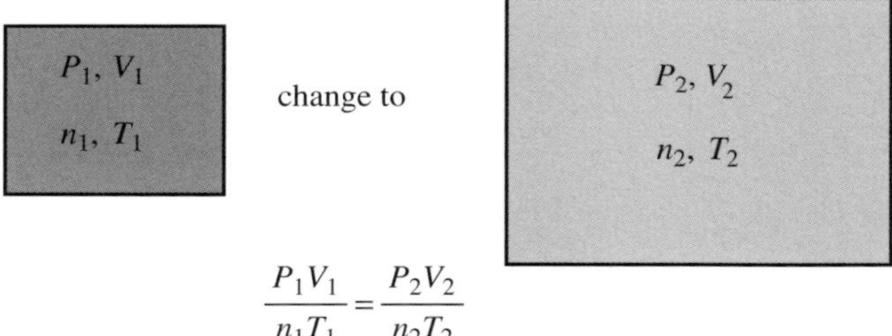

Figure 3.14 The equation of state.

Example questions

Q7

How many moles of gas are there in a gas of temperature 300 K, volume 0.02 m^3 and pressure 2×10^5 Pa?

Answer

$$n = \frac{PV}{RT} = \frac{2 \times 10^5 \times 0.02}{8.31 \times 300} = 1.60\ \text{mol}$$

Q8

A container of hydrogen of volume 0.1 m^3 and temperature 25 °C contains 3.20×10^{23} molecules. What is the pressure in the container?

Answer

The number of moles present is

$$n = \frac{3.20 \times 10^{23}}{6.02 \times 10^{23}} = 0.53$$

So

$$P = \frac{RnT}{V} = \frac{8.31 \times 0.53 \times 298}{0.1} = 1.3 \times 10^4\ \text{N m}^{-2}$$

Q9

A gas of volume 2 L, pressure 3 atm and temperature 300 K expands to a volume of 3 L and a pressure of 4 atm. What is the new temperature of the gas?

Answer

$$\frac{PV}{T} = \text{constant}$$

so

$$\frac{3 \times 2}{300} = 4 \times \frac{3}{T}$$

giving

$$T = 600\ \text{K}$$

Q10

Figure 3.15 shows two isothermal curves for the same quantity of gas. Which is at the higher temperature?

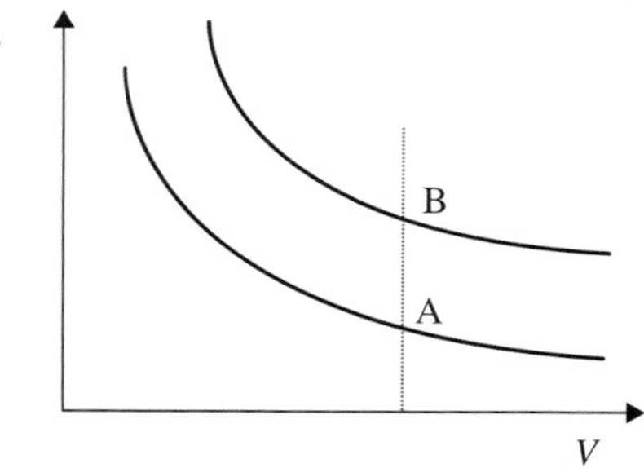

Figure 3.15.

Answer

Draw a vertical line that intersects the two isotherms at points A and B. Since B is at higher pressure than A and both have the same volume, it follows from $\frac{P}{T} = \text{constant}$ that B is at the higher temperature.

Q11

Figure 3.16 shows two curves obtained in an experiment to investigate the dependence of pressure on temperature at constant volume. Which straight line corresponds to the larger volume? (Both curves correspond to the same number of moles.)

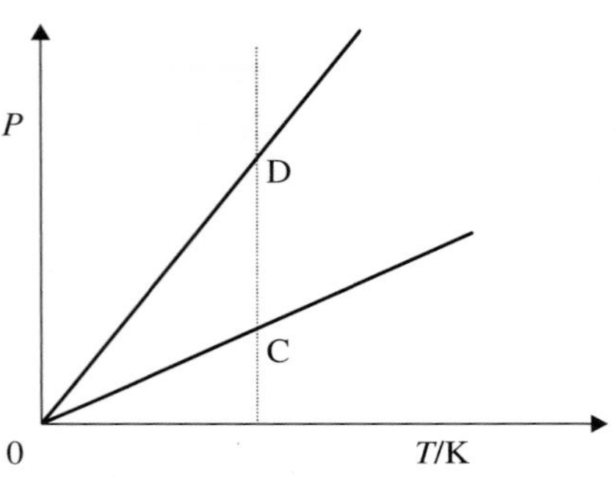

Figure 3.16.

Answer

Draw a vertical line which intersects the two straight lines at points C and D. Since D has higher pressure than C and both have the same temperature, it follows from $PV = \text{constant}$ that C is at higher volume.

Q12

Figure 3.17 shows how the pressure of a fixed quantity of gas depends on temperature in kelvin. As the temperature increases, is the volume of the gas changing?

Answer

If the volume is kept constant, a graph of pressure versus temperature will give a straight line *going through the origin*. Hence, in this problem, the volume must be changing.

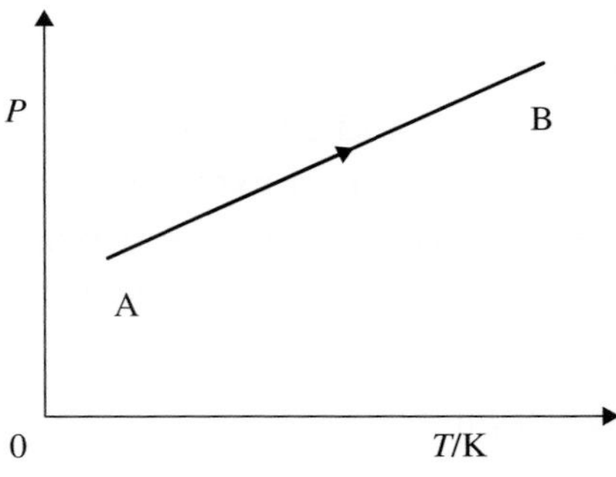

Figure 3.17.

Q13

Is the volume increasing or decreasing in Example question 12?

Answer

Draw the dotted lines through the origin and going through points A and B, as shown in Figure 3.18. These are isochoric lines, which means the volume is constant along each one. Also, draw a horizontal line from A to C as shown. Points A and C have the same pressure. Since C is at higher temperature, it must also be at higher volume. Hence point B also has a higher volume than A. The gas is therefore expanding.

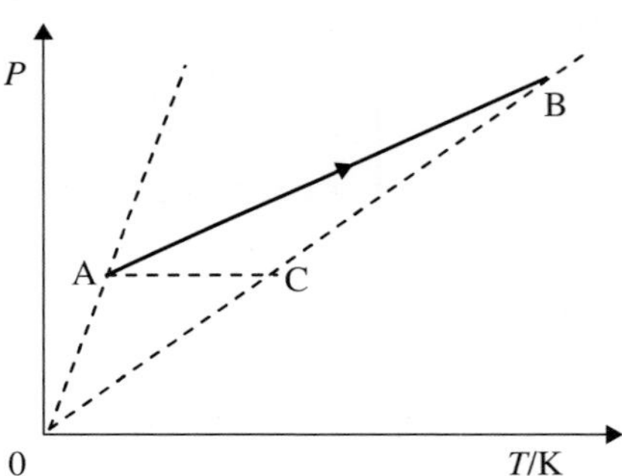

Figure 3.18.

Q14

If the temperature of a gas is increased by a factor of 4 and the density remains the same, what is the new pressure of the gas?

Answer

Since the density stays the same, the volume stays the same. Using $\frac{P}{T} = \text{constant}$ we deduce that the pressure must increase by a factor of 4.

QUESTIONS

1 A volume of 2.00 L of a gas is heated from 20.0 °C to 80.0 °C at constant pressure. What is the new volume?

2 A sealed bottle contains air at 22.0 °C and a pressure of 12.0 atm. If the temperature is raised to 120.0 °C, what will the new pressure be?

3 A gas is kept at a pressure of 4.00 atm and a temperature of 30.0 °C. When the pressure is reduced to 3.00 atm and the temperature raised to 40.0 °C, the volume is measured to be 0.45 L. What was the original volume of the gas?

4 An air bubble exhaled by a diver doubles in radius by the time it gets to the surface of the water. Assuming that the air in the bubble stays constant in temperature, find by what factor the pressure of the bubble is reduced.

5 12.0 kg of helium is required to fill a bottle of volume 5.00 L at a temperature of 20.0 °C. What pressure will the helium have?

6 What mass of carbon dioxide is required to fill a tank of volume 12.0 L at a temperature of 20.0 °C and a pressure of 4.00 atm?

7 A flask of volume 300.0 mL contains air at a pressure of 5.00×10^5 Pa, and a temperature of 27.0 °C. If the flask loses molecules at a rate of 3.00×10^{19} per second, after how much time will the pressure in the flask be reduced to half its original value? (Assume that the temperature of the air remains constant during this time.)

8 The point in Figure 3.19 represents the state of a *fixed quantity* of ideal gas in a container with a movable piston. The temperature of the gas in the state shown is 600 K. Copy the diagram. Indicate on it the point representing the new state of the gas after the following separate changes.
(a) The volume doubles at constant temperature.
(b) The volume doubles at constant pressure.
(c) The pressure halves at constant volume.

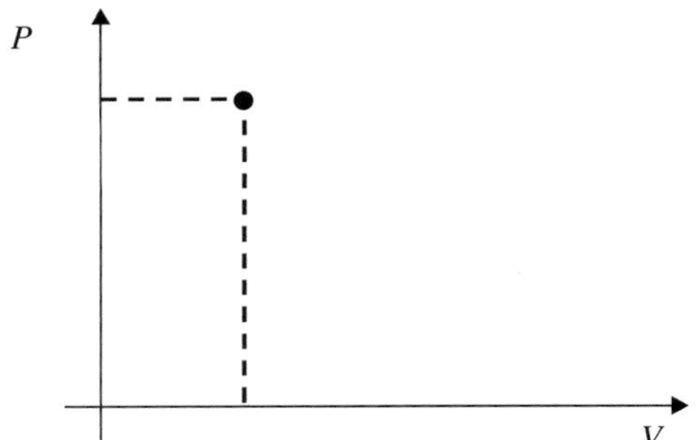

Figure 3.19 For question 8.

9 The point in Figure 3.20 shows the state of a fixed quantity of ideal gas kept at a temperature of 300 K. The state of the gas changes and is represented by the dotted route in the pressure–volume diagram. The gas is eventually returned to its original state.

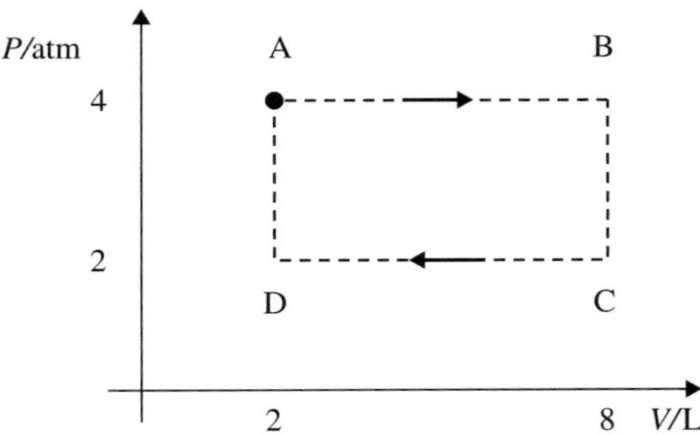

Figure 3.20 For question 9.

(a) Find the temperature of the gas at the corners of the rectangle on the pressure–volume diagram.
(b) At what point on the dotted path is the internal energy of the gas greatest?

10 Two ideal gases are kept at the same temperature in two containers separated by a valve as shown in Figure 3.21. What will the pressure be when the valve is opened? (The temperature stays the same.)

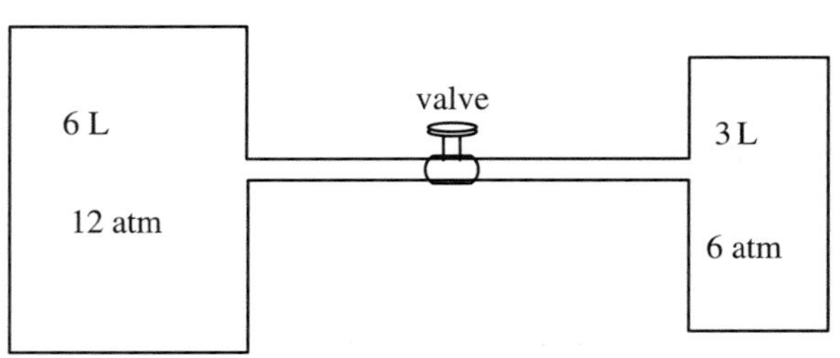

Figure 3.21 For question 10.

11 Figure 3.22 shows a cylinder in a vacuum, which has a movable, frictionless piston at the top. An ideal gas is kept in the cylinder. The piston is at a distance of 0.500 m from the bottom of the cylinder and the volume of the cylinder is 0.050 m^3. The weight on top of the cylinder has a mass of 10.0 kg. The temperature of the gas is 19.0 °C.

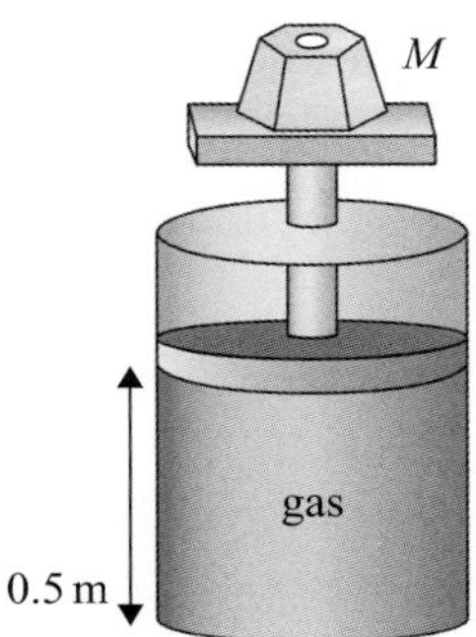

Figure 3.22 For question 11.

(a) What is the pressure of the gas?
(b) How many molecules are there in the gas?
(c) If the temperature is increased to 152.0 °C, what is the new volume of the gas?

12 The molar mass of a gas is 28 g mol^{-1}. A container has 2.00 mol of this gas at 0.00 °C and a pressure of 1.00 atm. What are the mass and volume of the gas?

13 A container with a volume of 1.25 m^3 is filled with hydrogen gas at pressure 2.35 atm and temperature 25.0 °C.
(a) How many molecules are there?
The container has a safety valve that opens releasing hydrogen whenever the pressure exceeds 2.50 atm. The container is now heated and then cooled down again. When the temperature has fallen to 21.0 °C the pressure is 2.05 atm.
(b) How many molecules escaped?
(c) What was the highest temperature the hydrogen achieved during heating?

14 A container with a volume of 1.07 m^3 is filled with a monatomic gas. The temperature is 140 °C and the pressure 1.47 atm.
(a) What will the pressure be if the temperature becomes 215 °C?
(b) If the temperature of the gas falls below 140 °C, a number of the atoms in the gas will join together to form diatomic molecules. When the temperature falls to 46.0 °C, the pressure is measured to be only 0.760 atm. How many moles of the diatomic molecules are there at 46.0 °C?

15 A balloon has a volume of 404 m^3 and is filled with helium of mass 70.0 kg. If the temperature inside the balloon is 17.0 °C, find the pressure inside the balloon.

16 A flask has a volume of 5.0×10^{-4} m^3 and contains air at a temperature of 300 K and a pressure of 150 kPa.
(a) Find the number of moles of air in the flask.
(b) Find the number of molecules in the flask.
(c) Find the mass of air in the flask. You may take the molar mass of air to be 29 g mol^{-1}.

17 The molar mass of helium is 4.00 g mol^{-1}.
(a) Calculate the volume of 1 mol of helium at stp (T = 273 K, P = 1 atm).
(b) What is the density of helium at stp?
(c) What is the density of oxygen gas at stp (the molar mass is 32 g mol^{-1})?

18 (a) By finding the volume of 1 mol of helium (molar mass 4 g mol^{-1}) at stp, 1 mol of water (molar mass 18 g mol^{-1}, density 1.0×10^3 kg m^{-3}) and 1 mol of uranium (molar mass 238 g mol^{-1}, density 18.7×10^3 kg m^{-3}), find what volume corresponds to each molecule.
(b) Assuming this volume to be a cube, find the size of the side of this cube for each of the three cases.
(c) How does this size compare with the actual size of each molecule?

19 The density of an ideal gas is 1.35 kg m^{-3}. If the temperature in kelvin and the pressure are both doubled, find the new density of the gas.

Thermodynamics

Thermodynamics deals with the conditions under which thermal energy can be transformed into mechanical work. The first law of thermodynamics states that the amount of thermal energy given to a system is used to increase that system's internal energy and to do work. The second law invokes limitations to how much thermal energy can actually be transformed into mechanical work.

Objectives

By the end of this chapter you should be able to:

- understand the meaning of *internal energy*;
- calculate *work* when a gas expands or compresses using $\delta W = P\,\delta V$;
- state the relationship between changes in the internal energy, the work done and the thermal energy supplied through the *first law of thermodynamics*, $\Delta U = Q - W$;
- define the terms *adiabatic*, *isothermal*, *isobaric* and *isochoric* and show these on a pressure–volume diagram;
- understand what is meant by *irreversibility* and *disorder*;
- understand that *entropy* is a measure of disorder;
- state the *second law of thermodynamics*;
- understand the meaning of *energy degradation*.

Internal energy

In Chapter 3.1 we defined the internal energy of a gas as the total kinetic energy of the molecules of the gas plus the potential energy associated with the intermolecular forces. If the gas is ideal, the intermolecular forces are assumed to be strictly zero, and the internal energy of the gas comes from the random kinetic energy of the molecules of the gas. The average kinetic energy of the molecules is given by

$$\bar{E}_k = \tfrac{1}{2}m\overline{v^2} = \tfrac{3}{2}kT$$

where $k = R/N_A = 1.38 \times 10^{-23}\ \mathrm{J\,K^{-1}}$ is the Boltzmann constant (see page 169).

Supplementary material

It follows that the internal energy U of an ideal gas with N atoms is given by $N\bar{E}_k$, so

$$U = \tfrac{3}{2}NkT$$

or, since $k = R/N_A$ and $PV = nRT$,

$$U = \tfrac{3}{2}nRT = \tfrac{3}{2}PV$$

where n is the number of moles. The change in internal energy due to a change in temperature is thus given by

$$\Delta U = \tfrac{3}{2}nR\,\Delta T$$

This formula shows that the internal energy of a fixed number of moles of an ideal gas depends only on temperature and not on the nature of the gas, its volume or other variables. In a classic experiment, James Prescott Joule allowed a gas to expand freely from container A into container B as shown in Figure 4.1.

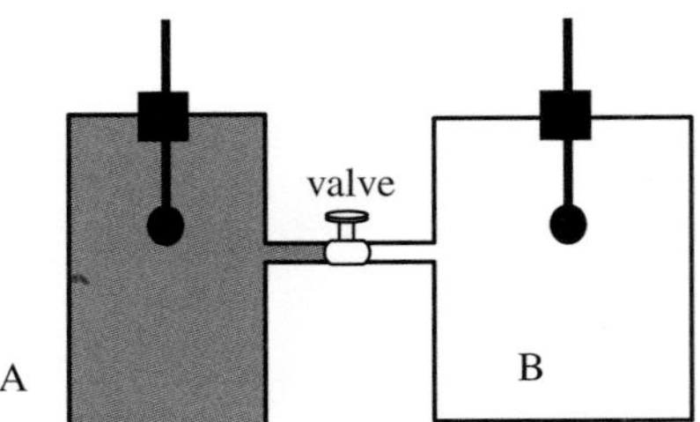

Figure 4.1 Joule's experiment in which internal energy is shown to depend only on temperature.

When the valve separating the two containers is opened, the gas fills the entire volume available to it. The containers are well insulated so no thermal energy enters or leaves the system. Joule tried to observe a temperature difference as the gas expanded and found none. Despite its increased volume and reduced pressure, the internal energy stayed the same. Actually, in a real gas a small drop in temperature is expected, since the molecules must do a certain amount of work against the attracting intermolecular forces which, although very small, are not exactly zero. With more accurate measurements than those available to Joule, this temperature drop can be detected.

Example question

Q1

A flask contains a gas at a temperature of 300 K. If the flask is taken aboard a fast-moving aeroplane, will the temperature of the gas increase as a result of the molecules moving faster?

Answer

No. The temperature of the gas depends on the random motion of the molecules and not on any additional uniform motion imposed on the gas as a result of the motion of the container.

Systems

In thermodynamics we often deal with *systems*, which simply means the complete set of objects under consideration. Thus, a gas in a container is a system, as is a certain mass of ice in a glass. A system can be large – for example, it can be the entire earth. Perhaps we may even consider the entire universe as a system. A system can be *open* or *closed*: mass can enter and leave an open system but not a closed system. An *isolated* system is one in which no energy in any form enters or leaves. If all the parameters defining the system are given, we speak of the system being in a particular *state*. For example, an ideal gas is specified if its pressure, volume and temperature are specified. Any processes that change the state of a system are called *thermodynamic processes*. Thus, heating a gas may result in changed pressure, temperature or volume and is thus a thermodynamic process. Doing work on the gas by compressing it is also a thermodynamic process.

It is important to realize that internal energy is a property of the particular state of the system under consideration, and for this reason internal energy is called a *state function*. Thus, if two gases originally in different states are brought to the same state (i.e. same pressure, volume and temperature), they will have the same internal energy irrespective of what the original state was and how the gas was brought to that final state. By contrast, thermal energy and work are not state functions. We cannot speak of the thermal energy content of a system or of its work content. Thermal energy and work are related to *changes* in the state of the system not to the state itself.

Work done on or by a gas

Imagine that we are given a quantity of a gas in a container with a frictionless, movable piston and that the gas is compressed slightly by exerting a force on the piston from the outside, as in Figure 4.2.

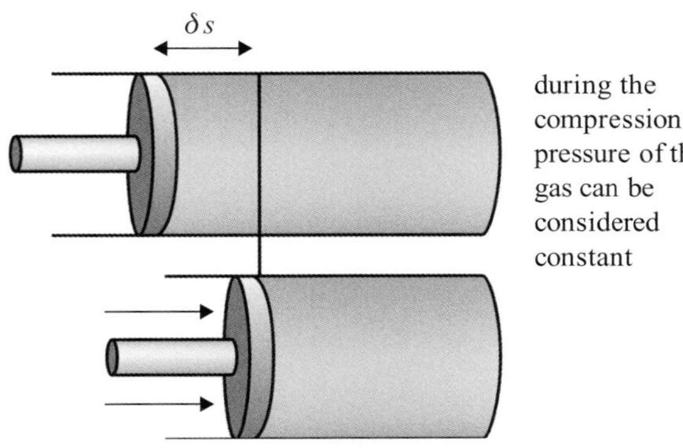

Figure 4.2 When the piston is pushed in by a small amount, work is being done *on* the gas.

If the pressure in the gas initially is P, and the cross-sectional area of the piston is A, then the force with which one must push is PA. If the piston moves an infinitesimal distance δs, the work done is

$$\begin{aligned}\delta W &= F\,\delta s \\ &= PA\delta s\end{aligned}$$

But $A\delta s$ is the amount by which the volume of the gas has been reduced, δV.

▶ Hence the (small) work done is

$$\delta W = P\,\delta V$$

Note that, as soon as the piston is moved, the pressure in the gas will, in general, change. This is why it is necessary to give the expression for work done in the form of infinitesimal quantities, as above. To find the work done under a large change of volume one must use calculus to integrate the expression given above; the pressure, and hence the force that must be exerted, is not constant. We will not be concerned with this here.

The work done has a simple interpretation on a pressure–volume diagram: in Figure 4.3a, the volume of a gas changes by an infinitesimal amount δV, so the work done is $P_0\delta V$. (Even though the pressure changes during the change of volume δV, it can be considered constant if δV is small enough.) The work done, $P_0\delta V$, is equal to the area of the strip whose width is δV and height P_0. If the change in volume $\Delta V = V_2 - V_1$ is not small, the work done may be found by adding the areas of vary many such narrow strips, so it is given by the area between the graph and the V-axis from V_1 to V_2 (Figure 4.3b).

▶ The *total* work done when the gas expands by an arbitrary amount is the area under the graph in the pressure–volume diagram.

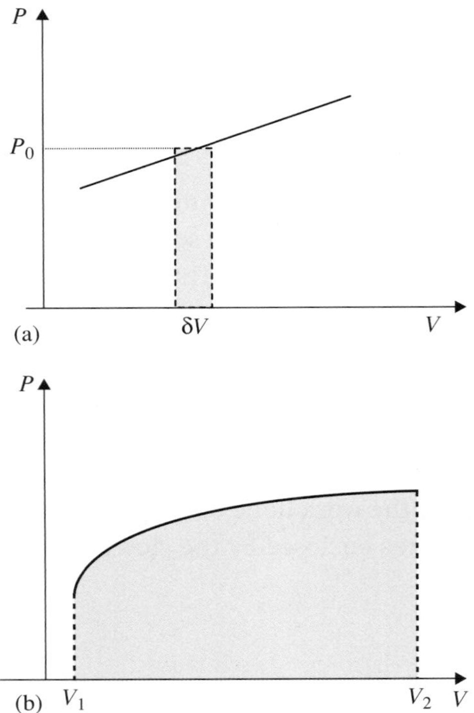

Figure 4.3 (a) Even though the pressure is not constant, the work done can be calculated for an infinitesimal volume change by considering that for such a small change the pressure is constant. (b) For a change in volume that is not small, the work done is found from the area under the curve in the pressure–volume diagram.

The pressure–volume diagrams in Figure 4.4 show an arbitrary series of changes on an ideal gas that begin and end in the state A (diagram (c)). The gas expands from A to B and thus the work done by the gas is the area between the curve

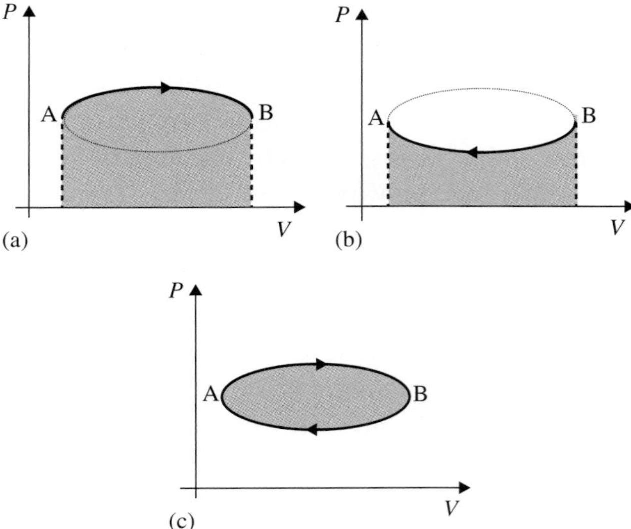

Figure 4.4 For a closed loop in a pressure–volume diagram, the work done is the area of the loop.

and the V axis from A to B (diagram (a)). From B to A, the gas is being compressed so the work is being done by an outside agent. That work equals the area between the curve and the V axis (diagram (b)).

▶ The net work done is the work done by the gas minus the work done on the gas. It equals the area enclosed by the closed loop.

A number of interesting processes can be identified on a pressure–volume diagram. A process in which the gas expands or contracts at constant pressure is called an *isobaric* process. On a pressure–volume diagram it is represented by a horizontal straight line (Figure 4.5a). A process in which the volume of the gas stays fixed is called *isochoric* and is represented by a vertical line (Figure 4.5b).

Since pressure is fixed in an isobaric process, the work done is easy to calculate, $W = P\Delta V$. Note that in an isochoric process no work is done on or by the gas.

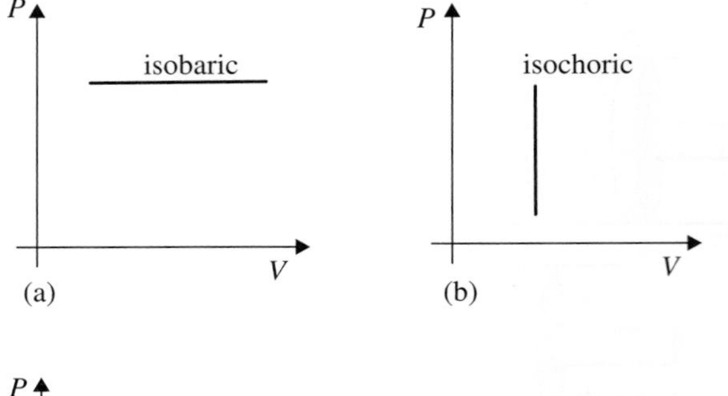

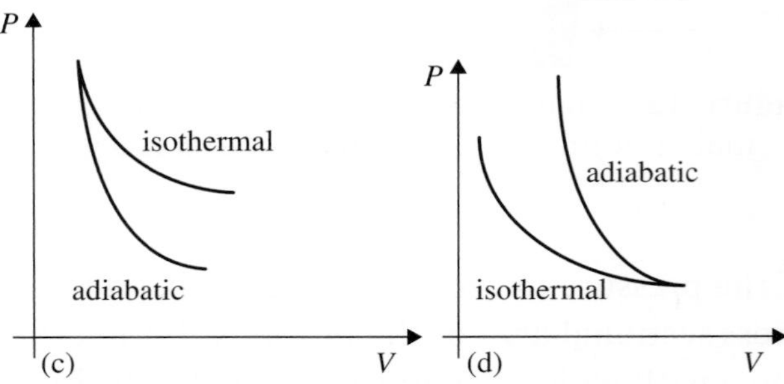

Figure 4.5 Isobaric, isochoric, isothermal and adiabatic processes.

Example question

Q2

A gas is compressed at constant pressure 2.00×10^5 Pa from a volume of $2.00\ \text{m}^3$ to a volume of $0.500\ \text{m}^3$. What is the work done? If the temperature initially was 40 °C what is the final temperature of the gas?

Answer

Since the compression takes place under constant pressure, the work done is

$$P \times \text{change in volume} = 2.00 \times 10^5\ \text{Pa} \times 1.50\ \text{m}^3$$
$$= 3.00 \times 10^5\ \text{J}$$

The final temperature is found from

$$\frac{V}{T} = \text{constant}$$

that is

$$\frac{2}{313} = \frac{0.5}{T}$$

giving

$$T = 78.25\ \text{K} = -195\ ^\circ\text{C}.$$

Apart from *isothermal* processes, which we met on page 176, the last process of interest is called *adiabatic* and is a process during which the gas does not absorb or give out any thermal energy, so $Q = 0$ (Figure 4.5c, d). We have also drawn an isotherm to show that the adiabatic curve is steeper than an isotherm going through the same point. In general, an isothermal process takes place slowly and the system must be in thermal equilibrium with its surroundings; an adiabatic process takes place very fast and the system is not in thermal equilibrium with its surroundings (see Figure 4.6). To help understand the difference between adiabatic and isothermal processes better, we will introduce the first law of thermodynamics here.

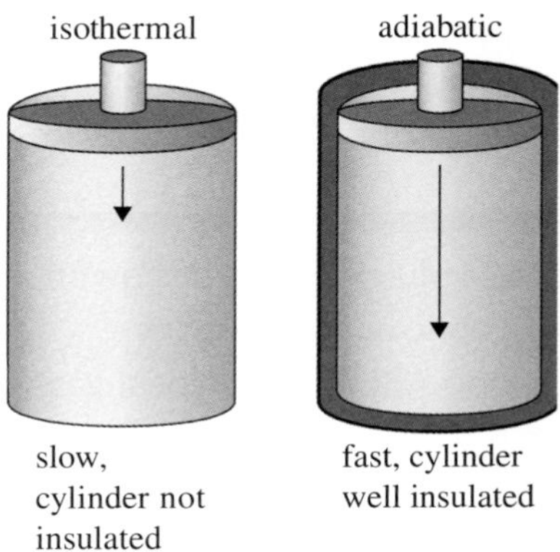

Figure 4.6 Isothermal and adiabatic systems.

The first law of thermodynamics

▶ When a small amount of thermal energy δQ is given to a gas, the gas will absorb that energy and use it to increase its internal energy and/or to do work by expanding. Conservation of energy demands that

$$\delta U = \delta Q - \delta W$$

where δU is the small change in internal energy and δW is the small amount of work done. In this formula, the convention is that a positive δQ denotes thermal energy absorbed by the gas while a negative δQ stands for thermal energy lost by the gas. Similarly, a positive δW stands for work done by the gas (the gas is expanding) and negative δW work done on the gas (the gas is being compressed). A positive δU thus represents an increase in the temperature and a negative δU represents a decrease in the temperature.

If the amounts of thermal energy and work are not small, then

$$\Delta U = Q - W$$

where Q is the thermal energy and W the work done.

This formula is known as the first law of thermodynamics and is a consequence of the law of conservation of energy. This law also incorporates what we stated earlier: namely that internal energy is a state function whereas thermal energy and work are not.

Example questions

Q3

A gas in a container with a piston expands isothermally (i.e. the temperature stays constant). If thermal energy $Q = 10^5$ J is given to the gas, what is the work done by the gas?

Answer

The pressure is not kept constant during the expansion, so we cannot use the formula we derived for work done. But since $T =$ constant, it follows that $\Delta U = 0$ and since

$$\Delta U = Q - W$$

we must have

$$W = Q$$

So, the work done by the gas in this case is equal to the thermal energy supplied to it: 10^5 J.

Q4

A gas expands adiabatically (i.e. it does not receive or lose thermal energy). Will its temperature increase or decrease?

Answer

Again using the first law with $\delta Q = 0$ we find

$$\delta U = -\delta W$$

The gas expands and so it is the gas that does the work, that is

$$\delta W > 0$$

Therefore

$$\delta U < 0$$

That is, the internal energy and thus temperature decrease. Similarly, if the gas is compressed adiabatically, the temperature will increase.

This explains why the adiabatic curve starting from a point on the pressure–volume diagram is steeper than the isothermal curve starting from that same point (see Figure 4.7). Consider an adiabatic and an isothermal process, both starting from the same point and bringing the gas to the same (expanded) final volume. Since the adiabatic process will reduce the temperature and the isothermal process will not, it follows that the pressure of the final state after the adiabatic expansion will be lower than the pressure of the state reached by the isothermal expansion. Hence, the adiabatic is steeper.

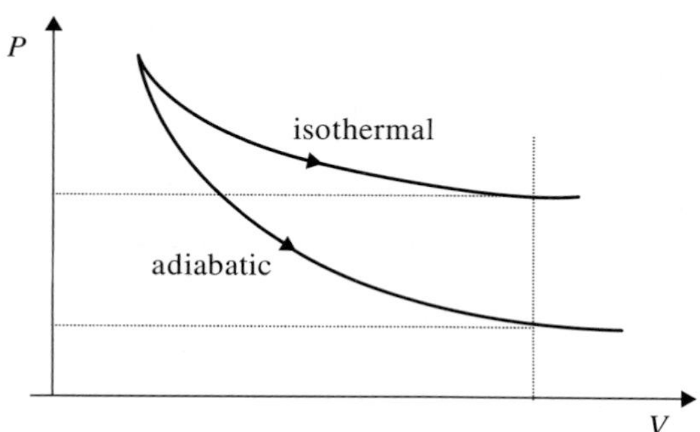

Figure 4.7.

Q5

An ideal gas, kept at constant pressure 3.00×10^6 Pa, has initial volume 0.100 m^3 and temperature 300 K. If the gas is compressed at constant pressure down to a volume of 0.080 m^3, find:

(a) the work done on the gas;

(b) the thermal energy taken out of the gas.

Answer

(a) The work done is

$$3.00 \times 10^6 \times 0.020 = 6.00 \times 10^4 \text{ J}$$

(b) From the first law

$$Q = \Delta U + W$$

so to find the thermal energy taken out we must first find the change in the internal energy of the gas. Since

$$U = \tfrac{3}{2}NkT \quad \text{or} \quad U = \tfrac{3}{2}PV$$

it follows that

$$\Delta U = \tfrac{3}{2}(PV)_{\text{final}} - \tfrac{3}{2}(PV)_{\text{initial}}$$
$$= -9.00 \times 10^4 \text{ J}$$

Finally

$$Q = -9.00 \times 10^4 - 6.00 \times 10^4$$
$$= -1.5 \times 10^5 \text{ J}$$

The negative sign in Q means that this thermal energy was removed from the gas.

Q6

Figure 4.8 is a pressure–volume diagram showing two adiabatics, an isochoric and an isobaric process making up a loop ABCD for an ideal gas.

(a) Along which legs is thermal energy supplied (Q_{in}) to or removed (Q_{out}) from the gas?

(b) What is the relation between Q_{in}, Q_{out} and the net work done in the loop?

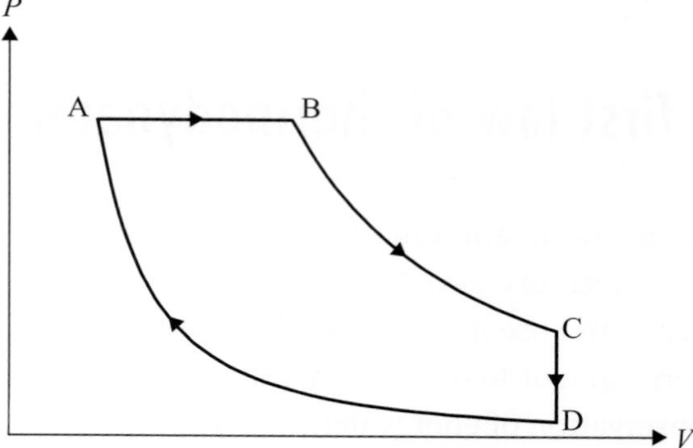

Figure 4.8.

Answer

(a) There is no thermal energy exchanged along the adiabatics BC and DA. Along AB, work is done by the gas so that $W > 0$ and $\Delta U > 0$ since the temperature at B is higher than that at A. Hence $Q > 0$ and energy is supplied to the gas. Along CD, $W = 0$ (the volume does not change) and $\Delta U < 0$ because the temperature at D is lower than that at C. Hence $Q < 0$ and energy is removed from the gas.

(b) Applying the first law for the total change A → A, we see that $\Delta U = 0$ so

$$0 = Q - W$$
$$= (Q_{\text{in}} - Q_{\text{out}}) - W$$

leading to $W = Q_{\text{in}} - Q_{\text{out}}$. ($W$ is the area of the loop.)

Q7

The loop ABC in Figure 4.9 consists of an isobaric, an isochoric and an isothermal process for a fixed quantity of an ideal gas.

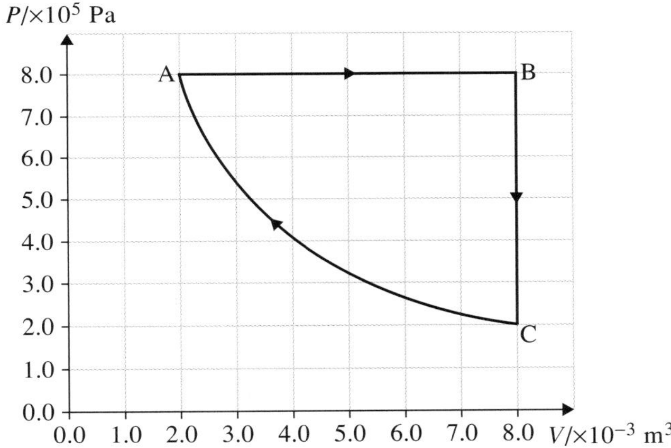

Figure 4.9.

The temperature of the gas at A is 400 K and the change in internal energy from A to B is 7.2 kJ. Calculate

(a) the temperature at B;

(b) the thermal energy transferred from A to B;

(c) the thermal energy transferred from B to C.

The work done on the gas from C to A is 2.2 kJ.

(d) Calculate the net work done in one cycle.

Answer

(a) The temperature at B is found from

$$\frac{V_A}{T_A} = \frac{V_B}{T_B}$$

that is,

$$\frac{2 \times 10^{-3}}{240} = \frac{8 \times 10^{-3}}{T_B}$$

$$\Rightarrow T_B = 960 \text{ K}$$

(b) The work done by the gas as it expands from A to B is

$$W_{AB} = P_A \Delta V$$
$$= 8.0 \times 10^5 \times (8.0 \times 10^{-3} - 2.0 \times 10^{-3})$$
$$= 4800 \text{ J} = 4.8 \text{ kJ}$$

Therefore, from the first law,

$$Q_{AB} = \Delta U_{AB} + W_{AB}$$
$$= 4.8 + 7.2 = +12 \text{ kJ}$$

(c) $Q_{BC} = \Delta U_{BC}$ since $W = 0$ for the change from B to C (the volume is constant). The magnitude of the temperature change from B to C is the same as that from A to B, so the changes in internal energy have the same magnitude (but opposite sign). Therefore $Q = -7.2$ kJ.

(d) The net work is therefore $W = 4.8 - 2.2 = 2.6$ kJ.

The second law of thermodynamics

There are many processes in thermodynamics that are consistent with the first law but are nonetheless impossible. A few of these processes involve:

- the spontaneous (i.e. without the action of another agent) transfer of thermal energy from a cold body to a hotter body;
- the air in a room suddenly occupying just one half of the room and leaving the other half empty;
- a glass of water at room temperature suddenly freezing, causing the temperature of the room to rise.

These processes do not happen because they are forbidden by a very special law of physics – the second law of thermodynamics.

Order and disorder

To begin our discussion of this law, consider a 1 kg mass moving at 10 m s^{-1}. Friction brings it to rest and so the initial kinetic energy of 50 J has been lost. Suppose that all of this energy went into the internal energy of the body. This means that the molecules now vibrate about their equilibrium positions faster than before. The original kinetic energy of the ball was associated with the *ordered* motion of the body as a whole. Every molecule of the body moved forward with the same component of velocity in addition to the random or disordered motion associated with the vibrations of the atoms. (See Figure 4.10.)

mass travelling at 10 m s^{-1} to the right

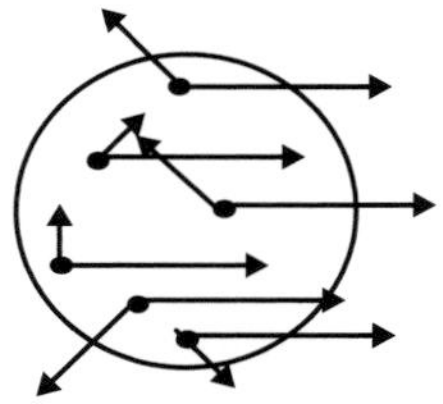

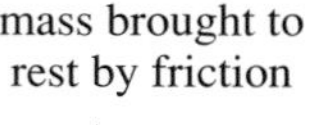

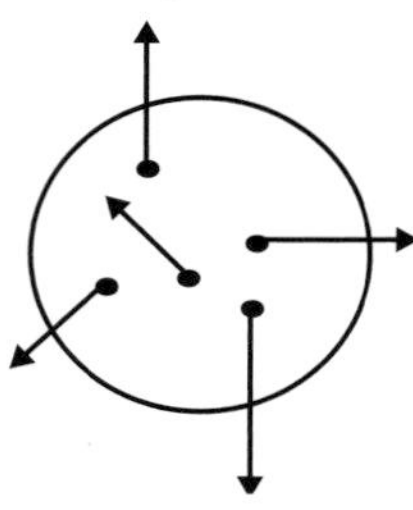

Figure 4.10 The ordered mechanical energy of the mass has been converted into disordered internal energy.

The mechanical (i.e. kinetic) energy of the ball was totally converted into *disordered* energy as a result of friction. There is an irreversibility in this conversion of energy. The ball that has been brought to rest by friction is not expected to convert part of this disordered motion into ordered motion and start accelerating back towards the direction it came from. The original kinetic energy cannot be *recovered* from the internal energy of the ball: we say that it has been *degraded*. Nothing in the laws of physics we have seen so far actually prevents the ball from accelerating backwards. What does prevent it is the second law of thermodynamics.

▶ The second law of thermodynamics deals with the limitations imposed on heat engines, devices whose aim is to convert thermal energy (disordered energy) into mechanical energy (ordered energy).

Reversibility

All natural processes are irreversible – they lead towards states of increased disorder. An irreversible process captured on film would look absurd if the film were to be run backwards. A glass of water looks ordered just before it slips from your hand and falls to the floor, breaking into many pieces. Capturing this on film and then running it in reverse would show the pieces of glass and drops of water assembling themselves into an unbroken glass full of water. It looks like thermodynamics is related to the *arrow of time* – the direction in which natural processes take place. A reversible process for a system consisting of a large number of molecules is reversible only as an idealized approximation.

Irreversibility can be quantified. There exists a quantity called *entropy* which, like internal energy, is a *state function*: that is, once the state of the system is specified, so is its entropy. Entropy depends only on the state of the system and not on how it got there.

▶ The definition of *change* in entropy is

$$\delta S = \frac{\delta Q}{T}$$

This gives the *small* change in the entropy of a system when a *small* quantity of thermal energy is given to or removed from the system at a temperature T (in kelvin). The unit of entropy is J K^{-1}.

If thermal energy is given to the system, $\delta Q > 0$ and entropy increases. If thermal energy is removed, $\delta Q < 0$ and entropy decreases. For a reversible process that returns the system to its original state, $\delta S = 0$. One such reversible process is the isothermal expansion of a gas and the subsequent isothermal compression back to the initial state. Since the expansion and compression are isothermal, leaving the temperature constant, we may write

$$\delta S_1 = \frac{|\delta Q|}{T}$$

during expansion and

$$\delta S_2 = -\frac{|\delta Q|}{T}$$

during compression. (The gas receives thermal energy upon expanding and discards thermal energy upon compressing – use the first law of thermodynamics.) The net entropy change is thus zero.

Let us apply the expression for δS given above to the case of the flow of thermal energy between a hot body at temperature T_h and a cold body at temperature T_c (Figure 4.11a). If a very small quantity of thermal energy δQ flows from the hot to the cold body, the total entropy change of the two bodies is

$$\begin{aligned}\delta S &= -\frac{\delta Q}{T_h} + \frac{\delta Q}{T_c} \\ &= \delta Q\left(\frac{1}{T_c} - \frac{1}{T_h}\right) \\ &\Rightarrow \delta S > 0\end{aligned}$$

(the temperature of each body is assumed unchanged during this infinitesimal exchange of thermal energy) and in fact thermal energy will flow from the hot body into the cold one. The opposite (Figure 4.11b) does not happen. It corresponds to a decrease in the entropy of the system:

$$\begin{aligned}\delta S &= \frac{\delta Q}{T_h} - \frac{\delta Q}{T_c} \\ &= \delta Q\left(\frac{1}{T_h} - \frac{1}{T_c}\right) \\ &\Rightarrow \delta S < 0\end{aligned}$$

These examples involve the isolated system of two bodies at different temperatures in thermal contact with each other. We have seen that the

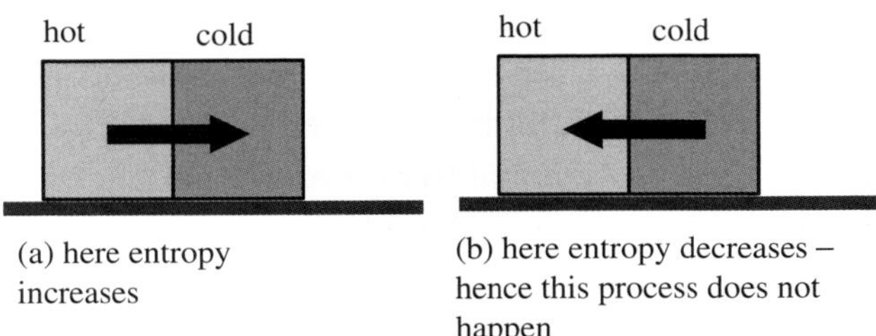

Figure 4.11 (a) When thermal energy flows from a hot to a cold body, the entropy of the universe increases. (b) If the reverse were to happen without any performance of work, the entropy would decrease, violating the second law.

(irreversible) flow of thermal energy from the warmer to the colder body results in an increase in the entropy of the system. In fact, any natural (irreversible) process in an isolated system results in an increase in the entropy of the system. On the other hand, in an isolated system any theoretical *reversible* process would leave the entropy of the system unchanged.

Similarly, when thermal energy is given to a solid at its melting temperature, the solid will use that thermal energy to turn into a liquid at the same temperature. The entropy formula again shows that the entropy increases as the solid absorbs the latent heat of fusion. The same is also true for vaporization.

This allows us to state the second law of thermodynamics in its general form:

▶ The entropy of an isolated system never decreases.

A number of equivalent statements of the second law also exist. If one of these statements is accepted, the others can be proved from it. The statement due to Clausius is:

▶ It is impossible for thermal energy to (spontaneously) flow from a cold to a hot object.

Supplementary material

The second law of thermodynamics leads, as we have seen, to an increase in the entropy in the universe, a state of increased disorder. Many processes that are possible under the first law (i.e. the law of energy conservation) do not happen because they would violate the second law. For example, a glass of water at 0 °C has never been observed to freeze into ice by giving thermal energy into the warm surroundings, making them even warmer. To say that this violates the second law does not imply that such a process is impossible – only very unlikely. The probability of this happening is

$$p \approx e^{\frac{\Delta S}{k}}$$
$$= e^{-\frac{\Delta Q}{kT}}$$
$$= e^{-\frac{mL}{kT}}$$

For 1 kg of water this is about $e^{-10^{26}}$ – an infinitesimal number.

Life has evolved from less ordered to more ordered species. This does not violate the second law. Although the entropy of any one particular species has decreased, the metabolic processes that have led to the growth of that species involve a larger entropy increase, so the overall entropy has increased.

Degradation of energy

Thermal energy flows, as we have seen, from hot to cold bodies. The difference in temperature between the two bodies initially offers us the opportunity to run a heat engine between those two temperatures, extracting useful mechanical work in the process. With time, the two bodies will approach the same temperature and the opportunity for using those two bodies to do work will be lost. Thus, the flow of thermal energy from the hotter to the colder body tends to equalize the two temperatures and deprives us of the opportunity to do work.

▶ It is a consequence of the second law that energy, while always being conserved, becomes less useful – this is called *energy degradation.*

The energy of the universe tends to move from highly ordered, useful forms to disordered, useless forms. If the second law is applied to the universe as a whole, then since it has nowhere to receive thermal energy from or give thermal energy away to, its expansion is adiabatic. Despite the small-scale non-uniformity of the universe (planets, solar systems, stars, galaxies, clusters of galaxies) we can still think of it on a very large scale as an expanding gas. If so, then by the first law of thermodynamics

$$\Delta U = 0 - W < 0$$

and so the temperature of the universe is decreasing. The universe is filled with electromagnetic radiation, produced during the original explosion (the Big Bang) that created the universe some 14 billion years ago. The spectrum of this radiation (i.e. how much energy is stored per interval of wavelength) is a direct function of the ambient temperature that this radiation finds itself in equilibrium with. Today, measurements of this temperature through the spectrum of the ambient radiation give it a value of only 2.7 K. The temperature of the universe, which originally was enormous, is constantly decreasing as a result of the expansion of the universe. If this expansion continues, the temperature will keep approaching absolute zero, leading to the 'heat death of the universe'.

? QUESTIONS

1 A gas expands at a constant pressure of 5.4×10^5 Pa from a volume of 3.6×10^{-3} m^3 to a volume of 4.3×10^{-3} m^3. How much work does the gas do?

2 A gas is compressed isothermally so that an amount of work equal to 6500 J is done on it.
(a) How much thermal energy is removed from or given to the gas?
(b) If the same gas were compressed adiabatically to the same final volume as in (a), would the work done on the gas be less than, equal to or greater than 6500 J? Explain your answer.

3 An ideal gas expands isothermally from pressure P and volume V to volume $2V$. Represent this change of the gas on a pressure–volume diagram. An equal quantity of an ideal gas at pressure P and volume V expands adiabatically to a volume $2V$.

Represent this change on the same axes. In which case is the work done by the gas larger?

4 An ideal gas is compressed isothermally from pressure P and volume $2V$ to a volume V. Represent this change of the gas on a pressure–volume diagram. An equal quantity of an ideal gas at pressure P and volume $2V$ is compressed adiabatically to a volume V. Represent this change on the same axes. In which case is the work done on the gas larger?

5 A quantity of thermal energy Q is supplied to three ideal gases, X, Y and Z. Gas X absorbs Q isothermally, gas Y isochorically and gas Z isobarically. Complete the table below by inserting the words positive, zero or negative for the work done W, the change in internal energy ΔU and the temperature change ΔT of each gas.

	W	ΔU	ΔT
gas X			
gas Y			
gas Z			

6 An ideal gas is compressed adiabatically.
(a) Use the first law of thermodynamics to state and explain the change, if any, in the temperature of the gas.
(b) Explain your answer to (a) by using the kinetic theory of gases.

7 An ideal gas is kept at constant pressure 6.00×10^6 Pa. Its initial temperature is 300 K. The gas expands at constant pressure from a volume of 0.200 m^3 to a volume of 0.600 m^3. The change in the internal energy of the gas during the change is 3.60×10^6 J. Calculate
(a) the work done by the gas;
(b) the temperature of the gas at the new volume;
(c) the thermal energy taken out of or put into the gas.

8 An amount Q of thermal energy is supplied to a system. Explain how it is possible that this addition of thermal energy may *not* result in an increase of the internal energy of the system.

9 An ideal gas undergoes a change from state P to state Q as shown in Figure 4.12. (The temperature is in kelvins.) For this change, state and explain
(a) whether work is done on the gas or by the gas;
(b) whether thermal energy is supplied to the gas or taken out of the gas.

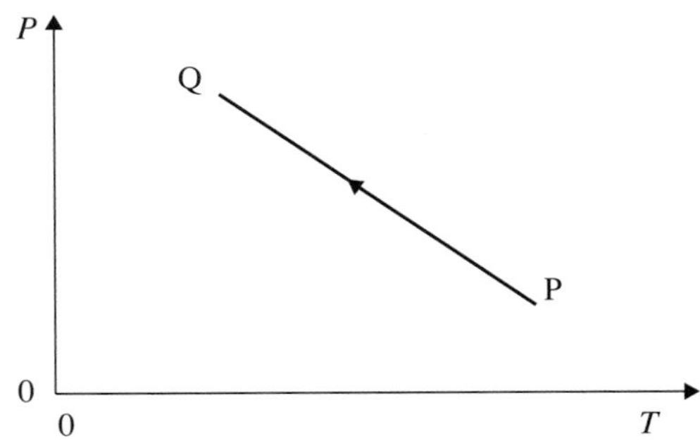

Figure 4.12 For question 9.

10 Two ideal gases, X and Y, have the same pressure, volume and temperature. The same quantity of thermal energy is supplied to both gases. Gas X absorbs the thermal energy at constant volume whereas gas Y absorbs the thermal energy at constant pressure. State and explain which of the two gases will have the largest final temperature.

11 Two ideal gases, X and Y, have the same pressure, volume and temperature. A quantity of thermal energy is supplied to both gases. Gas X absorbs the thermal energy at constant volume whereas gas Y absorbs the thermal energy at constant pressure. The increase in temperature of both gases is the same. State and explain which of the two gases received the largest quantity of thermal energy.

12 The *molar specific heat capacity* of an ideal gas is defined as the amount of thermal energy required to change the temperature of one mole of a gas by one kelvin. When n moles of gas absorb thermal energy Q at constant pressure,

$$Q = nc_P\Delta T$$

where c_P is the molar specific heat capacity at constant pressure.

When n moles of gas absorb thermal energy Q at constant volume,

$Q = nc_V\Delta T$

where c_V is the molar specific heat capacity at constant volume.
Using the first law of thermodynamics and $U = \frac{3}{2}nRT$, show that $c_P - c_V = R$, where R is the universal gas constant.

13 Consider the loop ABCD in Figure 4.13. The temperature at A is 800 K. The internal energy changes along the four legs of the loop are:

$\Delta U_{AB} = 180$ kJ, $\Delta U_{BC} = -120$ kJ, $\Delta U_{CD} = -90$ kJ, $\Delta U_{DA} = 30$ kJ

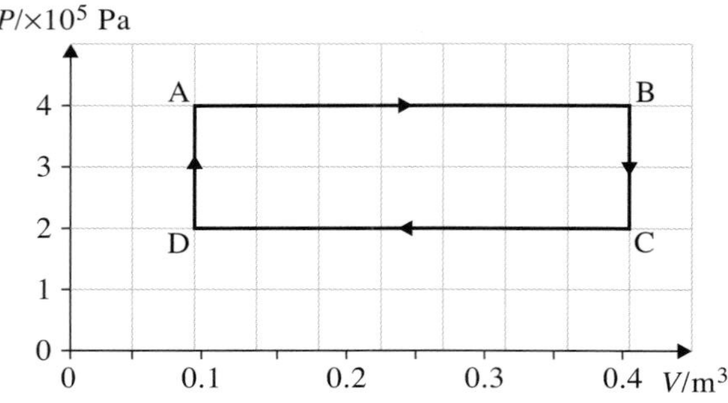

Figure 4.13 For question 13.

Calculate

(a) the temperature at points B, C and D;
(b) the amount of thermal energy given to and taken from the gas along each leg.

HL only

14 In calculus, the work done when a gas expands from volume V_1 to volume V_2 is given by

$$W = \int_{V_1}^{V_2} P\,dV$$

Use this expression to show that the work done by n moles of gas at temperature T during an isothermal expansion from volume V_1 to V_2 is

$$W = nRT\ln\left(\frac{V_2}{V_1}\right)$$

15 A quantity of ice at −10 °C is dropped in water. All the ice eventually melts and the final temperature of the water is +15 °C. Describe and compare the entropy changes taking place in the ice and in the water during the following processes. (Assume that there are no thermal energy exchanges between the ice and water system and the surroundings.)

(a) The temperature of the ice increases from −10 °C to 0 °C.
(b) The ice is melting.
(c) The water is approaching its final temperature of +15 °C.

Simple harmonic motion

Oscillations are a very common phenomenon in all areas of physics. They are interesting in their own right, but they are also needed to understand many diverse phenomena, from sound to light. This chapter introduces a very special and important type of oscillatory motion, called simple harmonic motion (SHM). We discuss the case of free oscillations in detail, and qualitatively discuss the effect of damping and of an external periodic force on the oscillations.

Objectives

By the end of this chapter you should be able to:

- recognize the occurrence of simple harmonic motion through the *defining relation*, $a = -\omega^2 x$;
- understand the terms *amplitude, displacement, angular frequency, frequency, period* and *phase*;
- use the equations $x = A\cos(\omega t + \phi)$, $v = -\omega A\sin(\omega t + \phi)$, $v = \pm\omega\sqrt{A^2 - x^2}$ and $T = \frac{2\pi}{\omega}$;
- discuss the *properties* of simple harmonic motion from *graphs*;
- solve problems with *kinetic energy* and *elastic potential energy* in simple harmonic motion;
- understand that in simple harmonic motion there is a *continuous transformation of energy*, from kinetic energy into elastic potential energy and vice versa;
- describe the effect of *damping* on an oscillating system;
- understand the meaning of *resonance* and give examples of its occurrence;
- discuss qualitatively the effect of a *periodic external force* on an oscillating system.

Oscillations

A typical example of an oscillation is provided by the simple pendulum, i.e. a mass attached to a vertical string. When the mass is displaced slightly sideways and then released, the mass will begin to oscillate. In an oscillation the motion is *repetitive*, i.e. *periodic*, and the body moves back and forth around an equilibrium position. A characteristic of oscillatory motion is the time taken to complete one full oscillation. This is the time taken to move from one extreme position of the motion and back to the same position. This is called the **period** (see Figure 1.1). We will mostly be interested in those oscillations where the period stays constant, i.e. when successive oscillations take the same time to complete. Many oscillations do not share this property. For example, the leaf of a tree blowing in the wind oscillates, but its oscillations do not have a fixed period, and the amount by which the leaf moves away from its

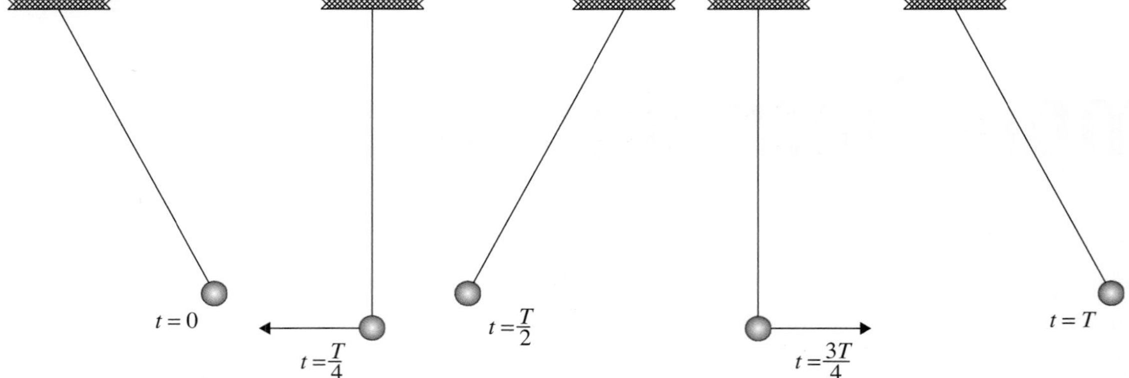

Figure 1.1 A full oscillation lasts for one period. At the end of a time interval equal to one period T, the system is in the same state as at the beginning of that time interval.

equilibrium position is not a regular function of time.

Examples of oscillations include:

- the motion of a mass at the end of a horizontal or vertical spring after the mass is displaced away from its equilibrium position;
- the motion of a ball inside a bowl after it has been displaced away from its equilibrium position at the bottom of the bowl;
- the motion of a body floating in a liquid after it has been pushed downwards and then released;
- a tight guitar string that is set in motion by plucking the string;
- the motion of a diving board as a diver prepares to dive;
- the motion of an aeroplane wing;
- the motion of a tree branch or a skyscraper under the action of the wind.

The examples mentioned above are all mechanical, but there are of course other kinds of oscillation, for example electrical.

A very special periodic oscillation is called **simple harmonic motion** (**SHM**) and is the main topic of this chapter. We shall consider three examples of SHM in the main text, and some others in the example questions.

Kinematics of simple harmonic motion

A mass at the end of a horizontal spring

We consider first a particle of mass m that is attached to a horizontal spring of spring constant k (Figure 1.2). If the particle is moved a distance A to the right and is then released, oscillations will take place because the mass will be pulled back towards the equilibrium position by a *restoring force*, the tension in the spring. The particle will perform oscillations about its equilibrium position (the vertical dotted line) between the extreme positions of the second and last diagrams in Figure 1.2.

Consider the particle when it is in an arbitrary position, as in the third diagram in Figure 1.2. At that position, the extension of the spring is x. The magnitude of the tension F in the spring is therefore (by Hooke's law) equal to $F = kx$, where k is the spring constant. The tension force is directed to the left. Assuming that **displacement** (i.e. distance moved) to the right of the equilibrium position is taken as positive, then

$$ma = -kx$$

since the tension force is directed to the left and so is taken as negative. This equation can

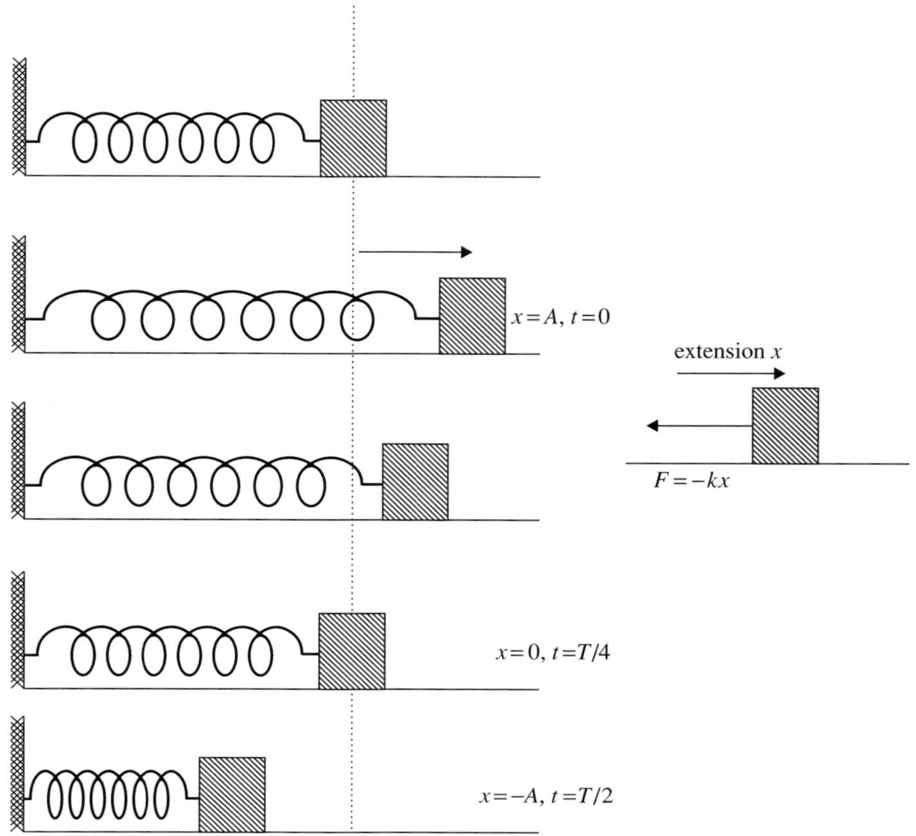

Figure 1.2 The mass–spring system. The net force on the body is proportional to the displacement and opposite to it.

be rewritten as

$$a = -\frac{k}{m}x$$

If we define $\omega^2 = \frac{k}{m}$ we then have the generic form:

$$a = -\omega^2 x$$

The constant ω is known as the **angular frequency** of the motion. Its unit is the inverse second, s^{-1}. The equation $a = -\omega^2 x$ is the defining relation for SHM. Thus we can say the following:

▶ Simple harmonic motion takes place when a particle that is disturbed away from its *fixed* equilibrium position experiences an *acceleration that is proportional and opposite to its displacement.*

Therefore, in general, to check whether SHM will take place, we must check that: (1) we have a fixed equilibrium position; and (2) when the particle is moved away from equilibrium, the acceleration of the particle must be both proportional to the amount of displacement and in the opposite direction to it.

Supplementary material

SHM is defined by the relation $a = -\omega^2 x$. In calculus, the acceleration is written as $a = \frac{d^2x}{dt^2}$ and so the defining relation becomes

$$\frac{d^2x}{dt^2} = -\omega^2 x \quad \Rightarrow \quad \frac{d^2x}{dt^2} + \omega^2 x = 0$$

This is a second-order differential equation whose general solution is

$$x = A\cos(\omega t + \phi)$$

where A and ϕ are constants. To check that $x = A\cos(\omega t + \phi)$is a solution, we calculate both

$$\frac{dx}{dt} = -A\omega\sin(\omega t + \phi)$$

and

$$\frac{d^2x}{dt^2} = -A\omega^2\cos(\omega t + \phi)$$

so that

$$\frac{d^2x}{dt^2} + \omega^2 x = -A\omega^2\cos(\omega t + \phi) + \omega^2[A\cos(\omega t + \phi)] = 0$$

The meaning of the constants A and ϕ is the following:

- The maximum value of the cosine function is 1, and so the maximum value of x is A. Thus A is the **amplitude** of the motion, the maximum displacement.
- The value of ϕ determines the displacement at $t = 0$. At $t = 0$ we have that $x = A\cos\phi$. If $\phi = 0$, then at $t = 0$ we have $x = A$. If $\phi = \frac{1}{2}\pi$, then at $t = 0$ we have $x = A\cos\frac{\pi}{2} = 0$, and so on. The angle ϕ is called the **phase** of the motion.

Given two oscillations with phases ϕ_1 and ϕ_2, the difference $|\phi_1 - \phi_2|$ is called the **phase difference** between the two oscillations.

The velocity is given by $v = \frac{dx}{dt} = -A\omega\sin(\omega t + \phi)$. Given that $x = A\cos(\omega t + \phi)$, we know from mathematics that this is a periodic function with period T given by

$$T = \frac{2\pi}{\omega}$$

The **period** is the time to complete one full oscillation. We have the important result that the period in SHM depends only on ω and not on the amplitude or the phase.

▶ The treatment above implies that, whenever we have $a = -\omega^2 x$, we can deduce that the displacement x, velocity v and period T of the SHM that takes place are given by

$$x = A\cos(\omega t + \phi)$$
$$v = -\omega A\sin(\omega t + \phi)$$
$$T = \frac{2\pi}{\omega}$$

where A, the amplitude, is the maximum displacement, and ϕ, the phase angle, determines the initial displacement. It is a characteristic of SHM that the period is independent of the amplitude A and the phase ϕ. We will mostly be working with situations where the phase angle is zero, in which case

$$x = A\cos(\omega t) \qquad v = -\omega A\sin(\omega t)$$

The typical behaviour of the displacement, velocity and acceleration as functions of time when $\phi = 0$ is shown in Figures 1.3 and 1.4.

We can see how the three graphs are related without using calculus as follows. We must recall that the gradient of the displacement–time graph gives the velocity, and the gradient of the velocity–time graph gives the acceleration. Let us begin with the graph showing the variation with time t of the displacement x. We must examine how the gradient of this graph changes as time goes on.

At $t = 0$, the gradient is zero, and so at $t = 0$ the velocity v is zero as well.

From $t = 0$ to $t = T/4$, the gradient is negative, so the velocity is negative. The gradient assumes its most negative value at $t = T/4$, which means that at this time the velocity is most negative. (The gradient is decreasing in this interval, so the velocity is decreasing as well.)

From $t = T/4$ to $t = T/2$, the gradient of the displacement graph is negative and becomes zero at $t = T/2$. The velocity is therefore negative in this interval and becomes zero at $t = T/2$. (The gradient is increasing in this interval because it is getting less negative, so the velocity is increasing.)

From $t = T/2$ to $t = 3T/4$, the gradient is positive and reaches its most positive value at

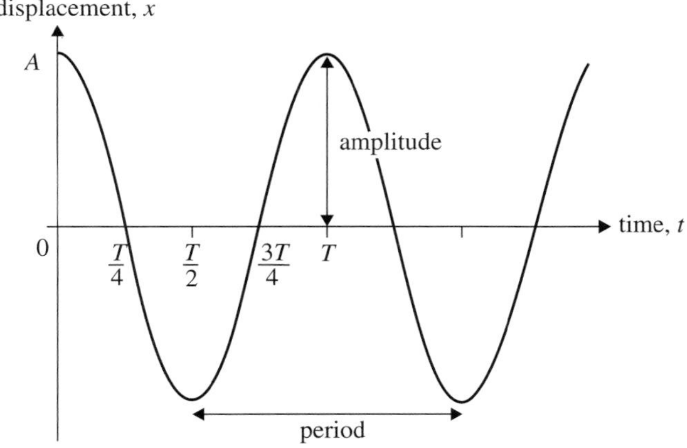

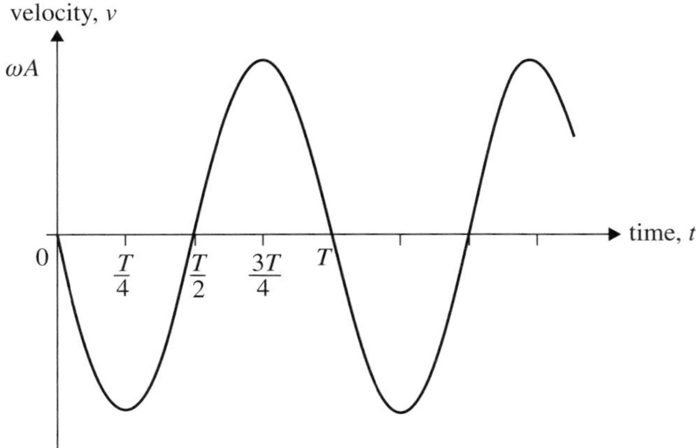

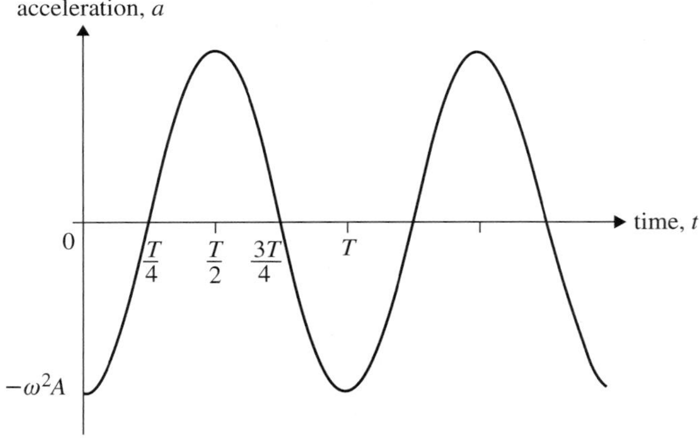

Figure 1.3 Graphs showing the variation with time of the displacement, velocity and acceleration in SHM.

$t = 3T/4$. The velocity in this interval is therefore positive and has a maximum value at $t = 3T/4$. (The gradient is increasing in this interval and so is the velocity.)

From $t = 3T/4$ to $t = T$, the gradient is positive but decreases to zero at $t = T$. In this interval the velocity is therefore positive and becomes

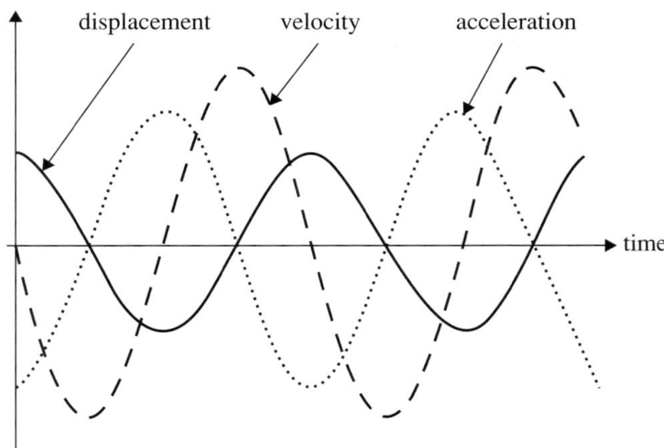

Figure 1.4 The variation of displacement, velocity and acceleration in SHM on the same axes.

zero at $t = T$. (In this interval, the gradient is decreasing and so is the velocity.)

In this way we begin to build up the graph showing the variation with time t of the velocity v. Having established the velocity–time graph, we may repeat the process above to determine the graph showing the variation with time of the acceleration a. This is left as an exercise.

Example questions

Note: In this chapter, all calculations performed with the calculator must be done with the calculator in *radian mode.*

Q1

A particle undergoes SHM with an amplitude of 4.0 mm and angular frequency of 2.0 s^{-1}. At $t = 0$, the displacement is $\frac{4.0}{\sqrt{2}}$ mm. Write down the equation giving the displacement for this motion.

Answer

We use $x = A\cos(\omega t + \phi)$, with $\omega = 2.0$ s^{-1} and $A = 4.0$ mm. So we have

$$x = 4.0\cos(2.0t + \phi)$$

where t is in seconds and x is in millimetres. At $t = 0$ we have

$$\frac{4.0}{\sqrt{2}} = 4.0\cos\phi$$

which implies

$$\cos\phi = \frac{1}{\sqrt{2}}$$

or

$$\phi = \frac{\pi}{4}$$

Hence the equation is

$$x = 4.0\cos\left(2.0t + \frac{\pi}{4}\right)$$

Q2

A particle undergoes SHM with an amplitude of 8.00 cm and an angular frequency of 0.250 s^{-1}. At $t = 0$, the velocity is 1.24 cm s^{-1}.

(a) Write down the equations giving the displacement and velocity for this motion.
(b) Calculate the initial displacement.
(c) Calculate the first time at which the particle is at $x = 2.00$ cm and $x = -2.00$ cm.

Answer

(a) We have that $x = A\cos(\omega t + \phi)$ and therefore $v = -\omega A\sin(\omega t + \phi)$. At $t = 0$ we therefore deduce that

$$1.24 = -0.250 \times 8.00\sin\phi$$

which gives

$$\phi = -0.669 \text{ rad}$$

Hence the displacement is

$$x = 8.00\cos(0.250t - 0.669)$$

and the velocity is

$$v = -2.00\sin(0.250t - 0.669)$$

(b) At $t = 0$, we have

$$x = 8.00\cos(-0.669) = 6.28 \text{ cm}$$

(c) From

$$2.00 = 8.00\cos(0.250t - 0.669)$$

we find

$$\cos(0.250t - 0.669) = 0.25$$

and thus

$$0.250t - 0.669 = \cos^{-1}(0.25) = 1.32$$

which gives

$$t = 7.95 \text{ s}$$

From

$$-2.00 = 8.00\cos(0.250t - 0.669)$$

we find

$$\cos(0.250t - 0.669) = -0.25$$

and thus

$$0.250t - 0.669 = \cos^{-1}(-0.25) = 1.82$$

which gives

$$t = 9.97 \text{ s}$$

It is convenient also to define the **frequency** f of the motion. This is defined as the number of oscillations per second. Since we have one oscillation in a time equal to the period T, the number of oscillations per second is $\frac{1}{T}$ and so

$$f = \frac{1}{T}$$

The unit of frequency is the inverse second, which is called the hertz (Hz). It follows from $T = \frac{2\pi}{\omega}$ that

$$\omega = 2\pi f$$

A particle in a bowl

We consider now a particle of mass m that is placed inside a spherical bowl of radius r, as shown in Figure 1.5. The first diagram shows the particle at its equilibrium position E at the bottom of the bowl. In the second diagram the particle is shown displaced away from equilibrium. The particle will be let go from that position P. In the absence of friction, the particle will perform oscillations about the equilibrium position. Will these oscillations be simple harmonic? To answer this question, we must relate the acceleration to the displacement.

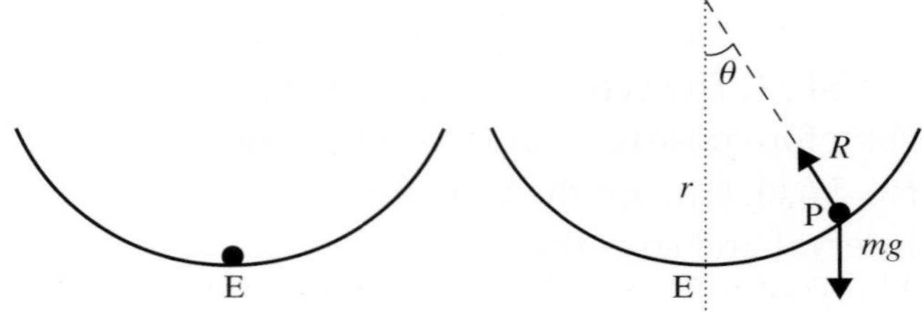

Figure 1.5 A particle in a bowl. The equilibrium position E is at the bottom of the bowl. The particle is released from P.

The forces on the particle are its weight mg and the reaction force R from the bowl, as shown in Figure 1.5. The displacement of the particle is the length of the arc joining points E and P, i.e. $x = r\theta$, where θ is as shown in the diagram. The force trying to bring the particle back towards the equilibrium position is found by taking components of the weight along the dashed set of axes shown in Figure 1.6.

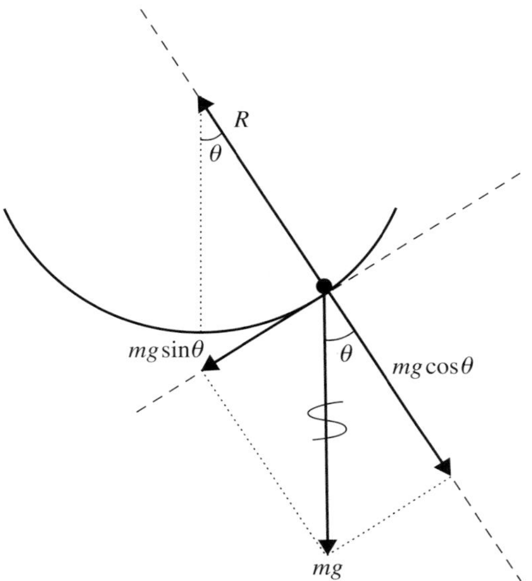

Figure 1.6 The forces on the particle in a bowl.

The force trying to bring the mass back is the component $mg \sin\theta$:

$$F = ma = -mg \sin\theta$$

which implies that

$$a = -g \sin\theta$$

Bringing in the displacement we see that

$$a = -g \sin\left(\frac{x}{r}\right)$$

The acceleration is opposite to the displacement x, but it is *not proportional* to it. We will have oscillations, but they will *not* be simple harmonic.

Let us now assume that the amount of displacement x is actually quite small compared to the radius of the bowl r. Then $\frac{x}{r}$ is a small number and we know that $\sin\left(\frac{x}{r}\right) \approx \frac{x}{r}$ in that case. Then, approximately,

$$a = -g\frac{x}{r} = -\frac{g}{r}x$$

and so

$$a = -\omega^2 x$$

where in this case $\omega^2 = \frac{g}{r}$. So we will have SHM but only for *very small amplitudes*. For small oscillations the period is then

$$T = 2\pi\sqrt{\frac{r}{g}}$$

The simple pendulum

We consider next a mass m that is attached to a vertical string of length L that hangs from the ceiling. The first diagram in Figure 1.7 shows the equilibrium position of the mass. In the second diagram, the particle is displaced away from the vertical and is then released.

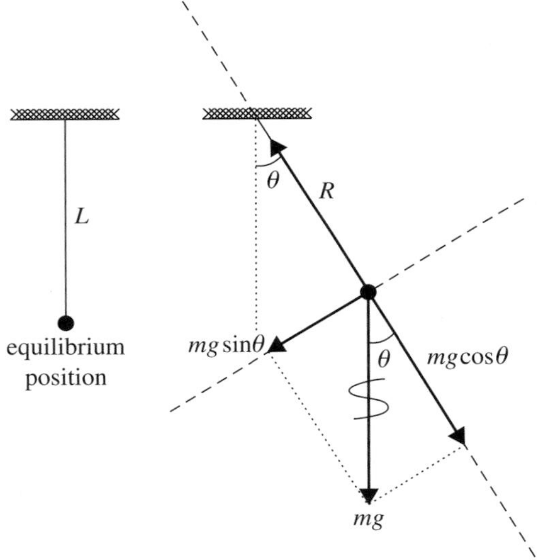

Figure 1.7 The equilibrium position of the pendulum, and the forces on the mass when the pendulum is displaced.

The force pushing the particle back towards the equilibrium position is $mg \sin\theta$ and so we have

$$ma = -mg \sin\theta \quad \Rightarrow \quad a = -g \sin\theta$$

The displacement is $x = L\theta$, where L and θ are as shown in Figure 1.7, and so

$$a = -g \sin\left(\frac{x}{L}\right)$$

Again, the acceleration is *not proportional* to the displacement, x. But if x is small compared to L, then $\sin\left(\frac{x}{L}\right) \approx \frac{x}{L}$ and so

$$a = -g\frac{x}{L} = -\frac{g}{L}x$$

that is,

$$a = -\omega^2 x \qquad \text{with} \qquad \omega^2 = \frac{g}{L}$$

For small oscillations the period of the pendulum is then

$$T = 2\pi\sqrt{\frac{L}{g}}$$

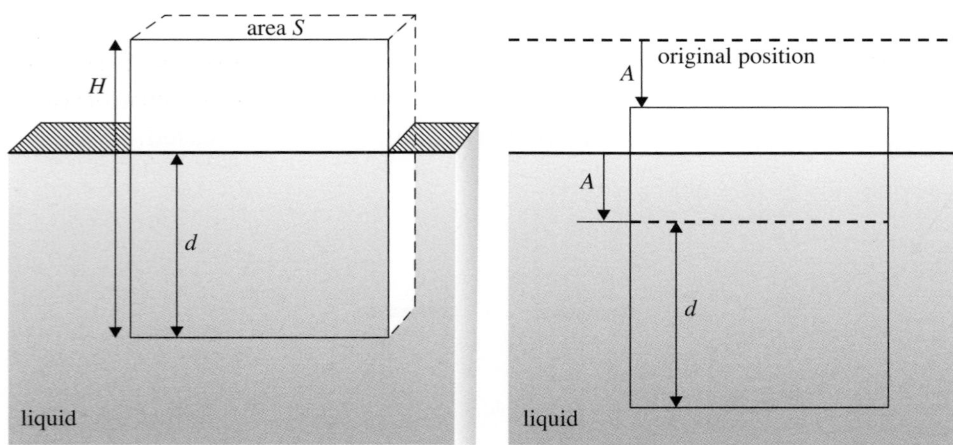

Figure 1.8 (a) A rectangular body floating in a liquid, with depth d immersed. (b) The body after it has been pushed down by a distance A.

Example questions

Q3

(a) Calculate the length of a pendulum that has a period equal to 1.00 s.

(b) Calculate the percentage increase in the period of a pendulum when the length is increased by 4.00%. What is the new period?

Answer

(a) From the text, the period of the pendulum is given by $T = 2\pi\sqrt{\frac{L}{g}}$ and so

$$L = \frac{T^2 g}{4\pi^2} = \frac{1.00^2 \times 9.81}{4\pi^2} = 0.248 \text{ m}$$

(b) Using the propagation of errors as in Chapter 1, we have $\frac{\Delta T}{T} \approx \frac{1}{2}\frac{\Delta L}{L}$. From this we find $\frac{\Delta T}{T} = \frac{1}{2} \times 4.00\% = 2.00\%$. Hence

$$\Delta T = \frac{2.00}{100} \times T = \frac{2.00}{100} \times 1.00 = 0.02 \text{ s}$$

The new period is then $T = 1.02$ s.

Q4

When a body is immersed in a liquid of density ρ it experiences an upward force called the upthrust, which is given by

$$U = \rho g V_{\text{imm}}$$

where V_{imm} is the volume of the body immersed in the liquid. A rectangular body is floating in a liquid of density ρ as shown in Figure 1.8. The body is pushed downwards by a distance A and is then released. Show that the body will perform simple harmonic oscillations, and find the period of the motion.

Answer

The diagram in Figure 1.9 shows the body after it has moved up a bit, so that it is now a distance x below its original equilibrium position.

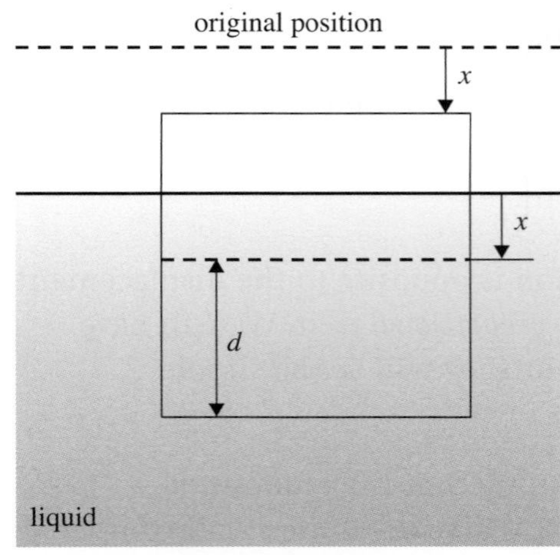

Figure 1.9 The floating body after it has moved back up a bit from its maximum displacement.

The forces on the body are its weight mg downwards and the upthrust U upwards. The upthrust is given by

$$U = \rho g V_{imm} = \rho g S(d + x)$$

where S is the base area of the body. The net force is upwards and equals

$$F_{net} = U - mg = \rho g S(d + x) - mg$$

At the equilibrium position $x = 0$, we have that

$$\rho g S d = mg$$

Substituting this value of mg in the net force, we find

$$F_{net} = \rho g S(d + x) - \rho g S d = \rho g S x$$

The net force on the body is upwards, i.e. opposite to the displacement x. We therefore have that

$$ma = -\rho g S x$$

and so

$$a = -\frac{\rho g S}{m} x$$

i.e. the oscillations are simple harmonic, with $\omega^2 = \frac{\rho g S}{m}$. The period of the oscillations is therefore

$$T = 2\pi\sqrt{\frac{m}{\rho g S}}$$

Q5

The graph in Figure 1.10 shows the variation with displacement x of the acceleration a of a body.

(a) Explain how it may be deduced that the body executes SHM.

(b) Use the graph to determine the period of oscillations.

(c) Determine the maximum speed of the body during the oscillations.

Answer

(a) The graph is a straight line through the origin with negative slope, and so fits the defining relation for SHM, $a = -\omega^2 x$, where $-\omega^2$ is the slope of the graph.

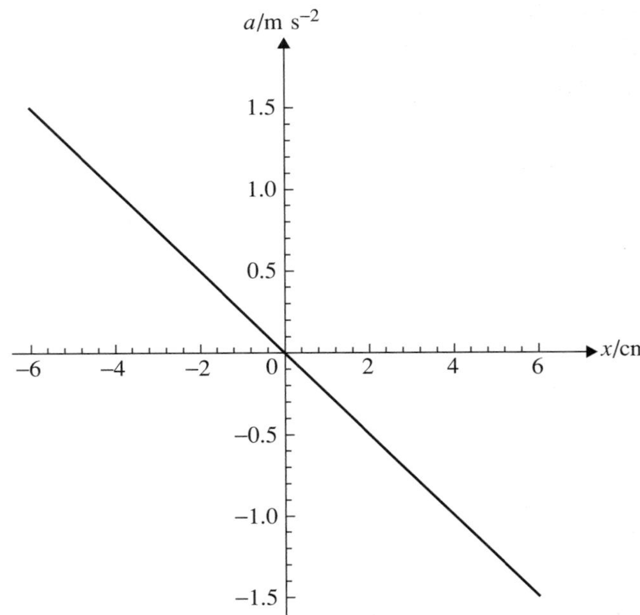

Figure 1.10 Graph showing the variation with time of the acceleration of a body performing SHM.

(b) From the graph we find that the slope is

$$-\omega^2 = -0.25\,\frac{\text{m s}^{-2}}{\text{cm}}$$

$$\omega^2 = 0.25\,\frac{\text{m s}^{-2}}{10^{-2}\,\text{m}}$$

$$\omega^2 = 25\,\text{s}^{-2}$$

$$\omega = 5.0\,\text{s}^{-1}$$

The period is thus $T = \frac{2\pi}{\omega} = \frac{2\pi}{5.0}\,\text{s} \approx 1.3\,\text{s}$.

(c) The amplitude of the motion is $A = 6.0\,\text{cm}$. The maximum speed is

$$v_{max} = \omega A = 5.0 \times 6.0 \times 10^{-2} = 0.30\,\text{m s}^{-1}$$

Q6

The graph in Figure 1.11 shows the displacement of a particle from a fixed equilibrium position.

(a) Use the graph to determine: (i) the period of the motion, (ii) the maximum velocity of the particle during an oscillation, and (iii) the maximum acceleration experienced by the particle.

(b) On a copy of the diagram, mark: (i) a point where the velocity is zero (label this with the letter Z), (ii) a point where the velocity is positive and has the largest magnitude (label this with the letter V), and (iii) a point where the acceleration is positive and has the largest magnitude (label this with the letter A).

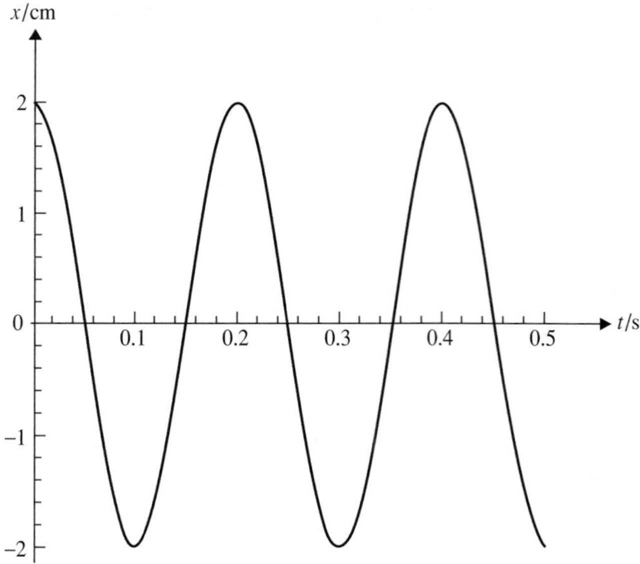

Figure 1.11 Graph showing the variation with time of the displacement of a particle performing SHM.

Answer

(a) (i) The period is read off the graph as $T = 0.20$ s. Since $T = \frac{2\pi}{\omega}$ we have that

$$\omega = \frac{2\pi}{T} = 31.4 \approx 31\ \mathrm{s}^{-1}$$

(ii) The maximum velocity is then

$$v_{max} = \omega A = 31.4 \times 0.020 = 0.63\ \mathrm{m\,s}^{-1}$$

(iii) The maximum acceleration is found from

$$a_{max} = |-\omega^2 A| = 31.4^2 \times 0.020 = 20\ \mathrm{m\,s}^{-2}$$

(b) (i) The velocity is zero at any point where the displacement is at a maximum or a minimum.

(ii) For example at $t = 0.15$ s.

(iii) For example at $t = 0.10$ s or $t = 0.30$ s.

Q7

A body of mass m is placed on a horizontal plate that undergoes vertical SHM (Figure 1.12). The amplitude of the motion is A and the frequency is f.

(a) Derive an expression for the reaction force on the particle from the plate when the particle is at its highest point.

(b) Using the expression in (a), deduce that the particle will lose contact with the plate if the frequency is higher than $\sqrt{\frac{g}{4\pi^2 A}}$.

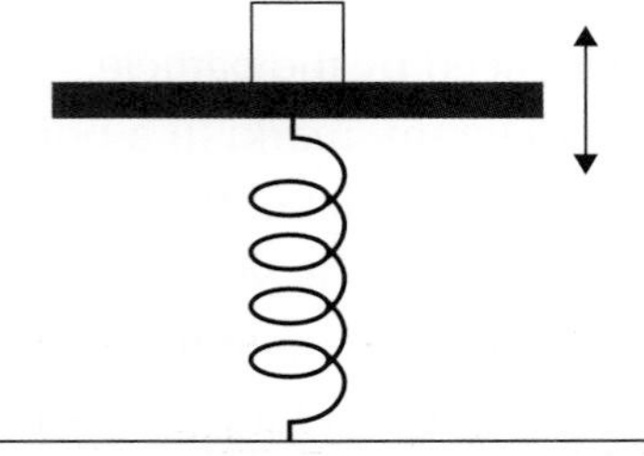

Figure 1.12 A particle on a horizontal plate executing SHM.

Answer

(a) At the highest point $x = A$ we have $a = -\omega^2 A$, so

$$R - mg = ma = -m\omega^2 A$$

and substituting $\omega = 2\pi f$ gives

$$R - mg = -m(2\pi f)^2 A$$

$$= -4\pi^2 f^2 mA$$

$$R = mg - 4\pi^2 f^2 mA$$

(b) The particle will lose contact with the plate when $R \leq 0$, i.e. when

$$mg - 4\pi^2 f^2 mA \leq 0$$

$$mg \leq 4\pi^2 f^2 mA$$

$$4\pi^2 f^2 mA \geq mg$$

$$f \geq \sqrt{\frac{g}{4\pi^2 A}}$$

Energy in simple harmonic motion

Consider again a mass at the end of a horizontal spring. Let the extension of the spring be x at a particular instant of time, and let the velocity of the mass be v at that time. The elastic potential energy stored in the spring is

$$E_p = \tfrac{1}{2}kx^2$$

and the kinetic energy of the mass is

$$E_k = \tfrac{1}{2}mv^2$$

These are shown separately in Figure 1.13, and on the same axes in Figure 1.14.

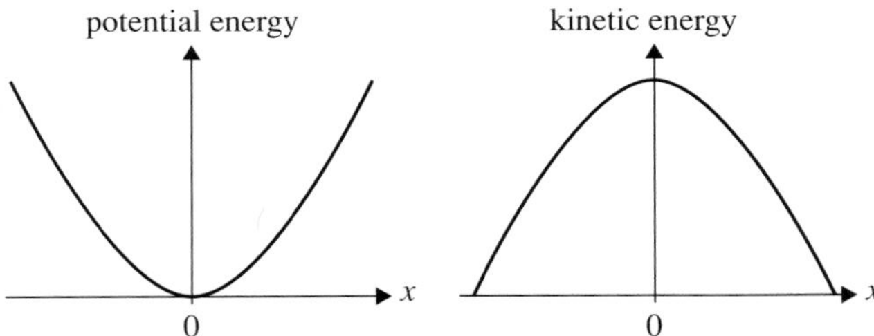

Figure 1.13 Graphs showing the variation with displacement of the potential energy and kinetic energy of a mass on a spring.

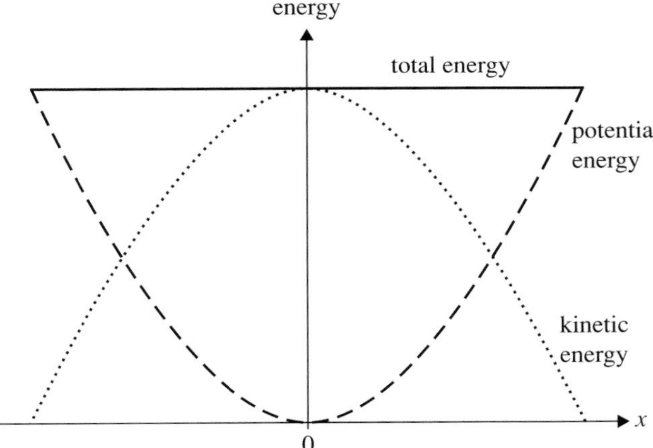

Figure 1.14 Graphs showing the variation with displacement of the potential energy and kinetic energy of a mass on a spring. The total energy is a horizontal straight line.

The total energy of the system is then

$$E = E_p + E_k = \frac{1}{2}kx^2 + \frac{1}{2}mv^2$$

In the absence of frictional and other resistance forces, this total energy is conserved, and so

$$E = \frac{1}{2}kx^2 + \frac{1}{2}mv^2 = \text{constant}$$

If the mass is released from rest when the extension is the amplitude of the motion A, then

$$\frac{1}{2}kx^2 + \frac{1}{2}mv^2 = \frac{1}{2}kA^2$$

Solving for the velocity v we find

$$v = \pm\sqrt{\frac{k}{m}}\sqrt{A^2 - x^2}$$

We need both signs since the mass passes any one position twice, once going to the right (positive velocity) and once going to the left (negative velocity).

Recalling that for this motion $\omega^2 = \frac{k}{m}$, we see that

$$v = \pm\omega\sqrt{A^2 - x^2}$$

The maximum velocity is achieved when $x = 0$, i.e. as the mass moves past its equilibrium position. The value of the maximum velocity is then

$$v_{\text{max}} = \omega A$$

At the extremes of the motion, $x = \pm A$, and so $v = 0$ as we expect.

At $x = \pm A$ the system has elastic potential energy only, and at $x = 0$ it has kinetic energy only. At intermediate points the system has both forms of energy: elastic potential energy and kinetic energy. During an oscillation, we therefore have transformations from one form of energy to another.

Example questions

Q8

The graph in Figure 1.15 shows the variation with the square of the displacement (x^2) of the potential

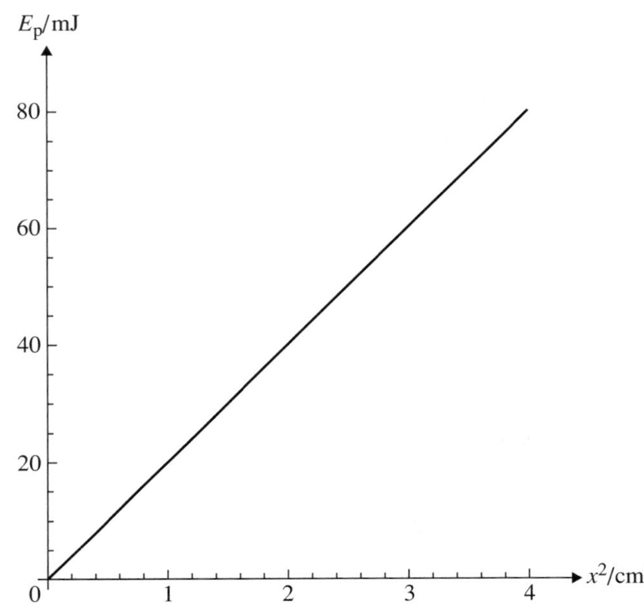

Figure 1.15 Graph showing the variation with the square of the displacement of the potential energy of a particle in SHM.

energy of a particle of mass 40 g that is executing SHM. Using the graph, determine:
(a) the period of oscillation;
(b) the maximum speed of the particle during an oscillation.

Answer

(a) The maximum potential energy is $E = \frac{1}{2}m\omega^2A^2$. From the graph the maximum potential energy is 80.0 mJ (80×10^{-3} J) and the amplitude is 2.00 cm (2.00×10^{-2} m). Thus

$$\omega^2 = \frac{2E}{mA^2}$$

$$= \frac{2 \times 80 \times 10^{-3}}{0.040 \times (2.00 \times 10^{-2})^2}$$

$$= 10^4 \text{ s}^{-2}$$

$$\omega = 100 \text{ s}^{-1}$$

(b) The maximum speed is found from

$$v_{max} = \omega A = 100 \times 2.00 \times 10^{-2} = 2.00 \text{ m s}^{-1}$$

Q9

The graph in Figure 1.16 shows the variation with displacement of the kinetic energy of a particle of mass 0.40 kg performing SHM. Use the graph to determine:
(a) the total energy of the particle;
(b) the maximum speed of the particle;
(c) the amplitude of the motion;

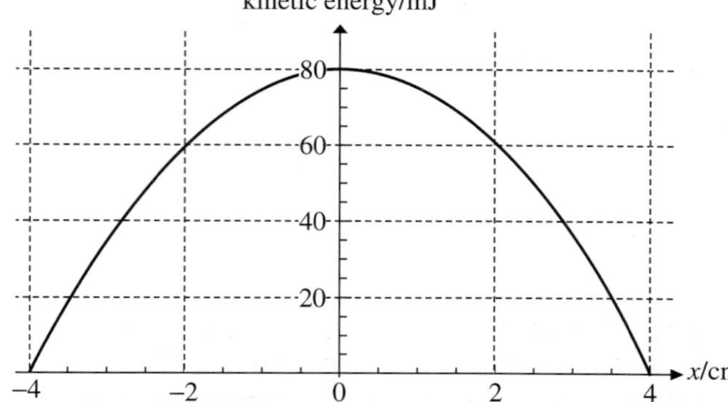

Figure 1.16 Graph showing the variation with displacement of the kinetic energy of a particle.

(d) the potential energy when the displacement is 2.0 cm;
(e) the period of the motion.

Answer

(a) The total energy is equal to the maximum kinetic energy, i.e. 80 mJ.
(b) The maximum speed is found from

$$\frac{1}{2}mv_{max}^2 = E_{max}$$

$$v_{max}^2 = \frac{2E_{max}}{m}$$

$$v_{max} = \sqrt{\frac{2 \times 80 \times 10^{-3}}{0.40}}$$

$$v_{max} = 0.63 \text{ m s}^{-1}$$

(c) The amplitude is 4.0 cm.
(d) When $x = 2.0$ cm, the kinetic energy is 60 mJ and so the potential energy is 20 mJ.
(e) The maximum potential energy is 80 mJ and equals $\frac{1}{2}kA^2$. Hence

$$\frac{1}{2}kA^2 = E_{max}$$

$$k = \frac{2E_{max}}{A^2}$$

$$k = \frac{2 \times 80 \times 10^{-3}}{(4.0 \times 10^{-2})^2}$$

$$k = 100 \text{ N m}^{-1}$$

and then

$$\omega^2 = \frac{k}{m}$$

$$= \frac{100}{0.40}$$

$$\omega = \sqrt{250}$$

$$= 15.81 \text{ s}^{-1}$$

and so the period is $T = \frac{2\pi}{\omega} = 0.40$ s.

Q10

A particle of mass 0.50 kg undergoes SHM with angular frequency $\omega = 9.0 \text{ s}^{-1}$ and amplitude 3.0 cm. For this particle, determine:
(a) the maximum velocity;
(b) the velocity and acceleration when the particle has displacement 1.5 cm and moves

towards the equilibrium position from its initial position at $x = 3.0$ cm;

(c) the total energy of the motion.

Answer

(a) The maximum velocity is given by

$$v_{max} = \omega A$$
$$= 9.0 \times 3.0 \times 10^{-2}$$
$$= 0.27\ \text{m s}^{-1}$$

(b) At $x = 1.5$ cm, the velocity is

$$v = \pm\omega\sqrt{A^2 - x^2} = \pm 9.0\sqrt{(3.0^2 - 1.5^2) \times 10^{-2}}$$
$$= \pm 0.23\ \text{m s}^{-1}$$

We must choose the negative sign since the particle is moving to the left, so $v = -0.23\ \text{m s}^{-1}$. The acceleration is

$$a = -\omega^2 x$$
$$= -9.0^2 \times 1.5 \times 10^{-2}$$
$$= -1.2\ \text{m s}^{-2}$$

(c) The total energy is

$$E = \tfrac{1}{2} m v_{max}^2$$
$$= \tfrac{1}{2}(0.50)\,0.27^2$$
$$= 18\ \text{mJ}$$

Damping

The SHM described above is unrealistic in that we have completely ignored frictional and other resistance forces. The effect of these forces on an oscillating system is that the oscillations will eventually stop and the energy of the system will be dissipated mainly as thermal energy to the environment and the system itself.

Oscillations taking place in the presence of resistance forces are called **damped oscillations**. The behaviour of the system depends on the degree of damping. We may distinguish three distinct cases: under-damping, critical damping and over-damping.

Under-damping

Whenever the resistance forces are small, the system will continue to oscillate but with a frequency that is somewhat smaller than that in the absence of damping. The amplitude gradually decreases until it approaches zero and the oscillations stop. The amplitude decreases exponentially. Typical examples of under-damped SHM are shown in Figure 1.17. The case represented by (b) corresponds to heavier damping than (a) and the oscillations die out faster. Note that the period of oscillation in the case of the heavier damping (b) is larger than that in the case of lighter damping (a).

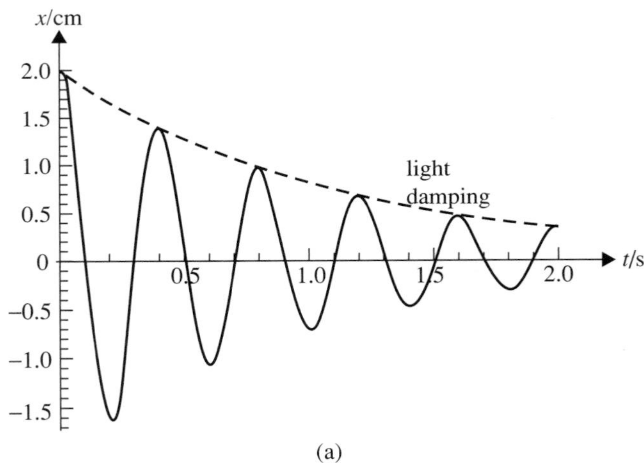

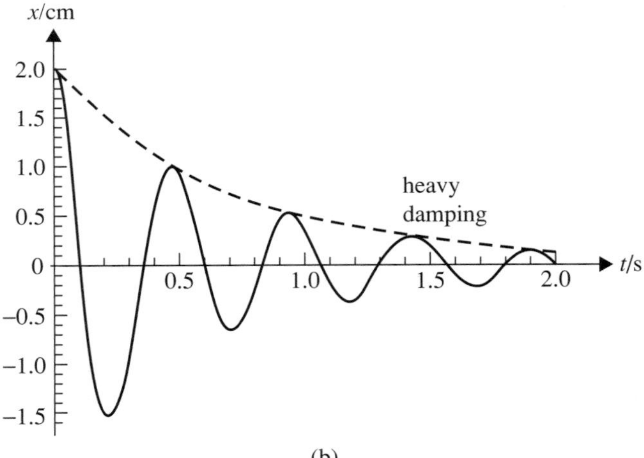

Figure 1.17 Graphs showing the variation with time of the displacement of a particle in damped SHM. The curve in (b) corresponds to heavier damping than in (a), and has a slightly longer period.

Critical damping

In this case the amount of damping is large enough that the system returns to its equilibrium state as fast as possible *without* performing oscillations. A typical case of critical damping is shown in Figure 1.18.

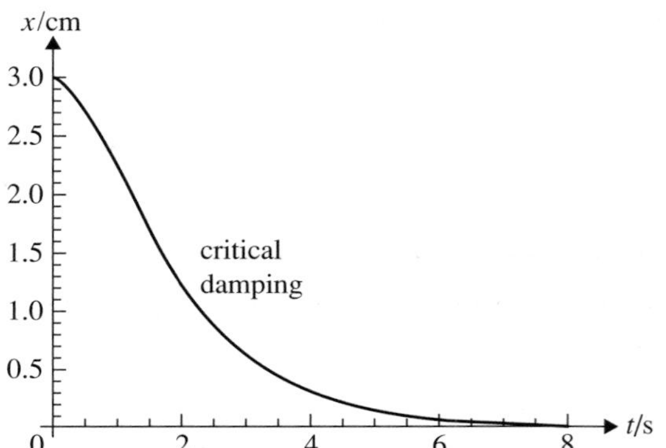

Figure 1.18 Critical damping. The displacement goes to zero without oscillations.

Over-damping

In this case the degree of damping is so great that the system returns to equilibrium without oscillations (as in the case of critical damping) but *much slower* than in the case of critical damping. The system shown in Figure 1.18 if over-damped would behave as the upper curve in Figure 1.19.

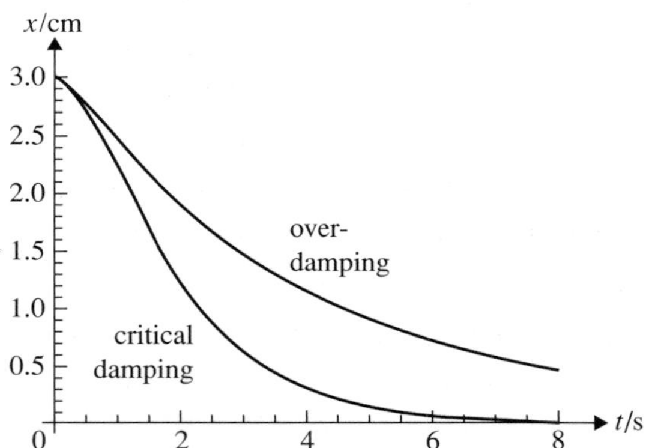

Figure 1.19 A system that is over-damped. The displacement goes to zero slower than in the case of critical damping.

Forced oscillations and resonance

We will now examine qualitatively the effect of an externally applied force F on a system that is free to oscillate with frequency f_0. The force F will be assumed to vary periodically with time with a frequency (the driving frequency) f_D, for example as $F = F_0 \cos(2\pi f_D t)$. The question is how the oscillating system will respond to the presence of the external driving force. The oscillations that take place in this case are called **forced oscillations**.

In general, some time after the external force is applied, the system will switch to oscillations with a frequency equal to the driving frequency f_D. However, the amplitude of the oscillations will depend on the relation between f_D and f_0, and the amount of damping. We might expect that, because the system wants to oscillate at its own natural frequency, when the external force has the same frequency as the natural frequency, large oscillations will take place. On the other hand, at very low frequencies, $f_D \approx 0$, and so $F = F_0 \cos(2\pi f_D t) \approx F_0$, i.e. it is constant. A constant force applied to a spring, for example, will extend the spring by a constant amount.

A detailed analysis produces the graph in Figure 1.20 showing how the amplitude of oscillation of a system with natural frequency f_0 varies as it is subjected to a periodic force of frequency f_D. The degree of damping increases as we move from the top curve down.

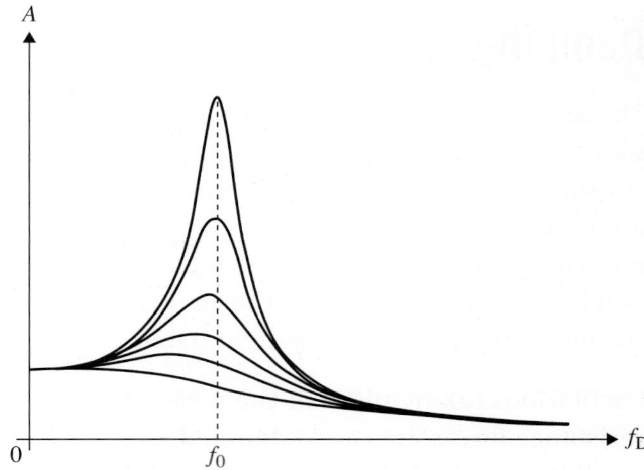

Figure 1.20 Graph showing the variation with driving frequency of the amplitude of forced SHM when the system is driven by an external periodic force.

The general features of the graph in Figure 1.20 are as follows:

- For a small degree of damping, the peak of the curve occurs at the natural frequency of the system, f_0.
- The lower the degree of damping, the higher and narrower the curve.
- As the amount of damping increases, the peak shifts to lower frequencies.
- At very low frequencies, the amplitude is essentially constant.

If f_D is very different from f_0, the amplitude of oscillation will be small. On the other hand, if f_D is approximately the same as f_0, and the degree of damping is small, the resulting driven oscillations will have large amplitude. The largest amplitude is obtained when f_D is equal to f_0, in which case we say that the system is in **resonance**.

▶ The state in which the frequency of the externally applied periodic force equals the natural frequency of the system is called *resonance*. This results in oscillations with large amplitude.

Resonance can be disastrous: we do not want an aeroplane wing to resonate; nor is it good for a building to be set into resonance by an earthquake. Resonance can be irritating: if the car in which you drive is set into resonance by bumps on the road or a poorly tuned engine. But resonance can also be a good thing: resonance is used by a microwave oven to warm food; and your radio uses resonance to tune into one specific station and not another. Another useful example of electrical resonance is the quartz oscillator, a crystal made out of quartz that can be made to vibrate at a specific frequency. The resonant frequency of the quartz oscillator depends on how it is cut from the original crystal. These crystals are used as the timing device in electronic watches and many other devices in electronics. They are cheap and keep their characteristics with time. The operation of the quartz oscillator uses a phenomenon called *piezoelectricity* in which an electrical signal applied to the crystal forces the crystal to vibrate. In turn, the mechanical vibration is fed back as another electrical signal at the crystal's resonant frequency.

? QUESTIONS

1 State what is meant by oscillation and simple harmonic motion.

2 State two ways in which an SHM oscillation is different from a general oscillation.

3 A ball goes back and forth along a horizontal floor bouncing off two vertical walls. Is the motion an example of an oscillation? If yes, is the oscillation simple harmonic?

4 A ball bounces vertically off the floor. Is the motion of the ball an example of an oscillation? If yes, is the oscillation simple harmonic?

5 Explain how you would use a spring of known spring constant to measure the mass of a body when in a spacecraft in outer space.

6 Explain why the oscillations of a pendulum are, in general, not simple harmonic. What condition must be satisfied for the oscillations to become approximately simple harmonic?

7 Show explicitly that, if $x = A\cos(\omega t + \phi)$, the period of the motion is given by $T = \frac{2\pi}{\omega}$ independently of A and ϕ.

8 The displacement of a particle executing SHM is given by $y = 5.0\cos(2t)$, where y is in millimetres and t is in seconds. Calculate:
(a) the initial displacement of the particle;
(b) the displacement at $t = 1.2$ s;
(c) the time at which the displacement first becomes –2.0 mm;
(d) the displacement when the velocity of the particle is 6.0 mm s^{-1}.

9 (a) Write down an equation for the displacement of a particle undergoing SHM with an amplitude equal to 8.0 cm and a frequency of 14 Hz, assuming that at $t = 0$ the displacement is 8.0 cm and the particle is at rest.

(b) Find the displacement, velocity and acceleration of this particle at a time of 0.025 s.

10 A point on a guitar string oscillates in SHM with an amplitude of 5.0 mm and a frequency of 460 Hz. Determine the maximum velocity and acceleration of this point.

HL only

11 A guitar string, whose two ends are fixed so that they cannot move, oscillates as shown in Figure 1.21.

Figure 1.21 For question 11.

The vertical displacement of a point on the string a distance x from the left end is given by $y = 6.0\cos(1040\pi t)\sin(\pi x)$, where y is in millimetres, x is in metres and t is in seconds. Use this expression to:

(a) deduce that all points on the string execute SHM with a common frequency and common phase, and determine the common frequency;

(b) deduce that different points on the string have different amplitudes;

(c) determine the maximum amplitude of oscillation;

(d) calculate the length L of the string;

(e) calculate the amplitude of oscillation of the point on the string where $x = \frac{3}{4}L$.

12 A body performs SHM along a horizontal straight line between the extremes shown by the dashed lines in Figure 1.22.

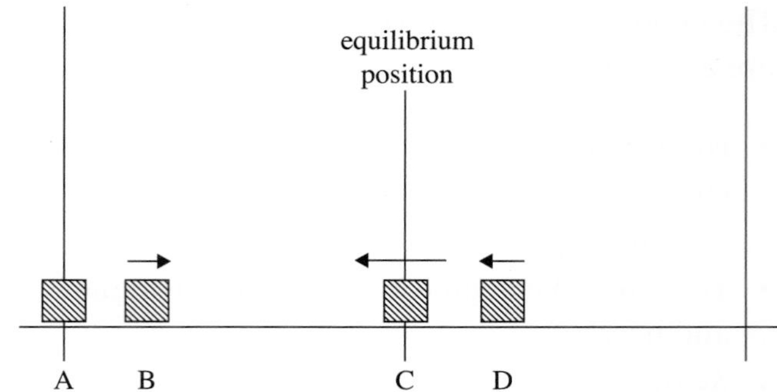

Figure 1.22 For question 12.

The arrows represent the direction of motion of the body. The body is shown in four positions, A, B, C and D. Copy the diagram and, in each position, draw arrows to represent the direction and relative magnitude of (a) the acceleration of the body, and (b) the net force on the body.

13 The piston (of mass 0.25 kg) of a car engine has a *stroke* (i.e. distance between extreme positions) of 9.0 cm and operates at 4500 rev min^{-1}, as shown in Figure 1.23.

(a) Calculate the acceleration of the piston at maximum displacement.

(b) Calculate the velocity as the piston moves past its equilibrium point.

(c) What is the net force exerted on the piston at maximum displacement?

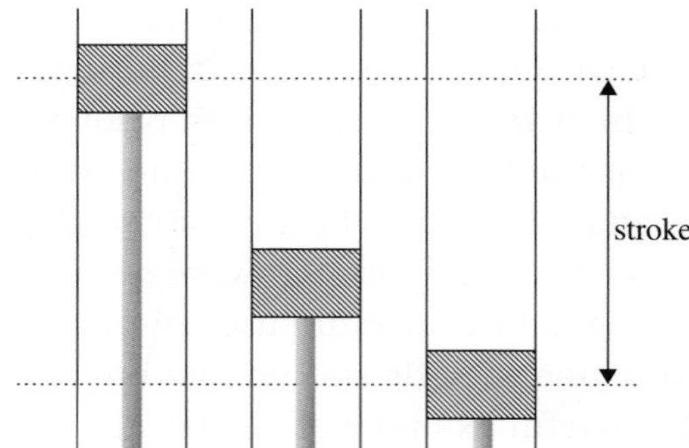

Figure 1.23 For question 13.

14 The graph in Figure 1.24 shows the variation with time t of the velocity v of a particle executing SHM.

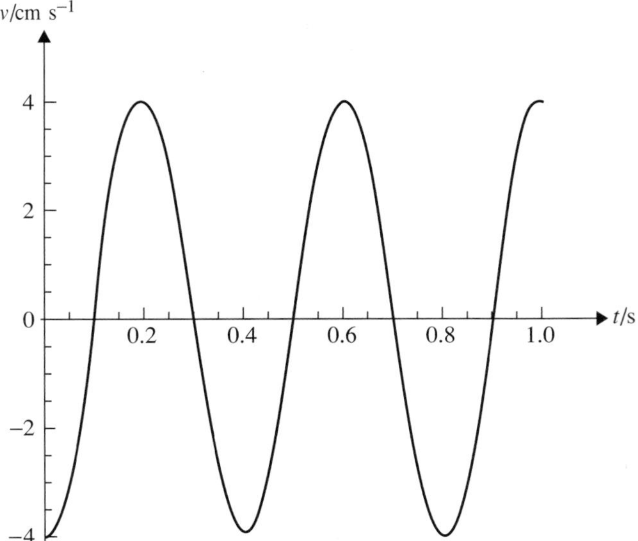

Figure 1.24 For question 14.

(a) Using the graph, estimate the area between the curve and the time axis from 0.10 s to 0.30 s.

(b) State what this area represents.

(c) Hence write down an equation giving the displacement of the particle as a function of time.

15 The graph in Figure 1.25 shows the variation with time t of the displacement x of a particle executing SHM.

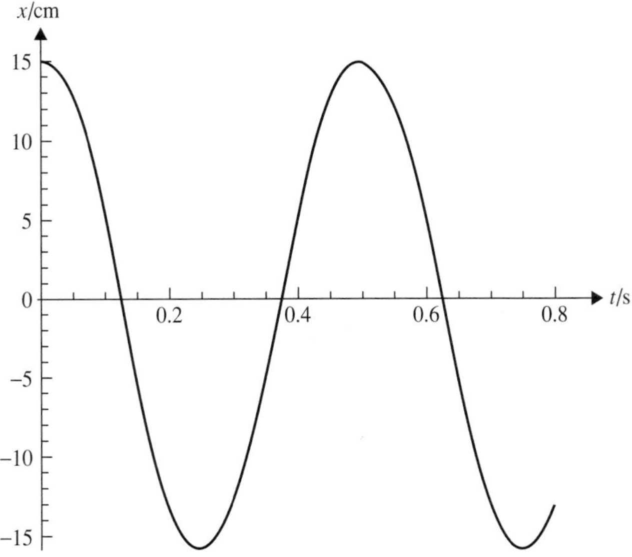

Figure 1.25 For question 15.

Draw a graph to show the variation with displacement x of the acceleration a of the particle (put numbers on the axes).

16 The graph in Figure 1.26 shows the variation with displacement x of the acceleration a of a body of mass 0.150 kg.

(a) Use the graph to explain why the motion of the body is SHM. Determine the following:

(b) the period of the motion;

(c) the maximum velocity of the body during an oscillation;

(d) the maximum net force exerted on the body;

(e) the total energy of the body.

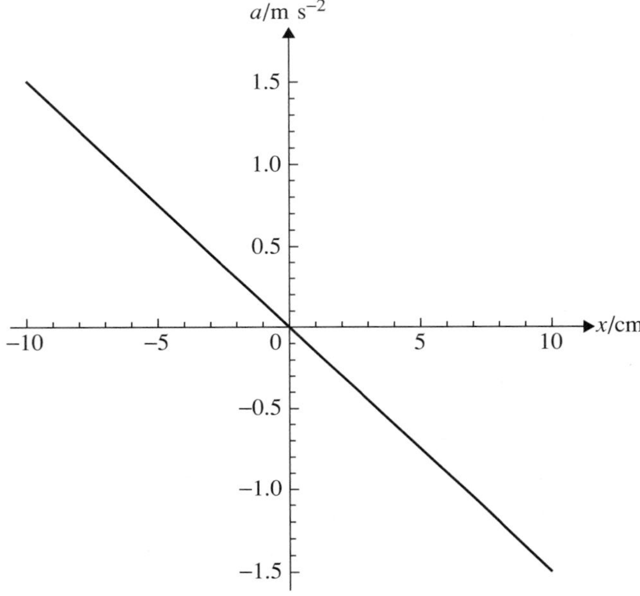

Figure 1.26 For question 16.

17 A body of mass 0.120 kg is placed on a horizontal plate. The plate oscillates vertically in SHM making five oscillations per second.

(a) Determine the largest possible amplitude of oscillations such that the body never loses contact with the plate.

(b) Calculate the normal reaction force on the body at the lowest point of the oscillations when the amplitude has the value found in (a).

18 A passenger on a cruise ship in rough seas stands on a set of 'weighing scales'. The reading R of the scales (in kilograms) as a function of time is shown in Figure 1.27.

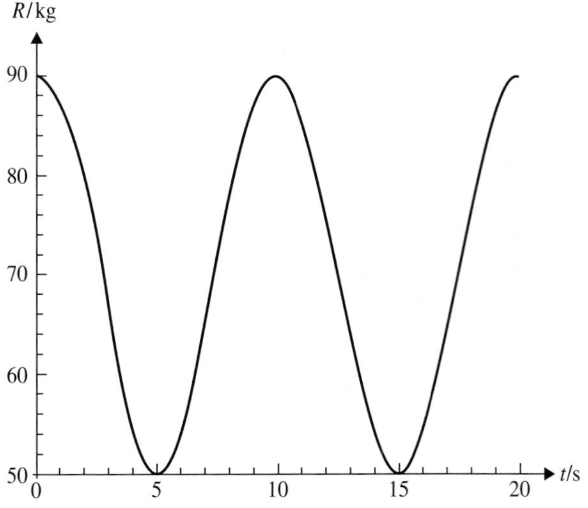

Figure 1.27 For question 18.

Use the graph to determine:
(a) the mass of the passenger;
(b) the amplitude of the waves in the sea.

HL only

19 This is a very unrealistic but interesting 'thought experiment' involving SHM. Imagine boring a straight tunnel from one place (A) on the surface of the earth to another place (B) diametrically opposite, and then releasing a ball of mass m at point A (Figure 1.28). To answer the following questions, you need to know that gravitation implies that, when the ball is at the position shown in Figure 1.28, it experiences a force of gravitation from the mass inside the dotted circle *only*. Further, this mass inside the dotted circle may be considered to be concentrated at the centre of the earth. Assume that the density of the earth is uniform.

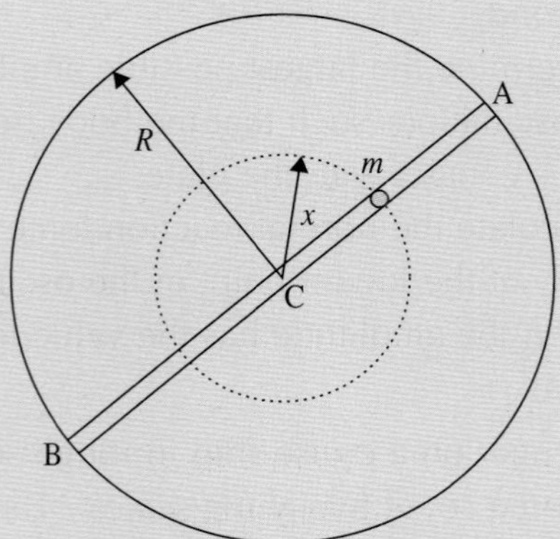

Figure 1.28 For question 19.

(a) Denoting the mass of the earth by M and its radius by R, derive an expression for the mass inside the dotted circle (of radius x).
(b) Derive an expression for the gravitational force on the ball when at the position shown in Figure 1.28, a distance x from the centre.
(c) Hence deduce that the motion of the ball is simple harmonic.
(d) Determine the period of the motion.
(e) Evaluate this period using $M = 6.0 \times 10^{24}$ kg, $R = 6.4 \times 10^{6}$ m and $G = 6.67 \times 10^{-11}$ N kg^{-2} m^{2}.
(f) Compare the period of this motion with the period of rotation of a satellite around the earth in a circular orbit of radius R.

20 A particle of mass m is attached to the middle of a horizontal string of constant tension T. The length of the string is L. The tension in the string is so large that the string is essentially horizontal at the equilibrium position. The particle is displaced vertically by a small distance A and is then released (Figure 1.29).

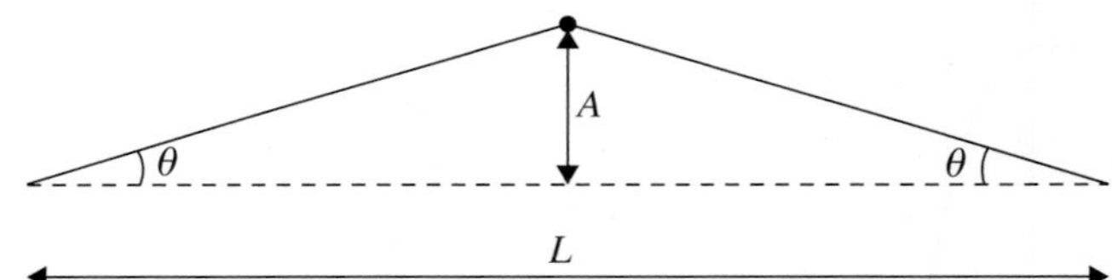

Figure 1.29 For question 20.

(a) Deduce that the net force on the particle at the position shown is $2T \sin\theta$.
(b) Hence deduce that the particle's acceleration is given by $a = -\frac{4T}{mL}x$, where x is the vertical distance of the particle from the horizontal line.
(c) Determine the period of oscillations of this particle.

21 A body is suspended vertically at the end of a spring that is attached to the ceiling of an elevator (Figure 1.30). The elevator moves with constant acceleration. Discuss

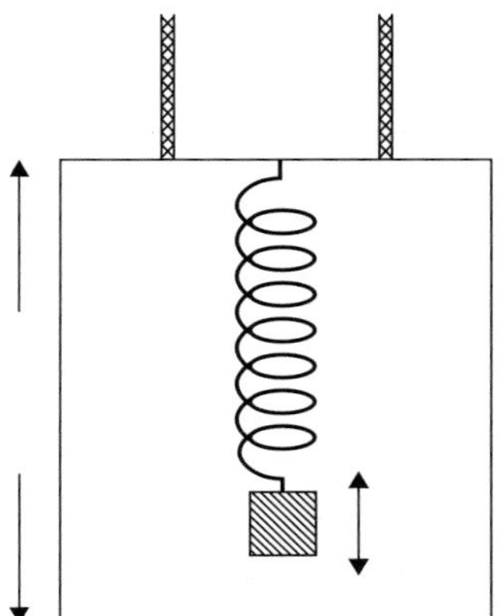

Figure 1.30 For question 21.

qualitatively the effect, if any, of the acceleration on the period of oscillations of the mass when the acceleration is (a) upwards and (b) downwards.

HL only

22 A particle undergoes SHM with angular frequency ω. The initial displacement is x_0 and the initial velocity is v_0. Deduce that an expression for the amplitude of this motion is

$$A = \sqrt{x_0^2 + \frac{v_0^2}{\omega^2}}.$$

23 A block is attached to a spring and performs SHM along a horizontal straight line. A piece of putty is dropped vertically so that it sticks to the block when it lands on it (Figure 1.31).

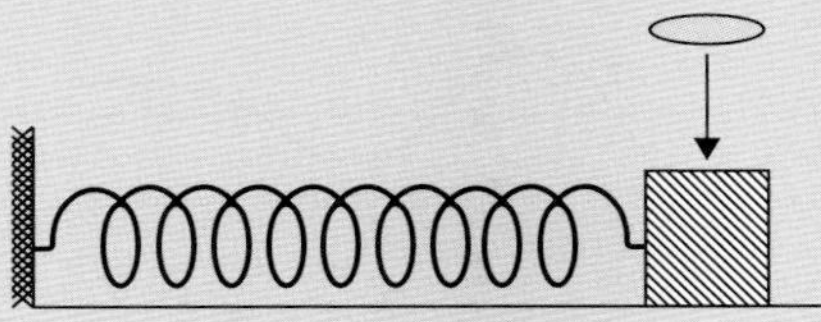

Figure 1.31 For question 23.

Discuss *qualitatively* the effects of this, if any, on the amplitude and the period of oscillation in the following two separate cases in which the putty lands on the block:

(a) when the block moves past its equilibrium position;

(b) when the block is momentarily at rest at maximum displacement.

24 A body of mass 1.80 kg executes SHM such that its displacement from equilibrium is given by $x = 0.360\cos(6.80t)$, where x is in metres and t is in seconds. Determine:

(a) the amplitude, frequency and period of the oscillations;

(b) the total energy of the body;

(c) the kinetic energy and the elastic potential energy of the body when the displacement is 0.125 m.

25 A body of mass 2.0 kg is connected to two springs, each of spring constant $k = 120\ \text{N m}^{-1}$ (Figure 1.32).

(a) When the springs are connected as in Figure 1.32(a), calculate the period of the oscillations of this mass when it is displaced from its equilibrium position and then released.

(b) When the springs are connected instead as in Figure 1.32(b), would the period change?

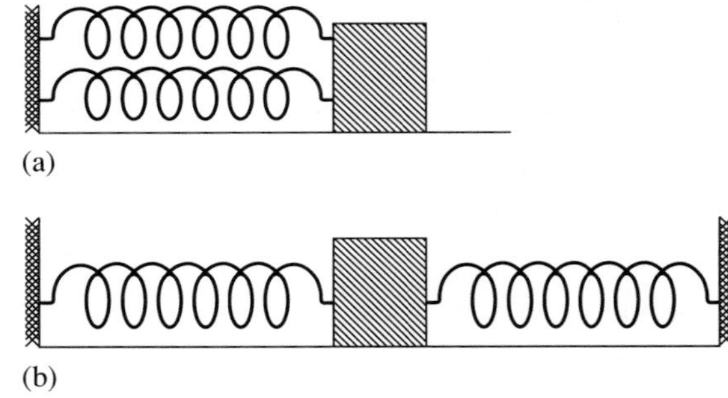

Figure 1.32 For question 25.

26 A woman bungee-jumper of mass 60 kg is attached to an elastic rope of natural length 15 m. The rope behaves like a spring of spring constant $k = 220\ \text{N m}^{-1}$. The other end of the spring is attached to a high bridge. The woman jumps from the bridge.

(a) Determine how far below the bridge she falls, before she instantaneously comes to rest.

(b) Calculate her acceleration at the position you found in (a).

(c) Explain why she will perform SHM, and find the period of oscillations.

(d) The woman will eventually come to rest at a specific distance below the bridge. Calculate this distance.

(e) Explain whether her oscillations are under-damped, critically damped or over-damped.

(f) The mechanical energy of the woman after she comes to rest is less than the woman's total mechanical energy just before she jumped. Explain what happened to the 'lost' mechanical energy.

27 State what is meant by under-damping, critical damping and over-damping in the context of SHM oscillations.

28 State two examples of oscillating systems where damping is desirable and two examples where it is undesirable.

29 The graph in Figure 1.33 shows the variation with time t of the displacement x of a particle undergoing SHM that is under-damped.

(a) By making measurements on the diagram, determine whether the ratio of successive amplitudes stays constant.

(b) The amount of energy stored in the oscillation is proportional to the square of the amplitude. Determine, for these oscillations, the amount of energy lost in one oscillation as a percentage of the energy stored in the previous oscillation.

(c) On the same axes, draw a graph to show the changes, if any, to the variation of displacement if the amount of damping were to increase (but still keep the oscillations under-damped).

30 The graph in Figure 1.34 shows the variation with time t of the displacement x of a particle performing critically damped SHM. On the

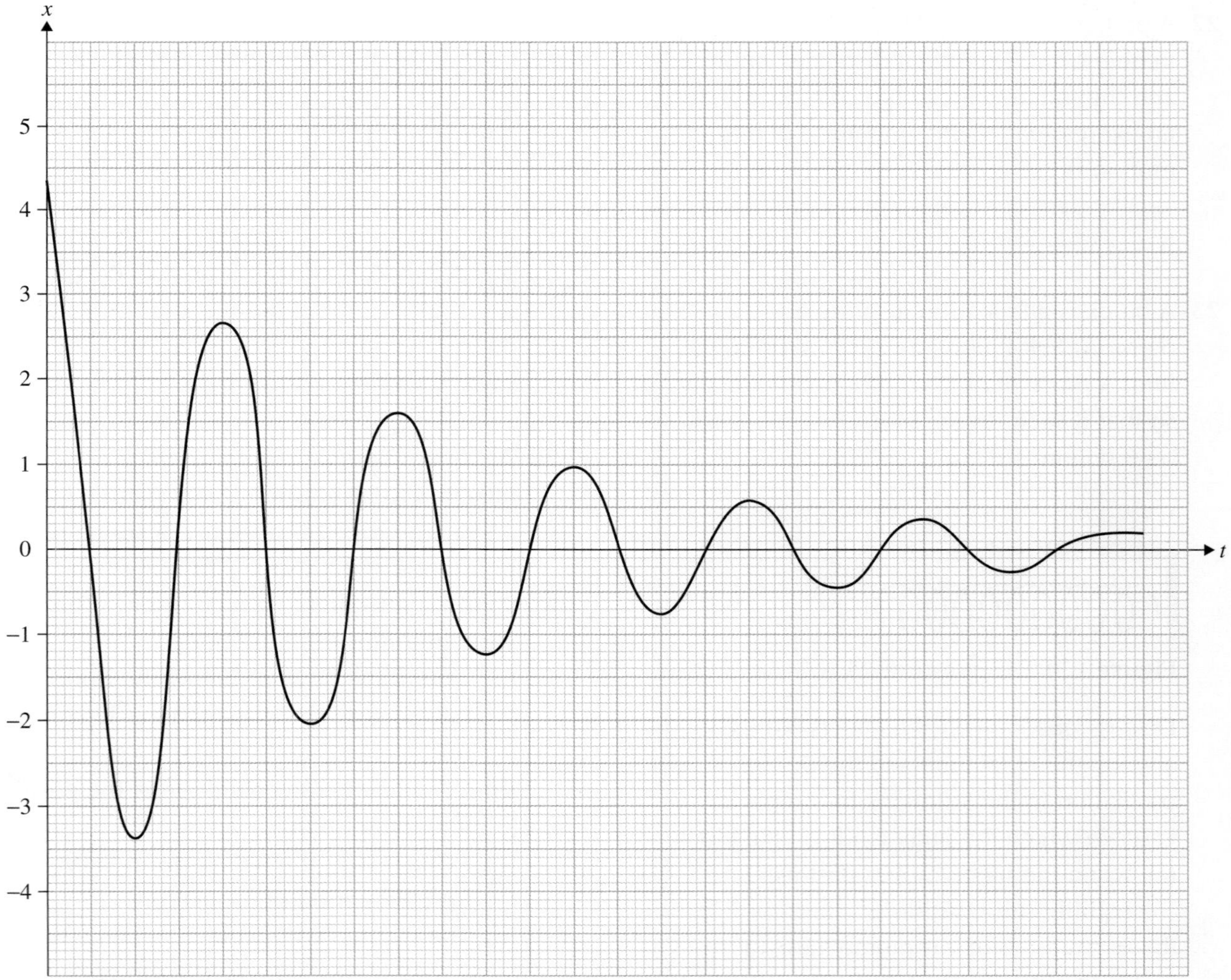

Figure 1.33 For question 29.

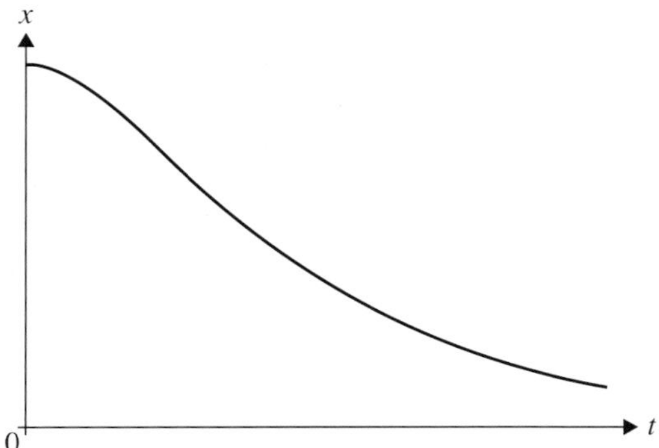

Figure 1.34 For question 30.

same axes, draw sketch graphs to show the variation of the displacement when the same system is (a) under-damped and (b) over-damped. (Note: no numbers are required on the axes.)

31 The shock absorbers of a car protect the passengers by absorbing the impact felt by the car when going over bumps on the road. Should the shock absorbers be under-damped, critically damped or over-damped? Discuss your answer.

32 State one advantage and one disadvantage of over-damped car shock absorbers.

33 A particle performs SHM. Draw sketch graphs on the same axes (no numbers are required) to show the variation with time t of the amplitude A of the motion for (a) no damping, (b) light damping and (c) heavy damping.

HL only

34 A particle of mass m is attached to a horizontal spring of spring constant k and executes SHM of amplitude A.

(a) State the angular frequency of oscillations of the particle.

(b) Deduce that the velocity and displacement of the particle satisfy the relation

$$\frac{v^2}{\omega^2 A^2} + \frac{x^2}{A^2} = 1$$

(c) Sketch a graph to show the variation with displacement x of the velocity v of the particle. Your graph must represent one full oscillation.

(d) The area of the ellipse $\frac{y^2}{b^2} + \frac{x^2}{a^2} = 1$ is given by πab. Determine the area of the graph you have drawn in (c).

(e) The mass is now subject to light damping. Suggest how the graph in (c) changes.

35 Distinguish between free oscillations and forced oscillations.

36 State what you understand by the term 'resonance'. Give one example of resonance.

37 It is said that soldiers marching over a bridge will break their step. What might be a reason for this?

38 A body of mass m is attached to a spring of spring constant k and unstretched length L. The other end of the spring is attached to a frictionless horizontal table. The spring is free to rotate as shown in Figure 1.35. The body moves along a circle on the table with frequency f.

(a) State the natural frequency of the spring–mass system.

(b) Calculate the extension of the spring.

(c) Comment on your answer to (b) when the frequency of rotation becomes equal to the natural frequency you stated in (a).

(d) How is the difficulty discovered in (c) resolved?

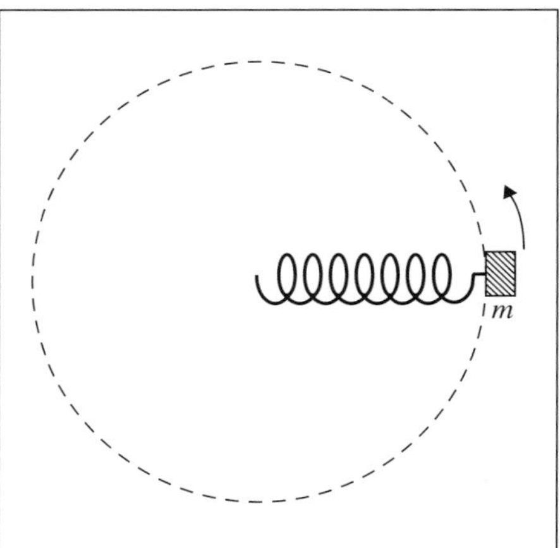

Figure 1.35 For question 38.

Travelling-wave characteristics

This chapter introduces a new and special kind of motion: wave motion. There are two large classes of waves: mechanical and electromagnetic waves. Waves can be further classified into transverse and longitudinal waves.

Objectives

By the end of this chapter you should be able to:

- state what is meant by *wave motion*;
- distinguish between *longitudinal* and *transverse* waves;
- define *amplitude*, *wavelength*, *period* and *frequency* and state the relationship between them, $f = \frac{1}{T}$;
- state what is meant by *crest* and *trough* and identify these on a graph;
- find amplitude and period from a *displacement–time* graph;
- find amplitude and wavelength from a *displacement–position* graph;
- understand the meaning of the terms *wavefront* and *ray*;
- use $v = \lambda f$.

What is a wave?

Waves are a very special kind of motion that differs significantly from the motion we have studied in earlier chapters. To understand the difference, and to appreciate this new kind of motion, let us look at what we have learned in a somewhat different way. If a stone is thrown at a window and the window breaks, this is because the stone transferred its kinetic energy from the point at which it was thrown onto the window. The stone exerted a force on the window (transfer of momentum) and broke it. A wave is also a way of transferring energy and momentum from one place to another but *without the actual large-scale motion of a material body.* For example, light (a kind of wave) from the sun arrives on earth having travelled a large distance in a vacuum, and upon arrival warms up the earth. A soprano singing can break a crystal glass because energy and momentum have been transferred through air by a sound wave.

Light is an example of a wave that does not need a medium in which to travel. It can travel in a vacuum as well as in solids (e.g. glass) or liquids (e.g. water). Light is part of a large family of waves called *electromagnetic waves.* Sound, along with water waves, string waves, etc., belongs to a family called *mechanical waves.* These do require a medium for their propagation. Sound, for example, cannot travel in a vacuum. Sound can travel in solids and liquids as well as, of course, in gases. Similarly, water waves travel, not surprisingly, in water.

How do we describe a wave? A wave is always associated with a *disturbance* of some kind. A rope held tight is horizontal when no wave is travelling on it. By moving one end up and down, we create a disturbance and individual points on the rope are now higher or lower than their original undisturbed positions. In the case of sound, the density of air becomes successively higher or lower when a sound wave travels through the air compared with when there is no sound wave. (The case of light is a bit more complicated and we will not discuss it here.)

▶ A wave is a disturbance that travels in a medium (which can be a vacuum in the case of electromagnetic waves) transferring energy and momentum from one place to another. The direction of energy transfer is the direction of propagation of the wave.

Note that in all the examples we have talked about, there is no large-scale motion of the medium. Points on a rope oscillate up and down, and molecules in air move back and forth along the direction of a sound wave that is travelling through the air. This is local, small-scale motion; the material of the medium does not itself travel large distances.

Transverse and longitudinal waves

In addition to the division into mechanical and electromagnetic, waves can be further divided into two classes. The first class is called **transverse** and consists of those waves in which the disturbance is *at right angles* to the direction of energy transfer. A typical example is a wave on a string: the direction of energy transfer is along the string but the disturbance is at right angles to the string (see Figure 2.1). Electromagnetic waves are also transverse.

The second class is called **longitudinal** and consists of those waves in which the disturbance is *along* the direction of energy transfer. A typical example is sound: if we imagine that a sound wave is moving from left to right in a thin tube, the disturbance is the motion of air molecules back and forth along the tube. Figure 2.2 shows a longitudinal wave. Molecules at $x = 0$, 2.0 and 4.0 cm have not moved ($y = 0$); those between $x = 0$ and 2.0 cm and between $x = 4.0$ and 5.0 cm have moved to the right ($y > 0$); and those between $x = 2.0$ and 4.0 cm have moved to the left ($y < 0$). The molecule at $x = 2.0$ cm is therefore at the centre of a *compression* (a region of higher than normal density), while that at $x = 4.0$ cm is at the centre of a *rarefaction* (a region of lower than normal density): see Figure 2.3.

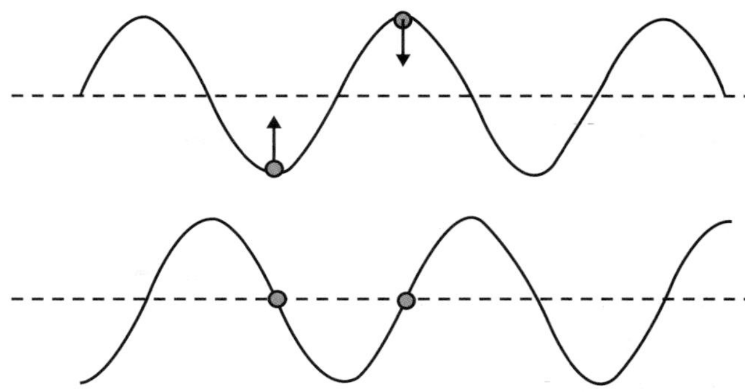

Figure 2.1 A transverse wave on a string travelling to the right. At the early time of the top picture, the parts of the string marked are at their maximum displacement above and below the equilibrium position of the string. Some time later the left part has moved up and the right part down – their motion is at right angles to the direction of motion of the wave.

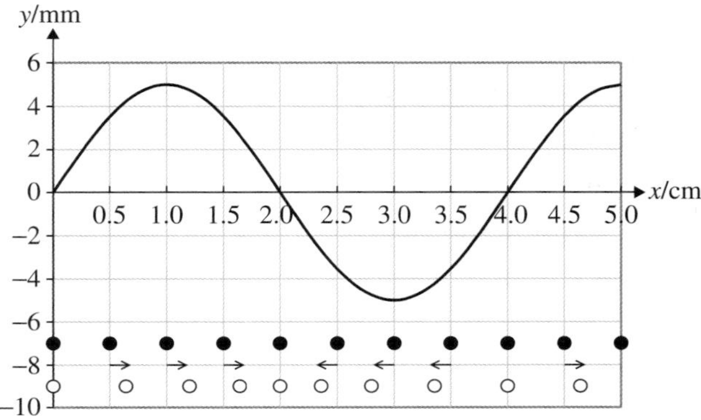

Figure 2.2 The black dots represent air molecules when no wave is present. The uncoloured dots below represent the positions of these molecules at the instant the wave shown by the graph passes.

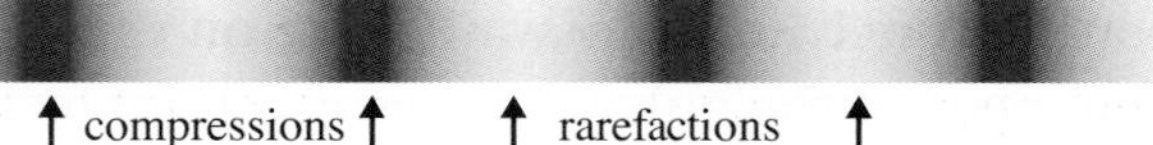

Figure 2.3 The motion of the molecules causes compressions and rarefactions in the medium in which the wave moves.

Wave pulses

To help us to understand waves we will start with a simple case, that of a wave pulse. If you tie one end of a rope to a wall and move the other end sharply up and then back down to its starting position, you will produce a wave pulse that will travel along the rope. It looks like Figure 2.4 (this is idealized to a triangular pulse – the real pulse would be curved):

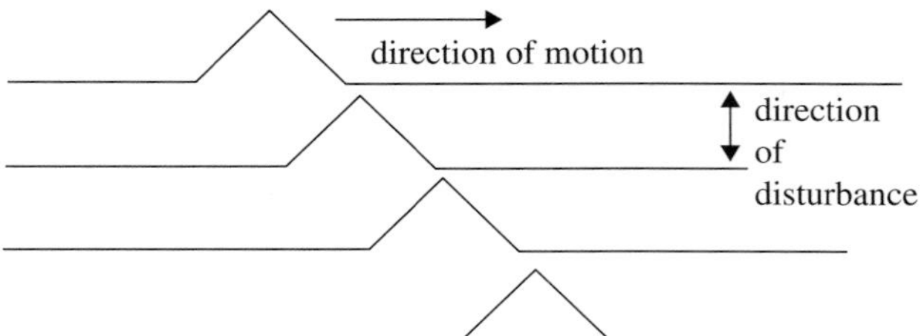

Figure 2.4 The pulse is moving to the right. The disturbance is normal to the direction of motion.

If your hand is first moved down below the rope then back up to the starting point, continues up above the rope and finally back down to the starting point, the pulse will look like Figure 2.5.

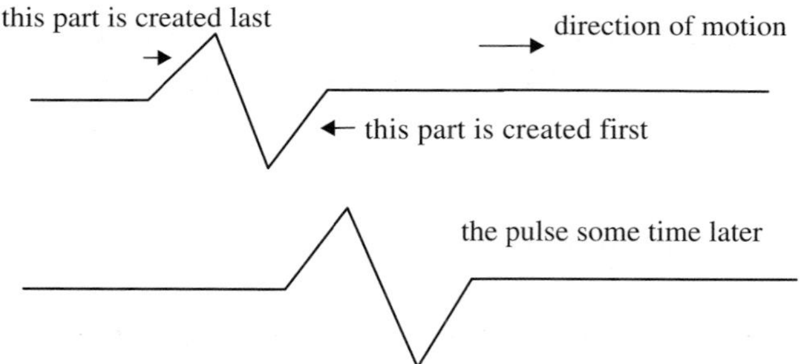

Figure 2.5 A full pulse travelling to the right.

It takes a certain time for this disturbance to move along the rope (i.e. for this wave pulse to reach another point in the rope). The wave pulse travels with a certain **speed** down the rope. In the case of the wave pulse on the rope, the speed of the pulse is determined not by the way in which the pulse was created (big or small pulse, wide or narrow) nor by how fast or slow your hand moved the rope; rather, it is determined by the tension T in the rope and the mass per unit length $\mu = \frac{m}{L}$ of the rope. Although not required for examination purposes, it is good to know the following:

▶ The speed of the pulse on the string is given by

$$v = \sqrt{\frac{T}{\mu}}$$

The speed of the wave is determined by the properties of the medium and not by how the wave is created.

The greater the tension in the medium, the greater the speed of the wave produced. You can convince yourself that the speed is greater when the tension is greater by creating pulses on a slinky, which can be kept at various tensions by having it stretched by different amounts. You will then also see that v is independent of the shape of the pulse you produce and of how fast you produced it.

The statement that the speed of the pulse is independent of the amplitude is true provided the amplitude is not too big. If the amplitude is big, then the string is more stretched and thus the tension is greater, implying a greater pulse speed. Not too big an amplitude means not big compared with the length of the string.

Travelling waves

In the previous section we saw how a single pulse can be produced on a stretched rope. We can create a *travelling wave* if we now produce one pulse after another. If, in addition, the agent forcing the rope up and down executes simple harmonic motion, then the wave will look like a sine wave (also called a harmonic wave) – see Figure 2.6 (top).

If the sequence of pulses produced are square pulses, then the wave generated is a travelling square wave – see Figure 2.6 (bottom).

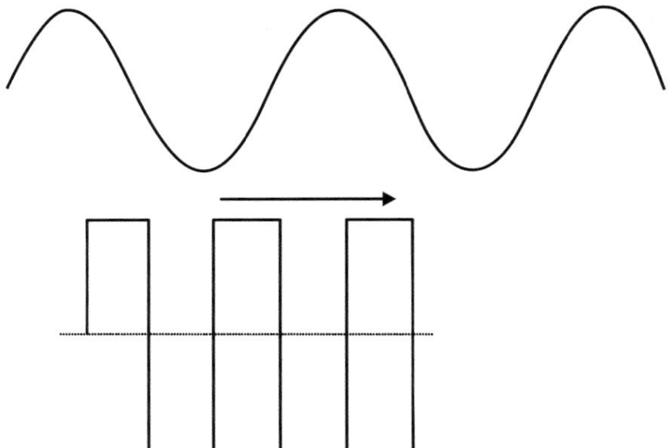

Figure 2.6 A periodic sine wave and a periodic square wave.

Harmonic waves are very important because any periodic disturbance can be expressed as a sum (superposition) of a number of harmonic waves. This is a general theorem in mathematics known as Fourier's theorem.

Harmonic waves

A simple way of producing harmonic waves is to attach one end of a rope to a tuning fork, as shown in Figure 2.7. If the tuning fork is then made to oscillate, one full wave will be produced on the rope after a time equal to the **period** of the tuning fork.

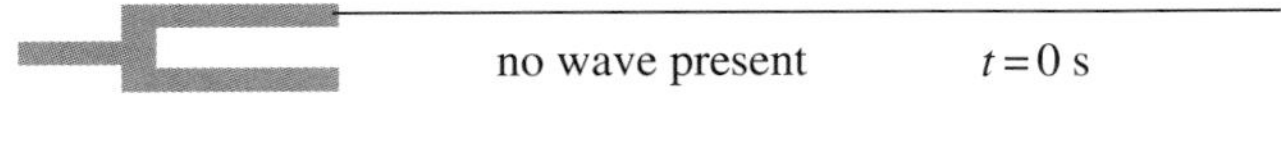

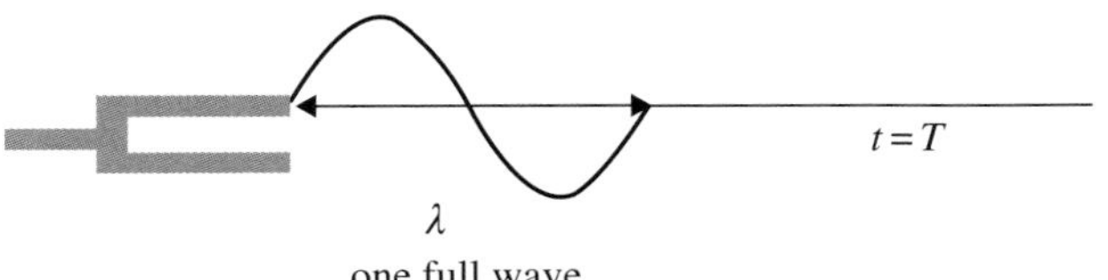

Figure 2.7 A full wave is produced in a time equal to one period.

▶ The length of a full wave is called the wavelength, λ, and the time needed to produce one full wave (or the duration of a full wave) is the period, T.

After a second full period, a second full wave will be produced (see Figure 2.8). The original full wave has moved forward a distance equal to the **wavelength**.

Figure 2.8 Two full waves are produced in sequence by the oscillating tuning fork.

▶ It thus follows that, since the wave moves forward a distance equal to a wavelength in a time equal to one period, the speed of the wave is given by

$$v = \frac{\lambda}{T}$$

Since one full wave is produced in a time of T s, it follows that the number of full waves produced in 1 s is $1/T$. This is the **frequency**.

▶ The number of full waves produced in 1 s is called the frequency of the wave, $f = \frac{1}{T}$. The unit of frequency is the inverse second, which is given the special name hertz (Hz). In terms of frequency the wave speed is thus

$$v = \lambda f$$

Waves can be represented graphically. This is a bit complicated because a wave depends on distance (where along the wave are we looking?) as well as time (at what time are we looking at the wave?). First we have to decide how we will quantify the 'disturbance' of the wave. For a wave on a string the obvious choice is to measure the height of a point on the string above or below the undisturbed position of the string. The disturbance here is thus the *displacement* of a point on the string and is measured in units of length. We normally denote this displacement by y, which will be a function of distance (x) and time (t).

In the case of sound, the disturbance may be associated with the density of the medium through which sound propagates. We may then define the difference $y_\rho = \rho - \rho_0$ as the *displacement* of density (ρ) relative to the equilibrium density of the medium when no sound is present in it (ρ_0). The displacement here has units of density and is also a function of position and time. In the case of sound, we could equally well define displacement as the difference $y_p = p - p_0$, which is the difference between the pressure of the medium when sound is present and the equilibrium pressure when no sound is present. Displacement would then have units of pressure.

This discussion can be generalized to all waves. All waves have a displacement that is the difference of some quantity and the equilibrium value of that quantity when no wave is present. The displacement of any wave is a function of position and time. We may therefore represent waves in graphs of displacement versus position (distance) and graphs of displacement versus time.

Let us consider a wave propagating along a string from left to right. The left end of the string is represented by $x = 0$ m and any other point on the string is specified by giving its corresponding x coordinate (see Figure 2.9).

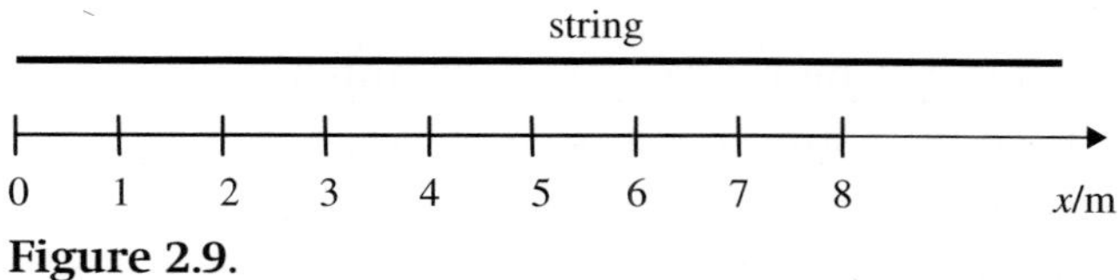

Figure 2.9.

As the wave propagates along the string, we would like to know the displacement at each point on the string *at a specific point in time.* This is given by a graph of displacement versus position – Figure 2.10.

The first important piece of information from such a graph is the wavelength.

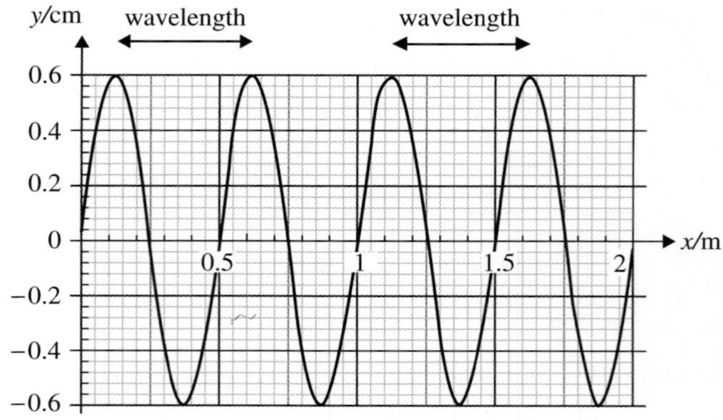

Figure 2.10 A graph of displacement versus position tells us the disturbance of any point on the string at a specific moment in time.

▶ Graphs showing the variation of displacement with position enable us to determine the wavelength of the wave as the distance from peak to next peak (or the length of a full wave).

This graph also tells us that at the point on the string that is 0.5 m from the string's left end the displacement is zero at some point in time. At that *same point in time* at a point 1.125 m from the left end the displacement is 0.6 cm, etc. Thus, a graph of displacement versus position is like a *photograph* of the string taken at a particular time. If we take a second photograph of the string some time later, the string will look different because the wave has moved in the meantime. It might look like Figure 2.11.

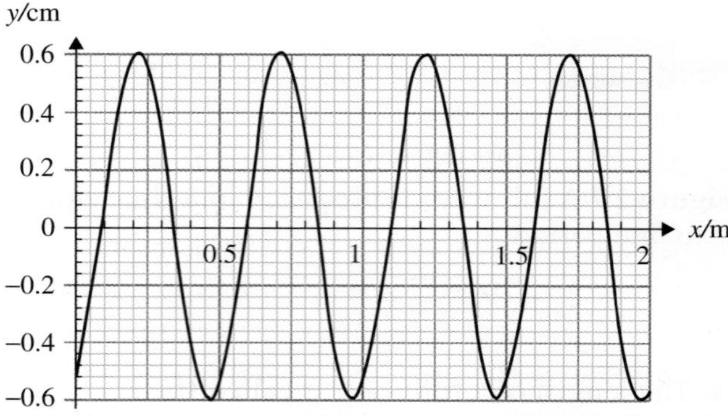

Figure 2.11 A graph of the disturbance of any point on the string at a later moment in time. Note that every point has a different disturbance from that shown in Figure 2.10.

We see that the displacement at $x = 0$ m that was zero in the first photograph is not zero now. It is about -0.5 cm. The displacement at a particular point on the string changes as time goes on and thus we can graph it as a function of time.

Figure 2.12 shows how the displacement of a particular point on the string (the point $x = 0$ m to be precise) varies as time goes on. This is a graph that shows the variation of displacement with time.

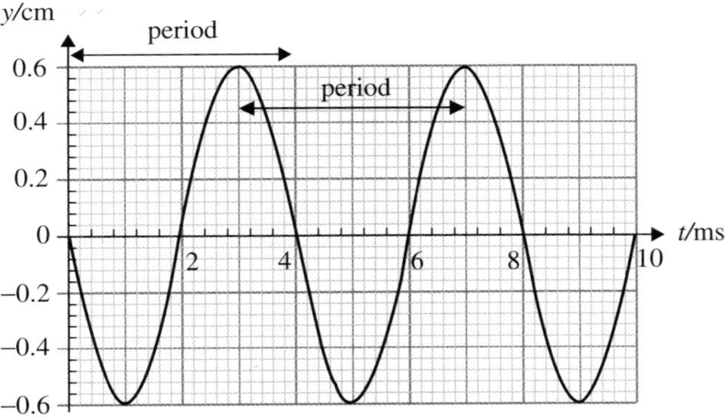

Figure 2.12 A graph of displacement versus time tells us the disturbance of a specific point on the string as time goes on.

▶ Graphs showing the variation of displacement with time enable us to determine the period of the wave as the time from peak to next peak (or the duration of a full wave).

From these graphs we can deduce the following information about the wave. From *any* graph we see that the maximum displacement of the wave is 0.6 cm. The *wavelength* of the wave can be determined by looking at a *displacement–position graph.* From Figure 2.10 it thus follows that $\lambda = 0.5$ m. To find the *period* we must look at a *displacement–time graph.* From Figure 2.12 we find $T = 4.0$ ms. Hence, the frequency is 250 Hz and the speed of the wave is 125 m s^{-1}. (Note that by comparing Figures 2.10 and 2.11 we see that the wave moved forward a distance of 0.1 m. Since the speed of the wave is 125 m s^{-1}, it follows that the photograph of Figure 2.11 was taken $0.1/125$ s $= 0.8$ ms later than that of Figure 2.10.)

Consider now the wave of Figure 2.13. We deduce that the disturbance is a pressure measured in kPa. However, in this graph the experimenter has not plotted the difference of pressure and the equilibrium value of the pressure. We may then deduce that the pressure in the medium when no wave travels through (the equilibrium pressure) is 4.0 kPa. We may also deduce that the maximum displacement (the amplitude) is 0.5 kPa. The wavelength is 4.0 m and in the absence of a displacement–time graph we can say nothing about the period or frequency, and hence speed, of this wave. On the other hand, if we are given the additional information that this is a sound wave of speed 340 m s^{-1}, then we deduce that the frequency is 85 Hz and so the period is 11.8 ms.

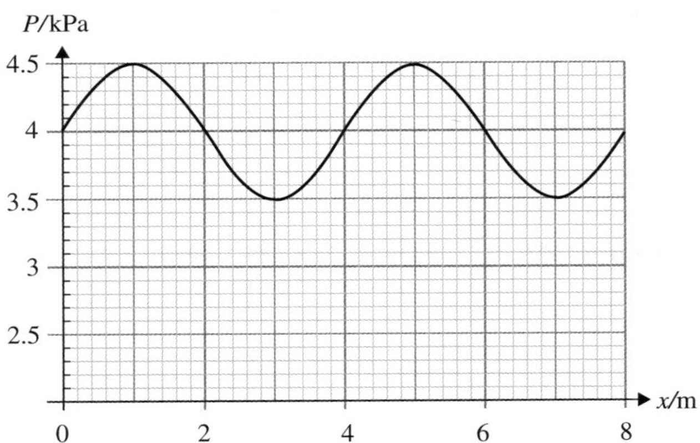

Figure 2.13 A wave in which the disturbance is about a non-zero value.

The wave of Figure 2.14 is an electromagnetic wave in which the displacement is the electric field measured in volts per metre. The amplitude is 0.2 V m^{-1} and the period is 3×10^{-15} s. The frequency is thus 3.33×10^{14} Hz. If we are told further that this wave moves in a vacuum then we know that the speed of such a wave

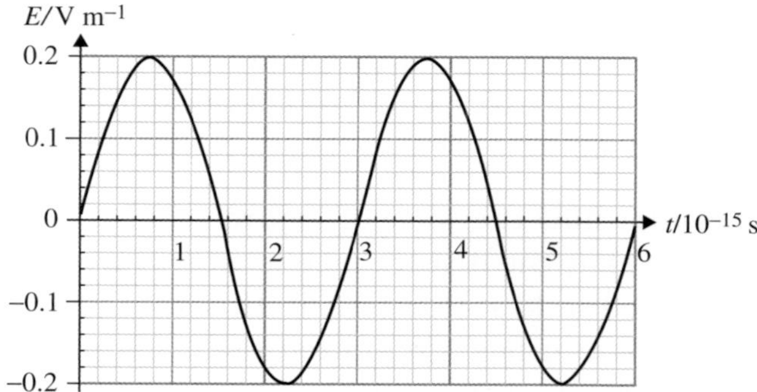

Figure 2.14 An electromagnetic wave as a function of time.

is 3×10^8 m s^{-1} and so the wavelength is 9.0×10^{-7} m.

▶ The wavelength (which we defined to be the length of one full wave) is also equal to the distance between successive crests or successive troughs in a displacement–position graph.

The period (which we defined to be the duration of one full wave) is also equal to the time between successive crests or successive troughs in a displacement–time graph.

The wavelength and frequency are two of the characteristics of a wave. A third characteristic is **amplitude**.

▶ The amplitude of a wave is defined to be the maximum displacement of the wave away from the position when no wave is present.

The amplitude of a wave is a measure of the energy the wave carries. In general, the energy carried is proportional to the square of the amplitude, which means that (all other things being equal) a water wave of amplitude 2.0 m carries four times as much energy as a water wave of amplitude 1.0 m.

In the first diagram of Figure 2.15 the amplitude of the wave is 2.0 cm. In the second it is 2.0 cm as well. The dotted line at 4.0 cm shows the equilibrium position, when no wave is present. The 4.0 cm might represent the height of a bit of water in a container. When no waves are present on the surface of the water, all points on the surface are 4.0 cm from the bottom of the container. When a small water wave is established in the container, the distance of various points on the surface varies as shown in the diagram. As the amplitude is the maximum displacement away from the equilibrium position, it is thus 2.0 cm.

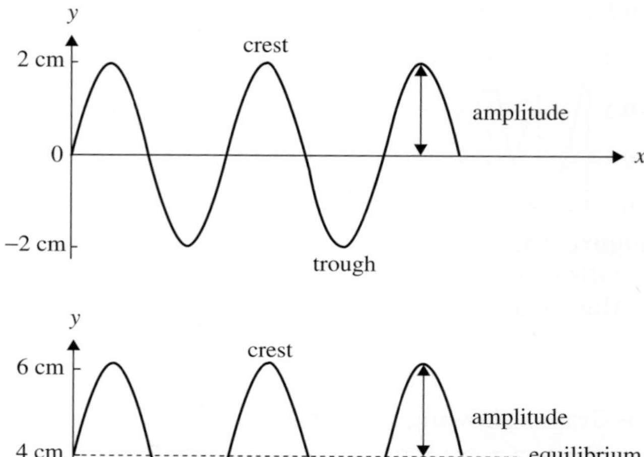

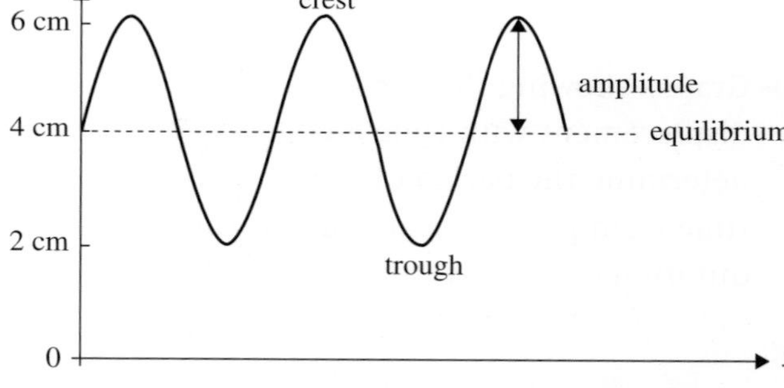

Figure 2.15 Diagrams showing the amplitude, crests and troughs of a travelling wave. In the second case, the equilibrium value is not at zero.

▶ Points on the wave with maximum displacement are called crests while those at minimum displacement are called troughs.

The diagrams in Figure 2.16 show the variation of displacement with position at various times. We see the meaning of the term travelling wave. The crests of the wave move forward.

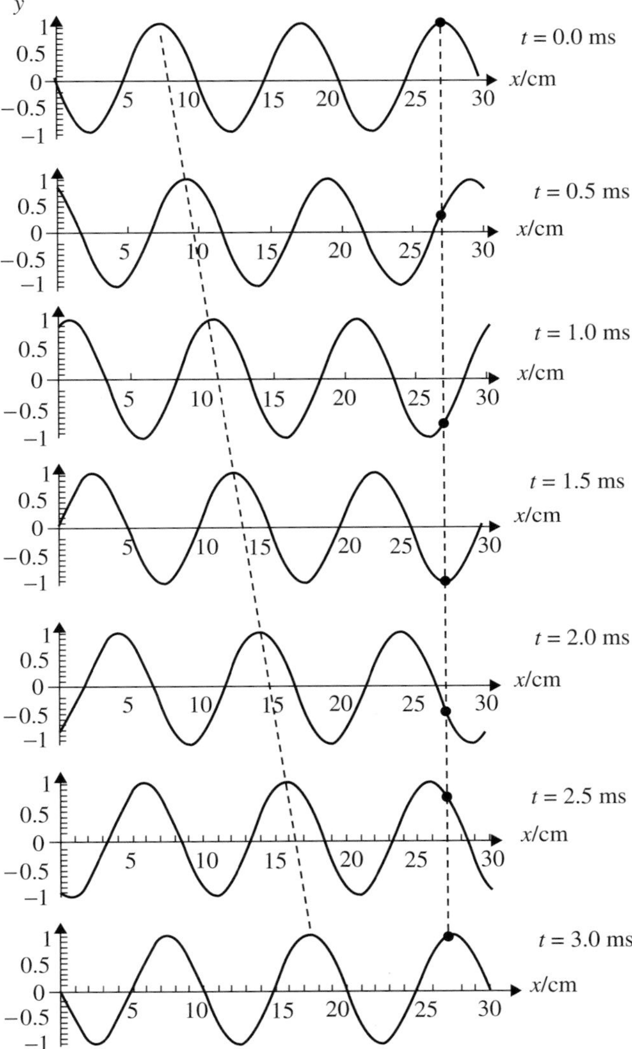

Figure 2.16 A sequence of pictures taken every 0.5 ms showing a travelling harmonic wave. Note how the peaks move forward. We have marked a point on the string to show that in a transverse wave points on the string move perpendicularly to the direction of the wave. After a full period ($T = 3.0$ ms) a picture of the rope looks like it did at the beginning ($t = 0$ ms), which is what allowed us to determine the period of the wave in the first place. The speed of the wave is 33.3 m s^{-1} (found by dividing the wavelength by the period) and the frequency is 333 Hz.

Example questions

Q1

A radio station emits at a frequency of 90.8 MHz. What is the wavelength of the waves emitted?

Answer

The waves emitted are electromagnetic waves and move at the speed of light (3×10^8 m s^{-1}). Therefore, from $v = \lambda f$ we find $\lambda = 3.3$ m.

Q2

A sound wave of frequency 450 Hz is emitted from A and travels towards B, a distance of 150 m away. Take the speed of sound to be 341 m s^{-1}. How many wavelengths fit in the distance from A to B?

Answer

The wavelength is

$$\lambda = \frac{341}{450}\text{ m}$$
$$= 0.758\text{ m}$$

Thus the number of wavelengths that fit in the distance 150 m is

$$N = \frac{150}{0.758}$$
$$= 198 \text{ wavelengths (approximately)}$$

Q3

The noise of thunder is heard 3 s after the flash of lightning. How far away is the place where lightning struck? (Take the speed of sound to be 340 m s^{-1}.)

Answer

Light travels so fast that we can assume that lightning struck exactly when we see the flash of light. If thunder is heard 3 s later, it means that it took 3 s for sound to cover the unknown distance, d. Thus

$$d = vt$$
$$= 340 \times 3\text{ m}$$
$$= 1020\text{ m}$$

Q4

Water wave crests in a lake are 5.0 m apart and pass by an anchored boat every 2.0 s. What is the speed of the water waves?

Answer

$$v = \frac{5.0}{2.0}\,\text{m s}^{-1}$$
$$= 2.5\,\text{m s}^{-1}$$

Q5

A toothed wheel has 300 teeth on its circumference. It rotates at 30 rpm (revolutions per minute). A piece of cardboard is placed such that it is hit by the teeth of the wheel as the wheel rotates. What is the frequency of the sound produced?

Answer

In 1 min the cardboard will be hit by a tooth $30 \times 300 = 9000$ times, which is 150 times in 1 s. The frequency of the sound is thus 150 Hz.

Q6

A railing consists of thin vertical rods a distance of 2 cm apart. A boy runs past the railing at a speed of 3 m s^{-1} dragging a stick against the rods. What is the frequency of the sound produced?

Answer

In 1 s the boy moves a distance of 3 m, or past $300/2 = 150$ rods. The frequency of the sound is thus 150 Hz.

Wavefronts

Imagine a wave propagating in some direction, for example, water waves approaching the shore (see Figure 2.17).

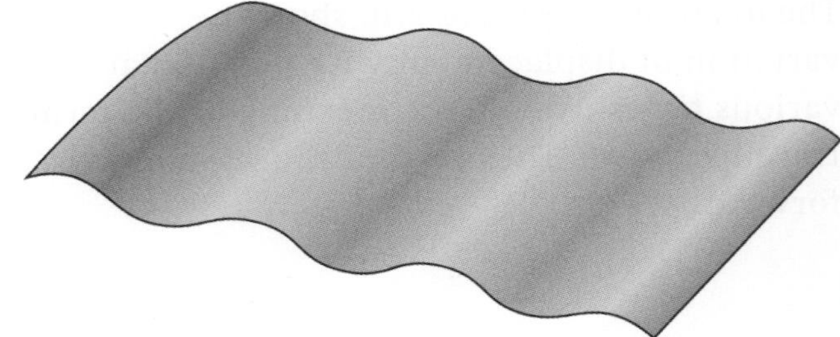

Figure 2.17 A two-dimensional wave.

The direction of the waves is horizontal, so if we imagine vertical planes going through the crests, the planes will be normal to the direction of the wave. These planes are called **wavefronts**; and lines at right angles to them are called **rays**.

▶ A *wavefront* is a surface through crests and normal to the direction of propagation of the wave. Lines in the direction of propagation of the wave (and hence normal to the wavefronts) are called *rays*. (See Figure 2.18.)

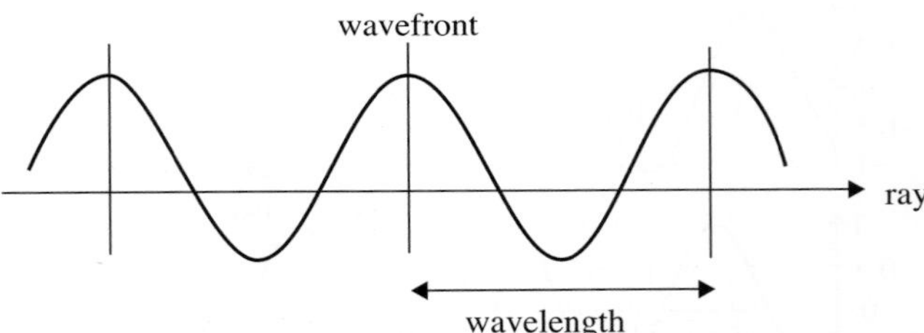

Figure 2.18 Surfaces through crests and normal to the direction of energy propagation of the wave are called wavefronts or wavecrests. Rays are mathematical lines perpendicular to the wavefronts in the direction of propagation of the wave.

(A wavefront is properly defined through the concept of *phase*. All points on a wavefront have the same phase. This will be discussed in Option G3.)

On the other hand, if we consider the surfaces going through crests of water waves caused by a stone dropped in the water, we would find that in this case the wavefronts are cylindrical surfaces (see Figure 2.19).

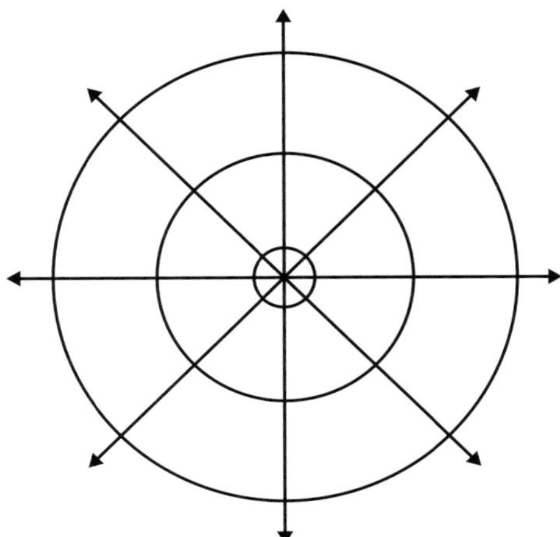

Figure 2.19 Example of cylindrical wavefronts. The cylinders go through the crests and are normal to the plane of the paper. The rays are radial lines.

Example question

Q7

A stone dropped in still water creates circular ripples that move away from the point of impact. The initial height of the ripple is about 2.4 cm and the wavelength is 0.5 m. Draw a sketch of the displacement of the ripples as a function of the distance from the point of impact.

Answer

The energy carried by the wave is distributed along the (circular) wavefronts. As the wave moves away from the point of impact, the length of the wavefront increases and so the energy per unit wavefront length decreases. Thus, the amplitude has to decrease as well. So we get the graph shown in Figure 2.20.

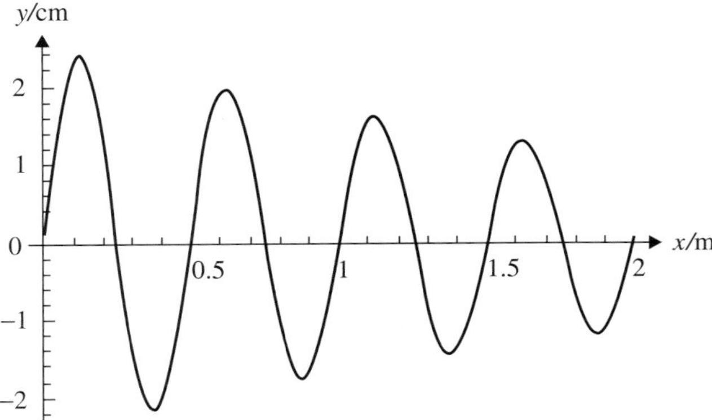

Figure 2.20.

The wavefronts of light waves leaving a point source (a very small lamp) would be spherical. We can thus speak of plane, cylindrical and spherical waves, according to the shape of the wavefronts. Note that cylindrical and spherical waves tend to become plane waves very far away from their source.

QUESTIONS

1 In football stadiums fans often create a 'wave' by standing up and sitting down again. What determines the speed of the 'wave'?

2 A number of dominoes are stood next to each other along a straight line. A small push is given to the first domino and one by one the dominoes fall over. How is this an example of wave motion? How can the speed of the wave pulse be increased? Design an experiment in which this problem can be investigated.

3 What is the wavelength that corresponds to a sound frequency of:
(a) 256 Hz;
(b) 25 kHz?
Take the speed of sound to be 330 m s^{-1}.

4 By making suitably labelled diagrams explain the terms:
(a) wavelength;
(b) period;
(c) amplitude;
(d) crest;
(e) trough.

5 The tension in a steel wire of length 0.800 m and mass 150.0 g is 120.0 N. What is the speed of transverse waves on this string? (Use $v = \sqrt{\frac{T}{\mu}}$.)

6 A string has a length of 20.0 m and is kept at a tension of 50.0 N. Its mass is 400.0 g. A transverse wave of frequency 15.0 Hz travels on this string.
(a) What is its wavelength?
(b) If the same wave is created on the same kind of string (same mass per unit length and same tension) but of double the length, what will the wavelength of the wave be? (Use $v = \sqrt{\frac{T}{\mu}}$.)

7 A stone is dropped on a still pond at $t = 0$. The wave reaches a leaf floating on the pond a distance of 3.00 m away. The leaf then begins to oscillate according to the graph shown in Figure 2.21.

(a) Find the speed of the water waves.

(b) Find the period and frequency of the wave.

(c) Find the wavelength and amplitude of the wave.

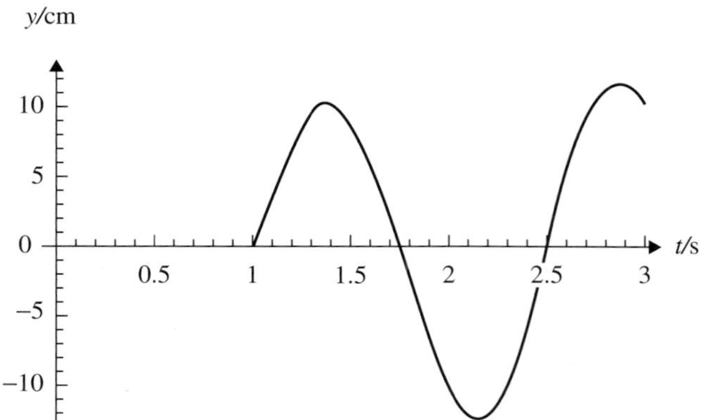

Figure 2.21 For question 7.

8 A sound wave of frequency 500 Hz travels from air into water. The speed of sound in air is 330 m s^{-1} and in water 1490 m s^{-1}. What is the wavelength of the wave in:

(a) air;

(b) water?

9 The speed of ocean waves approaching the shore is given by the formula $v = \sqrt{gh}$, where h is the depth of the water. It is assumed here that the wavelength of the waves is much larger than the depth (otherwise a different expression gives the wave speed). What is the speed of water waves near the shore where the depth is 1.0 m? Assuming that the depth of the water decreases uniformly, make a graph of the water wave speed as a function of depth from a depth of 1.0 m to a depth of 0.30 m.

10 (a) Explain, in the context of wave motion, what you understand by the term *displacement*.

(b) Using your answer in (a), explain the difference between longitudinal and transverse waves.

(c) A rock thrown onto the still surface of a pond creates circular ripples moving away from the point of impact. Why is more than one ripple created?

(d) Why does the amplitude decrease as the ripple moves away from the centre?

11 A ship sends a sonar pulse of frequency 30 kHz and duration 1.0 ms towards a submarine and receives a reflection of the pulse 3.2 s later. The speed of sound in water is 1500 m s^{-1}. Find the distance of the submarine from the ship, the wavelength of the pulse and the number of full waves emitted in the pulse.

12 Figure 2.22 shows three points on a string on which a transverse wave propagates to the right. Indicate how these three points will move in the next instant of time.

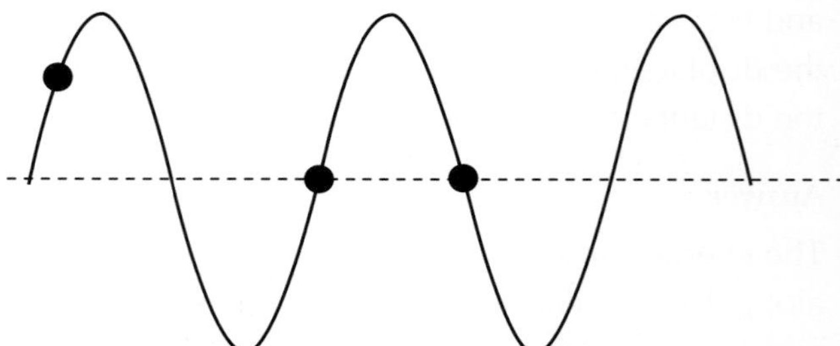

Figure 2.22 For question 12.

13 How would your answers change if the wave in question 12 were moving to the left?

14 Figure 2.23 shows a piece of cork floating on the surface of water when a wave travels through the water. On the same diagram draw the position of the cork half a wave period later.

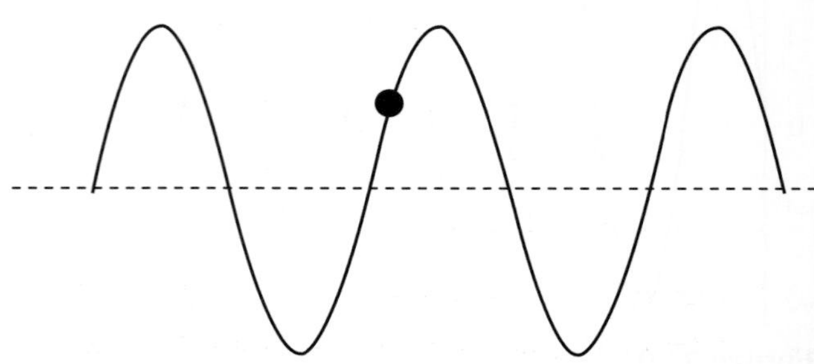

Figure 2.23 For question 14.

15 Figure 2.24 shows the same wave at two different times. The wave travels to the right and the bottom diagram represents the wave 0.2 s after the time illustrated in the top diagram. For this wave determine:

(a) the amplitude;
(b) the wavelength;
(c) the speed;
(d) the frequency.
(e) Can the graph be used to determine whether the wave is transverse or longitudinal?

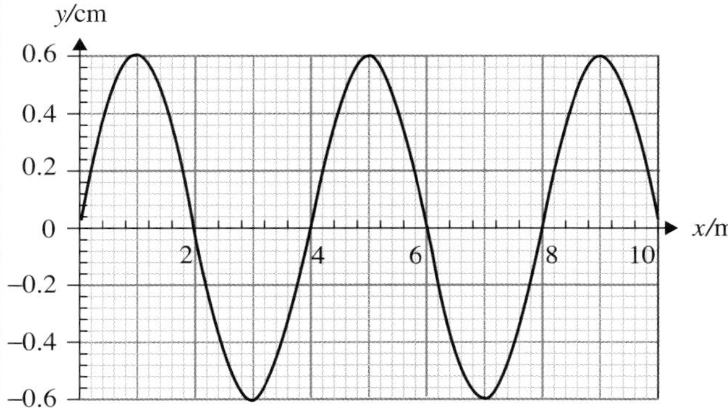

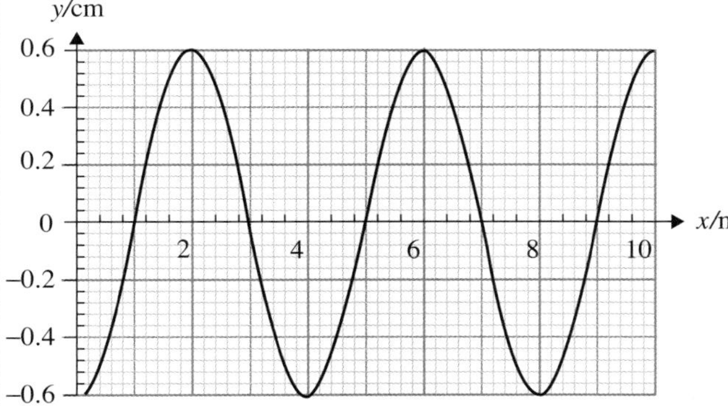

Figure 2.24 For question 15.

16 Figure 2.25 is a picture of a longitudinal wave travelling to the right taken at a specific time. The density of the lines is proportional to the density of the medium the wave travels through.

(a) Draw this wave a very short time later.
(b) Indicate on the diagram the wavelength.

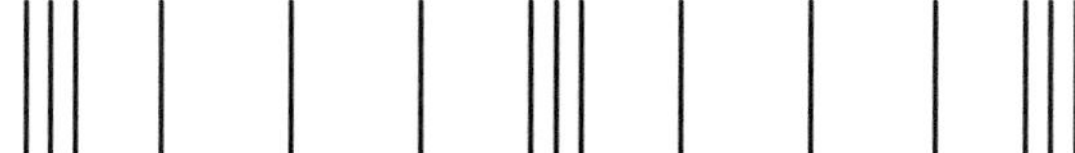

Figure 2.25 For question 16.

17 Figure 2.26 shows the variation with distance x of the displacement y of air molecules as a sound wave travels to the right through air. Positive displacement means motion to the right. The speed of sound in air is 340 m s^{-1}.

(a) Determine the frequency of the sound wave.
(b) State a distance x at which (i) a compression and (ii) a rarefaction occurs.

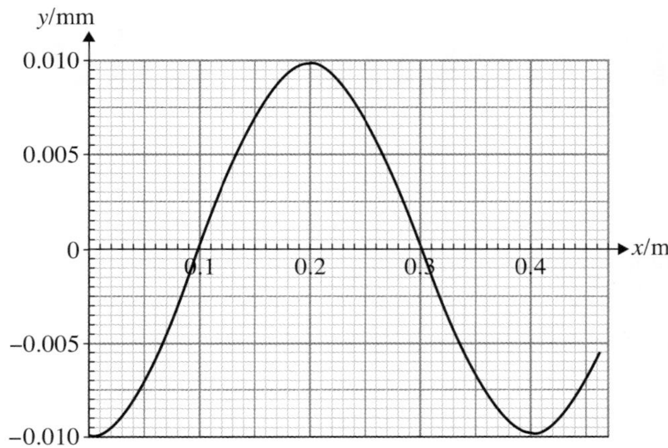

Figure 2.26 For question 17.

Figure 2.27 shows the variation with time t of the displacement y of a particular molecule of air as the sound wave travels through air.

(c) State a time at which this molecule is at the centre of (i) a compression and (ii) a rarefaction.

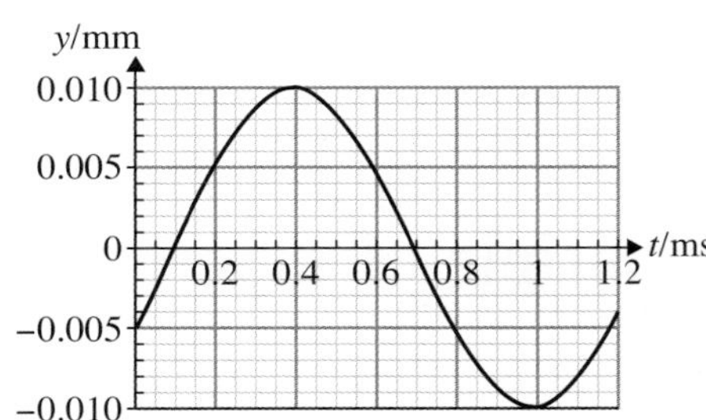

Figure 2.27 For question 17.

18 Draw diagrams to help explain the difference between transverse and longitudinal waves.

19 In the context of wave motion explain, with the aid of a diagram, the terms:

(a) wavefront;
(b) ray.

20 An earthquake creates waves that travel in the earth's crust; these can be detected by seismic stations. Explain why three seismic stations must be used to determine the position of the earthquake. Describe *two* differences in the signals recorded by three seismic stations, assuming they are at different distances from the centre of the earthquake.

Wave phenomena I: reflection and refraction

This chapter introduces the principle of superposition, which allows us to find the wave disturbance when two or more waves arrive at the same point in space at the same time. Two basic wave phenomena, reflection and refraction, are discussed. We also introduce Huygens' principle, which determines the evolution of a wavefront and explains reflection and refraction.

Objectives

By the end of this chapter you should be able to:

- state the principle of *superposition* and apply it to pulses and waves;
- state the laws of *reflection* and *refraction* and solve problems involving these phenomena;
- give the definition of *index of refraction*, $n = \frac{c_{\text{vacuum}}}{c_{\text{medium}}}$;
- state *Snell's law* $\frac{\sin\theta_1}{c_1} = \frac{\sin\theta_2}{c_2}$ and $n_1 \sin\theta_1 = n_2 \sin\theta_2$ for light;
- understand *Huygens' principle*.

The principle of superposition

Suppose that two pulses are produced in the same rope and are travelling towards each other from opposite ends. Something truly amazing happens when the two pulses meet. Figure 3.1 shows what happens in a sequence of pictures. For simplicity we have drawn idealized square pulses.

The disturbance gets bigger when the two pulses meet but subsequently the two pulses simply 'go through each other' as if nothing had happened. You should contrast this with what happens in the ordinary kind of motion: when two balls collide they *bounce off* each other.

What happens when two (or more) pulses meet at some point in space is described by the principle of **superposition**, which states that the displacement at that point is the algebraic sum of the individual displacements. As we can see in Figure 3.1, when the two pulses meet, the displacement is quite large; it is, in fact, the sum of the displacements of the two pulses. Note the word 'algebraic'. This means that if one pulse is 'up' and the other is 'down', then the resulting displacement is the difference of the individual ones.

▶ Mathematically, the principle of superposition states that if y_1 and y_2 are the individual displacements, then at the point where the two meet the total displacement has the value

$$y = y_1 + y_2$$

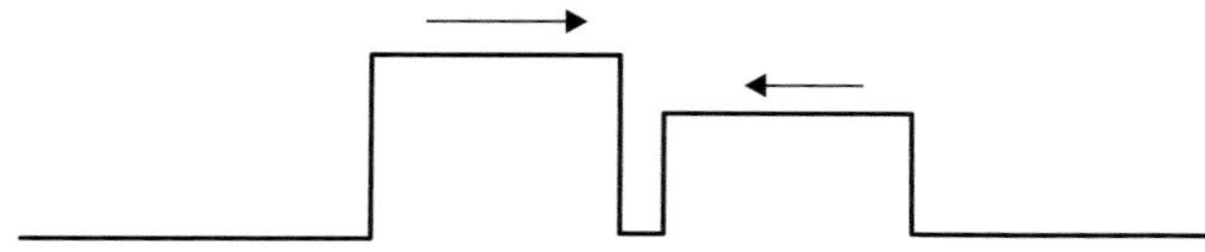

(a) The pulses are approaching each other.

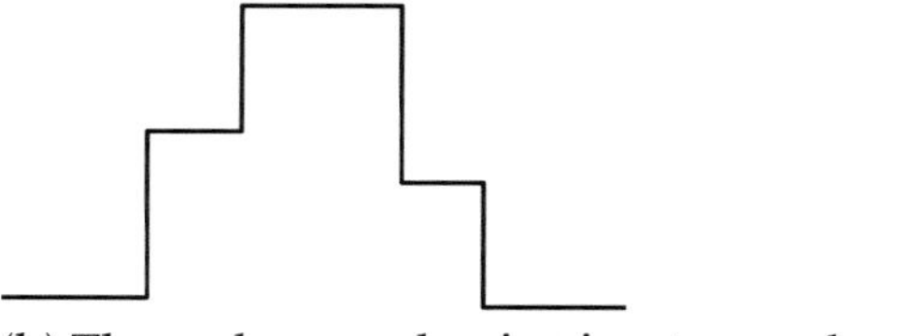

(b) The pulses are beginning to overlap.

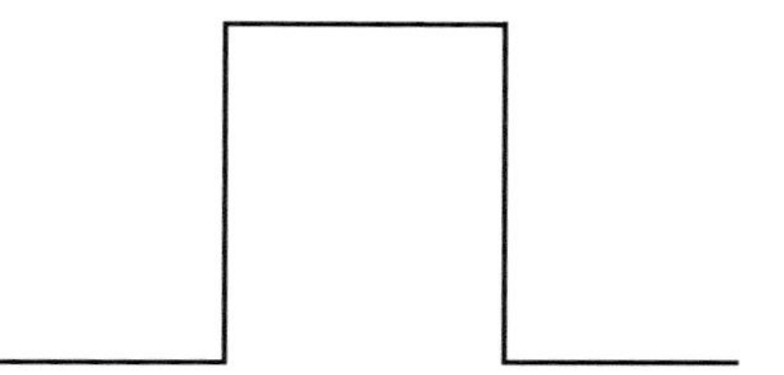

(c) The overlap is complete; the pulses are on top of each other.

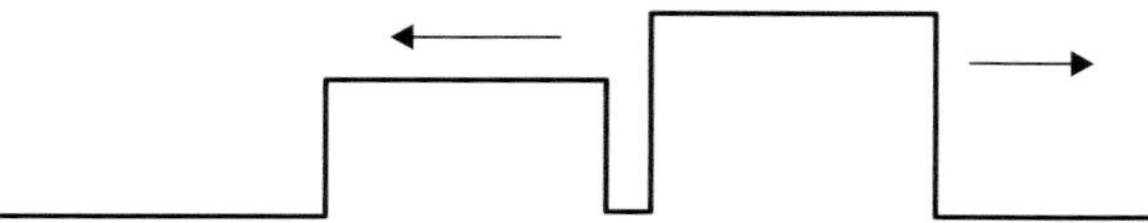

(d) The pulses move through each other.

Figure 3.1 The superposition of two positive pulses.

Let us look at Figures 3.1b and c in detail. In Figure 3.1b the two pulses are partially overlapping – Figure 3.2 shows both of them separately (the pulse moving toward the right is drawn in black and the one moving to the left in grey). There are five regions to consider. In region a, both pulses are zero. In region b, the black pulse is non-zero and the grey is zero. In region c, both are non-zero. In region d, the black is zero and the grey is not. In region e, both are zero. The shape of the resulting pulse is simply the sum of the two pulses. Thus, in region a, we get zero. In region b, we get the height of just the black pulse. In region c, we get a pulse whose height is the sum of the heights of the black and grey pulses. In region d, the height equals the height of just the grey pulse. In region e, we get zero.

In Figure 3.1c we have three regions to consider (see Figure 3.3). In a and c, both pulses are zero,

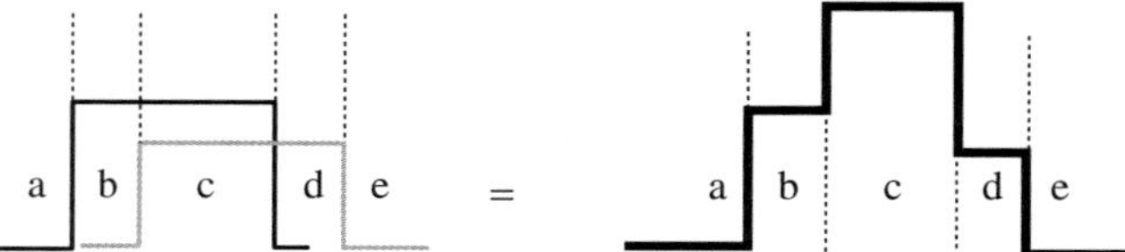

Figure 3.2 The situation in Figure 3.1b analysed.

so the resulting pulse is also zero. In region b, both are non-zero and the resulting pulse is the sum of the individual pulse heights.

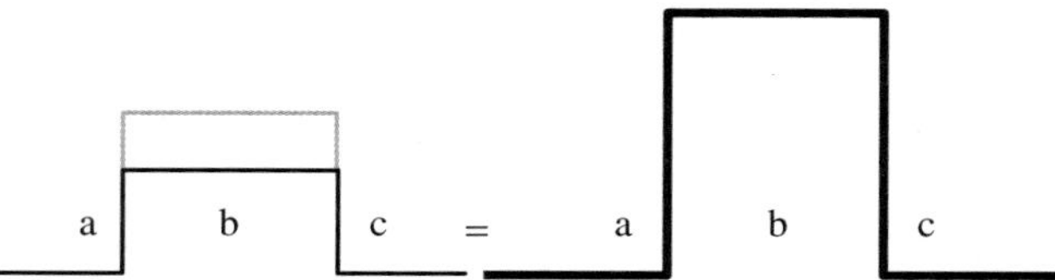

Figure 3.3 The situation in Figure 3.1c analysed.

If the two pulses are like the ones shown in the sequence in Figure 3.4, the resulting pulse when the two meet is momentarily zero. The situation in Figure 3.4b is analysed in Figure 3.5.

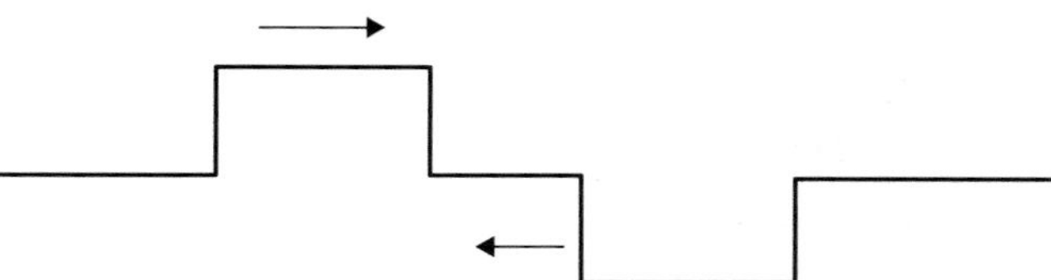

(a) Positive and negative pulses are approaching each other.

(b) The positive and negative pulses momentarily cancel each other out when they totally overlap.

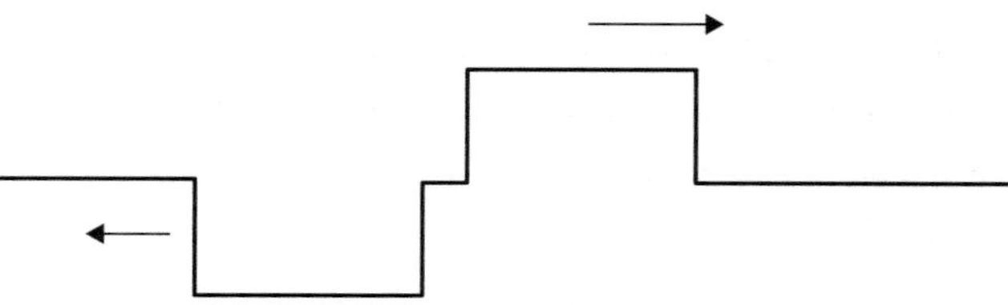

(c) The positive and negative pulses move through each other.

Figure 3.4 The superposition of a positive and a negative pulse.

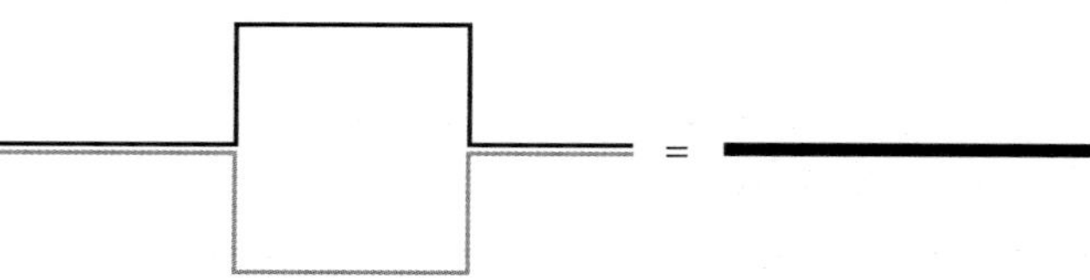

Figure 3.5 The situation in Figure 3.4b analysed.

At that instant when there is complete cancellation of the two pulses, the rope looks flat but it is moving as shown in Figure 3.6.

Figure 3.6 Parts of the rope are moving when the two pulses cancel each other out.

You should be able to convince yourself that when the rope looks like the first diagram in Figure 3.7 it is because the individual pulses are only partially overlapping, as in the second diagram.

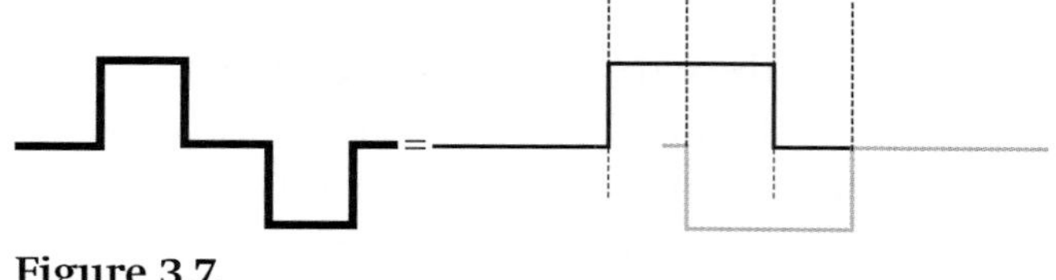

Figure 3.7.

Reflection of pulses

What happens when a pulse created in a rope with one end fixed approaches that fixed end? Consider the pulse of Figure 3.8. The instant the pulse hits the fixed end, the rope attempts to move the fixed end upward: that is, it exerts an upward force on the fixed end. By Newton's third law, the wall will then exert an equal but opposite force on the rope. This means that a displacement will be created in the rope that will be negative and will start moving towards the left.

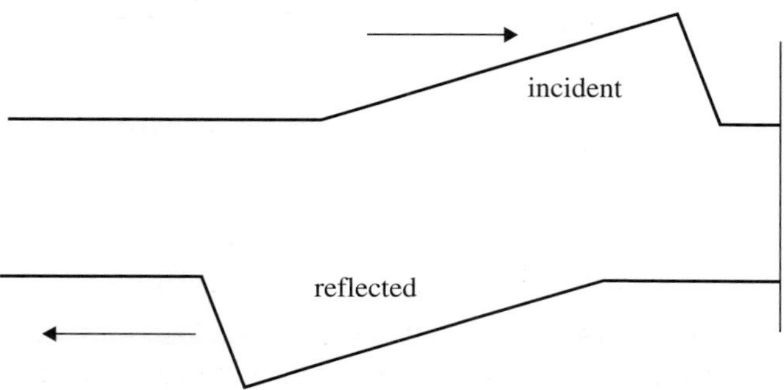

Figure 3.8 A pulse reflecting from a fixed end is inverted.

The pulse has been reflected by the wall and has been *inverted*. We can understand this in a different, more abstract, way as follows. The fixed end of the rope must remain fixed at all times. Imagine a pulse travelling along an imaginary rope that is an extension of the real rope into the wall. This imaginary pulse is moving from right to left. Using the principle of superposition, we ask: what is the shape of the imaginary pulse in order that when the real and imaginary pulses meet, the end of the rope (that tied to the wall) always stays fixed? The answer is a pulse that is identical to the real pulse but is inverted (see Figure 3.9). It is as if the real and imaginary pulses exchange places upon reflection.

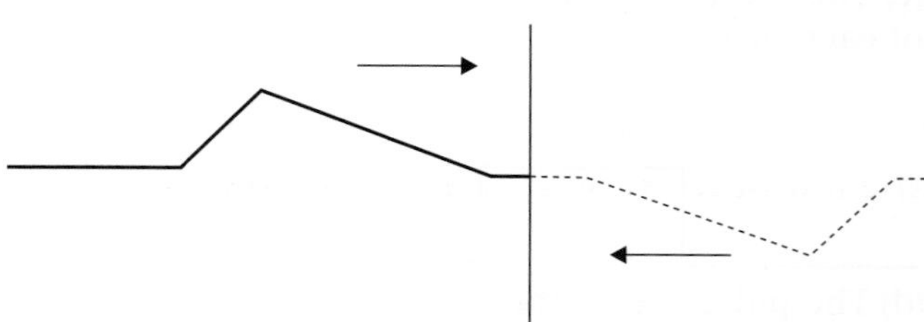

Figure 3.9 The real and imaginary pulses meet, keeping the end of the rope fixed.

If the end of the rope is not fixed but free to move (imagine that the end of the rope is now tied to a ring that can slide up and down a vertical pole), the situation is different (see Figure 3.10). Here the reflected pulse is the same as the original pulse. There is a change of direction but no inversion here. Can you see why?

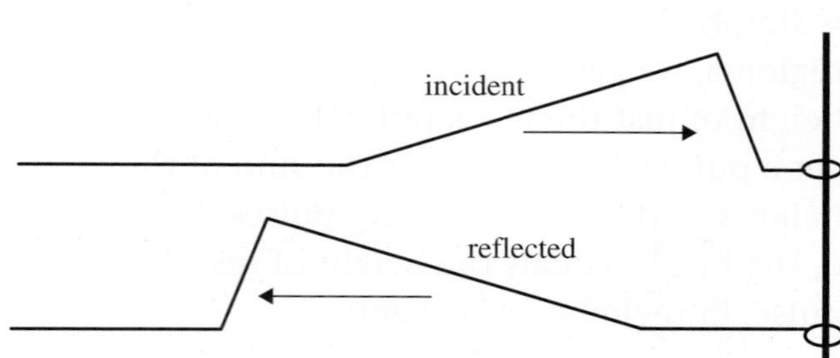

Figure 3.10 A pulse reflecting from a free end is not inverted.

Reflection and refraction of waves

This section deals with the wave phenomena of reflection and refraction as they apply to waves, especially light. The study of light has played a crucial role in the history of science. Newton discovered that ordinary white light is composed of different colours when he let sunlight go through a prism and saw the colours of the rainbow emerging from the other side. The wave nature of light was put forward by the Dutch physicist Christiaan Huygens in his book *A Treatise on Light* published in 1690. A bitter controversy between Huygens and Newton (Newton had postulated a particle theory of light) ended in Huygens' favour.

The law of reflection

The law of reflection states the following:

▶ The angle of incidence i (angle between the ray and the normal to the reflecting surface at the point of incidence) is equal to the angle of reflection r (angle between the normal and the reflected ray).

The reflected and incident rays and the normal to the surface lie on the same plane, called the plane of incidence.

(See Figure 3.11.)

Reflection can be demonstrated experimentally in a variety of ways. For light, this is most easily done by placing two pins in front of a mirror and then looking at the mirror from such a position that the image of one pin is behind the image of the other. Two additional pins are then placed along the line of sight of the first two pins. If one line is drawn joining the first pair of pins and a second line joining the other two, it will be found that the two lines intersect at a point on the surface of the mirror such that the normal to the mirror at that point bisects the angle between the original lines.

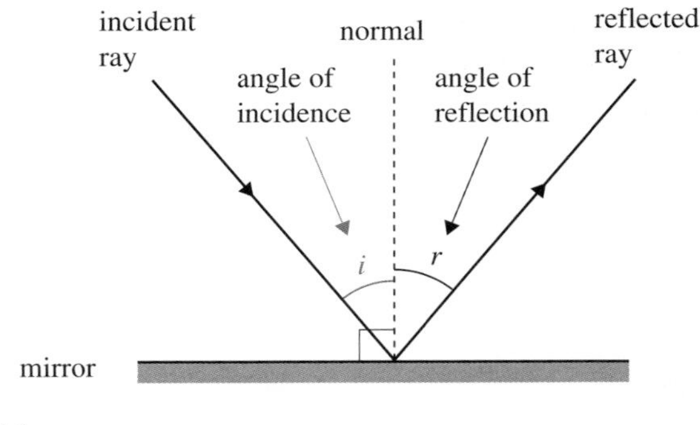

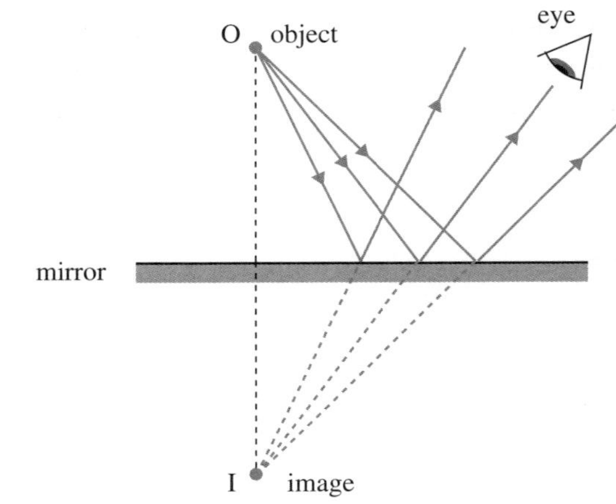

Figure 3.11 (a) Reflection at a plane (flat) surface. (b) The position of an image seen in a plane mirror.

This shows that the angle of incidence $\angle i$ is equal to the angle of reflection $\angle r$. This is illustrated in Figure 3.12.

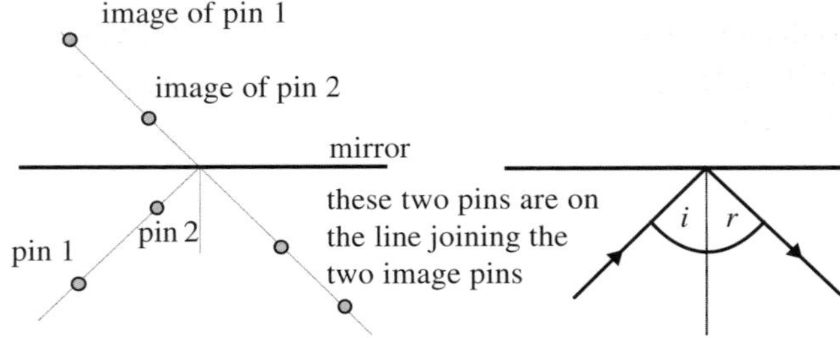

Figure 3.12 Demonstration of reflection for light.

In the case of sound, a source of sound can be directed at a solid surface and the reflected sound picked up by a microphone connected to an oscilloscope. The microphone is moved until it is in the position that gives the maximum reading on the oscilloscope. When this position is recorded, it is again found that the angle of incidence equals the angle of reflection. This is illustrated in Figure 3.13.

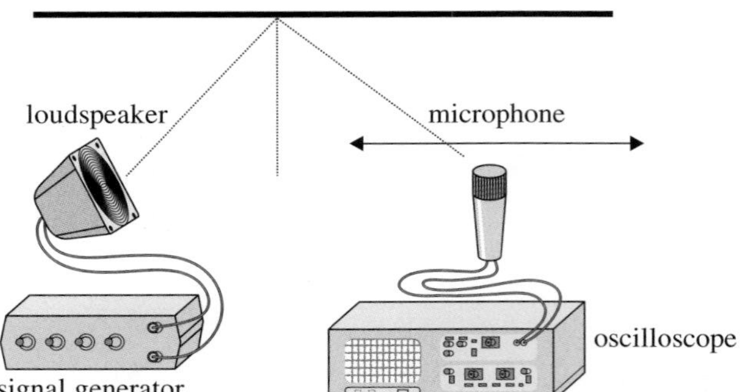

Figure 3.13 Demonstration of reflection for sound.

Reflection takes place when the reflecting surface is sufficiently smooth. This means that the wavelength of the incident wave has to be larger than the size of any irregularities of the surface.

Refraction

Light travels with a velocity of 3×10^8 m s^{-1} in a vacuum. In all other media, the velocity of light is smaller. The difference in the speed of propagation of light in different media is responsible for an effect called **refraction.** (In fact, any wave whose speed of propagation is different in different media will experience the same effect.) When a ray of light travelling in a given medium, say air, strikes an interface with another medium, say the surface of water in a pond, it will change direction as it enters the second medium.

Usually, when a ray of light strikes an interface between two media, there is both reflection and refraction (see Figure 3.14).

▶ Referring to Figure 3.14, it can be shown that

$$\frac{\sin\theta_1}{c_1} = \frac{\sin\theta_2}{c_2}$$

This is known as Snell's law (see also page 236). This law relates the sines of the angles of incidence and refraction to the speed of the wave in the two media, c_1 and c_2.

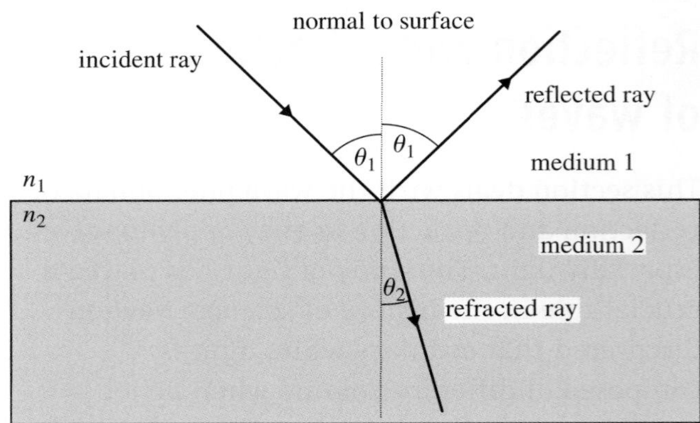

Figure 3.14 A ray of light incident on the interface of two media partly reflects and partly refracts.

In the case of *light only*, we usually define a quantity called the **index of refraction** of a given medium as

$$n = \frac{c}{c_m}$$

where c is the speed of light in vacuum and c_m is the speed of light in the medium in question.

▶ In terms of the index of refraction, Snell's law for *light* then reads

$$n_1 \sin\theta_1 = n_2 \sin\theta_2$$

(see Figure 3.14).

Since the speed of light is always largest in a vacuum, the index of refraction is always larger than one. By definition, the index of refraction of a vacuum (and approximately of air) is one. Thus, if we are given the index of refraction of a medium we can find the speed of light in that medium. For example, in a glass with $n = 1.5$, the speed of light is

$$c_g = \frac{c}{n_g} = \frac{3 \times 10^8}{1.5}\ \text{m s}^{-1} = 2 \times 10^8\ \text{m s}^{-1}$$

The index of refraction depends slightly on wavelength, so rays with the same angle of incidence but of different wavelength are refracted by different angles. This phenomenon is called **dispersion**.

Example questions

Q1

Light of wavelength 680 nm in air enters water making an angle of 40° with the normal. Find the angle of refraction and the wavelength of light in water. The index of refraction of water is 1.33.

Answer

By straightforward application of Snell's law we find

$$1 \times \sin 40^\circ = 1.33 \times \sin\theta$$
$$\Rightarrow \theta = 28.9^\circ$$

The wavelength in air is 680 nm, so the frequency in air is

$$f = \frac{3.00 \times 10^8}{680 \times 10^{-9}}$$
$$= 4.41 \times 10^{14}\ \text{Hz}$$

The frequency cannot change as the wave moves into the second medium. Imagine an observer right at the interface of the two media. The frequency can be found from the number of wavefronts that cross the interface per second. This number is the same for both media. Since the speed of light in water is

$$c_w = \frac{3.00 \times 10^8}{1.33}$$
$$= 2.26 \times 10^8\ \text{m s}^{-1}$$

it follows that the wavelength in water is

$$\lambda = \frac{2.26 \times 10^8}{4.41 \times 10^{14}}$$
$$= 512\ \text{nm}$$

Q2

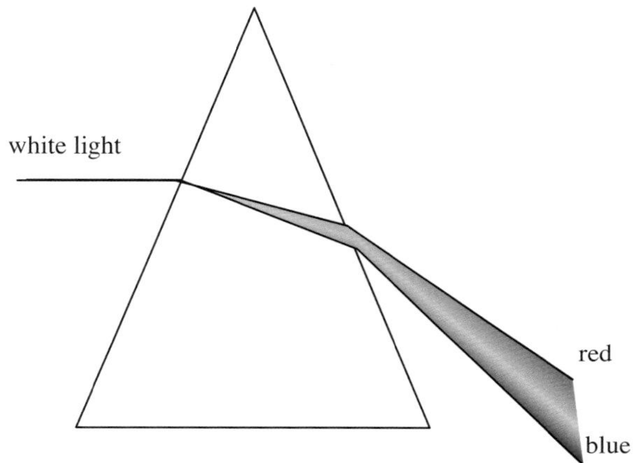

Figure 3.15.

The paths of rays of red and blue light passing through a glass prism are as shown in Figure 3.15. What can be deduced about the index of refraction of glass for red and blue light?

Answer

Considering the first refraction when the rays first enter the glass, we see that blue makes a smaller angle of refraction (draw the normal at the point of incidence to see that this is so). Hence its index of refraction must be larger.

Refraction for other waves

We have talked at length about refraction of light. Refraction, of course, is a phenomenon that applies to all waves. It happens whenever the wave changes its speed when going from one medium to another. For example, water waves will move more slowly when they enter a region of shallow water. Since the frequency is always unchanged, this means that the water waves will have a shorter wavelength in the shallow water (see Figure 3.16).

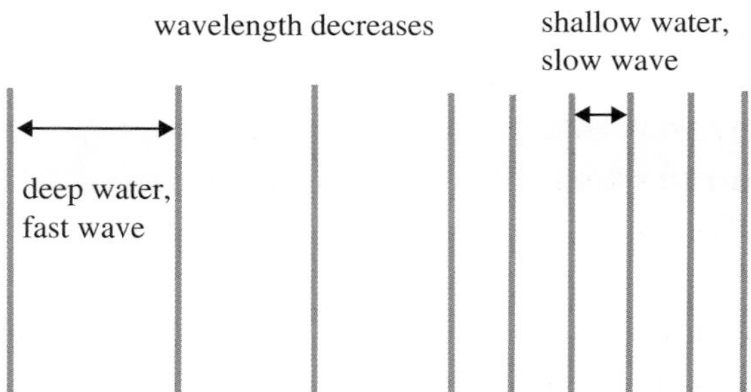

Figure 3.16 Water waves travel more slowly in shallow water. Thus refraction takes place when a water wave travels in water of variable depth.

It is a common observation that water waves approach the shore almost always parallel to the shoreline, even though when they were first created their direction was arbitrary. This is because as the waves approach the shore they refract into a medium of lower wave speed (shallow water). Thus, the direction of motion of the wave bends toward the normal, so the waves tend to become parallel to the shore (see Figure 3.17).

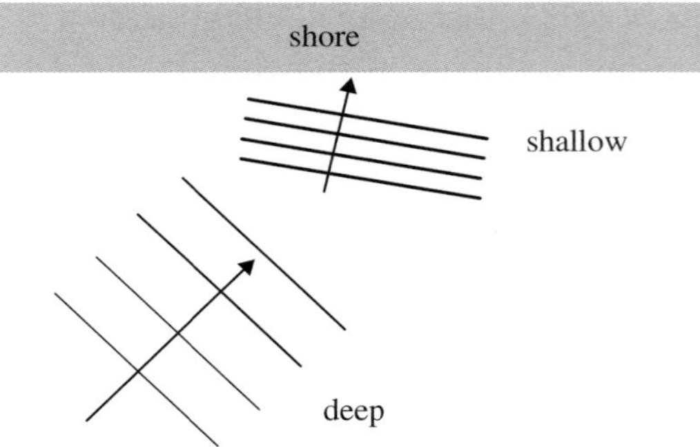

Figure 3.17 Wavefronts approaching the shore where the water is shallow slow down and so refract parallel to the shore.

A sound wave directed at a balloon filled with hydrogen will change its direction (i.e. refract) because the speed of sound in hydrogen is different from the speed of sound in air. The same is true when sound enters a liquid from, say, air. The speed of sound is greater in liquids than in gases, so sound entering a liquid will increase its wavelength. Finally, sound travels even faster in solids, metals, rock, etc. Typically, the speed of sound in a solid is a few thousand metres per second, compared with a few hundred metres per second in gases. The speed in liquids is in between. Table 3.1 gives the speed of sound in various media.

Medium	Speed/m s^{-1}
Air (0 °C)	331
Air (100 °C)	366
Helium (0 °C)	972
Oxygen (0 °C)	332
Water	1480
Sea water	1530
Mercury	1454
Aluminium	5100

Table 3.1 The speed of sound in various media.

Supplementary material

Huygens' principle

(Huygens' principle is not on the IBO examination syllabus. It is included here for completeness and because it is needed later.)

How does a wavefront propagate in space? Huygens' idea was to consider every single point on the wavefront of the wave as itself a source of waves. This is now known as **Huygens' principle**.

- Every point on the wavefront emits a spherical wavelet or secondary wave, of the same velocity and wavelength as the original wave. The wavelet is assumed to be emitted in the forward direction only. The amplitude of the wavelet is maximum in the forward direction and decreases rapidly away from that direction. The new wavefront is then the surface that is tangent to all the wavelets.

We can easily see that a plane or circular wavefront moving undisturbed forward easily obeys this construction (see Figure 3.18). The same is true for a spherical wave.

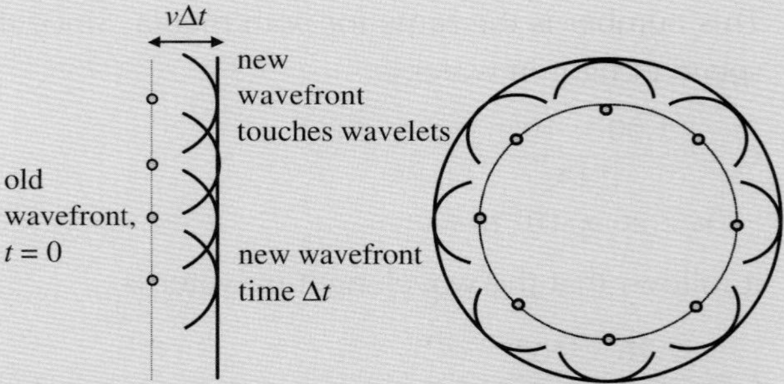

Figure 3.18 Each point on the old wavefronts acts as a source of spherical wavelets in the forward direction. The new wavefront touches all these wavelets.

The test comes when the wavefront encounters an obstacle of some kind or another. As we will soon see, the principle allows us to understand the phenomena of reflection and refraction.

Reflection

Huygens' principle allows us to theoretically understand the law of reflection in the following way. Consider a wave that is incident on a plane surface. Figure 3.19 shows two incident wavefronts, I_1 and I_2. The first wavefront to touch

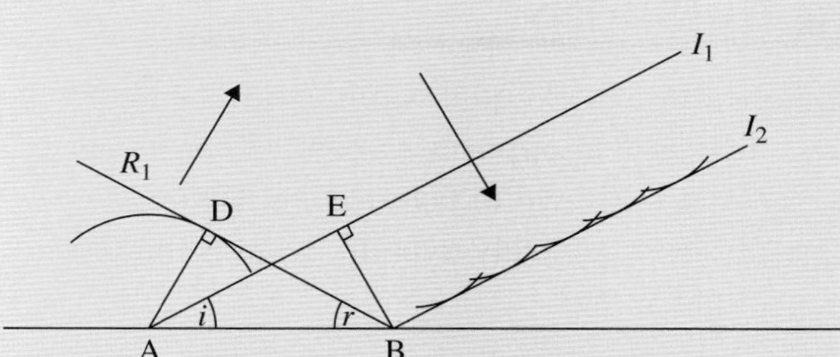

Figure 3.19 Huygens' construction applied to reflection.

the surface is I_1 and it touches at point A. I_2 touches later, say a period T later, at B. We have drawn a wavelet centred at A. All points on this wavelet have been emitted one period after those on I_1 and the same is true for point B. Thus, there must be a wavefront that contains both point B and a point on the wavelet. This wavefront is found by drawing a tangent from B to the wavelet. We call this the reflected wavefront R_1.

It is then clear from simple geometry that the angle of incidence ($\angle i$) equals the angle of reflection ($\angle r$): lengths AD and EB are equal since they both represent a wavelength. Thus, triangles ADB and AEB are equal, being right-angled and having two equal sides. Hence $\angle$EAB ($= \angle i$) equals $\angle$DBA ($= \angle r$); that is, the angle of reflection equals the angle of incidence.

Notice that the angle of incidence is defined as the angle between the normal to the surface and the incident ray. This angle is exactly the same as the angle between the *surface* and the incident *wavefront*. The same is true for the angle of reflection.

Figure 3.20 shows the effects of various barriers on waves in a ripple tank.

Refraction

The law of refraction is a consequence of Huygens' principle as follows. Figure 3.21 shows a wavefront (AB) that has hit the interface at A. A previous wavefront (CD) has already hit the interface at C at a time equal to one period earlier. (Since we are plotting wavefronts one wavelength apart it means that wavefront CD hit the interface a time equal to one wave period earlier.)

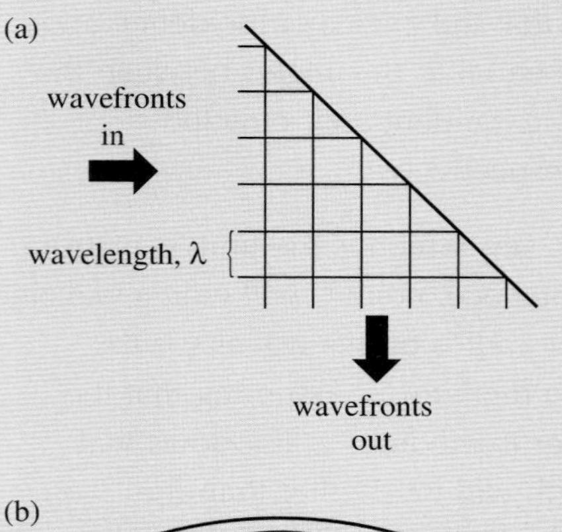

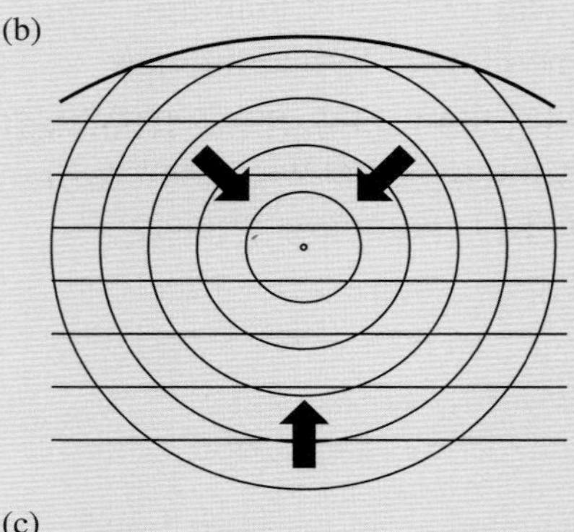

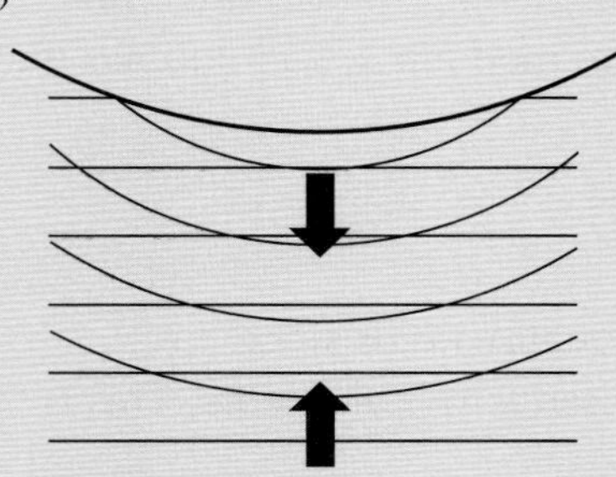

Figure 3.20 Waves in a ripple tank. (a) Waves reflected from a 45° barrier. Their wavelength stays the same. (b) Straight (plane) waves approach a concave barrier. The reflected waves are focused to a point. (c) Plane waves approach a convex barrier. The reflected waves spread out.

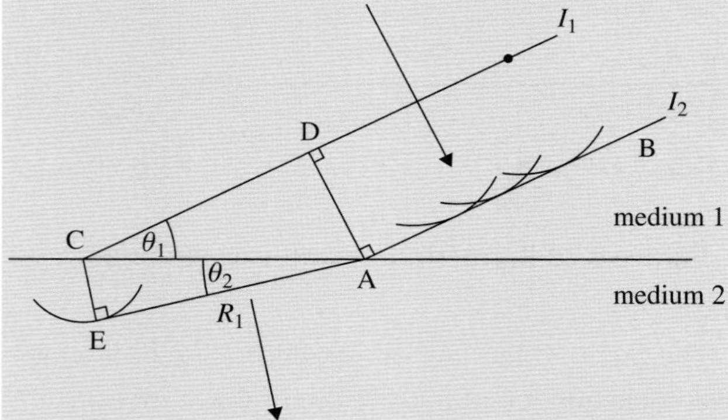

Figure 3.21 Huygens' construction applied to refraction.

Notice again that the angles of incidence and refraction are equal to the angles between the *surface* and the incident and refracted *wavefronts*, respectively.

At time $t = 0$, say, which is the time wavefront CD hits the interface, point C will emit a wavelet as shown. The radius of this wavelet is the wavelength in medium 2. Assuming that the wave is slower in medium 2, it follows that the wavelength will be smaller than the wavelength in medium 1. To find the new wavefront we must draw a tangent from A to this wavelet. Hence, the refracted wavefront is R_1 as shown in Figure 3.21. From trigonometry

$$\sin\theta_1 = \frac{DA}{AC}$$

$$\sin\theta_2 = \frac{CE}{AC}$$

But DA is the wavelength in medium 1 and CE the wavelength in medium 2, so it follows that

$$\frac{\sin\theta_1}{\sin\theta_2} = \frac{\lambda_1}{\lambda_2} = \frac{c_1}{c_2}$$

where the last equality holds since the frequency is the same in both media. This is Snell's law.

Figure 3.22 shows refraction of water waves in a ripple tank as the waves move from deep to shallower water. In shallower water the waves have a lower speed.

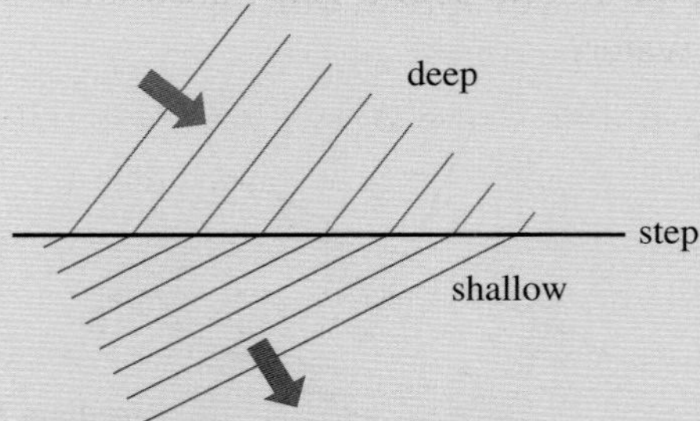

Figure 3.22 Refraction of water waves at a 'step'.

The fact that the law of refraction (Snell's law) is a consequence of a principle of wave motion (Huygens' principle) is strong evidence that light is indeed a kind of a wave.

QUESTIONS

1 Two pulses of equal width and height are travelling in opposite directions on the same string as shown in Figure 3.23. When the pulses completely overlap, what is the shape of the string?

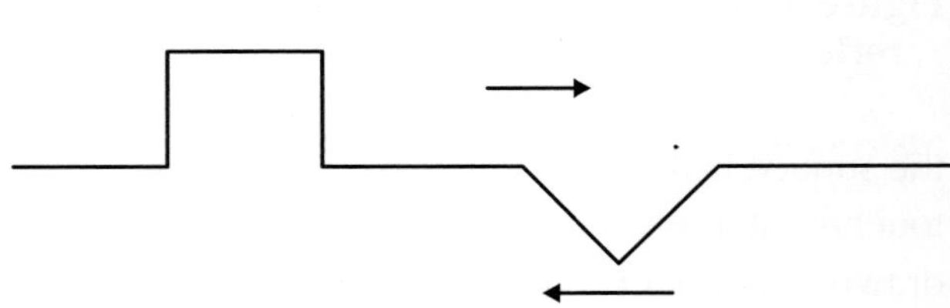

Figure 3.23 For question 1.

2 Two pulses of equal width and height are travelling in opposite directions on the same string as shown in Figure 3.24. When the pulses completely overlap, what is the shape of the string?

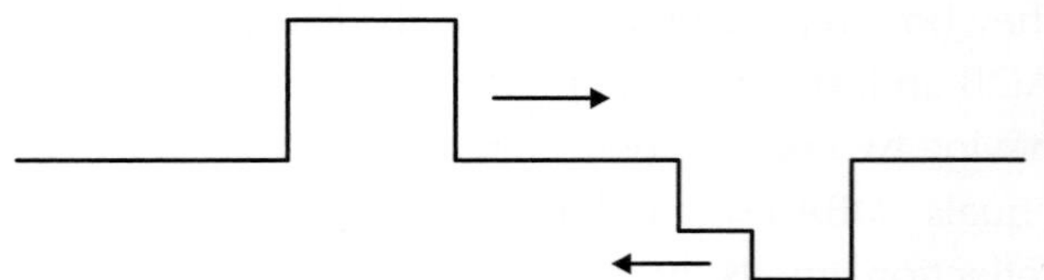

Figure 3.24 For question 2.

3 The wave pulses shown in Figure 3.25 travel at 1 cm s^{-1} and both have width 2 cm. The heights are indicated on the diagram. In each case, draw the shape of the resulting pulse according to the principle of superposition at times $t = 0.5$ s, $t = 1.0$ s and $t = 1.5$ s. Take $t = 0$ s to be the time when the pulses are about to meet each other.

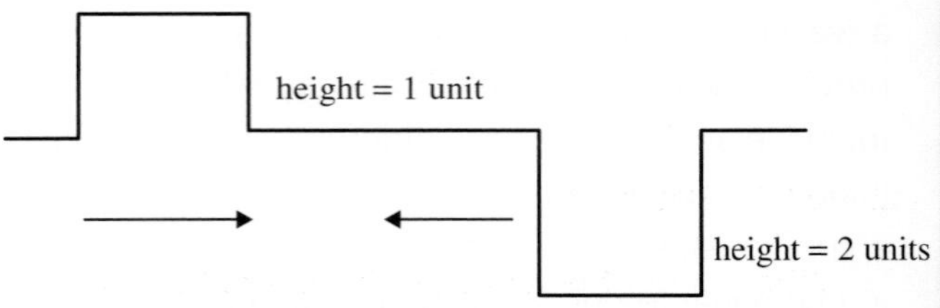

Figure 3.25 For question 3.

4 Two waves are simultaneously generated on a string as shown in Figure 3.26. Draw the actual shape of the string.

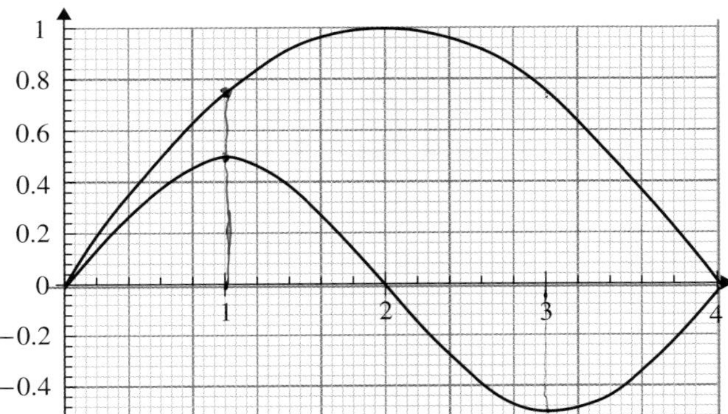

Figure 3.26 For question 4.

5 Red light of wavelength 6.8×10^{-7} m enters glass with an index of refraction of 1.583 from air, with an angle of incidence of 38°. Find:
(a) the angle of refraction;
(b) the speed of light in the glass;
(c) the wavelength of light in the glass.

6 Light of frequency 6.0×10^{14} Hz is emitted from point A and is directed toward point B a distance of 3.0 m away.
(a) How long will it take light to get to B?
(b) How many waves fit in the space between A and B?

7 A ray of light is incident on a rectangular block of glass of index of refraction 1.450 at an angle of 40°, as shown in Figure 3.27. If the thickness of the block is 4.00 cm, find the amount d by which the ray is deviated.

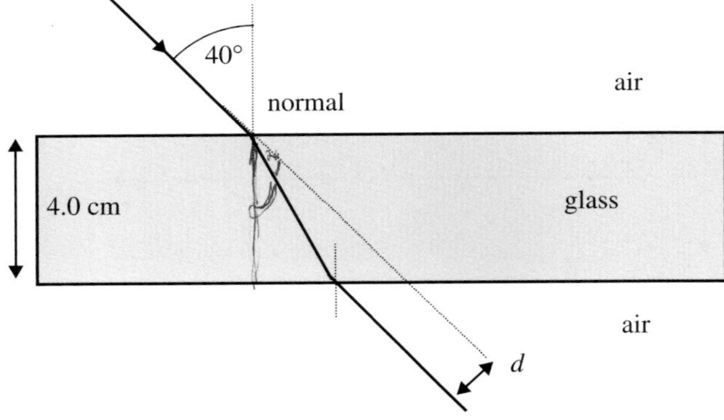

Figure 3.27 For question 7.

8 A ray of light enters glass from air at an angle of incidence equal to 45°, as shown in Figure 3.28. Draw the path of this ray assuming that the glass has an index of refraction equal to 1.420 and the plastic has an index of refraction of 1.350.

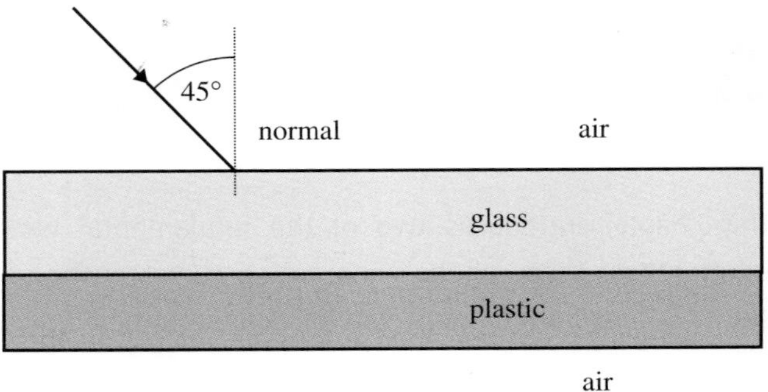

Figure 3.28 For question 8.

9 A ray of light moving in air parallel to the base of a glass prism of angles 45°, 45° and 90° enters the prism, as shown in Figure 3.29. Investigate the path of the ray as it enters the glass. The index of refraction of glass is 1.50.

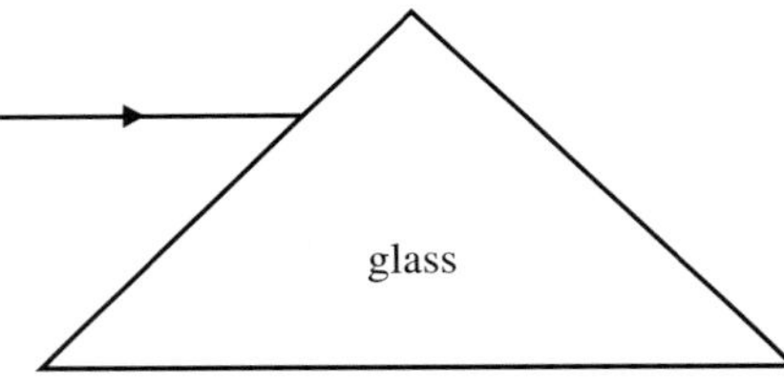

Figure 3.29 For question 9.

10 The speed of sound in air is 340 m s^{-1} and in water it is 1500 m s^{-1}. At what angle must a beam of sound waves hit the air–water interface so that no sound gets transmitted into the water?

11 A pulse with the shape shown in Figure 3.30 travels on a string at 40 m s^{-1} towards a fixed end. Taking $t = 0$ s to be when the front of the pulse first arrives at the fixed end, draw the shape of the string at: $t = 1.0$ ms; $t = 1.5$ ms; $t = 2.0$ ms; $t = 2.5$ ms; $t = 3.0$ ms; $t = 4$ ms.

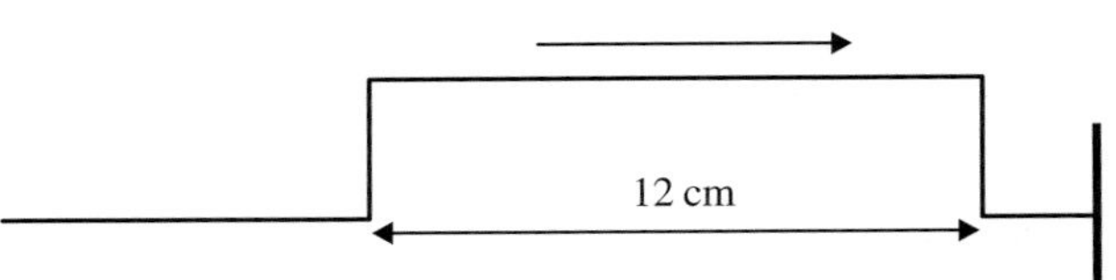

Figure 3.30 For question 11.

Wave phenomena II: diffraction and interference

This chapter introduces two of the fundamental wave phenomena, diffraction and interference. These phenomena are so characteristic of wave behaviour that anything showing these phenomena can be defined to be a wave.

Objectives

By the end of this chapter you should be able to:

- understand that diffraction is the *spreading* of a wave through an opening or past an obstacle;
- appreciate that *significant diffraction* takes place only if the *wavelength is comparable to or bigger than the size of the opening*;
- decide if *diffraction* for a given wave will take place in a given situation;
- understand that, as a result of *superposition*, when two identical waves arrive at the same place they will experience *constructive interference* if the crest of one matches the crest of the other, or *destructive interference* if the crest of one matches the trough of the other;
- appreciate the significance of the *path difference* in the phenomenon of interference.

Diffraction

The spreading of a wave as it goes past an obstacle or through an aperture is called **diffraction**. Let us consider a plane wave of wavelength λ propagating towards an aperture of size a.

▶ What will the wavefronts look like after the wave has gone through the aperture? As we will see, the value of the wavelength in relation to the aperture size will be crucial in determining what answer we get.

Let us first assume that the wavelength is very small compared with a (see Figure 4.1).

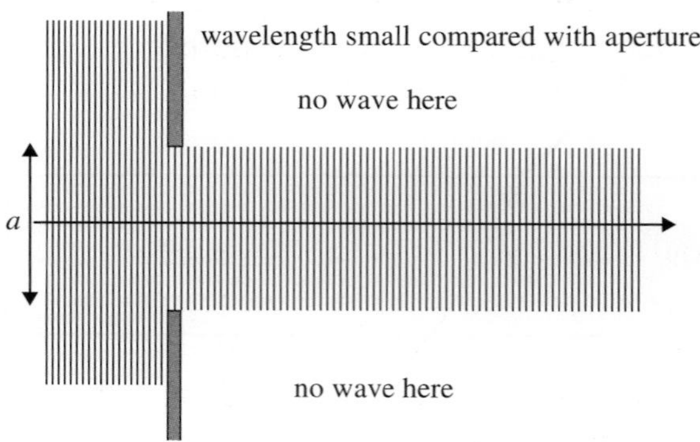

Figure 4.1 When the wavelength is small compared with the opening of the aperture, the amount of diffraction is negligible.

That part of the wave that is blocked by the screen does not propagate through and only the part which is free to go through does so. If the wave in question is light, this picture says that light goes through the opening, so that if we put a screen beyond the aperture we will see light on an area of the screen identical to the opening and darkness around it. Light travels in straight lines and does not bend as it goes through the aperture. There is no diffraction.

On the other hand, if the wavelength is comparable to or bigger than a, the new wavefronts are curved and the wave spreads around the edges of the opening (see Figure 4.2).

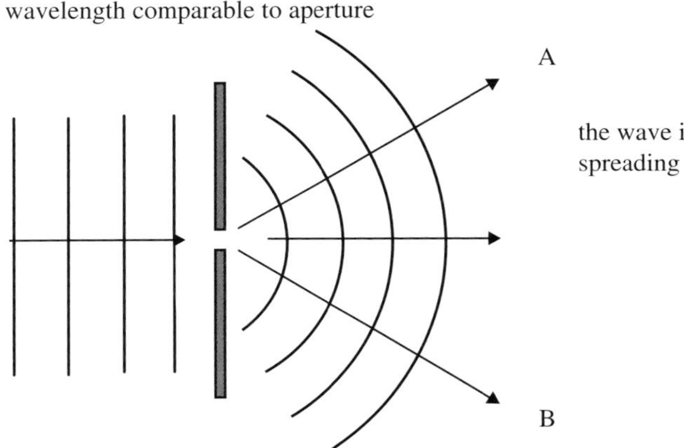

Figure 4.2 When the wavelength is comparable to the opening of the aperture, diffraction takes place.

If we put a screen some distance away from the aperture, we would see light in places where we would not expect any, such as at points A and B. This is the phenomenon of diffraction.

▶ Diffraction takes place whenever a wave whose wavelength is comparable to or bigger than the size of an aperture or an obstacle attempts to move through or past the aperture or obstacle.

(Note that here 'comparable to' can mean that the wavelength is a few times smaller than the aperture size.)

Supplementary material

Application of Huygens' principle helps to understand the phenomenon of diffraction. If the aperture size is very small, it is as if only one point on the wavefront will act as a source of waves and these will be circular: that is, the wave will spread. If the aperture is large, then many points on the wavefront will act as sources of secondary waves and these will tend to be planar: that is, there will not be appreciable diffraction.

(It must be realized, though, that Huygens' principle works in the same way for small and large wavelengths, so the principle by itself would give the same answer in both cases. It is a refined and much more sophisticated principle, the Huygens–Fresnel principle, that gives the correct wavefronts past the aperture. This principle is, however, beyond the scope of this book.)

Diffraction explains why we can hear, but not see, around corners. For example, a person talking in the next room can be heard through the open door because sound diffracts around the opening of the door – the wavelength of sound for speech is roughly the same as the door size. On the other hand, light does not diffract around the door since its wavelength is much smaller than the door size.

Other examples of diffraction are shown in Figures 4.3 and 4.4. Figure 4.3 shows diffraction around an obstacle.

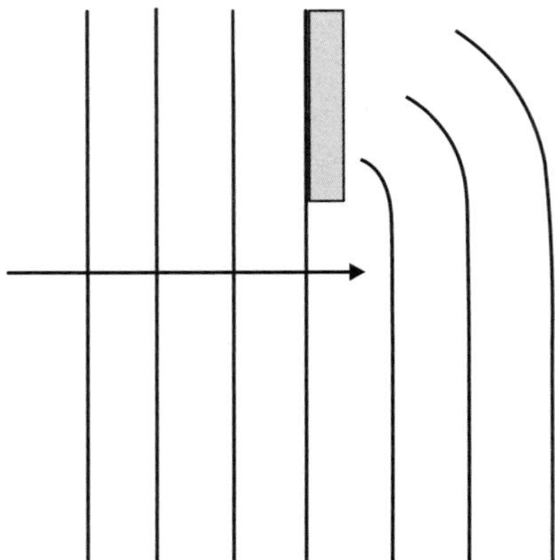

Figure 4.3 Diffraction also takes place when a wave moves past an obstacle.

If the wavelength is much smaller than the obstacle size, no diffraction takes place, as seen in Figure 4.4a. Diffraction does takes place if the wavelength is comparable to the obstacle size as seen in Figure 4.4b.

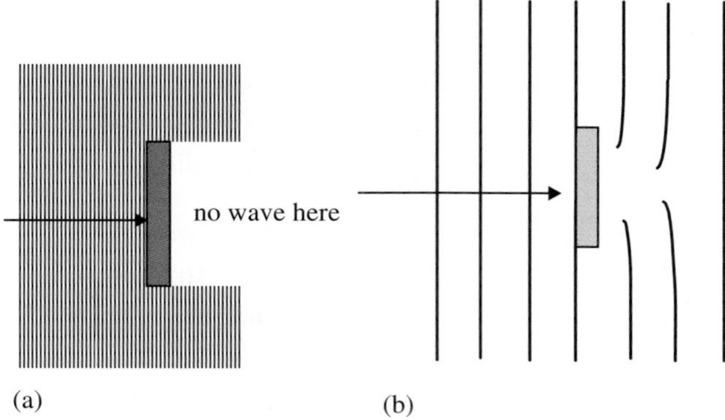

Figure 4.4 (a) If the wavelength is much smaller than the obstacle, no diffraction takes place and a shadow of the object is formed. (b) If the wavelength is comparable to the obstacle size, diffraction takes place and the wave appears far from the object in the region where the shadow was expected.

Interference

The most characteristic property of waves is their ability to interfere and diffract. The fact that light exhibits these phenomena is evidence that light is a wave. **Interference** is the result of superposition of two waves. We have met this principle of superposition in the previous chapter where we applied it mainly to individual pulses. Interference for light was demonstrated in 1801 by Thomas Young, an English scholar who also came close to deciphering hieroglyphics.

Let us be specific by considering two sources S_1 and S_2. Waves from the two sources meet at some point, say P, some distance away (see Figure 4.5).

Suppose that at time $t = 0$ both sources emit identical waves (same amplitude A, wavelength λ and frequency f). The wave from S_1 will take a certain time to arrive at P. From Figure 4.6, we read off this time as 2 s. The wave from the second source will take longer. Suppose that it takes 4 s (see Figure 4.7).

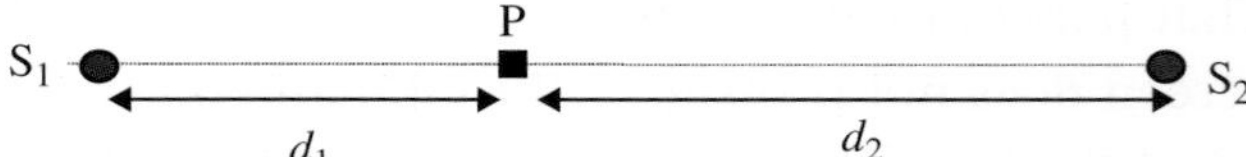

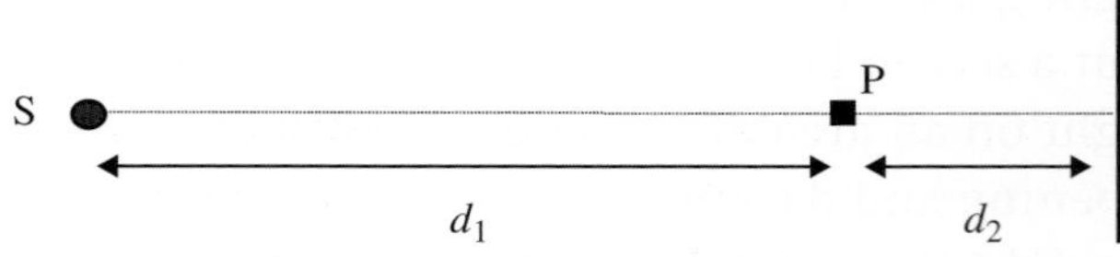

Figure 4.5 Interference from two sources. In the top diagram the waves arrive at P from the two sources and travel different distances in getting there. In the bottom diagram there is really only one source but the point P receives two waves. The first comes from the source S directly and the second wave is first reflected off the screen and then travels to P.

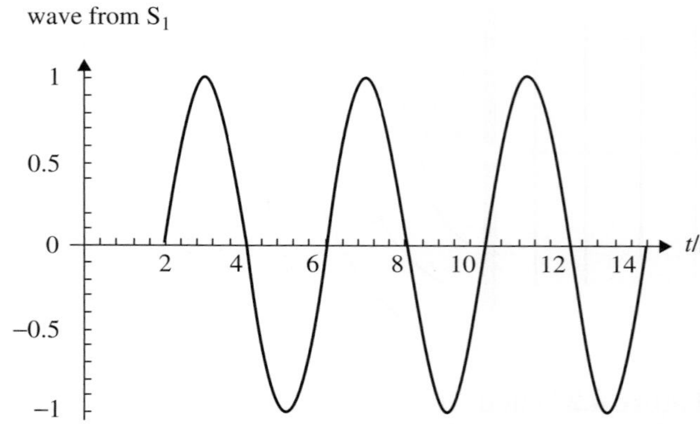

Figure 4.6 The first wave arrives at P 2 s after emission from the source.

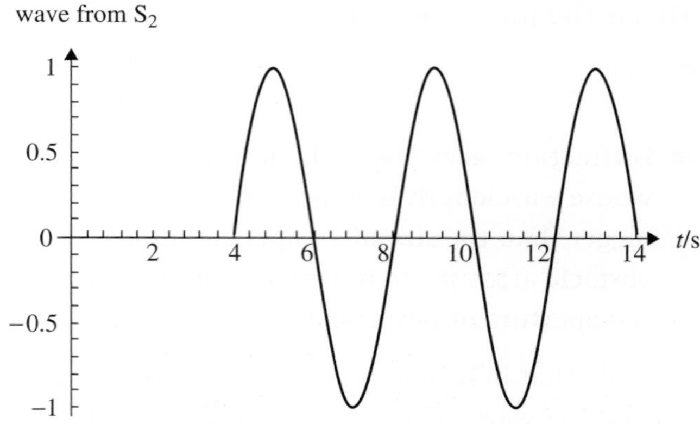

Figure 4.7 The second wave arrives at P 4 s after emission.

We see that, even though the waves are identical at emission, when they arrive at the observation point P, the crest of one matches the trough of the other. Thus, when they are added, according to the principle of superposition the resulting wave will be zero. We have a case of *destructive interference*: the two waves have cancelled each other out. If the two waves are sound waves, it means that at point P we hear no sound at all.

Suppose that we now change the distances of the two sources from P and the two waves arrive at P as shown in Figures 4.8 and 4.9.

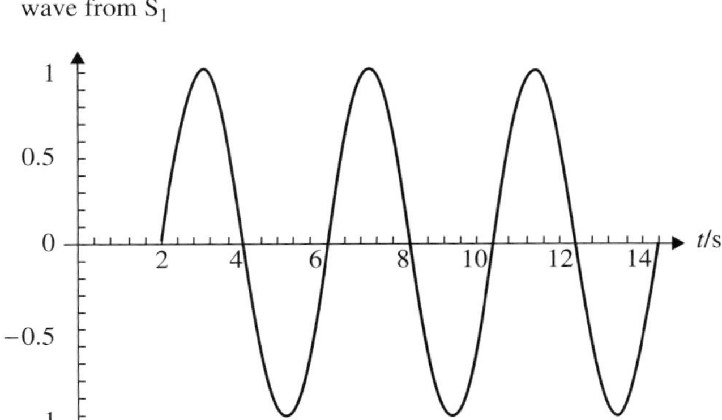

Figure 4.8 The first wave arrives at P 2 s after emission.

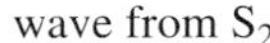

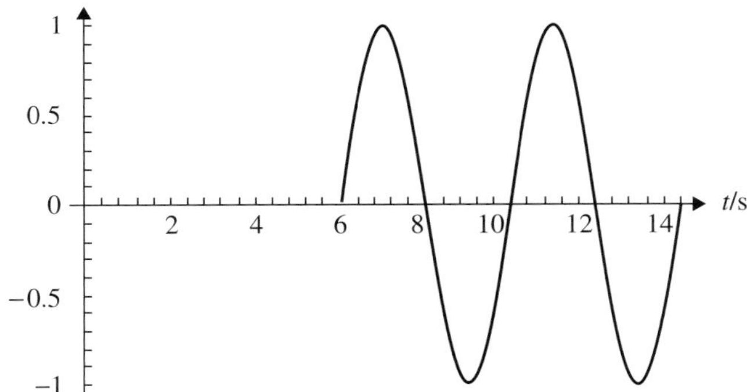

Figure 4.9 The second wave arrives at P 6 s after emission.

The arrival time from the first source is still 2 s but that from the second source is 6 s. Now the crests of one wave match the crests of the other. Thus, when we add them, we obtain a wave with double the amplitude of the individual waves (from 6 s on), as shown in Figure 4.10.

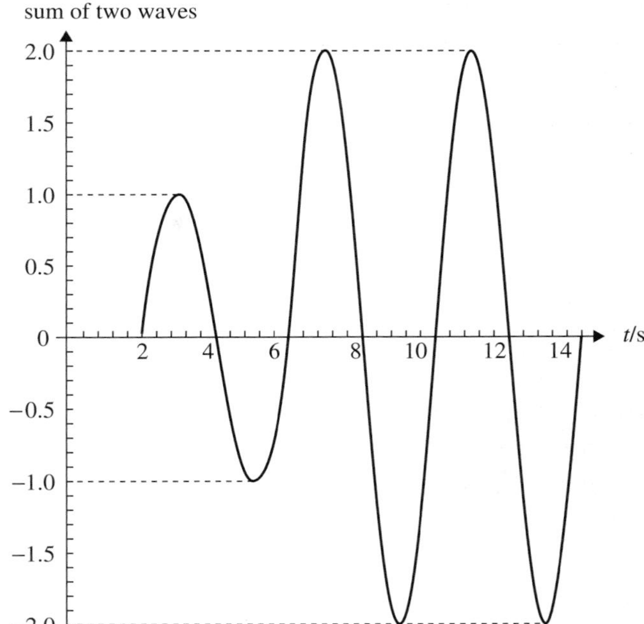

Figure 4.10 The sum of the waves from 6 s on (when both waves are present) has an amplitude that is double that of the individual waves.

This is a case of *constructive interference*. If the waves are sound waves, we would hear a very loud sound at point P. (Since loudness is proportional to the energy carried by the wave, and energy is proportional to the *square* of the amplitude, the loudness would be *four* times as great as the loudness of one wave alone.)

Note that the period of the individual waves is 4 s. In the first case of destructive interference the difference in arrival times was 2 s. In the case of constructive interference the difference in arrival times was 4 s. You must be able to convince yourself that, we would get destructive interference also when the difference in arrival times is 6 s, 10 s, 14 s, and so on (i.e. half-integral multiples of the period). Similarly, we would get constructive interference for differences in arrival times of 0 s, 4 s (as in the example), 8 s, 12 s, and so on (i.e. integral multiples of the period).

What is the general rule? If the distance from S_1 to P is d_1 and the distance from S_2 to P is d_2 (as shown in Figure 4.5), then the time of arrival of the first wave is d_1/v, where v is the wave velocity. Similarly, the wave from S_2 will arrive at P after a time d_2/v. The difference in arrival times is thus

$$\frac{d_1}{v} - \frac{d_2}{v}$$

There are two extreme cases: in case (i), the difference $\frac{d_1}{v} - \frac{d_2}{v}$ is an *integral multiple of the period* T of the wave. Then the crests of the wave from S_1 match the crests of the wave from S_2. The resultant wave has therefore the maximum possible amplitude, twice the amplitude of one of the waves. In case (ii), the difference $\frac{d_1}{v} - \frac{d_2}{v}$ is a *half-integral multiple of the period*. Then the maxima of one wave match the minima of the other. The two waves cancel each other out completely. The wave observed is zero. In case (i) we have constructive interference, and in case (ii) we have destructive interference.

▶ The condition for constructive interference is

$$\frac{d_1}{v} - \frac{d_2}{v} = nT$$

$$\Rightarrow d_1 - d_2 = nTv$$

but $Tv = \lambda$ so

$$d_1 - d_2 = n\lambda$$

$$n = 0, \pm 1, \pm 2, \pm 3, \ldots$$

that is, the *path difference* must be an integral multiple of the wavelength.

The condition for destructive interference is

$$d_1 - d_2 = \left(n + \tfrac{1}{2}\right)\lambda$$

$$n = 0, \pm 1, \pm 2, \pm 3, \ldots$$

As we already mentioned, if the wave is a sound wave, points of constructive interference are points of high intensity of sound. Points of destructive interference are points of no sound at all. If the wave involved is light, and then constructive interference means bright light, and destructive interference means points of darkness.

▶ If the path difference is anything other than an integral or half-integral multiple of the wavelength, then the resultant amplitude of the wave at P will be some value between zero and $2A$, where A is the amplitude of one of the waves.

Example question

Q1

Waves leaving two sources arrive at point P. Point P is 12 m from the first source and 16.5 m from the second. The waves have a wavelength of 3 m. What is observed at P?

Answer

The path difference is 4.5 m. It equals $(1 + \frac{1}{2}) \times 3$ m: that is, it is a half-integral multiple of the wavelength. We thus have destructive interference.

? QUESTIONS

1 Planar waves of wavelength 1.0 cm approach an aperture whose opening is also 1.0 cm. Draw the wavefronts of this wave as they emerge through the aperture.

2 Repeat question 1 for waves of wavelength 1 mm approaching an aperture of size 20 cm.

3 In the corridor shown in Figure 4.11 an observer at point P can hear someone at point Q but cannot see them. What physical phenomena may account for this? How could P *see* Q?

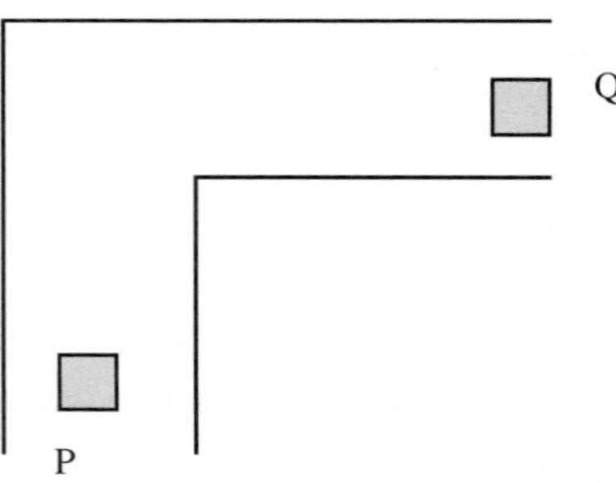

Figure 4.11 For question 3.

4 Two loudspeakers are connected to the same audio oscillator. An observer walks along the straight line joining the speakers (see Figure 4.12). At a point M halfway between the speakers he hears a loud sound. By the time he gets to point P a distance of 2.00 m from M he hears no sound at all. Explain how this is possible. Find the largest possible wavelength of sound emitted by the loudspeakers.

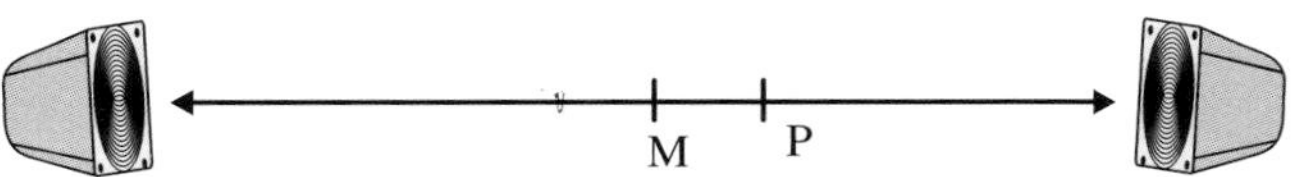

Figure 4.12 For question 4.

5 A radio station, R, emits radio waves of wavelength 1600 m which reach a house, H, directly and after reflecting from a mountain, M, behind the house (see Figure 4.13). If the reception at the house is very poor, what is the shortest possible distance between the house and the mountain? (Assume, for simplicity, no phase changes.)

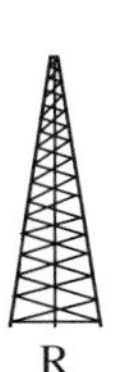

M

Figure 4.13 For question 5.

6 A car moves along a road that joins the twin antennas of a radio station that is broadcasting at a frequency of 90.0 MHz (see Figure 4.14). When in position A, the reception is good but it drops to almost zero at position B. What is the minimum distance AB?

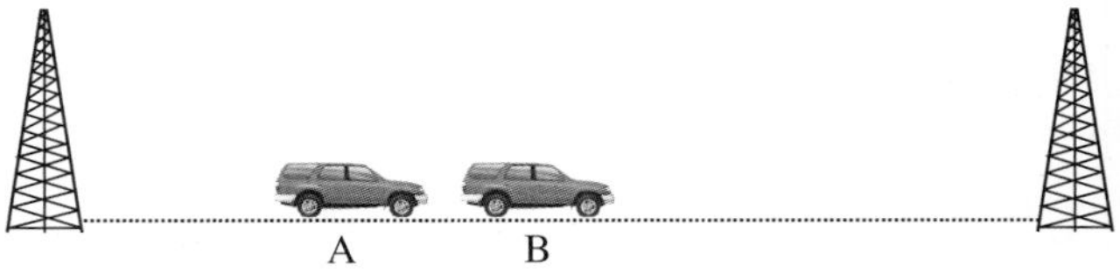

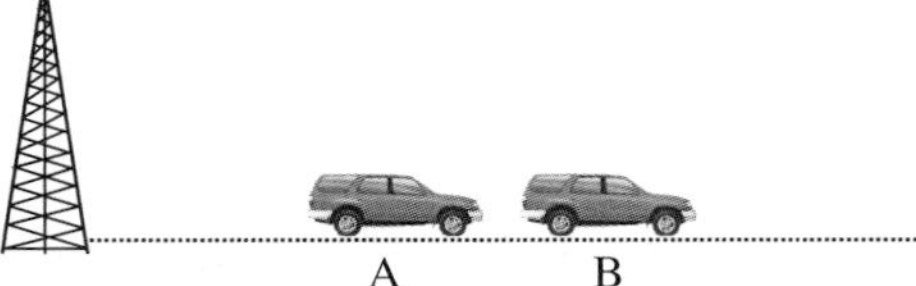

Figure 4.14 For question 6.

7 Two sources emit identical sound waves with a frequency of 850 Hz.

(a) An observer is 8.2 m from the first source and 9.0 m from the second. Describe and explain what this observer hears.

(b) A second observer is 8.1 m from the first source and 8.7 m from the second. Describe and explain what this observer hears.

(Take the speed of sound to be 340 m s^{-1}.)

8 In the context of wave motion, state what you understand by the term superposition. Illustrate constructive and destructive interference by suitable diagrams.

The Doppler effect

This chapter looks at the Doppler effect, the change in frequency of a wave when there is relative motion between the source and the observer. The Doppler effect is a fundamental wave phenomenon with many applications. This chapter discusses this phenomenon quantitatively. The phenomenon applies to all waves but sound waves only are considered here.

Objectives

By the end of this chapter you should be able to:

- understand the *Doppler effect* in a qualitative way and explain it by drawing appropriate diagrams for a moving source or a moving observer;
- derive the *Doppler formula* for a moving source $f_o = \frac{f_s}{1-(v_s/c)}$ and a moving observer $f_o = f_s(1 + \frac{v_o}{c})$, and use these in solving problems;
- qualitatively *explain* the Doppler effect by suitable *wavefront diagrams*.

The Doppler effect

Consider a source of waves and an observer who receives them. If there is relative motion between the observer and the source (i.e. the source or the observer, or both, move) then, in general, the observer will receive the wave at a frequency that is *different* from the emitted frequency. This is a phenomenon of everyday life. For example, if an approaching car creates a high-pitched sound, as it goes past us and recedes the frequency of the sound becomes lower.

▶ The Doppler effect is the change in the frequency of a wave received by an observer, compared with the frequency with which it was emitted. The effect takes place whenever there is motion between the emitter and receiver.

We can understand the Doppler effect in terms of wavefront diagrams. Consider first a stationary source of waves emitting circular wavefronts (Figure 5.1). Suppose for simplicity that the source emits a wave of frequency f that travels with speed c. This means that f wavefronts are emitted per second. An observer who is also stationary will clearly receive f wavefronts every second as well, so there is no Doppler effect.

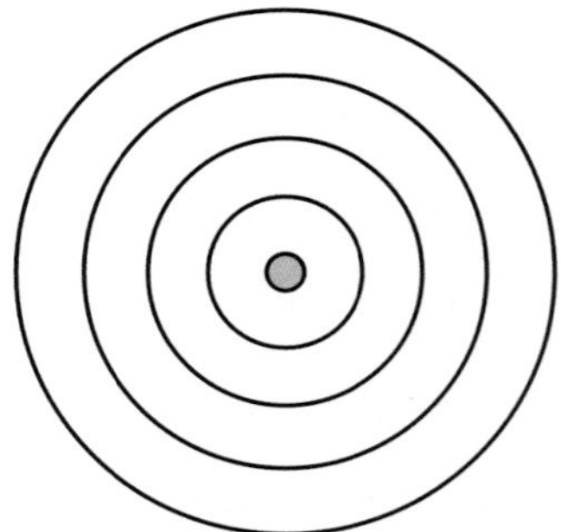

Figure 5.1 The wavefronts emitted by a stationary source are concentric. The common centre is the position of the source.

Now consider a stationary observer and a source of sound that moves with speed v_s ($<c$) towards the observer (Figure 5.2). The source emits sound of a single frequency f_s as measured by an

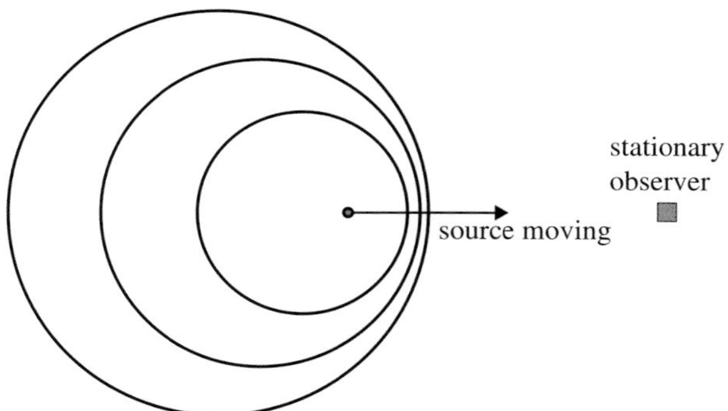

Figure 5.2 A source is approaching the stationary observer with speed v_s.

observer moving along with the source. (In what follows c stands for the speed of the wave, i.e. here for the speed of sound in still air and later on for the speed of light in a vacuum.)

In a time equal to one second, the source will therefore emit f_s wavefronts. In that same time interval, the source will move a distance equal to v_s towards the stationary observer (Figure 5.3).

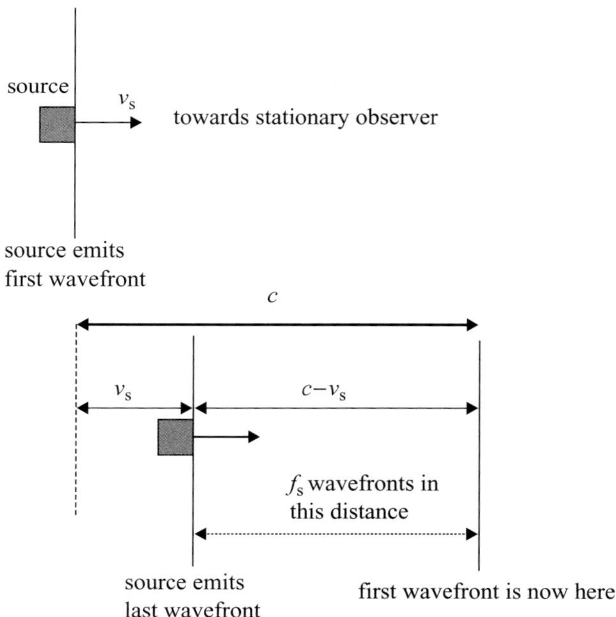

Figure 5.3 Determining the Doppler frequency.

Therefore, these f_s wavefronts are within a distance of $c - v_s$, and so the stationary observer will measure a wavelength (separation of wavefronts) equal to

$$\lambda_o = \frac{c - v_s}{f_s}$$

The frequency measured by the stationary observer is therefore

$$f_o = \frac{c}{\lambda_o}$$
$$= \frac{c}{(c - v_s)/f_s}$$
$$= f_s \frac{c}{c - v_s}$$

Dividing through by c gives

$$f_o = \frac{f_s}{1 - \frac{v_s}{c}} \quad \text{source moving towards observer}$$

As the source approaches, the stationary observer thus measures a higher frequency than that emitted by the source.

A similar calculation for the case of the source moving away from the stationary observer gives

$$f_o = \frac{f_s}{1 + \frac{v_s}{c}} \quad \text{source moving away from observer}$$

In the case of a stationary source and a moving observer we may argue as follows. First let us consider the case of the observer moving towards the source. The observer who moves with speed v_o with respect to the source may claim that he is at rest and that it is the source that approaches him with speed v_o. The observer will then measure a higher wave speed, equal to $c + v_o$. We are now back to the case of a moving source, and so the frequency measured by the observer is

$$f_o = \frac{f_s}{1 - \frac{v_o}{c + v_o}}$$
$$= \frac{f_s(c + v_o)}{c + v_o - v_o}$$
$$= \frac{f_s(c + v_o)}{c}$$

Dividing through by c gives

$$f_o = f_s\left(1 + \frac{v_o}{c}\right) \quad \text{observer moving towards source}$$

Similarly, if the observer moves away from the source we get

$$f_o = f_s\left(1 - \frac{v_o}{c}\right) \quad \text{observer moving away from source}$$

Notice carefully that, in the case of the moving source and the stationary observer, the wavelength measured by the observer, λ_o, is *different* from that measured by the source, λ_s. Consider the case of a source moving towards the observer:

$$\lambda_o = \frac{c}{f_o}$$

$$= \frac{c}{f_s/(1 - \frac{v_s}{c})}$$

$$= \frac{c}{f_s}\left(1 - \frac{v_s}{c}\right)$$

$$\lambda_o = \lambda_s\left(1 - \frac{v_s}{c}\right)$$

because

$$\lambda_s = \frac{c}{f_s}$$

However, in the case of the *moving observer* (towards the source for example):

$$\lambda_o = \frac{c + v_o}{f_o}$$

$$= \frac{c + v_o}{f_s/(1 + \frac{v_o}{c})}$$

$$= \frac{c}{f_s}$$

$$\lambda_o = \lambda_s$$

and is the *same* as that measured by the source.

This is why in defining the Doppler effect we refer to the change in *frequency* measured by the observer and not the change in wavelength.

The Doppler effect has many applications. One of the most common is to determine the speed of moving objects from cars on a highway (as the next Example question shows). Another application is to measure the speed of flow of blood cells in an artery.

Example questions

Q1

A sound wave of frequency 300 Hz is emitted towards an approaching car. The wave is reflected from the car and is then received back at the emitter at a frequency of 315 Hz. What is the velocity of the car? (Take the speed of sound to be 340 m s^{-1}.)

Answer

The car is approaching the emitter so the frequency it receives is

$$f_1 = 300 \times \frac{340 + u}{340}\ \text{Hz}$$

where u is the unknown car speed. The car now acts as an emitter of a wave of this frequency (f_1), and the original emitter will act as the new receiver. Thus, the frequency received (315 Hz) is (car is approaching)

$$315 = \left(300 \times \frac{340 + u}{340}\right) \times \frac{340}{340 - u}$$

from which we find $u = 8.29$ m s^{-1}.

Q2

A train with a 500 Hz siren on is moving at a constant speed of 8.0 m s^{-1} in a straight line. An observer is in front of the train and off its line of motion. What frequencies does the observer hear? (Take the speed of sound to be 340 m s^{-1}.)

Answer

What counts is the velocity of the train along the *line of sight* between the train and the observer. When the train is *very far away* (Figure 5.4) it essentially comes straight towards the observer

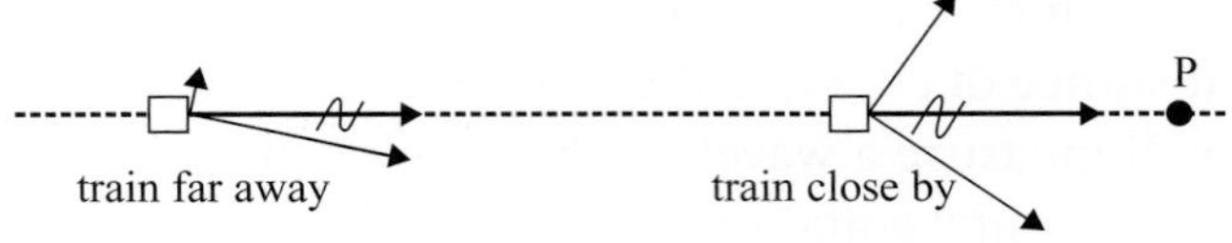

Figure 5.4.

and so the frequency received is

$$\begin{aligned} f_o &= f_s \frac{c}{c - v_s} \\ &= 500 \times \frac{340}{340 - 8} \\ &\approx 510 \text{ Hz} \end{aligned}$$

When the train is again *very far away* to the right, the train is moving away from the observer and the frequency received will be

$$\begin{aligned} f_o &= f_s \frac{c}{c + v_s} \\ &= 500 \times \frac{340}{340 + 8} \\ &\approx 490 \text{ Hz} \end{aligned}$$

As the train approaches, we take components of the train's velocity vector in the direction along the line of sight and the direction normal to it (see Figure 5.4).

As is seen from the diagram, the component along the line of sight is decreasing as the train gets closer to the observer. Thus, the observer will measure a *decreasing* frequency. It starts at 510 Hz and falls to 500 Hz when the train is at position P. As the train moves past P to the right, the observer will hear sound of *decreasing* frequency starting at 500 Hz and ending at 490 Hz.

Thus, the observer hears frequencies in the range of 510 Hz to 490 Hz, as shown in Figure 5.5.

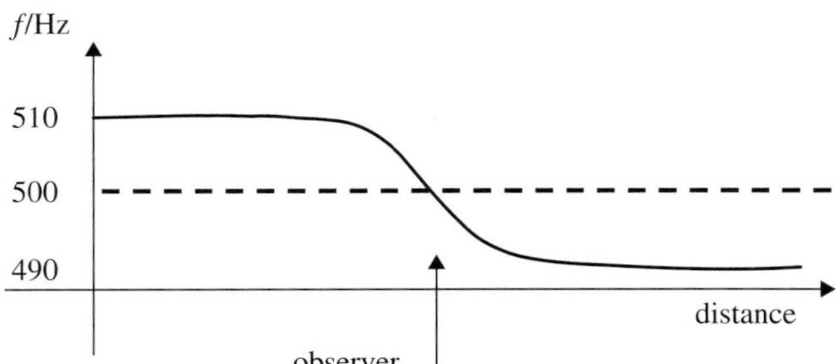

Figure 5.5.

The Doppler effect also applies to light, but the equation giving the frequency observed is more complicated. However, in the case in which the speed of the source or the observer is *small* compared to the speed of light, the equation takes a simple form:

$$\Delta f = \frac{v}{c} f \quad \text{for light only}$$

In this formula v is the speed of the source or the observer, c is the speed of light and f is the emitted frequency. Then Δf gives the change in the observed frequency.

Example question

Q3

Hydrogen atoms in a distant galaxy emit light of wavelength 658 nm. The light received on earth is measured to have a wavelength of 689 nm. State whether the galaxy is approaching the earth or moving away, and calculate the speed of the galaxy.

Answer

The received wavelength is longer than that emitted, and so the galaxy is moving away from earth.

The emitted frequency is

$$\begin{aligned} f &= \frac{c}{\lambda} \\ &= \frac{3.00 \times 10^8}{658 \times 10^{-9}} \\ &= 4.56 \times 10^{14} \text{ Hz} \end{aligned}$$

and the received frequency is

$$\begin{aligned} f &= \frac{c}{\lambda} \\ &= \frac{3.00 \times 10^8}{689 \times 10^{-9}} \\ &= 4.35 \times 10^{14} \text{ Hz} \end{aligned}$$

giving a shift of $\Delta f = 0.21 \times 10^{14}$ Hz. Hence the speed is found as follows:

$$\Delta f = \frac{v}{c} f \Rightarrow v = \frac{c\Delta f}{f}$$

$$v = \frac{3.00 \times 10^8 \times 0.21 \times 10^{14}}{4.56 \times 10^{14}}$$

$$v = 1.4 \times 10^7 \text{ m s}^{-1}$$

? QUESTIONS

Take the speed of sound to be 343 m s^{-1} in all the problems that follow.

1 A source of sound is directed at an approaching car. The sound is reflected by the car and is received back at the source. *Carefully* explain what changes in frequency the observer at the source will detect.

2 Light from a nearby galaxy is emitted at a wavelength of 657 nm and is observed on earth at a wavelength of 654 nm. What can we deduce about the motion of this galaxy?

3 Explain, with the help of diagrams, the Doppler effect. Show clearly the cases of a source that (a) moves towards and (b) goes away from a stationary observer as well the case of a moving observer.

4 A source approaches a stationary observer at 40 m s^{-1} emitting sound of frequency 500 Hz. What frequency does the observer measure?

5 A source is moving away from a stationary observer at 32 m s^{-1} emitting sound of frequency 480 Hz. What frequency does the observer measure?

6 A sound wave of frequency 512 Hz is emitted by a stationary source toward an observer who is moving away at 12 m s^{-1}. What frequency does the observer measure?

7 A sound wave of frequency 628 Hz is emitted by a stationary source toward an observer who is approaching at 25 m s^{-1}. What frequency does the observer measure?

8 A sound wave of frequency 500 Hz is emitted by a stationary source toward a receding observer. The signal is reflected by the observer and received by the source, where the frequency is measured and found to be 480 Hz. What is the speed of the observer?

9 A sound wave of frequency 500 Hz is emitted by a moving source toward a stationary observer. The signal is reflected by the observer and received by the source, where the frequency is measured and found to be 512 Hz. What is the speed of the source?

10 A disc rotates about its axis with constant angular velocity. A point on the rim moves with a speed of 7.5 m s^{-1}. Sound of frequency 500.0 Hz is emitted from a source on the circumference of the disc in directions parallel to the source's velocity as shown in Figure 5.6, and is received by an observer very far away from the disc. What frequencies does the observer measure?

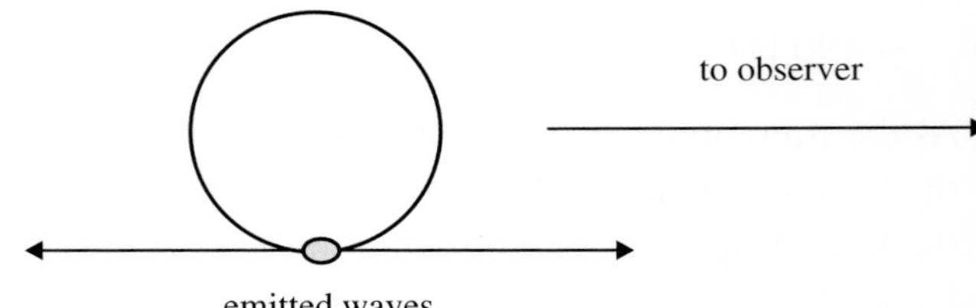

Figure 5.6 For question 10.

11 Consider the general case when both the source and the observer move towards each other. Let v_s be the velocity of the source and v_o that of the observer. In the frame of reference in which the observer is at rest, the waves appear to move with velocity $c + v_o$ and the source appears to move with velocity $v_s + v_o$. Thus, show that the frequency received by the observer is

$$f_o = f_s \frac{c + v_o}{c - v_s}$$

12 Consider a source moving away from a stationary observer with speed v. The source emits waves of speed c and wavelength λ_s. Explain why the observer will measure a *longer* wavelength for the waves received and show that the *shift* in wavelength $\Delta\lambda = \lambda_o - \lambda_s$ obeys $\frac{\Delta\lambda}{\lambda_s} = \frac{v}{c}$.

13 A source of sound emits waves of frequency f towards an object moving away from the source. The waves are reflected by the object and are received back at the source. The speed of the object is v.

(a) Deduce that the frequency of the reflected waves as measured by an observer at the source is given by

$$f' = f\frac{1-\frac{v}{c}}{1+\frac{v}{c}}$$

(b) If $\frac{v}{c}$ is small, it can be shown in mathematics that

$$\frac{1}{1+\frac{v}{c}} \approx 1 - \frac{v}{c}$$

Deduce that the magnitude of the frequency shift measured by the observer at the source becomes

$$\Delta f = \frac{2v}{c}f$$

(c) Ultrasound of frequency 5.000 MHz reflected from red blood cells moving in an artery is found to show a frequency shift of 2.4 kHz. The speed of ultrasound in blood is 1500 m s^{-1}.
(i) Estimate the speed of the blood cells.
(ii) In practice, a range of frequency shifts is observed. Explain this observation.

14 The sun rotates about its axis with a period that may be assumed to be constant at 27 days. The radius of the sun is 7.00×10^8 m. Discuss the shifts in frequency of light emitted from the sun's equator and received on earth. Assume that the sun emits monochromatic light of wavelength 5.00×10^{-7} m.

15 The human ear can detect frequencies in the range of about 20 Hz to 20 kHz. A source of sound moves towards and then away from a stationary observer. Describe qualitatively the changes, if any, in the frequency of sound heard by the observer when the source emits
(a) sound of a single frequency 500 Hz;
(b) sound with frequency in the range 500 Hz to 1000 Hz;
(c) all frequencies covering the entire audible range of the observer.

16 In a binary star system, two stars orbit a common point and move so that they are always in diametrically opposite positions. Light from both stars reaches an observer on earth. Assume that both stars emit light of wavelength 6.58×10^{-7} m.

(a) When the stars are in the position shown in Figure 5.7, the observer on earth measures a wavelength of light of 6.58×10^{-7} m from both stars. Explain why there is no Doppler shift in this case.

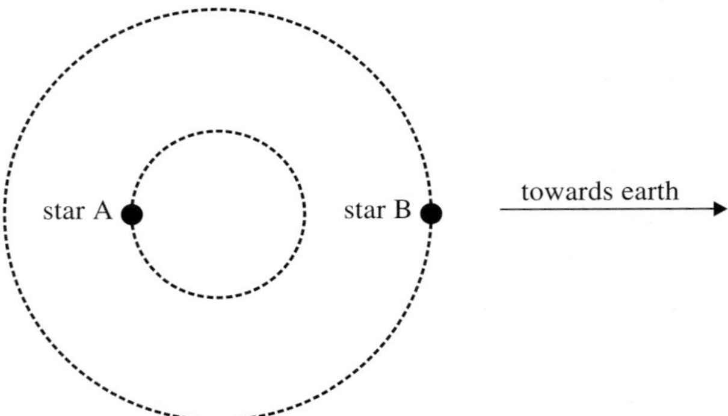

Figure 5.7 For question 16(a).

(b) When the stars are in the position shown in Figure 5.8, the earth observer measures two wavelengths in the received light, 6.50×10^{-7} m and 6.76×10^{-7} m. Determine the speed of each of the stars.

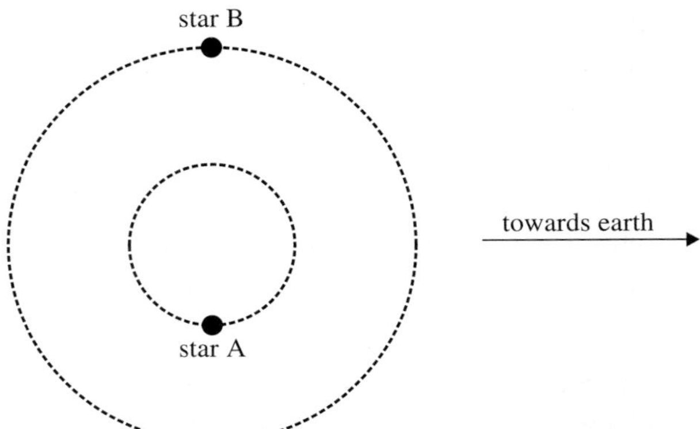

Figure 5.8 For question 16(b).

17 A source of sound emits waves of frequency 850 Hz in all directions as it approaches and then recedes from an observer close to its path. The power of the sound emitted is constant.
(a) Draw a sketch graph (no numbers required) to show the variation with time of the intensity of the sound heard by the observer.

The observer is 4.0 m away from the line of motion of the source. The source moves at a constant speed of 12 m s^{-1}, and its initial position is 24 m away, as shown in Figure 5.9.

(b) Draw a detailed graph to show the variation with time of the frequency of the sound heard by the observer.

(c) How does your graph in (b) change if the source is moving with constant acceleration? (Assume that the acceleration is 2.0 m s^{-2}, the initial position is the same (24 m away) and the initial velocity is 10 m s^{-1}.) Draw a detailed graph and explain the shape you have drawn.

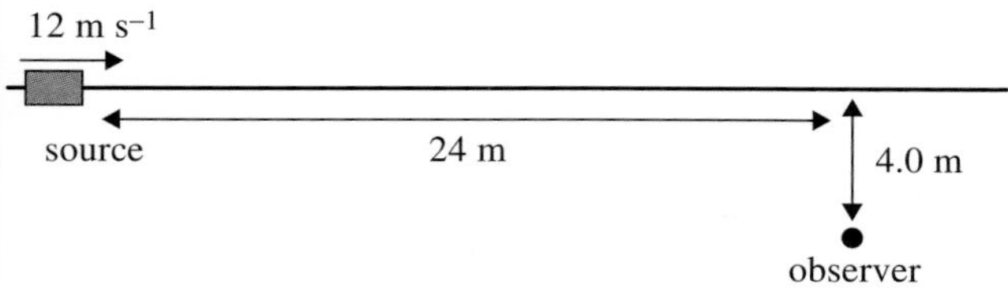

Figure 5.9 For question 17.

18 Sound of frequency 530 Hz is emitted by a stationary source. An observer approaching the source at high speed receives the sound and measures a frequency of 580 Hz.

(a) Determine the speed of the observer.

(b) Calculate the wavelength of the sound as measured by

(i) the source;

(ii) the observer.

Take the speed of sound in still air to be 340 m s^{-1}.

19 (a) The shift in frequency due to a source of light moving at speed v and emitting light of frequency f is given by

$$\Delta f = \frac{v}{c} f$$

Using the approximation (valid if $\frac{v}{c}$ is small)

$$\frac{1}{1 \pm \frac{v}{c}} \approx 1 \mp \frac{v}{c}$$

show that the shift in wavelength is given by

$$\Delta \lambda = \frac{v}{c} \lambda$$

where λ is the emitted wavelength.

(b) Calculate the speed of a galaxy emitting light of wavelength 5.48×10^{-7} m which when received on earth is measured to have a wavelength of 5.65×10^{-7} m.

Standing waves

A special wave is formed when two ordinary identical waves travelling in opposite directions meet. The result is a standing (stationary) wave: a wave in which the crests do not move.

Objectives

By the end of this chapter you should be able to:

- state the differences between a *standing* wave and a *travelling* wave;
- describe how *a standing wave is formed*;
- draw the *various harmonics on strings and tubes* and find the *wavelength in terms of the string or tube length*;
- state the meaning of the terms *fundamental* and *harmonics*;
- state the meaning of the term *resonance*;
- solve problems with *standing waves*.

Standing waves on strings and tubes

▶ When two waves of the same speed and wavelength and equal or almost equal amplitudes travelling in opposite directions meet, a standing wave is formed. This interesting wave is the result of the superposition of the two waves travelling in opposite directions.

The main difference between a standing wave and a travelling wave is that in the former no energy or momentum is transferred. A standing wave is characterized by having a number of points at which the displacement is *always* zero. These are called nodes. (In a travelling wave, there are no points where the displacement is *always* zero.) The points at which the displacement is a maximum are called antinodes. (Note that the nodes always have zero displacement whereas the antinodes are at maximum displacement for an instant of time only.) In Figure 6.1 a string of length L has been plucked in the middle and is about to be released.

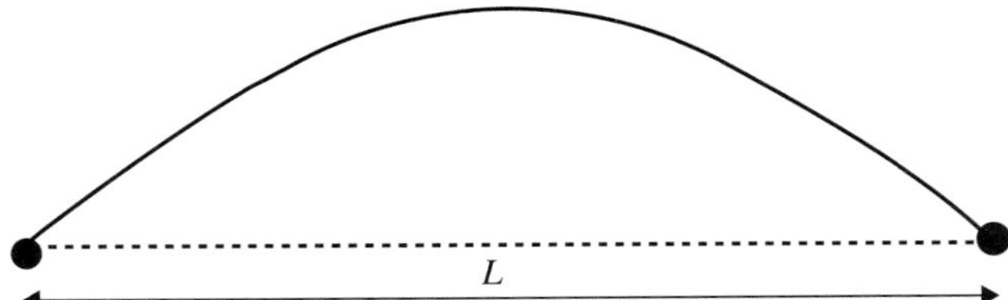

Figure 6.1 A standing wave on a string with both ends fixed. The string is held in this position and then released. A standing wave like this with a single antinode is known as a fundamental standing wave.

Successive pictures of the string will then look like Figure 6.2: the end points of the string remain fixed at all times (nodes) but the rest of the string oscillates. The middle point is the point on the string with the largest displacement (antinode). The string will return to its original position after a time equal to the period of the wave. In the absence of friction,

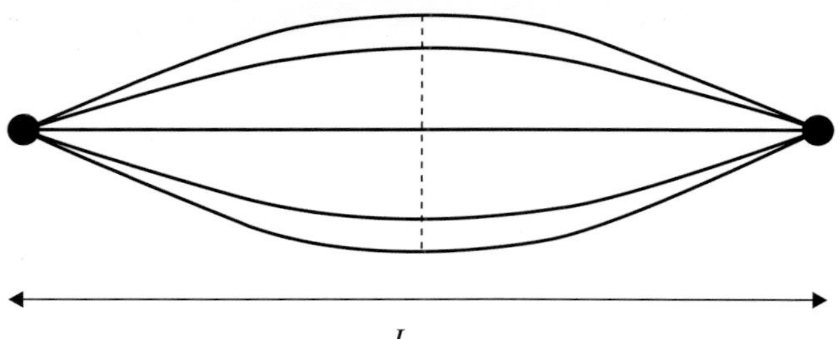

Figure 6.2 Positions of the string at various time intervals after being released. The dark circles show the positions of the nodes. The dotted line shows the position of the antinode.

this oscillation will continue forever. When the string is in its original position ($t = 0$) all the energy of the wave is in the form of potential energy of the stretched string. When the string assumes its undisturbed position, all the energy is in the form of kinetic energy. At all other positions the energy of the string consists of both potential and kinetic energy. Note that the crest of this wave (i.e. the antinode) does not move to the right or left as a crest does in a travelling wave.

The standing wave depicted above has a specific wavelength. Note that we have fitted half a full wave on the length of the string. This means that

$$\frac{\lambda}{2} = L$$
$$\Rightarrow \lambda = 2L$$

The wave with $\lambda = 2L$ is not the only standing wave that can exist on this string, however. Figure 6.3 shows the next standing wave. Note

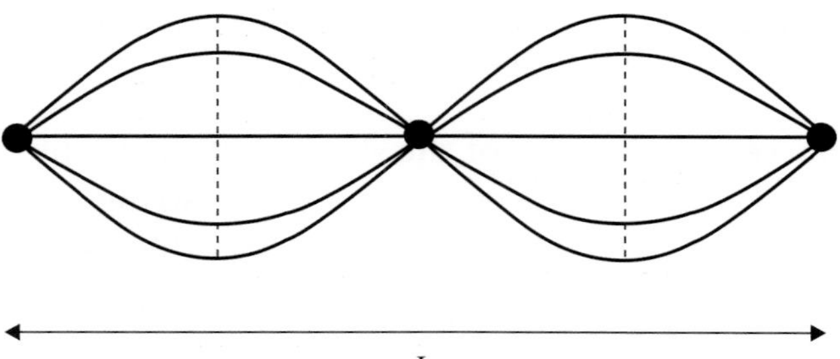

Figure 6.3 A standing wave with three nodes and two antinodes. A standing wave like this is known as the second harmonic.

that the only constraint we have is that the ends of the string are nodes. Here, we have fitted one full wave on the string. Thus, $\lambda = L$. This standing wave has three nodes and two antinodes.

An infinity of standing waves can thus exist on the string by 'fitting' waves with the constraint that the ends are nodes. The next standing wave is shown in Figure 6.4.

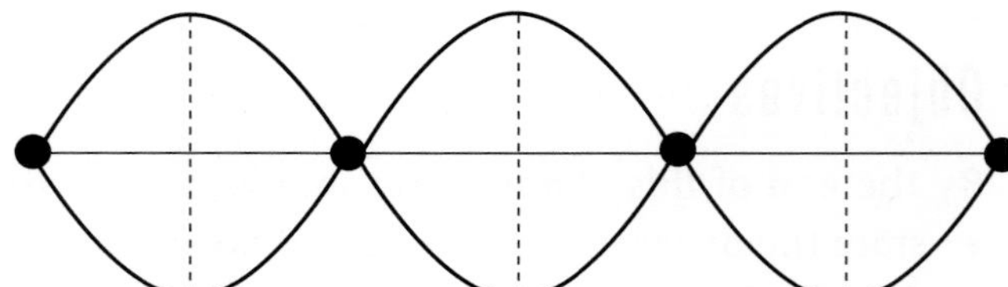

Figure 6.4 A standing wave with four nodes and three antinodes. A standing wave like this is known as the third harmonic.

For the third harmonic, we have fitted one and a half full waves on the string. Thus,

$$\frac{3}{2}\lambda = L$$
$$\Rightarrow \lambda = \frac{2L}{3}$$

In general, we find that the wavelengths satisfy

$$\lambda = \frac{2L}{n}, \quad n = 1, 2, 3, 4, \ldots$$

The wave with wavelength corresponding to $n = 1$ is called the fundamental mode of the string or the first harmonic. All other modes are called higher harmonics. So, for example, the mode with $n = 3$ is the third harmonic. The fundamental mode has the largest wavelength and thus the smallest frequency ($f = \frac{v}{\lambda}$, where v is the speed of the wave).

▶ If f_0 is the fundamental's frequency, then all other harmonics have frequencies that are integral multiples of f_0.

Note that the distance between two successive nodes is half a wavelength. The same is true for successive antinodes. The distance between a node and the next antinode is a quarter of a wavelength.

Figure 6.5 shows that particles between two consecutive nodes move in the same direction. Particles between the adjacent pair of nodes move in the opposite direction.

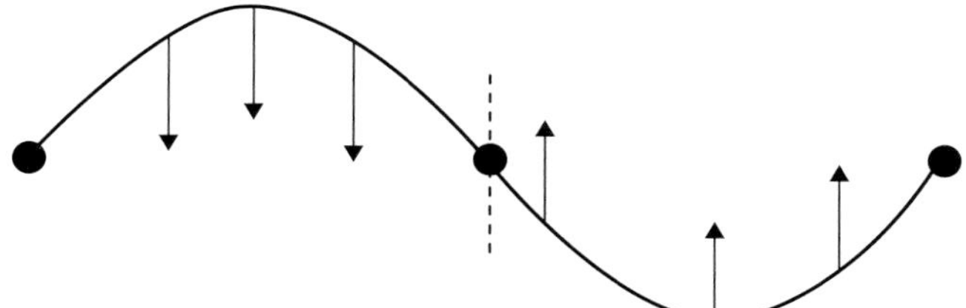

Figure 6.5 All points between two consecutive nodes are in phase: that is to say, they move in the same direction. They differ in phase by 180° with those between the next pair of nodes, which are moving in the opposite way.

If one end of the string is free and the other fixed, then the free end must be an antinode and the fixed end a node. The allowed wavelengths are then

$$\lambda = \frac{4L}{n}, \quad n = 1, 3, 5, \ldots$$

(Here n is an odd integer.) Examples of these standing waves are shown in Figures 6.6–6.8.

You must convince yourself that the wavelengths of these harmonics are indeed those given by the formula $\lambda = \frac{4L}{n}, n = 1, 3, 5, \ldots$

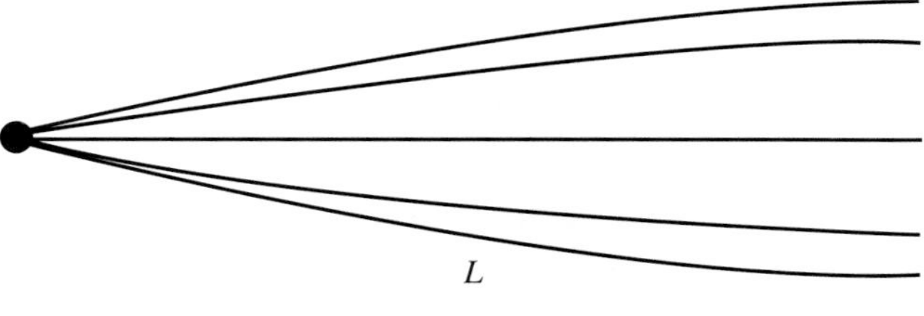

Figure 6.6 The fundamental standing wave on a string with one end fixed and the other free.

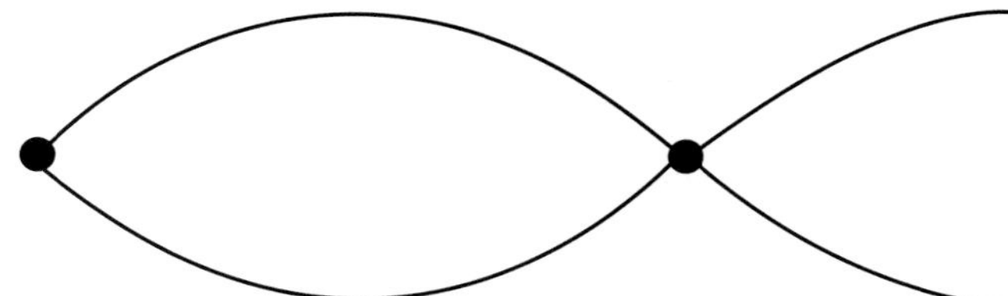

Figure 6.7 The second harmonic.

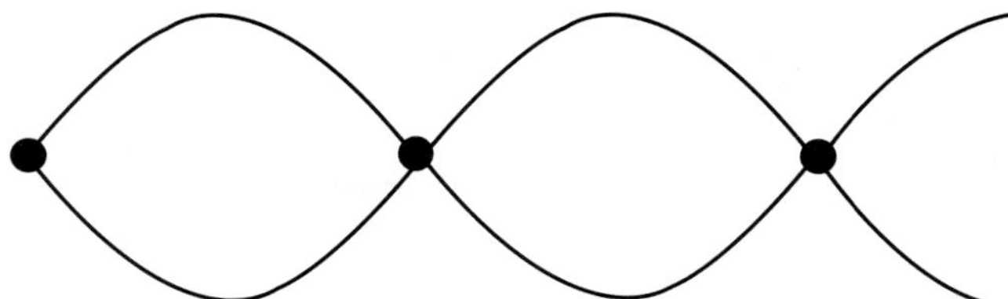

Figure 6.8 The third harmonic.

When both ends are free, the condition is

$$\lambda = \frac{2L}{n}, \quad n = 1, 2, 3, 4, \ldots$$

The situation here is entirely analogous to that with both ends fixed with the roles of node and antinode interchanged (see Figure 6.9).

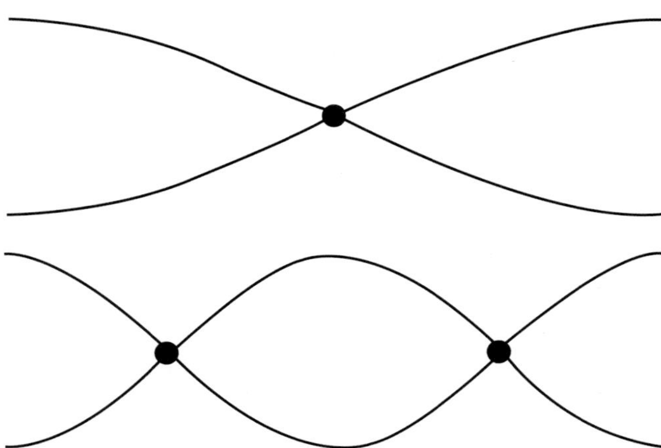

Figure 6.9 Standing waves on a string with both ends free are similar to those for both ends fixed except that nodes and antinodes are interchanged. The fundamental and second harmonic are shown here.

We have discussed standing waves exclusively in terms of waves on a string whose ends are fixed or free. Exactly the same results apply to sound standing waves formed in a pipe (such as a musical instrument) whose ends are open (corresponding to free string ends) or closed (corresponding to fixed string ends) – see Figure 6.10. Nodes exist at closed ends and antinodes at open ends.

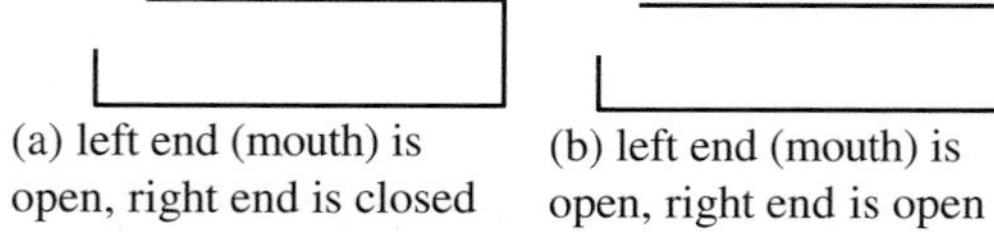

Figure 6.10 (a) A pipe with one end closed and one open. (b) A pipe with both ends open.

Supplementary material

Nodes in this case correspond to points in the pipe where the air molecules are not moving whereas antinodes correspond to points where the air molecules move with maximum displacement (see Figure 6.11). These are called displacement nodes and antinodes. Note, however, that at a displacement node the pressure of the gas varies the most (i.e. we have a pressure antinode), and at a displacement antinode the pressure variation is zero (i.e. we have a pressure node).

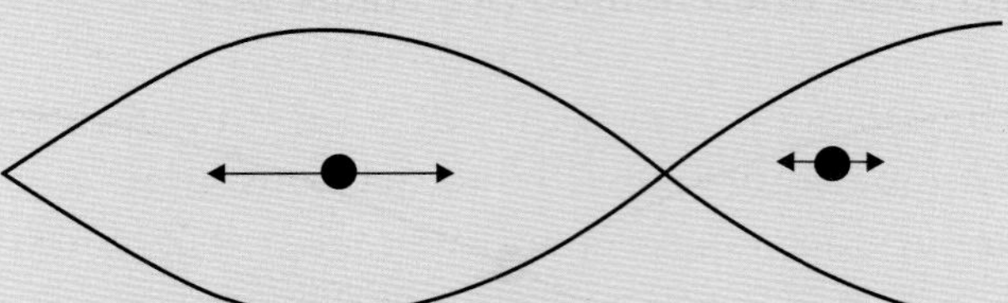

Figure 6.11 Air molecules in the pipe vibrate the most at antinodes and not at all at nodes.

You don't need to memorize the formulae for wavelength in terms of string or tube length. Rather, you should note that in all cases the distance between successive nodes or antinodes is half a wavelength and that the distance between a node and the next antinode is a quarter of a wavelength. This should allow you to figure out what kind of standing wave you can fit in the particular case you are examining. We see from these formulae that, as the length of the tube becomes smaller, the allowed wavelengths also get smaller, which means that the corresponding frequencies get larger. This is seen when you put a bottle under a tap and start to fill it with water. The falling water excites a standing wave in the bottle whose length of air column is getting smaller as the bottle fills. This means that the frequency of the sound emitted by the bottle becomes high pitched, as we know from experience.

Example questions

Q1

A standing wave is set up on a string kept under tension T. What must be done to the tension in order to double the fundamental frequency of the wave?

Answer

Since $f = \frac{v}{\lambda}$, and the wavelength is fixed in terms of the length of the string $\lambda = 2L$, we can double f by doubling the velocity of the wave. This means that the tension must increase by 4.

Q2

What is the ratio of the frequencies of the fundamental to the second harmonic for a standing wave set up on a string, both ends of which are kept fixed?

Answer

The frequencies are

$$f_0 = \frac{v}{2L} \quad \text{and} \quad f_1 = \frac{v}{L}$$

hence

$$\frac{f_0}{f_1} = \frac{1}{2}$$

Q3

A tube has one end open and the other closed. What is the ratio of the wavelengths of the fundamental to the second harmonic?

Answer

The fundamental and second harmonic have wavelengths

$$\lambda_0 = 4L \quad \text{and} \quad \lambda_1 = \frac{4L}{3}$$

hence

$$\frac{\lambda_0}{\lambda_1} = 3$$

Q4

A standing wave is set up in a tube with both ends open. The frequency of the fundamental is 300 Hz. What is the length of the tube? Take the speed of sound to be 340 m s^{-1}.

Answer

The wavelength is

$$\frac{340}{300}\text{ m} = 1.13\text{ m}$$

The fundamental's wavelength is equal to $2L$ and so $L = 0.57$ m.

Resonance and the speed of sound

When a vibrating tuning fork is brought near to the end of a long tube partially filled with water, a buzzing sound may be heard from the tube. When that happens, addition of more water in the tube will ruin the effect. This is an example of resonance. The tuning fork will excite the air in the tube and force it to vibrate with a frequency equal to the tuning fork's frequency. The amplitude of this standing wave will be appreciable, though, only if the frequency of the standing wave that the tube can support is equal to the tuning fork's frequency. When these two frequencies are the same, we hear the buzzing sound from the tube. Pouring more water in the tube changes the frequency of the tube and so the amplitude is now very small – no sound is heard from the tube.

This actually provides a simple method for measuring the speed of sound in air. A set of tuning forks of known frequencies are each sounded over a column of air in a long tube partially filled with water. The height of the column of water is adjusted (by pouring water in or out) until resonance is obtained (i.e. the tube emits a sound). The corresponding height of the air column and the frequency are recorded and this is repeated with the other tuning forks. The standing wave inside the tube must have a wavelength such that $\lambda = 4L$, where L is the length of the air column. But $\lambda = \frac{v}{f}$, where f is the corresponding frequency, which equals the known frequency of the tuning fork. Thus, v, which is the speed of sound, can be determined by repeating this procedure for various different tuning forks and then plotting L versus $1/f$. One must get a straight line with slope $v/4$.

Supplementary material

This discussion ignores end corrections. End corrections are necessary in practice because the standing wave may have a wavelength that does not satisfy $\frac{\lambda}{4} = L$ but rather $\frac{\lambda}{4} = L + e$, where e is a constant depending on the diameter of the tube. In an experiment to measure the speed of sound by resonance the end correction *must* be included.

Resonance is a general phenomenon. It occurs whenever a system that is capable of oscillation or vibration is subjected to an external disturbance with a frequency equal to the natural frequency of the system itself. In that case, the system oscillates with a large amplitude. If the frequencies do not match, the system still vibrates but the amplitude is very small. Clearly, resonance can be a dangerous phenomenon. A system that is set into vibration by something external and develops large amplitudes may eventually break or fall apart. Aeroplane wings, engines, bridges, tall buildings, etc., must all be protected against resonance from external vibrations due to wind, other vibrating objects, etc. Soldiers always break their step when walking over a bridge, in case the force that they exert on the bridge starts uncontrollable oscillations of the bridge. An earthquake may set a building into oscillation if the frequency of the longitudinal wave created by the earthquake is equal to the natural frequency of vibration of the building. This frequency is $\frac{c}{2L}$, where c is the speed of sound in the structure of the building and L is its height. (See Figures 6.12–6.14.)

Figure 6.12 The Tacoma Narrows bridge collapsed in 1940, a victim of resonant failure.

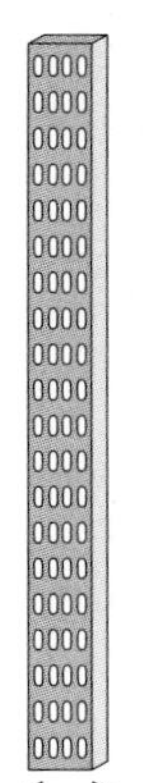
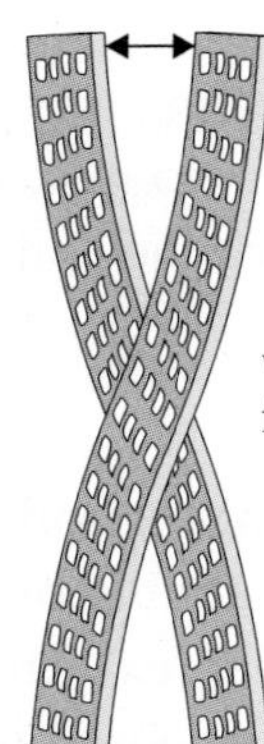

Figure 6.13 A building will be made to oscillate in a standing wave mode if the frequency of the earthquake wave matches the natural frequency of oscillation of the building.

Figure 6.14 The severe earthquake that struck northern Turkey in August 1999 released vast amounts of energy. Hundreds of buildings toppled and tens of thousands of people were killed.

? QUESTIONS

1 Describe what is meant by a standing wave. In what ways does a standing wave differ from a travelling wave?

2 How is a standing wave formed?

3 In the context of standing waves describe what is meant by:
(a) node;
(b) antinode.

4 Describe how you would arrange for a string that is kept under tension, with both ends fixed, to vibrate in its second harmonic mode. Draw the shape of the string when it is vibrating in its second harmonic mode.

5 Explain what is meant by resonance and give two examples where it occurs.

6 Car drivers occasionally experience a 'shaking steering wheel' when travelling at a particular speed. The shaking disappears at lower or higher speeds. Suggest a reason for this observation.

7 A string is held under tension, with both ends fixed, and has a fundamental frequency of 250 Hz. If the tension is doubled, what will the new frequency of the fundamental mode be?

8 A string has both ends fixed. What is the ratio of the frequencies of the first to the second harmonic?

9 The fundamental mode on a string with both ends fixed is 500 Hz. What will the frequency become if the tension in the string is increased by 20%?

10 The wave velocity of a transverse wave on a string of length 0.500 m is 225 m s^{-1}.
(a) What is the fundamental frequency of a standing wave on this string if both ends are kept fixed?
(b) While this string is vibrating in the fundamental harmonic, what is the wavelength of sound produced in air?
(Take the speed of sound in air to be 330 m s^{-1}.)

11 Figure 6.15 shows a tube with one end open and the other closed. Draw the standing wave representing the third harmonic standing wave in this tube.

Figure 6.15 For question 11.

12 A glass tube is closed at one end. The air column it contains has a length that can be varied between 0.50 m and 1.50 m. If a tuning fork of frequency 306 Hz is sounded at the top of the tube, at which lengths of the air

column would resonance occur? (Take the speed of sound to be 330 m s^{-1}.)

13 A glass tube with one end open and the other closed is used in a resonance experiment to determine the speed of sound. A tuning fork of frequency 427 Hz is used and resonance is observed for air column lengths equal to 17.4 cm and 55.0 cm.

(a) What speed of sound does this experiment give?

(b) What is the end correction for this tube?

14 A tube with both ends open has two consecutive harmonics of frequency 300 Hz and 360 Hz.

(a) What is the length of the tube?

(b) What are the harmonics?

(Take the speed of sound to be 330 m s^{-1}.)

15 A string of length 0.50 m is kept under a tension of 90.0 N and vibrates in its fundamental mode. The mass of the string is 3.0 g.

(a) What is the frequency of the sound emitted? (Take the speed of sound to be 330 m s^{-1}.)

(b) The same string now vibrates in water. What is the wavelength of the sound emitted? (Take the speed of sound in water to be 1500 m s^{-1}.)

16 A container of water of length 12 cm is placed on top of a vibration generator (Figure 6.16). When the generator is turned on, the water in the container sloshes back and forth.

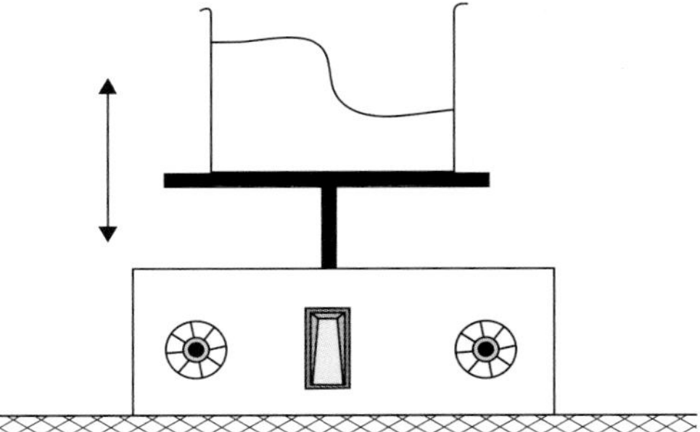

Figure 6.16 For question 16.

When the frequency is adjusted to about 0.75 Hz, the water actually spills out of the container.

(a) Suggest a reason for this.

(b) Estimate the speed of water waves in the container.

17 Do the following experiment at home. Take a styrofoam cup (top diameter approximately 8 cm) and fill it with cold coffee or tea. Now drag it slowly over a surface that is neither too smooth nor too rough, for example a kitchen counter.

(a) Observe and explain what you see on the surface of the liquid as the speed at which you drag the cup is varied.

(b) Knowing that the speed of water waves in the cup is about 0.15 m s^{-1}, estimate the frequency that makes the water vibrate.

(c) Is this frequency related to the speed of the cup?

18 Consider a string with both ends fixed. A standing wave in the second harmonic mode is established on the string, as shown in Figure 6.17. The speed of the wave is 180 m s^{-1}.

(a) Explain the meaning of wave speed in the context of standing waves.

(b) Consider the vibrations of two points on the string, P and Q. The displacement of point P is given by the equation $y = 5.0 \cos (45\pi t)$, where y is in mm and t is in seconds. Calculate the length of the string.

(c) State the phase difference between the oscillation of point P and that of point Q. Hence write down the equation giving the displacement of point Q.

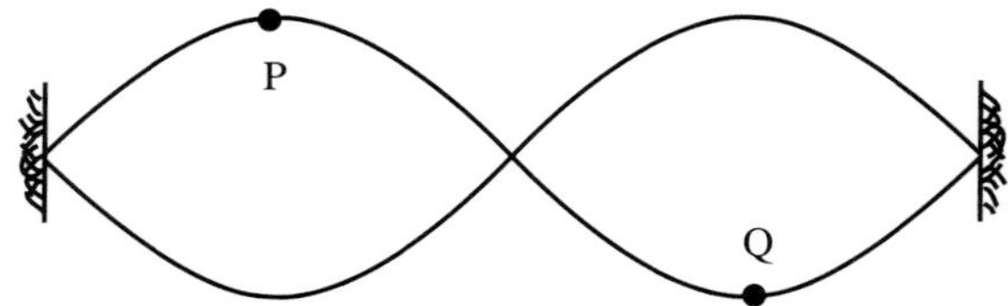

Figure 6.17 For question 18.

19 A sound wave of wavelength 1.7 m passes through air, where the speed of sound is 330 m s^{-1}. Assume that a molecule of air has mass 4.8×10^{-26} kg and that, as a result of the sound wave, it oscillates with an amplitude of 4.0×10^{-7} m. Calculate the maximum kinetic energy of the molecule due to its oscillations.

20 A string with both ends fixed vibrates in the third harmonic mode, as shown in Figure 6.18. The length of the string is 6.0 m and the speed of the wave is 120 m s^{-1}.

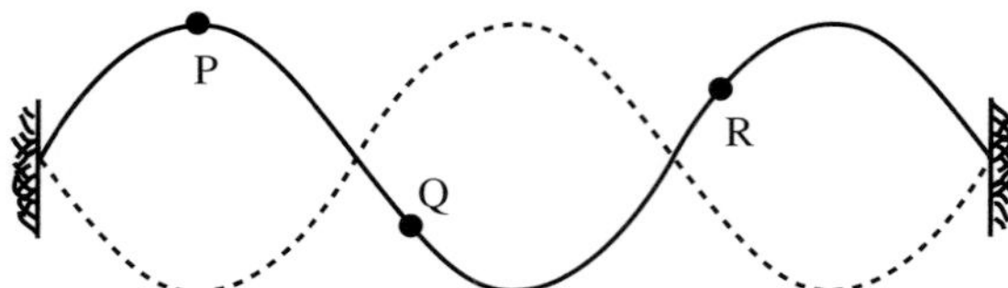

Figure 6.18 For question 20.

(a) Calculate the wavelength of the wave on the string.

(b) The amplitude of oscillation of point P is 4.0 mm. Explain why the displacement of point P is given by the equation $y = 4.0\cos(60\pi t)$, where y is in millimetres and t is in seconds.

(c) The amplitude of oscillation of points Q and R is 2.0 mm. State the equation giving the displacement of (i) point Q and (ii) point R.

(d) Calculate the average speed of (i) point P and (ii) point Q from to $t = 0$ to $t = \frac{T}{4}$, where T is the period of the wave.

(e) Calculate the maximum speed of (i) point P and (ii) point Q.

Diffraction

In previous chapters, we saw the behaviour of light in the *geometrical approximation*, which is when the important phenomena of diffraction and interference are neglected so that we can treat light propagation along straight lines. This chapter deals in detail with the problem of single-slit diffraction and the effect of slit width in the interference pattern.

Objectives

By the end of this chapter you should be able to:

- understand *diffraction* and draw the *diffraction patterns* from a rectangular slit, a sharp edge, a thin tube and a circular aperture;
- appreciate that the *first minimum* in single-slit diffraction past a slit of width b is approximately at an angle $\theta = \frac{\lambda}{b}$;
- draw the *intensity patterns* for a *single slit* of finite width and for *two slits* of negligible width;
- show the effect of *slit width* on the intensity pattern of two slits.

Diffraction

Diffraction, as we have seen earlier, is the spreading of a wave as it goes past an obstacle or through an aperture.

Let us consider a plane wave of wavelength λ propagating toward the right, where an aperture of size b is waiting. What will the wavefronts look like after the wave has gone through the aperture? The answer is not so straightforward. As we will see, the value of the wavelength in relation to the aperture size will be crucial in determining what answer we get. In the first case let us assume that the wavelength is very, very small compared with b (see Figure 7.1).

That part of the wave which is blocked by the screen does not propagate through and only that part which is free to go through does so. If the wave in question is light, this picture says

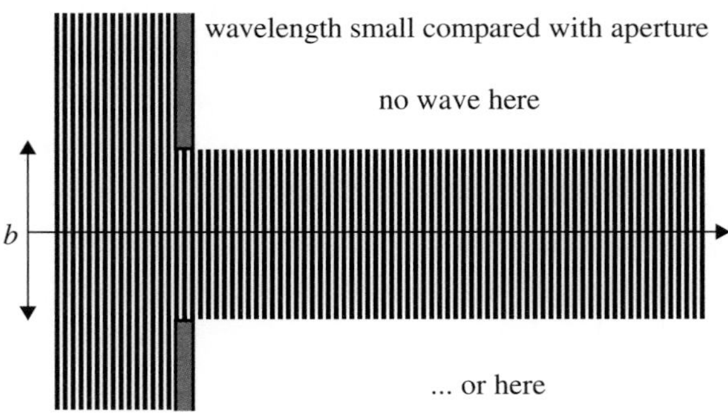

Figure 7.1 When the wavelength is small compared with the size of the opening of the aperture, the amount of diffraction is negligible.

that light goes through the opening, so that if we put a screen beyond the aperture we will see light on an area of the screen identical to the opening and darkness around it. Light travels in straight lines and does not bend as it goes through the aperture. There is no diffraction.

On the other hand, if the wavelength is comparable to or bigger than b, the new wavefronts are curved and the wave manages to go around the edges (see Figure 7.2).

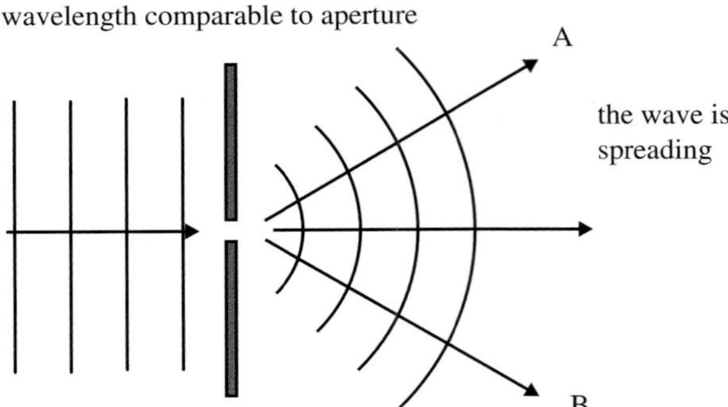

Figure 7.2 When the wavelength is comparable to the opening of the aperture, diffraction takes place.

If we put a screen some distance away from the aperture, we would see light in places where we would not expect any, such as points A and B, for example. This is the phenomenon of diffraction. It takes place whenever a wave whose wavelength is comparable to or bigger than the size of an aperture (or an obstacle – see Figure 7.3) attempts to move through or past the aperture or obstacle. (Note that here 'comparable to' means that the wavelength can be a few times smaller than the aperture size.)

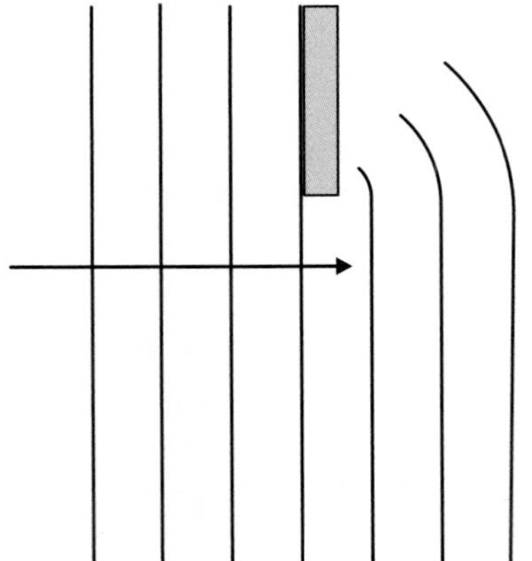

Figure 7.3 Diffraction also takes place when a wave moves past an obstacle.

Diffraction explains how we can hear, but not see, around corners. For example, a person talking in the next room can be heard through the open door because sound diffracts around the opening of the door; the wavelength of sound for speech is roughly the same as the door size. On the other hand, light does not diffract around the door since its wavelength is much smaller than the door size.

If the wavelength is much smaller than the obstacle size, no diffraction takes place, as seen in Figure 7.4(a). Diffraction does takes place if the wavelength is comparable to the obstacle size, as seen in Figure 7.4(b).

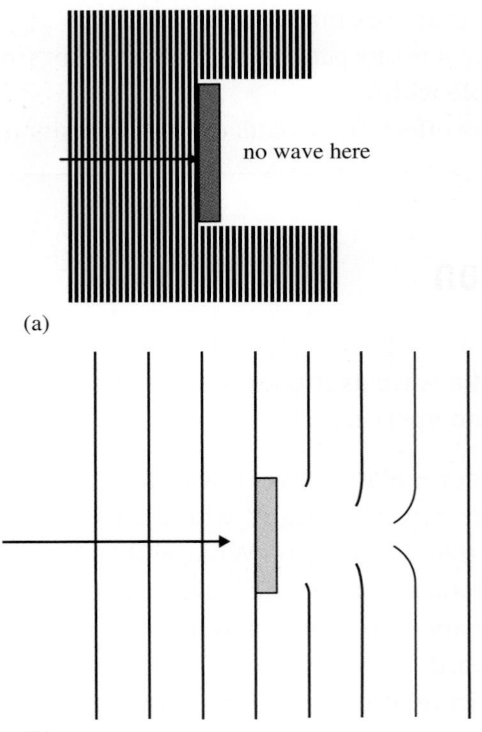

Figure 7.4 (a) If the wavelength is much smaller than the obstacle, no diffraction takes place and a shadow of the object is formed. (b) If the wavelength is comparable to the obstacle size, diffraction takes place and the wave appears far from the object in the region where the shadow was expected.

Diffraction of light is significant when the aperture or obstacle is small enough. The diffracted waves can interfere with each other, producing a pattern of light and dark areas. Figure 7.5 shows interference patterns due to (a) a single slit; (b) another single slit, wider than the first; (c) a circular aperture. All three apertures were illuminated by light of the same wavelength. Comparison of the single-slit diffraction patterns shows that the central maximum is narrower for the wider slit (b), and the spacing of the fringes is also smaller.

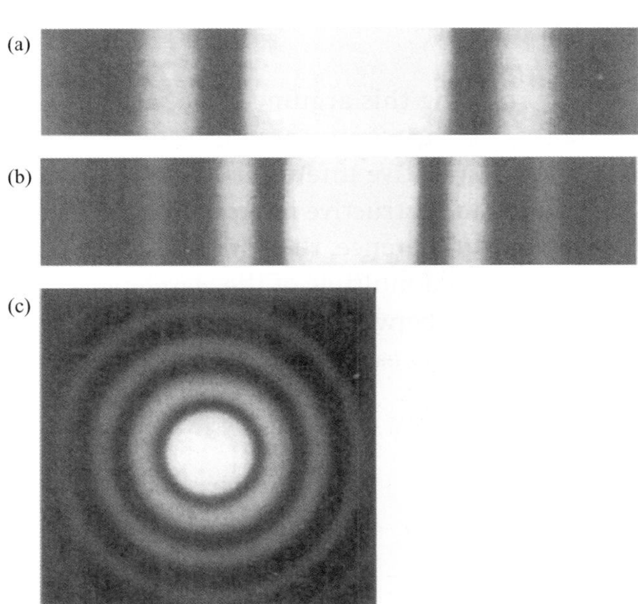

Figure 7.5 Interference patterns due to (a) a single rectangular slit; (b) another single slit, wider than the first; (c) a circular aperture.

Single-slit diffraction

When a wave of wavelength λ falls on an aperture whose opening size is b, an important wave phenomenon called diffraction takes place. As we saw earlier:

▶ Diffraction is appreciable if the wavelength is of the same order of magnitude as the opening or bigger.

$$\lambda \geq b$$

Diffraction is negligible, however, if the wavelength is much smaller than the opening size.

$$\lambda \ll b$$

To investigate this phenomenon we use Huygens' principle (see pp. 234–6) and say that every point on the wavefront that hits the slit will act as a source of secondary coherent radiation. Then what we see at a point P on a screen a large distance away will be the result of the interference of the waves arriving at P from each of the points on the wavefront. Figure 7.6 shows 10 such points labelled A_1, A_2, A_3, A_4, A_5 and B_1, B_2, B_3, B_4 and B_5.

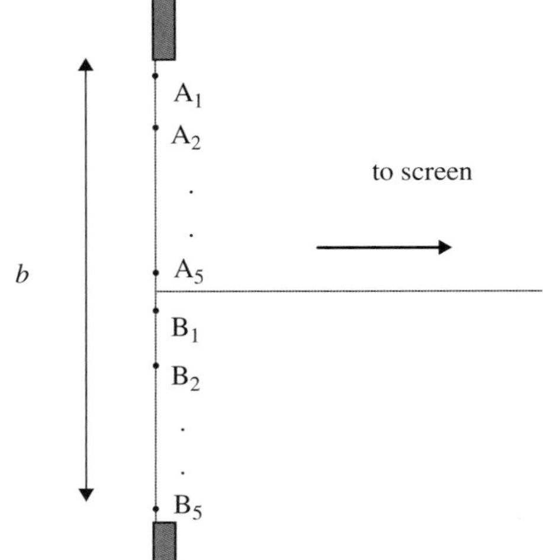

Figure 7.6 In the case of finite slit width each point on the wavefront entering the slit acts as a source of waves according to Huygens' principle and so interference will, in general, result on a screen some distance away.

We choose the Bs in such a way that they are symmetrically placed relative to the As.

All these points are on the same wavefront and therefore are coherent. But, in general, the wave from A_1 will travel a different distance in order to get to P than the wave from B_1 (see Figure 7.7). This path difference will, as in our discussion of interference, result in a phase difference between these two waves at P.

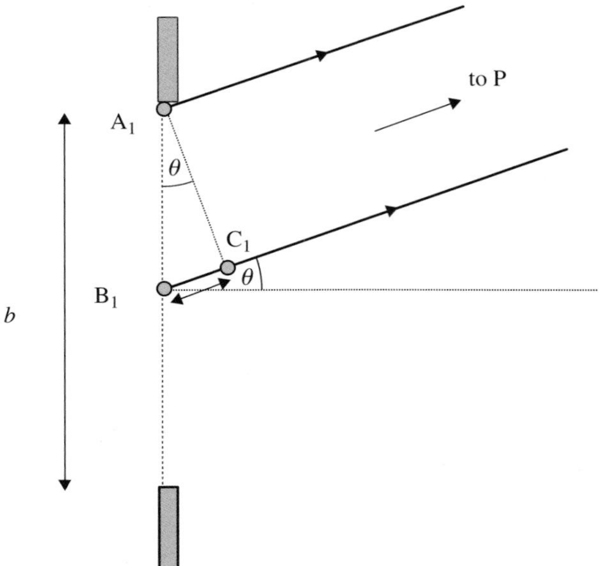

Figure 7.7 Diagram used to calculate the path difference. The path difference equals the distance B_1C_1 . Lines A_1P and B_1P are approximately parallel since P is far away. Thus, triangle $A_1B_1C_1$ is approximately right angled and angle $B_1A_1C_1$ equals θ. The path difference is the length B_1C_1.

If the path difference is half a wavelength, the two waves arrive at P with a 180° phase difference,so the maxima of one wave match the minima of the other. The result is destructive interference, or no wave at P. But remember, we still have to consider the other points, not just A_1 and B_1. What about A_2 and B_2? Triangles $A_1B_1C_1$ and $A_2B_2C_2$ are equal since they are right angled, that is $A_1B_1 = A_2B_2$ and $\angle B_1A_1C_1 = \angle B_2A_2C_2$ (see Figure 7.8). Thus, we see that whatever phase difference exists at P from A_1 and B_1, the same will be true for A_2 and B_2, and so on.

Thus, if we get zero wave at P from the first pair, we will get the same from the second as

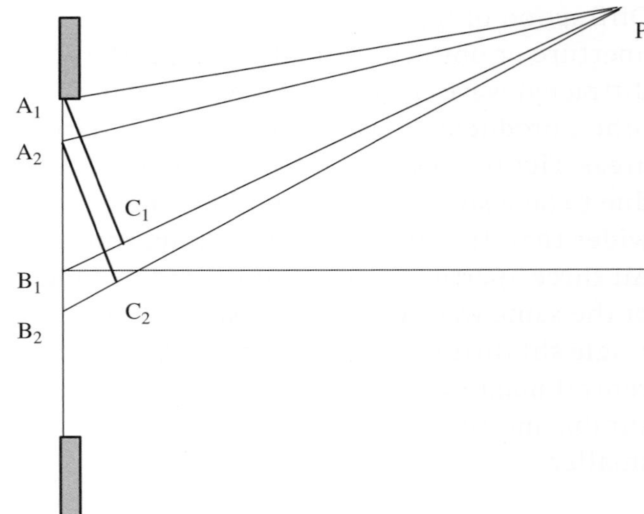

Figure 7.8 Triangles $A_1C_1B_1$ and $A_2C_2B_2$ are equal.

well. Continuing this argument we see that all the points on the wavefront will result in complete destructive interference if the first pair results in destructive interference. To get destructive interference, the path difference must be a half-integral multiple of the wavelength. The path difference between waves arriving at P from A_1 and B_1 is $\frac{b}{2}\sin\theta$ (see Figure 7.6) and so this means that if

$$\frac{b}{2}\sin\theta = \frac{\lambda}{2}$$
$$\Rightarrow b\sin\theta = \lambda$$

we get a minimum at P. If we split the aperture into four equal pieces instead of two and repeat this argument, we will find that the condition for destructive interference is also

$$\frac{b}{4}\sin\theta = \frac{\lambda}{2}$$
$$\Rightarrow b\sin\theta = 2\lambda$$

▶ In general, in interference from a single slit we get *destructive* interference at points P if

$$b\sin\theta = n\lambda \qquad n = 1, 2, 3, \ldots$$

This equation gives the angle θ at which minima are observed on a screen behind the aperture of size b on which light of wavelength λ falls. Since the angle θ is typically small, we may approximate $\sin\theta \approx \theta$ (if the angle is in radians) and so the first minimum is observed at an angle

$$\theta \approx \frac{\lambda}{b}$$

If the slit is circular, then the formula is

$$\theta \approx 1.22\frac{\lambda}{b}$$

In practice, it makes no difference which one is used as both are approximate anyway.

The maxima of the pattern are approximately half-way between minima. This equation is very important in understanding the phenomenon of diffraction so let us take a closer look.

The first minimum ($n = 1$) occurs at $b \sin\theta = \lambda$. If the wavelength is comparable to or bigger than b, appreciable diffraction will take place, as we said earlier. How do we see this from this formula? If $\lambda > b$, then $\sin\theta > 1$ (i.e. θ does not exist). The wave has spread so much around the aperture, the central maximum is so wide, that the first minimum does not exist. (Remember that diffraction is the spreading of the wave around the aperture, not necessarily the existence of interference maxima and minima.)

If now the wavelength is comparable to b, then again appreciable diffraction takes place and a number of minima and maxima are visible (*comparable* means that λ can be a bit less than b). If, on the other hand, $\lambda \ll b$, then from $\theta \approx \frac{\lambda}{b}$ it follows that θ is approximately zero. So the wave goes through the aperture along a straight line represented by $\theta = 0$. There is no wave at any point P on the screen for which θ is not zero. This means that the passage of the wave leaves a shadow of the aperture on the screen. There is no spreading of the wave and hence no diffraction, as we expected.

The intensity of light observed on a screen some distance from the slit is shown in Figure 7.9(a) for the case $b = 2\lambda$ and in Figure 7.9(b) for $b = 3\lambda$ (the vertical units are arbitrary). Note that the narrower slit (a) has a *wider* central maximum.

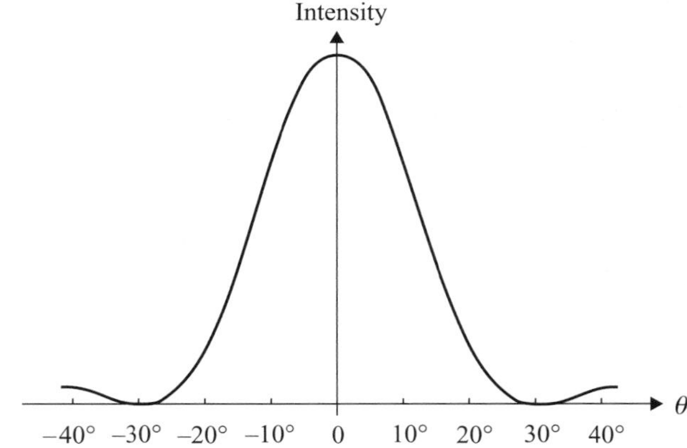

(a)

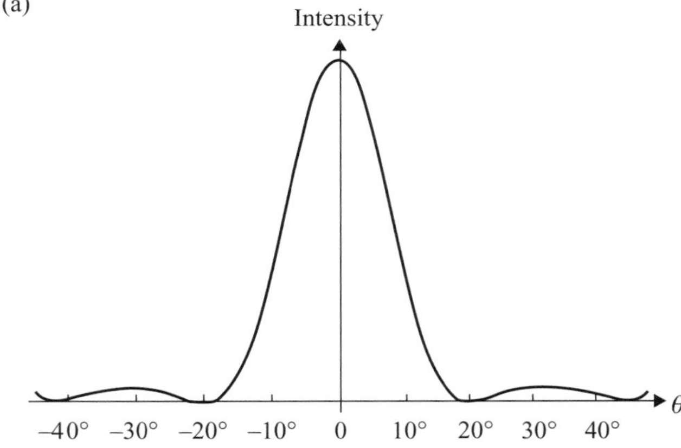

(b)

Figure 7.9 The single-slit intensity pattern for (a) a slit of size $b = 2\lambda$, and (b) a slit of size $b = 3\lambda$.

Supplementary material

The effect of slit width

This discussion of single-slit diffraction has an impact on the problem of two-slit interference, which is discussed in detail in option G (page 626). In option G we will see that, when coherent light is incident on two slits, an interference pattern will be formed – light from one slit interferes with light from the other slit. In option G the two slits will be assumed to be *very narrow*. In the realistic case of slits of finite width, however, there will be interference not only between light from the two different slits but also between light from different points within each slit. In the case of two very narrow slits, the latter does not occur, so covering one would make the interference pattern disappear.

On the other hand, the case of two slits whose widths cannot be so neglected will result in a more complicated pattern on the screen. This pattern will be the combined effect of (a) the interference pattern from one slit alone and (b) the interference from waves coming from different slits. Let us consider the intensity pattern for two very narrow slits separated by $d = 16\lambda$ shown in Figure 7.10.

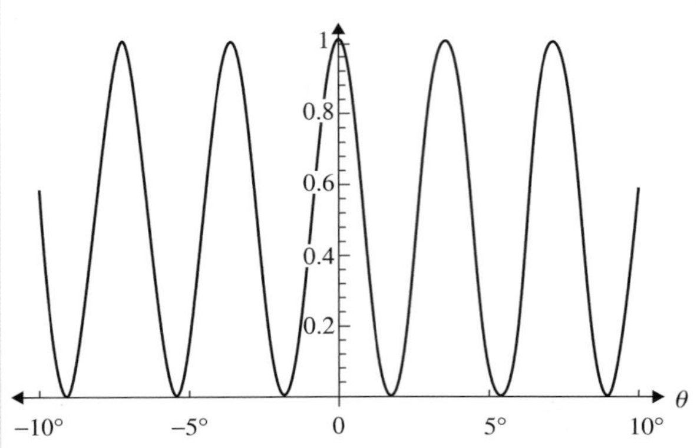

Figure 7.10 The two-slit interference intensity pattern for slits of negligible width separated by $d = 16\lambda$.

The intensity pattern for a single slit of width $b = 3\lambda$ was shown in Figure 7.9(b).

Finally, the intensity pattern for two slits separated by $d = 16\lambda$ as before, but whose width is not negligible, $b = 3\lambda$, is shown in Figure 7.11.

We have shown the single-slit pattern again, which is in fact the envelope curve for the two-slit pattern. The position of the maxima is the same as in the case of the narrow slits but the effect of the slit width is to *modulate* the intensity by the single-slit diffraction pattern.

Missing orders

If the slit width is ignored in a Young-type two-slit interference pattern, we observe a number of equally bright maxima, as in Figure 7.10. If the slit width is not ignored, this intensity pattern will be modulated by the diffraction effects of the slits. It sometimes happens that the first diffraction minimum in the one-slit diffraction pattern coincides with one of the maxima in the two-slit interference pattern. If that happens, the

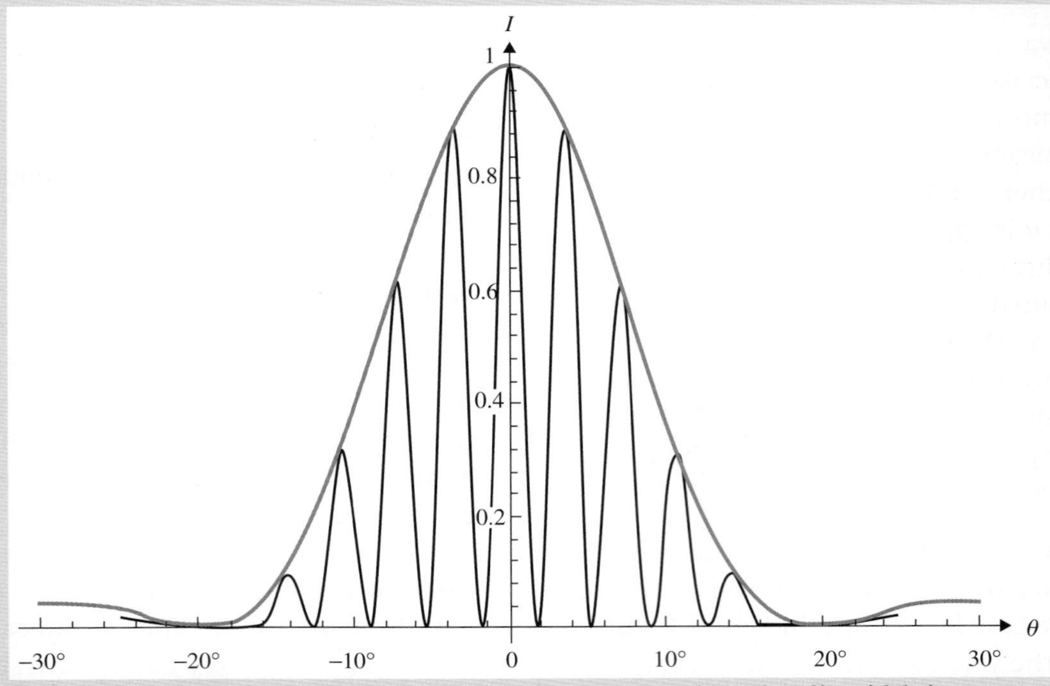

Figure 7.11 The modulated two-slit intensity pattern when the slit width is not negligible. Shown here is the case for $b = 3\lambda$ and $d = 16\lambda$. The heavy curve is the one-slit diffraction curve for a slit width of $b = 3\lambda$.

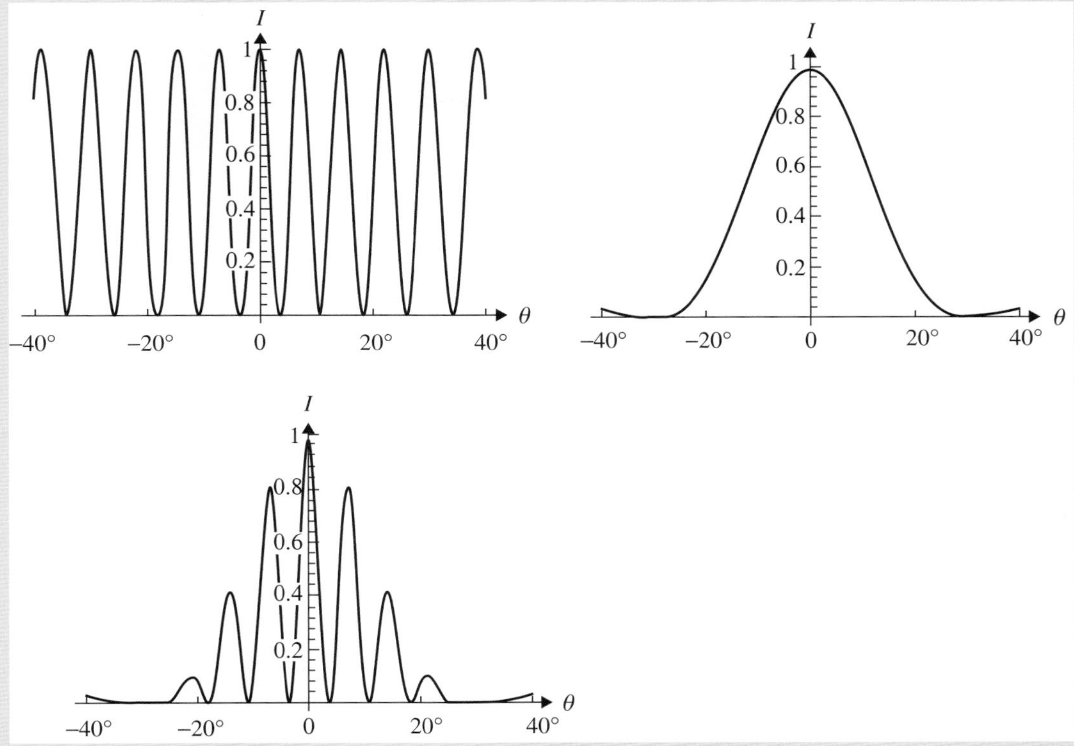

Figure 7.12 The fourth maximum in the two-slit pattern is missing because it coincides with the first diffraction minimum of the one-slit pattern. We can conclude that $d = 4b$.

maximum will be reduced to a point of zero intensity and we then speak of a missing order. Suppose that the first diffraction minimum occurs at an angle θ. Then $b \sin\theta = 1 \times \lambda$. Suppose that the nth maximum of the two-slit pattern coincides with the first diffraction minimum. Then $d \sin\theta = n\lambda$. Combining the two equations we see that

$$\left.\begin{aligned} d \sin\theta &= n\lambda \\ b \sin\theta &= \lambda \end{aligned}\right\} \Rightarrow d = nb$$

that is, the slit separation is n times the slit width where n is the missing order. Figure 7.12 is an example of this where the missing order is $n = 4$.

QUESTIONS

1 A single slit of width 1.50 μm is illuminated with light of wavelength 500.0 nm. Find the angular width of the central maximum.

2 Microwaves of wavelength 2.80 cm fall on a slit and the central maximum at a distance of 1.0 m from the slit is found to have a half-width (i.e. distance from middle of central maximum to first minimum) of 0.67 m. Find the width of the slit.

3 The intensity pattern for single-slit diffraction is shown in Figure 7.13. (The vertical units are arbitrary.)

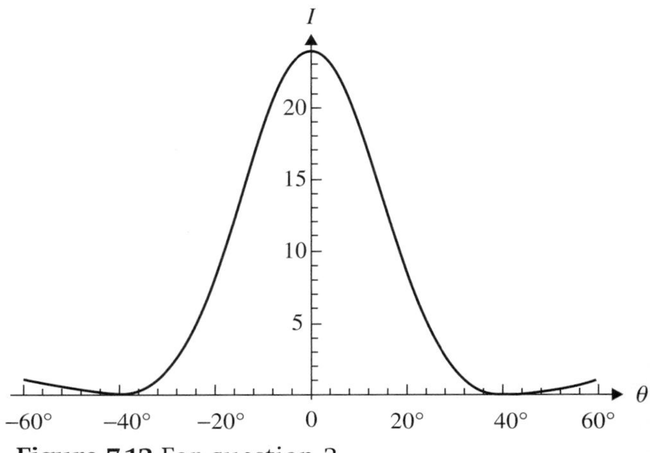

Figure 7.13 For question 3.

(a) Find the width of the slit in terms of the wavelength used.

(b) On a copy of the diagram, draw the intensity pattern for two such slits placed parallel to each other and separated by a distance equal to 10 wavelengths. How many interference maxima fall within the central diffraction maximum?

4 From the information in Figure 7.14, determine the wavelength used to obtain the single-slit diffraction pattern shown. The screen is 0.60 m from the slit and the slit width is 2.30 cm. What kind of wave is most likely being used?

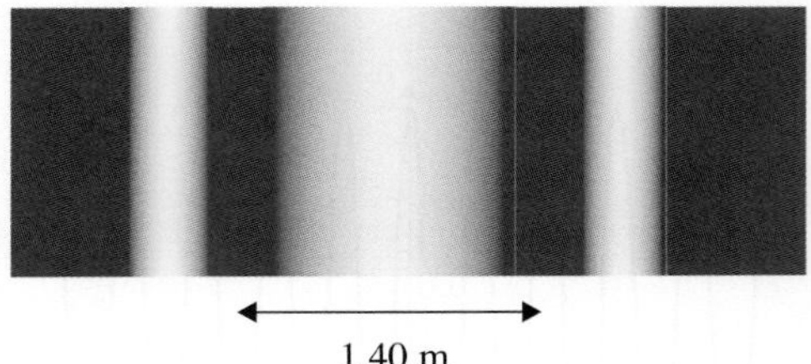

Figure 7.14 For question 4.

Resolution

This short chapter deals in detail with the limits to resolution imposed by diffraction.

Objectives

By the end of this chapter you should be able to:

- understand what is meant by *resolution;*
- apply the *Rayleigh criterion.*

The Rayleigh criterion

In the previous chapter, we discussed in some detail the diffraction of a wave through a slit of linear size b. One application of diffraction is in the problem of the resolution of the images of two objects that are close to each other.

Light from a distant star will, upon passing through a lens, diffract around the circular aperture of the lens. The image of a star is an extended disc with diffraction rings around it. Two distant objects that are very close to each other will, in general, produce diffraction patterns that will merge with each other, making it difficult to distinguish the pattern as one belonging to two separate objects (see Figure 8.1).

Figure 8.1 Diffraction limits our ability to distinguish two separate sources. In the first diagram the diffraction patterns have merged.

Rayleigh suggested that a useful criterion for deciding whether the two objects can be resolved is that the central maximum of one of the sources is formed at the position of the first minimum in the diffraction pattern of the other (see Figure 8.2).

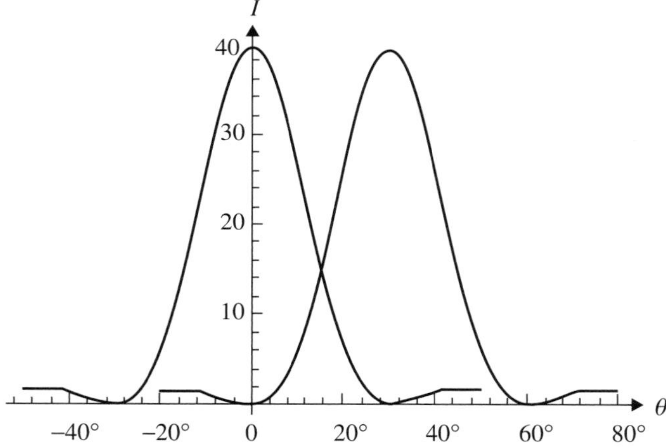

Figure 8.2 The Rayleigh criterion states that two sources are just resolved if the central maximum of the diffraction pattern of one source falls on the first minimum of the other.

Figure 8.3 shows two unresolved and two well-resolved sources.

▶ Recall that the first minimum in the diffraction pattern through a circular aperture of size b is formed at an angle θ given by

$$\theta = 1.22\frac{\lambda}{b}$$

and for a rectangular slit of width b by

$$\theta = \frac{\lambda}{b}$$

It then follows that the two objects can be resolved if their angular separation is larger than the θ given by the diffraction formulae above.

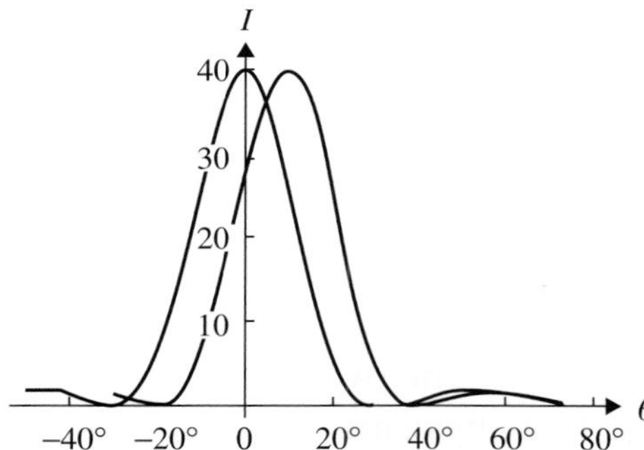

(a)

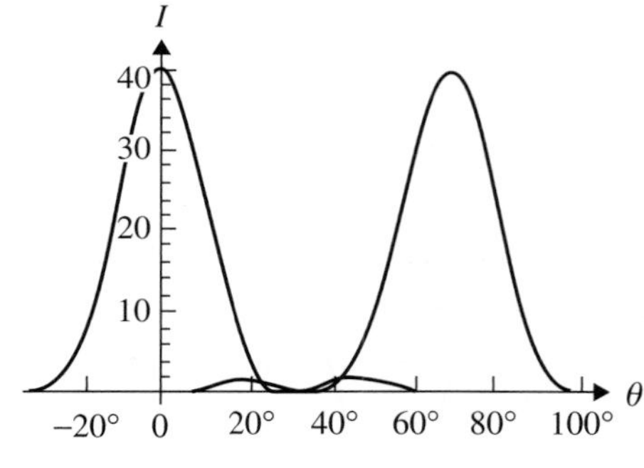

(b)

Figure 8.3 (a) Two unresolved sources. (b) Two well-resolved sources.

In Figure 8.4 the two objects are separated by a distance s and their distance from the observer is d. Their angular separation θ is given by $\theta = s/d$ in radians.

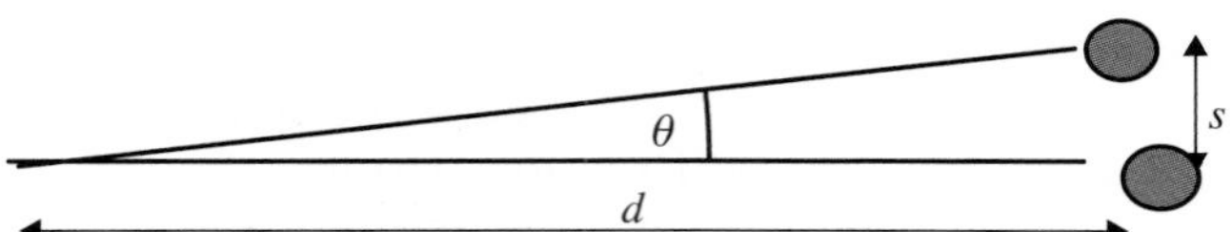

Figure 8.4 To see the two objects as distinct we need a lens that can resolve the angle θ.

Example questions

Q1

The camera of a spy satellite orbiting at 200 km has a diameter of 35 cm. What is the smallest distance this camera can resolve on the surface of the earth? (Assume a wavelength of 500 nm.)

Answer

Using Rayleigh's criterion and a wavelength of 5.0×10^{-7} m, we find that the distance s that can be resolved is given by $s = r\theta$ where

$$\theta \approx \frac{1.22 \times 5 \times 10^{-7}}{0.35}$$
$$\approx 1.74 \times 10^{-6} \text{ rad}$$
$$\Rightarrow s = r\theta$$
$$= 2 \times 10^{5} \times 1.74 \times 10^{-6} \text{ m}$$
$$= 0.34 \text{ m}$$

Q2

The headlights of a car are 2 m apart. The pupil of the human eye has a diameter of about 2 mm. Suppose that light of wavelength 500 nm is being used. What is the maximum distance at which the two headlights are seen as distinct?

Answer

The resolution of the eye is

$$\theta \approx \frac{1.22 \times 5 \times 10^{-7}}{2 \times 10^{-3}}$$
$$\approx 3 \times 10^{-4} \text{ rad}$$
$$\Rightarrow r = \frac{s}{\theta}$$
$$= \frac{2}{3 \times 10^{-4}}$$
$$= 0.67 \times 10^{4}$$
$$\approx 7000 \text{ m}$$

The car should be no more than this distance away.

Q3

The pupil of the human eye has a diameter of about 2 mm and the distance between the pupil and the back of the eye (the retina) where the image is formed is about 20 mm. Suppose the eye uses light of wavelength 500 nm. Use this information to estimate the distance between the receptors in the eye.

Answer

The angular separation, θ, of two objects that can be resolved is, from the answer to Example question 2 above, 3×10^{-4} rad. From Figure 8.5 this is also the angular separation between two receptors on the retina. Thus, the linear separation of the two receptors must be *smaller* than about

$$\begin{aligned} l &= r\theta \\ &= 20 \times 10^{-3} \times 3 \times 10^{-4} \\ &= 6 \times 10^{-6} \text{ m} \end{aligned}$$

As we have seen, the Rayleigh criterion states that two objects are just resolvable as distinct objects if their angular separation is not smaller than the angle θ given by

$$\theta = 1.22\frac{\lambda}{b}$$

In the case of a microscope, the object is placed a distance from the lens (see Figure 8.6) equal to the focal length f of the lens, and so

$$s = f\theta$$

Then the condition for resolution on the object becomes

$$s = 1.22\frac{\lambda f}{b}$$

In practice, $f \approx b$, i.e. these two lengths are of the *same order of magnitude*, and this means that

$$s \approx \lambda$$

(In writing down this formula we neglect the factor of 1.22 because the expression above is only meant to be understood at the level of orders of magnitude.) This states the very important *general result* that:

▶ To resolve a small object of size s, the wavelength λ of light used must be of the same order of magnitude as s or smaller.

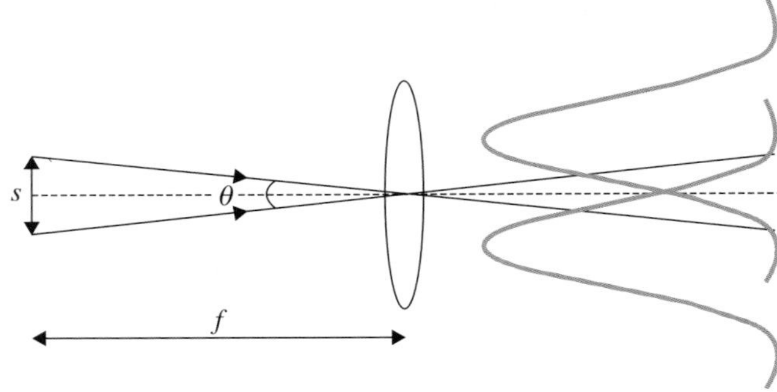

Figure 8.6 The Rayleigh resolution criterion applied to a microscope used to view a very small object.

This illustrates, for example, the operating principle of the electron microscope. To 'see', i.e. resolve, a small object of size, say, 0.01 nm, waves of roughly this wavelength must be used. This means that visible light cannot be used. On the other hand, according to de Broglie, electrons have a wave nature and so they are used in an electron microscope. If the electrons are accelerated to, say, 10^5 V, their kinetic energy will be $E_k = 10^5 \text{ eV} = 1.6 \times 10^{-14}$ J. Using

$$E_k = \frac{p^2}{2m}$$

we find a momentum p of

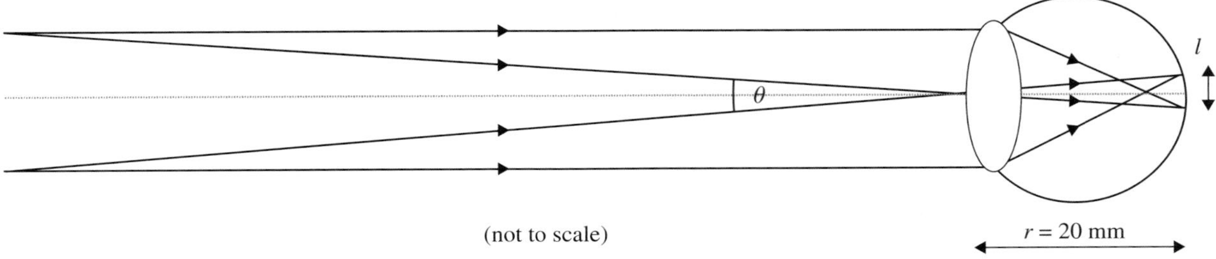

Figure 8.5 For example question 3. If the two receptors had a separation l larger than 6 μm, the two images would fall on the same receptor and would then appear as one.

$$p = \sqrt{2mE_k}$$
$$= \sqrt{2 \times 9.1 \times 10^{-31} \times 1.6 \times 10^{-14}}$$
$$= 1.71 \times 10^{-22} \text{ N s}$$

and hence a de Broglie wavelength of

$$\lambda = \frac{h}{p}$$
$$= \frac{6.63 \times 10^{-34}}{1.71 \times 10^{-22}}$$
$$= 4 \times 10^{-12} \text{ m}$$

This is small enough to resolve the size of 0.01 nm. An extension of this general principle of resolution therefore implies that, to resolve the structure of elementary particles, where separations as small as 10^{-18} m are involved, one must use a wavelength of this order of magnitude. If electrons are used, the energy required for the electron is in excess of 1000 GeV. This means that particle physics requires accelerators!

? QUESTIONS

1 Could a telescope with an objective lens of diameter 20 cm resolve two objects a distance of 10 km away separated by 1 cm? (Assume we are using a wavelength of 600 nm.)

2 The headlights of a car are separated by a distance of 1.4 m. At what distance would these be resolved as two separate sources by a lens of diameter 5 cm if a wavelength of 500 nm is being used? What effect would decreasing the wavelength used have on the distance you just found?

3 Assume that the pupil of the human eye has a diameter of 4.0 mm and receives light of wavelength 5.0×10^{-7} m.
   (a) Calculate the smallest angular separation that can be resolved by the eye at this wavelength.
   (b) What is the least distance between features on the moon (a distance of 3.8×10^8 m away) that can be resolved?

4 The Jodrell Bank radio telescope has a diameter of 76 m. Assume that it receives electromagnetic waves of wavelength 21 cm.
   (a) Calculate the smallest angular separation that can be resolved by this telescope.
   (b) Determine whether this telescope can resolve the two stars of a binary star system that are separated by a distance of 3.6×10^{11} m and are 8.8×10^{16} m from earth (assume a wavelength of 21 cm).

5 The Arecibo radio telescope has a diameter of 300 m. Assume that it receives electromagnetic waves of wavelength 8.0 cm. Determine if this radio telescope will see the Andromeda galaxy (a distance of 2.5×10^6 light years away) as a point source of light or an extended object. Take the diameter of Andromeda to be 2.2×10^5 light years.

6 A spacecraft is returning to earth after a long mission far from earth. At what distance from earth will an astronaut in the spacecraft first see the earth and the moon as distinct objects with a naked eye? Take the separation of the earth and the moon to be 3.8×10^8 m, and assume a pupil diameter of 4.5 mm and light of wavelength 5.5×10^{-7} m.

7 The Hubble Space Telescope has a mirror of diameter 2.4 m.
   (a) Estimate the resolution of the telescope assuming that it operates at a wavelength of 5.5×10^{-7} m.
   (b) Suggest why the Hubble Space Telescope has an advantage over earth-based telescopes of similar mirror diameter.

Polarization

This chapter introduces polarization, a property of transverse waves. A wave is polarized if the displacement of the wave always lies in the same plane. This chapter discusses how a wave can be polarized and introduces Malus's law for the intensity of light transmitted through a polarizer. We also discuss Brewster's law and close with a few applications of polarized light.

Objectives

By the end of this chapter you should be able to:

- explain the meaning of the term *polarization*;
- understand how *light can be polarized*;
- state and apply *Malus's law*;
- state and apply *Brewster's law*;
- understand the terms *optical activity* and *optically active substances*;
- outline some *applications of polarized light*, including the structure and operation of liquid crystal displays.

What is polarization?

Light (like all other transverse waves) has the important property of **polarization**. Before discussing the case of light, let us look at a simpler mechanical wave, a wave on a string. Figure 9.1 shows a string that is made to oscillate so that a transverse wave propagates along the string. In Figure 9.1(a) the string is always in the same vertical plane. In Figure 9.1(b) the string is always in a horizontal plane. The string waves here are said to be *plane polarized* because in each case the string is always in a fixed plane.

Now imagine a vertically polarized string wave. If an obstacle with a vertical slit is placed in the path of this wave (see Figure 9.2), the wave will simply go through the slit unimpeded. However, if the obstacle has a horizontal slit, the wave will be stopped, and no wave will be transmitted beyond the obstacle.

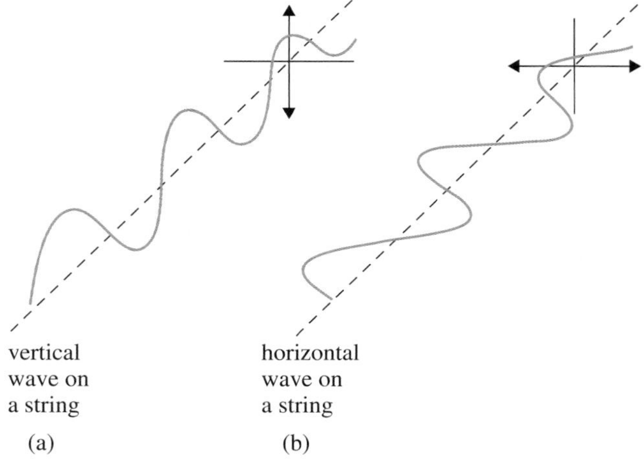

Figure 9.1 A string wave that is (a) vertically polarized and (b) horizontally polarized.

Like all other electromagnetic waves, light is a transverse wave in which an electric field and a magnetic field at right angles to each other propagate along a direction that is normal to both fields. For the discussion of the

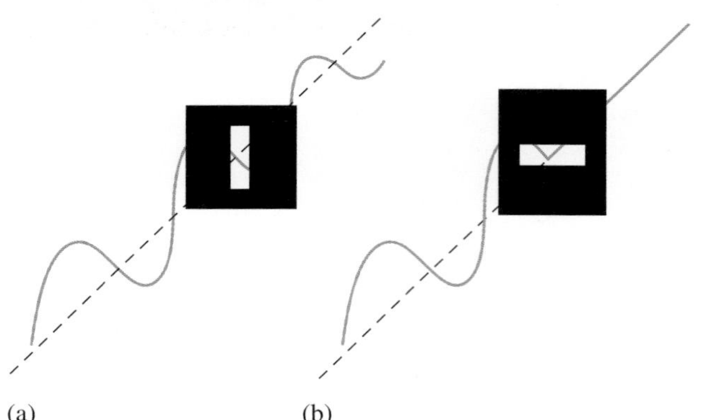

Figure 9.2 A vertical string wave passes through a vertical slit (a) . . . but not through a horizontal slit (b).

polarization of light, it is sufficient to concentrate only on the electric field in the electromagnetic wave and to ignore the magnetic field.

An electromagnetic wave is said to be **plane polarized** if the electric field always lies in the same plane, as the wave propagates. Thus in Figure 9.3(a) the wave is plane polarized, but in Figure 9.3(b) the wave is unpolarized. In both cases the wave is propagating along the direction into the plane of the page.

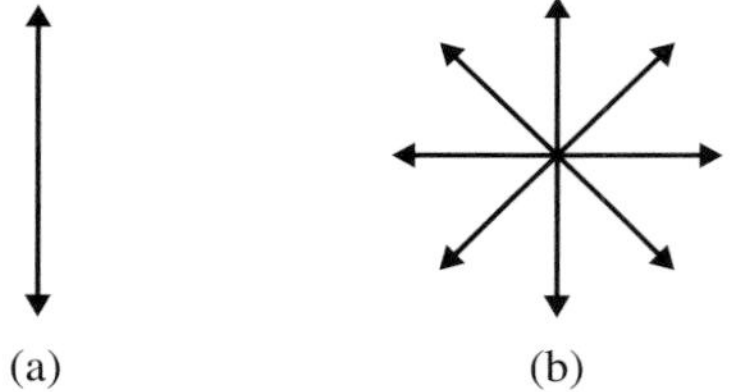

Figure 9.3 Electric field vectors of (a) polarized and (b) unpolarized light. Both waves are propagating into the plane of the page.

Most of the light around us, for example light from the sun or a light bulb, is unpolarized light. Unpolarized light can be polarized by letting it go through a **polarizer**. A polarizer is a sheet of material with a molecular structure that only allows a specific orientation of the electric field to go through (see Figure 9.4). The most common polarizer is a plastic called Polaroid invented by Edwin Land, a 19-year-old undergraduate at Harvard, in 1928. Thus a sheet of Polaroid with a vertical transmission axis

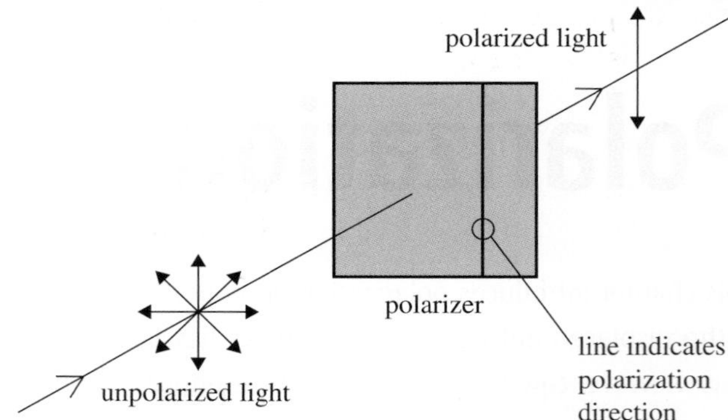

Figure 9.4 This polarizer only allows components of electric fields parallel to the vertical transmission axis to go through. Vertically polarized light is transmitted through this polarizer.

(this means only vertical electric fields can go through) placed in the path of unpolarized light will transmit only vertically polarized light. In diagrams, the transmission axis of the polarizer is indicated with a line.

Malus's law

Thus, consider an electromagnetic wave whose electric field E_0 makes an angle θ with the transmission axis of a polarizer. We may resolve the electric field into a component along the transmission axis and a component at right angles to it. Only the component along the axis will go through (see Figure 9.5).

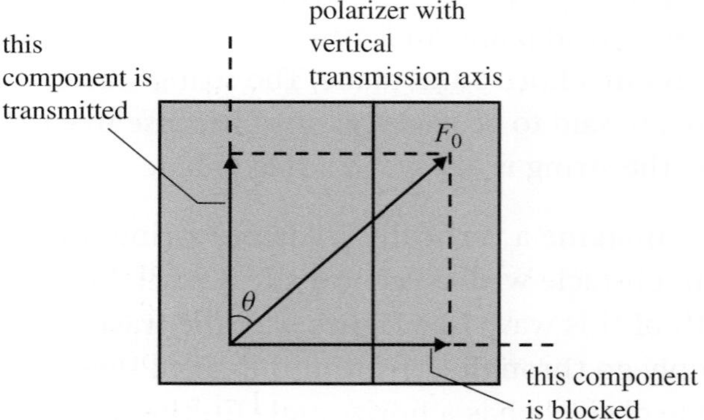

Figure 9.5 This polarizer has a vertical transmission axis. Therefore, only the component of the electric field along the vertical axis will be transmitted.

This component of the electric field along the transmission axis is

$$E = E_0 \cos\theta$$

The transmitted intensity I is proportional to the square of the electric field. So we have that

$$I = I_0 \cos^2\theta$$

where I_0 is the incident intensity. This is **Malus's law**, named after the Frenchman Etienne Malus, who studied this effect in 1808. The polarizer reduces the intensity of the transmitted light. We see that when the electric field is along the transmission axis ($\theta = 0$) then $I = I_0$, and when the electric field is at right angles to the transmission axis ($\theta = 90°$) then $I = 0$.

Example question

Q1

Vertically polarized light of intensity I_0 is incident on a polarizer that has its transmission axis at $\theta = 30°$ to the vertical. The transmitted light is then incident on a second polarizer whose axis is at $\theta = 60°$ to the vertical. Calculate the factor by which the transmitted intensity is reduced.

Answer

After passing through the first polarizer the intensity of light is

$$I = I_0 \cos^2\theta = I_0 \cos^2 30° = \frac{3I_0}{4}$$

The second polarizer has its transmission axis at $\theta = 30°$ to the first polarizer, and so the final transmitted light has intensity

$$I = \frac{3I_0}{4}\cos^2 30° = \frac{9I_0}{16}$$

The intensity is thus reduced by a factor of $\frac{9}{16}$.

Polarizers and analysers

A polarizer can be used to produce polarized light. It can also be used to determine if light is polarized. A polarizer used for this purpose is called an **analyser**. Unpolarized light passing through a polarizer (analyser) will have its intensity reduced by the same amount (by 50% in fact – see below) no matter what the orientation of the polarizer (analyser). Polarized light, on the other hand, will have its intensity reduced by an amount that depends on the orientation of the polarizer (analyser).

When unpolarized light is incident on a polarizer, the transmitted light will have its intensity reduced (since part of the light will be blocked by the polarizer). We can calculate the factor by which the intensity is reduced as follows. We think of the incident unpolarized light as having two electric fields, of equal magnitude, in directions along and normal to the transmission axis of the polarizer. The incident intensity is then proportional to $E^2 + E^2 = 2E^2$, where E is the magnitude of either the vertical or the horizontal electric field component. One of these components will be blocked, and so the transmitted intensity will be proportional to just E^2. Thus the intensity is reduced by a factor of 2 or 50% (Figure 9.6).

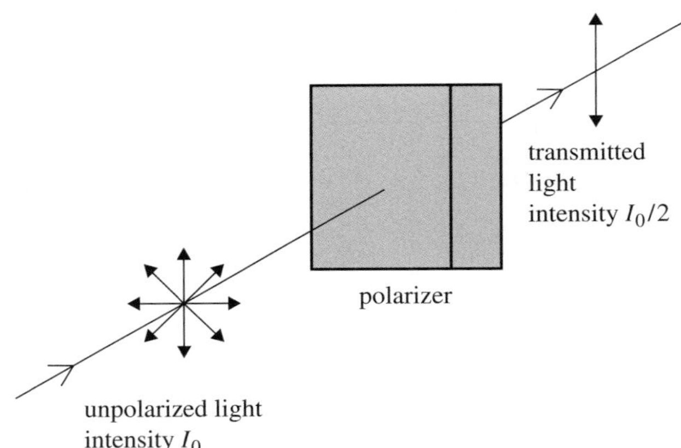

Figure 9.6 Unpolarized light has its intensity reduced by a factor of 2 after passing through a polarizer (analyser).

Supplementary material

For the more mathematically minded, the transmitted intensity will be, using Malus's law, $I = I_0 \cos^2\theta$. But each component of the incident unpolarized light will make a different angle θ with the transmission axis. Since we have a very large number of randomly chosen angles θ, we must find the average value of $\cos^2\theta$. This is just $\frac{1}{2}$, and so the transmitted intensity is half of the incident intensity.

When two polarizers are placed with their transmission axes at right angles to each other, no light emerges from the second polarizer (Figure 9.7).

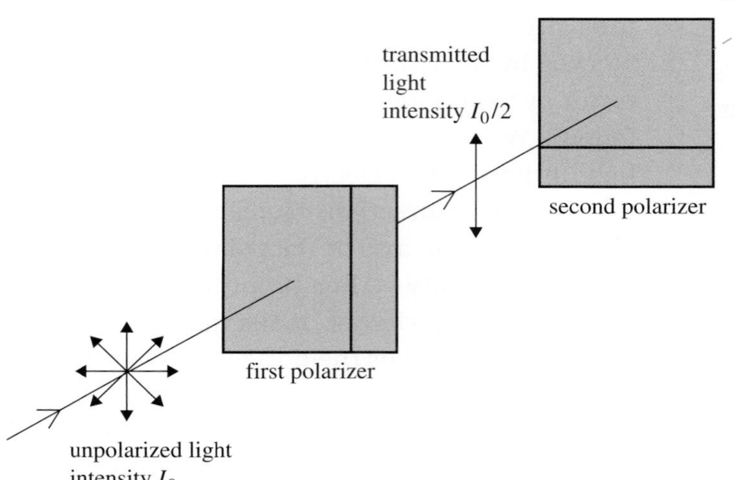

Figure 9.7 No light gets transmitted by an arrangement of two polarizers at right angles to each other.

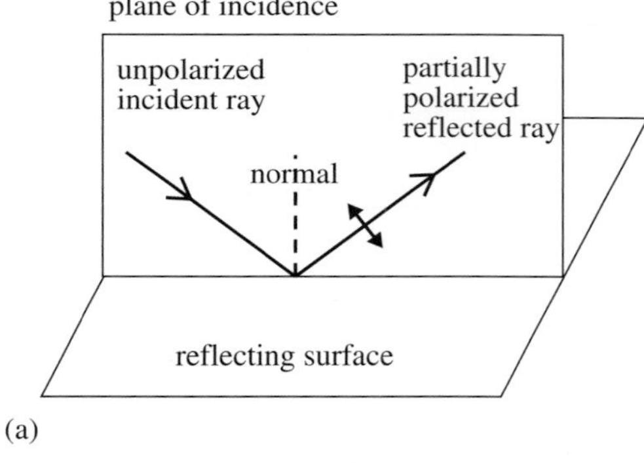

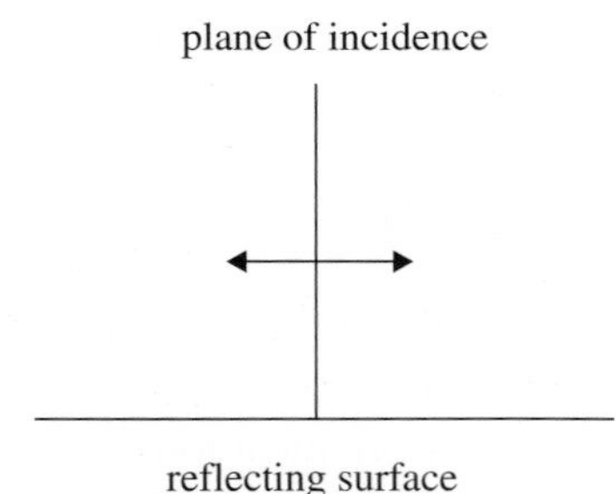

Figure 9.8 Partial polarization by reflection. (a) There is a small electric field component in the plane of incidence. (b) There is a larger electric field component in the plane parallel to the reflecting surface, as shown in this edge view.

Polarization by reflection

Polarized light can be obtained not only by passing light through a polarizer but also by reflection. When unpolarized light reflects off a non-metallic surface, the reflected ray is partially polarized (Figure 9.8). The 'glare' from reflections off the sea is partially polarized, and can be reduced by wearing Polaroid sunglasses (which have polarizing plastic lenses). The plane of polarization is parallel to the reflecting surface. Partially polarized light in this case means that the reflected light has various components of electric field of unequal magnitude. The component with the greatest magnitude is found in the plane parallel to the surface, and so the light is said to be partially polarized in this plane.

The two diagrams in Figure 9.8 can be combined into one, as shown in Figure 9.9. In this diagram, a dot indicates an electric field into or out of the page, and a double-headed arrow an electric field along the plane of incidence.

The degree to which the reflected ray is polarized depends on the angle of incidence. Consider an unpolarized light ray incident

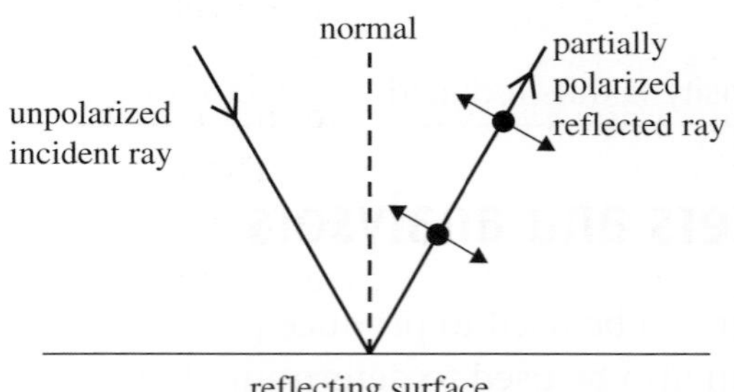

Figure 9.9 A double-headed arrow represents an electric field in the plane of incidence. A dot represents an electric field into or out of the page (i.e. polarizations parallel to the reflecting surface).

on a partly reflecting non-metallic surface (which is transparent to some extent, so that some light is transmitted). There exists a particular angle of incidence, called the polarizing angle or **Brewster angle**, for which the reflected ray is 100% polarized along a plane parallel to the reflecting surface (see Figure 9.10).

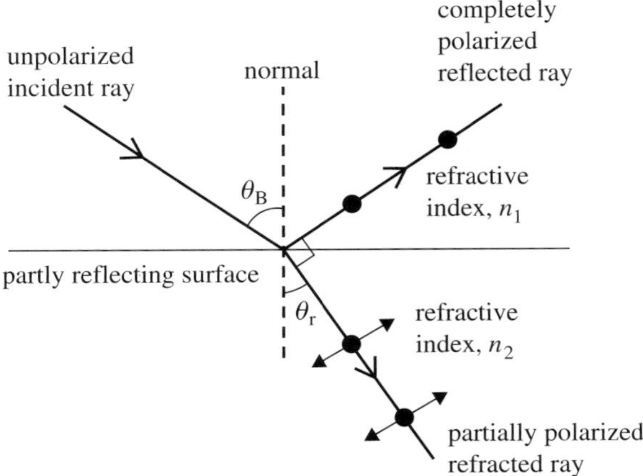

Figure 9.10 When the angle of incidence equals the Brewster angle (polarizing angle), the reflected ray is totally polarized in a plane parallel to the reflecting surface. Notice that the refracted ray is partially polarized.

In 1812, Sir David Brewster (who also invented the kaleidoscope) found experimentally that, when the reflected ray is 100% polarized, *the angle between the reflected ray and the refracted ray is 90°.*

The Brewster angle θ_B is determined by the refractive indices of the two media separated by the partly reflecting surface. Let the refractive index in the medium from which the ray is incident be n_1 and the refractive index of the medium the ray is entering be n_2. Then, the angle of incidence is θ_B and the angle of refraction is $90° - \theta_B$. Applying Snell's law we find:

$$\begin{aligned} n_1 \sin\theta_B &= n_2 \sin(90° - \theta_B) \\ &= n_2 \cos\theta_B \\ \Rightarrow \tan\theta_B &= \frac{n_2}{n_1} \end{aligned}$$

▶ Brewster's law states that

$$\tan\theta_B = \frac{n_2}{n_1}$$

In particular, if the ray is incident from air ($n_1 = 1$), then $\tan\theta_B = n_2$.

Example question

Q2

Calculate the Brewster angle for light incident on the surface of water. The refractive index of water is 1.33.

Answer

Applying $\tan\theta_B = \frac{n_2}{n_1}$ we find

$$\tan\theta_B = \frac{1.33}{1.00} \Rightarrow \theta_B = \tan^{-1} 1.33 = 53.1°$$

The angle of refraction θ_r for an angle of incidence equal to the Brewster angle θ_B is expected to be $90° - \theta_B = 36.9°$. Indeed, from Snell's law

$$n_1 \sin\theta_B = n_2 \sin\theta_r$$

$$1.00 \times \sin 53.1° = 1.33 \times \sin\theta_r$$

$$\sin\theta_r = 0.601$$

$$\theta_r = 36.9°$$

Optical activity

Consider two polarizers (analysers) whose transmission axes are at right angles to each other, as shown in Figure 9.11. No light is expected to be transmitted through the second polarizer (analyser). However, if we place certain sugar solutions between the two polarizers (analysers), light does get transmitted.

This is because the sugar solution has *rotated* the plane of polarization of the light entering it, so that this light, entering the second polarizer (analyser), has a component of electric field along the second transmission axis.

▶ The rotation of the plane of polarization is called *optical activity* and materials showing this phenomenon are said to be *optically active.*

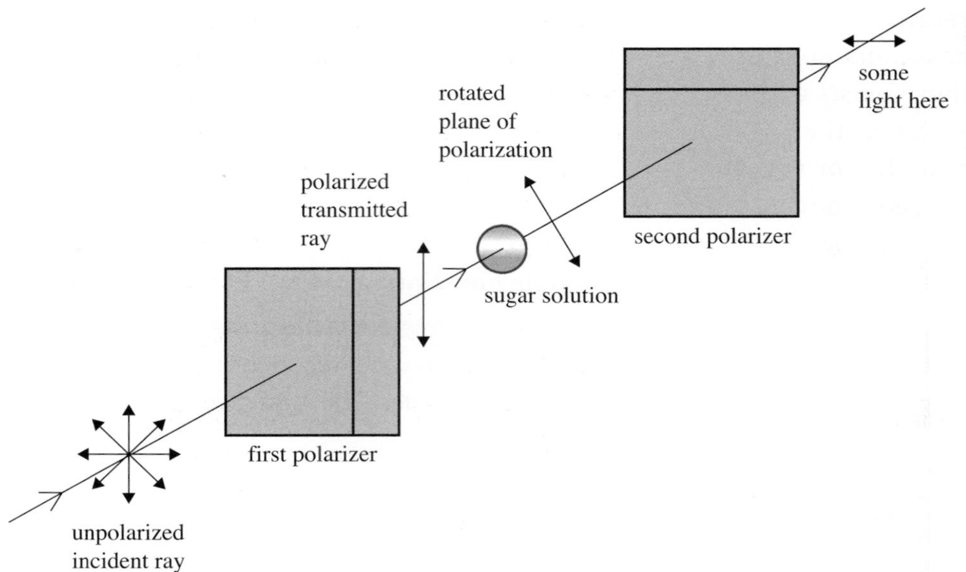

Figure 9.11 No light would normally pass through the two polarizers at right angles to each other. The presence of the sugar solution rotates the plane of polarization, so that light does get through.

The phenomenon of **optical activity** was first studied by the French physicist Dominique Arago in 1811. The phenomenon is exhibited by very many substances, such as organic compounds, notably sugar solutions, tartaric acid and turpentine, as well as many substances in crystal form, such as quartz. The angle by which the plane of polarization rotates depends on the distance travelled within the material and the wavelength of light used. In quartz, the angle rotates by approximately 22° for every millimetre travelled by yellow light. It is an interesting fact that some substances will rotate the plane of polarization clockwise (as we face the source of light) and others in an anticlockwise sense. This has fascinating applications in biology and biochemistry.

In the simple arrangement of Figure 9.11, the angle by which the plane of polarization rotates can easily be measured simply by rotating the second polarizer (analyser) until no light gets transmitted. The angle by which the polarizer (analyser) must be turned is equal to the angle of rotation by the optically active substance.

Practical applications of polarization

Stress analysis

It has been discovered (by Sir David Brewster in 1816) that certain materials that are not normally optically active become so if subjected to stresses. The degree to which the substance becomes optically active is proportional to the stress. A complicated pattern will be seen when a piece of plastic, under stress, is placed in between two polarizers at right angles to each other (Figure 9.12). Examination of the pattern reveals information about how the stress varies in the material. You can sometimes see patterns of coloured light on the windshield of a car if the glass has not been properly installed and is under stress.

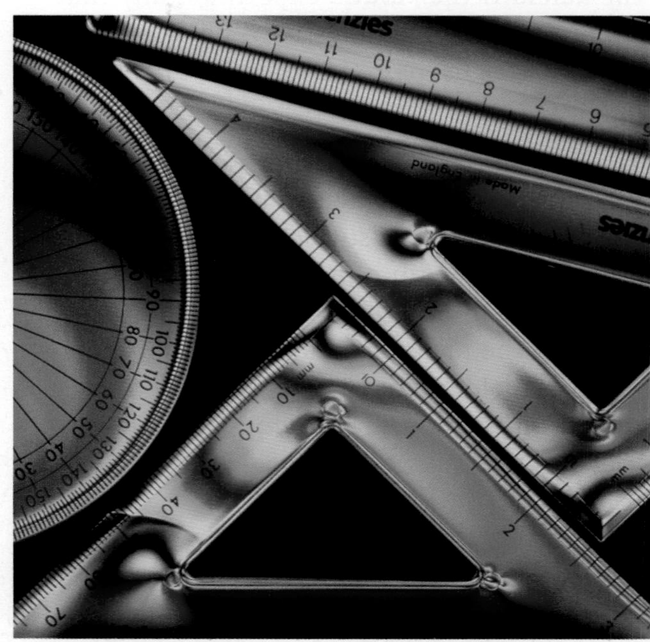

Figure 9.12 Plastic under stress.

Measuring solution concentrations

The amount of rotation of the plane of polarization in a sugar solution depends on the concentration of the solution. An early application of polarization has been to measure concentrations in solutions by measuring the angle of rotation of the polarization plane.

Liquid crystal displays

A more modern application is in liquid crystal displays (LCDs). These can be seen on calculators, watches and the elegant, thin, flat computer and TV screens available today.

An LCD consists of a surface of tiny rectangles called pixels (picture elements). Each pixel has liquid crystals in between two glass plates. The liquid crystals are relatively long, thin molecules that attract each other rather weakly. The first glass plate has very thin (the order of magnitude is 1 nm) slits or scratches along its surface so that the long, rod-like molecules align themselves with the slits. The other glass plate has similar slits but is rotated by 90° with respect to the first. Thus if the molecules next to the first glass plate are, say, vertical, those in contact with the other plate will be horizontal. The molecules in between will therefore, because of the forces between them, slowly change orientation from vertical to horizontal (see Figure 9.13).

Figure 9.13 The liquid crystal molecules are long and attract each other weakly. Here they form a line that gradually twists as we move into the plane of the page. The orientation of the molecules eventually becomes horizontal at the back plate.

Suppose now that a polarizer with its axis vertical is placed in front of the top glass plate. The transmitted light will be vertically polarized. As the light moves from molecule to molecule, its plane of polarization changes so as to be aligned with the orientation of the molecules. By the time the light reaches the back plate, the plane of polarization has rotated by 90°. If a second polarizer is placed behind the back plate with an axis of transmission at 90° with respect to the first polarizer, the light will simply go through and the pixel will be bright.

However, if a potential difference is established between the two glass plates, the molecules will tend to align their long axes with the electric field. The light reaching the back polarizer will therefore not be able to go through since it will still be vertically polarized. The pixel will then be dark (Figure 9.14).

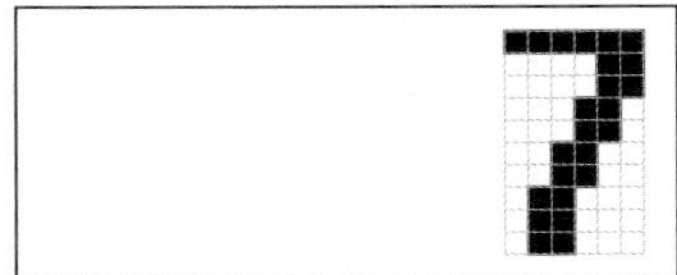

Figure 9.14 The number 7 on a calculator LCD is formed from dark pixels to which a voltage has been applied. The rest of the pixels are bright.

The idea, then, is to apply a voltage to certain pixels so they will appear black against the bright background of those pixels where no voltage is applied. The background can be made to look bright by placing a mirror there to reflect the light that went through the bottom polarizer (Figure 9.15).

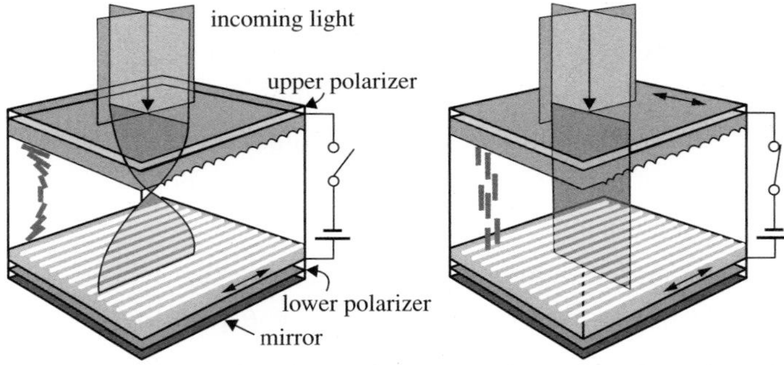

Figure 9.15 In the absence of a voltage between the plates, the light has its plane of polarization rotated, so it can transmit through the lower polarizer. With a voltage, the light is blocked.

Colour can be introduced into LCDs by using green, red and blue filters on sub-pixels. Depending on the relative brightness of the individual sub-pixels, various other colours can be perceived. Computer and TV LCD screens are substantially more sophisticated than the description given above, but the basic principle is the same.

? QUESTIONS

1 (a) State what is meant by polarized light.
(b) State two methods by which light can be polarized.

2 Explain why only transverse waves can be polarized.

3 Light is incident on an analyser. The transmitted intensity is measured as the orientation of the analyser is changed. In each of the following three outcomes, determine whether the incident light is polarized, partially polarized or completely unpolarized, explaining your answers.
(a) The intensity of the transmitted light is the same no matter what the orientation of the analyser.
(b) The intensity of the transmitted light varies depending on the orientation of the analyser. At a particular orientation, the transmitted intensity is zero.
(c) The transmitted intensity varies as the orientation varies, but it never becomes zero.

4 (a) State Malus's law.
(b) Polarized light is incident on a polarizer whose transmission axis makes an angle of 25° with the direction of the electric field of the incident light. Calculate the fraction of the incident light intensity that gets transmitted through the polarizer.

5 Polarized light is incident on a polarizer whose transmission axis makes an angle θ with the direction of the electric field of the incident light. Sketch a graph to show the variation with angle θ of the transmitted intensity of light.

6 Unpolarized light of intensity I_0 is incident on a polarizer. Calculate, in terms of I_0, the intensity of light transmitted through the polarizer.

7 Unpolarized light of intensity I_0 is incident on a polarizer. The transmitted light is incident on a second polarizer whose transmission axis is at 60° to that of the first. Calculate, in terms of I_0, the intensity of light transmitted through the second polarizer.

8 Unpolarized light of intensity I_0 is incident on a polarizer. A number of other polarizers will be placed in line with the first so that the final transmitted intensity is $\frac{I_0}{100}$. If each polarizer has its transmission axis rotated by 10° with respect to the previous one, how many additional polarizers are required?

9 Light is incident on two analysers whose transmission axes are at right angles to each other. No light gets transmitted. Determine whether it can be deduced if the incident light is polarized or not.

10 Unpolarized light is incident on two polarizers whose transmission axes are parallel to each other. Calculate the angle by which one of them must be rotated so that the transmitted intensity is half of the intensity incident on the *second* polarizer.

11 Unpolarized light is incident on two polarizers. The angle between the transmission axes of the two polarizers is 50°. What fraction of the incident intensity gets transmitted?

12 Two polarizers have their transmission axes at right angles to each other.
(a) Explain why no light will get transmitted through the second polarizer.
(b) A third polarizer is inserted in between the first two. Its transmission axis is at 45° to the other two. Determine whether any light will be transmitted by this arrangement of three polarizers.
(c) If the third polarizer were placed in front of the first rather than in between the two, would your answer to (b) change?

13 (a) State what is meant by the term *Brewster angle* (polarizing angle).
(b) Calculate the Brewster (polarizing) angle for light incident on a liquid of refractive index 1.40.

(c) Calculate the angle of refraction for a ray of light incident on the liquid with an angle of incidence equal to the value you found in (b).

14 Calculate the Brewster (polarizing) angle for light that is
(a) incident on a water–air surface from air;
(b) incident on a water–air surface from water.
Take the refractive index for water to be 1.33.

15 A fisherman is fishing in a lake. Explain why it would be easier for him to see fish in the lake if he was wearing Polaroid sunglasses.

16 Describe the advantage of Polaroid over ordinary sunglasses.

17 You stand next to a lake on a bright morning with one sheet of Polaroid glass. You don't know the orientation of its transmission axis. Suggest how you can determine it. (You may not use other Polaroid sheets with known transmission axes.)

18 State what is meant by
(a) optical activity;
(b) an optically active substance.

19 State two factors that affect the angle of rotation of the plane of polarization by an optically active substance.

20 Plan an experiment that will allow you to measure the concentration of a sugar solution. What do you need to have? What measurements must you make? How will the concentration of an unknown sugar solution be deduced?

21 State practical applications of polarization.

22 Outline the operation of liquid crystal displays.

Electric charge

Electricity is the study of electric charge, of which there are two kinds: positive and negative. Electric charge is a quantity that is conserved; like total energy, electric charge cannot be created or destroyed. It is believed that the total charge of the universe is zero – there is exactly as much positive charge as there is negative. Another important property of electric charge is that it is quantized, which means the charge on a body is always an integral multiple of a basic unit. Basic investigations into the nature and interactions of electric charge were carried out in the 1780s by Charles Coulomb, who discovered the law for the force between electric charges. Ingenious experiments in electrostatic induction and many other aspects of electricity were performed by Michael Faraday in the nineteenth century.

Objectives

By the end of this chapter you should be able to:

- appreciate that there is *a force between electric charges* and that vector methods must be used to find the net force on a given charge;
- describe the methods of charging by *friction* and *electrostatic induction* and outline their differences;
- understand the use of the *electroscope*;
- understand that charge resides on the *outside* surface of a conductor – the net charge *inside* a conductor is *zero*;
- use the formula for the *electric force between point charges* (Coulomb's law)

$$F = \frac{1}{4\pi\varepsilon_0}\frac{Q_1Q_2}{r^2} \quad \text{or} \quad F = k\frac{Q_1Q_2}{r^2}$$

Properties of electric charge

Negative charge resides on particles called electrons (and on many others – but we will only deal with electrons here). Positive charge resides on protons (and others), which exist in the nuclei of atoms. Electrons are much lighter than nuclei and so it is much easier for electrons to move than nuclei. This means that in solid bodies the motion of electric charge is brought about by the motion of electrons, but in liquids and especially in gases positive ions can also transport charge. As we will see later, the electron carries the smallest unit of electric charge. (Quarks, particles found in protons and neutrons, carry charges that are 1/3 or 2/3 of the electron charge. These particles cannot be observed as free particles so the electron can still be thought of as the carrier of the smallest unit of charge.) Electric charge is measured in a unit called the coulomb (C), and the electron's charge is (negative) 1.6×10^{-19} C. Materials can be classified into two large classes. The first class is *conductors*, which are materials that contain many free electrons inside them (free electrons are those that do not belong to one particular atom). The second class is *insulators*, which do not have many such free electrons. This means that in an electric field (explained later) the free electrons of a conductor will begin to move parallel to the electric field whereas no motion takes place in an insulator. This distinction between conductors and insulators is not completely clear-cut. There also exist materials called *semiconductors*, which have intermediate properties.

▶ A very important property of electric charge is that it is conserved. The total charge of an isolated system cannot change.

Example question

Q1

Two separated, identical conducting spheres are charged with charges of 4 μC and $-12\,\mu$C, respectively. If the spheres are allowed to touch and then separated again, what will be the charge on each sphere?

Answer

The net charge on the two spheres is $-8\,\mu$C. When the spheres are allowed to touch they will end up with the same charge since they are identical. When they separate, each will therefore have a charge of $-4\,\mu$C.

The electric force

Simple experiments allow us to deduce that there is a force between electric charges. This is the electric force. The details of this force were discovered by Coulomb and Henry Cavendish and are presented later in this chapter. For our purposes in this section it will be sufficient to know that the force is attractive between charges of opposite sign and repulsive for charges of similar sign.

Charging by friction

When a glass rod is rubbed with silk, it will develop a positive charge. This is because frictional forces between the silk and the glass remove electrons from the glass rod and deposit them on the silk. This method is called *charging by friction*.

Charging by induction

Suppose that a charged rod is brought near to, but does not touch, a conductor that rests on an insulating stand. Let us assume that the charge on the rod is negative. Then, electrons in the conductor nearest the charged rod will be repelled towards the other side of the conductor. This means that the side of the conductor nearest the rod will have a positive charge and the side furthest from it a negative charge. Note that since the conductor was originally electrically neutral, it remains so: the negative and positive charges on the sides of the conductor are equal. This is illustrated in Figure 1.1.

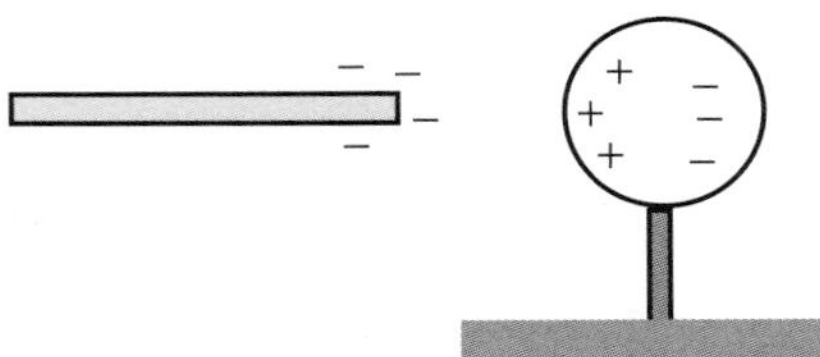

Figure 1.1 A negatively charged rod brought near to an insulated conductor forces electrons in the conductor to the side furthest from the rod.

Now imagine that, with the charged rod still nearby, you touch the conductor with your finger. What happens is that the electrons will flow to the earth through your body, leaving the conductor with a surplus of positive net charge (see Figure 1.2). If the charged rod is now removed, this positive charge will distribute itself on the surface of the conductor and we are left with a charged conductor. This method of charging is called *electrostatic induction*. We have *induced* charge on a body without actually touching that body with a charged object.

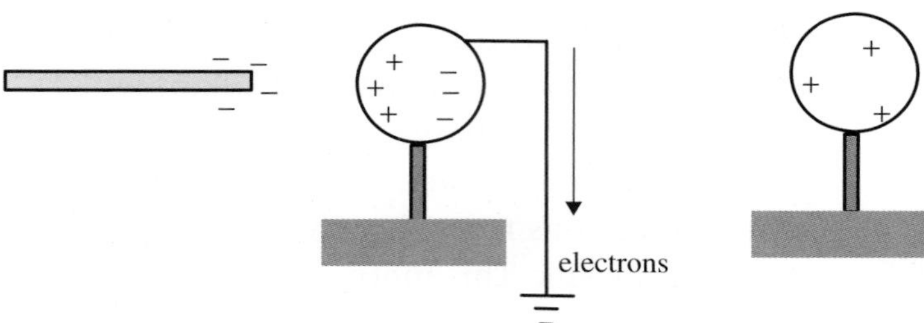

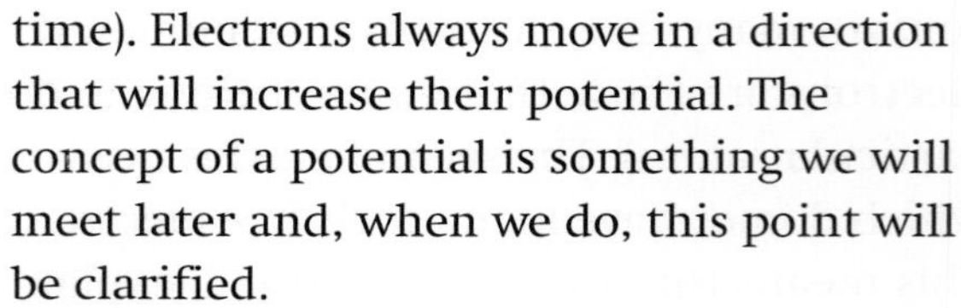

Figure 1.2 If the conductor is earthed, electrons from the conductor flow into the earth, leaving the conductor positively charged.

The induced charge in this case was positive, which is *opposite to the charge of the charging body*. This is always the case. Suppose, for example, that the external charge was positive. Then electrons would move towards this external charge, leaving a positive charge behind. By touching the conductor, we allow electrons from the earth to move *up to the conductor* and neutralize this positive charge, leaving the conductor with a net negative charge. You may wonder what determines which way the electrons will move. (In our example here, electrons moved toward the earth the first time, and on to the body from the earth the second time). Electrons always move in a direction that will increase their potential. The concept of a potential is something we will meet later and, when we do, this point will be clarified.

Here is another example of electrostatic induction. A charged body is brought near to two touching conducting spheres, each resting on insulating stands, as shown on the left of Figure 1.3.

If the external charge is negative, then electrons in the left sphere will be pushed away, leaving a positive charge on the left sphere. If *we now separate* the two spheres, as on the right of Figure 1.3, we will find that the left sphere has a net positive charge while the right sphere has a net negative charge. Again, the amount of positive charge on one body equals the amount of negative charge on the other, as required by the law of conservation of charge.

The electroscope

The electroscope is a simple and useful device for investigating electrostatic properties. A metallic rod with a metallic sphere on the top end is inserted through a piece of plastic into a glass cage (the cage may also be conducting, in which case it is earthed). The lower end of the rod has a strip of aluminium foil attached to it so it can move (in the original instruments a gold leaf was used instead). Figure 1.4 illustrates how an electroscope is used.

Figure 1.3 A negatively charged rod brought near two touching conductors will induce equal and opposite charges when the conductors are separated (in the presence of the rod).

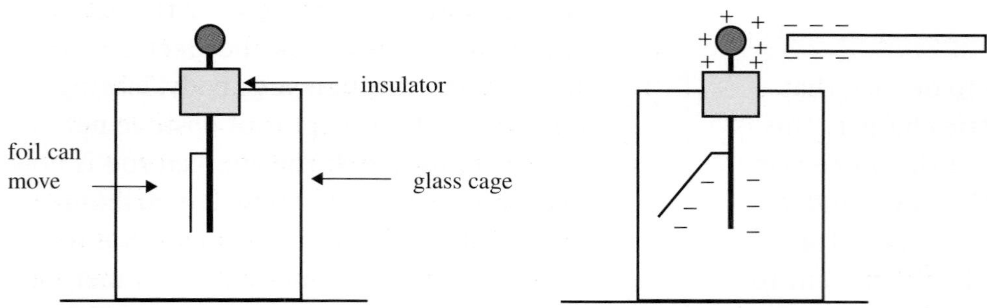

Figure 1.4 A negatively charged rod placed near the ball of the electroscope forces electrons from the ball down to the foil, causing it to diverge.

When an electric charge is placed near to (but not touching) the ball, the foil diverges. Let us assume that the charge is negative. This negative charge pushes electrons away from the ball. These electrons collect at the lower end of the rod and on the foil, and so the repulsive electric force between the similar charges causes the foil to diverge. (Note: If the cage had been made of a conducting material, a positive charge would be induced on the inside surface of the cage.)

The metal ball of the electroscope is thus left with a positive charge. Note that the net charge on the electroscope is still zero (conservation of charge). If we remove the external charge, the electrons will move back up to the ball, cancel the positive charge there and the foil will collapse completely.

If, when the foil is diverged, we keep the external charge nearby and then touch the ball of the electroscope, the foil will again collapse (Figure 1.5a). What happens is that the electrons from the foil and the lower end of the electroscope flow to the earth, leaving the electroscope with a net positive charge. *It is important to observe that even though the electroscope is now charged, the foil is collapsed*. Therefore, the electroscope *does not* measure the amount of charge on it. Rather, it measures its electric potential, relative to the zero potential of the earth. The concept of potential will be introduced in the next chapter. When the electroscope is connected to the earth, it has the earth's potential (i.e. zero) and so the foil is collapsed.

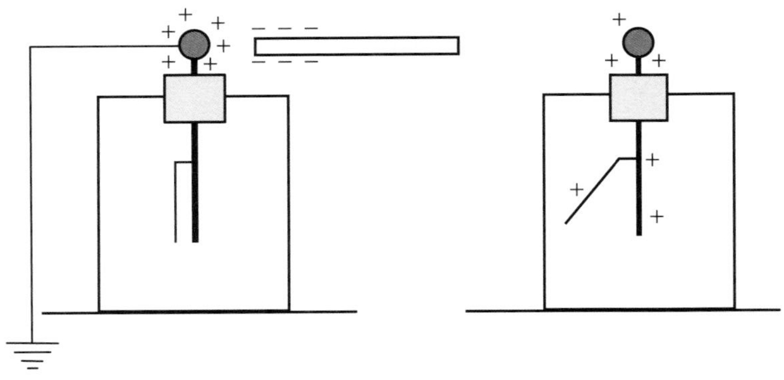

Why did the electrons move to the earth? This is because electrons always tend to move to a place of higher potential. The earth is at zero potential whereas the electrons on the lower end of the rod and the aluminium leaf are at some negative potential. Thus, by moving to the earth, the electrons increase their potential.

After earthing the electroscope, the rod can be moved away. The electroscope foil again diverges and stays raised (Figure 1.5b). This is because now there is a positive charge everywhere in the electroscope and so the foil is pushed away from the electroscope rod. Equivalently, the electroscope is now at a positive potential, higher than the potential of the earth. Note that the original external charge was negative. Charging the electroscope in this way always results in a charge opposite to the external one. It is another example of electrostatic induction.

Actually, we can test the sign of the charge of a charged electroscope in the following way. Suppose that we have charged our electroscope with an external negative charge as described above. Now bring the negative external charge close to the ball of the electroscope again. This negative charge will push electrons towards the lower end of the rod and the aluminium leaf. But these already have positive charge on them. The arrival of these extra electrons will reduce the amount of positive charge on the rod and leaf and will therefore cause the leaf to diverge less. On the other hand, if we bring a positive charge close to this positively charged electroscope, then electrons will be attracted to the top, leaving the lower end of the rod and the leaf even more positive, thus causing the leaf to diverge even further. Thus, the general rule for testing the sign of an unknown charge is to first charge the electroscope with a known charge. (You need that much to begin with.) Then bring the unknown

(a) (b)

Figure 1.5 If the electroscope is earthed (a) and the rod then removed (b), the electroscope stays positively charged. A positively charged rod would result in a negatively charged electroscope.

charge near to the ball of the electroscope. If the leaf diverges more, the unknown charge is of the same sign as the charge on the electroscope (which, remember, is opposite to the external charge that charged it). If the leaf collapses, then the unknown charge is opposite to that of the electroscope. (See, however, the first question at the end of the chapter.)

Electrostatic experiments

In static electricity, the charge that is deposited on a conductor always stays on the *outside* surface of the conductor. The net charge inside any conductor is zero. This amazing result was deduced experimentally by Benjamin Franklin, and later by Michael Faraday, in the following simple but ingenious experiment (see Figure 1.6). A metal sphere, on which an amount of charge was placed, was lowered into an ordinary metal bucket. The outside of the bucket was connected to an electroscope. With the sphere inside the bucket, the electroscope leaf diverged.

The charge on the sphere (assumed positive) attracted electrons to the inside surface of the bucket, leaving the outside surface of the bucket (and hence also the electroscope) with a positive charge, which caused the leaf to diverge. The sphere was then allowed to move inside the bucket but the amount of divergence of the electroscope leaf never changed. The sphere was then allowed to touch the inside of the bucket (Figure 1.7a). It was then taken out (Figure 1.7b) and connected to a second electroscope (Figure 1.7c).

The second electroscope's leaf did not diverge, indicating that the sphere was not charged: the sphere's positive charge was cancelled by the negative charge of the inside of the bucket. But the charge on the outside of the bucket did not change, since the leaf of the first electroscope did not change its divergence. Thus, the amount of charge on the sphere must have been exactly equal and opposite to the charge on the inside of the bucket. *The amount of net charge inside the bucket was thus zero all along.*

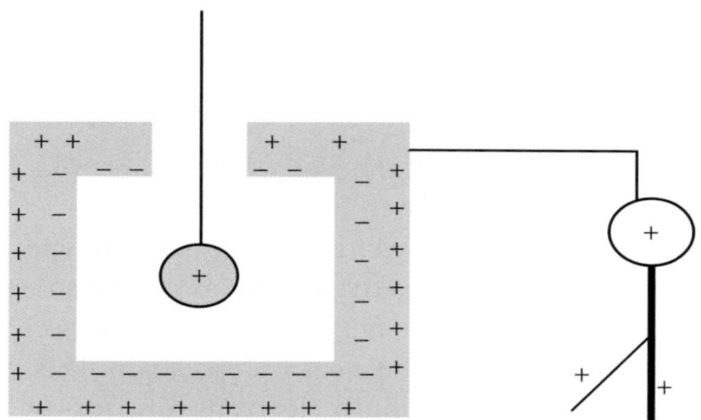

Figure 1.6 A positively charged sphere is lowered into a conducting bucket. Negative charge is induced in the interior of the bucket and an equal amount of positive charge is induced on the outside.

▶ This is a general result: in static situations the net charge inside a conductor is zero.

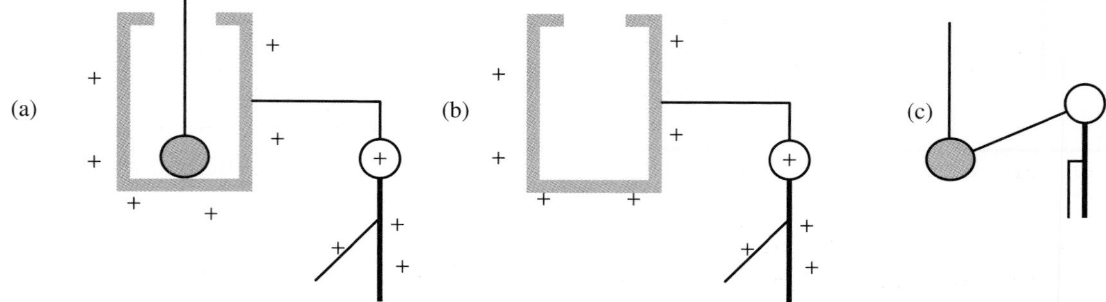

Figure 1.7 If the sphere is allowed to touch the interior of the bucket, its positive charge is completely cancelled by the negative charge in the bucket's interior. The sphere is completely neutral, as can be checked by connecting it to another electroscope.

Coulomb's law for the electric force

The electric force between two electric charges, Q_1 and Q_2, was investigated by Coulomb and, independently, by Cavendish. They discovered that this force is inversely proportional to the square of the separation of the charges and is proportional to the product of the two charges. It is attractive for opposite-sign charges and repulsive for similar-sign charges.

▶ In equation form, Coulomb's law states that the electric force between two point charges Q_1 and Q_2 is given by

$$F = \frac{1}{4\pi\varepsilon_0}\frac{Q_1 Q_2}{r^2}$$

where r is the separation of the two charges (see Figure 1.8). The two charges are assumed to be point charges.

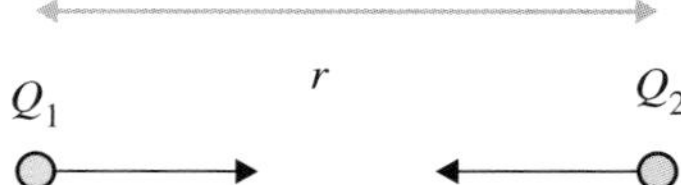

Figure 1.8 The force between two point electric charges is given by Coulomb's law. Shown here is the case of opposite charges.

We may call the factor $\frac{1}{4\pi\varepsilon_0}$ simply k, so that Coulomb's law reads

$$F = k\frac{Q_1 Q_2}{r^2}$$

The numerical value of the factor $\frac{1}{4\pi\varepsilon_0}$ or k is 8.99×10^9 N m^2 C^{-2} (we will often approximate the 8.99 to 9). The constant ε_0 is called the electric permittivity of a vacuum and $\varepsilon_0 = 8.85 \times 10^{-12}$ C^2 N^{-1} m^{-2}. The index zero in ε_0 signifies that we are considering the two charges to be in a vacuum. If the charges are in a medium, such as plastic or water, then we must use the value of ε appropriate to that medium in the formula above. Air has roughly the same value of ε as a vacuum. Note that this law is very similar to Newton's law of gravitation. Both forces are proportional to products of masses or charges and both are inversely proportional to the square of the separation. This means that many problems in electricity have the same solution as corresponding problems in gravitation; the big difference is, of course, that there are two kinds of electric charge but only one kind of mass. Also, the gravitational force is always attractive whereas the electrical force can be either attractive or repulsive.

Example questions

Q2

Two charges, $q_1 = 4\ \mu$C and $q_2 = 6\ \mu$C, are placed along a straight line separated by a distance of 2 cm. Find the force exerted on each charge.

Answer

This is a straightforward application of the formula $F = \frac{1}{4\pi\varepsilon_0}\frac{Q_1 Q_2}{r^2}$. We find that

$$F = \frac{9 \times 10^9 \times 4 \times 6 \times 10^{-12}}{4 \times 10^{-4}}\,\text{N}$$

$$= 540\ \text{N}$$

This is the force that q_1 exerts on q_2 and vice-versa.

Q3

At what distance from q_1 of example question 2 would a third positive charge experience no net force?

Answer

Let that distance be x. A positive charge Q at that point would experience a force from q_1 equal to $F_1 = \frac{1}{4\pi\varepsilon_0}\frac{q_1 Q}{x^2}$ and a force in the opposite direction from q_2 equal to $F_2 = \frac{1}{4\pi\varepsilon_0}\frac{q_2 Q}{(d-x)^2}$, where $d = 2$ cm is the distance between q_1 and q_2 (see Figure 1.9).

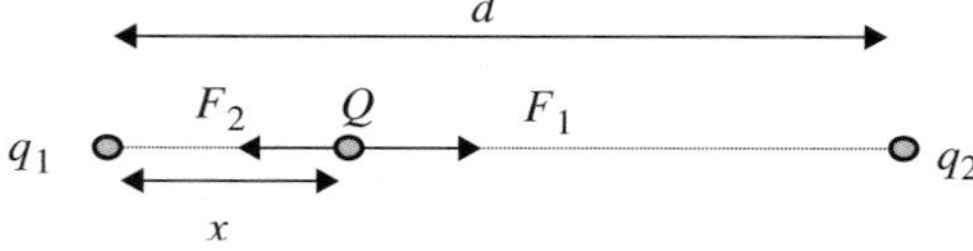

Figure 1.9.

Charge Q will experience no *net* force when $F_1 = F_2$, so

$$\frac{1}{4\pi\varepsilon_0}\frac{q_1 Q}{x^2} = \frac{1}{4\pi\varepsilon_0}\frac{q_2 Q}{(d-x)^2}$$

that is (substituting $q_1 = 4$ and $q_2 = 6$)

$$4(d - x)^2 = 6x^2$$
$$\Rightarrow x^2 + 4dx - 2d^2 = 0$$
$$\Rightarrow x = -2d \pm \sqrt{4d^2 + 2d^2}$$
$$= -2d \pm d\sqrt{6}$$

The two values of x are $x = 0.90$ cm and $x = -8.90$ cm. The second value is meaningless, so $x = 0.90$ cm.

Q4

Three charges $q_1 = 2\ \mu\text{C}$, $q_2 = 2\ \mu\text{C}$ and $q_3 = -3\ \mu\text{C}$ are at the vertices of an equilateral triangle, of side 3 cm. Find the net force on q_1.

Answer

q_1 experiences a force F_2 from q_2 and a force F_3 from q_3. Finding the magnitudes of F_2 and F_3 is easy: $F_2 = 40$ N and $F_3 = 60$ N. To find the net force (see Figure 1.10) we take horizontal and vertical components of the forces.

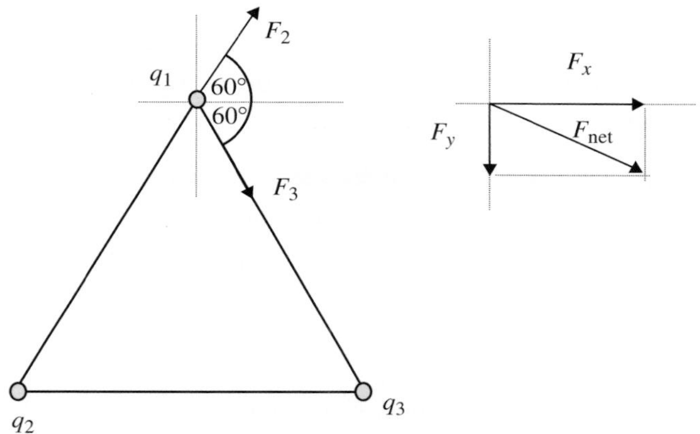

Figure 1.10.

Then

$$F_{2x} = F_2 \cos 60^\circ$$
$$= 20 \text{ N}$$

$$F_{2y} = F_2 \sin 60^\circ$$
$$= 34.64 \text{ N}$$

$$F_{3x} = F_3 \cos 60^\circ$$
$$= 30 \text{ N}$$

$$F_{3y} = F_3 \sin 60^\circ$$
$$= 51.96 \text{ N}$$

Thus, the net force in the x-direction is 50 N and that in the y-direction 17.32 N down. The magnitude of the net force is therefore 52.9 N making an angle of 19.1° with the horizontal, as shown on the right of Figure 1.10.

Q5

Two equal charges q are suspended from strings as shown in Figure 1.11. Show that $\tan\theta = \frac{kq^2}{mgr^2}$.

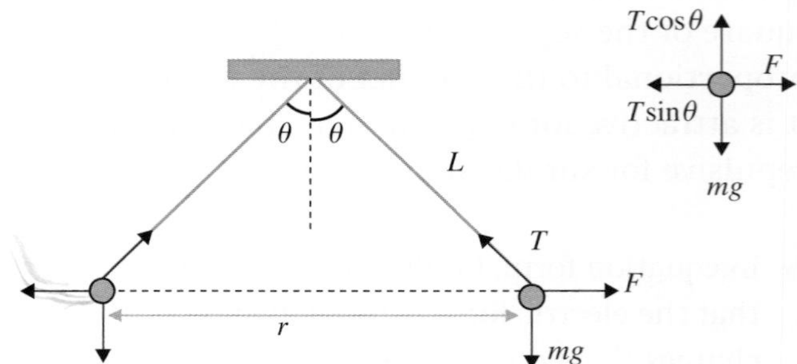

Figure 1.11.

Answer

Equilibrium demands that

$$T\cos\theta = mg$$
$$\Rightarrow T = \frac{mg}{\cos\theta}$$

and that

$$T\sin\theta = F$$
$$\Rightarrow F = \frac{mg}{\cos\theta}\sin\theta$$
$$= mg\tan\theta$$
$$\Rightarrow \tan\theta = \frac{F}{mg}$$

The electric force F is given by Coulomb's law as

$$F = k\frac{q^2}{r^2}$$

and so

$$\tan\theta = \frac{kq^2}{mgr^2}$$

Q6

Two identical conducting spheres are kept a certain distance r apart. One sphere has a positive charge Q on its surface and the other is neutral. The spheres are allowed to touch and are then separated. Write down an expression for the electric force between the spheres. One of the spheres is discharged. The spheres are then allowed to touch and then are separated again. Write down an expression for the electric force between the spheres now.

Answer

After touching each sphere has a charge $Q/2$ and so the force is

$$F = k\frac{(Q/2)(Q/2)}{r^2} = k\frac{Q^2}{4r^2}$$

After discharging one of the spheres and then allowing the spheres to touch again, the charge on each sphere will be $Q/4$. The force is then

$$F = k\frac{(Q/4)(Q/4)}{r^2} = k\frac{Q^2}{16r^2}$$

that is, one-quarter of the original force.

? QUESTIONS

1 A positively charged electroscope is found to diverge even further when a body of unknown charge is brought near to (but does not touch) the electroscope. What sign does this charge have? A second body brought into the vicinity of the electroscope makes the electroscope leaf diverge less. If this body is known to be charged, what is the sign of the charge? How would the leaf of the positively charged electroscope react if the body were neutral?

2 When a flame is brought near a charged electroscope, the foil collapses. How is this explained?

3 Three identical conducting spheres have charges of $+3$ C, -2 C and -7 C. If all three are allowed to touch and are then separated, what will be the charge on each sphere?

4 (a) What is the force between two charges of 2.0 μC and 4.0 μC separated by 5.0 cm?
(b) What does the force become if the separation is doubled?

5 Three charges are placed on a straight line as shown in Figure 1.12. Find the net force on the middle charge.

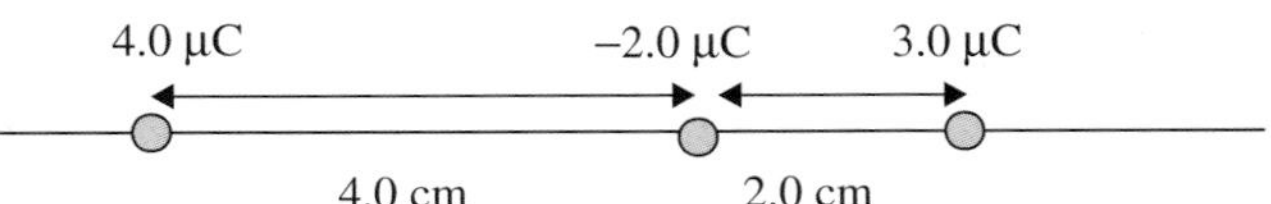

Figure 1.12 For question 5.

6 (a) In the previous question, where should the middle charge be placed so that it is in equilibrium?
(b) Is this a position of stable or unstable equilibrium?

7 Find the force (magnitude and direction) on the charge Q in Figure 1.13 where $Q = 3\ \mu$C.

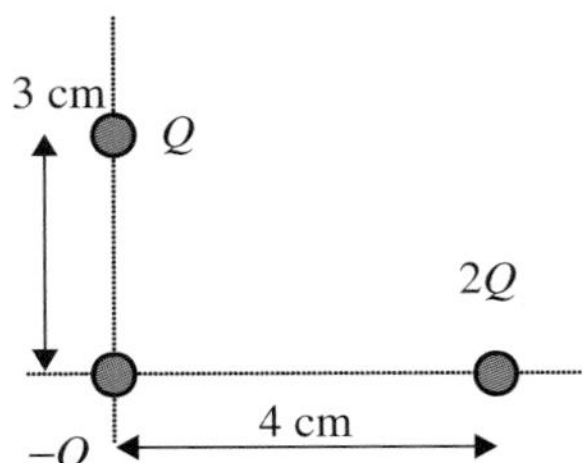

Figure 1.13 For question 7.

8 Four equal charges $Q = -5\ \mu$C are placed at the vertices of a square of side 12 cm, as in Figure 1.14. Find the force on the charge at the top right vertex.

Figure 1.14 For question 8.

9 Two plastic spheres each of mass 100.0 mg are suspended from very fine insulating strings of length 85 cm. When equal charges are placed on the spheres, the spheres repel and are in equilibrium when 10 cm apart.
(a) What is the charge on each sphere?
(b) How many electron charges does this correspond to?

10 A small plastic sphere is suspended from a fine insulating thread near, but not touching, the sphere of a Van de Graaff generator that is being charged. It is observed that the plastic sphere is slowly attracted toward the Van de Graaff sphere and eventually touches it, at which point it is violently repelled. Carefully explain these observations.

11 Consider two people, each of mass 60 kg, a distance of 10 m apart.

(a) Assuming that all the mass in each person is made out of water, estimate how many electrons there are in each person.

(b) Hence, *estimate* the electrostatic force of repulsion between the two people due to the electrons.

(c) What other simplifying assumptions have you made to make your estimate possible?

(d) No such force is observed in practice. Give one reason why this is so.

12 A negatively charged rod is allowed to touch the sphere of an electroscope that is initially uncharged. The rod is then removed. Draw the charge distribution of the electroscope and explain your drawing.

13 A positively charged rod is allowed to come close to, but not touch, the sphere of an electroscope that is initially uncharged.

(a) Draw the charge distribution of the electroscope and explain your drawing.

(b) The electroscope sphere is earthed while the rod is still nearby. Draw the charge distribution of the electroscope and explain your drawing.

(c) The rod is now removed. Draw the charge distribution of the electroscope and explain your drawing.

14 Repeat the previous question but now assume that the cage of the electroscope is conducting and earthed.

15 A negatively charged sphere is lowered inside a hollow metallic container and is allowed to touch the inside of the container. The sphere is then removed. What is the charge on the sphere? How is the law of conservation of charge satisfied in this experiment?

Electric field and electric potential

Electric charges create electric fields in space. The notion of electric field and the related concept of electric potential are introduced in this chapter.

Objectives

By the end of this chapter you should be able to:

- appreciate that a charge q in an *electric field of magnitude E* will experience a force of magnitude $F = qE$;
- understand that the electric field of a point or spherical charge Q a distance r away has a magnitude given by $E_P = k\frac{Q}{r^2}$ and is radial in direction – the *field is zero inside* a charged conductor;
- understand that the *electric field inside parallel plates is uniform* and its magnitude is given by $E = \frac{V}{d}$;
- understand that the work done in moving a charge q across a *potential difference ΔV* is $W = q\Delta V$;
- understand that a charge q that is at a point where there is potential V will have an *electric potential energy* of $U = qV$;
- understand that a charge moving in an electric potential satisfies the *law of conservation of energy:* $\frac{1}{2}mv_A^2 + qV_A = \frac{1}{2}mv_B^2 + qV_B$.

Electric field

The space around a charge or an arrangement of charges is different from space in which no charges are present. We say that it contains an **electric field**. We can test whether a space has an electric field by bringing a small positive charge q into the space. If this small charge q experiences a force, then there exists an electric field there. If no force is experienced, then there is no electric field (the electric field is zero). This small charge is called a test charge, because it tests for the existence of electric fields. It has to be small so that its presence does not disturb other charges in its vicinity.

▶ We define the electric field as the force per unit charge experienced by a small positive test charge q:

$$\vec{E} = \frac{\vec{F}}{q}$$

Note that the electric field is a vector, its direction being the same as that of the force a positive charge would experience at the given point. It follows that the unit of electric field is N C^{-1}.

The concept of electric field allows us to understand how a force is transmitted from one charge to another. A charge q placed at a point where the electric field is $\vec{E}$ will experience a force given by $\vec{F} = q\vec{E}$.

▶ The electric field from a single point charge Q at a point a distance r away is

$$E_P = k\frac{Q}{r^2}$$

This is because the force experienced by a test charge q placed at point P a distance r from Q is (by Coulomb's law)

$$F = k\frac{Qq}{r^2}$$

and so the electric field is

$$\begin{aligned} E_P &= \frac{F}{q} \\ &= \frac{k(Qq/r^2)}{q} \\ &= k\frac{Q}{r^2} \end{aligned}$$

(see Figure 2.1).

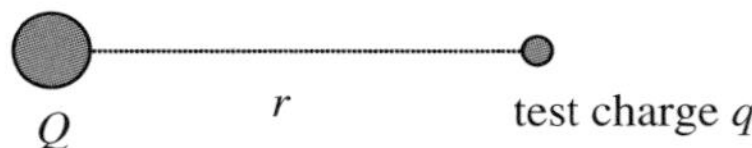

Figure 2.1.

Similarly, at a distance r from the centre of a sphere on which a charge Q has been placed, the electric field is given by the same formula as above. On the *surface* of the sphere of radius R the electric field is

$$E_P = k\frac{Q}{R^2}$$

but inside the sphere the electric field is zero.

▶ In electrostatics, the electric field is zero inside any conducting body (see Figure 2.2). This is because electrostatics deals with situations in which electric charge does not move. If an electric field existed inside a conductor it would force charges to move.

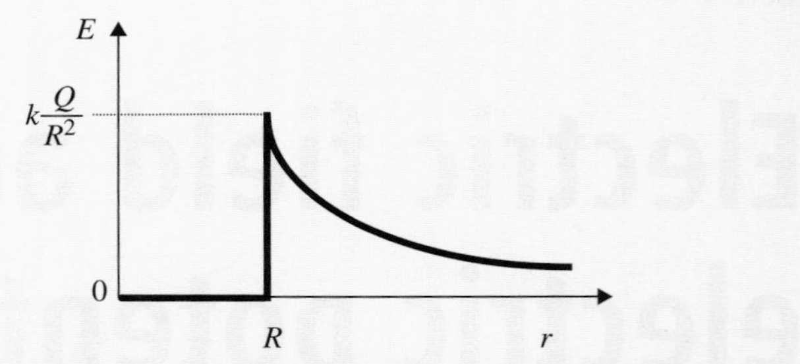

Figure 2.2 The electric field inside a conductor is zero.

Electric field lines

A very useful concept in dealing with electric fields is that of electric field lines. These are imaginary lines (curved or straight) with the property that the tangent to a field line at some point P gives the direction of the electric field at P. A single positive charge creates an electric field that is directed radially out of the charge. Thus the electric field lines in this case are straight lines coming radially out of the charge. In the case of a negative charge, the lines are directed into the charge. Figures 2.3–2.6 show the field lines for various arrangements of charges.

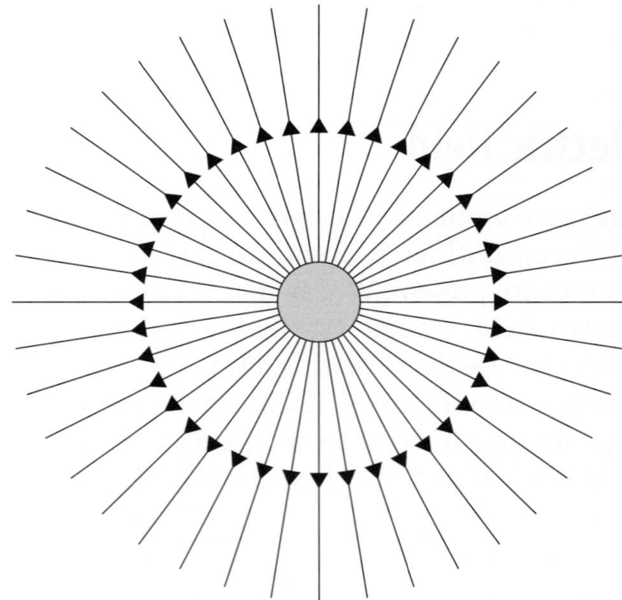

Figure 2.3 The electric field of a point or spherical charge is radial. The field of a negative charge would be directed inward.

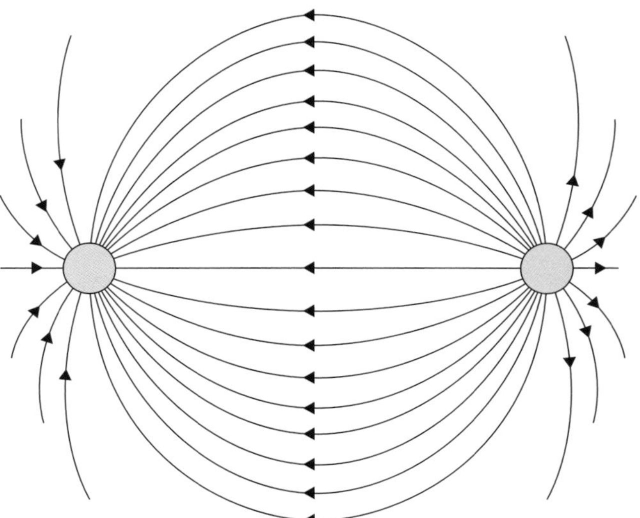

Figure 2.4 Electric field lines for two equal and opposite charges.

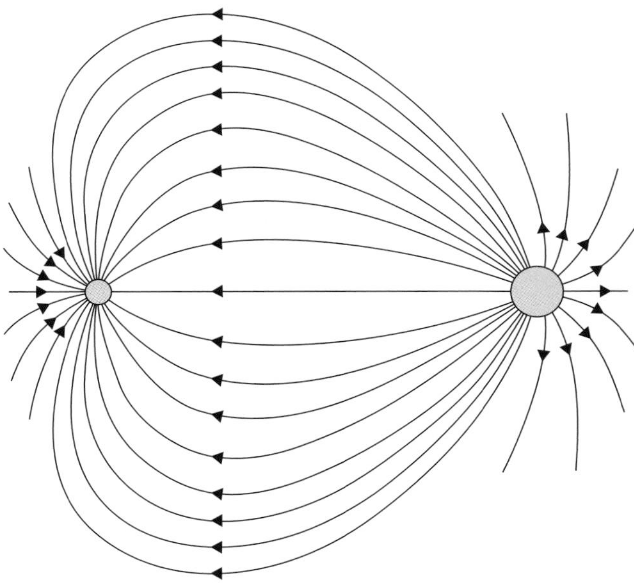

Figure 2.5 The electric field of two opposite and unequal charges. The charge to the right is three times larger than the left charge.

Electric field lines are usually drawn with the convention that the more lines starting from a charge, the larger the charge. The density of lines at a given point (i.e. the number of lines crossing a small area centred at the point) is proportional to the magnitude of the electric field at that point.

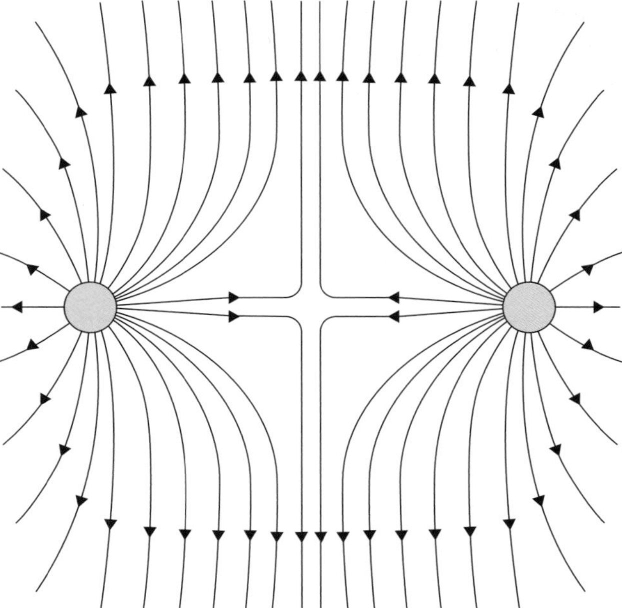

Figure 2.6 The electric field of two equal positive charges. The mid-point of the line joining the charges has zero electric field.

A *uniform* electric field is one that has constant magnitude and direction. Such a field is generated between two oppositely charged parallel plates (see Figure 2.7). Near the edges of the plates the field lines are curved, indicating that the field is no longer uniform there. This *edge effect* is minimized when the length of the plates is long compared with their separation.

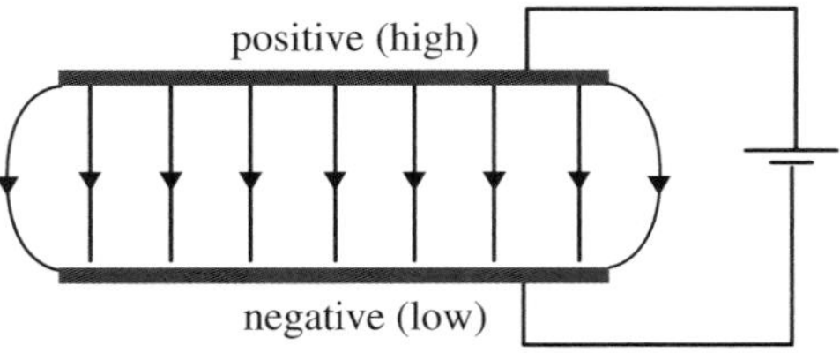

Figure 2.7 The electric field lines for two long, parallel charged plates.

Example question

Q1

The electric field between two parallel plates is 100.0 N C^{-1}. What acceleration would a charge of 2.0 μC and mass 10^{-3} kg experience if placed in this field? (Ignore its weight.)

Answer

The force is found from $F = Eq$ to be $F = 2.0 \times 10^{-4}$ N. Now, using $F = ma$, we find $a = 0.2$ m s^{-2}.

Electric potential

An electric charge creates an electric field in the space around it. It also creates a related quantity, an **electric potential**. Consider a positive charge Q and a positive test charge q. If the charge q is moved closer to Q, work must be done on q. This is because the two charges repel and so a force must be applied to q to make it move closer to Q.

▶ If the work done in moving the positive test charge q from very far away to some position P near Q is W, then the quantity

$$V = \frac{W}{q}$$

defines the potential at P. In other words, the potential at a point is the *work per unit charge* that must be done to bring the positive test charge from far away to the point of interest. The unit of potential is the volt, and 1 V = 1 J C^{-1}. (See Figure 2.8.)

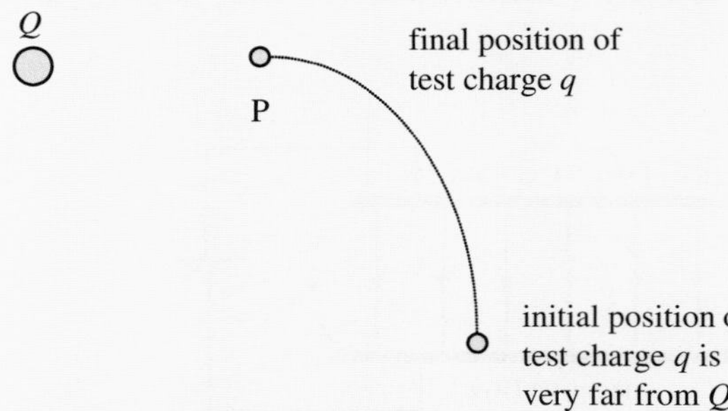

Figure 2.8 The work performed to bring the small positive charge from far away to a point near the charge Q goes into electric potential energy.

Example question

Q2

The work done in moving a test charge of 2.0 μC from very far away to a point P is 150×10^{-6} J. What is the potential at P?

Answer

From the definition, the electric potential at P is

$$V = \frac{W}{q} = \frac{150 \times 10^{-6}}{2 \times 10^{-6}} = 75 \text{ V}$$

The route taken by a charge q to get to P does not affect the amount of work that has to be done on the charge (see Figure 2.9).

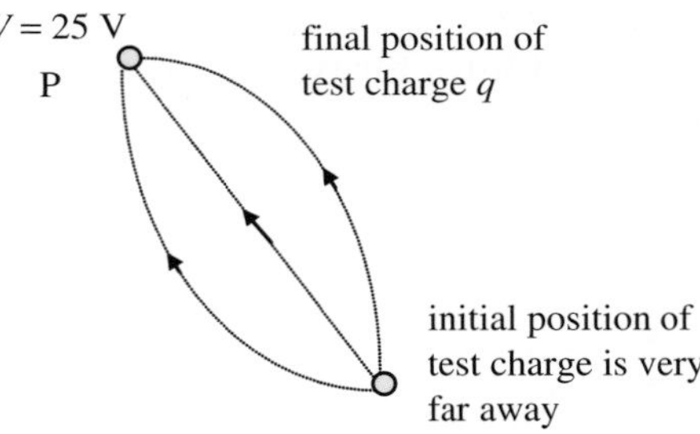

Figure 2.9 The work done in moving a charge q from far away to P is the same no matter what path is followed. If $q = 2$ C the work done is 50 J for all three paths.

The work that is done in moving the test charge q from far away to point P goes into electric potential energy of the charge q. Thus, if the potential at some point in space is V volts and a charge q is placed at that point, the electric potential energy of the charge is

$$U = qV$$

Example question

Q3

The potential at a point P is 12 V and a charge of 3 C is placed there. What is the electric potential energy of the charge? What is the electric potential energy if, instead, a charge of −2C is placed at P?

Answer

The electric potential energy of the charge is

$$U = qV = 3 \times 12 = 36 \text{ J}$$

If a negative charge is placed at P, the electric potential energy is

$$\begin{aligned} U &= qV \\ &= (-2) \times 12 \\ &= -24\ \text{J} \end{aligned}$$

Potential difference

Consider now an arrangement of charges that creates an electric potential in the space around it. What happens when a charge q is moved from one point to another? In Figure 2.10 the electric potential at point A is 15 V and at point B it is 28 V. A charge of 2 C initially at A is to be moved to B. What work must be done on the charge?

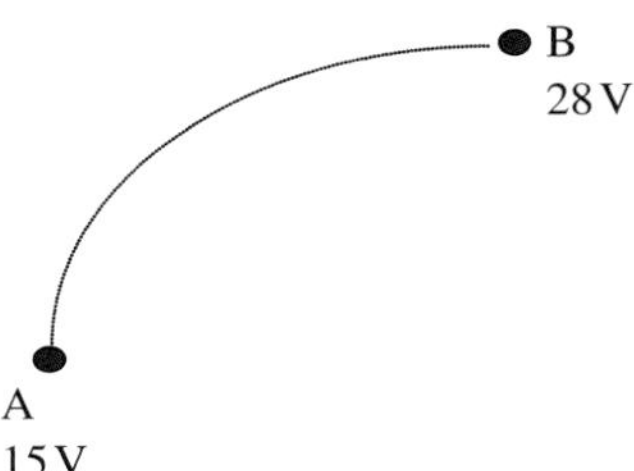

Figure 2.10 A charge moving across a potential difference.

The electric potential energy of the charge in position A is

$$\begin{aligned} U_A &= qV_A \\ &= 2 \times 15 \\ &= 30\ \text{J} \end{aligned}$$

The electric potential energy at position B is

$$\begin{aligned} U_B &= qV_B \\ &= 2 \times 28 \\ &= 56\ \text{J} \end{aligned}$$

The change in the potential energy is thus

$$\begin{aligned} \Delta U &= U_B - U_A \\ &= 56 - 30 \\ &= 26\ \text{J} \end{aligned}$$

This is the work that must be done.

▶ In general, the work that must be done *on* a charge q to move it from point A, where the potential is V_A, to point B, where the potential is V_B, is given by

$$\begin{aligned} W &= \Delta U \\ &= U_B - U_A \\ &= qV_B - qV_A \\ &= q(V_B - V_A) \end{aligned}$$

that is, it is the product of the charge times the potential difference between the two points.

Example question

Q4

What work must be performed in order to move a charge of 5.0 μC from the negative to the positive plate if a potential difference of 250 V is established between the plates? (See Figure 2.11.)

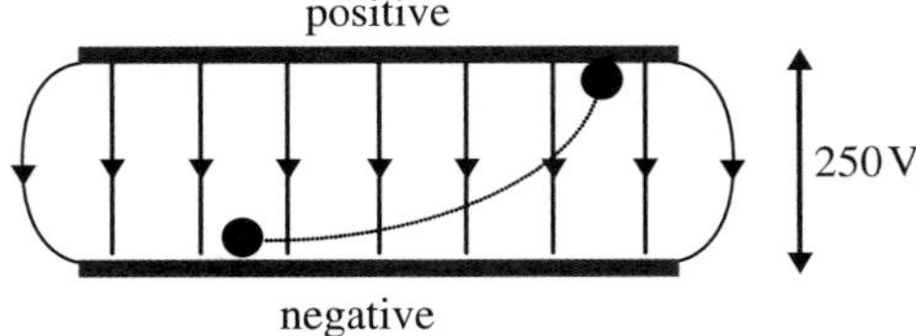

Figure 2.11.

Answer

The work done is simply

$$\begin{aligned} W &= q(V_B - V_A) \\ &= 5.0 \times 10^{-6} \times 250 \\ &= 1.25 \times 10^{-3}\ \text{J} \end{aligned}$$

Consider now a charge q that moves in a region of electric potential. Let the speed of the charge be v_A at position A and v_B at position B. The electric potential at point A is V_A and at point B it is V_B (see Figure 2.12). The mass of the charge is m.

At position A the total energy of the charge is

$$\tfrac{1}{2}mv_A^2 + qV_A$$

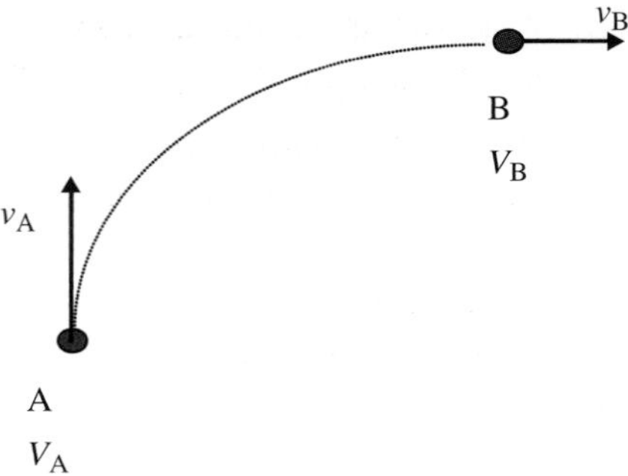

Figure 2.12.

At position B the total energy is

$$\frac{1}{2}mv_B^2 + qV_B$$

By the law of conservation of energy:

$$\frac{1}{2}mv_A^2 + qV_A = \frac{1}{2}mv_B^2 + qV_B$$

Example questions

Q5

A charge of 5 μC and mass 2×10^{-8} kg is shot with speed 3×10^2 m s^{-1} between two parallel plates kept at a potential of 200 V and 300 V, respectively, as shown in Figure 2.13. What will the speed be when the charge gets to the right plate?

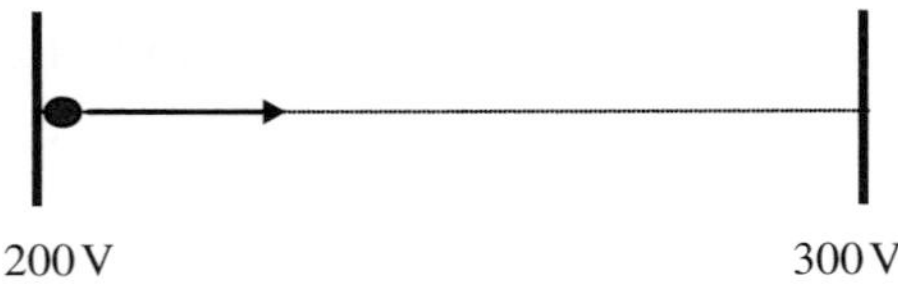

Figure 2.13.

Answer

We apply conservation of energy and so

$$\frac{1}{2}\left[2 \times 10^{-8} \times (3 \times 10^2)^2\right] + (5 \times 10^{-6} \times 200)$$
$$= \frac{1}{2}(2 \times 10^{-8} \times v_B^2) + (5 \times 10^{-6} \times 300)$$
$$\Rightarrow v_B = 200 \text{ m s}^{-1}$$

Q6

What must the initial velocity of an electron be if it is to reach the right plate of Figure 2.14 and momentarily stop there? (Charge of electron $= -1.6 \times 10^{-19}$ C; mass of electron $= 9.1 \times 10^{-31}$ kg.)

Figure 2.14.

Answer

We use conservation of energy again to find

$$\frac{1}{2}(9.1 \times 10^{-31} \times v^2) + (-1.6 \times 10^{-19}) \times 2 = 0$$
$$\Rightarrow v = 8.4 \times 10^5 \text{ m s}^{-1}.$$

The electric field between parallel plates

So far we only have a formula for the electric field of a point or spherical charge. In the case of parallel plates, the expression for the electric field is

$$E = \frac{V}{d}$$

where V is the potential difference between the plates and d is their separation. The electric field has this value at all points in between the plates. Its direction is from high to low potential (see Figure 2.15).

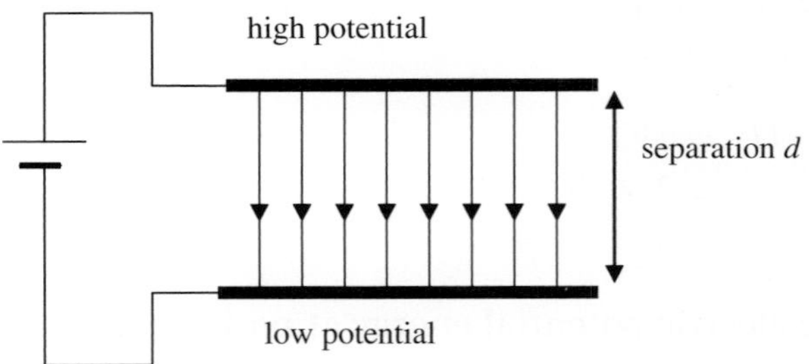

Figure 2.15.

Example question

Q7

Figure 2.16 shows two long, parallel, oppositely charged, vertical plates. Draw and explain the path followed by a positively charged sphere of charge q and mass m when:

(a) the sphere is released from rest at point P;

HL only

(b) the sphere is released from rest outside the plates at point Q above P.

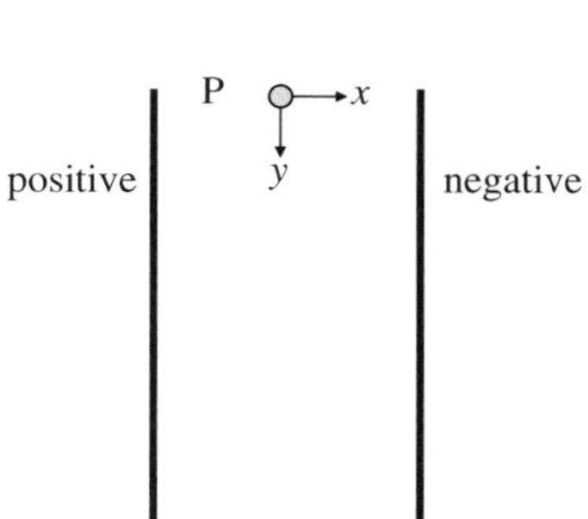

Figure 2.16.

Answer

The sphere is acted upon by two forces: the weight mg and the electrical force qE, where E is the horizontal electric field between the plates. Thus, the sphere has a vertical component of acceleration equal to g and a horizontal component of qE/m to the right.

(a) There is no initial velocity here and so the charge will follow a straight-line path along the direction of the resultant force.

(b) Between the two plates, the horizontal and vertical components of displacement are

$$x = \frac{1}{2}\frac{qE}{m}t^2 \qquad y = ut + \frac{1}{2}gt^2$$

(y is measured positive downward and t is measured from point P). u is the velocity the sphere acquires once it reaches point P. Eliminating time gives a curve

$$y = u\sqrt{\frac{2mx}{qE}} + \frac{mg}{qE}x$$

and not a straight line for the path.

The electronvolt

The study of atomic physics introduces us to a world of small scale. The energy scale that characterizes the atomic world is one of about 10^{-18} J. This is a tremendously small amount of energy by macroscopic standards; the joule is not the appropriate energy unit for atomic physics. A more convenient unit is the electronvolt, eV. When a charge q is moved from a point A to a point B between which a potential difference ΔV exists, then the work done is $W = q\Delta V$.

▶ This relationship allows us to define the electronvolt as the work done when a charge equal to one electron charge is taken across a potential difference of one volt. Thus

$$1 \text{ eV} = 1.6 \times 10^{-19} \text{ C} \times 1 \text{ V}$$
$$= 1.6 \times 10^{-19} \text{ J}$$

If a charge equal to two electron charges is taken across a potential difference of 1 V, the work done is 2 eV; a charge of three electron charges across a potential difference of 5 V results in work of 15 eV and so on.

Example question

Q8

What is the speed of a mass $m = 1.6 \times 10^{-27}$ kg whose kinetic energy is 5000 eV?

Answer

From

$$E_k = \tfrac{1}{2}mv^2$$

$$\Rightarrow v = \sqrt{\frac{2E_k}{m}}$$

$$= \sqrt{\frac{2 \times 5000 \times 1.6 \times 10^{-19}}{1.6 \times 10^{-27}}} \text{ m s}^{-1}$$

$$= 10^6 \text{ m s}^{-1}$$

The point being made here is that in calculations electronvolts must be changed to joules, the SI unit of energy.

? QUESTIONS

1 Draw the field lines for:
(a) two equal charges;
(b) two equal and opposite charges;
(c) two charges of the same sign, one double the other;
(d) two charges of opposite sign, one double the other.

2 Why must field lines be normal to conducting surfaces in electrostatics?

3 Copy the two diagrams in Figure 2.17 and draw the electric field at the points indicated, showing their relative size. The charges on the spheres are equal in magnitude.

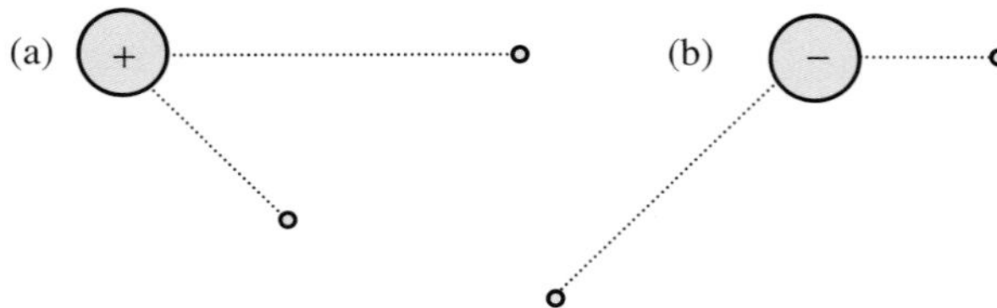

Figure 2.17 For question 3.

4 Two parallel plates are separated by 10.0 cm and a potential difference of 500.0 V is maintained between them. What is the force on an electron placed:
(a) 2.0 cm from the bottom plate;
(b) 4.0 cm from the bottom plate;
(c) 6.0 cm from the bottom plate?
(d) How much work is required to move an electron from a position 2.0 cm from the bottom plate to a position 2.0 cm from the top plate?

5 The electric field at a point in space has magnitude 100 N C^{-1} and is directed to the right. If an electron is placed at that point, what force and acceleration would it experience?

6 If a charge of magnitude $+5.0\ \mu C$ experiences an electric force of magnitude 3.0×10^{-5} N when placed at a point in space, find the electric field at that point.

7 The electric field is a vector and so two electric fields at the same point in space must be added according to the laws of vector addition. Consider two equal positive charges, each $2.00\ \mu C$, separated by $a = 10.0$ cm and a point P a distance of $d = 30.0$ cm as shown in Figure 2.18. The diagram shows the directions of the electric fields produced at P by each charge. Find the magnitude and direction of the net electric field at P.

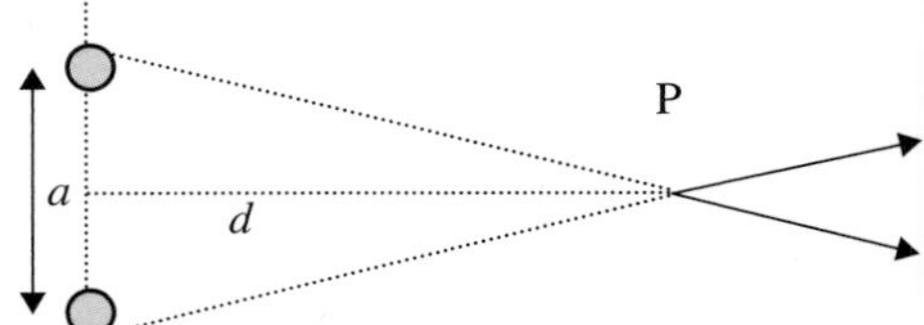

Figure 2.18 For question 7.

8 Repeat the calculation of question 7 for two charges that are unequal. Take the top charge to be $4.00\ \mu C$ and the other $2.00\ \mu C$.

9 Figure 2.19 shows lines along which the electric potential is constant and has the value given.
(a) Find the work that is required if a charge of 5.0 C is to be moved from the 100.0 V line to the 200.0 V line along path I.
(b) How much work would be required if the same charge were moved along path II?
(c) If the 5.0 C charge were first to move to the 300.0 V line along path II and then to the 200.0 V line along path III, how much work would be required then? Compare your answer to that in part (a).

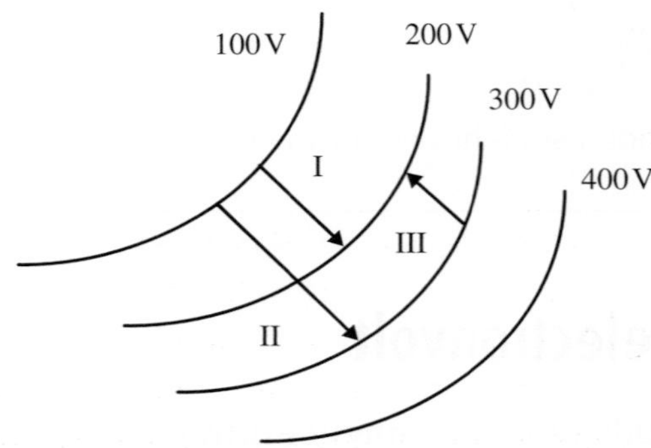

Figure 2.19 For question 9.

10 (a) An electron placed on the 100.0 V surface described in question 9 and released from rest would accelerate toward higher potential. What speed would it acquire by the time it reached the 200.0 V surface?

(b) If a proton were released from the 200.0 V surface, it would accelerate toward lower potential. What speed would it have when it reached the 100.0 V surface?

11 Two uniform electric fields of magnitude $E_1 = 115\ \text{N C}^{-1}$ and $E_2 = 125\ \text{N C}^{-1}$ are produced by two pairs of parallel plates as shown in Figure 2.20. Find the magnitude and direction of the net electric field at the points indicated.

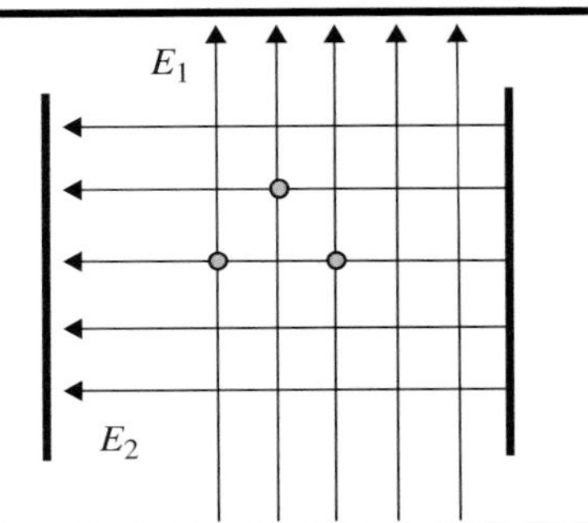

Figure 2.20 For question 11.

12 A conducting sphere of radius 15.0 cm has a positive charge of 4.0 μC deposited on its surface. Find the magnitude of the electric field produced by the charge at distances from the centre of the sphere of:

(a) 0.0 cm;
(b) 5.0 cm;
(c) 15.0 cm;
(d) 20.0 cm.

13 A particle of mass m and electric charge q is suspended vertically from the end of a spring of spring constant k. At equilibrium, the length of the spring extends by an amount x_0. The particle is now placed in a uniform electric field E, as shown in Figure 2.21. At the new equilibrium position, the spring is extended by an amount $2x_0$.

(a) Determine the sign of the charge.
(b) Determine the magnitude of the electric field strength E in terms of m, q and g.

The mass is now displaced by a small amount and is released.

(c) Explain why the oscillations that take place are simple harmonic.
(d) Is the period different from the period when the field was absent?

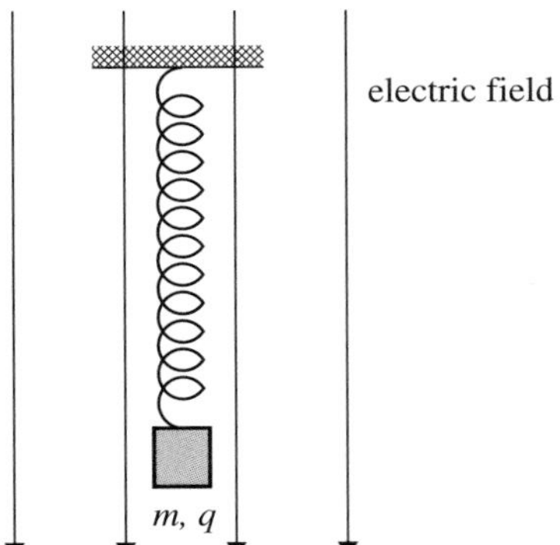

Figure 2.21 For question 13.

14 Two positive point charges of magnitude Q and $9Q$ are a distance d apart, as shown in Figure 2.22.

(a) Calculate the electric field strength at point P, a distance $\frac{d}{4}$ from Q.

A third positive point charge is placed at P and is then displaced a bit to the right.

(b) Explain why the charge will perform oscillations when released.
(c) Are the oscillations simple harmonic?
(d) How does your answer to (b) change if the third charge is negative?

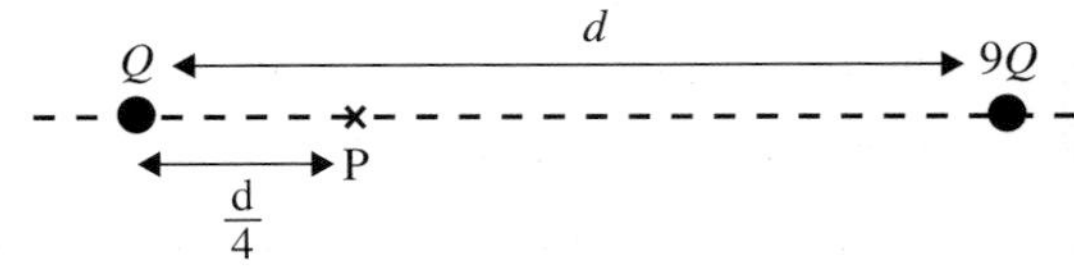

Figure 2.22 For question 14.

HL mathematics only

15 Consider again the previous problem. Suppose that the third positive charge placed at P has a magnitude q and mass m. It is displaced to the right of P by a *small* amount A.

(a) Find an expression for the net force on the charge q.

(b) In mathematics it can be proved that if x is small then

$$\frac{1}{(1+x)^2} \approx 1 - 2x$$

Use this approximation on the expression for the net force you found in (a) to show that it is approximately equal to

$$F \approx -\frac{256kQq}{3d^3}x$$

where x is the displacement from point P.

(c) Hence determine the nature of the oscillations that will take place when the charge q is released.

Electric field and electric potential

This chapter deals with more involved examples of electric fields and potentials and discusses the connection between electric field and electric potential. The concept of electric potential energy is introduced and discussed in simple situations.

Objectives

By the end of this chapter you should be able to:

- define the terms *electric field*, *electric potential* and *electric potential energy* ($U_{el} = qV_P$) and calculate these quantities in simple situations;
- define *equipotential surfaces* and *field lines* and state the *relationship between them*;
- understand that *electric fields* and *electric potentials* are *related* by $E = \frac{\Delta V}{\Delta r}$ or $E = -\frac{dV}{dr}$;
- understand that the *potential is constant inside a conductor* and the *electric field is zero*;
- understand that *work is done when a charge moves across a potential difference* $W_{B \to A} = q(V_A - V_B)$;
- state the similarities and differences between *gravitation* and *electricity*.

Electric fields

As we saw in Chapter 5.2, if a positive test charge q experiences an electric force $\vec{F}$, the electric field at the position of the test charge is defined as the ratio of the force to the charge:

$$\vec{E} = \frac{\vec{F}}{q}$$

The direction of the electric field is the same as the direction of the force (on the *positive* test charge q). At a point a distance r away from a charge Q, the magnitude of the electric field is

$$E_P = k\frac{Q}{r^2}$$

Vector methods can then be used to find the electric field due to an arrangement of point charges. An example is that of the dipole, which has two equal and opposite charges separated by a distance a (see Figure 3.1).

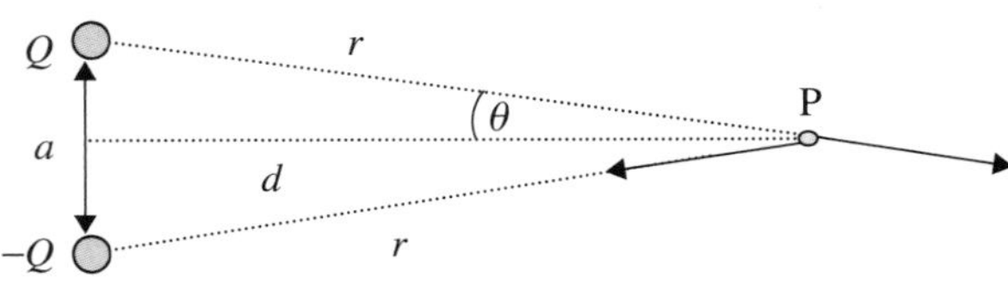

Figure 3.1 Two equal and opposite charges separated by a given distance form an electric dipole. The diagram shows the electric fields that must be added as vectors to get the net electric field at P.

We would like to find the electric field created by a dipole. It is easiest to find this field on the perpendicular bisector of the line joining the charges. At other points, the answer is more involved. Thus, consider a point a distance d from the midpoint of the line joining the charges. The electric field at P has a contribution of $E_P = \frac{1}{4\pi\varepsilon}\frac{Q}{r^2}$ from each charge, directed as shown. The horizontal components will cancel each other out but the vertical components add up. The vertical component of E_P is $E_P \sin\theta$ and since $\sin\theta = a/2r$ we find (recall $r^2 = d^2 + \frac{a^2}{4}$)

$$E = \frac{1}{4\pi\varepsilon_0}\frac{Qa}{\left(d^2 + \frac{a^2}{4}\right)^{\frac{3}{2}}}$$

This is directed vertically downwards, in the direction of the vector from Q to $-Q$. The quantity Qa is called the *dipole moment.*

If both charges were positive, the corresponding electric field would be given by

$$E = \frac{1}{4\pi\varepsilon_0}\frac{2Qd}{\left(d^2 + \frac{a^2}{4}\right)^{\frac{3}{2}}}$$

and would be horizontal (along the perpendicular bisector to the line joining the charges).

Electric potential and energy

Suppose that at some point in space we place a charge Q. Assume for concreteness that it is a positive charge. If we place another positive charge q nearby and try to move it even closer to the large charge Q, we will have to exert a force on q, since it is being repelled by Q (see Figure 3.2). That is, we have to do work in order to change the position of q and bring it closer to Q.

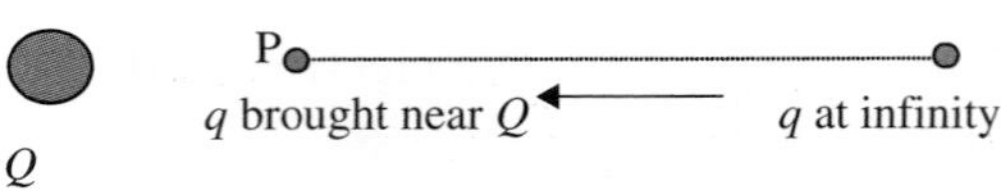

Figure 3.2.

▶ We have already defined (in the previous chapter) the electric potential at a point P as the amount of work done per unit charge as a small positive test charge q is moved from infinity to the point P, that is

$$V_P = \frac{W}{q}$$

The unit of potential is the volt (V), and $1\text{ V} = 1\text{ J C}^{-1}$.

The work done in moving a charge q from infinity to point P goes into *electric potential energy*. Thus

▶ If the potential at some point P is V_P, and we place a charge q at P, the quantity

$$U_{el} = qV_P$$

is the electric potential energy of the charge q.

Electric potential and electric potential energy are scalar quantities. Note the definition of potential, which involves taking a charge from infinity to some point P. This definition does not specify along which path the charge must be moved from infinity to point P. In fact, the properties of electric potential are such that the amount of work done would be the same irrespective of which path is taken. This is reminiscent of gravity: the change in gravitational potential energy when a mass m is moved from a position A to a position B is always mgh where h is the vertical separation of the two points A and B. The actual path followed by the mass is irrelevant. The gravitational and electric forces are called *conservative* for this reason. Friction is an example of a force where the amount of work done does depend on the path followed: it is obviously harder to push a heavy suitcase a long distance as opposed to a short distance. Such forces are called *dissipative*. An immediate property of conservative forces is that, if a body is moved along a closed path, the amount of work done is zero. This also means that, if the potential at point P is V volts, the amount of work done when a charge q is taken from P to infinity is $-qV$.

Consider now two points, A and B, in the vicinity of a charge Q (see Figure 3.3). The electric charge creates an electric potential everywhere in space, and at points A and B the potential is V_A and V_B, respectively. If we place a charge q at point B and move it from B to A, what is the work done? Since the amount of work done is independent of the path followed, we can calculate this work along paths for which we know the answer. We first take the charge from B to infinity and then from infinity to A.

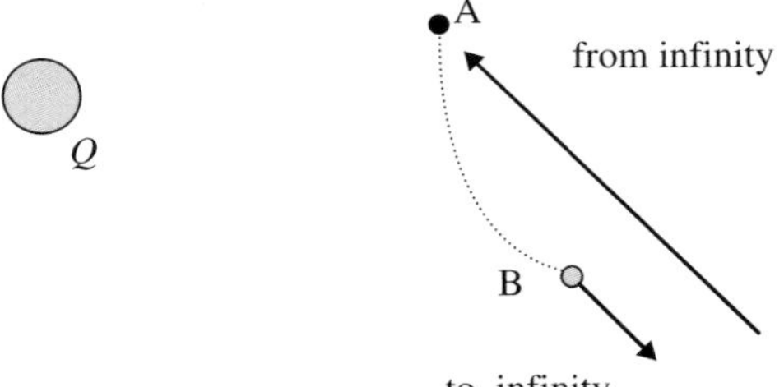

Figure 3.3 Work must be done in order to move a charge from one point to another where the potential is different.

On the first leg, the work done is $-qV_B$ and on the second leg it is qV_A. Thus, the total work done is

$$W_{B\to A} = q(V_A - V_B)$$

The quantity $V_A - V_B$ is the potential difference between A and B. Points at infinity are considered to be at zero potential. We have talked at some length about the electric potential that a charge Q creates in space. But how do we calculate this potential? To do this we need calculus, so what follows may be omitted and only the result may be noted.

Supplementary material

When the positive charge q is at some distance r from Q, it experiences a repulsive force

$$F = \frac{1}{4\pi\varepsilon_0}\frac{Qq}{r^2}$$

Thus, the force with which we must push the charge q to move it closer to Q is directed as shown in Figure 3.4. If we push a small distance dr, the work done is dW and

$$dW = -Fdr$$
$$= -\frac{1}{4\pi\varepsilon_0}\frac{Qq}{r^2}dr$$

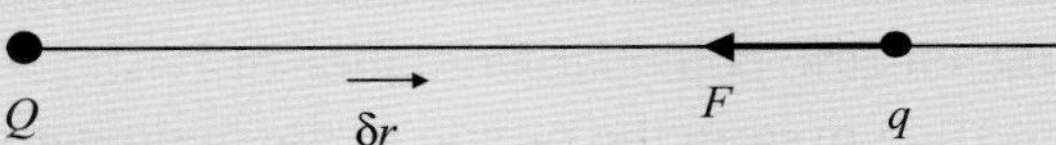

Figure 3.4 Diagram for calculating the work done in moving a positive charge from infinity to a point near another charge.

(The minus sign in dW is there because the force pushes the charge towards Q but dr is positive when directed away from Q.) The total work done is therefore

$$W = -\int_{\infty}^{R} \frac{1}{4\pi\varepsilon_0}\frac{Qq}{r^2}dr$$
$$= \frac{1}{4\pi\varepsilon_0}\frac{Qq}{r}\Bigg|_{\infty}^{R}$$
$$= \frac{1}{4\pi\varepsilon_0}\frac{Qq}{R}$$

But, by definition, $W = qV_P$, so

$$V_P = \frac{1}{4\pi\varepsilon_0}\frac{Q}{R}$$

Thus, the electric energy of a charge q a distance r from another charge Q is

$$U = \frac{1}{4\pi\varepsilon_0}\frac{Qq}{r}$$

In all these formulae, the charges must be entered with their correct sign.

Example questions

Q1

Find the electric potential energy between the proton in a hydrogen atom and an electron orbiting the proton at a radius 0.5×10^{-10} m. The proton has a charge 1.6×10^{-19} C, equal and opposite to that of the electron.

Answer

From the formula

$$U = \frac{1}{4\pi\varepsilon_0}\frac{Qq}{r}$$
$$= 9 \times 10^9 \times \frac{1.6 \times 10^{-19} \times (-1.6 \times 10^{-19})}{0.5 \times 10^{-10}}$$
$$= -46 \times 10^{-19}\ \text{J}$$

Q2

Find the electric potential a distance of 0.50×10^{-10} m from the proton of the hydrogen atom.

Answer

$$V_0 = \frac{1}{4\pi\varepsilon_0}\frac{Q}{r}$$

and so

$$V_P = 9 \times 10^9 \times \frac{1.60 \times 10^{-19}}{0.50 \times 10^{-10}}$$

$$= 29 \text{ V}$$

Q3

Find the electric potential energy for four charges of 2 μC each placed at the vertices of a square of side 10 cm.

Answer

Naming the charges as 1, 2, 3 and 4 (see Figure 3.5) we see that there are six pairs of charges: (1, 2), (1, 3), (1, 4), (2, 3), (2, 4) and (3, 4)

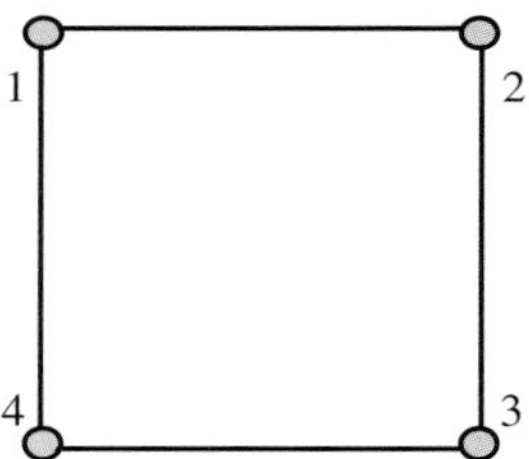

Figure 3.5.

Therefore

$$U = 9 \times 10^9 \times 4 \times 10^{-12} \times \left[\frac{1}{10} + \frac{1}{10} + \frac{1}{10} + \frac{1}{10} + \frac{1}{10\sqrt{2}} + \frac{1}{10\sqrt{2}}\right] \times 10^2 \text{ J}$$

Thus

$$U = 1.9 \text{ J}$$

Electric potential is a scalar quantity. So if we have not one but two charges, Q_1 and Q_2, the electric potential at a point P that is a distance r_1 from Q_1 and a distance r_2 from Q_2 is just

$$V_P = \frac{1}{4\pi\varepsilon_0}\frac{Q_1}{r_1} + \frac{1}{4\pi\varepsilon_0}\frac{Q_2}{r_2}$$

that is, we first find the potential at P from Q_1 alone then from Q_2 alone and add up the two (see Figure 3.6).

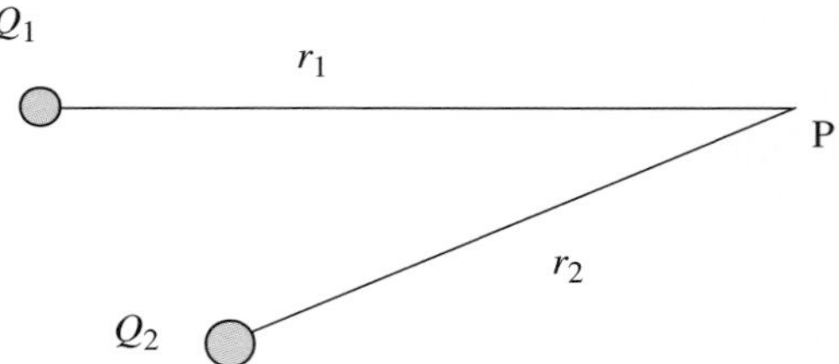

Figure 3.6 The potential at P is found by finding the potential there from the first charge, then finding the potential from the second charge, and finally adding the two.

Figure 3.7 shows the electric potential from one positive and one negative charge. In the absence of charges, the surface would be flat. The potential is represented by the height from the flat surface.

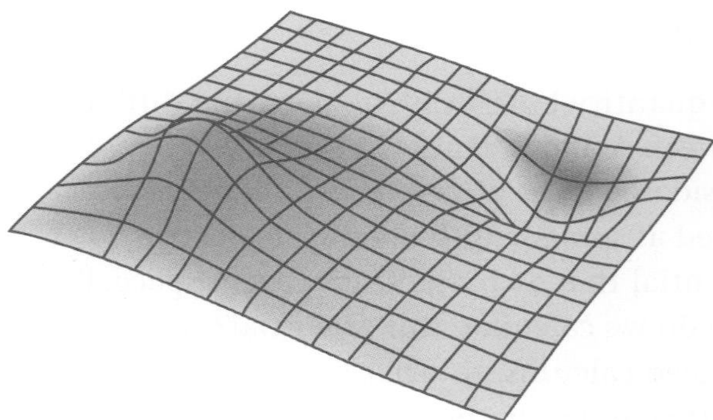

Figure 3.7 The electric potential due to two equal and opposite charges. The potential is proportional to the height of the surface.

The same procedure is followed for more than two charges. This simple formula for electric potential works in the case of point charges: that is, the objects on which the charges Q_i are placed are mathematical points or close to it. It also works in another special case. It works if the object on which the charge Q is placed is a sphere. But this is somewhat more delicate. If the point P is outside the sphere and at a distance r from the centre of the sphere, then the potential at P is indeed

$$V_P = \frac{1}{4\pi\varepsilon_0}\frac{Q}{r}$$

On the surface of the sphere the potential is

$$V_P = \frac{1}{4\pi\varepsilon_0}\frac{Q}{R}$$

where R is the radius of the sphere. But at any point inside the sphere the electric potential is constant and has the same value as the potential at the surface. (See Figure 3.8.)

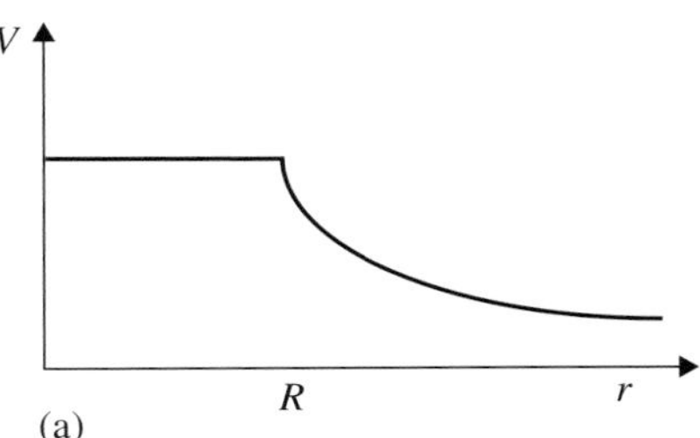

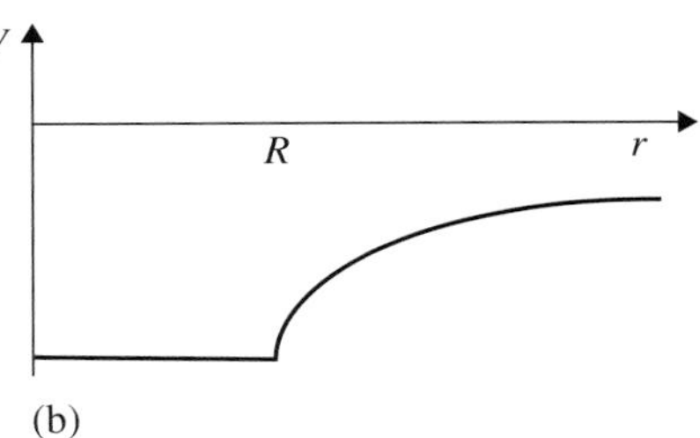

Figure 3.8 The electric potential is constant inside the sphere and falls off as $1/r$ outside. Shown here are (a) a positively charged sphere and (b) a negatively charged sphere.

Example questions

Q4

Two spheres of radii r and $R = 10r$ are connected by a long conducting wire. Before connecting, the big sphere had an amount of charge Q on it and the smaller sphere was uncharged. How much charge is there on each sphere now?

Answer

See Figure 3.9.

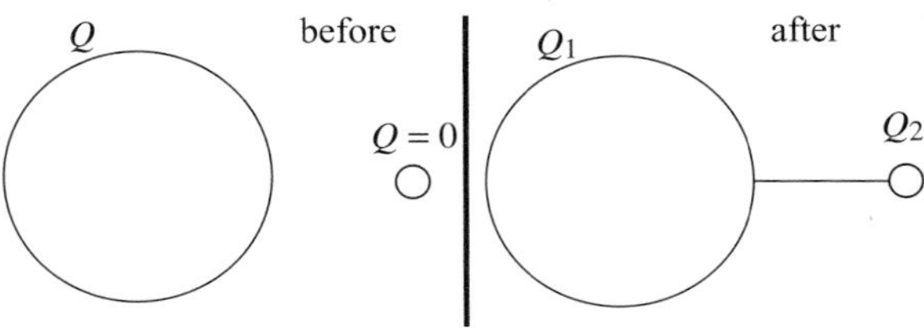

Figure 3.9.

The potential on the big sphere is $V_1 = \frac{Q_1}{4\pi\varepsilon_0 R}$ and on the small sphere $V_2 = \frac{Q_2}{4\pi\varepsilon_0 r}$. Here $Q_1 + Q_2 = Q$, by conservation of electric charge. When connected by the wire the two surfaces must be at the same potential, $V_1 = V_2$, and so

$$\frac{1}{4\pi\varepsilon_0}\frac{Q_1}{R} = \frac{1}{4\pi\varepsilon_0}\frac{Q_2}{r}$$

$$\Rightarrow \frac{Q_1}{R} = \frac{Q_2}{r}$$

Using $R = 10r$ we find $Q_1 = \frac{10}{11}Q$ and $Q_2 = \frac{1}{11}Q$. It can be seen that the big sphere has more charge than the small one even though they are both at the same potential.

Q5

Find the ratio of the electric field on the surface of the small sphere to that on the surface of the big sphere in Example question 4.

Answer

$$E_1 = \frac{Q_1}{4\pi\varepsilon_0 R^2}$$

$$= \frac{10Q/11}{4\pi\varepsilon_0(10r)^2}$$

$$= \frac{10Q/11}{4\pi\varepsilon_0 100r^2}$$

$$= \frac{Q}{4\pi\varepsilon_0 r^2} \times \frac{1}{10 \times 11}$$

$$E_2 = \frac{Q_2}{4\pi\varepsilon_0 r^2}$$

$$= \frac{Q/11}{4\pi\varepsilon_0 r^2}$$

$$= \frac{Q}{4\pi\varepsilon_0 r^2} \times \frac{1}{11}$$

and so

$$\frac{E_2}{E_1} = 10$$

that is, the small sphere has a bigger electric field on its surface. The small sphere is more curved than the big one and electric fields are largest near sharp objects.

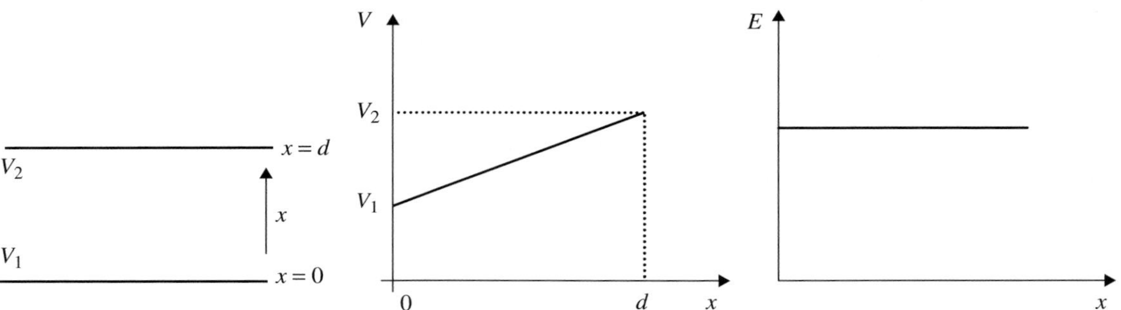

Figure 3.10 The potential increases uniformly as we move from the lower to the upper plate.

Parallel plates

There is one other case that is straightforward enough to allow us to write down a simple formula for the electric potential. This is the case of two long parallel plates separated by a distance d (see Figure 3.10).

If, for the sake of convenience, we take the top plate to have the higher potential, V_2, and the lower plate to have potential V_1, then the potential at any point with vertical distance x from the lower plate is

$$V(x) = V_1 + (V_2 - V_1)\frac{x}{d}$$

You can check that this formula gives the correct answers when $x = 0$ (lower plate) and $x = d$ (top plate). Halfway between the plates $x = \frac{d}{2}$ and $V = \frac{V_1 + V_2}{2}$. The potential increases uniformly from the lower plate to the top. The electric field between the plates is uniform, as we already know.

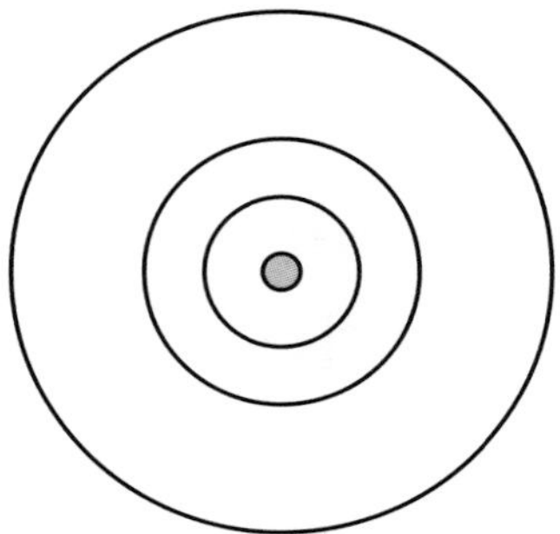

Figure 3.11 The equipotential surfaces of a point charge are concentric spheres.

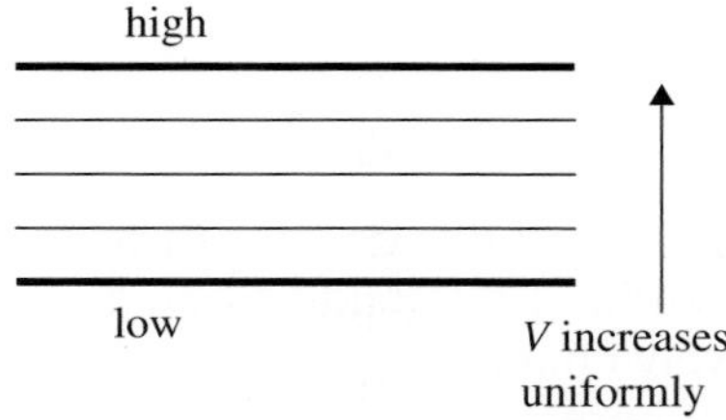

Figure 3.12 The equipotential surfaces for two parallel charged plates are planar.

Equipotential surfaces

Points in space that have the same potential are said to define equipotential surfaces. For example, for a single charge Q, the equipotential surfaces are concentric spheres centred at the charge, as shown in Figure 3.11.

All the points on a given sphere are at the same distance from the charge and hence at the same potential. For the two parallel plates, the equipotential surfaces are planes parallel to the plates (see Figure 3.12).

Figure 3.13 shows the equipotential lines for two charges: a positive charge of 4 C at point (−0.3, −0.3) and a negative one of −1 C at point (0.7, 0.7).

When a charge moves from one point of an equipotential surface to another point on the same equipotential surface, the work done is zero, since the potential difference between the two points is zero.

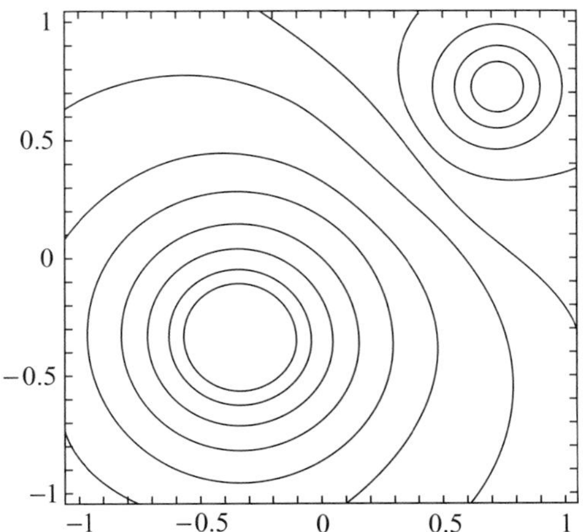

Figure 3.13 The equipotential surfaces of two opposite, unequal charges.

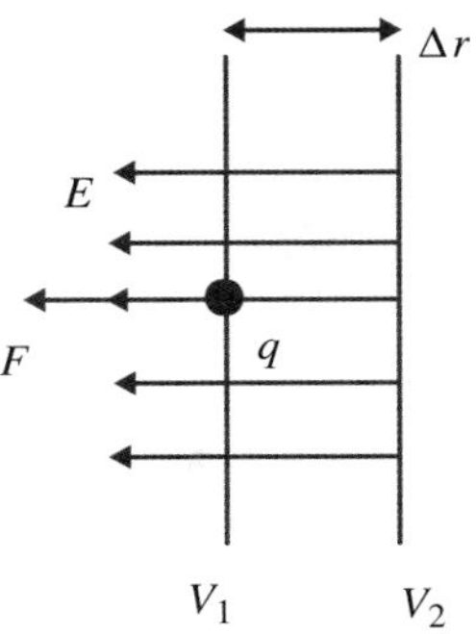

Figure 3.14 The electric field lines are directed to the left and so is the force on the positive charge q. If the charge is moved to the right, work must be performed.

The connection between electric potential and electric field

There is a deep connection between electric potential and electric field.

▶ If the electric potential at a point in space is V and the electric field at that same point has a magnitude E then

$$E = \frac{\Delta V}{\Delta r} \quad \left(\text{in calculus } E = -\frac{\mathrm{d}V}{\mathrm{d}r}\right)$$

(the minus sign is needed if we use calculus methods but not otherwise). This says that the electric field is the gradient of the electric potential. Thus, in a graph of electric potential versus distance, the slope is the electric field.

We can show this as follows (see Figure 3.14). Let a small positive charge q be placed at a point where the potential is V_1. We want to move it a distance Δr away to a position where the potential is at a higher value V_2. The force on the charge is $F = qE$ and so the work done is $W = F\,\Delta r = qE\,\Delta r$. But the work can also be found from $W = q\Delta V$, and so

$$qE\,\Delta r = q\Delta V$$
$$\Rightarrow E = \frac{\Delta V}{\Delta r}$$

This says, in particular, that if the electric potential is constant in some region of space, then the electric field is zero there. (Recall that the electric potential is constant inside a conducting sphere; the result above says therefore that the electric field is zero inside the sphere as we stated earlier.) This relationship also states that if the potential difference between two parallel plates is V and the separation between the plates is d then $E = \frac{V}{d}$ and is the same at all points inside the plates. It is perpendicular to the plates and is directed from high to low potential.

Example questions

Q6

A wire of length L has a potential difference V across its ends. Find the electric field inside the wire. Hence find the work done when a charge q is moved from one end of the wire to the other.

Answer

From $E = \frac{\Delta V}{\Delta r}$ it follows that $E = \frac{V}{L}$. The work done can be found in two ways. Either by using

$$W = q\Delta V = qV$$

or by

$$W = Fd = qEL = q\frac{V}{L}L = qV$$

as before.

Q7

The electric potential a distance r from a charge Q is $V = \frac{1}{4\pi\varepsilon_0}\frac{Q}{r}$. Use this expression to find the electric field at the same point.

Answer

Here we must use the calculus expression

$$E = -\frac{dV}{dr}$$
$$= -\frac{d}{dr}\left(\frac{1}{4\pi\varepsilon_0}\frac{Q}{r}\right)$$
$$= \frac{1}{4\pi\varepsilon_0}\frac{Q}{r^2}$$

as we expect.

The connection between electric potential and electric field extends to equipotential surfaces and electric field lines. It can be shown that electric field lines are always normal to equipotential surfaces. Figure 3.15 illustrates the equipotential surfaces due to a positive point charge and superimposed on these surfaces are arrows representing the electric field lines of the charge.

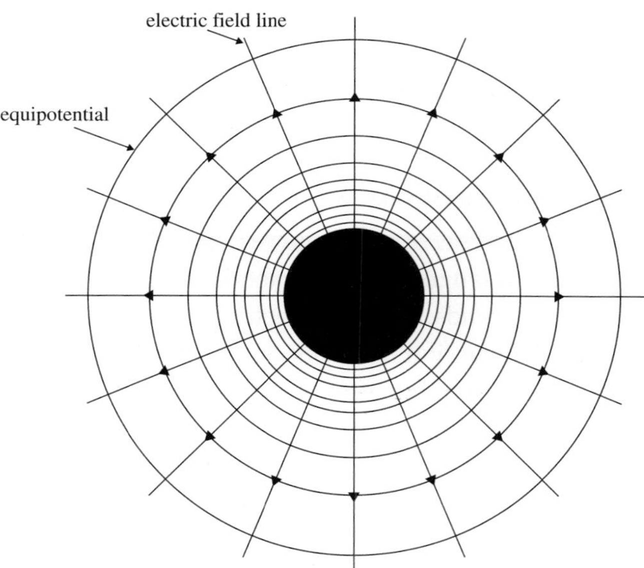

Figure 3.15 The electric field is normal to the equipotential surfaces.

The surfaces of conductors are equipotential surfaces, so electric field lines in the presence of conducting surfaces are normal to them, as in Figure 3.16. This can be explained as follows. If electric field lines were not normal to the conducting surface, there would be a component of electric field along the surface. Such a field would cause charges to move – an electric current would be established on the surface. This, however, is not consistent with the assumption that we are dealing with electrostatic situations, in which charges do not move. Hence the electric field lines must be normal to the conductor, and so the conductor surface must be an equipotential surface.

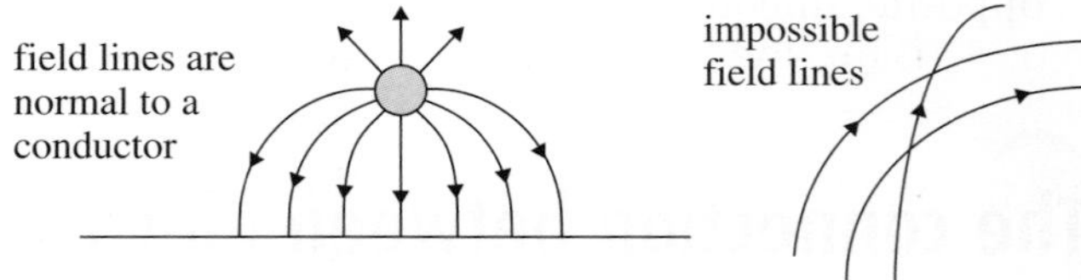

Figure 3.16 Properties of field lines. Field lines are normal to conducting surfaces. Field lines cannot cross.

Similarities between electricity and gravitation

As is clear from a comparison between Newton's law of gravitation and Coulomb's law, there are many similarities between electricity and gravitation. Table 3.1 shows a few of the

	Gravitation	Electricity
Acts on	Mass (positive only)	Charge (positive or negative)
Force	$F = G\frac{M_1M_2}{r^2}$ Attractive only Infinite range	$F = \frac{1}{4\pi\varepsilon_0}\frac{Q_1Q_2}{r}$ Attractive or repulsive Infinite range
Relative strength	1	10^{42}
Field	$g = G\frac{M}{r^2}$	$E = \frac{1}{4\pi\varepsilon_0}\frac{Q}{r^2}$
Potential	$V = -G\frac{M}{r}$	$V = \frac{1}{4\pi\varepsilon_0}\frac{Q}{r}$
Work done	Independent of path	Independent of path
Potential energy	$U = -G\frac{Mm}{r}$	$U = \frac{1}{4\pi\varepsilon_0}\frac{Qq}{r}$

Table 3.1 A comparison of gravitation and electricity.

similarities and differences between the two. The biggest difference is, of course, the existence of two kinds of electric charge, which implies that the electric force can be attractive or repulsive. The one kind of mass leads to only attractive forces.

Supplementary material

In some innovative work during the early part of the twentieth century, T. Kaluza and O. Klein considered that the universe has four space and one time dimensions instead of the usual three plus one. The extra dimension, they claimed, is curled up as a tiny circle and is essentially unobservable. They then showed that if gravitation is the only force in this five-dimensional universe and we now insist on looking at only its four-dimensional part, electricity arises naturally from gravitation in this reduction from five to four dimensions!

? QUESTIONS

1 A charged rod is brought near three conducting spheres resting on insulated stands, as shown in Figure 3.17. The spheres are originally touching. If they are now separated with the rod still nearby, what will be the sign of the charge on each sphere after the rod is taken away?

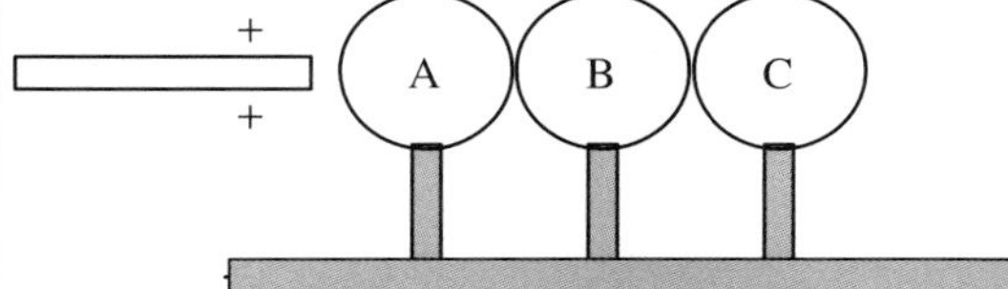

Figure 3.17 For question 1.

2 Four equal charges of 5 μC are placed at the vertices of a square of side 10 cm.
(a) What is the value of the electric potential at the centre of the square?
(b) What is the electric field there?
(c) How do you reconcile your answer with the fact that the electric field is the derivative of the potential?

3 (a) What is the electric potential at the mid-point of the line joining two equal positive charges Q ? Take their separation to be d.
(b) What is the electric potential at the mid-point of the line joining two equal but opposite charges?

4 Two charges, $Q_1 = 2\ \mu\text{C}$ and $Q_2 = -4\ \mu\text{C}$, are 0.3 m apart. Find the electric potential at a point P which is 0.4 m from Q_1 and 0.6 m from Q_2.

5 A charge Q of 10.0 C is placed somewhere in space. What is the work required to bring a charge of 1.0 mC from a point X, 10.0 m from Q, to a point Y, 2.0 m from Q? Does the answer depend on which path the charge follows?

6 An electron is brought from infinity to a distance of 10.0 cm from a charge of –10.0 C. How much work was done on the electron?

7 An electron moves from a point in space where the potential is 100.0 V to another point where the potential is 200.0 V. If it started from rest, what is its speed at the end of the trip?

8 Four charges are placed at the vertices of a square of side 5.00 cm, as shown in Figure 3.18.
(a) On the diagram, show the forces acting on the 2 μC charge. Find the magnitude and direction of the net force on the 2 μC charge.
(b) Calculate the value of the electric potential at the centre of the square.
(c) How much work must be done in order to move a charge of 1 nC initially at infinity to the centre of the square?

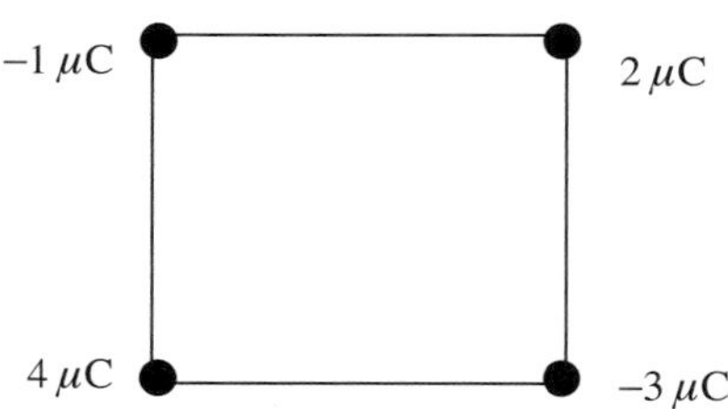

Figure 3.18 For question 8.

9 The electric dipole moment of a molecule is 6.2×10^{-30} C m and the charges are assumed to be $\pm 1.6 \times 10^{-19}$ C. The molecule finds itself in a uniform electric field of value 2.00×10^{6} V m^{-1} that is directed along the plane of the page (see Figure 3.19). The dipole also lies on the page.

(a) What is the separation of the charges?
(b) What is the net force on the dipole?
(c) What is the largest torque on the molecule about an axis through its middle and normal to the plane?

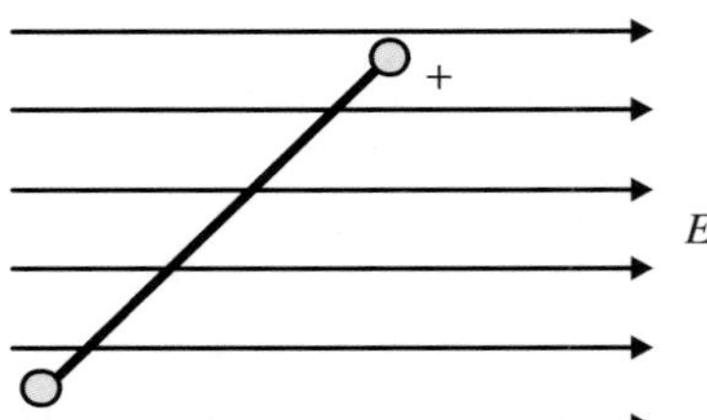

Figure 3.19 For question 9.

10 Two conducting spheres are separated by a distance that is large compared with their radii. The first sphere has a radius of 10.0 cm and has a charge of 2.00 μC on its surface. The second sphere has a radius of 15.0 cm and is neutral. The spheres are then connected by a long conducting wire.

(a) Find the charge on each sphere.
(b) Calculate the charge density on each sphere (charge density is the total charge on the sphere divided by the surface area of the sphere).
(c) Calculate the electric field on the surface of each sphere.
(d) Comment on your result in the light of your answer to part (b). Why is it stated that the wire is long?

11 Figure 3.20 shows the equipotential lines for two equal and opposite charges. Draw the electric field lines for these two charges.

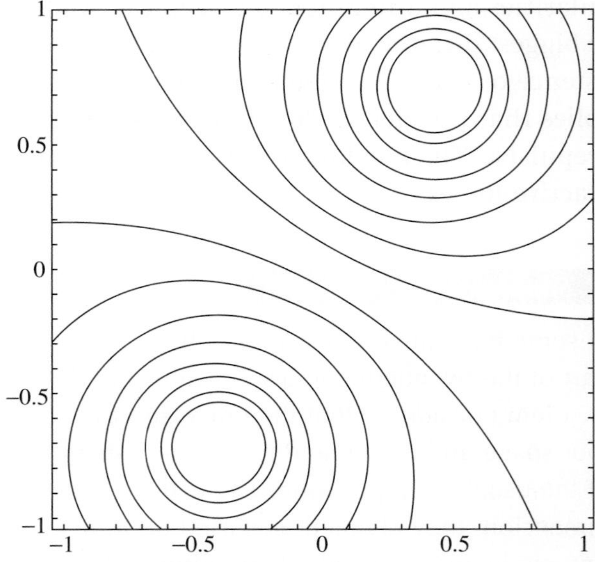

Figure 3.20 For question 11.

12 Two long parallel plates are separated by a distance of 15.0 cm. The bottom plate is kept at a potential of −250 V and the top at +250 V. A charge of −2.00 μC is placed at a point 3.00 cm from the bottom plate.

(a) Find the electric potential energy of the charge.

The charge is then moved vertically up to a point 3.00 cm from the top plate.

(b) What is the electrical potential energy of the charge now?
(c) How much work was done on the charge?

13 An electron is shot with a speed equal to 1.59×10^{6} m s^{-1} from a point where the electric potential is zero toward an immovable negative charge Q (see Figure 3.21).

(a) What should the potential at P be so that the electron stops momentarily at P and then turns back?
(b) What is the magnitude of Q?

Figure 3.21 For question 13.

14 Two equal and opposite charges are placed at points with coordinates $x = 0,\ y = a$ and $x = 0,\ y = -a$, as shown in Figure 3.22.
(a) Find the electric field at the point with coordinates $x = d,\ y = 0$.
(b) Repeat for two equal negative charges $-q$ on the y-axis.
(c) Plot these fields as functions of d.

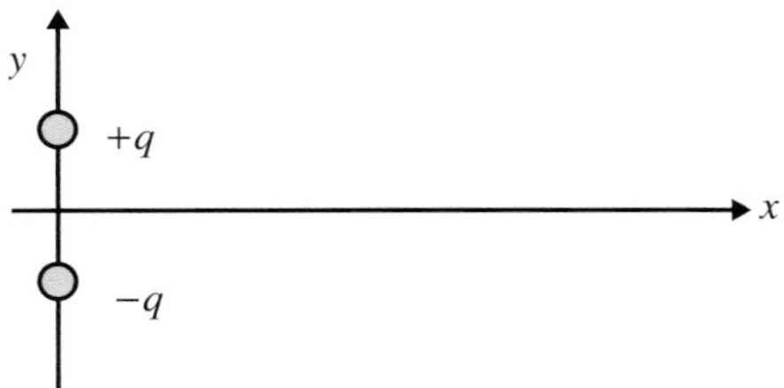

Figure 3.22 For question 14.

15 A charge Q is placed a distance d from a very large conducting plane. What is the electric field at a point P a distance $2d$ from the plane? (See Figure 3.23.)

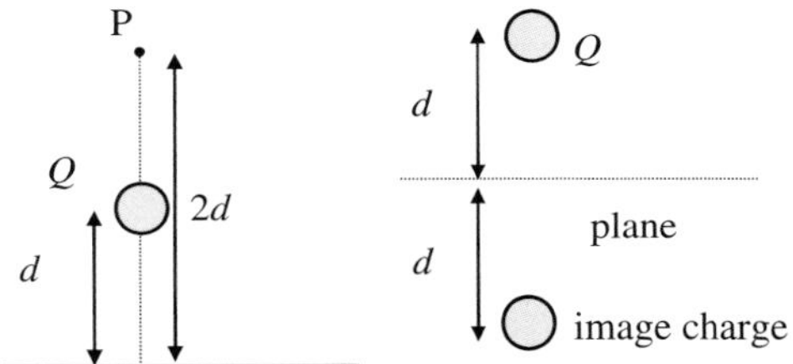

Figure 3.23 For question 15.

[*Hint*: Answer this as follows (the method of images). Draw field lines to convince yourself that the same lines would be obtained if, instead of the plane, an equal and opposite charge were placed at a position that is the mirror image of the charge in the plane. Thus, the electric field in the presence of the plane would be the same as the electric field of two equal and opposite charges without the plane. Thus, find this field at point P.]

16 A charge $-q$ whose mass is m moves in a circle of radius r around another stationary charge q located at the centre of the circle, as shown in Figure 3.24.
(a) Draw the force on the moving charge.
(b) Show that the velocity of the charge is given by $v^2 = \frac{1}{4\pi\varepsilon_0}\frac{q^2}{mr}$.
(c) Show that the total energy of the charge is given by $E = -\frac{1}{8\pi\varepsilon_0}\frac{q^2}{r}$.
(d) Hence find out how much energy must be given to the charge if it is to orbit around the stationary charge at a radius equal to $2r$.

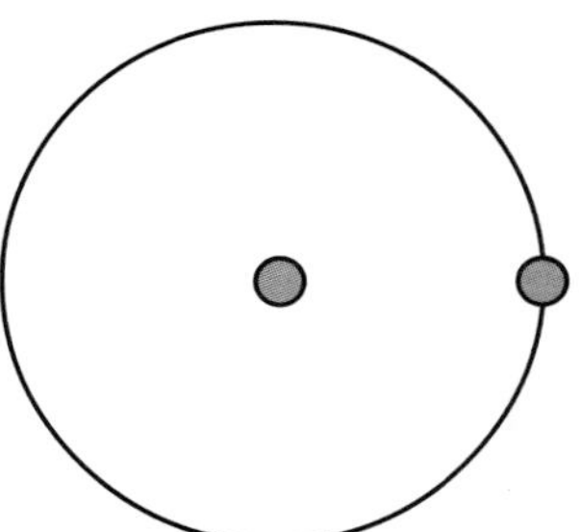

Figure 3.24 For question 16.

17 Three protons are initially very far apart. Calculate the work that must be done in order to bring these protons to the vertices of an equilateral triangle of side 5.0×10^{-16} m.

Electric current and electric resistance

The motion of electric charges creates electric currents. This chapter discusses the definition of electric current and electric resistance.

Objectives

By the end of this chapter you should be able to:

- state the definition of *electric current*, $I = \frac{\Delta Q}{\Delta t}$;
- state the definition of *electric resistance*, $R = \frac{V}{I}$;
- appreciate that metallic conductors at constant temperature satisfy *Ohm's law*, $I \propto V$;
- appreciate that the *potential* drops as one moves across a resistor in the direction of the current;
- understand that a resistor dissipates *power*, $P = VI$.

Electric current

Our study of electricity so far has dealt with stationary charges. New phenomena take place when electric charges are allowed to move, one of which is **electric current**.

▶ A moving charge creates an electric current. Electric current is the amount of charge that moves through the cross-sectional area of a wire per unit interval of time:

$$I = \frac{\Delta Q}{\Delta t}$$

The unit of electric current is the ampere, one of the fundamental units of the SI system, and $1\ \mathrm{A} = 1\ \mathrm{C\ s^{-1}}$. (The *definition* of the ampere is in terms of the magnetic force between two parallel conductors; this will be given in Chapter 5.6.)

Example question

Q1

Light falling on a metallic surface causes the emission of electrons from the surface at a rate of 2.2×10^{15} per second. What is the current leaving the surface?

Answer

The current is

$2.2 \times 10^{15} \times 1.6 \times 10^{-19}\ \mathrm{C\ s^{-1}} = 3.5 \times 10^{-4}\ \mathrm{A}$

In a conductor the 'free' electrons move randomly, much like gas molecules in a container. They do so with high speeds, of the order of $10^5\ \mathrm{m\ s^{-1}}$. This random motion, however, does not result in electric current – as many electrons move to the right as to the left (see Figure 4.1).

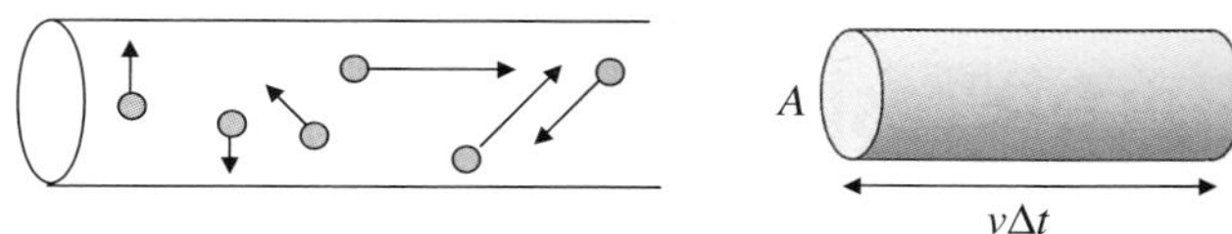

Figure 4.1 The random motion of the electrons inside a conductor takes place at high speeds but does not result in electric current. Current is the amount of charge that goes past a given point per unit interval of time.

▶ The presence of an electric field inside the conductor forces the electrons to accelerate in a direction opposite to the electric field (remember, the charge of the electron is negative) and this orderly motion of the electrons in the same direction is what makes electric current.

The electrons increase their kinetic energy as they move through the metal but soon they will suffer inelastic collisions with the atoms of the material, which means they will lose energy to the atoms. The electric field will again accelerate the electrons until the next collision and this process repeats. Thus, the electrons lose energy constantly, which the atoms of the material pick up. This means that these atoms will vibrate about their equilibrium positions more and this will show up *macroscopically* as increased temperature of the material. We can make a mechanical analogy of this (see Figure 4.2). Imagine a ball rolling down an inclined plane on which a number of pegs have been placed.

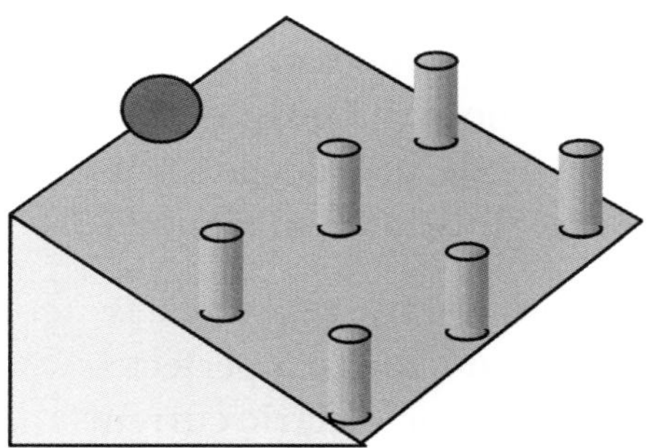

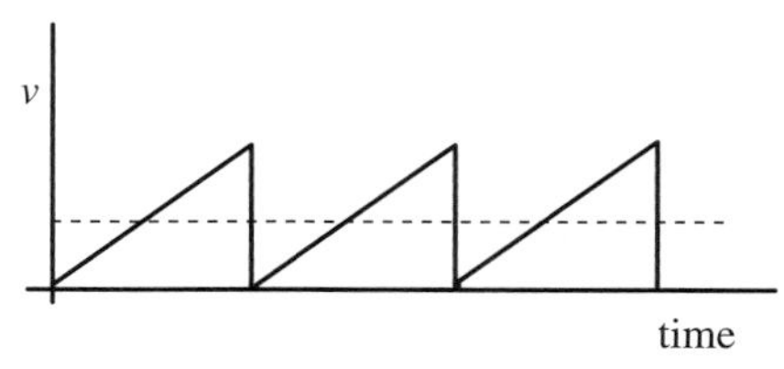

Figure 4.2 A mechanical model of the electron's motion inside a metal. The speed of the electron is increasing while the electric field is accelerating it, in between collisions. After a collision, the speed is reduced to zero and the electron begins to accelerate again. The electron's kinetic energy has been transferred to the atoms of the metal. The dotted line represents the drift velocity of the electron.

Gravity accelerates the ball down but as soon as a collision with a peg takes place, energy is lost and the ball will accelerate again from a reduced speed.

HL only

We can estimate the magnitude of the drift velocity as follows. Suppose that the conductor is a wire of cross-sectional area A and that there are n free electrons per unit volume in the material. If the electrons move with speed v, then in time Δt the number of electrons that have gone through the cross-section of the wire is simply the number of electrons inside the volume of a cylinder of cross-sectional area A and height $v\Delta t$. The number of electrons in this volume is $nAv\Delta t$, and hence the amount of charge that they carry is $enAv\Delta t$. This is the amount of charge that went past the wire in time Δt, and thus the current is

$$I = enAv$$

For a typical metal, $n = 10^{28}\ \text{m}^{-3}$; if the current is $I = 1$ A in a wire of cross-sectional area $10^{-6}\ \text{m}^2$ (a typical wire), we find $v = 6 \times 10^{-4}\ \text{m s}^{-1}$. This is quite a low speed, perhaps surprisingly so. If we turn on the switch for the lights in the classroom (which are about 5 m from the switch), we certainly do not have to wait for $\frac{5}{(6\times 10^{-4})}$ s = 139 min for the lights to come on! This is because, when the switch is turned on, an electric field is established within the wire. This happens at a speed close to the speed of light. As soon as the field is established, every free electron in the wire starts moving at the drift velocity, so the electric current is established in the conductor much faster than the velocity of the electrons making up the current.

It is a convention that the direction of electric current is taken to be opposite to the motion of the electrons, as shown in Figure 4.3.

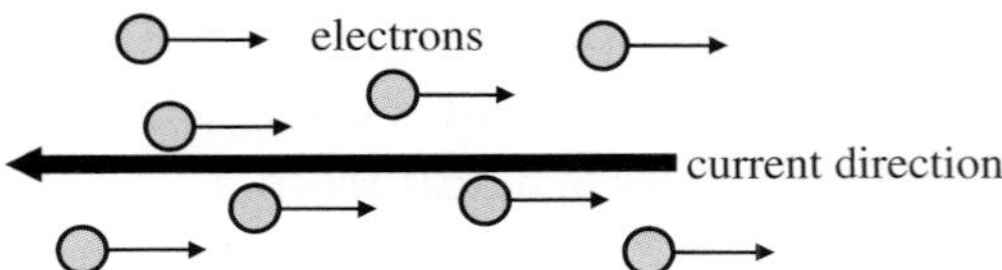

Figure 4.3 The direction of the current is taken to be opposite to the actual electron motion.

An electric current is also produced when a wire is heated so that it begins to emit electrons in a phenomenon known as thermionic emission. If the wire emits N electrons per second, the current leaving the hot wire is $I = eN$. Similarly, in the photoelectric effect, light or other electromagnetic radiation causes the emission of electrons from a metallic surface on which it falls. The emission of electrons is electric current that leaves the surface. Whereas in solid materials electric current consists exclusively of moving electrons, in liquids and especially gases positive ions may also be accelerated by electric fields, resulting in currents due to positive charges. In gases, even small electric fields can produce currents due to positive ions. This is because at low pressure electrons have a long mean free path, so they can be accelerated to high speeds by the electric field before colliding with gas molecules. These high-velocity electrons can then ionize atoms of the gas by knocking electrons out of the atoms, leaving behind positive ions, which also move under the influence of the electric field.

As a consequence of the law of conservation of charge, it follows that two devices connected in series will take the same current. When a wire comes to a junction, the current splits (not necessarily equally) so that the current entering the junction equals the total current leaving it. (See Figure 4.4.)

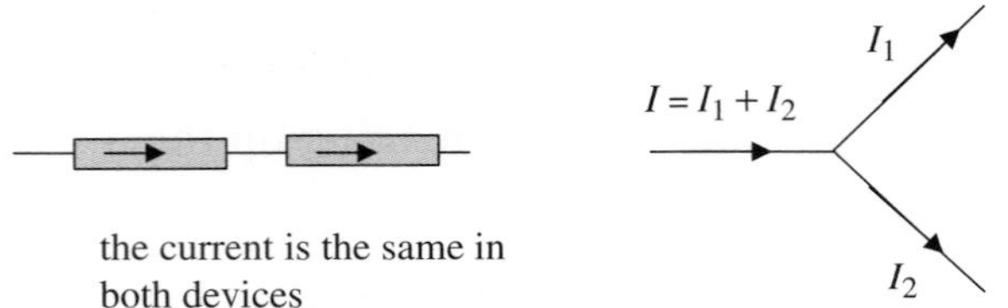

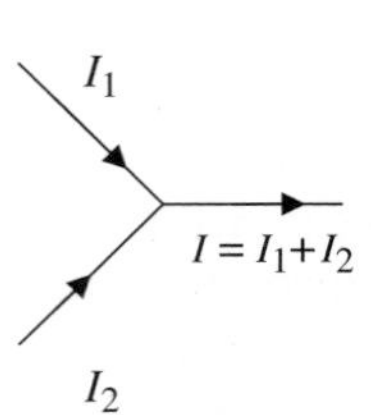

Figure 4.4 The current entering a junction equals the total current leaving it.

Electric resistance

Now we look at **electric resistance** and **Ohm's law**.

- The electric resistance of a conductor (for example, a wire of given length) is defined as the potential difference *across its ends* divided by the current flowing *through* it:

$$R = \frac{V}{I}$$

The unit of electric resistance is the volt per ampere and this is defined to be the ohm, symbol Ω. The equation above is the definition of resistance.

In 1826, Georg Ohm discovered that, when the temperature of a metallic conductor is kept constant, the current through the conductor is proportional to the potential difference across it

$$I \propto V$$

This statement is known as Ohm's law. Materials obeying Ohm's law thus have a constant resistance at constant temperature. A graph of I versus V gives a straight line through the origin if the material obeys Ohm's law.

Most materials obey Ohm's law at low temperatures, but as temperature increases, deviations from this law are seen. For example, an ordinary light bulb will obey Ohm's law as long as the current through it is small. As the current is increased, the temperature of the bulb increases and so does the resistance. Other devices, such as the diode, also deviate from Ohm's law. These are illustrated in Figure 4.5.

A conductor with zero electric resistance is known as a perfect conductor. In a perfect conductor, electric current can flow without a potential difference established at its ends. A class of materials known as *superconductors* have zero resistance below a certain temperature (known as the critical temperature) and are thus perfect conductors.

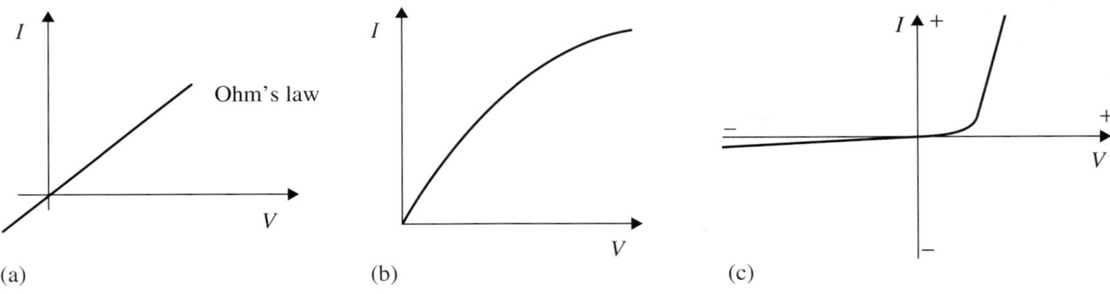

Figure 4.5 Graph (a) shows the current–voltage graph for a material obeying Ohm's law. A lamp filament (b) and a diode (c) do not obey this law.

Factors affecting the resistance of a wire

Three factors affect the resistance of a wire *kept at constant temperature*. They are the nature of the material, the length of the wire and the cross-sectional area of the wire. For metallic materials, an increase in the temperature results in an increase in the resistance.

▶ It is found from experiment that the electric resistance of a wire (at fixed temperature) is proportional to its length L and inversely proportional to the cross-sectional area A:

$$R \propto \frac{L}{A}$$

(see Figure 4.6).

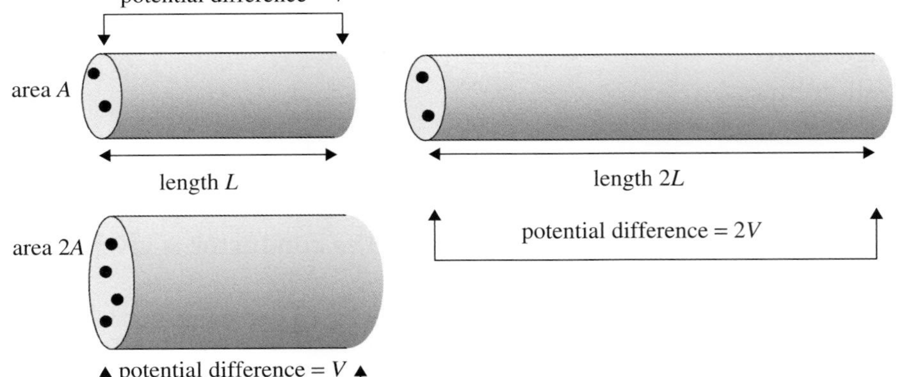

Figure 4.6 If we double the cross-sectional area A, the current that can flow through the metal for the same potential difference is doubled as well. Hence, the resistance R halves. If we double the length L, the potential difference at the ends of the wire will double while the current stays the same. Hence, the resistance R doubles.

Supplementary material

The dependence of resistance on length and cross-sectional area can also be understood as follows. If we combine the definition of resistance with $I = enAv$ and the fact that the potential difference across a length L of a wire is related to the electric field E in the wire through $V = EL$, we find that

$$R = \frac{L}{enAv}E$$

which explains the dependence on L and A.

Example question

Q2

A wire is subjected to a tension so that its length increases by 10% while the volume of the wire stays the same. How does the resistance of the wire change?

Answer

Let L and A be the original length and cross-sectional area of the wire. The new length is $1.1L$ and since the volume stays the same, the new cross-sectional area A' must satisfy

$$A'(1.1L) = AL$$

$$\Rightarrow A' = \frac{A}{1.1}$$

Since $R \propto \frac{L}{A}$, the new resistance is

$$R' = \frac{L'/A'}{L/A} = \frac{L'}{L}\frac{A}{A'} = 1.1 \times 1.1 = 1.21$$

$$\Rightarrow R' = 1.21\,R$$

that is, it increases by 21%.

Potential drop

The defining equation for resistance, $R = \frac{V}{I}$, can be looked at in the following way. Solving for the potential difference V we find

$$V = IR$$

which says that if a current flows through a resistor, then there must be a potential difference across the ends of that resistor given by the formula above. A resistor is thus said to drop the potential. (In an electric circuit we will often indicate a resistor by a box. The conducting wires also have resistance, but typically this is very small so we neglect it. The words potential difference and voltage will mean the same thing.) Suppose that in Figure 4.7, the potential at point A is 100 V, the current is 5 A and the resistance is 15 Ω. Then the *potential difference* at the ends of the resistor is $V = IR = 5 \times 15 = 75$ V. Thus, the potential at point B is 25 V. The resistance from B to C is zero, so the potential does not change as we move from B to C. The potential at all points from B to C is 25 V.

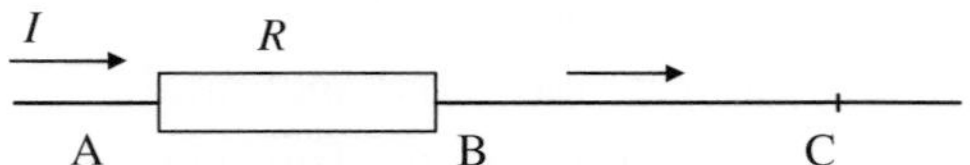

Figure 4.7 There is a potential difference across points A and B but not between B and C.

Example question

Q3

In Figure 4.8, two resistors are joined as shown. The top resistor receives a current of 3 A. What is the current in the other resistor? What is the current that enters at junction A?

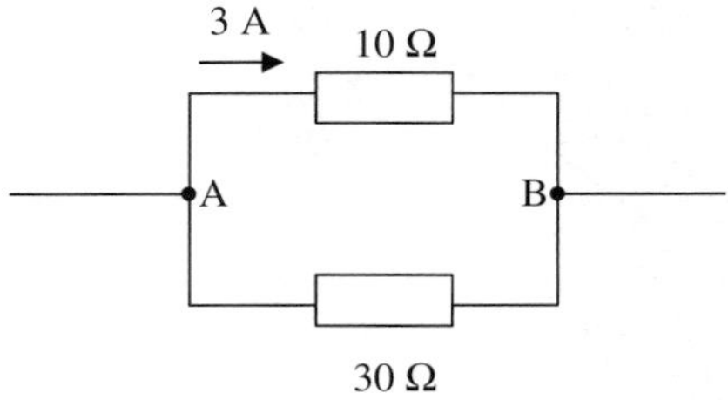

Figure 4.8.

Answer

Both resistors have the same potential difference across them (why?). The potential difference across the top resistor is

$$V = IR = 3 \times 10 = 30 \text{ V}$$

and so for the lower resistor we have

$$30 = I \times 30$$

$$\Rightarrow I = 1 \text{ A}$$

The current entering at A is 4 A.

Electric power

We saw earlier that whenever an electric charge ΔQ moves from a point A to a point B such that there exists a potential difference V between these points, work is being done. This work is $W = (\Delta Q)V$. Consider a conductor with a potential difference across its ends of V. In moving a charge ΔQ across the conductor in time Δt, the power dissipated in the conductor is

$$P = \frac{\text{work}}{\text{time}} = \frac{V\Delta Q}{\Delta t} = VI$$

since the current in the conductor is given by $I = \frac{\Delta Q}{\Delta t}$.

This power manifests itself in thermal energy and/or work performed by an electrical device (see Figure 4.9). In devices obeying Ohm's law (i.e. when the resistance is constant), we can use $R = \frac{V}{I}$ to rewrite the formula for power in equivalent ways:

$$P = RI^2 = \frac{V^2}{R}$$

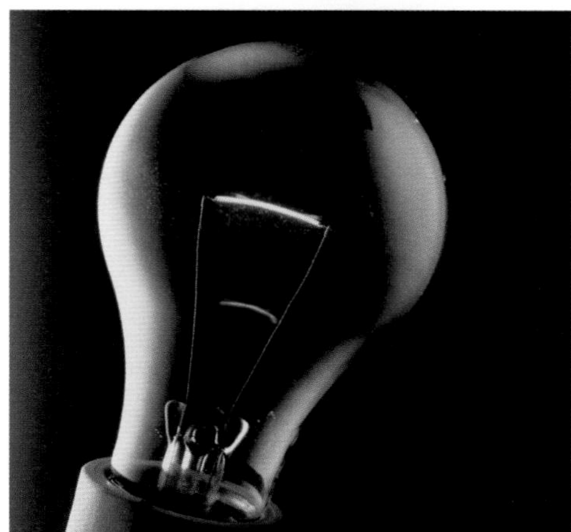

Figure 4.9 The metal filament in a light bulb glows as the current passes through it. It also feels warm. This shows that the bulb produces both heat and light.

Example question

Q4

A resistor of resistance 12 Ω has a current of 2.0 A flowing through it. How much energy is generated in the resistor in one minute?

Answer

The power generated in the resistor is

$$\begin{aligned} P &= RI^2 \\ &= 12 \times 4 \text{ W} \\ &= 48 \text{ W} \end{aligned}$$

Thus, in one minute (60 s) the energy generated is

$48 \times 60 \text{ J} = 2.9 \times 10^3 \text{ J}$

Electrical devices are usually rated according to the power they use. A light bulb rated as 60 W at 220 V means that it will dissipate 60 W *when a potential difference of* 220 V *is applied across its ends*. If the potential difference across its ends is anything other than 220 V, the power dissipated will be different from 60 W.

Example questions

Q5

A light bulb rated as 60 W at 220 V has a potential difference of 110 V across its ends. Find the power dissipated in this light bulb.

Answer

Let R be the resistance of the light bulb and P the power we want to find. Assuming R stays constant (so that it is the same when 220 V and 110 V are applied to its ends) we have

$$P = \frac{110^2}{R} \quad \text{and} \quad 60 = \frac{220^2}{R}$$

Dividing these equations side by side we find

$$\begin{aligned} \frac{P}{60} &= \frac{110^2/R}{220^2/R} \\ &= \frac{110^2}{220^2} \\ &= \frac{1}{4} \\ \Rightarrow P &= 60 \times \frac{1}{4} \\ &= 15 \text{ W} \end{aligned}$$

Q6

Figure 4.10 shows the variation of voltage across a conductor with the current through the conductor. Does it obey Ohm's law? What is the resistance of the conductor when the current through it is 0.6 A? What is the power dissipated in the conductor when the voltage across it is 1.5 V?

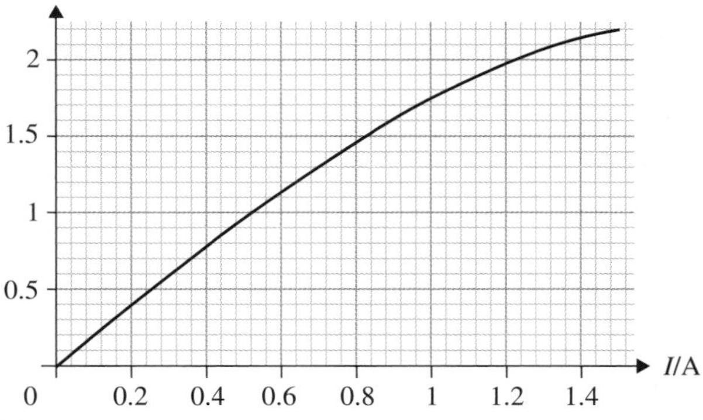

Figure 4.10.

Answer

The graph is straight only for small currents (less than about 0.5 A) and so the conductor obeys Ohm's law only for these small currents.

The resistance at 0.60 A is

$$\begin{aligned} R &= \frac{V}{I} \\ &\approx \frac{1.2}{0.60} \\ &= 2.0 \ \Omega \end{aligned}$$

When the voltage is 1.5 V, the current is about 0.82 A, so

$$P = VI$$
$$\approx 1.5 \times 0.82$$
$$= 1.2 \text{ W}$$

The cost of electricity

Electricity companies charge for electricity according to the amount of energy used by the consumer. A device that is rated at a power value of 60 W, for example an ordinary light bulb, uses 60 J of energy every second (when connected to the appropriate source of voltage). The energy used by the light bulb over a time of t s is thus $E = 60t$ J. In general, for a device of power rating P the energy used in t s is

$$E = Pt$$
$$= VIt$$

Electricity companies find it more convenient to use a different energy unit by which to charge consumers. They use the kilowatt-hour (kW h) as their energy unit, which is defined as the energy used by a device of power rating 1 kW in 1 h. This means that

$$1 \text{ kW h} = 1000 \text{ W} \times 60 \times 60 \text{ s} = 3.6 \times 10^6 \text{ J}$$

If the cost of 1 kW h is, say, \$0.1, then the cost of operating one 60 W light bulb over a 24 h period can be calculated as follows:

$$\text{energy used} = 60 \text{ W} \times 24 \text{ h} = 1440 \text{ W h}$$
$$\approx 1.4 \text{ kW h}$$

Hence

$$\text{cost} = 1.4 \times \$0.1 = \$0.14$$

? QUESTIONS

1 Outline the mechanism by which electric current heats up the material through which it flows.

2 Explain why a light bulb is most likely to burn out when it is first turned on rather than later.

3 State the factors that affect the resistance of a metal wire.

4 Explain why doubling the length of a wire will double its resistance.

5 By what factor does the resistance of a wire change if its radius is doubled?

6 Give an estimate for the number of free electrons per unit volume for gold (density 19 390 kg m^{-3}; molar mass 197 g mol^{-1}). Assume that each atom contributes just one electron to the set of free electrons.

7 Silver has 5.8×10^{28} free electrons per m^3. If the current in a 2 mm radius silver wire is 5.0 A, find the velocity with which the electrons drift in the wire.

8 (a) If a current of 10.0 A flows through a heater, how much charge passes through the heater in 1 h?
(b) How many electrons does this charge correspond to?

9 The graphs in Figure 4.11 show the current as a function of voltage across the same piece of metal wire which is kept at two different temperatures.
(a) Does the wire obey Ohm's law?
(b) Which of the two graphs corresponds to the higher temperature?

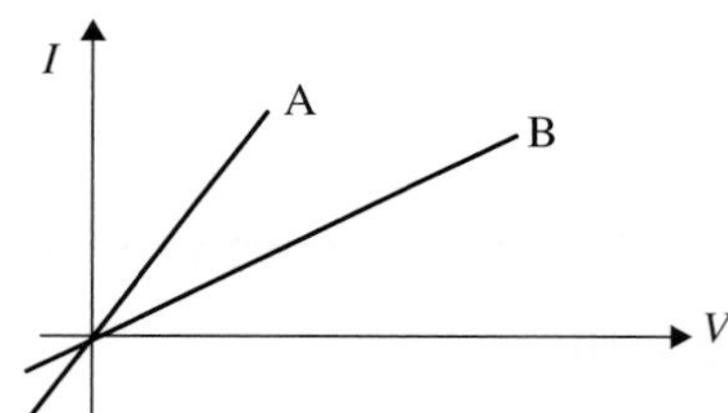

Figure 4.11 For question 9.

10 The current in a device obeying Ohm's law is 1.5 A when connected to a source of potential difference 6.0 V. What will the potential difference across the same device be when a current of 3.5 A flows in it?

11 In an experiment the current through and potential difference across a device were recorded as shown in Table 4.1. Does the device obey Ohm's law?

I/mA	5.0	9.8	11.5	14.0	17.2	21.2
V/mV	100	200	300	400	500	600

Table 4.1 For question 11.

12 A resistor obeying Ohm's law is measured to have a resistance of 12 Ω when a current of 3 A flows in it. What is the resistance when the current is 4 A?

13 The heating element of an electric kettle has a current of 15 A when connected to a source of potential difference 220V. What is its resistance?

14 The resistance of a fixed length of wire of circular cross-section is 10.0 Ω. What will be the resistance of a wire of the same length made of the same material but with only half the radius?

15 Look at Figure 4.12. The potential at point A is 24 V and a current of 2 A flows in the wire.
(a) What is the potential difference across each resistor?
(b) Find the potential at points B, C and D.

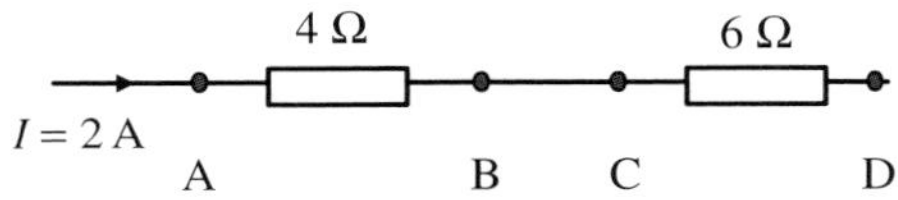

Figure 4.12 For question 15.

16 Look at Figure 4.13.
(a) Find the current in, and potential difference across, each resistor. The potential at A is 12 V.
(b) What is the potential difference between A and B?

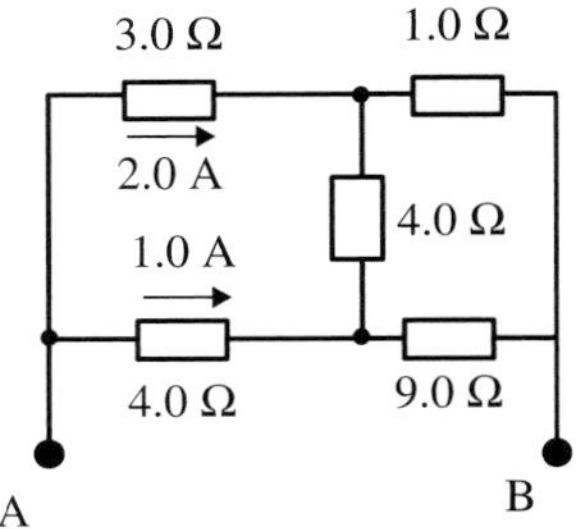

Figure 4.13 For question 16.

17 A light bulb is rated as 60 W at 220 V.
(a) How much current flows in the light bulb if it is connected to a 220 V source of voltage?
(b) If the light bulb is connected to a 110 V source of voltage, what current flows in it? (Assume the resistance stays the same.)
(c) What is the power output of the light bulb when it is connected to the 110 V source?

18 The resistance of a wire of length L and cross-sectional area A is given by $R = \rho\frac{L}{A}$, where ρ is a constant called the resistivity. The filament of an ordinary 120 W light bulb has a resistivity of 2.0×10^{-6} Ω m.
(a) What is its resistance when it is connected to a source of 220 V?
(b) If the radius of the filament is 0.03 mm, find its length.

19 Find the energy used when a 1500 W kettle is used for 4 minutes:
(a) in kW h;
(b) in joules.

20 In the USA the voltage supplied by the electricity companies is 110 V and in Europe it is 220 V. Consider a light bulb rated as 60 W at 110 V in the USA and a light bulb rated as 60 W at 220 V in Europe. Take the cost of electricity per kW h to be the same. Where does it cost more to operate a light bulb for 1 hour?

Electric circuits

This chapter explains how simple electric circuits can be solved: that is, how the current through and potential difference across resistors can be determined. The chapter begins with the concept of emf (which stands for electromotive force). The name is unfortunate, as emf is a potential difference and not a force. Hence, we always use the initials emf and never the full name. The chapter ends with a look at the potential divider circuit and sensors that use it.

Objectives

By the end of this chapter you should be able to:

- define *emf* and explain the role of *internal resistance* – the potential difference across a battery is $V = \mathcal{E} - Ir$;
- find the total resistance in *series* and *parallel* connections using $R_{\text{total}} = R_1 + R_2 + \cdots$ and $\frac{1}{R_{\text{total}}} = \frac{1}{R_1} + \frac{1}{R_2} + \cdots$;
- find the current through, and potential difference across, resistors in *simple circuits*;
- find the *power dissipated* by a resistor in a circuit using $P = VI$;
- describe the *potential divider*;
- explain the use of *sensors* in potential divider circuits.

Emf

Charges will not drift in the same direction inside a conductor unless a potential difference is established at the ends of the conductor. There are many ways of providing *a source of potential difference* to the circuit. The most common is the connection of a *battery* in the circuit. Others include a *generator*, a *thermocouple* and a *photosurface*. To understand the function of the battery, we can use the standard analogy in which the battery is likened to a pump that forces water through pipes up to a certain height and down again (see Figure 5.1). The gravitational force does work equal to $-mgh$ in lifting a mass m of water up to the height h, and work equal to $+mgh$ on the way down. The net work done by the gravitational force is thus zero. Because frictional forces are present, work must be done by the pump to compensate for the work done by these forces. In the absence of the pump, the water flow would stop.

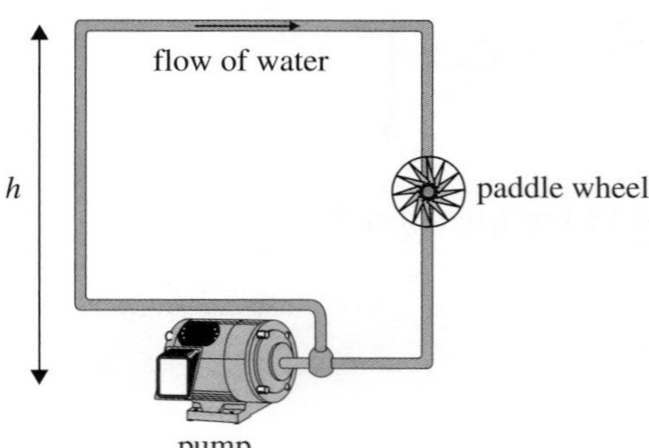

Figure 5.1 In the absence of the pump, the water flow would stop. The work done by the pump equals the work done to overcome frictional forces plus work done to operate devices, such as, for example, a paddle wheel.

If, in addition, the water drives a machine to perform useful work (for example, by turning a paddle wheel), then the pump would have to do work to allow for that as well.

In an electric circuit a battery performs a role similar to the pump's. A battery converts the energy it stores (chemical energy) into electrical energy. The work done by the electrical forces on a charge that moves in the circuit is zero, just as the net work done by gravitational force in the pump and water system described above is zero. Similarly, if a generator is used, the energy that gets converted into electrical energy is the mechanical energy that turns the coils of the generator. In the case of the thermocouple, it is thermal energy. In the case of the photosurface, it is solar energy.

In a battery, the electrons must be pushed from the positive to the negative terminal, which means work must be done *on the electrons* (see Figure 5.2).

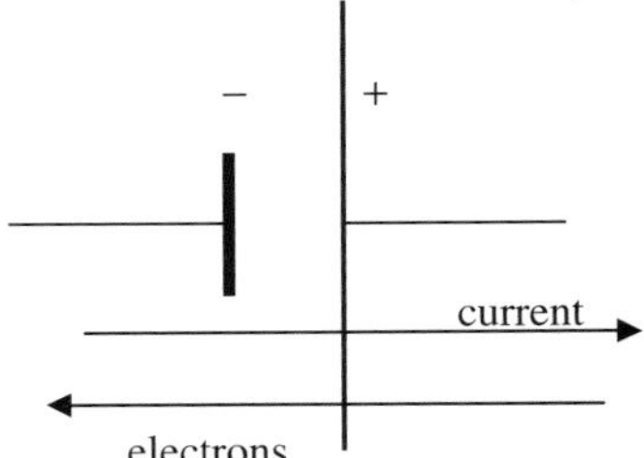

Figure 5.2.

▶ The total work done in moving a unit charge completely around the circuit is called the emf $\mathcal{E}$. Hence if a battery does work W in moving charge q around the circuit then

$$\mathcal{E} = \text{emf} = \frac{W}{q}$$

The unit of emf is the volt. (Emf may also be defined as the total power generated by the battery per unit current.)

Suppose we connect a voltmeter to the ends of a battery. We may assign the value of 0 V to the negative terminal of the battery. Then the positive terminal has a potential equal to the emf, $\mathcal{E}$. The chemicals inside the battery create a small resistance r, called the internal resistance of the cell. We cannot isolate this resistance – it is inside the battery and we may assume that it is connected in series to the cell. If the current that leaves the battery is I, then the potential difference across the internal resistance is Ir. In other words, the internal resistance reduces the voltage from a value of $\mathcal{E}$ on its left side to the value $\mathcal{E}-Ir$ on the right side. The potential difference across the battery is therefore

$$V = \mathcal{E} - Ir$$

We see that $V = \mathcal{E}$ when $I = 0$. This gives an alternative and less precise definition of the emf: the emf is the potential difference across the battery when the battery sends out zero current. (See Figure 5.3.)

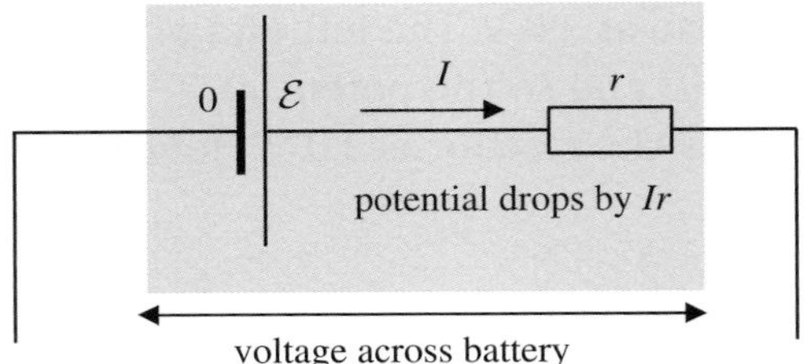

Figure 5.3 The potential difference across the battery terminals is less than the emf of the battery.

Example question

Q1

A battery of emf 12 V and internal resistance $r = 1.5\ \Omega$ produces a current of 3.0 A. What is the potential difference across the battery terminals?

Answer

We find

$$\begin{aligned} V &= \mathcal{E} - Ir \\ &= 12 - 3 \times 1.5 \\ &= 7.5\ \text{V} \end{aligned}$$

In Figure 5.4, a battery forces a current I into a circuit that contains a resistor of resistance R. The connecting wires are assumed to have zero resistance.

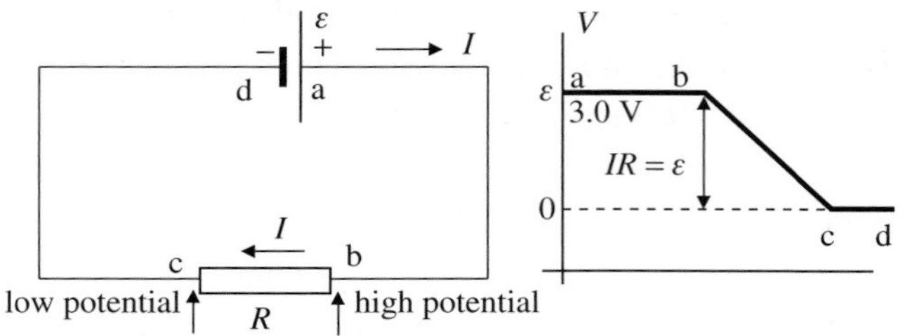

Figure 5.4 A battery connected to a circuit. The current flows into the circuit away from the positive terminal. This is the conventional definition of current. The electrons actually move in the opposite way.

If the emf of the battery in the circuit is 3.0 V (neglecting its internal resistance) and the resistance of the circuit is 1.5 Ω, the current can easily be determined. The positive terminal of the battery may be taken to be 3.0 V and so the negative terminal must be taken to be at 0 V (to give an emf of 3 V). Thus, the right end of the resistor is also at 3.0 V. The left end of the resistor is at 0.0 V and so the potential difference across the resistor is 3.0 V. Hence, the current is 2.0 A.

Simple electric circuits

A simple circuit will consist of a single battery and a number of resistors. When we talk about solving a circuit, we mean finding the current through and voltage across every resistor in the circuit. Here we will develop the methods to do just that. Table 5.1 shows the circuit symbols that you need.

Series circuits

First, let us consider a part of a circuit consisting of a number of resistors connected in *series*. This means that the resistors have the same current through them. An example with three resistors is shown in Figure 5.5. Let I be the common current in the three resistors.

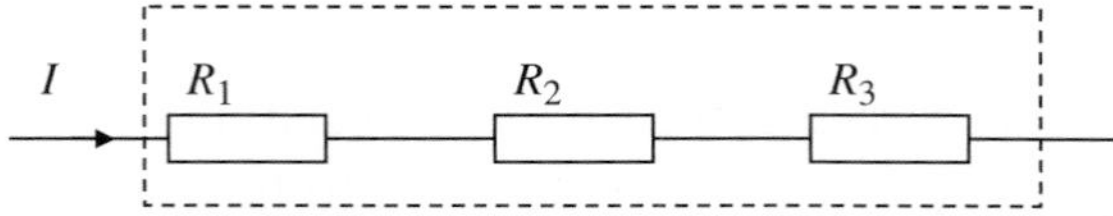

Figure 5.5 Three resistors in series.

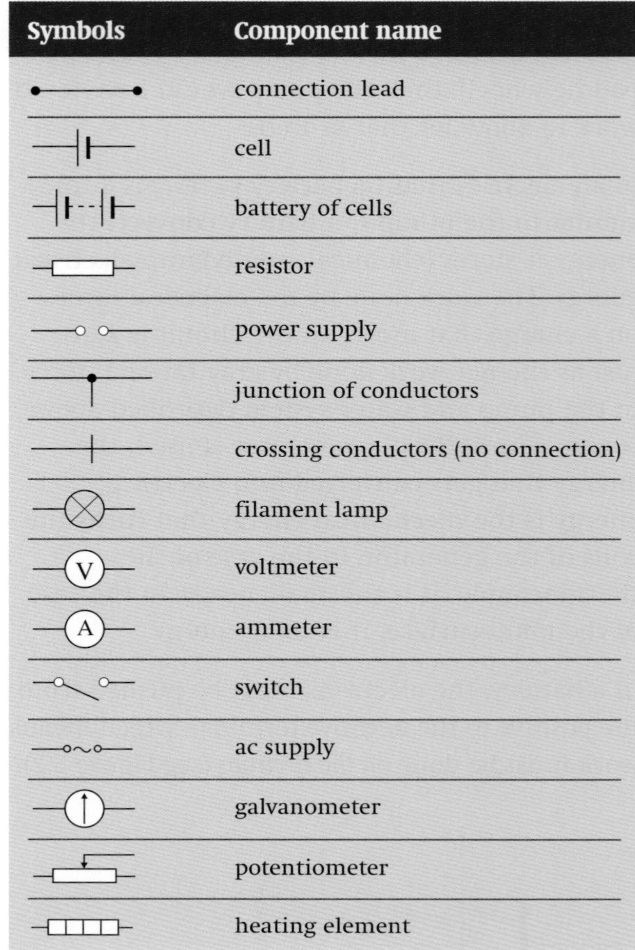

Symbols	Component name
	connection lead
	cell
	battery of cells
	resistor
	power supply
	junction of conductors
	crossing conductors (no connection)
	filament lamp
	voltmeter
	ammeter
	switch
	ac supply
	galvanometer
	potentiometer
	heating element

Table 5.1 Names of electrical components and their circuit symbols.

The potential difference across the resistors is

$$V_1 = IR_1, \quad V_2 = IR_2 \quad \text{and} \quad V_3 = IR_3$$

The sum of the potential differences is thus

$$V = IR_1 + IR_2 + IR_3 = I(R_1 + R_2 + R_3)$$

If we were to replace the three resistors by a *single* resistor of value $R_1 + R_2 + R_3$ (in other words, if we were to replace the contents of the dotted box in Figure 5.5 with a single resistor, as in the circuit shown in Figure 5.6), we would not be able to tell the difference. The *same current* flows into the dotted box and the *same potential difference* exists across its ends. We thus define the equivalent or total resistance of the three resistors of Figure 5.5 by

$$R_{total} = R_1 + R_2 + R_3$$

(If more than three were present, we would simply add all of them. The formula shows that the total resistance is larger than the individual ones being added.)

In a circuit, the combination of resistors of Figure 5.5 is equivalent to the single total or equivalent resistor. Suppose we now connect the three resistors to a battery of negligible internal resistance and emf equal to 24 V. Suppose that $R_1 = 2\,\Omega$, $R_2 = 6\,\Omega$ and $R_3 = 4\,\Omega$. The circuit is shown in the top diagram of Figure 5.6. Note that we know that the potential at point A is 24 V and at point B it is 0 V. (We *do not* know the potential difference across any of the three resistors individually.) In the bottom diagram, we have replaced the three resistors by the equivalent resistor of $R_{\text{total}} = 2 + 6 + 4 = 12\,\Omega$. We now observe that the potential difference across the equivalent resistor is known. It is simply 24 V and hence the current through the equivalent resistor is found as follows:

$$R = \frac{V}{I}$$

$$\Rightarrow I = \frac{V}{R} = \frac{24}{12} = 2\,\text{A}$$

This current, therefore, is also the current that enters the dotted box: that is, it is the current in each of the three resistors of the original circuit. We may thus deduce that the potential differences across the three resistors are

$$V_1 = IR_1 = 4\,\text{V}$$
$$V_2 = IR_2 = 12\,\text{V}$$
$$V_3 = IR_3 = 8\,\text{V}$$

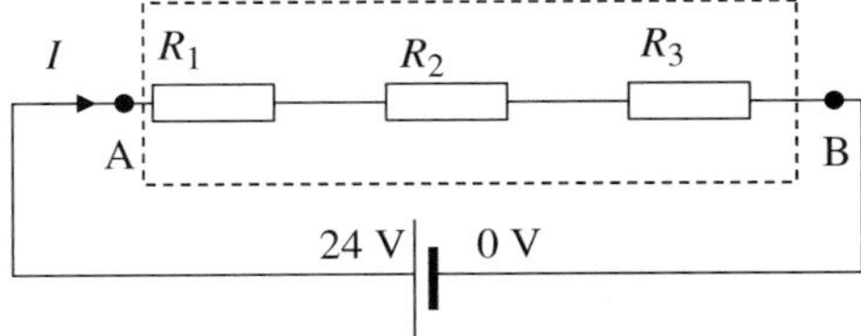

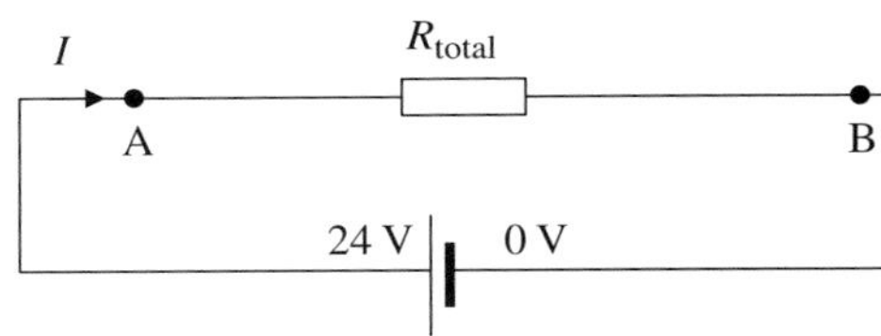

Figure 5.6 The top circuit is replaced by the equivalent circuit containing just one resistor.

Suppose now that we cannot neglect the internal resistance of the battery. The internal resistance is connected in series to the other resistances and so, if its value is $r = 1.0\,\Omega$, the total circuit resistance is $1 + 2 + 6 + 4 = 13\,\Omega$. The current leaving the battery is thus $\frac{24}{13} = 1.85$ A. The potential difference across the battery terminals is

$$\begin{aligned} V &= \mathcal{E} - Ir \\ &= 24 - 1.85 \times 1 \\ &= 22.15\,\text{V} \end{aligned}$$

which is less than the emf, as we expected.

Parallel circuits

Consider now part of another circuit, in which the current splits into three other currents that flow in three resistors, as shown in Figure 5.7. The current that enters the junction at A must equal the current that leaves the junction, by the law of conservation of charge. Furthermore, we note that the left ends of the three resistors are at the same potential (the potential at A) and the right ends are all at the potential of B. Hence, the three resistors have the same potential difference across them. This is called a *parallel* connection.

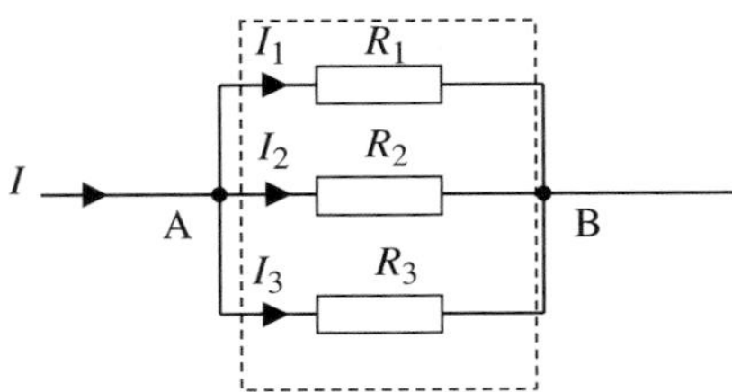

Figure 5.7 Three resistors connected in parallel.

We must then have that

$$I = I_1 + I_2 + I_3$$

Let V be the common potential difference across the resistors. Then

$$I_1 = \frac{V}{R_1}, \quad I_2 = \frac{V}{R_2} \quad \text{and} \quad I_3 = \frac{V}{R_3}$$

and so

$$\begin{aligned} I &= \frac{V}{R_1} + \frac{V}{R_2} + \frac{V}{R_3} \\ &= V\left(\frac{1}{R_1} + \frac{1}{R_2} + \frac{1}{R_3}\right) \end{aligned}$$

If we replace the three resistors in the dotted box with a single resistor, the potential difference across it would be V and the current through it would be I. Thus

$$I = \frac{V}{R_{\text{total}}}$$

Comparing with the last equation, we find

$$\frac{1}{R_{\text{total}}} = \frac{1}{R_1} + \frac{1}{R_2} + \frac{1}{R_3}$$

The formula shows that the total resistance is *smaller* than any of the individual resistances being added.

▶ We have thus learned how to replace resistors that are connected in series (same current) or parallel (same potential difference across) by a single resistor in each case, thus greatly simplifying the circuit.

A typical circuit will contain both series and parallel connections. In Figure 5.8, the two top resistors are in series. They are equivalent to a single resistor of 12 Ω. This resistor and the 6 Ω resistor are in parallel, so together they are equivalent to a single resistor of

$$\frac{1}{R_{\text{total}}} = \frac{1}{12} + \frac{1}{6} = \frac{1}{4}$$

$$\Rightarrow R_{\text{total}} = 4\ \Omega$$

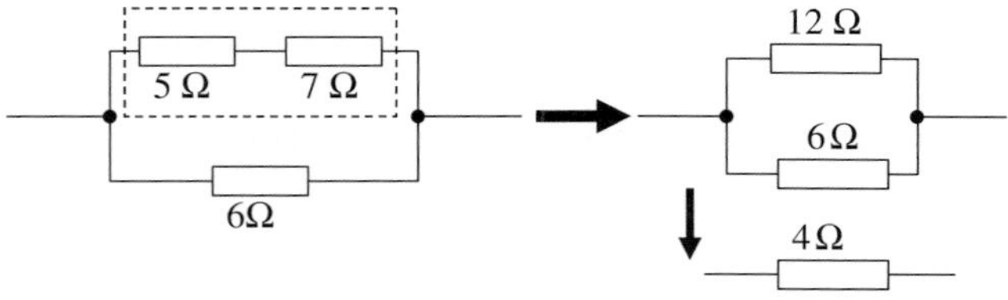

Figure 5.8 Part of a circuit with both series and parallel connections.

Consider now Figure 5.9. The two top 6 Ω resistors are in series, so they are equivalent to a 12 Ω resistor. This, in turn, is in parallel with the other 6 Ω resistor, so the left block is equivalent to

$$\frac{1}{R_{\text{total}}} = \frac{1}{12} + \frac{1}{6} = \frac{1}{4}$$

$$\Rightarrow R_{\text{total}} = 4\ \Omega$$

Let us go to the right block. The 12 Ω and the 24 Ω resistors are in series, so they are equivalent to 36 Ω. This is in parallel with the top 12 Ω, so the equivalent resistor of the right block is

$$\frac{1}{R_{\text{total}}} = \frac{1}{36} + \frac{1}{12} = \frac{1}{9}$$

$$\Rightarrow R_{\text{total}} = 9\ \Omega$$

The overall resistance is thus

$$4 + 9 = 13\ \Omega$$

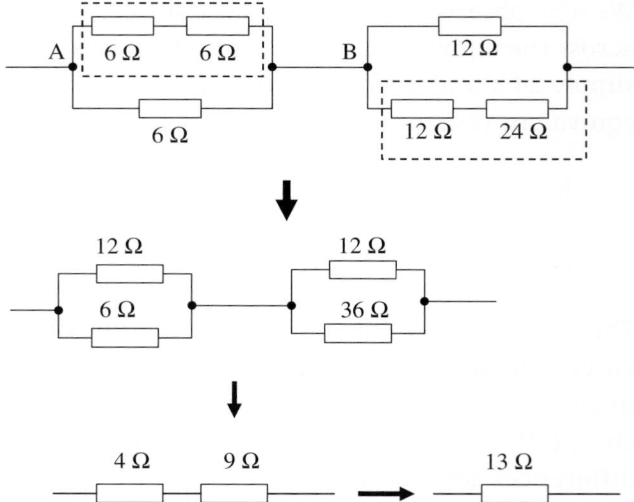

Figure 5.9 A complicated part of a circuit containing many parallel and series connections.

Suppose now that this part of the circuit is connected to a source of emf 156 V (and negligible internal resistance). The current that leaves the source is $I = \frac{156}{13} = 12$ A. When it arrives at point A, it will split into two parts. Let the current in the top part be I_1 and that in the bottom part I_2. We have $I_1 + I_2 = 12$ A. We also have that $12I_1 = 6I_2$, since the top and bottom resistors of the block beginning at point A are in parallel and so have the same potential difference across them. Thus, $I_1 = 4$ A and $I_2 = 8$ A. Similarly, in the block beginning at point B the top current is 9 A and the bottom current is 3 A.

Example questions

Q2

Find the total resistance in each of the circuits shown in Figure 5.10.

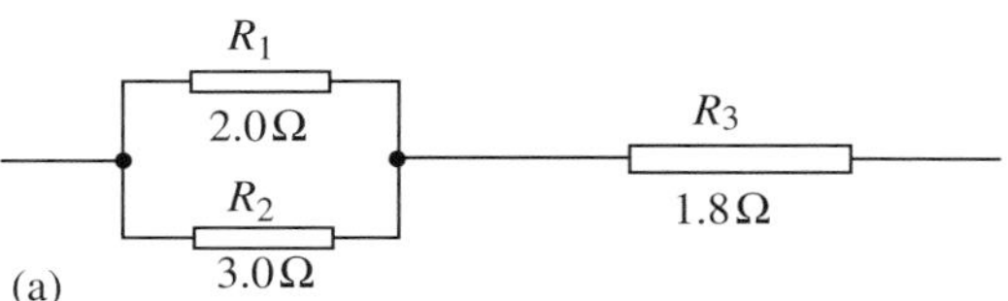

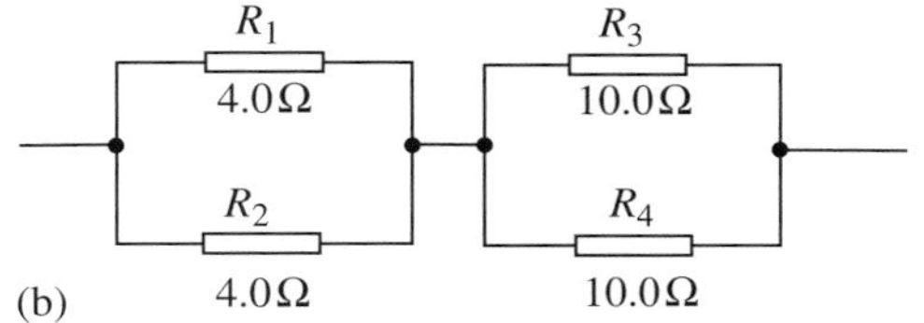

Figure 5.10.

Answer

(a) R_1 and R_2 are in parallel, so together they are equivalent to a resistor R where

$$\frac{1}{R} = \frac{1}{2.0} + \frac{1}{3.0}$$
$$= \frac{5.0}{6.0}$$
$$\Rightarrow R = \frac{6.0}{5.0}$$
$$= 1.2\ \Omega$$

Now, this R is in series with R_3, so together they are equivalent to

$$R_{\text{total}} = (1.2 + 1.8)\ \Omega$$
$$= 3.0\ \Omega$$

(b) R_1 and R_2 are in parallel, so together they are equivalent to a resistor R where

$$\frac{1}{R} = \frac{1}{4.0} + \frac{1}{4.0}$$
$$= \frac{1.0}{2.0}$$
$$\Rightarrow R = \frac{2.0}{1.0}$$
$$= 2.0\ \Omega$$

Similarly, R_3 and R_4 are in parallel so they are equivalent to a resistor of 5.0 Ω. The 2.0 Ω and 5.0 Ω are in series, so the overall total is 7.0 Ω.

Q3

What is the total current in the circuit in Figure 5.11?

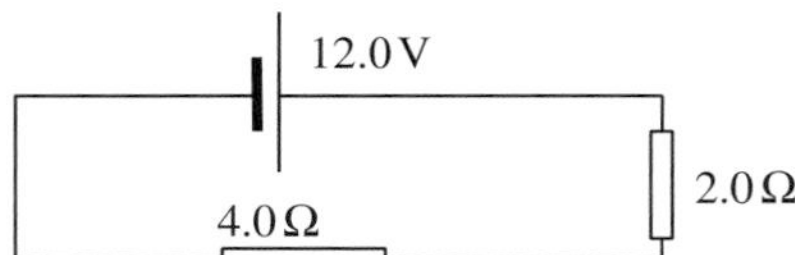

Figure 5.11.

Answer

The emf of the battery is 12 V. The total resistance of the circuit is 2.0 + 4.0 = 6.0 Ω. Thus, the total current is

$$I = \frac{12.0}{6.0}\text{A}$$
$$= 2.0\ \text{A}$$

Q4

What is the potential difference across each resistor in Example question 3?

Answer

The current through the 2.0 Ω resistor is 2.0 A, so the potential difference across it is $RI = 4.0$ V. Across the other resistor it is $RI = 4.0 \times 2.0\ \text{V} = 8.0$ V. Note that the sum of the potential differences across each resistor adds up to the emf of the battery.

Q5

Find the current in each of the resistors in the circuit shown in Figure 5.12.

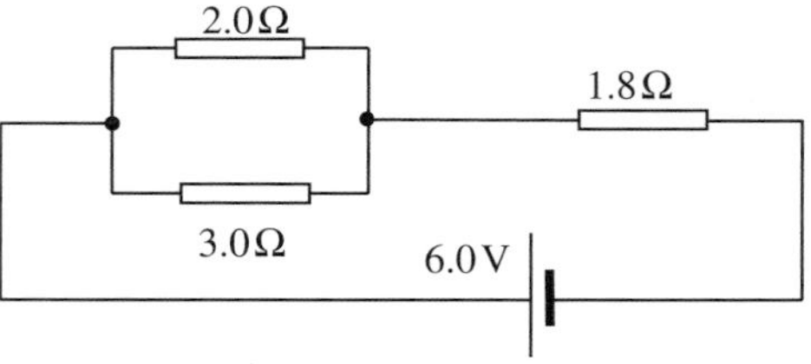

Figure 5.12.

Answer

The resistors of 2.0 Ω and 3.0 Ω are connected in parallel and are equivalent to a single resistor of resistance R found from

$$\frac{1}{R} = \frac{1}{2} + \frac{1}{3}$$
$$= \frac{5}{6}$$
$$\Rightarrow R = \frac{6}{5}$$
$$= 1.2\ \Omega$$

In turn, this is in series with the resistance of 1.8 Ω, so the total equivalent circuit resistance is 1.8 + 1.2 = 3.0 Ω. The current that leaves the battery is thus

$$I = \frac{6.0}{3.0}$$
$$= 2.0\ \text{A}$$

The potential difference across the 1.8 Ω resistor is thus $V = 1.8 \times 2.0 = 3.6$ V, leading to a potential difference across the two parallel resistors of $V = 6.0 - 3.6 = 2.4$ V. Thus the current in the 2 Ω resistor is

$$I = \frac{2.4}{2.0}$$
$$= 1.2\ \text{A}$$

and in the 3 Ω resistor is

$$I = \frac{2.4}{3.0}$$
$$= 0.80\ \text{A}$$

As a check, we see that 1.2 + 0.80 = 2.0 A, as it should be.

Q6

Find the current in each resistor in the circuit in Figure 5.13.

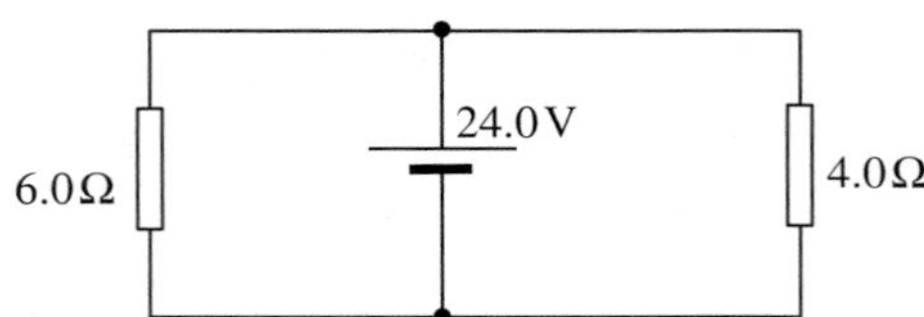

Figure 5.13.

Answer

The voltage across the 4.0 Ω resistor is 24.0 V and thus the current is 6.0 A. The voltage is 24.0 V across the other resistor as well, and so the current through it is 4.0 A. The current leaving the battery is 10.0 A.

Q7

Look at Figure 5.14. What is the potential difference between A and B? What is the current leaving the battery?

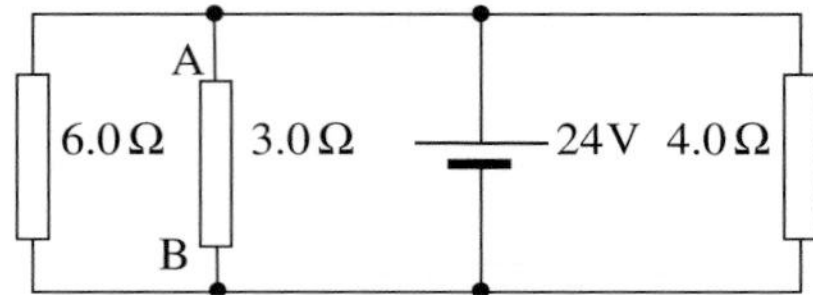

Figure 5.14.

Answer

The potential difference is 24 V for all resistors. The currents in the resistors are 8 A, 6 A and 4 A, respectively. The total current is thus 18 A.

Q8

Look at Figure 5.15. What is the current in the 2.0 Ω resistor when the switch is open and when the switch is closed? What is the potential difference across the two marked points, A and B, when the switch is open and when the switch is closed?

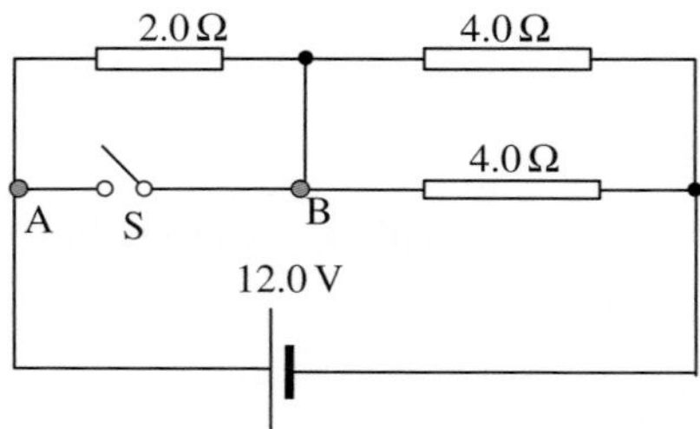

Figure 5.15.

Answer

When the switch is open, the total resistance is 4.0 Ω and thus the total current is 3.0 A. This is the current through the 2.0 Ω resistor. The potential at A is 12 V. The potential difference across the 2.0 Ω resistor is $2 \times 3 = 6$ V and so the potential at its right end, and hence at B, is 6 V. The potential difference across points A and B is thus 6 V.

When the switch is closed, no current flows through the 2.0 Ω resistor, since all the current takes the path through the switch, which offers no resistance. (The 2.0 Ω resistor has been *shorted out*.) The resistance of the circuit is then 2.0 Ω and the current leaving the battery is 6 A. The potential difference across points A and B is now zero. There is current flowing from A to B, but the resistance from A to B is zero. Hence the potential difference is 6 × 0 = 0 V.

Q9

Four light bulbs each of constant resistance 60 Ω are connected as shown in Figure 5.16. Find the power in each light bulb. If light bulb A burns out, find the power in each light bulb and the potential difference across the burned-out light bulb.

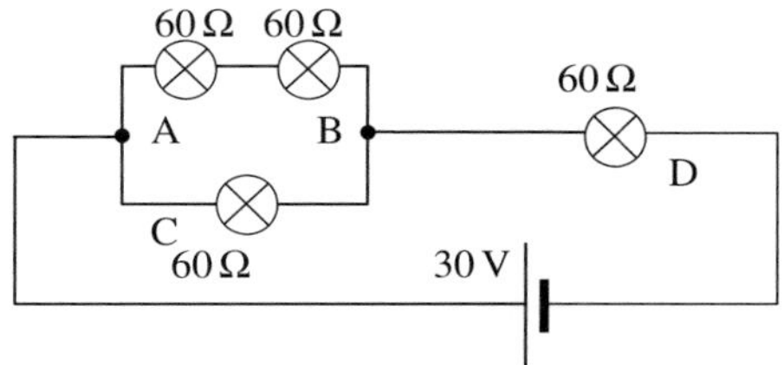

Figure 5.16.

Answer

A and B are connected in series so they are equivalent to one resistor of value $R = 60 + 60 = 120\ \Omega$. This is connected in parallel to C, giving a total resistance of

$$\frac{1}{R} = \frac{1}{120} + \frac{1}{60}$$
$$= \frac{1}{40}$$
$$\Rightarrow R = 40\ \Omega$$

Finally, this is in series with D, giving a total circuit resistance of $R = 40 + 60 = 100\ \Omega$. The current leaving the battery is thus $I = \frac{30}{100} = 0.3$ A. The current through A and B is 0.1 A and that through C is 0.2 A. The current through D is 0.3 A. Hence the power in each light bulb is

$$P_A = P_B$$
$$= 60 \times (0.1)^2$$
$$= 0.6\ \text{W}$$
$$P_C = 60 \times (0.2)^2$$
$$= 2.4\ \text{W}$$
$$P_D = 60 \times (0.3)^2$$
$$= 5.4\ \text{W}$$

With light bulb A burnt out, the circuit is as shown in Figure 5.17.

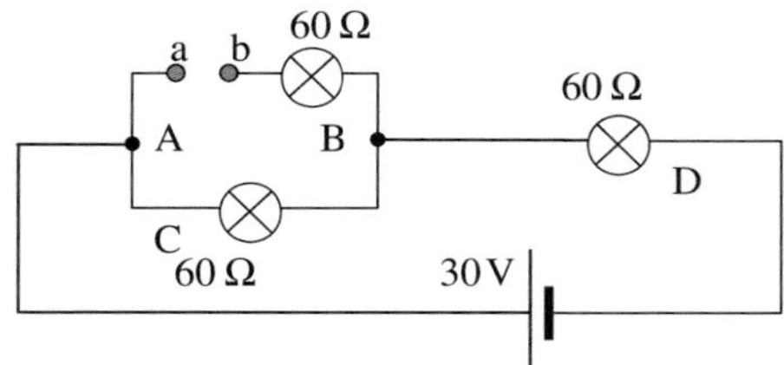

Figure 5.17.

Light bulb B gets no current, so we are left with only C and D connected in series, giving a total resistance of $R = 60 + 60 = 120\ \Omega$. The current is thus $I = 0.25$ A. The power in C and D is thus

$$P_C = P_D$$
$$= 60 \times (0.25)^2$$
$$= 3.75\ \text{W}$$

We see that D becomes dimmer and C brighter. The potential at point a is 30 V. The potential difference across light bulb C is

$$V = IR$$
$$= 0.25 \times 60$$
$$= 15\ \text{V}$$

and so the potential at the right end of C is 15 V. Light bulb B takes no current, so the potential difference across it is zero. Thus, the potential at point b is also 15 V. The potential difference across points a and b is therefore 15 V.

Ammeters and voltmeters

The current through a resistor is measured by an instrument called an ammeter, which is connected in series to the resistor as shown in Figure 5.18.

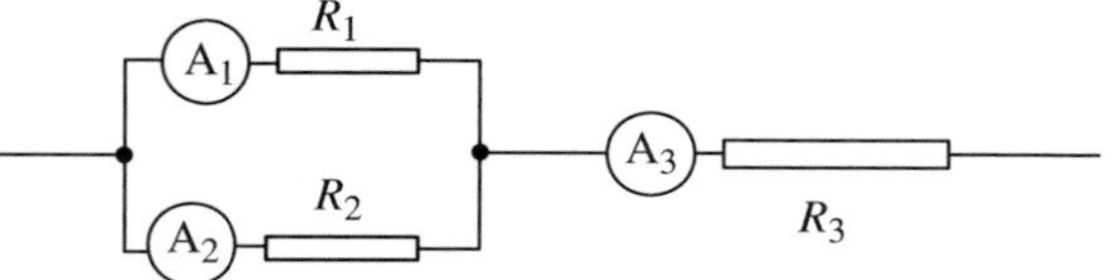

Figure 5.18 An ammeter measures the current in the resistor connected in series to it.

The ammeter itself has a small electric resistance. However, an *ideal ammeter has zero resistance* and throughout this book we are assuming that we are dealing with ideal ammeters.

Example question

Q10

How are the readings of the ammeters of Figure 5.18 related?

Answer

$I_3 = I_1 + I_2$

The potential difference across the ends of a resistor is measured by a voltmeter, which is connected in parallel to the resistor, as shown in Figure 5.19.

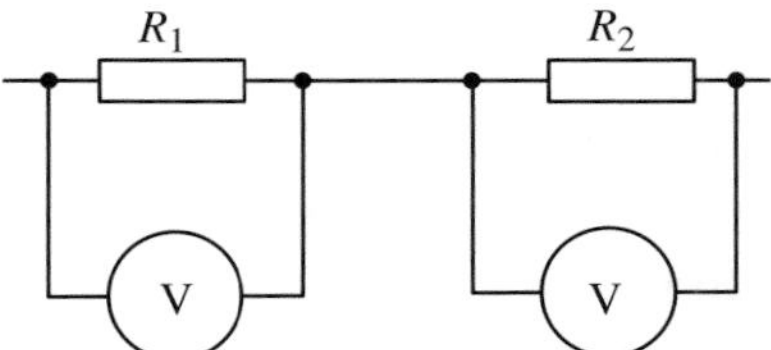

Figure 5.19 A voltmeter measures the potential difference across a resistor it is connected in parallel to.

Thus, to measure the potential difference across and current through a resistor, the arrangement shown in Figure 5.20 is used.

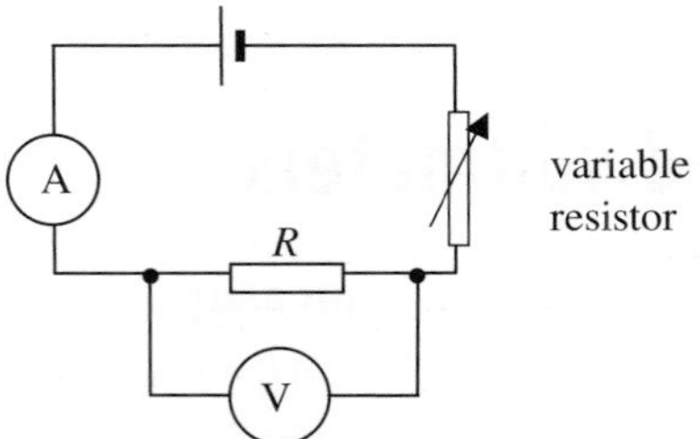

Figure 5.20 The correct arrangement for measuring the current through and potential difference across a resistor. The variable resistor allows the current in the resistor R to be varied.

An ideal voltmeter has infinite resistance (in practice about 50 000 Ω), which means that it takes no current when it is connected to a resistor.

Supplementary material

Voltmeters and ammeters are both based on a current sensor called a galvanometer. An ammeter has a small resistance connected in parallel to the galvanometer and a voltmeter is a galvanometer connected to a large resistance in series.

Example question

Q11

In the circuit in Figure 5.21, the emf of the battery is 9.00 V and the internal resistance is assumed negligible. A voltmeter whose resistance is 500 Ω is connected in parallel to a resistor of 500 Ω. What is the reading of the ammeter? If we assume that the current registered by the ammeter actually flows into the resistor, what value of the resistance would we measure? Repeat this calculation, this time assuming that the voltmeter's resistance is 5000 Ω.

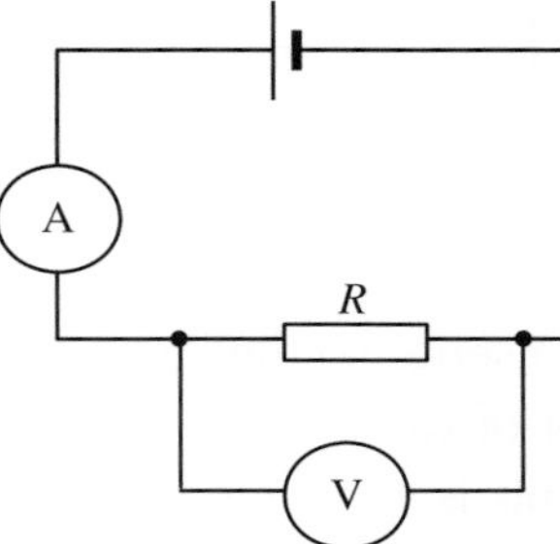

Figure 5.21.

Answer

The total resistance of the circuit is 250 Ω and so the current that leaves the battery is 36.0 mA. If this current is assumed to flow in the resistor, the resistance would be measured as $\frac{9.0\text{ V}}{36\text{ mA}} = 250\ \Omega$. With the higher voltmeter resistance, the total circuit resistance is 454.5 Ω. The current flowing is then $\frac{9.0\text{ V}}{454.5\ \Omega} = 19.8$ mA. If we assume all of this current goes into the resistance, the resistance would be measured as 454.5 Ω. In other words, what the experimental arrangement actually measures is not the resistance of the resistor R but the total resistance of R and the voltmeter's resistance. The higher the voltmeter resistance, the closer the total is to R.

Sensors based on the potential divider

The potential divider

The circuit in Figure 5.22(a) shows a potential divider. It can be used to investigate, for example, the current–voltage characteristic of some device denoted by resistance R. This complicated-looking circuit is simply equivalent to the circuit in Figure 5.22(b). In this circuit, the resistance R_1 is the resistance of the variable resistor XY from end X to the slider S, and R_2 is the resistance of the variable resistor from S to end Y. The current that leaves the battery splits at point M. Part of the current goes from M to N, and the rest goes into the device with resistance R. The right end of the resistance R can be connected to a point S on the variable resistor XY.

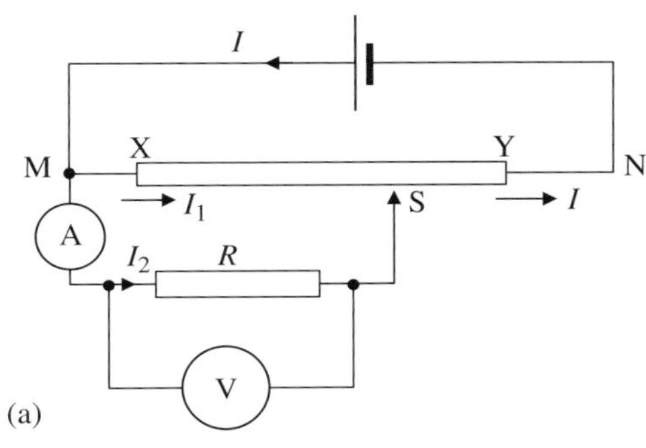

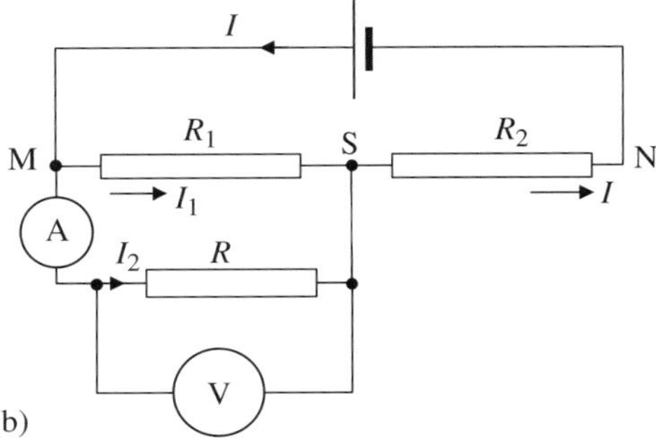

Figure 5.22 (a) This circuit uses a potential divider. The voltage and current in the device with resistance R can be varied by varying the point where the slider S is attached to the variable resistor. (b) The potential divider circuit is equivalent to this simpler-looking circuit.

By varying where the slider S connects to XY, different potential differences and currents are obtained for the device R. The variable resistor XY could also be just a wire of uniform diameter. One advantage of the potential divider over the conventional circuit arrangement (Figure 5.20) is that now the potential difference across the resistor can be varied from a minimum of zero volts, when the slider S is placed at X, to a maximum of $\mathcal{E}$, the emf of the battery (assuming zero internal resistance), by connecting the slider S to point Y. In the conventional arrangement of Figure 5.20, the voltage can be varied from zero volts up to some maximum value *less than* the emf.

Example question

Q12

In the circuit in Figure 5.23, the battery has emf $\mathcal{E}$ and negligible internal resistance. Derive an expression for the potential difference V across resistor R_1.

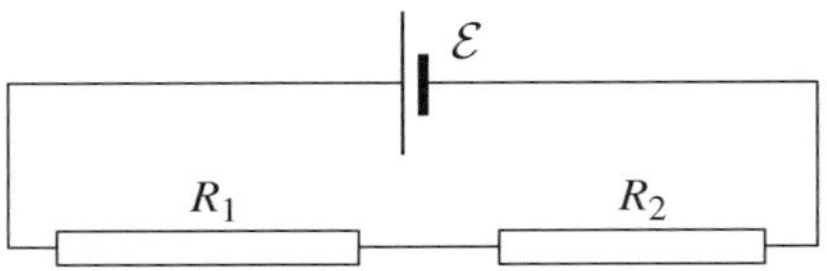

Figure 5.23.

Answer

Since $V = IR_1$ and $I = \frac{\mathcal{E}}{R_1+R_2}$,

we have that

$$V = \frac{R_1}{R_1 + R_2}\mathcal{E}$$

Using sensors

This section includes a use of a particular sensor, a light-dependent resistor in a circuit. Other examples using the potential divider circuit discussed earlier can also be used with various other types of sensor, for example strain gauges and temperature-dependent resistors. A few examples are given in the questions at the end of the chapter.

Consider the circuit in Figure 5.24 that contains a light-dependent resistor (LDR). An LDR is a resistor whose resistance decreases as the light falling on the resistor increases. Typically, the resistance is 100 Ω in bright light and more than 1.0 MΩ in the dark. A voltmeter is connected across the LDR. Because the resistance of the LDR

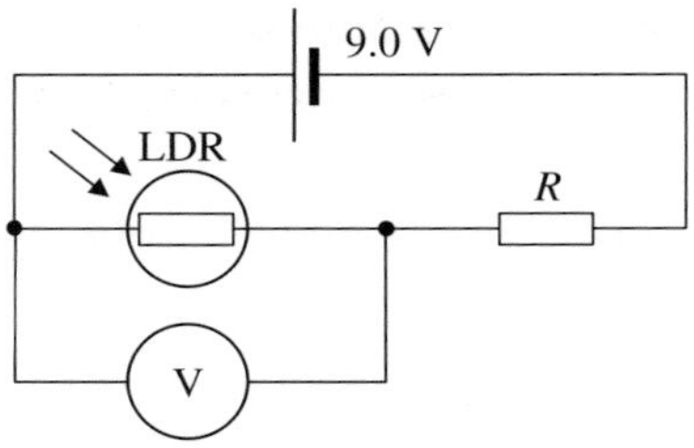

9.0 V
LDR
R
V

Figure 5.24 A light-dependent resistor in a potential divider circuit.

changes with varying intensity of incident light, the reading of the voltmeter across the LDR also changes as in a potential divider circuit.

The reading of the voltmeter across the LDR is

$$V = \frac{R_{\text{LDR}}}{R_{\text{LDR}} + R} \times 9.0 \text{ volts}$$

Assume that the LDR has a resistance of 900 kΩ when dark and 100 Ω when bright. With a fixed resistor of resistance $R = 500$ kΩ, the reading of the voltmeter is then:

- Dark

$$V = \frac{900 \times 10^3}{900 \times 10^3 + 500 \times 10^3} \times 9.0 \text{ volts}$$
$$= 5.8 \text{ volts}$$

- Bright

$$V = \frac{100}{100 + 500 \times 10^3} \times 9.0 \text{ volts}$$
$$= 1.8 \times 10^{-3} \text{volts}$$

The reading of the voltmeter is a measure of the illumination of the LDR and can therefore be used as a light sensor. A high value means the LDR is dark, and a very small value means the LDR is bright.

To have a sensitive sensor, we would like to have as large a difference as possible in the readings of the voltmeter for a dark and a bright LDR. This depends on the particular value of the fixed resistor chosen in relation to the dark and bright resistances of the LDR. Using your graphics calculator, you should be able to show that, with the numbers used here, the value of R resulting in the largest difference in the dark and bright readings of the voltmeter is about 9.5 kΩ.

Supplementary material

The mathematically inclined should be able to show that the value of R resulting in the largest possible difference in the dark and bright readings of the voltmeter equals $R = \sqrt{R_D R_B}$, where R_D and R_B are the resistances of the LDR in the dark and bright.

? QUESTIONS

1 Find the total resistance for each of the circuit parts in Figure 5.25.

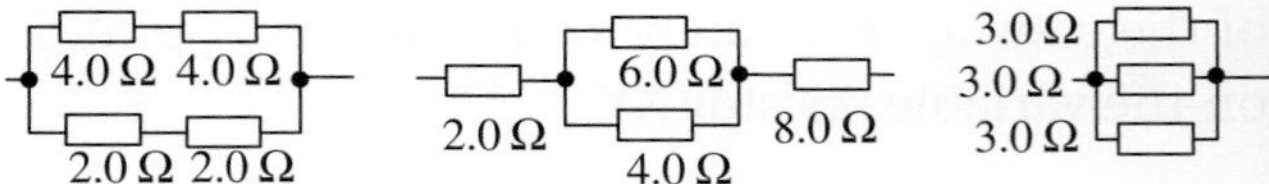

Figure 5.25 For question 1.

2 What is the resistance between A and B in Figure 5.26?

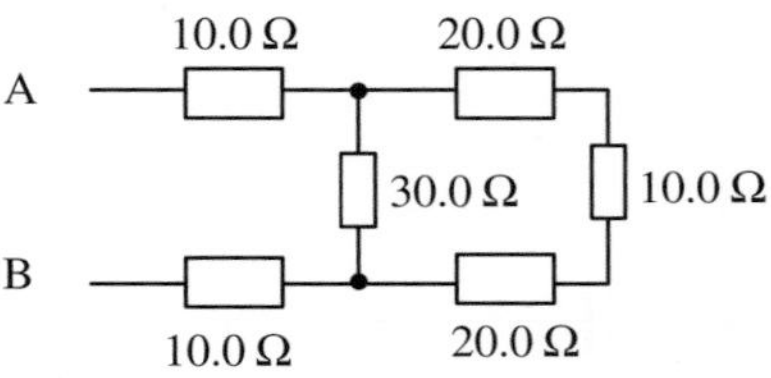

Figure 5.26 For question 2.

3 Each resistor in Figure 5.27 has a value of 6.0 Ω. Calculate the resistance of the combination.

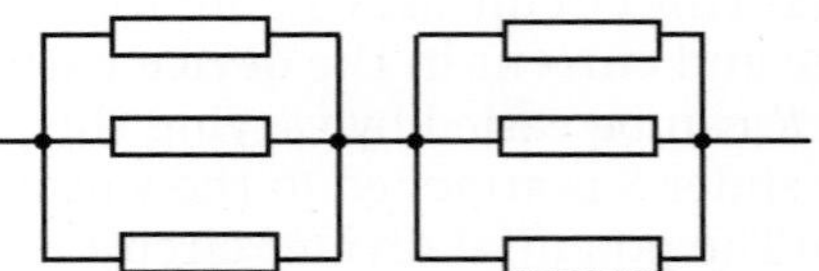

Figure 5.27 For question 3.

4 You are given one hundred 1 Ω resistors. What is the smallest and largest resistance you can make in a circuit using these?

5 A wire that has resistance R is cut into two equal pieces. The two parts are joined in parallel. What is the resistance of the combination?

6 Find the current in, and potential difference across, each resistor in the circuits shown in Figure 5.28.

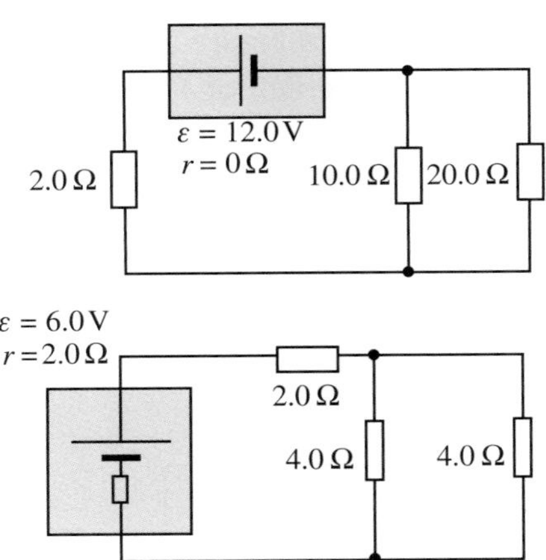

Figure 5.28 For question 6.

7 A battery has emf = 10.0 V and internal resistance 2.0 Ω. The battery is connected in series to a resistance R. Make a table of the power dissipated in R for various values of R and then use your table to plot the power as a function of R. For what value of R is the power dissipated maximum?

8 Six light bulbs, each of constant resistance 3.0 Ω, are connected in parallel to a battery of emf = 9.0 V and negligible internal resistance. The brightness of a light bulb is proportional to the power dissipated in it. Compare the brightness of one light bulb when all six are on, to that when only five are on, the sixth having burned out.

9 A toaster is rated as 1200 W and a mixer as 500 W, both at 220 V.

(a) If both appliances are connected (in parallel) to a 220 V source, what current does each appliance draw?

(b) How much energy do these appliances use if both work for one hour?

10 Find the current in each of the resistors in the circuit shown in Figure 5.29. What is the total power dissipated in the circuit?

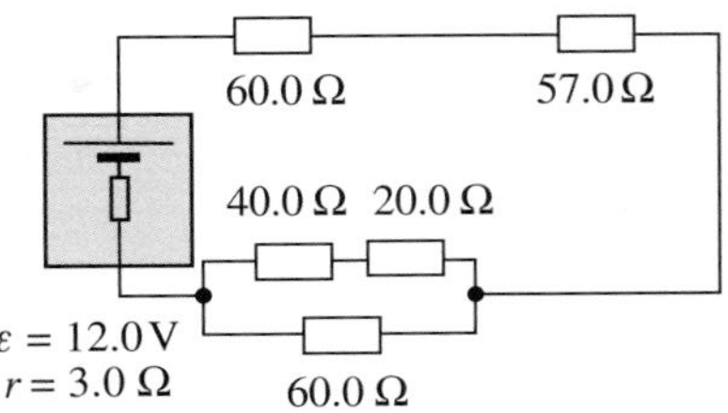

Figure 5.29 For question 10.

11 An electric kettle rated as 2000 W at 220 V is used to warm 2.0 L of water from 15 °C to 90 °C.

(a) How much current flows in the kettle?

(b) What is the resistance of the kettle?

(c) How long does it take to warm the water? (Specific heat capacity of water = 4200 J kg^{-1} K^{-1}.)

(d) How much does this cost if the power company charges $0.10 per kW h?

12 One light bulb is rated as 60 W at 220 V and another as 75 W at 220 V.

(a) If both of these are connected in parallel to a 110 V source, find the current in each light bulb. (Assume that the resistances of the light bulbs are constant.)

(b) Would it cost more or less (and by how much) to run these two light bulbs connected in parallel to a 110 V or a 220 V source?

13 Three appliances are connected (in parallel) to the same outlet, which provides a voltage of 220 V. A fuse connected to the outlet will blow if the current drawn from the outlet exceeds 10 A. If the three appliances are rated as 60 W, 500 W and 1200 W at 220 V, will the fuse blow?

14 An electric kettle rated as 1200 W at 220 V and a toaster rated at 1000 W at 220 V are both connected in parallel to a source of 220 V. If the fuse connected to the source blows when the current exceeds 9.0 A, can both appliances be used at the same time?

15 The graph in Figure 5.30a shows the temperature dependence of a special resistor *R*. The resistance drops with increasing temperature.

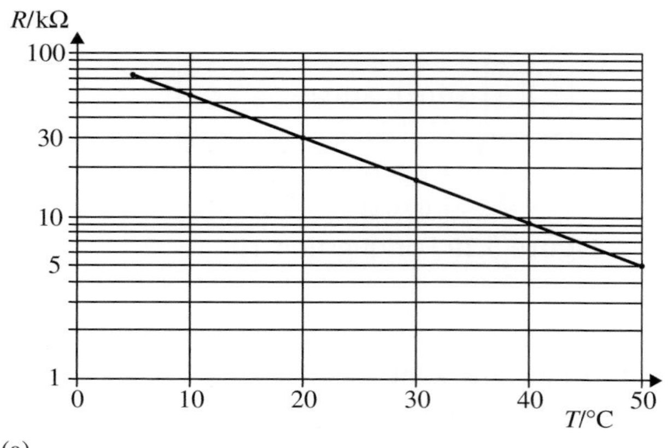

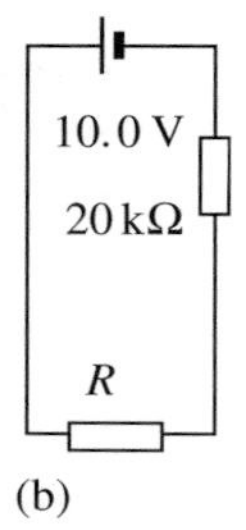

Figure 5.30 For question 15.

(a) Estimate the resistance of this resistor at 20 °C.

(b) If this resistor is connected in a circuit as shown in Figure 5.30b, find the current in the resistor when the temperature is 20 °C.

16 The temperature-dependent resistor of question 15 is connected in a circuit to a lamp of resistance 10 kΩ as shown in Figure 5.31. What will happen to the brightness of the lamp if the temperature of the room increases from 20 °C to 30 °C?

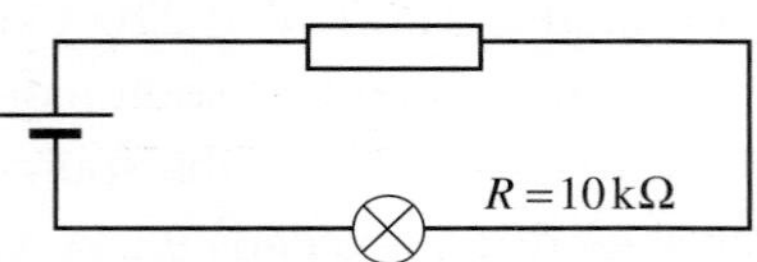

Figure 5.31 For question 16.

17 A clothes dryer operates at 220 V and draws a current of 20.0 A.

(a) What is the power of the machine?

(b) If the dryer is filled with wet clothes that contain 2.0 kg of water at 40 °C, how long will it take to dry them? (The specific heat capacity of water is 4200 J kg^{-1} K^{-1} and the specific latent heat of vaporization of water is 2257 kJ kg^{-1}.) Ignore any heat absorbed by the clothes themselves.

18 In the *potentiometer* in Figure 5.32 wire AB is uniform and has a length of 1.00 m. When contact is made at C with BC = 54.0 cm, the galvanometer G shows zero current. What is the emf of the second cell?

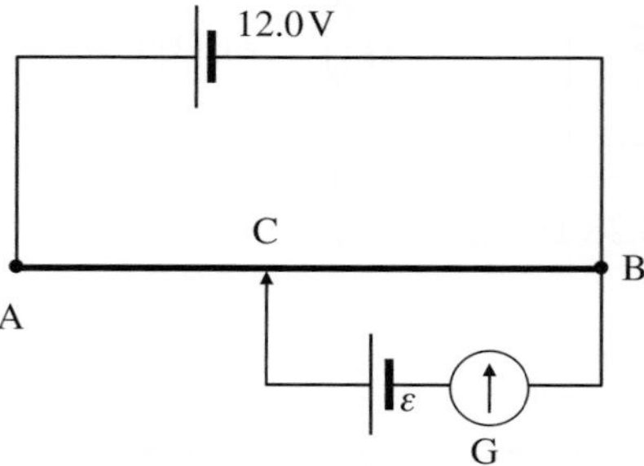

Figure 5.32 For question 18.

19 Two light bulbs are rated as 60 W and 75 W at 220 V. If these are connected in series to a source of 220 V, what will the power in each be? Assume a constant resistance for the light bulbs.

20 At a given time a home is supplied with 100.0 A at 220 V. How many 75 W (rated at 220 V) light bulbs could be on in the house at that time, assuming they are all connected in parallel?

21 (a) What is the reading of the voltmeter in the circuit shown in Figure 5.33 if both resistances are 200 Ω and the voltmeter also has a resistance of 200 Ω?

(b) What is the reading of the ammeter?

(c) If the voltmeter was ideal, what would the readings of the voltmeter and ammeter be?

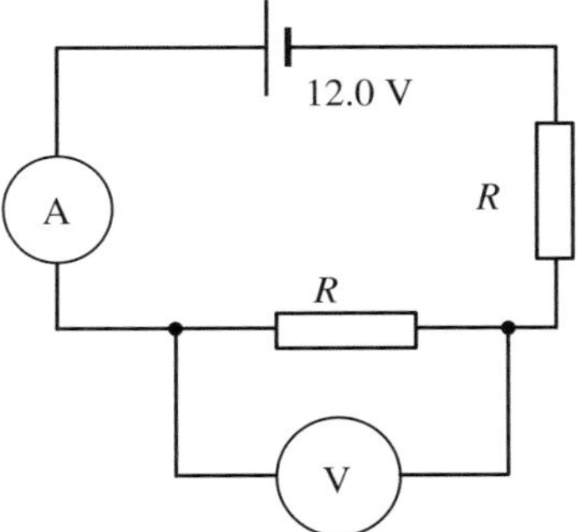

Figure 5.33 For question 21.

22 For the circuit shown in Figure 5.34, find the current taken from the supply.

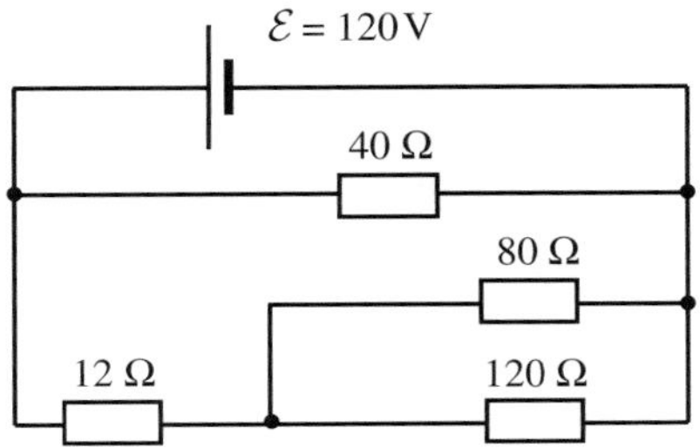

Figure 5.34 For question 22.

23 A direct current supply of constant emf 12.0 V and internal resistance 0.50 Ω is connected to a load of constant resistance 8.0 Ω. Find (a) the power dissipated in the load resistance and (b) the energy lost in the internal resistance in 10 min.

24 Consider the circuit in Figure 5.35, where A, B and C are three identical light bulbs of constant resistance. The battery has negligible internal resistance.

(a) Order the light bulbs in order of increasing brightness.

(b) If C burns out, what will be the brightness of A now compared with before?

(c) If B burns out instead, what will be the brightness of A and C compared with before?

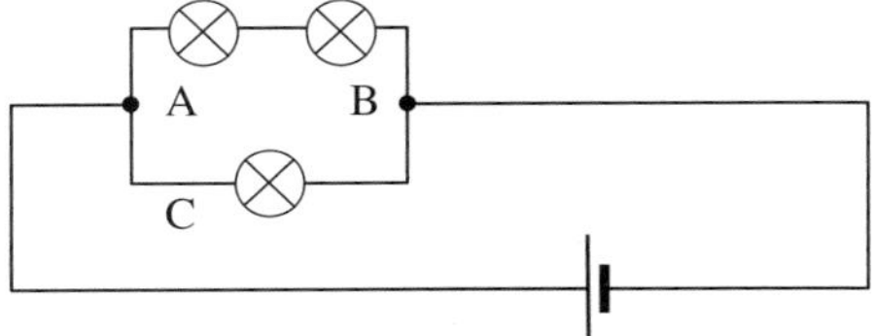

Figure 5.35 For question 24.

25 (a) Determine the potential difference across each resistor in the circuit in Figure 5.36.

(b) A voltmeter of resistance 2 kΩ is connected in parallel across the 3 kΩ resistor. What is the reading of the voltmeter?

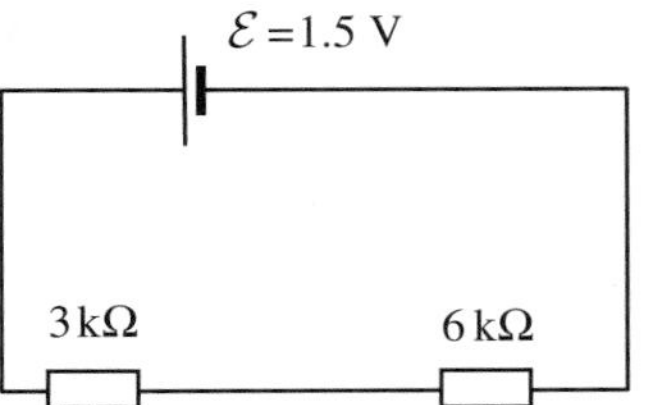

Figure 5.36 For question 25.

26 A battery of emf $\mathcal{E}$ and internal resistance r sends a current I into a circuit.

(a) Sketch the potential difference across the battery as a function of the current.

(b) What is the significance of (i) the slope and (ii) the vertical intercept of the graph?

HL only

27 Each resistor in the circuit shown in Figure 5.37 has value R and the circuit extends to the right forever. Find the total resistance between A and B.

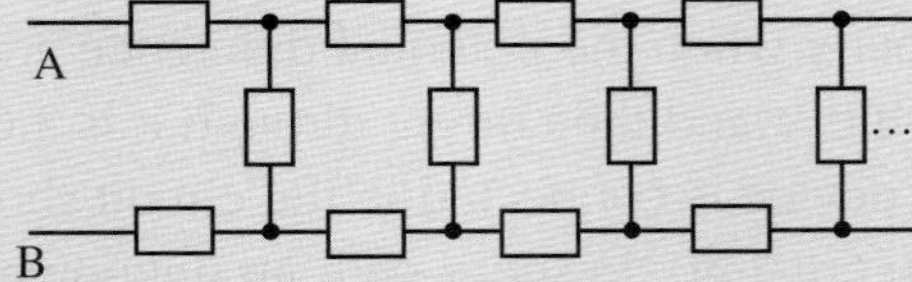

Figure 5.37 For question 27.

28 Twelve 1.0 Ω resistors are placed on the edges of a cube and connected to a 5.0 V battery, as shown in Figure 5.38. What is the current leaving the battery?

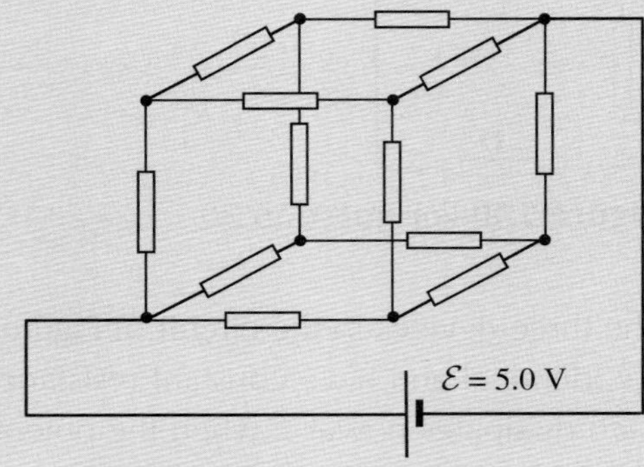

Figure 5.38 For question 28.

29 Two identical lamps, each of constant resistance *R*, are connected as shown in the circuit on the left in Figure 5.39. A third identical lamp is connected in parallel to the other two.

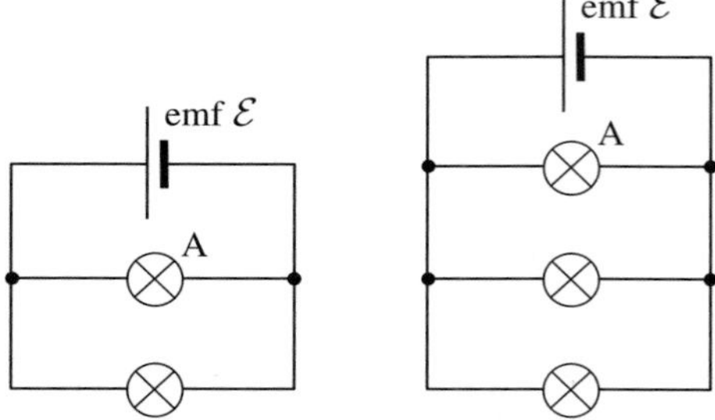

Figure 5.39 For question 29.

Compare the brightness of lamp A in the original circuit (left) with its brightness in the circuit with three lamps (right), when

(a) the battery has no internal resistance, and

(b) the battery has an internal resistance equal to *R*.

30 A device D, of constant resistance, operates properly when the potential difference across it is 8.0 V and the current through it is 2.0 A. The device is connected in the circuit shown in Figure 5.40, in series with an unknown resistance *R*. Calculate the value of the resistance *R*. (The battery has negligible internal resistance.)

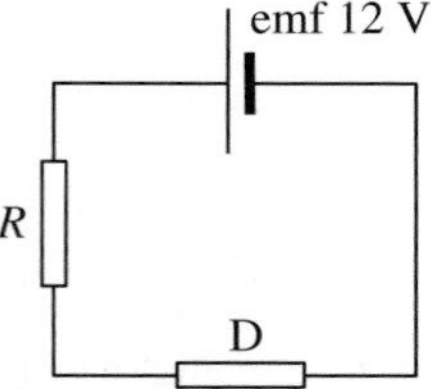

Figure 5.40 For question 30.

31 The three devices in the circuit in Figure 5.41 are identical and have constant resistance. Each dissipates power *P* when the potential difference across it is $\mathcal{E}$. (The battery has negligible internal resistance.)

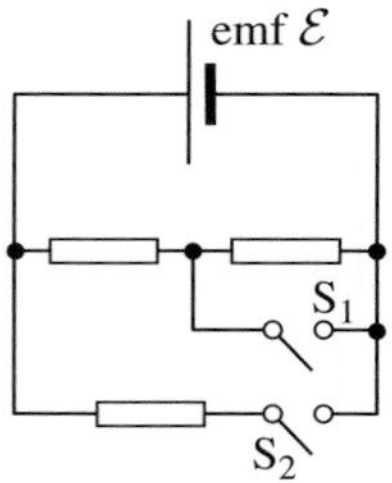

Figure 5.41 For question 31.

Calculate the total power dissipated in the circuit when

(a) S_1 is closed and S_2 is open;

(b) S_1 is closed and S_2 is closed;

(c) S_1 is open and S_2 is open;

(d) S_1 is open and S_2 is closed.

32 Two identical lamps are connected to a battery of emf 12 V and negligible internal resistance, as shown in Figure 5.42. Calculate the reading of the (ideal) voltmeter when lamp B burns out.

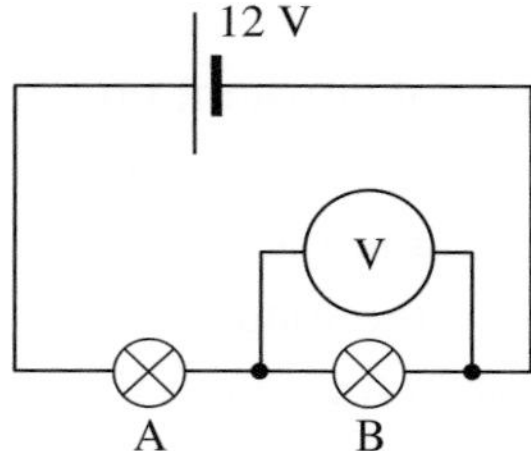

Figure 5.42 For question 32.

33 State the reading of the ideal voltmeter in the circuit in Figure 5.43.

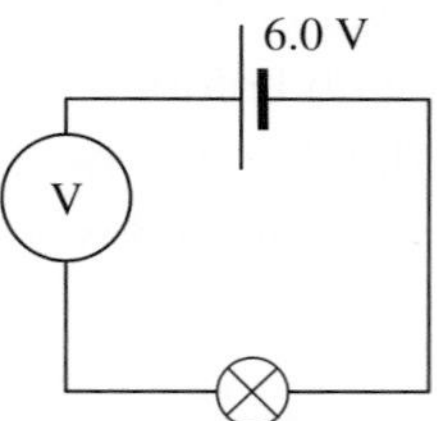

Figure 5.43 For question 33.

34 In an experiment, a voltmeter was connected across the terminals of a battery as shown in Figure 5.44.

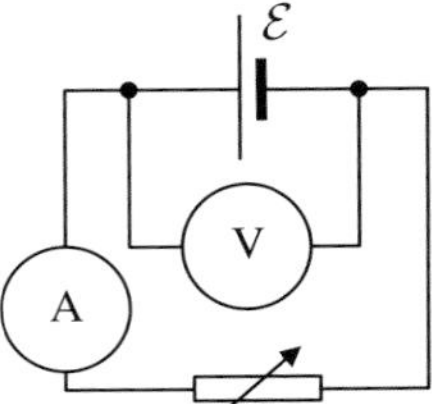

Figure 5.44 For question 34.

The current in the circuit is varied using the variable resistor. The graph in Figure 5.45 shows the variation with current of the reading of the voltmeter.

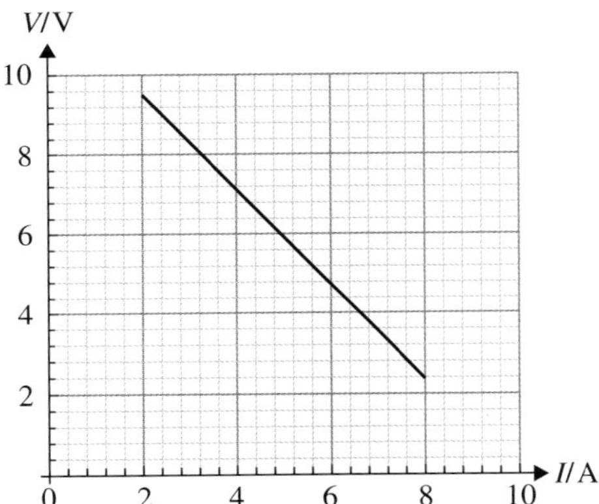

Figure 5.45 For question 34.

(a) Calculate the internal resistance of the battery.

(b) Calculate the emf of the battery.

35 Two resistors are connected in series as shown in Figure 5.46. The battery has negligible internal resistance. Resistor R has a constant resistance of 1.5 Ω.

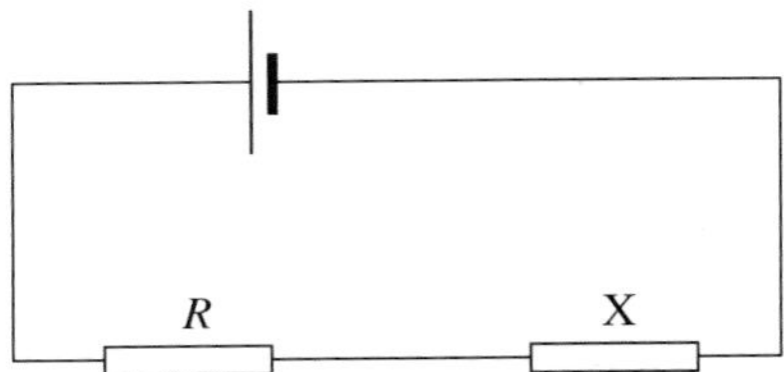

Figure 5.46 For question 35.

The current–voltage (I–V) characteristic of resistance X is shown in Figure 5.47.

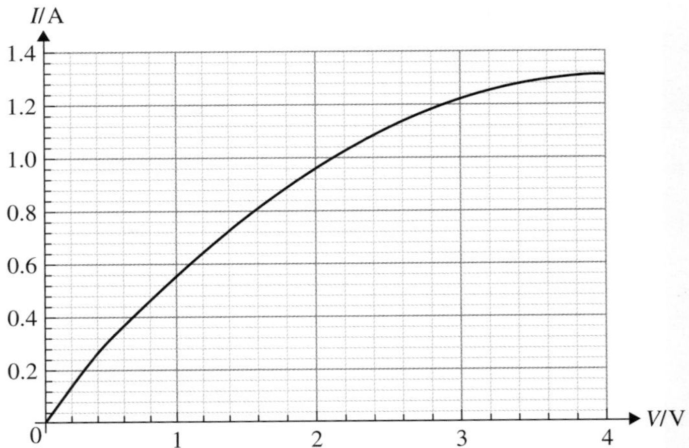

Figure 5.47 For question 35.

The potential difference across resistor R is 1.2 V. Calculate the emf of the battery.

36 When two resistors, each of resistance 4.0 Ω, are connected in parallel with a battery, the current leaving the battery is 3.0 A. When the same two resistors are connected in series with the battery, the total current in the circuit is 1.4 A. Calculate

(a) the emf of the battery;

(b) the internal resistance of the battery.

37 Two resistors, X and Y, have I–V characteristics given by the graph in Figure 5.48.

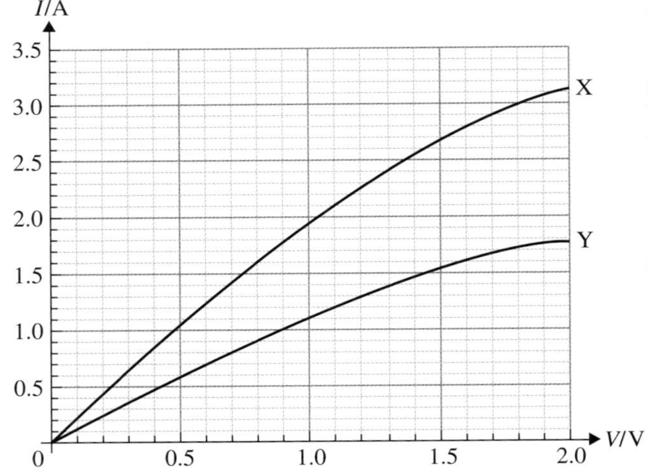

Figure 5.48 For question 37.

(a) The resistors X and Y are connected in parallel to a battery of emf 1.5 V and negligible internal resistance, as shown in Figure 5.49(a). Calculate the total current leaving the battery.

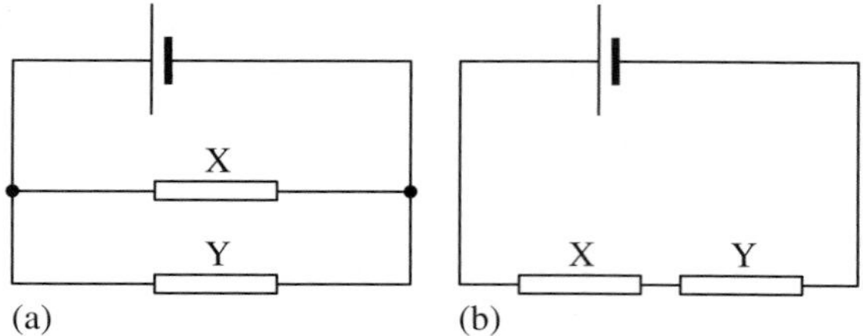

Figure 5.49 For question 37.

(b) In Figure 5.49(b) the resistors X and Y are connected in series. Estimate the total current leaving the battery in this circuit.

38 The circuit in Figure 5.50 contains a positive temperature coefficient (PTC) resistor whose resistance increases with increasing temperature, and a negative temperature coefficient (NTC) resistor whose resistance decreases with increasing temperature.

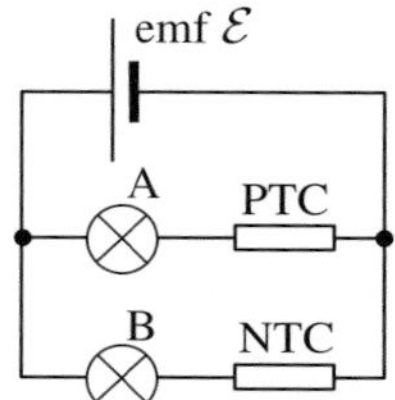

Figure 5.50 For question 38.

At room temperature the lamps (which are identical) are equally bright. Determine the changes, if any, in the brightness of lamps A and B when the temperature is increased. (The battery has negligible internal resistance.)

39 Figure 5.51 shows an NTC resistor (the resistance decreases with increasing temperature) in a circuit.

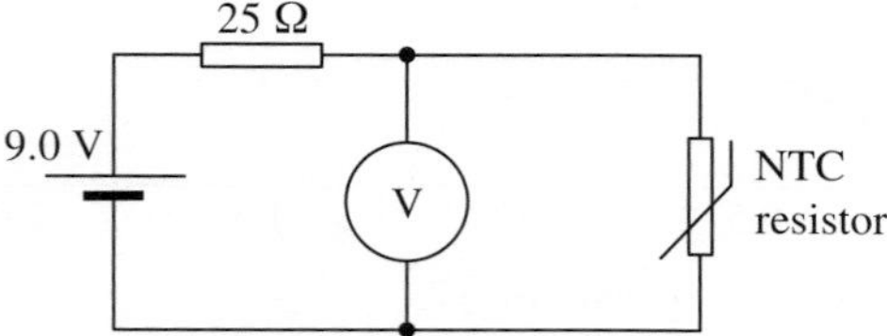

Figure 5.51 For question 39.

Figure 5.52 shows the variation with temperature T of the resistance of the NTC resistor.

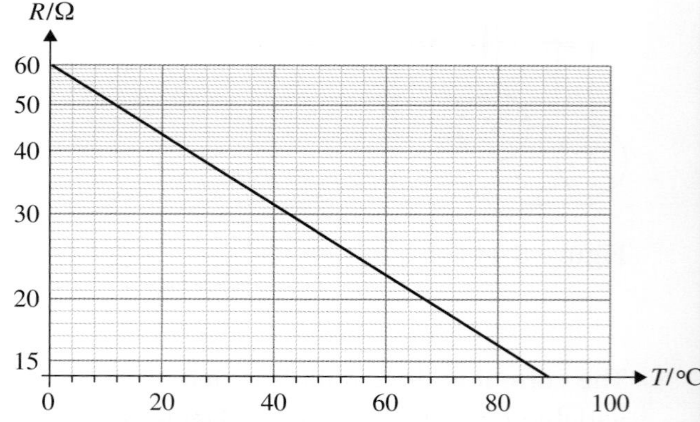

Figure 5.52 For question 39.

(a) State the resistance of the NTC resistor at a temperature of 25 °C.

(b) Deduce that the reading of the voltmeter, in volts, is given by

$$V = \frac{9.0 \times R_{\text{NTC}}}{R_{\text{NTC}} + 25}$$

where R_{NTC} is the resistance of the NTC resistor in ohms.

(c) Calculate the reading of the (ideal) voltmeter at 25 °C.

(d) The NTC resistor may be used as a temperature sensor. Describe how this circuit may be used to measure the temperature to which the NTC resistor is exposed.

40 (a) Calculate the potential difference between points A and B in the circuit in Figure 5.53. (The battery has negligible internal resistance.)

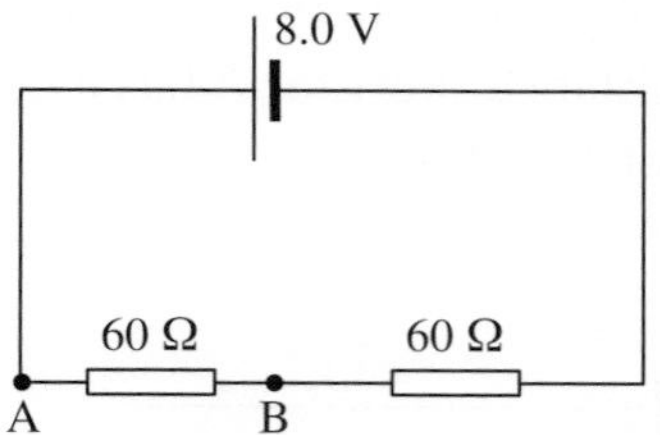

Figure 5.53 For question 40.

A lamp of constant resistance operates at normal brightness when the potential difference across it is 4.0 V and the current through it is 0.20 A. To light up the lamp, a student uses the circuit shown in Figure 5.54.

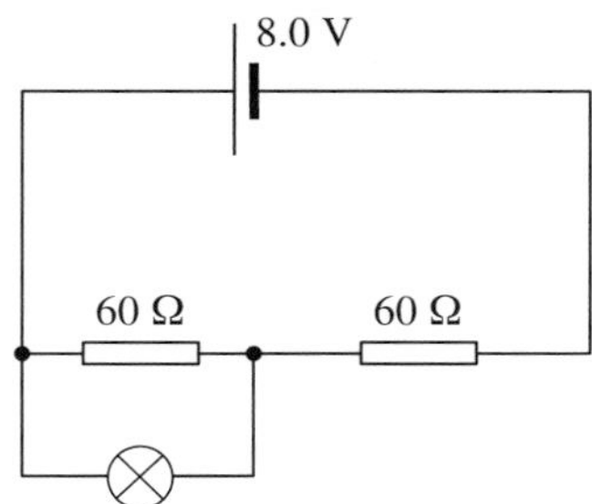

Figure 5.54 For question 40.

(b) Calculate the resistance of the light bulb at normal brightness.
(c) Calculate the potential difference across the light bulb in the circuit in Figure 5.54.
(d) Calculate the current through the light bulb.
(e) Hence explain why the light bulb will not light.

41 The circuit in Figure 5.55 contains a strain gauge, S. The resistance of S when it is not under stress is 100 Ω. The emf of the battery is 6.00 V. (The battery has negligible internal resistance.)

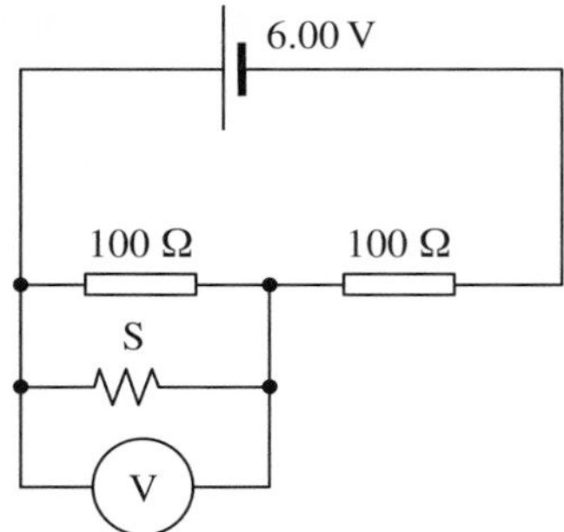

Figure 5.55 For question 41.

(a) Calculate the reading of the voltmeter when the strain gauge S is not under stress.
(b) When the strain gauge is under a certain load, its resistance increases to 110 Ω. Calculate the reading of the voltmeter now.

Magnetic fields

We have all observed with fascination how magnets attract or repel each other and we are familiar with compasses, which align with the magnetic field of the earth (a fact that has been used for navigation for hundreds of years). But it was only in 1820 that scientists began to understand the cause of magnetism, when the Danish scientist H. C. Ørsted discovered that a wire in which electric current was flowing influenced a magnetic needle placed near the wire. It was thus discovered that the origin of magnetism is electrical. The magnetic field of the earth is presumably caused by moving charges in the interior of the earth and the magnetic field of an iron bar magnet is caused by the motion of electrons in the atoms of the iron. Thus, electric currents cause forces on magnets and, as we will see in this chapter, magnets cause forces on electric currents as well – a result that we might expect from Newton's third law.

Objectives

By the end of this chapter you should be able to:

- understand the meaning of *magnetic field* and find its magnitude and direction in simple situations involving *straight-line conductors* ($B = \frac{\mu_0}{2\pi}\frac{I}{r}$) and *solenoids* ($B = \mu_0 \frac{NI}{L}$) using the right-hand rule where appropriate;
- find the *force on moving charges* ($F = qvB \sin\theta$) and *currents* ($F = BIL \sin\theta$) in magnetic fields and appreciate the definition of the *ampere* as a fundamental SI unit, using the right-hand rule for forces where appropriate.

Magnetic field

In the chapters on electricity, it was useful to introduce the concept of an electric field. A charge creates an electric field around itself and any other charge that enters this electric field will experience, as a result, an electric force. The same idea can be extended to magnetism. Both magnets and electric currents create magnetic fields around themselves and when another magnet or electric current (or moving charge in general) enters this magnetic field it will experience a *magnetic* force. The magnetic field is a vector quantity just like the electric field – it has magnitude and direction.

The direction of the magnetic field

The magnetic field direction is determined by the effect it has on a compass needle (i.e. a small bar magnet), as shown in Figure 6.1. A magnetic needle aligns itself in the direction of the magnetic field vector.

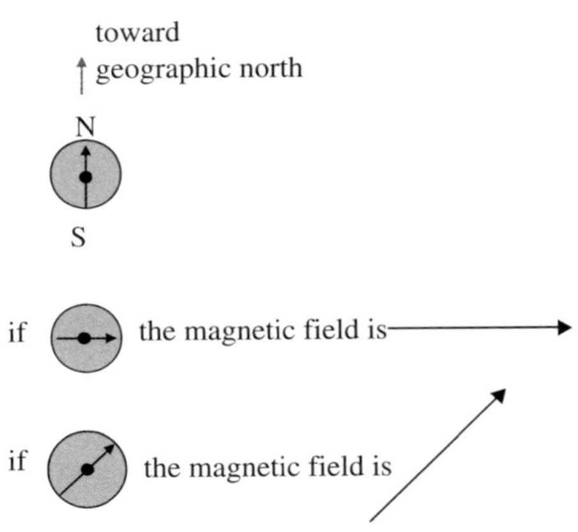

Figure 6.1 A magnetic needle is a small bar magnet whose north pole points in the direction of the geographic north pole of the earth. In the presence of another strong magnet, the needle will align itself with the magnetic field.

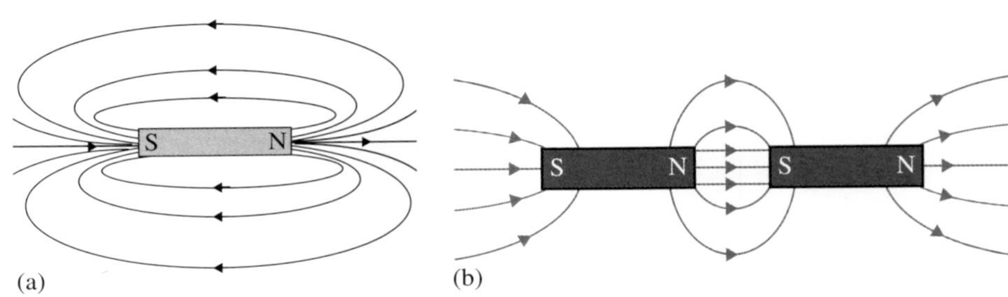

Figure 6.2 (a) The magnetic field lines of a bar magnet. The field is strongest near the poles of the magnet where the lines crowd together. (b) A uniform magnetic field is obtained if two opposite poles are placed near each other.

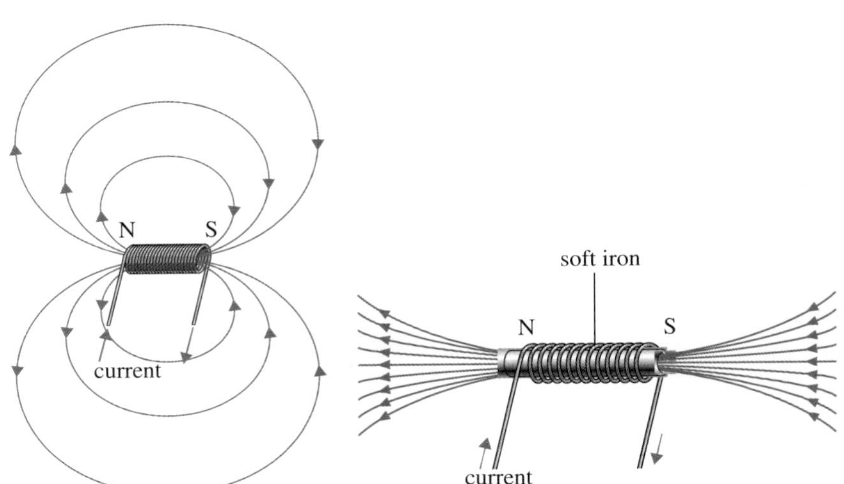

Figure 6.3 The magnetic field lines of a solenoid. The field is fairly uniform in the interior of the coil. Outside it resembles that of a bar magnet.

Magnetic field lines

Just like electric field lines, magnetic field lines are defined as imaginary lines around magnets and currents, tangents to which give the direction of the magnetic field. The magnetic field lines of permanent magnets and the field created by a solenoid (a coil of wire in which electric current flows) are shown in Figures 6.2 and 6.3.

In Figure 6.3, current is flowing in a solenoid and a magnetic field is created inside and outside the solenoid. The current is flowing in the clockwise direction if we look along the axis of the solenoid from right to left.

The magnetic field of a single loop of wire in which current flows is somewhat more complicated and is shown in Figure 6.4. In the right-hand diagram, we are looking at the loop 'from above'; the crosses indicate that the magnetic field is directed into the page while the dots indicate a magnetic field coming out of the page.

Figure 6.5 shows the magnetic field lines of a long straight wire. In Figure 6.5a, the current is coming out of the page. The magnetic field lines are circles centred at the wire. In Figure 6.5b, the current goes into the page. Remember that the magnetic field direction is tangent to the magnetic field lines and the arrows on the lines tell us which tangent to take.

The magnetic field of the earth resembles that of a bar magnet except that the bar magnet does not coincide with the line through the geographic north and south poles of the earth.

The direction of the magnetic field caused by a given current (a few examples of which we have seen in this section) is given by a right-hand rule, which we will describe later.

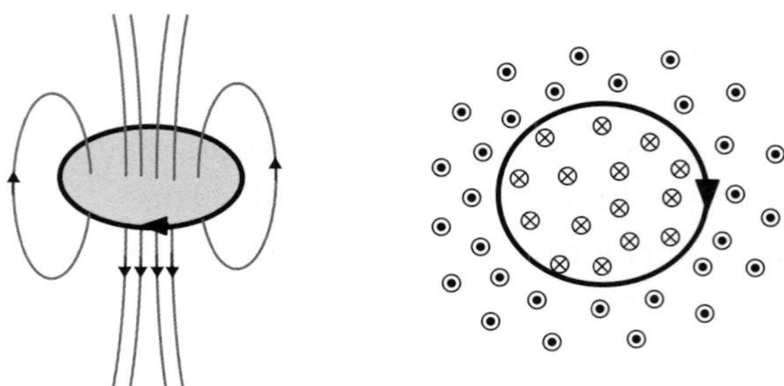

Figure 6.4 The magnetic field lines of a single turn of wire. In the plane of the loop the magnetic field is going into the page inside the loop and out of the page outside the loop. The current in the loop is flowing in the clockwise direction.

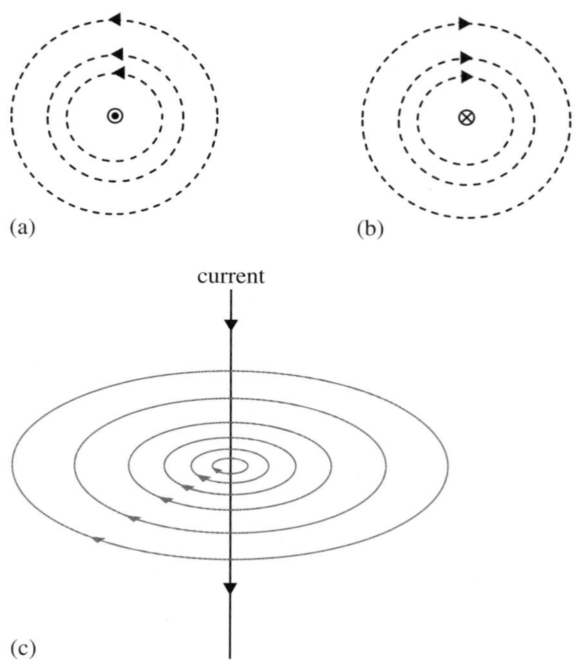

Figure 6.5 Magnetic field lines for straight current wires. The magnetic field magnitude is largest near the wire.

Example question

Q1

A magnetic monopole is a particle that is a pure north or pure south magnetic pole. (These are predicted to exist by modern theories of elementary particle physics but none have been found.) Suppose that a *south* magnetic monopole is placed at various positions in the vicinity of a bar magnet, as shown in Figure 6.6. Draw the force experienced by the monopole at the positions shown.

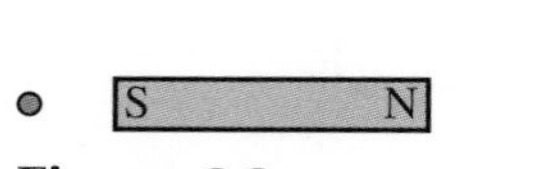

Figure 6.6.

Answer

The force on a north monopole would be in the same direction as the magnetic field direction at the position of the monopole. The force on a south monopole would be opposite to the direction of the magnetic field. Thus, the forces on the south monopole are as shown in Figure 6.7.

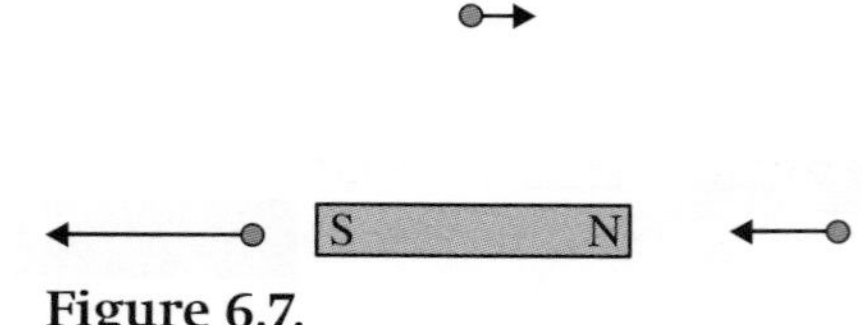

Figure 6.7.

The magnetic force on a current

If a current is placed in a region of magnetic field, it will experience a magnetic force. In Figure 6.8 a magnetic field is established out of the page and a wire carries a current from left to right, perpendicular to the magnetic field. The magnitude of the force is proportional to the current I, the magnetic field magnitude B and the length L of the wire that is in the magnetic field.

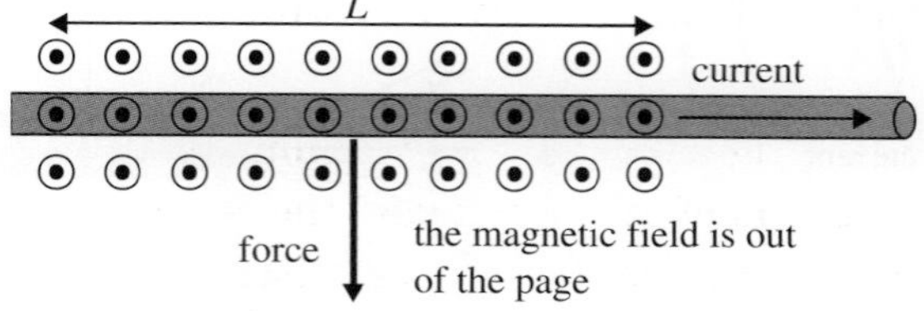

Figure 6.8 A current in a magnetic field experiences a magnetic force. The force is on that part of the wire that is in the magnetic field.

Mathematically

$$F \propto BIL$$
$$\Rightarrow F = kBIL$$

where k is a constant of proportionality. This constant can be made to equal one by proper choice of the unit of magnetic field. We can make $k = 1$ by saying that when the force on 1 m of wire carrying a current of 1 A is 1 N, then the magnitude of the magnetic field is defined to be 1 tesla (so $1\ \text{T} = 1\ \text{N A}^{-1}\ \text{m}^{-1}$). So the force on the current-carrying wire is

$$F = BIL$$

Remember, though, that the magnetic field was at right angles to the wire. If there is an angle between them then:

▶ The force on a length L of the wire is given by

$$F = BIL \sin\theta$$

where θ is the angle between the current and the direction of the magnetic field

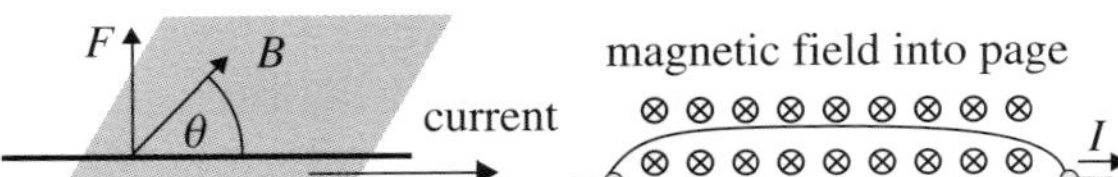

Figure 6.9 The force on a current-carrying wire in a magnetic field is normal to the plane containing the field and the current. If the ends of the wire are kept fixed, the wire will bend.

The formula above gives the magnitude of the force on the wire. The direction of the magnetic force is always normal to both the current and the magnetic field: that is, it is normal to the plane containing the current and the magnetic field vectors (see Figure 6.9). To find this direction we use a right-hand rule for force which says:

▶ Using the right hand place the thumb in the direction of the current and the fingers in the direction of the magnetic field. The direction *away* from the palm is the direction of the magnetic force. (See Figure 6.10.)

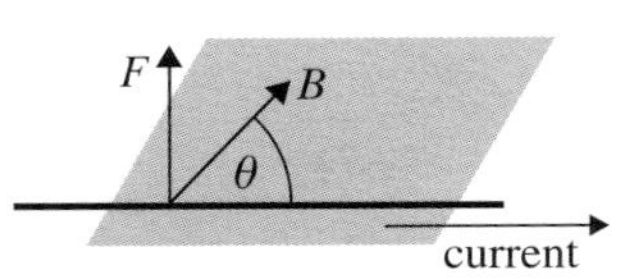

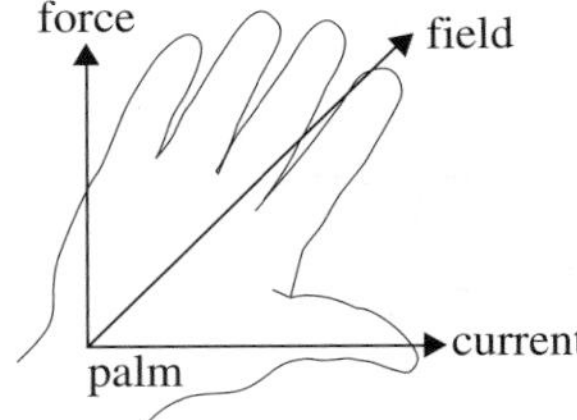

Figure 6.10 The magnetic force on a current is normal to both the magnetic field and the current direction. Its direction is given by a right-hand rule for force.

Supplementary material

Those familiar with the vector product of two vectors may recognize that the equation for the magnetic force is

$$\vec{F} = I\vec{L} \times \vec{B}$$

This equation correctly gives the magnitude as well as the direction of the force.

The magnetic force on a moving charge

An electric current that is in a magnetic field will experience a force as we just saw. But an electric current is just moving charges, so a moving charge will experience a magnetic force as well.

Consider a positive charge q that moves with speed v to the right. In time Δt the charge will move a distance $L = v\Delta t$. The current created by this charge is $I = \frac{q}{\Delta t}$, so the force on this current is

$$F = BIL \sin\theta$$
$$= B\frac{q}{\Delta t}v\Delta t \sin\theta$$
$$= qvB \sin\theta$$

▶ A charge q moving with speed v in a magnetic field of magnitude B will experience a force F given by

$$F = qvB \sin\theta$$

where θ is the angle between the direction of the velocity and the magnetic field. (See Figure 6.11.)

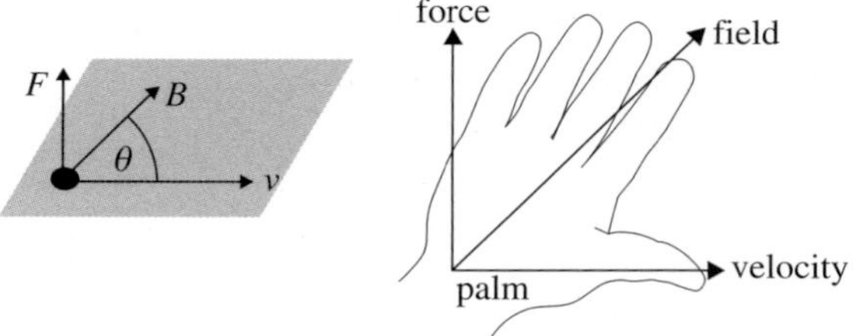

Figure 6.11 An electric charge moving in a magnetic field experiences a magnetic force. The charge shown is positive. The right hand is placed palm up on the page with the thumb pointing in the direction of the velocity and the fingers pointing in the direction of the magnetic field. The direction away from the palm (i.e. out of the page) is the direction of the force on a positive charge.

This implies that the magnetic force is zero if the charge moves parallel or antiparallel to the magnetic field. There is also no magnetic force if the charge is not moving. This is to be contrasted with the electric force on a charge, which is always non-zero irrespective of whether the charge moves or not. The magnetic force on particles that are electrically neutral ($q = 0$) is, of course, zero.

Supplementary material

Those familiar with the vector product of two vectors may recognize that the equation for the magnetic force is

$$\vec{F} = q\vec{v} \times \vec{B}$$

This equation correctly gives the magnitude as well as the direction of the force.

Example question

Q2

An electron approaches a bar magnet as shown in Figure 6.12. What is the direction of the force on the electron?

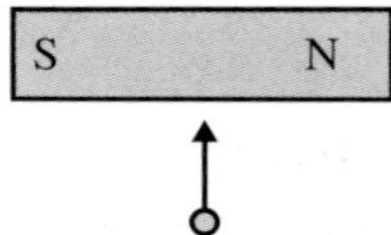

Figure 6.12.

Answer

The magnetic field at the position of the electron is to the left. Placing the right hand such that the thumb points up the page (velocity direction) and the fingers to the left (field direction), the palm is pointing out of the page. But the charge is negative and so the force is into the page.

Motion of charges in magnetic fields

The fact that the magnetic force on a charge is always normal to the velocity means that the path of a charge in a magnetic field must be a circle, as shown in Figure 6.13 (the path can also be helical – see question 21 at the end of the chapter).

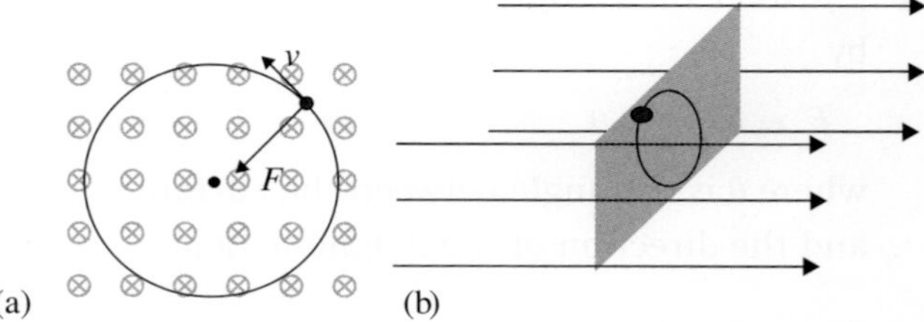

Figure 6.13 A charge in a magnetic field moves in a circle, as shown in (a). The plane of the circle is normal to the magnetic field, as shown in (b). (The charge here is positive.) The magnetic field is into the page in (a).

Consider a charge q moving with speed v in a magnetic field B. Assume that the charge's velocity is normal to the magnetic field, then the force on the charge is $F = qvB$ and so by Newton's second law

$$qvB = m\frac{v^2}{R}$$

where R is the radius of the circle the charge will move on. Therefore

$$R = \frac{mv}{qB}$$

Very massive or very fast charges will move on large circles; large charges and large magnetic fields will result in small circles. The time to make one full revolution in a magnetic field is found from

$$T = \frac{2\pi R}{v} = \frac{2\pi}{v}\frac{mv}{qB} = \frac{2\pi m}{qB}$$

and is thus independent of the speed. This is an important result in experimental particle physics and forms the basis for an accelerator called the cyclotron.

Work done and magnetic forces

Since the magnetic force is always normal to the velocity of the charge, it follows that it cannot do any work. The big magnets in particle accelerators are used only to deflect particles not to increase the particles' kinetic energy (this job is done by electric fields).

Ørsted's discovery

A current in a straight long wire produces a magnetic field around it. The Danish scientist H. C. Ørsted found that:

▶ The magnitude of the magnetic field B created by the current in a wire varies linearly with the current in the wire and inversely with the perpendicular distance from the wire (see Figure 6.14). In equation form

$$B = \frac{\mu_0}{2\pi}\frac{I}{r}$$

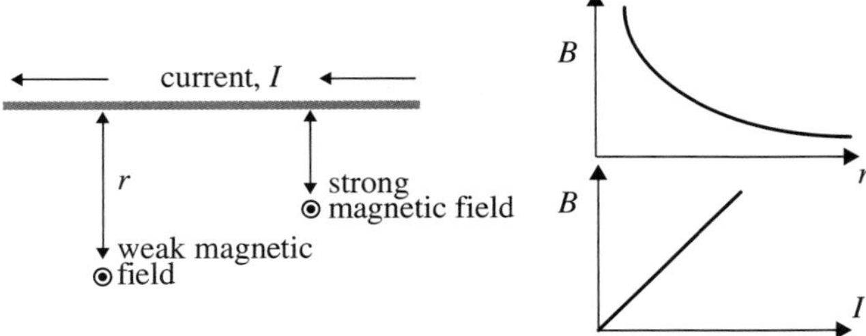

Figure 6.14 The magnitude of the magnetic field vector is inversely proportional to the distance from the wire. The magnetic field is directly proportional to the current.

The constant of proportionality involves the new physical constant μ_0, which is called the *magnetic permeability of vacuum*. If the wire is surrounded by something other than a vacuum, the appropriate permeability of that medium must be used in the formula above. The value of the magnetic permeability of the vacuum is (exactly)

$$\mu_0 = 4\pi \times 10^{-7}\ \mathrm{N\,A^{-2}}$$

It is the analogue in magnetism of the electric permittivity ε in electricity. The unit of the magnetic field is the tesla (T). The tesla is a big unit. The magnetic field of the earth is about 10^{-4} T on the earth's surface. A wire carrying a current of about 2000 A (as in some high-voltage transmission lines) produces a magnetic field of 8×10^{-5} T at a distance of 5 m from the wire.

Whereas the magnitude of the magnetic field is straightforward to investigate, its direction is less so. Let us consider a wire that carries a current normal to the page. The direction of the magnetic field at a given point in space is found by placing magnetic needles around the wire and seeing how they align themselves. Figure 6.15 shows the result of this simple experiment for various points around the wire.

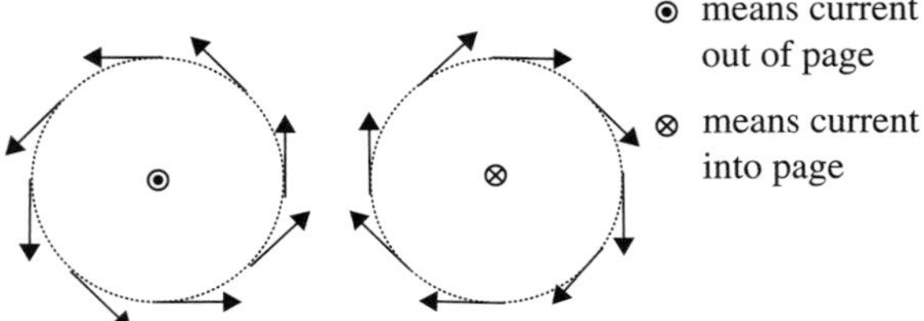

Figure 6.15 The direction of the magnetic field at various points around straight wires carrying current out of the page (left) and into the page (right).

The structure of the magnetic field direction is thus vectors that are tangent to a circle centred on the wire and 'flow' around the circle in the counter-clockwise sense (as looked at from above) if the current comes out of the page (shown by the full circle) and clockwise if the current goes into the page (shown by the cross in the circle).

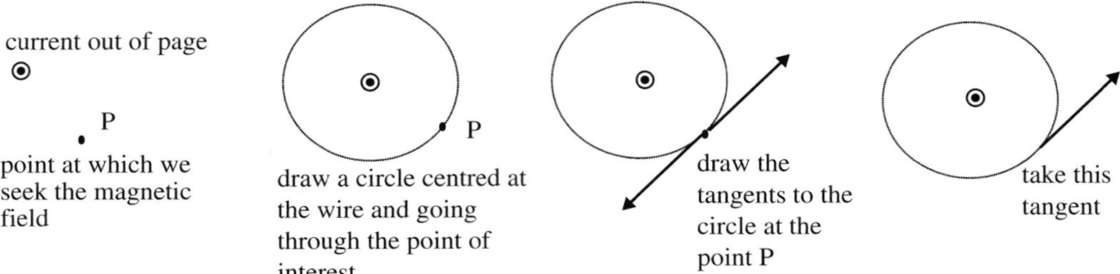

Figure 6.16 To find the magnetic field at a point near a straight wire, draw the imaginary circle centred at the wire, and going through the point of interest. Grip the wire with the fingers of the right hand with the thumb pointing in the direction of the current. Draw the tangent to the circle at the point of interest so that the vector drawn follows the curl of the fingers.

We can formalize this finding into a 'right-hand rule'.

▶ Grip the wire with the fingers of the right hand in such a way that the thumb points in the direction of the current. Then the direction in which the fingers curl is the direction of the 'flow' of the magnetic field vectors. (See Figures 6.16–6.18.)

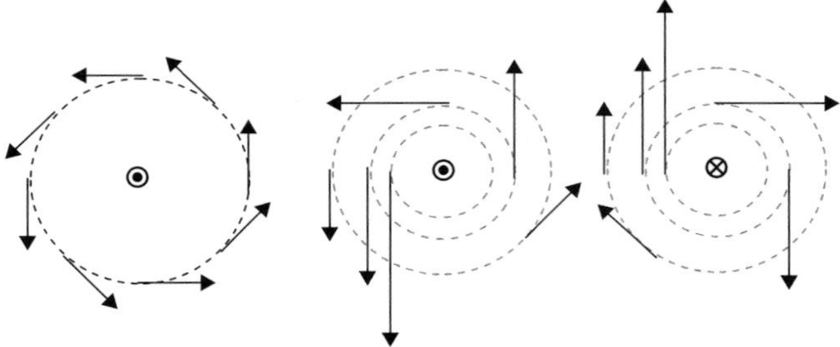

Figure 6.17 The magnetic field around a straight wire at various distances from the wire. Note that as the distance gets bigger the length of the arrow representing the magnetic field gets smaller.

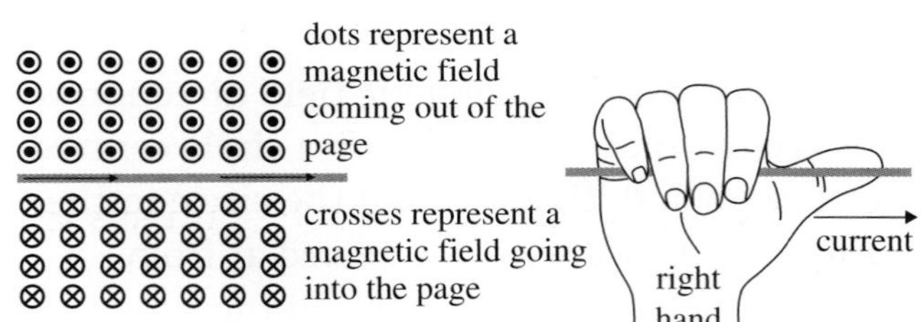

Figure 6.18 The magnetic field of a straight current-carrying wire looked at from a different point of view.

Example question

Q3

Find the magnetic field at point P in Figure 6.19.

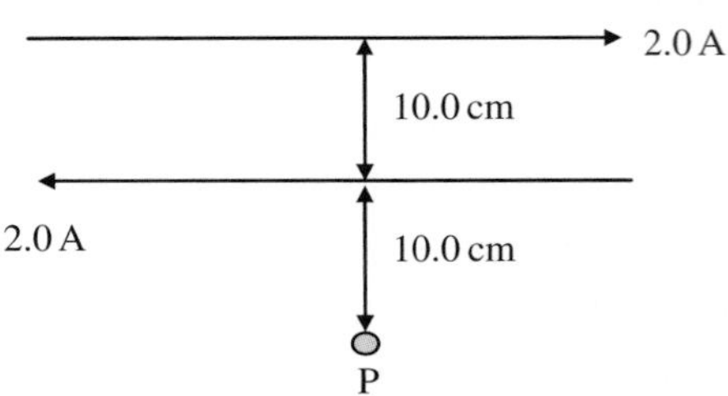

Figure 6.19.

Answer

The top wire produces a magnetic field into the page of magnitude

$$B_1 = 4\pi \times 10^{-7} \frac{2.00}{2\pi \times 0.200}\ \text{T}$$
$$= 2.00 \times 10^{-6}\ \text{T}$$

and the second wire produces a magnetic field out of the page of magnitude

$$B_2 = 4\pi \times 10^{-7} \frac{2.00}{2\pi \times 0.100}\ \text{T}$$
$$= 4.00 \times 10^{-6}\ \text{T}$$

resulting in a net magnetic field of 2.00×10^{-6} T out of the page.

The single current loop

The magnetic field of a single current loop was shown in Figure 6.4 on page 338. The magnetic field strength B at the centre of a circular loop of radius R carrying current I is

$$B = \frac{\mu_0 I}{2R}$$

The solenoid

In various applications it is necessary to have a uniform magnetic field – one that has the same magnitude and direction in a region of space. A

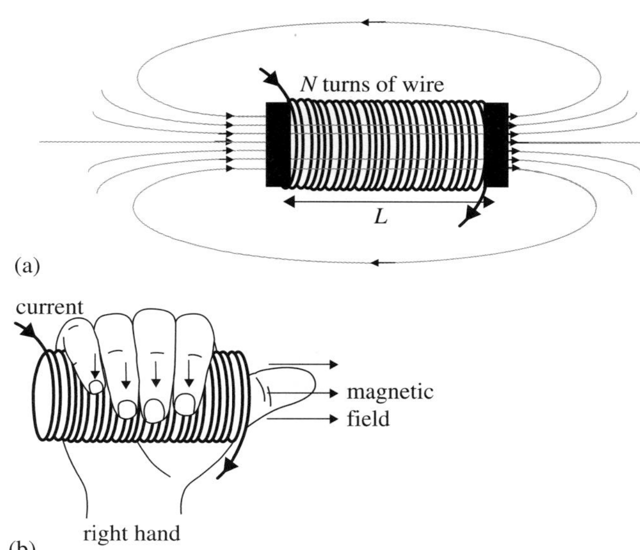

Figure 6.20 (a) A solenoid. If it has an iron core, a much stronger magnetic field results. (b) The second right-hand rule giving the direction of the solenoid magnetic field.

way of achieving such a field is through a solenoid, which is a wire wound tightly many times around an axis (see Figure 6.20a).

▶ In the *interior* of the solenoid the magnetic field is uniform in magnitude and direction and is given by

$$B = \mu_0 \frac{NI}{L}$$

where N is the number of turns, L the length of the solenoid and I the current through it.

A much stronger magnetic field can be obtained if the solenoid has an iron core.

The direction of the magnetic field of a solenoid is found by a second right-hand rule (see Figure 6.20b).

▶ Hold the solenoid with the right hand so that the fingers curl in the direction of the current in the coils of the solenoid. Then the thumb points in the direction of the magnetic field.

The solenoid magnetic field outside the solenoid resembles that of a bar magnet.

The force between two current-carrying wires

Consider now two long, straight, parallel wires each carrying current, say I_1 and I_2. The first wire (wire 1) creates a magnetic field in space, and in particular at the position of the second wire (wire 2). Thus, wire 2 will experience a magnetic force. Similarly, wire 2 will produce a magnetic field at the position of wire 1, so that wire 1 will also experience a magnetic force. By Newton's third law, the forces experienced by the two wires are equal and opposite (see Figure 6.21). If the currents are parallel, the forces are attractive and if they are antiparallel, the forces are repulsive.

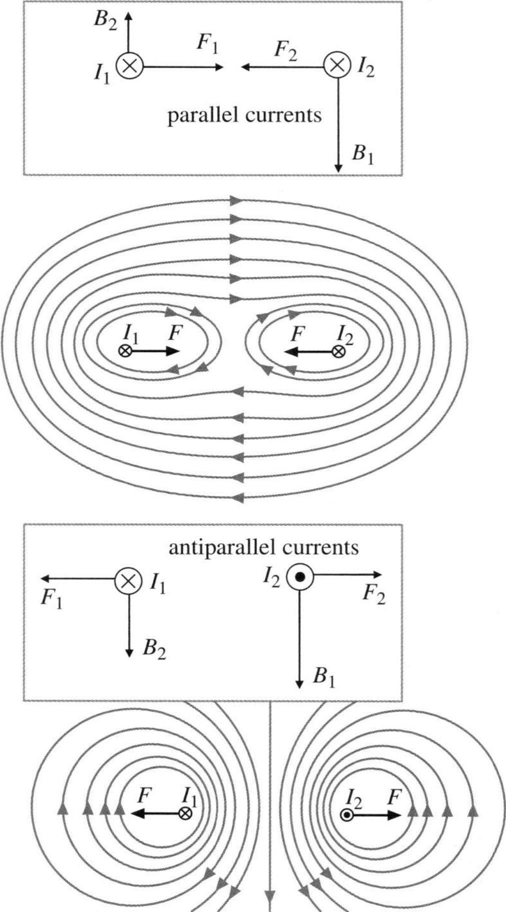

Figure 6.21 The forces on two parallel currents are equal and opposite.

Let us look at the problem of the forces between the two wires in more detail. Consider two long, straight, parallel wires each carrying electric current, say I_1 and I_2. The first wire (wire 1) creates a magnetic field B_1 and the second wire a magnetic field B_2. This means that wire 2 is in the magnetic field of wire 1 (B_1), and so will experience a force. Similarly, wire 1 is in the magnetic field of wire 2 (B_2), and so it too will experience a force. If the two parallel wires are separated by a distance r, then

$$B_1 = \mu_0 \frac{I_1}{2\pi r}$$

$$B_2 = \mu_0 \frac{I_2}{2\pi r}$$

Note that since the currents are different, the magnetic fields are different too. Now, the force on a length L of wire 2 is

$$F_2 = B_1 I_2 L$$

$$\Rightarrow F_2 = \mu_0 \frac{I_1}{2\pi r} I_2 L$$

and similarly the force on an equal length of wire 1 is

$$F_1 = B_2 I_1 L$$

$$\Rightarrow F_1 = \mu_0 \frac{I_2}{2\pi r} I_1 L$$

so, the two forces are equal in magnitude even though the magnetic fields are different. The equality of the forces is expected. The force that wire 1 exerts on wire 2 must be accompanied (Newton's third law) by an equal and opposite force. Let us now use the right-hand rule to find the directions of these forces. Assume first that the currents are flowing into the page. Then the magnetic fields are as shown and the forces are therefore attractive. If wire 1 carries current into the page and wire 2 carries current out of the page, the forces are repulsive. In both cases, we are consistent with Newton's third law. This is how it should be.

This fact is used to define the ampere, the unit of electric current. The ampere *equals* a coulomb divided by a second but it is no longer defined this way.

► The ampere is defined through the magnetic force between two parallel wires. If the force on a 1 m length of two wires that are 1 m apart and carrying equal currents is 2×10^{-7} N, then the current in each wire is defined to be 1 A.

The coulomb is defined in terms of the ampere as the amount of charge that flows past a certain point in a wire when a current of 1 A flows for 1 s.

? QUESTIONS

1 Draw the magnetic field lines for two parallel wires carrying equal currents into the page. Repeat for antiparallel currents.

2 Find the direction of the missing quantity from B, v and F in each of the cases shown in Figure 6.22. The circle represents a positive charge.

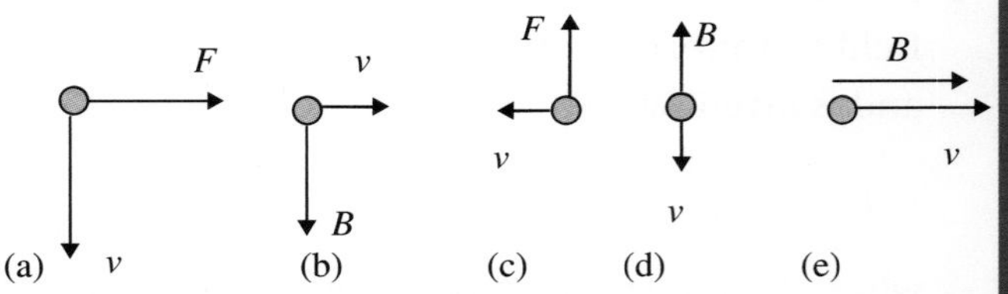

Figure 6.22 For question 2.

3 Two long, straight wires lie on the page and carry currents of 3.0 A and 4.0 A as shown in Figure 6.23. Find the magnetic field at point P.

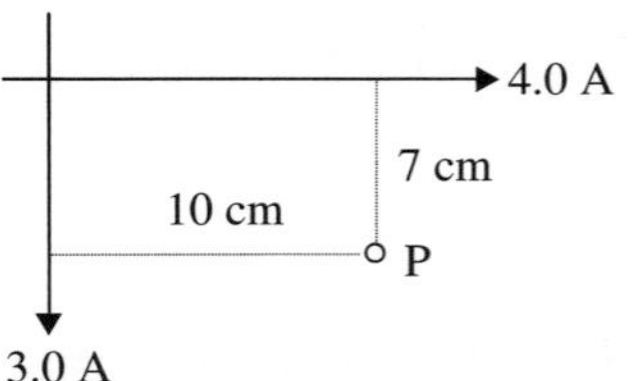

Figure 6.23 For question 3.

4 Find the magnetic field at points P, Q and R in Figure 6.24. The currents are parallel and each carry 5.00 A. Point Q is equidistant from the wires. (The three points lie on the same plane as the wires.)

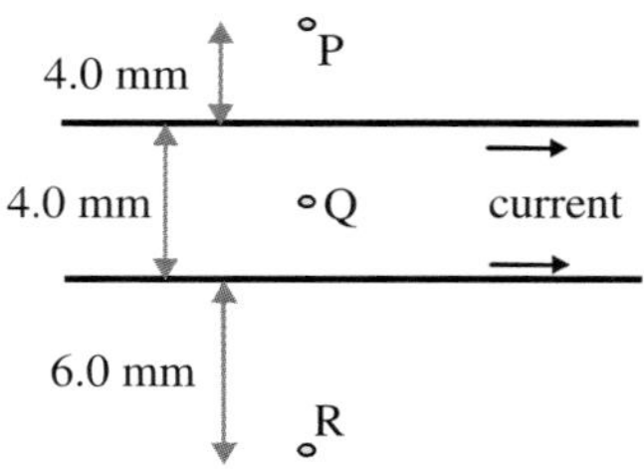

Figure 6.24 For question 4.

5 Draw the magnetic field lines that result when the magnetic field of a long straight wire carrying current into the page is superimposed on a uniform magnetic field pointing to the right that lies on the page. (See Figure 6.25.)

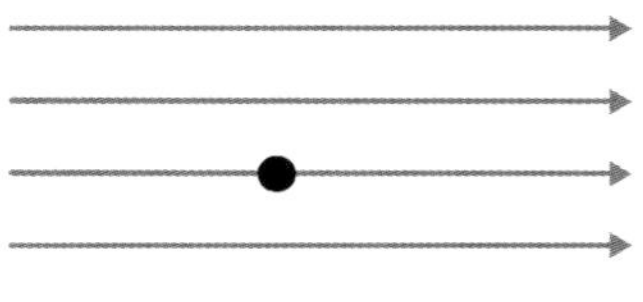

Figure 6.25 For question 5.

6 A long straight wire carries current as shown in Figure 6.26. Two electrons move with velocities that are parallel and perpendicular to the current. Find the direction of the magnetic force experienced by each electron.

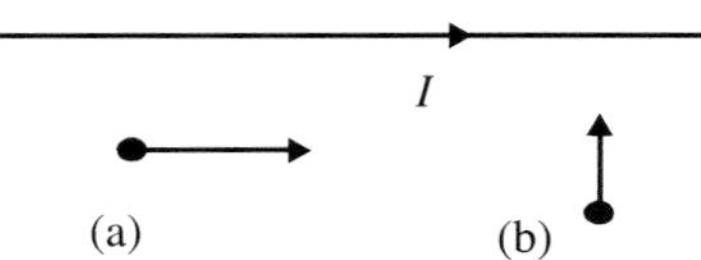

Figure 6.26 For question 6.

7 A proton moves past a bar magnet as shown in Figure 6.27. Find the direction of the force it experiences in each case.

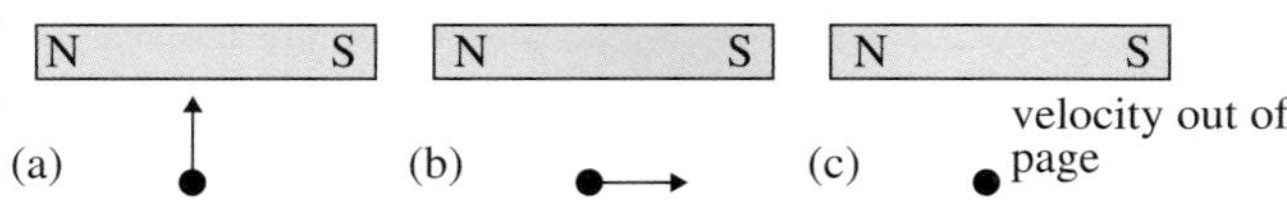

Figure 6.27 For question 7.

8 An electron is shot along the axis of a solenoid that carries current. Will it experience a magnetic force?

9 What is the direction of a magnetic field in each of the four cases in Figure 6.28 that results in a force on the current as shown?

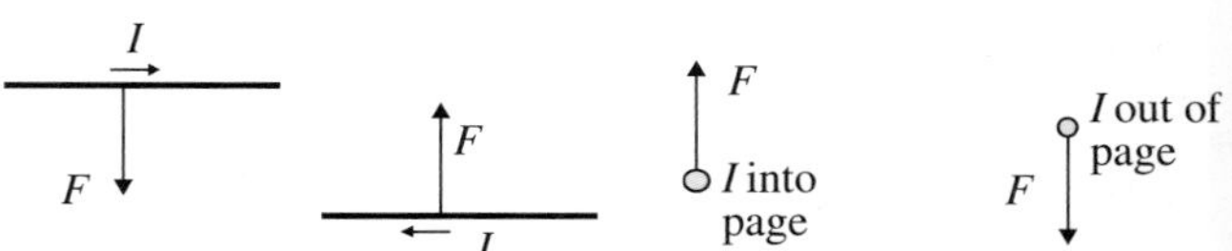

Figure 6.28 For question 9.

10 A rectangular loop of wire of size 5 cm × 15 cm is placed near a long straight wire with side CD at a distance of 5 cm from it, as shown in Figure 6.29. What is the net force exerted on the loop (magnitude and direction)? How does your answer change if the current in the loop is reversed?

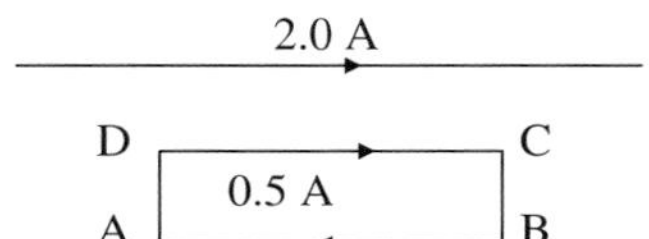

Figure 6.29 For question 10.

11 A rectangular coil of size 20 cm × 10 cm is placed in a horizontal uniform magnetic field of magnitude 0.050 T, as shown in Figure 6.30. A current of 2.0 A flows in the coil in a counter-clockwise direction as shown.
(a) Find the force on sections AB, BC, CD and DA.
(b) What is the net force on the coil?

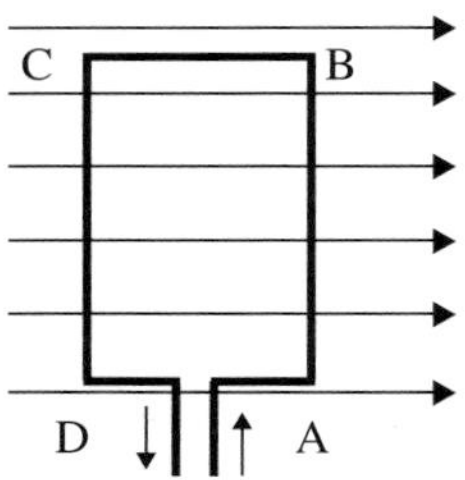

Figure 6.30 For question 11.

12 A tightly wound solenoid of length 30 cm is to produce a magnetic field of 2.26×10^{-3} T along its axis when a current of 15.0 A flows in it. If the radius of the solenoid is 12.0 cm, what length of wire is required to make the solenoid?

13 What is the direction of the magnetic field at points P and Q in the plane of a circular loop carrying a counter-clockwise current, as shown in Figure 6.31?

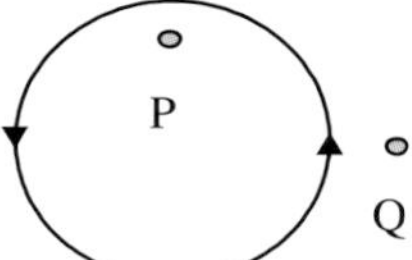

Figure 6.31 For question 13.

14 Two parallel wires a distance of 20.0 cm apart carry currents of 2.0 A and 3.0 A as shown in Figure 6.32.

(a) At which points is the magnetic field zero?

(b) How would your answer change if the direction of the 3.0 A current were reversed?

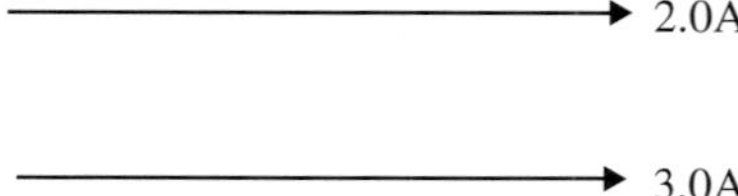

Figure 6.32 For question 14.

15 Figure 6.33 shows two parallel plates with a potential difference of 120 V a distance 5.0 cm apart. The top plate is at the higher potential and the shaded region is a region of magnetic field normal to the page.

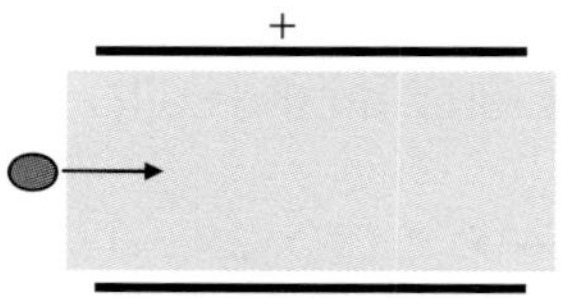

Figure 6.33 For question 15.

(a) What should the magnetic field magnitude and direction be such that an electron experiences zero net force when shot through the plates with a speed of 2×10^5 m s^{-1}.

(b) Would a proton shot with the same speed through the plates experience zero net force?

(c) If the electron's speed were doubled, would it still be undeflected if the magnetic field took the value you found in (a)?

16 A bar magnet is placed in a uniform magnetic field as shown in Figure 6.34.

(a) Is there a net force on the bar magnet?

(b) Will it move? If so, how?

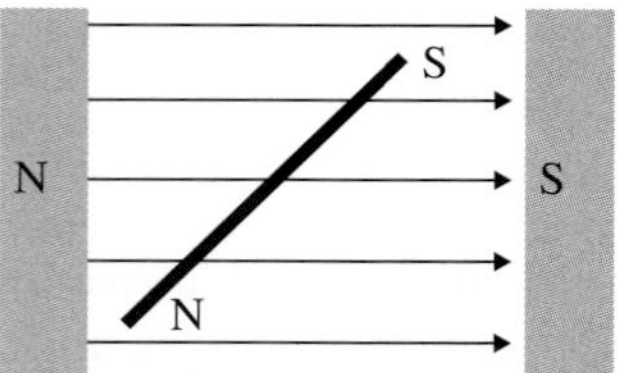

Figure 6.34 For question 16.

17 A high-tension electricity wire running along a north–south line carries a current of 3000.0 A. If the magnetic field of the earth at the position of the wire has a magnitude of 5.00×10^{-5} T and makes an angle of 30° below the horizontal, what is the force experienced by a length of 30.0 m of the wire?

HL only

18 Two circular loops of wire have their planes parallel and one is directly below the other, as shown in Figure 6.35. Current flows in a counter-clockwise direction (when looked at from above the loops) in both loops. Will there be a force between the loops? If yes, what will its direction be. If not, why is the force zero?

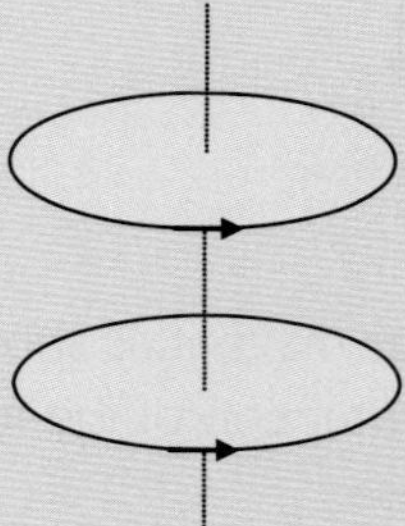

Figure 6.35 For question 18.

19 Figure 6.36 shows two parallel conductors carrying current out of the page. Conductor 1 carries double the current of conductor 2. Draw to scale the magnetic fields created by each conductor at the position of the other and the forces on each conductor.

Figure 6.36 For question 19.

20 An electron of speed v enters a region of magnetic field B directed normally to its velocity and is deflected into a circular path. Find an expression for the number of revolutions per second the electron will make. If the electron is replaced by a proton, how does your answer change?

HL only

21 A proton of velocity 1.5×10^6 m s^{-1} enters a region of uniform magnetic field $B = 0.50$ T. The magnetic field is directed vertically up (along the positive z direction) and the proton's velocity is initially on the z–x plane making an angle of 30° with the positive x axis. (See Figure 6.37.)

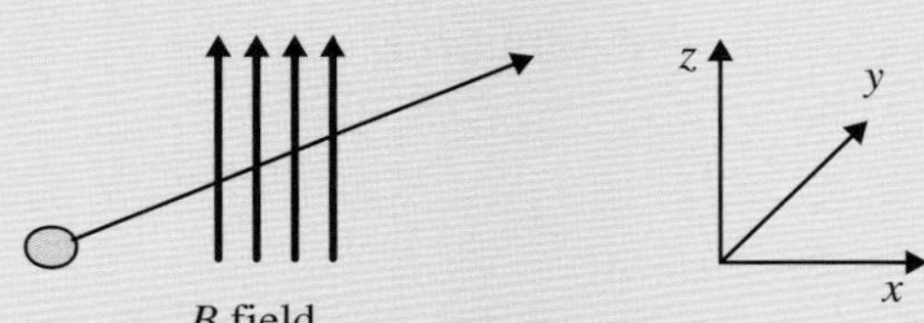

Figure 6.37 For question 21.

(a) Show that the proton will follow a helical path around the magnetic field lines.
(b) What is the radius of the helix?
(c) How many revolutions per second does the proton make?
(d) How fast is the proton moving along the field lines?
(e) What is the vertical separation of the coils of the helix?

22 An electron enters a region of uniform magnetic field $B = 0.50$ T, its velocity being normal to the magnetic field direction. The electron is deflected into a circular path and leaves the region of magnetic field after being deflected by an angle of 30° with respect to its original direction. How long was the electron in the region of magnetic field?

23 Find the magnetic field at point P due to three currents as shown in Figure 6.38.

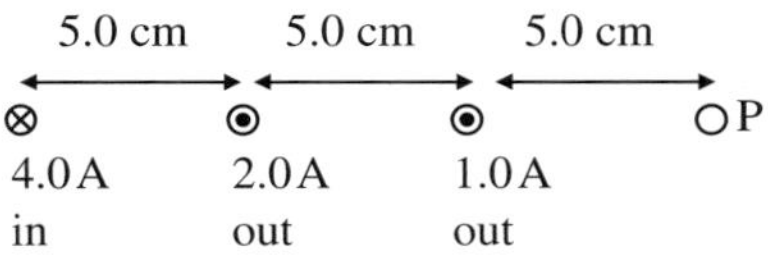

Figure 6.38 For question 23.

HL only

24 Find the magnetic field at point P due to the currents shown in Figure 6.39.

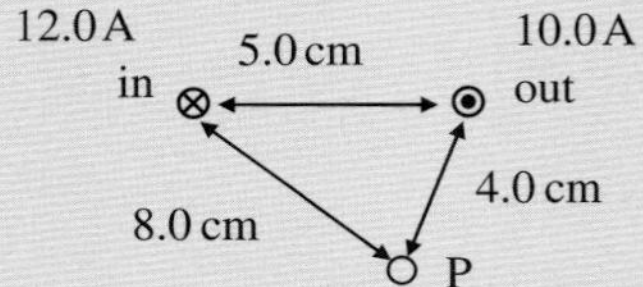

Figure 6.39 For question 24.

25 Three parallel wires carry currents as shown in Figure 6.40. Find the force per unit length that wires 1 and 3 exert on wire 2.

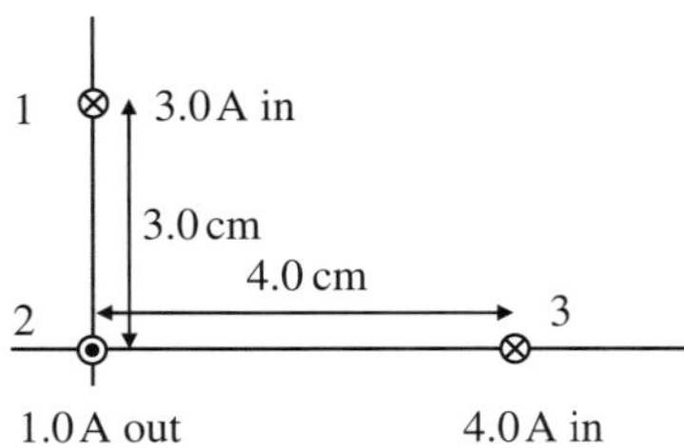

Figure 6.40 For question 25.

26 The magnetic field at the centre of a circular loop of wire of radius r carrying current I is given by the formula

$$B = \mu_0 \frac{I}{2r}$$

Use this expression to find the magnetic field created by an electron as it rotates with speed v in a circular orbit of radius r around a nucleus.

HL only

27 A tightly wound solenoid is to be made with wire from a fixed quantity (mass) of copper. It will then be connected to a source of *fixed* potential difference. How should the solenoid be made in order to produce the largest magnetic field?

28 Two parallel wires separated by a distance d carry the same current I, as shown in Figure 6.41.

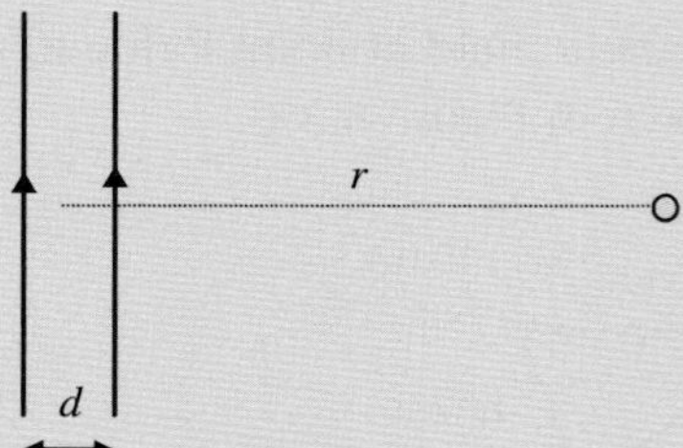

Figure 6.41 For question 28.

(a) Calculate the magnitude of the magnetic field at a point in the plane of the wires a distance r from the middle of the wires.

(b) By using the binomial expansion when r is much larger than d, show that the leading term in the expansion is $B = \mu_0 \frac{2I}{2\pi r}$. Why is this so?

(c) Repeat for the case where the currents are antiparallel. This time show that the leading term is $B = \mu_0 \frac{Id}{2\pi r^2}$. Why are the two expansions so different?

29 In a particle accelerator called the cyclotron, a charged particle is accelerated by an electric field and bent into a circular path by a magnetic field. The magnetic field is assumed uniform and the north and south poles are separated by a small gap. The particles to be accelerated originate from a source at the centre of the bottom magnet pole (the south pole in Figure 6.42) and begin to move outward in a circular path. The bottom magnet pole is split into two pieces called dees. An alternating potential difference is set up between the two dees so that every time the particle crosses from one dee to the other it increases its kinetic energy and thus moves on a circle of larger radius.

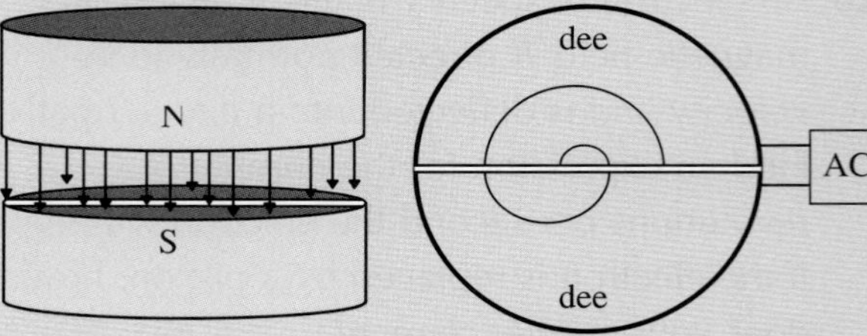

Figure 6.42 For question 29.

(a) Explain why the particle follows a spiral path.

(b) Show that the operation of the cyclotron depends on the frequency of the alternating voltage source, being equal to the frequency of revolution of the particle to be accelerated.

(c) If the mass and charge of the particle are m and q, respectively, show that the period of revolution is

$$T = \frac{2\pi m}{qB}$$

where B is the magnetic field, and is thus independent of the speed of the particle.

(d) Find the frequency (i.e. the number of revolutions per second) of an electron assuming that the magnetic field has a value of 0.50 T.

(e) If the potential difference between the dees at the instant the electrons cross is 120 kV, what would the kinetic energy of the electrons be after 100 revolutions?

30 A uniform magnetic field is established in the plane of the paper and has magnitude 0.3 mT. Two parallel wires separated by 5.0 cm carry currents of 200 A and 100 A into the plane of the paper as shown in Figure 6.43. Find the magnetic force per unit length on the 100 A wire.

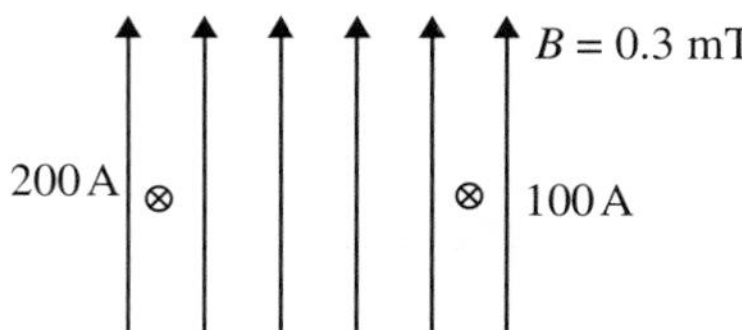

Figure 6.43 For question 30.

31 A uniform magnetic field is established in the plane of the paper as shown in Figure 6.44. Two wires carry *parallel* currents of equal magnitudes normally to the plane of the paper at P and Q. Point R is on the line joining P to Q and closer to Q. The magnetic field at position R is zero.

(a) Are the currents going into the paper or out of the paper?

(b) If the current is increased slightly, will the point where the magnetic field is zero move to the right or to the left of R?

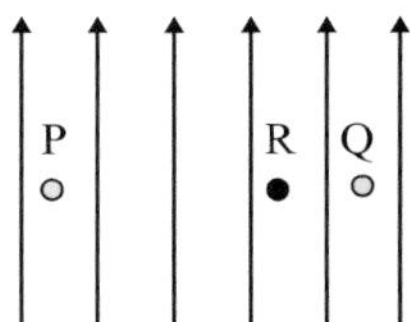

Figure 6.44 For question 31.

32 Two identical charged particles move in circular paths at right angles to a uniform magnetic field as shown in Figure 6.45. The radius of particle 2 is twice that of particle 1.

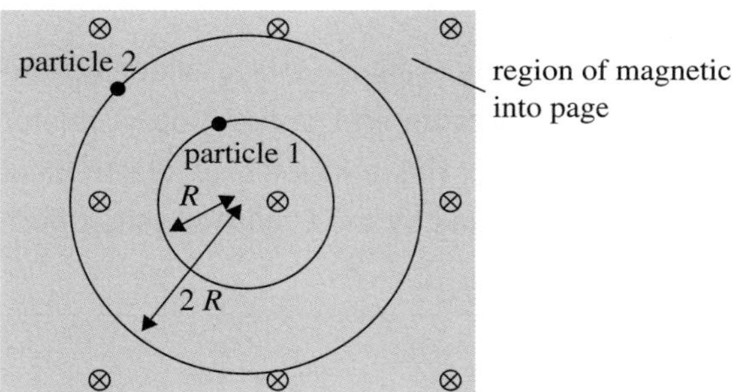

Figure 6.45 For question 32.

Determine the following ratios:

(a) $\dfrac{\text{period of particle 2}}{\text{period of particle 1}}$;

(b) $\dfrac{E_k \text{ of particle 2}}{E_k \text{ of particle 1}}$.

Electromagnetic induction

This chapter deals with Faraday's law, which dictates how a changing magnetic flux through a loop induces an emf in the loop. A related law, Lenz's law, determines the direction of this emf. The principles of electromagnetic induction are the result of ingenious experimenting by the English physicist Michael Faraday.

Objectives

By the end of this chapter you should be able to:

- calculate *flux* or *flux linkage* using $\Phi = BA\cos\theta$ or $\Phi = NBA\cos\theta$;
- identify situations in which an emf is *induced* and determine the magnitude of the emf by using *Faraday's law*, $\mathcal{E} = \frac{\Delta\Phi}{\Delta t}$ or $\mathcal{E} = -\frac{d\Phi}{dt}$; included are cases of a *changing area*, a *changing magnetic field* or a *changing angle between magnetic field and normal to loop*;
- find the direction of the induced current using *Lenz's law*.

A wire moving in a magnetic field

Let us imagine that a wire of length L is moved with velocity v in a region of a magnetic field of constant magnitude B. Assume for convenience that the magnetic field is coming out of the page and that the wire moves from top to bottom (see Figure 7.1).

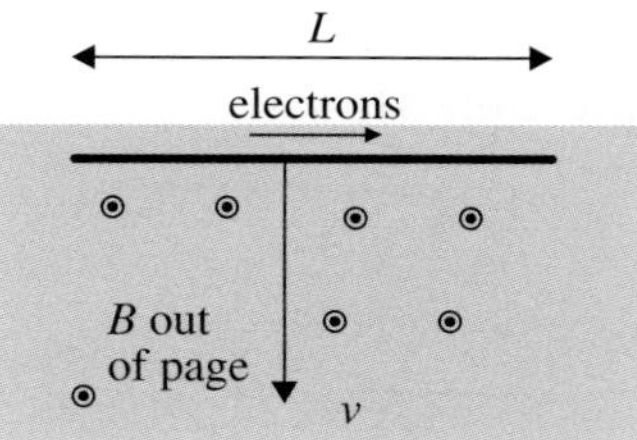

Figure 7.1 The wire is made to move normally to the magnetic field at constant speed. An emf develops between the ends of the wire.

The wire is conducting: that is, it has many 'free' electrons. As the wire moves, the electrons also move from top to bottom. Thus, the magnetic field will exert a force on these moving electrons. (We are talking here about the force on a moving charge, not the force on a current in the wire. There is no current in the wire since the wire is not part of any closed circuit.) The force on the electrons is directed from left to right and therefore the electrons are pushed to the right. This means that the left end of the wire has a net positive charge and the right end has an equal net negative charge accumulated there. (The net charge of the wire is zero.) The flow of electrons towards the right end of the wire will stop when the electrons already there are numerous enough to push any new electrons back by electrostatic repulsion. There is, in other words, an electric field established in the wire whose direction is from left to right. The value of this electric field is

$$E = \frac{\Delta V}{\Delta x} = \frac{V}{L}$$

where V is the potential difference between the ends of the wire that is established because of the accumulation of electric charge at its ends. The flow of electrons will thus stop when the electric force eE pushing the electrons back equals the magnetic force evB pushing them towards the right end. Thus

$$eE = evB$$

and so (substituting for the electric field)

$$V = vBL$$

We have found the extraordinary result that a conducting wire of length L moving with speed v normally to a magnetic field B will have a potential difference vBL across its ends. This is called a *motional emf*: it has been induced as a result of the motion of the conductor in the magnetic field. It is instructive to check that the quantity vBL really has the units of potential difference, namely volts:

$$[vBL] = \mathrm{m\,s^{-1}\,T\,m} = \mathrm{m\,s^{-1}}\frac{\mathrm{N}}{\mathrm{A\,m}}\mathrm{m}$$
$$= \mathrm{s^{-1}}\frac{\mathrm{J}}{\mathrm{C\,s^{-1}}} = \frac{\mathrm{J}}{\mathrm{C}} = \mathrm{V}$$

It is worthwhile pointing out that, whereas in electrostatics the electric field inside a conductor is zero, this is no longer the case when charges are allowed to move. Instead, the condition of zero electric field is replaced by a more general condition, namely that $eE = evB$ on a moving charge e.

Faraday's law

As we saw earlier, an electric current creates a magnetic field. In the previous section we saw that a wire that moves in a magnetic field has an induced emf at its ends. Actually producing a current by a magnetic field was a difficult problem in nineteenth-century physics.

Consider the following experiment. A magnet is moved towards a loop of wire whose ends are connected to a sensitive galvanometer and in a direction normal to the plane of the loop, as shown in Figure 7.2. The galvanometer registers a current.

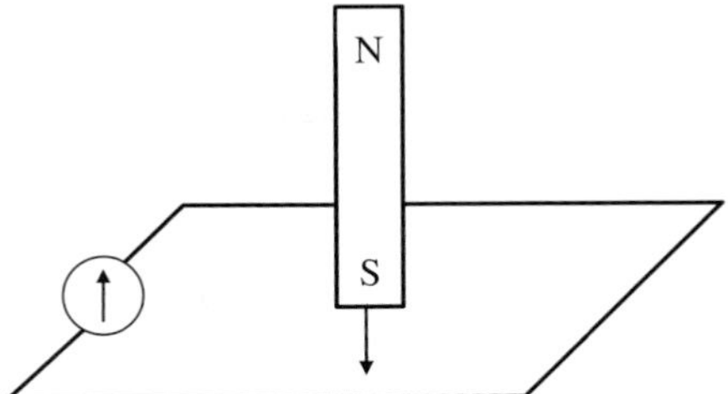

Figure 7.2 A bar magnet moving through a loop of wire connected to a galvanometer. An emf is induced in the loop and the galvanometer registers a current.

If the magnet is simply placed near the coil but does not move relative to it, nothing happens. The current has been created as a result of the motion of the magnet relative to the loop of wire. If we now move the magnet toward the coil faster, the reading on the galvanometer is greater. If we move the coil toward the magnet, we again find a reading. This indicates that it is the relative motion of the coil and magnet that is responsible for the effect. If a magnet of greater strength is used, the current produced is greater. If we try a different loop of wire, one with the same area but a larger number of turns of wire we find a greater current when a magnet is moved toward the wire. We also observe that if the area of the loop is increased, the current also increases. If the magnet is moved at an angle to the plane of the loop other than a right angle, the current decreases. Our problem is now to find the common thread in all these observations. To summarize, the observations are that the current registered by the galvanometer increases when:

- the relative speed of the magnet with respect to the coil increases;
- the strength of the magnet increases;
- the number of turns increases;
- the area of the loop increases;
- the magnet moves at right angles to the plane of the loop.

Faraday found that the common thread behind all these observations is the concept of *magnetic flux*. Imagine a loop of wire, which for simplicity we take to be planar (i.e. the entire loop lies on one plane). If this loop is in a region of magnetic field whose magnitude and direction is constant, then we define magnetic flux as follows.

▶ The *magnetic flux* Φ through the loop is

$$\Phi = BA\cos\theta$$

where A is the area of the loop and θ is the angle between the magnetic field direction and the direction *normal to the loop area.* (See Figure 7.3.) If the loop has N turns of wire around it, the flux is given by

$$\Phi = NBA\cos\theta$$

in which case we speak of *flux linkage*. The unit of magnetic flux is the Weber (Wb): 1 Wb = 1 T m^2.

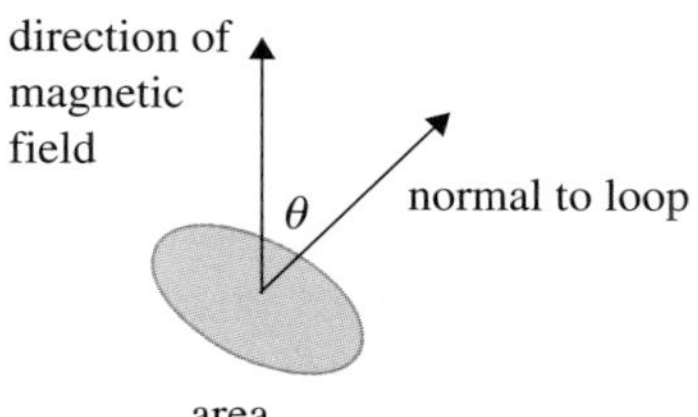

Figure 7.3.

This means that if the magnetic field is along the plane of the loop, then $\theta = 90°$ and hence $\Phi = 0$ (see Figure 7.4a). The maximum flux through the loop occurs when $\theta = 0°$, when the magnetic field is normal to the loop area and its value is then BA (see Figure 7.4b).

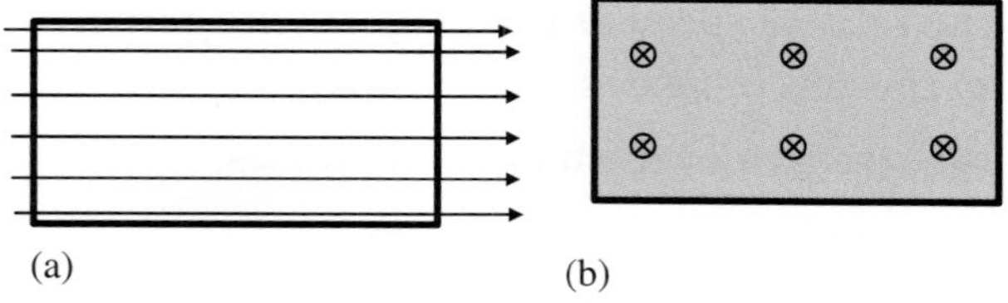

Figure 7.4 (a) The loop is not pierced by any magnetic field lines, so the flux through it is zero. (b) The magnetic field is normal to the loop, so the flux through it is the largest possible.

The intuitive picture of magnetic flux is the number of magnetic field lines that cross or pierce the loop area. Note that if the magnetic field went through only half the loop area, the other half being in a region of no magnetic field, then the flux in that case would be $\Phi = \frac{BA}{2}$. In other words, what counts is the part of the loop area that is pierced by magnetic field lines. Thus, to increase the magnetic flux of a loop of wire we must:

- increase the loop area that is exposed to the magnetic field;
- increase the value of the magnetic field;
- have the loop normal to the magnetic field.

The loop area has two sides (excluding Möbius strips!). Which of the two sides do we choose in order to define the normal direction to the loop? There are clearly two vectors normal to the loop and they point in opposite directions (see Figure 7.5). The answer is that it does not matter: the choice is a question of convention. But once the choice has been made, we must stick with it.

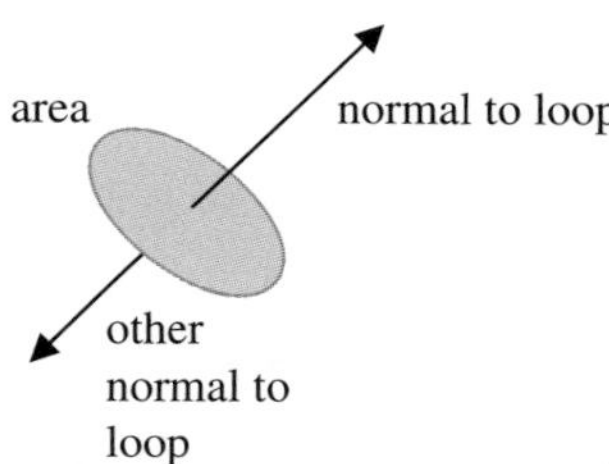

Figure 7.5.

Example question

Q1

A loop of area 2 cm^2 is in a constant magnetic field of $B = 0.10$ T. What is the magnetic flux through the loop when:

(a) the loop is perpendicular to the field;
(b) the loop is parallel to the field;
(c) the normal to the loop and the field have an angle of 60° between them?

Answer

(a) In this case $\theta = 0°$ and $\cos 0° = 1$, so

$$\text{flux} = 0.10\ \text{T} \times 2 \times 10^{-4}\ \text{m}^2 = 2 \times 10^{-5}\ \text{Wb}$$

(b) In this case $\theta = 90°$ and $\cos 90° = 0$, so

flux = 0

(c) In this case $\theta = 60°$, so

$$\text{flux} = 0.10\ \text{T} \times 2 \times 10^{-4}\ \text{m}^2 \times 0.5$$
$$= 10^{-5}\ \text{Wb}$$

What does magnetic flux have to do with the problem of how a magnetic field can create an electric field? The answer lies in a *changing magnetic flux*. In all the cases we described when looking at Figure 7.2 we had a magnetic flux through the loop, which was changing with time. As a magnet is brought closer to the loop area, the value of the magnetic field at the loop position is increasing and so is flux. If the magnet is held stationary near the loop, there is flux through the loop but it is not changing – so nothing happened. If the number of turns is increased, so is the flux linkage. Thus, there seems to be a connection between the amount of current induced and the rate of change of magnetic flux linkage through the loop. This is known as **Faraday's law.**

▶ Faraday found that the induced emf is equal to the (negative) rate of change of magnetic flux, that is

$$\mathcal{E} = -N\frac{\Delta\Phi}{\Delta t}$$

The minus sign need not concern us, as we will be finding the *magnitude* of the induced emf. However, if we use calculus (i.e. $\mathcal{E} = -N\frac{d\Phi}{dt}$), then the minus sign must be included. We will use calculus only in Chapter 5.8.

Example questions

Q2

The magnetic field through a single loop of area 0.2 m^2 is changing at a rate of 4 T s^{-1}. What is the induced emf?

Answer

The magnetic flux through the loop is changing because of the changing magnetic field, hence

$$\Phi = BA$$
$$\Rightarrow \mathcal{E} = \frac{\Delta\Phi}{\Delta t}$$
$$= \frac{\Delta B}{\Delta t}A$$
$$= 4 \times 0.2$$
$$= 0.8\ \text{V}$$

Q3

A uniform magnetic field $B = 0.40$ T is established into the page, as shown in Figure 7.6. A rod of length $L = 0.20$ m is placed on a railing and pushed to the right at constant speed $v = 0.60$ m s^{-1}. What is the induced emf in the loop?

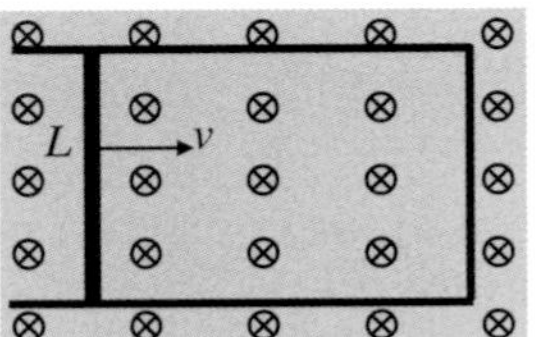

Figure 7.6.

Answer

The flux in the loop is clearly changing since the area of the loop decreases. Thus, there will be an emf induced. In a time interval Δt the rod will move to the right a distance $v\Delta t$ and so the area will decrease by $\Delta A = Lv\Delta t$, thus

$$\Phi = BA$$
$$\Rightarrow \mathcal{E} = \frac{\Delta\Phi}{\Delta t}$$
$$= B\frac{\Delta A}{\Delta t}$$
$$= B\frac{Lv\Delta t}{\Delta t}$$
$$= BLv$$
$$= 0.40 \times 0.20 \times 0.60$$
$$= 48\ \text{mV}$$

We began this chapter with a discussion of a wire that is dragged in a region of magnetic field. We saw, by considering the forces acting on the electrons of the wire, that a potential difference was induced at its ends that is given by

$$\mathcal{E} = BLv$$

We may re-derive this result by making use of the concept of changing flux and Faraday's law. The wire cuts magnetic field lines as it moves in the magnetic field. In time Δt it will move a distance of $v\,\Delta t$ and so the flux through *the area swept by the wire* is

$$\begin{aligned}\Delta\Phi &= BLv\Delta t\\ \Rightarrow \mathcal{E} &= \frac{\Delta\Phi}{\Delta t}\\ &= BLv\end{aligned}$$

(see Figure 7.7).

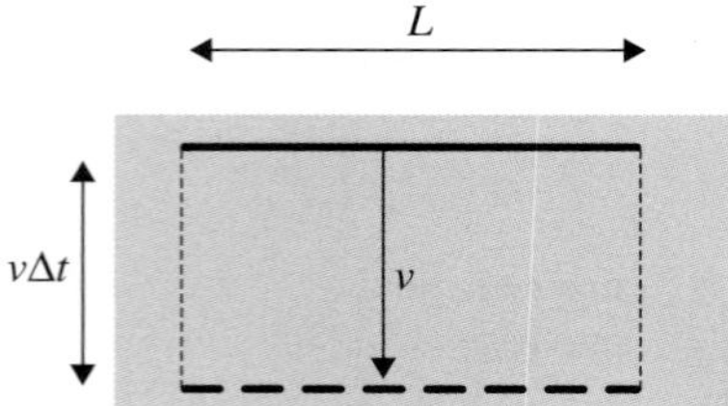

Figure 7.7 The wire sweeps out an area pierced by magnetic field lines as it moves.

Lenz's law

Having seen that a changing magnetic flux will produce an emf and therefore a current in a conducting loop of wire, we now move to the interesting problem of determining the direction of this induced current. We can guess the answer on the following intuitive grounds. Let us look again at example question 3. Which will be the direction of the induced current? There are two possibilities, the current will either flow in a clockwise or a counter-clockwise fashion in the loop. In either case, there will be a force on the rod because it is a current-carrying wire in a magnetic field.

If the current flows in the counter-clockwise direction:

By the right-hand rule, the force is directed towards the right – in the direction of motion of the rod.

If the current flows in the clockwise direction:

By the right-hand rule, the force is directed towards the left – in the direction opposite to the motion of the rod.

Which choice makes physical sense? If we decide that the current flows in the counter-clockwise direction, the magnetic force will accelerate the rod to the right, thereby increasing its speed. An increased speed leads to an increased emf (recall that $\mathcal{E} = BLv$) and thus increased current. This in turn means that the force on the rod will also get bigger and thus the acceleration will get bigger. And we go on forever. The rod accelerates forever without anyone providing the necessary energy. This choice is absurd. It violates the law of conservation of energy.

The current *must* flow in the clockwise direction. The force now is to the left and it opposes the motion of the rod. If we want the rod to move at constant speed, then we must apply on the rod a force equal and opposite to the magnetic force on the rod. If we do not apply any force on the rod, then the magnetic force will bring it to rest.

The reasoning applied above involves analysing forces. It can be used in almost any situation involving Faraday's law to find the direction of the induced current, but it would be good if we had a very general principle that would give us the answer. Such a general statement has been given by the Russian physicist Emil Lenz, and is called **Lenz's law**.

▶ Lenz's law states that the induced current will be in such a direction as to *oppose the change in the magnetic flux* that created the current.

This is a rather subtle and tricky formulation. Let us apply it to example question 3. The change in the magnetic flux has been a *decrease* in magnetic flux (area gets smaller). Lenz's law states that the induced current will be in a direction so as to oppose this *decrease*. The induced current will create *its own magnetic field*, as we learned from Ørsted's discovery. (This magnetic field has nothing to do with the magnetic field whose changing flux created the current.) But the magnetic field created by the induced current will also have a magnetic flux through the same loop. If the created magnetic field is in the same direction as the original magnetic field, its flux will add to the original flux (which, remember, is decreasing) and will thus prevent it from decreasing as fast. In this case the induced current is opposing the decrease in flux and this is what Lenz's law demands. If the induced magnetic field is to be in the same direction as the external magnetic field, the current must flow in a clockwise direction, as we found earlier. (It is assumed that you can find the direction of the current given the direction of the magnetic field it produces – the right-hand rule that allows us to do this is discussed in the previous chapter.)

Let us make sure that we understand what is going on by looking at another example.

Example question

Q4

A loop of wire has its plane horizontal and a bar magnet is dropped from above so that it falls through the loop with (a) the north pole first and (b) the south pole first, as shown in Figure 7.8. Find the direction of the current induced in the loop in each case.

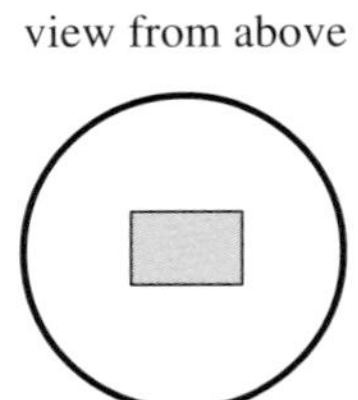

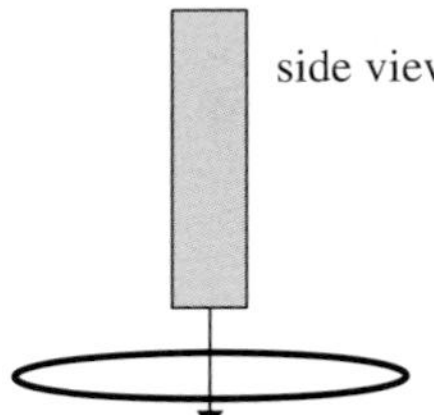

Figure 7.8.

Answer

(a) In this case, the north pole of the magnet enters first. The flux in the loop is *increasing* because the magnetic field at the loop is getting bigger as the magnet approaches. (We are taking the normal to the loop to be in the vertically down direction. This means that the flux is getting more and more positive.) The induced current must then oppose the *increase* in the flux. This can be done if the induced current produces a magnetic field in the *opposite* direction to that of the bar magnet. Thus, the current will flow in a counter-clockwise direction when looked at from above.

(b) In this case, the south pole of the magnet enters first. This time let us take the normal to the loop plane to be vertically up. Then the flux in the loop is again increasing and so the current will again produce a magnetic field opposite to the field of the bar magnet. This means that the induced magnetic field will be vertically down, thus the induced current is clockwise.

It is left as an exercise for you to show that the current (in both cases) flows in the opposite direction when the magnet is on its way out of the loop. You should also show that these conclusions are *independent* of the choice of the normal to the loop.

A good example that illustrates many of the principles of electromagnetic induction follows. Consider the motion of a rectangular loop of conducting wire of size $L \times L$ that moves with velocity v and enters a region of magnetic field of constant value B. The plane of the loop is normal to the magnetic field. This is illustrated in Figure 7.9.

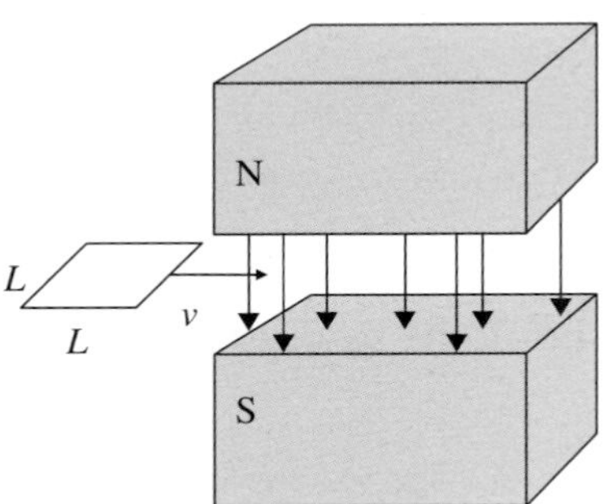

Figure 7.9 A horizontal loop entering a vertical magnetic field at constant speed.

As the loop begins to enter the region of magnetic field, the magnetic flux through the loop is increasing and so an emf will be induced in the loop. The flux equals $\Phi = BLx$ where x is the length of the loop that has entered the magnetic field region and so the rate of change of magnetic flux (and hence the emf) is BLv. A current then flows in the loop of value

$$I = \frac{\mathcal{E}}{R} = \frac{BLv}{R}$$

where R is the loop's resistance. By Lenz's law, the direction of the current is counter-clockwise (looked at from above). Therefore, there is a force acting on the part of the loop of length L that is inside the magnetic field. (The rear part of the loop is not inside the magnetic field and so experiences zero force.) The magnitude of the force is

$$F = BIL = \frac{B^2L^2v}{R}$$

and is directed against the velocity of the loop. Thus, if the loop is to maintain a constant velocity, a force pushing it to the right and equal to F must be applied to the loop. This means that this force does work. The rate at which work is being done (power dissipated) is

$$P = Fv = \frac{B^2L^2v^2}{R}$$

Where does this work go? It does *not* go into changing the kinetic energy of the loop since the loop is made to move at constant speed. The work goes into heating the wire. The wire has resistance and current flows in it. The power dissipated in the loop as a result of the current in it is

$$P = \mathcal{E}I = \frac{B^2L^2v^2}{R}$$

and is identical to the power dissipated by the external force, as it should be by energy conservation.

Faraday's disc

An interesting example of induced emf is provided by *Faraday's disc*. Like the example of the rod moving in a magnetic field, an emf is induced even though no magnetic flux is changing. This is a motional emf. A conducting disc of radius R rotates about an axis normal to its plane and going through its centre (see Figure 7.10). A magnetic field of constant value is established everywhere in space and is directed along the axis of rotation, which means it is also normal to the plane of the disc.

There is magnetic flux though the disc but it is constant in time. Imagine that the disc rotates with constant angular velocity in a counter-clockwise direction.

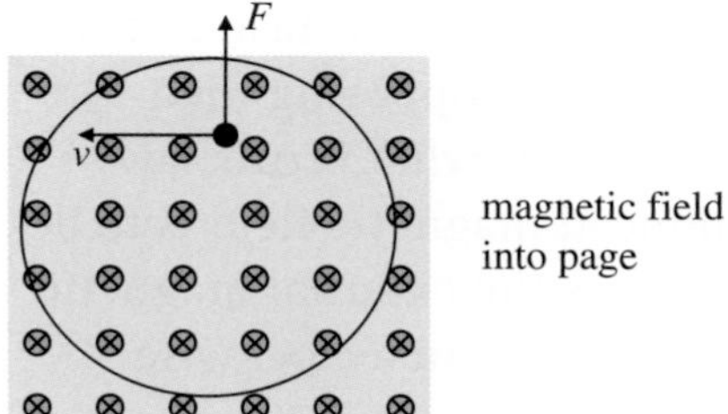

Figure 7.10 The disc is rotating at right angles to the magnetic field. A potential difference develops between the centre and the circumference.

This means that electrons in the disc experience a magnetic force that pushes them towards the circumference of the disc. The accumulation of electrons on the rim means that there is potential difference between the circumference and the centre of the disc. The flow of electrons will stop when the electric force on electrons trying to move to the circumference equals the magnetic force. The magnetic force on an electron at a distance r from the centre is

$$F = evB = e\omega rB$$

The magnitude of the electric field is $\frac{dV}{dr}$ and so

$$e\frac{dV}{dr} = e\omega rB$$

which can be integrated to give

$$\Delta V = \tfrac{1}{2}\omega R^2 B$$

for the potential difference between the centre and the circumference.

As with the case of the wire that moved in a magnetic field, the potential difference above can also be obtained through the concept of *flux through a swept area*. Thus, consider a radius of the disc. As the disc rotates, the radius can be thought to rotate too, and thus sweeps out an area given by

$$\Delta A = \tfrac{1}{2}R^2\Delta\theta$$

where $\Delta\theta$ is the angle the radius rotates by in a time equal to Δt. This is just the formula for the area of a sector of a circle of radius R and angle $\Delta\theta$. (See Figure 7.11.)

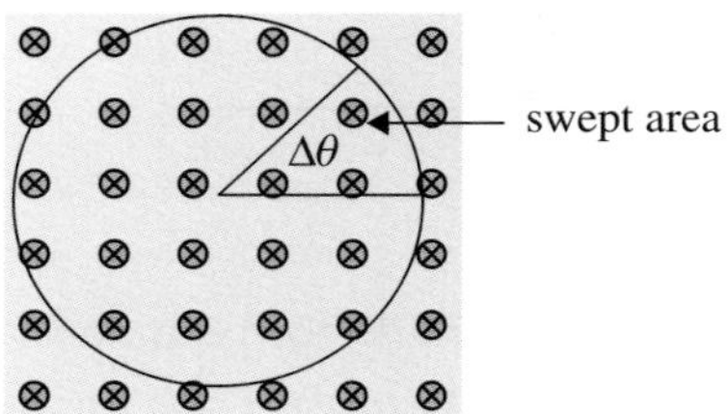

Figure 7.11 As a disc rotates, the radius can be thought to rotate too, sweeping out an area.

If the angular velocity of rotation is ω, then $\Delta\theta = \omega\Delta t$ and the flux through the swept area is $\Delta\Phi = B\frac{1}{2}R^2\omega\Delta t$. This means that the potential difference at the ends of the radius is

$$\begin{aligned}\mathcal{E} &= \frac{\Delta\Phi}{\Delta t}\\ &= \frac{B\frac{1}{2}R^2\omega\Delta t}{\Delta t}\\ &= \tfrac{1}{2}BR^2\omega\end{aligned}$$

as we found previously.

? QUESTIONS

1 The flux through a loop as a function of time is given by the graph in Figure 7.12. Make a sketch of the emf induced in the loop as a function of time.

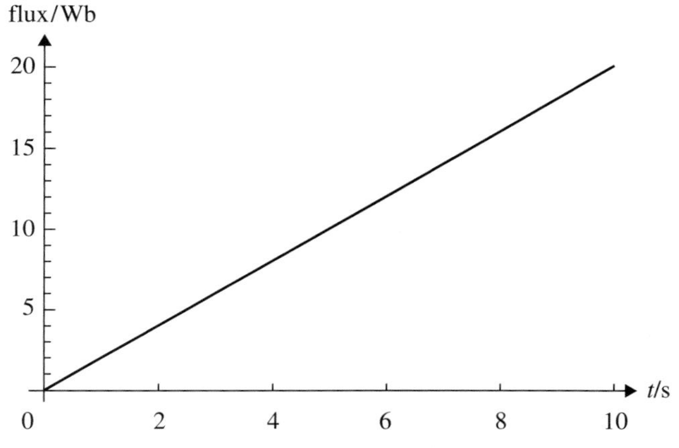

Figure 7.12 For question 1.

2 The flux through a loop as a function of time is given by the graph shown in Figure 7.13. Make a sketch of the emf induced in the loop as a function of time.

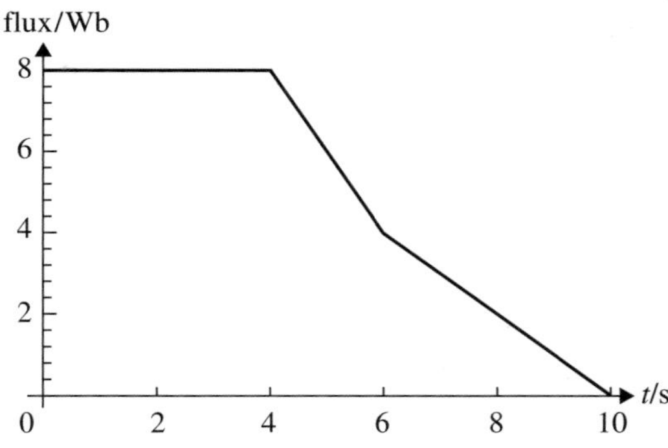

Figure 7.13 For question 2.

3 Figure 7.14 shows the emf induced in a loop as a result of a changing flux in the loop.
(a) What is a *possible* flux versus time graph that would give rise to such an emf?
(b) Why isn't there a unique answer?

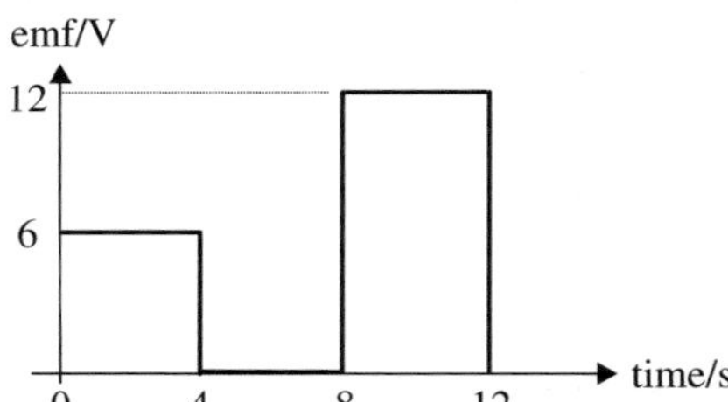

Figure 7.14 For question 3.

4 Figure 7.15 shows a top view of two solenoids with their axes parallel, one with a smaller diameter so that it fits inside the other. If the bigger solenoid has a current flowing in the clockwise direction (looked at from above) and the current is increasing in magnitude, find the direction of the induced current in the smaller solenoid.

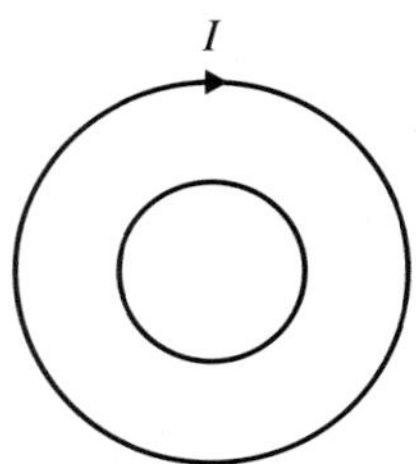

Figure 7.15 For question 4.

5 A metallic ring is dropped from a height above a bar magnet as shown in Figure 7.16. Determine the direction of the induced current in the ring as the ring falls over the magnet in each case, giving full explanations for your choices.

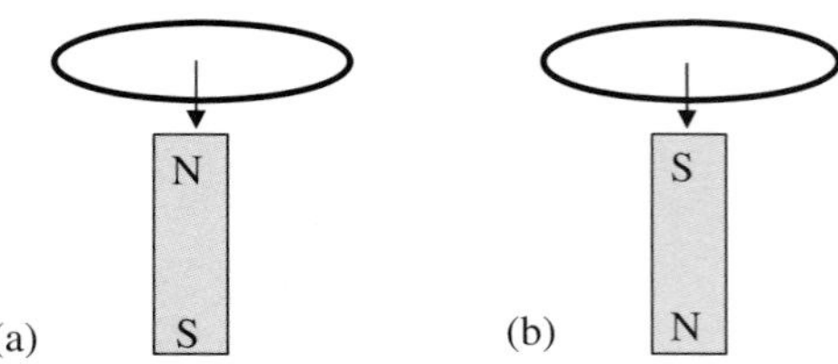

Figure 7.16 For question 5.

6 A magnet is dropped from above into a metallic ring as shown in Figure 7.17. Determine the direction of the current induced in the ring in each case.

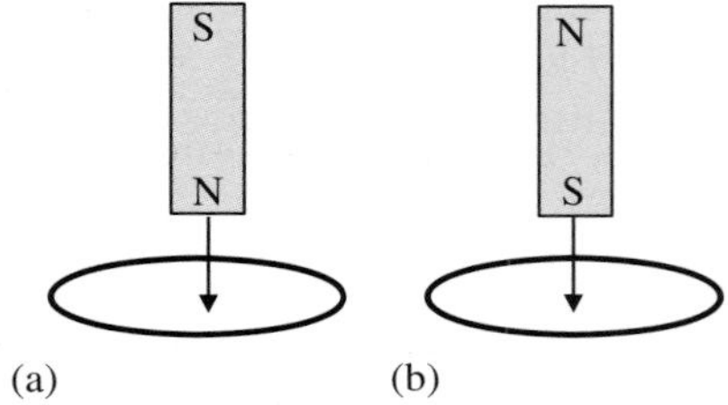

Figure 7.17 For question 6.

7 For question 5(a) determine the direction of the magnetic force on the ring as it (a) enters and (b) leaves the magnetic field.

8 A metallic rod of length L is dragged with constant velocity v in a region of magnetic field directed into the page (shaded region), as shown in Figure 7.18. By considering the force on electrons inside the rod, show that the ends of the rod will become oppositely charged. Which end is positively charged?

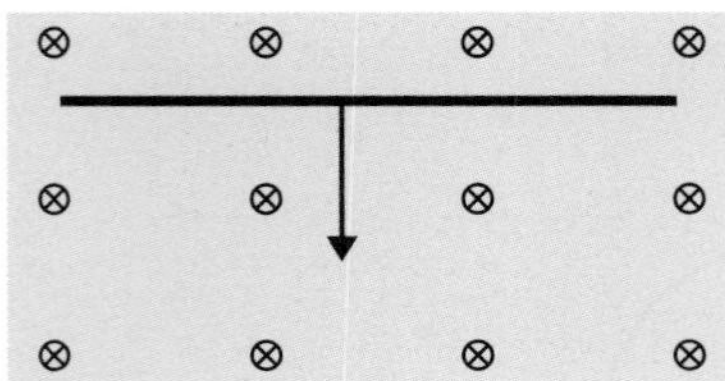

Figure 7.18 For question 8.

9 Find the direction of the current in the loop shown in Figure 7.19 as the current in the straight wire:

(a) increases;

(b) decreases.

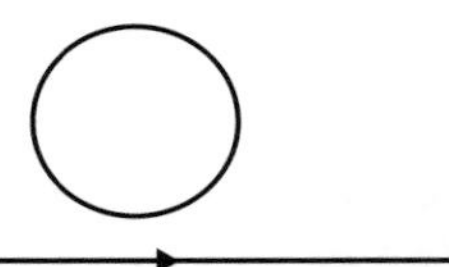

Figure 7.19 For question 9.

10 A coil of 1000 turns and length 20.0 cm has a smaller coil of diameter 2.0 cm and 200 turns inserted inside it. If the current in the big coil is changing at 150 A s^{-1}, find the emf induced in the smaller coil.

11 How can the Faraday disc be connected to an outside circuit to provide it with electric current? Is the current provided AC or DC?

12 Look at Figure 7.20, which we used earlier in the text. If the magnetic field is increasing, what will happen to the rod AB?

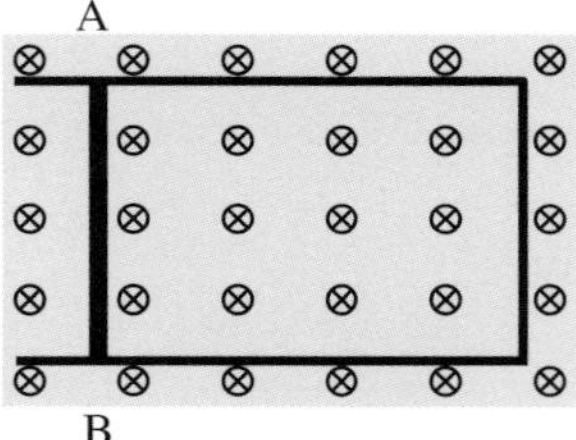

Figure 7.20 For question 12.

HL Mathematics only

13 The problem of the rod sliding over a wire in the shape of a Π that we met in example question 3 and question 12 will now be re-examined for the case in which the railing is no longer horizontal but is inclined by an angle θ, as shown in Figure 7.21. The rod has mass m, length L, resistance R and the

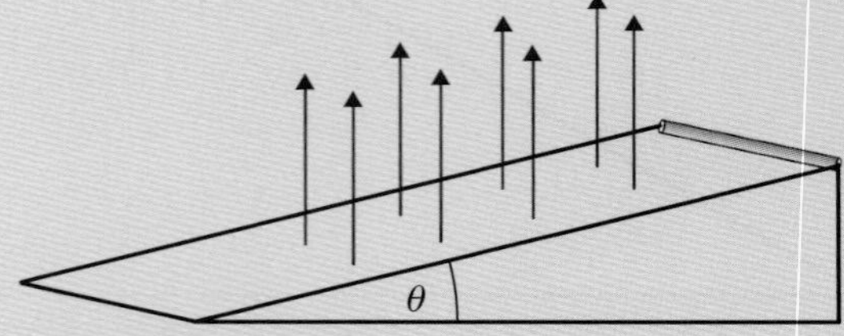

Figure 7.21 For question 13.

magnetic field B is uniform and directed vertically upward. The rod starts from rest; find the terminal velocity reached by the rod.

Hint: Do this in steps as follows.

Part A: (a) Find the flux of the magnetic field through the loop. (b) Find the rate of change of this flux and hence the induced emf. (c) What is the direction of the induced current? (d) Find the magnitude and direction of the magnetic force on the rod. (e) Assume terminal velocity is reached and find an expression for it.

Part B: To find the precise dependence of the velocity on time, write down an expression for the acceleration of the rod down the plane by applying Newton's second law. Realize that the acceleration is the time derivative of velocity and hence solve the differential equation to find the velocity as a function of time. Verify that the rod reaches the terminal velocity you found in (e).

14 A square conducting loop of wire of side a, mass m and resistance R falls under gravity normally to a uniform, horizontal magnetic field B, as shown in Figure 7.22. The area of the loop is small enough so that it can be contained totally within the region of the field.

(a) While the loop is entering the magnetic field, find the magnitude and direction of the induced current.

(b) Write down an expression for the acceleration of the loop as it is entering the field.

(c) Write the acceleration as the time derivative of the velocity and hence show that after time t the velocity of the loop is

$$v = \frac{gmR}{B^2a^2}\left[1 - \exp\left(-\frac{B^2a^2}{mR}t\right)\right]$$

where we have assumed for simplicity that the loop is dropped from rest from a position where the bottom leg is just about to enter the region of magnetic field.

(d) Show that the quantity $\frac{gmR}{B^2a^2}$ has units of velocity and $\frac{mR}{B^2a^2}$ units of time.

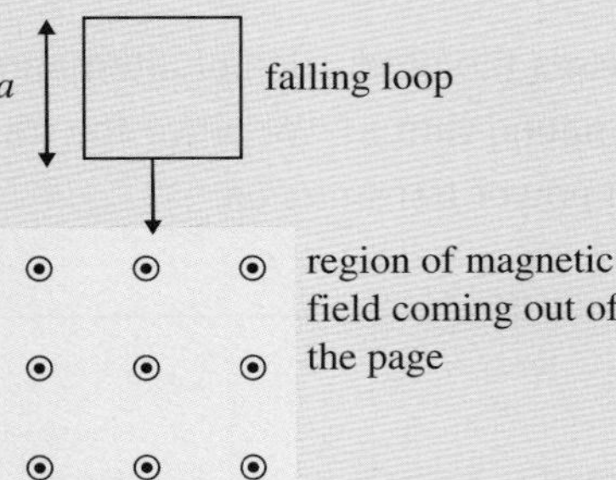

Figure 7.22 For question 14.

15 It was shown in the text that the potential difference between the centre and a point on the circumference of a metallic disc of radius r that rotates with constant angular velocity ω normally to a magnetic field B is $\Delta V = \frac{1}{2}\omega r^2 B$.

Assume the disc shown in Figure 7.23 is rotating in a clockwise sense and that the magnetic field is directed into the page.

(a) Which point is at the higher potential, the centre or a point on the circumference?

(b) If an external circuit of resistance R is connected between the centre and a point on the circumference, show that the current that will flow is $I = \frac{\omega r^2 B}{2R}$.

(c) What will be the direction of the current?

(d) Show that the power dissipated in the resistor is $P = \frac{\omega^2 r^4 B^2}{4R}$.

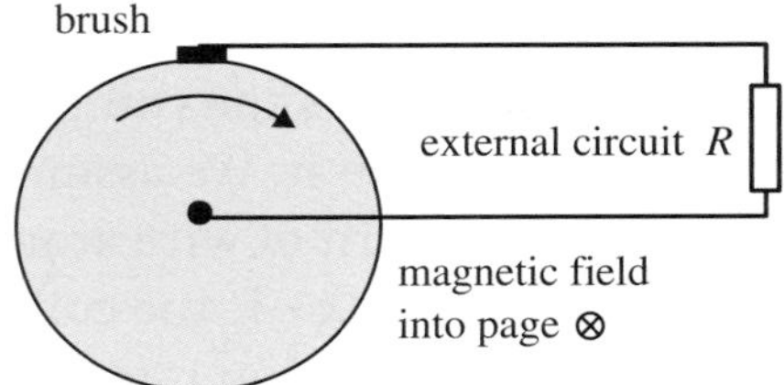

Figure 7.23 For question 15.

Alternating current

This chapter discusses the production of alternating current by the AC generator and the properties of alternating current. We prove the transformer equation and discuss the use of transformers in power transmission.

Objectives

By the end of this chapter you should be able to:

- appreciate that the induced emf in a uniformly rotating coil is sinusoidal;
- explain the operation and importance of the *AC generator*;
- understand the operation of the *transformer*;
- apply the *transformer equation*, $\frac{V_p}{V_s} = \frac{N_p}{N_s}$, and explain the use of transformers in power transmission;
- understand the terms *rms* and *peak current* ($I_{rms} = \frac{I_0}{\sqrt{2}}$) and *voltage* ($\mathcal{E}_{rms} = \frac{\mathcal{E}_0}{\sqrt{2}}$) and calculate the average power in simple AC circuits ($\langle P \rangle = \frac{\mathcal{E}_0 I_0}{2} = \mathcal{E}_{rms} I_{rms}$).

The AC generator

One very important application of electromagnetic induction is the AC (alternating current) generator – the method used universally to produce electricity (see Figure 8.1). The generator is in some sense a motor in reverse. A coil is made to rotate in a region of magnetic field. This can be accomplished in a variety of ways: by a diesel engine burning oil, by falling water in a hydroelectric power station, by wind power, etc.

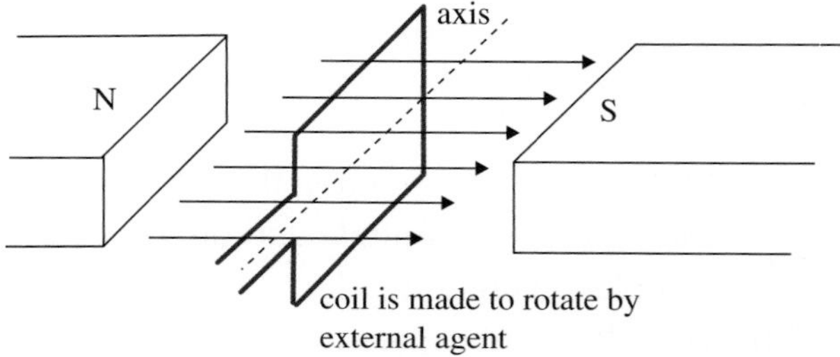

Figure 8.1 A coil that is forced to turn in a region of magnetic field will produce an emf.

The flux in the coil changes as the coil rotates and so an emf is produced in it. We assume that the coil has a single turn of wire around it, the magnetic field is $B = 0.4$ T, the coil has an area of 0.318 m^2 and a rotation rate of 50 revolutions per second. Then the flux in the coil changes as time goes on according to a cosine function as shown in Figure 8.2. (Time zero is taken to correspond to the coil in the

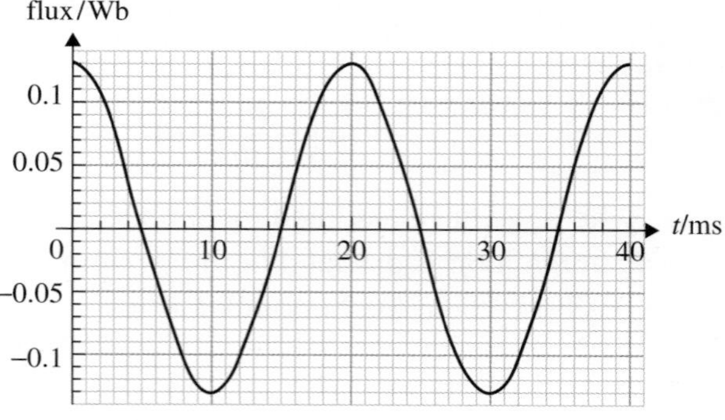

Figure 8.2 The flux in the coil is changing with time.

position of Figure 8.1 so that the flux is a maximum.)

The equation of the flux (linkage) is, in general,

$$\Phi = NBA \cos\theta$$

where θ is the angle between the magnetic field and the normal to the coil and N is the number of turns in the coil. Assuming that the coil rotates at a constant angular velocity ω, it follows that $\theta = \omega t$ and so the flux becomes

$$\Phi = NBA \cos(\omega t)$$

▶ By Faraday's law, the emf induced in the coil is (minus) the rate of change of the flux linkage and thus is given by

$$\mathcal{E} = -\frac{d\Phi}{dt}$$
$$\Rightarrow \mathcal{E} = \omega NBA \sin(\omega t)$$

The quantity $\mathcal{E}_0 = \omega NBA$ is the peak voltage produced by the generator. For the same numerical values as in the previous example, the emf induced is given by the graph shown in Figure 8.3 ($\omega = 2\pi f = 314\ \text{s}^{-1}$).

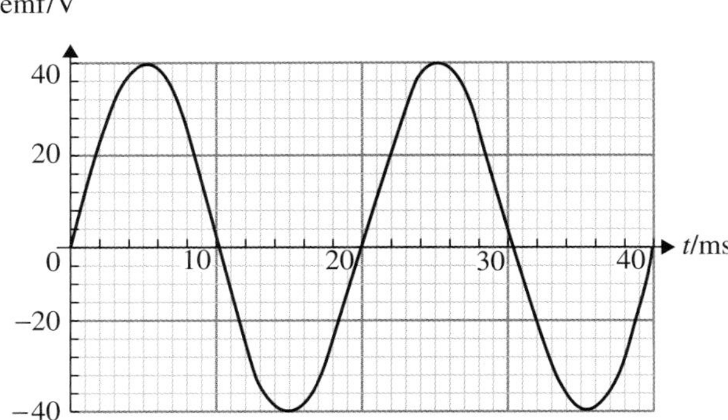

Figure 8.3 The emf induced in the loop as a function of time. The peak voltage is 40 V.

Note that the emf induced is zero whenever the flux assumes its maximum or minimum values and, conversely, it is a maximum or minimum whenever the flux is zero. The noteworthy thing here is that the voltage can be negative as well as positive. This is what is called *alternating voltage* and the current that flows in the coil is alternating current (AC). This means that, unlike the ordinary direct current (DC) that flows in a circuit connected to a battery, the electrons do not drift in the same direction but oscillate back and forth with the same frequency as that of the voltage.

The current that will flow in a circuit of resistance R can be found from

$$I = \frac{\mathcal{E}}{R} = \frac{\mathcal{E}_0 \sin(\omega t)}{R} = I_0 \sin(\omega t)$$

where $I_0 = \frac{\mathcal{E}_0}{R}$ is the peak current. For the emf of Figure 8.3 and a resistance of 16 Ω the current is shown in Figure 8.4.

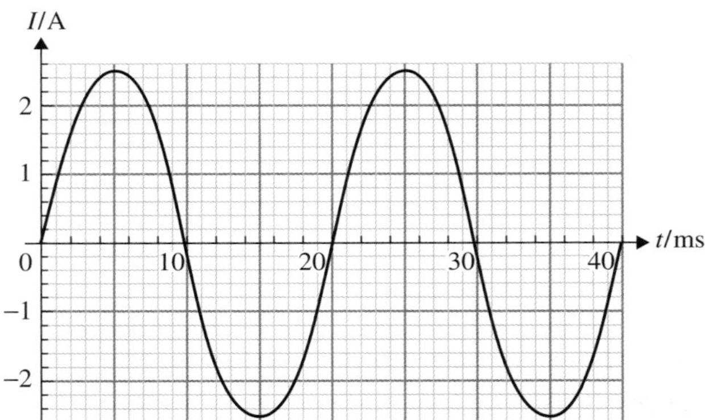

Figure 8.4 The induced current in the rotating loop. Note that the current is in phase with the emf. The peak current is found from peak voltage divided by resistance, i.e. $40/16 = 2.5$ A.

Power in AC circuits

The power generated in an AC circuit is

$$P = \mathcal{E}I = \mathcal{E}_0 I_0 \sin^2(\omega t)$$

and, just like the current and the voltage, is not constant in time. It has a peak value given by the product of the peak voltage and peak current (i.e. $40 \times 2.5 = 100$ W, for the previous example). The power as a function of time is shown in Figure 8.5.

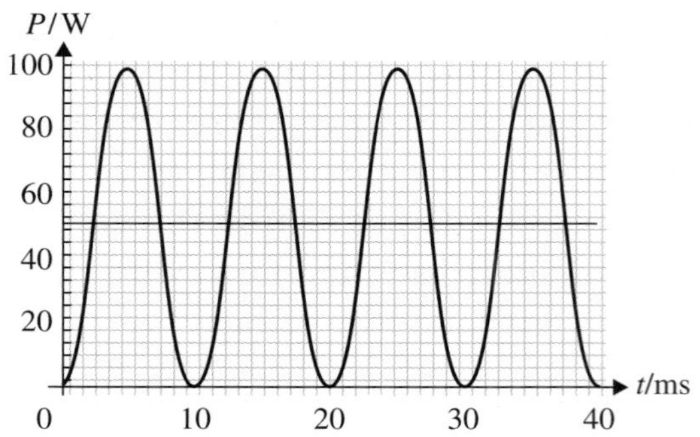

Figure 8.5 The power dissipated in a resistor as a function of time. Note that the period of one rotation of the coil is 20 ms. The power becomes zero every half rotation of the coil. The peak power is 100 W. The horizontal line indicates the average power of 50 W.

▶ It is instructive to write the expression for power in terms of the parameters of the rotating coil:

$$\begin{aligned} P &= \mathcal{E}I \\ &= \omega NBA \sin(\omega t) \times \frac{\omega NBA \sin(\omega t)}{R} \\ &= \frac{(\omega NBA)^2}{R} \sin^2(\omega t) \end{aligned}$$

This shows, for example, that if the speed of rotation of the coil is doubled, the power is increased by a factor of 4.

Root mean square (rms) quantities

It would be convenient to define an average voltage, average current and average power. For power this is not difficult, as power is always positive. Trying to find the average of the current or voltage, though, would give zero. In any one cycle, the voltage and current are as much positive as they are negative and so average to zero. To get around this problem we use the following trick. First, we square the current, getting a quantity that is always positive during the entire cycle. Then we find the average of this positive quantity. Finally, we take its square root. The result is called the rms value of the current (from root mean square).

How do we evaluate an rms quantity? Squaring the current gives

$$\begin{aligned} I^2 &= I_0^2 \sin^2(\omega t) \\ &= \frac{I_0^2}{2}[1 - \cos(2\omega t)] \end{aligned}$$

where in the last step we used the identity

$$\sin^2\theta = \frac{1 - \cos 2\theta}{2}.$$

Over one cycle, the cosine term averages to zero and so the average of the square of the current is

$$\langle I^2 \rangle = \frac{I_0^2}{2}$$

(angular brackets denote an average). Thus

$$I_{\text{rms}} = \frac{I_0}{\sqrt{2}}$$

Doing exactly the same thing for the voltage results in an rms voltage of

$$\mathcal{E}_{\text{rms}} = \frac{\mathcal{E}_0}{\sqrt{2}}$$

Since

$$\begin{aligned} P &= \mathcal{E}_0 I_0 \sin^2(\omega t) \\ &= \frac{\mathcal{E}_0 I_0}{2}[1 - \cos(2\omega t)] \end{aligned}$$

we get the following:

▶ The *average* power is

$$\begin{aligned} \langle P \rangle &= \left\langle \frac{\mathcal{E}_0 I_0}{2}[1 - \cos(2\omega t)] \right\rangle \\ &= \frac{\mathcal{E}_0 I_0}{2} \\ &= \frac{\mathcal{E}_0}{\sqrt{2}} \frac{I_0}{\sqrt{2}} \\ &= \mathcal{E}_{\text{rms}} I_{\text{rms}} \end{aligned}$$

(again the term with the cosine averages to zero over one period).

On a very non-rigorous level, we might say that dealing with rms quantities turns AC circuits into DC circuits. The product of the rms current times the rms voltage gives the *average* power in the circuit.

▶ We may also use the alternative formulae for average power

$$\langle P \rangle = R I_{\text{rms}}^2 = \frac{\mathcal{E}_{\text{rms}}^2}{R}$$

Example question

Q1

Find the rms quantities corresponding to the current and voltage of Figures 8.3 and 8.4.

Answer

The peak voltage is 40 V giving

$$\mathcal{E}_{\text{rms}} = \frac{40}{\sqrt{2}} \approx 28 \text{ V}$$

Similarly, the peak current is 2.5 A, giving

$$I_{\text{rms}} = \frac{2.5}{\sqrt{2}} \approx 1.8 \text{ A}$$

From Figure 8.5, the peak power is 100 W and the average power is 50 W. The product of the rms current times the rms voltage is indeed

$1.8 \times 28 = 50$ W

The slip-ring commutator

The current must now be fed from the rotating coil into an external circuit where it can be put to use. The rotating coil is connected to the outside circuit, to which it provides current, through *slip rings*, as shown in Figure 8.6. Each of the wires leading into the coil is firmly connected to its own ring S. As the coil rotates, the ring rotates along with it, but each ring is always in contact with the same brush (B) that connects to the outside circuit. This means that since AC current is produced in the coil, AC current will be fed to the external circuit as well.

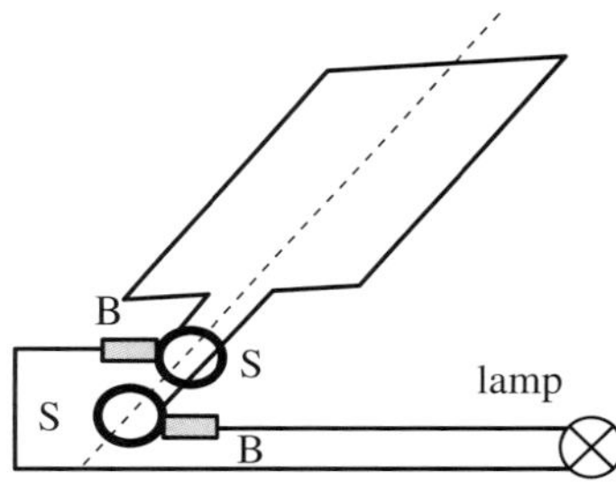

Figure 8.6 The slip-ring connection of the rotating coil to the outside circuit.

(What current would flow in an external circuit if the generator were connected to it via a *split* ring?)

The great advantage of AC voltage and current is that they allow the use of the transformer (see below).

Back-emf in the DC motor

In the DC motor, current fed into a loop that is in a magnetic field makes the coil turn as a result of the forces that develop on the sides of the loop. Because of Faraday's law an emf (the back-emf) will be induced in the loop as it begins to rotate, since there is a changing magnetic flux in the loop. By Lenz's law, this emf will oppose the change in the flux that created it. This means that a current will flow in the loop that is opposite to the current that the external battery feeds into the loop. The current in the loop will thus be less when the coil is rotating than initially, when the rotation had not yet started. The back-emf is the reason that lights sometimes dim when the motor of the refrigerator turns on. Initially the current drawn by the motor is large and only after the coil of the motor achieves a constant speed of rotation does the current drop to lower values.

The transformer

Consider two coils placed near each other as shown in Figure 8.7. The turns of both coils are wrapped around an iron core.

The first coil (the primary) has N_p turns of wire and the second (the secondary) N_s turns. If the

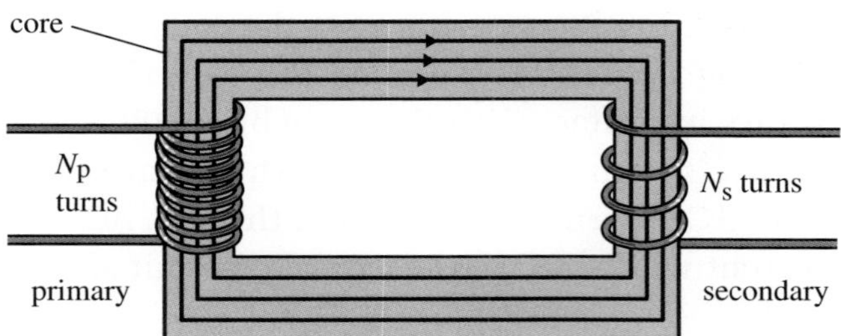

Figure 8.7 The changing flux in the secondary coil produces an emf in that coil.

primary coil is connected to an AC source of voltage, an alternating current will pass through this coil. The magnetic field this current will create will be changing in both magnitude and direction, since the current is. As the two coils are near each other, the magnetic field of the first coil enters the second coil and thus there is magnetic flux in this second coil. The purpose of the iron core is to ensure that as much of the flux produced in the primary coil as possible enters the secondary coil. Iron has the property that it confines magnetic flux and so no magnetic field lines spread out into the region outside the core. Since the magnetic field is changing, the flux is also changing and thus, by Faraday's law, there will be an *induced* emf in the secondary coil.

If the flux is changing at a rate $\frac{\Delta\Phi}{\Delta t}$ through one turn of wire, then the rate of change of flux linkage in the second coil is $N_s\frac{\Delta\Phi}{\Delta t}$, and that, therefore, is the emf induced in the secondary coil, $V_s = N_s\frac{\Delta\Phi}{\Delta t}$. Similarly, the emf, V_p, in the first coil is $V_p = N_p\frac{\Delta\Phi}{\Delta t}$. Hence

$$\frac{V_p}{V_s} = \frac{N_p}{N_s}$$

The arrangement just described is called a *transformer*. What we have achieved is to make a device that takes in AC voltage (V_p) in the primary coil and delivers in the secondary coil a *different* AC voltage (V_s). If the secondary coil has more turns than the primary, the secondary voltage is bigger than the primary voltage (if the secondary coil has fewer turns, the secondary voltage is smaller). *Note that the transformer works only when the voltage in the primary coil is changing*. Direct (i.e. constant) voltage fed into the primary coil would result in zero voltage in the secondary (except for the short interval of time it takes the current in the primary coil to reach its final steady value). In the case of standard AC voltage, there is a sine dependence on time with a frequency of 50 or 60 Hz. The frequency of the voltage in the secondary coil stays the same – the transformer cannot change the frequency of the voltage.

If the primary coil has a current I_p in it, then the power dissipated in the primary coil is V_pI_p. Assuming no power losses, the power dissipated in the secondary coil is the same as that in the primary and thus

$$V_pI_p = V_sI_s$$

Therefore, using $\frac{V_p}{V_s} = \frac{N_p}{N_s}$ the relationship between the currents is

$$\frac{I_p}{I_s} = \frac{N_s}{N_p}$$

(Power losses are reduced by having a laminated core rather than a single block for the core – this reduces power losses by eliminating eddy currents. Eddy currents are created in the core because the free electrons of the core move in the presence of a magnetic field. Thus these electrons are deflected into circular paths and they create small currents in the core. See Figure 8.8.)

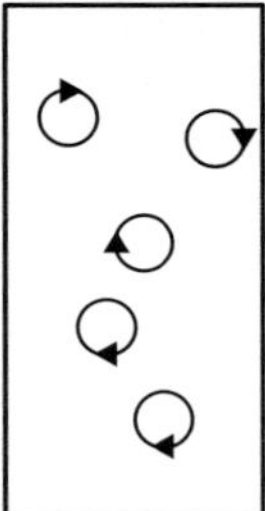

a solid core will have eddy currents

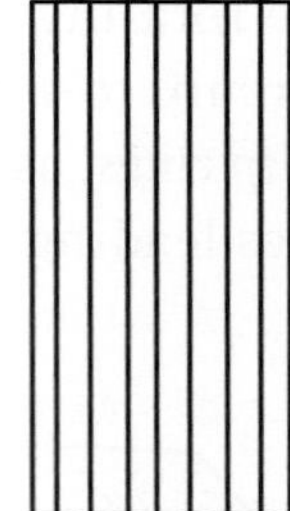

a laminated core with insulation between layers reduces eddies

Figure 8.8 Free electrons move in circular paths creating eddy currents in the magnetic field that is established in the core. Nearly all of these currents are eliminated if the core is laminated.

Transformers and power transmission

Transformers are used in the transport of electricity from power stations, where electricity is produced, to the consumer. At any given time, a city will have a power demand, P, which is quite large (many megawatts for a large city). If the power station sends out electricity at a voltage V and a current I flows in the cables from the power station to the city and back, then

$$P = VI$$

The cables have resistance, however, and thus there is power loss $P_{loss} = RI^2$ where R stands for the total resistance of the cables. To minimize this loss it is necessary to minimize the current (there is not much that can be done about minimizing R). However, small I (I is still a few thousand amperes) means large V (recall, $P = VI$), which is why power companies supply electricity at large voltages. Transformers are then used to reduce the high voltage down to that required for normal household appliances (220 V or 110 V). (See Figure 8.9.)

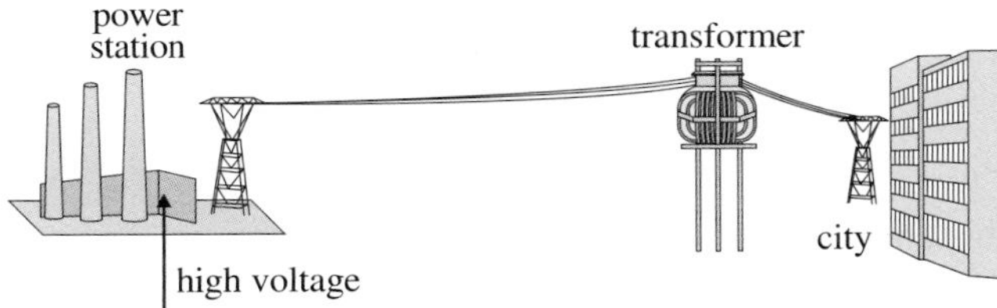

Figure 8.9 The voltage produced in the power station is high in order to reduce losses during transmission. Transformers are used to step down the voltage to what the consumer requires.

Example question

Q2

A power company produces 500 MW of electricity at a voltage of 1.2×10^5 V. The total resistance of the cables leading to and from a town is 4 Ω. How much current flows from the power station? What is the percentage loss of power in the cables? If the electricity were transmitted at the lower voltage of 0.8×10^5 V, what would the power loss be?

Answer

From $P = VI$ the current is

$$I = \frac{500 \times 10^6}{1.2 \times 10^5} = 4.2 \times 10^3 \text{A}$$

The power loss in the cables is

$$\begin{aligned} P_{loss} &= RI^2 \\ &= 4.0 \times (4.2 \times 10^3)^2 \\ &= 7.1 \times 10^7 \text{ W} \\ &= 71 \text{ MW} \end{aligned}$$

This corresponds to a power loss of $71/500 \times 100\% = 14\%$ of the produced power. With the lower voltage the current is

$$I = \frac{500 \times 10^6}{0.8 \times 10^5} = 6.2 \times 10^3 \text{A}$$

The power lost is then

$$\begin{aligned} P &= RI^2 \\ &= 4.0 \times (6.2 \times 10^3)^2 \\ &= 1.5 \times 10^8 \text{ W} \\ &= 150 \text{ MW} \end{aligned}$$

The percentage of power lost is now $150/500 \times 100\% = 30\%$.

? QUESTIONS

1 A transformer has 500 turns in its primary coil and 200 in the secondary coil.
  (a) If an AC voltage of 220 V and frequency 50 Hz is established in the primary coil, find the voltage and frequency induced in the secondary coil.
  (b) If the primary current is 6.0 A, find the current in the secondary coil assuming an efficiency of 70%.

2 A 300 MW power station produces electricity at 80 kV, which is then supplied to consumers along cables of total resistance 5.0 Ω.
  (a) What percentage of the produced power is lost in the cables?
  (b) What does the percentage become if the electricity is produced at 100 kV?

3 The rms voltage output of a generator is 220 V. The coil is a square of side 20.0 cm, has 300 turns of wire and rotates at 50 revolutions per second. What is the magnetic field?

4 Figure 8.10 shows the variation, with time, of the magnetic flux linkage through a loop. What is the rms value of the emf produced in the loop?

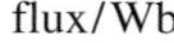

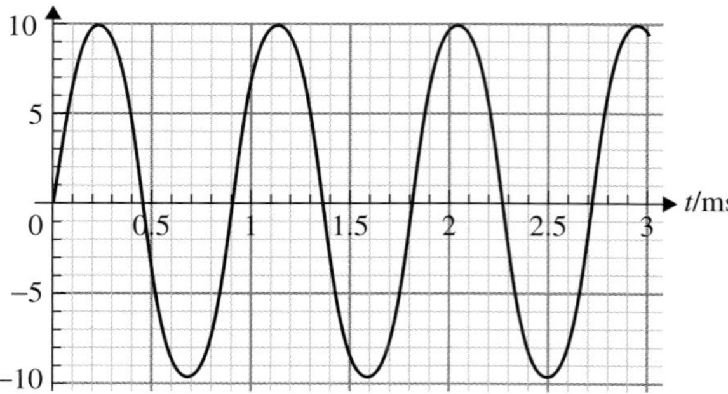

Figure 8.10 For question 4.

5 A power station produces 150 kW of power, which is transmitted along cables of total resistance 2.0 Ω. What fraction of the power is lost if it is transmitted at:

(a) 1000 V;

(b) 5000 V?

6 If the connection of a rotating generator coil to the outside circuit were made through a split ring (as discussed in the case of the DC motor), what sort of current would flow in the external circuit?

7 Figure 8.11 shows the variation with time of the power dissipated in a resistor when an alternating voltage from a generator is established at its ends. Assume that the resistance is constant at 2.5 Ω.

(a) Find the rms value of the current.

(b) Find the rms value of the voltage.

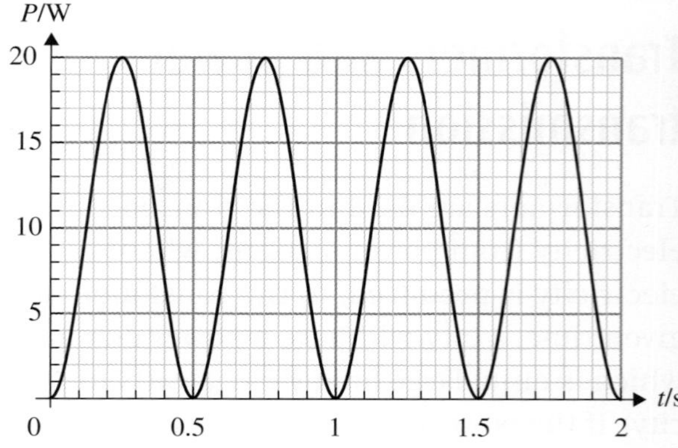

Figure 8.11 For question 7.

(c) Find the period of rotation of the coil.

(d) The coil is now rotated at double the speed. Draw a graph to show the variation with time of the power dissipated in the resistor.

8 Figure 8.12 shows the variation of the flux in a coil as it rotates in a magnetic field with the angle between the magnetic field and the normal to the coil.

(a) Draw a graph to show the variation of the induced emf with angle.

The same coil is now rotated at double the speed in the same magnetic field. Draw graphs to show:

(b) the variation of the flux with angle;

(c) the variation of the induced emf with angle.

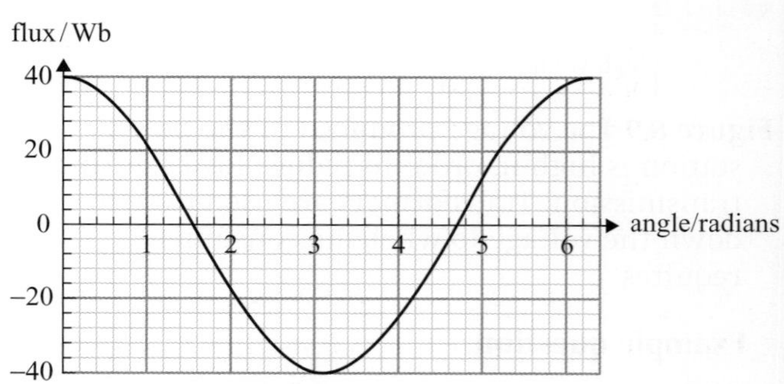

Figure 8.12 For question 8.

The atom and its nucleus

In ancient times, the Greek philosopher Demokritos asserted that all matter is made out of indivisible units. This chapter introduces the basic ideas and models that have given rise to our present understanding of the atom and its nucleus. We begin with Rutherford's experiment that provided the evidence for the existence of a small, massive and positively charged atomic nucleus and close with a discussion of the fundamental forces that operate within the nucleus.

Objectives

By the end of this chapter you should be able to:

- appreciate that *atomic spectra* provide evidence for an atom that can only take *discrete values in energy*;
- explain what *isotopes* are and how their existence implies that neutrons are present inside the nucleus;
- state the meaning of the terms *nuclide*, *nucleon*, *mass number* and *atomic number* (proton number);
- outline the properties of the *forces* that operate within the nucleus.

The discovery of the nuclear atom

In 1909, Geiger and Marsden, working under Rutherford's direction, performed a series of experiments in which they studied the scattering of alpha particles shot at a thin gold foil. Alpha particles have a mass approximately four times that of the hydrogen atom and a positive electric charge of two units ($2e$). Alpha particles are emitted when unstable elements decay; we will study them in more detail later.

Geiger and Marsden used radon as their source of alpha particles, which they directed in a fine beam toward the thin gold foil. The scattered alpha particles were detected (through a microscope) by the glow they caused on a fluorescent screen at the point of impact. As expected, most of the alpha particles were detected at very small scattering angles, such as at positions A, B and C in Figure 1.1.

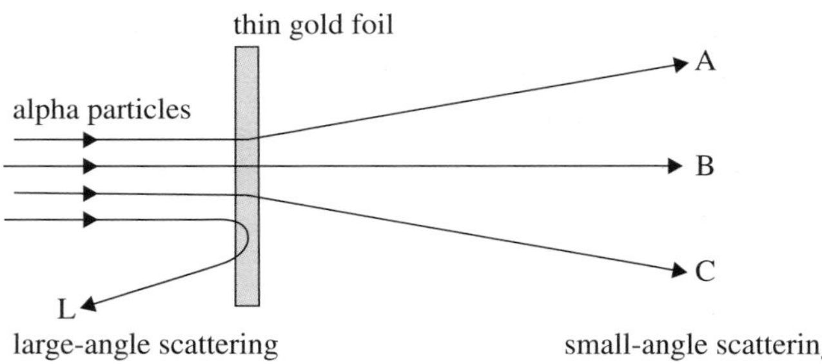

Figure 1.1 The majority of alpha particles are slightly deflected by the gold foil. Very occasionally, large-angle scatterings take place. The small deflections could be understood in terms of alpha particles approaching the nucleus at large distances. The large deflections were due to alpha particles approaching very close to the nucleus.

These small deflections could be understood in terms of the electrostatic force of repulsion between the positive charge of the gold atoms and the positive charge of the alpha particles. (Note that an alpha is about 8000 times more massive than the electron and so the effect of the electrons of the gold atoms on the path of the alphas is negligible.)

▶ To their great surprise, Rutherford, Geiger and Marsden found that, occasionally, alpha particles were detected at *very large scattering angles*, as can be seen in Figure 1.1. These large-angle scattering events could not be understood in terms of the prevailing model of the time – Thomson's model of the atom.

Consequences of the Rutherford (Geiger–Marsden) experiment

The very large deflection was indicative of an enormous force of repulsion between the alpha particle and the carrier of the positive charge of the atom. Such a large force could not be produced if the positive charge was distributed over the entire atomic volume, as Thomson had suggested earlier (see Figure 1.2). Rather, it suggested that the positive charge resided on an object that was tiny (thus the alpha particle could come very close to it) but massive (because there is no recoil of the gold atoms) (see Figure 1.3). In this way, the alpha particle could approach the positive charge at a very small distance, and the Coulomb force of repulsion, being proportional to the inverse of the square of the separation, would then be enormous. This force causes the large deflection in the alpha particle's path.

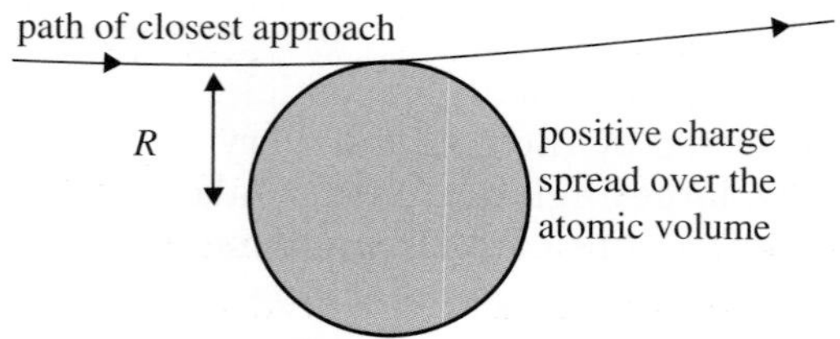

Figure 1.2 In Thomson's model, the closest an alpha particle can come to the atom's centre is a distance equal to the atomic radius.

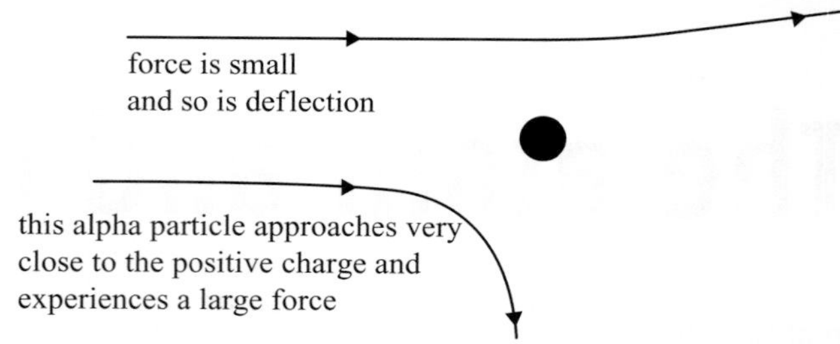

Figure 1.3 In Rutherford's model, the alpha particle can approach much closer if the nucleus is very small.

Rutherford calculated theoretically the number of alpha particles expected at particular scattering angles based on Coulomb's force law. He found agreement with his experiments if the positive atomic charge was confined to a region of linear size approximately equal to 10^{-15} m. This and subsequent experiments confirmed the existence of a nucleus inside the atom – a small, massive object carrying the positive charge of the atom.

Example question

Q1

Calculate the electric field at the surface of a nucleus of one unit of positive charge and radius 10^{-15} m. Compare this with the value of the electric field of the same charge that is now spread over a sphere of radius 10^{-10} m.

Answer

Applying the formula for the electric field $E = k\frac{Q}{r^2}$ we find

$$E = 9 \times 10^9 \times \frac{1.6 \times 10^{-19}}{(10^{-15})^2}$$
$$= 1.4 \times 10^{21}\ \mathrm{N\,C^{-1}}$$

Near the larger sphere, the electric field is $E = 1.4 \times 10^{11}\ \mathrm{N\,C^{-1}}$, which is a factor of 10^{10} smaller. This is why the deflecting forces in *Rutherford's model* are so large compared with what one might expect from *Thomson's model*.

The Rutherford model of the atom

These discoveries led to a new picture of the atom. A massive, positively charged nucleus occupied the centre of the atom and electrons orbited this nucleus in much the same way that planets orbit the sun: this was the Rutherford model (see Figure 1.4). The force keeping the electrons in orbit was the electrical force between the negative electron charge and the positive nuclear charge.

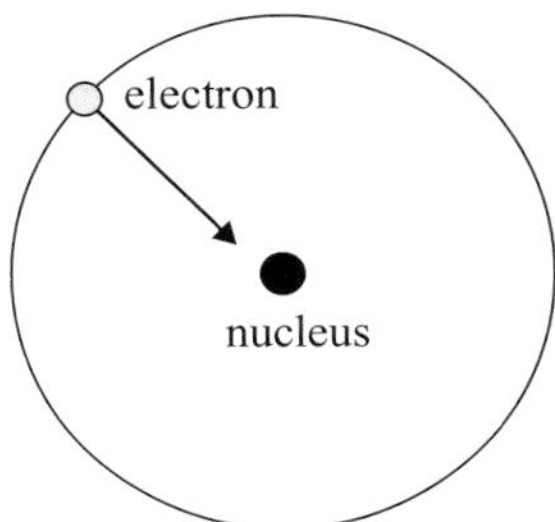

Figure 1.4 Rutherford's atomic model has the electrons orbiting the nucleus like planets orbiting the sun.

Immediately after these discoveries, difficulties arose with the Rutherford model.

▶ The main difficulty was that, according to the theory of electromagnetism, an accelerated charge should radiate electromagnetic waves and thus lose energy. The electrons in Rutherford's atom move in circular paths around the nucleus and so suffer centripetal acceleration. If they radiate and lose energy, it can be shown that this would lead to electron orbits that would spiral into the nucleus. The time required for the electron to fall into the nucleus is of the order of nanoseconds. Thus, the Rutherford model cannot explain why matter is stable, i.e. why atoms exist.

The Bohr model

The first attempt to solve this problem came from the Danish physicist Niels Bohr in 1911. These are the **Bohr postulates.**

▶ Bohr examined the simplest atom, that of hydrogen, and realized that the electron could exist in certain specific states of definite energy, without radiating away energy, if a certain condition was met by the orbit radius. The electron energy is thus *discrete* as opposed to continuous. The electron can only lose energy when it makes a transition from one state to another of lower energy. The emitted energy is then the difference in energy between the initial and final states. (See Figure 1.5.) The strongest piece of evidence in support of Bohr's idea is the existence of *emission* and *absorption spectra*.

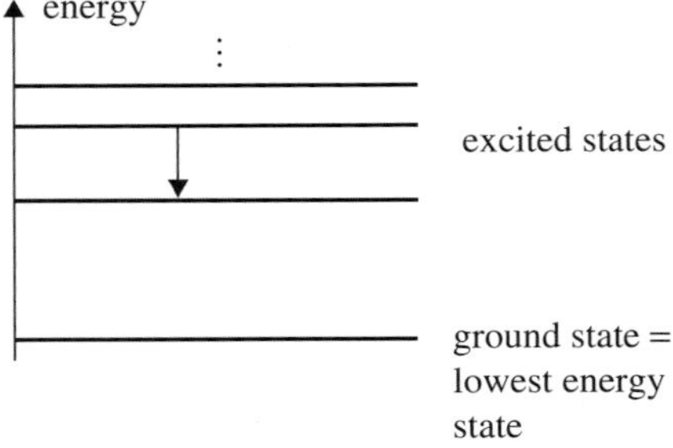

Figure 1.5 In the Bohr model the electron occupies one of a number of specific states each with a well-defined energy. While it is in one of these states, the electron does not radiate away energy.

Spectra

Consider hydrogen as an example. Under normal conditions (i.e. normal temperature, pressure, etc.) the electron in each hydrogen atom occupies the lowest energy state or **energy level** (the ground state). If the atoms are somehow excited (by increasing their temperature, for example) the electrons leave the ground state and occupy one of the higher energy, excited states. As soon as they do so, however, they make a transition back down to lower energy states, radiating energy in the process. The energy of the light emitted is very well defined since it corresponds to the difference in energy between the states involved in the transition. Knowing this energy difference allows us to calculate the wavelength of the emitted light, and so the wavelength, too, is well defined since the energy is. In this way it is found, for example, that hydrogen emits light of wavelengths 656 nm, 486 nm and 410 nm. Only hydrogen emits light of these wavelengths since only hydrogen has states whose energy differences lead to these wavelengths. Helium, for example, has energy states of different energy, so the wavelengths of light emitted when helium atoms are heated are different from those of hydrogen.

▶ The set of wavelengths of light emitted by the atoms of an element is called the *emission spectrum* of the element.

Conversely, consider atoms of hydrogen that are in their ground states and imagine sending light of a specific wavelength through a given quantity of hydrogen. If the wavelength of light does not correspond to any of the wavelengths in the emission **spectrum** of hydrogen, the light is transmitted through the atoms of hydrogen without any absorption. If, however, it matches one of the emission spectrum wavelengths, then this light is absorbed.

▶ The electrons simply take this energy and use it in order to make a transition to a higher energy state. The wavelengths that are so absorbed make up the *absorption spectrum* of the element and (as indicated above) they are the same wavelengths as those in the emission spectrum.

Thus, if white light (i.e. light containing all wavelengths) is sent through the gas and the transmitted light is analysed through a spectrometer, dark lines will be found at the position of the absorbed wavelengths.

Nuclear structure

Nuclei are made up of smaller particles, called protons and neutrons. The word *nucleon* is used to denote a proton or a neutron.

▶
- The number of protons in a nucleus is denoted by Z, and is called the atomic (or proton) number.
- The total number of nucleons (protons + neutrons) is called the mass (or nucleon) number, and is denoted by A.

Then the electric charge of the nucleus is $Z|e|$. The number of neutrons in the nucleus (the neutron number N) is thus $N = A - Z$. We will use the atomic and mass numbers to denote a nucleus in the following way: the symbol ${}^{A}_{Z}\text{X}$ stands for the nucleus of element X, whose atomic number is Z and mass number is A. Thus ${}^{1}_{1}\text{H}$, ${}^{4}_{2}\text{He}$, ${}^{40}_{20}\text{Ca}$, ${}^{210}_{82}\text{Pb}$ and ${}^{238}_{92}\text{U}$ are, respectively, the nuclei of hydrogen, helium, calcium, lead and uranium, with one, two, twenty, eighty-two and ninety-two protons. A nucleus with a specific number of protons and neutrons is also called a *nuclide*.

We can apply this notation to the nucleons themselves. For example, the proton (symbol p) can be written as ${}^{1}_{1}\text{p}$ and the neutron (symbol n) as ${}^{1}_{0}\text{n}$. We can even extend this notation to the electron, even though the electron has nothing to do with the nucleus and nucleons. We note that the atomic number is not only the number of protons in the nucleus but also its electric charge in units of $|e|$. In terms of this unit, the charge of the electron is -1 and so we represent the electron by ${}^{0}_{-1}\text{e}$. The mass number of the electron is zero – it is so light with respect to the protons and neutrons that it is, effectively, massless. The photon (the particle of light) can also be represented in this way: the photon has the Greek letter gamma as its symbol, and since it has zero electric charge and (strictly) zero mass it is represented by ${}^{0}_{0}\gamma$. Table 1.1 gives a summary of these particles and their symbols.

Particle	Symbol
Proton	${}^{1}_{1}\text{p}$
Neutron	${}^{1}_{0}\text{n}$
Electron	${}^{0}_{-1}\text{e}$
Photon	${}^{0}_{0}\gamma$
Alpha particle	${}^{4}_{2}\text{He}$ or ${}^{4}_{2}\alpha$

Table 1.1.

Isotopes

Nuclei that have the same number of protons (and therefore the same atomic number Z) but different number of neutrons (i.e. different N and mass number A) are called *isotopes* of each other. Since isotopes have the same number of protons, their atoms have the same number of electrons as well. This means that isotopes have identical chemical but different physical properties. The existence of isotopes can be demonstrated with an instrument called the mass spectrometer (this is discussed further in Chapter 6.6). The existence of isotopes is evidence for the existence of neutrons inside atomic nuclei.

The forces within the nucleus

The nucleons (i.e. protons and neutrons) are bound together in the nucleus by a force we have not yet met – *the strong nuclear force*. It is necessary to have a new force inside the nucleus, because otherwise the electrical repulsion between the positively charged protons would break the nucleus apart (see Figure 1.6).

▶ The strong nuclear force is an attractive force and much stronger than the electrical force if the separation between two nucleons is very small (i.e. about $r = 10^{-15}$ m or less). For larger separations, the nuclear force becomes so small as to be negligible – we say that the nuclear force has a *short range*.

The experimental evidence for the properties of the nuclear force comes from scattering

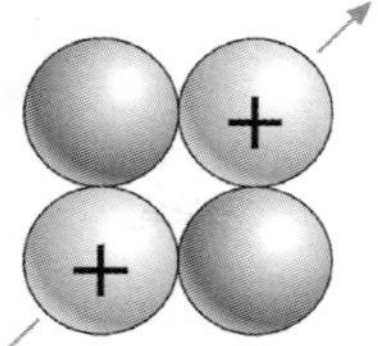

In a helium-4 nucleus, Coulomb forces push the protons apart.

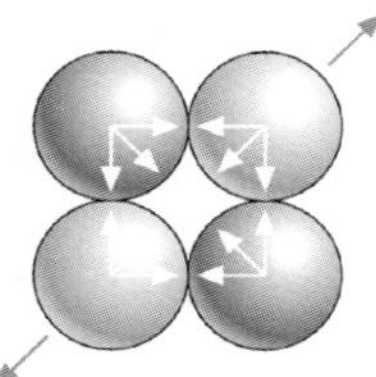

There must be forces between nucleons pulling them together. Gravitational forces are far too small.

Figure 1.6 There is an attractive force between nucleons that keeps them bound inside the nucleus.

experiments in which electrons of energy equal to about 200 MeV (in later experiments neutrons were also used) are allowed to hit nuclei and their scattering is studied. If we make the assumption of short-range forces, we obtain agreement with the data. A result of these experiments is that the nuclear radius R is given by

$$R = 1.2 \times A^{1/3} \times 10^{-15} \text{ m}$$

where A is the total number of protons and neutrons in the nucleus (the mass number). This implies that the nuclear density is the same for all nuclei (you will look at this further in the questions at the end of this chapter). The short range of the force implies that a given nucleon can only interact with a few of its immediate neighbours and not with all of the nucleons in the nucleus (see Figure 1.7).

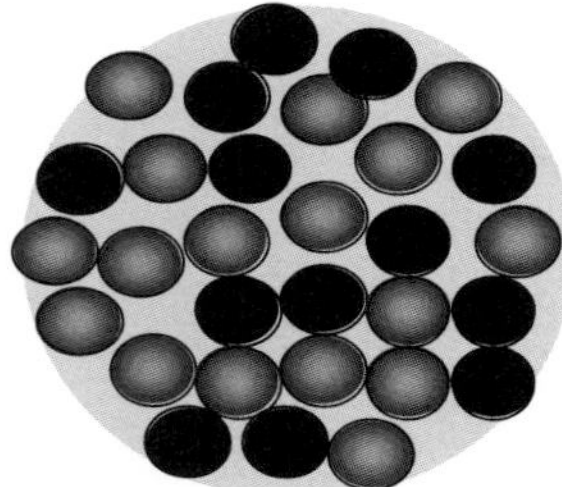

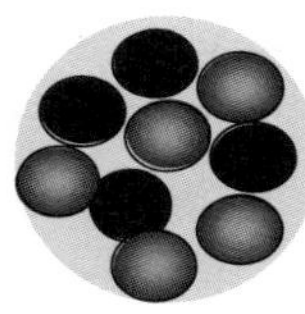

Figure 1.7 Irrespective of the size of the nucleus, any one nucleon is surrounded by the same number of neighbours, and only those act on it with the nuclear force.

Force	Electromagnetic	Strong nuclear	Weak nuclear
Acts on	Protons only	Protons and neutrons	Protons and neutrons
Nature	Repulsive	Attractive (mainly)	Attractive/repulsive
Range	Infinite	Short (10^{-15} m)	Short (10^{-17} m)
Relative strength	$\frac{1}{137}$	1	10^{-6}

Table 1.2 Forces operating in the nucleus.

There is one other force acting in the nucleus apart from the electrical and strong nuclear forces. This is the weak nuclear force, a force that is responsible for the decay of a neutron into a proton. The details of this decay (beta decay) will be examined in the next chapter. The forces acting in the nucleus are summarized in Table 1.2.

(Since the masses of subatomic particles are so small, the gravitational force is irrelevantly small compared with the other three forces.)

? QUESTIONS

1 The radius of an atomic nucleus is given by the expression

$R = 1.2 \times A^{1/3} \times 10^{-15}$ m

where A is the mass number of the nucleus.

(a) Use this expression to find the density of a nucleus of iron ($^{56}_{26}$Fe) in kg m^{-3}.

(b) How does this density compare with the normal density of iron?

(c) If a star with a mass equal to 1.4 times the mass of our sun (solar mass = 2.0×10^{30} kg) were to have this density, what should its radius be? (Such stars are formed in the end stage of the evolution of normal stars and are called neutron stars.)

2 Use the expression for the radius of a nucleus to show that all nuclei have the same density.

3 Describe carefully how the Geiger–Marsden–Rutherford experiment gave rise to the Rutherford model of the atom. Why is the experiment you just described inconsistent with Thomson's model of the atom?

4 Explain why the dark lines of an absorption spectrum have the same wavelengths as the bright lines of an emission spectrum for the same element.

5 What is an isotope? How do we know that isotopes exist?

6 Find the number of neutrons in these nuclei: $^{1}_{1}$H; $^{4}_{2}$He; $^{40}_{20}$Ca; $^{210}_{82}$Pb.

7 What is the electric charge of the nucleus $^{3}_{2}$He?

8 What is meant by the statement that the energy of atoms is discrete? What evidence is there for this discreteness?

9 What do you understand by the statement that the strong nuclear force has a short range?

10 What is the dominant force between two protons separated by a distance of:

(a) 1.0×10^{-15} m;

(b) 1.0×10^{-14} m?

11 Explain why a nucleon feels the strong force from roughly the *same number* of other nucleons, irrespective of the size of the nucleus.

HL only

12 Compare the gravitational force between two electrons a distance of 10^{-10} m apart with the electrical force between them when at the same separation.

Radioactivity

At the end of the nineteenth century and in the early part of the twentieth, it was discovered, mainly due to the work of Henri Becquerel and Marie and Pierre Curie, that some nuclei are unstable. That is to say, nuclei spontaneously emit a particle or particles, they decay, and become different nuclei. This phenomenon is called radioactivity. It was soon realized that three distinct emissions take place, called alpha, beta and gamma radiations.

Objectives

By the end of this chapter you should be able to:

- describe the properties of *alpha*, *beta* and *gamma* radiations;
- explain why some nuclei are *unstable* in terms of the relative number of neutrons to protons;
- define *half-life* and find it from a graph;
- solve problems of *radioactive decay*.

The nature of alpha, beta and gamma radiations

Early experiments with radioactive sources confirmed that three separate kinds of emissions took place. Called alpha, beta and gamma radiations, or particles, these emissions could be distinguished on the basis of their different ionizing and penetrating power.

Ionization

Alpha, beta and gamma radiations ionize air as they pass through it; this means they knock electrons out of the atoms of the gases in the air. An alpha particle of energy 2 MeV will produce about 10 000 ion pairs per mm along its path in air. A beta particle of the same energy will only produce about 100 ion pairs per mm in air. A gamma ray will produce about one ion pair per mm.

By letting these **ionizing radiations** pass through regions of magnetic (or electric) fields, it was seen that two of the emissions were oppositely charged and the third electrically neutral (see Figure 2.1).

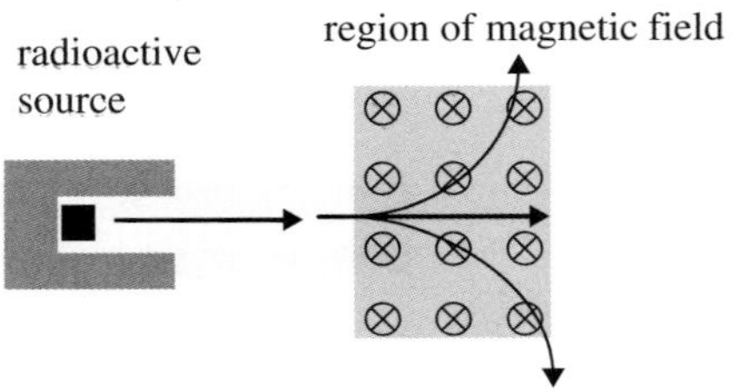

Figure 2.1 The existence of three distinct emissions is confirmed by letting these pass through a magnetic field and observing the three separate beams.

Alpha particles

The positive emissions were called alpha particles and were soon identified as nuclei of helium in an experiment by Rutherford and Rhoyd. By collecting the gas that the alpha particles produced when they came in contact with electrons and analysing its spectrum, its properties were found to be identical to those of helium gas. Thus, the alpha particles have a mass that is about four times the mass of the hydrogen atom and an electric charge equal to $+2e$.

Beta particles

The negative emissions (beta particles) were identified as electrons (charge $-e$) by experiments similar to Thomson's e/m experiment, which measured the charge-to-mass ratio. (Actually, the measured charge-to-mass ratio for the beta particles decreased slightly from the standard value as the speed of the betas increased. This is consistent with the theory of special relativity, which states that the mass of an object increases as the speed becomes comparable to the speed of light. This was an early test of the theory of relativity.)

Gamma rays

The electrically neutral emissions are called gamma rays and are photons (just like the photons of ordinary electromagnetic radiation) with very small wavelengths. Typically these wavelengths are smaller than 10^{-12} m, which is smaller than X-ray wavelengths. This identification was made possible through diffraction experiments in which gamma rays from decaying nuclei were directed at crystals and a diffraction pattern was observed on a photographic plate placed on the other side of the crystal.

Absorption

Alpha particles are the easiest to absorb. A few centimetres of air will stop most alpha particles (see Figure 2.2). Beta particles will be stopped by a few centimetres of paper or a thin sheet of metal (a few millimetres in thickness) while gamma particles will easily penetrate metallic foils; if they are energetic enough they will be stopped only by many centimetres of lead.

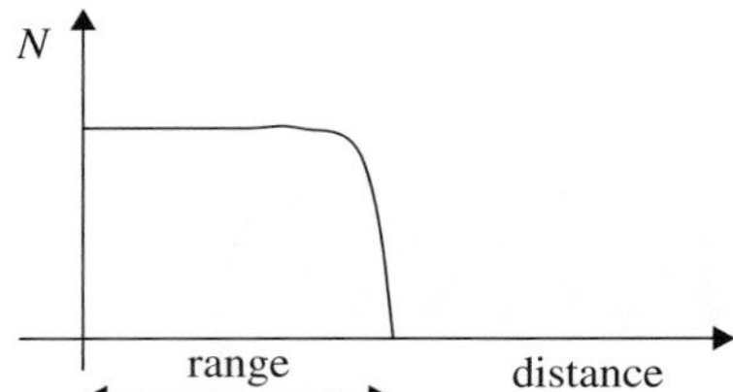

Figure 2.2 The penetration of matter by alpha particles of a fixed energy. The number of particles transmitted falls sharply to zero after a distance called the range. Particles of higher energy will have a larger range.

Further studies show that alpha particles have specific energies, whereas beta particles have a continuous range of energies. Gamma rays from a particular nucleus also have a few discrete values with maximum energies of about 1 MeV or so. Alphas are rather slow (about 6% of the speed of light) whereas betas are very fast (about 98% of the speed of light). Gammas, being photons, travel at the speed of light. These findings are summarized in Table 2.1.

Characteristic	Alpha particle	Beta particle	Gamma ray
Nature	Helium nucleus	(Fast) electron	Photon
Charge	$+2e$	$-e$	0
Mass	6.64×10^{-27} kg	9.1×10^{-31} kg	0
Penetrative power	A few cm of air	A few mm of metal	Many cm of lead
Ions per mm of air for 2 MeV particles	10 000	100	1
Detection	Causes strong fluorescence Affects photographic film Is affected by electric and magnetic fields	Causes fluorescence Affects photographic film Is affected by electric and magnetic fields	Causes weak fluorescence Affects photographic film Is not affected by electric and magnetic fields

Table 2.1 Properties of alpha, beta and gamma radiations.

Detecting radiation

One way to detect radiation is to take advantage of their ionizing effect. In the Geiger–Müller (GM) tube (Figure 2.3), radiation enters a chamber through a thin window. The chamber is filled with a gas, which is ionized by the incoming radiation. The positive ions accelerate toward the earthed casing and the electrons toward the positive electrode (kept at a few hundred volts) and so more ions are created as a result of collisions with the gas molecules. This registers as a current in the counter connected to the GM tube. The counter can also turn the current into an audible sound, giving a 'click' whenever an ionizing particle enters the tube.

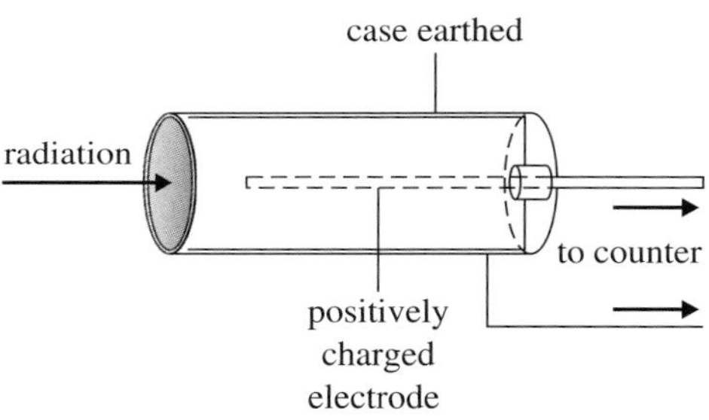

Figure 2.3 A Geiger–Müller tube for detecting ionizing radiation.

A similar principle is also used in the *ionization chamber*. Gas contained in the chamber is ionized by incoming radiation and the current so produced is a measure of the amount of radiation entering the chamber.

Segre plots

There are about 2500 nuclides (nuclei with a specific number of protons and neutrons), but only about 300 of them are stable; the rest are unstable (i.e. radioactive). Figure 2.4 is a plot of neutron number versus proton number (called a Segre plot) for the stable nuclei. The straight line corresponds to nuclei that have the same number of protons and neutrons. The plot shows that stable nuclei have, in general, more neutrons than protons. As the number of protons in the nucleus increases, the electrostatic repulsion between them grows as well, but the strong nuclear force does not grow proportionately since it is a short-range force. Thus, *extra* neutrons must be put in the nucleus in order to ensure stability through an increased nuclear force without participating in the repulsive electric force. (On the other hand, *too many* neutrons will also make the nucleus unstable by energetically favouring decays of neutrons into protons – hence there is a limit as to how large a nucleus can get).

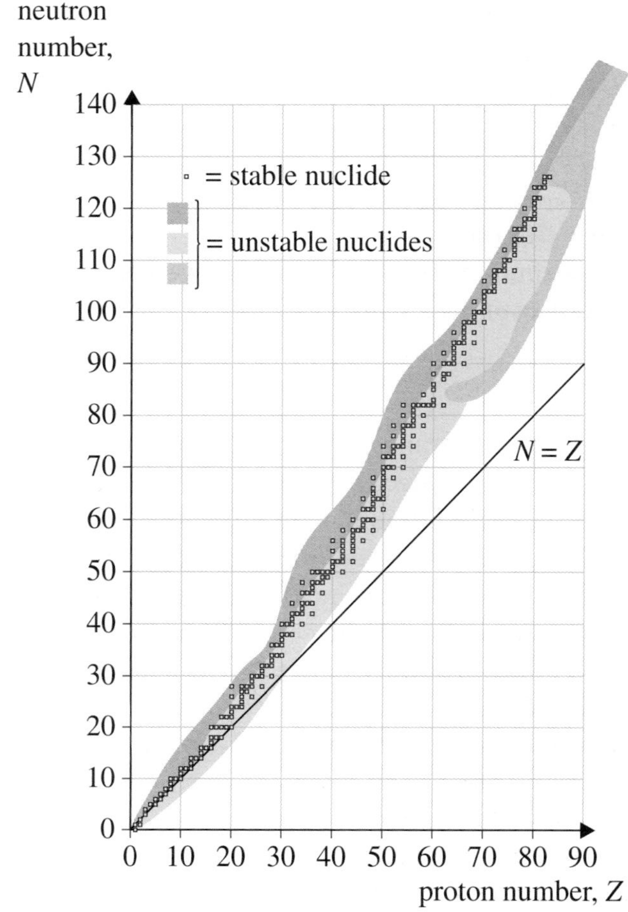

Figure 2.4 A Segre plot of stable nuclides.

Radioactive decay equations

Alpha decay

An example of alpha decay is that of uranium decaying into thorium:

$$^{238}_{92}\text{U} \rightarrow {}^{234}_{90}\text{Th} + {}^{4}_{2}\alpha$$

We say that the nucleus of uranium, being unstable, decayed into a nucleus of thorium and a nucleus of helium. Helium nuclei, being much lighter than thorium, actually move away from the uranium nucleus with a certain amount of kinetic energy. The energy of the alpha particle emitted can be either one specific value or a series of specific energy values (a discrete spectrum of energies). Note that in the reaction representing this decay, the total atomic number on the right-hand side of the arrow matches the atomic number to the left of the arrow. The same holds also for the mass number. This is true of all nuclear decays. Other examples are

$$^{224}_{88}\text{Ra} \rightarrow {}^{220}_{86}\text{Rn} + {}^{4}_{2}\alpha$$

$$^{212}_{84}\text{Po} \rightarrow {}^{208}_{82}\text{Pb} + {}^{4}_{2}\alpha$$

Beta decay

The second example of a radioactive decay is that of beta decay, such as

$$^{234}_{90}\text{Th} \rightarrow {}^{234}_{91}\text{Pa} + {}^{0}_{-1}\text{e} + {}^{0}_{0}\bar{\nu}_\text{e}$$

Note the appearance of the electron (the beta particle) in this decay. The last particle (the electron antineutrino) is included for completeness and need not concern us further here. Unlike alpha decay, the energy of the emitted beta particle has a continuous range of energy, a continuous spectrum. Note again how the atomic and mass numbers match. This is a decay of a nucleus of thorium into a nucleus of protactinium. Other examples are

$$^{214}_{82}\text{Pb} \rightarrow {}^{214}_{83}\text{Bi} + {}^{0}_{-1}\text{e} + {}^{0}_{0}\bar{\nu}_\text{e}$$

$$^{14}_{6}\text{C} \rightarrow {}^{14}_{7}\text{N} + {}^{0}_{-1}\text{e} + {}^{0}_{0}\bar{\nu}_\text{e}$$

Gamma decay

The third example of a decay involves the emission of a photon:

$$^{238}_{92}\text{U}^* \rightarrow {}^{238}_{92}\text{U} + {}^{0}_{0}\gamma$$

The star on the uranium nucleus on the left side of the arrow (the decaying nucleus) means that the nucleus is in an excited state, very much like a hydrogen atom in an energy state above the ground state. Nuclei, like atoms, can only exist in specific energy states. There exists a lowest energy state, the ground state, and excited states with energies larger than that of the ground state. Whenever a nucleus makes a transition from a high to a lower energy state, it emits a photon whose energy equals the energy difference between the initial and final energy states of the nucleus. The typical energies of nuclear states are a few million electronvolts (MeV). This means that the emitted photon in a nuclear transition will have an energy of the order of a few million electronvolts and will thus have a wavelength of

$$\lambda = \frac{hc}{\Delta E}$$

where ΔE is the photon's energy, h is Planck's constant (6.63×10^{-34} J s) and c is the speed of light. Substituting, say, 1 MeV for this energy, we find $\lambda = 1.2 \times 10^{-12}$ m. In contrast to the photons in atomic transitions, which can correspond to optical light, these photons have very small wavelengths. They are called gamma rays.

The changes in the atomic and mass numbers of a nucleus when it undergoes radioactive decay can be represented in a diagram of mass number against atomic number. A radioactive nucleus such as thorium ($Z = 90$) decays first by alpha decay into the nucleus of radium ($Z = 88$). Radium, which is also radioactive, decays into actinium ($Z = 89$) by beta decay. Further decays take place until the resulting nucleus is stable. The set of decays that takes place until a given nucleus

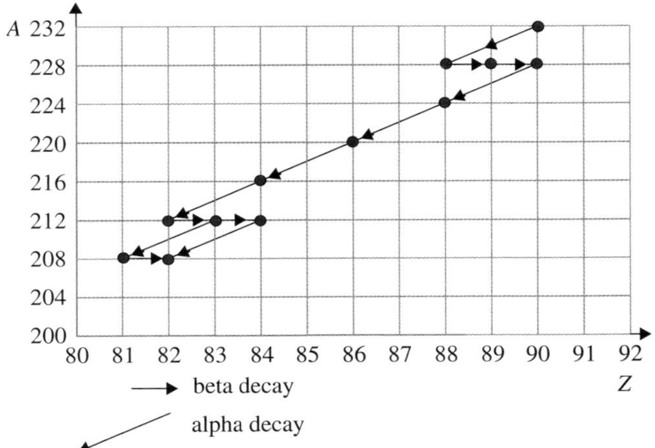

Figure 2.5 The decay series of thorium ($Z = 90$, $A = 232$). One alpha decay reduces the mass number by 4 and the atomic number by 2. One beta decay increases the atomic number by one and leaves the mass number unchanged. The end result is the nucleus of lead ($Z = 82$, $A = 208$).

ends up as a stable nucleus is called the *decay series* of the nucleus. Figure 2.5 shows the decay series for thorium. Successive decays starting with thorium end with the stable nucleus of lead.

Example question

Q1

A nucleus $^{A}_{Z}X$ decays by alpha decay followed by two successive beta decays. Find the atomic and mass numbers of the resulting nucleus.

Answer

The decay equation is

$$^{A}_{Z}X \rightarrow {}^{A-4}_{Z}Y + {}^{4}_{2}\alpha + 2\,{}^{0}_{-1}e$$

so the atomic number is Z and the mass number is $A - 4$.

The law of radioactive decay

We now come to the details of a decay. Suppose we concentrate on the particular decay $^{238}_{92}U \rightarrow {}^{234}_{90}Th + {}^{4}_{2}\alpha$, and that we are given a container with a specific number of atoms of uranium.

▶ The law of radioactive decay states that the number of nuclei that will decay per second (i.e. the rate of decay) is proportional to the number of atoms present that have not yet decayed.

This is a form of a physical law implying a *statistical* or *random* nature. This means that we cannot predict exactly when a *particular* nucleus will decay. But, given a large number of nuclei, the radioactive decay law can be used to predict the number of atoms that will have decayed after a given interval of time. The radioactive decay law leads to an exponential decrease of the number of decaying nuclei. Figure 2.6 shows an example of a radioactive decay in which the initial number of nuclei present is 200×10^{26}. As time passes, the number of undecayed nuclei is decreased. After a certain interval of time (5 s in this example), the number of undecayed nuclei left behind is half of the original number. If another 5 s goes by, the number of undecayed nuclei is reduced by another factor of 2, which is a factor of 4 relative to the original number at $t = 0$. This **half-life** is a general property of the decay law.

▶ There exists a certain interval of time, called the half-life, such that after each half-life the number of nuclei that have not yet decayed is reduced by a factor of 2.

Thus, consider a decay in which nuclei X decay into nuclei Y (the daughter nuclei) by, say, alpha emission. Assume that nuclei Y are stable. Then as time goes by, the number of X nuclei is reduced (Figure 2.6a). The number of Y nuclei is increasing with time, as shown in Figure 2.6b.

The half-life can be found from the graph as follows. The initial value is 200×10^{26} nuclei. We find half of this value, i.e. 100×10^{26}, and see that 100×10^{26} corresponds to a time of 5 s. This is the half-life.

We may also define a concept useful in experimental work: that of decay rate or

nuclei X/×10^26

200 150 100 50 0 5 10 15 20 t/s

(a)

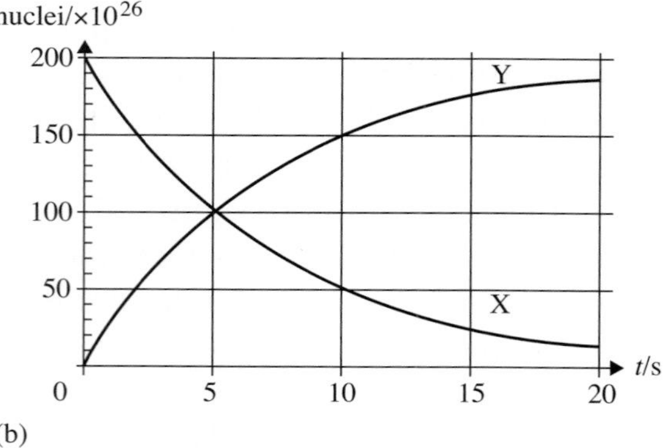

(b)

Figure 2.6 (a) The number of nuclei X that have not yet decayed as a function of time. This is an exponential decay curve. (b) The number of the daughter nuclei Y is increasing.

activity A – the number of nuclei decaying per second. It can be shown that activity obeys the same decay law as the number of nuclei, so in a period equal to a half-life the initial activity is reduced by a factor of 2. The unit of activity is the becquerel (Bq): 1 Bq is equal to one decay per second.

Example questions

Q2

An isotope has a half-life of 20 min. If initially there is 1024 g of this isotope, how much time must go by for there to be 128 g left?

Answer

The nuclei have been reduced by a factor of 8. Thus, 3 half-lives or 60 min must have gone by.

Q3

The activity of a sample is initially 80 decays per minute. It becomes 5 decays per minute after 4 h. What is the half-life?

Answer

The activity is reduced from 80 to 5 decays in 4 half-lives. The half-life is 1 h.

Q4

The activity of a sample is 15 decays per minute. The half-life is 30 min. When was the activity 60 decays per minute?

Answer

One half-life before the sample was given to us the activity was 30 decays per minute and one half-life before that it was 60 decays per minute, that is 60 minutes before.

The meaning of a half-life can also be understood in the following sense. Any given nucleus has a 50% chance of decaying within a time interval equal to the half-life. If a half-life goes by and the nucleus has not decayed, the chance of a decay in the next half-life is still 50%. Thus, the probability that a nucleus will have decayed by the second half-life is (see the tree diagram in Figure 2.7) $\frac{1}{2} + \frac{1}{2} \times \frac{1}{2} = \frac{3}{4} = 0.75$ or 75%.

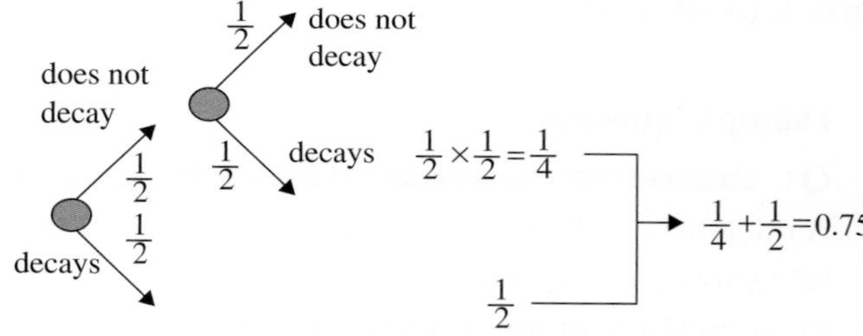

Figure 2.7 Tree diagram for nuclear decay.

(There is more on radioactive decay in Chapter 6.6.)

? QUESTIONS

1 In a study of the intensity of gamma rays from a radioactive source it is suspected that the counter rate C at a distance d from the source should behave as

$$C \propto \left(\frac{1}{d + d_0}\right)^2$$

where d_0 is an unknown constant. If a set of data for C and d is given, how should these be plotted in order to get a straight line?

2 The intensity of gamma rays of a specific energy (monochromatic rays) falls off exponentially with the thickness x of the absorbing material

$$I = I_0 \, e^{-\mu x}$$

where I_0 is the intensity at the face of the absorber and μ a constant depending on the material. (See Figure 2.8.)

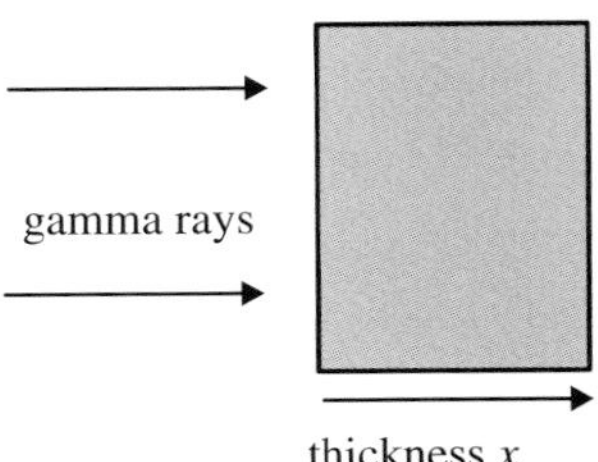

Figure 2.8 For question 2.

How should intensity I and thickness x be plotted in order to allow an accurate determination of the constant μ?

3 A radioactive source has a half-life of 3.00 min. At the start of an experiment there was 32.0 mg of the radioactive material present. How much will there be after 18.0 min?

4 The initial activity of a radioactive sample is 120 Bq. If after 24 h the activity is measured to be 15 Bq, find the half-life of the sample.

5 Beryllium-8 ($^{8}_{4}$Be) decays into two identical particles. What are they?

6 The only stable nuclei with more protons than neutrons are those of hydrogen and helium-3 ($^{3}_{2}$He). Why do you think there are so few?

7 An alpha particle and an electron with the same velocity enter a region of a uniform magnetic field at right angles to the velocity. Explain why they are deflected in opposite directions. Find the ratio of the radii of the circular paths the particles are deflected into.

8 Tritium ($^{3}_{1}$H) is a radioactive isotope of hydrogen and decays by beta decay. Write down the equation for the reaction and name the products of the decay.

9 Nitrogen ($^{14}_{7}$N) is produced in the beta decay of a radioactive isotope. Write down the reaction and name the particles in the reaction.

10 Bismuth ($^{210}_{83}$Bi) decays by beta and gamma emission. Write down the reaction and name the nucleus bismuth decays into.

11 Plutonium ($^{239}_{94}$Pu) decays by alpha decay. Write down the reaction and name the element produced in the decay.

12 A nucleus ($^{A}_{Z}$X) decays by emitting two electrons and one alpha particle. Find the atomic and mass numbers of the produced nucleus.

13 Name the two missing particles in the reaction $^{22}_{11}\text{Na} \rightarrow {}^{22}_{10}\text{Ne} + ? + ?$.

14 Discuss how one could confirm that a particular element emits:
(a) alpha particles;
(b) beta particles;
(c) gamma rays.

15 The track of an alpha particle in a cloud chamber was measured to be 30 mm. The energy required to produce an ion pair is about 32 eV, on average. Assuming that alpha particles create 6000 ions per mm along their path, estimate the energy of the alpha particle.

16 Many of the most stable nuclei have an even number of protons and an even number of neutrons. Can you suggest a reason why this might be so?

17 Explain why the heavy stable nuclei tend to have many more neutrons than protons.

18 Referring to the Segre plot in the text (Figure 2.4), what would be a likely decay for an unstable nucleus that has a large neutron-to-proton ratio? Where on the plot would such a nucleus be? What would be the likely decay for an unstable nucleus that has a small neutron-to-proton ratio? Where on the plot would this nucleus be?

Nuclear reactions

This chapter is an introduction to the physics of atomic nuclei. We will see that the sum of the masses of the constituents of a nucleus is not the same as the mass of the nucleus itself, which implies that the nucleus has enormous amounts of energy stored in it. Methods used to calculate energy released in nuclear reactions are presented.

Objectives

By the end of this chapter you should be able to:

- define the *unified mass unit*;
- state the meaning of the terms *mass defect* and *binding energy* and solve related problems;
- write *nuclear reaction equations* and balance the atomic and mass numbers;
- understand the meaning of the graph of *binding energy per nucleon* versus *mass number*;
- state the meaning of and difference between *fission* and *fusion*;
- understand that nuclear fusion takes place in the *core of the stars*;
- solve problems of *fission* and *fusion reactions*.

The unified mass unit

In nuclear physics, it is convenient to use a smaller unit of mass than the kilogram. We define a new unit called the *unified atomic mass unit*, u for short. It is defined to be $\frac{1}{12}$ of the mass of an atom of carbon-12, ${}^{12}_{6}\mathrm{C}$. The mass of a mole of ${}^{12}_{6}\mathrm{C}$ is 12 g and the number of molecules is the Avogadro constant, therefore the carbon-12 atom has a mass M given by

$$6.0221367 \times 10^{23} \times M = 12\,\mathrm{g}$$

$$M = \frac{12}{6.0221367 \times 10^{23}} \times 10^{-3}\,\mathrm{kg}$$

$$= 1.992648 \times 10^{-26}\,\mathrm{kg}$$

Hence

$$1\,\mathrm{u} = \frac{1}{12}(1.992648 \times 10^{-26}\,\mathrm{kg})$$

$$= 1.6605402 \times 10^{-27}\,\mathrm{kg}$$

Example question

Q1

Find in units of u the masses of the proton, neutron and electron (use Table 3.1).

Unified mass unit	$1.6605402 \times 10^{-27}$ kg
Electron	$9.1093897 \times 10^{-31}$ kg
Proton	$1.6726231 \times 10^{-27}$ kg
Neutron	$1.6749286 \times 10^{-27}$ kg

Table 3.1.

Answer

From the table of the masses in kilograms (Table 3.1) we find

$m_p = 1.007276$ u
$m_n = 1.008665$ u
$m_e = 0.0005486$ u

The mass defect and binding energy

To find the mass of a particular nucleus we have to subtract the mass of the electrons in the atom from the mass of the atom. If there are Z electrons in the atom, then

$$M_{\text{nucleus}} = M_{\text{atom}} - Zm_e$$

The mass of the atom is obtained from the periodic table and m_e is given above. We can find, for example, that the mass of the nucleus of helium is

$$M_{\text{nucleus}} = 4.0026 - 2 \times 0.0005486$$
$$= 4.0015\ \text{u}$$

We now recall that the helium nucleus is made up of two protons and two neutrons. If we add up their masses we find

$$2m_p + 2m_n = 4.0319\ \text{u}$$

which is *larger* than the mass of the nucleus by 0.0304 u. This leads to the concept of **mass defect.**

▶ We can see by examining each nucleus that this is generally true: the mass of the protons plus the mass of the neutrons is larger than the mass of the nucleus. We define their difference as the mass defect δ:

$$\delta = \text{total mass of nucleons} - \text{mass of nucleus}$$

or

$$\delta = Zm_p + (A - Z)m_n - M_{\text{nucleus}}$$

(remember that $A - Z$ is the number of neutrons in the nucleus). This formula allows us to calculate the mass defect for any nucleus.

Example question

Q2

Find the mass defect of the nucleus of gold, $^{197}_{79}\text{Au}$.

Answer

From the periodic table, the mass of the *atom* of gold is 196.967 u, and since it has 79 electrons the *nuclear* mass is

$$196.967\ \text{u} - 79 \times 0.0005486\ \text{u} = 196.924\ \text{u}.$$

The nucleus has 79 protons and 118 neutrons, so

$$\delta = (79 \times 1.007276 + 118 \times 1.008665 - 196.924)\ \text{u}$$
$$= 1.67\ \text{u}$$

Einstein's mass–energy formula

Where is the missing mass? The answer is given by Einstein's theory of special relativity, which states that mass and energy are equivalent and can be converted into each other. Einstein's famous formula from 1905 reads

$$E = mc^2$$

where c stands for the speed of light. The mass defect of a nucleus has been converted into energy and is stored in the nucleus. This energy is called the **binding energy** of the nucleus, and is denoted by E_b. Thus:

▶ $E_b = \delta c^2$

The binding energy of the nucleus is the work (energy) required to completely separate the nucleons of a nucleus.

The work required to remove one nucleon from the nucleus is *very roughly* the binding energy divided by the total number of nucleons.

At a more practical level, the binding energy of a nucleus is a measure of how stable it is – the higher the binding energy, the more stable the nucleus is.

It is convenient to find out how much energy corresponds to a mass of 1 u. Then, given a nuclear mass in u, we will immediately be able to find the energy that corresponds to it. Thus, an energy of 1 u is

$$\begin{aligned} 1\,\text{u} \times c^2 &= 1.6605402 \times 10^{-27} \times (2.9979 \times 10^8)^2\,\text{J} \\ &= 1.4923946316 \times 10^{-10}\,\text{J} \end{aligned}$$

Changing this to electronvolts, using

$$1\,\text{eV} = 1.602177 \times 10^{-19}\,\text{J}$$

gives an energy equivalent to a mass of 1 u of

$$\begin{aligned} \frac{1.4923946316 \times 10^{-10}}{1.602177 \times 10^{-19}} \frac{\text{J}}{\text{J eV}^{-1}} &= 931.5 \times 10^6\,\text{eV} \\ &= 931.5\,\text{MeV} \end{aligned}$$

(one MeV is one million electronvolts, $1\,\text{MeV} = 10^6\,\text{eV}$). So

$$1\,\text{u} \equiv 931.5\,\text{MeV}$$

Example questions

Q3

Find the energy equivalent to the mass of the proton, neutron and electron.

Answer

The masses in terms of u are $m_p = 1.0073$ u, $m_n = 1.0087$ u and $m_e = 0.0005486$ u. Hence the energy equivalents are, respectively, 938.3 MeV, 939.6 MeV and 0.511 MeV.

Q4

Find the binding energy of the nucleus of carbon-12.

Answer

The nuclear mass is

$$12.00000\,\text{u} - 6 \times 0.0005486\,\text{u} = 11.99671\,\text{u}$$

The mass defect is

$$\begin{aligned} &6 \times 1.007276\,\text{u} + 6 \times 1.008665\,\text{u} - 11.99671\,\text{u} \\ &= 0.09894\,\text{u} \end{aligned}$$

(the nucleus has 6 protons and 6 neutrons). Hence the binding energy is

$$0.09894 \times 931.5\,\text{MeV} = 92.2\,\text{MeV}$$

The binding energy curve

We saw on the previous page that the mass defect of helium is 0.0304 u, which corresponds therefore to a binding energy of

$$0.0304 \times 931.5\,\text{MeV} = 28.32\,\text{MeV}$$

(The alpha particle has an unusually large binding energy compared with nuclei of roughly the same mass. This accounts for its exceptional stability and the fact that unstable nuclei decay by emitting alpha particles.) There are four nucleons in the helium nucleus so the binding energy per nucleon is $28.32/4 = 7.1$ MeV. For carbon, we found a binding energy of 92.159 MeV, giving a binding energy per nucleon of 7.68 MeV.

▶ We find that most nuclei have a binding energy per nucleon of approximately 8 MeV.

This is shown in Figure 3.1.

This curve is at the heart of nuclear physics. The curve has a maximum for $A = 62$ corresponding to nickel. As we shall soon see, this curve tells us that if a heavy nucleus (heavier than nickel) splits up into two lighter ones or if two light nuclei (lighter than nickel) fuse together, then energy is released as a result. This is of fundamental importance and is the basis for nuclear fission and nuclear fusion, respectively. To understand all this we must first see what happens from the energy point of view when a nucleus decays.

Energy released in a decay

Let us consider the decay of radium by alpha particle emission (see Figure 3.2):

$$^{226}_{88}\text{Ra} \rightarrow {}^{222}_{86}\text{Rn} + {}^{4}_{2}\alpha$$

For any decay, the total energy to the left of the arrow must equal the total energy to the right of the arrow. Here total energy means the energy corresponding to each mass

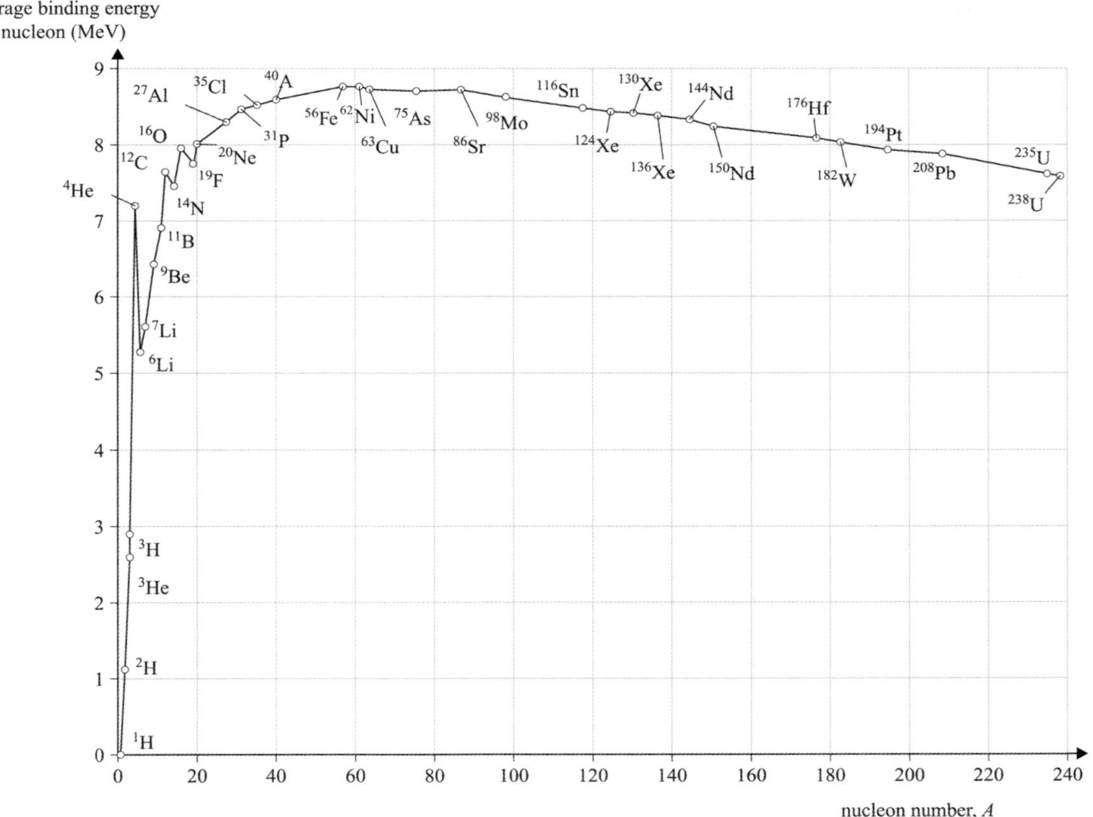

Figure 3.1 The binding energy per nucleon is almost constant for most nuclei.

according to Einstein's formula plus whatever kinetic energy each mass has. If the decaying radium nucleus is at rest, then the total energy available is simply Mc^2, where M is the mass of the nucleus of radium. To the right of the arrow, we have the energies corresponding to the masses of the radon and helium nuclei plus any possible kinetic energy: the produced nuclei are moving.

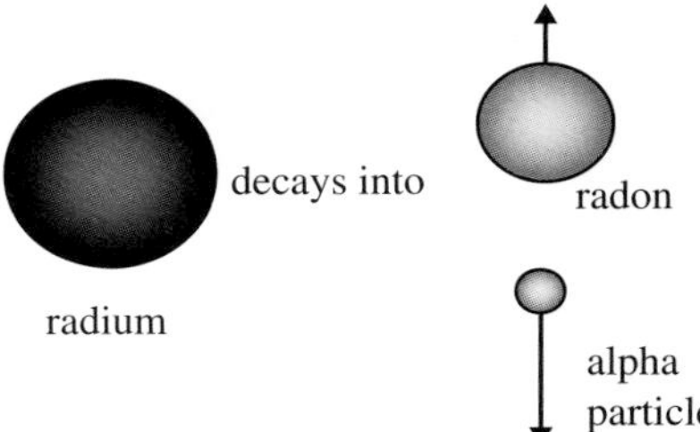

Figure 3.2 The energy released in a nuclear reaction is in the form of kinetic energy of the products.

Thus, to be at all possible, the decay must be such that at the very minimum the energy corresponding to the radium mass is larger than the energies corresponding to the radon plus alpha particle masses. Let us check if this is true. We need the *masses of the nuclei* that appear in the reaction, namely radium, radon and helium.

If we use the periodic table to find the masses, we must remember that the periodic table gives atomic masses not nuclear masses. Thus, we must subtract from each atomic mass the mass of the electrons in the atom.

However, the atomic number is conserved (i.e. it is the same before and after the decay) and equals the number of electrons in the atom. It follows that the number of electron masses that must be subtracted from the atomic mass to the left of the arrow is the same as the number of electron masses that must be subtracted from the right. Thus, as long as we are interested in *mass differences*, as we are here, it is enough to use atomic masses instead of nuclear masses.

According to the periodic table:

$$\text{mass of radium} = 226.0254\ \text{u}$$

$$\begin{array}{rrl} & \text{mass of radon} = & 222.0176\ \text{u} \\ + & \text{mass of helium} = & 4.0026\ \text{u} \\ \hline & \text{sum} = & 226.0202\ \text{u} \end{array}$$

We see that the mass of radium exceeds that of radon plus helium by 0.0052 u. Thus, there is an amount of energy released in the form of kinetic energy of radon and helium given by

$$0.0052 \times 931.5\ \text{MeV} = 4.84\ \text{MeV}$$

If 50 g of radium were to decay in this way, the total energy released would be $N \times 4.84$ MeV where N is the total number of nuclei in the 50 g of radium. In 50 g of radium there are $\frac{50}{226} = 0.22$ mol and so

$$N = 0.22 \times 6 \times 10^{23} = 1.3 \times 10^{23}$$

Hence the total energy released is

$$\begin{aligned} E &= 1.3 \times 10^{23} \times 4.84\ \text{MeV} \\ &= 6.3 \times 10^{23}\ \text{MeV} \\ &\approx 10^{11}\ \text{J} \end{aligned}$$

The momenta of radon and helium are opposite in direction and equal in magnitude by the law of conservation of momentum. (We assume that the decaying radium nucleus is at rest, so its momentum is zero.) Thus

$$M_{\text{radon}} v_{\text{radon}} = M_{\text{helium}} v_{\text{helium}}$$

Therefore

$$\begin{aligned} \frac{v_{\text{helium}}}{v_{\text{radon}}} &= \frac{M_{\text{radon}}}{M_{\text{helium}}} \\ &\approx \frac{222}{4} \\ &\approx 55 \end{aligned}$$

the velocity of radon is smaller than the velocity of helium by the ratio of the masses: approximately 55. (As an exercise you can show that the ratio of kinetic energies of the helium to the radon nuclei is also 55.)

Let us now re-examine these findings in terms of the binding energy curve. For the decay to take place, the mass of the decaying nucleus has to be greater than the combined masses of the products. This means that the binding energy of the decaying nucleus must be less than the binding energies of the product nuclei. This is why radioactive decay is possible for heavy elements lying to the right of nickel in the binding energy curve.

Nuclear reactions

If the total mass on the left-hand side of a reaction is smaller than the total mass on the right-hand side, the reaction may still take place. Consider the reaction in which an alpha particle collides with a nucleus of nitrogen:

$$^{14}_{7}\text{N} + {}^{4}_{2}\alpha \rightarrow {}^{17}_{8}\text{O} + {}^{1}_{1}\text{p}$$

(see Figure 3.3). This is an example of a nuclear reaction. Note how the atomic and mass numbers match as they did in nuclear decays. This is a famous reaction called the transmutation of nitrogen; it was studied by Rutherford in 1909. Note that if we add up the masses to the left of the arrow we find 18.0057 u, whereas the masses to the right are 18.0070 u (i.e. larger). Thus, this reaction will only take place if the alpha particle has enough kinetic energy to make up for the imbalance in mass between the two sides.

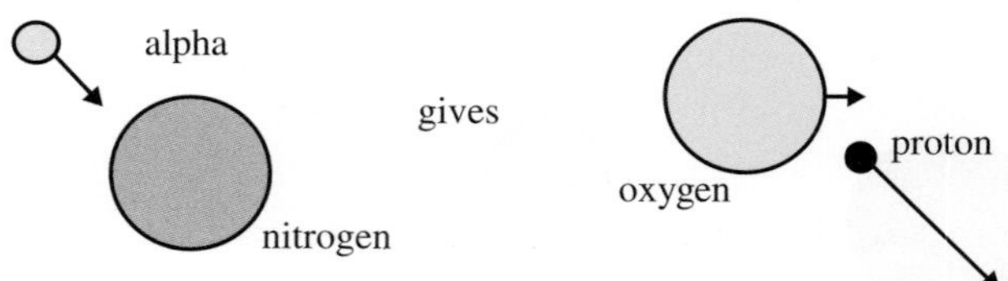

Figure 3.3 An alpha particle colliding with nitrogen produces oxygen and a proton

(Actually, the required minimum kinetic energy of the alpha particle has to be bigger than the energy equivalent of the mass difference between the two sides of the reaction. This is because the products of the reaction themselves will have kinetic energy.)

In a reaction in which four particles participate

$$A + B \to C + D$$

energy will be released if the quantity Δm given by

$$\Delta m \to (m_A + m_B) - (m_C + m_D)$$

is positive (i.e. if the total mass on the left is larger than the total mass on the right). The amount of energy released is then equal to

$$\Delta E = (\Delta m)c^2$$

There are two kinds of energy-producing nuclear reactions and we consider them separately in the following sections.

Nuclear fission

Nuclear fission is the process in which a heavy nucleus splits up into lighter nuclei. When a neutron is absorbed by a nucleus of uranium-235, uranium momentarily turns into uranium-236 according to the reaction

$$^{1}_{0}\text{n} + ^{235}_{92}\text{U} \to ^{236}_{92}\text{U}$$

Uranium-236 then splits into lighter nuclei. This is the fission reaction. A number of possibilities exist as to what these nuclei are. One possibility is

$$^{144}_{56}\text{Ba} + ^{89}_{36}\text{Kr} + 3^{1}_{0}\text{n}$$

The production of neutrons is a feature of fission reactions. The produced neutrons can be used to collide with other nuclei of uranium-235 in the reactor, producing more fission, energy and neutrons. The reaction is thus self-sustaining – it is called a *chain reaction*. For the chain reaction to get going a certain minimum mass of uranium-235 must be present, otherwise the neutrons escape without causing further reactions – this is called the *critical mass*.

The energy released can be calculated as shown in Table 3.2.

mass of uranium plus neutron	= 236.0526 u
mass of products = 143.92292 u + 88.91781 u + 3 × 1.008665 u	= 235.8667250 u
mass difference	= 0.185875 u
energy released	= 0.185875 × 931.5 MeV = 173.14 MeV

Table 3.2.

This energy appears as kinetic energy of the products.

Thus, an energy of about 173 MeV per fissioning nucleus of uranium is released. This is a lot of energy! A mass of 1 kg of uranium-235 undergoing fission would produce an amount of energy that can be found as follows: 1 kg is 1000/235 mol of uranium and thus contains $(1000/235) \times 6 \times 10^{23}$ nuclei. Each nucleus produces about 173 MeV of energy and thus the total is $(1000/235) \times 6 \times 10^{23} \times 173$ MeV or about 7×10^{13} J. In a nuclear reactor, the release of energy is done in a controlled way. If the rate of neutron production is too high, too much energy is produced in a very short time. This is what happens in a nuclear bomb.

Note that the fission process begins when a neutron collides with a nucleus of uranium-235. An alpha particle cannot be used to start this process because its positive charge would be repelled by the positive charge of the uranium nucleus and so would not lead to the capture of the alpha. An electron, on the other hand, would easily be captured but its small mass would not perturb the heavy nucleus sufficiently for fission to start.

Nuclear fusion

Nuclear fusion is the joining of two light nuclei into a heavier one with the associated production of energy. An example of this reaction is:

$$^{2}_{1}\text{H} + ^{2}_{1}\text{H} \to ^{3}_{2}\text{He} + ^{1}_{0}\text{n}$$

where two deuterium nuclei (isotopes of hydrogen) produce helium-3 (an isotope of helium) and a neutron. Computing masses to the left and right of the reaction arrow as in Table 3.3 we can find the energy released.

2 × mass of deuterium	= 4.0282 u
mass of helium + neutron	= 4.0247 u
mass difference	= 0.0035 u
energy released	= 0.0035 × 931.5 MeV = 3.26 MeV

Table 3.3.

A kilogram of deuterium would thus release energy of about 10^{13} J, which is comparable to the energy produced by a kilogram of uranium in the fission process.

Example question

Q5

Another fusion reaction is $4{}^1_1\text{H} \rightarrow {}^4_2\text{He} + 2{}^0_1\text{e} + 2\nu_e + {}^0_0\gamma$, where four hydrogen nuclei fuse into a helium nucleus plus two positrons (the antiparticle of the electron – same mass, opposite charge), two electron neutrinos and a photon. Calculate the energy released in this reaction.

Answer

We must find the masses before and after the reaction.

Mass of 4 protons (hydrogen nuclei)
$= 4 \times 1.007276 \text{ u} = 4.029104 \text{ u}$

Mass on right-hand side
$= (4.0026 - 2 \times 0.0005486) \text{ u}$
$+ 2 \times 0.0005486 \text{ u} = 4.002600 \text{ u}$

Mass difference $= 0.026504$ u

This gives an energy of 24.7 MeV. The two positrons annihilate into energy by colliding with two electrons giving an additional 2 MeV (= 4 × 0.511 MeV), for a total of 26.7 MeV.

For the light nuclei to fuse, very large temperatures are required. This is so that the electrostatic repulsion between the two nuclei that fuse is overcome. The enormous temperature (recall the kinetic theory of gases) causes the nuclei to move fast enough so as to approach each other sufficiently for fusion to take place. The very hot material (over ten million kelvin) undergoing fusion is in a state called plasma (ionized atoms). Plasma, being very hot, cannot come into contact with anything else (either because it causes it to melt or because it will result in heat losses) and therefore has to be contained by unusual methods such as magnetic fields in big machines called tokamaks. There are serious unsolved problems with the prolonged confinement of plasmas and this is one reason why nuclear fusion, still, is not a commercially viable source of energy. Commercial energy from the nucleus comes now only from the fission process, which unlike fusion, however, is environmentally suspect.

Fusion in stars

The high temperatures and pressures in the interior of stars make stars ideal places for nuclear fusion. As we saw in the previous section, high temperatures are required so that the nuclei have sufficiently large kinetic energy to approach each other, overcoming the electrostatic repulsion due to their positive charges. The high pressure ensures that sufficient numbers of nuclei are found close to each other, thus increasing the probability of them coming together and fusion taking place.

The reaction $4{}^1_1\text{H} \rightarrow {}^4_2\text{He} + 2{}^0_1\text{e} + 2\nu_e + {}^0_0\gamma$ is a typical reaction that takes place in stellar cores. Nuclear fusion is the source of energy for a star; it prevents the star from collapsing under its own weight and provides the energy the star sends out in the form of light and heat, for example. Stars are, in fact, element factories, producing, for example, all the elements that our bodies are made of. More details on this can be found in Option E on Astrophysics.

Fusion and fission processes are summarized in Figure 3.4.

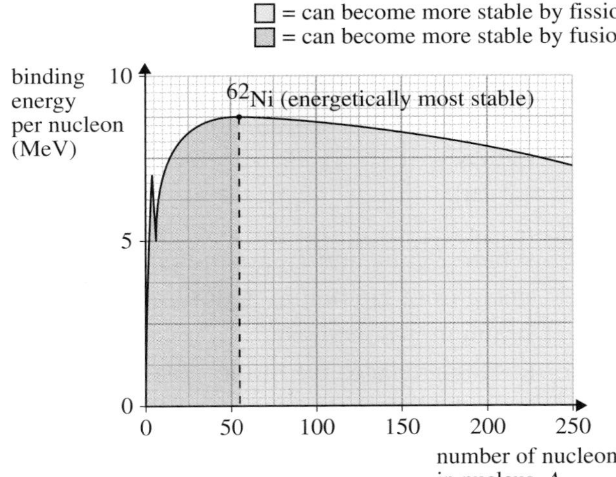

Figure 3.4 When a heavy nucleus splits up, energy is released because the produced nuclei have a higher binding energy than the original nucleus. When two light nuclei fuse, energy is produced because the products again have a higher binding energy.

QUESTIONS

1 Find the binding energy and binding energy per nucleon of the nucleus $^{62}_{28}\text{Ni}$. The atomic mass of nickel is 61.928348 u.

2 How much energy is required to remove one proton from the nucleus of $^{16}_{8}\text{O}$? A rough answer to this question is obtained by giving the binding energy per nucleon. A better answer is obtained when we write a reaction that removes a proton from the nucleus. In this case $^{16}_{8}\text{O} \rightarrow {}^{1}_{1}\text{p} + {}^{15}_{7}\text{N}$. Find the energy required for this reaction to take place. This is the proton separation energy. Get both values and compare them. (The atomic mass of oxygen is 15.994 u; that of nitrogen is 15.000 u.)

3 What is the energy released in the beta decay of a neutron?

4 The first excited state of the nucleus of uranium-235 is 0.051 MeV above the ground state.

(a) What is the wavelength of the photon emitted when the nucleus makes a transition to the ground state?

(b) What part of the spectrum does this photon belong to?

5 Calculate the energy released in the alpha decay $^{234}_{90}\text{Th} \rightarrow {}^{230}_{88}\text{Ra} + {}^{4}_{2}\text{He}$. (The atomic mass of thorium is 234.043596 u; that of radium is 230.03708 u.)

6 Assume uranium-236 splits into two nuclei of palladium-117 (Pd). (The atomic mass of uranium is 236.0455561 u; that of palladium is 116.9178 u.)

(a) Write down the reaction.

(b) What other particles must be produced?

(c) What is the energy released?

7 One possible outcome in the fission of a uranium nucleus is the reaction

$^{235}_{92}\text{U} + {}^{1}_{0}\text{n} \rightarrow {}^{95}_{42}\text{Mo} + {}^{139}_{57}\text{La} + 2{}^{1}_{0}\text{n} + ?$

(a) What is missing in this reaction?

(b) How much energy is released?

(Atomic masses: U = 235.043922 u; Mo = 94.905841 u; La = 138.906349 u.)

8 Another fission reaction involving uranium is

$^{235}_{92}\text{U} + {}^{1}_{0}\text{n} \rightarrow {}^{98}_{40}\text{Zr} + {}^{135}_{52}\text{Te} + 3{}^{1}_{0}\text{n}$

Calculate the energy released. (Atomic masses: U = 235.043922 u; Zr = 97.91276 u; Te = 134.9165 u.)

9 Calculate the energy released in the fusion reaction ${}^{2}_{1}\text{H} + {}^{3}_{1}\text{H} \rightarrow {}^{4}_{2}\text{He} + {}^{1}_{0}\text{n}$. (Atomic masses: ${}^{2}_{1}\text{H}$ = 2.014102 u; ${}^{3}_{1}\text{H}$ = 3.016049 u; ${}^{4}_{2}\text{He}$ = 4.002603 u.)

10 In the text, it was stated that the reaction $4{}^{1}_{1}\text{H} \rightarrow {}^{4}_{2}\text{He} + 2{}^{0}_{1}\text{e} + 2\nu_e + {}^{0}_{0}\gamma$ is the mechanism by which hydrogen in stars is converted into helium and that the reaction releases about 26.7 MeV of energy. The sun radiates energy at the rate of 3.9×10^{26} W and has a mass of about 1.99×10^{30} kg, of which 75% is hydrogen. Find out how long it will take the sun to convert 12% of its hydrogen into helium.

11 In the first nuclear reaction in a particle accelerator, hydrogen nuclei were accelerated and then allowed to hit nuclei of lithium according to the reaction ${}^{1}_{1}\text{H} + {}^{7}_{3}\text{Li} \rightarrow {}^{4}_{2}\text{He} + {}^{4}_{2}\text{He}$. Find the energy released. (The atomic mass of lithium is 7.016 u.)

12 Outline the role in nuclear fusion reactions of: (a) temperature; (b) pressure.

13 Show that an alternative formula for the mass defect is $\delta = ZM_H + (A - Z)\,m_n - M_{atom}$ where M_H is the mass of a hydrogen atom and m_n is the mass of a neutron.

14 Consider the nuclear *fusion* reaction involving the deuterium ($^2_1$D) and tritium ($^3_1$T) isotopes of hydrogen:

$$^2_1\text{D} + ^3_1\text{T} \rightarrow ^4_2\text{He} + ^1_0\text{n}$$

The energy released, Q_1, may be calculated in the usual way, using the masses of the particles involved, from the expression

$$Q_1 = (M_D + M_T - M_{He} - m_n)c^2$$

Similarly, in the *fission* reaction of uranium

$$^{235}_{92}\text{U} + ^1_0\text{n} \rightarrow ^{98}_{40}\text{Zr} + ^{135}_{52}\text{Te} + 3^1_0\text{n}$$

the energy released, Q_2, may be calculated from

$$Q_2 = (M_U - M_{Zr} - M_{Te} - 2m_n)c^2$$

(a) Show that the expression for Q_1 can be rewritten as

$$Q_1 = E_{He} - (E_D + E_T)$$

where E_{He}, E_D and E_T are the binding energies of helium, deuterium and tritium, respectively,

(b) Show that the expression for Q_2 can be rewritten as

$$Q_2 = (E_{Zr} + E_{Te}) - E_U$$

where E_{Zr}, E_{Te} and E_U are the binding energies of zirconium, tellurium and uranium, respectively.

(c) Results similar to the results obtained in (a) and (b) apply to all energy-releasing fusion and fission reactions. Use this fact and the binding energy curve in Figure 3.1 to explain carefully why energy is released in fusion and fission reactions.

Interactions of matter with energy

The photoelectric effect was one of the first signs that classical physics was inadequate when applied to the microscopic world. This chapter discusses the photoelectric effect and other aspects of the interaction of matter with energy, leading to the duality of matter and energy.

Objectives

By the end of this chapter you should be able to:

- describe the *photoelectric effect*;
- describe which aspects of this effect cannot be explained by classical physics and how the *new physics* introduced by Einstein provides explanations for them;
- understand the meaning of the terms *stopping voltage*, *threshold frequency* and *work function*;
- state the meaning of the term *photon* and use the equation for its energy, $E = hf$;
- solve problems on the photoelectric effect, $eV_s = hf - \phi$;
- state the meaning of the term *wave–particle duality*;
- state *de Broglie's* formula, $\lambda = \frac{h}{p}$, and use it in problems;
- describe the *Davisson–Germer experiment* and understand its significance.

The photoelectric effect

When light (or other electromagnetic radiation) falls on a metallic surface, electrons may be emitted from that surface in a phenomenon known as the **photoelectric effect**. An electroscope connected to the surface becomes positively charged when light falls on the metal (see Figure 4.1).

It is not difficult to imagine that electrons will be emitted, because electromagnetic radiation contains energy that can be transferred to electrons of the atoms of the photosurface, thus enabling them to pull themselves away from the attraction of the nuclei and leave the surface altogether. An apparatus to investigate this effect (first used by R. Millikan) is shown in Figure 4.2.

It consists of an evacuated tube, inside which is the photosurface and across from that a collecting plate where the emitted electrons arrive. The photosurface and the collecting plate are part of a circuit as shown. Light passes through an opening in the tube and falls on the photosurface, and the emitted electrons move toward the right, completing the circuit; thus, an electric current flows. The magnitude of the current can be detected

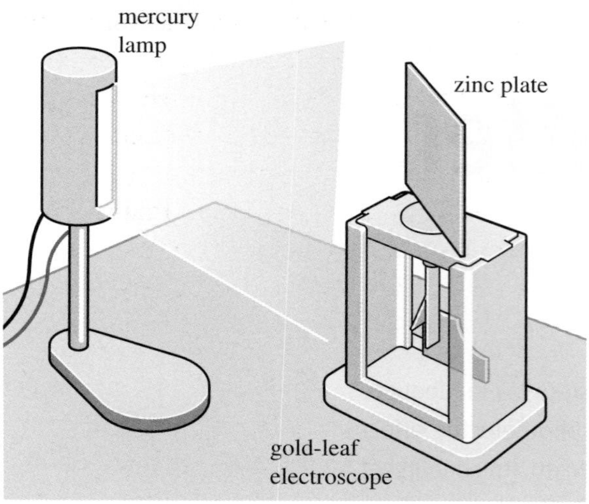

Figure 4.1 A photosurface becomes positively charged when light falls on it.

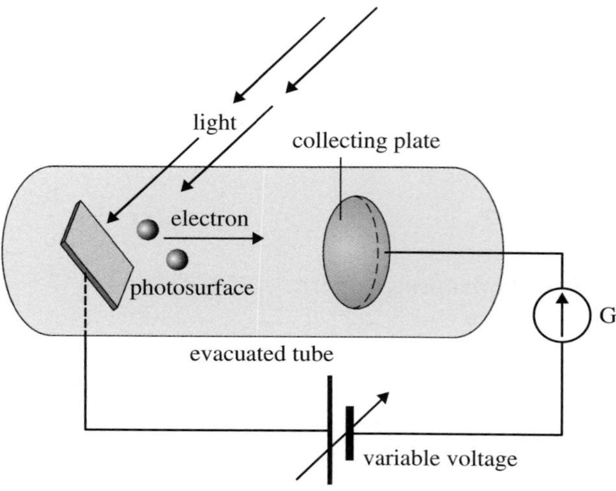

Figure 4.2 Apparatus for investigating the photoelectric effect. The variable voltage decelerates the emitted electrons and eventually stops them.

by the galvanometer G. It is readily found that, as the intensity of the light source increases, the current also increases. In fact, current and intensity are directly proportional to each other. A larger current can be due to either a larger number of electrons being emitted per second or electrons with higher speed (or both). To distinguish between the two cases we need a method to measure the energy (and hence speed) of the emitted electrons. This can be done by connecting a battery between the photosurface and the collecting plate as shown in Figure 4.3 (*note*: pay attention to where the negative terminal of the battery goes). By increasing the voltage of the battery

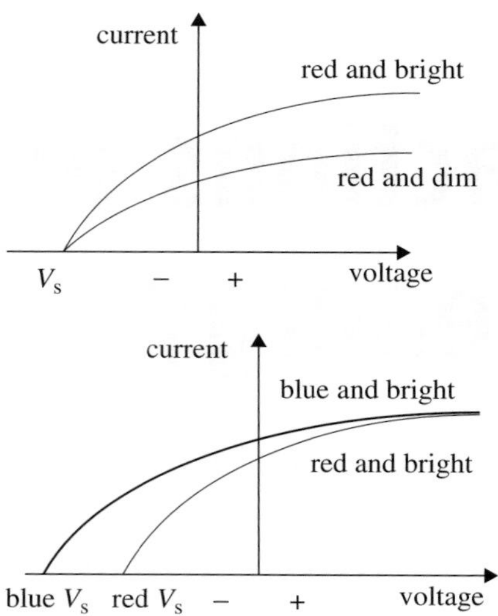

Figure 4.3 The photocurrent is larger for larger intensity light source. The stopping voltage depends on the frequency not the intensity.

we can make the current in the circuit zero. This is called the stopping voltage, V_s. It follows that the maximum kinetic energy of the emitted electrons must be eV_s. We see this as follows: Let the maximum kinetic energy of the electrons be E_k; then the work done in moving an electron from the cathode to the collecting plate is eV_s, and from mechanics we know that the work done is the change in the kinetic energy of the electron. So

$$eV_s = E_k$$

▶ We find that the stopping voltage stays the same no matter what the intensity of the light source is. Thus, the increase in the current is due to more electrons being emitted. The intensity of light has no effect on the maximum energy of the electrons (see Figure 4.3).

This is a very surprising result and we shall return to it soon. Another surprise awaits us if we allow monochromatic light (light of one specific frequency) to fall on the photosurface. We find that the stopping voltage depends on the frequency of the light source. The larger the frequency, the larger the stopping voltage (i.e. the larger the energy of the emitted electrons). If the polarity of the battery is now reversed so that the emitted electrons are actually *attracted* to the collecting plate, we find that the current increases but reaches a saturation value. This is because every single emitted electron is now collected.

If we plot the kinetic energy of the electrons (which equals eV_s) versus frequency, we find a straight line as shown in Figure 4.4a.

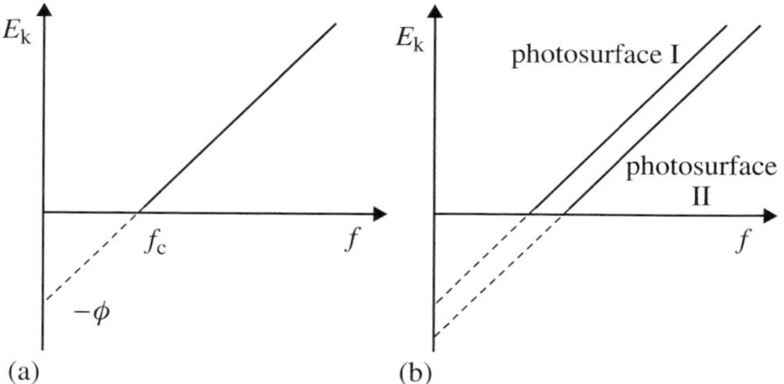

Figure 4.4 (a) The graph of kinetic energy versus frequency is a straight line. The horizontal intercept is the critical frequency. (b) When another photosurface is used, a line parallel to the first is obtained.

The puzzling feature of this graph is that there exists a frequency, called the critical (or threshold) frequency f_c, such that no electrons at all are emitted if the frequency of the light source is less than f_c, even if very intense light is allowed to fall on the photosurface. If the experiment is repeated with a different photosurface and the kinetic energy of the electrons is plotted versus frequency, a line parallel to the first is obtained, as shown in Figure 4.4b.

Another puzzling observation is that the electrons are emitted immediately after the light is incident on the photosurface, with no apparent time delay.

▶ We now have three surprising observations:

1 The intensity of the incident light does not affect the energy of the emitted electrons.
2 The electron energy depends on the frequency of the incident light, and there is a certain minimum frequency below which no electrons are emitted.
3 Electrons are emitted with no time delay.

These three observations are in violation of the standard laws of physics. According to the laws of classical electromagnetism, a more intense beam of light contains more energy and therefore should cause the emission of more energetic electrons. Classical electromagnetism offers no explanation as to why the frequency of light should affect the electron energy, nor does it explain why there should exist a critical frequency.

A very low-intensity beam of light carries little energy. So an electron might have to wait for a considerable length of time before it accumulated enough energy to escape from the metal. This would cause a delay in its emission.

The explanation of all these strange observations was provided by Albert Einstein in 1905.

▶ Einstein suggested that light (like any other form of electromagnetic radiation) consists of quanta, which are *packets of energy and momentum*. The energy of one such quantum is given by the formula

$$E = hf$$

where f is the frequency of the electromagnetic radiation and $h = 6.63 \times 10^{-34}$ J s is a constant, known as Planck's constant.

These quanta of energy and momentum are called *photons*, the particles of light.

(Max Planck had introduced h a few years earlier in his investigation of the spectrum of a black body. It is worth pointing out here that the spectrum of a black body could not be explained in terms of conventional physics, just as the photoelectric experiment could not.)

This suggestion implies, therefore, that light behaves in some cases as particles do, but in addition the energy of one of the particles making up light depends only on the frequency and not on the intensity. Thus, if a photon of frequency f is absorbed by an electron in the photosurface, the electron's energy will increase by hf. Now, it takes a certain amount of energy, let us say ϕ, to free the electron from the pull of the nuclei of the atoms of the photosurface. The electron will be emitted (become free) if hf is bigger than ϕ; the difference $hf - \phi$ will simply be the kinetic energy of the (now) free electron (see Figure 4.5). That is

$$E_k = hf - \phi$$

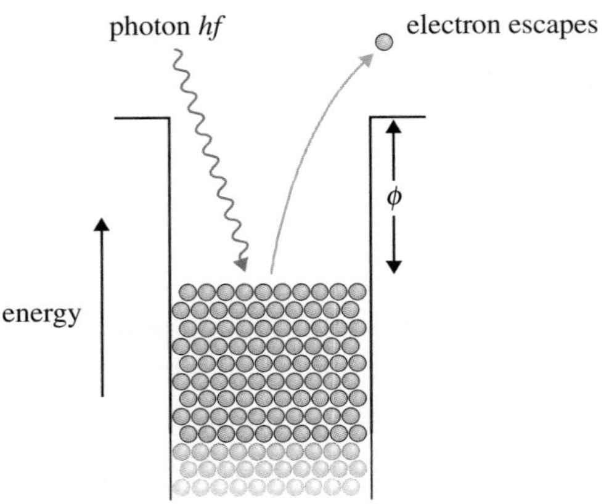

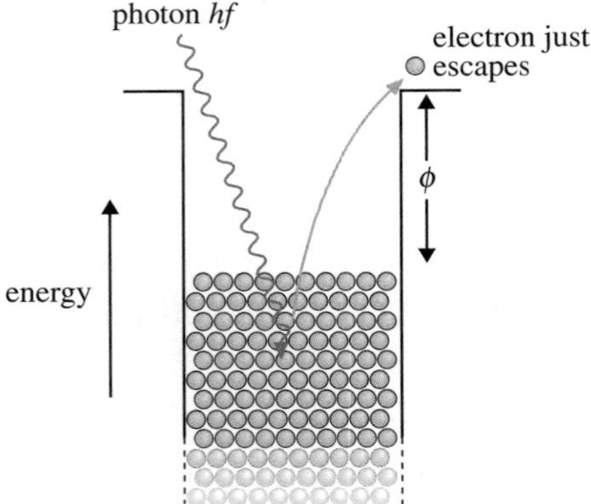

Figure 4.5 (a) A single photon of light may release a single electron from a metal. (b) A more tightly bound electron needs more energy to release it from the metal.

But this is exactly what our discussion of the photoelectric experiment gave. The value of ϕ (called the work function) is read off the graph, from the intercept of the straight line with the vertical axis. Note that the work function and the critical frequency are related by

$$hf_c = \phi$$

since $E_k = 0$ in that case.

Recalling that the kinetic energy of the electrons is measured in the photoelectric effect apparatus to be $eV_s = E_k$, it follows that:

► $eV_s = hf - \phi$

$$\Rightarrow V_s = \frac{h}{e}f - \frac{\phi}{e}$$

that is, in a graph of stopping voltage versus frequency, one obtains a straight line with slope h/e.

Example questions

Q1

A photosurface has a work function of 1.50 eV. Find the critical frequency. If light of frequency 6.1×10^{14} Hz falls on this surface, what is the energy and speed of the emitted electrons?

Answer

The critical frequency f_c is given in terms of the work function by $hf_c = \phi$ and thus

$$f_c = \frac{\phi}{h} = \frac{1.5 \times 1.6 \times 10^{-19}}{6.63 \times 10^{-34}}\ \text{Hz}$$
$$= 3.62 \times 10^{14}\ \text{Hz}$$

The kinetic energy of the electron is given by $E_k = hf - \phi$, that is

$E_k = 1.64 \times 10^{-19}\ \text{J} = 1.03\ \text{eV}$

From $E_k = \frac{1}{2}mv^2$ we find $v = 6.0 \times 10^5\ \text{m s}^{-1}$. (*Note*: use joules for E_k to find v.)

Q2

Monochromatic light of intensity 4 W and wavelength 4×10^{-7} m falling on a photosurface whose critical frequency is 6×10^{14} Hz releases 10^{10} electrons per second. What is the current collected in the anode? If the intensity of the light is increased to 8 W, what will the current be? If light of intensity 8 W and wavelength 6×10^{-7} m falls on this photosurface, what will the current be in that case?

Answer

From $I = \frac{\Delta Q}{\Delta t}$, the definition of electric current, we find

$I = e \times 10^{10}$

that is

$I = 1.6 \times 10^{-9}$ A

If the intensity doubles, so will the current, giving

$I = 3.2 \times 10^{-9}$ A

We note that the critical wavelength is

$$\frac{3 \times 10^{8}}{6 \times 10^{14}} \text{ m} = 5 \times 10^{-7} \text{ m}$$

and so if the wavelength becomes 6×10^{-7} m, no electrons will be emitted at all, hence $I = 0$ then.

Q3

Light of wavelength 5×10^{-7} m falls on a spherical photosurface whose critical frequency is 5×10^{14} Hz. The photosurface is in an insulated enclosure. What is the electric potential that the sphere will develop?

Answer

The kinetic energy of the emitted electrons will be

$$\begin{aligned} E_k &= hf - \phi \\ &= \frac{hc}{\lambda} - hf_c \\ &= 6.63 \times 10^{-20} \text{ J} \\ &= 0.4 \text{ eV} \end{aligned}$$

Hence electrons will be emitted until the electric potential on the sphere becomes 0.4 V, in which case the attraction of the electrons to the sphere will be strong enough to prevent further electrons from escaping.

More on the photon

The energy of the photon is given by the equation $E = hf$, which is a relation that is being directly tested in the photoelectric effect. The photon also carries momentum, given by

$$p = \frac{E}{c} = \frac{hf}{c} = \frac{h}{\lambda}$$

The existence of a photon momentum is supported by the Compton effect: the scattering of photons off electrons or protons. The photon, although a 'particle' with energy and momentum, has no mass (it also has zero electric charge). This implies (because of the theory of relativity – see Option H) that it always travels at the speed of light. For such particles (they are called relativistic), a more general definition of momentum allows zero-mass particles to have momentum.

Example questions

Q4

How many photons of wavelength 5×10^{-7} m are emitted per second by a 75 W lamp, assuming that 1% of the energy of the lamp goes into photons of this wavelength?

Answer

Let there be N photons per second emitted. Then the energy is $N\frac{hc}{\lambda}$ and this has to be 1% of 75 J, that is 0.75 J. So, $N = 0.19 \times 10^{19}$ photons per second.

Q5

If all the photons from example question 4 hit a mirror and are reflected by it, what pressure do these photons exert on the mirror? Take the area of the mirror to be 0.5 m^2.

Answer

Each photon has a momentum of $\frac{E}{c}$ or $\frac{h}{\lambda}$. The momentum change upon reflection is $2\frac{h}{\lambda}$. Since there are N such reflections per second, the force F on the mirror is $2N\frac{h}{\lambda}$, which is 0.5×10^{-8} N. The pressure is thus

$$\frac{F}{A} = 1.0 \times 10^{-8} \text{ N m}^{-2}$$

(Note that if the photons were absorbed rather than reflected the pressure would be half of what we got.)

We close this section with an observation made by G. I. Taylor in 1924. Imagine that light (i.e. a stream of photons) is directed at two slits in a Young-type experiment. Interference at a screen some distance away gives the familiar fringes of high and low intensity. Taylor now argues that if the intensity of light is reduced sufficiently, a stage will be reached when only one photon at a time arrives at the slits. We are now faced with the problem that a single photon, *which will go through either one slit or the other*, somehow produces the interference pattern on the screen. Taylor's observation is a sign that even when we treat light as photons, its wave nature is not completely forgotten.

De Broglie's wavelength

In 1923, Louis de Broglie suggested that to a particle of momentum p there corresponds a wave of wavelength given by the formula

$$\lambda = \frac{h}{p}$$

The de Broglie hypothesis, as this is known, thus assigns wave-like properties to something that is normally thought to be a particle. This state of affairs is called the duality of matter.

Example question

Q6

Find the de Broglie wavelength of a proton that has been accelerated from rest by a potential difference of 500 V.

Answer

The kinetic energy of the proton is given by

$$E_k = \frac{p^2}{2m}$$

The work done in accelerating the proton through a potential difference V is qV and this work goes into kinetic energy. Thus

$$\frac{p^2}{2m} = qV$$

$$\Rightarrow \quad p = \sqrt{2mqV}$$

Hence

$$\lambda = \frac{h}{\sqrt{2mqV}}$$

$$= \frac{6.63 \times 10^{-34}}{\sqrt{2 \times 1.67 \times 10^{-27} \times 1.60 \times 10^{-19} \times 500}} \text{ m}$$

$$= 1.3 \times 10^{-12} \text{ m}$$

The electron as a wave

The question is, given an electron, when do we treat it as a particle and when as a wave? Remember that if we call something a wave then it must show wave-like properties – in particular, diffraction. A wave of wavelength λ will diffract around an obstacle of size d if and only if λ is comparable to or bigger than d. To find a typical electron wavelength, consider an electron moving at a speed of 10^5 m s^{-1}. It has a momentum $p = 9.1 \times 10^{-26}$ kg m s^{-1} and therefore $\lambda = 7.2 \times 10^{-9}$ m. This is quite small. To see the wave-like nature of this electron we would need an 'obstacle' or an 'opening' of about this size. This is provided in nature by crystals. In a crystal, the atoms are regularly placed and the distance between them is typically of the order of 10^{-8} m. The spacing between the atoms is the 'opening' we are looking for. The reason the electron microscope can resolve small distances (down to 10^{-8} m) is precisely because these distances are of the same order of magnitude as the de Broglie wavelength of the electrons used.

A beam of electrons directed at such a crystal would scatter off the crystal in much the same way that X-rays do. The scattering of X-rays off the periodic arrangement of atoms in a crystal had been shown earlier (by Sir William Henry Bragg) to be the result of diffraction. Bragg derived a relation (the Bragg formula) between the spacing of the atoms in the crystal and the wavelength of the X-rays, so knowing one quantity made the calculation of the other possible. (See Figure 4.6.)

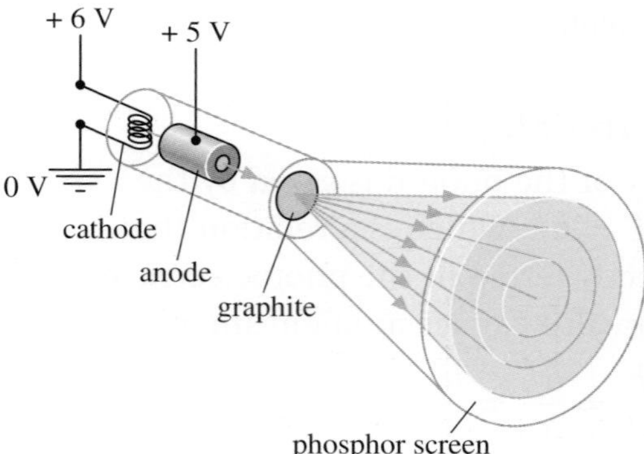

Figure 4.6 Electrons are accelerated from the cathode to the anode: they form a beam, which is diffracted as it passes through the graphite.

▶ Experiments showing the wave nature of the electron were carried out in 1927 by Clinton J. Davisson and Lester H. Germer, and also by George Thomson, son of J. J. Thomson, the discoverer of the electron. In the Davisson–Germer experiment, electrons of kinetic energy 54 eV were directed at a surface of nickel where a single crystal had been grown and were scattered by it (see Figure 4.7). Using the Bragg formula and the known separation of the crystal atoms allowed the determination of the wavelength, which was then seen to agree with the de Broglie formula.

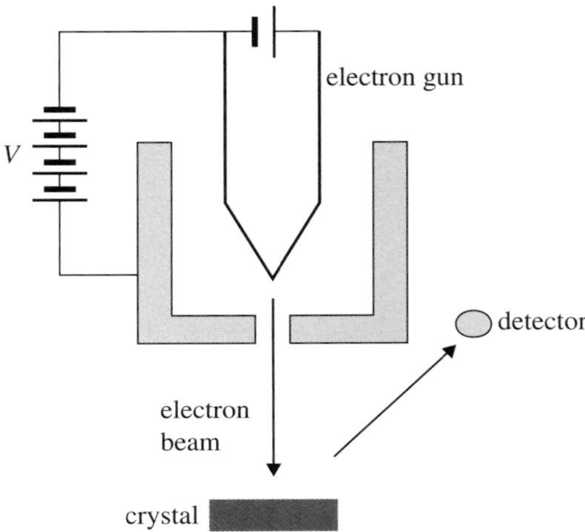

Figure 4.7 The apparatus of Davisson and Germer. Electrons emitted from the hot filament of the electron gun are accelerated through a known potential difference V and are then allowed to fall on a crystal. The positions of the scattered electrons are recorded by a detector.

On the other hand, if the wavelength is much smaller than d, then a particle-like description would be the appropriate one. Only when an electron moves inside a crystal whose interatomic spacing has similar dimensions as the de Broglie wavelength will diffraction take place.

Thus, one can perform a Young-type two-slit experiment with both photons and electrons. What is quite extraordinary about these experiments is that an interference pattern is observed beyond the two slits even if the intensity of light or the electrons is so low that only one photon or electron goes through the slits at a time. The photon or electron 'knows' of the existence of both slits.

Example question

Q7

In a neutron diffraction experiment, a beam of neutrons of energy 85 MeV are incident on a foil made out of lead and diffracted. The first diffraction minimum is observed at an angle of 16° relative to the central position where most of the neutrons are observed. From this information, determine the size of the lead nucleus.

Answer

The neutrons are diffracted from the lead nuclei, which act as 'obstacles' of size b. From our knowledge of diffraction, the first minimum is given by $\sin\theta = \frac{\lambda}{b}$, where λ is the de Broglie wavelength of the neutron. The mass of a neutron is $m = 1.67 \times 10^{-27}$ kg and, since its kinetic energy is 85 MeV, the wavelength is $\lambda = \frac{h}{p}$ where

$$p = \sqrt{2E_k m}$$
$$= \sqrt{2 \times 85 \times 10^6 \times 1.6 \times 10^{-19} \times 1.67 \times 10^{-27}}$$
$$= 21.3 \times 10^{-20} \text{ kg m s}^{-1}$$

Hence

$$\lambda = \frac{6.6 \times 10^{-34}}{21.3 \times 10^{-20}} \text{ m}$$
$$= 0.31 \times 10^{-14} \text{ m}$$

Therefore the size of the nucleus is given by

$$b = \frac{0.31 \times 10^{-14}}{\sin 16°} \text{ m}$$
$$= 1.12 \times 10^{-14} \text{ m}$$

? QUESTIONS

1 (a) Explain what is meant by the photoelectric effect.
(b) A photosurface has a work function of 3.00 eV. What is the critical frequency?

2 (a) What evidence is there for the existence of photons?

(b) A photosurface has a critical frequency of 2.25×10^{14} Hz. What is the voltage required to stop electrons emitted from a photosurface when radiation of frequency 3.87×10^{14} Hz falls on this surface?

3 Light of wavelength 5.4×10^{-7} m falls on a photosurface and causes the emission of electrons of maximum kinetic energy 2.1 eV at a rate of 10^{15} per second. The light is emitted by a 60 W light bulb.

(a) Explain why light causes the emission of electrons.

(b) Calculate the electric current that leaves the photosurface.

(c) Find the work function of the surface.

(d) Find the maximum kinetic energy of the electrons if the intensity of the light becomes 120 W.

(e) Find the current from the photosurface when the intensity is 120 W.

4 (a) State three aspects of the photoelectric effect that cannot be explained by the wave theory of light. For each, outline how the photon theory provides an explanation.

(b) When light of wavelength 2.08×10^{-7} m falls on a photosurface, a voltage of 1.40 V is required to stop the emitted electrons from reaching the anode. What is the largest wavelength of light that will result in emission of electrons from this photosurface?

5 (a) What is the effect of the intensity of light in the photoelectric experiment?

(b) To determine the work function of a given photosurface, light of wavelength 2.3×10^{-7} m is directed at the surface and the stopping voltage, V_s, recorded. When light of wavelength 1.8×10^{-7} m is used, the stopping voltage is twice as large as the previous one. Find the work function.

6 Light falling on a metallic surface of work function 3.0 eV gives energy to the surface at a rate of 5×10^{-4} W per square metre of the metal's surface. Assume that an electron on the metal surface can absorb energy from an area of about 1.0×10^{-18} m^2.

(a) How long will it take the electron to absorb an amount of energy equal to the work function?

(b) What does this imply?

(c) How does the photon theory of light explain the fact that electrons are emitted almost instantaneously with the incoming photons?

7 From the graph of electron kinetic energy E_k versus frequency of incoming radiation (Figure 4.8), deduce:

(a) the critical frequency of the photosurface;

(b) the work function.

(c) What is the kinetic energy of an electron ejected when light of frequency $f = 8.0 \times 10^{14}$ Hz falls on the surface?

(d) Another photosurface has a critical frequency of 6.0×10^{14} Hz. Sketch on Figure 4.8 the variation with frequency of the emitted electrons' kinetic energy.

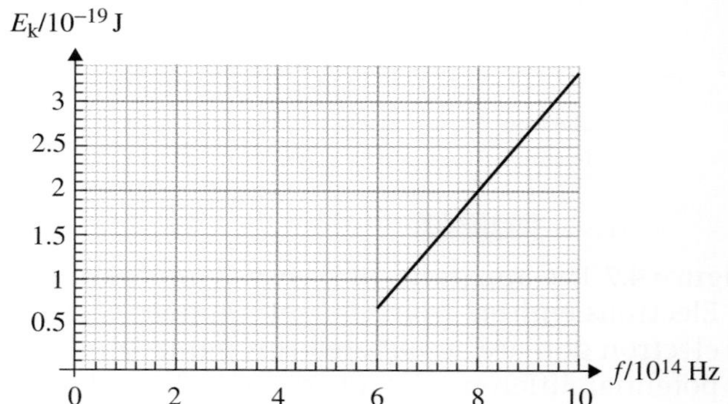

Figure 4.8 For question 7.

8 Consider a brick of mass 0.250 kg moving at 10 m s^{-1}.

(a) What is its de Broglie wavelength?

(b) Does it make sense to treat the brick as a wave? Explain.

9 (a) Describe an experiment in which the de Broglie wavelength of an electron can be measured directly.

(b) What is the speed of an electron whose de Broglie wavelength is equal to that of red light (680 nm)?

10 (a) Show that the de Broglie wavelength of an electron that has been accelerated from rest through a potential difference V is given by

$$\lambda = \frac{h}{\sqrt{2meV}}$$

(b) Calculate the ratio of the de Broglie wavelength of a proton to that of an alpha particle when both have been accelerated from rest by the same potential difference.

(c) Calculate the de Broglie wavelength of an electron accelerated from rest through a potential difference of 520 V.

11 This question will look at the intensity of radiation in a bit more detail. The intensity of light, I, incident normally on an area A is defined to be $I = \frac{P}{A}$, where P is the power carried by the light.

(a) Show that $I = \Phi hf$, where Φ is the *photon flux density*, i.e. the number of photons incident on the surface per second per unit area and f is the frequency of the light.

(b) Calculate the intensity of light of wavelength $\lambda = 5.0 \times 10^{-7}$ m incident on a surface when the photon flux density is $\Phi = 3.8 \times 10^{18}\ \text{m}^{-2}\,\text{s}^{-1}$.

(c) The wavelength of the light is decreased to $\lambda = 4.0 \times 10^{-7}$ m. Calculate the new photon flux density so that the intensity of light incident on the surface is the same as that found in (b).

(d) Hence explain why light of wavelength $\lambda = 4.0 \times 10^{-7}$ m and of the *same intensity* as that of light of wavelength $\lambda = 5.0 \times 10^{-7}$ m will result in *fewer* electrons being emitted from the surface per second.

(e) State one assumption made in reaching this conclusion.

Quantum theory and the uncertainty principle

This chapter introduces the discrete atomic world. We will see that, contrary to what occurs in the macroscopic world, the energy of an atom cannot be arbitrary, but rather assumes values from a discrete set. An elementary introduction to the Schrödinger theory is given. The Heisenberg uncertainty principle is also discussed.

Objectives

By the end of this chapter you should be able to:

- describe *emission* and *absorption spectra* and understand their significance for atomic structure;
- explain the origin of *atomic energy levels* in terms of the 'electron in a box' model;
- describe the hydrogen atom according to Schrödinger;
- do calculations involving *wavelengths* of spectral lines and *energy level differences*;
- outline the *Heisenberg uncertainty principle* in terms of position–momentum and time–energy.

Atomic spectra

When hydrogen gas is heated to a high temperature or exposed to a high electric field, it will glow, emitting light. In the laboratory, this can be seen with a tube of hydrogen whose ends are at a high potential difference, as shown in Figure 5.1.

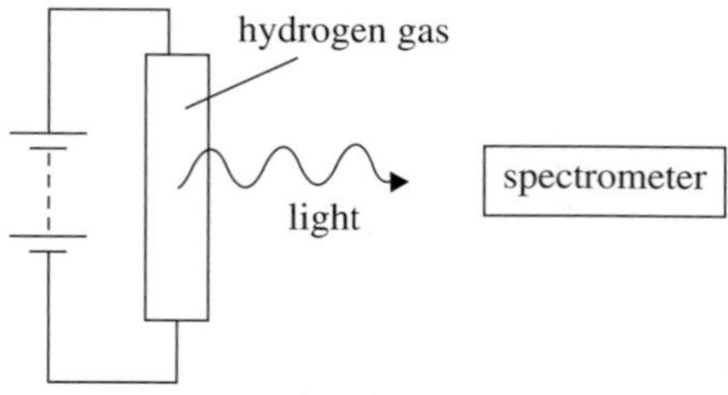

Figure 5.1 Hydrogen gas emits light when exposed to a high potential difference.

The emitted light may be analysed by letting it go through a *spectrometer*. The spectrometer splits the light that enters it into its component wavelengths. In the case of hydrogen, the emitted light consists of a series of bright lines. A few of the prominent lines and their wavelengths are shown in Figure 5.2. This is the **emission spectrum** of hydrogen. The line with wavelength 656 nm is red (the H_α line), the line with wavelength 486 nm is blue-green (the H_β line), and so on.

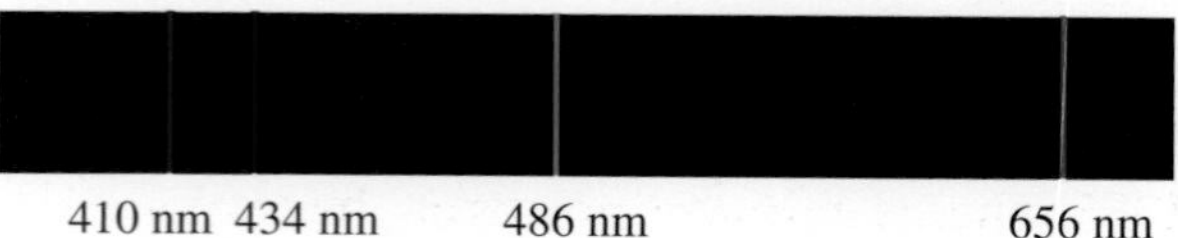

Figure 5.2 A few of the emission lines of hydrogen.

Similar results are obtained when other gases replace hydrogen in the tube. The striking result is that different gases have emission lines at different wavelengths. Knowing the precise wavelengths of the emission lines allows the identification of the gas – emission spectra are like 'fingerprints'.

▶ The spectrum of light that has been emitted by a gas is called the *emission spectrum* of the gas.

A similar phenomenon takes place when white light (consisting of all wavelengths in the visible region) is allowed to pass through hydrogen gas (Figure 5.3). White light analysed with a spectrometer would reveal a continuous band of the colours of the rainbow. But when the light that has been transmitted through hydrogen is analysed, a series of dark lines superimposed on the continuous band of colours is seen. This is the **absorption spectrum** of hydrogen. The dark lines in the absorption spectrum are at precisely the same wavelengths as the coloured bright lines in the emission spectrum of hydrogen.

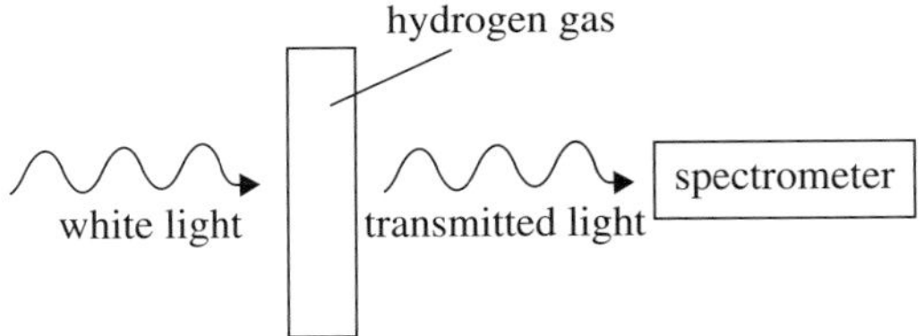

Figure 5.3 White light transmitted through a gas gives rise to the absorption spectrum of the gas.

▶ The spectrum of light that has been transmitted through a gas is called the **absorption spectrum** of the gas.

The striking feature of emission and absorption spectra is the fact that the emission and absorption lines are at *specific* wavelengths for a particular gas.

Attempts to explain these curious features occupied many physicists during the second half of the nineteenth century, without much success. In 1885 Johann Balmer discovered, by trial and error, that the wavelengths in the emission spectrum of hydrogen were given by the formula

$$\frac{1}{\lambda} = R\left(\frac{1}{4} - \frac{1}{n^2}\right)$$

where n may take the integer values 3, 4, 5, ... and R is a constant number. It thus became a serious challenge to explain the origin of the Balmer formula using the basic laws of physics. All such attempts failed as well.

Since the emitted light from a gas carries energy, it is reasonable, based on conservation of energy, to assume that the emitted energy is equal to the difference between the total energy of the atom before and after the emission. Since the emitted light consists of photons of a specific wavelength, it follows that the emitted energy is also of a specific amount, since the energy of a photon is given by

$$E = hf = \frac{hc}{\lambda}$$

These considerations point to the fact that the energy of an atom is *discrete*, i.e. not continuous. If the energy of an atom were continuous, then it would not make sense for the difference in energies before and after the emission of light to be always a set of specific amounts. The idea, then, was to try to see how the idea of discreteness could be introduced into the problem.

As a first attempt to see how this might come about, consider the following simple model.

The 'electron in a box' model

Imagine that an electron is confined within a box of linear size L (Figure 5.4). The electron, treated as a wave, according to de Broglie, has a wavelength associated with it given by

$$\lambda = \frac{h}{p}$$

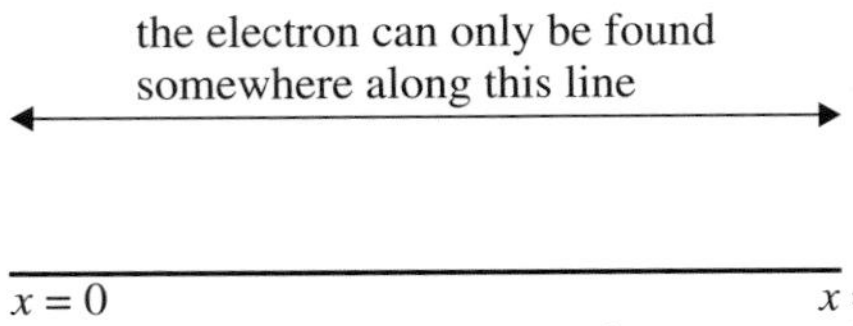

the electron can only be found somewhere along this line

$x = 0$ $x = L$

Figure 5.4 The electron is assumed to be confined within a linear region of length L.

Since the electron cannot escape from the box, it is reasonable to assume that the electron wave is zero at the edges of the box. In addition, since the electron cannot lose energy, it is also reasonable to assume that the wave associated with the electron in this case is a standing wave. So we want a standing wave that will have nodes at $x = 0$ and at $x = L$. This implies that the wavelength must be related to the size L of the box through

$$\lambda = \frac{2L}{n}$$

where n is an integer.

Therefore the momentum of the electron is

$$\begin{aligned} p &= \frac{h}{\lambda} \\ &= \frac{h}{\frac{2L}{n}} \\ &= \frac{nh}{2L} \end{aligned}$$

The kinetic energy is then

$$\begin{aligned} E_{\mathrm{k}} &= \frac{p^2}{2m} \\ &= \frac{\left(\frac{nh}{2L}\right)^2}{2m} \\ &= \frac{n^2h^2}{8mL^2} \end{aligned}$$

This result shows that, because we treated the electron as a standing wave in a 'box', we deduce that the electron's energy is 'quantized' or discrete, i.e. it cannot have any arbitrary value. The electron's kinetic energy can only be

$$E_{\mathrm{k}} = \begin{cases} 1 \times \dfrac{h^2}{8mL^2} & n = 1 \\ 4 \times \dfrac{h^2}{8mL^2} & n = 2 \\ 9 \times \dfrac{h^2}{8mL^2} & n = 3 \end{cases}$$

and so on.

It is very interesting that this simple model has given us what we have been looking for, namely a *discrete* set of energies. Of course, the electron in a 'box' is not a realistic model for an electron in the atom. This is just an example that shows the discrete nature of the electron energy when the electron is treated as a wave. The model points the way to the correct answer.

The Schrödinger theory

After early, and only partially successful, attempts by Niels Bohr to solve the problem of the spectrum of hydrogen, in 1926 the Austrian physicist Erwin Schrödinger (Figure 5.5) provided a realistic, quantum model for the behaviour of electrons in atoms. The Schrödinger theory assumes as a basic principle that there is a wave associated to the electron (very much like de Broglie had assumed). This wave is called the **wavefunction**, $\psi(x,t)$, and is a function of position x and time t. Given the forces that act on the electron, it is possible, in principle, to solve a complicated differential equation obeyed by the wavefunction (the Schrödinger equation) and obtain $\psi(x,t)$. For example, there is one wavefunction for a free electron, another for an electron in the hydrogen atom, etc.

Figure 5.5 Erwin Schrödinger.

▶ The interpretation of what $\psi(x,t)$ really means came from the German physicist Max Born. He suggested that $|\psi(x,t)|^2$ (the square of the absolute value of $\psi(x,t)$) can be used to find the *probability* that an electron will be found near position x at time t.

The theory only gives probabilities for finding an electron somewhere – it does not *pinpoint* an electron at a particular point in space. This is a radical change from ordinary, i.e. classical, physics, where objects have well-defined positions.

When the Schrödinger theory is applied to the electron in a hydrogen atom, it gives results similar to the simple 'electron in a box' example of the previous section. In particular, it predicts that the total energy of the electron (the sum of the kinetic energy and the electric potential energy) is given by the formula

$$E = -\frac{C}{n^2}$$

where n is an integer and C is a constant equal to

$$C = \frac{2\pi^2 m e^4 k^2}{h^2}$$

Here k is the constant in Coulomb's law, m is the mass of the electron, e is the charge of the electron and h is Planck's constant. Numerically (using slightly more accurate values than those listed in Appendix 1) C therefore equals

$$C = \frac{2\pi^2(9.109 \times 10^{-31})(1.602 \times 10^{-19})^4(8.988 \times 10^9)^2}{(6.626 \times 10^{-34})^2}$$

$$= 2.179 \times 10^{-18}\,\text{J}$$

$$= 13.6\ \text{eV}$$

so that finally we obtain

$$E = -\frac{13.6}{n^2}\ \text{eV}$$

In other words, the theory predicts that the electron in the hydrogen atom has quantized energy. The electron can be found in one of the **energy levels** of the atom, depending on the value of the integer n (Figure 5.6a). The model then also predicts that, if it finds itself at a high energy level, the electron can make a **transition** to a lower level, in the process emitting a photon of energy equal to the difference in energy between the levels of the transition (Figure 5.6b). Because the energy of the photon is given by $E = hf$, it follows that knowing the energy level difference we can calculate the frequency and wavelength of the emitted photon. Furthermore, the theory also predicts the probability that a particular transition will occur. (This is necessary in order to understand why some spectral lines are brighter than others.) Thus the Schrödinger theory explains atomic spectra.

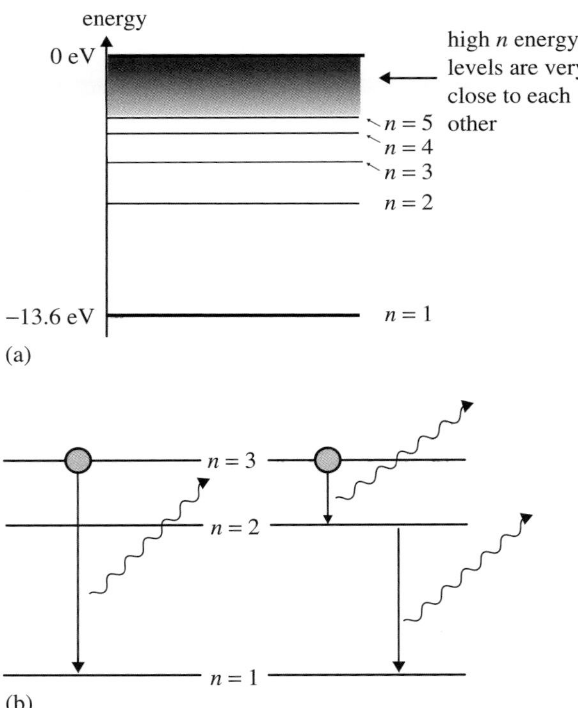

Figure 5.6 (a) The energy level diagram for the hydrogen atom according to the Schrödinger theory. (b) One photon is emitted for each transition from a high to a lower energy level. The Schrödinger theory predicts the probabilities for each transition.

Example questions

Q1

Show how the formula for the electron energy in the Schrödinger theory can be used to derive the empirical Balmer formula mentioned earlier.

Answer

We assume that Balmer considered transitions from an energy level n down to the energy level 2. Then the energy emitted is equal to the difference

$$-\frac{C}{n^2}-\left(-\frac{C}{2^2}\right)$$

which, in turn, is equal to the energy of the emitted photon, i.e. $\frac{hc}{\lambda}$. Thus,

$$\frac{hc}{\lambda}=-\frac{C}{n^2}-\left(-\frac{C}{2^2}\right)$$

$$\frac{1}{\lambda}=\frac{C}{hc}\left(\frac{1}{4}-\frac{1}{n^2}\right)$$

This is precisely Balmer's formula given earlier, with $R=\frac{C}{hc}$.

Q2

Calculate the wavelength of the photon emitted in the transition from $n=3$ to $n=2$.

Answer

The energy of the level $n=3$ is

$$-\frac{13.6}{3^2}\text{ eV}=-1.51\text{ eV}$$

The energy of the level $n=2$ is

$$-\frac{13.6}{2^2}\text{ eV}=-3.40\text{ eV}$$

The energy difference is then 1.89 eV, and that is the energy of the emitted photon. Then (note the necessary conversion from eV to joule)

$$hf=1.89\text{ eV}$$

$$f=\frac{1.89\text{ eV}}{6.63\times10^{-34}\text{ J s}}$$

$$=\frac{1.89\times1.6\times10^{-19}\text{ J}}{6.63\times10^{-34}\text{ J s}}$$

$$=4.56\times10^{14}\text{ Hz}$$

The wavelength is then

$$\lambda=\frac{c}{f}$$

$$=\frac{3.00\times10^{8}}{4.56\times10^{14}}$$

$$=6.58\times10^{-7}\text{m}$$

This agrees well with the red H_α line in the emission spectrum of hydrogen.

The graph of Figure 5.7 shows the variation of the probability distribution function (what you have learned in mathematics as a pdf) with distance r from the nucleus for the energy level $n=1$ (the lowest) of the hydrogen atom. The height of the graph is proportional to $|\psi(x,t)|^2$. The *shaded area* is the probability for finding the electron at a distance from the nucleus between $r=a$ and $r=b$.

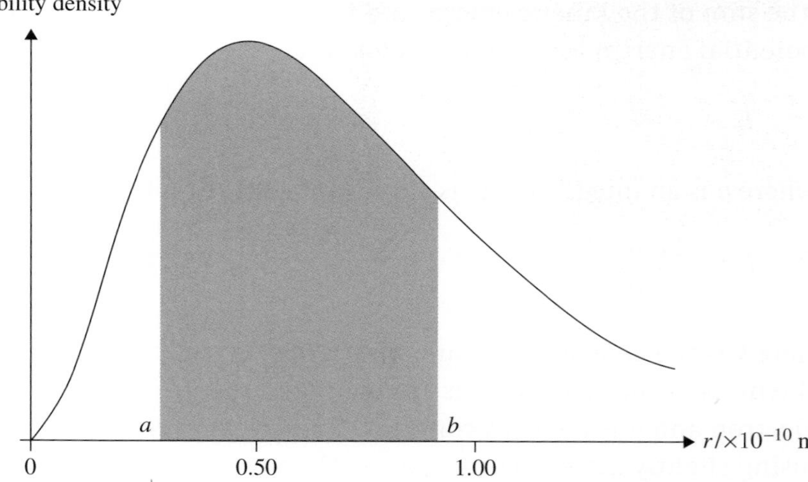

Figure 5.7 The shaded area gives the probability for finding an electron at a distance from the nucleus between $r=a$ and $r=b$, for the ground state of hydrogen. The peak in the graph corresponds to the *most likely* distance of the electron from the nucleus, and is about 0.50×10^{-10} m. The *average* distance of the electron from the nucleus is about 0.75×10^{-10} m.

The Heisenberg uncertainty principle

The Heisenberg uncertainty principle is named after Werner Heisenberg (1901–1976), one of the founders of quantum mechanics (Figure 5.8), who discovered the principle in 1927. The basic idea behind it is the wave–particle duality. Particles sometimes behave like waves and waves sometimes behave like particles, so that we cannot cleanly divide physical objects as *either* particles *or* waves.

Figure 5.8 Werner Heisenberg.

▶ The Heisenberg uncertainty principle applied to position and momentum states that it is not possible to measure simultaneously the position *and* momentum of something with indefinite precision. This has nothing to do with imperfect measuring devices or experimental errors. It represents a fundamental property of nature. The uncertainty Δx in position and the uncertainty Δp in momentum are related by

$$\Delta x\,\Delta p \geq \frac{h}{4\pi}$$

where h is Planck's constant.

This says that making momentum as accurate as possible makes position inaccurate, whereas accuracy in position results in inaccuracy in momentum. In particular, if one is made zero, the other has to be infinite.

Imagine that electrons are emitted from a hot wire in a cathode ray tube and that we try to make them move in a horizontal straight line by inserting a metal with a small opening of size a. We can make the electron beam as thin as possible by making the opening as small as possible. Making the beam very thin means that we know fairly accurately the vertical position of the electron. The electron must be somewhere within the opening and so the uncertainty in its vertical position will be no bigger than a, so $\Delta x \leq a$.

However, we will run into a problem as soon as the opening becomes of the same order as the de Broglie wavelength of the electrons. Recall that a wave of wavelength λ will *diffract* when going through an aperture of about the same size as the wavelength. Here, too, the electron will diffract through the opening, which means that a few electrons will emerge from the opening with a direction that is no longer horizontal.

We can describe this phenomenon by saying that there is an uncertainty in the electron's momentum in the vertical direction, of magnitude Δp. Figure 5.9 shows that there is a spreading of the electrons within an angular size 2θ.

The angle by which the electron is diffracted is given by (recall diffraction)

$$\theta \approx \frac{\lambda}{a}$$

where a is the opening size. But from Figure 5.9, $\theta \approx \frac{\Delta p}{p}$. Therefore,

$$\frac{\lambda}{a} \approx \frac{\Delta p}{p}$$

If we now take the opening size a as the uncertainty in the electron's position in the

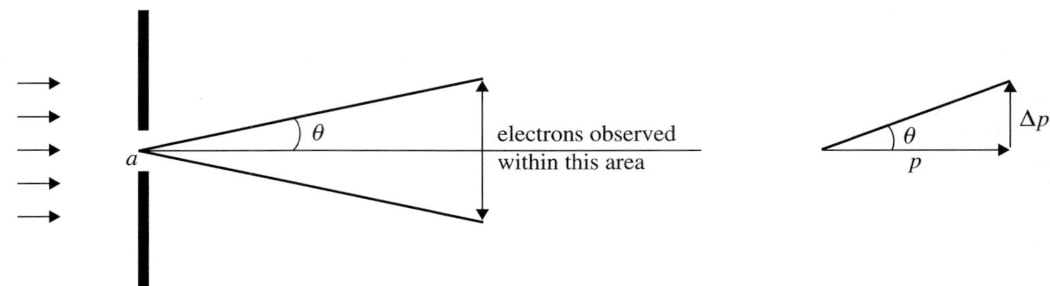

Figure 5.9 An electron passing through a slit suffers a deflection in the vertical direction.

vertical direction, we have

$$\Delta p \Delta x \approx \lambda p = h$$

This is a simple explanation of where the uncertainty formula comes from.

As an application of the uncertainty principle, consider an electron, which is known to be confined within a region of size L. Then the uncertainty in position must satisfy $\Delta x < L$, and so the uncertainty in momentum must be

$$\Delta p \approx \frac{h}{4\pi \Delta x} \approx \frac{h}{4\pi L}$$

The electron must then have a kinetic energy of

$$E_{\text{K}} = \frac{p^2}{2m} > \frac{\Delta p^2}{2m} \approx \frac{h^2}{32\pi^2 m L^2}$$

If we apply this result to an electron in the hydrogen atom, we see that the size of the region within which the electron is confined is about $L \approx 10^{-10}$ m. Then

$$E_{\text{K}} \approx \frac{h^2}{32\pi^2 m L^2} = \frac{(6.6 \times 10^{-34})^2}{32\pi^2 (9.1 \times 10^{-31})(10^{-10})^2}$$

$$\approx 1.5 \times 10^{-19}\ \text{J} \approx 1\ \text{eV}$$

which is in fact the correct order of magnitude value of the electron's kinetic energy.

Note the close resemblance of this formula to the formula for the energy obtained in the earlier section based on the 'electron in a box' model. Apart from a few numerical factors (of order 1), the two are the same, indicating the basic connection between the uncertainty principle and duality.

The uncertainty principle also applies to measurements of energy and time. If a state is measured to have energy E with uncertainty ΔE, then there must be an uncertainty Δt in the time during which the measurement is made, such that

$$\Delta E\, \Delta t \geq \frac{h}{4\pi}$$

For more applications of the uncertainty principle, see Option J, Particle physics.

? QUESTIONS

1 State what you understand by the terms:
(a) energy level;
(b) atomic transition;
(c) spectrum of an element.

2 An absorption spectrum is formed when photons of specific wavelengths are absorbed by the electrons of an atom, which then make transitions to higher energy levels. But as soon as the electrons reach the higher energy level they will fall back to the state they came from, re-radiating photons of precisely the same wavelength as those they absorbed. So there should not be any dark lines. What do you say?

3 An electron of kinetic energy 11.5 eV collides with a hydrogen atom in its ground state. With

what possible kinetic energy can this electron rebound off the atom?

4 (a) What is the evidence for the existence of energy levels in atoms?
(b) Electrons of kinetic energy (i) 10.10 eV, (ii) 12.80 eV and (iii) 13.25 eV collide with hydrogen atoms and can excite these to higher states. In each case, find the largest n corresponding to the state the atom can be excited to. Assume that the hydrogen atoms are in their ground state initially.

5 (a) What do you understand by the term ionization energy?
(b) What is the ionization energy for a hydrogen atom in the state $n = 3$?

6 (a) Find the smallest wavelength that can be emitted in a transition in atomic hydrogen.
(b) What is the minimum speed an electron must have so that it can ionize an atom of hydrogen in its ground state?

7 (a) Find the de Broglie wavelength of a proton (mass 1.67×10^{-27} kg) whose kinetic energy is 200.0 MeV.
(b) What is the de Broglie wavelength of an electron in the $n = 2$ state of hydrogen?

8 Using the uncertainty principle, show that an electron in a hydrogen atom will have a kinetic energy of a few eV.

9 Assume that an electron can exist within a nucleus (size 10^{-15} m) such that its associated wave forms a fundamental mode standing wave with nodes at the edges of the nucleus.
(a) Estimate the wavelength of this electron.
(b) Calculate the kinetic energy of the electron in MeV.
(c) Using your answer in (b), comment on whether the electron emitted in beta-minus decay could have existed within the nucleus before the decay.

10 A few of the lines in the emission spectrum of hydrogen may be represented as in Figure 5.10. Discuss how the spectrum diagram would differ if the hydrogen atom could be described by the 'electron in a box' model.

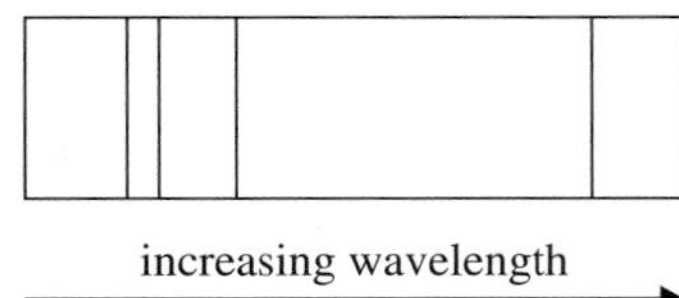

Figure 5.10 For question 10.

11 (a) State the de Broglie hypothesis.
(b) Calculate the de Broglie wavelength of an electron that has been accelerated by a potential difference of 5.0 V.
(c) Explain why precise knowledge of the wavelength of an electron implies imprecise knowledge of its position.

12 An experimenter wishes to make a very narrow beam of electrons. To do that, she suggests the arrangement of Figure 5.11. She expects that the beam can be made as narrow as possible by reducing the size d of the aperture through which the electrons will pass.
(a) Explain why in principle it is not possible to make a perfectly narrow beam.
(b) Are her chances of producing a narrow beam better with slow or fast electrons?

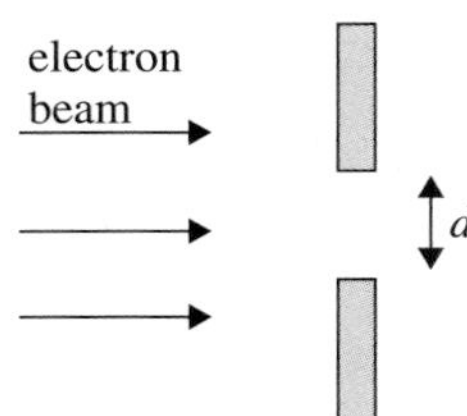

Figure 5.11 For question 12.

13 A tennis ball is struck so that it moves with momentum 6.0 N s straight through an open square window of side 1.0 m. Because of the uncertainty principle, the tennis ball may deviate from its original path after going through the window. *Estimate* the angle of deviation of the path of the tennis ball. Comment on your answer.

14 *Theoretically* it is possible in principle to balance a pencil on its tip so that it stands vertically on a horizontal table. Explain why in quantum theory this is impossible in principle. (You can turn this problem into a good theoretical extended essay if you try to estimate the time the pencil will stay up after it has been momentarily balanced!)

15 The graphs in Figure 5.12 represent the wavefunctions of two electrons. Identify the electron with

(a) the least uncertainty in momentum and

(b) the least uncertainty in position.

Explain your answers.

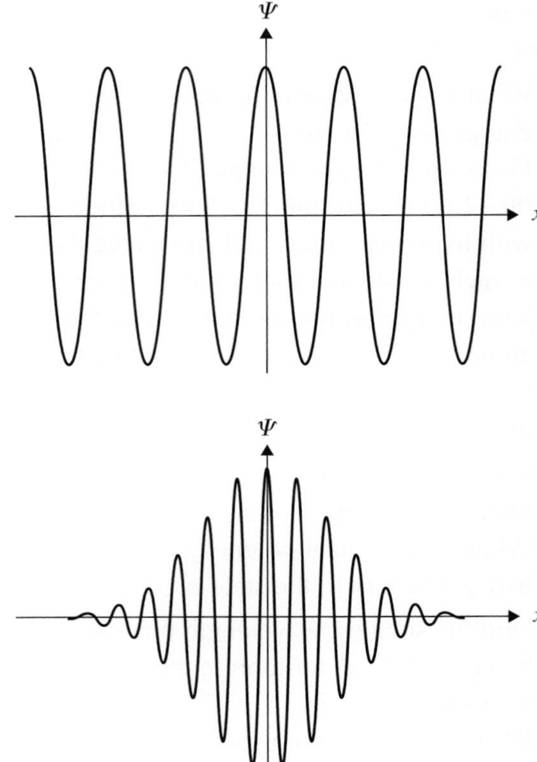

Figure 5.12 For question 15.

Nuclear physics

This chapter provides a more detailed discussion of the radioactive decay law and scattering experiments in which nuclear sizes may be determined. The mass spectrometer is discussed as well as the existence of isotopes. The prediction of the neutrino in beta decays on the basis of energy and momentum conservation is also discussed.

Objectives

By the end of this chapter you should be able to:

- solve problems of *closest approach* using the law of conservation of energy and appreciate that nuclei have well-defined radii;
- describe a *mass spectrometer* and its implications for *isotope* existence;
- state the theoretical arguments that have been used to postulate the existence of the *neutrino*;
- state the *radioactive decay law*, $N = N_0\,e^{-\lambda t}$, $A = -\frac{dN}{dt} = (N_0\lambda)\,e^{-\lambda t}$;
- state the meaning of *half-life* and *decay constant* and derive the relationship between them;
- appreciate that the decay constant is the *probability of decay per unit time*;
- understand that the *initial activity* of a sample is $A_0 = N_0\lambda$;
- obtain *short* and *long* half-lives from experimental data;
- solve problems with *activities* and the *radioactive decay law*.

Scattering experiments and distance of closest approach

In scattering experiments such as Rutherford's, simple energy considerations can be used to calculate the distance of closest approach of the incoming particle to the target. Thus, consider, as an example, an alpha particle (of charge $q = 2e$) that is shot head-on toward a stationary nucleus of charge $Q = Ze$ (see Figure 6.1). Initially the system has a total energy consisting of the alpha particle's kinetic energy $E = E_k$. We take the separation of the alpha and the nucleus to be large so no potential energy exists. At the point of closest approach, a distance d from the centre of the nucleus, the alpha particle stops and is about to turn back. Thus, the total energy now is the electric potential energy of the alpha and the nucleus, given by

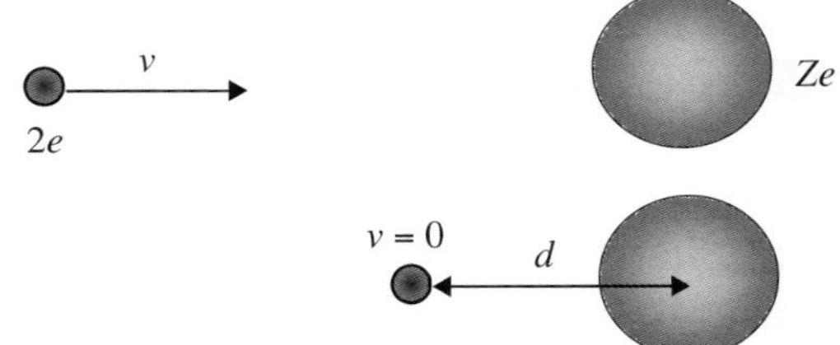

Figure 6.1 The closest approach of an alpha particle happens in a head-on collision.

$$E = k\frac{Qq}{d}$$
$$= k\frac{(2e)(Ze)}{d}$$
$$= k\frac{2Ze^2}{d}$$

(We are assuming that the nucleus does not recoil so its kinetic energy is ignored.)

Then, by conservation of energy

$$E_k = k\frac{2Ze^2}{d}$$
$$\Rightarrow d = k\frac{2Ze^2}{E_k}$$

Assuming a kinetic energy for the alpha particle equal to 2.0 MeV directed at a gold nucleus ($Z = 79$) gives $d = 1.1 \times 10^{-13}$ m. This is outside the range of the nuclear force, so the alpha particle is simply repelled by the electrical force.

As the energy of the incoming particle is increased, the distance of closest approach decreases. The smallest it can get is, however, of the same order as the radius of the nucleus. Thus, experiments of this kind have been used to estimate the nuclear radii. A result of these experiments is that the nuclear radius R depends on mass number A through

$$R = 1.2 \times A^{1/3} \times 10^{-15}\ \text{m}$$

The mass spectrometer

The existence of isotopes (i.e. atoms of the same element having slightly different masses due to differing number of neutrons in the nucleus) can be demonstrated with an instrument called a mass spectrometer. Imagine that singly ionized ions of an element are emitted from the black box in Figure 6.2. Singly ionized means that each atom has lost a single electron and thus has a net positive charge of e. The ions move through a pair of slits (S_1), which collimates the beam. They then enter a region of electric and magnetic fields at right angles to each other. The magnetic field is directed into the page in the region shaded grey. The positive

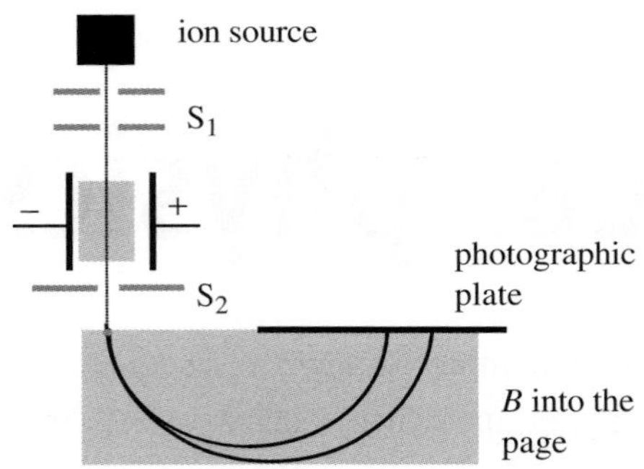

Figure 6.2 A mass spectrometer. Ions enter through the collimating slits S_1. They then enter a region of magnetic and electric fields and approach a second slit, which only allows ions of a given velocity to pass. A second magnetic field bends these ions into circular paths according to their mass.

ions are deflected to the left by the electric field and to the right by the magnetic field. By choosing a suitable value for the magnetic field, the ions can continue through undeflected if the magnetic and electric forces are equal. This means that $eE = evB$ or simply that

$$v = \frac{E}{B}$$

Thus, only ions with this specific velocity can pass through the second slit S_2. Ions with other velocities will be deflected and so will be prevented from going through this second slit. This arrangement acts as a velocity selector for the ions. The selected ions then enter a second region of magnetic field (also directed into the page) and are thus deflected into a circular path, hitting a photographic plate where they are recorded.

▶ The radius of the circular path is given by

$$R = \frac{mv}{eB}$$

If the beam contains atoms of equal mass, all atoms will hit the plate at the same point. If, however, isotopes are present, the heavier atoms will follow a longer radius circle and will hit the plate further to the right. Measurement of the radius of each isotope's path thus allows for the determination of its mass.

Beta decay and the neutrino

The process of beta decay described earlier originates from a decay of a neutron inside an atomic nucleus:

$$^{1}_{0}\mathrm{n} \rightarrow {}^{1}_{1}\mathrm{p} + {}^{0}_{-1}\mathrm{e} + {}^{0}_{0}\bar{\nu}_{\mathrm{e}}$$

The neutron decays into a proton (thus increasing the atomic number of the nucleus by 1), an electron and an antineutrino. A free neutron (i.e. one not inside a nucleus) decays into a proton according to the reaction equation above, with a half-life of about 11 min. A related decay is that of *positron emission*, in which a proton inside a nucleus turns itself into a neutron accompanied by the emission of a positron (the antiparticle of the electron) and a neutrino:

$$^{1}_{1}\mathrm{p} \rightarrow {}^{1}_{0}\mathrm{n} + {}^{0}_{+1}\mathrm{e} + {}^{0}_{0}\nu_{\mathrm{e}}$$

Unlike a free neutron, a free proton cannot decay into a neutron since the rest energy of a neutron is larger than that of a proton. Inside a nucleus the reaction is, however, possible (because binding energy is used to make up for the difference). These reactions must be understood as the disappearance of one particle and the appearance or creation of the three particles on the right-hand side of the decay equation. We must *not* think that the decaying particle actually consists of the three particles into which it somehow splits in the decay.

There is an unfamiliar particle in beta decay, the electron antineutrino, $\bar{\nu}_{\mathrm{e}}$, a particle that went undetected until 1953. Its presence in beta decay was predicted on theoretical grounds as follows. Consider the decay $^{1}_{0}\mathrm{n} \rightarrow {}^{1}_{1}\mathrm{p} + {}^{0}_{-1}\mathrm{e} + {}^{0}_{0}\bar{\nu}_{\mathrm{e}}$. The mass of the neutron is larger than that of the proton and electron together by

$$1.008665\ \mathrm{u} - (1.007276 + 0.0005486)\ \mathrm{u} = 0.00084\ \mathrm{u}$$

corresponding to an energy of

$$0.00084 \times 931.5\ \mathrm{MeV} = 0.783\ \mathrm{MeV}$$

This is the available energy in the decay, which will show up as kinetic energy of the products. If only the electron and the proton are produced, then the electron being the lighter of the two will carry most of this energy away as kinetic energy. Thus, we should observe electrons with kinetic energies of about 0.783 MeV. In experiments, however, the electron has a *range* of energies from zero up to 0.783 MeV. The question is then, where is the missing energy?

Figure 6.3 shows two ways in which a neutron may decay.

▶ Wolfgang Pauli and Enrico Fermi hypothesized the existence of a third particle in the products of a beta decay in 1933. Since the energy of the electron in beta decay has a *range* of possible values, it means that a third very light particle must also be produced so that it carries the remainder of the available energy. Enrico Fermi coined the word neutrino for the 'little neutral one'.

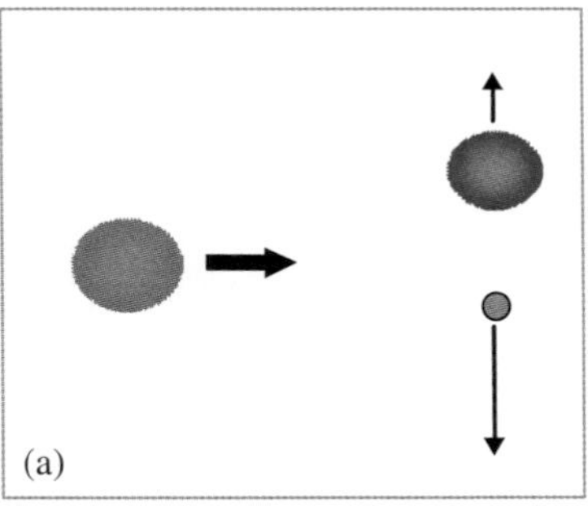

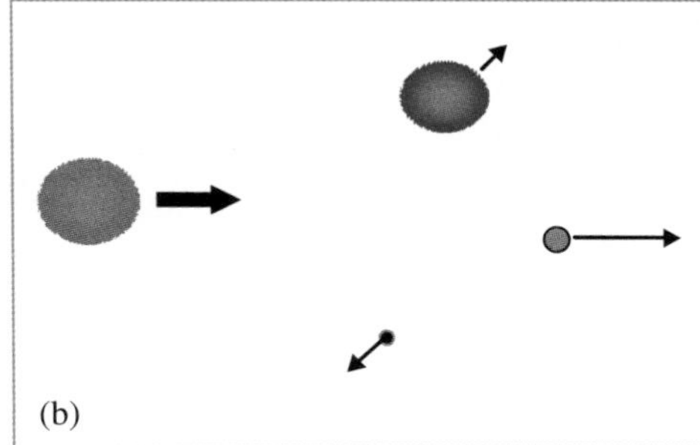

Figure 6.3 (a) A neutron at rest decaying into just two particles. The two particles must have equal and opposite momentum so they move in opposite directions. (b) A neutron at rest decaying into three particles. There are now many possibilities as to how the three particles move.

Electron capture

A process related to beta decay is electron capture, in which a proton inside a nucleus captures an electron and turns into a neutron and a neutrino:

$$^{1}_{1}\mathrm{p} + {}^{0}_{-1}\mathrm{e} \rightarrow {}^{1}_{0}\mathrm{n} + {}^{0}_{0}\nu_{\mathrm{e}}$$

The creation of a neutron star rests on this process, in which the huge pressure inside the star drives electrons into protons in the nuclei of the star, turning them into neutrons.

Table 6.1 gives some examples of beta decays.

Decay	Half-life	Maximum energy
${}^{3}_{1}H \rightarrow {}^{3}_{2}He + {}^{0}_{-1}e + {}^{0}_{0}\bar{\nu}_e$	12.3 yr	0.0186 MeV
${}^{14}_{6}C \rightarrow {}^{14}_{7}N + {}^{0}_{-1}e + {}^{0}_{0}\bar{\nu}_e$	5730 yr	0.156 MeV
${}^{22}_{11}Na \rightarrow {}^{22}_{10}Ne + {}^{0}_{+1}e + {}^{0}_{0}\nu_e$	2.60 yr	0.546 MeV
${}^{13}_{7}N \rightarrow {}^{13}_{6}C + {}^{0}_{+1}e + {}^{0}_{0}\nu_e$	9.99 min	1.19 MeV

Table 6.1 Examples of beta decay.

Nuclear energy levels

The nucleus, like the atom, exists in discrete energy levels. The main evidence for the existence of nuclear energy levels comes from the fact that the energies of the alpha particles and gamma ray photons that are emitted by nuclei in alpha and gamma decays are *discrete*. (This is to be contrasted with beta decays, in which the electron has a continuous range of energies.)

Figure 6.4 shows the lowest nuclear energy levels of the magnesium nucleus ${}^{24}_{12}Mg$. Also shown

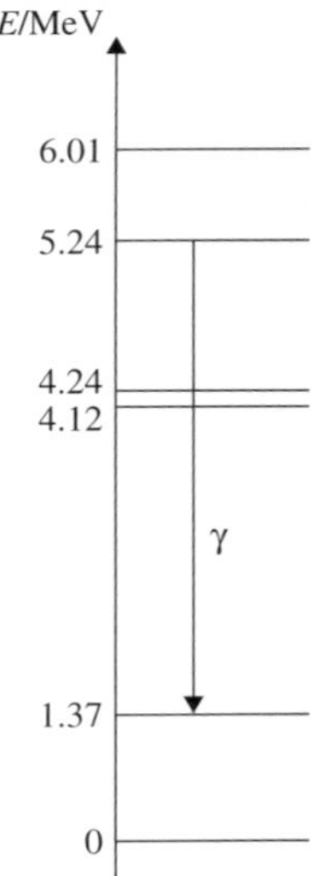

Figure 6.4 Nuclear energy levels of magnesium ${}^{24}_{12}Mg$. Notice the difference in scale between these levels and atomic energy levels.

is a gamma decay from the level with energy 5.24 MeV to the first excited state. The emitted photon has energy 5.24 − 1.37 = 3.87 MeV.

Figure 6.5 shows an energy level of plutonium (${}^{242}_{94}Pu$) and a few of the energy levels of uranium (${}^{238}_{92}U$). Also shown are two transitions from plutonium to uranium energy levels. These are alpha decays:

$$ {}^{242}_{94}Pu \rightarrow {}^{238}_{92}U + {}^{4}_{2}\alpha $$

The energies of the emitted alpha particles are 4.983 − 0.148 = 4.835 MeV and 4.983 − 0.307 = 4.676 MeV.

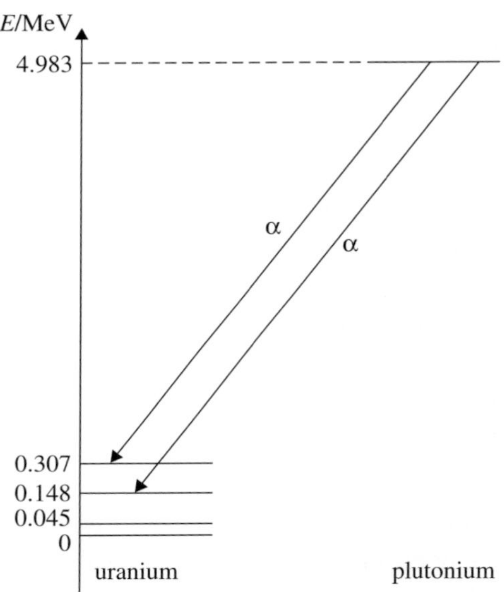

Figure 6.5 Energy levels for plutonium and uranium. Transitions from plutonium to uranium energy levels explain the discrete nature of the emitted alpha particle in the alpha decay of plutonium.

The following example applies these ideas to beta decay.

Example question

Q1

The nucleus of bismuth (${}^{211}_{83}Bi$) decays into lead (${}^{207}_{82}Pb$) in a two-stage process. In the first stage, bismuth decays into polonium (${}^{211}_{84}Po$). Polonium then decays into lead. The nuclear energy levels that are involved in these decays are shown in Figure 6.6.

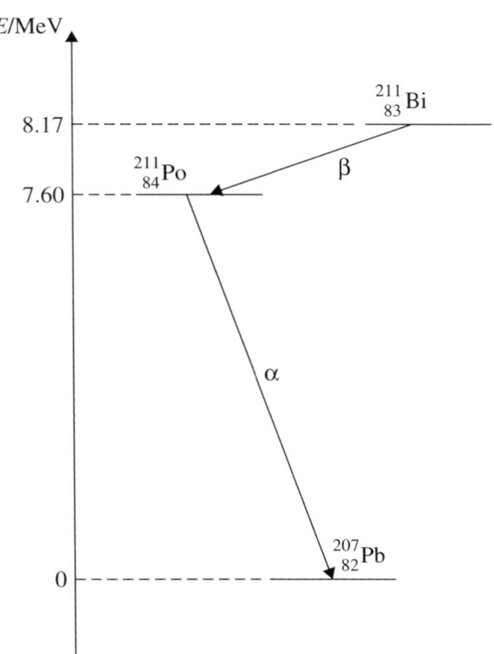

Figure 6.6 The two-stage decay of bismuth into lead.

(a) Write down the reaction equations for each decay.
(b) Calculate the energy released in the beta decay.
(c) Explain why the electron does not always have this energy.

Answer

(a) $^{211}_{83}\text{Bi} \rightarrow {}^{211}_{84}\text{Po} + {}^{0}_{-1}\text{e} + {}^{0}_{0}\bar{\nu}$ and

$^{211}_{84}\text{Po} \rightarrow {}^{207}_{82}\text{Pb} + {}^{4}_{2}\alpha$.

(b) The energy released is the difference in the energy levels involved in the transition, i.e. 0.57 MeV.

(c) The energy of 0.57 MeV must be shared between the electron, the antineutrino and the polonium nucleus. So the electron does not always have the maximum energy of 0.57 MeV. Depending on the angles (between the electron, the antineutrino and the polonium nucleus), the electron energy can be anything from zero up to the maximum value found in (b).

The radioactive decay law

▶ The law of radioactive decay states that the number of nuclei that will decay per second is proportional to the number of atoms present that have not yet decayed,

$$\frac{dN}{dt} = -\lambda N$$

Here λ is a constant, known as the decay constant. Its physical meaning is that it represents the probability of decay per unit time (see page 412 for an explanation of this statement).

If the number of nuclei originally present (at $t = 0$) is N_0, by integrating the previous equation it can be seen that the number of nuclei of the decaying element present at time t is

$$N = N_0 \, e^{-\lambda t}$$

As expected, the number of nuclei of the decaying element is decreasing exponentially as time goes on (see Figure 6.7). This form of the decay law can be shown to be equivalent to the simpler version described earlier. After one half-life, $T_{1/2}$, half of the nuclei present have decayed, so

$$\frac{N_0}{2} = N_0 \exp\left(-\lambda T_{1/2}\right)$$

On taking logarithms we find

$$\begin{aligned} \lambda T_{1/2} &= \ln 2 \\ &= 0.693 \end{aligned}$$

This is the relationship between the decay constant and the half-life.

(This means that an equivalent and more convenient formula for the decay equation is $N = N_0 \left(\frac{1}{2}\right)^{t/T_{1/2}}$. Can you see how?)

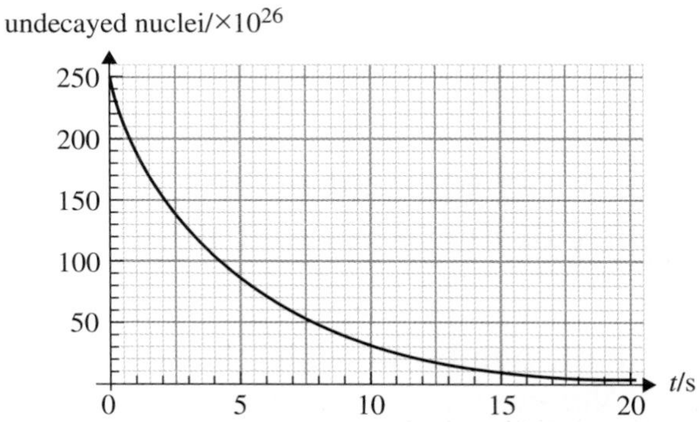

undecayed nuclei/×10^{26}

250, 200, 150, 100, 50

0, 5, 10, 15, 20 t/s

Figure 6.7 The decay of radioactive nuclei obeys an exponential law.

The number of decays per second is called activity. It follows from the exponential decay law that activity also satisfies an exponential law:

$$N = N_0 \, e^{-\lambda t}$$
$$A = -\frac{dN}{dt}$$
$$= (N_0 \lambda) \, e^{-\lambda t}$$

Thus, the initial activity of a sample is given by the product of the decay constant and the number of atoms initially present, $A_0 = N_0 \lambda$.

Example question

Q2

Carbon-14 has a half-life of 5730 yr and in living organisms it has a decay rate of 0.25 Bq g^{-1}. A quantity of 20 g of carbon-14 was extracted from an ancient bone and its activity was found to be 1.81 Bq. What is the age of the bone?

Answer

The decay constant is

$$\lambda = \frac{\ln 2}{5730} \text{ yr}^{-1}$$
$$= 1.21 \times 10^{-4} \text{ yr}^{-1}$$

When the bone was part of the living body the 20 g would have had an activity of 5 Bq. If the activity now is 1.81 Bq, then

$$A = A_0 \, e^{-\lambda t}$$
$$\Rightarrow 1.81 = 5e^{-1.21 \times 10^{-4} t}$$
$$\Rightarrow -1.21 \times 10^{-4} t + \ln 5 = \ln 1.81$$
$$\Rightarrow -1.21 \times 10^{-4} t = -1.016$$
$$\Rightarrow t = \frac{1.016}{1.21 \times 10^{-4}}$$
$$\approx 8400 \text{ yr}$$

Why the decay constant is the probability of decay per unit time

Since $\frac{dN}{dt} = -\lambda N$, we know that in a short time interval dt the number of nuclei that will decay is $dN = \lambda N dt$ (we ignore the minus sign by considering dN to be positive). The probability that any one nucleus will decay within the time interval dt is thus

$$\text{probability} = \frac{dN}{N} = \lambda dt$$

and so the probability of decay per unit time is equal to the **decay constant**:

$$\frac{\text{probability}}{dt} = \lambda$$

? QUESTIONS

1 With what velocity should an alpha particle be fired head-on at a stationary gold nucleus so that the distance of closest approach is 8.5×10^{-15} m? (Take the alpha mass to be 6.64×10^{-27} kg.)

2 A particle of mass m and charge $+e$ is directed from very far away toward a massive ($M >> m$) object of charge $+Ze$ with a velocity v, as shown in Figure 6.8. The distance of closest approach is d. Sketch (on the same axes) a graph to show the variation with separation of:
(a) the particle's kinetic energy;
(b) the particle's electric potential energy.

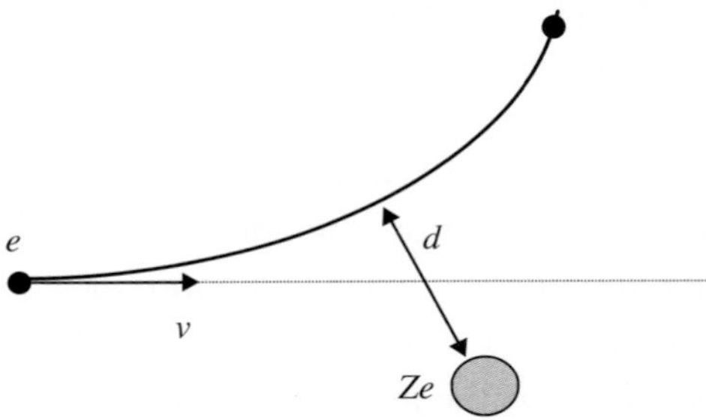

Figure 6.8 For question 2.

3 Singly ionized atoms of neon-20 of velocity 2.0×10^5 m s^{-1} enter the velocity selector of a mass spectrometer, where the magnetic field has the value 0.15 T.
(a) What electric field is established in the velocity selector?
(b) The ions then enter the region where a second magnetic field of value 0.50 T

deflects them into circular paths. What is the radius of the circular path?

(c) If the beam of ions also contains traces of neon-22, what would the detection radius for this isotope be?

(Molar masses: neon-20 = 19.992 g mol^{-1}; neon-22 = 21.99 g mol^{-1}.)

4 What might be a reason for the high penetrating power of neutrons?

5 Show that in an elastic collision between a neutron of mass m and a nucleus of mass M (with the nucleus initially at rest), M will recoil with a velocity given by

$$w = \frac{2m}{m + M}v$$

where v is the initial velocity of the incoming neutron.

6 (a) Find the decay constant for krypton-92, whose half-life is 3.00 s.

(b) Suppose that you start with 1/100 mol of krypton. How many undecayed atoms of krypton are there after (i) 1 s, (ii) 2 s, (iii) 3 s?

7 (a) What is the probability that a radioactive nucleus will decay during a time interval equal to a half-life?

(b) What is the probability that it will have decayed after the passage of three half-lives?

(c) A nucleus has remained undecayed after the passage of four half-lives. What is the probability it will decay during the next half-life?

8 What is the activity of 1.0 g of radium-226 (molar mass = 226.025 g mol^{-1}). The half-life of radium-226 is 1600 yr.

9 The half-life of an unstable element is 12 days. Find the activity of a given sample of this element after 20 days if the initial activity was 3.5 MBq.

10 A radioactive isotope of half-life 6.0 days used in medicine is prepared 24 h prior to being administered to a patient. If the activity must be 0.50 MBq when the patient receives the isotope, what number of atoms of the isotope should have been prepared?

11 The age of very old rocks can be found from uranium dating. Uranium is suitable because of its very long half-life: 4.5×10^9 yr. The final stable product in the decay series of uranium-238 is lead-206. Find the age of rocks that are measured to have a ratio of lead to uranium atoms of 0.80. You must assume that no lead was present in the rocks other than that due to uranium decaying.

12 The isotope $^{40}_{19}K$ of potassium is unstable, with a half-life of 1.37×10^9 yr. It decays into the stable isotope $^{40}_{18}Ar$. Moon rocks were found to contain a ratio of potassium to argon atoms of 1:7. Find the age of the moon rocks.

13 (a) In an experiment to measure the half-life of an isotope it is found that the readings of the counter never become zero no matter how long one waits, as shown in Figure 6.9. Why?

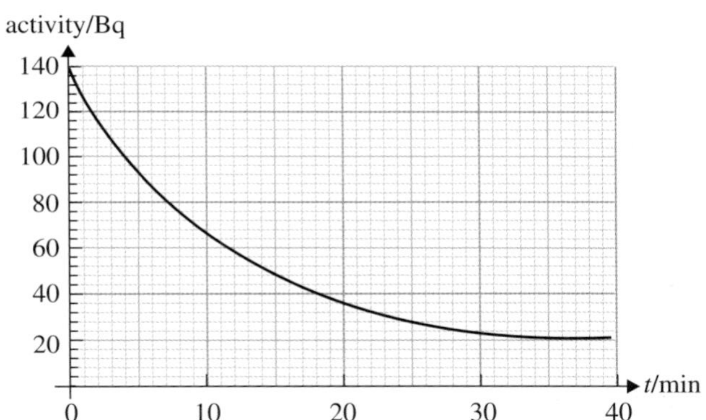

Figure 6.9 For question 13(a).

(b) The experimenter then 'corrects' the data and obtains the graph shown in Figure 6.10. What has he done and what half-life does he obtain for this isotope?

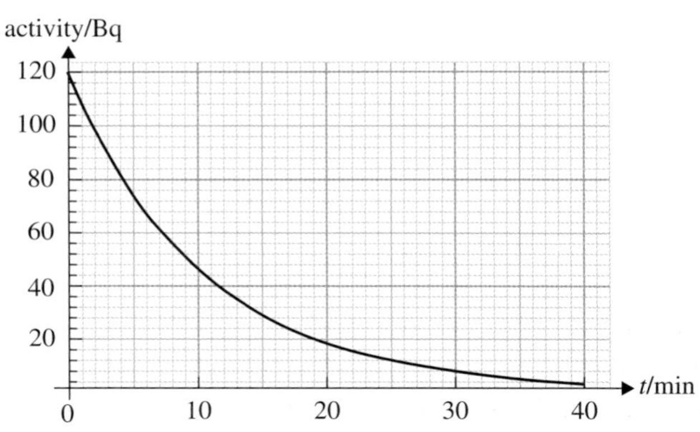

Figure 6.10 For question 13(b).

14 Two unstable isotopes are present in equal numbers (initially). Isotope A has a half-life of 4 min and isotope B has a half-life of 3 min. What is the ratio of the activity of A to that of B after:

(a) 0 min;

(b) 4 min;

(c) 12 min?

15 A sample contains two unstable isotopes and a counter placed near it is used to record the decays. How would you determine each of the half-lives of the isotopes from the data?

16 The half-life of an isotope with a very long half-life cannot be measured by observing its activity as a function of time, since the variation in activity over any reasonable time interval would be too small to be observed. Let m be the mass in grams of a given isotope of long half-life.

(a) Show that the number of nuclei present in this quantity is $N_0 = \frac{m}{\mu} N_A$ where μ is the molar mass of the isotope in g mol^{-1} and N_A is the Avogadro constant.

(b) From $A = -\frac{dN}{dt} = (N_0\lambda)e^{-\lambda t}$ show that the initial activity is $A_0 = \frac{mN_A}{\mu}\lambda$ and hence that the half-life can be determined by measuring the initial activity (in Bq) and the mass of the sample (in grams).

17 Show that the nuclear density is the same for all nuclei. (Take the masses of the proton and neutron to be the same.)

18 Figure 6.11 shows the nuclear force between two protons as a function of their separation.

(a) What is the range of the nuclear force that can be deduced from this graph?

(b) What would the nuclear force between two protons be when they are separated by a distance of 10^{-15} m?

(c) What is the electrical force between these two particles at this separation?

(d) What is the gravitational force between two protons at this separation?

(e) What is the ratio of the electrical to the gravitational force between the two protons?

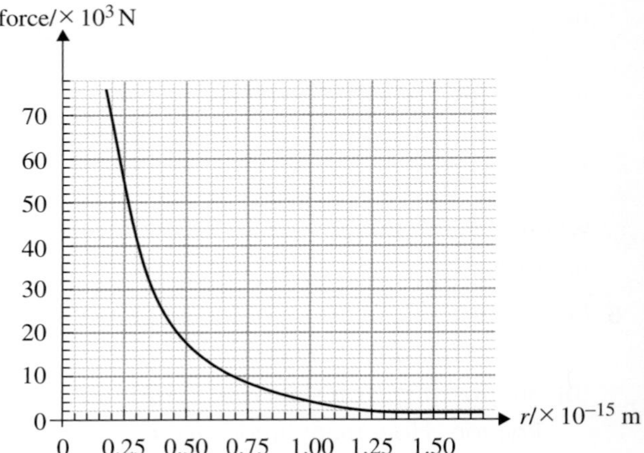

Figure 6.11 For question 18.

19 In electron capture, ${}^1_1\text{p} + {}^{\ 0}_{-1}\text{e} \rightarrow {}^1_0\text{n} + {}^0_0\nu$, the only emitted particle is the neutrino, which, being extremely weakly interacting, cannot be observed. So how do we know when electron capture takes place?

20 Radium's first excited nuclear level is 0.0678 MeV above the ground state.

(a) Write down the reaction that takes place when radium decays from the first excited state to the ground state.

(b) What is the wavelength of the photon emitted?

Energy degradation and power generation

This chapter deals with energy sources and how the energy content of each source can be extracted. We make the important distinction between renewable (will not run out) and non-renewable (will run out) sources of energy. The chapter introduces the basic physics associated with nuclear fission, solar, wind, wave and wind power.

Objectives

By the end of this chapter you should be able to:

- explain the meaning of the term *energy degradation*;
- understand that, in the cyclic operation of an engine, *not all the available thermal energy can be transformed* to mechanical work;
- outline *how electricity is produced*;
- understand the difference between *renewable* and *non-renewable* forms of energy;
- state the meaning of the term *energy density*;
- understand how energy is produced by *nuclear fuels*;
- describe the function of the *main elements of a nuclear reactor*;
- appreciate the problems with *nuclear fusion*;
- understand the basics of *solar, wind, hydroelectric* and *wave power*;
- state the meaning of the term *solar constant*;
- discuss the relative *advantages* and *disadvantages* of various energy sources.

Degradation of energy

Thermal energy flows, as we have seen, from hot to cold bodies. The difference in temperature between two bodies offers the opportunity to run a 'heat engine' between those two temperatures, extracting useful mechanical work in the process. That is to say, some of the thermal energy that is transferred from the hot to the cold body can be transformed into mechanical work. This is shown in Figure 1.1. The diagram to the right in this figure is a **Sankey diagram** representing the energy flows. The *width* of each arrow in the diagram is proportional to the energy carried by that arrow. The input energy is 800 J and the useful mechanical work done is 200 J, giving an efficiency of

$$e = \frac{200}{800} = 0.25$$

With time, the two bodies will approach the same temperature, and the opportunity for using those two bodies to do work will be lost.

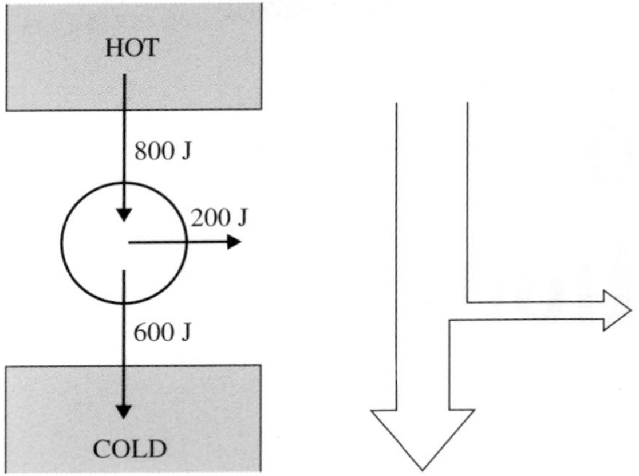

Figure 1.1 Schematic energy flow diagram for a heat engine. The diagram to the right is a Sankey diagram for the engine. The width of the arrow is proportional to the energy it carries.

▶ Thus the flow of thermal energy from the hot to the colder body tends to equalize the two temperatures and deprives us of the opportunity to do work.

Suppose, then, that we do have two places ('reservoirs') at different temperatures. The thermal energy that can now flow from the hot to the colder reservoir can be used to perform work. The hot reservoir is the hot interior of the cylinders where gasoline or some other fuel is burned. The cold reservoir is the exhaust system of the engine. It must be understood that any *practical* heat engine must work in a *cycle*. That is to say, the engine begins in some state, absorbs thermal energy and does work. The engine must now be returned to its initial state so that the process can be *repeated*. For example, consider a gas that is kept in a container with a piston (Figure 1.2). The gas absorbs thermal energy and so expands. The motion of the piston can be used to perform mechanical work.

If all that happens is to expand the gas, then *all* the thermal energy absorbed can be transformed into mechanical work. To make the engine practical, the gas must be returned to its initial state (Figure 1.3), so that it can again absorb energy and perform more work. The piston must then be pushed back in to return the gas to its initial state.

The price to pay for operating in a cycle is that *not all* of the thermal energy transferred can be transformed into mechanical work. Some of this

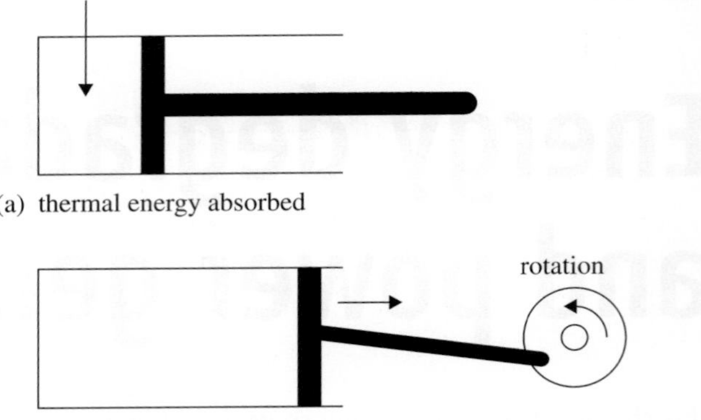

Figure 1.2 An expanding gas performs mechanical work.

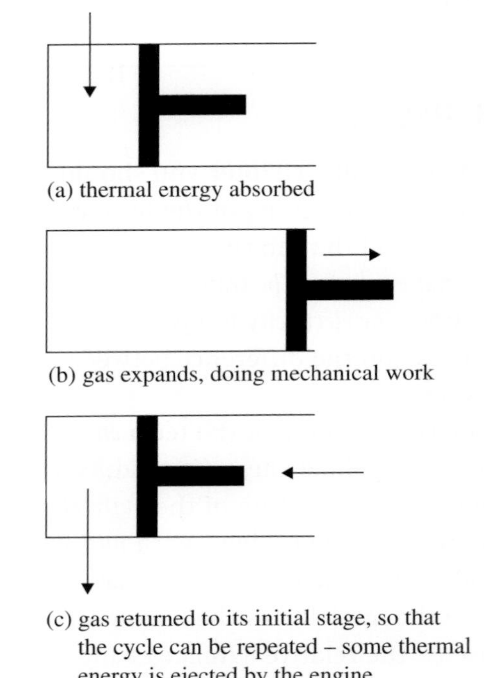

Figure 1.3 The engine must work in a cycle and so must be returned to its initial state.

energy must be returned to the cold reservoir. While not lost, this energy is less useful. To use it to perform mechanical work, another *colder* reservoir must be found. This energy has become **degraded**. The necessity of losing some energy to the colder reservoir in a cyclic process is a consequence of a fundamental law of physics, the second law of thermodynamics.

▶ Energy, while always being conserved, becomes less useful, i.e. it cannot be used to perform mechanical work – this is called *energy degradation*.

Electricity production

We are heavily dependent on electricity, and many of the energy sources that are available to us today are used to produce electricity. The production of electricity (almost universally) takes place in *electric generators*, such as the one described in Chapter 5.8. The main idea is to rotate a coil in a magnetic field so that magnetic field lines are cut by the moving coil. According to Faraday's law an emf (voltage) will be created in the coil, which can then be delivered to consumers. A generator thus converts mechanical energy (the rotational energy of the coil) into electrical energy. The various other sources of energy available are used to provide the mechanical energy of the rotating coil (Figure 1.4).

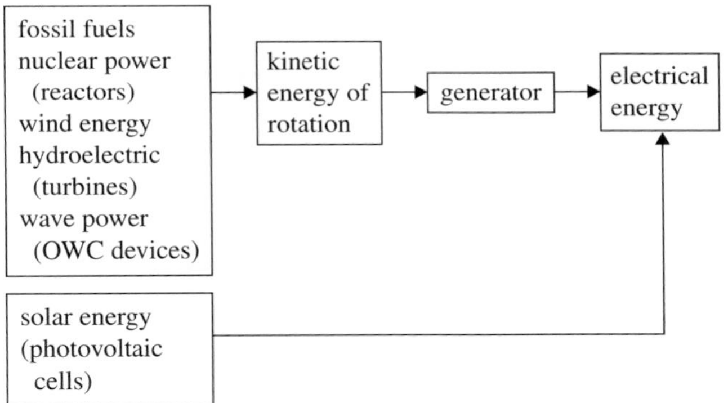

Figure 1.4 Methods of electricity production.

Energy sources

The development of civilization has gone hand in hand with an increase in the use of energy. Whereas ancient peoples had food and sunlight as their only sources of energy, consuming no more than about 8 MJ of energy per day, modern humans depend on energy for food, shelter, transportation, communication, manufacture of goods, services and entertainment. The average world use of energy per person amounts today to about 300 MJ per day in the more developed countries, giving a power consumption per person of about $300 \times 10^6/(24 \times 60 \times 60) = 3.5$ kW. In the USA, the power consumption per person is at a high of 10 kW, whereas in parts of Africa it is below 0.1 kW. The world average is about 0.8 kW per person. Taking 3 kW as an estimate for living in comfortable conditions, and a world population of 6.7 billion (6.7×10^9), results in a total world energy demand for one year of about 6.3×10^{20} J. This is very close to the total annual world production of energy, which is estimated to be about 1.5×10^{21} J. Taking into account that the world's population is increasing, it is obvious that we are faced with an extremely serious problem. We need *sources of energy*. We may classify energy sources into two large classes, **non-renewable** and **renewable**.

- *Non-renewable sources* of energy are finite sources, which are being depleted, and will run out. They include fossil fuels (e.g. oil, natural gas and coal) and nuclear fuels (e.g. uranium). The energy stored in these sources is, in general, a form of potential energy, which can be released by human action.
- *Renewable sources* include solar energy (and the other forms indirectly dependent on solar energy, such as wind energy and wave energy) and tidal energy.

The main sources of energy, and the percentage of the total energy produced of each, is given in Table 1.1. The figures are world averages and are approximate. Data for individual countries vary. World averages also vary, as different countries rely on different energy sources and change their dependence on any one particular fuel.

As mentioned earlier, most renewable sources are directly or indirectly linked to the sun.

Fuel	Percentage of total energy production (%)	Carbon dioxide emission (g MJ^{-1})
Oil	40	70
Natural gas	23	50
Coal	23	90
Nuclear	7	–
Hydroelectric	7	–
Others	<1	–

Table 1.1 Energy sources and the percentage of the total energy production for each. The third column gives the mass of carbon dioxide emitted per unit of energy produced from a particular fuel. Fossil fuels account for about 86% of the total energy production.

Energy density

A useful characteristic of fuels is their **energy density**.

▶ The *energy density* of a fuel is the energy that can be obtained from a unit mass of the fuel. Energy density is measured in J kg^{-1}.

If the energy is obtained by burning the fuel (as in fossil fuels), the energy density is simply the heat of combustion (see Table 1.2).

In a nuclear fission reaction, mass is converted *directly* into energy through Einstein's formula $E = mc^2$. As discussed in Chapter 6.3, one kilogram of uranium-235 releases a quantity of energy equal to 7×10^{13} J $= 7 \times 10^4$ GJ. Natural uranium (mainly uranium-238) contains about 0.7% of uranium-235, and so the energy density of natural uranium as a nuclear fuel is $\frac{0.7}{100} \times 7 \times 10^4 = 490$ GJ kg^{-1}, substantially higher than that of fossil fuels. Enriched uranium containing 3% uranium-235 has an energy density of $\frac{3}{100} \times 7 \times 10^4 = 2100$ GJ kg^{-1}.

Substance	Heat of combustion
Coal	30 MJ kg^{-1}
Wood	16 MJ kg^{-1}
Diesel oil	45 MJ kg^{-1}
Gasoline	47 MJ kg^{-1}
Kerosene	46 MJ kg^{-1}
Natural gas	39 MJ m^{-3} (at stp)

Table 1.2 Energy density of fossil fuels.

To calculate the energy density of water used in a hydroelectric power plant, imagine that 1 kg of water falls from a height of 100 m and that *all* the kinetic energy so gained is converted into the rotational motion that is used to produce electricity. The gain in kinetic energy is

$$\begin{aligned} E &= \frac{1}{2}mv^2 \\ &= mgh \\ &\approx 1 \times 10 \times 100 \\ &= 10^3 \text{ J} \end{aligned}$$

This implies that the energy density of water used as a 'fuel' in a hydroelectric power plant is 10^3 J kg^{-1}, substantially below the energy density of fossil and nuclear fuels.

Energy density is a major consideration in the choice of a fuel. Obviously, *all other factors being equal*, the higher the energy density, the more desirable the fuel.

Fossil fuels

Fossil fuels (oil, coal and natural gas) have been created over millions of years. They are produced by the decomposition of buried animal and plant matter under the combined action of the high pressure of the material on top and bacteria.

Burning coal and oil have been the traditional ways of producing electricity. The thermal energy released in combustion is used to power steam engines, which, in turn, power generators. Gasoline in internal combustion engines has been powering automobiles for over a century.

Although generally efficient (30–40%), these engines are primarily responsible for atmospheric pollution and contribute greenhouse gases to the atmosphere. In electricity-producing power plants using coal, the efficiency is typically around 30%, depending on the technology level of the plant and the precise cycles of operation. Natural gas produces somewhat higher efficiencies, typically 42%.

Example question

Q1

A power plant produces electricity by burning coal, using the thermal energy produced as input to a steam engine, which makes a turbine turn, producing electricity. The plant has a power output of 400 MW and operates at an overall efficiency of 35%.

(a) Calculate the rate at which thermal energy is provided by the burning coal.

(b) Hence calculate the rate at which coal is being burned (use a coal energy density of 30 MJ kg^{-1}).

(c) The thermal energy discarded by the power plant is removed by water (Figure 1.5). The temperature of the water must not increase by more than 5 °C. Calculate the rate at which the water must flow.

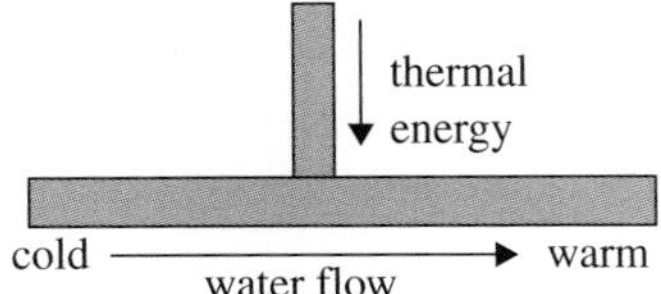

Figure 1.5.

Answer

(a) The efficiency is the ratio of power output to power input, and so thermal energy must be provided at a rate of

$$\frac{400}{0.35} = 1.14 \times 10^3 \approx 1.1 \times 10^3 \text{ MW}$$

(b) The amount of mass of coal that must be burned per second is found from

$$\frac{\Delta m}{\Delta t} \times 30 \times 10^6 = 1.14 \times 10^9 \Rightarrow \frac{\Delta m}{\Delta t} = 38 \text{ kg s}^{-1}$$

or

$$38 \times 60 \times 60 \times 24 \times 365 = 1.2 \times 10^9 \text{ kg yr}^{-1}$$

(c) The thermal energy discarded enters the water at a rate of

$$\frac{\Delta Q}{\Delta t} = 1.14 \times 10^3 - 0.400 \times 10^3 = 740 \text{ MW}$$

This thermal energy warms up the water according to $\Delta Q = (\Delta m)c\Delta T$, where Δm is the mass of water into which the thermal energy goes, c is the specific heat capacity of water (4200 J kg^{-1} K^{-1}) and ΔT is the temperature increase of the water (5 °C). The rate at which thermal energy enters the water is

$$\frac{\Delta Q}{\Delta t} = \frac{\Delta m}{\Delta t} c\Delta T = 740 \text{ MW}$$

Thus, we find that

$$\frac{\Delta m}{\Delta t} = \frac{740 \times 10^6}{4200 \times 5}$$

$$= 35 \times 10^3 \text{ kg s}^{-1}$$

Fossil fuel mining

Coal is obtained by mining. The mining process produces a large number of toxic substances, and the coal itself, which is stored in large quantities near the mines, is high in sulphur content and traces of heavy metals. Rain can wash away the sulphur and heavy metal traces, creating serious environmental problems if this acidic water enters underground water reserves. The sites of coal-mining are also considered to be environmental disaster areas, which is why many countries have strict laws requiring mining companies to have plans for reclaiming the area after the mining is over. Drilling for oil also has adverse environmental effects, with many accidents leading to leakage of oil both at sea and on land.

▶ Advantages of fossil fuels

- Relatively cheap (while they last)
- High power output (high energy density)
- Variety of engines and devices use them directly and easily
- Extensive distribution network is in place

▶ **Disadvantages of fossil fuels**

- Will run out
- Pollute the environment
- Contribute to greenhouse effect by releasing greenhouse gases into atmosphere

In the overall considerations over choice of fuel, one must take into account the cost of transporting the fuel from its place of production to the place of distribution. Fossil fuels have generally high costs because the mass and volume of the fuel tend to be large. Similarly, one needs extensive storage facilities. Fossil fuels, especially oil, pose serious environmental problems due to leakages at various points along the production–distribution line.

Nuclear power

Nuclear **fission** is the process in which a heavy nucleus splits into lighter nuclei. The details of the process and the methods used to calculate the energy produced have been presented in detail in Chapter 6.3, which you should review.

Nuclear reactors

A nuclear reactor is a machine in which nuclear reactions take place, producing energy. The **fuel** of a nuclear reactor is typically uranium-235. The isotope of uranium that is most abundant in nature is uranium-238. Natural uranium contains only about 0.7% of uranium-235. The uranium fuel in a reactor is thus **enriched**, i.e. is made to contain more uranium-235, about 3% or even higher. When a nucleus of uranium-235 captures a neutron, it turns into uranium-236, which then decays, releasing energy and more neutrons. In addition to the common reaction discussed in Chapter 6.3, we also have the reaction:

$$^{1}_{0}\text{n} + {}^{235}_{92}\text{U} \rightarrow {}^{236}_{92}\text{U} \rightarrow {}^{140}_{54}\text{Xe} + {}^{94}_{38}\text{Sr} + 2{}^{1}_{0}\text{n}$$

These are examples of *induced* fission. The fission does not proceed by itself – neutrons must initiate it. (Some nuclei undergo *spontaneous* fission, i.e. no neutrons are necessary to initiate it, but this is rare.)

The neutrons produced can be used to collide with other nuclei of uranium-235 in the reactor, producing more fission, more energy and more neutrons. The reaction is thus self-sustaining; it is called a **chain reaction**. For the chain reaction to get going, a certain minimum mass of uranium-235 must be present, otherwise the neutrons escape without causing further reactions – this is called the **critical mass**. Uranium-235 will only capture neutrons if the neutrons are not too fast. The neutrons produced in the chain reaction are much too fast to be captured by uranium-235 (they have typical kinetic energies of about 1 MeV whereas to be absorbed the kinetic energy must be less than about 1 eV) and must therefore be slowed down.

The slowing down of neutrons is achieved through collisions of the neutrons with atoms of the **moderator**, a material surrounding the **fuel rods** (the tubes containing uranium-235). The moderator material can be graphite or water, for example. The rate of the reaction is determined by the number of neutrons available to be captured by uranium-235. Too few neutrons would result in the reaction stopping, while too many neutrons would lead to an uncontrollably large release of energy.

Thus **control rods**, i.e. a material that can absorb excess neutrons whenever this is necessary, are introduced into the moderator. The control rods can be removed when not needed and reinserted when necessary again. The control rods ensure that the energy from the nuclear reactions is released in a slow and controlled way as opposed to the uncontrolled release of energy that would take place in a nuclear weapon.

Schematic diagrams of the cores of two types of nuclear reactors are shown in Figure 1.6.

The energy released in the reaction is in the form of kinetic energy of the produced neutrons (and gamma ray photons). This kinetic energy is converted into thermal energy (in the

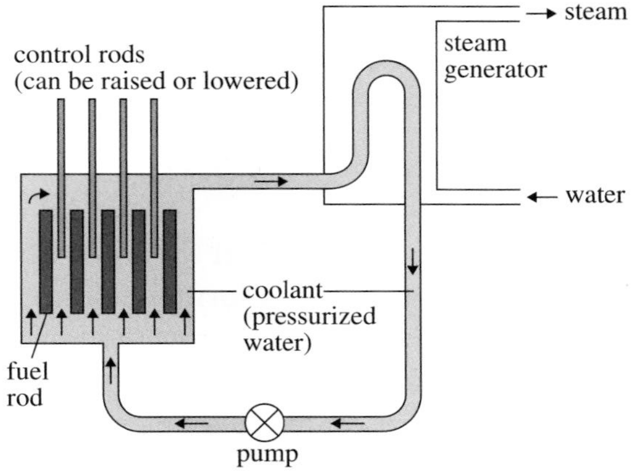

(a) pressurized water reactor (PWR)

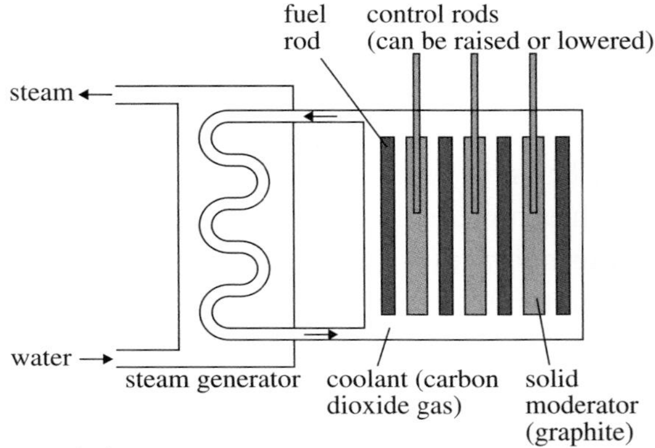

(b) gas-cooled reactor

Figure 1.6 Schematic diagrams of two types of fission reactors.

moderator) as the neutrons are slowed down by collisions with the moderator atoms. A coolant (for example, water or liquid sodium) passing through the moderator can extract this energy, and use it in a heat exchanger to turn water into steam at high temperature and pressure. The steam can then be used to turn the turbines of a power station, finally producing electricity. These energy transformations are summarized in Figure 1.7.

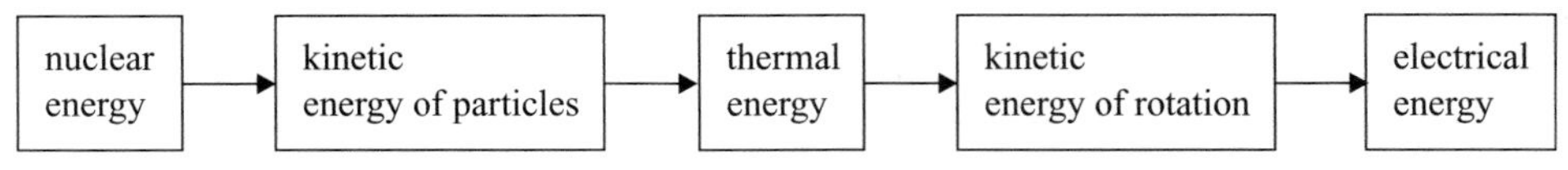

Figure 1.7 The main energy transformations that take place in a nuclear power station.

Plutonium production

The fast neutrons produced in a fission reaction may be used to bombard uranium-238 and produce plutonium-239. This isotope of plutonium does not occur naturally. The reactions are:

$$^{1}_{0}\text{n} + {}^{238}_{92}\text{U} \rightarrow {}^{239}_{92}\text{U}$$

$$^{239}_{92}\text{U} \rightarrow {}^{239}_{93}\text{Np} + {}^{0}_{-1}\text{e} + \overline{\nu}$$

$$^{239}_{93}\text{Np} \rightarrow {}^{239}_{94}\text{Pu} + {}^{0}_{-1}\text{e} + \overline{\nu}$$

The importance of these reactions is that non-fissionable material (uranium-238) is being converted to fissionable material (plutonium-239) as the reactor operates. The plutonium-239 produced can then be used as the nuclear fuel in other reactors. (It can also be used in the production of nuclear weapons.)

Problems with nuclear reactors

The spent fuel in a nuclear reactor together with the products of the reactions are all highly radioactive, with long half-lives. The problem of how to dispose of this material safely is a serious disadvantage of the fission process in commercial energy production. At present, this material is buried deep underground in containers that are supposed to avoid leakage to the outside. In addition, there is always the possibility of an accident due to uncontrolled heating of the moderator. This might increase the temperature (in the case of a graphite moderator, it would also start a fire) and hence the pressure in the cooling pipes, resulting in an explosion. (This would be a conventional explosion – the reactor cannot explode in the way a nuclear weapon does.) In this case, radioactive material would leak from the sealed core of a reactor, dispersing radioactive material into the environment. Even worse, it may lead to the meltdown of the entire core. These are serious concerns with nuclear fission as a source of commercial power. On the positive side, nuclear power does not produce large amounts of greenhouse gases.

The nuclei produced in a fission reaction are typically unstable and decay usually by beta decay. The beta decay produces an additional amount of energy. Even if the reactor is shut down, production of thermal energy continues because of the beta decay of the product nuclei. The energy produced in this way is enough to melt the entire core of the reactor if the cooling system breaks down.

An additional worry about nuclear reactors is that the fissionable material produced (for example, plutonium-239) can be recovered and be used in a nuclear weapons programme.

Uranium mining

Like all forms of mining, uranium mining is dangerous, and in fact even more so. Uranium produces radon gas, a known strong carcinogen. Inhalation of this gas as well as of radioactive dust particles is a major hazard in the uranium mining business. Mine shafts require good ventilation and must be closed to avoid direct contact with the atmosphere. The disposal of waste material from the mining processes is also a problem, since the material is radioactive.

▶ **Advantages of nuclear energy**

- High power output
- Large reserves of nuclear fuels
- Nuclear power stations do not produce greenhouse gases

▶ **Disadvantages of nuclear energy**

- Radioactive waste products difficult to dispose of
- Major public health hazard should 'something go wrong'
- Problems associated with uranium mining
- Possibility of producing materials for nuclear weapons

Nuclear fusion

A typical energy-producing nuclear **fusion** reaction is

$$^{2}_{1}\text{H} + ^{3}_{1}\text{H} \rightarrow ^{4}_{2}\text{He} + ^{1}_{0}\text{n} + 17.6\ \text{MeV}$$

In this reaction, deuterium and tritium (two isotopes of hydrogen) fuse to form a helium nucleus and a neutron plus energy. Deuterium ($^{2}_{1}$H) can be obtained by separating it from ordinary hydrogen in water using electrolysis. Tritium ($^{3}_{1}$H) is obtained by bombarding lithium with neutrons. There are ample supplies of both water and lithium.

The problem with fusion is that, since they are both positively charged, the reacting nuclei repel. Thus, in order to get them close enough to each other for the reaction to take place, high temperatures must be reached. In this way the kinetic energy of the nuclei can be used to overcome the electrical repulsion. The temperatures required are of the order of 10^8 K. At this temperature, hydrogen atoms are ionized and so we have a **plasma** (a mixture of positive nuclei and electrons). The hot plasma must be confined in such a way that it does not come into contact with anything else. This is because contact with other materials would result in both (a) a reduction of temperature and (b) contamination of the plasma with other materials. These two effects would cause the fusion reaction to stop. The plasma is therefore confined magnetically in a *tokamak* (a Russian word for toroidal magnetic chamber) machine. This has specially designed magnetic fields that allow the plasma to move around magnetic field lines without touching the container walls.

Energy must be supplied to the fusion process to reach the high temperatures required. It has not yet been possible to produce more energy out of fusion than has first been put in, for sustained periods of time. For this reason, fusion as a source of commercially produced energy is not yet feasible. There are also technical problems with using the energy produced in fusion to produce electricity.

Compared to nuclear fission, nuclear fusion has the advantage of plentiful fuels, substantial amounts of energy produced, and much fewer problems with radioactive waste.

Solar power

The nuclear fusion reactions in the sun send out an incredible, and practically inexhaustible, amount of energy, at a rate of about 3.9×10^{26} W. This means that, on average, the earth receives about 1400 W per square metre of the surface of the outer atmosphere. Some of this radiation is reflected back into space, some is trapped by the atmosphere's gases, and about 1000 W m^{-2} (1 kW m^{-2}) is received on the surface of the earth. This amount assumes direct sunlight on a clear day and thus is the *maximum* that can be received at any one time. Averaged over a 24-hour time period, the intensity of sunlight is about 340 W m^{-2}. This high-quality, free and inexhaustible energy can be put to various uses.

Active solar devices

An early application of solar energy has been in what are called 'active solar devices'. In these, sunlight is used directly to heat water or air for heating in a house, for example. The collecting surface is usually flat and covered by glass for protection; the glass should be coated to reduce reflection. A blackened surface below the glass collects sunlight, and water circulating in pipes underneath gets heated. This hot water can then be used for household purposes, such as in bathrooms (the heated water is kept in well-insulated containers) or, with the help of a pump, it can circulate through a house, providing a heating effect.

In other schemes, the pipes can be exposed to sunlight directly, in which case they are blackened to increase absorption (Figure 1.8). The surface underneath the pipes is then reflecting so that more radiation enters the pipes. Such a collector works not only with direct sunlight but also with diffuse light, e.g. on partially cloudy days.

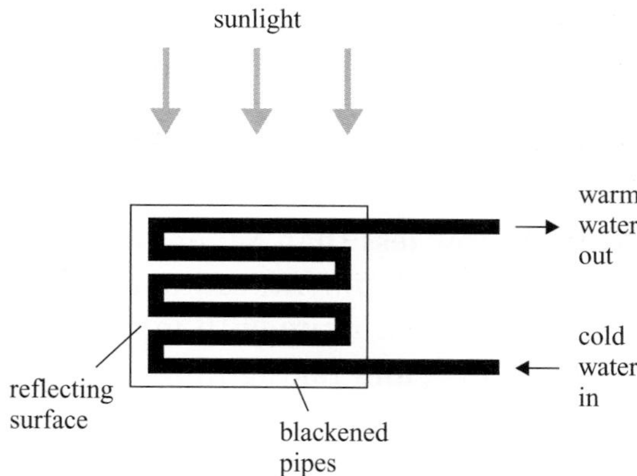

Figure 1.8 A device for collecting sunlight. The water in the pipes becomes heated and can be put to use.

These simple collectors are cheap and are usually put on the roof of a house. Their disadvantage is that they tend to be bulky and cover too much space.

More sophisticated collectors include a concentrator system in which the incoming solar radiation is focused, for example by a parabolic mirror, before it falls on the collecting surface. Such systems can heat water to much higher temperatures (500 °C to 2000 °C) than a simple flat collector. These high temperatures can be used to turn water into steam, which can drive a turbine, producing electricity (Figure 1.9). Obviously, back-up systems must be available in case of cloudy days, etc.

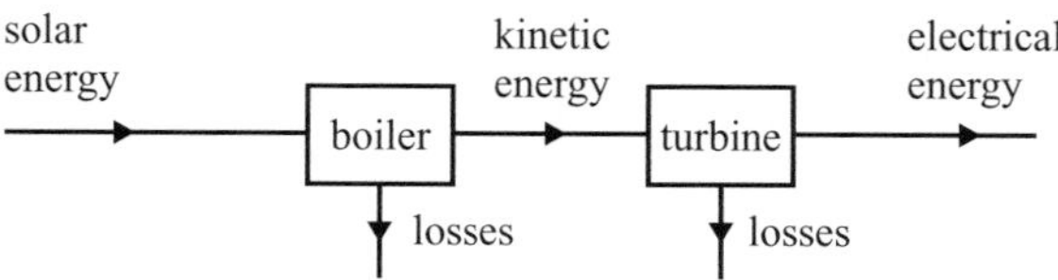

Figure 1.9 Energy flow diagram for electricity production by solar collectors.

Photovoltaic cells

A promising method for producing electricity from sunlight is that provided by photovoltaic cells. The photovoltaic cell was developed in 1954 at Bell Laboratories and is used extensively in the space programme. A photovoltaic cell converts sunlight into DC current at an efficiency of about 30% at present. In the past, the major cost of photovoltaic systems has been the cost of manufacturing the actual cell, but this cost is decreasing. From a cost of about \$100 per watt of power produced per cell, the price is now less than \$4. Adding on the price of related equipment, estimated at \$2 per watt, and used at a site with medium sunshine, 400 W m^{-2}, and taking into account a lifetime of the cell of about 20 years, this works out to a cost per kWh only slightly higher than that produced by diesel-powered generators.

The actual workings of the photovoltaic cell depend on the physics of semiconductors. However, it must be understood that the photovoltaic principle of electricity generation from sunlight is not the same as the photoelectric effect, where sunlight falling on certain surfaces also produces electric current. In the photoelectric effect, the electrons are actually ejected from the metal; whereas in the photovoltaic phenomenon, electrons, having absorbed photons of the right energy, make a transition from the valence band energy levels across the gap and into the conduction band energy levels (Figure 1.10).

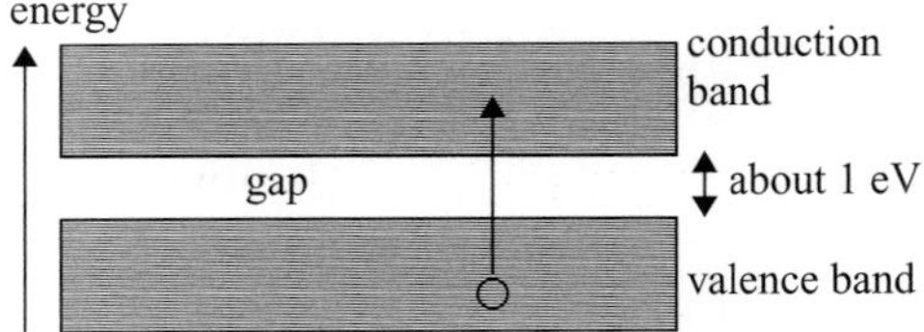

Figure 1.10 Energy level diagram for a silicon semiconductor.

As the price of photovoltaic systems drops, they are bound to become more dominant in electricity production around the world. Already, in places far from major power grids, their use is more economical than grid expansion, and these systems can usefully be used to power small remote villages, pump water in agriculture, power warning lights, etc. Their environmental ill-effects are practically zero, with the exception of chemical pollution at the place of their manufacture.

▶ **Advantages of solar energy**

- 'Free'
- Inexhaustible
- Clean

▶ **Disadvantages of solar energy**

- Works during the day only
- Affected by cloudy weather
- Low power output
- Requires large areas
- Initial costs high

The solar constant

The sun's total power output is $P = 3.9 \times 10^{26}$ W (this is also known as the sun's luminosity). On earth, we receive only a very small fraction of this total power output. The average distance between the sun and the earth is $r = 1.50 \times 10^{11}$ m. The sun's power is distributed uniformly over the surface of an imaginary sphere of radius $r = 1.50 \times 10^{11}$ m.

The power that is collected by area A (Figure 1.11) is the fraction $\frac{A}{4\pi r^2}$ of the total power P. (Note that $4\pi r^2$ is the surface area of the imaginary sphere.) The power through the area A is simply $P\frac{A}{4\pi r^2}$.

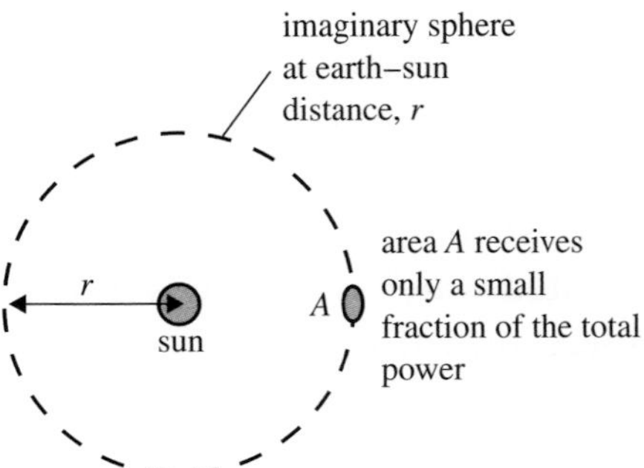

Figure 1.11.

▶ The *power per unit area* received at a distance r from the sun is called the intensity, I, and so

$$I = \frac{P}{4\pi r^2}$$

This amounts to about 1400 W m^{-2}, and is known as the *solar constant*. It is the power received by one square metre placed normally to the path of the incoming rays a distance of 1.50×10^{11} m from the sun.

This actual amount received varies somewhat due to the fact that the power output of the sun is not entirely constant. This gives variations of ±1.5%. In addition, the earth does not keep a constant distance from the sun (the orbit is slightly elliptical) and this gives additional variations of ±4.0%. To find the radiation received on the earth's *surface*, we must take into account reflection of the radiation from the atmosphere and the earth's surface itself, latitude, angle of incidence and average between day and night.

It is useful to define the total amount of energy received by one square metre of the earth's surface in the course of one day. This is called the **daily insolation**. Figure 1.12 shows the daily insolation at two different latitudes as a function of time. The curve with the big dip corresponds to a latitude of 60°. The other is for a latitude of 36°. At zero latitude (the equator), the insolation is almost constant at about 25 MJ m^{-2} day^{-1}.

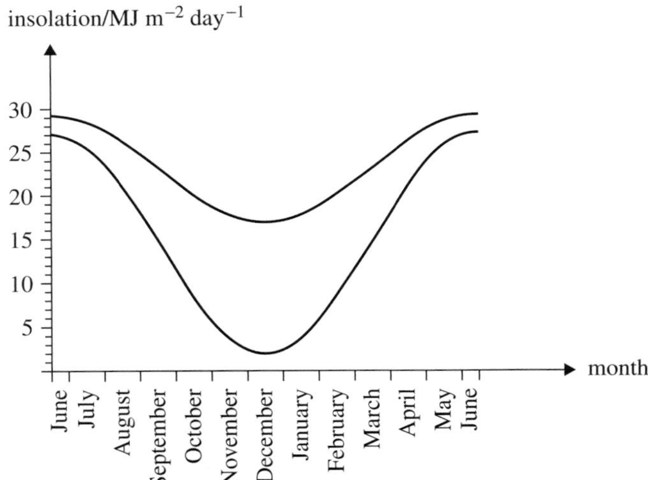

Figure 1.12 The daily insolation at two latitudes in the northern hemisphere. The curve with the big dip corresponds to a latitude of 60°. The other is for a latitude of 36°.

The reduction of the daily insolation in the winter for high latitudes can be explained by the shorter length of daylight and the oblique incidence of light (Figure 1.13).

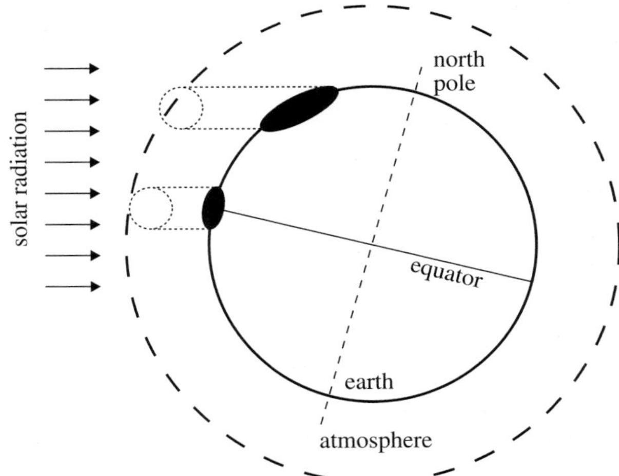

Figure 1.13 At higher latitudes, the energy is spread over a larger area and so the intensity is less. In addition, the radiation has to go through a greater depth of atmosphere and so some of the energy is absorbed.

Hydroelectric power

Hydropower, the power derived from moving water masses, is one of the oldest and most established of all renewable energy sources. This highly site-dependent energy source is capable of producing very cheap electricity. Its use has expanded very rapidly, with power output from hydroelectric plants doubling every 15 years. Turbines driven by falling or moving water have a long working life without major maintenance costs. Also, despite the high costs of the initial construction, hydropower is very promising for many parts of Africa and South America. It is widely used in Norway. Hydropower stations are, however, associated with massive changes in the ecology of the area surrounding the plants. To create a reservoir behind a newly constructed dam, a vast area of land must be flooded.

The principle behind hydropower is simple. Consider a mass m of water that falls down a vertical height h (Figure 1.14). The potential energy of the mass is mgh, and this gets converted into kinetic energy when the mass descends the vertical distance h. The mass is given by $\rho\Delta V$, where ρ is the density of water (1000 kg m^{-3}) and ΔV is the volume it occupies (see Figure 1.15).

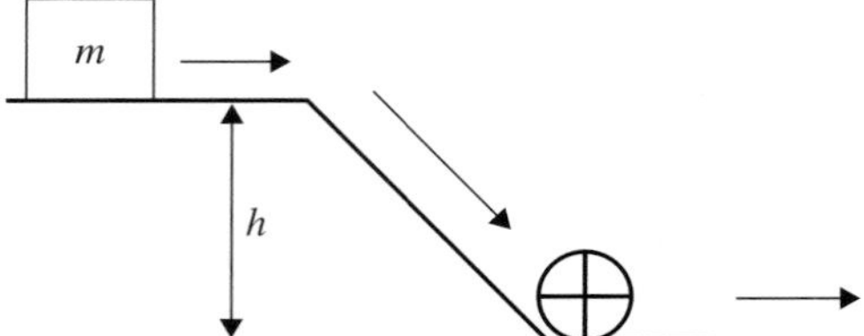

Figure 1.14 Water falling from a vertical height h has its potential energy converted into kinetic energy, which can be used to drive turbines.

The rate of change of this potential energy, i.e. the power P, is given by the change in potential energy divided by the time taken for that change, so

$$P = \frac{mgh}{\Delta t} = \frac{\rho\Delta Vgh}{\Delta t} = \rho\frac{\Delta V}{\Delta t}gh$$

The quantity $Q = \frac{\Delta V}{\Delta t}$ is known as the volume flow rate (volume per second) and so

$$P = \rho Qgh$$

Within a time equal to Δt, the mass of water that will flow through the tube (Figure 1.15) is $m = \rho\Delta V = \rho Q\Delta t$.

Figure 1.15.

This is the power available for generating electricity (or to convert into some other mechanical form) and it is thus clear that hydropower requires large volume flow rates, Q, and large heights, h.

Example question

Q2

Find the power developed when water in a stream with a flow rate 50 L s^{-1} falls from a height of 15 m.

Answer

Applying the power formula, we find (remembering to do all the conversions)

$$P = \rho Qgh = 1000 \times (50 \times 10^{-3}) \times 9.8 \times 15$$
$$= 7.4 \text{ kW}$$

A number of different schemes are available for extracting the power of water. Water can be stored in a *lake*, which should be at as high an elevation as possible to allow for energy release when the water is allowed to flow to lower heights. In a *pump storage system*, the water that flows to lower heights is again pumped back to its original height by using the generators of the plant as motors to pump the water. Obviously, to do this requires energy (more energy, in fact, than can be regained when the water is again allowed to flow to lower heights). This energy has to be supplied from other sources of electrical energy. But it is the only way to *store* energy on a large scale for use when demand is high. In other words, *excess* electricity from somewhere else can be provided to the plant to raise the water so that energy can be produced *later* when it is needed. Finally, there are schemes that take advantage of the tides, *tidal storage systems*. The general idea here is to have the flow of water during a tide turn turbines, producing electricity.

▶ Advantages of hydroelectric energy
- 'Free'
- Inexhaustible
- Clean

▶ Disadvantages of hydroelectric energy
- Very dependent on location
- Requires drastic changes to environment
- Initial costs high

Wind power

This ancient method for extracting energy is particularly useful for isolated small houses and agricultural use, where small wind turbines extracting 3 kW of power from the wind can provide all the energy needed for simple living conditions. Small wind turbines have vanes no larger than about 1 m long. Modern large wind turbines are capable of producing up to a few megawatts of power and, of course, they tend to be big, with vanes larger than 30 m.

Wind power devices have no adverse effects (though there is some evidence that low-frequency sound emitted during the operation of wind turbines affects people's sleeping habits). However, a very large number of them in wind parks is not an attractive sight to many people, and there is a noise problem. The cost of wind energy conversion systems varies from about \$500 to \$5000 per kilowatt of power produced. The blades are susceptible to stresses in high winds, and damage due to metal fatigue frequently occurs. The design must also take into account gale-force winds, which may be very rare for a particular site, but would certainly result in very serious damage to an inadequately designed system. Generally, about one-quarter of the power carried by the wind can be converted into electricity (Figure 1.16).

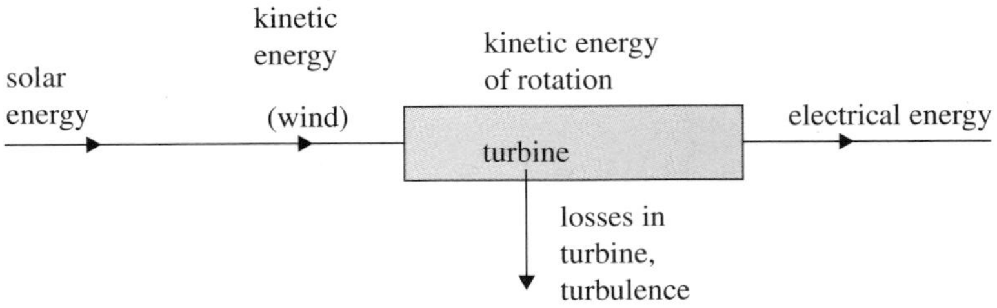

solar energy → kinetic energy (wind) → turbine (kinetic energy of rotation) → electrical energy

↓ losses in turbine, turbulence

Figure 1.16 Energy flow diagram for wind energy extraction.

Wind speed is the crucial factor for these systems, the power extracted being proportional to the cube of the wind speed. Wind speeds of up to about 4 m s^{-1} are not particularly useful for energy extraction. Serious power production from wind occurs at speeds from 6 to 14 m s^{-1}. The dependence of the power on the area of the blades and the cube of the wind speed can be understood as follows (Figure 1.17).

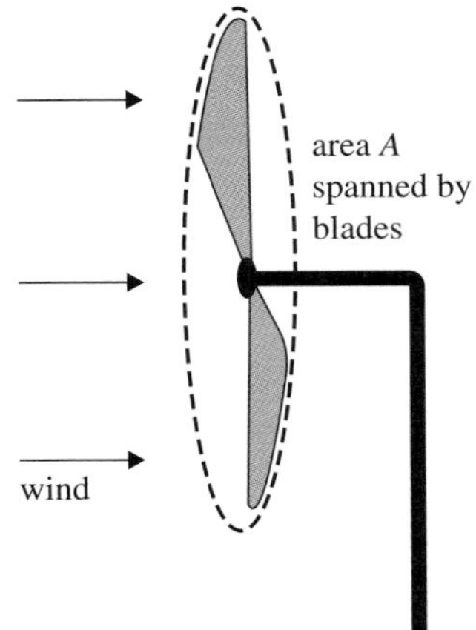

Figure 1.17 A horizontal axis wind turbine with two blades.

Let us consider the mass of air that can pass through a tube of cross-sectional area A with velocity v in time Δt (Figure 1.18). Let ρ be the density of air. Then the mass enclosed in a tube of length $v\Delta t$ is $\rho A v \Delta t$. This is the mass that will exit the right end of the tube *within* a time interval equal to Δt. The kinetic energy of this mass of air is thus

$$\frac{1}{2}(\rho A v \Delta t)v^2 = \frac{1}{2}\rho A \Delta t v^3$$

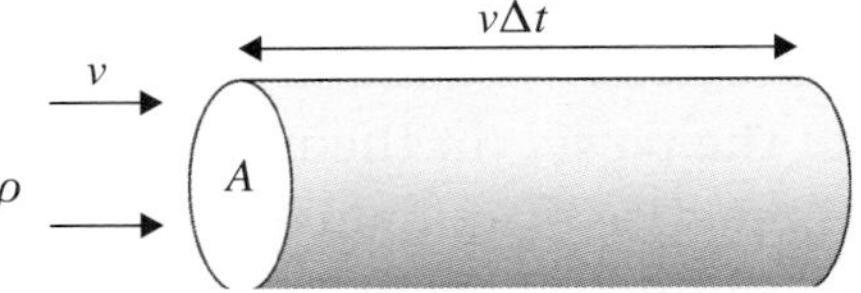

Figure 1.18 The mass of air within this cylinder will exit the right end within a time of Δt.

▶ The kinetic energy per unit time is the power, and so dividing by Δt we find

$$P = \frac{1}{2}\rho A v^3$$

which shows that the power carried by the wind is proportional to the cube of the wind speed and proportional to the area spanned by the blades.

If this stream of air meets a wind turbine, then A stands for the area presented to the air stream by the blades of the wind turbine. The power that can be extracted is thus

$$P = C_p \frac{1}{2} \rho A v^3$$

where C_p is known as the power coefficient. It is simply an efficiency factor that determines how much of the available wind power the wind turbine can extract. Theoretically, C_p is between 0.35 and 0.45.

Assuming a wind speed of 12 m s^{-1}, an air density of 1.2 kg m^{-3} and an efficiency coefficient of 0.40, we find

$$\frac{P}{A} = C_p \frac{1}{2} \rho v^3$$
$$= 0.40 \times \frac{1}{2} \times 1.2 \times 12^3$$
$$= 4.1 \times 10^2 \text{ W m}^{-2}$$

as the theoretical power extracted per unit wind turbine area. A 2 m^2 wind turbine area will thus extract about 820 W of power from the wind.

Doubling the wind turbine area doubles the power extracted, but doubling the wind speed increases the power (in theory) by a factor of eight. In practice, frictional and other losses (mainly turbulence) result in a smaller power increase. The calculations above also assume that all the wind is actually *stopped* by the wind turbine, extracting all of the wind's kinetic energy, which in practice is not the case.

Advantages of wind power

- The source is the wind and so 'free'
- For practical purposes it is inexhaustible
- Clean, without carbon emissions
- Ideal for remote island locations

Disadvantages of wind power

- Works only if there is wind – not dependable
- Low power output
- Aesthetically unpleasant (and noisy)
- Best locations far from large cities
- Maintenance costs high

Wave power

It has been realized that deep-water, long-wavelength sea waves carry a lot of energy. Water waves are very complex and belong to a class of waves called *dispersive*, i.e. the speed of the wave depends on the wavelength.

A water (sea) wave of amplitude A carries an amount of power *per unit length of its wavefront* equal to

$$\frac{P}{L} = \frac{\rho g A^2 v}{2}$$

where ρ is the density of water and v stands for the *speed of energy transfer* in the wave.

For waves of amplitude 1.5 m and wave energy transfer speed $v = 4.0$ m s^{-1}, the formula above gives (here it is worth paying attention to the units)

$$\frac{P}{L} = \frac{1}{2} \rho g A^2 v$$
$$= \frac{1}{2} \times 10^3 \times 9.8 \times 1.5^2 \times 4.0$$
$$= 44 \text{ kW m}^{-1}$$

The units are:

$$(\text{kg m}^{-3})(\text{N kg}^{-1})(\text{m})^2(\text{m s}^{-1})$$
$$= (\text{N m})\,\text{s}^{-1}\,\text{m}^{-1}$$
$$= (\text{J})\,\text{s}^{-1}\,\text{m}^{-1}$$
$$= \text{W m}^{-1}$$

This is a substantial amount of power.

Supplementary material

In advanced books you may see this formula also written with a denominator of 4 rather than 2, i.e.

$$\frac{P}{L} = \frac{\rho g A^2 c}{4}$$

Here $c = \frac{\lambda}{T}$ is the speed of the wave, which, because the wave is dispersive, is not equal to the energy transfer speed v; in fact $c = 2v$. So the wave speed in the example above is $c = 2 \times 6.25\,\mathrm{m\,s^{-1}} = 12.5\,\mathrm{m\,s^{-1}}$. This is a technical point that we will not discuss further.

Many devices have been proposed to extract the power out of waves. The one to be discussed here is called the oscillating water column (Figure 1.19). As a crest of the wave approaches the cavity in the device, the column of water in the cavity rises and so pushes the air above it upwards. The air passes through a turbine, turning it, and is then released into the atmosphere. As a trough of the wave approaches the cavity, the water in the cavity falls and thus draws in air from the atmosphere, which again turns the turbine.

Wave patterns are irregular in wave speed, amplitude and direction, and it is difficult to achieve reasonable efficiency of wave devices over all the variables. For many wave devices, it is difficult to couple the low frequency of the water waves (typically 0.1 Hz) to the much higher generator frequencies (50–60 Hz) required for electricity production. The OWC solves this problem. The great advantage of the OWC device is that the speed of the air through the column can be increased by adjusting the diameter of the valves though which the air passes. In this way very high air speeds can be attained, thus coupling the low-frequency water waves with the high-frequency turbine motion.

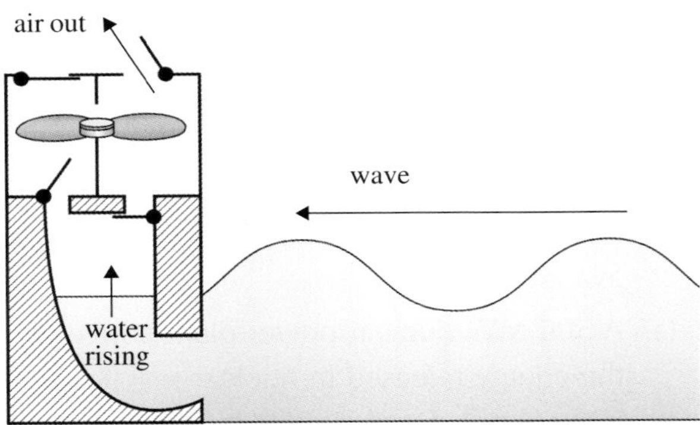

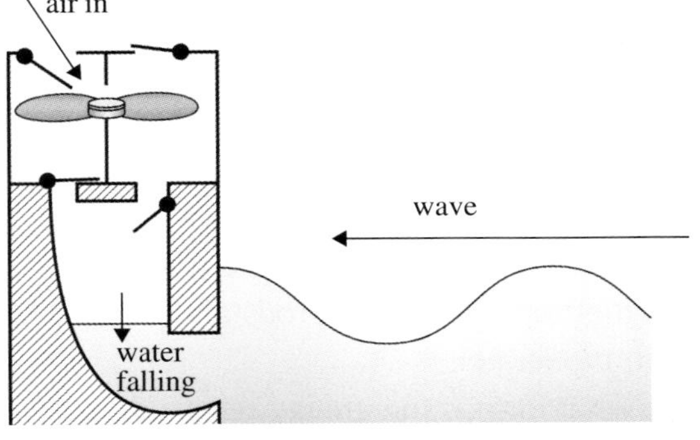

Figure 1.19 An oscillating water column (OWC) plant.

▶ Advantages of wave power

- The source is waves and so 'free'
- Reasonable energy density
- For practical purposes it is inexhaustible
- Clean, without carbon emissions

▶ Disadvantages of wave power

- Works only in areas with large waves
- Irregular wave patterns make it difficult to achieve reasonable efficiency
- Difficult to couple low-frequency water waves with high-frequency turbine motion
- Maintenance and installation costs very high
- Transporting the produced power to consumers involves high costs
- Devices must be able to withstand hurricane and gale-force storms

? QUESTIONS

1 Consider a scheme in which thermal energy is extracted from the ocean. Some of the extracted energy is used to perform mechanical work (run the ship) and the rest is discarded back into the ocean. Why will this not work?

2 Explain what is meant by *degradation of energy*. Give one example of energy degradation.

3 (a) Define *energy density* of a fuel.
(b) Estimate the energy density of water that falls from a waterfall of height 75 m and is used to drive a turbine.

4 A power plant produces 500 MW of power.
(a) How much energy is produced in one second? Express your answer in (i) joules, (ii) kWh and (iii) MWh.
(b) How much energy (in joules) is produced in one year?

5 A power plant operates in four stages. The efficiency in each stage is 80%, 40%, 12% and 65%.
(a) What is the overall efficiency of the plant?
(b) Make a Sankey diagram for the energy flow in this plant.

6 A coal power plant with 30% efficiency burns 10 million kilograms of coal a day. (Take the heat of combustion of coal to be 30 MJ kg^{-1}.)
(a) What is the power output of the plant?
(b) At what rate is thermal energy being discarded by this plant?
(c) If the discarded thermal energy is carried away by water whose temperature is not allowed to increase by more than 5 °C, calculate the rate at which water must flow away from the plant.

7 One litre of gasoline releases 35 MJ of energy when burned. The efficiency of a car operating on this gasoline is 40%. The speed of the car is 9.0 m s^{-1} when the power developed by the engine is 20 kW. Calculate how many kilometres the car can go with one litre of gasoline when driven at this speed.

8 A coal-burning power plant produces 1.0 GW of electricity. The overall efficiency of the power plant is 40%. Taking the energy density of coal to be 30 MJ kg^{-1}, calculate the amount of coal that must be burned in one day.

9 In the context of nuclear fission reactors, state what is meant by
(a) uranium enrichment;
(b) moderator;
(c) critical mass.

10 (a) Calculate the energy released in the fission reaction

$${}^{1}_{0}n + {}^{235}_{92}U \rightarrow {}^{236}_{92}U \rightarrow {}^{140}_{54}Xe + {}^{94}_{38}Sr + 2{}^{1}_{0}n$$

(b) How many fission reactions per second must take place if the power output is 200 MW? (The atomic masses are: uranium-235, ${}^{235}_{92}U$ = 235.043 923 u; xenon-140, ${}^{140}_{54}Xe$ = 139.921 636 u; strontium-94, ${}^{94}_{38}Sr$ = 93.915 360 u; neutron, ${}^{1}_{0}n$ = 1.008 665 u.)

11 The energy released in a typical fission reaction involving uranium-235 is 200 MeV.
(a) Calculate the energy density of uranium-235.
(b) How much coal (heat of combustion 30 MJ kg^{-1}) must be burned in order to give the same energy as that released in nuclear fission with 1 kg of uranium-235 available?

12 (a) A 500 MW nuclear power plant converts the energy released in nuclear reactions into electrical energy with an efficiency of 40%. Calculate how many fissions of uranium-235 are required per second. Take the energy released per reaction to be 200 MeV.
(b) What mass of uranium-235 is required to fission per second?

13 (a) Make a schematic diagram of a fission reactor, explaining the role of (i) fuel rods, (ii) control rods and (iii) moderator.
(b) In what form is the energy released in a fission reactor?

14 By looking up appropriate sources, write an essay about the problem of radioactive waste disposal.

15 Distinguish between a solar panel and a photovoltaic cell.

16 The typical energy of photons in the visible spectrum is 2 eV. Explain why a semiconductor with an energy gap between the valence and conduction bands of more than 2 eV would not be suitable in a photovoltaic cell.

17 Sunlight of intensity 700 W m^{-2} is captured with 70% efficiency by a solar panel, which then sends the captured energy into a house with 50% efficiency.

(a) If the house loses thermal energy through bad insulation at a rate of 3.0 kW, find the area of the solar panel needed in order to keep the temperature of the house constant.

(b) Make a Sankey diagram for the energy flow.

18 A solar heater is to heat 300 L of water initially at 15 °C to a temperature of 50 °C in a time of 12 hours. The amount of solar radiation falling on the collecting surface of the solar panel is 240 W m^{-2} and is collected at an efficiency of 65%. Calculate the area of the collecting panel that is required.

19 A solar heater is to warm 150 kg of water by 30 K. The intensity of solar radiation is 600 W m^{-2} and the area of the panels is 4.0 m^2. The specific heat capacity of the water is 4.2×10^3 J kg^{-1} K^{-1}. Estimate the time this will take, assuming a solar panel efficiency of 60%.

20 The graph in Figure 1.20 shows the variation with incident solar power P of the temperature of a solar panel used to heat water when thermal energy is extracted from the water at a rate of 320 W. The area of the panel is 2.0 m^2 and the intensity of the solar radiation incident on the panel is 400 W m^{-2}. Calculate

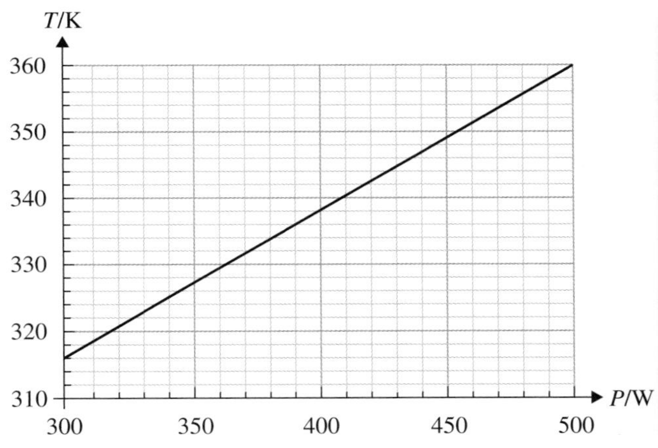

Figure 1.20 For question 20.

(a) the temperature of the water;

(b) the power incident on the panel;

(c) the efficiency of the panel.

21 The graph in Figure 1.21 shows the power curve of a wind turbine as a function of the wind speed. If the wind speed is 10 m s^{-1}, calculate the energy produced in the course of one year, assuming that the wind blows at this speed for 1000 hours in the year.

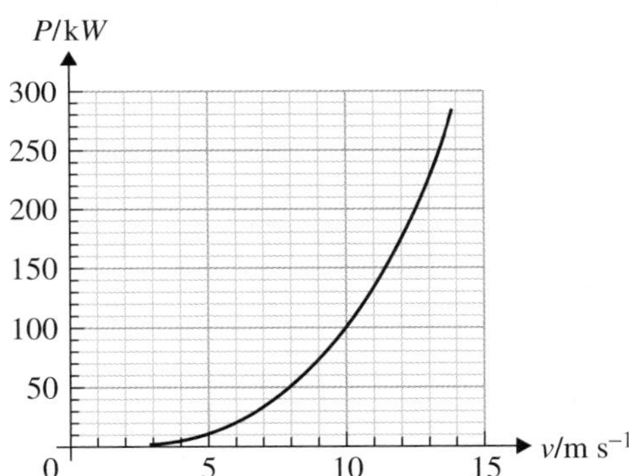

Figure 1.21 For question 21.

22 State the expected increase in the power extracted from a wind turbine when

(a) the length of the blades is doubled;

(b) the wind speed is doubled;

(c) both the length of the blades and the wind speed are doubled.

(d) Outline reasons why the actual increase in the extracted power will be less than your answers.

23 Wind of speed v is incident on the blades of a wind turbine. The blades present the wind with an area A.

(a) Deduce that the maximum theoretical power that can be extracted is given by

$$P = \frac{1}{2}\rho A v^3$$

(b) State any assumptions made in deriving the relation in (a).

24 Air of density 1.2 kg m^{-3} and speed 8.0 m s^{-1} is incident on the blades of a wind turbine. The radius of the blades is 1.5 m. Immediately after passing through the blades, the wind speed is reduced to 3.0 m s^{-1} and the density of air is 1.8 kg m^{-3}. Calculate the power extracted from the wind.

25 Calculate the blade radius of a wind turbine that must extract 25 kW of power out of wind of speed 9.0 m s^{-1}. The density of air is 1.2 kg m^{-3}. State any assumptions made in this calculation.

26 Find the power developed when water in a waterfall with a flow rate of 500 L s^{-1} falls from a height of 40 m.

27 Water falls from a vertical height h at a flow rate (volume per second) Q. Deduce that the maximum theoretical power that can be extracted is given by $P = \rho Q g h$.

28 A student explaining pumped storage systems says that the water that is stored at a high elevation is allowed to move lower, thus producing electricity. Some of this electricity is used to raise the water back to its original height, and the process is then repeated. What is wrong with this statement?

29 (a) Supply the details for the derivation of the equation

$$\frac{P}{L} = \frac{\rho g A^2 v}{2}$$

for a wave with a square profile.

(b) Calculate the power per unit wavefront length that can be obtained from deep-sea waves of amplitude 5.0 m and wave speed $v = 4.8\,\mathrm{m\,s^{-1}}$.

(c) What wavefront length is required for a total power output of 1.0 MW.

30 Describe the operation of an oscillating water column (OWC) device. State the main advantage of the OWC device.

31 Make an annotated energy flow diagram showing the energy changes that are taking place in each of the following:

(a) a conventional electricity-producing power station using coal;
(b) a hydroelectric power plant;
(c) an electricity-producing wind turbine;
(d) an electricity-producing nuclear power station.

HL only

32 Sunlight of intensity 800 W m^{-2} is captured by a tank containing 100 kg of water with an efficiency of 80%. The tank is rectangular in shape and has dimensions $1.0 \times 1.0 \times 0.10\,\mathrm{m^3}$. It has walls of thickness 5.0 mm. The surrounding air has a temperature of 20 °C. Assume that the tank is well insulated from all sides except the top surface (of area 1.0 m^2). The material of the tank has a thermal conductivity of $k = 0.30\,\mathrm{W\,m^{-1}\,K^{-1}}$, its density is 1200 kg m^{-3} and its specific heat capacity is 450 J kg^{-1} K^{-1}.

The rate of flow of thermal energy through a surface of area A and thickness x separated by temperatures T_1 and T_2 is given by

$$\frac{\Delta Q}{\Delta t} = kA\frac{T_1 - T_2}{x}$$

(a) Calculate the mass of the tank.
(b) By equating the energy received from the sunlight to the thermal energy lost by conduction to the surrounding air, estimate the final temperature of the water.

(c) Find the heat capacity, C, of the tank–water system.

(d) Show that the temperature T of the water in °C is increasing at a rate $\frac{\Delta T}{\Delta t}$ that can be found from the equation

$$C\frac{\Delta T}{\Delta t} = AI_{in} - kA\frac{T - 20}{x}$$

where I_{in} is the intensity of sunlight captured by the tank, C is the heat capacity of the system, k is the thermal conductivity of the tank, A is the area of the top surface of the tank, and x is the thickness of the tank wall.

(e) Evaluate the rate of temperature increase when the temperature is the average of the initial temperature of 20 °C and the final temperature you found in part (b).

(f) Assuming that the temperature is increasing at this rate, calculate how long it will take the water to reach its final temperature.

CHAPTER 7.2

The greenhouse effect and global warming

This chapter deals with the physical mechanisms that control the energy balance of the earth. The important phenomenon of black-body radiation is introduced along with the associated Stefan–Boltzmann and Wien displacement laws. The 'greenhouse effect' is introduced as the trapping by gases in the atmosphere of radiation emitted by the earth. The enhanced greenhouse effect is also discussed. As much as possible, the chapter stays close to the physics of the problem, and does not enter into judgements based on political or moral grounds.

Objectives

By the end of this chapter you should be able to:

- understand and apply the *black-body radiation law*;
- understand the meaning of the terms *emissivity* and *albedo*;
- work with a simple *energy balance equation*;
- understand the meaning of the term *greenhouse effect* and distinguish this effect from the *enhanced greenhouse effect*;
- name the main *greenhouse gases* and their natural and anthropogenic sources and sinks;
- understand the molecular mechanism for *infrared radiation absorption*;
- state the evidence linking *global warming* to the increased concentrations of greenhouse gases in the atmosphere;
- understand the definition of *surface heat capacity* and apply it in simple situations;
- discuss the *expected trends on climate* caused by changes in various factors and appreciate that these are interrelated;
- state *possible solutions* to the enhanced greenhouse effect and *international efforts* to counter global warming.

The black-body law

One of the great advances in physics of the nineteenth century was the realization that all bodies that are kept at some *absolute* (kelvin) temperature T radiate energy in the form of electromagnetic waves. For example, the energy from the sun that warms the earth, thereby sustaining life on earth, is the energy radiated by the hot surface of the sun that arrives on earth through the vacuum of space. The power radiated by a body is governed by the **Stefan–Boltzmann law**.

▶ The amount of energy per second (i.e. the power) radiated by a body depends on its surface area A, absolute temperature T, and the properties of the surface:

$$P = e\sigma A T^4$$

This is known as the *Stefan–Boltzmann law*. The constant σ is known as the *Stefan–Boltzmann constant* and equals $\sigma = 5.67 \times 10^{-8}\ \mathrm{W\,m^{-2}\,K^{-4}}$.

The constant e appearing in this formula is called the **emissivity** of the surface. It is a dimensionless number that varies from 0 to 1. The special case $e = 1$ corresponds to what is called a **black body**, a theoretical body that is a 'perfect' emitter. A real body is a good approximation to the theoretical black body if its surface is black and dull. For example, a piece of charcoal is a better approximation to a black body than a shiny silver surface. In other words, surfaces differ in the value of the emissivity e. Dark and dull surfaces have e close to 1, whereas light and shiny surfaces have e close to 0. Table 2.1 gives values for the emissivity of various surfaces.

Surface	Emissivity
Black body	1
Ocean water	0.8
Ice	0.1
Dry land	0.7
Land with vegetation	0.6

Table 2.1 Emissivity of various surfaces.

A body of emissivity e that is kept at some temperature T_1 will *radiate* power at a rate $P_{\text{out}} = e\sigma A T_1^4$ but will also *absorb* power at a rate $P_{\text{in}} = e\sigma A T_2^4$ if its surroundings are kept at a temperature T_2. Hence the net power *lost* by the body is

$$P_{\text{net}} = P_{\text{out}} - P_{\text{in}} = e\sigma A\left(T_1^4 - T_2^4\right)$$

At equilibrium, $P_{\text{net}} = 0$, i.e. the body loses as much energy as it gains, and so the body's temperature stays constant and equals that of the surroundings, $T_1 = T_2$.

Surfaces that are black and dull, as opposed to light and shiny, are also good *absorbers* of radiation. Thus we wear dark clothes in the winter to absorb the radiation from the sun. Light-coloured surfaces are good *reflectors* of radiation, which is why we wear light-coloured clothes in the summer.

The energy radiated by a body is electromagnetic radiation and is distributed over an infinite range of wavelengths. However, most of the energy is radiated at a specific wavelength that is determined by the temperature of the body – the higher the temperature, the shorter the wavelength. For a body at ordinary room temperature (20 °C, 293K) the wavelength at which most of the energy is radiated is an infrared wavelength. This is why we associate infrared radiation with 'heat'.

Figure 2.1 shows how the power is radiated from 1 m² of the same surface as the temperature of the surface is varied (T = 350 K, 300 K and 273 K).

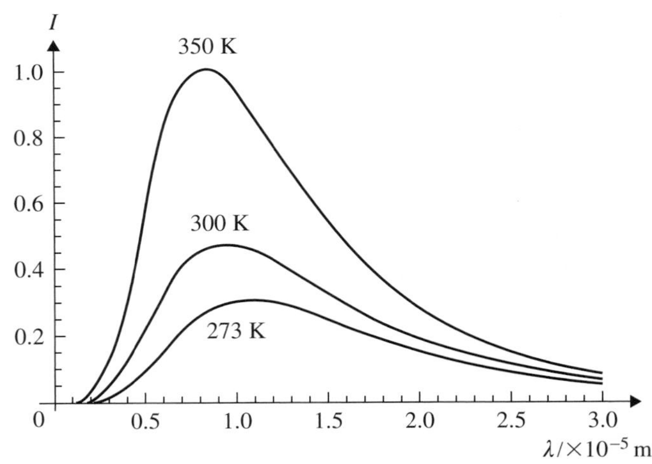

Figure 2.1 Black-body spectra for a body at the three temperatures shown. The units on the vertical axis are arbitrary. (The curves appear to start from a finite value of wavelength. This is not the case. The curves start at zero wavelength but are too small to appear on the graphs.)

We see that, with increasing temperature, the peak of the curve occurs at lower wavelengths and the height of the peak increases. The relation between the temperature and the peak wavelength, the wavelength at which most of the energy is emitted, is given by **Wien's law**:

$$\lambda T = 2.90 \times 10^{-3} \text{ m K}$$

(Note that the unit here is metre kelvin, not millikelvin.)

The earth's surface emits infrared radiation because the earth's surface is at a temperature of 288 K (global day and night average):

$$\lambda = \frac{2.90 \times 10^{-3}}{288} = 1.0 \times 10^{-5} \text{ m}$$

which is a typical infrared wavelength. The sun, by contrast, with a surface temperature of 5800 K emits at

$$\lambda = \frac{2.90 \times 10^{-3}}{5800} = 5.0 \times 10^{-7} \text{ m}$$

which is in the wavelength range of visible light.

Figure 2.2 shows the power emitted from 1 m^2 of various different surfaces kept at the same temperature (300 K). The difference in the curves is due to the different emissivities ($e = 1.0$, 0.8 and 0.2). The curves are identical apart from an overall factor that shrinks the height of the curve as the emissivity decreases.

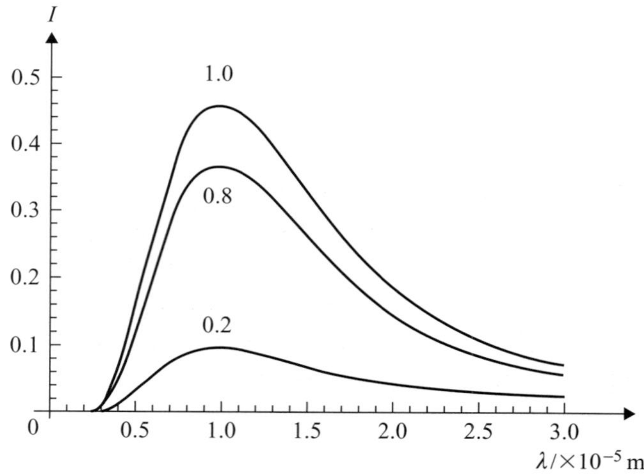

Figure 2.2 The spectrum of three bodies with different emissivities at the same temperature (300 K). The units on the vertical axis are arbitrary.

Example questions

Q1

By what factor does the power emitted by a body increase when the temperature is increased from 100 °C to 200 °C?

Answer

The temperature increases (on the kelvin scale) from 373 K to 473 K, and so the emitted power, being proportional to the fourth power of the temperature, will increase by a factor

$$\left(\frac{473}{373}\right)^4 = 2.59$$

Q2

The emissivity of the naked human body may be taken to be $e = 0.90$. Assuming a body temperature of 37 °C and a body surface area of 1.60 m^2, calculate the total amount of energy lost by the body when exposed to a temperature of 0.0 °C for 30 minutes.

Answer

From $P_{net} = P_{out} - P_{in} = e\sigma A(T_1^4 - T_2^4)$ we find that the net power lost by the body is (notice that we must use kelvins)

$$P_{net} = 0.90 \times 5.67 \times 10^{-8} \times 1.60 \times (310^4 - 273^4)$$
$$= 301 \text{ W}$$

Hence the energy lost is

$$E = P_{net}t$$
$$= 301 \times 30 \times 60$$
$$= 5.4 \times 10^5 \text{ J}$$

(For the purposes of an estimate, assume that the body has mass 60 kg and is made out of water, so that the specific heat capacity is $c = 4200 \text{ J kg}^{-1} \text{ K}^{-1}$. This would result in a drop in body temperature of $\Delta T = \frac{5.4\times10^5}{60\times4200} = 2.1$ K. This would be serious! However, it ignores the fact that respiration provides a source of energy.)

Solar radiation

The sun may be considered to radiate as a perfect emitter (i.e. as a black body). The sun emits a total power of $P = 3.9 \times 10^{26}$ W. The average earth–sun distance is $d = 1.5 \times 10^{11}$ m. So, at the distance of the earth, we may imagine that the power radiated by the sun is distributed uniformly on the surface of a sphere centred at the sun of radius d (see Figure 1.11 on page 424). The earth receives only a very small fraction of this power, equal to $\frac{a}{4\pi d^2}$, where a is the area used to collect the power. Thus the *power per unit area* (i.e. the **intensity**) received by earth is

$$I = \frac{P}{4\pi d^2}$$

▶ *Intensity* is the power of radiation received per unit area of the receiver.

Substituting the numerical values gives

$$I = \frac{3.9 \times 10^{26}}{4\pi(1.5 \times 10^{11})^2} \approx 1400 \text{ W m}^{-2}$$

This is the intensity of the solar radiation at the top of the earth's atmosphere. It is called the **solar constant** and is denoted by S.

If we know that radiation of intensity I is incident on a surface of area A, we can calculate the **power** delivered to that area from:

$$P = IA$$

Albedo

The **albedo** (from the Latin for 'white'), α, of a body is defined as the ratio of the power of radiation reflected or scattered from the body to the total power incident on the body:

$$\alpha = \frac{\text{total scattered/reflected power}}{\text{total incident power}}$$

The albedo is a dimensionless number. Snow has a high albedo (0.85), indicating that snow reflects most of the radiation incident on it, whereas charcoal has an albedo of only 0.04, meaning that it reflects very little of the light incident on it. The earth as a whole has an average global albedo that is about 0.3. The albedo of the earth varies. The variations depend on the time of the year (many or few clouds), latitude (a lot of snow and ice or very little), on whether one is over desert land (high albedo, 0.3–0.4), forests (low albedo, 0.1), or water (low albedo, 0.1), etc.

The calculation of the solar constant as $S = 1400 \text{ W m}^{-2}$ is the value at a particular point in the upper atmosphere. At any one moment in time, the earth offers a 'target' area of πR^2, where R is the radius of the earth (see Figure 2.3). As the target area is only a quarter of the total surface area of the earth ($4\pi R^2$), the power of the radiation received per square metre of the earth's surface is $\frac{S}{4} = 350 \text{ W m}^{-2}$. Since 30% is reflected, this means that the earth receives a net radiation intensity of $350 \times 0.7 = 245 \text{ W m}^{-2}$.

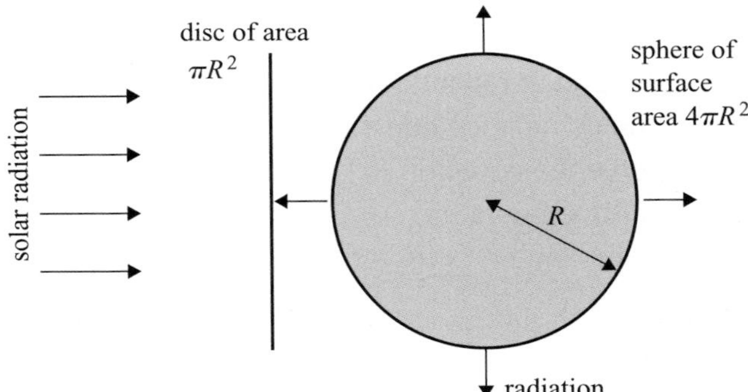

Figure 2.3 The radiation reaching the earth falls on a disc of area πR^2, where R is the radius of the earth.

Energy balance

The earth has a constant average temperature and behaves as a black body. So the energy input to the earth must equal (balance) the energy output by the earth. Taking account of albedo, the power delivered to surface area A (Figure 2.4) is

$$P = (1 - \alpha)IA$$

The next example introduces a first example of an **energy balance equation**.

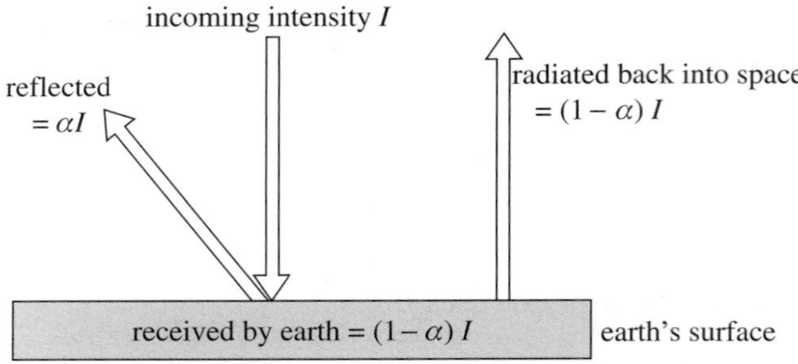

Figure 2.4 Energy diagram showing energy transfers in a model without an atmosphere. Note that the energy in equals the energy out.

Example question

Q3

Assume that the earth has a fixed temperature T and that it radiates as a black body. The average incoming solar radiation has intensity $I = \frac{S}{4} = 350\ \text{W m}^{-2}$. Take the albedo of the earth to be $\alpha = 0.30$. Ignore the effect of the atmosphere.

(a) Write down an equation expressing the fact that the power received by the earth equals the power radiated by the earth into space (an energy balance equation).

(b) Solve the equation to calculate the constant earth temperature.

(c) Comment on your answer.

Answer

(a) The power *received* by an area A of the earth's surface is

$$P_{in} = (1 - \alpha)IA = (1 - \alpha)\frac{S}{4}A$$

This is because a power $\alpha\frac{S}{4}A$ has been reflected back into space. The earth radiates power from the entire surface area of its spherical shape, and so the power *radiated* (by the Stefan–Boltzmann law) is

$$P_{out} = \sigma A T^4$$

(Here we are assuming that the earth is a black body, so $e = 1$; and the surrounding space is taken to have a temperature of 0 K.) Equating the above two equations gives

$$(1 - \alpha)\frac{S}{4}A = \sigma A T^4$$

$$(1 - \alpha)S = 4\sigma T^4$$

(b) Hence we find

$$T = \sqrt[4]{\frac{(1 - \alpha)S}{4\sigma}}$$

This evaluates to

$$T = \sqrt[4]{\frac{(1 - 0.30) \times 1400}{4(5.67 \times 10^{-8})}} \approx 256\ \text{K}$$

This temperature is –17 °C.

(c) It is perhaps surprising that this extremely simple model has given an answer that is not off by orders of magnitude! But a temperature of 256 K is 32 K lower than the earth's average temperature of 288 K, and so obviously the model is just too simplistic. One reason this model is too simple is precisely because we have not taken into account the fact that not all the power radiated by the earth actually escapes. Some of the power is absorbed by the gases in the atmosphere and is re-radiated back down to the earth's surface, causing further warming that we have neglected to take into account. In other words, this model neglects the *greenhouse effect*. This simple model also points to the general fact that increasing the albedo (more energy reflected) results in lower temperatures.

Another drawback of the simple model presented above is that the model is essentially a zero-dimensional model. The earth is treated as a point without interactions between the surface and the atmosphere. (Latent heat flows, thermal energy flow in oceans through currents, thermal energy transfer between the surface and the atmosphere due to temperature differences between the two, are all ignored.) Realistic models must take all these factors (and many others) into account, and so are very complex.

The greenhouse effect

This effect applies to any planet with an atmosphere, but in this discussion the planet will be assumed to be the earth.

The solar radiation reaching the earth is mainly radiation in the visible region of the electromagnetic spectrum (with small amounts in the ultraviolet and infrared). About 30% of this radiation is reflected back into space, and the rest arrives at the earth's atmosphere and the surface, warming both. The earth's surface radiates back as all warm bodies do. But the earth's surface is at an average temperature of 288 K and, using Wien's law, we see that the wavelengths at which this energy is radiated are infrared wavelengths. Unlike visible light wavelengths, which pass through the atmosphere unobstructed, infrared radiation is strongly absorbed by various gases in the atmosphere, the so-called *greenhouse gases*. This radiation is in turn re-radiated by these gases in all directions. This means that some of this radiation is received by the earth's surface again, causing additional warming (Figure 2.5). This is radiation that would be lost in space were it not for the greenhouse gases. Without this **greenhouse effect**, the earth's temperature would be 32 K lower than what it is now. This effect would be absent if there was no atmosphere.

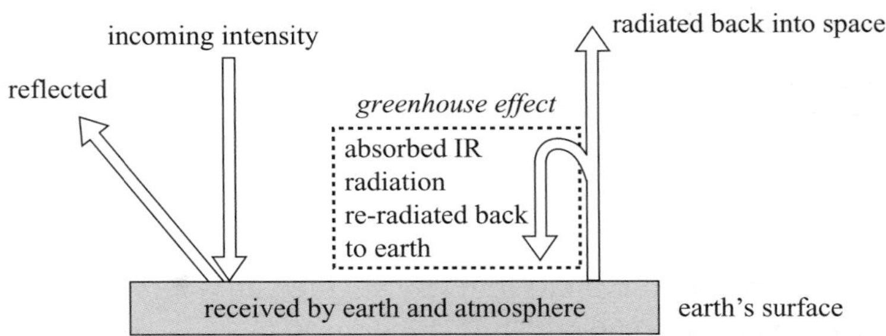

Figure 2.5 A simplified energy flow diagram to illustrate the greenhouse effect.

▶ The *greenhouse effect* may be described as the warming of the earth caused by infrared radiation, emitted by the earth's surface, which is absorbed by various gases in the earth's atmosphere and is then partly re-radiated towards the surface. The gases primarily responsible for this absorption (the *greenhouse gases*) are water vapour, carbon dioxide, methane and nitrous oxide.

A more detailed energy flow diagram is shown in Figure 2.6. The total incoming intensity is represented by 100 in arbitrary units or percentages. (The diagram does not include

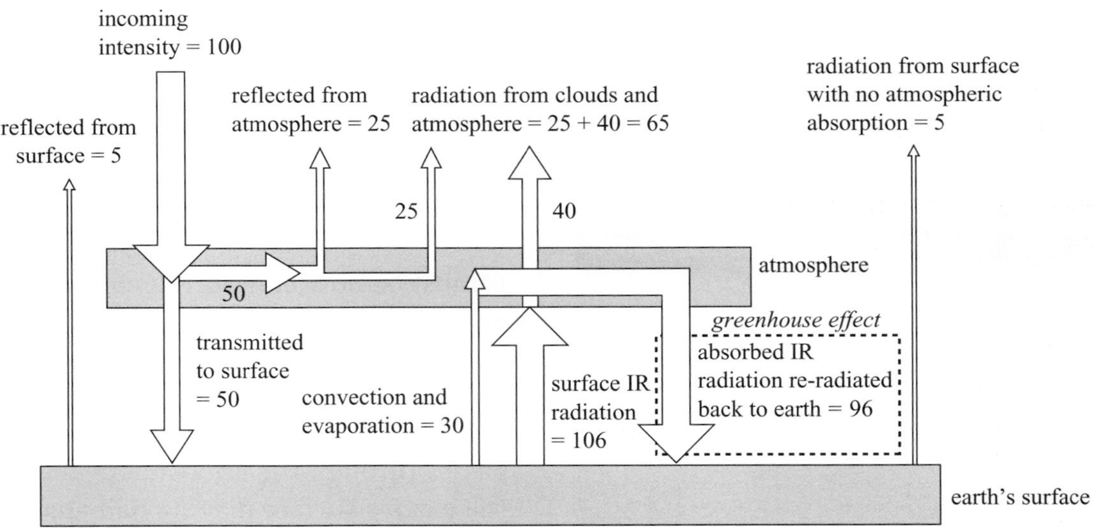

Figure 2.6 A more detailed energy flow diagram for the earth–atmosphere system.

energy associated with winds, ocean waves and currents and transfers of energy across the earth's surface. These are important but are too complicated for our purposes here.) Notice that the energy in and the energy out balance separately, as indicated in Tables 2.2 and 2.3 for the entire earth system and the surface. It is left as an exercise to check that the energy also balances for the atmosphere.

Mechanism	Intensity in (arbitrary units)
Radiation from sun	100
Total for entire earth system	100
Mechanism	**Intensity out (arbitrary units)**
Reflected from surface	5
Reflected from atmosphere	25
Radiation from clouds and atmosphere	65
Radiation from surface with no atmospheric absorption (the IR 'window')	5
Total for entire earth system	100

Table 2.2 Energy balance for the entire total earth system.

Mechanism	Intensity in (arbitrary units)
Transmitted to surface from sun	50
Absorbed IR radiation re-radiated back to earth (greenhouse effect)	96
Total for earth's surface	146
Mechanism	**Intensity out (arbitrary units)**
Reflected from surface	5
Convection and evaporation	30
IR radiation from surface	106
Radiation from surface with no atmospheric absorption (the IR 'window')	5
Total for earth's surface	146

Table 2.3 Energy balance for the earth's surface.

For the earth as a whole, the total reflected radiation is thus $5 + 25 = 30$, consistent with an albedo of 0.3. The total outgoing radiation is 100, consistent with energy conservation.

Notice that, for the surface, the amount of radiation emitted is $106 + 5 = 111$, compared to the incoming amount of 100. This represents 111% of the average incoming intensity $I = \frac{S}{4} = 350\ \text{W m}^{-2}$, so is

$$111\% \times 350 = \frac{111}{100} \times 350 = 390\ \text{W m}^{-2}$$

This must be consistent with the earth's surface temperature of 288 K. Indeed, the radiation per unit area from a surface at this temperature is

$$\sigma T^4 = 5.67 \times 10^{-8} \times (288)^4 \approx 390\ \text{W m}^{-2}$$

The greenhouse effect is thus a *natural* consequence of the presence of the atmosphere. There is, however, also the *enhanced* greenhouse effect, which refers to additional warming due to *increased* quantities of the greenhouse gases in the atmosphere. The increases in the gas concentrations are due to human activity.

The greenhouse gases in the atmosphere have natural as well as man-made (anthropogenic) origins (Table 2.4). Along with these sources of the greenhouse gases, we have 'sinks' as well, that is to say, mechanisms that reduce these concentrations. For example, carbon dioxide is absorbed by plants during photosynthesis and is dissolved in oceans. Methane is destroyed in the lower atmosphere by chemical reactions involving free hydroxyl radicals (·OH). Nitrous oxide is also destroyed in the atmosphere by photochemical reactions.

It must be noticed that the radiation incident on the earth is mainly visible light. Photons of visible light, unlike photons of infrared radiation, are *not* absorbed by the gases of the atmosphere. Therefore, the incident radiation passes through the atmosphere and arrives at the earth's surface (having had about 25% of the radiation *reflected* back into space from the upper atmosphere).

Greenhouse gas	Natural sources	Anthropogenic sources
H_2O (water vapour)	evaporation of water from oceans, rivers and lakes	
CO_2 (carbon dioxide)	forest fires, volcanic eruptions, evaporation of water from oceans	burning fossil fuels in power plants and cars, burning forests
CH_4 (methane)	wetlands, oceans, lakes and rivers	flooded rice fields, farm animals, termites, processing of coal, natural gas and oil, and burning biomass
N_2O (dinitrogen oxide, nitrous oxide)	forests, oceans, soil and grasslands	burning fossil fuels, manufacture of cement, fertilizers, deforestation (reduction of nitrogen fixation in plants)

Table 2.4 Sources of greenhouse gases.

Mechanism of photon absorption

Consider a molecule of carbon dioxide (one of the many gases that are capable of absorbing infrared photons). We already know from atomic physics that the energy of electrons within atoms is quantized (i.e. it assumes discrete values). The same effect (i.e. the existence of discrete energy values) applies to the energy of molecules due to their vibrational and rotational motion. This energy is also quantized, and there are vibrational and rotational energy levels (Figure 2.7) just as there are atomic energy levels. The big difference between the two kinds of energy level (vibrational/rotational versus atomic) is that the difference in energy between the vibrational/rotational energy levels is approximately the same as the energies of infrared photons. (Atomic energy levels, in general, differ in energy by amounts far greater than the energy of infrared photons.)

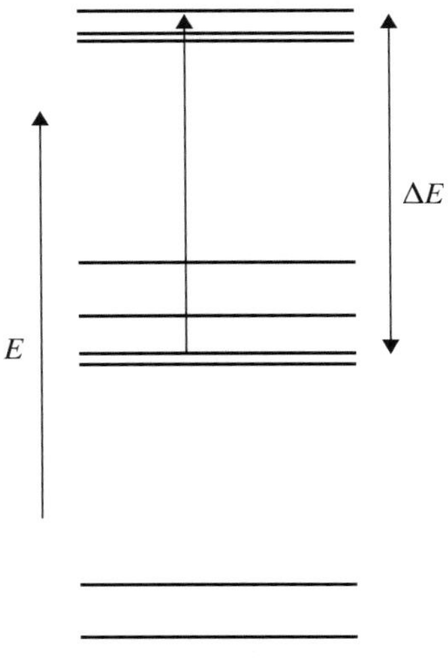

Figure 2.7 Combined vibrational and rotational energy levels of a diatomic molecule. The absorption of a photon of energy ΔE results in the transition indicated.

This means that infrared photons travelling through these gases will be absorbed. Absorbing photons means that the gas molecules will now be excited to higher energy levels. But the molecules prefer to be in low-energy states, and so they will immediately make a transition to a lower-energy state by emitting the photons they absorbed. But these photons are *not all* emitted outwards into space. Some are emitted *back towards the earth*, thereby warming the earth's surface.

The precise mechanism for photon absorption by the greenhouse gases is complex and requires quantum mechanics. Here we will try to understand the absorption by making use of the concept of resonance that we met in our study of simple harmonic motion (Chapter 4.1).

Consider two atoms forming a diatomic molecule (we concentrate on diatomic molecules – this discussion would get very complicated for molecules with three or more atoms). The force between the atoms may be very loosely modelled as a mass–spring system (Figure 2.8). The atoms

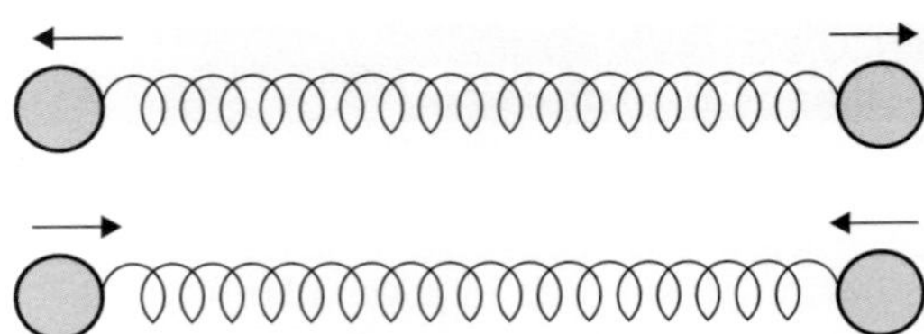

Figure 2.8 The atoms of a diatomic molecule vibrate. The energy associated with the vibration is quantized.

may be thought to be connected by a spring, and simple harmonic oscillations take place when the atoms are disturbed from their equilibrium positions.

The frequency of oscillation is given by

$$f = \frac{1}{2\pi}\sqrt{\frac{k}{m}}$$

where m is related to the masses of the two atoms, m_1 and m_2, through

$$m = \frac{m_1 m_2}{m_1 + m_2}$$

For carbon monoxide (CO), the 'spring' constant has a value $k = 1900\ \text{N m}^{-1}$ and $m = 1.14 \times 10^{-26}$ kg. Therefore the frequency is

$$f = \frac{1}{2\pi}\sqrt{\frac{1900}{1.14 \times 10^{-26}}}$$

$$= 6.5 \times 10^{13}\ \text{Hz}$$

This frequency is the *natural frequency* of the molecule. Photons travelling through the gas will be in resonance with the molecule if they have a frequency equal to the natural frequency. A typical infrared photon has an energy of 0.25 eV and so its frequency is

$$f = \frac{E}{h}$$

$$= \frac{0.25 \times 1.6 \times 10^{-19}}{6.6 \times 10^{-34}}$$

$$= 6.1 \times 10^{13}\ \text{Hz}$$

This is approximately the same as the natural frequency of the molecule. This means that the photons will be absorbed by the molecule.

Transmittance curves

Consider infrared radiation passing through the atmosphere. The intensity of radiation after passing through the atmosphere will be less than the incident intensity because some of the radiation will be absorbed. We may then make a transmittance curve that shows the variation with wavelength of the percentage of radiation that actually gets through the gas. The transmittance curve of Figure 2.9 indicates that all photons of wavelength less than about $\lambda = 4 \times 10^{-6}$ m and larger than $\lambda = 8 \times 10^{-6}$ m are transmitted through the gas, whereas photons of wavelengths between $\lambda = 4 \times 10^{-6}$ m and $\lambda = 8 \times 10^{-6}$ m are absorbed to varying degrees. The curve implies that *all* the photons of wavelength $\lambda = 6 \times 10^{-6}$ m are absorbed. The amount of absorption depends on the concentration of the absorbing gas.

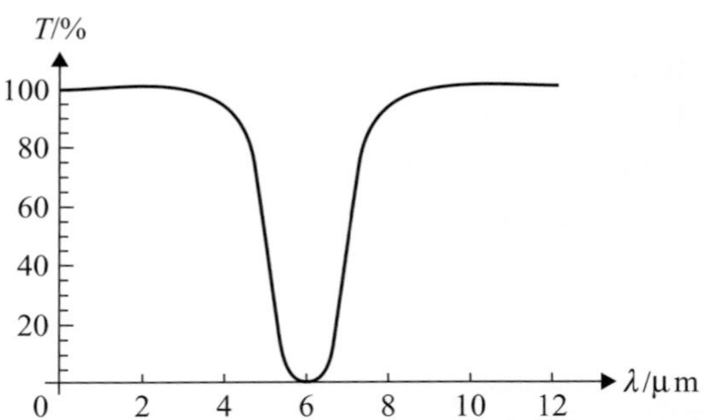

Figure 2.9 A typical transmittance curve for a gas, showing absorption at wavelengths around 6 μm.

Figure 2.10 shows the theoretical black-body spectrum of the sun and the actual spectrum due to absorption by gases in the atmosphere. A realistic transmittance curve is shown in Figure 2.11. It shows the transmittance, through the earth's atmosphere at sea level, for infrared radiation in the wavelength range 1×10^{-6} m to 15×10^{-6} m. There are very strong absorption bands at wavelengths of 1.1×10^{-6} m, 2.8×10^{-6} m and 4.1×10^{-6} m, and between 5.5×10^{-6} m and 7.5×10^{-6} m.

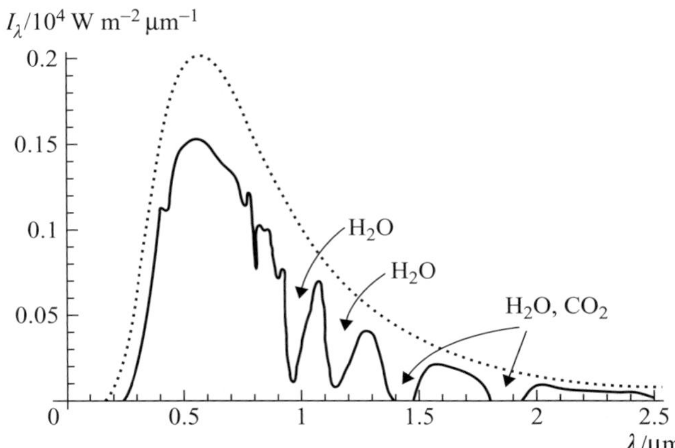

Figure 2.10 The dotted line shows the black-body spectrum of the sun. The solid line is the actual spectrum observed at the surface of the earth due to absorption of the incoming radiation by gases in the atmosphere.

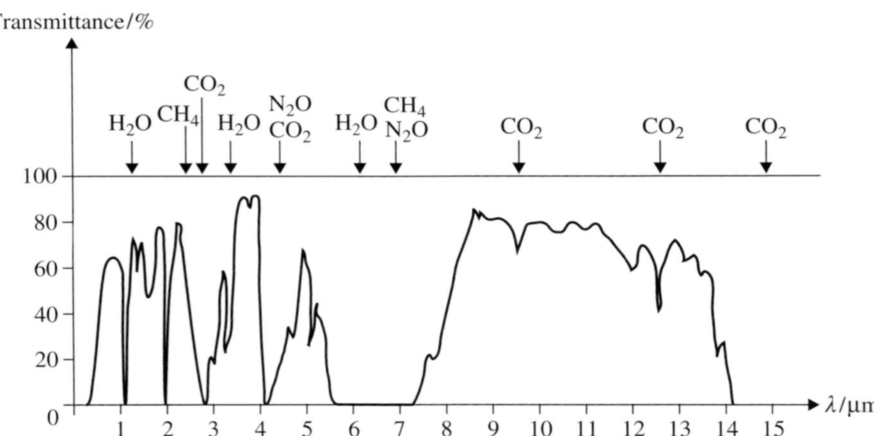

Figure 2.11 Transmittance curve showing absorption from various gases.

Surface heat capacity

We define C_S, the surface heat capacity of the body, to be the energy required to increase the temperature of 1 m^2 of the surface by 1 K. The concept is useful in the context of bodies radiating and absorbing energy, since it is the surface that is responsible for the energy lost and gained. The units of C_S are J m^{-2} K^{-1}. Thus, for a surface of surface heat capacity C_S and area A, the amount of thermal energy needed to increase its temperature by ΔT is given by

$$Q = AC_S\Delta T$$

Example question

Q4

Show that the surface heat capacity is related to the ordinary specific heat capacity c, through $C_S = \rho hc$, where ρ is the density of the material and h is the depth of the surface.

Answer

We have $Q = AC_S\Delta T$ and $Q = mc\Delta T$, and so $AC_S\Delta T = mc\Delta T$. But $m = \rho V = \rho Ah$, and hence

$$AC_S\Delta T = \rho Ahc\Delta T$$

$$C_S = \rho hc$$

This example shows that, in order to calculate the surface heat capacity, one must make estimates of the relevant depth h that will go into the expression. In addition, one has to take an average over various surface heat capacities corresponding to different materials on the surface, for example water, ice, dry land, etc. Thus, if we consider a surface of water of depth 100 m we would have

$$C_S = \rho hc = 10^3 \times 100 \times 4200 = 4.2 \times 10^8 \text{ J m}^{-2} \text{ K}^{-1}$$

The surface heat capacity of dry land is smaller by a factor of about 10.

Example question

Q5

Radiation of intensity 340 W m^{-2} is incident on the surface of a lake of surface heat capacity $C_S = 4.2 \times 10^8$ J m^{-2} K^{-1}. Calculate the time t required to increase the temperature by 2.0 K. Comment on your answer.

Answer

The thermal energy needed to increase the temperature by ΔT is given by $Q = AC_S\Delta T$.

This happens in time t and so

$$\frac{Q}{t} = AC_S\frac{\Delta T}{t}$$

$$\frac{Q/A}{t} = C_S\frac{\Delta T}{t}$$

$$I = C_S\frac{\Delta T}{t}$$

$$340 = 4.2 \times 10^8 \times \frac{2.0}{t}$$

$$t = \frac{4.2 \times 10^8 \times 2.0}{340}\ \text{s}$$

$$= 29 \text{ days}$$

We are assuming (unrealistically) that the lake receives the radiation for the entire duration of a day. The answer would be twice as long if the lake received the radiation for only 12 hours per day.

We can make use of the concept of surface heat capacity to make a very simple model of energy balance for a planet. Assume that a planet has surface heat capacity C_S. The planet receives a solar intensity of I_{in} and loses energy into space at a rate I_{out}. The net influx of power on the planet is then $I_{in} - I_{out}$. Over a time t the energy received by an area A of the planet's surface is then $(I_{in} - I_{out})At$, and so $(I_{in} - I_{out})At = AC_S\Delta T$. The increase of the planet's surface temperature after a time t is then

$$\Delta T = \frac{(I_{in} - I_{out})t}{C_S}$$

If $I_{in} > I_{out}$ then the temperature of the planet will increase.

This model is very unrealistic, of course, since even the smallest imbalance between I_{in} and I_{out} would result, over time, in an enormous temperature increase. The model assumes, for example, that the rate of temperature change is constant. A more realistic model would involve a variable rate and so would read

$$\frac{dT}{dt} = \frac{(I_{in} - I_{out})}{C_S}$$

Clearly, if $I_{in} = I_{out}$, the temperature stays constant. Because I_{out} certainly depends on the planet's temperature, this becomes a differential equation, which usually requires a computer to solve it.

Global warming

We have seen that the natural greenhouse effect works in order to keep the earth's temperature at 288 K. This makes life, as we know it, possible on earth. Due to human activities, the concentration of the greenhouse gases in the atmosphere is increasing, and this will lead to additional warming due to the enhanced greenhouse effect. Figure 2.12 shows the variation of the deviations of the earth's average temperature from the expected long-term average since 1880. The deviations are positive and increasing over the last 25 years.

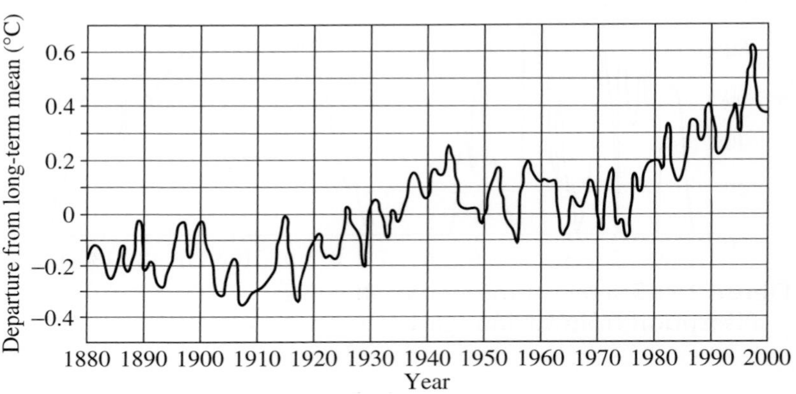

Figure 2.12 The deviation of the earth's global average surface temperature from the expected long-term average since 1880. (Source: US National Climatic Data Center, 2001.)

Figure 2.13 shows the variation with time of the concentrations of the main greenhouse gases over geological, recent and present time periods. The concentrations are all increasing. For carbon dioxide, in particular, the present concentrations are almost double those in pre-industrial times (before approximately the nineteenth century).

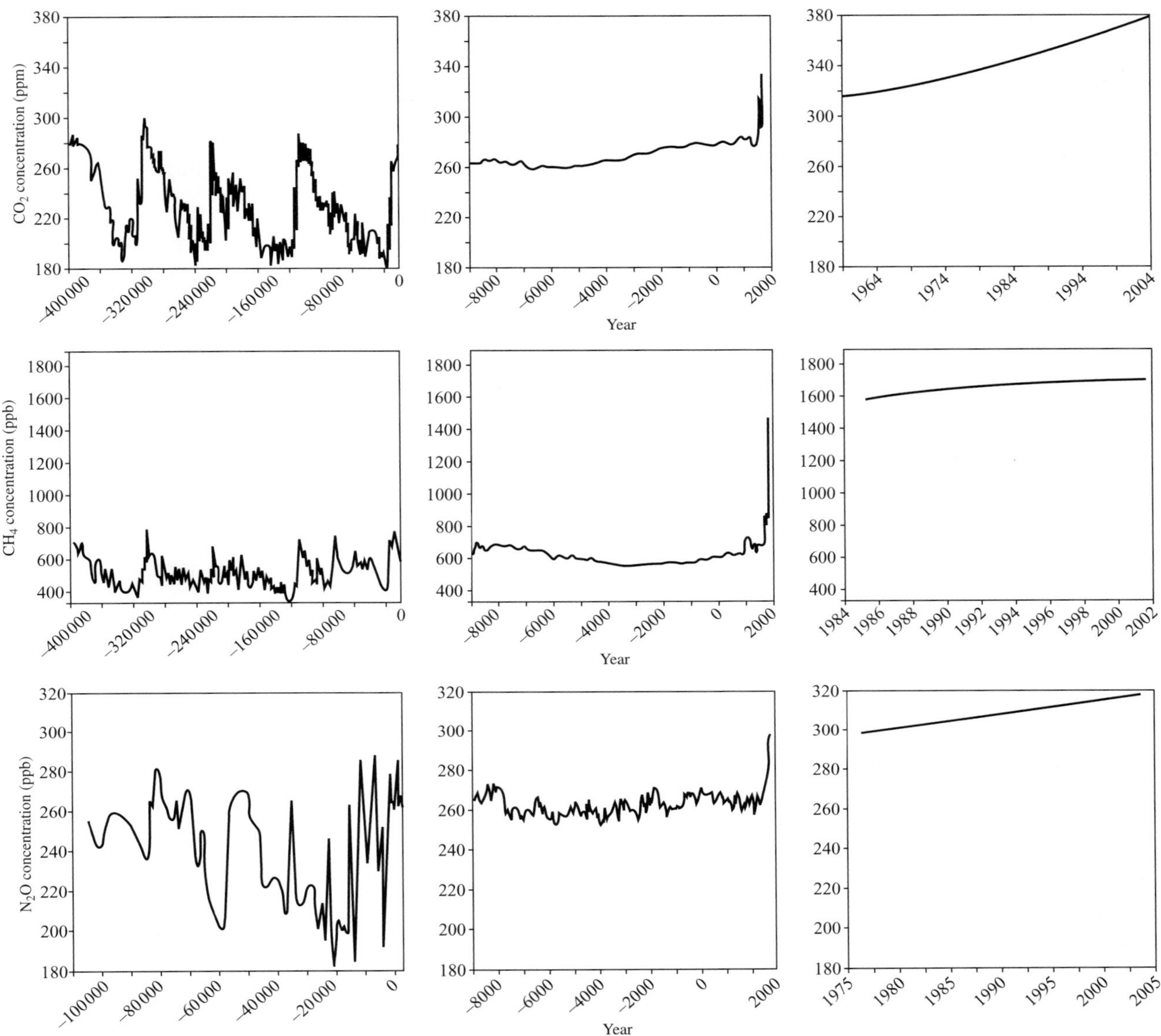

Figure 2.13 The concentrations of carbon dioxide, methane and nitrous oxide in the atmosphere. (Source: US Environmental Protection Agency.)

The graph of temperature in Figure 2.12 and the gas concentration graphs in Figure 2.13 are strong evidence of the connection between global warming and greenhouse gases. A criticism of the conclusion linking the two has been that the data do not cover a large enough time span. Countering this argument is the very impressive body of evidence collected from ice cores in Antarctica and Greenland. Analysing very old ice core samples gives, among many other things, information about gas concentrations and atmospheric temperature at the time of freezing. The results of this analysis are that there is a very close link between global warming and increased greenhouse gas concentrations.

The Antarctic ice cores, in particular, extracted from a depth of about 3600 m over (frozen) lake Vostok in East Antarctica in 1998, have been thoroughly analysed to reveal a connection between temperature changes and changes in carbon dioxide and methane concentrations. The ice cores give a detailed account of global climatic conditions over a time period spanning some 420 000 years.

Figure 2.14 shows the variation with time of the change in average world temperature relative to the present temperature. The curve indicates that the earth has been cooler for most of the last 400 000 years. The graph also shows that the earth was warmest whenever the levels of carbon dioxide in the atmosphere increased. Therefore, it is certain that the average global temperature of the earth will increase. What is uncertain is the *detailed* effect of this temperature increase on the global climate – in magnitude (How big will these effects be?) and in time scale (How soon will they happen?). Predicting these effects is a central problem for both scientists and policy-makers around the world.

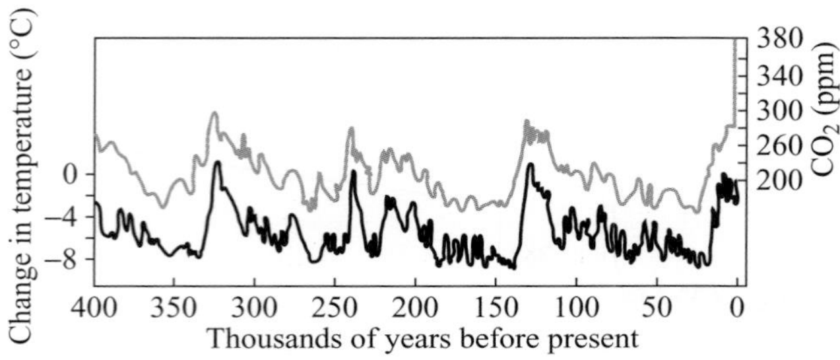

Figure 2.14 Changes in atmospheric carbon dioxide concentration (upper curve) and average temperature (lower curve) over the past 400 000 years show a strong correlation. Source: A. V. Fedorov et al., *Science*, **312**, 1485 (2006).

The questions that need answers are many. They include the following:

- What is the best estimate for the temperature increase, over a given time period?
- What will be the effects of a higher temperature on the amount of rainfall?
- How much ice will melt?
- What will be the rise in sea level?
- Will there be areas of extra dryness and drought and, if so, where will these areas be?
- Will the temperature of the oceans be affected and, if so, by how much?
- Will ocean currents be affected and, if so, how?
- Will there be periods of extreme climate variability?
- Will the frequency and intensity of tropical storms increase?
- What is the effect of sulphate aerosols in the atmosphere? Do they offset global warming?
- What are the feedback mechanisms affecting global climate?
- Can the observed temperature increase be blamed on greenhouse gases exclusively?
- Given the long lifetime of carbon dioxide in the atmosphere, can the process of global warming be reversed even if present emissions are drastically reduced?
- What are the ecological implications of the expected changes in the habitat of many species?
- What will be the effects on agriculture?
- Will there be more diseases?
- What are the social and economic effects of all of the above?

The majority of experts tend to agree that the enhanced greenhouse effect is behind global warming. Others have looked for different causes. One theory is that global warming may be due to increased solar activity, which results in an increased solar power output. It is known that the sun undergoes periodic changes in its total emitted power. These changes are complex phenomena and not very well understood. The general opinion is that the pattern of global warming is not consistent with the changes in solar activity. Other theories include increased concentrations of the greenhouse gases due to volcanic activity and changes in the earth's orbit around the sun (see end-of-chapter question 4 for a simple example). The changes involve variations in the *eccentricity* of the orbit as well as the 'tilt' of the orbit with respect to the sun. These are used to introduce variations in the received energy from the sun in order to account for changes in the temperature. These orbital phenomena occur over time scales ranging from 20 000 to 100 000 years. So, while they are relevant at these time scales, they are perhaps not so relevant for the climate changes of, say, the last 200 years.

Sea level

The level of water in the sea is always varying. Many reasons contribute to this, for example varying atmospheric pressure, plate tectonic movements, wind, tides, flow of large rivers into the sea, changes in water salinity and others.

What concerns us here are changes in sea level due to climate changes. The relation between climate and sea level is a complicated one. It is known that climate changes affect sea level through the fact that the temperature determines how much ice melts or how much water freezes. For example, it is known that, during the last ice age of 18 000 years ago, the sea level was lower than its present value by as much as 100 m.

▶ Changes in sea level affect the amount of water that can evaporate and the amount of thermal energy that can be exchanged with the atmosphere. In addition, changes in sea level affect ocean currents. The presence of these currents is vital in transferring thermal energy from the warm tropics to colder regions.

The melting of ice

To melt a mass m of ice at 0 °C requires an amount of thermal energy $Q = mL$, where L is the **specific latent heat of fusion** of ice. Thus, to melt ice, energy must be provided, and therefore cooling results at the place from where this energy is removed. For the purposes of discussing changes in sea level, we must distinguish between land ice (ice supported on land) and sea ice (ice floating in sea water). Sea ice, when melted, will not result in a change of sea level. This is a consequence of a principle of fluid mechanics known as Archimedes' principle. The weight of the ice is equal to the weight of the *displaced water* and so when the ice melts it will occupy a volume equal to the volume of the displaced water (i.e. no change in sea level will come about). By contrast, land ice, when melted, will result in an increased sea level.

Estimating changes in sea level

Overall, warming will, in general, result in a rise in sea level, not only because more land ice will melt but also because warmer water occupies a larger volume. The expansion of water is anomalous, however. Water will actually contract in volume as it is heated from 0 °C to 4 °C, and then will expand as the temperature is increased further from 4 °C. This means that the density of water is highest at 4 °C, a fact that is of considerable importance for life in lakes, rivers and oceans.

Given a volume V_0 at a temperature θ_0, the volume after a temperature increase of $\Delta\theta$ will increase by ΔV given by

$$\Delta V = \gamma V_0 \Delta\theta$$

where γ is a coefficient known as the **coefficient of volume expansion**.

▶ The *coefficient of volume expansion* is defined as the fractional change in volume per unit temperature change.

For water, the coefficient γ actually depends on temperature, and so a given volume of water will change by different amounts even for the same temperature changes $\Delta\theta$ depending on the initial temperature of the water.

The following example is a typical, rough estimate of the expected rise in sea level as a result of an increase in temperature.

Example question

Q6

The area of the oceans of the earth is about 3.6×10^8 km^2 and the average depth of water is about 3.7 km. Using a coefficient of volume expansion of water of 2×10^{-4} K^{-1}, estimate the expected rise in sea level after a temperature increase of 2 K. Comment on your answer.

Answer

The total volume of water in the oceans is approximately $V_0 = A \times d$, where A is the area and d is the average depth. So

$$V_0 = 3.6 \times 10^8 \times 3.7 = 1.33 \times 10^9 \text{ km}^3$$
$$= 1.33 \times 10^{18} \text{ m}^3$$

The increase in volume is then:

$$\Delta V = \gamma V_0 \Delta\theta$$
$$= 2 \times 10^{-4} \times 1.33 \times 10^{18} \times 2$$
$$= 5.3 \times 10^{14} \text{ m}^3$$

Sea level will increase by an amount h such that (converting A to m^2)

$$h = \frac{\Delta V}{A}$$
$$= \frac{5.3 \times 10^{14}}{3.6 \times 10^{14}}$$
$$= 1.5 \text{ m}$$

This estimate assumes a constant coefficient of expansion, uniform heating of all the water and does not take into account the initial water temperature. It also does not take into account the fact that, with a higher water temperature, more evaporation would take place, hence cooling the water. This estimate calculates the rise in sea level of the *existing* area of water. A rising sea would cover dry land and so the area of water would increase. This would *decrease* the height found in the estimate.

Effects of global warming on climate

A higher average earth temperature implies a rising sea level. One effect on climate of a rising sea level is the change in the albedo of the surface (more water as opposed to dry land). This effect is considered in the next example.

Example question

Q7

About 50% of the area of a certain large region of the earth's surface was covered by water. As a result of ice melting, 60% of this region is now covered by water. Estimate the change in the albedo of the region. Take the albedo of sea water to be $\alpha_S = 0.20$ and that of land to be $\alpha_L = 0.40$.

Answer

Let radiation of intensity I fall on the region. Then the total amount of radiation originally reflected was

$$\alpha_S \times 0.5I + \alpha_L \times 0.5I = (\alpha_S \times 0.5 + \alpha_L \times 0.5)I$$

The average albedo of the region was thus $\alpha_S \times 0.5 + \alpha_L \times 0.5$. With more water the albedo similarly becomes $\alpha_S \times 0.6 + \alpha_L \times 0.4$. The change in albedo is thus

$$\Delta\alpha = (\alpha_S \times 0.6 + \alpha_L \times 0.4) - (\alpha_S \times 0.5 + \alpha_L \times 0.5)$$
$$= 0.1 \times \alpha_S - 0.1 \times \alpha_L$$
$$= 0.1 \times (\alpha_S - \alpha_L)$$
$$= -0.1 \times 0.20$$
$$= -0.020$$

The albedo thus decreases, which means that a small additional warming can perhaps be expected. (This is an example of positive feedback – warming causes ice to melt, which in turn decreases the albedo, which results in additional warming.)

The expected changes in temperature due to a change in albedo, because of more water covering land, are actually small. A more significant effect of ice melting and the sea level rising is expected to be the fact that, with more water, and at a higher temperature, the evaporation rate will increase and therefore more water vapour will be released into the atmosphere. This means:

- cooling of the earth's surface (because latent heat is given to the water in order to evaporate);
- more cloud cover (and therefore more reflected radiation);
- more precipitation (i.e. rain, but not necessarily in the region of interest).

An additional effect of higher temperatures on climate is the fact that carbon dioxide solubility in the oceans decreases. This means that more carbon dioxide is left in the atmosphere.

The next example discusses another factor affecting global climate, deforestation.

Example question

Q8

Large areas of rainforests are being destroyed by cutting down (and burning) trees. Discuss the possible effects of this on the energy balance of the region.

Answer

Changing forests to dry land has three immediate consequences. The first is that the low albedo of the dark, moist forests is replaced by a higher albedo – this tends to reduce temperatures since more radiation is reflected rather than absorbed. The second is that the evaporation rate is decreased – this tends to increase temperatures since the surface no longer has to supply the latent heat for evaporation. The two are thus opposing effects. Models show that, regionally, there are no significant changes in temperature as a result of deforestation. The local precipitation rate, though, generally drops. The third factor is that by removing the forests and burning the trees a carbon dioxide sink is removed (the trees) and more carbon dioxide is produced (by burning the trees). It is estimated that two billion tonnes of carbon dioxide has been released into the atmosphere as a result of deforestation. This, as we have seen, enhances the greenhouse effect.

The issue of deforestation is still a bit controversial. Rainforests must, of course, be preserved in order to maintain the existing habitat and thus prevent the extinction of very many animal and plant species. However, the effect of deforestation on climate is uncertain because rainforests do produce methane and thus contribute to the increased concentrations of greenhouse gases. Forests do absorb carbon dioxide but that is returned to the atmosphere when the trees die and decompose.

Measures to reduce global warming

There is clearly an urgent need to stop the increase in all the greenhouse gases, and carbon dioxide in particular. Measures to achieve this include the following:

- using fuel-efficient cars and developing hybrid cars further;
- increasing the efficiency of coal-burning power plants;
- replacing coal-burning power plants with natural gas-fired plants;
- considering methods of capturing and storing the carbon dioxide produced in power plants (carbon capture and storage, CCS);
- increasing the amounts of power produced by wind and solar generators;
- considering nuclear power;
- being energy conscious, with buildings, appliances, transportation, industrial processes and entertainment;
- stopping deforestation.

The Kyoto protocol and the IPCC

An extremely important agreement towards cutting greenhouse gas emissions was reached in 1997, in Kyoto, Japan. The industrial nations agreed to reduce their emissions of greenhouse gases by 5.2% from the 1990 levels over the period from 2008 to 2012. The protocol allowed mechanisms for developed nations to use projects aimed at reducing emissions in developing nations as part of their own reduction targets. Endorsed by 160 countries, the protocol would become legally binding if at least 55 countries signed it. The non-ratification of the protocol by the USA and Australia has weakened the impact of the agreement.

Unlike the Kyoto protocol, which imposed mandatory limits for greenhouse gas emissions, the Asia–Pacific Partnership on Clean Development and Climate (APPCDC, or AP6) asked for voluntary reductions of these emissions. It was signed by the USA, Australia, India, the People's Republic of China, Japan and South Korea in 2005. It is an agreement in which the signatory nations agree to cooperate in reducing emissions. It has been criticized as worthless because the reductions are voluntary.

It has been defended because it includes China and India, major greenhouse gas producers, who are not bound by the Kyoto protocol.

A major, comprehensive, detailed and scientifically impartial analysis of global climate has been undertaken by the Intergovernmental Panel on Climate Change (IPCC). The IPCC was created by the World Meteorological Organization (WMO) and the United Nations Environment Programme (UNEP) in 1988. While conducting no research of its own, the IPCC reports on technical, scientific and socio-economic aspects of climate change using assessments of existing published scientific material. Its four reports in 1990, 1997, 2001 and 2007 have been instrumental in providing an accurate analysis of the global situation.

QUESTIONS

1 (a) State what you understand by the term *black body*.
(b) Give an example of a body that is a good approximation to a black body.
(c) By what factor does the rate of radiation from a body increase when the temperature is increased from 50 °C to 100 °C?

2 The graphs in Figure 2.15 show the variation with wavelength of the intensity of radiation emitted by two bodies of identical shape.

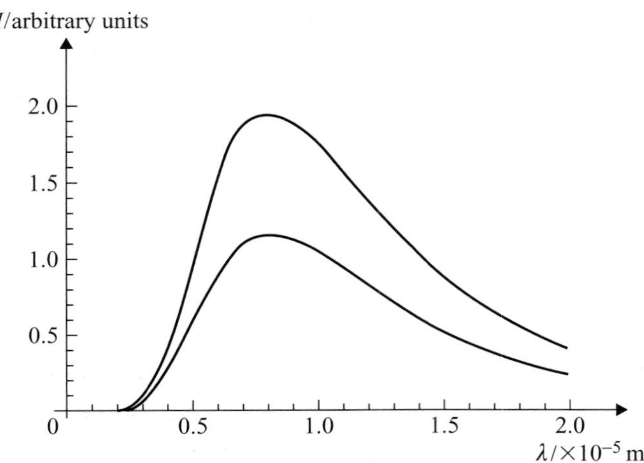

Figure 2.15 For question 2.

(a) Explain why the temperature of the two bodies is the same.
(b) The upper graph actually corresponds to a black body. Calculate the emissivity of the other body.

3 The total power radiated by a body of area 5.00 km^2 and emissivity 0.800 is 1.35×10^9 W. Assume that the body radiates into vacuum at temperature 0 K. Calculate the temperature of the body.

4 If the distance d between the sun and the earth decreases, the earth's average temperature T will go up. The fraction of the power radiated by the sun that is received on earth is proportional to $\frac{1}{d^2}$; the power radiated by the earth is proportional to T^4.
(a) Deduce the dependence of the temperature T of the earth on the distance d.
(b) Hence estimate the expected rise in temperature if the distance decreases by 1.0%. Take the average temperature of the earth to be 288 K.

5 (a) Define the term *intensity* in the context of radiation.
(b) *Estimate* the intensity of radiation emitted by a naked human body of surface area 1.60 m^2, temperature 37 °C and emissivity 0.90, a distance of 5.0 m from the body.

6 A body radiates energy at a rate (power) P.
(a) Deduce that the intensity of this radiation at distance d from the body is given by

$$I = \frac{P}{4\pi d^2}$$

(b) State one assumption made in deriving this result.

7 The graph in Figure 2.16 shows the variation with wavelength of the intensity of the radiation emitted by a black body.
(a) Determine the temperature of the black body.
(b) Copy the diagram, and, on the same axes, draw a graph to show the variation with wavelength of the intensity of radiation emitted by a black body of temperature 600 K.

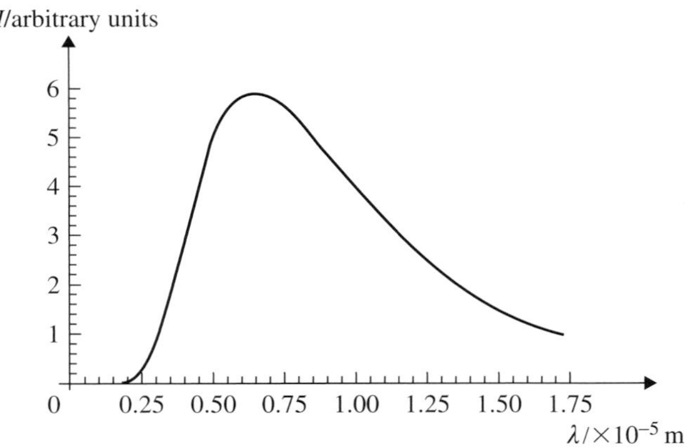

Figure 2.16 For question 7.

8 (a) Define the term *albedo*.
(b) State three factors that the albedo of a surface depends on.

9 A researcher uses the following data for a simple climatic model of an earth without an atmosphere (see Example question 3 in the text): incident solar radiation = 350 W m^{-2}, absorbed solar radiation = 250 W m^{-2}.
(a) Make an energy flow diagram for this data.
(b) Determine the average albedo for the earth that is to be used in the modelling.
(c) Determine the intensity of the outgoing long-wave radiation.
(d) Estimate the temperature of the earth according to this model, assuming a constant earth temperature.

10 Radiation of intensity 340 W m^{-2} is incident on a lake of depth 50 m.
(a) How much time is needed to increase the water temperature by 1 K?
(b) Estimate the heat capacity of the entire body of water on earth. (Use an average depth of 300 m if you cannot find a better estimate.)
(c) Then estimate the time needed to increase the water temperature by 1 K if solar radiation of intensity 340 W m^{-2} were incident on the water.

11 (a) Repeat the calculations of the simple model presented in Example question 3 for the planets Venus and Mars in order to predict their surface temperatures. Take the distances to the sun to be 1.08×10^{11} m (Venus) and 2.28×10^{11} m (Mars), and use a solar power output of 3.9×10^{26} W. Assume that the albedo α for Venus is 0.59 and that for Mars is 0.15.
(b) The actual surface temperatures are 740 K (Venus) and 213 K (Mars). What do your answers in (a) suggest about the atmospheres of Venus and Mars?

12 Make a simple model of the greenhouse effect as in Figure 2.17. Assume that only a fraction t of the energy radiated by the earth actually leaves the earth.
(a) Copy the diagram and complete the three boxes (i)–(iii) to show the intensities involved.
(b) Write the energy balance equation and calculate t so that the temperature is $T \approx 288$ K. Take $\frac{S}{4} = 350$ W m^{-2} and the earth albedo to be 0.30.

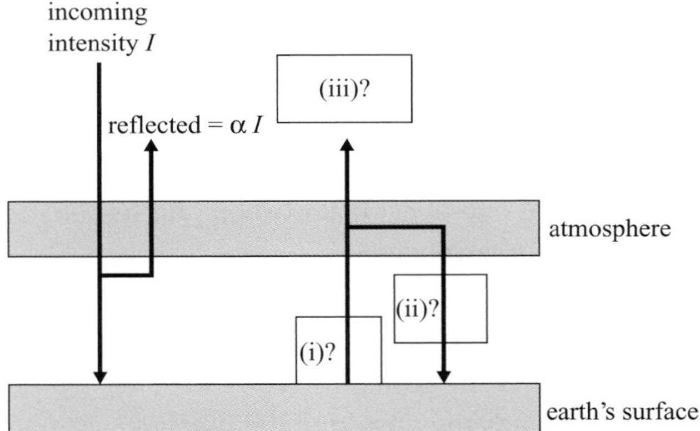

Figure 2.17 For question 12.

13 (a) Define *surface heat capacity*.
(b) State an order-of-magnitude estimate for the ratio $\frac{\text{surface heat capacity of water}}{\text{surface heat capacity of land}}$.
(c) Use your estimate to explain why the climate over water changes much more slowly than the climate over land.

14 Outline the main ways in which the surface of the earth loses thermal energy to the atmosphere and to space.

15 A researcher making climate simulations wants to investigate the effects of deforestation by changing the value of the albedo in her calculations. Should she increase or decrease the albedo?

16 (a) How does the albedo of a subtropical, warm, dry land compare to that of a tropical ocean?
(b) Suggest mechanisms through which the subtropical land and the tropical ocean lose thermal energy to the atmosphere.
(c) If the sea level were to increase, sea water would cover dry land. Suggest one change in the regional climate that might come about as a result.

17 Suggest a reason why covering dry land near the equator by water would have a smaller effect on climate than covering subtropical land with water. (*Hint*: Consider the fact that equatorial land is probably better covered by vegetation than subtropical land, and concentrate on the fact that the albedo of vegetation and water are almost the same.)

18 Evaporation is a method of thermal energy loss. Do you expect this method to be more significant for a tropical ocean or an arctic ocean? Explain your answer.

19 (a) State one effect that evaporation has on the earth's surface.
(b) State one effect that evaporation has on the atmosphere.

20 Radiation is incident on a planet with an atmosphere. Figure 2.18 shows the energy balance of the planet.
(a) What is the albedo of the planet?
(b) How can it be deduced that the planet's temperature is constant?

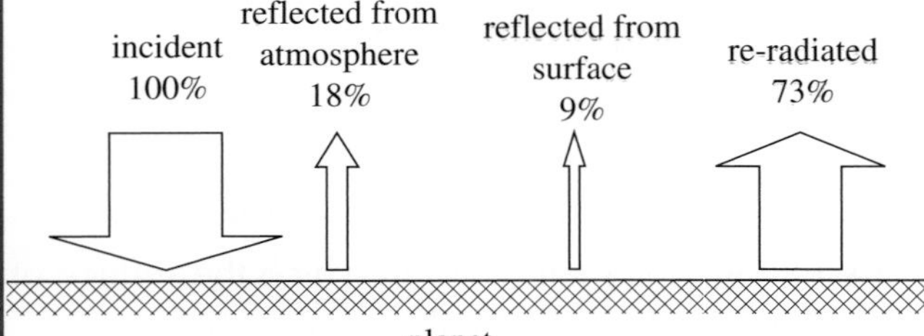

Figure 2.18 For question 20.

21 Figure 2.19 shows two energy flow diagrams for thermal energy transfer to and from specific areas of the surface of the earth.

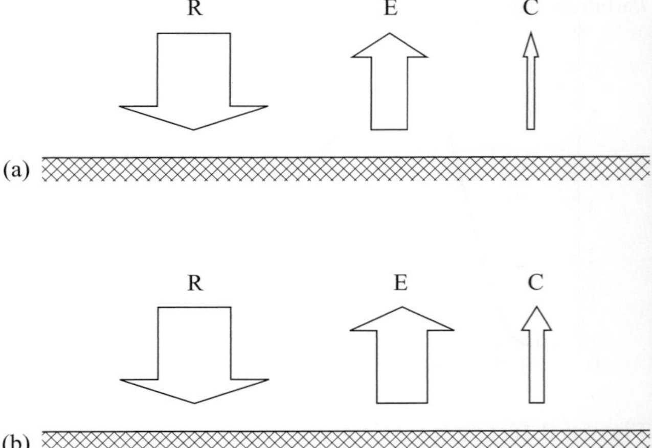

Figure 2.19 For question 21.

R represents the net energy incident on the surface in the form of radiation; E is the thermal energy lost from the earth due to evaporation; and C is the thermal energy conducted to the atmosphere because of the temperature difference between the surface and the atmosphere. Suggest, giving a reason, whether the earth area in each diagram is most likely dry and cool or moist and warm.

22 Draw a sketch graph to show how the latent heat flux from the earth's surface depends on latitude.

23 It is estimated that a change of albedo by 0.01 will result in a 1 °C temperature change. A large area of the earth consists of 60% water and 40% land. Calculate the expected change in temperature if melting ice causes a change in the proportion of the area covered by water from 60% to 70%. Take the albedo of dry land to be 0.30 and that of water to be 0.10.

24 (a) State what is meant by the *greenhouse effect*.
(b) State the main greenhouse gases in the earth's atmosphere, and for each give three natural and three man-made sources.

25 Distinguish between the *natural* greenhouse effect and the *enhanced* greenhouse effect.

26 Outline the evidence that links increased concentrations of carbon dioxide with global warming over a long period of time.

27 (a) Describe what is meant by a transmittance curve.

(b) Figure 2.20 shows a transmittance curve for IR radiation through the atmosphere. Discuss the changes you would expect to the general shape of this curve if the concentrations of carbon dioxide were to be reduced drastically.

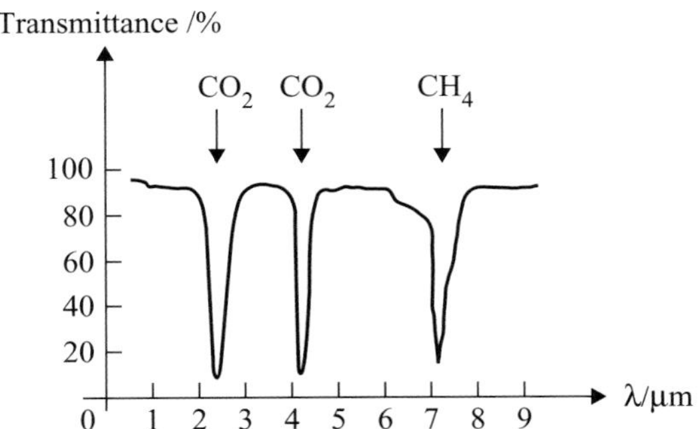

Figure 2.20 For question 27.

28 (a) State and explain two ways in which a rising sea level affects the global climate.

(b) State two physical mechanisms that may contribute to increased sea levels.

29 An iceberg of total mass 10^5 kg floats in water.

(a) Assuming a constant temperature of 0 °C for the iceberg, calculate the amount of energy required to melt it. Take the specific latent heat of fusion of ice to be 330 kJ kg^{-1}.

(b) State whether or not this will result in an increased sea level.

30 The area of the Mediterranean Sea is approximately 2.5×10^6 km^2 and the average depth of water is about 1.5 km. Using a coefficient of volume expansion of water of 2×10^{-4} K^{-1}, estimate the expected rise in sea level after a temperature increase of 3 K. State any assumptions made in your estimate.

31 The West Antarctic ice sheet, if it melts, will result in a 6 m sea level rise. Estimate the volume of this ice sheet. List any assumptions you make.

32 Suggest effects of deforestation on the global climate.

33 State two mechanisms, other than the enhanced greenhouse effect, which have been postulated to account for global warming.

34 List measures that might help to reduce global warming.

35 Outline the recommendations of the Kyoto protocol.

36 What is the IPCC and what does it do?

Analogue and digital signals

This chapter introduces binary numbers, and analogue and digital signals. Various storage devices using information in analogue or digital form are briefly discussed.

Objectives

By the end of this chapter you should be able to:

- convert *decimal numbers into binary numbers* and vice versa;
- understand the *difference* between an *analogue signal* and a *digital signal*;
- convert an *analogue signal into a digital signal*;
- outline the structure of a *compact disc*;
- appreciate the role of *interference* in reading a CD;
- calculate *pit depths* in terms of the *wavelength* of light used;
- outline the basic *structure* of various *storage devices*;
- outline the *advantages of digital storage*.

Binary numbers

In ordinary arithmetic, we use the decimal system to represent numbers, which means that we use the ten digits from 0 to 9. In the **binary system**, numbers are represented using only the two digits 0 and 1. Consider a decimal number like 5037. Its 'ones' digit is 7, its 'tens' digit is 3, its 'hundreds' digit is 0, and its 'thousands' digit is 5. Each digit is associated with a power of 10. The 'ones' digit is associated with 10^0, the 'tens' with 10^1, the 'hundreds' with 10^2, and the 'thousands' digit with 10^3. Then

$$5037 = \underline{5} \times 10^3 + \underline{0} \times 10^2 + \underline{3} \times 10^1 + \underline{7} \times 10^0$$

So the digits of a decimal number are just the coefficients of various powers of 10. These coefficients can be the digits from 0 to 9.

The same idea applies to binary numbers. The difference is that we will be using powers of 2 rather than 10, and the coefficients will be the digits 0 or 1 rather than the digits from 0 to 9.

For example, suppose we wanted to express the decimal number 5 in the binary system. First, we write the number 5 as a sum of powers of the number 2 with coefficients that are either 0 or 1 (the coefficients of the powers of 2 are shown underlined):

$$5 = \underline{1} \times 2^2 + \underline{0} \times 2^1 + \underline{1} \times 2^0$$

The binary representation of 5 is then given by the coefficients of the powers of 2, i.e. the underlined numbers. We use the notation 5_2 to mean the binary representation of the number 5. So

$$5_2 = 101$$

Similarly the number 12 is

$$12 = \underline{1} \times 2^3 + \underline{1} \times 2^2 + \underline{0} \times 2^1 + \underline{0} \times 2^0$$

$$12_2 = 1100$$

and the decimal number 14 in the binary system is

$$14 = \underline{1} \times 2^3 + \underline{1} \times 2^2 + \underline{1} \times 2^1 + \underline{0} \times 2^0$$

$$14_2 = 1110$$

These binary representations each used four digits. They are four-bit **words**. A decimal number like 5 is represented by 101 that has only three bits. We can make that into four bits by adding zeros in front. Thus decimal 5 becomes 0101. The decimal number 4 as a four-bit word is

$$4 = \underline{1} \times 2^2 + \underline{0} \times 2^1 + \underline{0} \times 2^0$$

$$4_2 = 100 = 0100$$

With four-bit words (i.e. four digits), we can represent only a finite number of numbers, namely $2^4 = 16$ numbers. (This is because for each of the four digits we have the choice of 0 or 1, i.e. two choices. The total number of choices is then $2 \times 2 \times 2 \times 2 = 2^4 = 16$.) These are the numbers from 0 to 15. To represent larger numbers, we have to increase the number of bits in the binary representation of the number.

Example questions

Q1

How many numbers can be represented with five-bit words?

Answer

With five bits we can have at most $2^5 = 32$ numbers. These are the numbers from 0 to 31.

Q2

Write the decimal number 65 as a binary number using eight bits.

Answer

First write the number in terms of its coefficients and powers of 2 as

$$65 = \underline{1} \times 2^6 + \underline{0} \times 2^5 + \underline{0} \times 2^4 + \underline{0} \times 2^3 + \underline{0} \times 2^2 + \underline{0} \times 2^1 + \underline{1} \times 2^0$$

$$65_2 = 1000001$$

This uses seven digits. As an eight-bit word, the number would be 01000001.

Q3

Express the eight-bit binary number 01010101 as a decimal.

Answer

The number is shown below. We have put the appropriate power of 2 under each digit.

01010101
76543210

So

$$01010101 \rightarrow \underline{0} \times 2^7 + \underline{1} \times 2^6 + \underline{0} \times 2^5 + \underline{1} \times 2^4 + \underline{0} \times 2^3 + \underline{1} \times 2^2 + \underline{0} \times 2^1 + \underline{1} \times 2^0$$

$$= 0 + 64 + 0 + 16 + 0 + 4 + 0 + 1 = 85$$

Q4

What is the least number of bits needed to express the decimal number 2008 as a binary number?

Answer

The *smallest* power of 2 that exceeds 2008 is 11, since $2^{11} = 2048 > 2008$. Hence we must use 11 bits in the binary representation of 2008 (in fact, $2008_2 = 11111011000$).

Given a number in binary form, we call the leftmost digit the **most significant bit** (MSB) and the last digit (the digit the number ends with) the **least significant bit** (LSB). Thus the binary number 01111 has 0 as its MSB and 1 as its LSB. The MSB is associated with the highest power of 2, and so it is the digit that mostly determines the value of the number.

Analogue and digital signals

When one speaks into a microphone, a voltage in created in the microphone. The voltage is proportional (directly related) to the actual physical movement of the diaphragm of the microphone. A large voltage is created when the diaphragm moves fast, and a small voltage when it moves slowly. The voltage signal so generated varies *continuously* between two extreme values. Such signals are called **analogue signals**. An example is shown in Figure 1.1.

▶ Analogue signals are continuous signals, varying between two extreme values in a way that is proportional to the physical mechanism that created the signal.

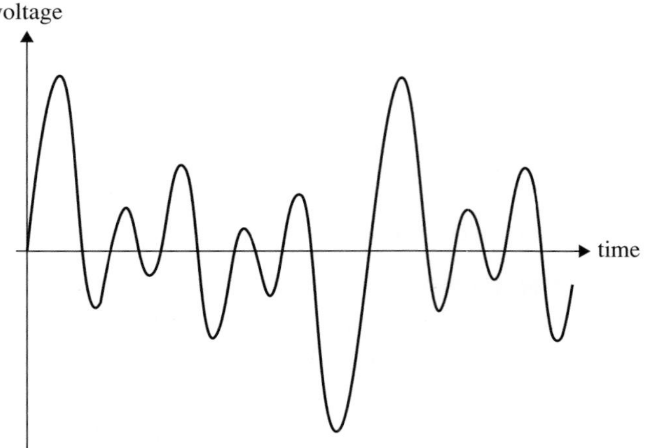

Figure 1.1 An analogue signal.

A **digital signal** by contrast is not continuous. It can only take a discrete set of values. An example is shown in Figure 1.2.

▶ A digital signal is a coded form of a signal that takes the discrete values 0 or 1 only.

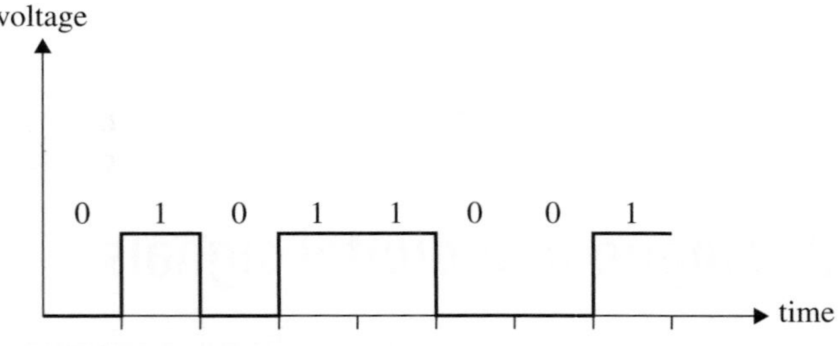

Figure 1.2 A digital signal.

Consider the potential divider circuit of Figure 1.3. The emf of the battery is 8 V. This means that the reading of the voltmeter V can be any number between 0 and 8 V depending on where the lead (indicated by the arrow) connects to the variable resistor R. Touching at the bottom of the resistor gives 0 V and touching at the top gives 8 V (assuming no internal resistance in the battery). The signal generated in the voltmeter is an analogue signal.

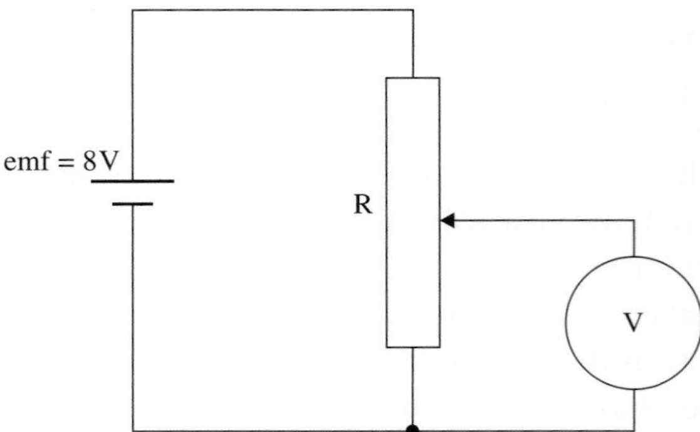

Figure 1.3 The voltmeter can have any reading from 0 V to 8 V.

Imagine that we move the point of contact from the bottom end of the resistor to the top at a constant speed. Assume further that this is done in 4 ms. Then, the reading of the voltmeter would be the time-dependent signal shown in Figure 1.4.

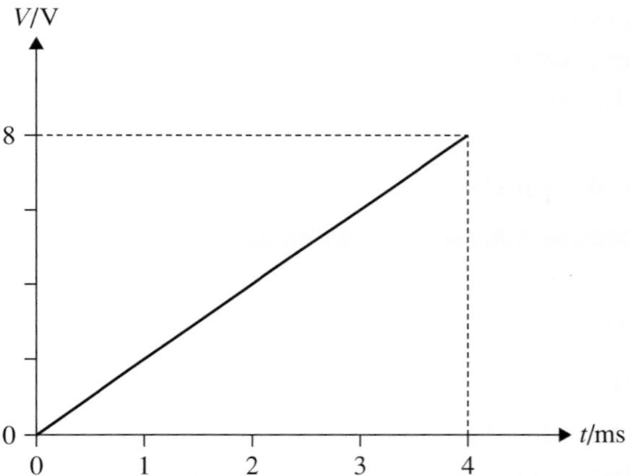

Figure 1.4 The reading of the voltmeter is an analogue signal.

This analogue signal must then be *sampled*, which means that it must be measured. This is done at regular intervals of time. The number of times per second the signal is sampled (measured) is called the *sampling rate* or *sampling frequency*. Sampling the signal means that we observe it for very short intervals of time, wait, and then sample it again. Thus we do not, in general, know how the signal behaves in between the instants of time when it is sampled. Typically, for audio signals, a sampling rate of 8000 times per second is used. This means that such an audio signal is sampled every $\frac{1}{8000} = 125\ \mu s$.

As an example, consider sampling the analogue signal of Figure 1.4 every 1 ms. This would result in the *pulse amplitude modulated* signal (PAM signal) in Figure 1.5. The result of this sampling is shown in Table 1.1.

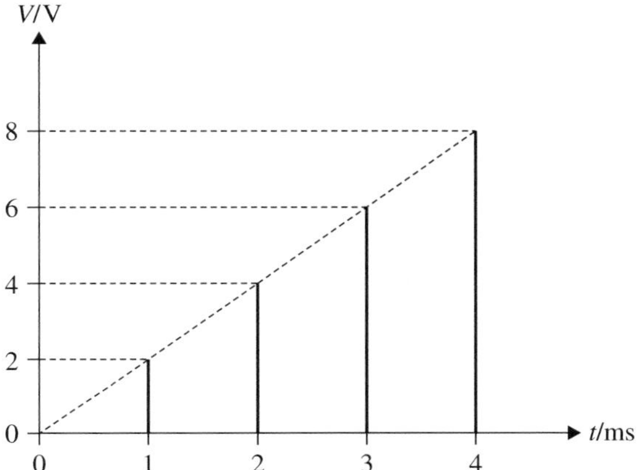

Figure 1.5 The analogue signal of Figure 1.4 is sampled every 1 ms.

Time/ms	PAM signal/V
0	0
1	2
2	4
3	6
4	8

Table 1.1 The analogue signal has been discretized by the PAM process.

Notice that the actual duration of one sample is very short (e.g. 2.0 μs, 1.0 μs or even much less), which is why we represent the sampled signal by vertical lines of practically zero width in Figure 1.5. The fact that the actual sampling time is very short compared to the time in between consecutive samplings will be important later on.

Now suppose we wish to convert the voltage readings into binary numbers using two-bit words. This means that we can handle at most $2^2 = 4$ words, namely 00, 01, 10 and 11. We can then split the range of the original voltage (0–8 V) into four levels (0–2, 2–4, 4–6, 6–8), and we will assign to each level a two-bit word. In each level there is a lower boundary and an upper boundary. The result is shown in Table 1.2.

PAM signal V/V	Binary code
$0 \le V < 2$	00
$2 \le V < 4$	01
$4 \le V < 6$	10
$6 \le V < 8$	11

Table 1.2 The analogue signal has been converted into a digital two-bit binary code.

What we have done is to take the lower boundary voltage in each level, divide it by 2 (because 2 = highest voltage divided by number of words) to get the voltages 0, 1, 2 and 3. We then convert these numbers into binaries with two digits. (Converting from binary numbers to decimals gives the voltages 0, 1, 2 and 3 V. The fact that we divided by 2 is not important, as it is the relative size of the signals that matters.)

Obviously there is a loss of information in this digitization of the original data. We can do better by using a higher sampling frequency (e.g. every 0.5 ms rather than every 1 ms) and use three-bit words (a maximum of $2^3 = 8$) and digitize the data as shown in Table 1.3.

PAM signal V/V	Binary code
$0 \le V < 1$	000
$1 \le V < 2$	001
$2 \le V < 3$	010
$3 \le V < 4$	011
$4 \le V < 5$	100
$5 \le V < 6$	101
$6 \le V < 7$	110
$7 \le V < 8$	111

Table 1.3 The same signal is now in three-bit binary code.

Here we have taken the lower boundary voltage and converted that into a binary number. It is not necessary to divide by anything here since the highest voltage is 8 V and the number of words is also eight.

The process of dividing the range of the analogue signal (highest value minus lowest value) into a set of levels is called **quantization**, and the levels themselves are called **quantization levels**. The number of quantization levels is determined, as we have seen, by the length of the word to be used, i.e. by the number of bits used. With n bits, the number of quantization levels is 2^n.

This gives rise to the notion of **quantization error**. Suppose that the analogue signal varies from a minimum value of m to a maximum value of M and we use n-bit words to digitize it. The number of quantization levels is 2^n, and so at each sampling the analogue signal will take one of these 2^n values. The quantity $q = \frac{M-m}{2^n}$ is known as the quantization error of the digitization process. In Table 1.2 the quantization error is 2 V and in Table 1.3 it is 1 V. Two analogue signal values that differ by less than the quantization error are assigned the same binary number.

Compact disks

A compact disk (CD) is a device on which information can be stored in digital form. The information can then be retrieved; for example, if it is music that is stored, the music can be played on a CD player or a computer. The CD is a disk of diameter 12 cm. Consider, for concreteness, a music CD. The analogue music signal is first converted into a digital signal (a series of '0's and '1's as described above). This sequence is now imprinted on the CD. This is done by making marks called **pits** on the CD. The parts of the path on the CD without pits are sometimes called **lands**. The *edge* of a pit corresponds to binary '1'. A series of pits is made along a path that spirals from the centre of the disk outwards (Figure 1.6).

Figure 1.6 The pits and the lands are placed along a spiral on the surface of the disk.

The distance between adjacent paths is very small, 1600 nm. The width of a pit is 500 nm, its length varies from 830 nm to 3560 nm, and its depth is about 125 nm (Figure 1.7). These are astonishingly small numbers. For example, the pit width is comparable to the wavelength of green light.

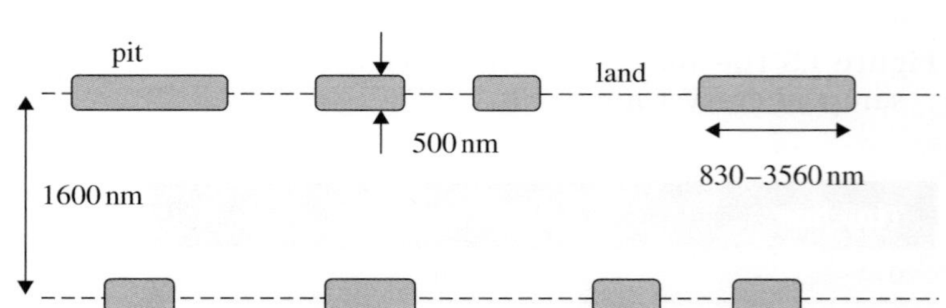

Figure 1.7 Two neighbouring tracks with pits and lands.

The bottom surface of the disk (the side that is actually being read) is covered with optically transparent material (a polycarbonate). The question now is how to extract the information from the CD. This means reading the '0's and the '1's that have been imprinted on the surface of the disk. This is done with a laser beam.

Consider a laser beam that is directed on the disk (bottom side). The beam cannot have a zero width. So when the beam is incident near the *edge* of a pit, a few of the rays in the beam will be reflected off the pit and the rest will be reflected off the land (Figure 1.8). This means that these rays will interfere, because they are coherent (they are part of the same laser beam). The light that gets reflected from a land travels an extra distance $2d$, and this is the path difference between the two sets of rays. If we choose $2d$ to be equal to half a wavelength, i.e.

$$d = \frac{\lambda}{4}$$

the interference will be destructive and the reflected light will have zero intensity. Thus when the detector of the reflected laser light (a photodiode) receives zero intensity, the laser is at a pit–land edge and this corresponds to binary '1'.

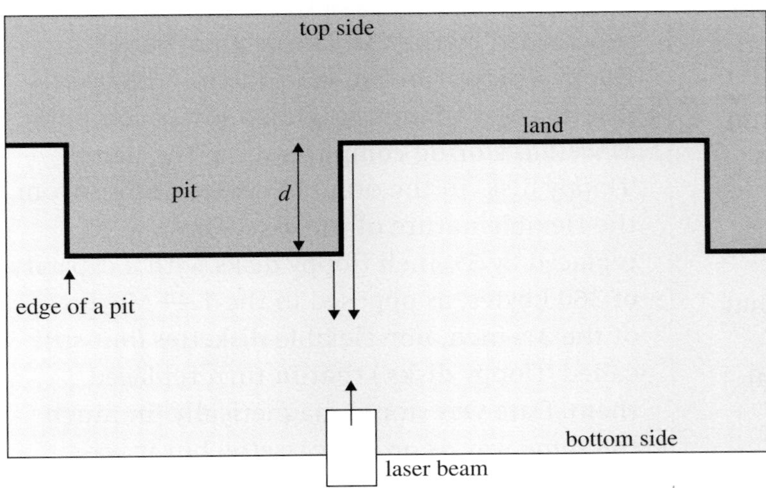

Figure 1.8 Destructive interference takes place when the laser light is reflected near a pit edge. (Note that a pit on the top surface becomes a bump when looked at from the bottom. For our purposes here it is largely irrelevant what we call a particular spot. The objective is to be able to tell the difference between the two. So we will call a pit/bump by the name *pit*.)

The wavelength of the laser light used is about 780 nm in air. The index of refraction of the polycarbonate material is about 1.55, which means that the wavelength of light in the polycarbonate is

$$\lambda = \frac{\lambda_{air}}{n} = \frac{780}{1.55} = 503 \text{ nm}$$

The pit depth must then be

$$d = \frac{\lambda}{4} = \frac{503}{4} = 126 \text{ nm}$$

The laser source moves outwards and so follows the spiral of the pits and lands as the disk rotates. Because the circumference is getting longer as we move outwards, the rate of rotation of the disk is reduced, so that the laser can sample the disk at the same rate. There are clearly many technical problems to be solved here, such as stability, focusing on the right part of the spiral, and timing.

Example questions

Q5

Calculate the pit depth for CDs that are to be read by a CD player operating with a laser (in the polycarbonate) of wavelength 600 nm.

Answer

The pit depth must be one-quarter of the wavelength, and so the depth should be 150 nm.

Q6

Information is imprinted on a CD at a rate of 44 100 words per second. The information consists of 32-bit words (actually two channels of 16-bit samples each). A CD lasts for 74 minutes. Calculate the storage capacity of a CD.

Answer

The number of bits imprinted on the CD is

$$44\,100 \times 32 \times 74 \times 60 = 6.27 \times 10^9 \text{ bits}$$

Since 1 byte = 8 bits this corresponds to

$$\frac{6.27 \times 10^9}{8} \approx 780 \times 10^6 \text{ bytes} = 780 \text{ Mbytes}.$$

Other storage devices

DVDs

The DVD (digital versatile disk) is similar to the CD in many ways. Here the pit length is shorter than on a CD, allowing more data to be stored along the spiral. In addition, data can be stored on both sides of the disk or in a double layer on the same side. Overall, this results in more than seven times the storage capacity compared to that of a CD.

LPs

In Edison's original sound recording in 1877, sound was incident on a diaphragm, which therefore began to vibrate. A needle attached to the diaphragm then made marks on a rotating tinfoil-covered cylinder. The 'marks' were a direct, mechanical copy of the actual audio signal. During playback, the needle retraces the pattern scratched on the cylinder surface and now makes the diaphragm move, thus reproducing the sound stored. In the later vinyl LPs the principle of recording is essentially the same, except that, instead of a rotating cylinder, a flat rotating disk is used. During playback, the signal is amplified electrically and fed into a loudspeaker, rather than directly making a diaphragm vibrate. LPs have a very limited storage capacity and are subject to damage (by scratches and dust). They have been mainly superseded by CDs. But some people insist that Maria Callas in Bellini's *Norma* is far more sublime in the original LP than in any digital version!

Cassettes

These devices, popular in the 1960s and 1970s, but now completely superseded by CDs, use *magnetic recording* to store data in analogue form. They are what are called *sequential* devices. For example, if ten songs are recorded on a cassette and you want to get to song number 6, you must wind the cassette until you get to the song you want. This takes time. The recording takes place on the ribbon of the cassette, which is made out of a strong plastic tape coated in ferric oxide, a ferromagnetic material, which means that it can be permanently magnetized when exposed to a magnetic field. The analogue audio signal of music, say, is converted to a varying electric current. The varying current produces its own varying magnetic field. When the tape of the cassette is exposed to this magnetic field, a 'copy' of this magnetic field is created on the tape. During playback, the magnetic field stored on the tape will induce an electric current in a coil, which can be converted into an audio signal playing the music that was recorded.

The advantages of the cassette have been its low price and availability, and the fact that the tape could be erased and new material recorded. Its disadvantages include the sequential nature of the device and its limited storage capacity. Cassettes are easily damaged by exposure to high temperatures and careless handling.

Floppy disks

The floppy disk, like the cassette, uses magnetic recording. Like the cassette, it has also been superseded by the CD. The original 8-inch floppy disk was invented in the mid-1960s at IBM as a way of inputting data into a computer, as well as storing computer data. The name 'floppy disk' in the original device derives from the flexible nature of the disk. These were replaced by 5¼-inch floppy disks with a capacity of 360 kbytes, as opposed to the 1.44 Mbytes of the 3½-inch, non-flexible diskettes (but still called 'floppy disks') that in turn replaced them. Data was stored magnetically (in much the same way as on the cassette) but it was arranged on concentric rings, which had the advantage that one could access data on an outer ring without having to go sequentially through the intermediate data as on a cassette. This provided a *direct access* storage device. After a 20-year period of dominance in the field of computer data storage, floppy disks are now, essentially, obsolete.

Hard disks

Once used only in computers, hard disks can now be found in digital cameras and digital video recorders, some mobile phones and other devices. They store data in large quantities. The device itself consists of a number of disks made out of aluminium or glass arranged on a spindle. The surface of the disks is covered with material that can be magnetized (usually cobalt). The surface may be thought to be divided into a very large number of tiny regions (the size is of order 10^{-6} m, i.e. 1 μm), and each such region is the seat of a '0' or a '1' of digitized data. The growth of hard disk capacity has been exponential. Whereas the early personal computers had a hard disk with a capacity of just a few megabytes, today's personal computers boast a hard disk capacity in the hundreds of gigabytes. The data is stored in *sectors* and *tracks*. Tracks are concentric rings and a sector is a part of the same track. The data can be accessed almost instantly irrespective of its position on the disk.

Advantages of digital storage

As indicated above, digital storage provides enormous advantages over analogue devices. These advantages include the following:

- The capacity for data storage is huge in digital devices.
- The access to particular stored data is fast.
- The retrieval of the data is fast.
- The storage is reliable.
- The stored data can be copied or erased easily.
- The stored data can be encrypted.
- The data can be processed and manipulated by a computer.
- The data can be transported easily physically as well as electronically.

On the negative side, whereas an analogue storage system, such as ordinary photographic film, degrades slowly with time, a serious error with a digital storage device is usually catastrophic, in the sense that the data may never be recoverable.

QUESTIONS

1 Express the following decimal numbers as binary numbers:

(a) 3; (b) 10; (c) 18; (d) 31.

For each, state the most significant bit and least significant bit.

2 Express the following binary numbers as decimal numbers:

(a) 110; (b) 1100; (c) 0101; (d) 11110.

3 (a) State what is meant by (i) an analogue signal and (ii) a digital signal.

(b) Give one example each of (i) an analogue signal and (ii) a digital signal.

4 Consider the analogue signal of Figure 1.9.

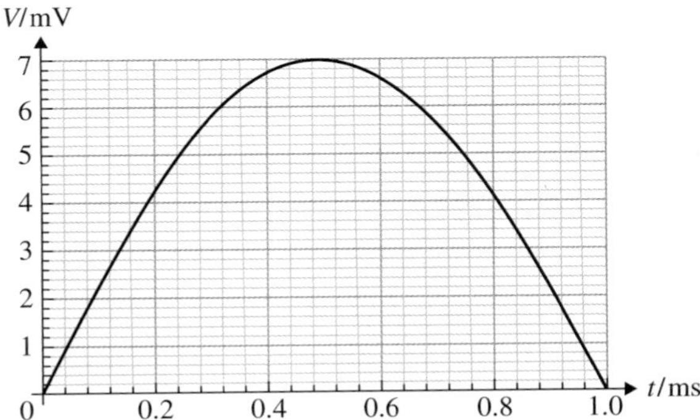

Figure 1.9 For question 4.

By sampling (i.e. measuring) the signal every 0.1 ms, express the signal as a digital signal. (Assign the nearest integer value to each signal measurement.) It would help to copy and fill in the following table.

Time/ms	Signal strength/mV	Three-bit binary code	Digital signal
0			
0.1			
0.2			
0.3			
0.4			
0.5			
0.6			
0.7			
0.8			
0.9			
1.0			

5 The binary code for a signal that is sampled eight times is shown in the table below.

Binary code	Digital signal	Signal strength
1100		
1001		
0010		
0000		
0010		
1000		
1110		
1111		

(a) Copy and complete this table.
(b) Put the individual signals together to construct the complete digital signal.
(c) Reconstruct the analogue signal.

6 *Estimate* the length of the spiral carrying pits and lands on an ordinary CD of diameter 12 cm. Assume that adjacent parts of the spiral are 1600 nm apart. Explain your method, listing the assumptions you have made.

7 It takes 4.0 minutes to record a song on a CD at a rate of 44 100 words per second. A word has a length of 32 bits. How many bytes does the song take?

8 Calculate the storage capacity of an 80-minute CD that was recorded at a rate of 44 100 bits per second using two channels of 16-bit words each.

9 (a) Explain how digital data is stored on a CD.
(b) Explain how interference of light can be used to distinguish a pit from a land.
(c) A CD player uses a laser of wavelength 680 nm. What is an appropriate pit depth?

10 A 12 cm diameter CD lasts for 80 minutes. The laser source of the CD player moves radially outwards as the CD rotates. The initial rate of rotation of the CD is 500 rpm and the final rate is 250 rpm.
(a) Calculate the average speed of the laser source.
(b) Calculate the radius of the innermost track at which the data is stored. Assume that neighbouring spirals are separated by 1600 nm.

11 The laser of a CD player has a wavelength of 740 nm in air. The lands and the pits on the CD are covered by a polycarbonate of index of refraction 1.52.
(a) Calculate the wavelength of the laser in the polycarbonate.
(b) Calculate a suitable pit depth, explaining your reasoning.

12 Beautiful colours appear when white light is incident on the underside of a CD. Suggest the mechanism that creates these colours.

13 Why does a DVD have a larger storage capacity than a CD.

14 List the features of a DVD recording of a film that are not available on an old-fashioned video cassette.

15 Suggest the role of the laser wavelength in the storage capacity of devices such as CDs and DVDs.

16 Explain why the recording of an LP is said to be an analogue recording.

17 Is the image on ordinary photographic film digital or analogue storage? Explain your answer.

18 State two similarities and two differences between a floppy disk and a hard disk.

19 State and explain three advantages of digital storage of data over analogue data storage.

Digital imaging with charge-coupled devices

This chapter introduces an important device, the charge-coupled device (CCD). The basic mechanism in the operation of the CCD is discussed, and various applications are briefly described.

Objectives

By the end of this chapter you should be able to:

- understand the definition of *capacitance*;
- understand the *basic operation of a charge-coupled device* (CCD);
- define *quantum efficiency*, *magnification* and *resolution*;
- solve problems with CCDs;
- name the *applications* of CCDs in *medical imaging*.

Capacitance

Any two conductors that are separated by either a vacuum or an insulator are called a *capacitor*. This might include two parallel plates a certain distance apart, two conducting spheres in a vacuum a certain distance apart or even a single conducting sphere isolated from the earth by an insulating stand.

Consider two parallel plates a distance d apart, as shown in Figure 2.1. The plates are connected to a source of potential difference V, provided, in this case, by a battery. When the switch S is closed, a current will flow for a short time and then stop. The current will flow in a anticlockwise direction (i.e. the electrons will move clockwise). This means that negative charge will accumulate on the bottom plate, leaving behind an equal amount (in magnitude) of positive charge on the top plate.

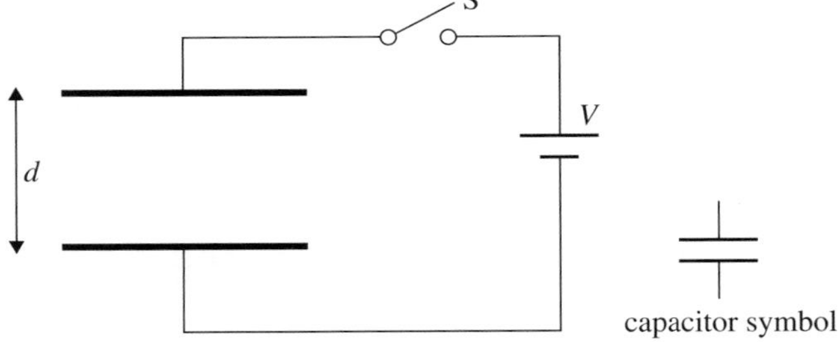

Figure 2.1 A simple circuit with a capacitor, and the symbol for a capacitor.

How much charge can accumulate on either plate, given the potential difference of the battery? This is determined by a property known as the **capacitance** of the parallel plates. The amount of charge Q that can accumulate on the plates is directly proportional to the potential difference between the plates (i.e. $Q \propto V$). The constant of proportionality in this relation is called the capacitance C of the plates,

$$Q = CV$$

▶ In other words, *capacitance* is the charge per unit potential difference that can accumulate on a conductor. The SI unit of capacitance is the farad (F), with one farad (1 F) being a capacitance of one coulomb per volt (1 C V^{-1}).

The farad is a large capacitance, and here we shall use smaller multiple units, the microfarad (1 μF = 10^{-6} F), nanofarad (1 nF = 10^{-9} F) and picofarad (1 pF = 10^{-12} F).

The capacitance of parallel plates depends on the surface area of the plates, their distance apart and the material between the plates. In an electric circuit, a capacitor is represented by the symbol shown in Figure 2.1.

Example question

Q1

The capacitance of two parallel plates is 4.5 pF. Calculate the charge on one of the plates when a potential difference of 8.0 V is established between the plates.

Answer

Applying the formula defining the capacitance gives

$Q = CV = 4.5 \times 10^{-12} \times 8.0 = 3.6 \times 10^{-11}\,\text{C} = 36\,\text{pC}$

The charge-coupled device

The charge-coupled device (CCD) (see Figure 2.2), invented at Bell Labs in 1969, has

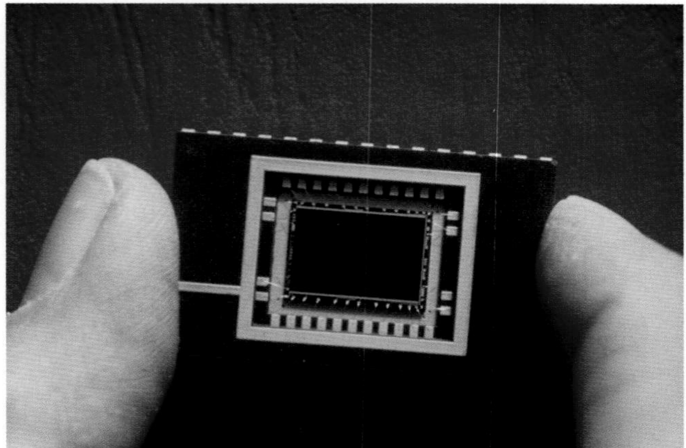

Figure 2.2 A charge-coupled device (CCD).

revolutionized image acquisition in astronomy by providing images of high resolution, in digital form, that can be easily manipulated and processed. These images can be obtained in a fraction of the time required using conventional means such as photographic film, and can be used to obtain images of very faint objects.

Soon after the introduction of the CCD in astronomy, many commercial applications followed, such as digital cameras and digital video recorders, scanners and many others. The image in Figure 2.3 is a photograph of exceptional clarity and detail of the galaxy M31 obtained using a CCD on the Hubble Space Telescope.

Figure 2.3 This Hubble Space Telescope image of the galaxy M31 was obtained with a CCD.

The CCD is a silicon chip varying in surface dimensions from 20 mm × 20 mm to 60 mm × 60 mm. This surface is covered with light-sensitive elements called **pixels** (picture elements), whose size varies from 5×10^{-6} m to 25×10^{-6} m. Each pixel releases electrons when light is incident on it by a process known as the photoelectric effect (strictly electron–hole production in a semiconductor). We may think of each pixel as a small capacitor. The electrons released in the pixel constitute a certain amount of electric charge Q and therefore a certain potential difference V develops at the ends of the pixel equal to $V = \frac{Q}{C}$, where C is the capacitance of the pixel. This potential difference can be measured with electrodes attached to the pixel.

The energy carried by a single photon of light of frequency f is given by

$$E = hf$$

where $h = 6.63 \times 10^{-34}$ J s is the Planck constant. Since $f = \frac{c}{\lambda}$, where λ is the wavelength of light, we also have

$$E = \frac{hc}{\lambda}$$

Imaging with a CCD is then made possible by the following fact:

▶ The number of electrons released when light is incident on a pixel is proportional to the intensity of light. This means that the charge and so the potential difference across a pixel are also proportional to the intensity of light on that pixel.

Example questions

Q2

Calculate the number of pixels on a 30 mm × 30 mm CCD where the pixel size is 22×10^{-6} m.

Answer

The collecting area of the CCD is

$$30 \times 30 = 9.0 \times 10^{2}\ \text{mm}^2$$
$$= 9.0 \times 10^{2} \times 10^{-6}\ \text{m}^2$$
$$= 9.0 \times 10^{-4}\ \text{m}^2$$

and that of a pixel is

$$22 \times 10^{-6} \times 22 \times 10^{-6} = 4.8 \times 10^{-10}\ \text{m}^2$$

The number of pixels is therefore

$$\frac{9.0 \times 10^{-4}}{4.8 \times 10^{-10}} = 1.9 \times 10^{6}$$

Q3

Light of intensity 6.8×10^{-6} W m^{-2} and wavelength 5.0×10^{-7} m is incident on the collecting area of the CCD of Example question 2. Calculate the number of photons incident on each pixel in a period of 25 ms.

Answer

The area of one pixel is 4.8×10^{-10} m^2 and so the power incident on this area is

$$P = 6.8 \times 10^{-6} \times 4.8 \times 10^{-10} = 3.3 \times 10^{-15}\ \text{W}$$

The energy deposited in 25 ms is then

$$E = 3.3 \times 10^{-15} \times 25 \times 10^{-3} = 8.2 \times 10^{-17}\ \text{J}$$

The energy of one photon is

$$E = \frac{hc}{\lambda} = \frac{6.63 \times 10^{-34} \times 3.0 \times 10^{8}}{5.0 \times 10^{-7}} = 4.0 \times 10^{-19}\ \text{J}$$

and so the number of photons per pixel is

$$\frac{8.2 \times 10^{-17}}{4.0 \times 10^{-19}} \approx 210$$

The diagram in Figure 2.4 shows rows of pixels on the collecting surface of a CCD. When the CCD surface is exposed to light for a certain period of time (by opening a shutter), charge and hence voltage begins to build up in each pixel. After the shutter closes, a potential difference is applied to each row of pixels in order to force the charge stored in each pixel to move to the row below (this is the origin of the name 'charge-coupled' – the charges in one row are coupled to those in the row below).

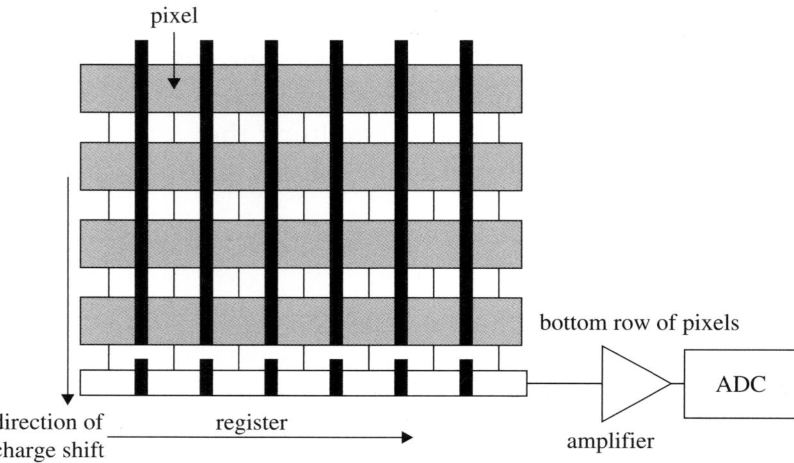

Figure 2.4 The charges in each row are moved to the row below until they reach the register. From there, they are read one by one, amplified and converted into digital form.

Starting from the bottom row, the charge of each pixel is moved vertically down into the register, and from there, one by one, the charge is moved horizontally, where the voltage is amplified, measured and passed through an analogue-to-digital converter (ADC) until the charge in the entire row is read. The computer that is processing all this now has two pieces of information stored. The first is the value of the voltage in each pixel and the second is the position of each pixel. The process is now repeated with the next row, until the voltage in each pixel in each row has been measured, converted and stored.

The charge, and hence voltage, in each pixel is proportional to the intensity of light incident on the pixel. A digital copy of the image is then stored since the intensity of light in each pixel is now known. The process so described would result in a black-and-white image. It can then be displayed on a computer screen or an LCD screen in general.

To form a coloured image, the pixels are arranged in groups of four, with green filters on two of them (the eye is most sensitive at green) and one red and one blue for the other two (see Figure 2.5). The intensity of light in pixels of the same colour, say green, is measured as outlined above. An algorithm (a computer software program) is then used to find the intensity of green light in each pixel by interpolation based on the intensity in neighbouring green pixels. In this way one has the intensity in each pixel for each of three colours: green, red and blue. Combining the different intensities for different colours gives a coloured image.

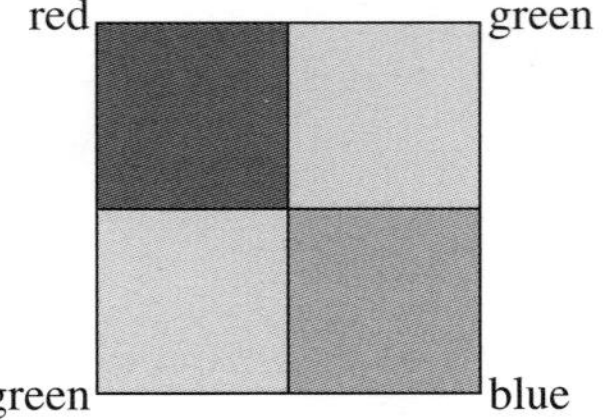

Figure 2.5 A group of four pixels with green, red and blue filters.

CCD imaging characteristics

Quantum efficiency

Not every photon incident on a pixel will result in an electron being released. Some may be reflected and others may simply go through the pixel. We use **quantum efficiency** to describe this.

▶ We define the *quantum efficiency* of a pixel as the ratio of the number of emitted electrons to the number of incident photons.

One of the great advantages of CCDs is their very high quantum efficiency. It ranges between 70% and 80%. This is to be compared to 4% for the best-quality photographic film and 1% for the human eye. (However, the quantum efficiency is not constant for all wavelengths.) CCDs are now routinely used to measure the apparent brightness of stars. The apparent brightness of a star is typically of order 10^{-12} W m^{-2}.

Example question

Q4

The area of a pixel in a CCD is 8.0×10^{-10} m^2 and its capacitance is 38 pF. Light of intensity 2.1×10^{-3} W m^{-2} and wavelength 4.8×10^{-7} m^2 is incident on the collecting area of the CCD for 120 ms. Calculate the potential difference established at the ends of a pixel, assuming that 70% of the incident photons cause the emission of electrons.

Answer

The energy incident on a pixel is

$$2.1 \times 10^{-3} \times 8.0 \times 10^{-10} \times 120 \times 10^{-3}$$
$$= 2.0 \times 10^{-13} \text{ J}$$

The energy of one photon is

$$E = \frac{hc}{\lambda} = \frac{6.63 \times 10^{-34} \times 3.0 \times 10^{8}}{4.8 \times 10^{-7}}$$
$$= 4.1 \times 10^{-19} \text{ J}$$

The number of incident photons is then

$$\frac{2.0 \times 10^{-13}}{4.1 \times 10^{-19}} = 4.9 \times 10^5$$

The number of absorbed photons is therefore

$$0.70 \times 4.9 \times 10^5 = 3.4 \times 10^5$$

The charge corresponding to this number of electrons is

$$3.4 \times 10^5 \times 1.6 \times 10^{-19} = 5.4 \times 10^{-14}\ \text{C}$$

The potential difference is then

$$V = \frac{Q}{C} = \frac{5.4 \times 10^{-14}}{38 \times 10^{-12}} = 1.4\ \text{mV}$$

Magnification

Consider a CCD that is used to obtain an image of an object. As usual in optics we define the **magnification** of the CCD to be the ratio of the length of the image as it is formed on the CCD to the actual length of the object. The magnification of a CCD system is determined by the overall properties of the lenses that are used to focus the light.

Example question

Q5

A digital camera is used to take a photograph of the eye of an insect. The area of the real eye is 1.4×10^{-6} m^2 and the area of the image eye is 9.5×10^{-6} m^2. Calculate the magnification.

Answer

The ratio of image to object *areas* is $\frac{9.5\times10^{-6}}{1.4\times10^{-6}} = 6.76$, and so the ratio of corresponding *linear* sizes, the magnification, is $\sqrt{6.76} = 2.6$.

Notice, of course, that for most applications with a digital camera, the size of the image will be smaller than the actual object (say a person, a building or a galaxy).

Resolution

A very important characteristic of a CCD is its ability to resolve two closely spaced points on the object whose image we seek (i.e. to see them as distinct). A rough measure of the resolution ability is that the images (on the CCD) of the two points do not fall on the same pixel. This means that the images must be at least one pixel length apart. A safer and more conservative measure is to demand that the images of the two points are two pixel lengths apart. In this way, we are sure to resolve the points without ambiguities.

▶ Two points are *resolved* if their images are more than two pixel lengths apart.

Example question

Q6

The magnification produced by a 3.0 megapixel digital camera with a collecting area of 12 mm^2 is 1.5. Determine if this camera can resolve two points a distance 3.2×10^{-3} mm apart.

Answer

The area of a pixel is found from

$$\frac{12}{3.0 \times 10^6} = 4.0 \times 10^{-6}\ \text{mm}^2$$

and so the length of a pixel is

$$\sqrt{4.0 \times 10^{-6}} = 2.0 \times 10^{-3}\ \text{mm}$$

The images of the two points are a distance apart of

$$1.5 \times 3.2 \times 10^{-3}\ \text{mm} = 4.8 \times 10^{-3}\ \text{mm}$$

This is larger than two pixel lengths and so the points are resolved.

The resolution is clearly better with a high pixel density (i.e. number of pixels per unit area). An image of high resolution is of better quality since the image includes more detail than an image of low resolution. A higher quantum efficiency means that the image will require less time to form if the incident light intensity is very low and is therefore of special importance in astronomical images.

Medical uses of CCDs

In medicine the CCD has had a major impact in **endoscopy**: an endoscope is a device (a thin tube) that can be inserted into a patient to make observation of internal organs possible. CCDs are now used in endoscopes so that real-time digital images can be obtained.

Driven by the needs of X-ray astronomers, special CCDs have been developed in which **X-rays** can be detected. These devices have been adapted by medical imaging researchers for medical use. For X-rays with energies below 150 keV (which is the case with most medical applications of X-rays), photons incident on a silicon pixel produce electrons via the photoelectric effect, as does visible light. The X-ray CCD can then act as a detector of X-rays, replacing the old X-ray pick-up tube. One extra advantage is that the sensitivity of the CCD allows for shorter exposure times, with an obvious benefit to the patient. The negative side is that these devices are still expensive.

? QUESTIONS

1 A parallel-plate capacitor of capacitance 12 μF has a potential difference of 24 V applied to it. Calculate the charge on each plate of the capacitor.

2 A charged parallel-plate capacitor of capacitance 2.0 nF has 24 nC of charge on each plate. The capacitor is included in the circuit of Figure 2.6. The value of the resistance R is 6.0 Ω. Calculate the *initial* current that will flow in the resistor when the switch is closed. Explain your reasoning.

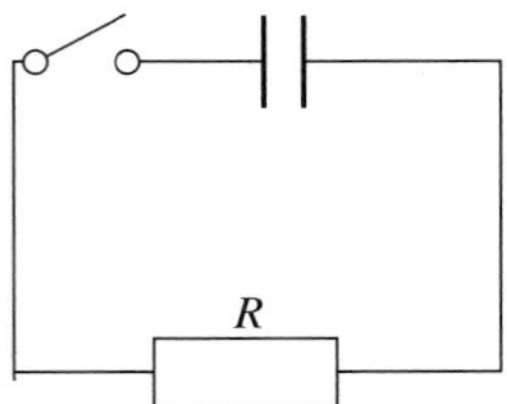

Figure 2.6 For question 2.

3 Consider a CCD with $500 \times 500 = 2.5 \times 10^5$ pixels (which is not a large number of pixels).

(a) Assuming that each pixel stores the potential difference across it as an eight-bit word, calculate the numbers of bits stored by the CCD.

(b) Give every letter of the alphabet (26 letters) a number from 1 to 26. How many bits do you need to express a letter as a binary number?

(c) Assume for the sake of an estimate that the average number of letters in a word is six. Calculate the number of words that have the same content of bits as the bits in the CCD of (a).

(d) Comment on the validity of the expression 'a picture is worth a thousand words'.

4 Calculate the energy of a photon of wavelength 5.8×10^{-7} m.

5 The collecting area of a CCD is 36 mm^2 and there are three million pixels on the surface. Calculate the linear size of a pixel.

6 Define the quantum efficiency and magnification of a CCD.

7 One-third of the photons incident on a CCD do not result in electrons being emitted. Calculate the quantum efficiency of the CCD.

8 (a) State what is meant by resolution in the context of imaging with a CCD.

(b) State the condition for two points to be resolved in the image by a CCD.

9 Explain why a CCD with a large pixel density will have a better resolution than one with a lower pixel density.

10 State three devices that use a CCD.

11 Outline how a CCD forms the image of an object.

12 One digital camera (X) has 1.0 megapixels and another (Y) has 8.0 megapixels. The collecting areas and quantum efficiencies are the same. Outline differences in the images of the same object obtained by the two cameras.

13 Two cameras have the same density of pixels on their collecting surfaces but one has a larger quantum efficiency. State and explain a situation where an image taken by the higher quantum efficiency camera would be superior to the image made by the other camera.

14 Suggest a difference, if any, in the images obtained by two digital cameras with the

same density of pixels and quantum efficiency but where one has a larger collecting area.

15 A digital camera is used to take a photograph of a flower seed. The area of the real seed is 6.2×10^{-6} m^2 and the area of the image seed is 9.4×10^{-6} m^2. Calculate the magnification.

16 The magnification produced by a 4.0 megapixel digital camera with a collecting area of 16 mm^2 is 1.3. Determine if this camera can resolve two points a distance 8.2×10^{-4} mm apart.

17 (a) Calculate the number of photons per second per unit area incident on the surface of a CCD when the intensity of light is 28 W m^{-2} and the light has wavelength 6.8×10^{-7} m.

(b) Repeat the calculation for light of the same intensity but wavelength 4.4×10^{-7} m.

18 The number of photons per pixel needed for an acceptable image in a certain digital camera is 6000. The wavelength of light used is 4.8×10^{-7} m and the intensity of the light incident on the collecting area of the digital camera is 1.4 mW m^{-2}. The area of a pixel is 5.0×10^{-10} m^2.

(a) Calculate the time the shutter must remain open in order to obtain an acceptable image.

(b) In practice, a longer time than that calculated in (a) will be needed. Suggest why this is so.

19 The collecting area of a CCD is 48 mm^2 and there are four million pixels on the surface. The capacitance of each pixel is 24 pF. Light of intensity 5.2×10^{-3} W m^{-2} and wavelength 6.3×10^{-7} m is incident on the collecting area of the CCD for 80 ms. Calculate the potential difference established at the ends of a pixel, assuming a quantum efficiency of 75%.

20 Suggest a justification for the phrase *charge-coupled* in the name of the CCD.

21 An energy of 3.65 eV is needed to create an electron–hole pair in silicon by X-rays. Calculate the number of electrons produced by X-rays of energy 5.0 keV.

22 State the advantages of imaging with a CCD compared to imaging with ordinary photographic film.

23 CCDs used for very accurate astronomical work are often cooled down to very low temperatures. Suggest a reason for this.

24 Discuss which characteristics of the CCD are of importance to astronomical imaging.

25 State one application of the CCD in medicine, outlining the advantage it offers.

Part II
Options

The eye and sight

This chapter introduces the basic features of the human eye and the important concepts of depth of vision and accommodation. The function of the two different light-sensitive cells in the eye, called rods and cones, is discussed, and their role in vision under different conditions is analysed. The role of cones in colour vision is also discussed. Primary colours are introduced, and colour addition and subtraction discussed. The chapter ends with a brief note on the role of colour in perception.

Objectives

By the end of this chapter you should be able to:

- make an annotated *diagram of the eye*;
- explain the *function* of the main parts of the eye;
- outline the differences in the *density of rods and cones* across the retina;
- define *scotopic vision* and *photopic vision*;
- account for the *differences in scotopic and photopic vision*;
- understand the terms *primary colour* and *secondary colour*;
- understand the difference between *addition and subtraction of colours*;
- solve simple problems with *colour mixing*;
- understand the role of light in the *perception* of objects.

The structure of the human eye

The human eye is a remarkable 'instrument'. Figure A1.1 shows the basic features of the human eye. The eye is almost spherical in shape, with a diameter of about 2.5 cm. Light enters the eye through the **cornea** (a transparent membrane), where most of the refraction takes place. The index of refraction of the cornea is about 1.37, substantially different from the index of refraction of air (1.00).

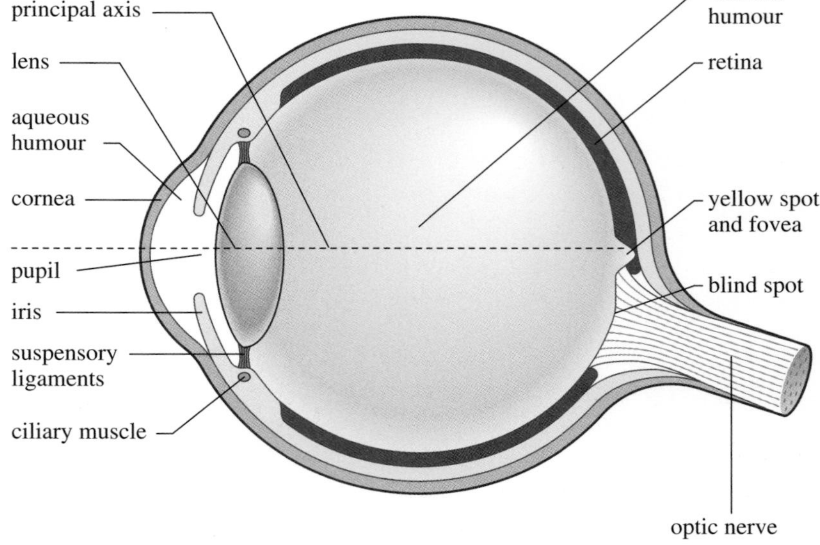

Figure A1.1 The human eye.

In between the cornea and the eye lens is a liquid-filled chamber called the **aqueous humour**. The liquid filling the chamber is clear, mainly water with small amounts of salts. Its index of refraction is 1.33, essentially equal to that of water. This chamber is separated into two parts by the **iris** (the coloured part of the eye). At the centre of the iris is the **pupil**, an aperture through which the light enters the eye **lens**. The pupil can increase or decrease in diameter in order to adjust to varying intensities of light. The eye lens is attached to the **ciliary muscle** by ligaments – the ciliary muscle controls the curvature of the lens.

Light passing through the lens then enters a second chamber filled with a jelly-like substance called the **vitreous humour**. The light finally reaches the back surface of the eye, the **retina**. The retina is covered with light-sensitive cells that record the arrival of light. There are two types of light-sensitive cells on the retina, called **rods** and **cones**. Light reaching the rods and the cones is converted into tiny electrical signals in nerve fibres attached to these cells. The nerve fibres all converge to the **optic nerve**, which transmits the electrical signals to the brain. Close to the beginning of the optic nerve, and essentially on the principal axis of the eye, is an area called the **fovea**, a spot of diameter of about 0.25 mm, where vision is exceptionally acute. This is filled with cones, each connected to a different nerve fibre (unlike elsewhere on the retina, where many different cones are connected to the same fibre).

The distribution of rods and cones is not constant along the surface of the retina. At the fovea we have many cones but no rods. The density of cones at the centre of the fovea reaches 150 000 per mm^2. The rods are mainly found at the edges of the retina (i.e. away from the principal axis of the eye), whereas the concentration of the cones increases as we approach the principal axis.

Depth of vision

Figure A1.2 shows a converging lens and a set of rays, all parallel to the principal axis of the lens, incident on the lens. The rays refract and all pass through the same point on the principal axis of the lens. This point is called the **focal point** of the lens, and its distance from the optical centre of the lens is called the **focal length**.

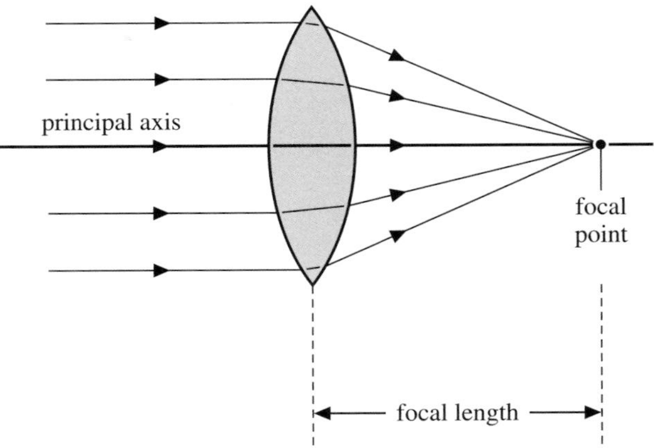

Figure A1.2 Focal point and focal length of a converging lens.

The eye cannot, at the same time, focus on two objects at two different distances from the eye. But if you focus on an object, O, far from the eye and straight ahead, so that the object is seen clearly, other objects closer and further than that object will also be seen clearly enough, even though the eye is not exactly focusing on them. If the furthest object that can be seen acceptably clearly is O_1 and the closest is O_2, then the distance O_1O_2 is called the **depth of vision** (or depth of field) (see Figure A1.3).

▶ The *depth of vision* is the range of object distances from the eye within which objects, or points on an object, can be seen acceptably clearly.

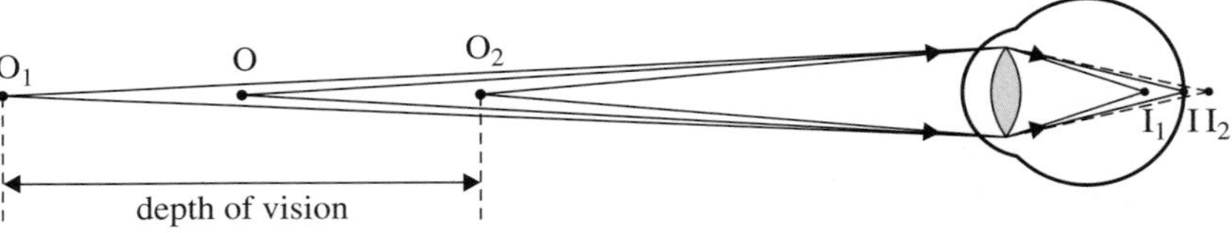

Figure A1.3 Diagram showing what is meant by depth of vision.

The depth of vision depends on the distance to the object. The further the object is from the eye, the larger the depth of vision. If the object is put close to the eye, the depth of vision is greatly reduced. However, if brighter light is used, the depth of vision will increase. This is because in brighter light the iris will reduce the pupil diameter. Figure A1.4 shows an increased depth of vision in the presence of a smaller aperture.

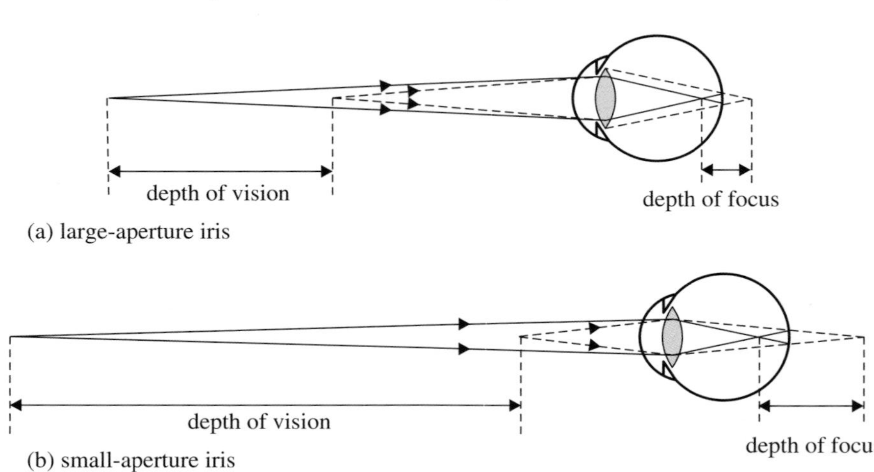

Figure A1.4 A reduced pupil diameter means that the rays entering the eye can be brought to focus.

Accommodation

The term **accommodation** refers to the ability of the eye lens to change its focal length. This is done by contractions of the ciliary muscle. When the muscle is relaxed, the eye has the shape shown in Figure A1.5(a) and the eye is said to be *unaccommodated*. The lens has its greatest focal length and the eye can focus on distant objects without fatigue. By contrast, when the muscle is contracted, the lens has the shape shown in Figure A1.5(b), its focal length is the least and the eye is said to be *accommodated*. The eye can then focus on nearby objects. This is an active process, leading to fatigue.

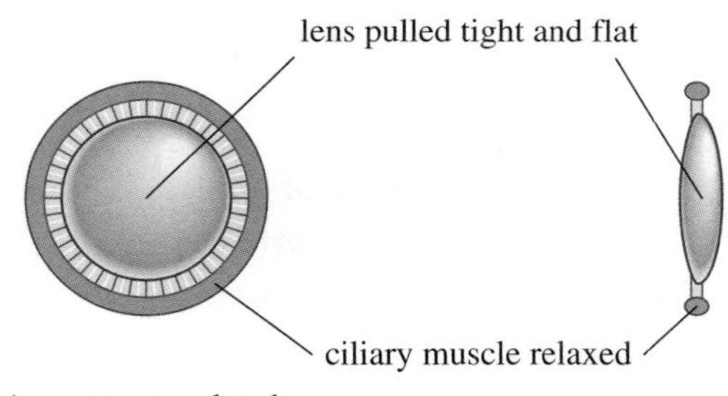

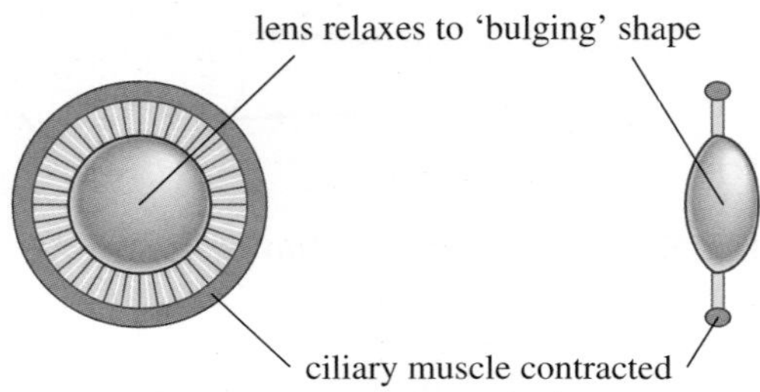

Figure A1.5 Changes in the eye lens in the case of an accommodated and an unaccommodated eye.

The nearest distance at which an object can be seen clearly, without undue strain on the eye, is called the *near point* of the eye. For a normal healthy eye, this distance is about 25 cm. The *far point* is the furthest distance the eye can focus on clearly. For a normal healthy eye, this is infinity.

Scotopic and photopic vision

There are major differences in the functioning of the rods and the cones. Even though the rods have different responses to different wavelengths of light, the rods do not transmit this difference in a way that the brain can interpret as a difference in colour. They are, however, sensitive to light of low intensity, because many different rods are connected to the same nerve fibre. This means that, even if the intensity of light in any one rod is low, the signal given to the nerve fibre will be the sum of the individual signals and therefore can be large. A disadvantage of connecting different rods to the same nerve fibre is that in this way we lose on detail in the image.

▶ Vision in which the rods are the main detectors of the incident light in the eye is called *scotopic* vision.

The cones, on the other hand, do distinguish different colours. There are three types of cone, each sensitive to a different colour. Fewer of them are connected to the same fibre, and this allows for more detailed images. The cones are only sensitive when the intensity of light is high (i.e. in bright light). This is why in very low-intensity light (in the dark) it is not possible to distinguish colours. Thus if you look at a galaxy through a large telescope, you will see a black-and-white image; you will not see the brilliant colours that published photographs of galaxies have in books and on posters.

▶ Vision in which the cones are the main detectors of the incident light in the eye is called *photopic* vision.

These facts are summarized in Table A1.1.

Scotopic vision	Photopic vision
Rods are used	Cones are used (mainly)
Used at night and when there is very little light available	Used during the day and when there is a lot of light available
Distinguishes shapes but not colours	Distinguishes shapes and colours
Distinguishes little detail	Distinguishes a lot of detail

Table A1.1 Differences between scotopic and photopic vision.

Example question

Q1

Explain why in low-intensity light it is easier to obtain a clear image of an object by looking at the object a bit sideways rather than directly at it.

Answer

Since the intensity of light is low, vision takes place mainly through the rods and not the cones. The highest concentrations of the rods are away from the principal axis, and so we look a bit sideways at the object for light to fall on the rods.

Figure A1.6 shows the relative sensitivity of cones and rods to light of different wavelengths. (Recall that rods do not distinguish colour.) We see that rods are more sensitive than cones for blue light.

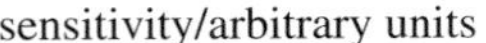

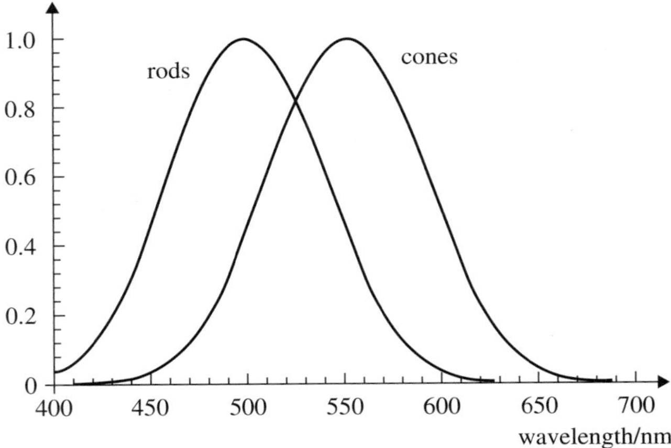

Figure A1.6 Overall relative sensitivity of cones and rods as a function of the wavelength of light.

Example question

Q2

Use the spectral response graph in Figure A1.6 to answer this question. An object reflecting red light of wavelength 640 nm is viewed in

(a) low-intensity light and

(b) high-intensity light.

Describe what the observer sees.

Answer

(a) In low-intensity light, vision is through rods. Light of wavelength 640 nm is beyond what the rods can detect, and so the object cannot be seen.

(b) In high-intensity light, the cones are used, and the object can be seen clearly.

Colour

The perception of colour is made possible by the fact that there are three types of cone cell, each type being sensitive to either blue, green or red light. This was suggested by Thomas Young as long ago as 1800. Figure A1.7 shows the spectral response curve for each type of cell. Adding together the three curves B, G and R for the cones produces the overall spectral response of the cones as already shown in Figure A1.6.

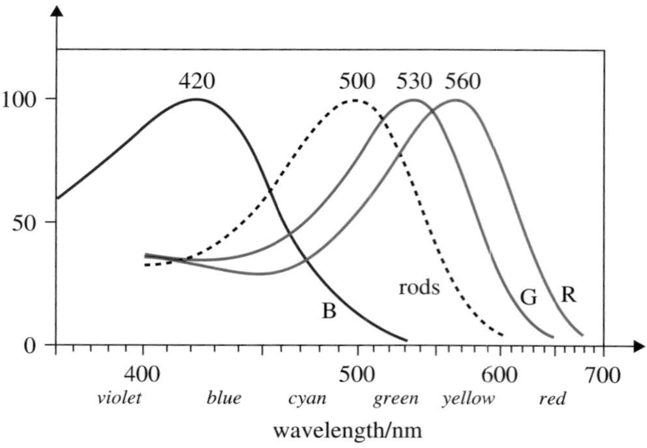

Figure A1.7 Relative sensitivity of the three types of cone cell.

It can be seen from Figure A1.7 that light of wavelength 550 nm will excite only the green- and red-sensitive cones. The combination of green and red (in equal quantities) gives yellow light, and so this is the colour that the brain understands for this wavelength of light.

Colour blindness

Colour blindness is a general term referring to people with deficiency in the perception of colour. It affects men more frequently than women. Complete colour blindness is rare. Since colour is perceived by the cone cells, colour blindness is associated with non-functioning cone cells or insufficient numbers of one or more types of cone cell. It can also be due to brain or nerve damage. The most common form of colour blindness involves the red and green cone cells, and the inability to distinguish between red and green colours. If one type of cone cell is non-functioning, the colours that can be perceived are only those that can be made by combining the colours to which the other two types of cone cell are sensitive. If two types of cone cell are not functioning, then the person is completely colour blind in the sense that he or she cannot distinguish between any two coloured objects.

Colour addition

It is an amazing fact that, by mixing light of just three colours, we can make a *very wide* range of other colours. Three is the minimum number of colours needed. With two colours, for example green and red, we cannot make blue. If we take the three colours to be blue (B), green (G) and red (R), the combination

$$X = bB + gG + rR$$

gives any desired colour, where b, g and r are the relative intensities of the blue, green and red light used in the mixture. The three colours used (in this case, blue, green and red) are called **primary colours**. (But others might also be used as primaries – see page 477.) In practice, this means that if you shine blue, green and red lights of various intensities onto a white screen, the colour X would appear where the three coloured beams overlap.

▶ *Primary colours* are colours which, when overlapped, give a wide range of other colours. No one primary can be made with the other two. Adding three primary colours of light, say B, G and R, in equal amounts gives white light, $W = B + G + R$.

To get the colour $X = bB + gG + rR$, the three primary colours are mixed with relative intensities b, g and r.

▶ Obtaining a colour of light by overlapping different amounts of three primary colours is called *colour addition.*

Adding the primaries (here taken as blue, green and red) two at a time results in the three **secondary colours**, of cyan, magenta and yellow:

$B + G = C$, cyan (bluish green, i.e. turquoise)

$B + R = M$, magenta (reddish purple)

$R + G = Y$, yellow

It follows that adding a specific primary colour to a secondary colour results in white light, W:

$$C + R = W \quad (\text{because } C = B + G)$$
$$M + G = W \quad (\text{because } M = B + R)$$
$$Y + B = W \quad (\text{because } Y = R + G)$$

The primary colour added to the secondary colour to give white light is called the **complementary colour** of the secondary; for example, red is complementary to cyan.

Example question

Q3

What colour of light is obtained when we overlap equal intensities of magenta with yellow?

Answer

We get

$$\begin{aligned} M + Y &= (R + B) + (R + G) \\ &= (R + B + G) + R \\ &= W + R \end{aligned}$$

This is red.

As mentioned earlier, there is no unique choice of the three primary colours. Blue, green and red are normally used because they give a very wide range of colours by colour addition. They correspond to the three sets of cones present in the eye. This system is also used in colour television and digital cameras. But other systems can be used as well. For example, consider the choice of red (R), yellow (Y) and blue (B) as the primaries. A wide range of colours is obtained by using colour addition with these three, but unfortunately it is not possible to obtain green light by adding any combination of these three. However, a mixture of yellow (Y) and blue (B) can be made identical to a mixture of red (R) and green (G). That is to say

$$yY + bB = gG + rR$$

This means that

$$gG = yY + bB - rR$$

$$G = \frac{y}{g}Y + \frac{b}{g}B - \frac{r}{g}R$$

In this way we have managed to get green out of the three primaries Y, B and R, but this time the coefficient of red is negative.

In other words, if we allow for negative coefficients in the mixture, any three colours can be used as primaries, and there is therefore no unique choice of primaries. (Notice that the standard choice of primaries, red, green and blue, also requires negative coefficients in order to obtain certain colours. There is, in fact, no choice of three primaries from which all other colours may be obtained with only positive coefficients in the mixture.)

Notice that the presence of negative coefficients in the mixture $yY + bB + rR$ is sometimes referred to as colour subtraction. The proper meaning of colour subtraction, however, is discussed below.

Colour subtraction

The term **colour subtraction** refers to white light being transmitted through a coloured filter. The transmitted light has the colour of the filter because the filter removes (subtracts) a certain colour from the white light. The three primary filters used are yellow, magenta and cyan filters (see Figure A1.8).

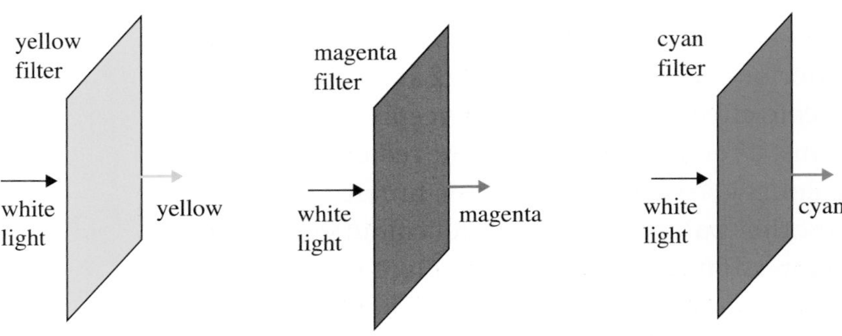

Figure A1.8 The three primary filters, yellow, magenta and cyan, remove blue, green and red colour, respectively, from white light.

White light transmitted through a yellow filter has the blue removed, so that the transmitted light has a colour given by

$$\begin{aligned} W - B &= (B + G + R) - B \\ &= G + R \\ &= Y \end{aligned}$$

i.e. yellow, as expected of a yellow filter.

Similarly, a magenta filter removes green, and a cyan filter removes red. In other words, the three filters each remove their respective complementary colour.

If light is transmitted through a magenta filter *and then* through a yellow filter, the transmitted colour will be

$$\begin{aligned} W - B - G &= (B + G + R) - B - G \\ &= R \end{aligned}$$

i.e. red.

If white light is transmitted through the three primary filters of yellow, magenta and cyan, the light will be absorbed and the three filters will look black where they all overlap. This is because

$$W - B - G - R = (B + G + R) - B - G - R = 0$$

Perception of colour and light

The perception of colour has, as we have seen, its physiological basis in the functioning of the cone cells in the eye. But the overall perception of colour extends into the realm of psychology. This has been exploited by architects, designers, interior decorators, advertisers and others, to create effects based on the perception of colour. Thus, a room painted in bright red or yellowish colours gives a sense of a busy, hurried place. Another painted in soft, pastel colours gives the impression of a relaxed, calm place. Soft reddish or orange colours create a 'warm' atmosphere, whereas bluish and violet colours give the impression of a cold or cool place. Small rooms can be made to 'look' bigger by painting them in light, soft colours, and a low ceiling can be 'raised' by painting it with a colour that is lighter than that used for the walls. A floor will look smaller if painted in dark colours rather than light colours.

Another effect is the inclusion of shadows. Deep shadows give the impression of a solid, massive object, whereas light shadows, or the absence of them, give the impression of a light and 'airy' structure.

? QUESTIONS

1 (a) Make an annotated diagram of the human eye.
(b) Explain the function of the parts you have annotated.

2 (a) Explain why you cannot see clearly under water.
(b) Why can you see clearly if you are wearing a diving mask?

3 (a) Describe the function of cones and rods in vision.
(b) State the distribution of cones and rods on the retina.

4 Many different rod cells are connected to the same nerve fibre. State and explain one advantage and one disadvantage of this in the context of the eye's ability to see.

5 (a) State what is meant by (i) depth of vision and (ii) accommodation.
(b) Outline why the depth of vision increases when the eye's aperture is reduced.
(c) Hence explain the effect on the depth of vision of an increase in the intensity of light.

6 Define what is meant by (a) scotopic vision and (b) photopic vision.

7 Suggest why it is difficult to observe colour in low-intensity light even though the outline of an object can be clearly seen.

8 Explain why in high-intensity light an object can be seen most clearly by looking directly at the object but as the intensity is reduced the object is most clearly seen when it is observed off the eye's principal axis.

9 (a) What is meant by colour blindness?
(b) State and explain whether colour blindness is associated with damage to rod cells or cone cells.

10 The density of cones on the fovea is 150000 cones per square millimetre. The fovea may be taken as a circle of diameter 0.25 mm.
(a) Calculate the average separation of cones in the fovea.
(b) The diameter of the eye is about 2.5 cm. Calculate the angle subtended at the pupil of the eye by the separation between two cones calculated in (a).
(c) Diffraction at the eye's aperture limits the resolution of the eye, i.e. whether two distinct objects are actually seen as distinct. The minimum angular separation between two objects that can be seen as distinct is given by $\theta \approx 1.22\frac{\lambda}{d}$, where λ is the wavelength of light used and d is the diameter of the aperture. Calculate θ by taking $\lambda = 5.5 \times 10^{-7}$ m and a pupil diameter of $d = 1.5 \times 10^{-3}$ m.
(d) By comparing the values obtained in (b) and (c), state and explain whether there would be any improvement in the resolution of the eye if the cones were closer to each other.

11 (a) Explain why the depth of vision is increased when looking at a page of text through a hole in a piece of cardboard.
(b) Suggest why there is a limit to the increase in the depth of vision that can be achieved in this way.

12 (a) Sketch graphs to show the variation with wavelength of the relative sensitivity of cones and rods.
(b) Use your graphs to explain why reducing the intensity of light shifts the wavelength at which the eye is most sensitive towards blue wavelengths.

13 (a) State what is meant by primary colours.
(b) How many primary colours are there?
(c) Explain why the choice of primary colours is not unique.

14 Using the spectral response curve of Figure A1.7 in the text, explain the colour perceived when light of wavelength (a) $\lambda = 400$ nm and (b) $\lambda = 680$ nm is incident on the eye.

15 State what is meant by (a) colour addition and (b) colour subtraction.

16 Determine the colour of light obtained when (a) cyan and yellow and (b) cyan and magenta are added with equal intensities.

17 Determine the colour of white light that is transmitted first through a magenta filter and then through a cyan filter.

18 What two primary filters (cyan, magenta and yellow) must be used so that white light will emerge green?

19 (a) Determine the colour obtained when cyan, yellow and magenta are added with equal intensities.
(b) Determine the colour obtained when white light is transmitted through overlapping cyan, yellow and magenta filters.

20 Comment on the statement: 'Colour is a construction of the mind and not the property of an object.'

21 Name one of your favourite buildings and describe how the use of colour makes the building special.

22 The three grey dots in Figure A1.9 are identical. Do they *look* equally bright? How do you explain your answer?

Figure A1.9 For question 22.

OPTION A2

The Doppler effect

The content of this option is identical to that in Chapter 4.5 of Topic 4, Oscillations and waves, in the Core and AHL Material, to which the reader is referred.

SL Option A – Sight and wave phenomena

OPTION A3

Standing waves

The content of this option is identical to that in Chapter 4.6 of Topic 4, Oscillations and waves, in the Core and AHL Material, to which the reader is referred.

SL Option A – Sight and wave phenomena

OPTION A4

Diffraction

The content of this option is identical to that in Chapter 4.7 of Topic 4, Oscillations and waves, in the Core and AHL Material, to which the reader is referred.

Resolution

The content of this option is identical to that in Chapter 4.8 of Topic 4, Oscillations and waves, in the Core and AHL Material, to which the reader is referred.

Polarization

The content of this option is identical to that in Chapter 4.9 of Topic 4, Oscillations and waves, in the Core and AHL Material, to which the reader is referred.

Quantum physics

The content of this option is identical to that in Chapters 6.4 and 6.5 of Topic 6, Atomic and nuclear physics, in the Core and AHL Material, to which the reader is referred.

Nuclear physics

The content of this option is identical to that in Chapter 6.6 of Topic 6, Atomic and nuclear physics, in the Core and AHL Material, to which the reader is referred.

Analogue and digital signals

The content of this option is identical to that in Chapter 8.1 of Topic 8, Digital technology waves, in the Core and AHL Material, to which the reader is referred.

Data capture and imaging using CCDs

The content of this option is identical to that in Chapter 8.2 of Topic 8, Digital technology waves, in the Core and AHL Material, to which the reader is referred.

Electronics

The content of this option is identical to that in Option F5 of Option F, Communications, to which the reader is referred.

The mobile phone system

The content of this option is identical to that in Option F6 of Option F, Communications, to which the reader is referred.

Introduction to relativity

The content of this option is identical to that in Option H1 of Option H, Special and general relativity, to which the reader is referred.

Concepts and postulates of special relativity

The content of this option is identical to that in Option H2 of Option H, Special and general relativity, to which the reader is referred.

Relativistic kinematics

The content of this option is identical to that in Option H3 of Option H, Special and general relativity, to which the reader is referred.

Particles and interactions

The content of this option is identical to that in Option J1 of Option J, Particle physics, to which the reader is referred.

Quarks

The content of this option is identical to that in Option J3 of Option J, Particle physics, to which the reader is referred.

Introduction to the universe

This chapter is an introduction to the basic properties of the solar system and an account of the main celestial objects we meet in a study of astrophysics. The motion of the stars as they appear to an observer on the moving earth is also briefly discussed.

Objectives

By the end of this chapter you should be able to:

- describe the main features of the *solar system*;
- name the *main objects* making up the universe;
- give the definition of a *light year*;
- state the *average distances between stars and between galaxies*;
- outline the main facts about the *motion of stars* as they appear to an observer on earth.

The solar system

We live in a part of space called the solar system: a collection of eight major planets bound in elliptical orbits around a star called the sun. (Pluto has been stripped of its status as a major planet, and is now called a 'dwarf planet.' We shall not consider it as a planet in this option.) The sun has a mass of 1.99×10^{30} kg and a radius of 6.96×10^{8} m. The elliptical orbits of the planets have the sun at one of the two foci of the ellipse (see Figure E1.1a). The orbit of the earth is almost circular; that of Mercury is the most elliptical. The planes of the orbits of the planets differ only slightly from the plane of the earth's orbit, with the exception of Mercury, which has an inclination of about 7°. All planets revolve around the sun in the same direction. This is also true of the comets, with a few exceptions, the most famous being Halley's comet. The motion of the planets and comets around the sun is dictated by Kepler's laws (we have seen Kepler's third law in Chapter 2.11). Kepler's laws are also obeyed by the moons in their orbits around their respective planets. Characteristics of the planets are given in Tables E1.1–E1.3.

All the planets except Mercury and Venus have moons orbiting them. The earth's moon has a mass of 7.35×10^{22} kg, a radius of 1.74×10^{6} m, an orbit radius around the earth of 3.84×10^{8} m and an orbital period of 27.3 days. Jupiter has 16 moons, four of which are as big as earth's moon. Saturn has 17 moons and a spectacular ring system of millions of objects moving around the planet in circular, coplanar orbits. Uranus has 15 moons and a ring system. Pluto's moon, Charon, is almost as large as Pluto itself, so we may actually speak of a binary system. Pluto's orbit crosses the orbit of Neptune, and at times Pluto is actually closer to the sun than Neptune is. Pluto would have a high probability of a collision with Neptune were it not for the fact that the planes of their orbits are different.

In a region of space between the orbits of Mars and Jupiter is the *asteroid belt*. It consists of thousands of small objects (small planets) in orbit around the sun. The largest is called Ceres and

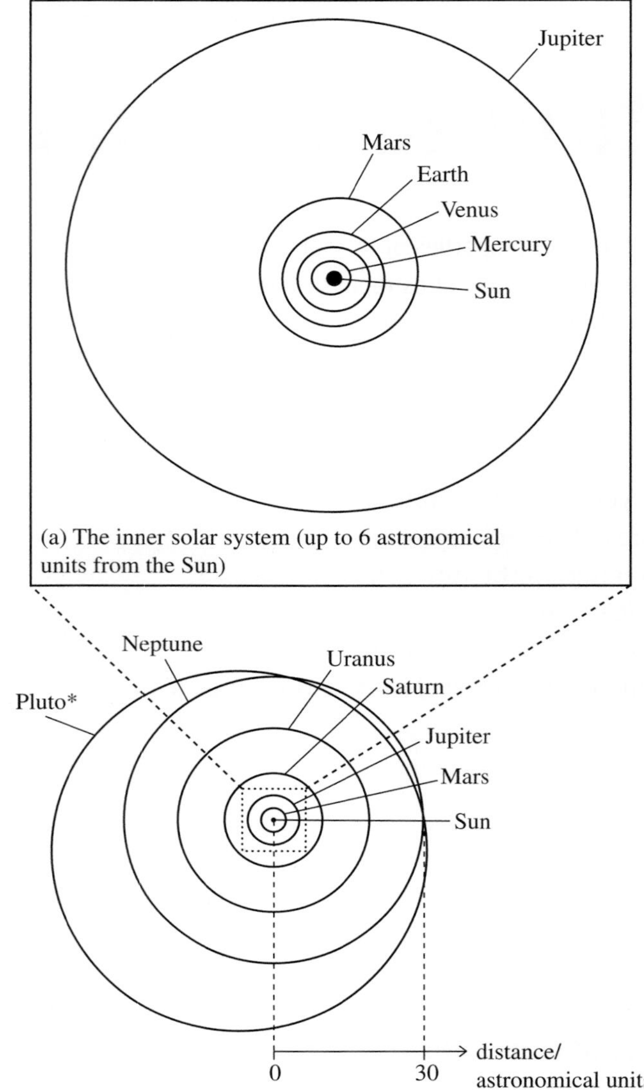

Figure E1.1 Planets orbit the sun in elliptical orbits. The sun is at one of the two foci of the ellipse. There is also a belt of small rocky asteroids between Mars and Jupiter.
*Pluto is no longer considered to be a planet.

Planet	Mass/kg	Radius/m	Orbit radius/m (average)	Orbital period
Mercury	3.30×10^{23}	2.44×10^{6}	5.79×10^{10}	88.0 days
Venus	4.87×10^{24}	6.05×10^{6}	1.08×10^{11}	224.7 days
Earth	5.98×10^{24}	6.38×10^{6}	1.50×10^{11}	365.3 days
Mars	6.42×10^{23}	3.40×10^{6}	2.28×10^{11}	687.0 days
Jupiter	1.90×10^{27}	6.91×10^{7}	7.78×10^{11}	11.86 yr
Saturn	5.69×10^{26}	6.03×10^{7}	1.43×10^{12}	29.42 yr
Uranus	8.66×10^{25}	2.56×10^{7}	2.88×10^{12}	83.75 yr
Neptune	1.03×10^{26}	2.48×10^{7}	4.50×10^{12}	163.7 yr

Table E1.1 The solar system. The distance between the sun and the earth (1.50×10^{11} m) is known as the astronomical unit (AU).

Planet	
Mercury	(smallest)
Mars	
Venus	
Earth	
Neptune	
Uranus	
Saturn	
Jupiter	(largest)

Table E1.2 The planets listed in order of increasing size.

Planet	Radius	Mass	Acceleration due to gravity
Mercury	0.379	0.056	0.36
Venus	0.972	0.817	0.87
Earth	1.000	1.000	1.00
Mars	0.533	0.108	0.38
Jupiter	11.190	318	2.64
Saturn	9.470	95.2	1.13
Uranus	3.689	14.6	1.07
Neptune	3.496	17.3	1.14

Table E1.3 The relative size, mass and acceleration due to gravity at the surface of the planets compared with earth, which is assigned a value of 1 for all these properties.

has a diameter of 770 km; many are under 10 km across. The asteroids revolve around their axes with periods under 12 h. There must have been many collisions between asteroids and the earth but traces of only a few such collisions remain. One theory about the asteroid belt involves the disruption of one planet into many pieces. Another invokes the effect of nearby Jupiter, whose large mass did not allow the material that was there at the time of the formation of the solar system to assemble into a planet.

Beyond the solar system

In the course of our study of the option on astrophysics, we will meet various objects making up the universe. Table E1.4 is an introduction to the meaning of the various terms. Most of these will be discussed in greater detail later on.

Example question

Q1

Take the density of interstellar space to be one atom of hydrogen per cubic centimetre of space. How much mass is there in a volume of interstellar space equal to the volume of the earth? Give an order-of-magnitude estimate without using a calculator.

Answer

The volume of the earth is

$$\begin{aligned} V &= \tfrac{4}{3}\pi R^3 \\ &\approx \tfrac{4}{3} \times 3 \times (6 \times 10^6)^3 \text{ m}^3 \\ &\approx 4 \times 200 \times 10^{18} \\ &\approx 10^{21} \text{ m}^3 \end{aligned}$$

Hence, the number of atoms in this volume is $10^{21} \times 10^6 = 10^{27}$ atoms of hydrogen. This corresponds to a mass of

$$10^{27} \times 1.6 \times 10^{-27} \text{ kg} \approx 1 \text{ kg}$$

The light year

As we move away from the solar system, we enter immense expanses of space. It is useful to have a more convenient unit of distance than the metre.

▶ We define the light year (ly) as the distance travelled by light in one year. Thus

$$\begin{aligned} 1 \text{ ly} &= 3 \times 10^8 \times 365 \times 24 \times 60 \times 60 \text{ m} \\ &= 9.46 \times 10^{15} \text{ m} \end{aligned}$$

Also convenient for measuring large distances is the *parsec* (pc), a unit that will be properly defined on page 507, 1 pc = 3.26 ly = 3.09×10^{16} m.

▶ The average distance *between stars* in a galaxy is about 1 pc, an easy number to remember. The distance to the nearest star (Proxima Centauri) is 4×10^{16} m, which is approximately 4.3ly = 1.3 pc. A simple message sent to a civilization on Proxima Centauri would thus take 4.3 yr to reach it and an answer would arrive on Earth another 4.3 yr later.

The average distance *between galaxies* varies from about 100 kpc for galaxies within the same cluster to a few Mpc for galaxies belonging to different clusters.

Binary star	Two stars orbiting a common centre
Black dwarf	The remnant of a white dwarf after it has cooled down. It has very low luminosity
Black hole	A singularity in space-time; the end result in the evolution of a very massive star
Brown dwarf	Gas and dust that did not reach high enough temperatures to initiate fusion. These objects continue to compact and cool down
Cepheid variable	A star of variable luminosity. The luminosity increases sharply and falls off gently with a well-defined period. The period is related to the absolute luminosity of the star and so can be used to estimate the distance to the star
Clusters of galaxies	Galaxies close to each other and affecting each other gravitationally, behaving as one unit
Comet	A small body (mainly ice and dust) orbiting the sun in an elliptical orbit
Constellation	A group of stars in a recognizable pattern that *appear* to be near each other in space
Dark matter	Generic name for matter in galaxies and clusters of galaxies that is too cold to radiate. Its existence is inferred from techniques other than direct visual observation
Galaxy	A collection of a very large number of stars mutually attracting each other through the gravitational force and staying together. The number of stars in a galaxy varies from a few million in dwarf galaxies to hundreds of billions in large galaxies. It is estimated that 100 billion galaxies exist in the observable universe
Interstellar medium	Gases (mainly hydrogen and helium) and dust grains (silicates, carbon and iron) filling the space in between stars. The density of interstellar mass is very low. There is about one atom of gas for every cubic centimetre of space. The density of dust is a trillion times smaller. The temperature of the gas is about 100 K
Main sequence star	A normal star that is undergoing nuclear fusion of hydrogen into helium. Our sun is a typical main sequence star
Neutron star	If a red giant is very large (a supergiant), the end result of the explosion throwing off mass will be a star even smaller than a white dwarf (a few tens of kilometres in diameter) and very dense. This is a star consisting almost entirely of neutrons. The neutrons form a superfluid around a core of immense pressure and density. A neutron star is an astonishing macroscopic example of microscopic quantum physics
Nova	The sudden increase in luminosity of a white dwarf caused by material from a nearby star falling into the white dwarf
Planetary nebula	The ejected envelope of a red giant star
Pulsar	A rapidly rotating neutron star emitting electromagnetic radiation in the radio region. Pulsars have very strong magnetic fields. Periods of rotation vary from a few milliseconds to seconds
Quasars	Powerful energy emitters. These are very active cores of young galaxies. The name stands for quasi-stellar radio-emitting objects, a name given since the first observations of quasars indicated a small, stellar-like size. The energy output from a quasar is greater than that of hundreds of galaxies combined. From redshift measurements, quasars are known to move away from us at very high speeds
Red dwarf	A very small star with low temperature, reddish in colour
Red giant	A main sequence star evolves into a red giant – a very large, reddish star. There are nuclear reactions involving the fusion of helium into heavier elements
Stellar cluster	A group of stars that are physically near each other in space, created by the collapse of the same gas cloud
Supernova	The explosion of a red supergiant star. The amount of energy emitted in a supernova explosion can be staggering – comparable to the total energy radiated by our sun in its entire lifetime!
White dwarf	A red giant at the end stage of its evolution will throw off mass and leave behind a very small (the size of the earth), very dense star in which no nuclear reactions take place. It is very hot but its small size gives it a very low luminosity

Table E1.4 Definitions of terms.

Example questions

Q2

The Local Group is a cluster of some 20 galaxies, including our own Milky Way and the Andromeda galaxy. It extends over a distance of about 1 Mpc. Estimate the average distance between the galaxies of the Local Group.

Answer

Assume that a volume of

$$V = \tfrac{4}{3}\pi R^3$$
$$\approx \tfrac{4}{3} \times 3 \times (0.5)^3\ \text{Mpc}^3$$
$$\approx 0.5\ \text{Mpc}^3$$

is uniformly shared by the 20 galaxies. Then to each corresponds a volume of

$$\frac{0.5}{20}\ \text{Mpc}^3 = 0.025\ \text{Mpc}^3$$

The linear size of each volume is thus

$$\sqrt[3]{0.025\ \text{Mpc}^3} \approx 0.3\ \text{Mpc}$$
$$= 300\ \text{kpc}$$

so we may take the average separation of the galaxies to be 300 kpc.

Q3

The Milky Way galaxy has about 2×10^{11} stars. Assuming an average mass equal to that of the sun, estimate the mass of the Milky Way.

Answer

The mass of the sun is 2×10^{30} kg and so the Milky Way galaxy has a mass of about

$$2 \times 10^{11} \times 2 \times 10^{31} = 4 \times 10^{41}\ \text{kg}$$

Q4

The observable universe contains some 100 billion galaxies. Assuming an average mass comparable to that of the Milky Way, estimate the mass of the observable universe.

Answer

The mass is

$$100 \times 10^9 \times 4 \times 10^{41}\ \text{kg} = 4 \times 10^{52}\ \text{kg}$$

The motion of the stars

The observation of the motion of the stars is greatly complicated by the fact that the earth is itself moving. In the course of a night, stars and constellations appear to move across the sky from east to west. The ancient astronomers noticed, however, that the *relative* positions of the stars and constellations remained unchanged. That gave rise to the notion of the *celestial sphere*, a huge sphere surrounding and rotating around the earth on whose surface the stars and constellations were firmly embedded (see Figure E1.2). We know now that the rotation of the stars and constellations is a consequence of the rotation of the earth about its axis. If the axis of rotation of the earth is extended, it intersects the celestial sphere at the north and south celestial poles. The star Polaris (the North Star) is right on the celestial north pole and so appears not to move at all. The rest of the stars and constellations appear to rotate about it.

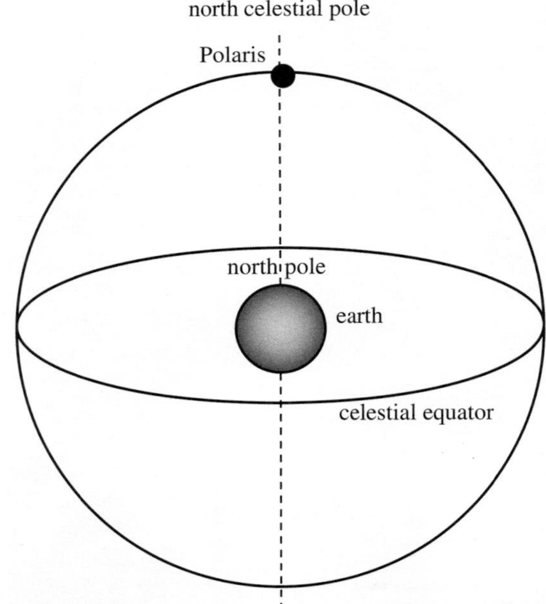

Figure E1.2 The celestial sphere upon which the stars seem to be embedded. The star Polaris is right on the celestial north pole.

As shown in Figure E1.3, the axis of rotation of the earth precesses in space. The axis of rotation that now points to the star Polaris will point to the star Vega in 12 000 years' time. Vega will then become the 'north star'.

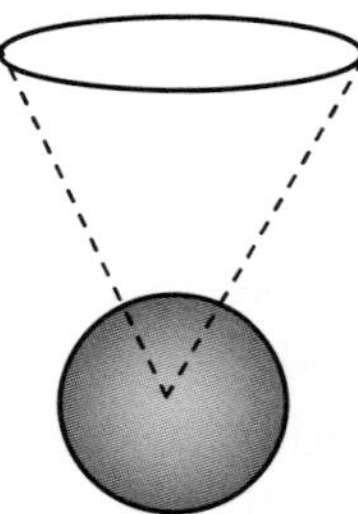

Figure E1.3 The axis of rotation of the earth precesses in space tracing out a cone. Now it points at the star Polaris. In the year AD 14 000 it will point at the star Vega. The period of precession is about 26 000 yr.

A long time exposure of the night sky would show arcs traced by stars as the 'celestial sphere rotates' – that is, as the earth rotates about its axis (see Figure E1.4).

Figure E1.4 A photograph of the night sky over a long period of time shows stars moving along arcs. Copyright: Anglo-Australian Observatory. Photograph taken by David Malin.

As the earth rotates around the sun, the night sky appears to be changing. As can be seen from Figure E1.5, at different times of the year the night hemisphere points along different directions in the sky and hence the view of stars and constellations is different as well. Since the earth completes one revolution in one year, it follows that the change in the direction from one night to the next is $\frac{360^\circ}{365} = 0.986^\circ$, or about one degree. This is too small to be detected by the unaided eye but in the course of a few weeks the changes can easily be detected.

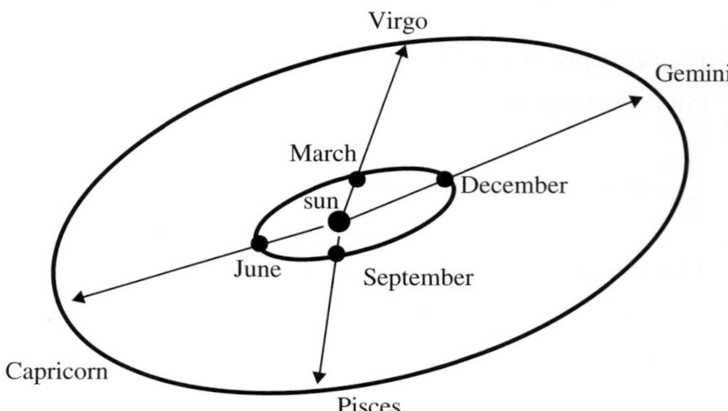

Figure E1.5 As the earth rotates around the sun, the earth's night hemisphere points at different constellations. Shown here are four of the twelve constellations making up the astrological zodiac.

QUESTIONS

1 The density of interstellar space is very low, yet light suffers significant absorption on its way to us from a distant star or galaxy. How can that be?

2 How would you distinguish the photograph of a star from that of a quasar?

3 A neutron star has an average density of about 10^{17} kg m^{-3}. Show that this is comparable to the density of an atomic nucleus.

4 A sunspot near the centre of the sun is found to subtend an angle of 4 arcseconds (1 arcsecond = 1/3600 of a degree). Find the diameter of the sunspot.

5 Draw appropriate diagrams to show how the phases of the Moon are created.

6 How many earth volumes fit into Jupiter?

7 Divide the planets among the students in your class and then calculate the density of each planet. List the planets in order of increasing density.

8 On which planet would you expect the escape velocity to be the greatest? Divide the planets among the students in your class and then calculate the escape velocity of each planet. List the planets in order of increasing escape velocity.

9 For the planets, make a graph of the logarithm of the period of revolution around the sun versus the logarithm of the distance to the sun. Draw a line of best fit and find the slope. What is the formula relating the period to the distance?

10 From Kepler's third law (see also question 9), it can be deduced that the distance of Venus from the sun is about 0.7 AU, where 1 AU is the distance of the earth from the sun. Assuming circular orbits, draw a diagram that shows Venus and the earth at their closest. A radar signal is emitted from earth, bounces off Venus, and is received back on earth 300 s later. From this information, find the value of 1 AU in metres.

11 The resolution of the Hubble Space Telescope is about 0.05 arcseconds (1 arcsecond = 1/3600 of a degree). What is the diameter of the smallest object on the moon that can be resolved by the telescope?

12 The moon never shows us its 'dark side'. What does this imply about its period of revolution about its axis and its period of revolution around the earth? Illustrate your answer by diagrams. Find out more about how this might come about.

13 Explain why the sun always rises in the east and sets in the west. Does the moon do the same? Do the stars do the same? Explain.

14 The speed of a body in orbit around another can be determined using Newton's law of gravitation. Let M be the mass of the body at the centre of a circular orbit and m the mass of the orbiting body. Then, the force on m is the force of gravity $F = \frac{GMm}{r^2}$. Equating this to mass times acceleration gives $v^2 = \frac{GM}{r}$. Use this to find the orbital speed of the earth around the sun.

15 Europa is a moon of Jupiter orbiting the planet in 3.55 days at a distance of 671 000 km. Find the mass of Jupiter.

16 The sun is at a distance of 28 000 ly from the centre of the Milky Way and revolves around the galactic centre with a period of 211 million years. Estimate from this information the orbital speed of the sun and the mass of the Milky Way. What assumption have you made in stating that your answer is indeed the mass of the galaxy? (See the two previous questions.)

17 Why are the planets Venus and Mercury always observed near the sun (for example, just after sunset or just before sunrise)?

Stellar radiation

This chapter introduces two main tools in the study of stellar structure: the black-body radiation law and the related Wien displacement law. The significance of stellar spectra is discussed as well as the properties of a few special star systems, such as binary stars. The chapter closes with a discussion of another major tool in astrophysics: the Hertzsprung–Russell diagram.

Objectives

By the end of this chapter you should be able to:

- understand that a star is in equilibrium under the action of two opposing forces, *gravitation* and the *radiation pressure of the star*;
- appreciate that *nuclear fusion* provides the energy source of a star;
- give the definitions of *luminosity*, $L = \sigma AT^4$, as the power radiated into space by a star and *apparent brightness*, $b = \frac{L}{4\pi d^2}$, as the power received per unit area on earth;
- state the *Wien displacement law*, $\lambda_0 T = 2.90 \times 10^{-3}$ K m, and solve problems using it;
- appreciate the kind of information a *stellar spectrum* can provide;
- state the main properties of *main sequence stars*, *red giants*, *white dwarfs* and *binary stars*;
- describe the structure of an *HR diagram* and place the main types of stars on the diagram.

The energy source of stars

A star such as our own sun radiates an enormous amount of energy into space – about 10^{26} J s^{-1}. The source of this energy is nuclear fusion in the interior of the star, in which nuclei of hydrogen fuse to produce helium and release energy in the process. Because of the *high temperatures* in the interior of the star, the electrostatic repulsion between protons can be overcome and hydrogen nuclei can fuse. Because of the *high pressure* in stellar interiors, the nuclei are sufficiently close to each other to give a high probability of collision and hence fusion. The sequence of nuclear fusion reactions that take place is called the *proton–proton cycle* and consists of

$$^1_1\text{H} + {}^1_1\text{H} \rightarrow {}^2_1\text{H} + {}^0_1\text{e}^+ + {}^0_0\nu_e$$
$$^1_1\text{H} + {}^2_1\text{H} \rightarrow {}^3_2\text{He} + {}^0_0\gamma$$
$$^3_2\text{He} + {}^3_2\text{He} \rightarrow {}^4_2\text{He} + 2{}^1_1\text{H}$$

Energy is released at each stage of the cycle but most of it is released in the third and final stage. The energy produced is carried away by the photons and neutrinos produced in the reactions. As these particles move outwards they collide with surrounding protons and electrons and give them some of the energy. Thus, gradually, most of the particles in the star will receive some of the kinetic energy produced. The motion of the particles inside the star, as a result of the energy they receive, can stabilize the star against gravitational collapse. Note that the net effect of these reactions is to turn four hydrogen nuclei into one helium:

$$4{}^{1}_{1}\mathrm{H} \rightarrow {}^{4}_{2}\mathrm{He} + 2\mathrm{e}^{+} + 2\nu_{\mathrm{e}} + 2\gamma$$

Helium, being heavier than hydrogen, collects in the core of the star. The energy released in the reactions above can be calculated by the methods of nuclear physics we studied earlier. The energy released per reaction is 26.7 MeV or 4.27×10^{-12} J.

▶ Nuclear fusion provides the energy that is needed to keep the star hot, so that the radiation pressure is high enough to oppose further gravitational contraction, and at the same time to provide the energy that the star is radiating into space (see Figure E2.1).

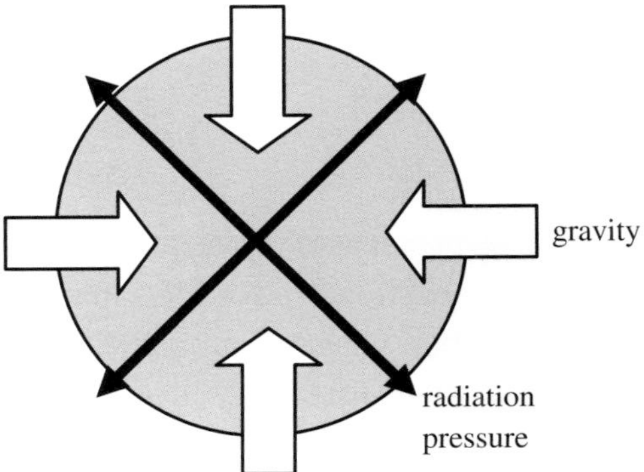

Figure E2.1 The stability of a star depends on equilibrium between two opposing forces: gravitation, which tends to collapse the star, and radiation pressure, which tends to make it expand.

Luminosity

▶ Luminosity is the amount of energy radiated by the star per second; that is, it is the power radiated by the star. As shown in the next section, luminosity depends on the surface temperature and surface area of the star.

Consider a star of luminosity L. Imagine a sphere of radius d centred at the location of the star. If the star is assumed to radiate uniformly in all directions, then the energy radiated in 1 s can be thought to be distributed over the surface of this imaginary sphere. A detector of area a placed somewhere on this sphere will receive a small fraction of this total energy (see Figure E2.2a). The fraction is equal to the ratio of the detector area a to the total surface area of the sphere; that is, the received energy per second will be $\frac{aL}{4\pi d^2}$.

▶ The received energy per second per unit area of detector is called the apparent brightness and is given by

$$b = \frac{L}{4\pi d^2}$$

The units of apparent brightness are W m^{-2}.

This shows that the apparent brightness is directly proportional to the intrinsic luminosity, and varies as the inverse square of the star's distance (see Figure E2.2b).

Apparent brightness is measured using a *charge-coupled device* (CCD), which offers many advantages over the conventional photographic film method (see Chapter 8.2). A CCD has a photosensitive silicon surface that releases an electron when it is hit by a photon. The number of electrons released is proportional to the number of photons that hit the surface. Thus, the amount of charge is a direct measure of the brightness of the object being observed. The

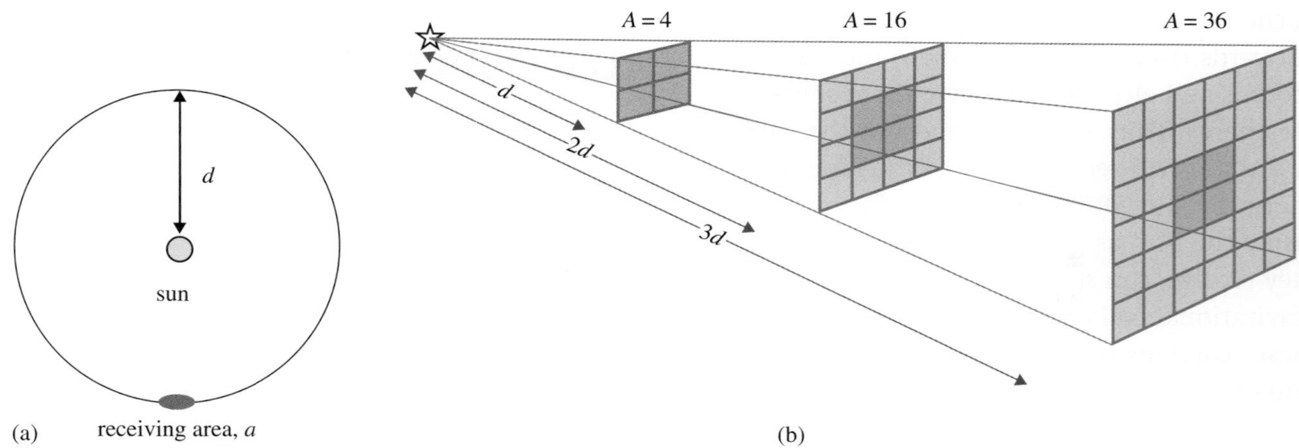

Figure E2.2 (a) The sun's energy is distributed over an imaginary sphere of radius equal to the distance between the sun and the observer. The observer thus receives only a very small fraction of the total energy, equal to the ratio of the receiver's area to the total area of the imaginary sphere. (b) The inverse square law:

$$\text{observed brightness} \propto \frac{1}{\text{area } A} \propto \frac{1}{(\text{distance } d)^2}$$

silicon surface is divided into many smaller areas, called *pixels*, and the charge released in each pixel can then be used (with digital techniques) to reconstruct an image of the object being observed. CCDs are more than 50 times more efficient in recording the photons arriving at the device than conventional photographic film.

Black-body radiation

A body of surface area A and *absolute* temperature T radiates energy away in the form of electromagnetic waves, according to the Stefan–Boltzmann law.

▶ The amount of energy per second radiated by a star of surface area A and absolute *surface* temperature T (i.e. the *luminosity*) is given by

$$L = \sigma A T^4$$

where the constant σ is called the Stefan-Boltzmann constant ($\sigma = 5.67 \times 10^{-8}\ \text{W m}^{-2}\ \text{K}^{-4}$).

If we now recall the definition of apparent brightness given in the previous section, we see that

$$b = \frac{\sigma A T^4}{4\pi d^2}$$

Example questions

Q1

The radius of star A is three times that of star B and its temperature is double that of B. Find the ratio of the luminosity of A to that of B.

Answer

$$\frac{L_A}{L_B} = \frac{\sigma 4\pi (R_A)^2 T_A^4}{\sigma 4\pi (R_B)^2 T_B^4}$$

$$= \frac{(R_A)^2 T_A^4}{(R_B)^2 T_B^4}$$

$$= \frac{(3R_B)^2 (2T_B)^4}{(R_B)^2 T_B^4}$$

$$= 3^2 \times 2^4 = 144$$

Q2

The stars in Example question 1 have the same apparent brightness when viewed from earth. Calculate the ratio of their distances.

Answer

$$\frac{b_A}{b_B} = 1$$

$$= \frac{L_A / (4\pi d_A^2)}{L_B / (4\pi d_B^2)}$$

$$= \frac{L_A}{L_B}\frac{d_B^2}{d_A^2}$$

$$= 144\frac{d_B^2}{d_A^2}$$

$$\Rightarrow \frac{d_A}{d_B} = 12$$

Q3

The apparent brightness of a star is $6.4 \times 10^{-8}\,\mathrm{W\,m^{-2}}$. If its distance is 15 ly, what is its luminosity?

Answer

We use $b = \frac{L}{4\pi d^2}$ to find

$$L = b4\pi d^2$$

$$= \left(6.4 \times 10^{-8}\,\frac{\mathrm{W}}{\mathrm{m}^2}\right) \times 4\pi \times (15 \times 9.46 \times 10^{15})^2\,\mathrm{m}^2$$

$$= 1.62 \times 10^{28}\,\mathrm{W}$$

Q4

A star has half the sun's surface temperature and 400 times its luminosity. How many times bigger is it?

Answer

We have that

$$400 = \frac{L}{L_{sun}}$$

$$= \frac{\sigma 4\pi (R)^2 T^4}{\sigma 4\pi (R_{sun})^2 T_{sun}^4}$$

$$= \frac{(R)^2 (T_{sun}/2)^4}{(R_{sun})^2 T_{sun}^4}$$

$$= \frac{R^2}{(R_{sun})^2 16}$$

$$\frac{R^2}{(R_{sun})^2 16} = 400$$

$$\Rightarrow \frac{R^2}{(R_{sun})^2} = 16 \times 400$$

$$\Rightarrow \frac{R}{R_{sun}} = 80$$

The energy radiated by a star is in the form of electromagnetic radiation and is distributed over an infinite range of wavelengths. Figure E2.3 shows what is called the spectrum of a black body, that is, the energy radiated per second per wavelength interval from a unit area of the body. The horizontal axis represents wavelength in micrometres. The vertical scale has units of $\mathrm{W\,m^{-3}}$.

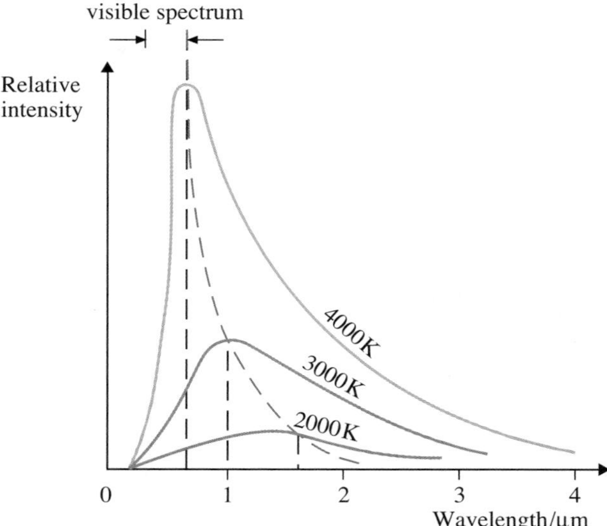

Figure E2.3 Radiation profiles at different temperatures. The broken lines show how the peak intensity, and the wavelength at which this occurs, vary with temperature. The overall intensity is represented by the area under the graph.

Most of the energy is emitted around the peak wavelength. Calling this wavelength λ_0, we see that the colour of the star is mainly determined by the colour corresponding to λ_0. The area under the black-body curve is the total power radiated from a unit area, irrespective of wavelength, and is thus given by σT^4.

▶ The Wien displacement law relates the wavelength λ_0 to *surface temperature* T:

$$\lambda_0 T = \text{constant} = 2.90 \times 10^{-3}\,\mathrm{K\,m}$$

which implies that the higher the temperature, the lower the wavelength at which most of the energy is radiated.

Example questions

Q5

The sun has an approximate black-body spectrum with most of the energy radiated at a wavelength of 5.0×10^{-7} m. Find the surface temperature of the sun.

Answer

From Wien's law

$5.0 \times 10^{-7}\ \text{m} \times T = 2.9 \times 10^{-3}\ \text{K m}$

that is

$T = 5800\ \text{K}$

Q6

The sun (radius $R = 7.0 \times 10^{8}$ m) radiates a total power of 3.9×10^{26} W. Find its surface temperature.

Answer

From $L = \sigma A T^4$ and $A = 4\pi R^2$ we find

$$T = \left(\frac{L}{\sigma 4\pi R^2}\right)^{1/4} \text{K} \approx 5800\ \text{K}$$

Stellar spectra

A great wealth of information can be gathered about a star from studies of its spectrum.

Temperature

The surface temperature of the star is determined by measuring the wavelength at which most of the radiation is emitted (see Figure E2.4).

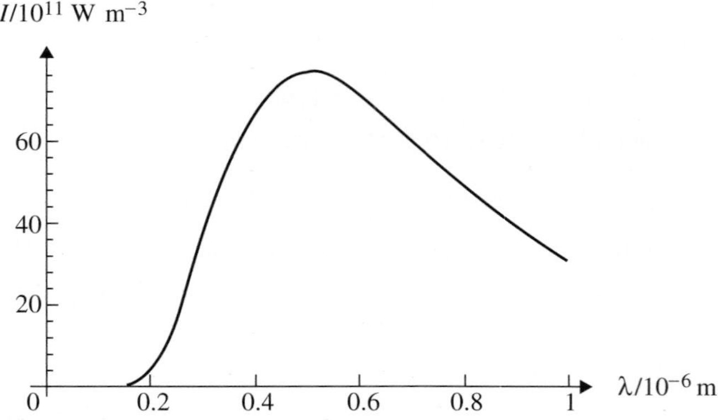

Figure E2.4 The spectrum of this star shows that most of the energy is emitted at a wavelength of about $\lambda = 5 \times 10^{-7}$ m. Use of Wien's law then allows the determination of the surface temperature of the star.

For the star of Figure E2.4, Wien's law gives

$$\lambda_0 T = 2.90 \times 10^{-3}\ \text{K m}$$
$$\Rightarrow T = \frac{2.90 \times 10^{-3}}{5 \times 10^{-7}}\ \text{K}$$
$$= 5800\ \text{K}$$

Chemical composition

In practice it is not always possible to obtain a spectrum like that of Figure E2.4. It is much more common to obtain an absorption spectrum in which dark lines are seen superimposed on a background of continuous colour (shown in black and white in Figure E2.5). Each dark line represents the absorption of light of a specific frequency by a specific chemical element in the star's atmosphere.

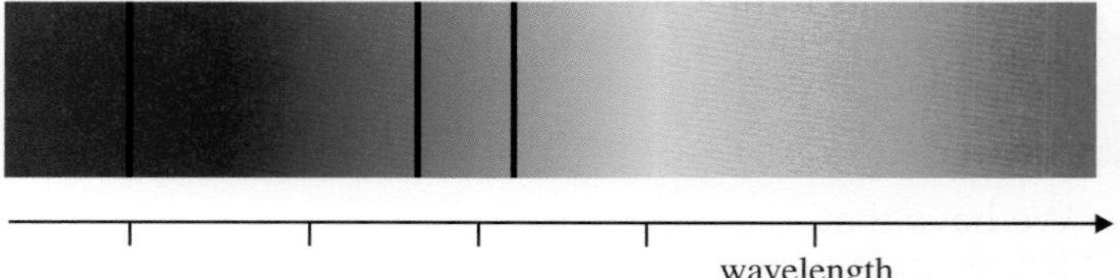

Figure E2.5 Absorption spectrum of a star showing three absorption lines. A real spectrum would show thousands of dark lines.

It has been found, however, that most stars have essentially the same chemical composition, yet show different absorption spectra. The reason for this difference is that different stars have different temperatures. Consider two stars with the same content of hydrogen. One is hot, about 25 000 K, and the other cool, about 10 000 K. The hydrogen in the hot star is ionized, which means the electrons have left the hydrogen atoms. These atoms cannot absorb any light passing through them, since there are no bound electrons that can absorb the photons and make transitions to higher energy states. Thus, the hot star will not show any absorption lines at hydrogen wavelengths. The cooler star, however, has many of its hydrogen atoms in the energy state $n = 2$. Electrons in this state can absorb photons to make transitions to states such as $n = 3$ and $n = 4$, giving rise to the characteristic hydrogen absorption lines. Similarly, an even cooler star of temperature, say, 3000 K will have most of its electrons in the ground state of hydrogen atoms and so can only absorb photons corresponding to ultraviolet wavelengths. These will not result in dark lines in an optical spectrum.

In this way, study of absorption spectra gives information about the temperature of the star and its chemical composition. Of course, as discussed in the last paragraph, the understanding is that absence of certain lines does not necessarily imply the absence of the corresponding chemical element.

Stars are divided into seven *spectral classes* according to their colour (see Table E2.1). As we have just seen, colour is related to surface temperature. The spectral classes are called O, B, A, F, G, K and M. (Remembered as Oh Be A Fine Girl/Guy Kiss Me!)

Spectral class	Colour	Temperature/K
O	Blue	25000–50000
B	Blue-white	12000–25000
A	White	7500–12000
F	Yellow-white	6000–7500
G	Yellow	4500–6000
K	Yellow-red	3000–4500
M	Red	2000–3000

Table E2.1 Colour and temperature characteristics of spectral classes.

It is known from spectral studies that hydrogen is the predominant element in normal main sequence stars (see next section), making up to 70% of their mass, followed by helium with 28%; the rest is made up of heavier elements.

Radial velocity

If a star moves away from or toward us, its spectral lines will show a Doppler shift. The shift will be toward the red if the star moves away, and toward the blue if it comes toward us. Measurement of the shift allows the determination of the radial velocity of the star.

Rotation

If a star rotates, then part of the star is moving toward the observer and part away from the observer. Thus, light from the different parts of the star will again show Doppler shifts, from which the rotation speed may be determined.

Magnetic fields

In a magnetic field a spectral line may split into two or more lines (the Zeeman effect). Measurement of the amount of splitting yields information on the magnetic field of the star.

The Hertzsprung–Russell diagram

Astronomers realized early on that there was a correlation between the luminosity of a star and its surface temperature. The higher the temperature, the higher the luminosity. In the early part of the twentieth century, the Danish astronomer, Ejnar Hertzsprung, and the American, Henry Norris Russell, independently pioneered plots of stellar luminosities. Hertzsprung plotted luminosities versus surface temperature and Russell plotted absolute magnitude versus spectral class. Such plots are now called Hertzsprung–Russell (HR) diagrams. In the HR diagram that follows (Figure E2.6), the vertical axis represents luminosity in units of the sun's luminosity (i.e. 1 on the vertical axis corresponds to the solar luminosity of 3.9×10^{26} W). The horizontal axis shows the surface temperature of the star (in thousands of kelvin). The temperature *decreases as we move to the right*. Also shown at the top of the diagram is the *spectral class* for each star, which is an alternative way to label the horizontal axis. The luminosity in this diagram varies from 10^{-5} to 10^{5}, a full 10 orders of magnitude, whereas the temperature varies from 3000 K to 25 000 K. For this reason, the scale on the axes is *not* linear.

As more and more stars were placed on the HR diagram, it became clear that a pattern was emerging. The stars were not randomly distributed on the diagram.

▶ Three clear features emerge from the HR diagram.

1 Most stars fall on a strip extending diagonally across the diagram from top left to bottom right. This is called the main sequence.

2 Some large stars, reddish in colour, occupy the top right – these are the *red giants* (large, cool stars).

3 The bottom left is a region of small stars known as *white dwarfs* (small and hot).

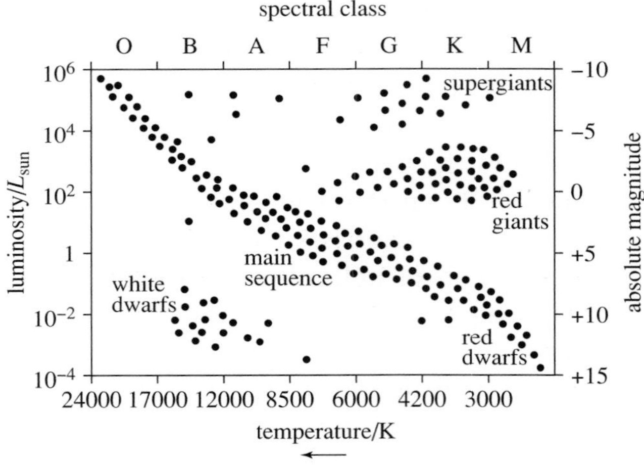

Figure E2.6 The Hertzsprung–Russell diagram. The (surface) temperature increases to the left. Note that the scales are not linear.

In fact, about 90% of all stars are main sequence stars, 9% are white dwarfs and 1% are red giants. Another feature of the HR diagram is that, as we move along the *main sequence* toward hotter stars, the mass of the stars increases as well. Thus, the right end of the main sequence is occupied by red dwarfs and the left by blue giants. Note that as we move up the main sequence (right to left), the mass of the stars increases.

Note that, once we know the temperature of a star (for example, through its spectrum), the HR diagram can tell us the luminosity of the star with an acceptable degree of accuracy, provided it is a main sequence star. (The main sequence is, after all, not a mathematical line but a broad band.) This observation is the basis for a method that determines the distance to a star called spectroscopic parallax (see Option E3).

Types of stars

As we have just seen, the HR diagram makes a clear division of stars into various types.

Main sequence stars

Our sun is a typical member of the main sequence. It has a mass of 2×10^{30} kg, a radius of 7×10^8 m, an average density of 1.4×10^3 kg m^{-3} and radiates at a rate of 3.9×10^{26} W. What distinguishes different main sequence stars is their mass. Main sequence stars produce enough energy in their core, from nuclear fusion of hydrogen into helium, to exactly counterbalance the tendency of the star to collapse under its own weight. The luminosity of stars on the main sequence increases as the mass increases.

Red giants

Red giants are another important class of stars. They are very large, cool stars with a reddish appearance. The luminosity of red giants is considerably greater than the luminosity of main sequence stars of the same temperature; they can, in fact, be a million or even a billion times bigger. Treating them as black bodies radiating according to the Stefan–Boltzmann law means that a luminosity of 10^6 times bigger corresponds to an area of 10^6 times bigger, which means a radius of 10^3 times bigger. This explains the name given to these stars. The mass of a red giant can be as much as 1000 times the mass of our sun, but their huge size also implies small densities. In fact, a red giant will have a central hot core surrounded by an enormous envelope of extremely tenuous gas.

White dwarfs

These are very common stars but their faintness makes them hard to detect. A well-known white dwarf is Sirius B, the second star in a binary star system (double star), the other member of which, Sirius A, is the brightest star in the evening sky. Sirius A and B have about the same surface temperature (about 10 000 K) but the luminosity of Sirius B is about 10 000 times smaller. This means that Sirius B has a radius that is 100 times smaller than that of Sirius A. Here is a star of mass roughly that of the sun with a size similar to that of the earth. This means that its density is about 10^6 times the density of the earth!

White dwarfs form when a star collapsing under its own gravitation stabilizes as a result of *electron degeneracy pressure*. This means that the electrons of the star are forced into the same quantum states. To avoid that, the Pauli exclusion principle forces them to acquire large kinetic energies. The large electron energies can then withstand the gravitational pressure of the star.

In addition, we may identify three other important star types.

Variable stars

Whereas the luminosity of our sun and other main sequence stars has remained constant over millions of years, stars exist that show a variation in their luminosity with time. These are called *variable stars*. The variation of luminosity with time (a graph showing the variation of luminosity with time is known as the *light curve* of the star) can be periodic or non-periodic. The reasons for the variable luminosity are mainly changes in the internal structure of the star. For example, a normal main sequence star will, as part of its evolutionary process, grow in size as its outer envelope expands. In doing so, it may eject mass from the outer layers, forming what is called a *planetary nebula*, with an ensuing increase in the star's luminosity. Similarly, if the star is substantially heavier than the sun, the release of mass and energy from the outer envelope is even more dramatic, resulting in a *supernova* with luminosity increases by factors of a million. In the case of binary stars (see later), matter can be transferred from one star to the other and, on being heated, this matter can radiate, again increasing the star's luminosity.

Cepheids

Most prominent among the class of *periodic* variables are the Cepheid stars, because there exists a relationship between the period of the light curve and the peak luminosity of these stars. Thus, observation of a Cepheid over time allows the determination of its period and hence its peak luminosity. Knowledge of the luminosity is important since comparison with the apparent brightness yields the distance of the star. Cepheids have periods from 1 to 50 days.

The study of variable stars is important since it provides much information about the internal structure of the star and is a testing ground for theories about stellar structure.

Binary stars

A system of two stars that orbit a common centre is called a binary star system. Depending on the method used to observe them, binaries fall into three classes:

- visual
- eclipsing
- spectroscopic.

Binaries are important because they allow for the determination of stellar masses as explained below.

Visual binaries – These appear as two separate stars when viewed through a telescope. They are in orbit around a common centre, the centre of mass of the two stars, as shown in Figure E2.7 in the simplified case of circular orbits.

It is shown in the chapter on gravitation that the common period of rotation for a binary is given by

$$T^2 = \frac{4\pi^2 d^3}{G(M_1 + M_2)}$$

where d is the distance between the two stars. Thus we can conclude that:

▶ Measurement of the separation distance and period gives the *sum* of the masses making up the binary.

To determine the masses individually, we need information about the orbit of each star. Note that the inner star is the more massive of the two.

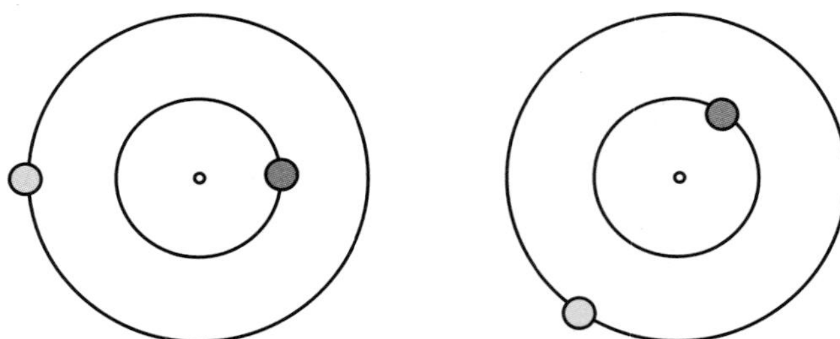

Figure E2.7 A binary star system. The stars rotate about their centre of mass. The two stars are always diametrically opposite each other.

Example question

Q7

A visual binary with a period of 50 yr is at a distance from earth of 8.79 ly. The distance between the stars subtends an angle at earth (the 'angular diameter') of 7.56 arcseconds. Find the sum of the masses in the binary.

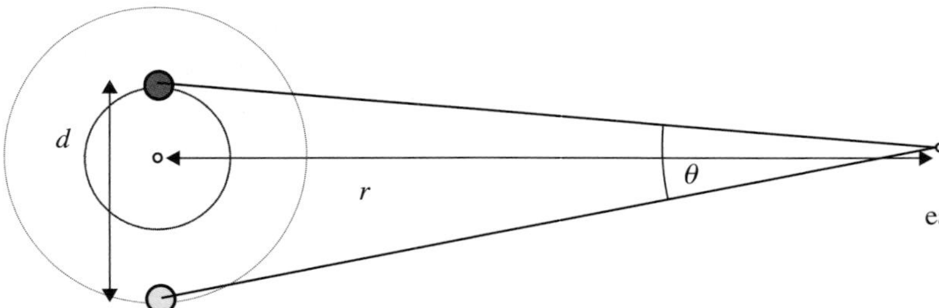

Figure E2.8 (Not to scale).

Answer

See Figure E2.8.

Figure E2.8 shows what is meant by 'angular diameter' – it is the angle θ that the separation of the stars subtends at earth. The distance separating the stars is $d = r\theta$ where r is the distance to the binary. The angle must be expressed in radians, that is (″ = arcseconds)

$$\theta = 7.56'' = \frac{7.56^\circ}{3600} = \frac{7.56^\circ}{3600} \times \frac{\pi}{180^\circ} = 3.665 \times 10^{-5}\ \text{rad}$$

The distance to the binary in metres is

$$r = 8.79 \times 9.46 \times 10^{15} = 8.31 \times 10^{16}\ \text{m}$$

Hence the separation of the stars is $d = 3.05 \times 10^{12}$ m. From the formula for the period

$$M_1 + M_2 = \frac{4\pi^2 d^3}{GT^2} = \frac{4\pi^2(3.05 \times 10^{12})^3}{6.67 \times 10^{-11} \times (50 \times 365 \times 24 \times 60 \times 60)^2} = 6.75 \times 10^{30}\ \text{kg}$$

or 3.4 solar masses.

Eclipsing binaries – If the plane of the orbit of the two stars is suitably oriented relative to that of the earth, the light from one of the stars in the binary may be blocked by the other, resulting in an eclipse of the star, which may be total or partial. If a bright star (light grey circle) is orbited by a dimmer companion (dark circle), the light curve has the pattern shown in Figure E2.9. Such an example is provided by the system of AR Cassiopeia.

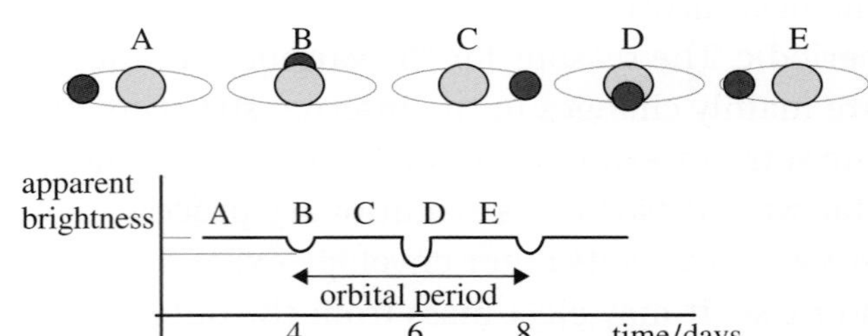

Figure E2.9 The light curve of AR Cassiopeia shows dips in brightness as the dimmer companion disappears behind the brighter star. When the dim star is in front, the dip is the largest.

Example question

Q8

Discuss the light curve of the eclipsing binary system Algol shown in Figure E2.10.

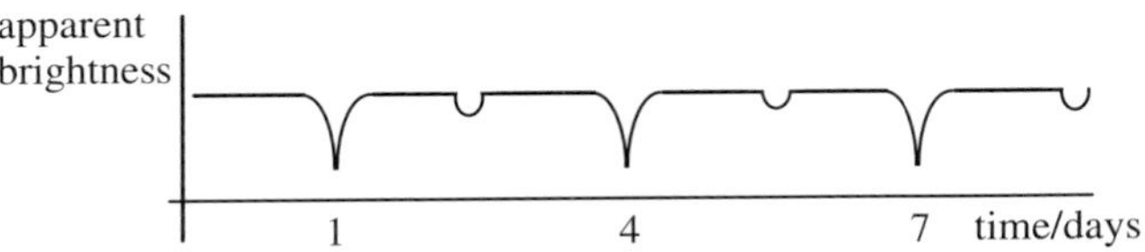

Figure E2.10.

Answer

This is an example of an eclipsing binary system in which the brighter of the two stars partially disappears from view every 3 days. The large dip in brightness occurs when the brighter star is behind the dimmer one. The small dip in brightness occurs when the brighter star is in front of the dimmer star.

Spectroscopic binaries – This system is detected by analysing the light from one or both of its members and observing that there is a periodic Doppler shifting of the lines in the spectrum. A blueshift is expected as the star approaches the earth and a redshift as it moves away from the earth in its orbit around its companion (Figure E2.11).

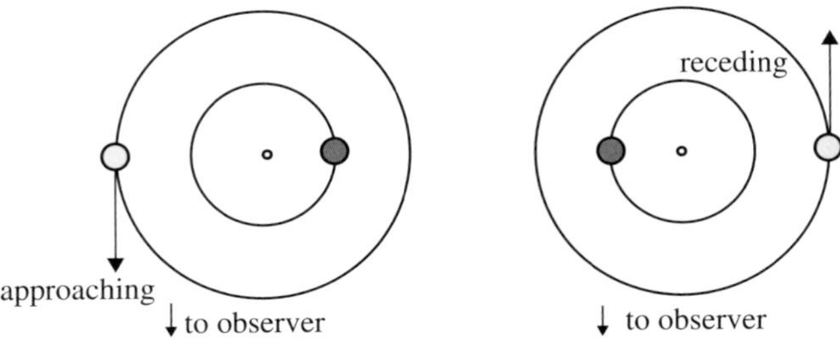

Figure E2.11 A binary star system. The stars rotate about their centre of mass. If the light grey star is the brighter, its light arrives at an observer blueshifted in the first diagram and redshifted in the second. In both positions shown, the stars are said to be in conjunction.

If λ_0 is the wavelength of a spectral line and λ the wavelength received on earth, the shift, z, of the star is defined as

$$z = \left|\frac{\lambda - \lambda_0}{\lambda_0}\right|$$

If the speed of the source is small compared with the speed of light, it can be shown that

$$z = \frac{v}{c}$$

which shows that the shift is indeed directly proportional to the source's speed.

The top diagram in Figure E2.12 shows a spectrum with one line and the other two diagrams show what this line would look like if it were blue- or redshifted.

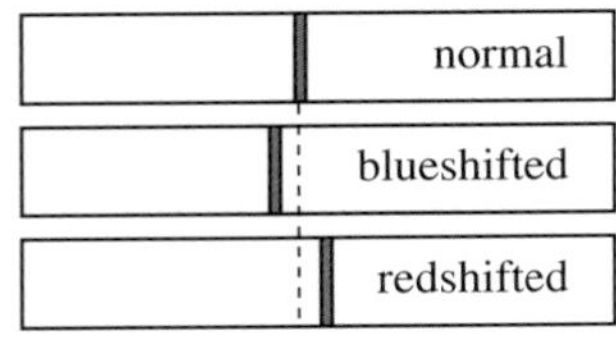

Figure E2.12 A normal spectral line (observed when the star's velocity is normal to the line of sight) is periodically blue- and redshifted as the star revolves in its orbit. In this example we are assuming that the second star is very dim so its light is not recorded. See questions 23 and 24 at the end of the chapter for the case in which light from both stars is analysed.

There is more discussion of the Doppler effect for light in Chapter 4.5 and on page 536.

Example question

Q9

The blueshifts and redshifts of the bright star in Figure E2.12 are 3.4×10^{-5}. If it is known that the two stars are equal in mass and the distance separating them is 2.8×10^{12} m, what are these masses?

Answer

From the Doppler formula, $v = zc = 10\,200\ \text{m s}^{-1}$. From

$$v^2 = \frac{GM_1{}^2}{d(M_1 + M_2)}$$

$$= \frac{GM}{2d}$$

it follows that

$$M = \frac{2v^2 d}{G}$$
$$= 4.4 \times 10^{30}\ \text{kg}$$

QUESTIONS

1 The light from a star a distance of 70 ly away is received on earth with an apparent brightness of $3.0 \times 10^{-8}\ \text{W m}^{-2}$. Calculate the luminosity of the star.

2 The luminosity of a star is 4.5×10^{28} W and its distance from earth is 88 ly. Calculate the apparent brightness of the star.

3 The apparent brightness of a star is $8.4 \times 10^{-10}\ \text{W m}^{-2}$ and its luminosity 6.2×10^{32} W. Calculate the distance to the star in light years.

4 Two stars have the same size but one has a temperature that is four times larger.
(a) How much more energy per second does the hot star radiate?
(b) The apparent brightness of the two stars is the same; what is the ratio of the distance of the cooler star to that of the hotter star?

5 Two stars are the same distance from earth and their apparent brightnesses are $9.0 \times 10^{-12}\ \text{W m}^{-2}$ (star A) and $3.0 \times 10^{-13}\ \text{W m}^{-2}$ (star B). Calculate the ratio of the luminosity of star A to that of star B.

6 Take the surface temperature of our sun to be 6000 K and its luminosity to be 3.9×10^{26} W. Find, in terms of the solar radius, the radius of a star with:
(a) temperature 4000 K and luminosity 5.2×10^{28} W;
(b) temperature 9250 K and luminosity 4.7×10^{27} W.

7 Two stars have the same luminosity. Star A has a surface temperature of 5000 K and star B a temperature of 10 000 K.
(a) Which is the larger star and by how much?
(b) If the apparent brightness of A is double that of B, what is the ratio of the distance of A to that of B?

8 Star A has apparent brightness $8.0 \times 10^{-13}\ \text{W m}^{-2}$ and its distance is 120 ly. Star B has apparent brightness $2.0 \times 10^{-15}\ \text{W m}^{-2}$ and its distance is 150 ly. The two stars have the same size. Calculate the ratio of the temperature of star A to that of star B.

9 Two stars A and B emit most of their light at wavelengths of 650 nm and 480 nm respectively. If it is known that star A has twice the radius of star B, find the ratio of the luminosities of the stars.

10 Explain how the surface temperature of a star determines the spectral class to which it belongs.

11 Describe how the colour of the light from a star can be used to determine the surface temperature of the star.

12 Explain why a star on the top left of the main sequence will spend much less time on the main sequence than another star on the lower right.

13 Describe the main features of the HR diagram. What quantities can be plotted on the vertical axis and which on the horizontal? Why are the scales non-linear?

14 Describe how a stellar absorption spectrum is formed.

15 Figure E2.13 shows the intensity of a particular spectral line emitted by a non-rotating star. On the same graph, draw what you would expect if the star were rotating.

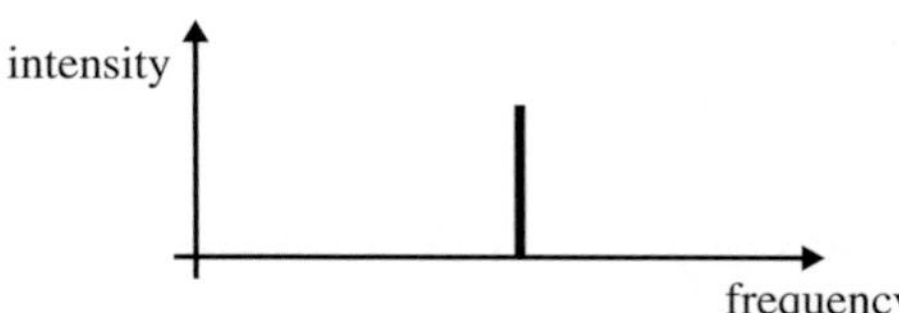

Figure E2.13 For question 15.

16 Show that, if the stars in a binary star system have the same mass, they share the same orbit.

17 Make a sketch of the light curve of an eclipsing binary of period 20 yr in which:
(a) both members are equally bright;
(b) the inner star is much brighter than the other.

(Assume that the line of sight is in the orbital plane.) In each case draw diagrams to show the relative position of the two stars for significant times during the period.

18 From redshift measurements in a spectroscopic binary, it is known that the ratio of the masses is 1.20. If the period of the binary is 40 yr, and from parallax measurements it is known that the two stars are separated by a distance of 2.4×10^{12} m, find the individual masses of each star in the binary.

19 A visual binary system is at a distance of 5.0 pc. The distance between the two stars subtends an angle of 4.5 arcseconds.
(a) What is this distance?
(b) The period of the binary is 87.8 yr. What is the sum of the masses of the stars making up the binary?
(c) The radius of the orbit of one of the stars subtends an angle of 1.91 arcseconds. What is the mass of each of the stars?

20 Describe what is meant by the term *white dwarf*. List two properties of the star. How does a white dwarf differ from a main sequence star of the same surface temperature?

21 A white dwarf, of mass half that of the sun and radius equal to one earth radius, is formed. What is the density of this white dwarf?

22 Where on the HR diagram would our sun lie at the time of its creation?

23 Figure E2.14 shows the spectrum of a spectroscopic binary.
(a) Explain the structure of this spectrum.
(b) Explain how it can be deduced that the stars are not equally massive.

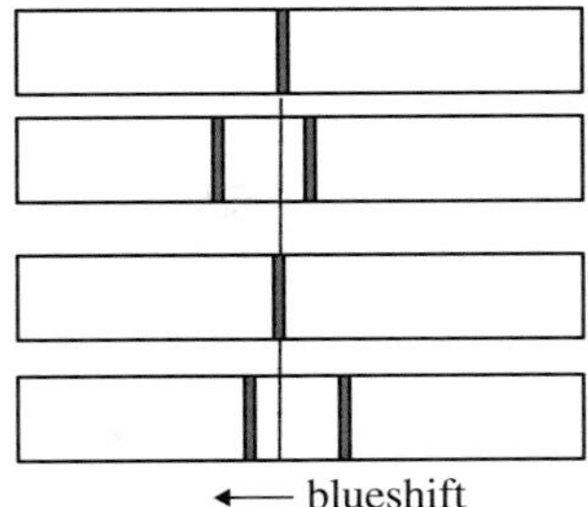

Figure E2.14 For questions 23 and 24.

(c) Show by appropriate diagrams the relative positions of the two stars that give rise to each of the four spectra shown.

24 For the binary star system described in question 23, assume that the redshift in the second diagram of Figure E2.14 is 3.4×10^{-5} and the blueshift is 4.7×10^{-5}. Find the ratio of the masses of the two stars in the binary.

25 A binary star system consists of two stars that have a ratio of apparent brightness equal to 10. Explain carefully how we can deduce that the ratio of the luminosities of the stars is also 10.

26 (a) Find the temperature of a star whose spectrum is shown in Figure E2.15.
(b) Assuming this is a main sequence star, what do you *estimate* its luminosity to be?

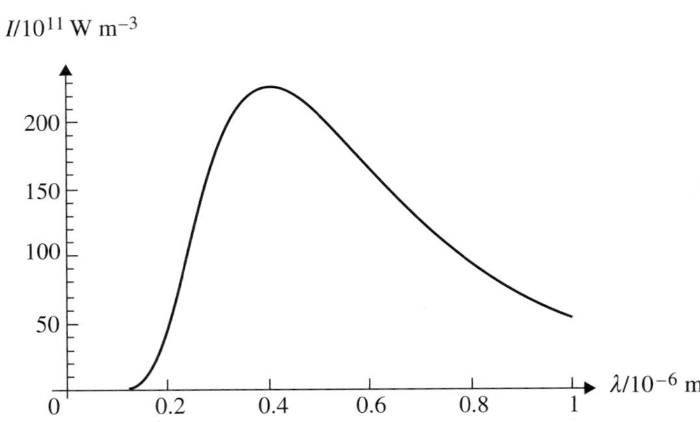

Figure E2.15 For question 26.

Stellar objects

A major problem in astrophysics is the accurate determination of the distance to a star. This chapter discusses three methods for measuring distances: the parallax method, the spectroscopic parallax method and the Cepheid star method. The main tools in the study of stellar luminosity, such as absolute and apparent luminosities, and absolute and apparent magnitudes, are also discussed.

Objectives

By the end of this chapter you should be able to:

- describe the method of *parallax*, $d \text{ (in parsecs)} = \frac{1}{p \text{ (in arcseconds)}}$, the method of *spectroscopic parallax* and the *Cepheids method* for determining distances in astronomy;
- define the *parsec*;
- state the definitions of *apparent brightness*, $b = \frac{L}{4\pi d^2}$, and *apparent* and *absolute magnitude*, $\frac{b}{b_0} = 100^{-m/5} = 2.512^{-m}$;
- solve problems using *apparent brightness* and *luminosity*;
- use the magnitude–distance formula.

The parallax method

The parallax method takes advantage of the fact that, when an object is viewed from two different positions, it appears displaced, relative to a fixed background. If we measure the angular position of a star and then repeat the measurement some time later, the two positions will be different, relative to a background of stars, because of the fact that in the intervening time the earth has moved in its orbit around the sun. We make two measurements of the angular position of the star six months apart; see Figure E3.1. The distance between the two positions of the earth is equal to $D = 2R$, the diameter of the earth's orbit around the sun ($R = 1.5 \times 10^{11}$ m). The distance to the star, d, is given by

$$\tan p = \frac{R}{d}$$

$$\Rightarrow d = \frac{R}{\tan p}$$

Since the parallax angle is very small, $\tan p \approx p$

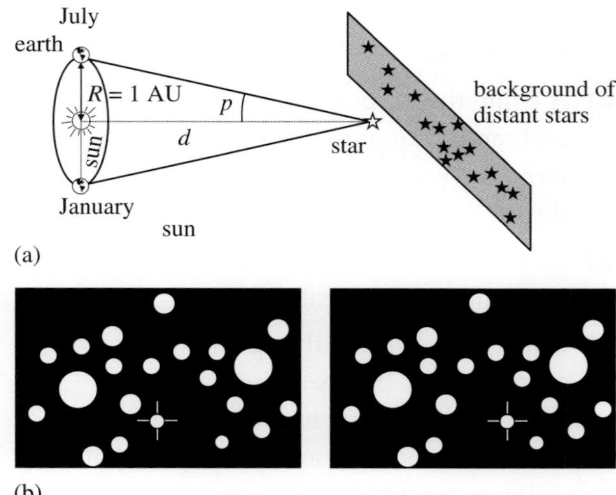

Figure E3.1 (a) The parallax of a star. (b) Two 'photographs' of the same region of the sky taken six months apart. The position of the star (indicated by a cross) has shifted, relative to the background stars, in the intervening six months.

where the parallax p is measured in radians, and so $d = \frac{R}{p}$

▶ The parallax angle is shown in Figure E3.1. It is the angle at the position of the star that subtends a distance equal to the radius of the earth's orbit around the sun, a distance known as one astronomical unit, 1 AU = 1.5×10^{11} m.

Parallaxes are measured quite accurately provided they are not too small. For example, parallaxes down to 1 arcsecond, symbol 1″ (or 1/3600 of a degree), are easily measured.

▶ If the star is too far away, however, the parallax is too small to be measured and this method fails. Typically, measurements from observatories on earth allow distances up to 300 ly (roughly 100 parsec) to be determined with the parallax method, which is therefore mainly used for nearby stars. (Using measurements from satellites above the earth's atmosphere, distances larger than 500 pc can be determined using the parallax method.)

The parallax method can be used to define a common unit of distance in astronomy, the parsec. One parsec (*parallax second*) is the distance to a star whose parallax is 1 arcsecond, as shown in Figure E3.2.

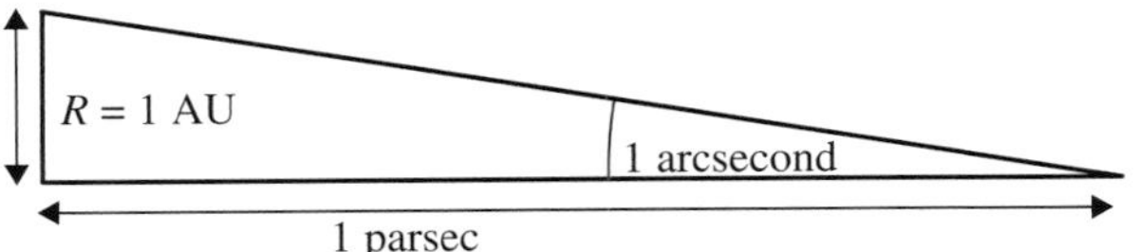

Figure E3.2 The definition of a parsec. A parsec is that distance at which 1 AU subtends an angle of 1 arcsecond.

In conventional units this means that

$$1\ \text{pc} = \frac{1.5 \times 10^{11}}{\left(\frac{2\pi}{360}\right)\left(\frac{1}{3600}\right)}\ \text{m}$$
$$= 3.09 \times 10^{16}\ \text{m}$$

(The factor of $2\pi/360$ converts degrees into radians.) In terms of a light year (1 ly = 9.46×10^{15} m), 1 pc = 3.26 ly. In summary:

- 1 AU = 1.5×10^{11} m
- 1 ly = 9.46×10^{15} m
- 1 pc = 3.09×10^{16} m = 3.26 ly

▶ This means that if the parallax of a star is known to be p arcseconds, the distance is $1/p$ parsecs, or

$$d\ (\text{in parsecs}) = \frac{1}{p\ (\text{in arcseconds})}$$

Table E3.1 shows the five nearest stars.

Star	Distance/ly
Proxima Centauri	4.3
Barnard's Star	5.9
Wolf 359	7.7
Lalande 21185	8.2
Sirius	8.6

Table E3.1 Distances to the five nearest stars.

Absolute and apparent magnitudes

The ancient astronomers devised a *relative* system of classifying stars according to how bright they *appeared* to an observer on earth. Each star was given a number called the *apparent magnitude m* – the higher the apparent magnitude, the dimmer the star. In the system of Hipparchos and Ptolemy, six classes of brightness were defined, and assigned numbers from 1 to 6. A magnitude 6 star was supposed to be 100 times *dimmer* than a magnitude 1 star. Thus, a magnitude 2 star is $100^{1/5} \approx 2.512$ times dimmer than a magnitude 1 star.

The modern system of assigning a measure to apparent brightness conforms roughly to that of the ancient astronomers. The modern magnitude scale is defined as follows.

▶ Given a star of apparent brightness b, we assign to that star an *apparent magnitude m* defined by

$$\frac{b}{b_0} = 100^{-m/5}$$

(The value

$$b_0 = 2.52 \times 10^{-8}\ \mathrm{W\,m^{-2}}$$

is taken as the reference value for apparent brightness.)

Taking logarithms (to base 10) gives the equivalent form

$$m = -\frac{5}{2}\log\left(\frac{b}{b_0}\right)$$

Since $100^{1/5} = 2.512$ the first equation above can also be written as

$$\frac{b}{b_0} = 2.512^{-m}$$

As an example, consider a star whose apparent brightness is $6.43 \times 10^{-9}\ \mathrm{W\,m^{-2}}$. Then

$$\begin{aligned} m &= -2.5\log\frac{6.43 \times 10^{-9}}{2.52 \times 10^{-8}} \\ &= -2.5\log 0.2552 \\ &= 1.48 \end{aligned}$$

Similarly, a star of apparent magnitude $m = 4.35$ has apparent brightness given by

$$\begin{aligned} \frac{b}{b_0} &= 2.512^{-m} \\ \Rightarrow b &= 2.52 \times 10^{-8} \times 2.512^{-4.35} \\ &= 4.58 \times 10^{-10}\ \mathrm{W\,m^{-2}} \end{aligned}$$

Note that a star of apparent brightness equal to the reference value $b_0 = 2.52 \times 10^{-8}\ \mathrm{W\,m^{-2}}$ is assigned an apparent magnitude $m = 0$.

▶ It is somewhat confusing so we repeat this point, namely that the magnitude scale is defined so that the larger the magnitude, the dimmer the star.

Consider now two stars of apparent magnitude m_1 and m_2 and apparent brightness b_1 and b_2. We have

$$\frac{b_1}{b_0} = 2.512^{-m_1} \quad \text{and} \quad \frac{b_2}{b_0} = 2.512^{-m_2}$$

and so taking ratios gives

$$\frac{b_1}{b_2} = 2.512^{m_2 - m_1}$$

This allows us to compare the apparent brightness of two stars given their apparent magnitudes.

Our sun has an apparent magnitude of −26.74. Sirius A, the brightest star in the night sky, has apparent magnitude −1.5, Proxima Centauri has 0.3 and Barnard's Star has 9.5. Thus, we find that the apparent brightness of Sirius A is

$$\begin{aligned} \frac{b}{b_0} &= 2.512^{-m} \\ \Rightarrow b &= 2.52 \times 10^{-8} \times 2.512^{-(-1.5)} \\ &= 1 \times 10^{-7}\ \mathrm{W\,m^{-2}} \end{aligned}$$

We may also compare the brightness of Sirius to that of Barnard's Star to find

$$\begin{aligned} \frac{b_{\text{Sirius}}}{b_{\text{Barnard's}}} &= 2.512^{(9.5+1.5)} \\ &= 2.512^{11} \\ &\approx 25\,000 \end{aligned}$$

which means that Sirius is about 25 000 times as bright. Comparing the brightness of Proxima Centauri to that of Barnard's Star gives

$$\begin{aligned} \frac{b_{\text{Proxima}}}{b_{\text{Barnard's}}} &= 2.512^{(9.5-0.3)} \\ &= 2.512^{9.2} \\ &\approx 5000 \end{aligned}$$

which means that Proxima Centauri is about 5000 times brighter than Barnard's Star.

The human eye can detect a star of apparent magnitude not larger than about 6. With simple binoculars the limit is raised to stars of magnitude 9. The largest telescopes can record images of objects of apparent magnitude as faint as 27. (See Figure E3.3.)

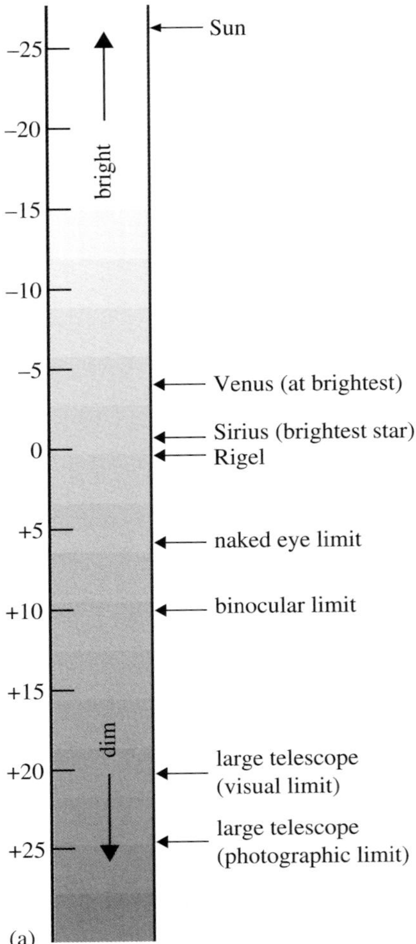

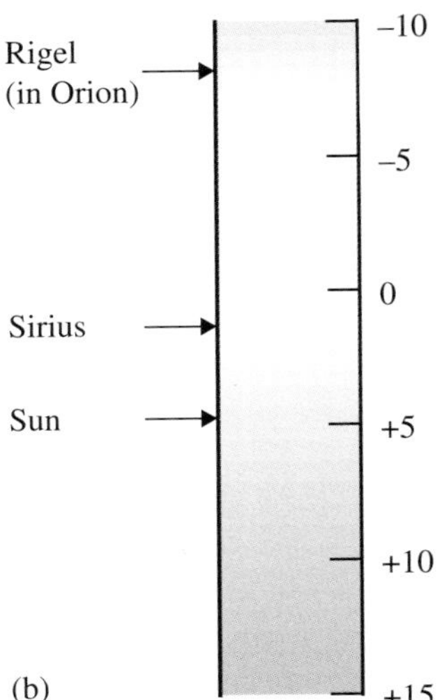

Figure E3.3 (a) Apparent magnitudes of stars. (b) Absolute magnitudes of stars.

Two stars that have the same apparent magnitude are not necessarily equally bright intrinsically, since they may be at different distances. To establish a system of absolute magnitudes that will tell us if one star is intrinsically brighter than another, we imagine that all stars are positioned at the *same* distance from earth. By convention, this distance is taken to be 10 pc.

▶ The apparent magnitude a star *would* have if placed at a distance of 10 pc from earth is called the *absolute magnitude M* of the star (see Figure E3.4).

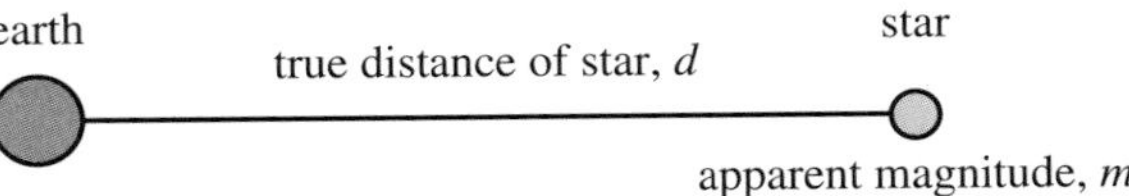

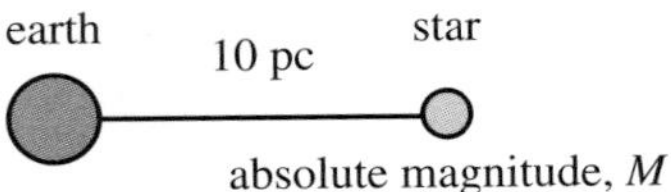

Figure E3.4 Diagram used for the definition of the absolute magnitude of a star.

Absolute and apparent magnitudes and distance are then related. Let us compare the apparent brightness b of a star to the apparent brightness B that it *would have* if it was placed at a distance of 10 pc. We have

$$\frac{b}{B} = 100^{-(m-M)/5}$$

But also we have

$$b = \frac{L}{4\pi d^2} \quad \text{and} \quad B = \frac{L}{4\pi (10\text{ pc})^2}$$

and so

$$\frac{L/(4\pi d^2)}{L/(4\pi 10^2)} = 100^{-(m-M)/5}$$

$$\left(\frac{d}{10}\right)^{-2} = 100^{-(m-M)/5}$$

Taking logarithms (to base 10) gives

$$2\log\left(\frac{d}{10}\right) = \left(\frac{m-M}{5}\right)\log 100$$

$$2\log\left(\frac{d}{10}\right) = \left(\frac{m-M}{5}\right)\times 2$$

Finally we obtain

$$m - M = 5\log\left(\frac{d}{10}\right)$$

where it must be stressed that d *is expressed in parsecs* (pc). If necessary we can solve for the distance d to obtain

$$d = 10^{(m-M)/5} \times 10 \text{ pc}$$

Table E3.2 shows the five brightest stars in the sky along with their apparent and absolute magnitudes. Sirius appears to be the brightest but, of the five stars shown, Canopus is the one with the largest luminosity.

Star	*m*	*M*
Sirius	−1.43	1.4
Canopus	−0.72	−4.5
Alpha Centauri	−0.27	4.7
Arcturus	−0.06	−0.1
Vega	0.02	0.5

Table E3.2 Apparent and absolute magnitudes of the five brightest stars.

Example questions

Q1

Calculate the absolute magnitude of a star whose distance is 25.0 ly and whose apparent magnitude is 3.45.

Answer

We must first change light years (ly) into parsecs (pc). Since

$$25 \text{ ly} = \frac{25}{3.26} \text{ pc} = 7.67 \text{ pc}$$

we have

$$m - M = 5\log\left(\frac{d}{10}\right)$$

$$M = m - 5\log\left(\frac{d}{10}\right)$$

$$M = 3.45 - 5\log(0.767)$$

$$M = 4.03$$

Q2

Calculate the distance to Sirius using the data in Table E3.2.

Answer

From

$$d = 10^{(m-M)/5} \times 10 \text{ pc}$$

we get

$$\begin{aligned} d &= 10^{(m-M)/5} \times 10 \text{ pc} \\ &= 10^{(-1.43-1.4)/5} \times 10 \text{ pc} \\ &= 10^{-2.83/5} \times 10 \text{ pc} \\ &= 10^{-0.566} \times 10 \text{ pc} \end{aligned}$$

$$d = 2.7 \text{ pc}$$

Spectroscopic parallax

▶ The term *spectroscopic parallax* refers to a method of finding the distance to a star given the star's luminosity and apparent brightness. The term is misleading in that no use of parallax is being made.

Assume that we know the luminosity, L, and apparent brightness, b, of a star. Since these two quantities are related by

$$b = \frac{L}{4\pi d^2}$$

it follows that

$$d = \sqrt{\frac{L}{4\pi b}}$$

The question is then how to determine the luminosity of the star. This is done by examining its spectrum, from which, as we saw in the last chapter, the temperature can be deduced. Knowing the temperature and using the HR diagram (*assuming the star is a main sequence star*) allow us to determine the luminosity as well.

Thus, the distance can be found. This method can be used to estimate distances to several thousand parsecs.

Example question

Q3

A main sequence star emits most of its energy at a wavelength of 2.4×10^{-7} m. Its apparent brightness is measured to be 4.3×10^{-9} W m^{-2}. How far is the star?

Answer

From Wien's law we find the temperature of the star to be

$$\lambda_0 T = 2.9 \times 10^{-3}\ \text{K m}$$
$$\Rightarrow T = \frac{2.9 \times 10^{-3}}{2.4 \times 10^{-7}}\ \text{K}$$
$$= 12\,000\ \text{K}$$

From the HR diagram on page 500, we see that such a temperature corresponds to a luminosity of about 100 times that of the sun, that is

$$L = 3.9 \times 10^{28}\ \text{W}$$

Thus

$$d = \sqrt{\frac{L}{4\pi b}}$$
$$= \sqrt{\frac{3.9 \times 10^{28}}{4\pi \times 4.3 \times 10^{-9}}}\ \text{m}$$
$$= 8.5 \times 10^{17}\ \text{m}$$
$$\approx 90\ \text{ly}$$
$$\approx 28\ \text{pc}$$

The Cepheids

Cepheid variable stars are stars whose luminosity is not constant in time but varies from a minimum to a maximum *periodically*, the periods being typically from a couple of days to a couple of months. The brightness of the star increases sharply and then fades off more gradually, as shown in the light curve of a Cepheid in Figure E3.5.

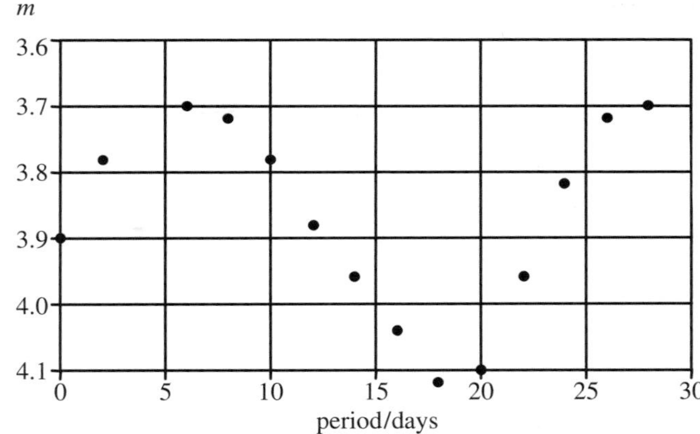

Figure E3.5 The apparent magnitude of a Cepheid star varies periodically with time.

The first Cepheid was discovered by the nineteen-year-old English astronomer John Goodricke in 1748, two years before his death.

The reason for the periodic behaviour of the brightness of Cepheid stars has to do with the interaction of radiation with matter in the atmosphere of the star. This interaction causes the outer layers of the star to undergo periodic expansions and contractions. The star is at its brightest when the surface of the star expands outward at high velocity. It is at its dimmest when the surface moves inward.

▶ At the beginning of the twentieth century, Henrietta Leavitt discovered a remarkable relationship between the peak luminosity of Cepheids and their period. The longer the period, the larger the luminosity (see Figure E3.6). This makes Cepheid stars 'standard candles' – observing a Cepheid and finding its period allows the determination of its luminosity. This, in turn, allows the determination of its distance, as explained below.

For example, the Cepheid whose light curve is shown in Figure E3.5 has a period of about 22 days. From Figure E3.6, this corresponds to a luminosity of about 7000 solar luminosities, or about $L = 2.73 \times 10^{30}$ W. The peak apparent

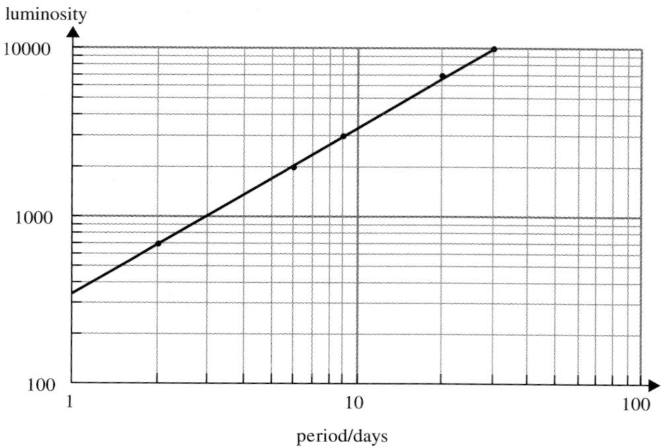

Figure E3.6 There is a relationship between the peak luminosity of a Cepheid star and its period. The luminosity is given in terms of the solar luminosity (see Appendix 3).

magnitude of the Cepheid from Figure E3.5 is about $m = 3.7$. The peak apparent brightness can be found from

$$\frac{b}{2.52 \times 10^{-8}} = 2.512^{-m}$$

$$\Rightarrow b = 2.52 \times 10^{-8} \times 2.512^{-3.7}$$

$$= 8.34 \times 10^{-10}\ \mathrm{W\,m^{-2}}$$

Now, using the relationship between apparent brightness, luminosity and distance,

$$b = \frac{L}{4\pi d^2}$$

$$\Rightarrow d = \sqrt{\frac{L}{4\pi b}}$$

$$= \sqrt{\frac{2.73 \times 10^{30}}{4\pi \times 8.34 \times 10^{-10}}}$$

$$= 1.6 \times 10^{19}\ \mathrm{m}$$

$$\approx 1700\ \mathrm{ly}$$

$$\approx 520\ \mathrm{pc}$$

Thus, one can determine the distance to the galaxy in which the Cepheid is assumed to be. The Cepheids method can be used to find distances up to a few Mpc.

Figure E3.7 summarizes the distances at which each of the methods of determining stellar distance is effective.

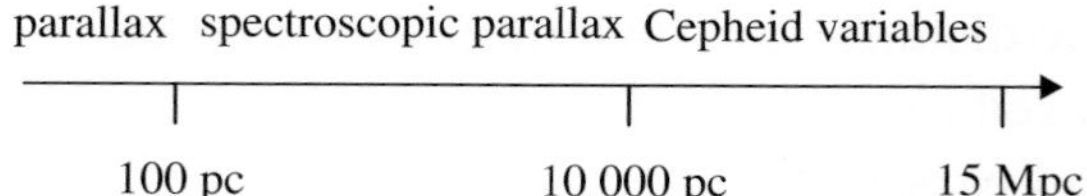

Figure E3.7 The ordinary parallax method allows the determination of distances up to about 100 pc. The spectroscopic parallax method extends distance measurements to about 10 000 pc. The Cepheid variable star method extends the scale further to 15 Mpc.

? QUESTIONS

1 Describe with the aid of a clear diagram what is meant by the parallax method in astronomy. Explain why the parallax method fails for stars that are very far away.

2 Give definitions of:
(a) apparent magnitude of a star;
(b) absolute magnitude of a star.

3 Find the distance to Procyon, which has a parallax of 0.285″.

4 The distance of Epsilon Eridani is 10.8 ly. What is its parallax?

5 Betelgeuse has an angular diameter of 0.016″ (i.e. the angle subtended by the star's diameter at the eye of an observer) and a parallax of 0.0067″.
(a) What is the distance of Betelgeuse from the earth?
(b) What is its radius in terms of the sun's radius?

6 The parallax of a star is 0.025″ and its absolute magnitude is $M = 0.8$. Is its apparent magnitude less than or greater than 0.8?

7 The parallax of Kapteyn's Star is 0.250″ and its apparent magnitude is 9.2.
(a) How far is it?
(b) Is this star visible to the human eye?

8 How many times brighter is a star of absolute magnitude 2 than a star of absolute magnitude 4?

9 Vega has an absolute magnitude of 0.5 and Capella an absolute magnitude of –0.6. Which is the brighter star and by how much?

10 Table E3.3 contains information on apparent magnitude and parallax for two stars.
(a) Which star appears brighter?
(b) Which star has the larger luminosity?

Star	Apparent magnitude	Parallax
A	4.82	0.022″
B	5.38	0.034″

Table E3.3 For question 10.

11 Table E3.4 contains information on absolute magnitude and parallax for two stars.
(a) Which star has the larger luminosity?
(b) Which star appears brighter?

Star	Absolute magnitude	Parallax
A	3.75	0.025″
B	3.75	0.040″

Table E3.4 For question 11.

12 The two stars making up a binary star system have apparent magnitudes of $m = 5.1$ (star A) and $m = 8.2$ (star B). Explain carefully how we can deduce that star A has the greater *luminosity*.

13 A main sequence star emits most of its energy at a wavelength of 2.42×10^{-7} m. Its apparent brightness is measured to be 8.56×10^{-12} W m^{-2}. How far is the star? (Use the HR diagram on page 500.)

14 What is the apparent brightness and apparent magnitude of a star of luminosity 2.45×10^{28} W and a parallax of 0.034″?

15 (a) Altair has an apparent magnitude of $m = 1.0$. Calculate its apparent brightness.
(b) Procyon has an apparent brightness of 1.78×10^{-8} W m^{-2}. Calculate its apparent magnitude.

16 Using Figure E3.6 in the text, calculate the distance of a Cepheid variable star whose period is 10 days and whose peak apparent brightness is 3.45×10^{-14} W m^{-2}.

17 Use the formula given on page 510 relating absolute and apparent magnitudes to distance to answer the following questions.
(a) Find the distance of the star Rigel, which has absolute magnitude -7.0 and apparent magnitude 0.1.
(b) Alpha Centauri has an apparent magnitude of -0.27 and a parallax of 0.760″. What is its absolute magnitude?
(c) Our sun has an apparent magnitude of -26.74. What is the greatest distance from which this would be visible to the unaided human eye?

Cosmology

This chapter introduces Olbers' paradox and its resolution, and the monumental discovery by Edwin Hubble that the universe is expanding. The basic idea of the Big Bang theory is introduced and the difficulties in determining the future evolution of the universe are discussed.

Objectives

By the end of this chapter you should be able to:

- describe *Olbers' paradox* in Newtonian cosmology and how it is resolved;
- describe the main features of the *Big Bang* and the *expansion of the universe*;
- understand the significance of the *cosmic background radiation*;
- state the meaning of the terms *open universe* and *closed universe*;
- outline the theoretical possibilities for the *evolution of the universe*;
- state the meaning and significance of the term *critical density*;
- appreciate the importance of various forms of *dark matter*.

Olbers' paradox

The universe appears to be full of *structures*. There are planets and moons in our *solar system*, stars in our *galaxy*, our galaxy is part of a *cluster* of galaxies and our cluster is part of an even bigger *supercluster* of galaxies. If we look at the universe on a very large scale, however, we no longer see any structures. If we imagine cutting up the universe into cubes of side 300 Mpc across, the interior of any one of these cubes would look the same as the interior of any other cube, anywhere else in the universe. This has led to what is called the *homogeneity principle* in cosmology. On a *large scale*, the universe looks *uniform*.

Similarly, if we look in different directions, we see essentially the same thing. If we look far enough in any one direction, we will count the same number of galaxies. No one direction is special in comparison with another. This has led to a second principle of cosmology, the *isotropy principle*.

▶ These two principles, homogeneity and isotropy, make up what is called the *cosmological principle* – a principle that has had a profound role in the development of cosmology.

The cosmological principle implies that the universe has no edge (for if it did, the part of the universe near the edge would look different from a part far from the edge, violating the homogeneity principle). Similarly, it implies that the universe has no centre (for if it did, observing from the centre would show a different picture from observing from any other point, violating the principle of isotropy).

Newton used an extreme version of the cosmological principle when he suggested that the universe is infinite in extent, has no beginning and is static, meaning it has been uniform and isotropic *at all times*. However, as early as the eighteenth and nineteenth centuries, serious theoretical problems were posed for cosmological models such as Newton's universe.

▶ The astronomers de Cheseaux and Olbers asked the very simple question of why the night sky is dark. Their argument, based on the prevailing static and infinite cosmology of the period, led to a night sky that would be bright!

Imagine a universe that is infinite and contains an infinite number of stars more or less uniformly distributed in space. The very distant stars contribute very little light to an observer on earth but there are very many of them. Mathematically, let n stand for the number density of stars, that is the number of stars per unit volume of space. At a distance d from a star of luminosity L, the received energy per area per second (the apparent brightness) is

$$b = \frac{L}{4\pi d^2}$$

(see Figure E4.1.)

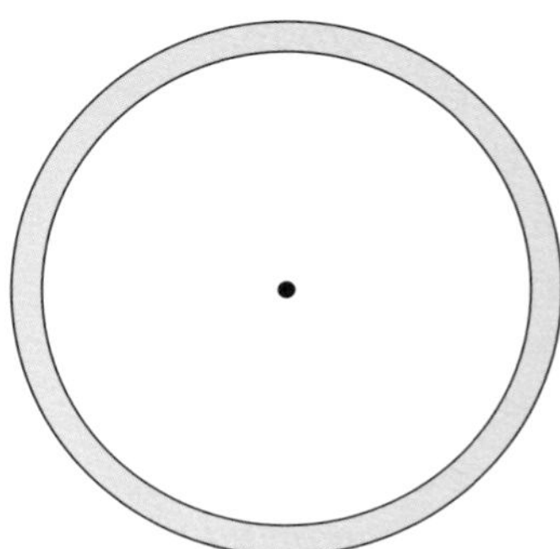

Figure E4.1 An observer (the black dot) in an infinite universe is surrounded by stars whose distribution is roughly uniform. The number of stars in a thin shell (marked) around the observer is proportional to the square of the radius of the shell and hence the energy emitted from those stars is independent of the size of the shell.

The number of stars in a thin shell of thickness t a distance d from the observer is number density × volume $= 4\pi d^2 nt$. Hence the received energy per second per area from all the stars in the thin shell is

$$\frac{L}{4\pi d^2} \times 4\pi d^2 nt = Lnt$$

This is a constant (i.e. it does not depend on the distance to the shell d). Since there is an infinite number of such shells surrounding the observer, and since each contributes a *constant amount of energy, the total energy* received must be infinite, making the night sky infinitely bright, which it is not. This is Olbers' paradox.

Newton's static universe

Olbers' paradox cannot be eliminated in Newton's universe. The obvious way to try to solve the puzzle is to invoke absorption of the radiation from the intervening stars and the interstellar medium. This does not work, however, because in an eternal universe the interstellar medium would, in time, be heated up by the radiation it absorbed and would then itself radiate as much energy as it received, leading to the same difficulty. There is, in fact, no natural way to avoid this paradox in static, infinite cosmological models.

In a finite, expanding universe (see next section), however, the radiation received by the observer is small and finite *for two main reasons*:

1 There is a finite number of stars and each has a finite lifetime. This means that stars have not been radiating forever, nor will they go on radiating forever. Their total radiation is thus small and finite compared with the infinite energy they would emit if there were an infinite number of them radiating for an infinite amount of time.

2 Because of the finite age of the universe, stars that are far away (beyond the 'event horizon') have not yet had time for their light to reach us.

An additional reason that helps resolve Olbers' paradox is the following:

3 The radiation received is redshifted (because of the expanding universe) and so contains less energy.

The expanding universe

The dark lines in the absorption spectra of distant galaxies correspond to wavelengths that have been absorbed by the chemical elements in the outer layers of the galaxies. The positions of the dark lines are well known from experiments on earth but the observed wavelengths from the galaxies, when compared to those measured on earth, were found to be a bit longer: they were redshifted (see Figure E4.2). The same applies to the emission spectrum of a galaxy, but that is usually too faint to be seen.

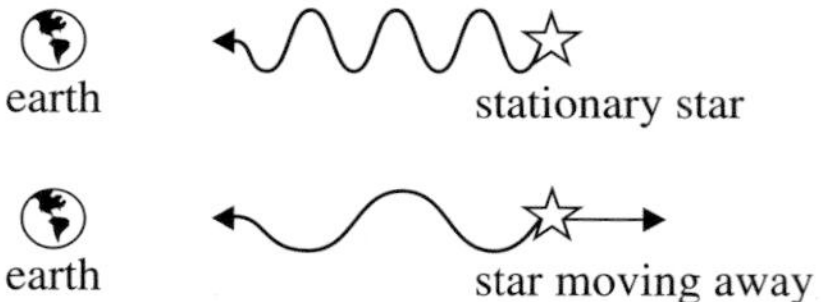

Figure E4.2 Light from the star received on earth has a longer than expected wavelength.

▶ Hubble interpreted the redshift of the spectral lines as evidence of a velocity of the galaxy *away from* us, as in the Doppler effect. The faster the galaxy, the larger the redshift. Hubble's observations thus suggest an expanding universe with galaxies moving away from us and from each other. It also suggests that in the past the universe was much smaller. The universe appears to have started from a kind of explosion that set matter moving outward. This is the idea of the Big Bang model of cosmology.

It is important to realize that the universe is not expanding into empty space. The expansion of the universe is not supposed to be like an expanding cloud of smoke that fills more and more volume in a room. The galaxies that are moving away from us are not moving into another, previously unoccupied, part of the universe. *Space is being created* in between the galaxies and so the distance between them increases, creating the illusion of motion of one galaxy relative to another.

The cosmic background radiation

In 1964, Penzias and Wilson, two radio astronomers working at Bell Laboratories, made a fundamental, if accidental, discovery. They used an antenna they had just designed to study radio signals from our galaxy. But the antenna was picking up a signal that persisted no matter what part of the sky the antenna was pointing at. The spectrum of this signal (i.e. the amount of energy as a function of the wavelength) turned out to be a black-body spectrum corresponding to a temperature of 2.7 K. The *isotropy* of this radiation (i.e. it was the same in all directions) indicated that it was not coming from any particular spot in the sky; rather it was radiation that was filling all space. Penzias and Wilson did not know that this kind of radiation had been predicted on the basis of the Big Bang theory 30 years earlier by George Gamow and his co-workers and more recently by Peebles and Dicke at Princeton. The Princeton group was in fact planning to start a search for this radiation when the news of the discovery arrived.

▶ With help from the Princeton group, Penzias and Wilson realized that the radiation detected was the remnant of the hot explosion at the beginning of time. It was the afterglow of the enormous temperature that existed in the very early universe. As the universe has expanded, the temperature has kept falling to reach its present value of 2.7 K.

Example question

Q1

Find the wavelength at which most of the cosmic background radiation is emitted.

Answer

From the Wien displacement law, $\lambda T = 2.9 \times 10^{-3}$ K m, it follows that most of the energy is emitted at a wavelength $\lambda = 1.07$ mm, which is a microwave wavelength.

The Big Bang: the creation of space and time

The discovery of the expanding universe by Hubble implies a definite beginning of the universe, some 14 billion years ago. The size of the universe at that time was infinitesimally small and the temperature and pressure enormous. These conditions create the picture of a gigantic explosion at $t = 0$, which set matter moving outwards. Billions of years later we see the remnant of this explosion in the receding motion of the distant galaxies. This is known as the Big Bang scenario in cosmology. It is important to understand that the Big Bang was not an explosion that took place at a specific time in the past somewhere in the universe. At the time of the Big Bang the space in which the matter of the universe resides was created as well. Thus, the Big Bang happened about 14 billion years ago everywhere in the universe (the universe then being a point).

The main experimental evidence in support of the Big Bang theory includes the following:

- **The expansion of the universe** – The universe is now observed to expand. Hence in the past the universe had a smaller size. Even further into the past the universe must have been a tiny object, which started to expand. This points to a picture of an 'explosion' that set the universe moving outward.
- **The cosmic background radiation** – Today we observe the background radiation at 2.7 K. This is consistent with a small, hot universe in the distant past, which began to cool down as it expanded.
- **Helium abundance** – It is a prediction of the Big Bang model that there should be an abundance of helium in the universe, of about 25% by mass. Measurements of helium abundance today, within our own galaxy, nearby galaxies and clusters of galaxies, as well as in newly born stars, give a number that is never less than 25%. It is very difficult to account for this lower bound on helium in such different measurements if we do not accept the cosmological explanation of helium formation.

The development of the universe

Mathematically, the expansion of the universe can be described in terms of a scale factor of the universe in the following way. If the distance between two galaxies was x_0 at some arbitrary time, then the separation of these two galaxies at some time t later is given by the expression

$$x(t) = R(t)x_0$$

The function $R(t)$ is called the *scale factor* of the universe and is of basic importance to cosmology. It is sometimes referred to loosely as the *radius of the universe*. Note that this is a scalar function, not a vector, indicating the standard assumption about the isotropy and homogeneity of the universe on a large scale.

It is a basic problem in cosmology to discover what this scale factor $R(t)$ is. Application of the laws of general relativity results in *three possibilities* for $R(t)$.

▶ The first possibility is that $R(t)$ starts from zero, increases to a maximum value and then decreases back to zero again. The universe collapses after an initial period of expansion. This is called a *closed universe*.

In the second possibility, the scale factor $R(t)$ increases without limit – the universe continues to expand forever. This is called an *open universe*.

The third possibility is that the universe expands forever, but the rate of expansion decreases, becoming zero after an infinite time. This is called a *flat universe*.

These three possibilities are shown in Figure E4.3.

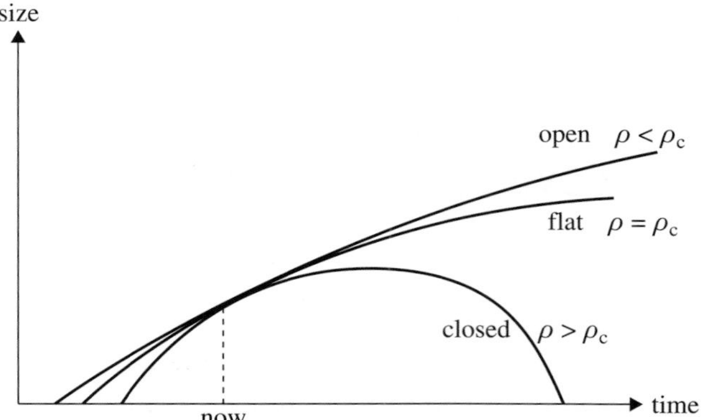

Figure E4.3 The three solutions of Einstein's equations for the evolution of the universe. The present time is indicated by 'now'. Notice that, depending on which solution is taken, the age of the universe is different. In other words, different solutions imply a different age.

Which of the three possibilities is actually realized depends on the value of the mass density of the universe, ρ, relative to a *critical density* whose value (as shown below) is about $\rho_c \approx 10^{-26}$ kg m^{-3}.

- If $\rho < \rho_c$, the universe expands forever at a slowing rate. The universe is called *open*.
- If $\rho = \rho_c$, the universe expands forever at a slowing rate that approaches zero. The universe is called *flat*.
- If $\rho > \rho_c$, the universe collapses after a period of expansion. The universe is called *closed*.

General relativity actually gives an additional interpretation to the three different scenarios for $R(t)$. General relativity says that the geometry of the universe (i.e. the rules of geometry) depend on the amount of mass in the universe. The mass in the universe bends or curves the space and time in the universe. The amount of bending depends on how much mass there is.

The case $\rho < \rho_c$ corresponds to an *open universe* of infinite volume, whose curvature is analogous to that of the surface of a saddle (a hyperboloid). The case $\rho > \rho_c$ corresponds to a *closed universe*, with a finite volume and a curvature similar to that of a sphere. This is a universe without edges. Finally, $\rho = \rho_c$ corresponds to an *open*, infinite, but *flat* universe, analogous to the surface of an ordinary plane.

These universes cannot be visualized. A closed universe means that its volume is finite and that it has no boundary. The *inside* of a sphere is a three-dimensional space of finite volume but it does have a boundary (the surface of the sphere). We therefore try to visualize these cases with two-dimensional analogies. For example, imagine dots on the surface of a balloon representing galaxies. As the balloon is inflated (the universe is expanding) the dots move further apart (the distance between the galaxies increases). (See Figure E6.5 on page 538.)

Table E4.1 summarizes this information about these three possible types of universe.

Geometry	Density	Type	Volume	Expansion
Hyperbolic	$\rho < \rho_c$	Open	Infinite	For ever, at slowing rate
Euclidean	$\rho = \rho_c$	Flat (open)	Infinite	For ever, but rate approaches zero
Spherical	$\rho > \rho_c$	Closed	Finite	Stops, followed by collapse

Table E4.1 Characteristics of different possible universes.

Supplementary material

Estimate of the critical density

The critical density can be calculated simply by using Newtonian mechanics. Consider a spherical cloud of dust of radius r and a mass m at the surface of this cloud which moves away from the centre with a velocity v that satisfies Hubble's law, $v = Hr$ (see Figure E4.4). Here the constant H stands for the Hubble constant. Its numerical value is 72 km s^{-1} Mpc^{-1}. This is discussed in detail in Option E6.

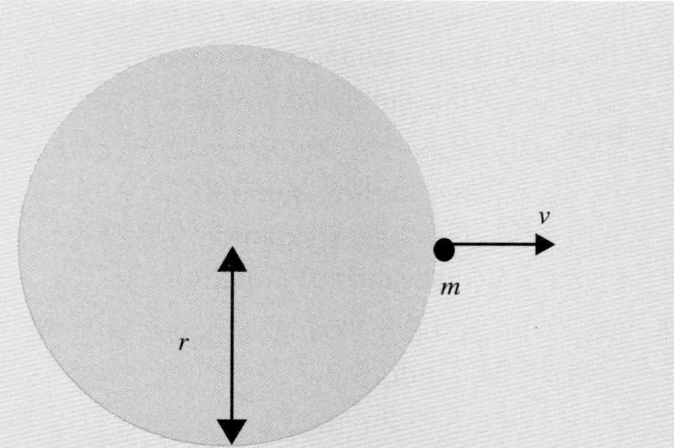

Figure E4.4 Estimating critical density.

The total energy of the mass is

$$E = \frac{1}{2}mv^2 - \frac{GMm}{r}$$

where M is the mass of the cloud. If we call the density of this cloud ρ, then $M = \rho\frac{4}{3}\pi r^3$ and using this together with $v = Hr$ we find

$$E = \frac{1}{2}mr^2\left(H^2 - \frac{8\pi\rho G}{3}\right)$$

The mass m will continue to move away if its total energy is positive. The expansion will halt at infinity if the energy is zero, and contraction will follow the expansion if the energy is negative.

▶ The criterion, therefore, is the value of the density relative to the quantity

$$\rho_c = \frac{3H^2}{8\pi G} \approx 10^{-26}\ \text{kg m}^{-3}$$

Determining the mass density of the universe – dark matter

To measure the mass density of the universe means measuring the mass of galaxies within a large volume of space and dividing that mass by the volume. There is an immediate problem in all of this in that we know there exists 'dark matter', matter that we cannot see (because it is too cold to radiate). The determination of the density of the universe, ρ, is difficult. The problem is made worse by the fact that neutrino masses are not yet determined, so their contribution to the density of the universe is unknown. Dark matter could be in the form of brown dwarfs and other similar cold objects, but the existence of more exotic possibilities is also hypothesized.

First are WIMPS (non-baryonic, weakly interacting massive particles). Neutrinos might be classified as such but so also are various other particles predicted by theories of elementary particle physics.

Second are MACHOS (massive compact halo objects), for example black and brown dwarfs.

Dark energy

The discussion of the previous sections is based on the standard Big Bang model of the universe and now appears to be outdated. Since 1998 it has been known that distant supernovas are moving away from us at much faster speeds than those expected based on the standard Big Bang model. Based on gravitation alone, we would expect a deceleration in the speed of recession of distant objects according to the graphs of Figure E4.3. The data says, instead, that the speed is increasing. What is causing this acceleration? It appears that the universe is filled with a kind of all-permeating vacuum energy called **dark energy**. The presence of this energy creates a kind of repulsive force that not only counteracts the effect of gravity on a large scale, but actually dominates it, causing acceleration in distant objects rather than the expected deceleration. The domination of the effects of dark energy over gravity appears to have started about 5 billion years ago.

It thus appears that, even though the present density of the universe is now believed to equal the critical density, the universe does not expand as the graph of Figure E4.3 would suggest for $\rho = \rho_c$, but instead follows the pattern shown in Figure E4.5.

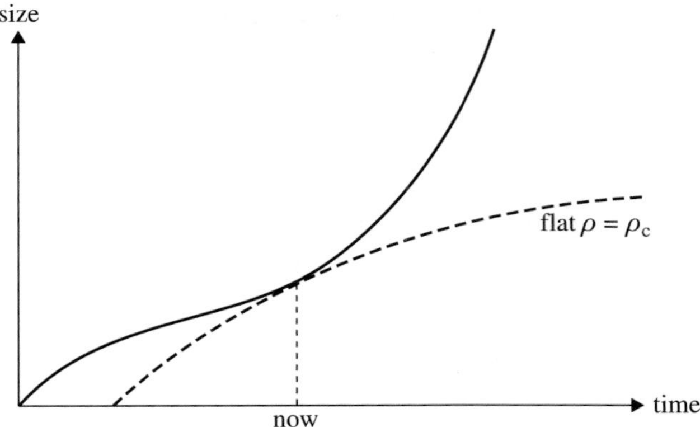

Figure E4.5 The rate of expansion of the universe is accelerating. The dotted line is the expected rate of expansion for $\rho = \rho_c$ based on the standard Big Bang model.

There is now convincing evidence that $\rho = \rho_c$ based on detailed studies of anisotropies in the cosmic background radiation undertaken by the Wilkinson Microwave Anisotropy Probe (WMAP). The mass–energy density of the universe is believed to be made out of approximately 73% dark energy and only 27% matter. And of this matter in the universe, 85% is estimated to be dark matter (i.e. 85% of the 27% matter), leaving a miniscule fraction (15% of the 27% matter) of $0.15 \times 0.27 \approx 0.04$, i.e. about 4%, accounted for by ordinary matter. These are clearly very exciting times for cosmology!

? QUESTIONS

1 State what you understand by the term *Olbers' paradox*. Why is this 'paradox' a problem for infinite cosmologies? How is the paradox resolved in the Big Bang model of cosmology?

2 How many hydrogen atoms per m^3 does the critical density $\rho_c \approx 10^{-26}\ \text{kg m}^{-3}$ correspond to?

3 Discuss three pieces of evidence that support the Big Bang model of the universe.

4 The temperature of the cosmic background radiation measured from earth is about 2.7 K.
(a) What is the significance of the cosmic background radiation?
(b) What temperature for the cosmic background radiation would an observer in a very distant galaxy measure? Why?

5 What will happen to the temperature of the cosmic background radiation if:
(a) the universe keeps expanding forever;
(b) the universe starts to collapse?

6 It is said that the Big Bang started everywhere in space. What does this mean?

7 In the context of the Big Bang theory, explain why the question 'what existed before the Big Bang?' is meaningless.

8 Explain, with the use of two-dimensional examples if necessary, the terms *open* and *closed* as they refer to cosmological models. Give an example of a space that is finite without a boundary and another that is finite with a boundary.

9 In the context of cosmology, what do you understand by the terms:
(a) *critical density*;
(b) *closed universe*;
(c) *open universe*?

10 A student explains the expansion of the universe as follows: 'Distant galaxies are moving at high speeds into the vast expanse of empty space.' What is wrong with this statement?

11 Explain what a comparison of the mass density of the universe with the critical density allows us to determine.

12 What is the main difficulty in determining the value of the mass density of the universe?

13 What do you understand by the term *dark matter*? Give three examples of dark matter.

14 What was the temperature of the universe when the peak wavelength of the background radiation was equal to the wavelength of red light (7×10^{-7} m)?

15 (a) Draw a sketch graph to show the variation with wavelength of the intensity of the cosmic background radiation.
(b) If the universe is in fact open, as recent evidence suggests, explain how the graph you drew in (a) will change many millions of years in the future.

Stellar evolution

This chapter is a detailed account of the nuclear fusion reactions that can take place in the interior of a star, and how the sequence of these reactions determines the evolution and death of a star. The Hertzsprung–Russell (HR) diagram is used to show the evolutionary paths of stars.

Objectives

By the end of this chapter you should be able to:

- describe how a star is *formed*;
- state the main sequences of *nuclear reactions* taking place in a star and say how the *mass* of the star determines which sequences actually take place;
- describe the *main stages in the evolution of a star* and say how the *mass* plays a determining role;
- describe the *end stages* of stellar evolution and appreciate the significance of the *Chandrasekhar limit*;
- state the main properties of a *black hole*;
- state the main properties of *pulsars*;
- state the main characteristics of *quasars*;
- state the meaning of the term *gravitational lensing*.

Nucleosynthesis

Interstellar space (the space between stars) consists of gas and dust at a density of about 10^{-21} kg m^{-3}. This amounts to about one atom of hydrogen in every cubic centimetre of space. The gas is mainly hydrogen (about 74% by mass) and helium (25%), with other elements making up the remaining 1%. Whenever the gravitational energy of a given mass of gas exceeds the average kinetic energy of the thermal random motion of its molecules, the gas becomes unstable and tends to collapse:

$$\frac{GM^2}{R} \geq \frac{3}{2}NkT$$

where k = Boltzmann's constant, T = temperature and N = number of molecules.

This is known as the Jeans criterion. Stars formed and continue to be formed when rather cool gas clouds in the interstellar medium ($T \approx 10$–100 K) of sufficiently large mass (large enough to satisfy the Jeans criterion) collapsed under their own gravitation. In the process of contraction, the gas heated up. Typically, the collapsing gas would break up into smaller clouds, resulting in the creation of more than one star. When the temperature rises sufficiently for visible light to be emitted, the star so formed is called a *protostar* (see Figure E5.1).

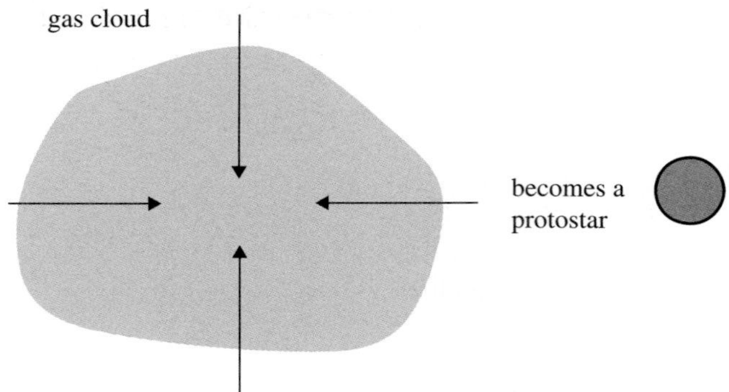

Figure E5.1 The formation of a protostar out of a collapsing cloud of gas.

Example questions

Q1

Show that the Jeans criterion can be rewritten as $M^2 = \frac{3}{4\pi\rho}\left(\frac{3kT}{2mG}\right)^3$, where ρ is the density of the gas and m is the mass of a molecule of the gas.

Answer

Cube each side of the Jeans criterion equation to find

$$\left(\frac{GM^2}{R}\right)^3 = \left(\frac{3kMT}{2m}\right)^3$$

$$\Rightarrow M^2 = \left(\frac{3}{4\pi\rho}\right)\left(\frac{3kT}{2mG}\right)^3$$

using the definition of density and $M = Nm$, where m is the mass of one molecule.

Q2

Take the density of interstellar gas to be about 100 atoms of hydrogen per cm^3. What is the smallest mass this cloud can have so that it becomes unstable and begins to collapse?

Answer

The density is

$$\frac{100 \times 1.67 \times 10^{-27}\ \text{kg}}{10^{-6}\ \text{m}^3} = 1.67 \times 10^{-19}\ \text{kg}^{-3}$$

With $T = 100$ K in the Jeans criterion (see example question 1) we find

$$M \approx 3.0 \times 10^{33}\ \text{kg}$$
$$= 1.5 \times 10^3 M_{\text{sun}}$$

This shows that the gas cloud is quite large and that it can break up, forming more than one star.

As the gas is compressed more (always under the action of gravity) its temperature rises and so does its pressure. The pressure in the core of the star is one way the star can become stable against gravity and stay at a fixed size. However, the core of the gas can get so hot ($T = 5 \times 10^6$ to 10^7 K) that nuclear fusion reactions take place, resulting in the release of enormous amounts of energy. The vast quantity of energy released can account for the sustained luminosity of stars such as our sun, for example, over the 4–5 billion years of its life so far. Thus, nuclear fusion provides the energy that is needed to keep the star hot, so that its pressure is high enough to oppose further contraction and at the same time to provide the energy that the star is radiating into space.

▶ While on the main sequence, the main nuclear fusion reactions taking place are those of the proton–proton cycle discussed in Option E2. The net effect of these reactions is to turn four hydrogen nuclei into one helium

$$4\,{}^1_1\text{H} \rightarrow {}^4_2\text{He} + 2\text{e}^+ + 2\nu_\text{e} + 2\gamma$$

with a release of about 26.7 MeV or 3.98×10^{-12} J of energy. Helium, being heavier than hydrogen, collects in the core of the star (see Figure E5.2).

The mass–luminosity relation

For stars on the main sequence, there exists a relation between the mass and the luminosity of the star. The mass–luminosity relation states that

$$L \propto M^\alpha$$

where the exponent α is between 3 and 4. This relation comes from application of the laws of nuclear physics to stars. The uncertainty in its value comes from the fact that the composition of the stars (the equation of state) is not precisely known.

One application of the mass–luminosity relation is to estimate the lifetime of the star on

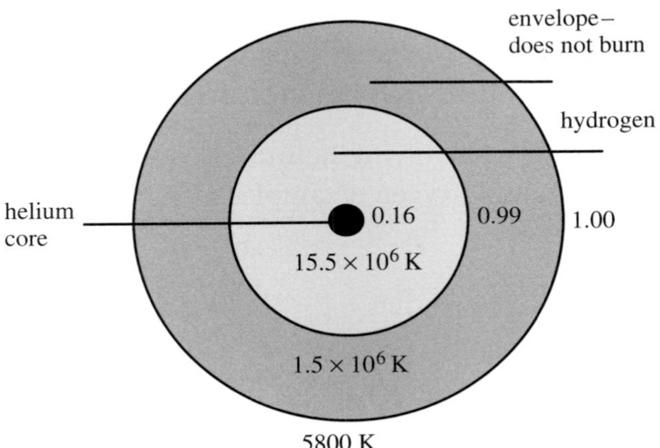

Figure E5.2 The structure of a main sequence star of one solar mass. The numbers 0.16, 0.99 and 1.00 represent the fraction of mass enclosed within each shell. The helium core consists of about 62% helium and 36% hydrogen, showing that nuclear fusion has already started converting hydrogen into helium. The rest of the star is predominantly hydrogen (73%) with 25% helium. The density in the core is about 164 kg m^{-3}, whereas in the outer levels the density falls to 90 kg m^{-3}.

the main sequence. Since luminosity is the power radiated by the star, we may write that

$$\frac{E}{T} \propto M^{\alpha}$$

where E is the total energy radiated by the star and T is the time in which this happens. Now, for the purposes of an estimate, we may assume that the total energy that the star can radiate will come from converting *all* its mass into energy according to Einstein's formula, $E = Mc^2$. Thus

$$\frac{E}{T} \propto M^{\alpha} \quad \Rightarrow \quad \frac{Mc^2}{T} \propto M^{\alpha}$$

$$\Rightarrow T \propto M^{1-\alpha}$$

Assuming for concreteness that $\alpha = 4$, we see that the lifetime of a star of mass M is proportional to

$$T \propto \frac{1}{M^3}$$

Typically, a star with mass equal to one solar mass will spend about 10^{10} years on the main sequence. A star with 10 times the mass of our sun will spend a time on the main sequence that is $\frac{1}{10^3} = 10^{-3}$ less than the time spent by the sun, i.e. 10^7 years.

Main sequence stars on the upper left-hand corner of an HR diagram have very high luminosity and therefore are very massive.

▶ After the star has used about 12% of its hydrogen (the *Schönberg–Chandrasekhar limit*), its core will contract but its outside envelope will expand substantially, making it a very large star. The star will begin to leave the main sequence and move over to the red giant branch.

A more detailed calculation of the lifetime is given in the answer to the example question below.

Example question

Q3

The lifetime of the sun. Our sun emits energy at a rate (luminosity) of about 3.9×10^{26} W. What mass of hydrogen undergoes fusion in a year? Assuming that the energy loss is maintained at this rate, find the time required for the sun to convert 12% of its hydrogen into helium. (Mass of sun = 1.99×10^{30} kg.)

Answer

Assuming the proton–proton cycle as the reaction releasing energy by fusing hydrogen, we have seen above that the energy released per reaction is about 3.98×10^{-12} J. Since the luminosity of the sun is 3.9×10^{26} W, it follows that the number of fusion reactions required per second is

$$\frac{3.9 \times 10^{26}}{3.98 \times 10^{-12}} = 9.8 \times 10^{37}$$

For every such reaction, four hydrogen nuclei turn into helium and thus the mass of the fused hydrogen is

$$9.8 \times 10^{37} \times 4 \times 1.67 \times 10^{-27} \text{ kg s}^{-1}$$
$$= 6.5 \times 10^{11} \text{ kg s}^{-1}$$

or 2×10^{19} kg per year.

At the time of its creation, the sun consisted of 75% hydrogen, corresponding to a mass of

$$0.75 \times 1.99 \times 10^{30}\ \text{kg} = 1.5 \times 10^{30}\ \text{kg}$$

The Schönberg–Chandrasekhar limit of 12% results in a hydrogen mass to be fused of 1.8×10^{29} kg. The time for this mass to fuse is thus

$$\frac{1.8 \times 10^{29}}{6.5 \times 10^{11}}\ \text{s} = 2.8 \times 10^{17}\ \text{s}$$

$$= 8.9 \times 10^{9}\ \text{yr}$$

Since the sun has existed for about 5 billion years, it still has about 4 billion years left in its lifetime as a main sequence star.

Nuclear reactions beyond the main sequence

With the hydrogen in the core exhausted, nuclear reactions there stop and hence the core contracts under its own weight. The contraction of the core releases gravitational potential energy, which heats up the core and the surrounding envelope of hydrogen. The hydrogen continues to fuse and the released energy forces the outer layers of the star to expand. At the same time, though, the outer layers are getting cooler because of the rapid expansion. The star is thus getting bigger and cooler on the surface – it is becoming a *red giant*. In the meantime, the core temperature is increasing.

What happens next depends on the *mass* of the star.

Low-mass stars (mass less than 0.25 solar masses)

No further nuclear reactions take place. The core stays a core of helium.

Mass between 0.25 and 4 solar masses

The temperature of the core reaches the 10^8 K required for nuclear reactions in the core involving helium to start. Since a helium nucleus has two units of positive charge as opposed to one for hydrogen, higher temperatures are required for helium nuclei to fuse. This is because the larger electric charge implies a larger electric force of repulsion that has to be overcome.

The reactions involving helium produce nuclei of carbon and oxygen. Examples of such reactions are

$$^{4}_{2}\text{He} + {}^{4}_{2}\text{He} \rightarrow {}^{8}_{4}\text{Be} + \gamma$$
$$^{4}_{2}\text{He} + {}^{8}_{4}\text{Be} \rightarrow {}^{12}_{6}\text{C} + \gamma$$
$$^{4}_{2}\text{He} + {}^{12}_{6}\text{C} \rightarrow {}^{16}_{8}\text{O} + \gamma$$

The first two reactions occur in rapid succession and have the net effect of converting three helium nuclei into one of carbon. This is called the *triple alpha process*. No further nuclear reactions take place and the core now consists of carbon and oxygen.

Mass between 4 and 8 solar masses

In this mass range, the core temperature rises further and nuclear reactions involving carbon and oxygen take place, producing a core of oxygen, neon and magnesium.

Mass over 8 solar masses

The evolution of such a massive star is very different from that of less massive stars. Because of the large mass of the star, the oxygen, neon and magnesium core will contract further, reaching a temperature high enough for these core elements to fuse, producing heavier elements. In the outer layers helium continues to produce more carbon, and hydrogen more helium. This process repeats, with ever heavier elements settling in the central core. Eventually iron will be produced by the fusing of silicon, and once this happens, the iron will settle at the core. Fusion cannot produce elements heavier than iron, since the binding energy per nucleon peaks with iron and further fusion is not energetically possible. Thus, a massive star ends its cycle of nuclear reactions with iron at its core surrounded by progressively lighter elements, as shown in Figure E5.3. The outer layers of the star have since expanded to a very large size, making the star a *red supergiant*.

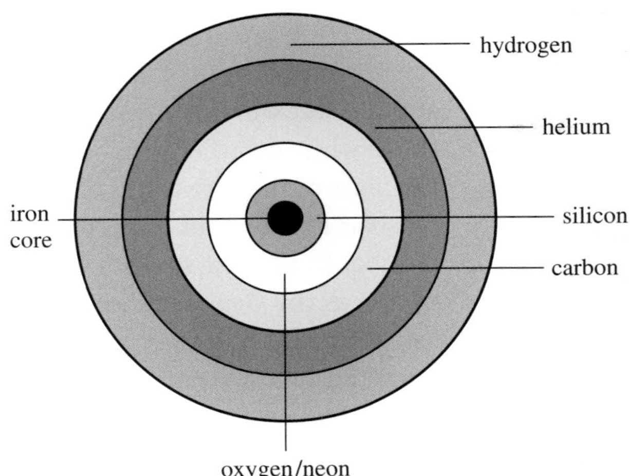

Figure E5.3 The central core of the star consists of iron with layers of lighter elements surrounding it.

Table E5.1 shows the temperatures at which various elements participate in fusion reactions.

Element	$T/10^6$ K	Where
Hydrogen	1–20	Main sequence
Helium	100	Red giant
Carbon	500–800	Supergiant
Oxygen	1000	Supergiant

Table E5.1 The temperatures at which elements participate in fusion reactions.

Evolutionary paths and stellar processes

Once a star is formed out of contracting gases, its surface temperature is not particularly high, but it has a large size, which means that the star starts out somewhere to the right of the main sequence in the HR diagram. As the star continues to contract, its temperature increases and the star moves toward the main sequence. The time spent moving toward the main sequence depends on the mass of the star. Heavier stars take less time. Our sun has taken about 20 to 30 million years to reach the main sequence. (See Figure E5.4.)

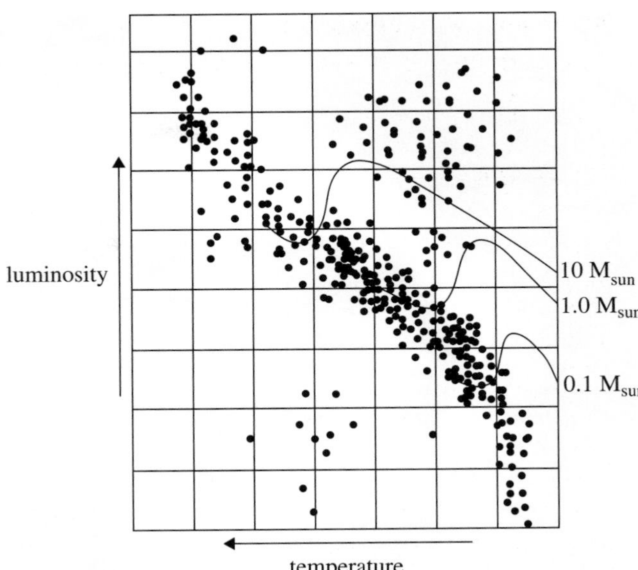

Figure E5.4 Evolutionary tracks of protostars as they approach the main sequence. M_{sun} stands for one solar mass. (Note that temperature is increasing towards the left.)

▶ The mass of the star is the factor that determines its final fate.

Table E5.2 shows the various outcomes for various stellar mass ranges. The table is explained in greater detail in what follows.

Initial mass of star (in terms of solar masses)	Outcome
<0.25	White dwarf with helium core
0.25–4	White dwarf with carbon/oxygen core
4–8	White dwarf with oxygen/neon/magnesium core
8–40	Neutron star
>40	Black hole

Table E5.2 The final fates of stars of various initial masses.

Case 1: Evolution of a star of mass under 8 solar masses

We saw in the last section that, depending on the mass of the star, nuclear reactions in the core stop when the core is made mainly out of helium or carbon/oxygen or oxygen/neon/ magnesium.

Figure E5.5 Helix: a planetary nebula. The star that produced this nebula can be seen at the exact centre. [Note: The name 'planetary nebula' is rather misleading, since it has no connection whatsoever with planets. Planetary nebulae were thought to resemble planets when first seen through a telescope, and the name has stuck.]

The energy released from the core contraction and the hydrogen or helium fusion in the outer layers may force the tenuous outer layers to be ejected from the star in what is called a *planetary nebula* (see Figure E5.5). This leaves behind the small core of the star. The mass of the core may thus be substantially reduced compared with the original mass of the star.

But the core is still contracting under its own weight and getting smaller. The conditions in the core mean that the electrons behave as a gas and the pressure they generate is what keeps the core from collapsing further under its weight. This pressure is generated because of a quantum mechanical principle, Pauli's principle, which states that no two electrons may occupy the same quantum mechanical state.

The core has now become a *white dwarf star*. Now exposed, and with no further energy source, the star is doomed to cool down to practically zero temperature and will then become a *black dwarf*.

▶ The electron pressure can stop the further collapse of the core and the star will become a stable white dwarf only if the mass of the core is less than 1.4 solar masses. This important number in astrophysics is known as the *Chandrasekhar limit*. If the mass of the core is more than 1.4 solar masses, the star will become a neutron star or a black hole.

The Chandrasekhar limit is named after the great Indian (and later American) astrophysicist, Subrahmanyan Chandrasekhar (Figure E5.6). His work on collapsed stars was presented in 1935 at a meeting of the Royal Astronomical Society in England. His ideas were publicly ridiculed by Sir Arthur Eddington, his colleague and mentor at Cambridge University. For his work, Chandrasekhar shared the 1983 Nobel prize in physics.

Figure E5.6 Subrahmanyan Chandrasekhar.

The best known white dwarf is Sirius B, a star that accompanies the star Sirius. It has a mass of 1.02 solar masses, a radius of 5400 km and a surface temperature of 10 000 K. Although hot, it is hard to see, mainly because of the small surface area from which the light is emitted (i.e. the luminosity is low).

The transition from a white to a black dwarf may be uneventful, but occasionally something dramatic may take place. If the white dwarf is part of a binary system, it may attract material from the companion star, which may then be drawn into the white dwarf. As this material falls into the white dwarf, it heats up and emits light. In this way the luminosity of the white dwarf may, briefly, increase by tens of thousands of times. This temporary increase in luminosity is called a *nova* (see Figure E5.7).

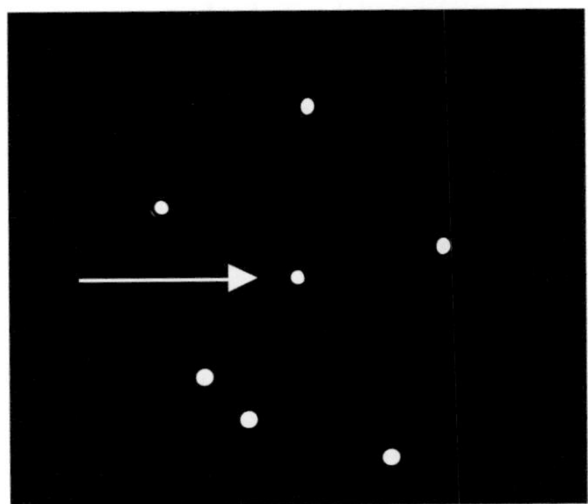

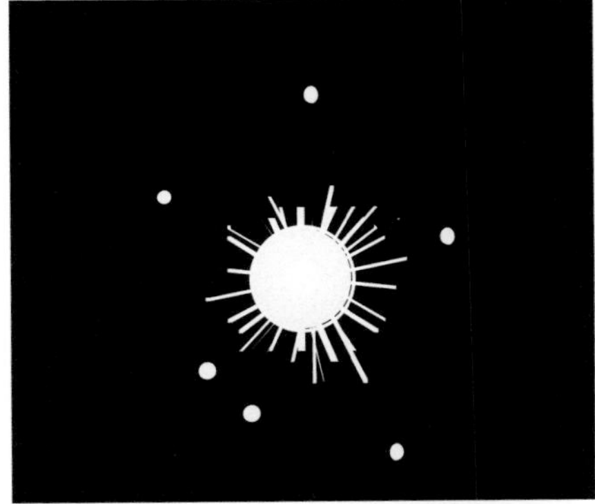

Figure E5.7 A white dwarf star increasing in luminosity during a nova.

Case 2: Evolution of a star of mass over 8 solar masses

As we saw in the last section, the end of nuclear reactions has left a massive star with an iron core. The star is full of photons that have been produced in the various nuclear fusion reactions. They are so energetic that they rip the iron nuclei apart into smaller nuclei. The smaller nuclei are in turn ripped apart into individual protons and neutrons, so that in a very short time the star is composed mainly of protons, electrons, neutrons and photons. Because of the high densities involved, the electrons are forced into the protons, turning them into neutrons and producing neutrinos that escape from the star ($e^- + p \rightarrow n + \nu_e$). The star's core is now made almost entirely of neutrons and it is still contracting rapidly. Pauli's principle is now applied to neutrons. The neutrons get too close to each other and a pressure develops to prevent them from getting any closer. But the neutrons have overshot. They have become too close together and the entire core will now rebound to a larger equilibrium size. The rebounding of the core is catastrophic for the star. It creates an enormous shockwave travelling outward that tears apart the outer layers of the star. The explosion that takes place is much more violent than a planetary nebula and is called a *supernova*. The core that is left behind is called a *neutron star*, and is more massive than the Chandrasekhar limit of 1.4 solar masses.

The first calculations showing the details of neutron star formation were performed by J. R. Oppenheimer (the 'father' of the American atomic bomb) and G. M. Volkoff in 1939. Neutron pressure keeps the star stable, provided the mass of the core is not more than about 3 solar masses – the *Oppenheimer–Volkoff limit.*

Black holes

If the mass of the collapsing star exceeds a few tens of solar masses, the gravitational collapse is unstoppable. The star will soon reach a radius at which the escape velocity from the surface of the sun equals the speed of light, and hence nothing can escape from the star. This radius is called the gravitational radius of the star, R_g, or the Schwarzschild radius or the event horizon radius. It can be found from

$$R_S = \frac{2GM}{c^2}$$

It can be calculated from this formula that for a star of one solar mass the gravitational radius is about 3 km. For the earth it is just 9 mm.

The fact that light cannot escape from a very massive object was known to Pierre Laplace as early as 1795. The first detailed calculations of how a star could actually collapse to form a black hole were performed by Oppenheimer and Snyder in 1939.

▶ If the mass of the core of a star is less than the Chandrasekhar limit of about 1.4 solar masses, the star will become a stable white dwarf in which electron pressure keeps the star from collapsing further.

If the core is more massive than the Chandrasekhar limit, the core will collapse further until electrons are driven into protons, turning them into neutrons. Neutron pressure now keeps the star from collapsing further and the star has become a neutron star.

If the core is substantially more massive than the Oppenheimer–Volkoff limit of about 2–3 solar masses, neutron pressure will not be enough to oppose the gravitational collapse and the star will become a black hole.

Evidence for black holes

Even though a black hole cannot be seen directly, its effects are observable. If it happens to be in the vicinity of other stars, then the strong gravitational field of the hole will influence the motion of nearby stars. Thus, one looks for binary star systems which are sources of X-rays and in which one star is invisible: gas forced into the black hole accelerates and becomes very hot, radiating X-rays on its way into the hole. There are now nine known examples of binary star systems in which the invisible member is a black hole. These include the oldest black hole candidate, the powerful X-ray binary Cygnus X-1, located near the centre of our galaxy. Much heavier black holes exist in other galactic centres. Fifteen of these are known and their masses are in the millions of solar masses.

Figure E5.8 shows a schematic summary of the life history of a star.

These evolutionary stages can be shown on an HR diagram (Figure E5.9).

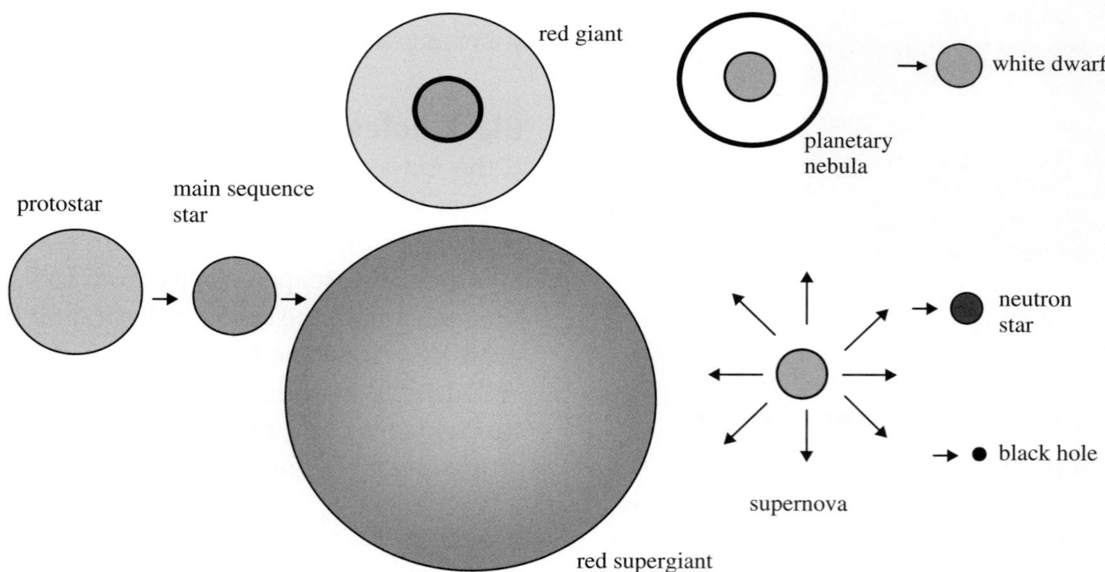

Figure E5.8 The birth and death of a star. The star begins as a protostar, evolves to the main sequence and then becomes a red giant or supergiant. After a planetary nebula or supernova explosion, the core of the star develops into one of the three final stages of stellar evolution, a white dwarf, a neutron star or a black hole.

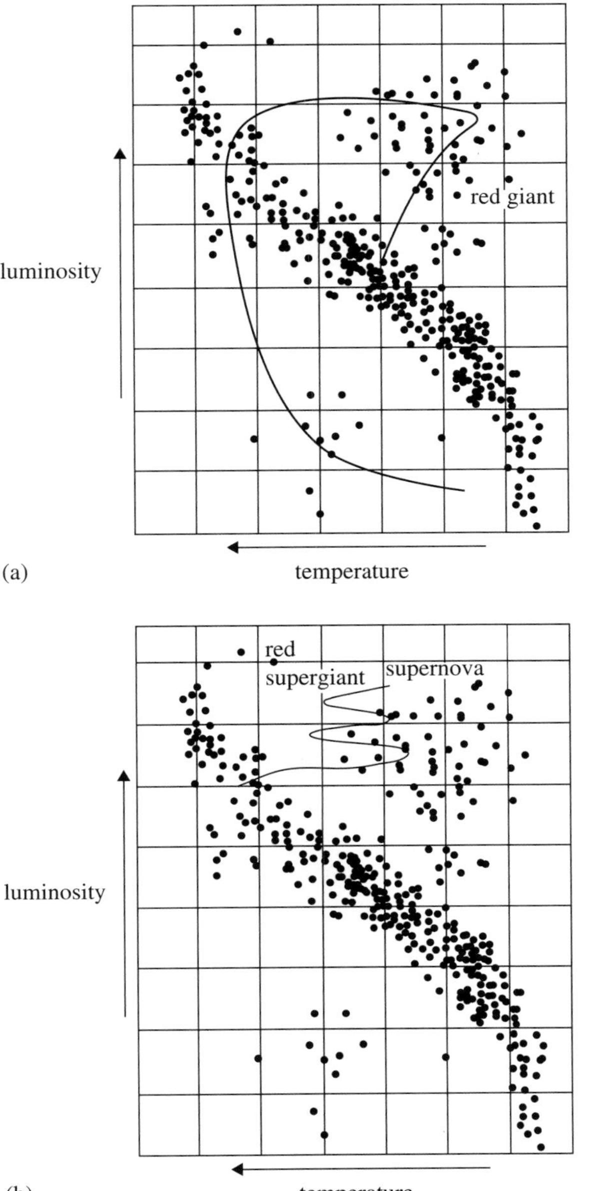

Figure E5.9 Evolutionary tracks of two stars. (a) This is the path of a star of one solar mass that ends up as a white dwarf, which continues to cool down, moving the star ever more to the right on the HR diagram. (b) This is the path of a star of 20 solar masses. It becomes a red supergiant that explodes in a supernova. After the supernova, the star becomes a neutron star, whose luminosity is too small to be plotted on the HR diagram.

Pulsars and quasars

Pulsars

A neutron star may have a magnetic field of quite large magnitude (10^8 T) and may rotate as well, with a period ranging from 30 ms to 0.3 s. Rotating neutron stars emit electromagnetic waves in the *radio* part of the spectrum and so neutron stars can be detected by radio telescopes. (They can also radiate in the X-ray part of the spectrum.) Rotating neutron stars that radiate in this way are called *pulsars*. Despite the name, it is rotation not pulsation that is responsible for the radiation. The radiation emitted by the pulsar is in a narrow cone around the magnetic field direction. If the magnetic field is not aligned with the axis of rotation, then, as the star rotates, the cone containing the radiation *precesses* around the rotation axis (see Figure E5.10). An observer who can receive some of this radiation will then do so every time the cone sweeps past. This explains the pulse nature of this radiation. Pulsars were discovered by Jocelyn Bell (now Professor J. Bell-Burnell), a graduate student at Cambridge University, in 1967.

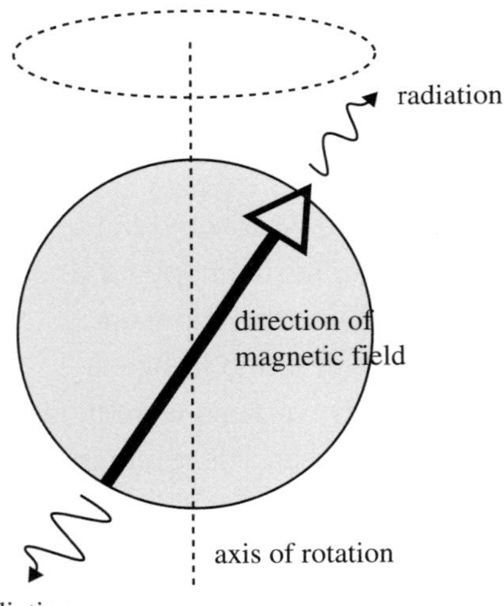

Figure E5.10 If the axis of rotation of a neutron star does not coincide with the direction of the magnetic field, the emitted radiation shows a beacon effect.

Supplementary material

Quasars

In the early days of radio astronomy, a few radio sources were discovered for which there was no obvious optical counterpart. Finally, a star-like object was identified to be at the position of one of these radio sources and its emission spectrum was obtained. The spectrum was mysterious in that it contained lines that could not be identified with any known element. The puzzle was resolved when it was realized that the lines did belong to familiar elements but they were redshifted by amounts never seen before. The largest redshift for a quasar is just under 5, which corresponds to a recession velocity of almost 95% of the speed of light. Using Hubble's law placed the quasar at a distance of about 4700 Mpc. The nearest quasar is at a distance of about 240 Mpc and most are more than 1000 Mpc away. This means that by observing quasars we observe the universe as it was a very long time ago. Quasars (the name stands for quasi-stellar radio sources) are believed to be the very active centres of very young galaxies.

The luminosity of quasars varies from 10^{38} W to 10^{42} W. A luminosity of 10^{42} W is equivalent to about 2×10^{15} suns or 10 000 Milky Ways! What powers a quasar? Most theories involve the presence of a huge black hole at the centre of the quasar that swallows up stars at a rate of perhaps 1000 each year. As the material falls into the black hole, it heats up and radiates, building the quasar's huge luminosity.

In 1979, two quasars were discovered in roughly the same region of space, raising hope for a binary quasar system. When the two were analysed further, they were found to have identical spectra. The 'two' quasars were in fact two images of just one quasar. The multiple images were created by gravitational lensing. Radio signals from the quasar travel past a massive galaxy on their way to earth and are bent by the galaxy in accordance with Einstein's theory of general relativity (see Figure E5.11). Such multiple images of quasars provide valuable information about the mass of the lensing body.

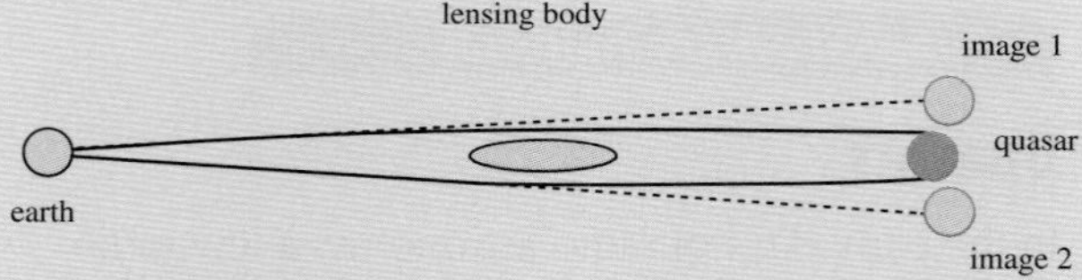

Figure E5.11 The radio signals from the distant quasar are bent as they travel past a massive galaxy. An observer on earth sees two images of the quasar.

QUESTIONS

1 What would the evidence be that a black hole exists at a particular point in space?

2 Using the known luminosity of the sun and assuming that it stays constant during the sun's lifetime, which is estimated to be 10^{10} yr, calculate the mass this energy corresponds to, according to Einstein's mass–energy formula.

3 A neutron star has a diameter of 20 km and makes 1000 revolutions per second.
(a) What is the speed of a point on its equator?
(b) What fraction of the speed of light is this?

4 Comparing two main sequence stars of mass 1 and 10 solar masses, which would you expect to stay longer on the main sequence? Why?

5 What is a planetary nebula? Why do most photographs show planetary nebulae as rings – doesn't the gas surround the core from all directions?

6 How would you react to a claim of the discovery of a star with a core of gold?

7 Assume that the luminosity of a main sequence star is given by $L \propto M^4$. Realizing that the available energy that can be radiated equals the rest mass of the star Mc^2, show that the lifetime of a star scales as $t \propto M^{-3}$. Hence show that a star that is twice as massive as the sun has a lifetime that is 8 times shorter than that of the sun.

8 How would you react to the discovery of a stellar cluster 100 million years old containing a large number of class O stars? (See question 7 above and page 499.)

9 Assume that no stars of mass greater than about 2 solar masses could form. Would life as we know it on earth be possible?

10 Describe the evolution of a main sequence star of mass:
(a) 1 solar mass;
(b) 10 solar masses.

11 Calculate the energy released in the reactions:
(a) ${}^4_2\text{He} + {}^8_4\text{Be} \rightarrow {}^{12}_6\text{C} + \gamma$;
(b) ${}^4_2\text{He} + {}^{12}_6\text{C} \rightarrow {}^{16}_8\text{O} + \gamma$.

(Atomic masses: He = 4.00260 u, Be = 8.0053 u, O = 15.9941 u.)

12 Why is the temperature at which helium nuclei fuse higher than that for hydrogen?

13 What causes:
(a) a planetary nebula;
(b) a supernova?

14 Describe the significance of the Chandrasekhar limit in stellar evolution.

15 Describe the formation of a red giant star.

16 Show on an HR diagram the evolution of a star of 5 solar masses.

17 Consider the reaction ${}^{4}_{2}\text{He} + {}^{4}_{2}\text{He} \rightarrow {}^{8}_{4}\text{Be} + \gamma$ and look at Figure E5.12. The electrostatic repulsion of the positive helium nuclei prevents them from fusing unless the temperature is very high. Estimate this temperature by setting the kinetic energy of a helium nucleus equal to $\frac{3}{2}kT$, where k is Boltzmann's constant. At the point of closest approach the helium nuclei stop and if they are close enough the strong nuclear force will take over and force them to fuse. At this point, set the electrostatic potential energy of the nuclei equal to the sum of the kinetic energies, and thus show that the temperature can be found from

$$3kT = \frac{1}{4\pi\varepsilon_0}\frac{4e^2}{d}$$

Taking the distance of closest approach to be $d = 1.0 \times 10^{-14}$ m, calculate T numerically.

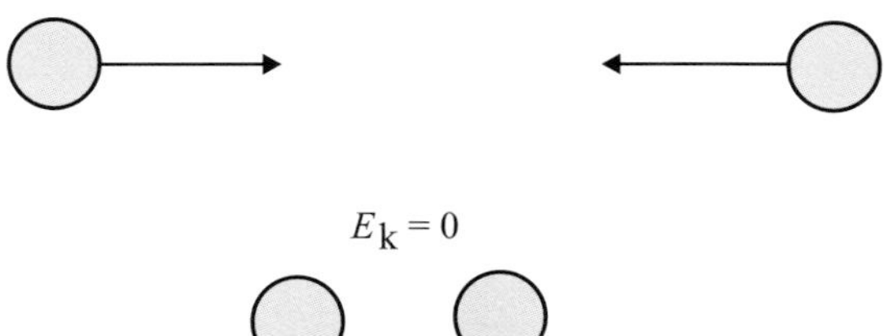

Figure E5.12 For question 17.

18 Table E5.3 shows the luminosity L of a star and the corresponding mass M of the star. By plotting the logarithm of the luminosity versus the logarithm of the mass, find the relationship between these quantities assuming a power law of the kind $L = kM^{\alpha}$, giving the numerical value of the parameter α.

Mass (in solar masses)	Luminosity (in solar luminosities)
1	1
3	42
5	238
12	4700
20	26500

Table E5.3 For question 18.

19 The light from a Cepheid star shows blue- and redshifts of varying magnitude. The blueshift is observed when the star is at its brightest and the redshift when at its dimmest. How can this be explained? When the shift is plotted against time, a periodic curve matching exactly the light curve of the Cepheid is obtained. How can this be explained? Theories of Cepheids as pulsating stars predict that the period T and density ρ are related by

$$T^2\rho = \text{constant}$$

Considering Cepheids of the same mass, show that this implies that the longer-period stars have larger luminosities.

20 Assume that the material of a main sequence star obeys the ideal gas law, $PV = NkT$. The volume of the star is proportional to the cube of its radius R, and N is proportional to the mass of the star, M. Show that $PR^3 \propto MT$. The star is in equilibrium under the action of its own gravity, which tends to collapse it, and the pressure created by the outflow of energy from its interior, which tends to expand it. It can be shown that this equilibrium results in the condition $P \propto \frac{M^2}{R^4}$. (Can you see how?) Combine these two proportionalities to show that $T \propto \frac{M}{R}$. Use this result to explain that, as a star shrinks, its temperature goes up. Conclude this rough analysis by showing that the luminosity of main sequence stars of the same density is given by $L \propto M^{3.3}$.

21 Compare the chemical composition of a young star with that of a star of similar mass but 10 billion years in age.

22 What is a mechanism for energy production in a quasar?

23 What was so unexpected in quasar spectra?

24 Why is the radiation observed from a pulsar pulsed and not continuous?

25 Is the energy emitted by a quasar much less than, about the same as or much larger than the energy emitted by a normal galaxy?

26 (a) Assuming a quasar swallows 1000 stars a year, how long would it take a quasar to consume the mass of the entire Milky Way galaxy? (Assume that the Milky Way contains 2×10^{11} stars.)

(b) What conclusion about a quasar's lifetime can you draw from your calculation?

Galaxies

This chapter discusses Hubble's scheme for the classification of galaxies and provides more details about the expanding universe and Hubble's law. The main events in the lifetime of the universe are outlined.

Objectives

By the end of this chapter you should be able to:

- understand the Hubble *classification scheme* of galaxies and describe the structure of the *Milky Way galaxy*;
- state the *Hubble law* and solve problems using this law, $v = Hd$;
- state the meaning of the *Hubble constant*;
- identify *significant epochs* in the life of the universe;
- understand the term *inflationary universe*.

This section is not required for examination purposes.

Types of galaxy

The Milky Way galaxy

Our sun is one of about 200 billion stars (2×10^{11}) making up the Milky Way, our galaxy, which is a spectacular object to scientist and non-scientist alike, that can be clearly seen on a clear, dark night. The Milky Way is a *spiral* galaxy with a central disc-like bulge (see Figure E6.1). The galaxy has a diameter of some 100 000 ly. At the edges it has a thickness of about 2000 ly. Our solar system occupies a position on one of the spiral arms a distance of about 30 000 ly from the centre, and orbits the galactic centre, completing one revolution every 225 million years. Assuming an average mass for stars equal to that of our sun (2×10^{30} kg) results in a mass for the galaxy of about 4×10^{41} kg.

Galaxies were classified by Edwin Hubble in 1924 into a scheme based mainly on appearance. Hubble identified three basic types of galaxies, *spiral* (with a subdivision into *barred spirals*), *elliptical* and *irregular*. The original scheme has since been modified but it is still being used today.

Spiral galaxies

Our own Milky Way and our close neighbour Andromeda are examples of spiral galaxies. A spiral galaxy consists of a central nucleus, a flattened disc in which the spiral arms are found and a halo of older faint stars. A spiral galaxy contains old as well as young stars. Spirals range in diameter from 6000 pc to 30 000 pc and from 10^9 to 10^{12} solar masses. Our own galaxy is a large spiral in both size and mass. New stars are formed mainly in the

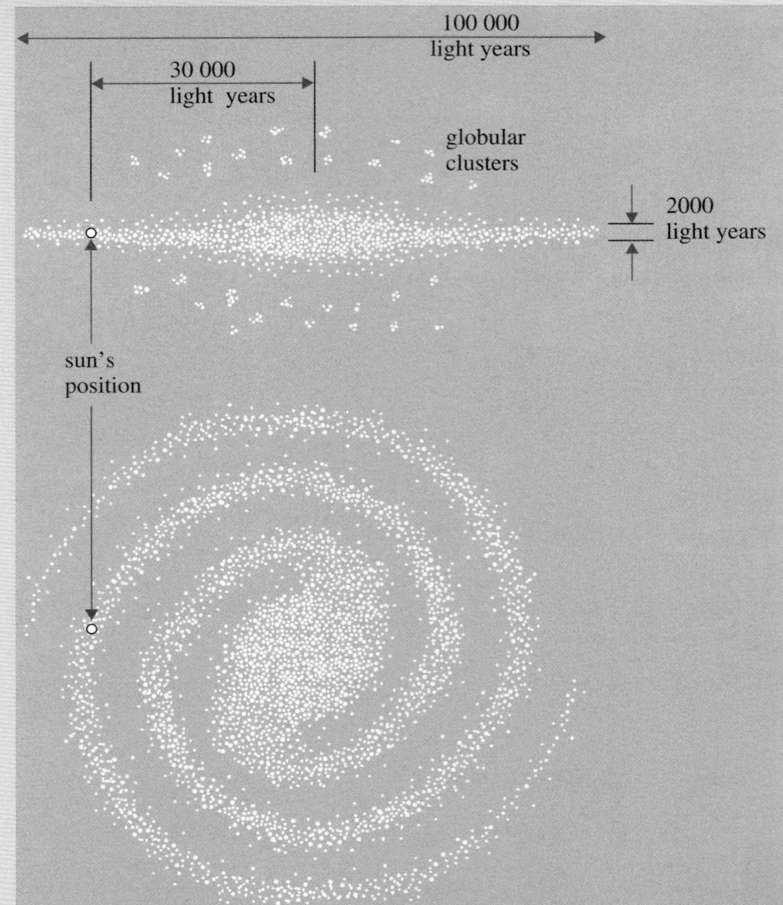

Figure E6.1 The size and structure of the Milky Way galaxy.

spiral arms where the density of interstellar dust is the greatest. The presence of interstellar gas is seen from detailed photographs as well as from the observed radiation at a wavelength of 21 cm that is indicative of such gas. The central nucleus consists mainly of older stars. The subdivision called *barred spirals* is a class of galaxies that is a variation of the spirals; some astronomers believe that they are essentially spirals and therefore don't need a new class to describe them. Like spirals they have spiral arms, but a 'bar' of stars and gas runs through the central bulge and extends into the disc. The spiral arms appear to start from the ends of the bar and not from the central bulge as is the case in the ordinary spirals. Spirals are the most common galaxies; perhaps more than 50% of all galaxies fall into this class.

Elliptical galaxies

These galaxies have a spherical or ellipsoidal shape and consist almost entirely of old stars. There are giant elliptical galaxies containing very massive stars (stars of mass equal to 10^{12} solar masses) and extend in size to a few Mpc. A good example of such a galaxy is M87. The most common ellipticals, however, are small galaxies containing only a few million stars that can be as small as 1 kpc in diameter. A good example of such a dwarf elliptical is the Leo II system, which is so near our own galaxy as to be influenced by the Milky Way's gravity. Ellipticals differ from spirals in that they have no, or very little, interstellar gas. This means that there is very little star formation activity. About 45% of all galaxies are ellipticals.

Irregular galaxies

About 5% of all galaxies fall into the class of irregular galaxies. They have no definite symmetry and are irregular or even chaotic in appearance. Irregular galaxies seem to be undergoing intense star-making activity with many young star clusters. Our closest extragalactic neighbours, the Large and Small Magellanic Clouds, are irregular galaxies. The irregular shape of these galaxies is believed to be (in some but not all cases) due to the collision or close encounter of two regular galaxies.

The characteristics of the three types of galaxy are summarized in Table E6.1, and they are shown in Figure E6.2.

	Spirals/barred spirals	Ellipticals	Irregulars
Shape	Flattened disc, central bulge from which spiral arms start. In barred galaxies, arms start from the ends of the bar. Halo	Spherical or ellipsoidal in shape with stars fairly uniformly distributed in the galaxy	No obvious structure
Star content	The disc contains both young and old stars. The halo has mainly old stars	Contain mainly old stars	Contain both young and old stars
Gas and dust	The disc contains significant amounts of both. The halo does not	Contain little or no gas and dust	Contain a lot of gas and dust
Star formation	Takes place in spiral arms	No significant new star formation in the last 10 billion years	Very significant star formation

Table E6.1 Properties of the three types of galaxy.

Figure E6.2 (a) Spiral galaxy. (b) Elliptical galaxy. (c) Irregular galaxy.

Galactic motion

As we leave our galaxy behind and enter intergalactic space, we find that our galaxy is part of a group of galaxies – the Local Group. There are about 20 galaxies in the Local Group, the nearest being the Large Magellanic Cloud at a distance of about 160,000 light years. In this group, we find the Andromeda galaxy, a spiral galaxy like our own and the largest member of the Local Group. The Local Group extends over a distance of about 10 million light years. This grouping of galaxies into *clusters* is very common. As we move even further out, we encounter collections of clusters of galaxies, known as *superclusters*. It is believed that our Local Group cluster belongs to a supercluster (or supergalaxy) of size 15×10^6 pc across. Contrary to what was believed until recently, the distribution of clusters in space is not uniform but there seem to be areas of linear size 10^8 ly that are empty.

As early as 1914, V. M. Slipher announced his measurements on 15 spiral galaxies. Thirteen of these showed redshifted absorption lines, indicating that these galaxies were moving away from us. By 1925, the number of galaxies studied by Slipher and his assistant, M. Humason, had climbed to 45 and all but the closest galaxies appeared to be moving away at enormous speeds.

▶ The velocity of recession is found by an application of the Doppler effect to light. Light from galaxies arrives on earth redshifted. This means that the wavelength of the light measured upon arrival is longer than the wavelength at emission. According to the Doppler effect, this implies that the source of the light – the galaxy – is moving away from the observers on earth.

The redshift in the light from distant galaxies is, strictly speaking, an effect of general relativity (the expanding universe) and is not due to the Doppler effect.

Light emitted from galaxies comes from atomic transitions in the hot gas in the interior of the galaxies, which is mostly hydrogen. Galaxies are surrounded by cooler gas and thus light travelling through is absorbed at specific wavelengths, showing a characteristic absorption spectrum. The wavelengths corresponding to the dark lines are well known from experiments on earth but the observed wavelengths from the galaxies, when compared to those measured on earth, were found to be a bit longer: they were redshifted. The same applies, of course, to the emission spectrum of the galaxy, but that is usually too faint to be seen.

If λ_0 is the wavelength of a spectral line and λ is the (longer) wavelength received on earth, the redshift, z, of the galaxy is defined as

$$z = \frac{\lambda - \lambda_0}{\lambda_0}$$

If the speed v of the receding galaxy is small compared with the speed of light c, then

$$z = \frac{v}{c}$$

which shows that the redshift is indeed directly proportional to the receding galaxy's speed (more correctly, the component of velocity along the line of sight – see Figure E6.3 and Chapter 4.5).

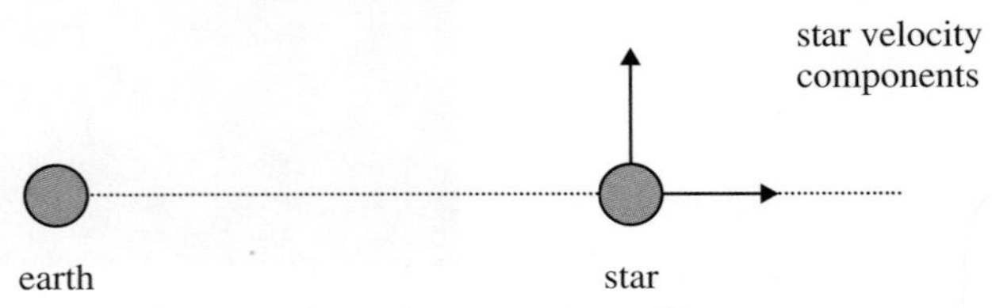

Figure E6.3 Using the Doppler effect we can only measure the component of the star's velocity along the line of sight not the total velocity.

Example question

Q1

A hydrogen line has a wavelength of 434 nm. When received from a distant galaxy, this line is measured on earth at 486 nm. What is the speed of recession of this galaxy?

Answer

The redshift is

$$\frac{486 - 434}{434} = 0.12$$

hence

$$\begin{aligned} v &= 0.12c \\ &= 3.6 \times 10^7 \text{ m s}^{-1} \end{aligned}$$

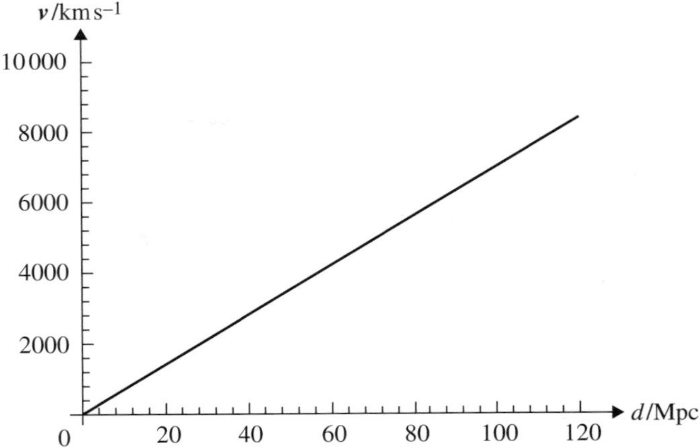

Figure E6.4 Hubble discovered that the velocity of recession of galaxies is proportional to their distance from us.

Hubble's law

In 1925, Edwin Hubble began a study to measure the distance to the galaxies for which Slipher and Humason had determined the velocities of recession. In 1929, Hubble (building on earlier work by V. M. Slipher, and C. Wirtz and K. Lundmark) could announce that galaxies move away from us with speeds that are proportional to their distance. This was a monumental discovery.

▶ Hubble studied a large number of galaxies and found that, the more distant the galaxy, the faster it moves away from us. This is Hubble's law, which states that the velocity of recession is directly proportional to the distance, or

$$v = Hd$$

where d is the distance between the earth and the galaxy, and v its velocity of recession (see Figure E6.4). The constant of proportionality, H, is the slope of the graph and is known as the Hubble constant.

H is the constant of proportionality, known appropriately as the Hubble constant. (It is constant in space but it varies with time.) This was a dramatic discovery – it made the universe a dynamic, evolving, expanding universe. There is considerable debate as to the value of the Hubble constant. The uncertainties come mainly from the enormous difficulties in measuring distances to remote galaxies accurately. The graph in Figure E6.4 assumes a value of 72 km s^{-1} Mpc^{-1}. This is the most recent value of the Hubble constant, established after a Hubble Space Telescope study of Cepheid stars in 18 galaxies.

Hubble's discovery implies that, in the past, the distances between galaxies were smaller and, moreover, that at a specific time in the past the entire universe had the size of a point. This specific point in time is taken to be the beginning of the universe. Not only was time created then but also the space in which the matter and energy of the universe reside. As the space expanded, the distance between clumps of matter increased, leading to the receding galaxies that Hubble observed. It is conventional to describe this three-dimensional expansion of the universe by a two-dimensional model that can be visualized. If we draw two points on the surface of a balloon, they will move apart from each other as the balloon is inflated, as shown in Figure E6.5.

Figure E6.5 A two-dimensional model of Hubble's law. The points on the balloon move away from each other as the balloon is inflated.

This two-dimensional model can easily be visualized since we can observe the expansion of the balloon into the three-dimensional space in which the balloon is embedded. The expansion of the universe, on the other hand, is three-dimensional and could be visualized only if we could similarly view it as embedded in a four-dimensional space. We cannot.

Figure E6.6 shows how the 'radius' of the universe changes in an expanding universe.

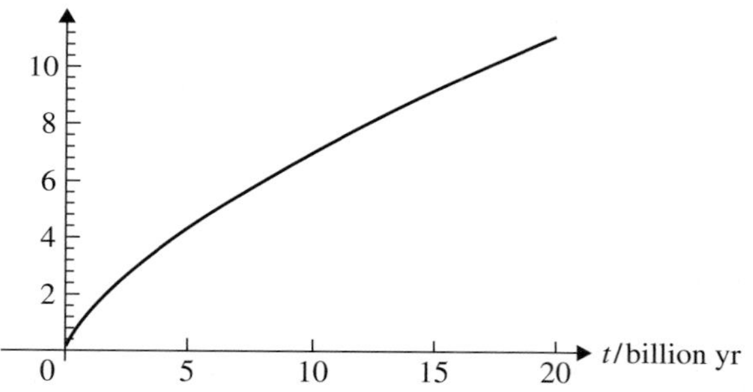

Figure E6.6 The 'radius' of the universe (in arbitrary units) as a function of time.

Hubble's law does not imply that the earth is at the centre of the universe even though the observation of galaxies moving away from us might lead us to believe so. An observer on a different star in a different galaxy would reach this (erroneous) conclusion about their location too. Suppose that a distant galaxy a distance r from the earth has speed v as measured by us. Let $\vec{r}$ be the vector joining the earth to the galaxy. Then $\vec{v} = H\vec{r}$. Now consider a different observer in a different galaxy a distance R from us and moving away at speed V (see Figure E6.7). Hubble's law applied to this galaxy states that $\vec{V} = H\vec{R}$.

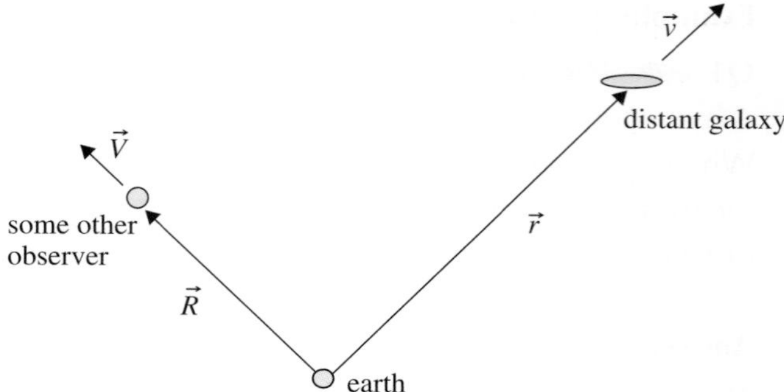

Figure E6.7 Observers on earth are not privileged when it comes to determining Hubble's law.

As far as this observer is concerned, the distant galaxy has velocity $\vec{v} - \vec{V}$, and position vector $\vec{r} - \vec{R}$. Clearly

$$\vec{v} - \vec{V} = H(\vec{r} - \vec{R})$$

that is, Hubble's law is satisfied by the other observer as well. Thus, all observers have the illusion that they are at the centre of the universe. The linear Hubble law is the only possible law for which this could happen.

▶ If we assume that the expansion of the universe has been constant up to now, then $1/H$ gives an upper bound to the age of the universe. This is only an upper bound since the expansion rate, having been faster at the beginning, implies a younger universe. The time $1/H$, known as the Hubble time, is about 14 billion years. The universe cannot be older than that. The more detailed argument that leads to this conclusion is as follows. Imagine a galaxy, which now is at a distance r from us. Its velocity is thus $v = Hr$. In the beginning the galaxy and the earth were at zero separation from each other. If the present separation of r is thus covered at the same *constant* velocity Hr, the time, T, taken to achieve this separation must be given by $v = \frac{r}{T} = Hr$, that is $T = \frac{1}{H}$. Time T is a measure of the age of the universe.

The numerical value of the Hubble time with $H = 72 \times 10^3$ m s^{-1} Mpc^{-1} is

$$T_H = \frac{1}{H}$$
$$= \frac{1}{72 \times 10^3 \text{ m s}^{-1} \text{ Mpc}^{-1}}$$
$$= \frac{1}{72 \times 10^3 \text{ m s}^{-1}} \times 10^6 \text{ pc}$$
$$= \frac{1}{72 \times 10^3 \text{ m s}^{-1}} \times 10^6 \times 3.09 \times 10^{16} \text{ m}$$
$$= 4.29 \times 10^{17} \text{ s}$$
$$= \frac{4.29 \times 10^{17} \text{ s}}{365 \times 24 \times 60 \times 60 \text{ s yr}^{-1}}$$
$$= 13.6 \times 10^9 \text{ yr}$$

The evolution of the universe

If we extrapolate backwards in time, starting with the present temperature of 2.7 K, we can find the temperature of the radiation and the matter filling the universe at earlier times.

Out of the fundamental constants of G, c and h we may define a quantity with units of time. This is known as the *Planck time* and is assumed to mark that time in the history of the universe before which quantum gravitational effects were dominant. Since no quantum theory of gravity exists, the Planck time can be taken as the furthest one can extrapolate backwards in time. It is given by the combination

$$t_P = \sqrt{\frac{hG}{c^5}} \approx 10^{-43} \text{ s}$$

At this early time after the Big Bang, the temperature was about 10^{32} K. The thermal energy associated with this temperature can be calculated from $E_k \approx \frac{3}{2}kT$, giving an energy of the order of 10^{19} GeV (1 GeV = 10^9 eV). Whatever particles existed then would have had a kinetic energy of this order of magnitude.

Forces are unified: time = 10^{-43} s

The strong nuclear force presumably joined with the electroweak into one unified force. During this period, leptons (i.e. electrons, muons, neutrinos, etc.) were indistinguishable from quarks, and under the action of the unified force these particles turned into each other.

Strong nuclear force separates: time = 10^{-35} s

The next milestone in the evolution of the universe occurred at a time of about 10^{-35} s, when the strong nuclear force decoupled from the electroweak force. The temperature by then had fallen to about 10^{27} K.

Inflation begins: time = 10^{-35} s

There followed an extremely rapid period of expansion, called the inflationary epoch. It lasted for no more than 10^{-32} s but in this brief time the size of the universe increased by a factor of 10^{50}!

Forces separate: time = 10^{-12} s

At a time of about 10^{-12} s after $t = 0$, the temperature was about 10^{16} K and the four fundamental forces, gravity, electromagnetism, strong nuclear and weak nuclear, behaved as separate forces. The size of the universe was about 10^{-16} of its present size.

Nucleons form: time = 10^{-2} s

At $t = 10^{-2}$ s, the temperature had fallen sufficiently (to 10^{11} K) for quarks to bind together and to form protons and neutrons and their antiparticles. The universe had a size of about 10^{-10} of its present size. At $t = 1$ s after the Big Bang, $T = 10^{10}$ K, and protons, neutrons, electrons and their antiparticles were in thermal equilibrium with each other.

Example question

Q2

Show that at temperature $T = 10^{10}$ K there is enough thermal energy to create electron–positron pairs.

Answer

The thermal energy corresponding to $T = 10^{10}$ K is $E_k \approx \frac{3}{2}kT$, that is

$1.5 \times 1.38 \times 10^{-13}$ J = 1.3 MeV

The rest energy of an electron is $m_e c^2 \approx 0.5$ MeV, so the thermal energy $E_k \approx 1.3$ MeV is enough to produce a pair.

Nuclei form: time = 3 min

At $t = 200$ s ('the first three minutes'), the temperature had fallen down to 10^9 K and the time was right for protons and neutrons to start combining, creating the nuclei of the light atoms. When the temperature was just over 10^9 K, the thermal motion of nucleons inside the nucleus was large enough to break the nucleus apart. Therefore, no nuclei could have existed prior to this time. This temperature sets the time when nuclei began to form – the period of *nucleosynthesis*. The relative numbers of protons, neutrons and electrons differ because of differences in mass, but can be determined by applying the laws of thermodynamic equilibrium. Using, in addition, the laws of nuclear physics, which determine how nucleons combine to form nuclei, one can predict the relative abundances of the nuclei so produced as the universe cools from 10^9 K to lower temperatures. For example, it can be shown that at this time there were seven protons for every neutron in the universe, or fourteen protons for every two neutrons. The two neutrons can combine with two protons to form one helium nucleus, the remaining twelve protons forming twelve hydrogen nuclei. The mass of twelve hydrogen nuclei is about 12 u and the mass of one helium nucleus about 4 u.

In this way, we can predict that there should exist an abundance of helium-4 in the universe of about 25% by mass. The fact that the measured abundance of helium is 25% is one of the strongest pieces of evidence in favour of the Big Bang scenario.

After the formation of light nuclei, 3 min or so after the Big Bang, the universe consisted mainly of electrons, photons and light nuclei (protons and deuterium and helium nuclei) up to a time of about 10^4 yr ($T = 10^4$ K). The universe then had a size of about 10^{-4} of its present size.

Atoms form: time = 3×10^5 yr

There followed a period of *recombination*, in which electrons joined with protons to form neutral atoms of hydrogen at about 3×10^5 yr, $T = 3000$ K. (The term *recombination* is misleading since atoms of hydrogen had not existed earlier.) The universe was cooling down sufficiently for matter and radiation to decouple. Previously, photons scattering off electrons kept the electrons (matter) in thermal equilibrium with radiation (photons). The fact that electrons were now in atoms and not free means that photons could move larger distances without being scattered by electrons. Earlier, the total energy carried by photons was greater than the energy carried by matter, but at these lower temperatures equality was reached. Soon afterwards, the energy carried by matter became the dominant energy in the universe; the universe became matter-dominated and continues to be so today.

First stars and galaxies form: time = 0.5×10^6 yr

About half a million years after $t = 0$, matter began to cool sufficiently to allow for the formation of stars and galaxies. Nuclear fusion in the interior of stars provided their energy and heavier nuclei were formed. Our solar system formed just over a billion years from the Big Bang.

Matter and antimatter

The universe we observe is made out of matter and not antimatter. Yet in the very early universe there were *almost* equal numbers of particles and antiparticles. Note the word 'almost', for if the numbers of particles and antiparticles had been exactly the same, we would not be here – no matter would exist. Theories of elementary particles predict that in the very early universe an asymmetry in their interactions produced a very slight excess of particles over antiparticles (one extra particle for every 10^9 particle–antiparticle pairs in the universe). The particles constantly collided with the antiparticles and turned themselves into photons. But the reverse process also occurred, with photons turning themselves into pairs of particles and antiparticles. When the universe cooled down to below 10^{10} K, the energy of the photons was so reduced that they could no longer produce pairs of particles and antiparticles. The annihilation of particles and antiparticles into photons continued, however, until all particle–antiparticle pairs were turned into photons (permanently). This left behind the one particle, in the 10^9 pairs, that was unmatched. This is the matter that we see today.

? QUESTIONS

1 What type of galaxy is the Milky Way according to Hubble's classification scheme.

2 Outline the structure of the Milky Way galaxy.

3 State and explain Hubble's law. Explain why this law is evidence for an expanding universe.

4 Some galaxies actually show a blueshift, indicating that they are moving toward us. Does this violate Hubble's law?

5 Galaxies are affected by the gravitational pull of neighbouring galaxies and this gives rise to what are called *peculiar* velocities. Typically these are about 500 km s^{-1}. How far away should a galaxy be so that its velocity of recession due to the expanding universe equals its peculiar velocity?

6 Suppose that sometime a detailed study of the Andromeda galaxy and all the nearby galaxies in our Local Group will be possible. Would this help in determining Hubble's constant more accurately?

7 Figure E6.8 shows two lines due to calcium absorption in the spectrum of five galaxies, ranging from the nearby Virgo to the very distant Hydra. Each diagram gives the wavelength of the H line (hydrogen line). The wavelength of the H line in the lab is 656.3 nm. Use the Doppler shift formula (non-relativistic version) to find the velocity of recession of each galaxy. Using Hubble's law, find the distance to each galaxy.
(Use $H = 72$ km s^{-1} Mpc^{-1}.)

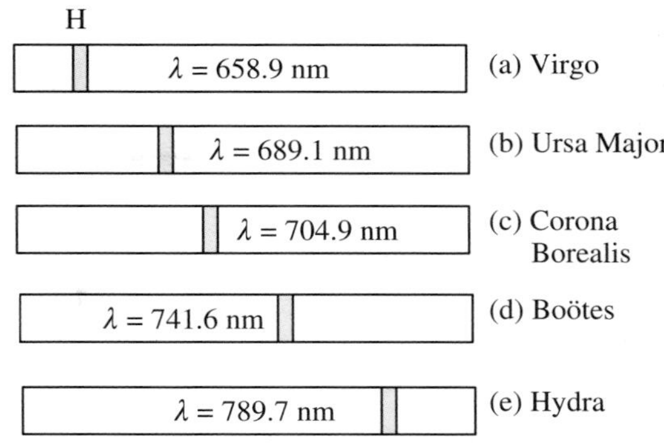

Figure E6.8 For question 7.

For those taking the Special and general relativity option

8 Take Hubble's constant now to be $H = 72$ km s^{-1} Mpc^{-1}.
(a) At what distance from the earth is the speed of a receding galaxy equal to the speed of light?
(b) What happens to galaxies that are beyond this distance?
(c) Is the theory of special relativity violated?

9 A spectral line, when measured on earth, corresponds to a wavelength of 4.5×10^{-7} m. When received from a distant galaxy, the wavelength of the same line is measured at 5.3×10^{-7} m.
(a) What is the redshift for this galaxy?
(b) How fast is this galaxy moving from us? Find the answer by using the non-relativistic formula
(c) How far is the galaxy?
(Take $H = 72$ km s^{-1} Mpc^{-1}.)

10 Explain why the inverse of the Hubble constant, $1/H$, is taken to be the 'age of the universe'. How old would the universe be if $H = 500$ km s^{-1} Mpc^{-1} (close to Hubble's original value)?

11 Explain how the Hubble constant sets an *upper bound* to the age of the universe.

12 Explain why the Hubble law does not imply that the earth is at the centre of the universe.

13 Consider a balloon and two points on its equator (see Figure E6.9). The radius of the balloon is R and is increasing with time. The distance between the two points is thus getting bigger. This distance is given by $r = R\theta$, where θ is the angle that the arc joining the two points subtends at the centre of the balloon. Assume that as the balloon expands the angle θ stays the same.

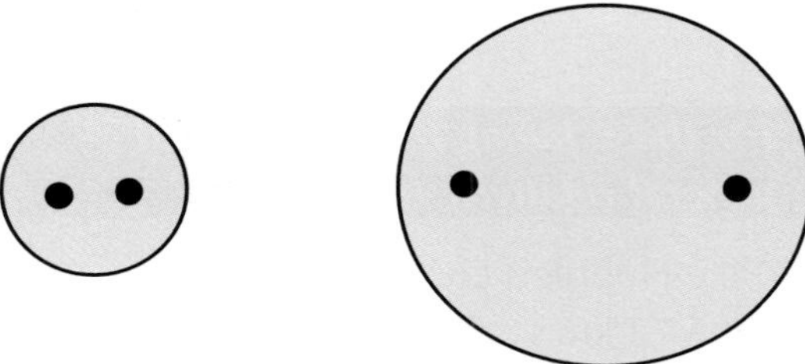

Figure E6.9 For question 13.

(a) Show that the velocity with which the two points move apart is proportional to their separation (i.e. show that $v = Hr$, where $H = \frac{1}{R}\frac{dR}{dt}$). This shows that Hubble's law is satisfied.

(b) Show that, if the radius of the balloon is expanding uniformly (i.e. if $R \propto t$), then the Hubble 'constant' is actually decreasing with time as $H = \frac{1}{t}$.

(c) How should the radius be increasing in order that H be really constant in time?

14 What do you understand by the term *nucleosynthesis*?

15 Suggest why no atoms existed at times prior to about 10^5 years after the Big Bang.

16 What significant event took place three minutes after the Big Bang?

17 The universe had almost equal quantities of matter and antimatter in its very early stages. Outline the reason why the universe today is made out of matter only.

18 All stars, regardless of age, contain *at least* 25% helium by mass. How is this significant?

19 An old theory of cosmology (the steady state theory) asserted that, as the universe expanded, matter was constantly being created so as to keep the density of the universe constant. Taking the density of the universe to be about 10^{-26} kg m^{-3}, find at what rate matter must be created in order that the density of an expanding universe be kept constant. Take $H = 72$ km s^{-1} Mpc^{-1}.

HL only

20 (The following very long problem is for mathematically inclined students who might enjoy it. It will certainly not be required in the IB examination!)
Imagine space to be filled with gas of density ρ. A galaxy of mass m at a distance r from the earth is thus attracted toward the earth by the mass enclosed in a sphere of radius r centred on the earth. Newton's laws (second law and gravitation) then imply that

$$m\frac{dv}{dt} = \left(\frac{4\pi}{3}\rho r^3\right)\frac{Gm}{r^2}$$

where the quantity in brackets represents the mass of the gas in the sphere of radius r. Use $v = HRr_0 = \frac{dR}{dt}r_0$, where R is the scale factor of the universe and r_0 is the separation of two points at some arbitrary time t_0. Substituting into Newton's law we find

$$\frac{d^2R}{dt^2} + \frac{4\pi}{3}G\rho R = 0$$

This is the equation obeyed by the scale factor $R(t)$, but it still cannot be solved because the density is also a function of time. But by the law of conservation of mass we must have (why?)

$$\rho R^3 = \rho_0 R_0^3$$

where the zero subscripts indicate the values of the density and the scale factor now. Thus, show that

$$2\frac{d^2R}{dt^2} + \frac{C}{R^2} = 0$$

where the constant C has the value $C = \frac{8\pi G}{3}\rho_0 R_0^3$. Show that the differential equation for R just derived is equivalent to

$$\left(\frac{dR}{dt}\right)^2 - \frac{C}{R} + k = 0$$

where k is a new constant of integration. (Just differentiate this last equation and show that you get the old one.) This last equation is known as the Friedmann equation. It describes how the scale factor varies with time. It was derived by Newtonian mechanics but it turns out that it is also valid in general relativity as well.

Solve this equation for the case of $k = 0$ to find $R(t) \propto t^{2/3}$. What does the rate of increase of R become as time gets large?

Hence show that $H \propto \frac{1}{t}$. The expansion will stop if $\frac{dR}{dt} = 0$. Using the Friedmann equation, show that this requires that $k > 0$. Assuming that $k > 0$, show that the solution of the Friedmann equation is given in parametric form as

$$R(\theta) = \frac{C}{2k}(1 - \cos\theta)$$

$$t(\theta) = \frac{C}{2k^{3/2}}(\theta - \sin\theta)$$

where the parameter θ varies from 0 to 2π. This is the equation of a cycloid. Sketch this curve. Show that the largest value of the scale of the universe is then $R = \frac{C}{k}$ and that this takes place at a time given by $\frac{\pi C}{2k^{3/2}}$. Show that R becomes zero again at a time given by $\frac{\pi C}{k^{3/2}}$. Show that, for small t, the solution for $k > 0$ of the previous problem agrees with the solution for $k = 0$, that is

$$R(t) \propto t^{2/3}$$

Why is there such an agreement? At which point in the lifetime of the universe was the expansion the fastest (i.e. largest rate of change of R)? What does this suggest? Attempt to apply the same analysis to the case $k < 0$. (*Hint*: You will have to replace sines and cosines by hyperbolic sines and cosines.) What do you guess k represents?

Radio communication

Communication, the transfer of information in many different forms from one place to another, is perhaps the dominant characteristic of our present global society. We are now all dependent on computers, modems and mobile telephones for very many aspects of our daily lives. Thanks to rapid advances in just the past two decades, the average person now has access to an unprecedented amount of information. This information can be retrieved, stored and retransmitted with astonishing ease and speed. This option is an introduction to the fascinating field of communications. Its proper study requires some physics, a lot of electronics and a lot of very advanced mathematics. The approach taken here is non-mathematical and is intended only as a brief introduction to the subject.

Objectives

By the end of this chapter you should be able to:

- understand the difference between a *carrier wave* and a *signal wave* (containing the information or message);
- sketch simple *power spectra*;
- understand that *modulation* of the carrier wave is necessary in order to *transmit information*;
- understand the process of *amplitude modulation* (AM);
- define what is meant by *sideband frequencies* and *bandwidth*;
- solve problems with amplitude-modulated waves;
- understand the process of *frequency modulation* (FM);
- describe the advantages and disadvantages of modulation by FM compared to AM;
- describe the components and function of a simple *AM radio receiver*.

Modulation

The most common form of communication involves two people talking to each other. The following example illustrates features common to all communication systems. To communicate we need a *source* (the first person speaks), a *carrier* (in this example, a sound wave) and a *receiver* (the second person). To produce the sound in the first place, a voice must be available; and to receive it, an ear is needed. To process everything, two brains are required as well.

Now imagine that the first person makes the same sound all the time, for example pronouncing the letter C repeatedly. Unless, by some prearrangement, this is supposed to signify something, the information submitted to the second person in this way is zero. To convey information, the signal (in this case the C) must be *modified* in some way. One way to modify the signal is to pronounce the letter C at various intensities, loud and soft, or to leave different intervals of time between one C and the next. Modifying the signal in this way can be used to transmit information if both the source and the receiver understand the rules by which the signal gets modified.

▶ Modifying a signal in some way so that it can be used to transmit information is called *modulation*. The modulation that takes place in modern communication systems is electrical in nature.

Signals

We must distinguish between two types of wave:

- **signal wave**, which contains the information or message to be transmitted, e.g. audio (sounds or voice), video (picture or movie) or data;
- **carrier wave**, the means by which the information is to be transmitted (usually an electromagnetic wave), e.g. a radio wave or visible light or alternating current.

The simplest wave is a sinusoidal wave of constant amplitude A and single frequency f. The displacement ('displacement' here usually refers to a voltage) of such a wave is

$$y = A\sin(2\pi ft)$$

Thus

$$y = 5\sin(200\pi t)$$

represents a wave of frequency $f = 100$ Hz and amplitude 5 units. Given a signal, we can find its **power spectrum**. This means plotting the power (amplitude squared) as a function of frequency. Since our simple signal contains just one frequency, we obtain the power spectrum shown in Figure F1.1.

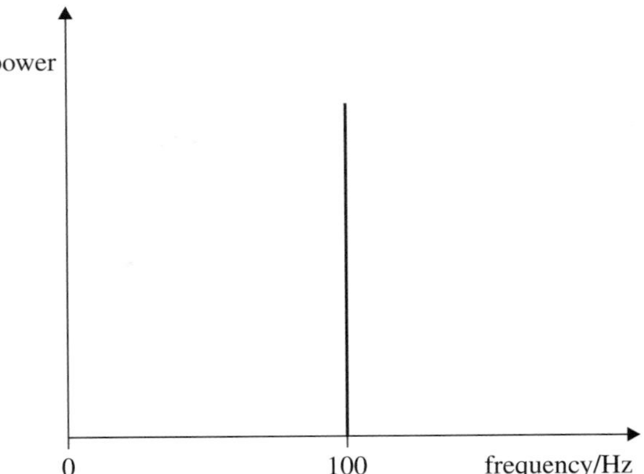

Figure F1.1 The power spectrum of a single-frequency wave.

Consider by contrast a more involved signal consisting of two sine waves:

$$y = 10\sin(200\pi t) + 5.0\sin(400\pi t)$$

The frequencies are 100 Hz and 200 Hz with corresponding amplitudes 10 and 5.0 units. Its power spectrum is shown in Figure F1.2.

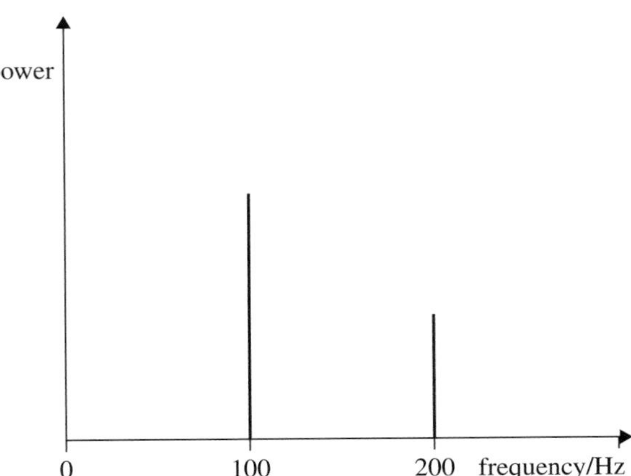

Figure F1.2 The power spectrum of a wave consisting of two components with different frequencies and amplitudes.

Most of the time we shall be concentrating on **harmonic** waves, i.e. waves of the form $\sin(2\pi ft)$ or $\cos(2\pi ft)$. A famous result in mathematics states that any periodic signal can be written as a sum (perhaps an infinite sum) of harmonic waves with specific coefficients. This is why the study of harmonic signals is important: through them, all other signals can be obtained. As an example of this, consider a periodic square wave, as in Figure F1.3.

This can be approximated with

$$y = \sin(2\pi ft) + \tfrac{1}{3}\sin(6\pi ft) + \tfrac{1}{5}\sin(10\pi ft) + \cdots$$

where $f = \frac{1}{T}$. Figure F1.4 shows the approximation with just six terms in this series.

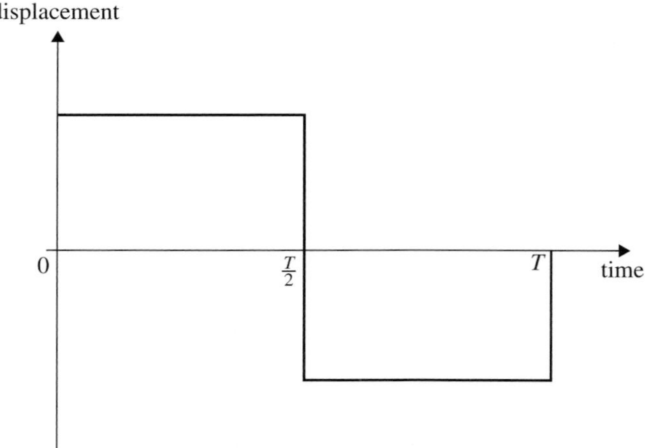

Figure F1.3 A periodic square wave.

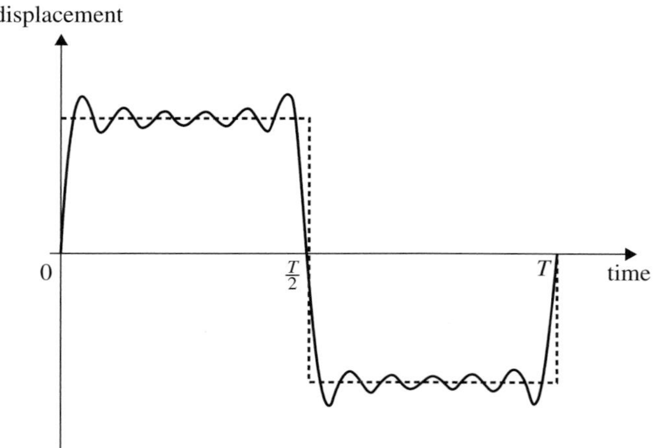

Figure F1.4 Approximation of the square wave with harmonic waves of odd frequency, f, $3f$, $5f$, etc. The approximation gets better when we include more terms in the series above.

Amplitude modulation (AM)

Consider two simple signal (information) and carrier waves. Assume that both are sinusoidal with displacements given by

$$y_S = A_S \sin(2\pi f_S t) \qquad \text{signal wave}$$
$$y_C = A_C \sin(2\pi f_C t) \qquad \text{carrier wave}$$

▶ In the process of amplitude modulation (AM), the *amplitude* of the carrier wave gets changed (i.e. modulated) by the addition of the instantaneous displacement of the signal wave.

So the modulated carrier wave becomes

$$y_M = [A_C + A_S \sin(2\pi f_S t)] \sin(2\pi f_C t) \qquad \text{modulated carrier wave}$$

With some trigonometry (the details are not required for examination purposes), this can be rewritten as

$$y_M = A_C \sin(2\pi f_C t) + \tfrac{1}{2} A_S [\cos(2\pi(f_C - f_S)t) - \cos(2\pi(f_C + f_S)t)]$$

This shows that the modulated carrier wave now has three components:

(a) the original carrier wave, $A_C \sin(2\pi f_C t)$;

(b) a wave of amplitude $\frac{1}{2}A_S$ and frequency $(f_C - f_S)$;

(c) a wave of amplitude $\frac{1}{2}A_S$ and frequency $(f_C + f_S)$.

Suppose that we have the sinusoidal signal (information) wave shown in Figure F1.5(a) and the carrier wave shown in Figure F1.5(b). The amplitude-modulated wave is then that shown in Figure F1.5(c). The power spectrum of the amplitude-modulated carrier wave is shown in Figure F1.6.

The frequencies $(f_C - f_S)$ and $(f_C + f_S)$ are known as the lower and upper **side frequencies**. The difference between the upper and lower side frequencies is known as the **bandwidth**:

$$\Delta f = (f_C + f_S) - (f_C - f_S)$$
$$= 2f_S$$

In practice, the information signal wave will carry more than one frequency. If the information signal wave carries a range of frequencies from f_L to f_H, then the modulated carrier wave will consist of a wave at the carrier frequency f_C and two **sidebands**. The lower sideband will contain frequencies in the range $(f_C - f_H)$ to $(f_C - f_L)$ and the upper sideband will contain frequencies in the range $(f_C + f_L)$ to $(f_C + f_H)$. The power spectrum is shown in Figure F1.7.

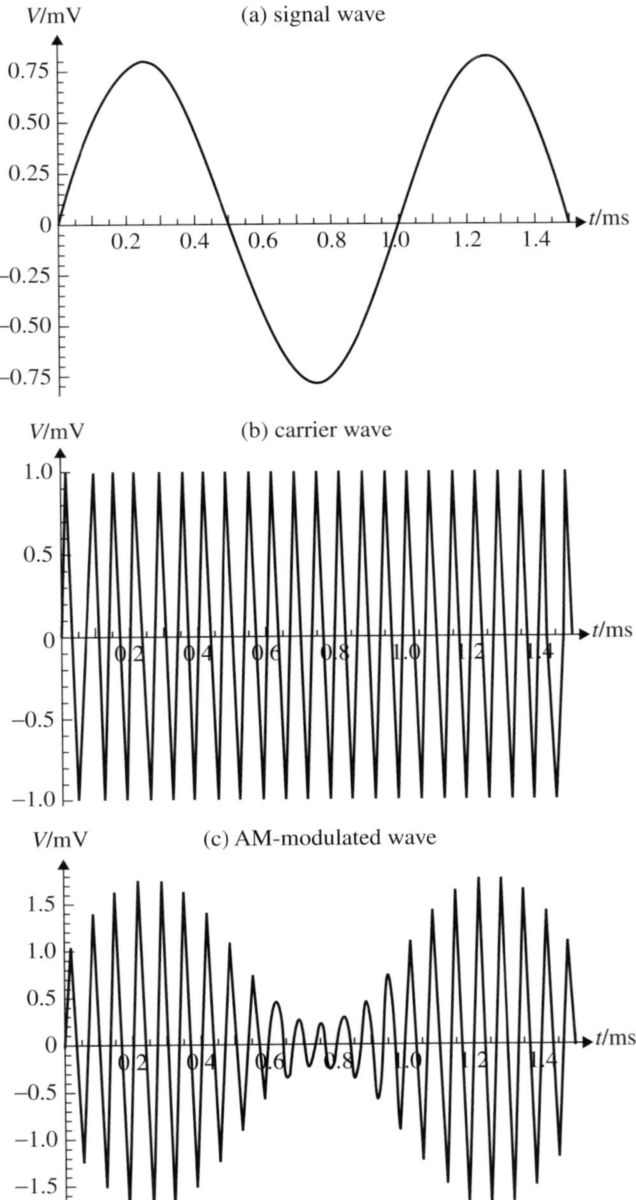

Figure F1.5 (a) A signal (information) wave, (b) a high-frequency carrier wave and (c) the amplitude-modulated carrier wave produced.

The **bandwidth** is defined as the range of the frequencies in the modulated signal and thus equals

$$\Delta f = (f_C + f_H) - (f_C - f_H)$$
$$= 2f_H$$

▶ We thus have the important result that, for amplitude modulation, the *bandwidth* is twice the highest signal wave frequency.

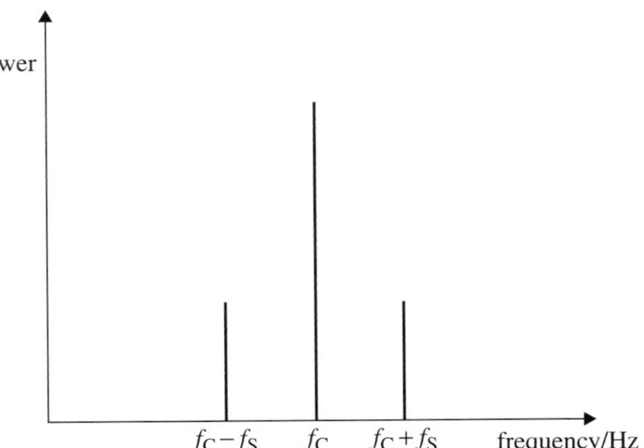

Figure F1.6 The power spectrum of the AM wave from Figure F1.5, which has been amplitude-modulated by a single frequency in the information signal.

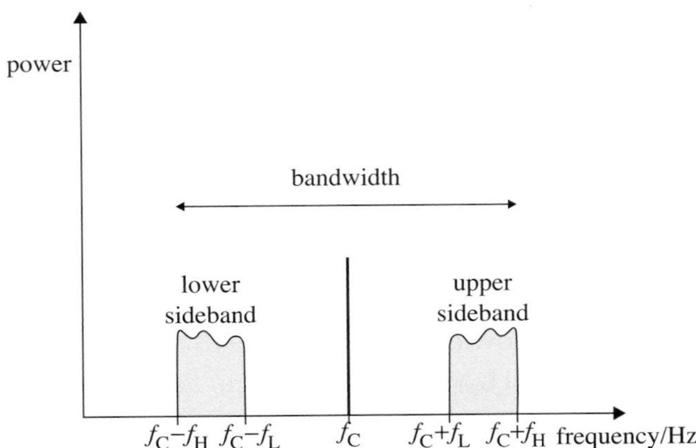

Figure F1.7 When the signal (information) wave has many frequencies, we have sidebands on both sides of the carrier frequency.

From the earlier formula for the amplitude-modulated carrier wave, we can see that the amplitude has a maximum value equal to $A_C + A_S$ and a minimum value of $A_C - A_S$. This means that the difference between the maximum and the minimum amplitude values is

$$(A_C + A_S) - (A_C - A_S) = 2A_S$$

i.e. twice the signal amplitude.

Example questions

Q1

(a) A 2 kHz information signal is used to amplitude-modulate a 1 MHz carrier. Calculate the bandwidth of the transmitted signal.

(b) The information signal is now changed to a signal with a range of frequencies from 0.20 kHz to 2.0 kHz. State the frequencies generated by the modulator for the 0.20 kHz and 2.0 kHz signals.

(c) Calculate the bandwidth for this transmitted signal.

(d) Radio stations have been allowed to broadcast in the frequency range 600 kHz to 1400 kHz. How many radio stations can broadcast in this range if the signal has the bandwidth calculated in (c)?

Answer

(a) There will be two side frequencies at (1 ± 0.002) MHz, i.e. at 1.002 MHz and 0.998 MHz. The bandwidth is $1.002 - 0.998 = 0.004\,\text{MHz} = 4\,\text{kHz}$.

(b) The frequencies for the 0.20 kHz signal are $(1 \pm 0.0002)\,\text{MHz}$, i.e. 1.0002 MHz and 0.9998 MHz. For the 2.0 kHz signal they are 1.002 MHz and 0.998 MHz, as before.

(c) The bandwidth is $1.002 - 0.998 = 0.004\,\text{MHz} = 4\,\text{kHz}$, as before, twice the highest frequency in the information signal.

(d) The frequency range is $1400 - 600 = 800\,\text{kHz}$. Thus we can have $\frac{800\,\text{kHz}}{4\,\text{kHz}} = 200$ radio stations in this frequency band.

Q2

The graph of Figure F1.8 shows a carrier wave modulated by a single audio frequency. Using the graph, determine:

(a) the frequency of the carrier;

(b) the frequency of the information signal;

(c) the amplitude of the information signal.

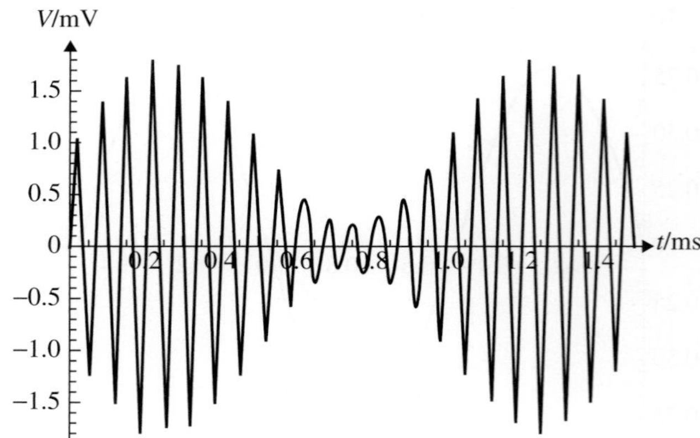

Figure F1.8 An amplitude-modulated carrier wave.

Answer

(a) There are three full waves in a time interval of 0.20 ms. Hence the carrier period is approximately $\frac{0.20}{3} = 0.067$ ms. The frequency is therefore $\frac{1}{0.067} = 15\,\text{kHz}$.

(b) To find the period of the information signal, look at the envelope of the carrier wave from peak to peak (or trough to trough if more convenient). This period is $1.30 - 0.30 = 1.0\,\text{ms}$. The frequency is then $\frac{1}{0.0010} = 1.0\,\text{kHz}$.

(c) The modulated signal has a maximum amplitude of 1.80 mV and a minimum amplitude of 0.20 mV. The difference in these is equal to twice the amplitude of the information signal, so amplitude of information signal $= \frac{1.80-0.20}{2} = \frac{1.60}{2} = 0.80\,\text{mV}$.

The modulation of a signal can be represented as a block diagram as shown in Figure F1.9. The result of mixing the original audio (information) signal with the carrier results in the three components mentioned above. The amplifier amplifies these three, but does not amplify the original audio signal.

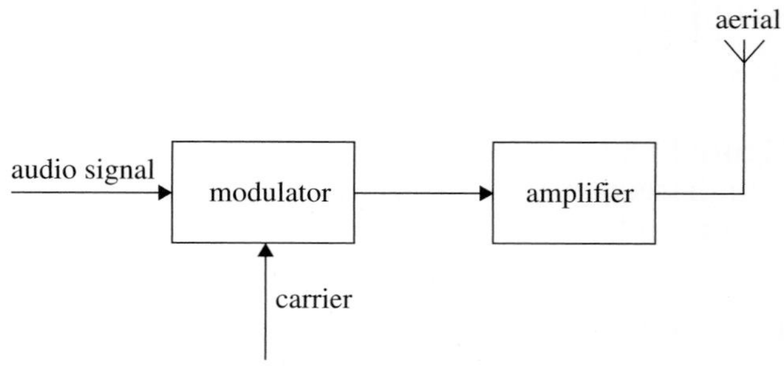

Figure F1.9 Block diagram for an amplitude modulator.

Frequency modulation (FM)

In frequency modulation (FM), the carrier wave's *frequency* is changed (modulated) according to the instantaneous displacement of the information *(message) signal* wave. The frequency of the modulated signal is greatest when the information signal has its greatest positive value, and the frequency is least when the information signal has its most negative value. (The information signal always has a much lower frequency than the carrier, as is also the case with AM.) Thus consider the information signal wave of Figure F1.10(a) and the carrier wave of Figure F1.10(b). The frequency-modulated carrier wave that results is given in Figure F1.10(c).

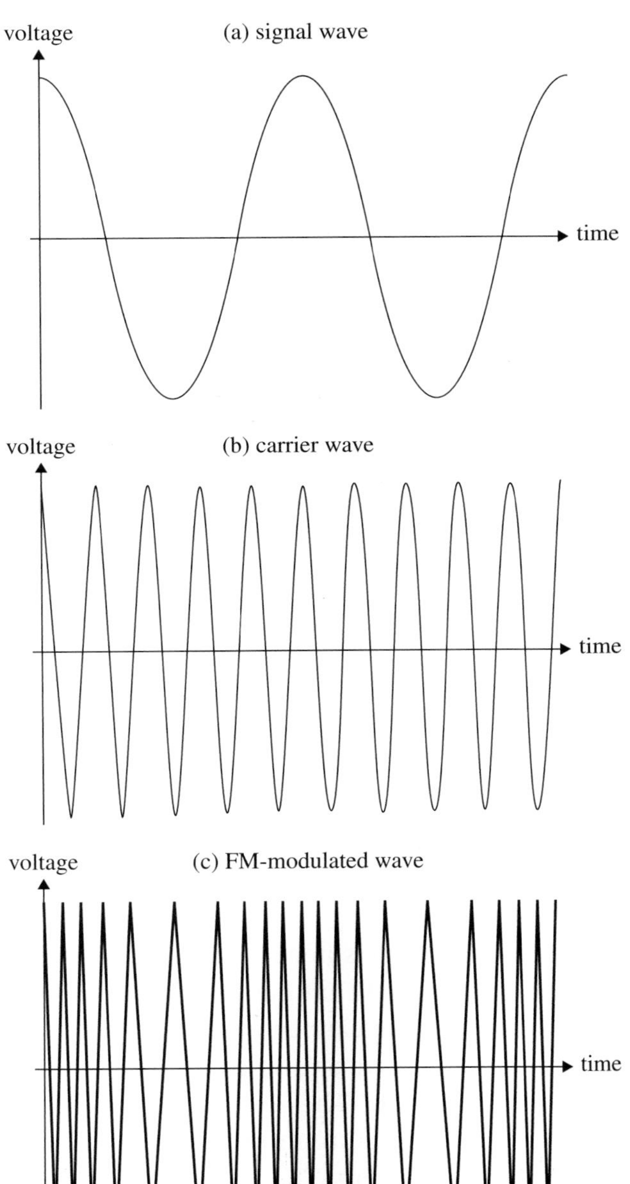

Figure F1.10 (a) A signal (information) wave modulating (b) a carrier wave, resulting in (c) a frequency-modulated carrier wave.

▶ Frequency modulation (FM) involves changing the *frequency* of the carrier signal according to the instantaneous value of the information signal.

Notice that in the frequency-modulated signal the frequency changes but the amplitude stays constant. This is important for the quality of FM transmissions – see page 550.

Supplementary material

The mathematics of frequency modulation is complex and beyond the scope of this book. For a carrier signal $y_C = A_C \sin(2\pi f_C t)$, the modulated FM signal may be written as $y_{FM} = A_C \sin(2\pi f_C t + \phi)$, i.e. the process of modulation introduces a *phase* ϕ (recall what we have learned about simple harmonic motion in Chapter 4.1). In frequency modulation, the phase is related to the information signal. The precise way they are related is that the rate of change with time of the phase ϕ is proportional to the instantaneous information signal $y_S(t)$, i.e. $\frac{d\phi}{dt} = k y_S(t)$. This defines frequency modulation. The parameter k is called the *frequency deviation constant* and is related to the *modulation index* β through the relation $\beta = \frac{kA_I}{2\pi f_I}$, where A_I and f_I are the amplitude and maximum frequency of the information signal. You can experiment on your graphics calculator, or preferably a computer, with various information signals and carrier waves to see what kind of frequency modulation you obtain as you vary k.

In frequency modulation we have a parameter β, called the modulation index:

$$\beta = \frac{\Delta f}{f_I}$$

Here, $\Delta f = f - f_C$ is the maximum deviation of the modulated carrier's frequency f relative to the unmodulated carrier frequency f_C. Also, f_I is the highest frequency in the information signal. The importance of this index is that it is related to bandwidth. The FM bandwidth is given (approximately) by

$$\text{FM bandwidth} \approx 2(\Delta f + f_I)$$

In radio FM broadcasts, $\Delta f = 75\,\text{kHz}$ and the modulation index β used is high, typically 5.

▶ In frequency modulation the *bandwidth* depends on the maximum information signal frequency f_I and the modulation index β.

Example question

Q3

A high-quality FM radio station has a frequency deviation of 75 kHz and contains audio signals varying from 50 Hz to 15 kHz. What is the modulation index and the bandwidth of the FM transmissions?

Answer

Applying the formulas in the text gives $\beta = \frac{75}{15} = 5$ and bandwidth $= 2(75 + 15) =$ 180 kHz (This is larger by 150 kHz compared to an AM transmission containing the same audio information.)

The power spectrum of frequency modulation is much more complex than that for amplitude modulation. Even with one frequency in the information signal the power spectrum has many sideband frequencies. The advantage of a high modulation index β is that in that case the amplitude of the carrier wave decreases relative to the amplitude of the sidebands. This means that most of the power (98%) is transmitted in the sidebands (where the information is) and not in the carrier.

Comparing AM and FM

- FM has a better signal-to-noise ratio. This is because noise adds to the amplitude of the carrier wave and so is not included in the received signal. Notice that, when amplifying an AM signal, the noise gets amplified as well.
- In FM, the amplitude of the carrier is small compared to the amplitude of the sidebands. This means that most of the power in transmission goes to the sidebands, which is where the information is.
- The same information can be transmitted with less power with FM compared with AM.
- The bandwidth for FM is greater than that for AM.
- The modulators and demodulators for FM are more complex compared with those for AM.

The AM radio receiver

An AM receiver may be represented schematically as in the block diagram of Figure F1.11. It consists of an aerial (antenna), a tuning circuit, an RF (radio-frequency) amplifier, a demodulator, an AF (audio-frequency) amplifier, and a loudspeaker. The role and function of each block is described below.

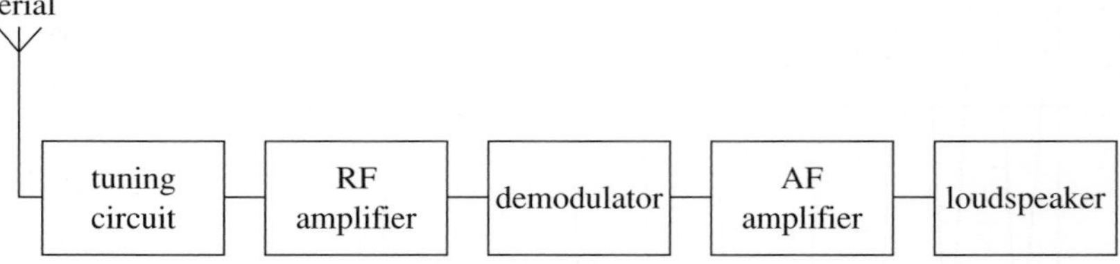

Figure F1.11 A block diagram of an AM radio receiver.

Aerial

The aerial (antenna) is needed in order to pick up the carrier signal that has been emitted by the transmitter. The carrier wave is an electromagnetic wave and so contains a time-varying electric field. The electric field forces electrons in the aerial to move, and this in turn creates a small current. The aerial is exposed to the carrier waves of many transmitters (radio stations, for example). In general, the electrons in the aerial move as a result of the electric fields of the very many carrier waves that the aerial picks up. So a way must be found to isolate the particular radio station one wants to tune to.

Tuning circuit

The role of the tuning circuit is to isolate the particular carrier wave that one wants to tune to. We may think of this circuit as an electrical oscillating system that has its own natural frequency. The natural frequency can be altered by changing the capacitance of a variable capacitor in the circuit. The situation is then analogous to a mechanical system that is driven by an external periodic force. The system will respond when it is in resonance with the external force. In other words, by making the natural frequency of the tuning circuit equal to the frequency of a particular carrier wave, we ensure that only that particular carrier will be picked up. Thus a copy of the modulated wave is now present in the tuning circuit as a small current. This current can be turned into a voltage and fed into the RF amplifier.

RF amplifier

This stands for radio-frequency amplifier. The voltages sent by the tuning circuit to the demodulator are generally extremely small. They have to be increased so that the demodulator can work. This is the function of the RF amplifier.

Demodulator

In this important part of the receiver the information carried by the carrier is extracted and the carrier rejected. In the first step the signal from the RF amplifier is fed into a diode. The diode only allows the passage of current in one direction and not the other. This means that the negative voltages in the graph in Figure F1.12 are ignored.

Recall that the carrier wave has a much larger frequency than that of the information signal wave. So the diode output is passed through a filter, which essentially cuts out the high-frequency carrier and leaves only the slowly

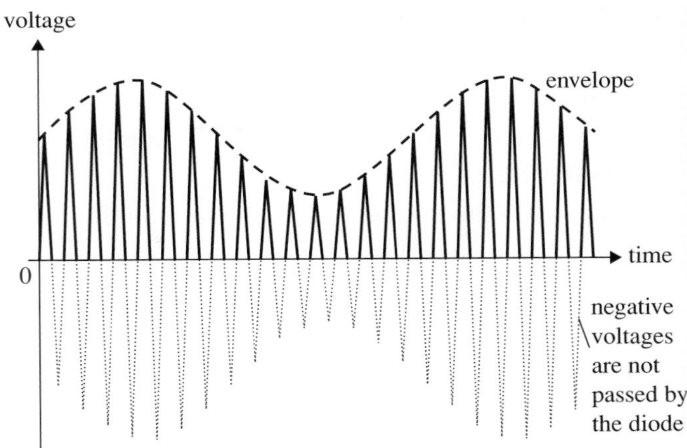

Figure F1.12 An amplitude-modulated (AM) wave.

oscillating audio-frequency information signal. This is the 'envelope' of the carrier wave shown in the graph in Figure F1.12 with the dashed line.

AF amplifier

This stands for audio-frequency amplifier. The signal sent by the demodulator is small and needs to be amplified before sending it to the loudspeaker; otherwise the loudspeaker cannot be driven.

Loudspeaker

The audio-frequency signal is still electrical in nature. This signal will then drive the diaphragm of the loudspeaker, so that the sound content of the information signal can be recovered.

? QUESTIONS

1 Calculate the frequency of the following signals, where the time t is measured in seconds:
(a) $3.0 \sin(2000\pi t + 0.1)$
(b) $4.0 \sin(6600t)$
(c) $12 \times 10^{-3} \sin\left(\frac{\pi t}{10^{-4}} + \frac{\pi}{4}\right)$

2 (a) In the context of communications, state the meaning of modulation.
(b) State and explain whether AM or FM transmissions are more likely to be affected by noise.

3 Describe the process of amplitude modulation.

4 A sinusoidal information signal has frequency of 5.0 kHz and is to amplitude-modulate a sinusoidal carrier of frequency 4.0 MHz.
   (a) State the frequencies in the amplitude modulated signal.
   (b) Sketch the power spectrum of the modulated signal.

5 In the context of modulated carrier waves, state the meaning of sideband frequencies.

6 Referring to the discussion of the square wave on page 545, draw a sketch graph of the power spectrum of a square wave.

7 Speech and music cover the frequency range from about 50 Hz to about 4.5 kHz. What is the bandwidth required by an AM radio station?

8 A 3 kHz information signal is used to amplitude-modulate a 1.5 MHz carrier.
   (a) Calculate the bandwidth of the transmitted signal.
   (b) The information signal is now changed to a signal with a range of frequencies from 0.20 kHz to 20 kHz. Calculate the range of frequencies in the lower sideband and in the upper sideband, and state the bandwidth for this transmitted signal.
   (c) Radio stations have been allowed to broadcast in the frequency range 800 kHz to 1200 kHz. How many radio stations can broadcast in this range if the signal has the bandwidth found in (b)?

9 In radio communications the frequency range 30 kHz to 300 kHz is known as LW (long wave). You are given permission to operate a radio station in the LW frequency range. Explain why you would not be given the choice between AM or FM modulation for your transmissions. What would you be forced to use?

10 The graph in Figure F1.13 shows a carrier wave modulated by a single audio frequency. Using the graph determine:
   (a) the frequency of the carrier;
   (b) the frequency of the information signal;
   (c) the amplitude of the information signal.

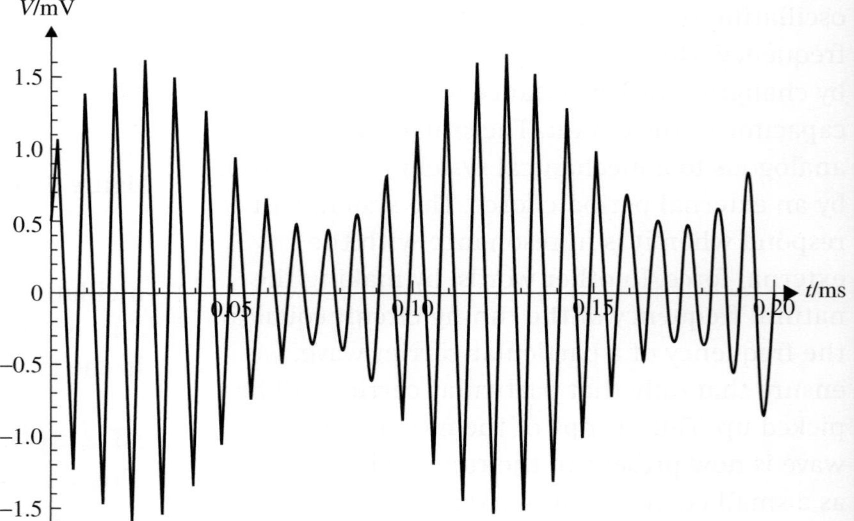

Figure F1.13 For question 10.

11 Describe the process of frequency modulation.

12 State and explain three advantages of frequency modulation over amplitude modulation in radio transmissions.

13 Outline the significance of bandwidth in the transmission of a radio station broadcast. What would happen, in practice, if the bandwidth allotted to a particular radio station were to be reduced to, say, half its original size.

14 In many countries, the range of frequencies used for FM radio station transmissions is 88 MHz to 108 MHz. The bandwidth required is about 1 MHz.
   (a) How many radio stations can one have in this frequency range?
   (b) In practice, many more radio stations use this frequency in any one country. Explain how this is possible.

15 The graphs in Figure F1.14 show a carrier wave modulated by a single-frequency audio wave.

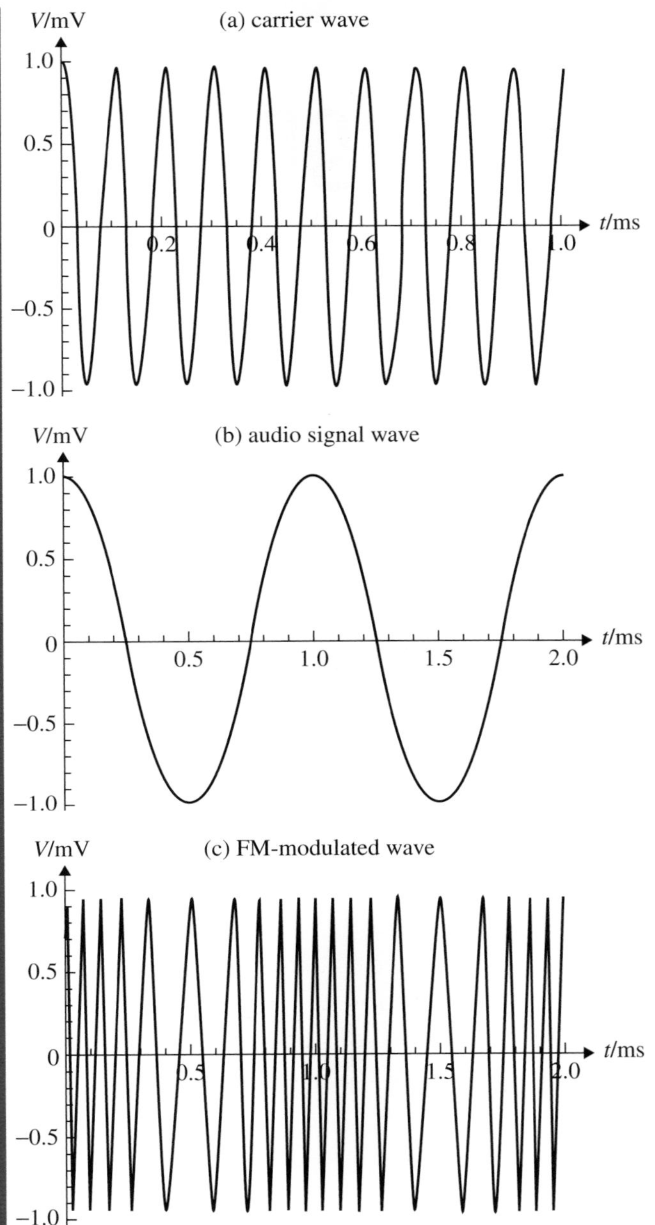

Figure F1.14 For question 15.

The graph in Figure F1.15 shows a detail of the frequency-modulated wave near $t = 0.5$ ms.

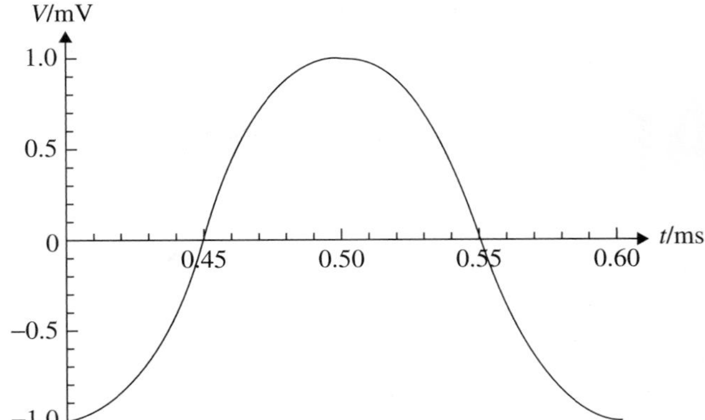

Figure F1.15 For question 15.

Use the graphs to *estimate*:

(a) the carrier frequency;

(b) the information signal frequency;

(c) the modulation index $\frac{\Delta f}{f_1}$, i.e. the ratio of the maximum deviation of the modulated carrier's frequency to the information signal frequency;

(d) an approximate value for the bandwidth available for this FM transmission.

(e) Discuss how the answers to the previous parts could have been obtained from the graph of the FM-modulated wave alone, i.e. just the graph in Figure F1.15.

16 An FM radio station has a frequency deviation of 75 kHz and contains audio signals varying from 100 Hz to 12 kHz. For the FM transmissions, calculate:

(a) the modulation index;

(b) the bandwidth.

17 Outline the operation of an AM receiver.

18 Explain the role of resonance in the tuning circuit of a simple AM receiver.

Analogue and digital signals

This chapter will introduce analogue and digital signals and the important concepts of sampling and sampling frequency. Binary numbers will be introduced, and the process of converting an analogue signal into a digital signal and vice versa discussed. We will discuss the transmission of digital signals and the advantages this offers compared to analogue signal transmission. The chapter will end with a discussion of time division multiplexing (TDM), which is commonly used to transmit many digital signals along the same channel at the same time.

Objectives

By the end of this chapter you should be able to:

- convert a decimal number into a *binary number* and vice versa;
- distinguish between an *analogue signal* and a *digital signal*;
- understand the meaning of *sampling* and the importance of *sampling frequency*;
- explain the significance of *bit rate*;
- understand the meaning of *quantization level* and *quantization error*;
- state the advantages of the *digital transmission* of a signal;
- solve problems in *analogue-to-digital conversion* of signals;
- describe the main processes involved in the *transmission and reception of a digital signal*;
- understand the importance of *time division multiplexing*.

Binary numbers

This section is identical to the corresponding section in Chapter 8.1 of Topic 8, Digital technology, in the Core and AHL Material, to which the reader is referred.

Analogue and digital signals

This section is identical to the corresponding section in Chapter 8.1 of Topic 8, Digital technology, in the Core and AHL Material, to which the reader is referred.

Bit rate of a digital signal

The **bit rate** refers to the number of bits that can be transmitted per second. If each bit has a duration of τ seconds, then the bit rate is given by

$$\text{bit rate} = \frac{1}{\tau}$$

Furthermore, if the number of bits per sample is n and the signal is sampled f times per second, we must also have

$$\text{bit rate} = f \times n$$

i.e.

$$\text{bit rate} = (\text{sampling rate}) \times (\text{number of bits per sample})$$

Example question

Q1

Calculate the bit rate for a signal that is sampled 8000 times per second and has 16 quantization levels.

Answer

Since $2^4 = 16$, we have four bits per sample and so the bit rate is

$$8000 \times 4 = 32\,000 \text{ bit s}^{-1} = 32 \text{ kbit s}^{-1}$$

The duration of one bit is

$$\frac{1}{32\,000} = 3.1 \times 10^{-5} \text{ s} = 31\ \mu\text{s}$$

The bit rate is important because it determines the bandwidth that will allow a given digital signal to pass through a channel of communication (e.g. a cable or an optic fibre – see Option F4). A small bandwidth will distort the pulses to such an extent that reconstructing the analogue signal from its digital form may be impossible.

▶ It can be shown that the bandwidth for the transmission of a digital signal is in fact equal to the bit rate.

The sampling rate (i.e. the sampling frequency) is of crucial importance when the time comes to reconstruct an analogue signal from the digitized signal. To see this point, consider an audio signal of frequency 500 Hz (Figure F2.1) that is being sampled at a sampling rate of 357 Hz, i.e. 357 times per second.

Since the sampling frequency is 357 Hz, the sampling will take place every $\frac{1}{357} = 2.80$ ms. The resulting pulse-amplitude modulation (PAM) signal is shown in Figure F2.2.

Fitting a smooth curve to these points results in the reconstructed analogue signal of Figure F2.3. Clearly this signal is not a faithful reproduction of the original. The frequency is much lower than that of the original signal. The appearance of this low-frequency signal is called *aliasing*. This happened because the sampling frequency was much too small.

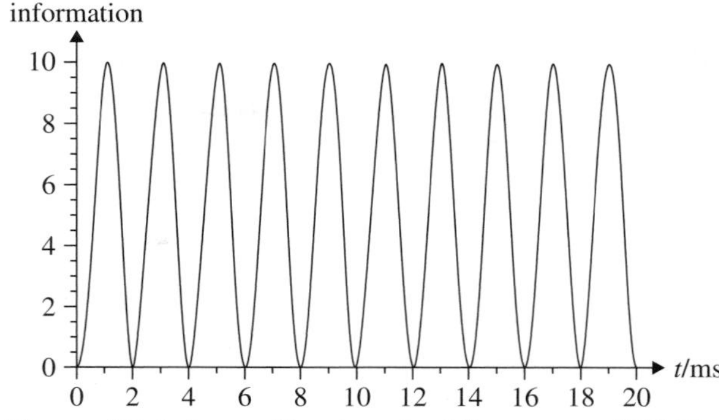

Figure F2.1 An audio signal of frequency 500 Hz.

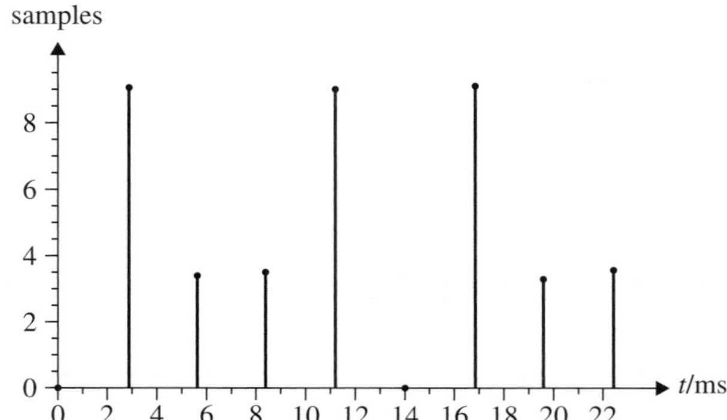

Figure F2.2 The PAM signal with a sampling frequency of 357 Hz.

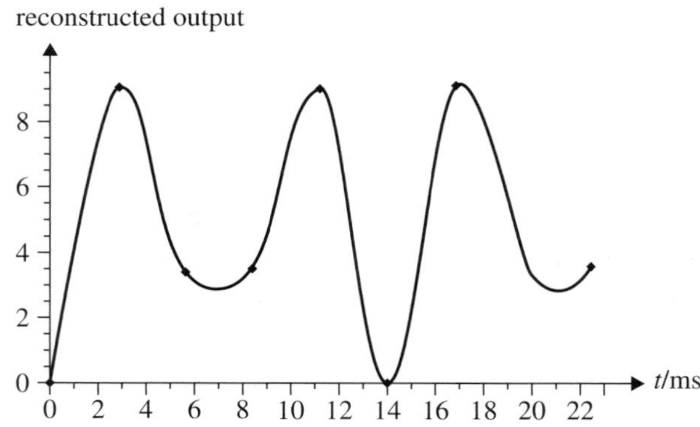

Figure F2.3 The reconstructed analogue signal after sampling at 357 Hz.

▶ A low sampling frequency (compared to the information signal frequency) results in *aliasing*, i.e. unfaithful reconstructions of the signal.

A mathematical theorem known as the **Shannon–Nyquist sampling theorem** states that, to avoid this problem, the sampling frequency must be at least twice as large as the largest frequency in the information signal. This is known as the **Nyquist frequency**.

Example questions

Q2

A signal has frequencies ranging from 400 Hz to 5.4 kHz. What is the minimum sampling frequency that will result in a faithful reproduction of this signal?

Answer

By the Shannon–Nyquist sampling theorem, any frequency higher than $2 \times 5.4 \approx 11$ kHz will do.

Q3

Consider the audio signal represented by the graph in Figure F2.1 above. Sample this signal with a frequency of 2.0 kHz (i.e. 2000 times per second), and plot a graph of the resulting reconstructed signal along a time axis. Compare the result with that obtained above when sampling at 400 Hz.

Answer

The result of the sampling and the reconstructed analogue signal are shown in Figures F2.4 and F2.5.

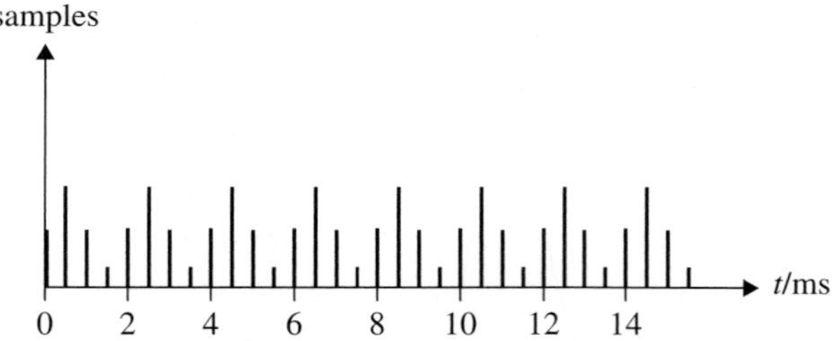

Figure F2.4 The PAM signal with a sampling frequency of 2.0 kHz.

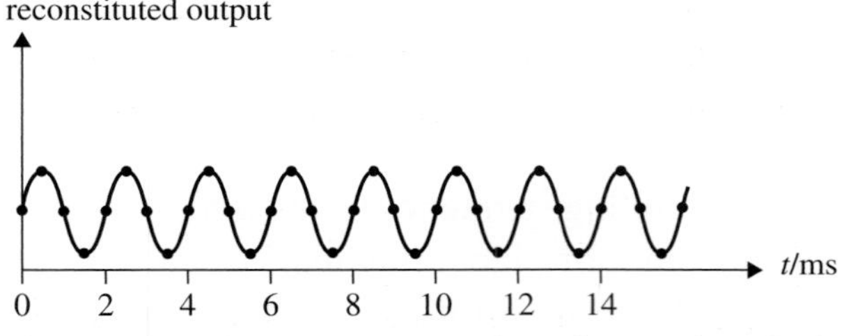

Figure F2.5 The reconstructed analogue signal after sampling at 2.0 kHz resembles the original signal.

The sampling frequency here is very high (the Shannon–Nyquist sampling theorem is more than satisfied), and as a result we have a very faithful reproduction of the original signal, unlike in the case of sampling at 400 Hz.

Q4

The signal in Figure F2.6 is sampled every millisecond with 16 sampling quantization levels.

(a) Construct the PAM signal out of this analogue signal.

(b) Express the signal as a binary code.

(c) Convert the signal into a digital signal.

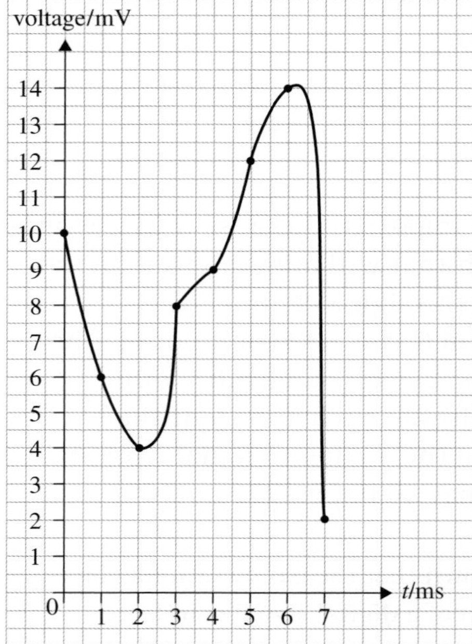

Figure F2.6 The analogue signal that has been sampled every 1.0 ms.

Answer

(a) The PAM signal is shown in Figure F2.7.

(b) The signal has values at the sampling times as shown in the second column of Table F2.1. These values are converted into four-bit binary code in the third column. We use four-bit words since there are 16 quantization levels.

(c) The binary code must now be converted into a digital signal. The codes 1010, 0110 and 0100 are represented by:

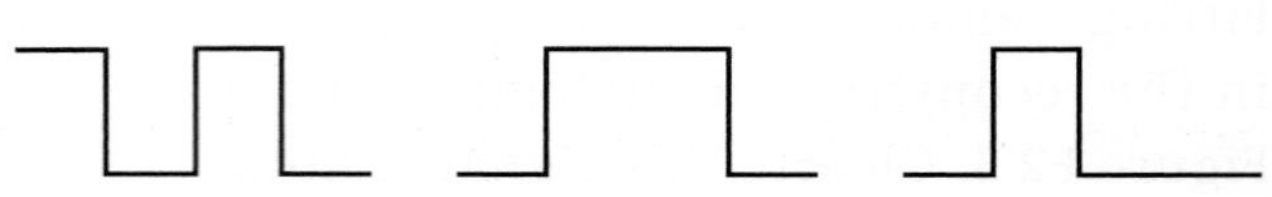

Working similarly with the rest of the binary codes, we obtain the digital signal shown in Figure F2.8.

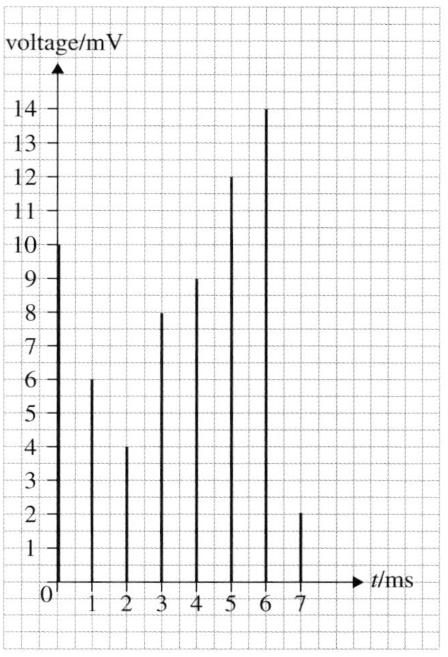

Figure F2.7 The PAM signal of the analogue signal in Figure F2.6.

Time/ms	Signal/V	Binary code
0	10	1010
1	6	0110
2	4	0100
3	8	1000
4	9	0100
5	12	1100
6	14	0110
7	2	0010

Table F2.1 The analogue signal has been discretized by the PAM process and converted into a digital four-bit binary code.

The transmission and reception of digital signals

The transmission and reception of a digital signal is shown schematically in the block diagram of Figure F2.9.

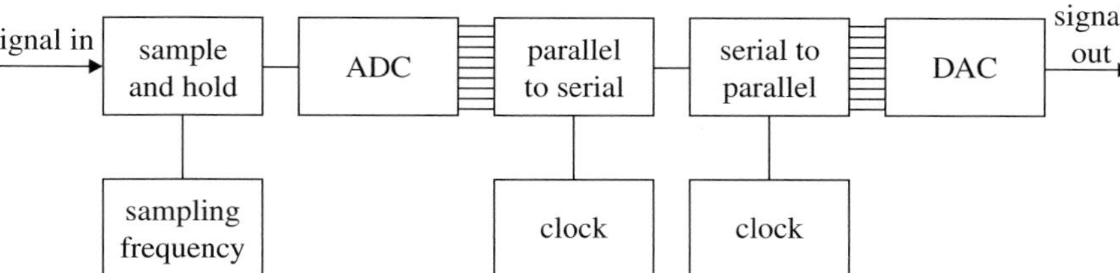

Figure F2.9 Block diagram for the transmission and reception of a digital signal.

The analogue signal arrives at the block called sample and hold. In this device, the signal is sampled according to the sampling frequency used and momentarily stored. (For the sake of discussion, we may take the sampling frequency to be 8 kHz, the frequency used universally in the telephone system.) In the next block, the ADC (analogue-to-digital converter), every sample of the signal is converted into an n-bit binary code. (For concreteness we take n to be 8.) The output of the ADC is a set of eight bits making up one sampled signal. The eight bits are registered in one step in the device called the parallel-to-serial converter. Each bit is then transmitted one by one from this device along a single conducting line. At the other end, the bits, arriving one by one, are registered in the device called the serial-to-parallel converter. Once all the bits have arrived, they are put together to make one eight-bit word. The eight bits are then simultaneously fed into the DAC (digital-to-analogue converter), where the digital signal is now turned into an analogue signal. The purpose of the devices labelled 'clocks' is to

Figure F2.8 The digital signal constructed out of the analogue signal of Figure F2.6.

control the process of transmitting the bits in the parallel-to-serial and the serial-to-parallel converters. The bits must be sent before the next batch of bits arrives.

Time division multiplexing

Time division multiplexing (TDM) is a method commonly used to transmit many digital signals along the same channel at the same time.

As noted earlier, the actual time required for sampling is very short compared to the time in between two consecutive samplings. Thus, consider the three signals of Figure F2.10. The time in between two pulses is wasted time. In TDM the same channel is used to transmit many different signals, as shown in Figure F2.11.

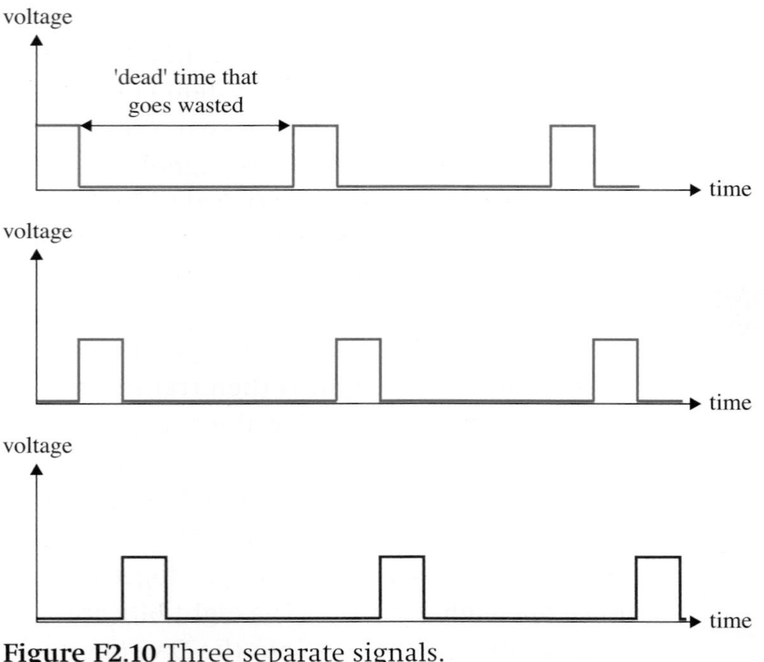

Figure F2.10 Three separate signals.

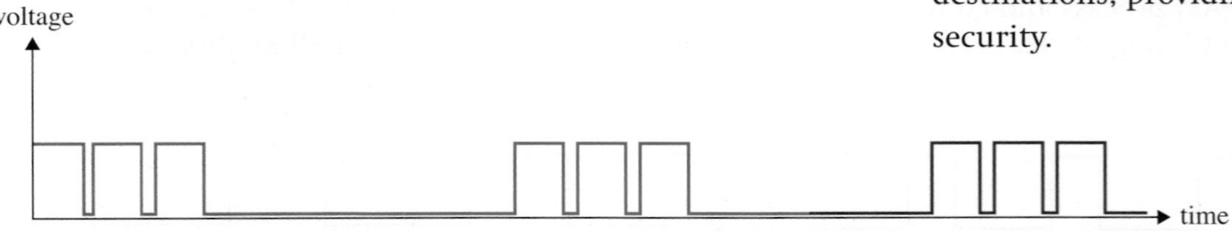

Figure F2.11 The time between signals can be used to transmit other signals along the same line.

Mixing of individual signals so that they can be fed along the transmission line is achieved in a device known as a multiplexer (Figure F2.12).

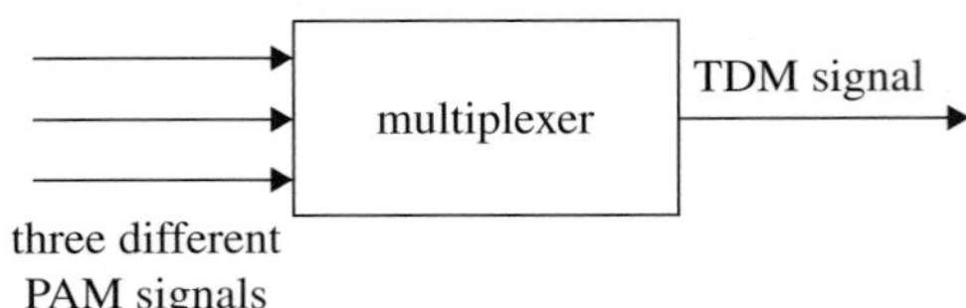

Figure F2.12 Block diagram for a time division multiplexer.

The advantages of digital communication

Communicating by the transmission of digital signals has a very large number of advantages over communication by the transmission of analogue signals. Whereas the initial (1970s) costs associated with the digital equipment necessary were high, and the transmissions themselves were unreliable, digital communications now are the standard because mass production and technical advances have made possible very low-cost, sophisticated, reliable integrated circuits. The advantages of digital communications include the following:

- Digital signals can be regenerated perfectly, i.e. noise and distortion can be eliminated, despite transfers over large distances.
- Digital circuits are relatively inexpensive, reliable and readily available.
- Error-correcting codes can be applied to digital signals to ensure that errors in the transmission of the signals are eliminated.
- The signals can be encrypted, by scrambling the bits in the signal, so that they can only be read at the desired destinations, providing privacy and security.

- The signals can be stored, processed and controlled by computers.
- Digital signals can be stored on devices such as CDs and DVDs that are readily available and inexpensive.
- Digital signals can be compressed.
- Time division multiplexing can be used with digital signals.

Supplementary material

There is very sophisticated physics and mathematics in error-correcting codes. The topic could be of interest to students taking either of those subjects or computer science. Astonishingly, there is a deep connection between a certain error-correcting code, a certain lattice of points in 24 dimensions, and the problem of the closest packing of spheres in 24 dimensions! Equally astonishingly, there is also a connection with string theories!

? QUESTIONS

1 Express the decimal numbers (a) 7, (b) 19 and (c) 67 in binary form.

2 Express the binary numbers (a) 01001, (b) 11101 and (c) 10101 in decimal form.

3 How many bits are needed to express the decimal numbers (a) 16, (b) 32 and (c) 64 as binary numbers?

4 How many bits do we need to express the decimal number 1453 in binary form?

5 How many quantization levels are there when we use five bits to represent a sampled signal?

6 An analogue signal varying from −10 mV to +10 mV is sampled with five-bit words. Estimate the quantization error involved.

7 A sampled signal will be represented with an *n*-bit binary number. State one advantage and one disadvantage of using a high value of *n*.

8 Distinguish between an analogue signal and a digital signal.

9 Give three examples of an analogue signal and three examples of a digital signal.

10 You listen to your favourite radio station by using the aerial (antenna) of your radio to pick up the signal. Is the signal that your aerial picks up an analogue or a digital signal. Explain. Is the signal transmitted by the loudspeaker of your radio an analogue or a digital signal?

11 Distinguish between a binary code and a digital signal.

12 (a) State what is meant by *sampling* and *sampling frequency*.
(b) Explain why the sampling frequency must be higher than the frequency of the signal being sampled.
(c) The graph in Figure F2.13 shows part of a 250 Hz signal that is to be sampled with a sampling frequency also of 250 Hz. The first sample is taken at $t = 0$.

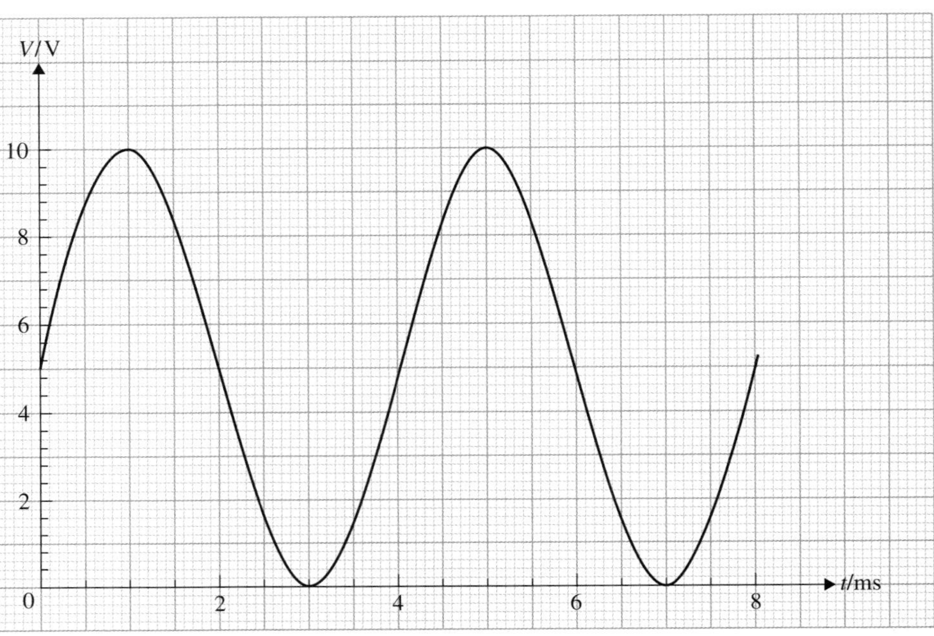

Figure F2.13 For question 12.

(i) Make a graph to show the pulse amplitude modulated signal.

(ii) Use the result of (c)(i) to reconstruct the analogue signal. Comment on your answer.

13 What do you understand by the term 'Shannon–Nyquist sampling theorem'? What is the significance of the Nyquist frequency?

14 A sampled signal is assigned the binary code 01001. Make a drawing to show the digital signal constructed out of this code.

15 Reconstruct the binary code for the digital signal shown in Figure F2.14. The sampling has produced three-bit words.

16 The graph in Figure F2.15 shows an analogue signal. Assume that the signal is sampled every 0.1 ms. Copy and complete the table below. Use the table to draw the digital signal so constructed using three-bit words.

Time/ms	Signal/mV	Binary code	Digital signal
0			
0.1			
0.2			
0.3			
0.4			
0.5			
0.6			
0.7			
0.8			
0.9			
1.0			

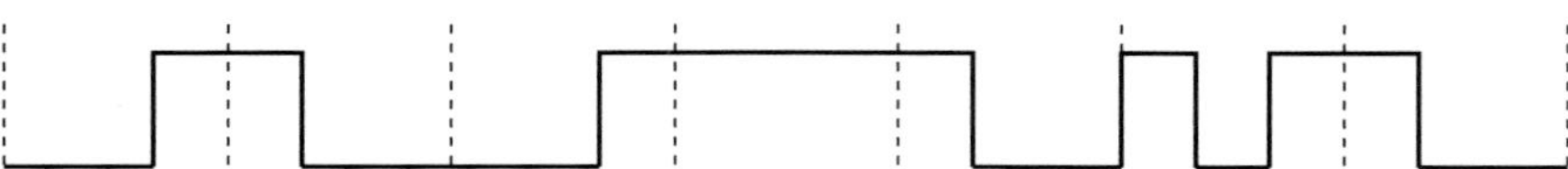

Figure F2.14 For question 15.

Figure F2.15 For question 16.

17 The table below has been obtained by sampling an analogue signal.
(a) Copy and complete this table.
(b) Put the individual signals together to construct the complete digital signal.
(c) Reconstruct the analogue signal.

Binary code	Digital signal	Signal strength
1111		
1001		
0011		
0001		
0101		
1010		
1100		
1101		

18 The digital signal in Figure F2.16 has been constructed using three-bit words. Reconstruct the analogue signal from this digital signal.

19 A signal is sampled with a frequency of 5.0 kHz and the sample is converted into an eight-bit word. Determine;
(a) the bit rate;
(b) the bit duration.

20 The sampling rate during the playback of a compact disc (CD) is 44.1 kHz. Each sample consists of a 32-bit word.
(a) Calculate the bit rate during playback.
(b) Estimate the duration of a single bit.

21 Calculate the time between samples transmitted along a line when the signal is sampled at a frequency of 4.0 kHz.

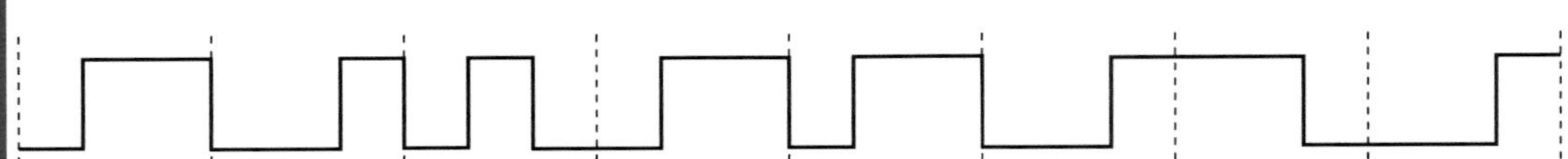

Figure F2.16 For question 18.

22 Make a block diagram to show the main features involved in
(a) the recording of a CD;
(b) the playback of a CD.

23 Make a block diagram to show the main features involved in the transmission and reception of a telephone call along an ordinary conducting line.

24 One of the elements in the transmission of a digital signal is a parallel-to-serial converter. Explain the role of this converter. Why is it not feasible to transmit a signal represented with, say, eight bits using eight parallel wires at the same time?

25 Explain what is meant by *time division multiplexing.*

26 A telephone call is sampled with a sampling frequency of 8.0 kHz in eight-bit words. The duration of one bit along the transmission line is 2.0 μs.
(a) Calculate the time between consecutive words on the transmission line.
(b) Estimate the number of different phone calls that can be transmitted on the same line.
(c) Would your answer to (b) increase, decrease or stay the same if the sampling frequency were to increase to 16 kHz?

27 Fast digital communications have made profound changes to the daily lives of many millions of people. State and discuss three such changes by referring once to (a) ethical, (b) social and (c) economic factors.

Optic fibre transmission

This chapter introduces one very important channel of communication, the optical fibre. We discuss the optics of the optic fibre and the concept of the critical angle. We introduce two types of optic fibres, multimode and monomode fibres, and discuss these in the context of dispersion and attenuation. The chapter ends with a discussion of signal-to-noise problems.

Objectives

By the end of this chapter you should be able to:

- understand the phenomenon of *total internal reflection*;
- calculate the *critical angle*;
- solve problems with total internal reflection;
- understand the structure of a *step-index optic fibre*;
- distinguish between *multimode* and *monomode* optic fibres;
- understand and distinguish between *material dispersion* and *modal dispersion*;
- appreciate the limitations on *bit rate* and *frequency* caused by dispersion;
- understand the terms *attenuation* and *specific attenuation*;
- sketch the variation with wavelength of the specific attenuation;
- solve problems with attenuation;
- understand the term *noise*;
- solve *signal-to-noise ratio* problems.

Total internal reflection

When a ray of light enters a medium of low refractive index from a medium of high refractive index, the refracted ray bends away from the normal, as shown in Figure F3.1.

This means that the angle of refraction θ_r (the angle between the refracted ray and the normal, in the medium with the lower refractive index) is always larger than the angle of incidence θ_i (the angle between the incident ray and the normal, in the medium with the higher refractive index). As the angle of incidence is increased, the angle of refraction will eventually become 90° (Figure F3.2). The angle of incidence for which this happens is called the **critical angle**.

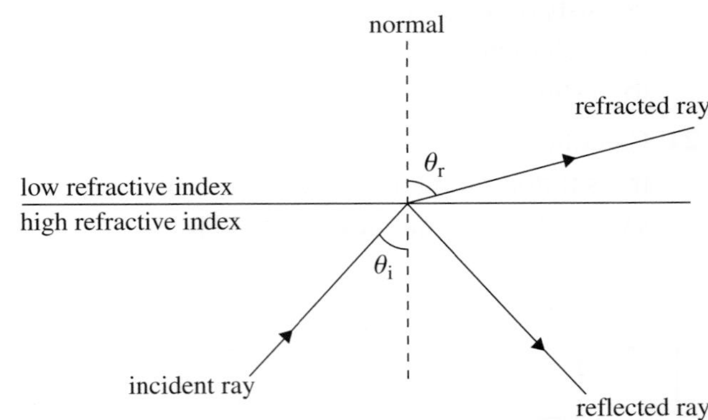

Figure F3.1 A ray of light incident on a boundary partly reflects and partly refracts. The angle of refraction is larger than the angle of incidence.

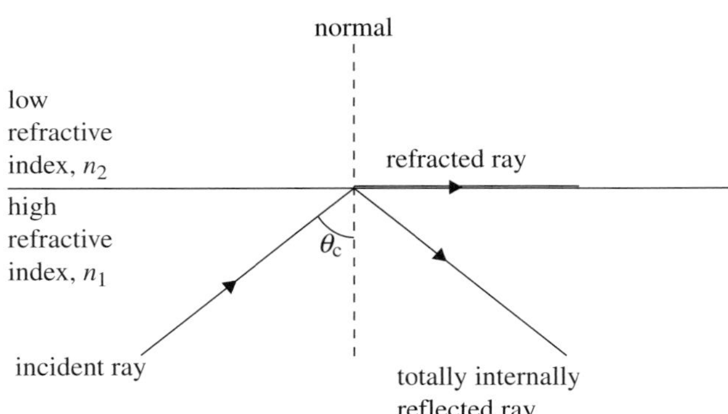

Figure F3.2 The angle of incidence is the critical angle θ_c when the angle of refraction is 90°.

▶ **The critical angle is that angle of incidence for which the angle of refraction is 90°.**

The critical angle θ_c can be found from Snell's law:

$$n_1 \sin\theta_c = n_2 \sin 90°$$

$$\sin\theta_c = \frac{n_2}{n_1}$$

$$\theta_c = \arcsin\frac{n_2}{n_1}$$

For an angle of incidence greater than the critical angle, no refraction takes place. The ray simply reflects back into the medium from which it came (Figure F3.3). This is called *total internal reflection*.

Example questions

Q1

A ray of light in water (refractive index 1.33) is incident from water on a water–air boundary. Calculate the critical angle of the water–air boundary.

Answer

From Snell's law, we have

$$1.33 \times \sin\theta_c = 1.00 \times \sin 90°$$

$$\sin\theta_c = \frac{1.00}{1.33}$$

$$\theta_c = \arcsin\frac{1.00}{1.33}$$

$$\theta_c = 48.8°$$

Q2

In Figure F3.4 the ray shown emitted at point P is totally internally reflected. What can we deduce about the refractive index of the liquid?

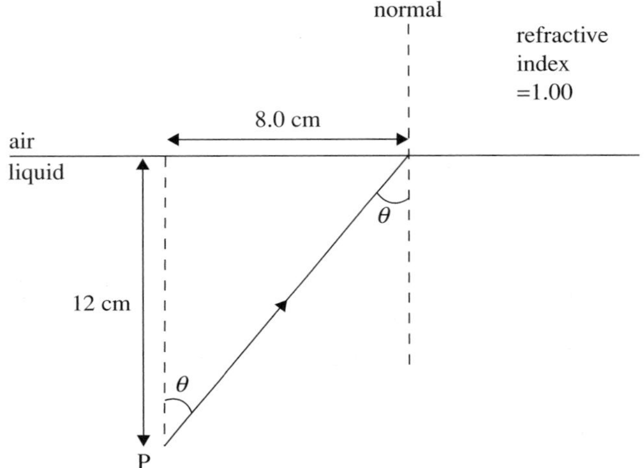

Figure F3.4.

Answer

From the diagram, the angle of incidence θ has a tangent equal to $\tan\theta = \frac{8}{12}$ and so

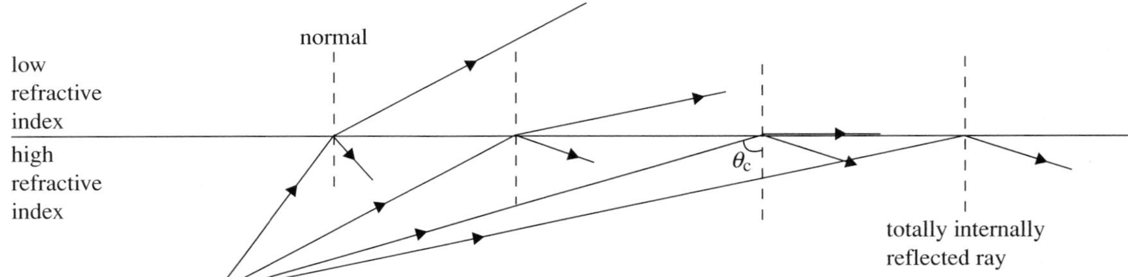

Figure F3.3 Four rays emitted from the same point in the medium with high refractive index. The angle of incidence increases as we move to the right. The angle of incidence for the rightmost ray is greater than the critical angle. There is no refracted ray. The ray just reflects.

$\theta = \arctan\frac{8}{12} = 34°$. The critical angle can be *at most* 34°. Then the refractive index must be greater than n, where $n \sin 34° = 1.00 \times \sin 90°$, i.e. greater than $n = \frac{1}{\sin 34°} = 1.8$.

Optical fibres

One important application of total internal reflection is a device known as an **optical fibre**. The optical fibre consists of a very thin glass core surrounded by a material of slightly lower refractive index (the cladding). Such a thin fibre can easily be bent without breaking, and a ray of light can be sent down the length of the fibre's core. For most angles of incidence, total internal reflection occurs (Figure F3.5), so that the light ray stays within the core and never enters the cladding.

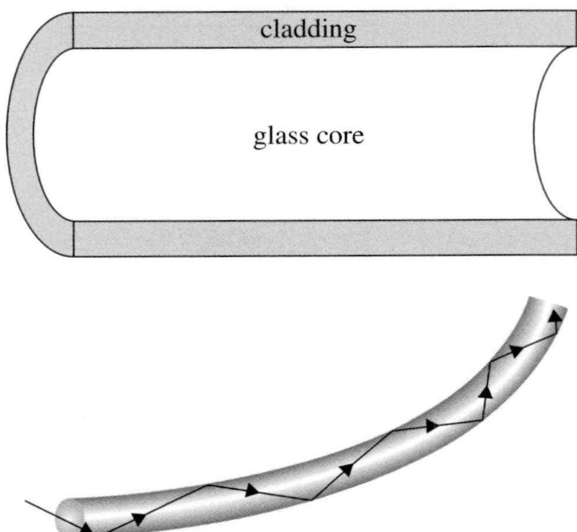

Figure F3.5 A ray of light follows the shape of the fibre by repeated internal reflections.

If n_1 and n_2 are the indices of refraction for the core and the cladding, respectively (so $n_1 > n_2$), the critical angle can be calculated as usual from

$$\sin\theta_c = \frac{n_2}{n_1} \qquad \theta_c = \arcsin\frac{n_2}{n_1}$$

It is convenient also to find an expression for $\cos\theta_c$. Since $\cos\theta_c = \sqrt{1 - \sin^2\theta_c}$, we find

$$\cos\theta_c = \sqrt{1 - \frac{n_2^2}{n_1^2}} = \frac{\sqrt{n_1^2 - n_2^2}}{n_1}$$

Acceptance angle

The maximum angle of incidence that a ray can make upon entering the fibre that will result in total internal reflection is called the **acceptance angle** of the fibre. Let us call this angle A (see Figure F3.6). It may be calculated as follows. Applying Snell's law at the entry point for this limiting maximum angle, we find

$$1.00 \times \sin A = n_1 \times \sin a$$

But $a = 90° - \theta_c$, so that

$$\begin{aligned}\sin A &= n_1 \sin(90° - \theta_c)\\ &= n_1 \cos\theta_c\\ &= \sqrt{n_1^2 - n_2^2}\end{aligned}$$

The acceptance angle is thus given by

$$A = \arcsin\sqrt{n_1^2 - n_2^2}$$

This means that, if we want to have *every* ray entering the fibre to suffer total internal reflection, we must have $A = 90°$ and so

$$\sin 90° = \sqrt{n_1^2 - n_2^2} = 1.$$

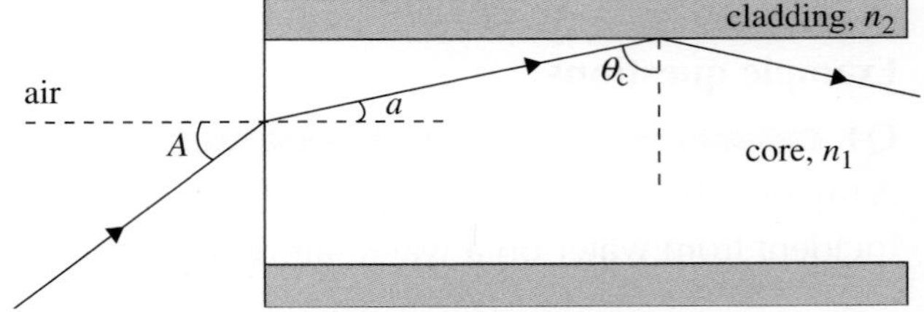

Figure F3.6 The acceptance angle A is the maximum angle of incidence for total internal reflection in the fibre.

Example questions

Q3

The refractive index of the core of an optical fibre is 1.50 and that of the cladding is 1.40. Calculate the acceptance angle of the fibre.

Answer

From the expression above, the acceptance angle (maximum angle of incidence for total internal reflection) is

$$A = \arcsin\sqrt{n_1^2 - n_2^2}$$
$$= \arcsin\sqrt{1.50^2 - 1.40^2}$$
$$= \arcsin\sqrt{2.25 - 1.96}$$
$$= \arcsin\sqrt{0.29}$$
$$= \arcsin 0.5385$$
$$A = 33°$$

Q4

The refractive index of the core of an optic fibre is 1.50 and the critical angle of the core–cladding boundary is 75°.

(a) Calculate the refractive index of the cladding.

(b) Calculate the acceptance angle of the fibre.

Answer

(a) Applying Snell's law at the core–cladding boundary, we find that the cladding refractive index n_2 is

$$1.50 \times \sin 75° = n_2 \times \sin 90°$$

This gives $n_2 = 1.45$.

(b) The acceptance angle is

$$A = \arcsin\sqrt{n_1^2 - n_2^2}$$
$$= \arcsin\sqrt{1.50^2 - 1.45^2}$$
$$A = 23°$$

Dispersion

Rays of light entering an optic fibre will in general follow different paths. Rays that undergo very many internal reflections over a given distance are said to follow *high-order mode* paths, while those suffering fewer reflections follow *low-order mode* paths (Figure F3.7).

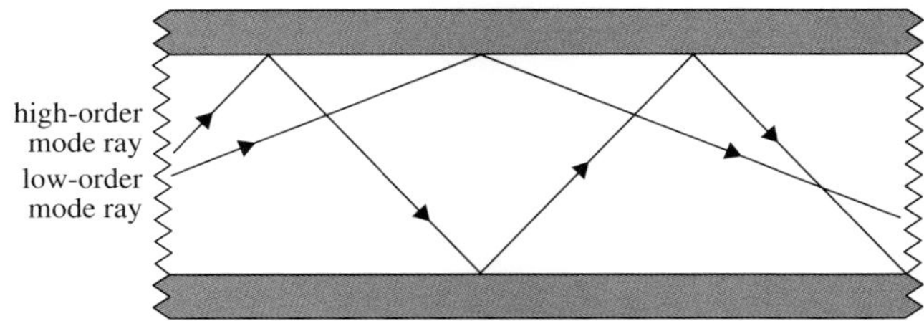

Figure F3.7 Low-order and high-order mode rays in an optic fibre.

Because the refractive index of a medium depends on the wavelength of the light travelling through it, light of different wavelengths will travel through the glass core of an optic fibre at different speeds. This is known as **material dispersion**. Therefore, a set of light rays of different wavelengths will reach the end of a fibre at different times even if they follow the same path.

Thus, consider a pulse of light created by turning on, say, a light-emitting diode (LED) for a short interval of time. The power of the signal as a function of time as it enters the fibre is represented on the left-hand side of Figure F3.8. The area under the pulse is the energy carried by the pulse. In the output pulse, on the right-hand side of Figure F3.8, the area is somewhat less because some energy has been lost along the transmission.

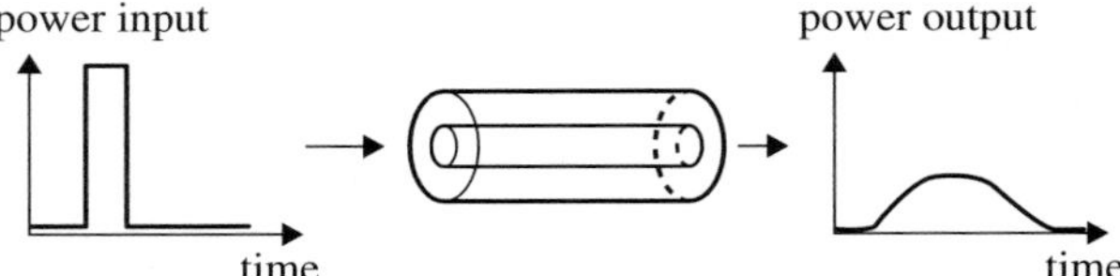

Figure F3.8 The effects of material dispersion.

Now consider another set of rays that have the same wavelength but follow different paths (i.e. they have different order mode paths). Those rays travelling along low-order paths are more 'straight', travel a shorter distance, and so will reach the end faster than higher-order rays. This leads to what is called **modal dispersion**. The effect on the input signal of Figure F3.8 is the same.

In practice, a set rays will have different wavelengths and will follow different paths, so they will be subject to both material and modal dispersion. This is the case in **multimode** fibres (Figure F3.9a). Multimode fibres have a core diameter of about 100 μm and the cladding is about 20 μm thick.

Of special interest are **monomode** fibres (Figure F3.9b), in which the light propagates (approximately) along the same path. The diameter of the core of a monomode fibre is

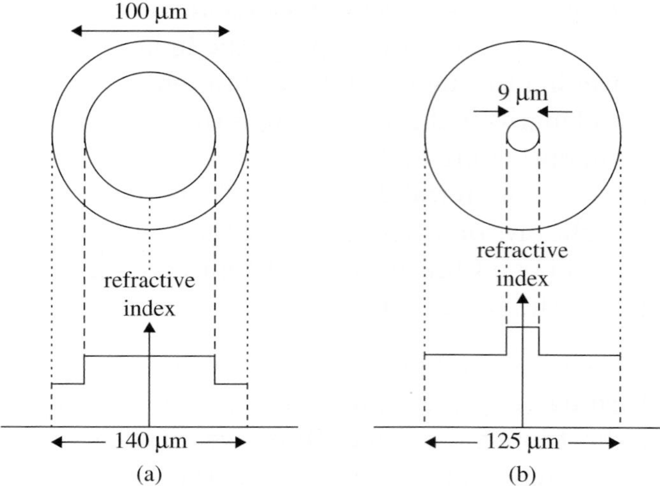

Figure F3.9 (a) A multimode optic fibre. (b) A monomode optic fibre.

very small, about 8–10 μm, only a few times larger than the wavelength of light entering it. The thickness of the cladding is correspondingly much larger, about 125 μm in diameter, in order to make connecting one fibre to another easier. The propagation of light in such a fibre is not governed by the conventional laws of optics that we are using in this chapter. The full electromagnetic theory of light must be used, which results in the conclusion that light follows, essentially, just one path down the fibre, eliminating modal dispersion. Monomode fibres are now used for long-distance transmission of both analogue and digital signals.

Figure F3.9 also illustrates the meaning of the term **step-index fibre**. This means that the refractive index of the core is constant and so is that of the cladding, but at a slightly lower value. The refractive index thus shows a 'step' (down) as we move from the core to the cladding. This type of fibre is to be contrasted with a **graded-index fibre**, in which the refractive index decreases smoothly from the centre of the core (where it reaches a maximum) to the outer edge of the core. The refractive index in the cladding is constant.

Example question

Q5

The length of an optic fibre is 5.0 km. The refractive index of the core of the optic fibre is 1.50 and the critical angle of the core–cladding boundary is 75°. Calculate the time taken for a ray of light to travel down the length of the fibre:

(a) along a straight line parallel to the axis of the fibre;

(b) by suffering the maximum number of internal reflections in the fibre.

Answer

The speed of light in the core of the fibre is determined by the refractive index:

$$c = \frac{3.00 \times 10^8}{1.50} = 2.00 \times 10^8\ \mathrm{m\,s^{-1}}$$

(a) The distance travelled by light in this case is 5.0 km and so the time taken is

$$t = \frac{5.0 \times 10^3}{2.00 \times 10^8} = 25\ \mu\mathrm{s}$$

(b) The ray must travel as shown in Figure F3.10 with the angle θ_c being infinitesimally larger than 75°.

Then $s = \frac{d}{\sin\theta}$. The total distance travelled by the ray is then

$$s = \frac{5.00}{\sin 75^\circ} = 5.18\ \mathrm{km}$$

and the time taken is

$$t = \frac{5.18 \times 10^3}{2.00 \times 10^8} = 26\ \mu\mathrm{s}$$

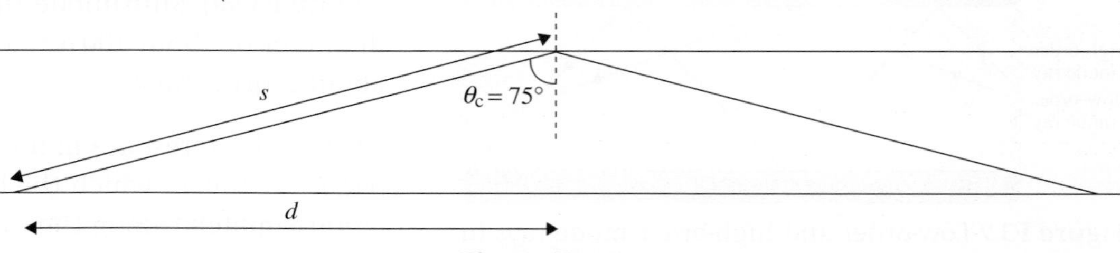

Figure F3.10.

This 'smearing' effect on the output pulse means that it is no longer exactly clear where the pulse ends and where it begins. Since the pulse width is wider in the output signal, the bit rate (the inverse of the bit width) is reduced as a result of dispersion. Also, to transmit a pulse of width τ, the associated carrier wave must have a period of at least 2τ so that bits do not overlap (Figure F3.11).

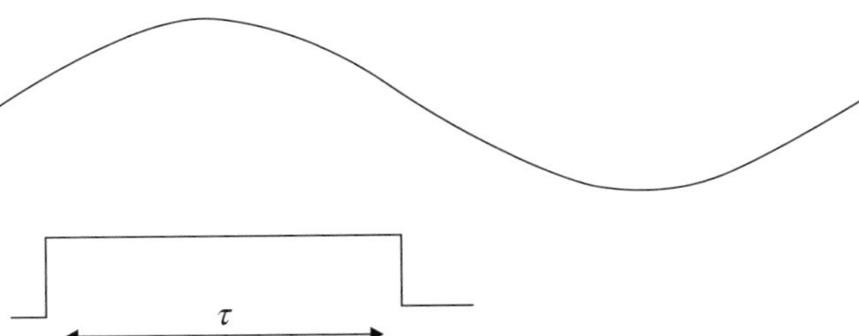

Figure F3.11 The period of the carrier is at least twice the pulse duration.

Since the width increases as a result of dispersion, the associated carrier wave period increases as well, and this implies that the maximum frequency that can be transmitted decreases.

▶ Dispersion limits the bit rate and the maximum frequency that can be transmitted.

Attenuation

Any signal travelling through a medium will suffer a power loss. This is called **attenuation**. It may be necessary to amplify the signal for further transmission. In the case of optic fibres, attenuation is mainly due to impurities in the glass core. The massive introduction of optic fibres in communications has been made possible by advances in the manufacture of very pure glass. For example, the glass in the window of a house appears to let light through without much absorption of energy. But the window pane is less than 1 cm thick. Glass of the same quality as that found in ordinary windows and of thickness of the order of kilometres would not transmit any light at all.

▶ Attenuation in an optic fibre is caused by the impurities of the glass core. The amount of attenuation depends on the wavelength of light being transmitted.

To quantify attenuation, we use a logarithmic scale. We define the *power loss in decibels* (dB) as

$$\text{power loss} = 10\log\frac{P_{\text{final}}}{P_{\text{initial}}}\ (\text{in dB})$$

This is a negative quantity.

Thus a *power loss* of 16 decibels means that the initial power of, say, 8.0 mW has been reduced to:

$$-16 = 10\log\frac{P_{\text{final}}}{P_{\text{initial}}}$$

$$-1.6 = \log\frac{P_{\text{final}}}{8.0}$$

$$\frac{P_{\text{final}}}{8.0} = 10^{-1.6} = \frac{1}{40}$$

Hence

$$P_{\text{final}} = \frac{1}{40}P_{\text{initial}}$$

$$= \frac{8.0}{40}$$

$$= 0.20\ \text{mW}$$

This idea can also be applied to signals that are amplified, as the next example shows.

Example question

Q6

An amplifier amplifies an incoming signal of power 0.34 mW to a signal of power 2.2 mW. Calculate the power *gain* of the amplifier in decibels.

Answer

The amplifier is shown schematically in Figure F3.12.

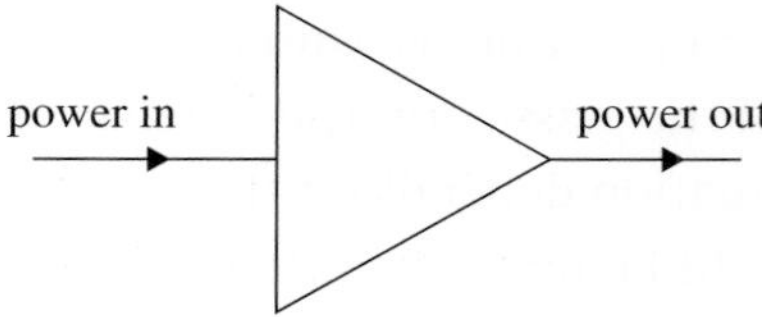

Figure F3.12.

For the amplifier we have

$$\text{gain} = 10 \log \frac{P_{\text{out}}}{P_{\text{in}}}$$

$$= 10 \log \frac{2.2}{0.34}$$

$$= 10 \times 0.81$$

$$= 8.1\,\text{dB}$$

It is worth remembering that an increase in power by a factor of 2 results in a power gain in decibels of approximately 3:

$$\text{gain} = 10 \log \frac{P_{\text{out}}}{P_{\text{in}}}$$

$$= 10 \log 2$$

$$= 3.01$$

$$\approx 3\text{dB}$$

Similarly, a decrease of power by a factor of 2 implies a 3 dB power loss in decibels.

Example question

Q7

Two amplifiers of gain 5.00 dB and 4.00 dB amplify a signal as shown in Figure F3.13. What is the overall amplification produced by the two amplifiers?

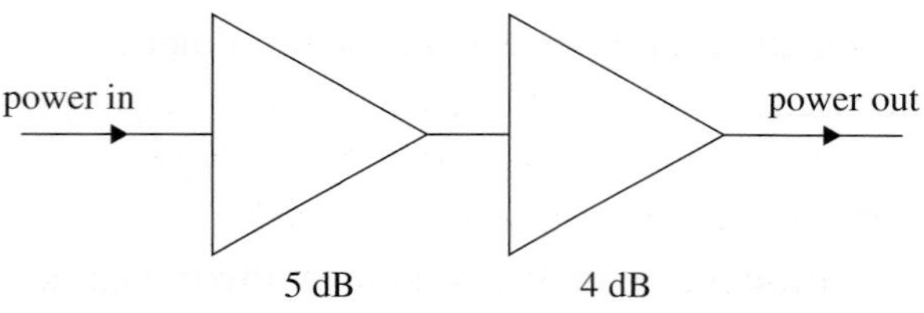

Figure F3.13.

Answer

Let the power input in the first amplifier be P. Then the power out is

$$5.00 = 10 \log \frac{P_{\text{out}}}{P}$$

$$\log \frac{P_{\text{out}}}{P} = 0.5$$

$$\frac{P_{\text{out}}}{P} = 10^{0.5}$$

$$P_{\text{out}} = 3.16P$$

This is the power input into the second amplifier, and so

$$4.00 = 10 \log \frac{P_{\text{out}}}{3.16P}$$

$$\log \frac{P_{\text{out}}}{3.16P} = 0.4$$

$$\frac{P_{\text{out}}}{3.16P} = 10^{0.4}$$

$$\frac{P_{\text{out}}}{3.16P} = 2.51$$

$$P_{\text{out}} = 2.51 \times 3.16P$$

$$P_{\text{out}} = 7.94P$$

There is a quicker way to get the answer though. Just add the gains in decibels from each amplifier to get 9.00 dB. This is going to be the overall gain, and so

$$9.00 = 10 \log \frac{P_{\text{out}}}{P}$$

$$\log \frac{P_{\text{out}}}{P} = 0.9$$

$$\frac{P_{\text{out}}}{P} = 10^{0.9}$$

$$\frac{P_{\text{out}}}{P} = 7.94$$

$$P_{\text{out}} = 7.94P$$

The proof that this is always true is left as an end-of-chapter problem (question 17). That is, the gain in the amplifier system of Figure F3.14 is $G_1 + G_2$.

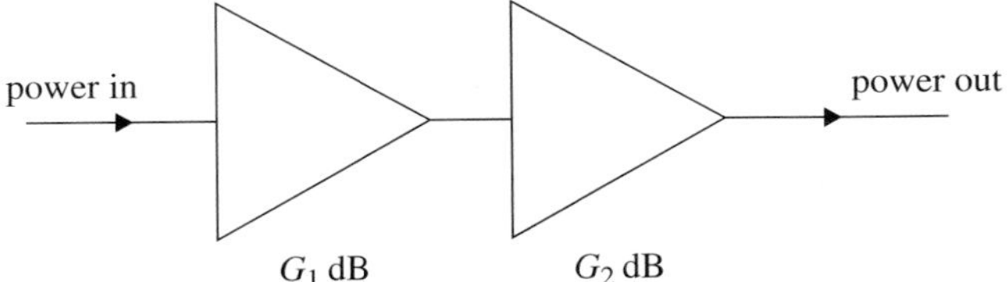

Figure F3.14 The overall gain in this arrangement of two amplifiers is the sum of the individual gains.

Also useful is the concept of the **specific attenuation**, i.e. the power loss in decibels per unit length travelled, i.e.

$$\text{specific attenuation} = \frac{10 \log \frac{P_{\text{final}}}{P_{\text{initial}}}}{L}$$

This is measured in decibels per kilometre (dB km^{-1}).

Example questions

Q8

A signal of power 12 mW is input to a cable of specific attenuation 4.0 dB km^{-1}. Calculate the power of the signal after it has travelled 6.0 km in the cable.

Answer

The loss is $4.0 \times 6.0 = 24$ dB. Then

$$-24 = 10 \log \frac{P_{\text{out}}}{P_{\text{in}}}$$

$$-2.4 = \log \frac{P_{\text{out}}}{P_{\text{in}}}$$

$$\frac{P_{\text{out}}}{P_{\text{in}}} = 10^{-2.4}$$

$$P_{\text{out}} = 3.98 \times 10^{-3} P_{\text{in}}$$

$$= 3.98 \times 10^{-3} \times 12$$

$$= 0.048 \text{ mW}$$

Q9

A signal travels along a monomode fibre of attenuation per unit length 5.0 dB km^{-1}. The signal enters a number of equally spaced amplifiers each providing a gain of 25 dB. How many amplifiers must be used so that, after having travelled a total distance of 300 km, the signal emerges from the last amplifier with no power loss?

Answer

The total power loss without any amplifiers would have been $-5.0 \times 300 = -1500$ dB. The net gain of the amplifiers must then be $+1500$ dB, and so we need $\frac{1500}{25} = 60$ amplifiers.

The specific attenuation (i.e. the power loss in dB per unit length) actually depends on the wavelength of the radiation travelling along the optic fibre. When the specific attenuation is plotted as a function of the wavelength, the graph of Figure F3.15 is obtained.

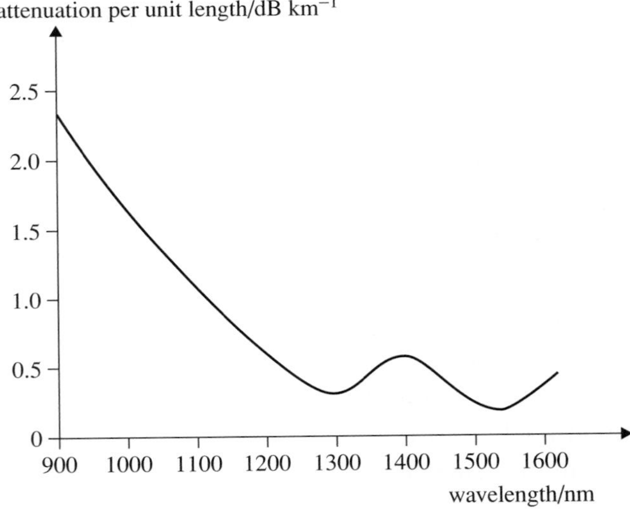

Figure F3.15 The variation with wavelength of the attenuation per unit length (the specific attenuation) in a monomode fibre.

The graph shows minima at wavelengths of 1310 nm and 1550 nm, which implies that these are the desirable wavelengths for optimal transmission. These are infrared wavelengths.

Detection

The light that enters an optic fibre will travel down the length of the fibre, and at some point the arrival of the light must be registered and detected. This is usually done with a photodiode. A simplified detection system is shown in Figure F3.16.

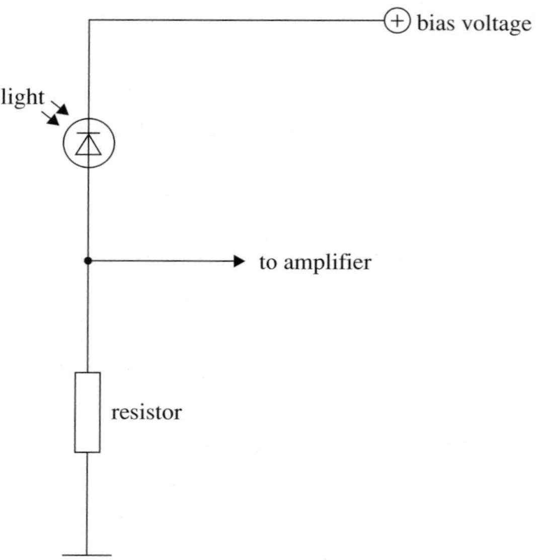

Figure F3.16 A light detector circuit with a photodiode.

The photodiode with zero bias works as a photovoltaic cell. In this case, for the purposes of detection, the reverse bias voltage is arranged so that, in the absence of any light falling on the photodiode, the current is zero. When light of a specific wavelength falls on the photodiode, a current is allowed to flow of a magnitude that is approximately proportional to the intensity of the incident light.

Noise

The term **noise** collectively refers to unwanted signals that travel along a given medium with the signal of interest. If the medium is a cable, the main source of noise is the random motion of electrons in the cable, which creates additional electric fields contaminating the signal. This increases with increasing temperature. Charged particles emitted by the sun during intense solar activity also create noise that can be picked up by a signal in a cable, as does lightning and other atmospheric disturbances.

The great advantage of the optic fibre over cables is that the fibre itself does not cause any appreciable noise. The causes of noise in an optic fibre include the contamination of the light entering the fibre from noise created by the transmitter of the light. But the *main* source of noise in an optic fibre is the *dark current* in the photodiode, i.e. the small current that exists even when the photodiode is dark. This current has to do with radiation falling on the photodiode other than the light it is intended to record, as well as the workings of the semiconductor junctions in the photodiode. The current depends on the bias voltage used as well as on temperature.

As with the everyday meaning of the word, noise is a nuisance. In a room full of people talking to each other, you cannot follow your conversation and you cannot make out conversations of other people (the famous 'cocktail-party effect' in acoustics). Communication becomes impossible when the power of the noise is comparable to the power of the signal.

We define the **signal-to-noise ratio** (SNR) in decibels (dB) to be

$$\text{SNR} = 10 \log \frac{P_{\text{signal}}}{P_{\text{noise}}}$$

where P_{signal} and P_{noise} are, respectively, the power of the signal and the power of the noise.

Example questions

Q10

The minimum SNR considered acceptable for a certain signal is 30 dB. If the power of the noise is 2.0 mW, calculate the least acceptable signal power.

Answer

From the definition of the signal-to-noise ratio we have

$$\text{SNR} = 10 \log \frac{P_{\text{signal}}}{P_{\text{noise}}}$$

$$30 = 10 \log \frac{P_{\text{signal}}}{2.0}$$

$$\log \frac{P_{\text{signal}}}{2.0} = 3.0$$

$$\frac{P_{\text{signal}}}{2.0} = 10^3$$

$$P_{\text{signal}} = 2.0 \times 10^3$$

$$= 2.0 \text{ W}$$

Q11

A given signal is fed into an amplifier of gain (in dB) G. Calculate the new signal-to-noise ratio after amplification in terms of the SNR before amplification.

Answer

The amplified signal and noise powers, P'_{signal} and P'_{noise}, will be related to the power before amplification through

$$G = 10 \log \frac{P'_{signal}}{P_{signal}}$$

$$\frac{P'_{signal}}{P_{signal}} = 10^{G/10}$$

$$P'_{signal} = P_{signal} \times 10^{G/10}$$

and

$$G = 10 \log \frac{P'_{noise}}{P'_{noise}}$$

$$P'_{noise} = P_{noise} \times 10^{G/10}$$

Thus the new signal-to-noise ratio SNR′ is

$$SNR' = 10 \log \frac{P'_{signal}}{P'_{noise}}$$

$$= 10 \log \frac{P_{signal} \times 10^{G/10}}{P_{noise} \times 10^{G/10}}$$

$$= 10 \log \frac{P_{signal}}{P_{noise}}$$

$$= \text{original SNR}$$

This example makes it clear that amplification is not of any use in improving the signal-to-noise ratio. The amplifier amplifies the signal but it amplifies the noise as well.

Regeneration

The transmission of analogue signals is plagued by noise. As we have seen, amplification does not improve the signal-to-noise ratio because the noise gets amplified along with the signal. This is shown in Figure F3.17.

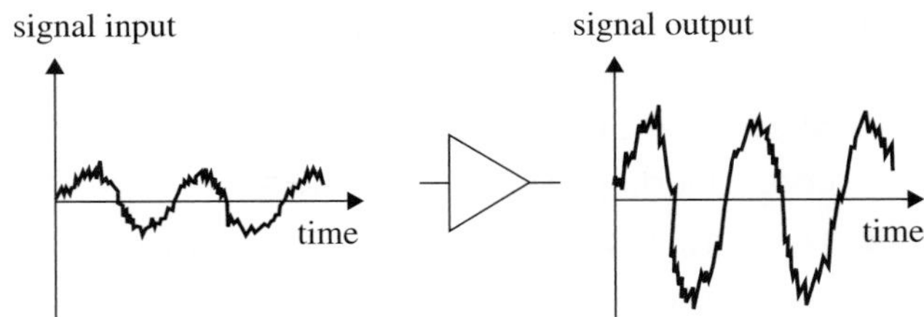

Figure F3.17 Amplification of an analogue signal with noise.

The transmission of digital signals, however, is inherently different because digital signals can be perfectly regenerated (reshaped and amplified). Figure F3.18 shows a digital signal that has been contaminated with noise. Amplification and regeneration results in a distortion-free digital signal without loss of information.

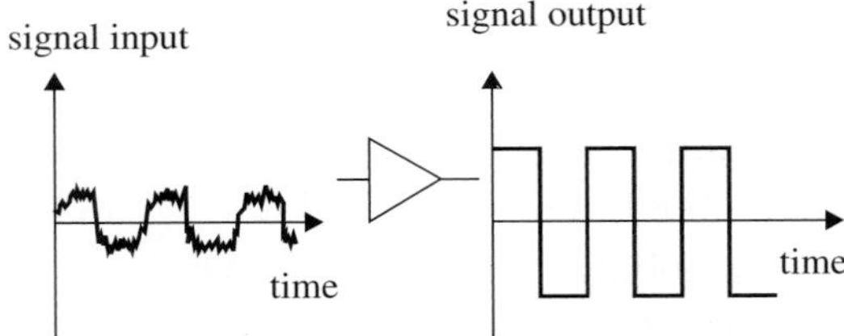

Figure F3.18 The digital signal can be perfectly regenerated.

Regeneration can be achieved with a device known as a Schmitt trigger, which is discussed in Option F5 on electronics (HL only). Optic fibres, with their ability to transmit digital signals in the form of light pulses, are therefore ideal for high-quality communications.

? QUESTIONS

1 Calculate the speed of light in the core of an optic fibre of refractive index 1.45.

2 (a) State what is meant by total internal reflection.
(b) Define the critical angle.
(c) Explain why total internal reflection can only occur for a ray travelling from a high to a low refractive index medium and not the other way around.

3 The refractive indices of the core and the cladding of an optic fibre are 1.50 and 1.46, respectively. Calculate the critical angle at the core–cladding boundary.

4 The refractive index of the cladding of an optic fibre is 1.42. What should the refractive index of the core be so that any ray entering the fibre gets totally internally reflected?

5 Calculate the acceptance angle of an optic fibre with core and cladding refractive indices equal to 1.52 and 1.44, respectively.

6 State one crucial property of the glass used in the core of an optic fibre.

7 (a) What is meant by dispersion in the context of optic fibres?
(b) Distinguish between modal and material dispersion.

8 Outline reasons why a laser is superior to a light-emitting diode for transmission along a fibre.

9 An optic fibre has length 8.00 km. The core of the optic fibre has refractive index 1.52, and the core–cladding critical angle is 82°.
(a) Calculate the speed of light in the core.
(b) Calculate the minimum and maximum times taken for a ray of light to travel down the length of the fibre.

10 The pulse shown in Figure F3.19 is input in a multimode optic fibre. Suggest the shape of the output pulse after it has travelled a long distance down the fibre.

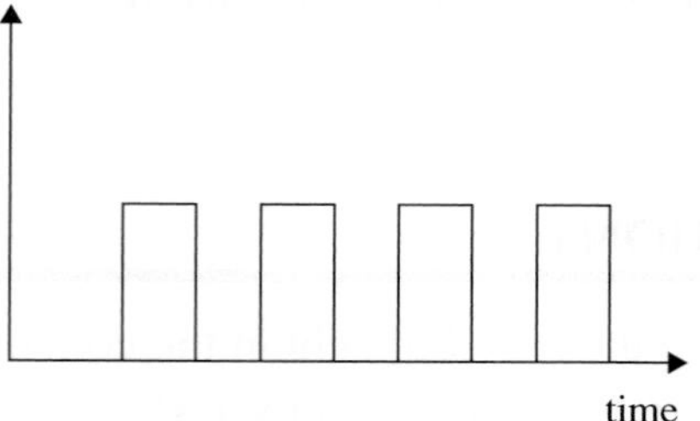

Figure F3.19 For question 10.

11 (a) Distinguish between monomode and multimode optic fibres.
(b) Discuss the effect of reducing the fibre core diameter on the bandwidth that can be transmitted by the fibre.

12 List the advantages of optic fibres in communications.

13 Outline the effect of dispersion on (a) the bit rate and (b) the frequency that can be transmitted along an optic fibre.

14 State the main cause of attenuation in an optic fibre.

15 A signal is said to have a signal-to-noise ratio of 30 dB. Explain what is meant by this statement.

16 The signal-to-noise ratio in a certain signal is 10 dB. The signal passes through an amplifier of gain 6.0 dB. What will be the signal-to-noise ratio after amplification?

17 Two amplifiers of gain (in dB) G_1 and G_2 amplify a signal as shown in Figure F3.20. Calculate the overall gain produced by the two amplifiers.

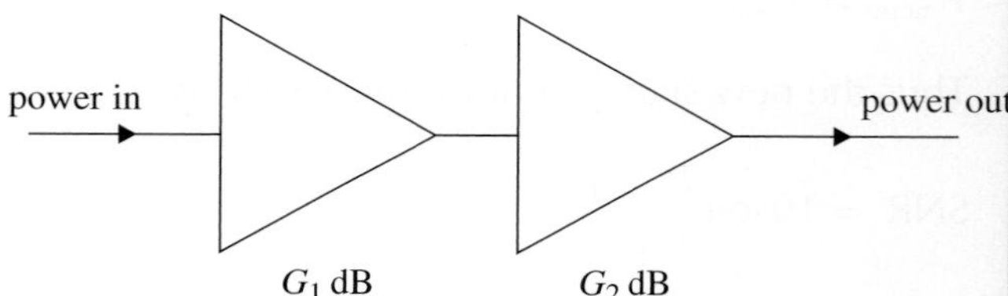

Figure F3.20 For question 17.

18 A signal of power 4.60 mW is attenuated to 3.20 mW. Calculate the power loss in decibels.

19 A signal of power 8.40 mW is attenuated to 5.10 mW after travelling a distance of 25 km in a cable. Calculate the attenuation per unit length of the cable.

20 A coaxial cable has a specific attenuation of 12 dB km^{-1}. The signal must be amplified when the power of the signal falls to 70% of the input power. After how much distance must the signal be amplified?

21 A signal is input to an amplifier of gain +15 dB. The signal then travels along a cable, where it suffers a power loss of 12 dB (Figure F3.21). Calculate the ratio of the output power to the input power.

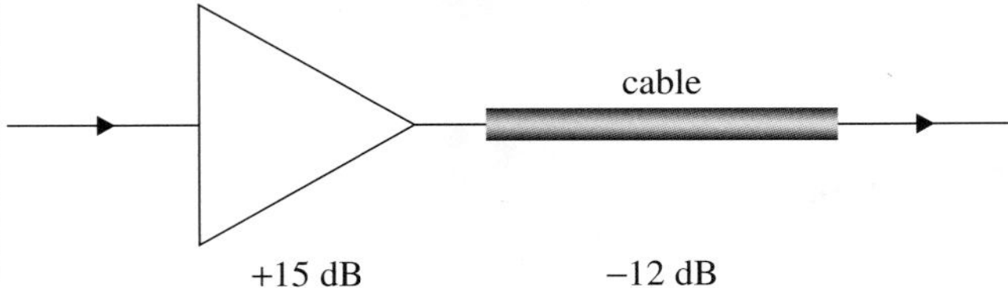

Figure F3.21 For question 21.

22 A signal is input to an amplifier of gain +7.0 dB (Figure F3.22). The signal then travels along a cable, where it suffers a power loss of 10 dB, and is then amplified again by an amplifier of gain +3.0 dB. Calculate the ratio of the output power to the input power.

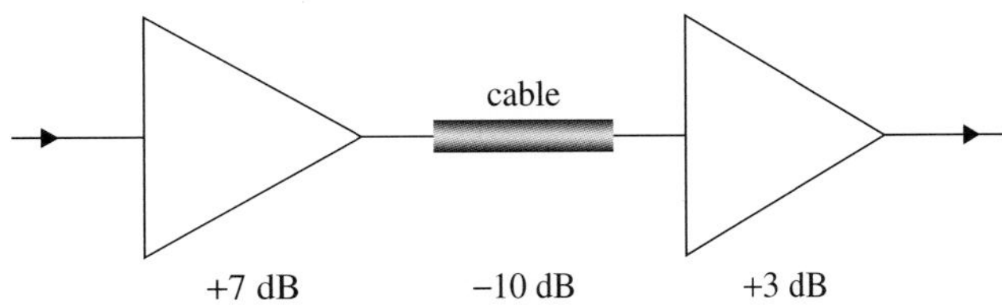

Figure F3.22 For question 22.

23 In the arrangement of Figure F3.23, the output power is twice the input power. Calculate the required gain G of the amplifier.

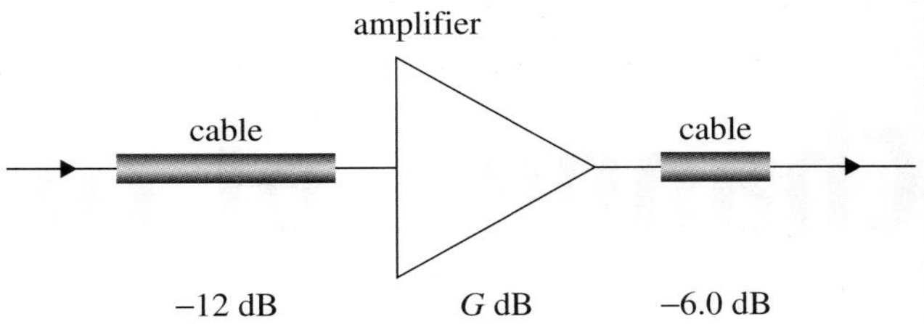

Figure F3.23 For question 23.

24 In a telephone cable, the power of the noise is measured to be 45 mW. The signal is considered barely acceptable if the signal-to-noise ratio is 20 dB. Calculate the least signal power for a signal to be barely acceptable.

25 (a) Sketch a graph (no numbers are required on the axes) to illustrate the variation with wavelength of the specific attenuation in an optic fibre.

(b) Explain why infrared wavelengths are preferred in optic fibre transmissions.

26 (a) State what is meant by *noise* in communications.

(b) State the main causes of noise in (i) copper wires and (ii) optic fibres.

(c) Suggest a way to reduce noise in (i) copper wires and (ii) optic fibres.

Channels of communication

In previous chapters we saw how a carrier wave can be modulated so that it can carry the information contained in an information signal. The carrier wave must then carry this information from the transmitter to its destination receiver. The carrier wave must thus propagate in a *medium*. There are many media or *channels of communication* available. Depending on the signal being transmitted, one or more channels may be used. In this chapter we will examine various channels of communication.

Objectives

By the end of this chapter you should be able to:

- recall the *main channels of communication* (i.e. copper wires, wire pairs, coaxial cables, optic fibres, radio waves, microwave links and satellite communications);
- understand the *characteristics and uses* of these channels of communication;
- solve simple problems involving *attenuation* in the channels mentioned above;
- understand the differences between *polar satellites* and *geosynchronous satellites*;
- solve simple problems with *satellite motion*.

Copper wires

When the telephone network was first established, copper wires were used to transmit the *electrical* signal sent by one's telephone to the local exchange (Figure F4.1). In many places around the world, copper wires are still in use. They can be seen stretching from telegraph pole to telegraph pole along roads. The wires carry current and the current is not constant. This means that the magnetic field it produces varies as well. A wire nearby will be affected by the magnetic field and this will result in *cross-talk*, i.e. noise and interference in the call carried by the nearby line. It is therefore desirable to have the wires as far apart as feasible in order to reduce the effects of interference of one wire on another. Other disadvantages of copper wires include the very low bandwidth that can be transmitted (about 20 kHz) and the frequent need for amplification of the signal (every 10 km).

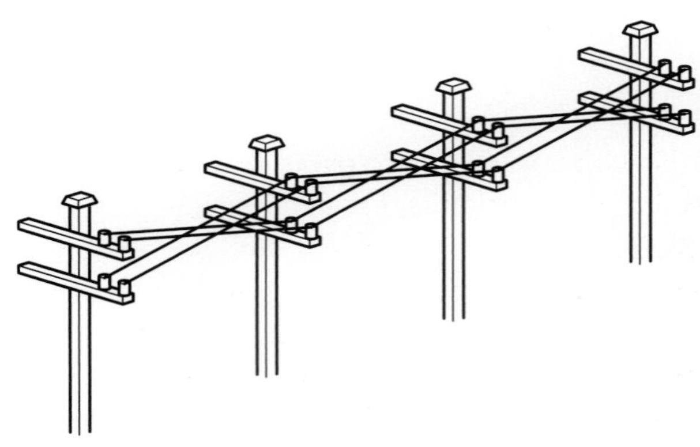

Figure F4.1 Copper wires.

Wire pairs

To reduce the effects of magnetic field interference from one wire to another, twisted wires were developed, in which two copper wires are twisted around each other so that, at any point, the currents in the two wires are in opposite directions, resulting therefore in a much reduced net magnetic field (Figure F4.2). In addition, twisted wires reduce the flux linkage (by minimizing the area exposed to magnetic fields) and so minimize the unwanted signals created by electromagnetic induction. Each wire is insulated before twisting, and both are then inserted into an insulated outer cover.

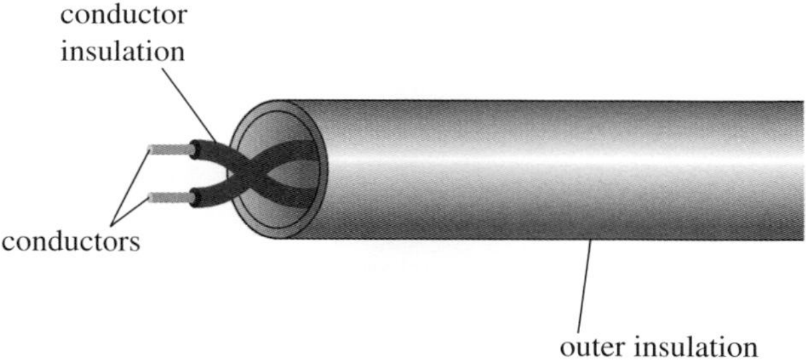

Figure F4.2 Wire pairs.

Wire pairs reduce but do not completely eliminate cross-talk. They suffer from serious attenuation (the average distance between amplification of the signal is of the order of 5 km), especially at high frequencies, and they distort the transmitted signal due to *dispersion*, i.e. due to the fact that radio waves of different frequencies travel at different speeds in the wires. Another disadvantage of wire pairs is the reduced bandwidth of the signal that can be carried along them (a maximum of the order of 500 kHz).

Coaxial cables

The problems of the wire pair were mostly solved with the development of the coaxial cable (Figure F4.3). This consists of a central copper wire surrounded by insulation and a second copper conductor, usually braided, that completely surrounds the inner copper wire. The inner and outer conductors thus have the same axis, hence the name coaxial.

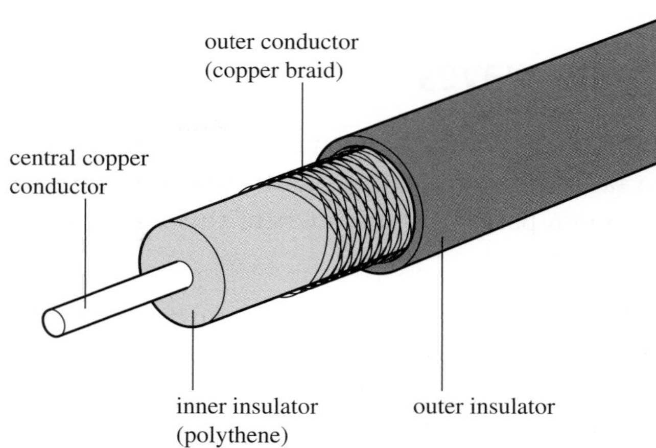

Figure F4.3 Coaxial cable.

The main advantage of the coaxial cable relative to the wire pair is the higher bandwidth that can be carried (up to 500 MHz) and the reduced (but not eliminated) attenuation and cross-talk effects. The average distance between amplification varies a lot with frequency. At frequencies of a few megahertz (used for telephone signals) amplification is needed every 10 km, whereas at 1 GHz (used for cable TV) amplification is necessary every 100 m or so.

Coaxial cables were used to carry high-frequency radio waves and were the standard in telecommunications until the appearance of the optic fibre and satellite links. Coaxial cables used for telephone call transmission are usually buried underground, and this adds to their cost and creates delays in their implementation. The main use of coaxial cable today is to carry cable TV signals to consumers.

Optic fibres

Optic fibres have been discussed in the previous chapter. They are now replacing the coaxial cable for most telephone communication needs. They can carry very high-frequency signals (approaching the terahertz range) and have a very large bandwidth (10 GHz). Attenuation is low, with amplification being required every 80 km or so.

Radio waves

Table F4.1 shows the vast radio spectrum used in radio communications and a few of the uses to which particular members of this family of waves are put.

A radio wave can travel from its emitting aerial to its destination receiver in essentially three forms. These are *surface* waves, *sky* waves and *space* waves. The following is a brief description of each.

Surface waves

These are waves of frequency below about 3 MHz. The associated wavelength is therefore $\frac{3\times10^8}{3\times10^6} = 100$ m or more. This is a large wavelength, which means that these waves are substantially diffracted by the earth's surface. These waves can therefore travel by following the curvature of the earth's surface and can travel large distances, well beyond the horizon of the transmitter (Figure F4.4). The actual distance travelled depends on many factors, such as the power of the transmitter, the actual frequency used, and the conductivity of the ground over which the wave travels. For AM radio transmissions the range is a few hundreds of kilometres, and for powerful transmitters at low frequencies (3 kHz) the range can be thousands of kilometres.

Frequency band	Classification	Abbreviation	Wavelength	Typical uses
3 Hz–30 Hz	extremely low	ELF	10^5–10^4 km	submarine communication
30 Hz–300 Hz	ultra-low	ULF	10^4–10^3 km	submarine communication
300 Hz–3 kHz	infra-low	ILF	10^3–10^2 km	baseband telephone signals
3 kHz–30 kHz	very low	VLF	10^2–10 km	long-range navigation
30 kHz–300 kHz	low	LF	10–1 km	long-range navigation AM radio broadcasting
300 kHz–3 MHz	medium	MF	1 km–100 m	maritime radio direction finding AM radio broadcasting
3 MHz–30 MHz	high	HF	100–10 m	international radio broadcasting amateur radio long-distance ship communication
30 MHz–300 MHz	very high	VHF	10–1 m	FM radio broadcasting television broadcasting aircraft communication aircraft navigational aids
300 MHz–3 GHz	ultra-high	UHF	1 m–10 cm	television broadcasting mobile phones microwave links navigational aids radar
3 GHz–30 GHz	super-high	SHF	10–1 cm	mobile phones microwave links radar satellite communications
30 GHz–300 GHz	extremely high	EHF	10–1 mm	radar radio astronomy
300 GHz–3 THz	tremendously high	THF	1–0.1 mm	research

Table F4.1 The radio wave spectrum.

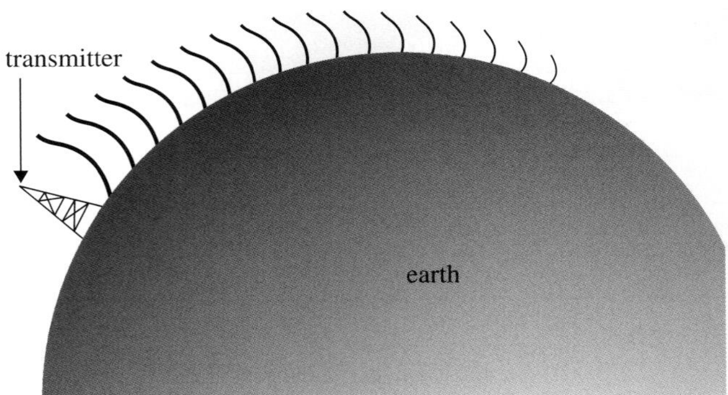

Figure F4.4 Surface wave propagation.

Sky waves

Radio waves in the frequency range 3 MHz to 30 MHz propagate as sky waves. This means that the waves are directed upwards towards the atmosphere where they suffer (a complicated) total internal reflection from a layer of the atmosphere called the *ionosphere* (Figure F4.5). The waves therefore return to the surface of the earth a certain distance away from the transmitter. This distance is called the **skip distance**. They are then reflected from the surface of the earth back into the atmosphere, where the process is repeated. The waves suffer substantial attenuation in the ionosphere. The ionosphere extends from a height of about 50 km above the earth's surface up to 500 km. This is a zone where ultraviolet radiation from the sun ionizes air molecules, creating electrons and positive ions. It has different layers with different concentrations of electrons. The actual electron concentration is affected by the sun's 11-year cycle of solar activity. The lowest layer disappears at night when the incoming ultraviolet radiation is not present.

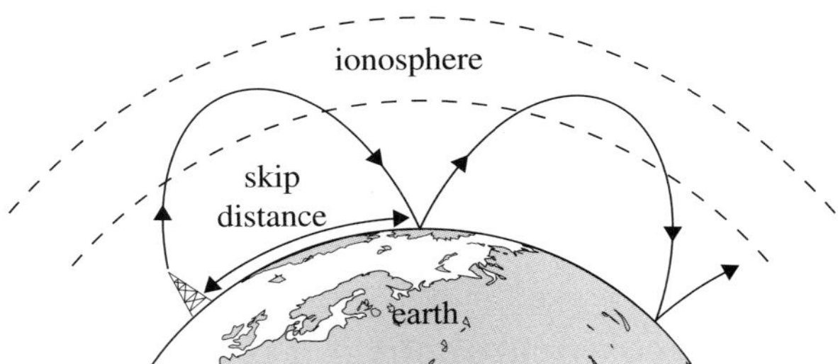

Figure F4.5 Sky wave propagation.

This form of radio wave transmission is used by amateur radio operators, international radio broadcasts and ship communications. Due to varying skip distances, unpredictable ionosphere conditions and interference, these communications tend to be unreliable.

Space waves

These are waves of frequency above 30 MHz. At these frequencies the wavelength is 10 m or less and the waves travel along straight lines (line-of-sight propagation) (Figure F4.6). The ionosphere has no effect on these waves. The range is then dictated by the height of the transmitting station and is typically a few tens of kilometres. This is the method used for radio FM transmissions as well as earth-bound and satellite TV transmissions.

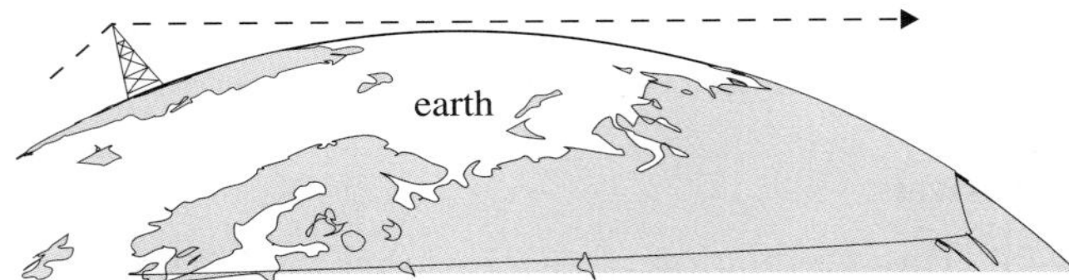

Figure F4.6 Space wave propagation.

Microwave transmission through free space

Microwaves have a higher frequency than radio waves (a few gigahertz) and so can carry a larger bandwidth (100 MHz), making multiplexing possible. They can travel along straight lines from one point to another, and suffer substantially less attenuation than coaxial cables (Figure F4.7).

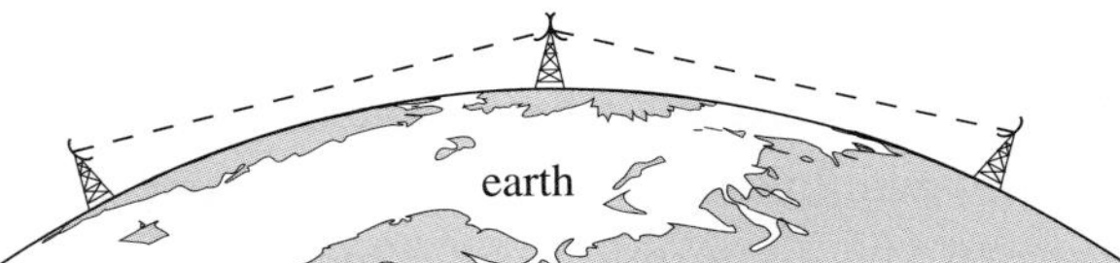

Figure F4.7 A microwave link.

The information above is summarized in Table F4.2.

Channel	Carrier frequency	Bandwidth	Average distance between amplifiers	Specific attenuation/dB km^{-1}
Copper wires	20 kHz	20 kHz	10 km	10
Wire pairs	10 MHz	500 kHz	5 km	25
Coaxial cable	2 MHz (telephone)	500 MHz	10 km	6
	1 GHz (TV)		100 m	200
Microwaves in free space	5 GHz	100 MHz	50 km	distance-dependent
Optic fibres	0.2 THz	10 GHz	80 km	0.20

Table F4.2 Typical characteristics of various channels of communication.

Example questions

Q1

The specific attenuation of a coaxial cable is 14 dB km^{-1}. A signal of initial power 200 mW is input to such a cable.

(a) Calculate the power of the signal after it has travelled a distance of 3.0 km along the cable.

(b) State whether a signal of similar power to that in (a) but of much higher frequency would suffer a larger or smaller attenuation.

Answer

(a) The attenuation after a distance of 3.0 km is $3.0 \times 14 = 42$ dB. The power is then found from

$$-42 = 10 \log\left(\frac{P}{200}\right)$$

$$\log\left(\frac{P}{200}\right) = -4.2$$

$$\frac{P}{200} = 10^{-4.2}$$

$$= 6.3 \times 10^{-5}$$

$$P = 0.013 \text{ mW}$$

(b) Attenuation in coaxial cables is very frequency-dependent. There is much more attenuation at higher frequencies.

Q2

A microwave link station emits microwaves of power 28 MW uniformly in all directions.

(a) Calculate the power received by an antenna dish of area $A = 1.2$ m^2 of this signal at a distance of 100 km.

(b) Determine the attenuation of the signal in dB.

Answer

The power is distributed uniformly over a sphere of radius *d*. The power *per unit sphere area* is therefore $\frac{P}{4\pi d^2}$ and so the power collected by the antenna is

$$\frac{P}{4\pi d^2} \times A = \frac{28 \times 10^6}{4\pi (10^5)^2} \times 1.2 = 0.27 \text{ mW}$$

(b) The power loss in dB is

$$10 \log\left(\frac{0.27 \times 10^{-3}}{28 \times 10^6}\right) = -110 \text{ dB}$$

This corresponds to a specific attenuation of $\frac{110}{100} = 1.1$ dB km^{-1}.

Satellite communications

In 1945, the science-fiction novelist Arthur C. Clarke published his pioneering essay 'Extra-terrestrial relays' (largely based on earlier work by other scientists), in which he suggested that geosynchronous satellites orbiting the earth could provide worldwide radio coverage. It wasn't until 1963 though that it became possible to launch the first satellite, Syncom 2, in such an orbit. Today, there are over 150 known satellites orbiting the earth, more than 100 of which are in geosynchronous orbits.

Geosynchronous (geostationary) satellites

An orbit is **geosynchronous** if it is directly above the equator and its period (the time for one complete revolution) is equal to the period of rotation of the earth around its axis, i.e. 24 hours. The reader with knowledge of gravitation should be able to show that this orbit must be a distance of approximately 42 000 km from the earth's centre. The great advantage of the geosynchronous satellite is that, since the satellite and the earth rotate with the same period, the satellite is always above the *same* point on the earth's surface (which is why they are also called geostationary), and that point must be on the equator. Because the orbit is above the equator, you can 'see' geosynchronous satellites if you look south from a place in the northern hemisphere and if you look north from a place in the southern hemisphere. Geosynchronous satellites are very far from the earth. Putting a satellite into such an orbit is very expensive (in addition to the cost of buying or renting the satellite).

Example question

Q3

The distance of a geosynchronous satellite from the centre of the earth is 42 000 km. How much of the earth can the satellite 'see'? Take the radius of the earth to be 6400 km.

Answer

Figure F4.8 shows the geosynchronous satellite in orbit. The dashed lines are tangent to the surface of the earth at points A and B.

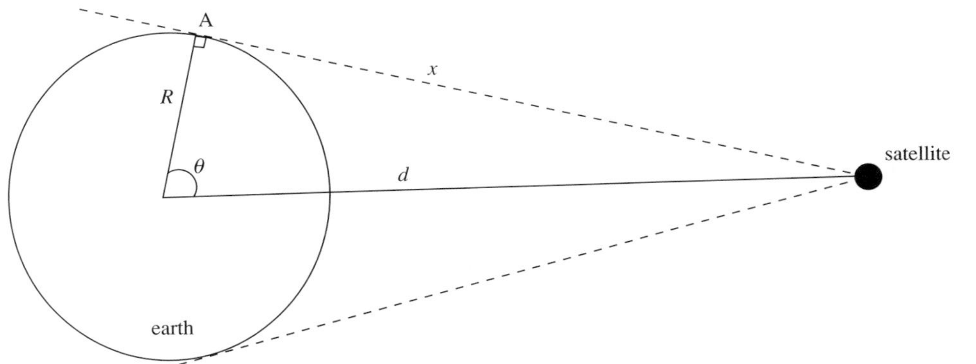

Figure F4.8.

From trigonometry, we have

$$\cos\theta = \frac{R}{d} = \frac{6400}{42\,000} = 0.152$$

This means that $\theta = \arccos(0.152) = 81°$.

With some more advanced geometry (see the 'just for fun' end-of-chapter question 17 in Option H5), it can be shown that this is about 42% of the entire surface area of the earth. This means that three satellites can more than cover the entire area of the earth's surface (except for the polar regions, of course, which are never accessible to a geosynchronous satellite).

Example question

Q4

(a) In the previous example, calculate the time between the emission of a signal at A and its arrival at B via the geosynchronous satellite.

(b) For what kind of transmission would this time delay, possibly, be annoying?

Answer

(a) By Pythagoras, the distance x can be found from $d^2 = R^2 + x^2$. So the distance travelled by the signal from A to B is $2x = 2\sqrt{d^2 - R^2} = 8.3 \times 10^7$ m. At the speed of light $c = 3 \times 10^8\ \text{m s}^{-1}$, the signal would then take

$$t = \frac{2\sqrt{d^2 - R^2}}{c} = \frac{8.3 \times 10^7}{3 \times 10^8} = 0.28\ \text{s}$$

(b) This is a small time delay, but it could, however, be annoying in a telephone conversation.

Geosynchronous satellites are obviously extremely important in communications. Data (telephone calls, images, video, etc.) can be transmitted from a transmitter at a particular place on the earth's surface towards the satellite, and the satellite can then redirect the signal to a receiver somewhere else. A TV station, for example, can use the satellite to redirect its signal to a vast geographic area.

The signal from the transmitter to the satellite must be very well focused so as to avoid loss of power in the signal when it arrives at the satellite. To make the expensive satellite operation worthwhile financially, a very large bandwidth must be available, so that a large number of different data can be transmitted simultaneously, using for example multiplexing. (This requires digital signals.) In addition, the satellite must be able to transmit the signal without using too much power, simply because the satellite has limited power supplies (solar cells that can produce only a few hundred watts of power). These considerations impose constraints on the range of frequencies that can be used.

▶ The requirements of a well-focused, large-bandwidth signal that can deliver reasonable power at a relatively low amplitude dictates that the frequencies that can be used for satellite communications must be in the gigahertz (GHz) range.

The frequency used to transmit to the satellite is called the *up-link* frequency. The frequency used by the satellite to transmit down to earth is called the *down-link* frequency. The up-link and down-link frequencies are always different, with the up-link frequency being the larger of the two (by convention).

The reason for this difference in frequencies is to avoid the following problem. The receiver on the satellite operates at the up-link frequency. It is designed to be able to pick up very small signals and so is very sensitive. The transmitter on the satellite operates at the down-link frequency, and is powerful. If the up-link and down-link frequencies were the same, resonance would occur. The arrival of a tiny signal would create a larger output signal at the same frequency. Because it is so sensitive, the receiver would also pick up this signal, and would create an even larger output signal, and so on. This is called positive feedback.

A typical up-link frequency is 10 GHz, in the microwave region of the electromagnetic spectrum. The corresponding wavelength is

$$\lambda = \frac{3 \times 10^8}{10 \times 10^9}$$

$$= 3 \times 10^{-2}\ \text{m}$$

i.e. 3 cm, a typical microwave wavelength. The bandwidth available is of the order of 500 MHz. Table F4.3 lists some typical values for satellite communications.

Up-link frequency/GHz	Down-link frequency/GHz	Bandwidth/MHz
6	4	500
14	11	500
30	20	1500

Table F4.3 Satellite frequencies and bandwidth.

Polar orbit satellites

These satellites have north–south orbits passing over the poles of the earth. They are typically in low orbits (a few hundred kilometres above the earth as opposed to the 42 000 – 6400 = 35 600 km of geosynchronous satellites above the surface).

At a height of 500 km the orbital period is about 95 minutes. A low polar orbit satellite will pass any one point on the earth's surface twice in the course of one day and will be 'visible' to an observer at that point for a period of approximately 10 minutes (see Example question 5).

Example question

Q5

A satellite is in a polar orbit at a height of 500 km from the earth's surface. The satellite completes one orbit in 95 minutes and has a speed of $7.6 \times 10^3\ \text{m s}^{-1}$.

(a) Calculate the angle by which the earth has rotated during one revolution of the satellite. Assume that at $t = 0$ the satellite is directly overhead the observer at O.

(b) Estimate the time for which the satellite is visible to an observer on the equator.

(c) Show that the satellite will pass any one point on the earth's surface twice in the course of one day, as claimed in the text.

Answer

In Figure F4.9 the dashed circle represents the orbit of the satellite at a height h from the surface. The observer is at O and the vertical line represents the horizon of the observer. (The observer can see what is to the right of the line.) The satellite therefore comes into view at A and disappears at B.

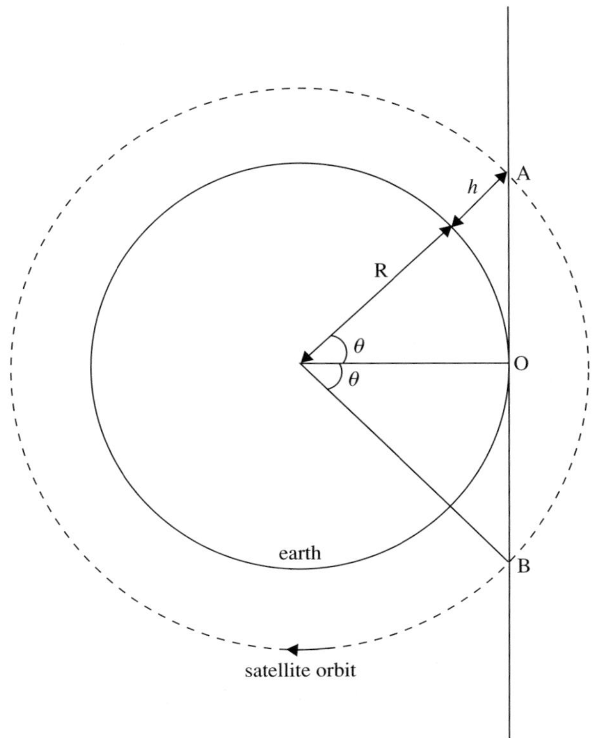

Figure F4.9.

(a) The earth rotates by 360° in 24 hours, and so in 95 minutes it will rotate by

$$360° \times \frac{95}{60 \times 24} = 24°$$

(b) The angle θ is given by

$$\cos\theta = \frac{R}{R+h}$$

$$= \frac{6400}{6900}$$

$$= 0.928$$

$$\theta = 22°$$

The arc length AB is equal to

$$\text{AB} = 2\pi(R+h)\frac{2\theta}{360°}$$

$$= 2\pi(6900)\frac{44°}{360°}$$

$$= 5300\ \text{km}$$

The time to cover this distance (remember to convert speed to km s^{-1}) is

$$t = \frac{5300}{7.6}\ \text{s}$$

$$= 697\ \text{s} \quad \approx 12\ \text{min}$$

This is the time for which the satellite is visible to the observer at O.

(c) We have seen that the earth moves by about 24° for every revolution of the satellite. If the satellite is above observer O at $t = 0$, then by the time the satellite returns to the same point in space the observer will have moved out of sight. The satellite and the observer *may* meet after the observer has made a 180° rotation; this takes 12 hours. In these 12 hours the satellite has made $\frac{60\times 12}{95} \approx 7.5$ full revolutions. This is a half-integral number. This means that the satellite is again directly overhead the observer and so the satellite and the observer meet twice a day, as claimed earlier, at diametrically opposite points on the equator.

This example makes it clear that polar orbit satellites, while having the advantage of being able to see the whole of the earth at some point or other, are visible to a particular observer for only about 12 minutes out of the 95 minutes of each orbit period. This means that the satellite has to pick up a signal from a transmission station underneath, store it, and then transmit it *later* when it passes over the destination receiver. This is not convenient for the transmission of a telephone call, unless many such satellites are involved. The advantage of the low orbit polar satellites is that they are cheaper to put into orbit, require less power to transmit up-link signals, and serve the polar regions that are unreachable by geosynchronous satellites.

In order to transmit to the satellite, one must know where the satellite is, and so tracking systems are necessary to pinpoint the position of the satellite at any one time.

Polar orbit satellites have many uses other than communication, for example, geological surveying and cartography, meteorology, oceanography, and military espionage.

? QUESTIONS

1 Identify the main sources of attenuation in copper wires, wire pairs, coaxial cable, optic fibres and microwave links.

2 A network of computers in a small business uses twisted wire pairs. Explain why wire pairs rather than coaxial cables or optic fibres are an acceptable solution in this case.

3 Explain why coaxial cable would be preferable over twisted wire pairs for connecting a computer modem to an internet provider.

4 State and explain the advantages of optic fibre transmissions over transmissions in ordinary cables. What is the physical nature of the signal transmitted in an optic fibre?

5 The strength of a signal in a coaxial cable varies with distance as shown in Figure F4.10. The highest signal-to-noise ratio during the transmission is 50 dB and the lowest is 20 dB. It may be assumed that the noise level is constant throughout the cable.

(a) Calculate the specific attenuation in the cable.

(b) Calculate the gain at each amplifier station.

(c) The input power of the signal is 600 mW. Calculate the power of the signal after 15 km if no amplifiers are used.

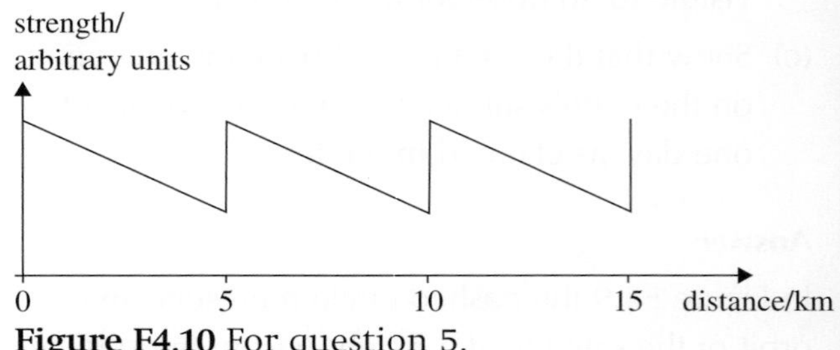

Figure F4.10 For question 5.

6 (a) State typical values of frequencies at which satellites emit and receive.

(b) Suggest why the up-link and down-link frequencies are different.

7 State three uses of satellites in the communications field.

8 Suggest a reason why a satellite should have as large a bandwidth as possible.

9 State the advantages of geosynchronous satellites over polar orbit satellites.

10 (a) State approximate values for the orbital radii of

(i) a geosynchronous satellite;

(ii) a low polar orbit satellite.

(b) Consider a transmitter that emits a total power P uniformly in all directions. Deduce that at a distance d from the transmitter the power received per unit area of the receiver is given by $\frac{P}{4\pi d^2}$.

(c) Assuming that a low polar orbit satellite and a geosynchronous satellite receive the same power per unit area from their respective transmitters, calculate, using your estimates in (a), the ratio $\frac{P_{\text{geosync}}}{P_{\text{polar}}}$ of the powers radiated by the respective transmitters.

(d) In practice the ratio $\frac{P_{geosync}}{P_{polar}}$ is much less than your answer in (c). Suggest reasons why this is so.

11 A satellite is in a polar orbit at a height of 600 km from the earth's surface. The satellite completes one orbit in 97 minutes and has a speed of $7.56 \times 10^3\ m\,s^{-1}$.

(a) Calculate the angle by which the earth has rotated during one revolution of the satellite. Assume that at $t = 0$ the satellite is directly overhead the observer at O.

(b) Estimate the distance that a point on the equator of the earth has moved during one period of the satellite.

(c) Estimate the time for which the satellite is visible to an observer on the equator.

Electronics

This chapter introduces a versatile and useful device in electronics, the operational amplifier (op-amp). The inverting and non-inverting amplifiers are discussed, as well as applications of the op-amp in simple circuits. The chapter ends with an important application of the op-amp, the Schmitt trigger, which may be used to reshape digital signals.

Objectives

By the end of this chapter you should be able to:

- understand the basic principles of the *operational amplifier* (op-amp);
- draw circuit diagrams for both *inverting* and *non-inverting amplifiers*;
- derive expressions for the *gain* of both inverting and non-inverting amplifiers;
- solve problems involving the op-amp;
- design simple circuits involving the op-amp as a *comparator*;
- describe the use of the *Schmitt trigger* in reshaping digital signals.

The operational amplifier (op-amp)

The op-amp is a very versatile device and one of the most useful integrated circuits in all of electronics. This is because of its simplicity and the fact that many interesting circuits result by connecting it to just a few external components. The op-amp was used in the old analogue computers because of its ability to perform mathematical operations such as addition, subtraction, differentiation and integration. This function has now been superseded in the modern digital computer.

The schematic diagram for an op-amp is shown in Figure F5.1(a) and even more simply in Figure F5.1(b). The op-amp can amplify both DC and AC voltages. Its main features are as follows:

- The op-amp has very high gain in the output voltage (up to 10^6).
- It has very high input resistance, which implies that it does not draw any appreciable current from the input signal.
- It has very low output resistance, which implies that any load can be driven no matter how low its resistance.
- It is a differential amplifier, meaning that it gives an output signal that is proportional to the difference between two input signals.

The commonly used op-amps come in a design with eight pins. We will be interested in only five of these eight available pins, as listed below.

1. The inverting input: an input here will be changed in sign; we call this input voltage V_-.
2. The non-inverting input: an input here will not be changed in sign; we call this input voltage V_+.
3. Output: this is the output signal of the op-amp; we call this output voltage V_0.

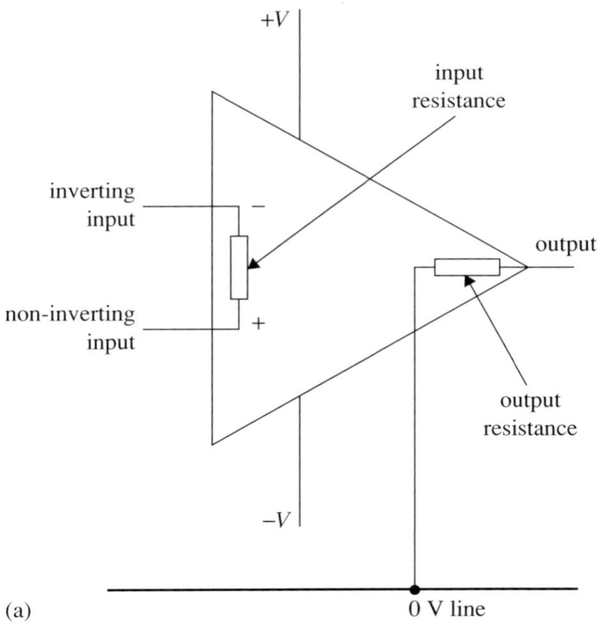

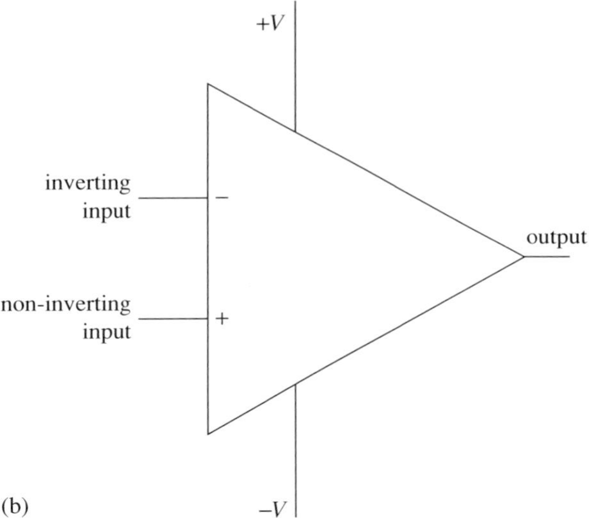

Figure F5.1 (a) The circuit diagram for an op-amp showing the high (2MΩ) input resistance and the low (200 Ω) output resistance. (b) Simplified diagram for the op-amp.

4 The positive supply of voltage: this is indicated by $+V$.

5 The negative supply of voltage: this is indicated by $-V$.

In most circuit diagrams involving the op-amp, the power supply voltages $\pm V$ are usually omitted. Figure F5.1 is a 'block diagram' for the op-amp. The internal circuit components are not shown – they are complex and beyond the scope of this book. An equivalent way of drawing the op-amp is shown in Figure F5.2.

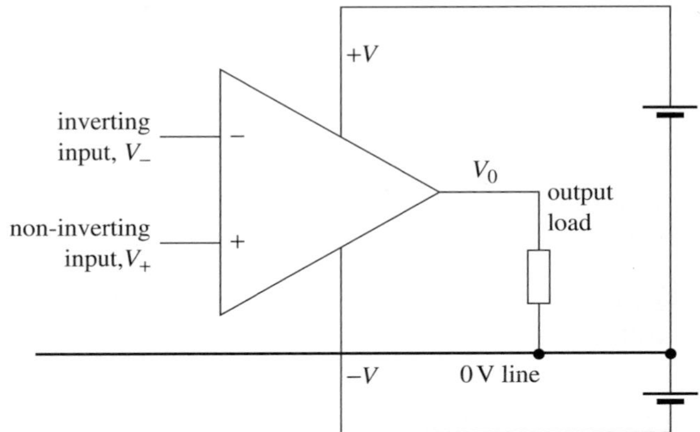

Figure F5.2 The circuit diagram for an op-amp showing the power supply voltages.

This shows more clearly the power supply voltages and also shows the output signal being fed into an external load. The thick line is the zero volt (0 V) line, i.e. the voltage of the earth. It is the voltage relative to which all other voltages are measured.

The first result about the op-amp is that the output voltage, V_0, is directly proportional to the difference between the two input voltages, V_+ and V_-. In equation form this is written as

$$V_0 = G_0(V_+ - V_-)$$

The variable G_0 is known as the **open loop gain** and, typically, $G_0 = 10^6$ for DC and low-frequency signals. The gain decreases with increasing input signal frequency.

Care must be taken with this equation. The graph in Figure F5.3 shows the variation of the output voltage V_0 with the input voltage difference $V_+ - V_-$. The formula can be used *only* for the non-horizontal part of the graph. This is because the output voltage can never exceed the power supply voltage $+V$ or be less than $-V$. (In practice, the saturation values of the output voltage are about $\pm 80\%\ V$.

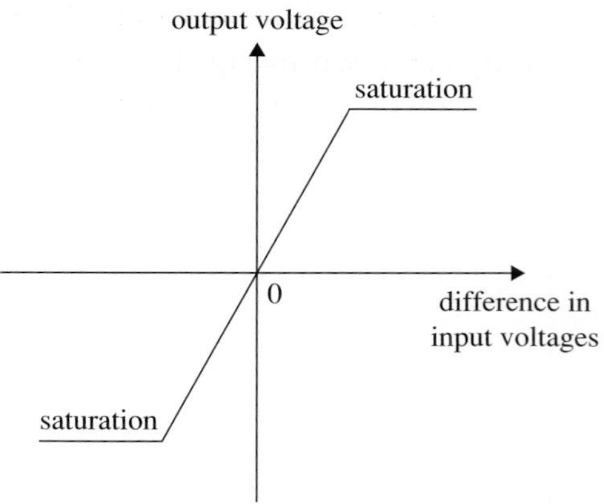

Figure F5.3 Variation of output voltage with input voltage difference for an op-amp.

Example question

Q1

An op-amp has an open loop gain of $G_0 = 10^6$. The power supply voltages are -15 V to $+15$ V.

(a) What is the largest voltage difference between the input signals for which the equation $V_0 = G_0\,(V_+ - V_-)$ can be used?

(b) What is the output voltage for (i) $V_+ - V_- = 8.0$ μV and (ii) $V_+ - V_- = 26$ μV.

Answer

(a) The maximum supply voltage (and therefore the maximum output voltage) is 15 V, so

$$\begin{aligned} V_+ - V_- &= \frac{V_0}{G_0} \\ &= \frac{15}{10^6}\,\text{V} \\ &= 15\ \mu\text{V} \end{aligned}$$

For an input voltage difference of at most 15 μV, we can use the equation $V_0 = G_0(V_+ - V_-)$ to calculate the output voltage. For input voltage differences larger than 15 μV, the output voltage will be saturated, i.e. constant at -15 V or $+15$ V.

(b) (i) Since 8.0 μV is *less* than the maximum of 15μV, we can use the equation to get

$$\begin{aligned} V_0 &= G_0(V_+ - V_-) \\ &= 10^6 \times 8.0\ \mu\text{V} \\ &= 8.0\ \text{V} \end{aligned}$$

(ii) Here 26 μV is *more* than the maximum and we have saturation, so $V_0 = 15$ V. (In a real op-amp, as opposed to an ideal one, the saturation voltage would be somewhat less than 15 V.)

The inverting amplifier

Figure F5.4 shows an op-amp acting as an **inverting amplifier**. The output voltage is V_0 and the input voltage is applied to the inverting input of the op-amp. The resistor labelled R_F is called the *feedback* resistor. Notice that part of the output (at X) is fed back as input to the op-amp. Because the input is through the inverting input of the op-amp, this signal is out of phase with the original input signal by 180° and the feedback is called a *negative feedback*. This means that the gain of the amplifier is reduced (which is a strange thing to do in an amplifier). The advantage of doing so is that in this way the gain is stable (constant) over a wide range of voltages and frequencies, and independent of the characteristics of the op-amp itself.

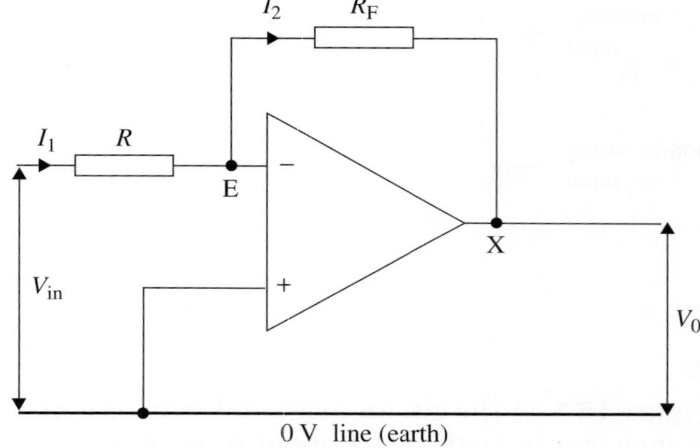

Figure F5.4 The inverting amplifier.

Let the open loop gain be G_0, which as we know is typically of the order of 10^6. We have $V_+ = 0$ V, so the voltage V_- at point E is $\frac{V_0}{G_0}$ and therefore very small, practically zero. Assuming that the voltage at E is zero means that we are making the *virtual earth approximation*, i.e. we are assuming that point E is connected to the earth, which has zero voltage. The potential difference across resistor R is then V_{in}, and the current flowing through this resistor is

$$I_1 = \frac{V_{in}}{R}$$

The current in resistor R_F is

$$I_2 = \frac{-V_0}{R_F}$$

The negative sign is there since the potential V_0 is negative. (Remember that current flows towards lower potential – since the potential at E is zero, the potential at X must be negative.) In this way the current I_2 is defined as a positive quantity.

The current in R flows towards E. Since practically no current flows in the op-amp, we must have that $I_1 = I_2$, i.e. that

$$\frac{V_{in}}{R} = -\frac{V_0}{R_F}$$

or

$$\frac{V_0}{V_{in}} = -\frac{R_F}{R}$$

The ratio $G = \frac{V_0}{V_{in}}$ is known as the **closed loop gain** of the inverting amplifier and so

$$G = \frac{V_0}{V_{in}} = -\frac{R_F}{R} \quad \text{closed loop inverting amplifier gain}$$

Example questions

Q2

(a) Calculate the closed loop gain of the inverting amplifier shown in Figure F5.4 when $R = 100\ \text{k}\Omega$ and $R_F = 1.0\ \text{M}\Omega$.

(b) The op-amp works with a power supply of ± 15 V. Calculate the input voltage for which the op-amp will saturate.

Answer

(a) From the equation above, the closed loop gain of this inverting amplifier is

$$G = -\frac{R_F}{R}$$

$$= -\frac{1.0 \times 10^6}{100 \times 10^3}$$

$$= -10$$

This means that a single input voltage of, say, 0.25 mV will result in an (inverted) output voltage of $V_0 = 2.5$ mV.

(b) In the ideal case the op-amp saturates at ± 15 V. The smallest positive input voltage that causes saturation is therefore 1.5 V (see Figure F5.5).

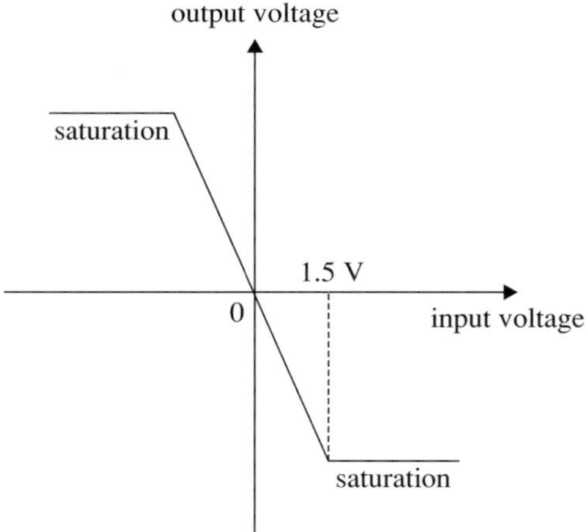

Figure F5.5 Variation of output voltage with input voltage for the inverting amplifier of Example question 2.

Q3

Calculate the closed loop gain of the inverting amplifier (such as that of Figure F5.4) whose output–input characteristic is as shown in Figure F5.6.

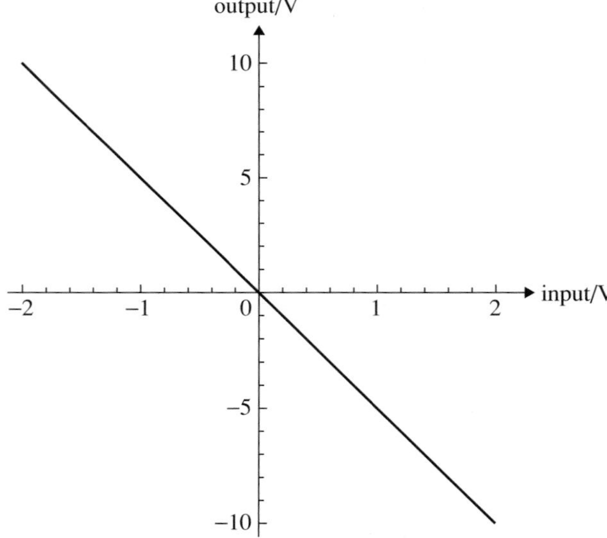

Figure F5.6 Output–input characteristic for the inverting amplifier of Example question 3.

Answer

From $V_0 = GV_{in}$, we see that the gain is the gradient of the graph and equals -5. (The negative sign indicates that this is an inverting amplifier.)

The non-inverting amplifier

Figure F5.7 shows an op-amp acting as a **non-inverting amplifier**. The two resistors R and R_F act as a potential divider (see Chapter 5.5) and so divide the potential difference V_0 in the ratio $R_F : R$. The voltage at point X is therefore $\frac{R}{R+R_F}V_0$ and hence this is also the voltage at Y, i.e. the input voltage at the inverting input.

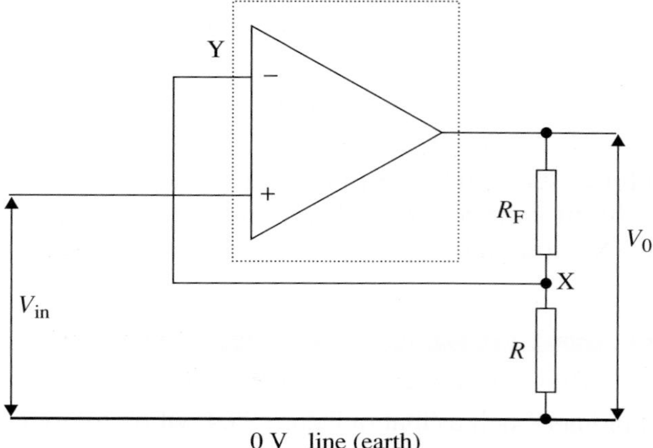

Figure F5.7 The non-inverting amplifier. The resistors R and R_F act as a potential divider.

To see this more precisely, we may argue as follows. Let the potential at X be V. Then the potential difference across R is V. The current I in R and R_F is the same and the total resistance of R and R_F is $R + R_F$. Then we get

$$V = IR \qquad \text{and} \qquad V_0 = I(R + R_F)$$

Eliminating the current gives

$$V = \frac{R}{R+R_F}V_0$$

So for the input voltages we now have

$$V_+ = V_{in} \qquad \text{and} \qquad V_- = \frac{R}{R+R_F}V_0$$

If the open loop gain is G_0 (we apply the definition of the open loop gain to the box in dotted lines), then $V_0 = G_0(V_+ - V_-)$, and so we get

$$V_0 = G_0\left(V_{in} - \frac{R}{R+R_F}V_0\right)$$

But by definition, $V_0 = GV_{in}$, where G is the closed loop gain, and so

$$GV_{in} = G_0\left(V_{in} - \frac{R}{R+R_F}GV_{in}\right)$$

Solving for G we find

$$G = \frac{G_0}{1 + \frac{R}{R+R_F}G_0}$$

In the denominator, $\frac{R}{R+R_F}G_0 \gg 1$ so we may neglect the term with just the 1. Then

$$\begin{aligned} G &= \frac{G_0}{1 + \frac{R}{R+R_F}G_0} \\ &\approx \frac{G_0}{\frac{R}{R+R_F}G_0} \\ &= \frac{R+R_F}{R} \\ &= 1 + \frac{R_F}{R} \end{aligned}$$

This is the **closed loop gain** of the non-inverting amplifier and so

$$G = 1 + \frac{R_F}{R} \qquad \text{closed loop non-inverting amplifier gain}$$

Example question

Q4

(a) Calculate the closed loop gain of the non-inverting amplifier shown in Figure F5.7 when $R = 10\,\text{k}\Omega$ and $R_F = 100\,\Omega$.

(b) The op-amp works with a power supply of $\pm 15\,\text{V}$. Draw and label the output–input characteristic for this non-inverting amplifier.

Answer

(a) From the equation above, the closed loop gain of this non-inverting amplifier is

$$\begin{aligned} G &= 1 + \frac{R_F}{R} \\ &= 1 + \frac{100}{10} \\ &= 11 \end{aligned}$$

(b) The output–input characteristic of the non-inverting amplifier is shown in Figure F5.8. The slope of the non-horizontal part of the graph is the closed loop gain.

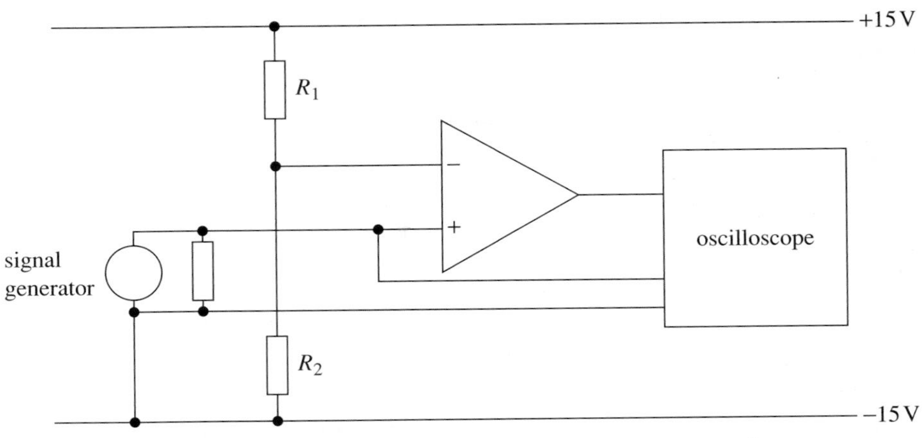

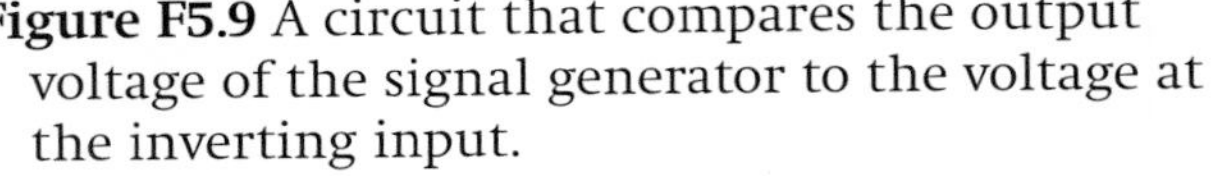
Figure F5.9 A circuit that compares the output voltage of the signal generator to the voltage at the inverting input.

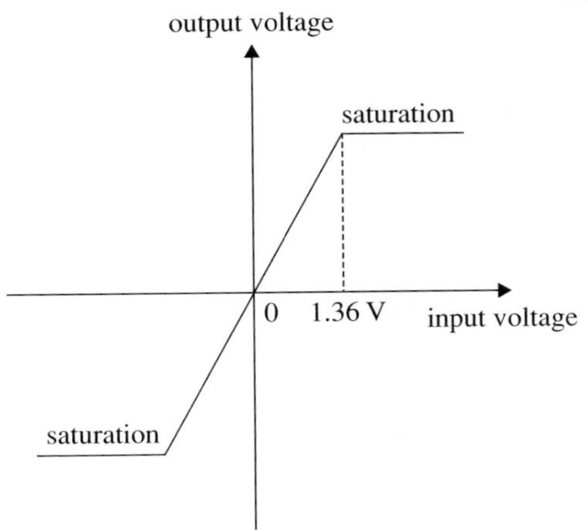

Figure F5.8 Output–input characteristic of the non-inverting amplifier of Example question 4.

Simple op-amp circuits

The op-amp is capable of comparing one voltage relative to another. Many simple circuits can be constructed that exploit this *comparator* property of the op-amp. Generally, the voltages to be compared are fed as inputs into the op-amp. Let's assume that we use a 15 V supply, so that the theoretical saturation voltage is $\pm 15\,\text{V}$. With the op-amp as in Example question 1, in the open loop state, we saw that the output will saturate when the absolute value of the difference between the two input voltages is greater than $\pm 15\,\mu\text{V}$. That is to say

$$V_0 = +15\,\text{V} \qquad V_+ - V_- > +15\,\mu\text{V}$$
$$V_0 = -15\,\text{V} \qquad V_+ - V_- < +15\,\mu\text{V}$$

In the circuit of Figure F5.9 the resistors R_1 and R_2 determine the voltage input to the inverting input of the op-amp. (If they are equal, then $V_- = 0$. To have a variable reference voltage, these two resistors can be replaced by a potentiometer.)

Assume that $V_- = 0$. The signal generator sends a sinusoidal signal to the non-inverting input. This means that V_+ varies as shown in Figure F5.10 (also shown in the figure is the reference voltage $V_- = 0$.

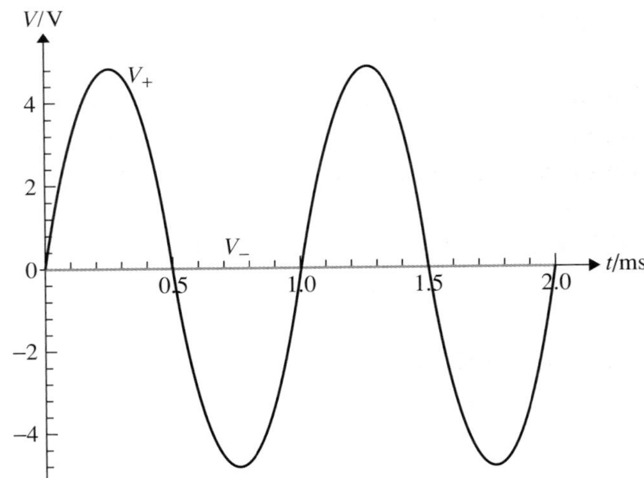

Figure F5.10 A sinusoidal input voltage V_+ that is to be compared to a zero reference voltage, $V_- = 0$.

The output fed into the oscilloscope is shown in Figure F5.11. In the first 0.5 ms the sinusoidal signal (V_+) is larger than the reference voltage ($V_- = 0$) by more than 15 μV, and so the output saturates at +15 V. In the next 0.5 ms signal V_+ is less than the reference voltage V_- by more than 15 μV, and so the output again saturates, but now at −15 V. This repeats again and again.

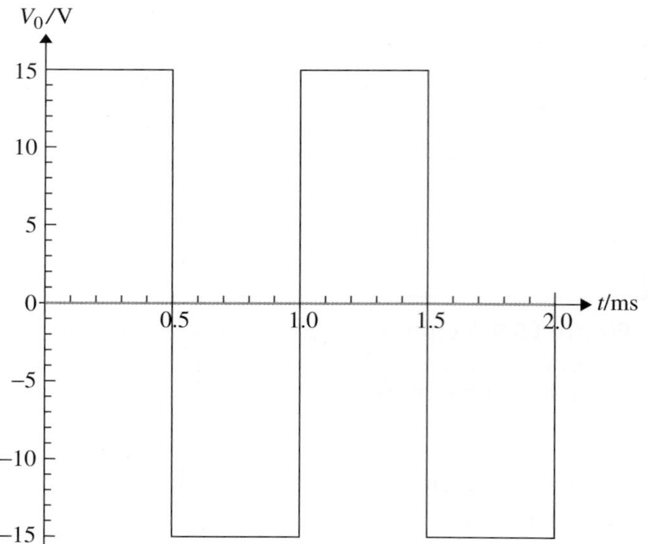

Figure F5.11 Oscilloscope reading for the circuit of Figure F5.9.

Consider now the circuit of Figure F5.12, where the output of the op-amp is connected to a buzzer that operates (is on) when the voltage across it is 30 V. There is a thermistor connected in the circuit. This is a resistor whose resistance decreases with increasing temperature. The voltage at the non-inverting input of the op-amp is determined by the voltage at point X, which can be taken as the reference voltage.

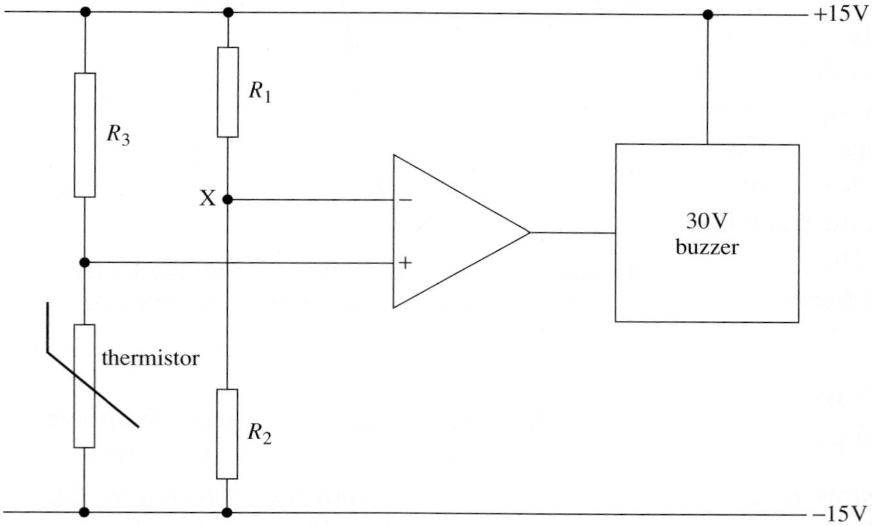

Figure F5.12 A circuit that activates the buzzer when the temperature increases above a predetermined level.

Assume that the resistors R_1 and R_2 are equal. Then the reference voltage at X is zero. When the thermistor is cold, its resistance is high, the voltage at the non-inverting input is high (positive) and so the output voltage saturates at +15 V. The potential difference across the buzzer is zero and so it is off. Now if the temperature increases, the voltage at the non-inverting input will decrease and will eventually become negative if the temperature rises sufficiently. The output voltage now will saturate at −15 V and the potential difference across the buzzer will become 30 V. The buzzer will then go off as a warning of the increased temperature. (A potentiometer can replace the resistors R_1 and R_2.)

In a variation of this circuit, we may replace the buzzer with two light-emitting diodes (LEDs), as in Figure F5.13. Depending on whether the output voltage saturates at a positive or a negative value, one or other of the LEDs will light. We may then use two different colour LEDs, say green and red, to indicate that the temperature is low or high.

Reshaping digital pulses – the Schmitt trigger

In the transmission of a digital signal, noise and other factors may contribute to a distortion of the signal. An example of such a distorted signal is shown in Figure F5.14.

Unlike analogue signals, however, a digital signal can easily be regenerated. This may be done with a device known as the **Schmitt trigger**. This device has an input–output characteristic that can be described by the graph of Figure F5.15. The graph shows the variation with input voltage of the output voltage of the device.

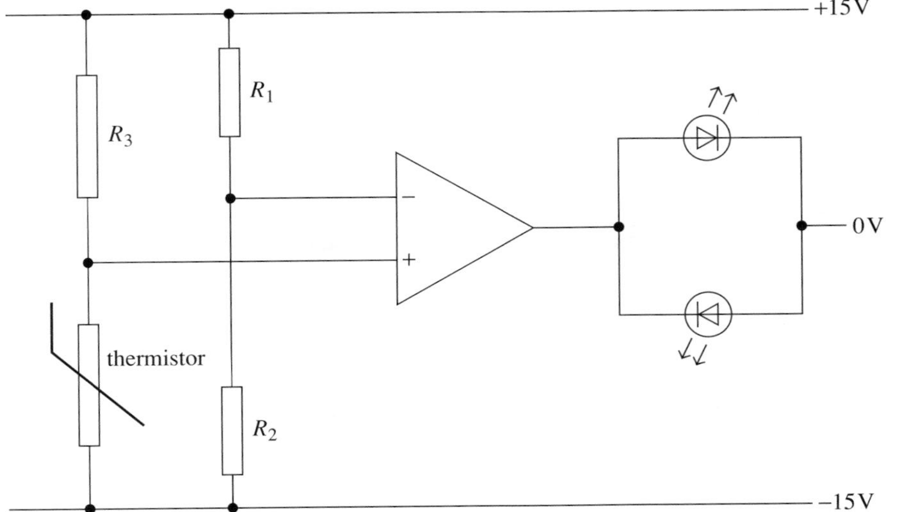

Figure F5.13 A variation of the previous circuit using LEDs.

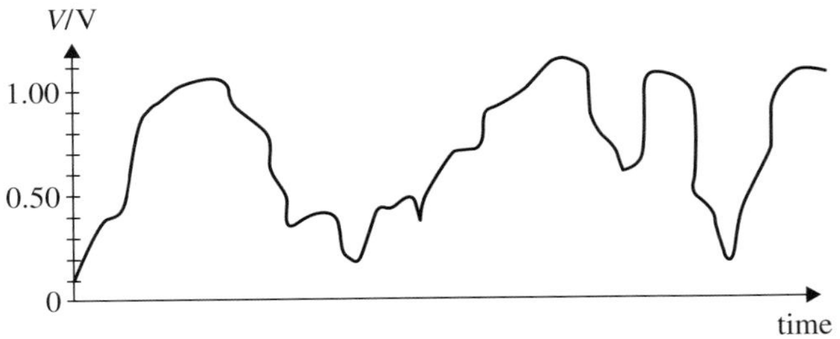

Figure F5.14 A very corrupt digital signal that must be reshaped.

For zero input voltage, the output is $-V_0$. As the input voltage increases, the output remains at $-V_0$ (follow the lower horizontal line) until the input reaches the threshold voltage V_2. The output then jumps abruptly to the value $+V_0$. If now the input signal decreases, the output stays at $+V_0$ until the lower threshold V_1 is reached, at which the output now jumps abruptly to $-V_0$. The output is thus determined by the two threshold voltages V_1 and V_2.

The Schmitt trigger therefore works as a standard comparator (it compares the input voltage to a reference value) but also has the behaviour of Figure F5.15, i.e. the reference value is different when the input is increasing (V_2) from when it is decreasing (V_1).

As an example, consider values $V_1 = 0.40$ V, $V_2 = 0.75$ V and $V_0 = 3.0$ V. Assume that the signal of Figure F5.14 is the input signal to the Schmitt trigger. The signal starts very low and the Schmitt trigger output will be $-V_0 = -3.0$ V. The output will remain at -3.0 V until the signal has a value just higher than the *upper* level of the trigger (here taken to be $V_2 = 0.75$ V). The output will then stay constant at a high value ($V_0 = +3.0$ V) until the signal falls below the lower level of the trigger (here taken to be $V_1 = 0.40$ V), at which point the output becomes -3.0 V again. This would result in the graph of Figure F5.16.

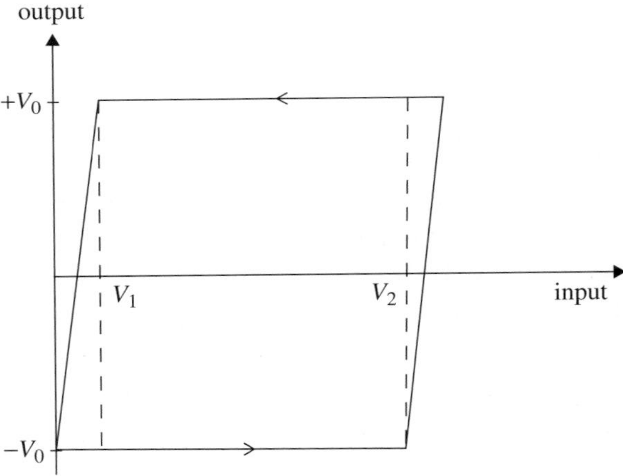

Figure F5.15 Input–output characteristic of the Schmitt trigger.

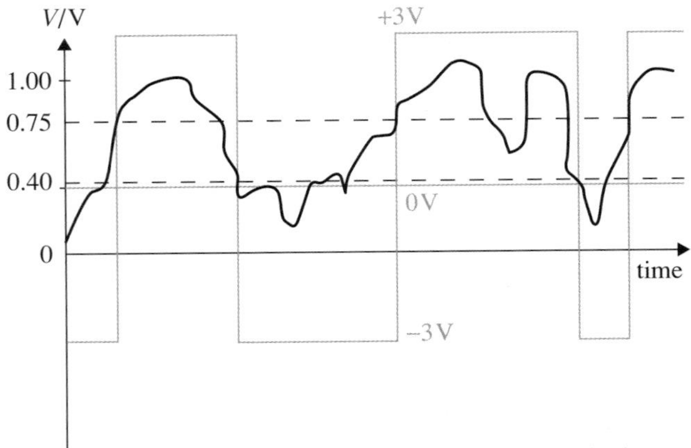

Figure F5.16 Regeneration of the digital signal. Note that the scale for the regenerated signal (in grey) is different from that for the original.

The Schmitt trigger is built around op-amps and uses the comparator properties of the op-amp. In the circuit of Figure F5.17 with $R_1 = 15\,\text{k}\Omega$, $R_2 = 10\,\text{k}\Omega$, $R_3 = 100\,\text{k}\Omega$ and a reference voltage of 3.0 V, the thresholds are 0.75 V and 0.40 V (see below).

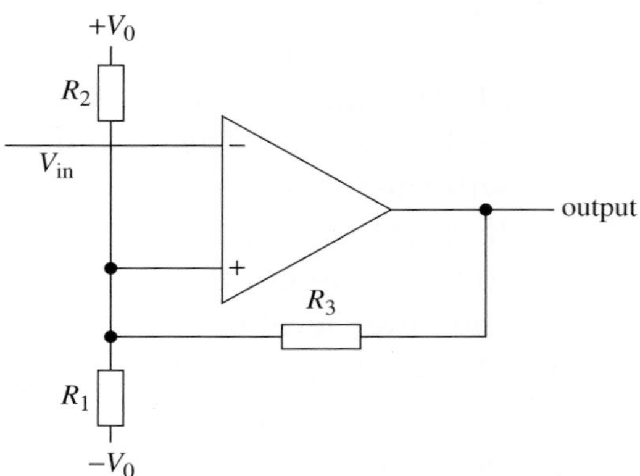

Figure F5.17 The op-amp as a Schmitt trigger.

Let us now calculate the threshold voltages. Consider first the case in which the input is less than the voltage at the non-inverting input, V_+. The output will then be V_0. The potential difference across resistor R_2 is $V_0 - V_+$. The current through R_2 is $I_2 = \frac{V_0 - V_+}{R_2}$. Similarly,the potential difference across R_3 is $V_0 - V_+$ and the current through R_3 is $I_3 = \frac{V_0 - V_+}{R_3}$. Finally, the potential difference across R_1 is $V_+ + V_0$ and the current through R_1 is $I_1 = \frac{V_+ + V_0}{R_1}$. The three currents are related by

$$I_1 = I_2 + I_3$$

which implies that

$$\frac{V_+ + V_0}{R_1} = \frac{V_0 - V_+}{R_2} + \frac{V_0 - V_+}{R_3}$$

Solving for the voltage V_+ at the non-inverting input we get the value for the high threshold

$$V_+ = V_0 \frac{R_1R_2 + R_3R_1 - R_2R_3}{R_1R_2 + R_2R_3 + R_3R_1} \quad \text{high threshold}$$

Working similarly we can find the value for the low threshold

$$V_+ = V_0 \frac{R_3R_1 - R_1R_2 - R_2R_3}{R_1R_2 + R_2R_3 + R_3R_1} \quad \text{low threshold}$$

With $R_1 = 15\,\text{k}\Omega, R_2 = 10\,\text{k}\Omega$, $R_3 = 100\,\text{k}\Omega$ and a reference (output) voltage of $V_0 = 1.0$ V, we get two possible values for V_+, 0.40 V and 0.75 V, for output voltages $V_0 = \pm 3.0$ V.

? QUESTIONS

1 The open loop gain of an op-amp is 10^5 and the supply voltage varies from -15 V to $+15$ V. Calculate the output voltage when the input voltage ($V_+ - V_-$) is: (a) 250 μV, (b) 120 μV, (c) -80 μV, and (d) -340 μV.

2 An op-amp operates with a supply voltage of ± 9.0 V and has an open loop gain of 10^5.

(a) State what is meant by *open loop gain* and *saturation*.

(b) The output voltage is a linear function of the input voltage difference only for a range of voltage differences. Calculate this range.

3 Calculate the theoretical gain of the amplifier circuit in Figure F5.18.

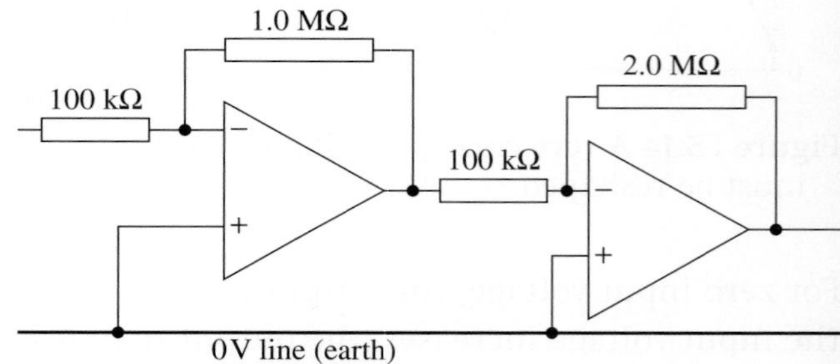

Figure F5.18 For question 3.

4 Show that an alternative drawing of the non-inverting amplifier is given by the diagram in Figure F5.19.

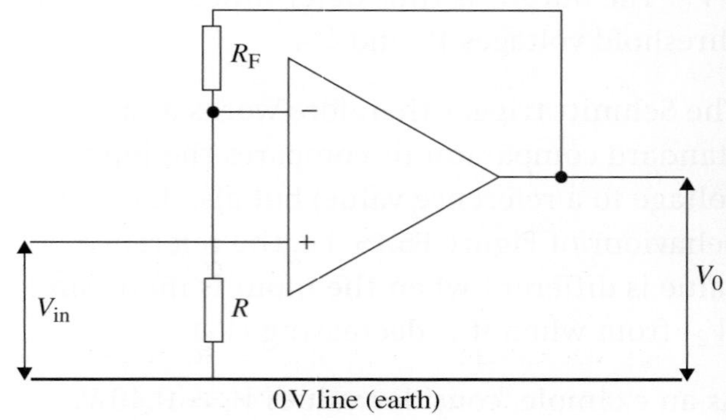

Figure F5.19 For question 4.

5 Compare the circuit of the previous problem (Figure F5.19) with the circuit in Figure F5.20.

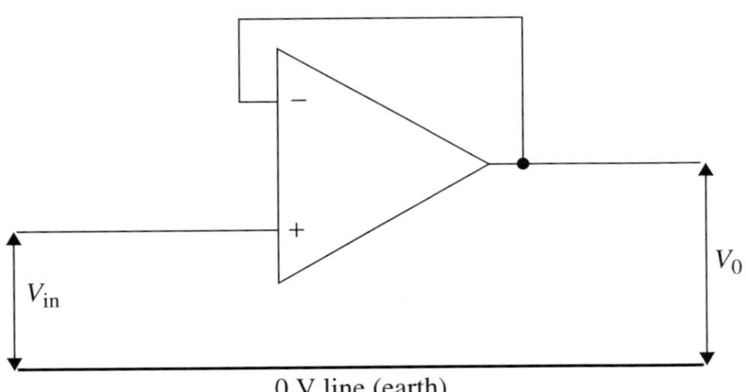

Figure F5.20 For question 5.

(a) What values of R and R_F are needed to convert Figure F5.19 to Figure F5.20?
(b) Calculate the gain of the circuit in Figure F5.20.
(c) Suggest a use of this circuit.

6 (a) In the circuit in Figure F5.21, both resistors have the value 1.0 kΩ. What is the voltage across resistor R_2?

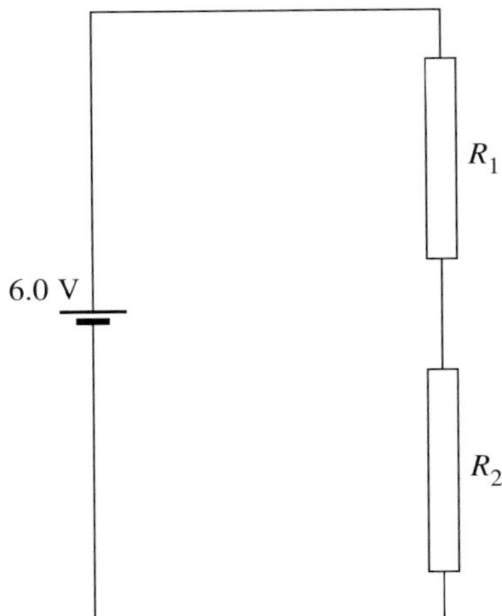

Figure F5.21 For question 6.

(b) A voltmeter of resistance 1.0 kΩ is connected across resistor R_2. What will be the reading of the voltmeter? Comment on your answer.
(c) The circuit is now changed to that in Figure F5.22. What is the reading of the voltmeter now?

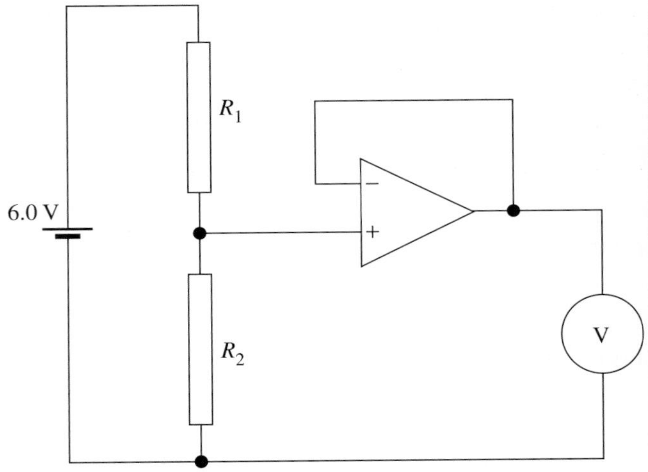

Figure F5.22 For question 6.

7 The diagram in Figure F5.23 shows an ideal op-amp. The point V is referred to as a virtual earth.

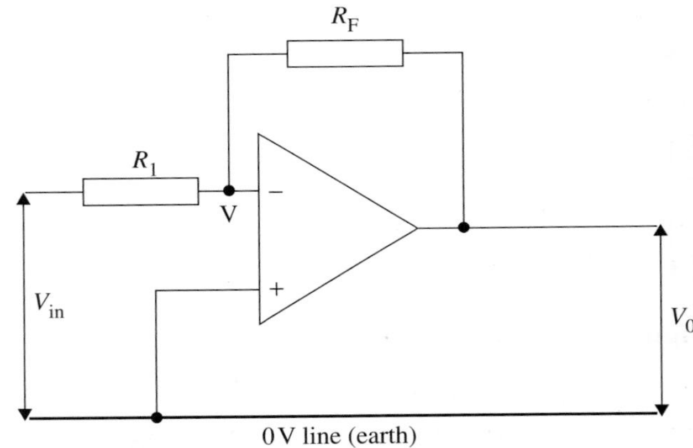

Figure F5.23 For question 7.

(a) Explain what is meant by the term *virtual earth*.
(b) Derive an expression for the voltage gain of this amplifier.
(c) The resistor R_F is replaced by another device. The current through the device is related to the potential difference across it by $I = I_0 e^{-kV}$. Deduce that

$$V_O = \frac{1}{k}\ln\left(\frac{V_{in}}{I_0 R_1}\right)$$

(d) Suggest one advantage of this inverting amplifier over the conventional one discussed in the text.

8 Explain how the circuit shown in Figure F5.24 can be used to measure the amount of charge on the capacitor C.

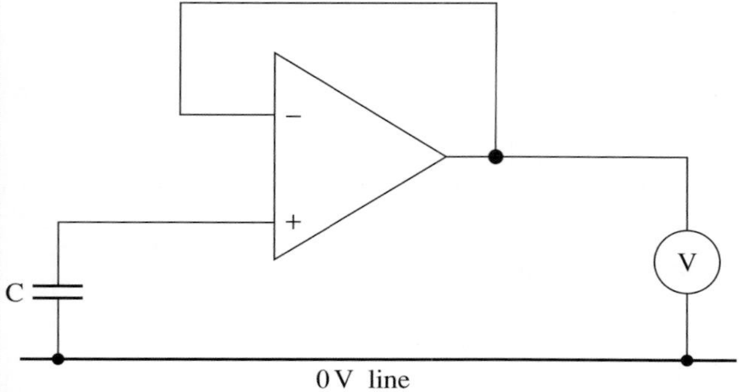

Figure F5.24 For question 8.

9 A signal of 4.0 mV is input in the circuit shown in Figure F5.25. The op-amp is assumed to be ideal.

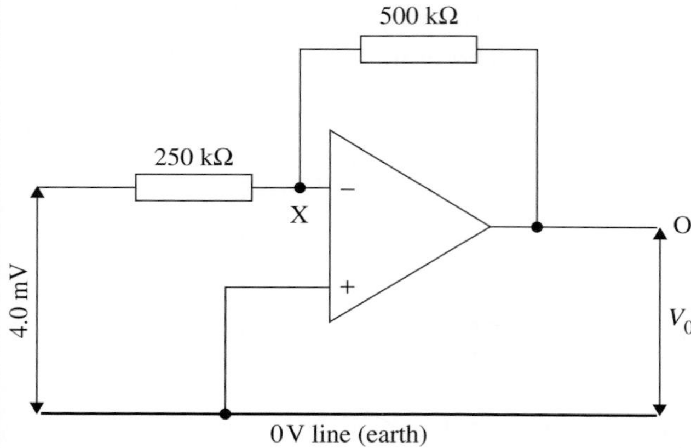

Figure F5.25 For question 9.

(a) State the voltage at X.

(b) Calculate the current in the 250 kΩ resistor.

(c) Calculate the output voltage at O.

10 Consider the circuit in Figure F5.26. The op-amp output voltage saturates at ±15 V.

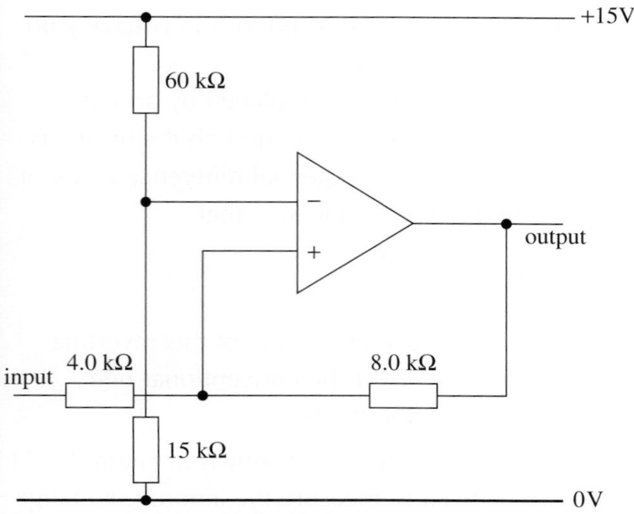

Figure F5.26 For question 10.

(a) Calculate the voltage at the inverting input of the op-amp.

(b) The input signal is 6.0 V and the output voltage is +15 V. What is the smallest input voltage change that will make the output voltage saturate at −15 V?

11 The circuit in Figure F5.27 contains a diode, which only allows the flow of current in one direction ('down' in this circuit). A positive voltage is fed into the non-inverting input of the op-amp.

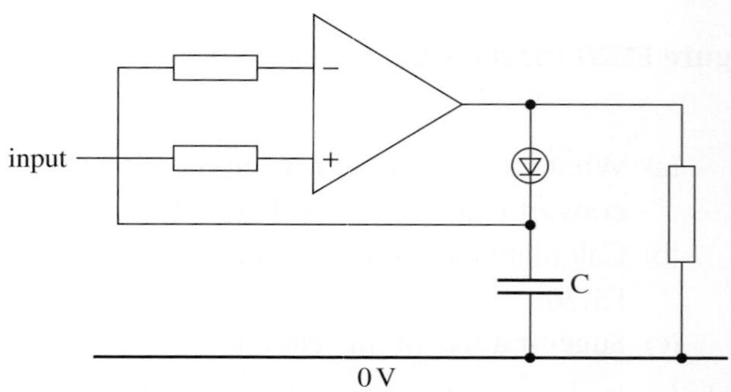

Figure F5.27 For question 11.

The input voltage varies with time according to the graph of Figure F5.28. Explain why the potential difference across the capacitor after 1 s will be equal to the *maximum* value of the applied input voltage.

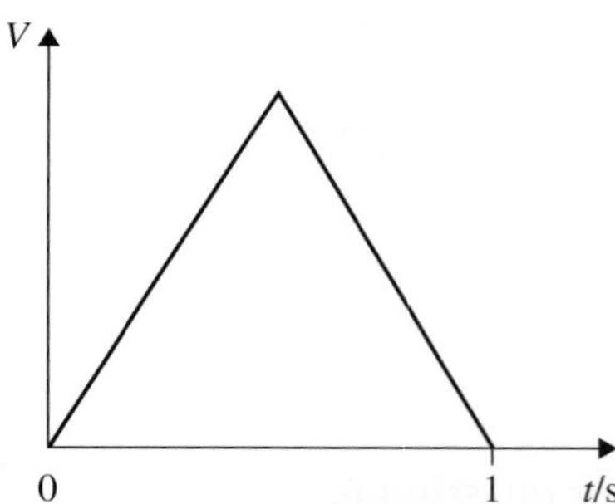

Figure F5.28 For question 11.

12 In the circuit in Figure F5.29, $R = 16\,\text{k}\Omega$, $R_F = 32\,\text{k}\Omega$ and the op-amp operates with a power supply voltage ranging from −15 V to +15 V.

(a) Calculate the output voltage when the input voltage is +4.0 V.

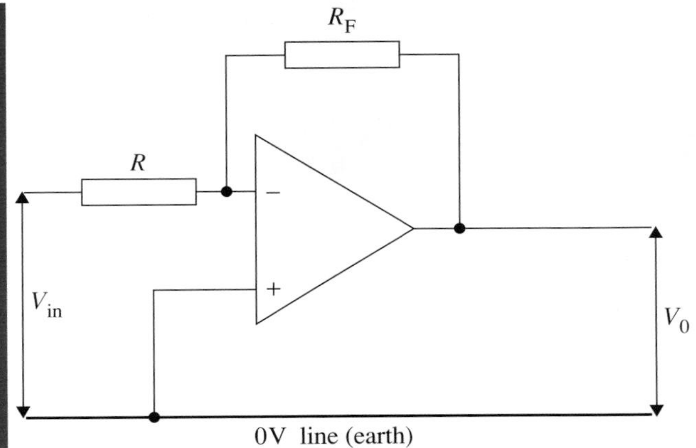

Figure F5.29 For question 12.

(b) The input voltage is replaced by the signal shown in Figure F5.30. Draw a sketch graph to show the variation with time of the output signal.

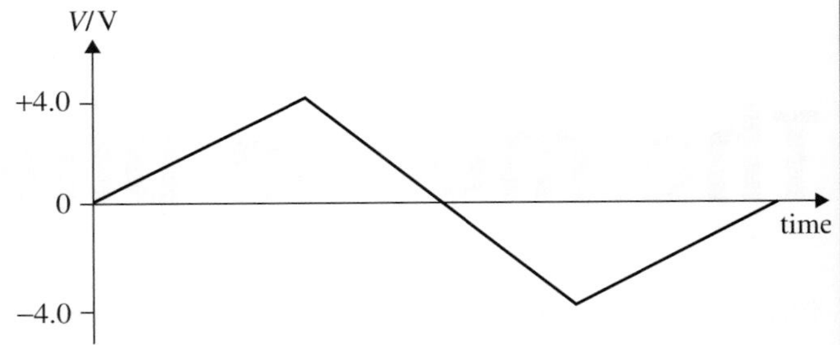

Figure F5.30 For question 12.

(c) What changes, if any, would come about in your answer to part (b) if the op-amp operated with a ±6.0 V power supply?

13 Outline the use of a Schmitt trigger in reshaping a digital signal.

The mobile phone system

This chapter is a very brief introduction to the mobile phone system. It discusses the main features of the structure of the system, namely the cellular organization of the base stations and the cellular exchange.

Objectives

By the end of this chapter you should be able to:

- state the role of the *cellular exchange* and *base stations* in the mobile phone system;
- understand that different frequencies are allocated to neighbouring *cells* to avoid overlap in calls.

Mobile phones have become an integral part of life in many parts of the world. The concept of the mobile phone system was developed by engineers at Bell Laboratories, in the USA, in 1947. The first mobile phone system was established in the Nordic countries in the early 1980s. Modern mobile phone systems are digital, which makes communications secure and difficult to tap into, unlike the early analogue systems.

The main ingredients of the mobile phone system include the **mobile phones** themselves, **base stations** and the **cellular exchange**. A mobile phone has the dual function of a receiver and a transmitter of radio waves. The frequencies used in modern digital systems are a few gigahertz (GHz). The wavelength associated with a radio wave of frequency 1 GHz is

$$\begin{aligned}\lambda &= \frac{c}{f}\\ &= \frac{3\times 10^8}{1\times 10^9}\\ &= 0.3\,\text{m}\end{aligned}$$

The handset (the mobile phone), when turned on, sends a radio signal that registers its presence to the nearest base station. Like the phone itself, the base station is a transmitter and a receiver of radio waves. The base station is located at the centre of a **cell**, an area from within which the base station can receive and transmit radio signals. The linear dimension of a cell varies from 0.5 km (in densely populated urban environments) up to 30 km in hill-free countryside. The base station is connected via cables to the cellular exchange, which controls the operation of very many base stations.

The idea is that very many adjacent cells provide coverage over a large geographical area. The shape of each cell is circular, since it contains an omnidirectional aerial (that of the base station) at its centre. The base stations are arranged in an approximately hexagonal array. In this way, a given geographical area can be covered without 'gaps'. This is shown in Figure F6.1. The cells are shown as hexagonal rather than circular. This is a convention to show a fully covered area without overlapping circles.

The cellular exchange offers entry into the regular (fixed) telephone system network. Consider a phone call to a fixed telephone number made from a mobile phone. The signal

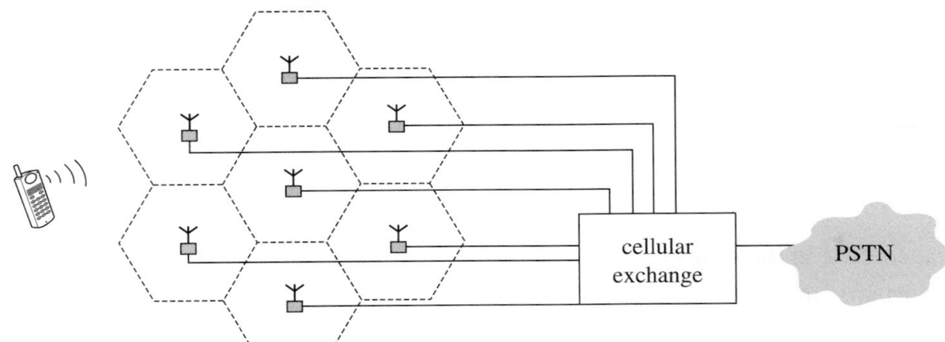

Figure F6.1 Base stations connected to a cellular exchange that gives access to the public switched telephone network (PSTN).

will leave the mobile phone and will be received by the base station in the cell where the mobile phone is located. From the base station it will travel to the cellular exchange, and from there to the destination fixed telephone number. If the mobile phone moves during the call, from one cell to another, the cellular exchange will automatically reroute the phone call to the base station at the centre of the new cell. The range of the base station is essentially equal to the linear dimension of the cell.

A main function of the cellular exchange is to allocate a range of frequencies to each cell, with neighbouring cells being allocated different frequency ranges in order to avoid overlap and interference between calls.

The base station within the cell will then select a frequency for a particular call. The same frequency can be used for other calls at the same time using the time division multiplexing technique. The frequencies emitted are different from those received and are usually separated by 50 MHz.

Mobile phones offer the user the ability to send text messages, pictures, video and music, and allow access to electronic mail and the internet, making them an unusually powerful tool of communication.

QUESTIONS

1 State one advantage and one disadvantage in making the cell radius very large, say 100 km.

2 Suggest a reason why mobile phone antennas are small.

3 Base stations have a power output that is small. Consider a power output of 5.0 W. Calculate the intensity of the radiation (power per unit area) a distance of 3.0 km from the base station.

4 The mobile phone, like base stations, emits at low power (less than 1 W today compared to about 3 W in the old analogue phones). State and explain one advantage of low-power transmissions, other than health considerations.

5 Describe the role of the cellular exchange in mobile phone communications.

6 The analogue signal that is input to a mobile phone is sampled 8000 times a second, and the digital signal created by the analogue-to-digital converter is an eight-bit word.
(a) Calculate the bit rate.
(b) The digital signal is actually compressed so that the bit rate is reduced to about 13 kbit s^{-1}. State one effect of this compression on the quality of the sound transmitted.

7 The base station transmission rate on one particular carrier frequency is about 270 kbit s^{-1} and the signal emitted by a mobile phone has transmission rate of 13 kbit s^{-1}. How many different calls can be multiplexed on the same carrier?

8 Based on your study of the earlier chapters, suggest a block diagram showing the main components of a mobile phone outlining the function of each part you include.

Light

This chapter describes Michelson's experiment to measure the speed of light, which is one of the most important physical constants. The various members of the large family of electromagnetic waves are introduced and their properties described. The dependence of the index of refraction on wavelength (the phenomenon of dispersion) is discussed and the chapter closes with a discussion of the laser and its applications.

Objectives

By the end of this chapter you should be able to:

- describe one experiment that measures the *speed of light*;
- understand the *nature of an electromagnetic wave* and how it is produced;
- name the *main members of the electromagnetic family of waves*;
- state the meaning of the term *dispersion* and calculate the *speed of light* from the *index of refraction* of the medium, $n = \frac{c_{vac}}{c_{med}}$;
- describe what the *laser* is and list a few of its uses;
- state the meaning of the terms *monochromatic* and *coherent*.

The speed of light

One of the most important physical constants is the speed of light in a vacuum. This is the limiting speed for all material objects according to Einstein's theory of relativity. A very early attempt to measure the speed of light was made by Galileo in 1600. A lantern was uncovered at a predetermined time and an observer some distance away was supposed to record the time that he first saw the lantern's light. Dividing his distance from the lantern by the time he recorded would give the speed of light. Obviously the experiment failed because the time taken by light to cover the known distance was so small that it could not be measured. The first measurement of the speed of light was made by the Danish astronomer Ole Roemer in 1676, who devised an ingenious method based on observations of eclipses of one of the moons of Jupiter. Roemer was thus the first to show that the speed of light is finite.

A very accurate terrestrial method to measure c was developed by the American physicist Albert Michelson in 1926. Michelson used a rotating octagonal prism whose rate of rotation could be very accurately controlled. A ray of light from a very strong source is reflected off face F_1 of the prism (see Figure G1.1) and allowed to move a very large distance (about 35 km) to a spherical mirror, from which it is reflected back to the prism. A final reflection off face F_2 of the prism brings the light into an observing telescope. If the prism begins to rotate, the light in the telescope disappears, since the prism has the wrong orientation relative to the rays from the mirror. As the speed of rotation is increased, light will again become visible in the telescope. This is because, in the time it has taken light to cover the distance from the prism to the spherical mirror and back, the prism has turned by exactly one-eighth of a revolution.

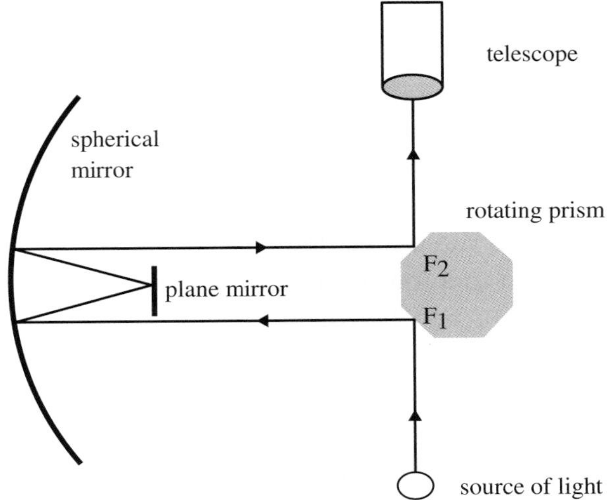

Figure G1.1 A simplified diagram of the arrangement used by Michelson to measure the speed of light. The distance of the prism to the spherical mirror was about 35 km so the diagram is very much out of scale.

Michelson saw light in the telescope with the prism rotating at a rate of 530 revolutions per second. Thus, he calculated a speed of light (in air) to be

$$c = \frac{2 \times 35}{(1/8) \times (1/530)} \frac{\text{km}}{\text{s}} = 2.97 \times 10^8 \text{ m s}^{-1}$$

Electromagnetic waves

There exists a very large family of waves called electromagnetic waves. This family has the following characteristics:

- they can travel in a vacuum;
- they travel at a speed of 3×10^8 m s^{-1} in a vacuum – the speed of light;
- they are transverse waves.

The displacement in electromagnetic waves is actually a pair of quantities: an electric and a magnetic field at right angles to each other, which vary with position and time. Both fields are at right angles to the direction of propagation of the wave, which makes electromagnetic waves *transverse*. In Figure G1.2 the electric field oscillates in the z–y plane and the magnetic field in the x–y plane. The direction of propagation is along the y

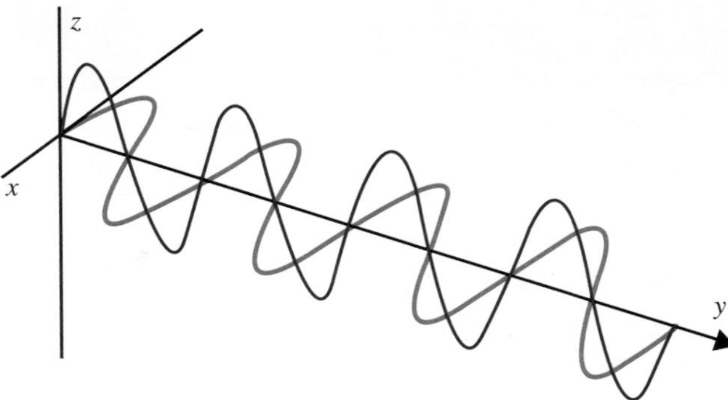

Figure G1.2 An electromagnetic wave has an electric and a magnetic field at right angles to each other and to the direction of motion of the wave.

direction (normal to both fields). As long as the plane along which the electric field oscillates stays the same, the wave is called plane *polarized*.

The theoretical prediction of electromagnetic waves was the crowning achievement of the Scottish theoretical physicist James Clerk Maxwell in 1867. The experimental verification of Maxwell's ideas came from the German physicist Heinrich Hertz in 1887, eight years after Maxwell's death.

The various members of this family of waves are distinguished by wavelength or frequency as well as their method of production. Electromagnetic waves include light, gamma and X-rays, ultraviolet and infrared light, microwaves, TV and radio waves. The wavelengths range from 10^{-14} m for very energetic gamma rays to 10^4 m for radio waves. Ordinary visible light occupies a small window in the electromagnetic spectrum: violet light at 400 nm (7.5×10^{15} Hz) to red light at 700 nm (4.3×10^{14} Hz) – see Table G1.1.

The entire electromagnetic spectrum is shown in Figure G1.3. The frequency increases as we move to the right. The photon energy increases from about 10^{-10} eV for a radio wave photon to 10^8 eV for an energetic gamma ray. This means that the photon, which represents the particle nature of light, becomes more dominant as we move toward the right in Figure G1.3.

Wavelength range/nm (= 10^{-9} m)	Frequency/ THz (= 10^{12} Hz)	Colour
390–455	659–769	Violet
455–492	610–659	Blue
492–577	520–610	Green
577–597	503–520	Yellow
597–622	482–503	Orange
622–780	384–482	Red

Table G1.1 Wavelengths and frequencies of visible light.

▶ Electromagnetic waves are produced when:

- an electric charge is accelerated;

or

- molecules, atoms or atomic nuclei make transitions to lower energy states.

Radio waves

These were the waves Hertz first observed. They are generally produced in various kinds of electrical circuits in which electrons are forced to accelerate. The emission antennas of radio and TV stations are typical examples of accelerated electron motion followed by radio wave emission.

Microwaves

Microwaves are now used extensively in communication, remote control devices and heating and cooking food. They are produced in molecular transitions. The energy associated with the rotational and vibrational motion of a molecule is quantized and the molecule finds itself in one of a number of energy levels, just as the electron's energy in a hydrogen atom is quantized, giving rise to molecular energy levels. When the molecule makes a transition from a high to a lower energy level, microwaves may be produced. Hydrogen gas emits microwave radiation with a wavelength of 21 cm – this has been detected from sources inside our galaxy, greatly increasing our knowledge of galactic structure. Microwave radiation with a wavelength of about 1 mm fills space and is a remnant of the Big Bang that created the universe.

Infrared

Just below the optical part of the spectrum (in frequency) is infrared (IR) radiation, first detected by Sir William Herschel in 1800. Commonly associated with this radiation is thermal radiation – the electromagnetic waves emitted by objects up to temperatures of order 10^4 K. IR radiation is emitted by human bodies, hot pieces of coal, light-bulb filaments and the sun. Some nocturnal hunting animals, such as pit viper snakes, are sensitive to IR radiation. IR radiation is produced in molecular transitions.

Light

Occupying a tiny window in the huge electromagnetic spectrum is the all-important visible light. The wavelengths range from (very

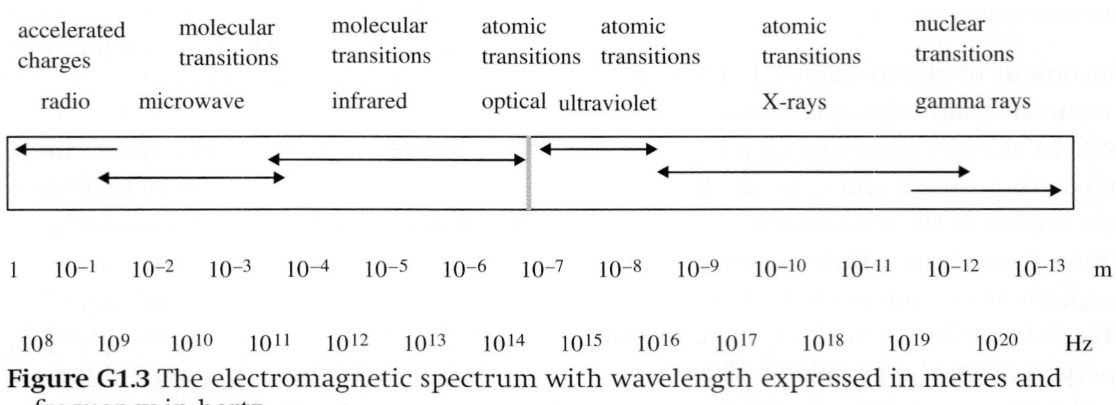

Figure G1.3 The electromagnetic spectrum with wavelength expressed in metres and frequency in hertz.

roughly) 400 nm for violet light to about 700 nm for red. Light is produced in atomic transitions (for example in a discharge tube) or by accelerated electric charges (for example in the hot filament of a lamp where electrons are accelerated in constant collisions). The human eye is a detector of optical light and can record the arrival of as few as just 10 photons of light.

Ultraviolet

Ultraviolet (UV) radiation was discovered by Johann Ritter in 1801. UV radiation is very energetic and can ionize air (producing the ionosphere). UV radiation is harmful but most UV rays from the sun are absorbed by ozone (O_3) in the atmosphere. UV radiation is produced in atomic transitions.

X-rays

These were discovered by Wilhelm Conrad Röntgen in 1895. They are produced when electrons are rapidly decelerated as they collide with atoms (*Bremsstrahlung*), or when electrons make transitions from very excited states down to the ground state in high atomic number elements. They are very penetrating and have important applications in medicine. X-rays have been observed from galaxies, stars and black holes, greatly increasing our understanding of the universe by complementing knowledge derived from optical observations.

Gamma rays

These are the most energetic members of the electromagnetic spectrum with wavelengths of 10^{-12} m or less. They are produced when nuclei make transitions to lower nuclear energy levels or when particles annihilate in collisions with their antiparticles.

Properties of EM waves

Dispersion

When a beam of white light falls on a triangular prism, the colours of the rainbow will emerge from the other side of the prism (see Figure G1.4). This is because the index of refraction of glass actually depends on the wavelength of light entering the glass. This is the phenomenon of dispersion. In fact, the index of refraction is slightly smaller for red light than it is for blue. This means that red light will be bent by a smaller amount than blue and so the beam that emerges splits into the colours of the rainbow. If the various colours are recombined, white light is again obtained. The graph in Figure G1.4 shows the variation with wavelength of the refractive index for two substances: acrylic plastic and flint glass. In both cases the refractive index is lower for red wavelengths.

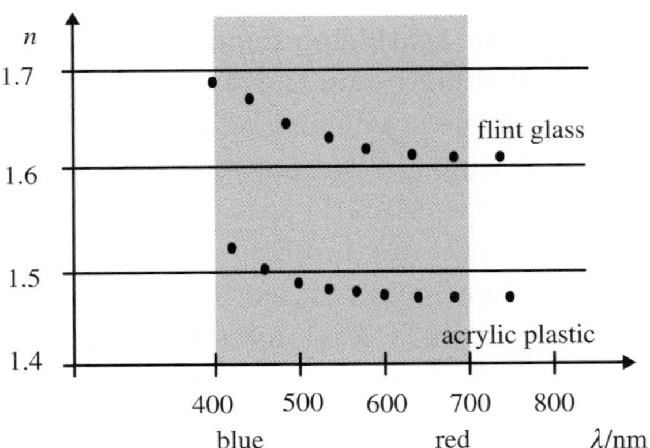

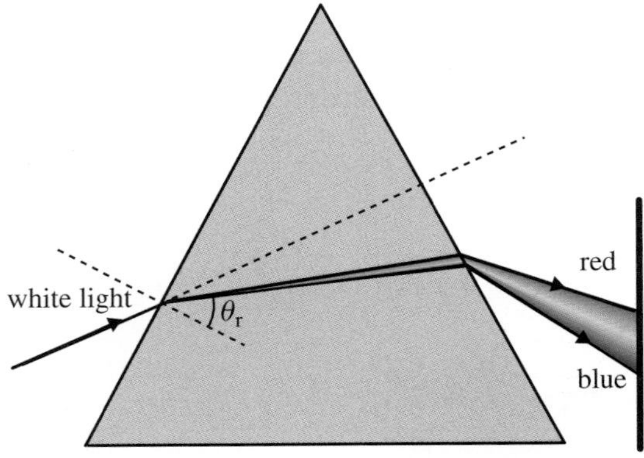

Figure G1.4 The index of refraction depends on wavelength and is smaller for red light. White light entering a prism splits into the colours of the rainbow in a phenomenon known as dispersion. The index of refraction for red light is smaller than that for blue and so a red ray has a larger angle of refraction θ_r.

Scattering of light

When electromagnetic radiation is travelling through a material medium, the electric field associated with the radiation will force electric charges (e.g. electrons) in the molecules of the medium to oscillate. These oscillating electric charges produce electromagnetic radiation in all directions. We call this phenomenon **scattering** of radiation.

▶ *Scattering* of electromagnetic radiation by matter is a general phenomenon involving the interaction of radiation with molecules of matter. Scattering results in the radiation being redirected without being altered in any other way.

In particular, light from the sun will scatter in the atmosphere, as shown in Figure G1.5. The details of the scattering depend on many factors, one of them being the size of the particles doing the scattering relative to the wavelength of light, λ. The scattering of light by particles that are small compared to the wavelength of light (i.e. molecules of the gases in the atmosphere) was studied long ago by Lord Rayleigh, in 1871. Rayleigh's law states that the amount of scattering is proportional to the inverse fourth power of the wavelength $\left(\propto \frac{1}{\lambda^4}\right)$. This means that sunlight entering the atmosphere will have its blue components scattered much more than other wavelengths because blue light has shorter wavelength than the other colours. Therefore, if one looks at the sky in a direction other than that of the incident light (i.e. away from the sun), the short wavelengths (i.e. blue) scatter the most, giving the sky its characteristic blue colour. (In the absence of an atmosphere, the sky would look black.) During sunsets and sunrises, the sun is low in the atmosphere, and so the light that reaches an observer is the one that is *least* scattered, i.e. red.

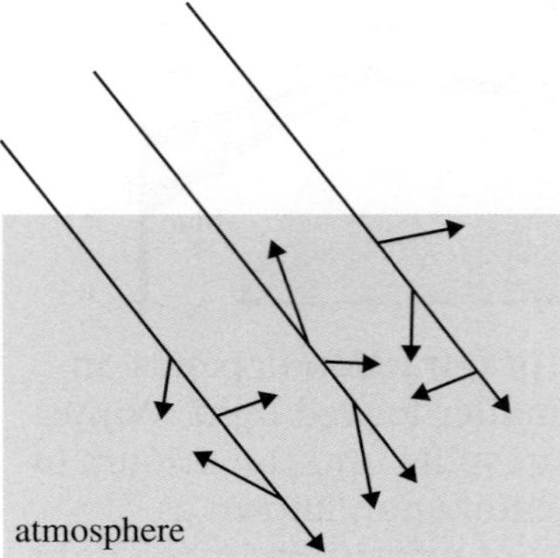

Figure G1.5 Scattering of sunlight in the atmosphere.

However, if the size of the particles scattering light is larger than the wavelength of light, then colours other than blue are dominant in scattering. This partly explains the reddish colour of the sky over deserts where the atmosphere contains large dust particles. (The explosion of the volcano on Krakatoa in 1883 produced large quantities of volcanic ash that stayed in the atmosphere for years, with reports of unusual colours for the sun, the moon, sunrises and sunsets.)

Absorption

If the energy of the photons in the electromagnetic radiation matches the energy difference between energy levels of the molecules of the matter, then those photons will be absorbed and will cause the excitation of the molecules to higher energy states. As we have discussed in Chapter 7.2 on the greenhouse effect, gases such as water vapour, carbon dioxide and methane have energy levels that differ in energy by amounts comparable to infrared photon energies. This means that infrared radiation gets absorbed by these gases, leading to the 'greenhouse effect' and increased global temperatures. Similarly, ozone, while capable of absorbing infrared radiation (and is therefore a greenhouse gas), also absorbs harmful ultraviolet radiation, and so forms a protective layer in the atmosphere.

Transmission

Finally, we have the phenomenon of transmission of electromagnetic radiation from one medium into another. As we have seen, when radiation is incident on the boundary between two different media, part of the radiation will be reflected and part will be refracted, i.e. transmitted into the second medium.

The laser

Physicists for a long time searched for powerful yet concentrated, coherent sources of light over very narrow ranges of frequency (i.e. monochromatic). The emission of light from the hot filament of an ordinary light bulb is incoherent in the sense that the emissions of photons from different atoms in the filament are totally uncorrelated. We have no control over the emission times of photons from the various atoms. One way to make the source of radiation more coherent is to reduce the area from which radiation is being emitted. Reducing the area, though, in general means that the intensity of the light is also reduced. For example, the sun emits an enormous amount of energy per second, about 3.9×10^{26} W from its entire surface area, but this energy is emitted over all frequencies. The power radiated within 1 MHz around a wavelength of 500 nm (the wavelength at which most of the sun's energy is emitted) is only 7.5×10^{-2} Wm^{-2}. Making the area 1 mm^2 means that the radiated power is an insignificant 7.5×10^{-8} W. The laser is the answer to this problem. The first laser was constructed by Theodore H. Maiman in 1960 following earlier work in the microwave region by Charles Townes in the USA and Aleksandr Prokhorov and Nikolai Basov in the USSR. The word laser is an acronym and stands for **L**ight **A**mplification by **S**timulated **E**mission of **R**adiation.

▶ The laser is a source of very intense, very directional, monochromatic, coherent radiation.

Figure G1.6 shows a cross-section of a laser beam. All points in the cross-section have the same phase.

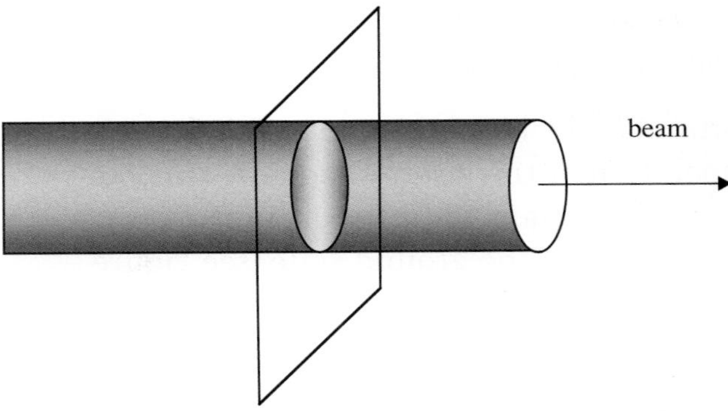

Figure G1.6 The meaning of coherent light: points on the same vertical plane through a laser beam have the same phase. The phase difference between widely separated points on the beam stays the same as time goes on.

The production of laser light

We know from atomic physics that, once an electron finds itself in an excited state, it will quickly return to a lower energy state, emitting one photon as it does so. The energy of the emitted photon is equal to the difference in energy between the levels involved in the transition. This emission of radiation from atoms is called *spontaneous* emission. If we imagine very many electrons performing the same transition in very many different atoms, we will get very many photons emitted that will have just one thing in common, their energy. They will differ in practically everything else; in particular, they will be moving in different directions, they will have different polarizations, and they will not be in phase.

There is another way to get photons emitted from atoms, and this is called *stimulated* emission. Imagine that an electron is in an excited state. (Assume, for simplicity, that this is the first excited state above the ground state, and that the energy of this state is E above the ground-state energy.) A photon of energy E incident on the electron will *stimulate*, i.e. force, the photon to make the transition to the ground state. In this way, we have two photons, the one incident on the electron and the one emitted in the transition. These two photons have the same energy, of course, but also move in the same direction *and* have the same phase.

Stimulated emission is the basis of the operation of the laser. To achieve this, we must have many more atoms in the excited state than in the ground state (see Figure G1.7). In the diagram, a line indicates an

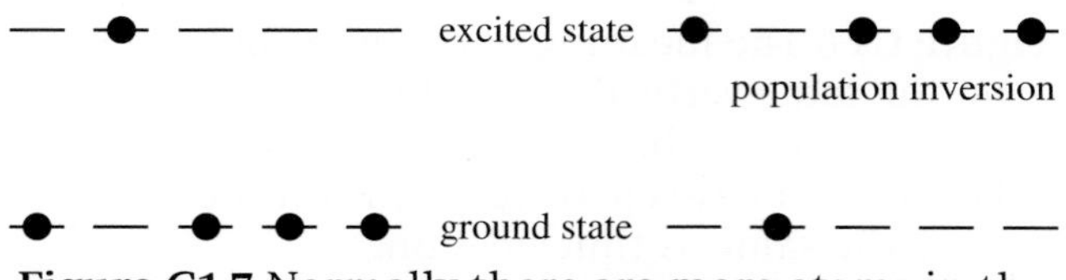

Figure G1.7 Normally there are more atoms in the ground state than in an excited state. With population inversion, the opposite is true.

unoccupied state in an atom, and a line with a dot on it signifies an occupied state. This is called **population inversion**. Normally, atoms are in the ground state, so any incident photons (of the right energy) will simply be absorbed and will not cause stimulated emission. To achieve population inversion, we must have *metastable* states. These are excited states where electrons stay for unusually long times. Normally, an electron in an excited state will make the transition to a lower state in a time of 10^{-8} s. In a metastable state, the lifetime of an excited electron may be as long as 10^{-3} s. The explanation for the existence of metastable states is beyond the level of this book.

In the helium–neon laser, helium is used to create population inversion in neon. The two gases are kept together at low pressure in the ratio of 85% helium to 15% neon. An electric field is used to excite helium atoms to a metastable state of energy 20.61 eV above the ground state of helium (Figure G1.8). Because this state is metastable, a helium atom stays in it long enough to collide with a neon atom, exciting it into a neon metastable state 20.66 eV above the ground state of neon. (This means that helium must provide an additional 0.05 eV from its kinetic energy and is now back in its ground state.) In this way there are more atoms in the neon metastable state than in the first excited state, which has energy 18.70 eV above the ground state. Population inversion has been achieved in neon.

Transitions from the neon state with energy 20.66 eV to the state with energy 18.70 eV result in photons with energy 1.96 eV being emitted. This corresponds to photons of wavelength 632.8 nm (calculated using the most accurate values available). These photons are reflected from mirrors at the ends of the laser tube, causing stimulated emission in other neon atoms in the metastable state. One of the mirrors is partially transparent to light, and so some of these photons exit the tube, producing the laser beam. In this way we produce light with unique characteristics: very monochromatic, very intense, very directional and coherent.

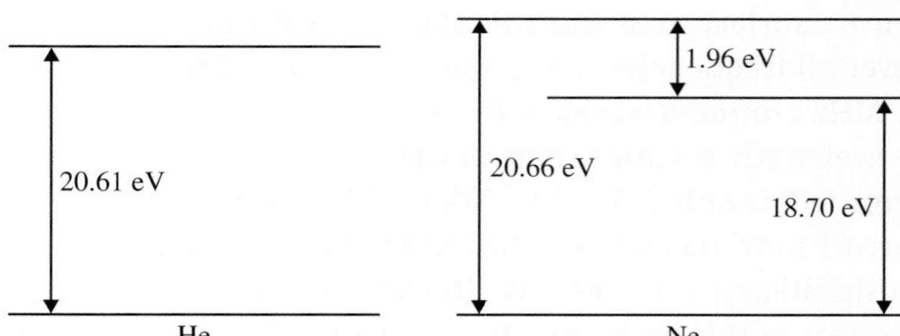

Figure G1.8 Energy levels for helium and neon, showing the metastable states in both atoms.

Uses of lasers

The introduction of lasers has revolutionized many areas of industry and medicine. In medicine, lasers are used to:

- destroy tumours;
- reattach damaged retinas (the laser damages part of the tissue so that the resulting scar welds the retina back into place);
- unblock arteries and heart valves (by destroying the plaque and other residues that clog them);

- cut and seal nerves in neurosurgery;
- correct vision defects such as myopia in cornea operations.

In industry and defence their uses include:

- welding;
- cutting and drilling metals;
- operating laser and compact discs;
- measuring distances accurately in surveying;
- measuring distances accurately between the earth and the moon by reflecting laser beams off mirrors left on the moon;
- reading barcodes;
- communication, where coded signals travel in optical fibres transmitting telephone conversations;
- sophisticated 'smart weapons', where a laser beam guides the weapon to its target.

? QUESTIONS

1 In Galileo's attempt to measure the speed of light, the two lanterns were about 8 km apart.
   (a) How long would light take to travel this distance?
   (b) How does it compare with a typical reaction time of 0.1 s?

2 In Armand Fizeau's measurement of the speed of light in 1849, a gear (toothed) wheel was used (see Figure G1.9). Light from a source falls on a plate P and part of it reflects through a hole H_1 in the gear wheel. The wheel is initially at rest. The light travels to a distant mirror and is reflected back through the same hole into the observer's eye. As the wheel begins to turn, the observer will no longer see light. This is because on its return trip, the light ray hits a tooth and is intercepted. If, however, the speed of rotation is increased to a critical value, the observer again sees light. This is because it takes light as much time to travel the distance *D and back* as it takes hole H_2 to take up the position previously held by H_1. In Fizeau's experiment, a wheel with 720 teeth was used. Light was seen when the wheel revolved at 25.2 revolutions per second and the distance D to the mirror was 8.65×10^3 m. Find the speed of light obtained by Fizeau.

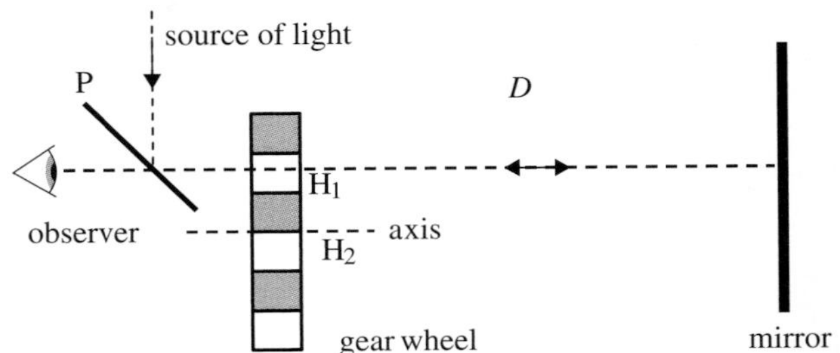

Figure G1.9 For question 2.

3 The index of refraction for blue light of wavelength 4.5×10^{-7} m for a particular kind of glass is 1.328 and for red light of wavelength 6.5×10^{-7} m it is 1.321. An equilateral triangular prism is made out of this glass and white light is incident on it parallel to one of its bases. Find the angles the blue and red rays make with the normal as they emerge from the prism. What is the deviation of each ray?

4 What is the difference between light emitted from a light bulb and light from a laser?

5 Find out in detail how exactly a laser is used in:
   (a) a CD;
   (b) surveying;
   (c) reading a barcode.

6 Distinguish between *spontaneous* emission and *stimulated* emission.

7 Outline how laser light is produced.

8 State what is meant by *population inversion*.

9 (a) Explain why a point source of ordinary light, of power P, will have an intensity (power per unit area) given by $I = \frac{P}{4\pi d^2}$ at a distance d away from the source.
   (b) Does the same result hold for a laser source? Explain your answer.

10 (a) Calculate the intensity of light from a 60 W ordinary light bulb a distance of 4.0 m away.

(b) A He–Ne laser has a power of 8.0 mW and exits a laser tube from an aperture of diameter 2.0 mm. Calculate the intensity of this laser beam.

11 (a) A He–Ne laser has wavelength $\lambda = 632.8$ nm and the beam diameter as it exits the laser tube is $d = 0.50$ mm. Determine that the angular spread of the beam is given by $\theta = \frac{\lambda}{d}$ using ideas based on (i) diffraction and (ii) the uncertainty principle.

(b) Calculate the numerical value of the angular spread.

(c) What is the diameter of the laser beam when it is incident on a target a distance of 500 km away?

Optical instruments

In this chapter we discuss the formation of images by lenses and two optical instruments – the compound microscope and the refracting telescope. The chapter closes with brief remarks about lens aberrations.

Objectives

By the end of this chapter you should be able to:

- find *images* of objects placed in front of lenses using the graphical method;
- find *images* of objects placed in front of lenses using the algebraic method, $\frac{1}{u}+\frac{1}{v}=\frac{1}{f}$, $m=-\frac{v}{u}$, and appreciate the *conventions* being used;
- understand how a *simple magnifying glass* works and find its magnification;
- understand how a *compound microscope* works and find its magnification;
- understand how a *refracting telescope* works and find its magnification;
- describe the two main *lens defects* and how those defects are corrected.

Lenses

Just as the behaviour of mirrors is determined by the law of reflection, the behaviour of lenses is determined by the law of refraction. A ray of light that enters a lens will, in general, be deviated from its original path.

The amount of deviation depends on the index of refraction of the glass making up the lens, the radii of the two spherical surfaces that the lens is polished to and the angle of incidence of the ray.

We will make the approximation that the lens is always very *thin*, which allows for simplifications. The two sides of the lens are not necessarily cut from the same curvature glass surface and may be convex, concave or planar. Various types of lens are illustrated in Figure G2.1.

▶ The straight line that goes through the centre of the lens at right angles to the lens surface is known as the *principal axis* of the lens.

Converging lenses

Lenses that are thicker at the centre than at the edges are *converging* lenses, which means that a ray of light changes its direction towards the axis of the lens (see Figure G2.2a). Rays of a parallel beam of light converge towards each other after going through the lens.

A beam of rays parallel to the principal axis will, upon refraction through the lens, pass through the same point on the principal axis on the other side of the lens (see Figure G2.3a).

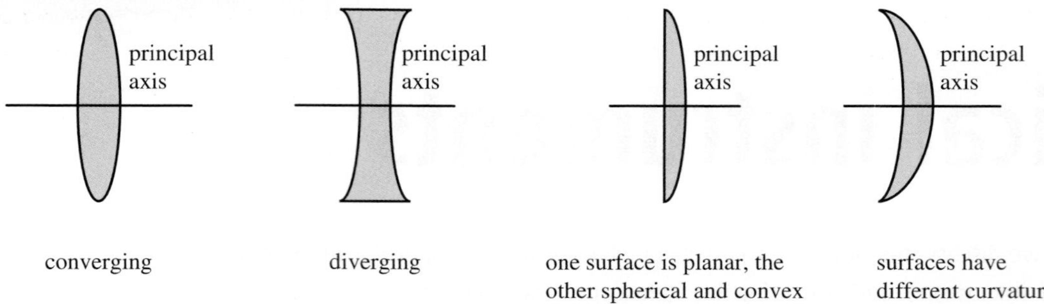

Figure G2.1 Various types of lens.

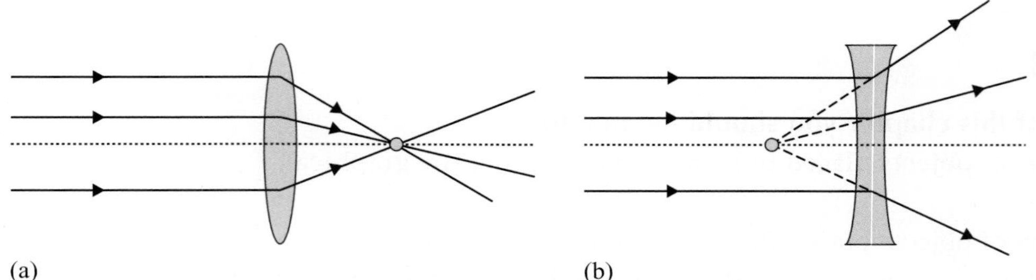

Figure G2.2 (a) A converging lens. (b) A diverging lens. A beam of rays parallel to the principal axis converges toward the principal axis in the case of a converging lens but diverges from it in the case of a diverging lens.

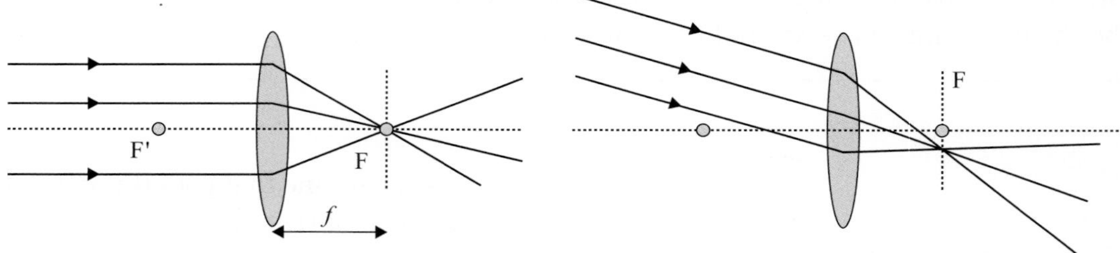

Figure G2.3 (a) Rays that are parallel to one another and are also parallel to the principal axis pass through the focal point of the lens, a point on the principal axis, after refraction. (b) If the rays are not parallel to the principal axis, the rays will go through a common point that is in the same plane as the focal point.

▶ Rays that are parallel to the principal axis will, after refraction in the lens, pass through a point on the principal axis called the *focal point*. The distance of the focal point from the centre of the lens is called the *focal length* and is denoted by f.

Optometrists usually use the inverse of the focal length to specify lenses. The power of a lens is defined as

$$P = \frac{1}{f}$$

When the focal length is expressed in metres, the power is expressed in dioptres (D), $1\ \text{D} = 1\ \text{m}^{-1}$.

If the parallel beam of rays is not parallel to the axis then the rays will again go through a single point. This point and the focal point of the lens are in the same vertical plane (see Figure G 2.3b).

For example, a lens with a focal length of $f = 25$ cm has a power of

$$P = \frac{1}{0.25} = 4.0\ \text{D}$$

(The point on the other side of the lens at a distance f from the lens is also a focal point. A ray parallel to the principal axis and entering the lens from right to left will pass through F′.)

We now know how one set of rays will refract through the lens. We may call a ray parallel to the principal axis 'standard ray 1'.

Another set of rays whose refraction through the lens is easy to describe is the set that first pass through the left focal point of the lens. They then emerge parallel to the principal axis on the other side of the lens, as shown in Figure G2.4. We may call such a ray 'standard ray 2'.

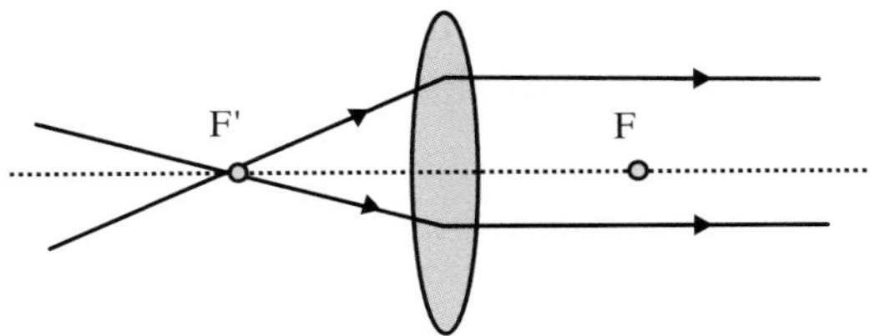

Figure G2.4 A ray passing through the focal point emerges parallel to the axis.

A third light ray whose behaviour we know something about is one that is directed at the centre of the lens. This ray will go through undeflected, as shown in Figure G2.5a. We may call such a ray 'standard ray 3'.

The reason for this behaviour is that near the mid-point of the lens the two lens surfaces are almost parallel. A ray of light going through glass with two parallel surfaces is shown in Figure G2.5b. The ray simply gets shifted parallel to itself. The amount of the parallel shift is proportional to the width of the glass block, which is the width of the lens. Since we are making the approximation of a very thin lens, this displacement is negligible, which proves our result.

With the help of these three 'standard rays' we can find the image of any object placed in front of a converging lens. These rays are shown together in Figure G2.6.

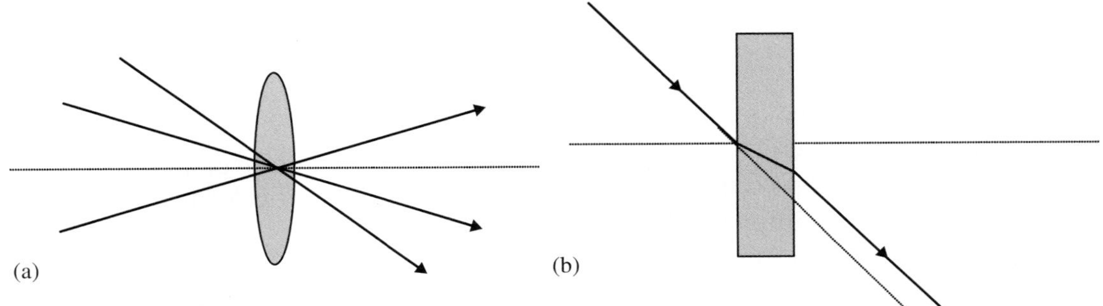

Figure G2.5 (a) A ray going through the centre of the lens is undeflected. (b) A ray entering a glass plate is shifted parallel to itself by an amount proportional to the thickness of the plate.

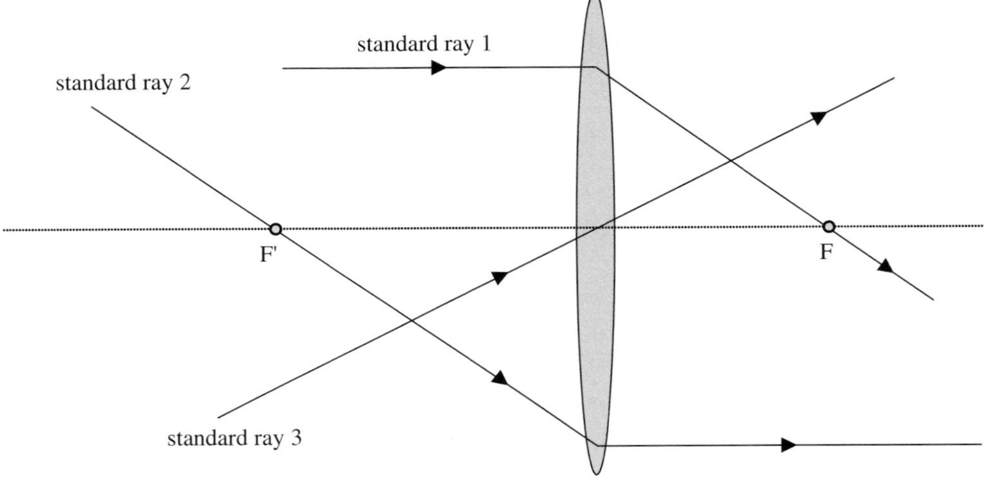

Figure G2.6 The refraction of the three standard rays in a converging lens.

We will get different kinds of images depending on the distance of the object from the lens. The distances of the object and the image are measured from the centre of the lens.

▶ An image can be real or virtual. A real image is one where actual rays of light pass through it. A real image can be projected and seen on a screen. A virtual image is one where no rays of light pass through, only their mathematical extensions. A virtual image cannot be projected onto a screen.

In describing the image we would like to know:

- its distance from the lens;
- if it is real or virtual;
- if it is inverted or upright;
- if it is larger or smaller than the object and by how much.

We consider first an object of height 1 cm that is a distance of 10 cm from a lens of focal length 5 cm. Using all three standard rays, starting from the top of the object we construct the image of the top point by finding where the refracted rays intersect. The image of the bottom of the object must be formed on the principal axis. By symmetry, the image will be at right angles to the principal axis and so if we find the image of the top, the full image can be drawn. (If the object is at an angle to the principal axis then rays from the bottom must also be considered.) The full image is then as shown in Figure G2.7.

We see that the image is inverted. It is also real since rays of light actually pass through it.

Measuring the distance from the lens to the image we find about 10 cm. The height of the image is about 1 cm. The image is the same size as the object. To see this image the eye must be put in a position where refracted rays enter the eye. Any position to the right of the lens will do. Note that if you cover any part of the lens, the image will still be formed. But because less light passes through the lens, the image will not be as bright. No other change in the image will be seen.

Consider next what happens when the object is placed at a distance from the lens equal to the focal length. Here we make use of standard rays 1 and 3 leaving the top of the object, as shown in Figure G2.8.

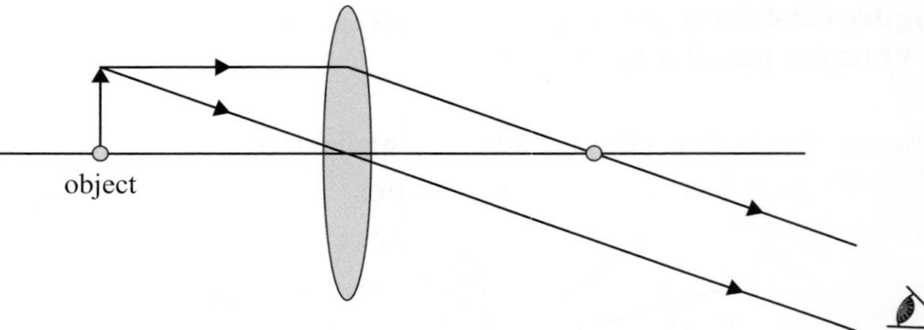

Figure G2.8 The image of an object that is placed at the focal point is formed at infinity.

Here the refracted rays are parallel and so do not meet. In this case we say that the image is formed at infinity.

For the final case, consider an object placed closer to the lens than the focal length, a distance of 3.5 cm from the lens. (The focal length is 5 cm). We again make use of standard rays 1 and 3 leaving the top of the object (see Figure G2.9).

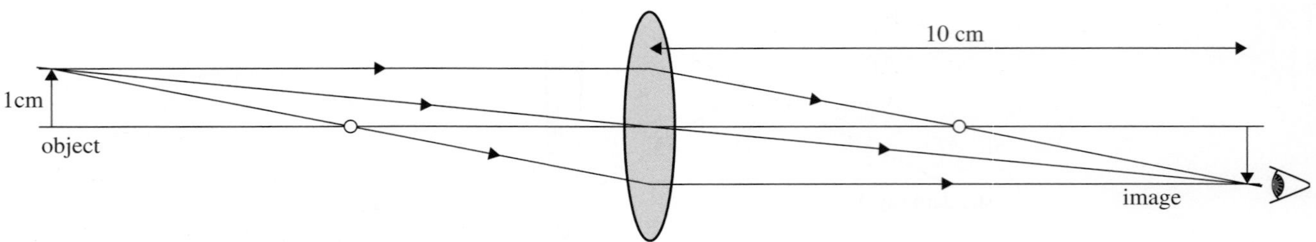

Figure G2.7 The image of an object that is further from the lens than the focal length.

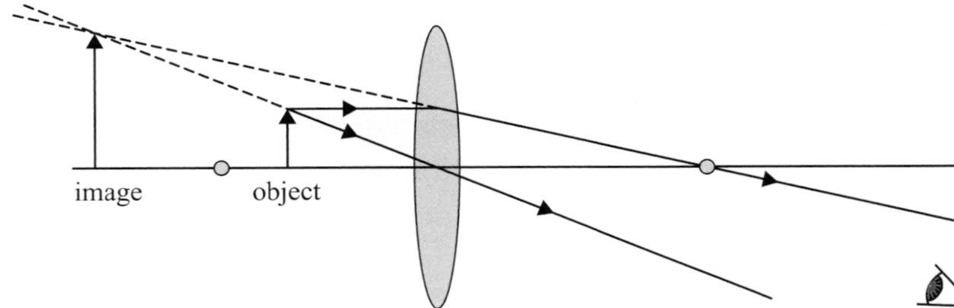

Figure G2.9 The object is placed closer to the lens than the focal length.

The refracted rays do not intersect. When extended backwards they do intersect to form a virtual image. The eye receiving the refracted rays is tricked into believing that they originated from the position where the extensions intersect. This is where the image is. The image is upright and larger than the object. Measuring the distance to the image we find about 11.7 cm. The height of the image is measured to be about 3.3 cm.

The methods described above are graphical methods for finding the image. These are very useful because they allow us 'to see the image being formed'. There is, however, also an algebraic method which is faster.

The algebraic method uses an equation that relates the object and image distances to the focal length of the lens. We derive this equation as follows. The object is placed in front of the lens as shown in Figure G2.10.

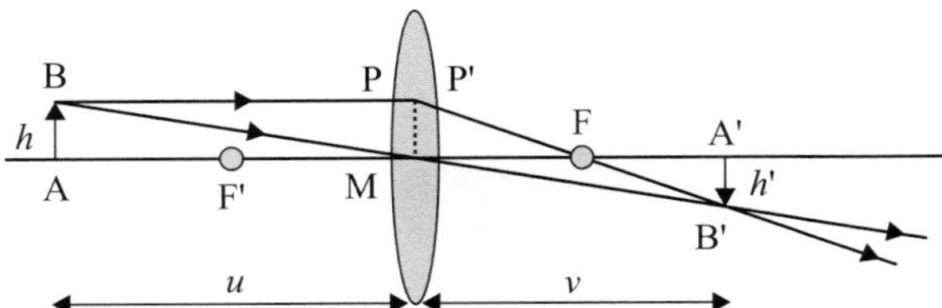

Figure G2.10 The image of an object placed in front of a converging lens.

Let u be the distance of the object from the lens and v that of the image. Triangles ABM and A′B′M are similar (angles are clearly equal) and so

$$\frac{h}{u} = \frac{h'}{v}$$
$$\Rightarrow \frac{h'}{h} = \frac{v}{u}$$

The lens is thin and so P and P′ may be considered to be the same point. Then, triangles MPF and A′B′F are also similar, so

$$\frac{h}{f} = \frac{h'}{v - f}$$
$$\Rightarrow \frac{h'}{h} = \frac{v - f}{f}$$

(note that MP $= h$). Combining the two equations gives

$$\frac{v}{u} = \frac{v - f}{f}$$
$$\Rightarrow vf = uv - uf$$
$$\Rightarrow vf + uf = uv \quad \text{(divide by } uvf\text{)}$$
$$\Rightarrow \frac{1}{u} + \frac{1}{v} = \frac{1}{f}$$

▶ The equation

$$\frac{1}{f} = \frac{1}{u} + \frac{1}{v}$$

is known as the thin lens equation and can be used to obtain image distances.

To examine whether the image is larger or smaller than the object we define the linear magnification, m, of the lens as the ratio of the image height to the object height:

$$m = \frac{\text{image height}}{\text{object height}}$$

Numerically, the linear magnification is $m = \frac{v}{u}$. It is much more convenient, though, to introduce a minus sign so that we define linear magnification as

$$m = \frac{\text{image height}}{\text{object height}}$$
$$= \frac{h'}{h}$$
$$= -\frac{v}{u}$$

The usefulness of the minus sign will be appreciated as soon as we look at an example.

The thin lens equation and the magnification formula allow a complete determination of the image without a ray diagram. But to do that a number of conventions must be followed.

The conventions used here are:

- f is positive for a converging lens;
- u is positive;
- v is positive for real images (i.e. those formed on the other side of the lens from the object);
- v is negative for virtual images (i.e. those formed on the same side of the lens as the object);
- $m > 0$ means the image is upright;
- $m < 0$ means the image is inverted;
- $|m| > 1$ means the image is larger than the object;
- $|m| < 1$ means the image is smaller than the object.

Example questions

Q1

A converging lens has a focal length of 15 cm. An object is placed 60 cm from the lens. Determine the image.

Answer

The object distance is $u = 60$ cm and the focal length is $f = 15$ cm. Thus,

$$\frac{1}{v} = \frac{1}{f} - \frac{1}{u}$$
$$= \frac{1}{15} - \frac{1}{60}$$
$$= \frac{1}{20}$$
$$\Rightarrow v = 20 \text{ cm}$$

The image is real (positive v) and is formed on the other side of the lens. The magnification is

$$m = -\frac{20}{60}$$
$$= -\frac{1}{3}$$

The negative sign in the answer for magnification tells us that the image is inverted. This is why we defined magnification in the way we did. The magnitude of the magnification is less than one. The image is 3 times shorter than the object. (Construct a ray diagram for this example.)

Q2

An object is placed 15 cm in front of a converging lens of focal length 20 cm. Determine the image.

Answer

Applying the lens equation again we have

$$\frac{1}{v} = \frac{1}{f} - \frac{1}{u}$$
$$= \frac{1}{20} - \frac{1}{15}$$
$$= -\frac{1}{60}$$
$$\Rightarrow v = -60 \text{ cm}$$

The image is virtual (negative v) and is formed on the same side of the lens as the object. The magnification is

$$m = -\left(\frac{-60}{20}\right)$$
$$= +3$$

Thus, the image is 3 times taller than the object and is upright (positive m). The lens here is acting as a magnifying glass. (Construct a ray diagram for this example.)

A converging lens can produce a real or a virtual image depending on the distance of the object relative to the focal length.

Supplementary material

Diverging lenses

(Diverging lenses are included here for completeness – they are not part of the IBO syllabus and will not be examined.)

Lenses that are thinner at the centre than at the edges are *diverging* lenses, which means that a ray of light changes its direction *away* from the axis of the lens (see Figure G2.2b). Rays of a parallel beam of light diverge from each other after going through the lens.

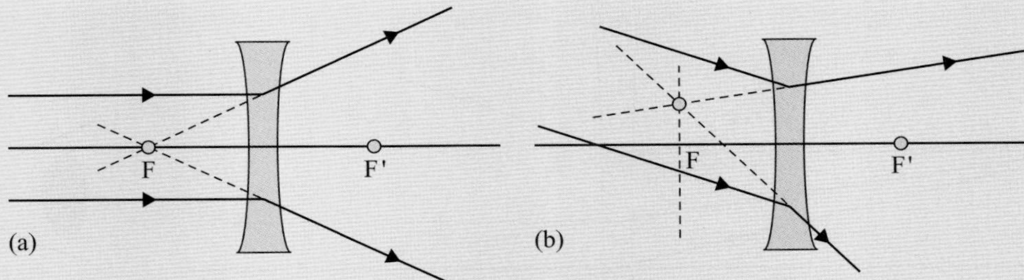

Figure G2.11 (a) Rays parallel to the principal axis diverge from the lens in such a way that the extensions of the rays pass through the focal point of the lens on the same side as the incoming rays. (b) Other parallel rays at an angle to the principal axis will appear to come from a point off the principal axis at a distance from the centre of the lens equal to the focal length.

With small but important changes, much of the discussion for converging lenses can be repeated for diverging lenses. We therefore need to know the behaviour of three standard rays in order to construct an image graphically.

First we need a definition of the focal point of a diverging lens. In a diverging lens, rays coming in parallel to the principal axis will, upon refraction, move away from the axis in such a way that their *extensions* go through a point on the principal axis called the focal point of the lens. The distance of the focal point from the centre of the lens is the focal length of the diverging lens (see Figure G2.11a). This is our 'standard ray 1' for diverging lenses.

If the beam is not parallel to the principal axis, the extensions of the refracted rays will all go through the same point a distance from the lens equal to the focal length (see Figure G2.11b).

The second standard ray is one that is directed at the focal point on the other side of the lens. This ray will refract parallel to the principal axis, as shown in Figure G2.12. This is 'standard ray 2'.

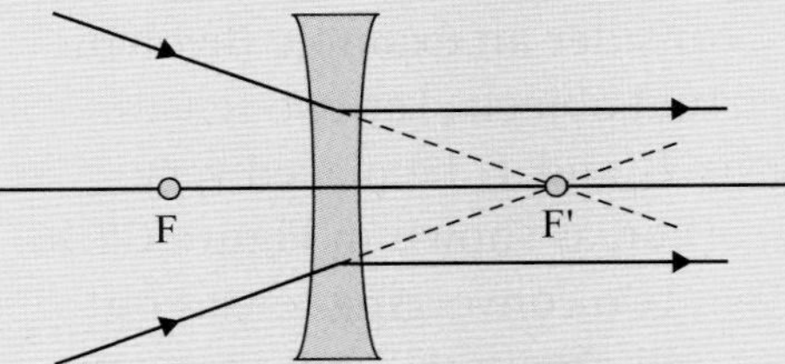

Figure G2.12 A ray directed towards the focal point on the other side of the lens emerges parallel to the principal axis.

Finally, a ray that passes through the centre of the lens is undeflected, as shown in Figure G2.13. This is 'standard ray 3'.

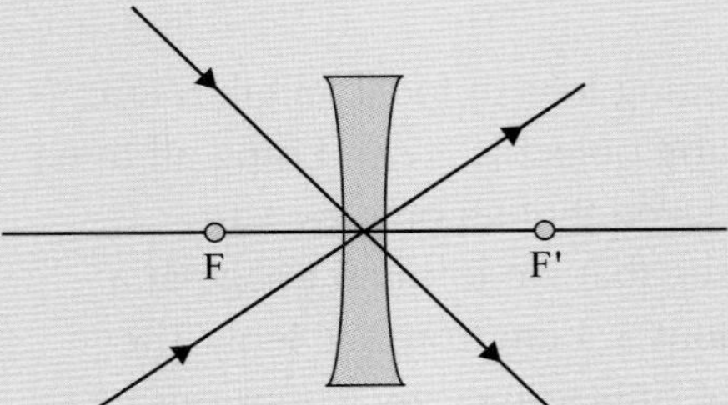

Figure G2.13 A ray directed at the centre of the lens passes through undeflected.

The behaviour of all three standard rays is shown in Figure G2.14.

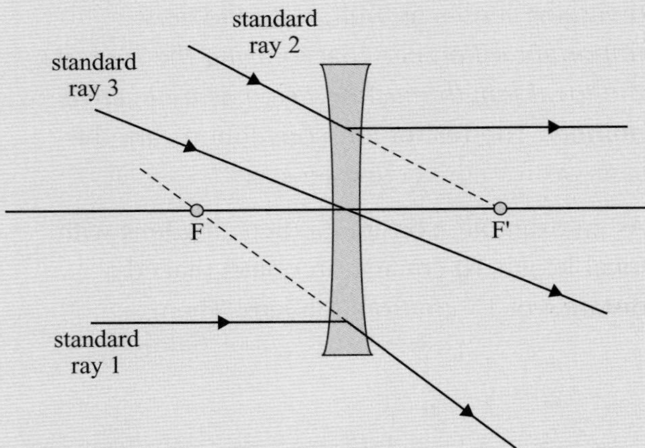

Figure G2.14 The refraction of the three standard rays in a diverging lens.

With this knowledge we can obtain the images of objects placed in front of diverging lenses. Consider an object placed a distance of 8 cm in

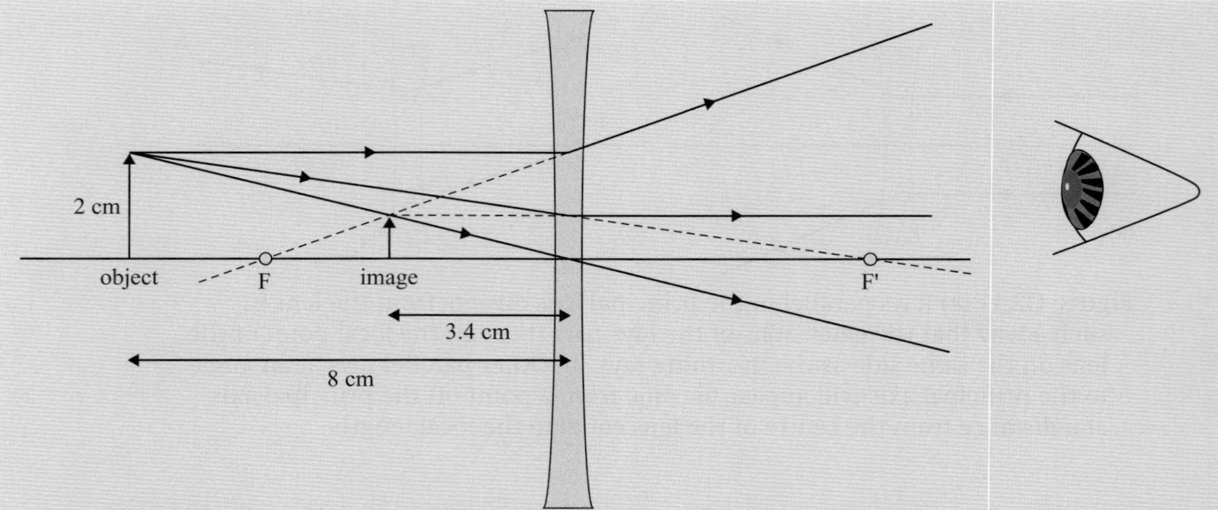

Figure G2.15 Formation of an image by a diverging lens. All three standard rays have been used here.

front of a diverging lens of focal length 6 cm. The height of the object is 2 cm. Using all three standard rays (even though only two are required) we see that we form an image at a distance of about 3.4 cm from the lens. The image is virtual (it is formed by extensions of rays). It is upright and has a height of about 0.86 cm. (See Figure G2.15.)

It can be shown that the same formula relating object and image distances and focal length that we used for converging lenses applies to diverging lenses as well, *with the very important difference that in using the formula the focal length must be taken as a negative number.* The rest of the conventions are the same as for converging lenses.

As an example, consider a diverging lens with focal length 10 cm and an object placed a distance of 15 cm from the lens. Then

$$\frac{1}{v} = \frac{1}{f} - \frac{1}{u}$$
$$= -\frac{1}{10} - \frac{1}{15}$$
$$= -\frac{25}{15 \times 10}$$
$$= -\frac{1}{6}$$
$$\Rightarrow v = -6 \text{ cm}$$

The negative sign for v implies that the object is virtual and is formed on the same side of the lens as the object. The magnification is

$$m = -\left(\frac{-6}{10}\right)$$
$$= +0.6$$

implying an image 0.6 of the height of the object and upright.

▶ When the object is real (i.e. $u > 0$), a diverging lens always produces a virtual image ($v < 0$). The magnification is then always positive implying an upright image.

Virtual objects

Let us finally consider an example involving non-real or virtual objects. Let two lenses of focal lengths f_1 and f_2 be placed very close to each other, as shown in Figure G2.16. (We have drawn two converging lenses but the results we will obtain will hold for any pair of lenses.) An object is placed a distance u from the centre of the two-lens combination.

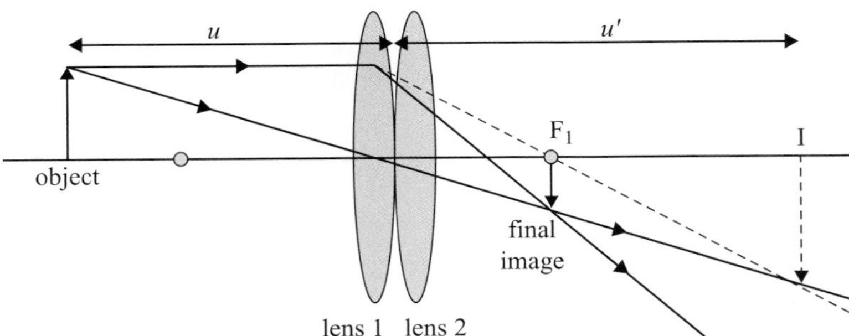

Figure G2.16 Image I is formed by completely ignoring the second lens. This image will act as the (virtual) object to the second lens.

Ignoring for a moment the second lens, the image will be formed at a distance v' given by

$$\frac{1}{v'} = \frac{1}{f_1} - \frac{1}{u}$$

This image serves as the object to the second lens. It is a virtual object, however. This is because the rays are actually entering the second lens from left to right but the 'object' is situated to the right of the second lens (i.e. on the 'wrong' side). As it is virtual, the distance of this object must be taken as negative, which means that u' of this virtual object is the negative of what we found for v'. Thus, the distance v of the final image is found from

$$\frac{1}{v} = \frac{1}{f_2} - \left[-\left(\frac{1}{f_1} - \frac{1}{u}\right)\right]$$

$$\Rightarrow \frac{1}{v} + \frac{1}{u} = \frac{1}{f_2} + \frac{1}{f_1}$$

Thus, the combination of the two lenses acts as a single lens of focal length f given by

$$\frac{1}{f} = \frac{1}{f_2} + \frac{1}{f_1}$$

Example questions

Q3

An object of length 9.5 cm lies on a table. A converging lens of focal length 75 cm is placed at a distance of 40 cm from the object. Determine the image formed by this lens. A second converging lens with the same focal length is now placed above the first lens at a distance of 6.5 cm from the first lens. Determine the image formed by this combination of lenses.

Answer

With just the first lens the image is formed at a distance found from

$$\frac{1}{v} + \frac{1}{u} = \frac{1}{f}$$

$$\Rightarrow \frac{1}{v} + \frac{1}{40} = \frac{1}{75}$$

$$\Rightarrow v = -85.7 \text{ cm}$$

The image is virtual and upright. This image acts as the object to the second lens. The distance of the object from the second lens is

$$85.7 + 6.5 = 92.2 \text{ cm}$$

The object is a real object for the second lens and so $u = +92.2$ cm. The new image is thus formed at a distance found from

$$\frac{1}{92.2} + \frac{1}{v} = \frac{1}{75}$$

$$\Rightarrow v = 402 \text{ cm}$$

The final image is thus real. The first lens produces a magnification of

$$m_1 = \frac{h'}{h} = -\left(\frac{-85.7}{40}\right)$$

$$\Rightarrow h' = +20.4 \text{ cm}$$

The second lens will magnify this image to a new size given by

$$m_2 = \frac{h''}{h'} = -\left(\frac{402}{92.2}\right)$$

$$\Rightarrow h'' = -88.7 \text{ cm}$$

The overall magnification is given by

$$m = \frac{h''}{h} = \frac{-88.7}{9.5} = -9.34$$

The image is inverted. It can be checked that the overall magnification is the product of the magnifications of each lens.

HL only

Q4

Figure G2.17 shows the formation of an image in a converging lens of focal length 4.0 cm, ignoring the presence of the diverging lens (of focal length 6.0 cm). Determine the position of the image when the diverging lens is taken into account and complete the ray diagram.

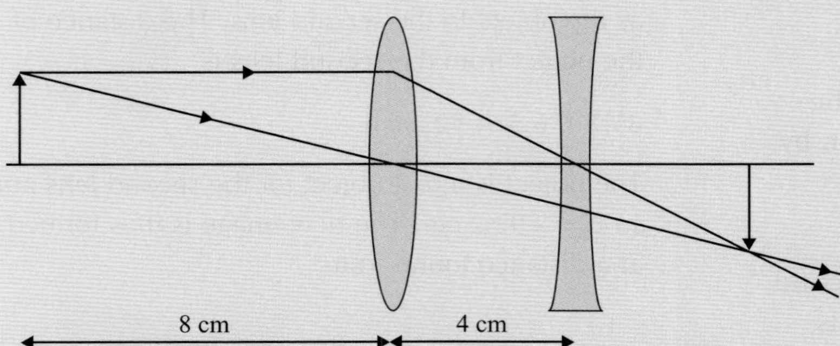

Figure G2.17.

Answer

Ignoring the diverging lens, the image is at a distance from the converging lens found from

$$\frac{1}{8}+\frac{1}{v}=\frac{1}{4}$$
$$\Rightarrow v = 8.0 \text{ cm}$$

Its distance from the diverging lens is therefore 4.0 cm. This image acts as the virtual object for the diverging lens. Hence $u = -4.0$ cm. The final image is therefore at a distance found from

$$\frac{1}{-4}+\frac{1}{v}=\frac{1}{-6}$$
$$\Rightarrow v = 12.0 \text{ cm}$$

The image is thus real. The magnification of the lens system is given by

$$-\frac{8}{8}\times -\frac{12}{-4} = -3$$

which implies that the final image is inverted and three times as large as the original object. Figure G2.18 is a ray diagram of the problem.

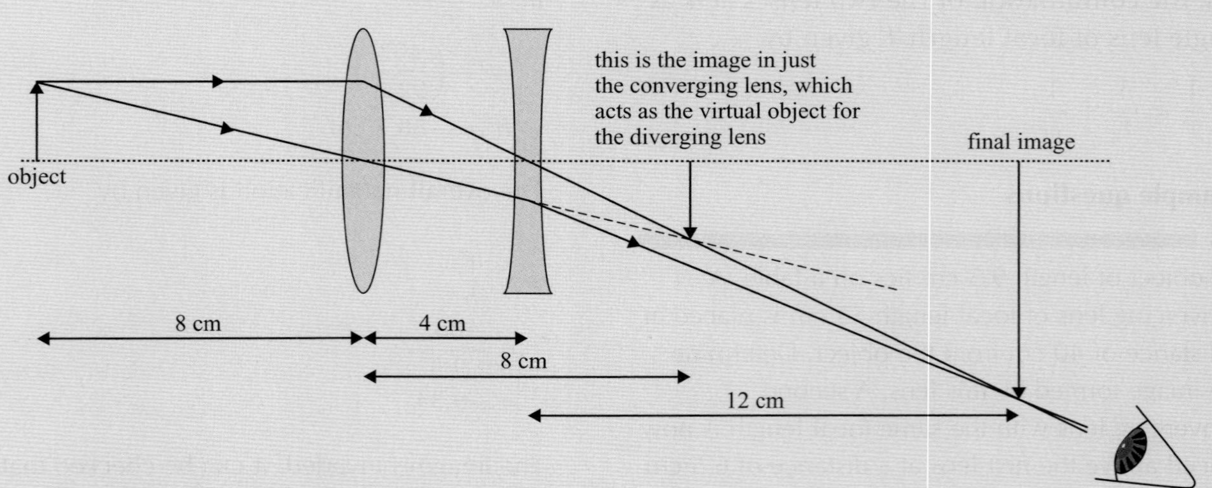

Figure G2.18 A ray diagram for question 4.

Optical instruments

Much of our knowledge about the natural world in which we live is owed to optical instruments based on mirrors and lenses. These have enabled the observation of very distant objects through telescopes and very small objects through microscopes. We have already seen how a single converging lens can produce an enlarged upright image of an object placed closer to the lens than the focal length, thus acting as a magnifying glass. The apparent size of an object depends on the size of the image that is formed on the retina. In turn, this size depends on the angle subtended by the object at the eye. This is why we bring a small object closer to the eye in order to view it – the angle subtended at the eye by the object increases.

▶ The closest point on which the human eye can focus without straining is known as the *near point* of the eye. This distance is taken to be about 25 cm for a normal eye, but it depends greatly on age. The largest distance the eye can focus on without straining is called the *far point*. The far point is taken to be infinity for a normal eye. In practice, infinity means anything larger than a few metres.

Thus, let an observer view a small object at a distance of 25 cm from the eye and let θ stand for the angle that the object subtends at the eye, as shown in Figure G2.19. Assuming the angle is small, we have approximately that $\theta = \frac{h}{25\text{ cm}}$ (the approximation involved is $\theta \approx \tan\theta$).

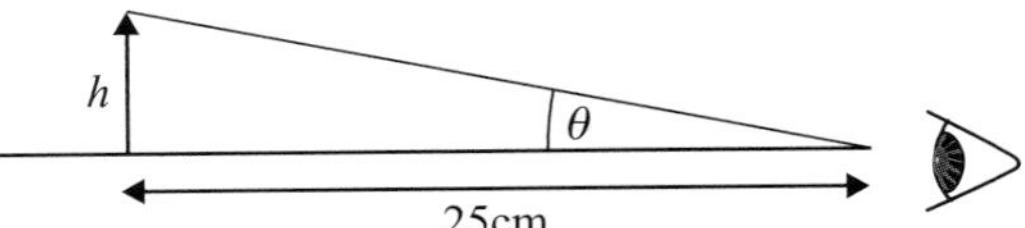

Figure G2.19 The apparent size of an object depends on the angle subtended at the eye.

If the object is now viewed through a lens and is placed closer to the lens than the focal length, a virtual, upright, enlarged image will be formed (see Figure G2.20).

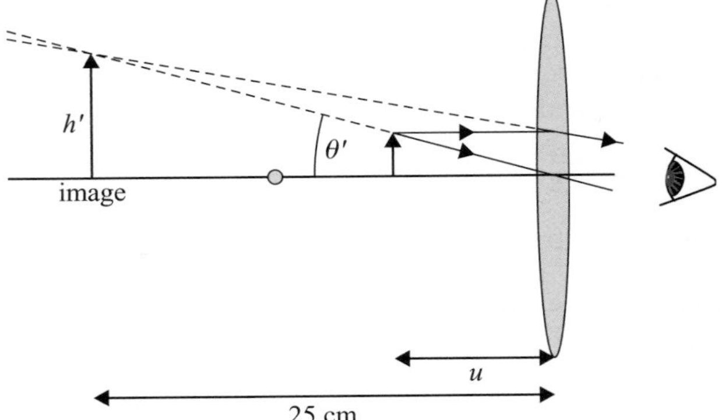

Figure G2.20 A converging lens acting as a magnifier.

Let the distance of the object to the lens be u. If the image is to be formed at a distance of 25 cm, then (remember the image is virtual, hence its distance is negative)

$$\frac{1}{f} = \frac{1}{u} + \frac{1}{-25}$$

$$\Rightarrow u = \frac{25f}{25+f}$$

Let θ' be the angle that the image subtends at the eye through the lens. From simple geometry we obtain

$$\theta' = \frac{h'}{25\text{ cm}} = \frac{h}{u} = \frac{h(25+f)}{25f}$$

The *angular magnification* M is defined as

$$M = \frac{\theta'}{\theta} = \frac{h(25+f)/25f}{h/25} \quad \left(\text{since } \theta = \frac{h}{25}\right) = \frac{25+f}{f} = 1 + \frac{25}{f}$$

This is the magnification of the magnifying glass when the image is formed 25 cm from the lens. The lens is assumed to be very close to the eye.

If the object is placed at the focal length of the lens, the image is formed at infinity and the eye viewing this image is said to be relaxed. In this case, $u = f$, and so the angular magnification is

$$M = \frac{h/f}{h/25} = \frac{25}{f}$$

(Here the lens need not be very close to the eye.)

In both cases, the magnification can be increased by decreasing the focal length of the lens. Lens defects known as aberrations (see page 620) limit the angular magnification to about 4.

The microscope

To increase the magnification more requires a microscope. A *compound microscope* (Figure G2.21) consists of two converging lenses. The object is placed at a distance from the first lens (the *objective*) slightly larger than the focal length f_o (the objective usually has a focal length that is less than 1 cm). A real inverted image is formed at a distance from the second lens (the *eyepiece*) that is equal to the focal length of the eyepiece (which is a few centimetres). This image acts as an object for the eyepiece and this lens now forms an enlarged, virtual, final image at infinity. The eyepiece thus acts as a simple magnifying glass on the image formed by the objective. The first image is formed a distance L to the right of the objective's focal point. Manufacturers arrange for this distance (known as the tube length) to be 16 cm. Let u be the distance of the object from the objective. The image formed by the objective is a distance of $f_o + 16$ from the objective and so (using the lens equation) u and f_o are related by

$$\frac{1}{u} + \frac{1}{f_o + 16} = \frac{1}{f_o}$$

$$\Rightarrow u = \frac{f_o(f_o + 16)}{16}$$

Thus, the objective produces a lateral magnification of

$$m = -\frac{16 + f_o}{u} = -\frac{16 + f_o}{\left[\frac{f_o(16+f_o)}{16}\right]} = -\frac{16}{f_o}$$

The magnification of the microscope is the product of the magnification produced by the objective times the magnification produced by the eyepiece.

The eyepiece has an angular magnification of $M = \frac{25}{f_e}$ (f_e is the focal length of the eyepiece – the final image is at infinity).

▶ The final magnification of the microscope is therefore

$$M = -\frac{16}{f_o}\frac{25}{f_e}$$

Note: If the image by the objective lens is formed at a distance past the objective focal point other than 16 cm, the magnification is

$$M = -\frac{d}{f_o}\frac{25}{f_e}$$

where d is the distance of the image in the objective past the objective focal point. In this formula the focal lengths must be expressed in centimetres.

A compound microscope is illustrated in Figure G2.21.

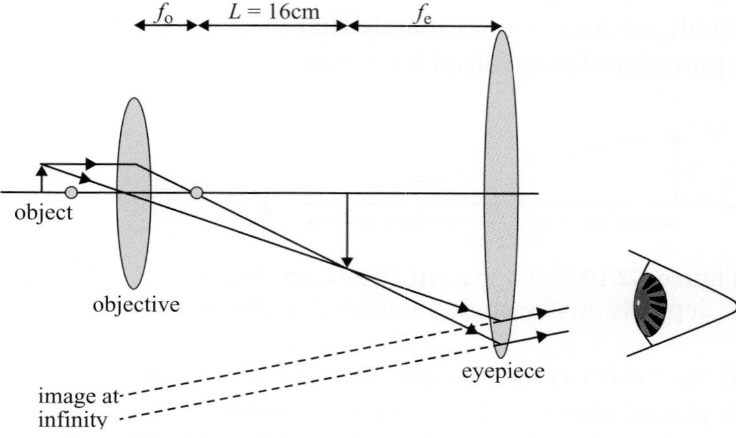

Figure G2.21 A compound microscope consists of two converging lenses.

Example question

Q5

A microscope has an objective of focal length 0.500 cm and an eyepiece of focal length 3.00 cm. What is the magnification of the microscope?

Answer

The magnification is

$$M = -\frac{16}{f_o}\frac{25}{f_e}$$
$$= -\frac{16}{0.500} \times \frac{25}{3.00}$$
$$= -267$$

The refracting telescope

The function of a telescope is to allow the observation of large objects that are very distant. A star is enormous but looks small because it is far away. The telescope is then used to increase the angle at which the star is observed relative to the angle at which the star is observed by the unaided eye. The telescope is thus not used to provide a *lateral* magnification of the star, since the image in that case would be many orders of magnitude larger than the earth. A refracting astronomical telescope (see Figure G2.22) consists of two converging lenses. Since the object observed is very far away, it follows that the image produced by the first lens (the objective) is at the focal plane of the objective lens. It is this image that is then magnified by the eyepiece, just as by a magnifying glass. The second lens (the eyepiece) forms a virtual, inverted image of the object. The final image is produced at infinity and so the distance between the two lenses is the sum of their focal lengths.

The angular magnification of the telescope is defined as the ratio of the angle the object subtends through the telescope divided by the angle subtended by the object at the unaided eye. Thus

$$M = \frac{\theta_2}{\theta_1}$$
$$= \frac{h/f_e}{h/f_o}$$
$$= \frac{f_o}{f_e}$$

The position of the eyepiece can be adjusted to provide clear images of objects other than very distant ones. The objective lens should be as large as possible in order to allow as much light as possible into the telescope. Because it is difficult to make very large lenses, telescopes have been designed to use mirrors rather than lenses.

Example question

Q6

A refracting telescope has a magnification of 70.0 and the two lenses are 60.0 cm apart when adjusted for a relaxed eye. What are the focal lengths of the lenses?

Answer

From

$$M = \frac{f_o}{f_e}$$
$$= 70$$
$$\Rightarrow f_o = 70\, f_e$$

and

$$f_o + f_e = 60 \text{ cm}$$
$$\Rightarrow 71\, f_e = 60 \text{ cm}$$
$$\Rightarrow f_e = 0.845 \text{ cm}$$
$$f_o = 59.2 \text{ cm}$$

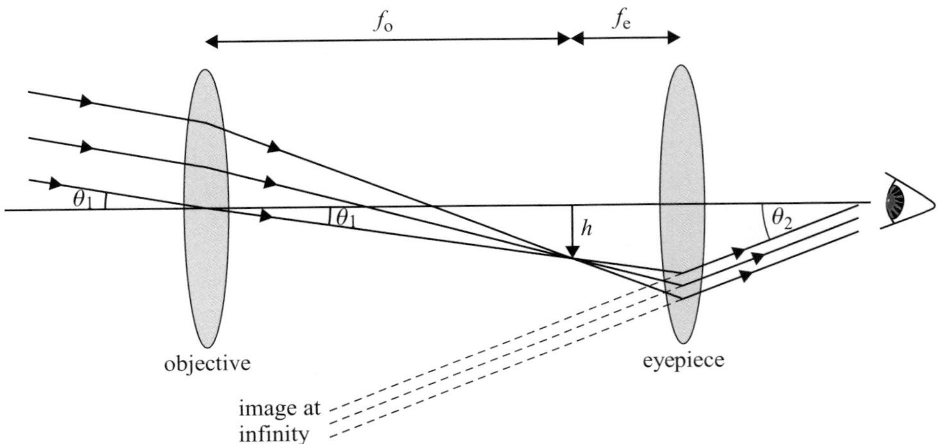

Figure G2.22 A refracting astronomical telescope. The final image is inverted.

Lens aberrations

Lenses do not behave exactly as described above – they suffer from *aberrations*. Two main types of aberration are important for lenses: *spherical* and *chromatic*.

▶ *Spherical aberrations* occur because rays that enter the lens far from the principal axis have a different focal length from rays entering near the axis.

In Figure G2.23, rays hitting the lens far from its mid-point refract through a point on the principal axis that is closer to the lens than rays that hit the lens closer to the middle. This means that the image of the point is not going to be a point image but a blurred patch of light. Spherical aberration can be reduced by reducing the aperture of the lens (its diameter – this is called stopping down), but that means that less light goes through the lens, which results in a less bright image. A lens with a smaller diameter would also suffer from more pronounced diffraction effects.

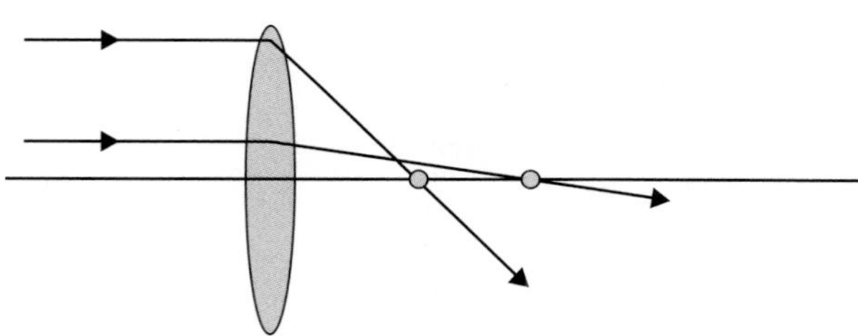

Figure G2.23 Spherical aberration. Rays from a distant point source are not brought to focus at a single point. The image is not a point image.

The fact that the focal point varies for rays that are further from the principal axis means that the magnification produced by the lens also varies. This leads to a *distortion* of the image, as shown in Figure G2.24.

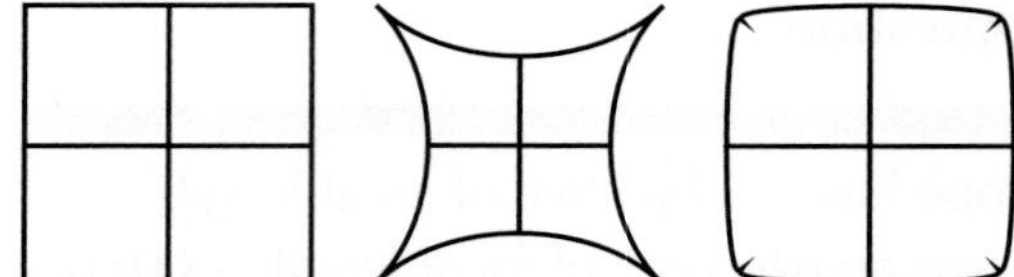

Figure G2.24 An example of distortion due to spherical aberration. The grid is distorted because the magnification varies as one moves away from the principal axis.

▶ The second aberration, *chromatic aberration*, arises because the lens has different refractive indices for different wavelengths. Thus, there is a separate focal length for each wavelength (colour) of light.

This makes images appear coloured – there are lines around the image in the colours of the rainbow (see Figure G2.25a). Chromatic aberration obviously disappears when monochromatic light is used. Chromatic aberrations can be reduced, again, by a combination of lenses. A diverging lens of different index of refraction placed near the first lens will eliminate the aberration for two colours and reduce it for the others (see Figure G2.25b).

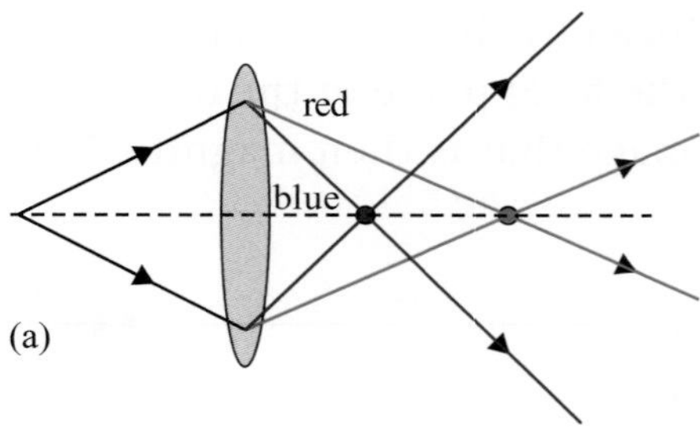

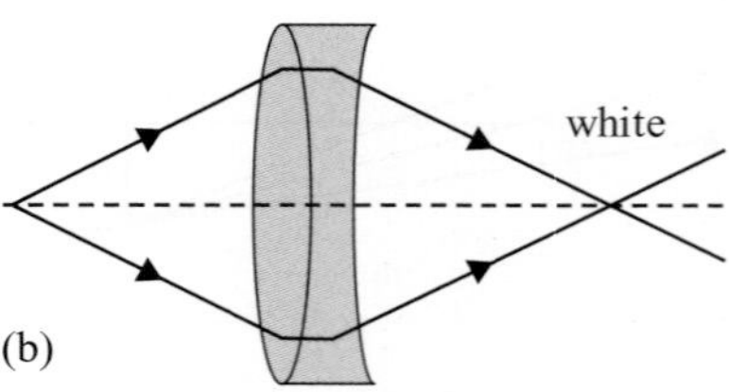

Figure G2.25 (a) Light of different colour bends by different amounts and hence different colours are focused at different places. (b) An achromatic doublet consists of a pair of lenses of different indices of refraction.

? QUESTIONS

1 Define:
(a) focal point of a converging lens;
(b) focal length of a converging lens.

2 Explain what is meant by:
(a) a real image formed by a lens;
(b) a virtual image formed by a lens.

3 Explain why a real image can be projected on a screen but a virtual image cannot.

4 A mirror appears to reverse left and right. Does a lens do the same? Explain your answer.

5 A student wants to buy lenses for a homemade telescope. Should she look for a short or long focal length objective lens?

6 A converging lens has a focal length of 6.0 cm. Determine the distance x in Figure G2.26.

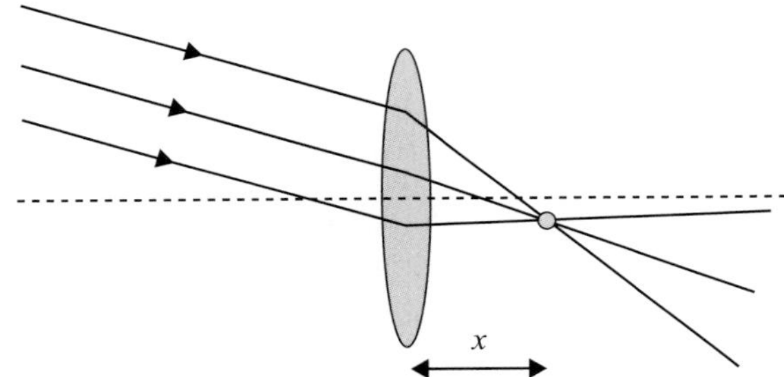

Figure G2.26 For question 6.

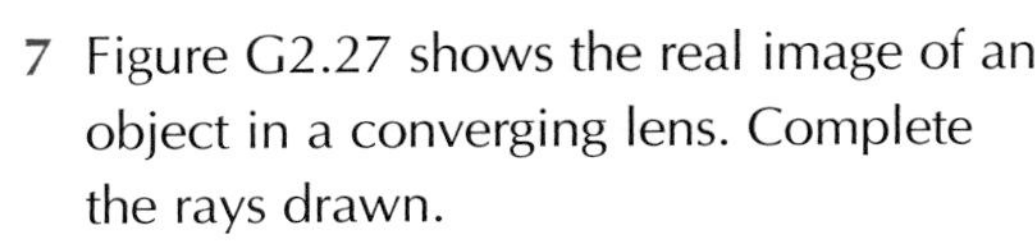

7 Figure G2.27 shows the real image of an object in a converging lens. Complete the rays drawn.

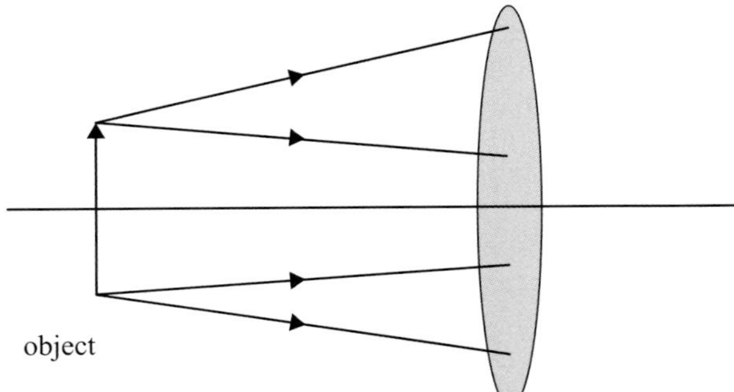

Figure G2.27 For question 7.

8 An object 2 cm tall is placed in front of a converging lens of focal length 10 cm. Using ray diagrams, construct the image when the object is at a distance of:
(a) 20 cm;
(b) 10 cm;
(c) 5 cm.
Confirm your ray diagrams by using the lens equation.

9 Using the graphical method, determine the image characteristics of an object of height 2.5 cm that is placed a distance of 8.0 cm in front of a converging lens of focal length 6.0 cm. Confirm your ray diagram by using the lens equation.

10 Using the graphical method, determine the image characteristics of an object of height 4.0 cm that is placed a distance of 6.0 cm in front of a converging lens of focal length 8.0 cm. Confirm your ray diagram by using the lens equation.

11 Consider a converging lens of focal length 5.00 cm. An object of length 2.236 cm is placed in front of the lens as shown in Figure G2.28 (not to scale) so that the middle of the object is on the principal axis. By drawing appropriate rays, determine the image in the lens. Is the angle the image makes with the principal axis the same as that of the object?

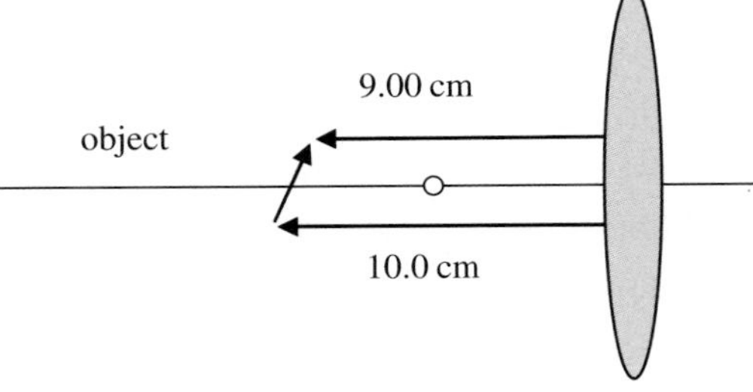

Figure G2.28 For question 11.

12 A student finds the position of the image created by a converging lens for various positions of the object. She constructs a table of object and image distances (Table G2.1).

(a) Explain how these data can be used to determine the focal length of the lens.
(b) Determine the focal length quoting the uncertainty in its value.

u/cm ± 0.1 cm	12.0	16.0	20.0	24.0	28.0
v/cm ± 0.1 cm	60.0	27.2	19.9	17.5	16.8

Table G2.1 For question 12.

13 An object is placed in front of a converging lens which rests on a plane mirror as shown in Figure G2.29. The object is moved until the image is formed exactly at the position of the object. Draw rays from the object to form the image in this case. Explain how the focal length of the lens can be determined from this arrangement.

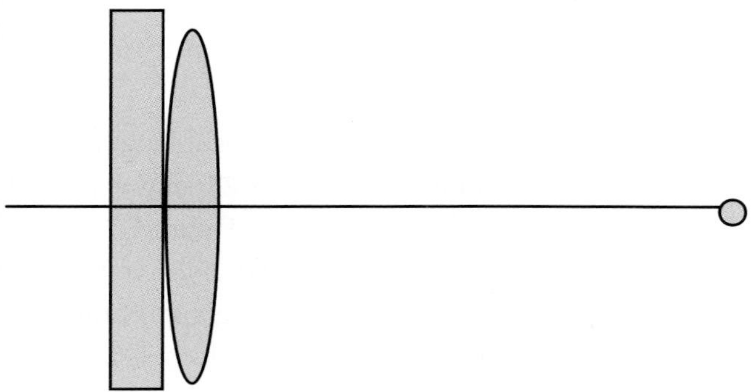

Figure G2.29 For question 13.

14 A converging lens has a focal length of 15 cm. An object is placed 20 cm from the lens.
(a) Determine the image (i.e. its position and whether it is real or virtual, upright or inverted) and find the magnification.
(b) Draw a ray diagram to confirm your results.

15 An object is at a distance of 5.0 m from a screen. A converging lens of focal length 60 cm is placed between the object and the screen so that an image of the object is formed on the screen.
(a) At what distance(s) from the screen should the lens be placed?
(b) Which choice results in the larger image?

16 Two converging lenses each of focal length 10.0 cm are 4.00 cm apart. Find the focal length of this lens combination.

17 An object is viewed through a system of two converging lenses L_1 and L_2 (to the right of L_1). L_1 has focal length of 15.0 cm and L_2 has focal length of 2.0 cm. The distance between the lenses is 25.0 cm and the distance between the object (placed to the left of L_1) and L_1 is 40.0 cm. Determine:
(a) the position of the image;
(b) the magnification of the image;
(c) the orientation of the image.

18 An object is viewed through a system of two lenses L_1 and L_2 (to the right of L_1). L_1 is converging and has a focal length of 35.0 cm; L_2 is diverging and has a focal length of 20.0 cm. The distance between the lenses is 25.0 cm and the distance between the object (placed to the left of L_1) and L_1 is 30.0 cm. Determine:
(a) the position of the image;
(b) the magnification of the image;
(c) the orientation of the image.

19 The pupil of the human eye through which light enters the eye is about 3 mm in radius. Find out how much more light a telescope with a radius of 5.0 m can collect.

20 A converging lens of focal length 10.0 cm is used as a magnifying glass. An object whose size is 1.6 mm is placed at some distance from the lens so that a virtual image is formed a distance of 25 cm in front of the lens.
(a) What is the distance between the object and the lens?
(b) Where should the object be placed if the image is to form at infinity?
(c) When the image is at infinity, find its angular size.

21 Your *IBO Data Booklet* lists the formula for the angular magnification of the simple magnifying glass as $M = \frac{\theta'}{\theta}$.
(a) By drawing suitable diagrams, show the angles that are entered into this formula.
(b) A simple magnifying glass produces an image at the near point. Explain what is meant by near point.
(c) Show that when a simple magnifying glass produces an image at the near point, the magnification is given by $M = 1 + \frac{25}{f}$, where f is the focal length of the lens.

22 The normal human eye can distinguish two objects a distance of 0.12 mm apart when they are placed at the near point. If a simple magnifying glass of focal length 5.00 cm is used to view the images at the near point, how close can the objects be and still be distinguished as distinct?

23 The objective of a microscope has a focal length of 0.80 cm and the eyepiece has a focal length of 4.0 cm. Find the magnification of the microscope. (The final image is at infinity.)

24 The moon is at a distance of about 3.8×10^8 m and its diameter is about 3.5×10^6 m.
(a) Determine that the angle subtended by the diameter of the moon at the eye of an observer on earth is about 0.53°.
(b) A very large telescope objective lens has a focal length of about 20 m. Calculate the diameter of the image of the moon formed by such a lens.

25 A telescope consists of an objective, L_1, which is a converging lens of focal length 80.0 cm and an eyepiece of focal length 20.0 cm. The object is very far from the objective (effectively an infinite distance away) and the image is formed at infinity.
(a) What is the angular magnification of this telescope?
(b) The telescope is used to view a building of height 65.0 m a distance of 2.50 km away. What is the angular size of the final image?

26 A refracting telescope has an eyepiece focal length of 3.0 cm and an objective focal length of 67.0 cm.
(a) What is the magnification of the telescope?
(b) What is its length? (Assume that the final image is produced at infinity.)

27 A refracting telescope has a distance between the objective and the eyepiece of 60 cm. The focal length of the eyepiece is 3.0 cm. The eyepiece has to be moved 1.5 cm further from the objective to provide a clear image of an object some finite distance away. What is this distance? (Assume that the final image is produced at infinity.)

28 (a) Describe the two main lens aberrations and indicate how these can be corrected.
(b) In an attempt to understand the distortion caused by spherical aberration, a student considers the following model. She places an object of height 4.00 cm at a distance of 8.00 cm from a converging lens. One end of the object is 1.00 cm below the principal axis and the other 3.00 cm above. She assumes that rays leaving the bottom of the object will have a focal length of 4.00 cm and the rays from the top a focal length of 3.50 cm. (See Figure G2.30.) (i) Under these assumptions, draw rays from the bottom and top of the object to locate the image. (ii) Draw the image again by using the 4.00 cm focal length for all rays and compare.

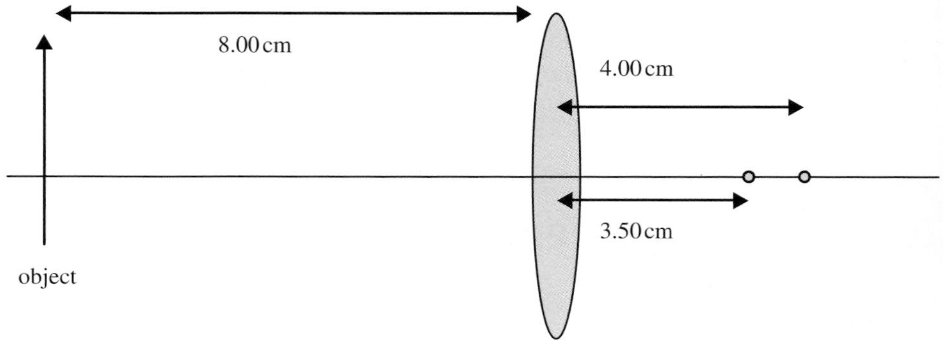

8.00 cm
4.00 cm
3.50 cm
object

Figure G2.30 For question 28.

29 An object is placed in front and to the left of a converging lens, and a real image is formed on the other side of the lens. If the distance of the object from the left focal point is x and the distance of the image from the right focal point is y, prove that $xy = f^2$.

Interference and diffraction

In Chapter 4.3 and the previous chapter, we saw the behaviour of light in the *geometrical approximation*, which is when the important phenomena of diffraction and interference are neglected, so that we can treat light propagation along straight lines. This chapter gives a detailed account of the phenomenon of interference from two coherent sources. It also deals with multiple-slit diffraction and the diffraction grating.

Objectives

By the end of this chapter you should be able to:

- appreciate the meaning of the terms *coherence* and *coherent sources*;
- give the meanings of the terms *phase difference* and *path difference*;
- describe *Young's two-slit experiment*;
- derive, understand and use the formula $d \sin \theta = n\lambda$ for *constructive interference*, and derive from this the formula

  $$s = \frac{\lambda D}{d};$$

- describe one method to measure the *wavelength of light*;
- appreciate that under the right conditions, *interference takes place for all waves*;
- show the effect on the intensity of light of adding *more narrow slits* with the same slit separation;
- solve problems with the *diffraction grating formula*, $d \sin \theta = n\lambda$, which gives the positions of the maxima.

Two-source interference

In Chapter 4.4 we saw that, when identical waves are emitted from two coherent sources and observed at the same point in space, interference will take place (see Figure G3.1). The principle of superposition allowed us to determine the following:

▶ If the path difference is an integral multiple of the wavelength, *constructive* interference takes place:

$$\text{path difference} = n\lambda, \quad n = 0, \pm1, \pm2, \pm3 \ldots$$

If the path difference is a half-integral multiple of the wavelength, *destructive* interference takes place:

$$\text{path difference} = \left(n + \tfrac{1}{2}\right)\lambda, \quad n = 0, \pm1, \pm2, \pm3 \ldots$$

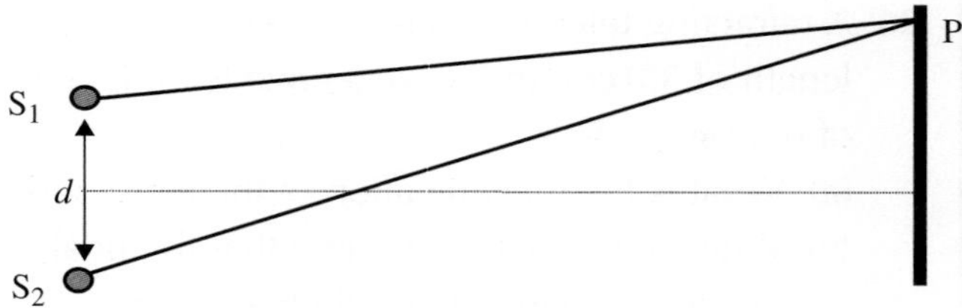

Figure G3.1 Interference from two coherent sources. The waves arriving at P from the two sources travel different distances in getting there and hence arrive with a path difference.

The two sources (black circles) in Figure G3.2 emit circular wavefronts (four are shown from each source). These represent crests. At points such as A, B and C crests of one source meet crests from the other and so constructive interference takes place. The path difference for each case is zero, since these are equidistant from the sources. Constructive interference also takes place for a point such as D, for which the path difference is three wavelengths (a distance of one wavelength from one source and four wavelengths from the other). On the other hand, for a point such as E, destructive interference takes place. This is because point E is a distance of two wavelengths from one source but three and a half from the other, resulting in a path difference of one and a half wavelengths.

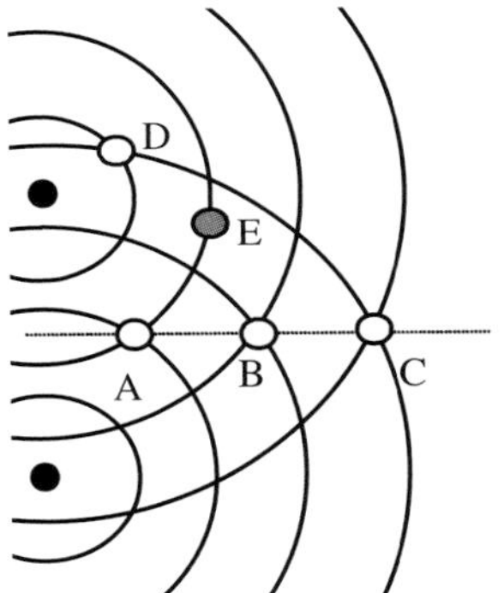

Figure G3.2 Interference between circular wavefronts.

Two-source interference for light, sound and water waves can be studied using the arrangements in Figure G3.3.

In the case of light, monochromatic light (i.e. light of one specific wavelength) from a laser is allowed to fall on two very thin slits separated by a small distance (0.1 mm or less). Interference fringes are observed on a screen some distance away. Constructive interference means bright light, and destructive interference means points of darkness.

Sound interference can be observed if sound from a signal generator is fed into two loudspeakers and an observer some distance away listens to both speakers, or if a microphone picks up the sound and feeds it into an oscilloscope. At points of constructive interference the oscilloscope signal will be large, corresponding to high intensity of sound, and at points of destructive interference it will be almost zero, corresponding to low intensity.

For water waves, two-source interference is observed if a signal generator drives two dippers in a ripple tank. Where destructive interference takes place, the water surface is almost flat.

If the path difference is anything other than an integral or half-integral multiple of the wavelength, then the resultant amplitude of the wave at P will be some value between zero and $2A$, where A is the amplitude of one of the waves.

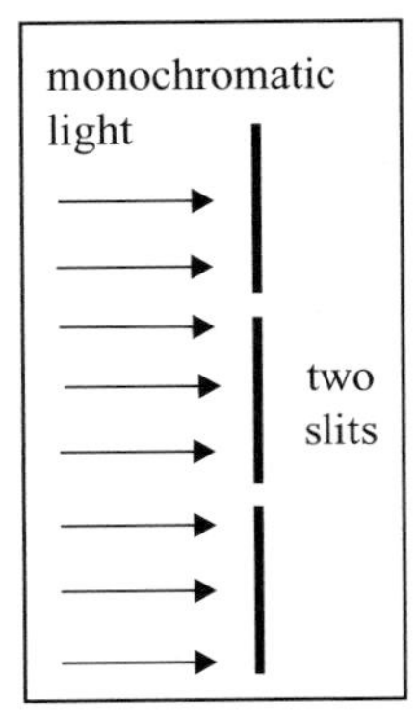

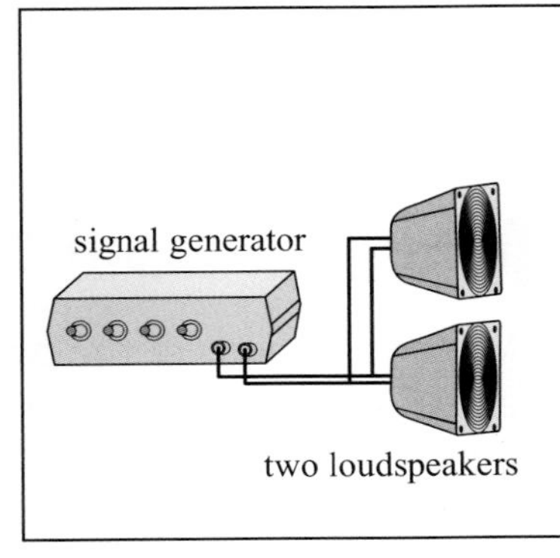

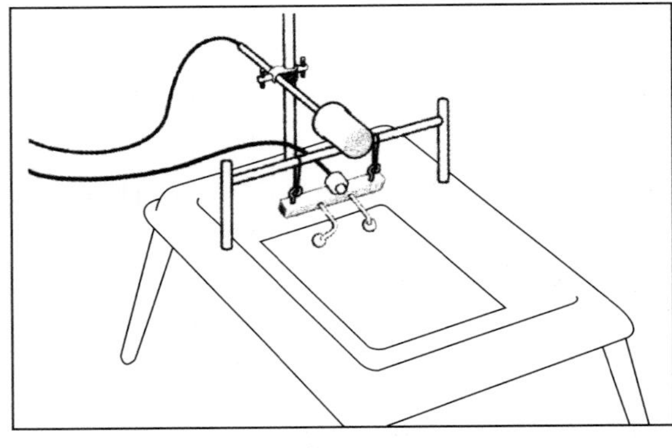

Figure G3.3 Experimental arrangements to observe interference for light, sound and water waves.

Interference for light

In Figure G3.4, monochromatic laser light falls on two slits, which then act as the two sources of coherent light. The precise meaning of coherence and coherent light will be given later. Point Z is such that the distance S_1P equals the distance ZP. The path difference is thus S_2Z. We want to calculate this path difference in order to derive the conditions for constructive interference at P. Note that, in practice, the distance between the slits, d, is only 0.1 mm and the distance to the screen is a few metres. This means that, approximately, the lines S_1P and ZP are parallel and the angles PS_1Z and PZS_1 are right angles. Thus, the angle S_2S_1Z equals θ, the angle defining point P (since these two angles have their sides mutually perpendicular).

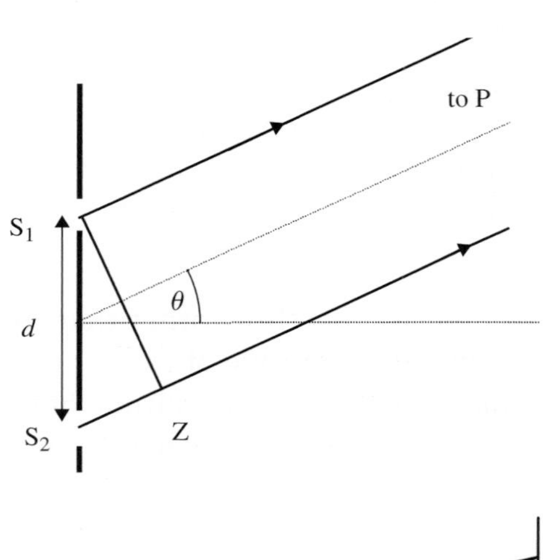

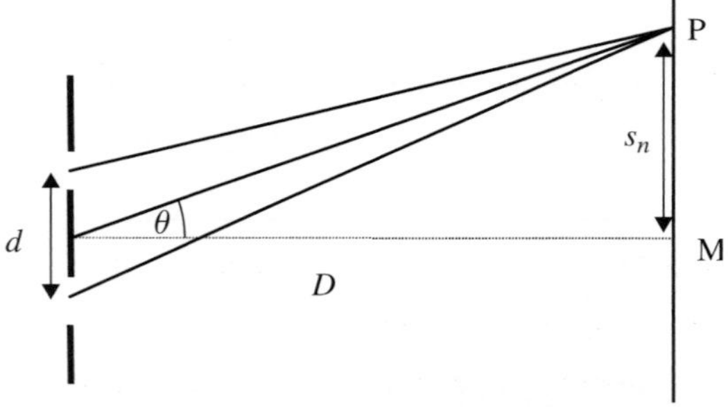

Figure G3.4 The geometry of the problem that enters in the calculation of the path difference. The nth maximum at P is a distance s_n from the centre of the screen.

The distance S_2Z (i.e. the path difference) is (by trigonometry) equal to $d \sin \theta$ and so:

▶ The condition for *constructive interference* at P becomes

$$d \sin \theta = n\lambda$$

Here, d is the separation of the two slits. As implied above, the angle θ is quite small, so $\sin\theta$ is small, which means we can approximate $\sin\theta$ by $\tan\theta$ (check on your calculator that for small angles θ, in radians, it is an excellent approximation that $\sin\theta \sim \tan\theta \sim \theta$). But $\tan\theta = \frac{s_n}{D}$ (see Figure G3.4) where D is the distance of the slits from the screen and s_n stands for the distance MP, i.e. the distance of the point P from the middle point of the screen. The suffix n in s_n signifies that we are considering the nth maximum in the interference pattern. Thus,

$$s_n = \frac{n\lambda D}{d}$$

▶ The linear separation, s, on a screen of *two consecutive maxima* is thus

$$s = s_{n+1} - s_n = (n+1)\frac{\lambda D}{d} - n\frac{\lambda D}{d}$$

$$s = \frac{\lambda D}{d}$$

Therefore, in an interference experiment, measurement of the separation s between two successive maxima, and of the distances D and d, gives a value for the wavelength λ of the wave.

This last formula shows that the maxima of the interference pattern are equally separated. Additional work shows that these maxima are also equally bright.

Young's two-slit experiment

Modern versions of the two-slit interference experiment are performed with laser light. This makes sure that the two slits act as coherent sources of light. An early demonstration of the phenomenon of interference for light was performed by Thomas Young in 1801.

Monochromatic light from a source S falls upon a small slit as shown in Figure G3.5. As a result of diffraction, the light spreads around the single slit, which acts as a coherent source illuminating two narrow, parallel slits separated by a very small distance. The interference pattern is observed on a screen placed some distance from the slits. A filter placed in front of the light source ensures the light hitting the slits is monochromatic. The lens between the source and the single slit is there to make sure that the wavefronts hitting the single slit are *planar* (this is a technicality known as Fraunhofer diffraction and need not concern us further). The lens, filter and single slit are unnecessary if a laser is used.

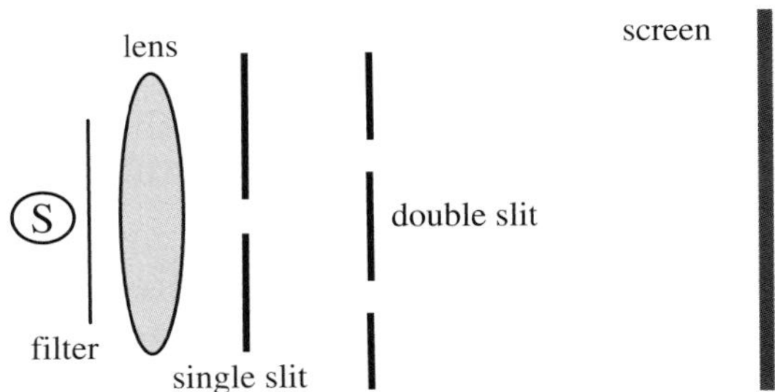

Figure G3.5 Young's two-slit experiment.

Example question

Q1

In a Young's two-slit experiment, a source of light of unknown wavelength is used to illuminate two very narrow slits a distance of 0.15 mm apart. On a screen at a distance of 1.30 m from the slits, bright spots are observed separated by a distance of 4.95 mm. What is the wavelength of light being used?

Answer

By straightforward application of the result $s = \frac{\lambda D}{d}$ we find a wavelength of 571 nm.

Why must the two sources be coherent?

We have postponed until the end a discussion of the very important fact that for interference to be observed the two sources must be **coherent**.

First, we introduce the concept of phase. The equation giving the displacement of a wave travelling toward the right with amplitude A, period T and wavelength λ is given by

$$y = A\sin\left(\frac{2\pi t}{T} - \frac{2\pi x}{\lambda} + \phi\right)$$

where the angle ϕ is known as the *phase* of the wave. Two waves given by the equations

$$y_1 = A\sin\left(\frac{2\pi t}{T} - \frac{2\pi x}{\lambda}\right)$$

and

$$y_2 = A\sin\left(\frac{2\pi t}{T} - \frac{2\pi x}{\lambda} + \frac{\pi}{4}\right)$$

are identical in that they have the same amplitude, frequency and wavelength but are said to have a *phase difference* between them of $\frac{\pi}{4}$.

▶ If the phase difference between the waves stays the same as time goes on, the sources are said to be coherent. Coherence means a constant phase difference between two sources.

Two loudspeakers connected to the same amplifier would produce sound waves with a constant phase difference between them (usually a zero phase difference); they would be coherent sources. Similarly, waves produced on two identical strings by two people shaking the ends of the strings in identical fashion without stopping would also produce coherent waves on the strings.

The case of light, however, is very different. Unlike a loudspeaker, which produces a continuous stream of sound waves, a source of light, such as a lamp, produces a non-continuous stream of light waves. Assume that the lamp is a point source of light, i.e. that just one point in the lamp filament produces the emitted light. If we could film that point while it is emitting light and then play the film in slow motion (slowed down by a factor of a few billion times) we would see the point being on for while, then off for a while, and so on. Consider now two such lamps. Even if the lamps are identical, the light emitted from one lamp will not be correlated with that from the other. Even if the on–off times coincide, there is no reason why the phase difference between the waves emitted will be the same as time goes on. The two lamps are incoherent sources of light.

The conditions derived earlier for two-slit interference hold for the case where the phase difference between the two sources initially is zero. If the sources are coherent but there is a phase difference ϕ between them, the relevant path difference now is $\frac{\phi}{2\pi}\lambda + (d_1 - d_2)$, where d_1 and d_2 are the distances from S_1 to P and from S_2 to P, respectively.

Working precisely as before, the condition for constructive interference is

$$d_1 - d_2 = n\lambda + \frac{\phi}{2\pi}\lambda$$
$$n = 0, 1, 2, 3, \ldots$$

and for destructive interference, we get

$$d_1 - d_2 = \left(n + \tfrac{1}{2}\right)\lambda + \frac{\phi}{2\pi}\lambda$$
$$n = 0, 1, 2, 3, \ldots$$

For $\phi = 0$, these conditions give the familiar ones derived earlier.

The conditions for arbitrary phase difference explain, finally, why the two sources must be coherent. Coherence between the two sources means that the phase difference between them, ϕ (whatever it is, not necessarily zero) stays the same as time goes on. If it does not remain constant (if ϕ is some function of time, $\phi(t)$), then at a particular point P the issue of whether we get a maximum or a minimum also depends on time. For example, if ϕ starts from zero, increases to 2π and then drops back to zero again periodically, with a period of, say, 10^{-9} s, then what is observed at P is a rapid succession of maxima and minima with a period of 10^{-9} s. The observer thus only sees an average of these effects – there is no interference pattern at all.

Intensity in two-slit interference

The fringes in a Young's two-slit experiment, *where the slit width is assumed negligible*, are equally bright.

The formula for intensity is a function of the angle θ, defined in Figure G3.4. This is graphed in Figure G3.6 for the case of $d = 2\lambda$. The horizontal variable is θ (in degrees). It is seen that the fringes are equally bright as mentioned earlier.

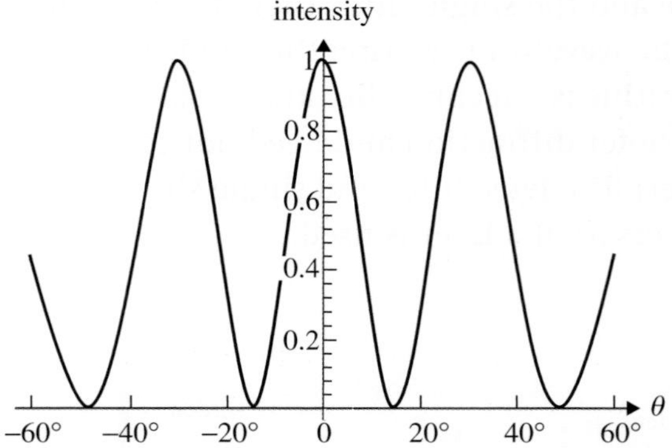

Figure G3.6 The intensity pattern for two slits of negligible width. The separation of the slits is $d = 2\lambda$.

For larger slit separations the maxima are closer to each other. Figure G3.7 shows the intensity for $d = 4\lambda$.

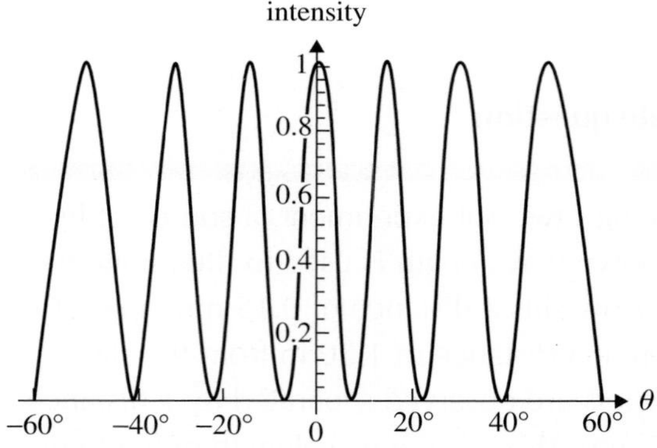

Figure G3.7 The intensity pattern for two slits of negligible width. The separation of the slits is $d = 4\lambda$.

▶ This shows that, for accurate measurement of the fringe separation, as small a slit separation as possible should be used.

Example question

Q2

Calculate the fringe separation for light of wavelength 680 nm that falls on two slits separated by 0.1 mm when the screen is placed 1.3 m from the slits.

Answer

$$s = \frac{\lambda D}{d}$$
$$= \frac{680 \times 10^{-9} \times 1.3}{0.1 \times 10^{-3}} \text{ m}$$
$$= 8.8 \text{ mm}$$

▶ The *width* of the slits has not entered in this discussion. This is because we are assuming that the two slits have a very small width compared with the wavelength of the wave. In this idealized case, the conclusions we stated are valid.

In a more realistic case, the width is also important and, because of diffraction at each slit, there is a *modulating effect* on the interference pattern (i.e. the fringes are no longer of equal intensity). In the thin-slit approximation, covering one of the slits would completely wipe out the interference pattern (no dark and bright fringes – just uniform illumination) – see Figure G3.8.

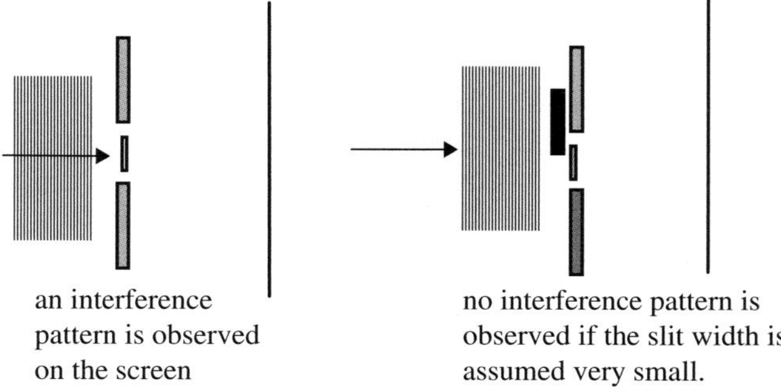

Figure G3.8 In the idealized case of negligible slit widths, covering one slit destroys the interference pattern.

In the realistic case, covering one slit would still result in a complicated diffraction pattern on the screen.

Two-slit experiments can also be performed with water waves in a ripple tank, sound waves (two speakers connected to a signal generator), microwaves, radio waves, etc. All waves show interference phenomena.

Multiple-slit diffraction

As the number of slits increases, the interference pattern increases in complexity. We will consider here the simplified case in which the width of each slit is very small compared with the wavelength being used. Consider the case of four slits separated by a distance d, as shown in Figure G3.9. If the path difference between the ray leaving slit 1 and the ray leaving slit 2 is an integral number of wavelengths, then by similar triangles the path difference between *any* two rays is also an integral number of wavelengths. The path difference between the rays from slits 1 and 2 is $d \sin\theta$ and so constructive interference takes place whenever

$$d \sin\theta = n\lambda, \quad n = 0, \pm1, \pm2, \pm3, \ldots$$

that is, the same condition as in the two-slit case. Here d is the separation of two successive slits.

▶ Thus the maxima of the multiple-slit interference pattern are observed at the same angles as the corresponding two-slit pattern with the same slit separation.

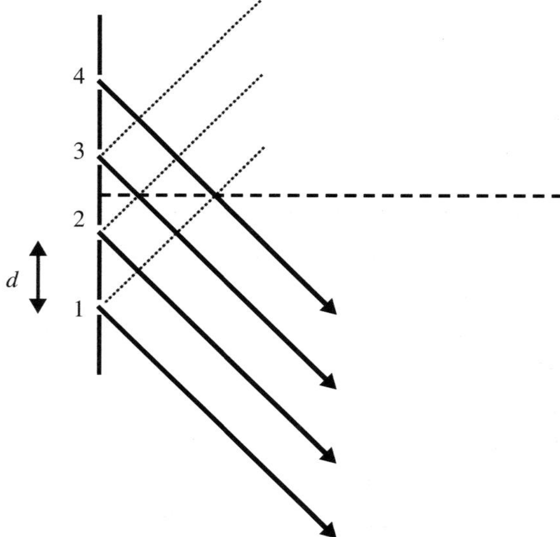

Figure G3.9 The path difference between the first slit and any other slit is an integral multiple of the path difference between the first and second slit. Thus, if the path difference between the first and second slit is an integral multiple of a wavelength, constructive interference from all slits takes place.

At points for which the condition above is *not* satisfied, there is cancellation of the waves from the four slits, but the cancellation is not always complete, giving rise to secondary maxima.

The number of secondary maxima is $N-2$ where N is the number of slits. The intensity of the principal maxima is proportional to N^2 and their width is proportional to $1/N$ Thus, as N increases, the intensity of the secondary maxima decreases and becomes completely negligible (see Figures G3.10 and G3.11). This means, therefore, that for large N the primary maxima are bright and thin, making the measurement of their separation easy.

The minima are observed at

$$d \sin\theta = \frac{m}{N}\lambda$$

where $m = 1, 2, 3, \ldots$, but $m = N, 2N, 3N, \ldots$ are excluded. Here N stands for the number of slits.

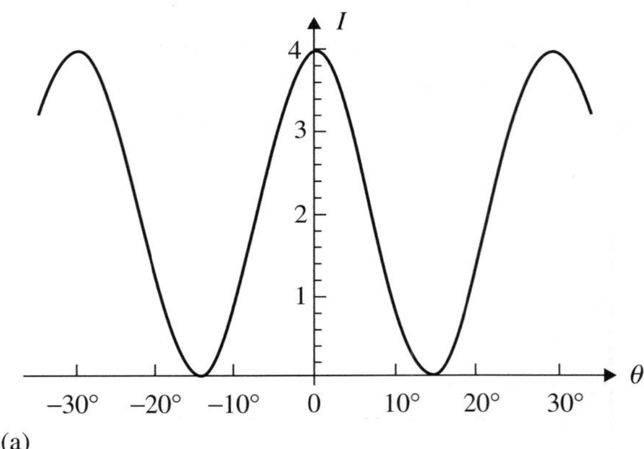

(a)

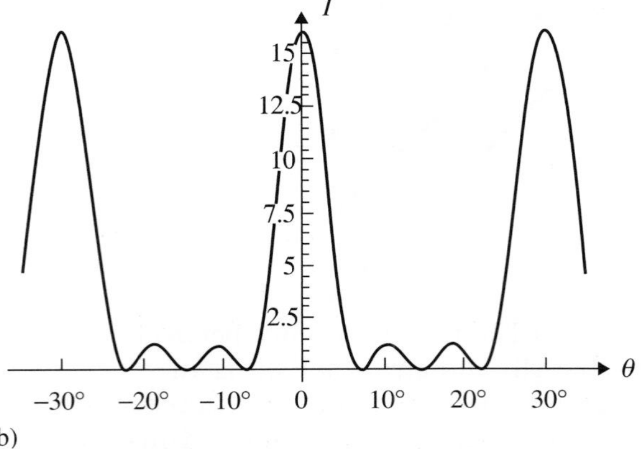

(b)

Figure G3.10 (a) The intensity distribution for two slits. (b) The intensity distribution for four slits. Note how the width of the maxima decreases but their position stays the same.

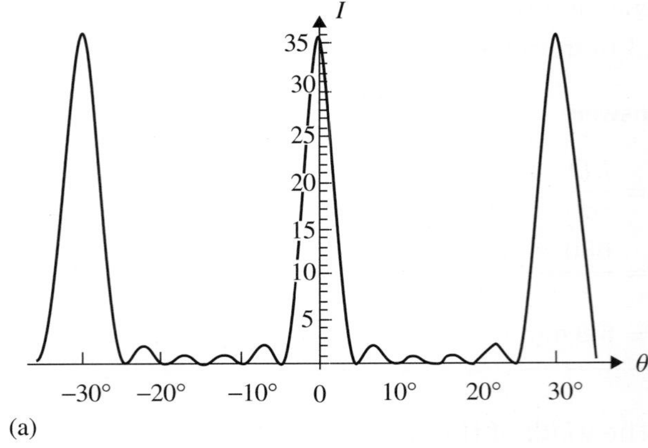

(a)

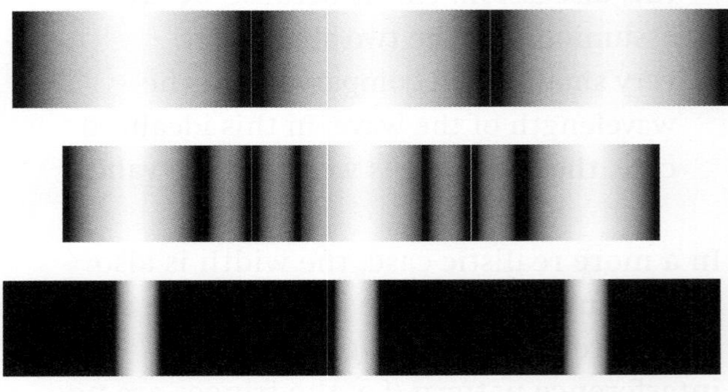

(b)

Figure G3.11 (a) The intensity distribution for six slits. Note how the width of the maxima decreases but their position stays the same. Note also how the relative importance of the secondary maxima decreases with increasing slit number. (b) The intensity pattern for two slits (top), four slits (middle) and very many slits (bottom). Note that the principal maxima are observed at the same positions. For $N = 4$ there are two secondary maxima. As N increases, the secondary maxima become unimportant and the primary maxima become very narrow. In all cases we assume the slit width to be negligible.

Example question

Q3

What is the slit separation for the intensity distribution patterns of Figure G3.11(a)?

Answer

The first primary maximum occurs at $\theta = 30°$ and since

$d \sin\theta = \lambda$

$\Rightarrow d = \dfrac{\lambda}{\sin 30°}$

$= 2\lambda$

The diffraction grating

The diffraction grating is an important device in spectroscopy (the analysis of light) whose main purpose is the measurement of the wavelength of light. A grating is simply a large number of parallel slits whose width we take to be negligible. Instead of actual slits, modern gratings consist of a transparent slide on which lines or grooves have been precisely cut. The first diffraction gratings were constructed by the American astronomer David Rittenhouse in 1785 and a few years later by the German Joseph von Fraunhofer, who made significant discoveries with it. The advantage of a large number of slits is that the maxima in the interference pattern are sharp and bright and can easily be distinguished from their neighbours. This makes measurement of their separation easier. The maxima of the pattern are observed at angles given by the formula

$$d \sin\theta = n\lambda, \quad n = 0, 1, 2, 3, \ldots$$

In practice, a diffraction grating is stated by its manufacturer to have 'X lines per centimetre (millimetre)'. This means that the separation of the slits is $d = \frac{1}{X}$ cm (mm). It is quite common to find diffraction gratings with 600 lines per mm corresponding to a slit separation of $d = 1.67 \times 10^{-6}$ m.

Example question

Q4

Light of wavelength 680 nm falls normally on a diffraction grating that has 600 lines per mm. What is the angle separating the central maximum ($n = 0$) from the next ($n = 1$)? How many maxima can be seen?

Answer

The separation between slits is

$$d = \frac{1}{600} \times 10^{-3} \text{ m}$$

With $n = 1$ we find

$$\sin\theta = 1 \times 680 \times 10^{-9} \times 600 \times 10^{3}$$
$$= 0.408$$

Hence

$$\theta = 24.1^\circ$$

For $n = 2$ we find $\theta = 54.7^\circ$ and no solution can be found for $n = 3$; the sine of the angle becomes larger than 1. Thus, we can see the central maximum and two orders on either side.

QUESTIONS

1 In a Young's two-slit experiment it is found that an nth-order maximum for a wavelength of 680.0 nm coincides with the $(n + 1)$th maximum of light of wavelength 510.0 nm. What is n?

2 Two loudspeakers are 1.00 m apart and are connected to the same audio oscillator. An observer walks along a straight line a distance of 12.0 m from the loudspeakers as shown in Figure G3.12. The observer hears a loud sound at M but almost no sound by the time she gets to point P a distance of 2.00 m from M. Explain how this is possible. Find the wavelength of sound emitted by the loudspeakers.

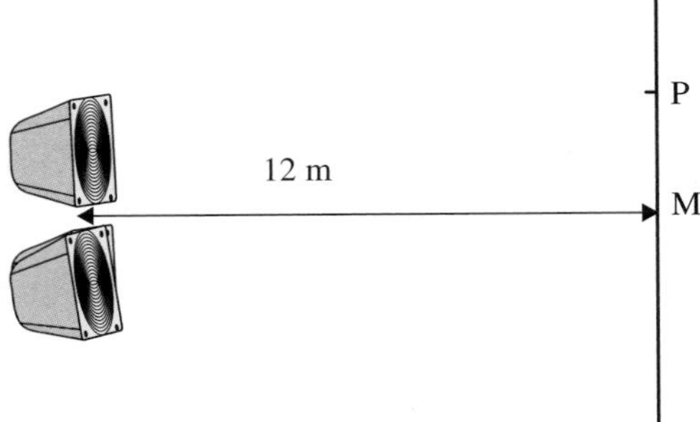

Figure G3.12 For question 2.

3 In a Young's two-slit experiment, a coherent source of light of wavelength 680 nm is used to illuminate two very narrow slits a distance of 0.12 mm apart. If a screen is placed at a distance of 1.50 m from the slits, find the separation of two successive bright spots.

4 Explain why two identical flashlights pointing light to the same spot on a screen will never produce an interference pattern.

5 Explain what will happen to the interference pattern in a Young's two-slit experiment if *one* of the slits is covered with transparent film that absorbs some of the light through it.

6 In a typical classroom demonstration, two loudspeakers are connected to the same audio signal generator and students are asked to stand at various positions in the room to listen to the sound produced. Depending on where they stand, the sound is sometimes loud and sometimes very soft. What wave phenomenon does this demonstrate? Give *three* reasons why there are no spots where the intensity of sound is completely reduced to zero.

7 Discuss the effect on the bright spots in a Young's two-slit experiment of:
(a) decreasing the separation of the slits;
(b) increasing the wavelength of light;
(c) increasing the distance to the screen;
(d) increasing the distance of the source from the slits;
(e) using white light as the source.

8 Light of wavelength 644 nm (in air) is incident normally on two narrow parallel slits a distance of 1 mm apart. A screen is placed a distance of 1.2 m from the slits.
(a) Determine the distance on the screen between the central maximum and the fifth bright spot.
(b) If this experiment were repeated in water (index of refraction 1.33), how would your answer change?

9 A car moves along a road that is parallel to the twin antennas of a radio station broadcasting at a frequency of 95.0 MHz (see Figure G3.13). The antennas are 30.0 m apart and the distance of A from the mid-point of the antennas is 2.0 km. When in position A, the reception is good, but it drops to almost zero at position B. What is the distance AB?

Figure G3.13 For question 9.

10 Two radio transmitters are 80.0 m apart on a north–south line. They emit coherently at a wavelength of 1.50 m. A satellite in a north–south orbit travelling at 7.50 km s^{-1} receives a signal that alternates in intensity with a frequency of 0.560 Hz. Assuming that the signal received by the satellite is the superposition of the waves from the individual transmitters, find:
(a) the distance between two consecutive points where the satellite receives a strong signal;
(b) the height of the satellite from the earth's surface.

11 Figure G3.14 is the intensity pattern from a two-slit interference experiment. Determine the separation of the slits in terms of the wavelength of light used.

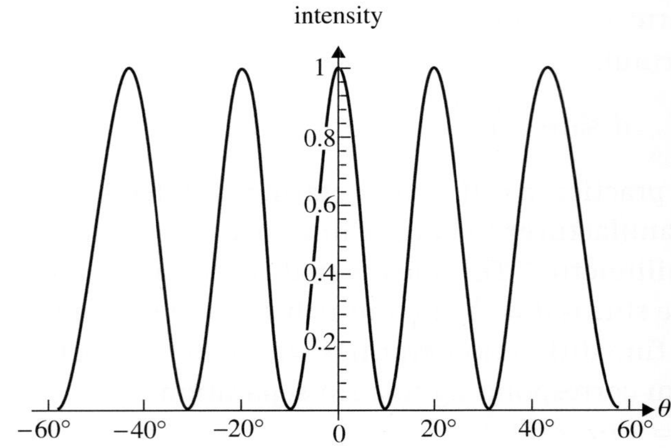

Figure G3.14 For question 11.

12 What will the intensity pattern for the two slits of question 11 be if the slit separation is halved?

HL only

13 In a two-slit interference experiment with slits of negligible width, five maxima are observed on each side of the central maximum. When the slits are replaced by two slits of finite width separated by the same distance as before, the third maximum on either side of the central maximum is missing (i.e. the intensity of light there is zero). Calculate the width of the slits in terms of their separation, *d*.

14 Two *very narrow*, parallel slits separated by a distance of 1.4×10^{-5} m are illuminated by coherent, monochromatic light of wavelength 7.0×10^{-7} m.

(a) Describe what is meant by coherent and monochromatic light.

(b) Draw a graph to show the intensity of light observed on a screen far from the slits.

(c) By drawing another graph on the same axes, illustrate the effect on the intensity distribution of increasing the width of the slits to 2.8×10^{-6} m.

15 A diffraction grating with 350 lines per mm produces first-order maxima at angles 8.34° and 8.56° for two separate wavelengths of light.

(a) What are these wavelengths?

(b) What angle separates the second-order maxima of these wavelengths?

16 A grating with 400 lines per mm is illuminated with light of wavelength 600.0 nm.

(a) At what angles are maxima observed?

(b) What is the largest order that can be seen with this grating and this wavelength?

17 Visible light ranging in wavelengths from 400.0 nm to 700.0 nm falls on a grating with 400 lines per mm. Describe the spectrum that is observed.

18 (a) Draw a graph to show the variation with angle of the intensity of light observed on a screen some distance from two very narrow, parallel slits when coherent monochromatic light falls on the slits.

(b) Illustrate by a graph on the same axis the effect on the intensity of light of replacing the two slits by five very narrow slits whose separation is the same as that of the original two slits.

X-rays

This brief chapter looks at X-rays, including their production, X-ray scattering and diffraction, and the Bragg condition.

Objectives

By the end of this chapter you should be able to:

- describe the mechanisms for the *production of X-rays*;
- predict the effect on the *X-ray spectrum* of changes in the *accelerating voltage* and the nature of the *target material*;
- explain how *X-ray diffraction* results from *scattering of X-rays* in a crystal;
- derive the *Bragg scattering condition* and solve problems involving it;
- outline how X-rays may be used to determine the *structure of crystals*.

The production of X-rays

Suppose that electrons emitted from a hot wire (as in a cathode-ray tube) are accelerated through a very large potential difference, say 30 kV. We then let these electrons hit a piece of material (e.g. tungsten) called the 'target'. (See Figure G4.1.)

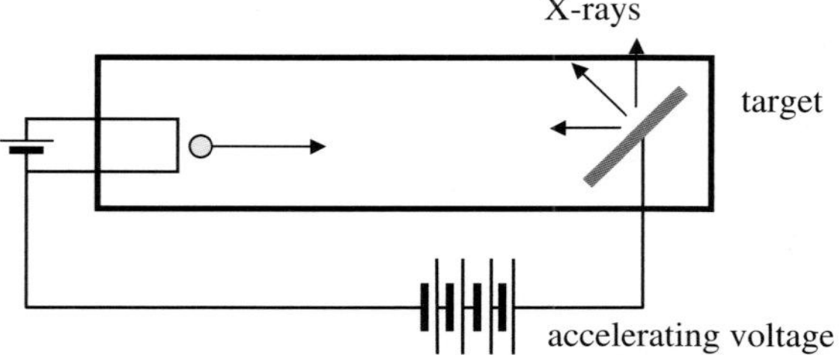

Figure G4.1 Apparatus for producing X-rays. The emitted electrons are accelerated toward the target by a high potential difference.

As we saw earlier, when charges accelerate, they emit electromagnetic radiation. Here the electrons are rapidly brought to rest by the collisions with the atoms of the target and thus radiate electromagnetic radiation. The radiation emitted will have a whole range of wavelengths.

Figure G4.2 gives the intensity of the radiation (i.e. the number of photons emitted for a given wavelength times the energy of one of those photons) as a function of the wavelength.

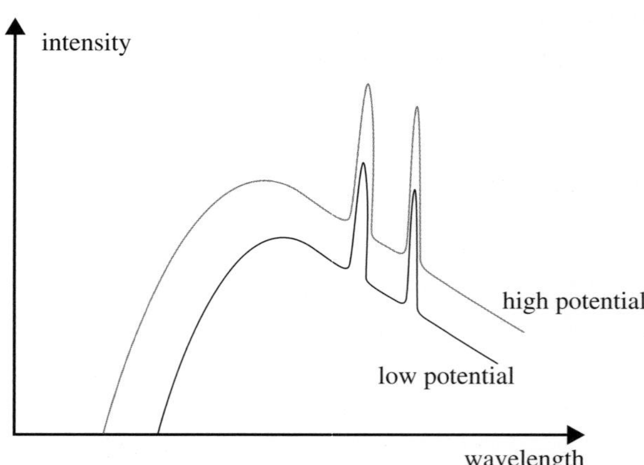

Figure G4.2 The spectrum of X-rays. Increasing the accelerating potential decreases the minimum wavelength.

The striking feature is the existence of a minimum wavelength below which no radiation is emitted. How is this explained? Let us imagine that the electrons have been accelerated through a potential difference of V volts. Then, just before hitting the target, the electrons have kinetic energy $E_k = eV$. When an electron converts all of this energy into a single photon, we must have, by conservation of energy, $\frac{hc}{\lambda} = eV$, and thus we obtain a minimum wavelength

$$\lambda = \frac{hc}{eV}$$

This shows that an increased accelerating voltage results in a smaller minimum wavelength. If the electron converts part of its kinetic energy to one photon and the rest to another, this results in photons of wavelengths larger than the minimum one we just found (see Figure G4.3).

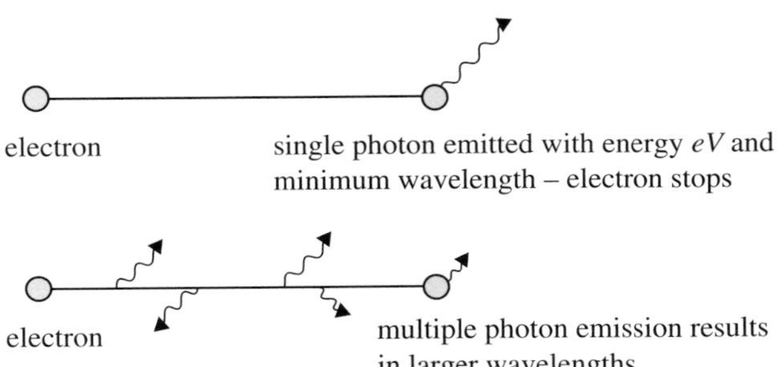

Figure G4.3 Ways in which an electron can give its energy to photons.

Of the total energy supplied to the electrons by the accelerating voltage, only a small part (a fraction of 1%) is radiated as energy of X-rays. The rest heats up the target, which means that it must be cooled if it is not to melt.

The spectrum of X-rays indicated in Figure G4.2 has two parts, the continuous spectrum whose origin we just discussed and the discrete spectrum, which is the set of spikes on top of the continuous spectrum, at specific wavelengths. If we increase the accelerating voltage, the positions of these wavelengths remain unchanged. This suggests that the spikes have to do only with the target material. What happens is that the incoming electrons knock electrons out of their ground state in the target atoms. Electrons in the atom in higher states then make the transition to occupy the now empty ground state, thus radiating photons (see Figure G4.4).

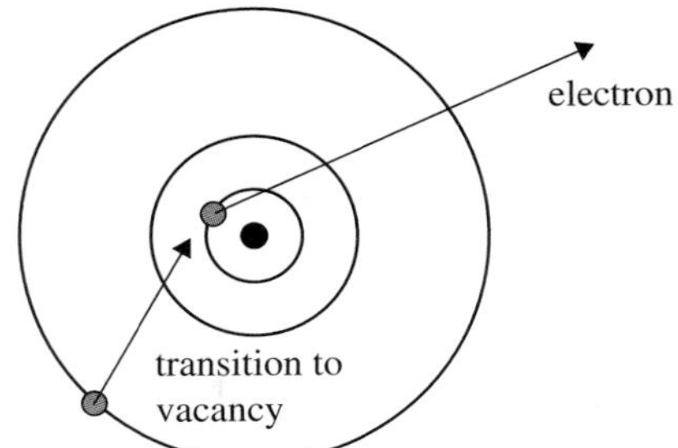

Figure G4.4 An inner-shell electron is ejected from the atom by the incoming electron. Its place is then taken by a higher-shell electron, which emits a photon in the transition.

These photons have wavelengths in the X-ray region. (In a big atom, the energy of the ground state can be many keV. Tungsten's ground state energy is −67 keV. This is why the emitted photons are in the X-ray region.) As we already know, these photons will have specific wavelengths corresponding to the energy difference between the ground state energy and the energy of the state they came from. This energy difference is, of course, characteristic of the atoms of the target and thus does not depend on the accelerating voltage V. If we change the target, we will find spikes at different wavelengths.

Example question

Q1

What is the minimum wavelength of X-rays emitted in a 50 kV tube?

Answer

The minimum wavelength is

$$\lambda = \frac{hc}{eV} = 2.49 \times 10^{-11}\ \text{m}.$$

X-ray diffraction

Soon after the discovery of X-rays by W. Röntgen, the German physicist Max von Laue suggested that a beam of X-rays directed at the regular arrangement of atoms (or ions) in a crystal would show interference effects in a way similar to light diffracting through a diffraction grating. In experiments performed in 1912, X-rays from an X-ray tube were directed at a crystal, as shown in Figure G4.5.

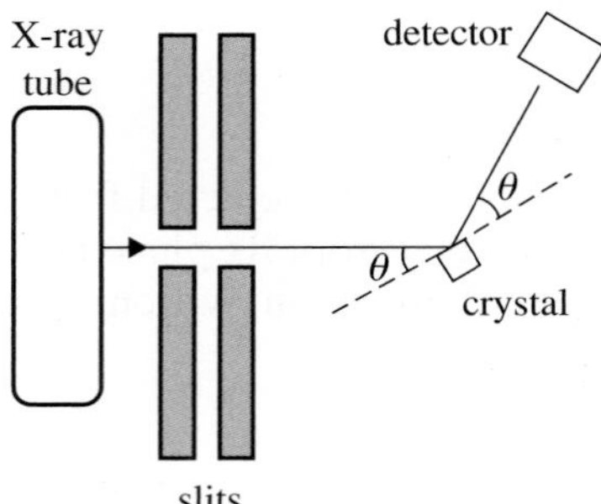

Figure G4.5 X-rays scattered by atoms in the crystal are observed at a detector. The intensity of the received X-rays is maximum at certain angles θ and minimum at others.

X-rays, scattered by the atoms in the crystal, were received at a detector, which at that time would have been photographic film. As the position of the detector was varied, it was found that there were certain angles at which the intensity of the X-rays reaching the detector was a maximum and others for which the intensity was practically zero. This is typically what happens in an interference pattern. These early experiments gave support to the idea that X-rays were electromagnetic waves. (The physical mechanism behind this effect is X-ray scattering. The incident X-rays are electromagnetic waves and so carry an electric field. This field causes the atoms it falls upon to vibrate, and therefore these radiate at the same frequency as the frequency of the incident waves. The radiated electromagnetic waves are the scattered/reflected/diffracted X-rays.)

The atoms (or ions) in a crystal are arranged in regular patterns. As von Laue suggested, the interatomic distances in the crystal are of the same order of magnitude as the wavelength of X-rays, and so could play the role of the slits in an ordinary diffraction grating used with visible light. Consider a cubic crystal, such as that of ordinary salt, sodium chloride (NaCl), in which the ions (Na^+ and Cl^-) are arranged at the vertices of cubes, as shown in Figure G4.6.

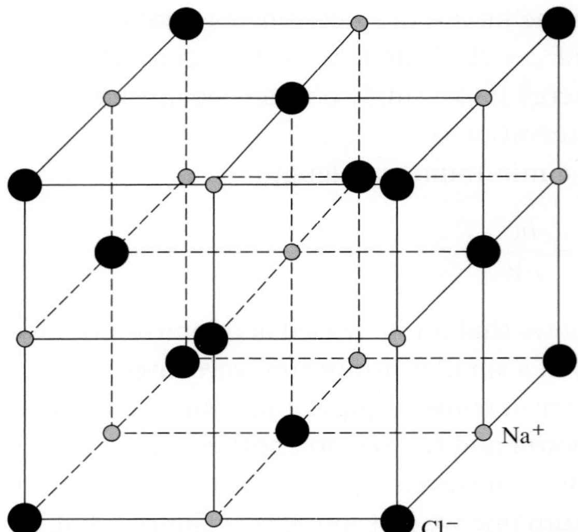

Figure G4.6 The arrangement of the ions of Na^+ and Cl^- in the crystal of ordinary salt, NaCl. (The chloride ion Cl^- is about five times bigger than the sodium ion Na^+, but for clarity it is drawn only about twice as big.)

To begin to understand the process of scattering of X-rays from a crystal, consider first a two-dimensional analogy in which atoms are arranged in rows, as shown in Figure G4.7 (two rows are shown). The figure shows X-rays scattering from adjacent atoms in the top row as well as from adjacent atoms in the second row. The angle of incidence is θ_1, which is defined as the angle between the incident ray and the row (and *not* the angle between the incident ray and the normal, as is customary in optics). Similarly the angle of scattering (reflection) is θ_2.

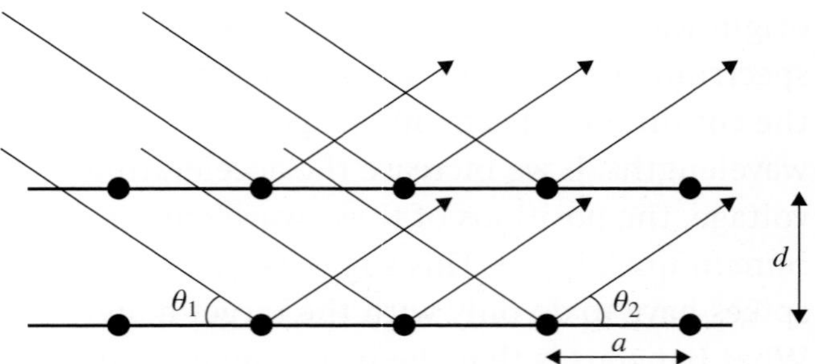

Figure G4.7 Two rows of atoms in a two-dimensional array. The distance between adjacent atoms in the same row is taken to be a, and the distance between two adjacent rows is taken to be d. In a cubic crystal, a and d would be equal.

From the geometry of Figure G4.8, we see that the scattered (reflected) rays from two adjacent atoms have a path difference between them of

$$\mathrm{AC} - \mathrm{BD} = a \cos \theta_2 - a \cos \theta_1$$

The two rays will therefore be in phase if $\theta_1 = \theta_2$.

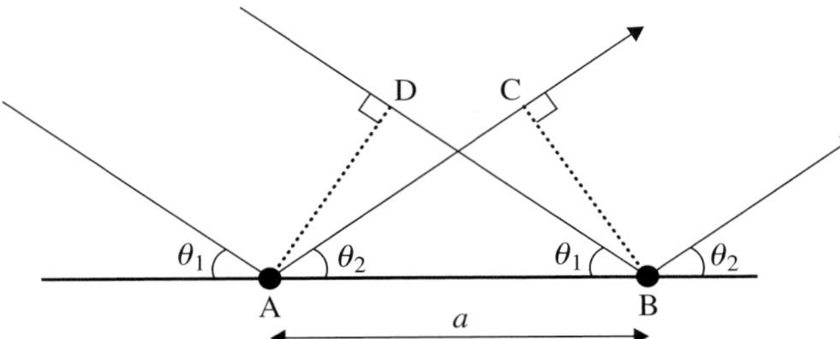

Figure G4.8 X-rays scattering from two adjacent atoms in the same row. The two rays shown will interfere constructively if the path difference between them, $a \cos \theta_2 - a \cos \theta_1$, is zero. This implies that $\theta_1 = \theta_2$. (The dotted lines are at right angles to the rays.)

Now consider the scattering involving an atom in the first row and one directly below it in the second row, as in Figure G4.9. The diagram assumes that the condition $\theta_1 = \theta_2$ is satisfied and we have set $\theta_1 = \theta_2 = \theta$.

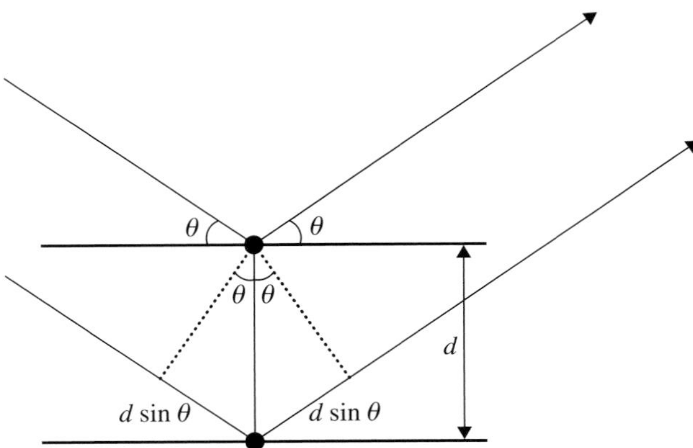

Figure G4.9 The path difference between the rays scattered from atoms in two adjacent rows is $2d \sin \theta$. (The dotted lines are at right angles to the rays.)

The path difference between the two scattered rays is

$$d \sin \theta + d \sin \theta = 2d \sin \theta$$

Therefore we will have constructive interference between the two rays if

$$2d \sin \theta = n\lambda$$

This is known as the **Bragg condition**, named in honour of William Bragg and his son Lawrence Bragg, who analysed X-ray diffraction in the manner described above.

In other words, we will get strong scattered (reflected) beams in those directions for which *both* conditions are satisfied:

1 $\theta_1 = \theta_2$ (rays scattered from atoms in first row are in phase);

2 $2d \sin \theta = n\lambda$ (rays scattered from atoms in first row and from atoms in second row are in phase).

The first condition is equivalent to saying that the angle of incidence is equal to the angle of reflection. The second is similar to the diffraction grating condition, but notice carefully the factor of 2 as well as the fact that the angle θ is defined differently here.

This discussion can be extended to a real three-dimensional crystal by now considering *planes* of atoms rather than rows. The same conditions may then be derived, except that now the distance d will stand for the distance between planes of atoms. Because we can have many different sets of parallel planes in a crystal, we will have many different values of d and many angles for which constructive interference will take place (see Figure G4.10). This means that the interference pattern will, in general, be quite complex.

Example question

Q2

X-rays of wavelength 1.45×10^{-10} m are reflected off a crystal. When the angle between the X-ray beam and the face of the crystal is increased from zero, a strong reflected beam is detected when the angle becomes 36.4°.

(a) Calculate the spacing of the crystal planes responsible for this reflection.

(b) Are there other angles at which strong reflection is observed?

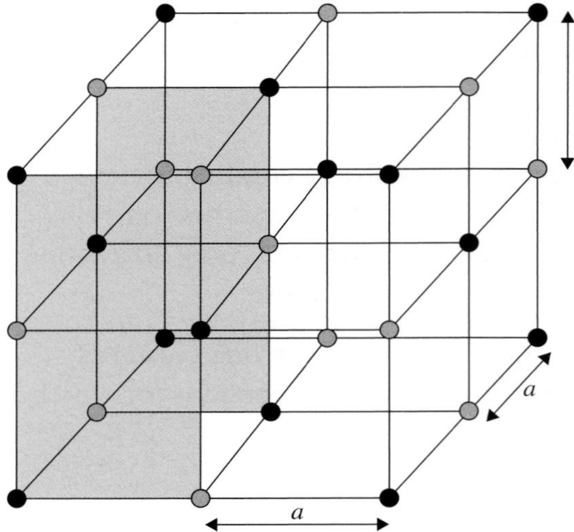

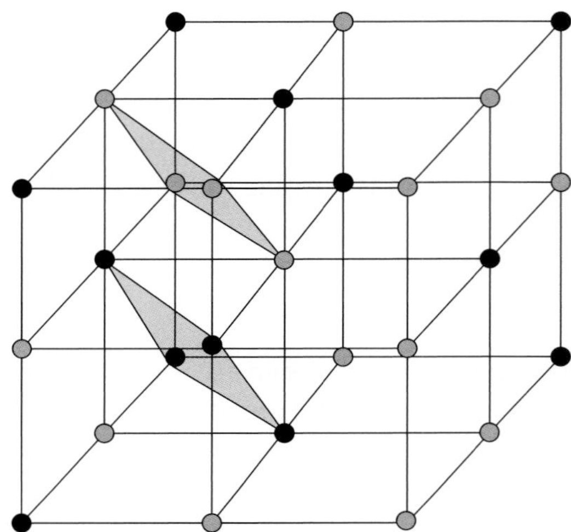

Figure G4.10 In a three-dimensional cubic crystal there are many parallel atomic planes. In the upper diagram the distance between the planes is a. In the lower diagram the distance between the planes is $\frac{a}{\sqrt{3}}$.

Answer

(a) Using the Bragg condition, we find

$$d = \frac{n\lambda}{2\sin\theta} = \frac{1 \times 1.45 \times 10^{-10}}{2\sin 36.4^\circ} = 1.22 \times 10^{-10}\,\text{m}$$

(b) With the value of d just calculated, we have

$$\sin\theta = \frac{n\lambda}{2d} = n\frac{1.45 \times 10^{-10}}{2 \times 1.22 \times 10^{-10}} = n \times 0.59$$

No other angles exist, since for $n = 2$ or higher we get $\sin\theta > 1$, which is impossible.

X-ray diffraction played a crucial role in the determination of the structure of the DNA molecule. Rosalind Franklin began studies of X-ray diffraction with the DNA molecule in the 1950s. James Watson and Francis Crick discovered the helical structure of DNA in 1963.

? QUESTIONS

1 (a) Describe how X-rays are produced.
(b) What is the minimum wavelength of X-rays emitted in a 67.0 kV machine?

2 (a) Describe what happens to the maximum frequency of the X-rays produced in an X-ray tube when the accelerating voltage is increased.
(b) In a television screen, electrons are accelerated by a potential difference of 30 kV. How fast are the electrons moving just before they hit the screen?
(c) What is the maximum frequency of the X-rays produced when the electrons in (b) are brought to rest?

3 It is said that the production of X-rays and the photoelectric effect are 'opposite' phenomena. Make this statement precise.

4 In an X-ray tube, the accelerating voltage is 40.0 kV and the current between the cathode and the anode is 20.0 mA.
(a) What is the smallest wavelength of X-rays produced in this tube.
(b) If only 0.50% of the total energy supplied is converted into X-rays, the rest going to heat up the anode, find the rate at which heat must be removed from the anode in order to keep it at a constant temperature.

5 X-rays of wavelength λ are incident on a crystal whose atomic planes are a distance d apart. The incident beam makes an angle θ with the face of the crystal. State and explain the *two* conditions that must be satisfied for a strong reflected beam to be observed at an angle θ to the face of the crystal.

6 The separation of the slits in a diffraction grating is about 10^{-6} m. Suggest why, though suitable for diffraction with visible light, this is unsuitable for diffraction with X-rays.

7 X-rays of wavelength 6.3×10^{-11} m are incident on a crystal whose atomic planes are separated by a distance of 4.4×10^{-10} m. Calculate the first two angles at which strong reflection is observed.

8 X-rays of wavelength 6.26×10^{-11} m are incident on a NaCl crystal. The first strong reflection is observed at an angle of 6.41°. Calculate the distance between the atomic (actually ionic) planes of NaCl.

9 First-order ($n = 1$) diffraction is observed at an angle of 12.4° between the direction of the incident X-ray beam and the crystal face. Assuming that the atomic planes responsible for this effect are separated by a distance of 2.5×10^{-10} m, calculate:
(a) the angle at which second-order diffraction takes place;
(b) the wavelength of the X-rays.

10 Figure G4.11 shows a cross-section of the arrangement of the atoms in a cubic crystal. The distance between adjacent atoms in the same row is d.
(a) Calculate, in terms of d, the distance between the planes indicated by pairs of dotted lines (i) and (ii).
(b) Outline, using your answer to (a), how X-ray diffraction can be used to determine the structure of a crystal.

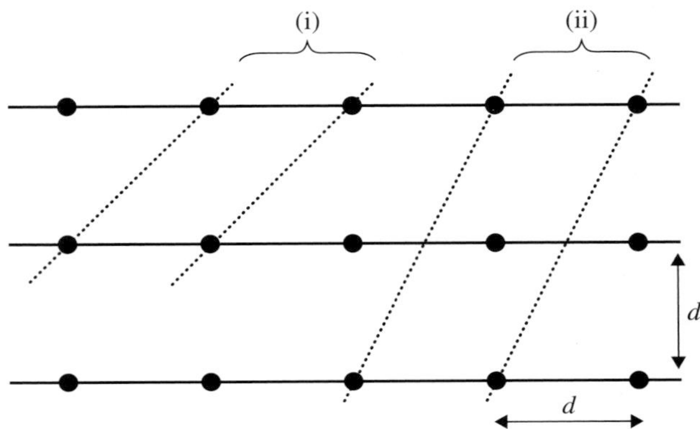

Figure G4.11 For question 10.

Thin-film interference

This short chapter looks at interference due to thin films, commonly seen as the coloured patches in soap bubbles and on thin layers of leaked oil floating on water. It also looks at the use of thin air wedges to measure small distances.

Objectives

By the end of this chapter you should be able to:

- appreciate that *phase changes* may be introduced upon *reflection* of a ray of light;
- explain the role of *phase difference* in interference;
- understand interference in thin films and thin air wedges by *division of amplitude*;
- describe how interference may be used to *measure small distances*.

Parallel films

This phenomenon is commonly seen as the coloured patches on thin layers of leaked oil floating on water on streets, on thin layers of grease floating on water in a cup and in soap bubbles. To understand this phenomenon we must first realize that, upon reflection, a ray of light may undergo a phase change (see Figure G5.1).

Consider now a thin film with parallel sides surrounded by air (see Figure G5.2).

Let d be the thickness of the film of oil. Then the path difference is $2d$ assuming we view the film normally from above. There will be a phase change of π at the first reflection at the air–oil interface since oil has a larger index of refraction than air. At the second reflection at the oil–air interface there is no phase change. Using the condition for *constructive interference* in the presence of a phase difference $\phi = \pi$ (with λ_o the wavelength in oil) we get

$$\text{path difference} = k\lambda_o + \frac{\phi}{2\pi}\lambda_o$$

$$k = 0, 1, 2, 3, \ldots$$

that is

$$\text{path difference} = \left(k + \frac{1}{2}\right)\lambda_o$$

$$k = 0, 1, 2, 3, \ldots$$

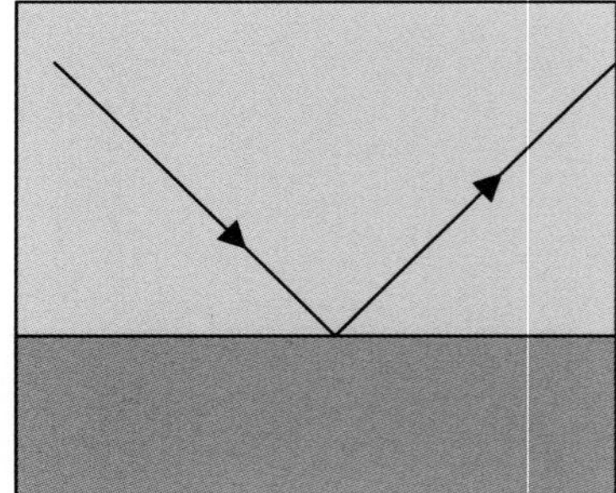

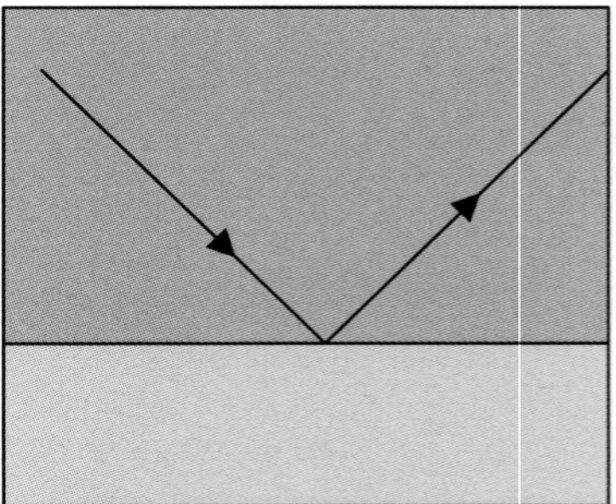

Figure G5.1 A ray of light reflecting off a medium with higher index of refraction will undergo a phase change of π.

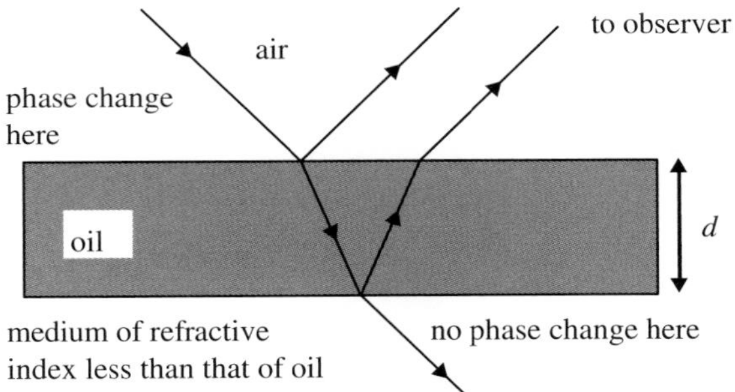

Figure G5.2 Thin-film interference in oil is explained by the phase difference due to the extra distance covered by one of the rays and by the phase change upon reflection at the top surface.

which means we get a maximum if this path difference is a half-integral multiple of the wavelength. However, the wavelength of light in oil (λ_o) is not the same as that in air. Rather, in oil $\lambda_o = \lambda/n$, where n is the index of refraction of oil and λ the wavelength of light in air.

The wavelength that shows constructive interference for a particular thickness of the film will lend its colour to the film.

▶ Thus, constructive interference takes place when

$$2d = \left(k + \frac{1}{2}\right)\frac{\lambda}{n}$$

that is

$$2dn = \left(k + \frac{1}{2}\right)\lambda, \quad k = \text{integer}$$

Example question

Q1

A solar cell must be coated in order that as little as possible of the light falling on it is reflected. A solar cell has a very high index of refraction (about 3.50). A coating of index of refraction 1.50 is placed on such a cell. What should its minimum thickness be in order to minimize reflection of light of wavelength 524 nm?

Answer

We will have phase changes of 180° at *both* reflections (from the top of the coating and the solar cell surface), hence the condition for a minimum is

$$2dn = \tfrac{1}{2}\lambda$$

$$\Rightarrow d = \frac{\lambda}{4n}$$

$$= \frac{524 \times 10^{-9}}{4 \times 1.50}$$

$$= 87.3 \text{ nm}$$

Thin air wedges

Another example of interference is provided by an arrangement in which two flat glass plates are put on top of each other with a thin piece of paper (of thickness D) in between them so that a very small angle is formed between the plates (see Figure G5.3). Air is trapped between the glass plates, forming an air wedge of variable thickness. Fringes are seen when the

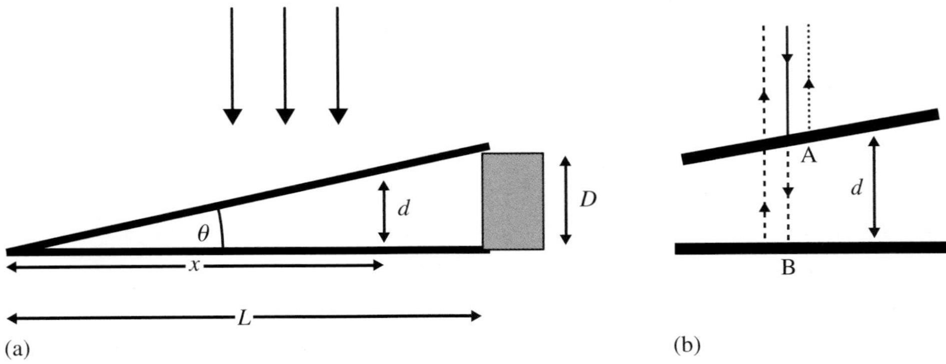

Figure G5.3 (a) Two flat glass plates have a thin wedge of air between them. (b) A ray of light coming down vertically (solid line) splits at A (the interface between the top plate and the air wedge underneath it). The ray is partially reflected upward (dotted line) and the other part (dashed line) traverses the air gap twice, undergoing reflection at B.

glass plates are observed from above after being illuminated by light from an extended source. The problem is essentially that of interference in thin films except that here the thickness of the film is variable.

We assume that the glass plates are coated so that no reflection takes place from the top surface of the top plate and the bottom surface of the bottom plate.

A ray of light coming vertically down will then partly reflect from point A (the interface of the top plate and the air wedge underneath it) and partly continue to point B. Point B is at the top face of the bottom plate. It will reflect from this point and move up where it will interfere with the ray that reflected from A. The path difference is thus $2d$, where d is the thickness of the air wedge at the point of impact of the light ray. The ray undergoes no phase change at A (A is on the inside of the top plate) but there is a phase change of π at B. Applying the condition for *constructive* interference we find

$$2d = \left(k + \frac{1}{2}\right)\lambda, \quad k = \text{integer}$$

Thus the *bright fringes* occur for thicknesses given by

$$d = \frac{\lambda}{4}, \frac{3\lambda}{4}, \frac{5\lambda}{4}, \text{ and so on}$$

We see that the fringes are equally separated (see Figure G5.4).

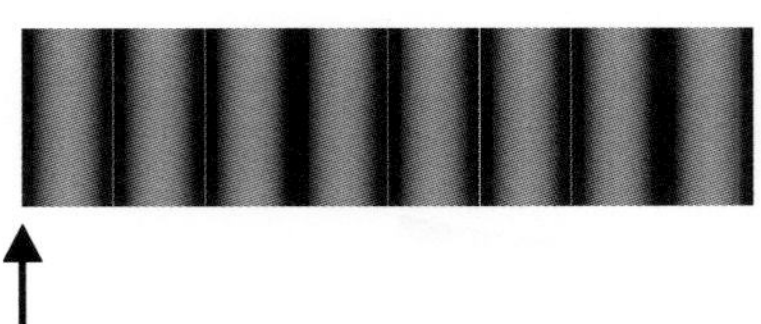

plates join here

Figure G5.4 The fringe pattern of the air-wedge system.

Measuring small distances

The air wedge can be used to measure small distances such as D in Figure G5.3. To do that we need to find the angle of the wedge. From Figure G5.3, $d = x \tan\theta$ and so the difference of air-wedge thicknesses corresponding to successive bright bands, Δd, obeys $\Delta d = \Delta x \tan\theta$. Since $\Delta d = \lambda/2$ it follows that

$$\frac{\lambda}{2} = \Delta x \tan\theta$$

$$\Rightarrow \tan\theta = \frac{\lambda}{2\Delta x}$$

But Δx is the bright fringe separation, which can be measured (by measuring the separation of many fringes and dividing appropriately), and hence the angle of the wedge can be determined. Having determined the angle, measurement of the length L allows the determination of the small distance D (see Figure G5.3).

Example question

Q2

A wire of diameter D is placed between two glass plates of length 4 cm forming a thin air wedge as shown in Figure G5.3. When the plates are illuminated with light of wavelength 590 nm, 20 dark fringes are observed across the top plate. Find the diameter of the wire.

Answer

The separation of the dark fringes is the same as that of the bright fringes. It is simply

$$\frac{4 \text{ cm}}{20} = 0.20 \text{ cm}$$

The angle of the wedge is thus found from

$$\tan\theta = \frac{\lambda}{2\Delta x}$$
$$= \frac{590 \text{ nm}}{2 \times 0.20 \text{ cm}}$$
$$= \frac{590 \times 10^{-9} \text{ m}}{2 \times 0.20 \times 10^{-2} \text{ m}}$$
$$= 1.48 \times 10^{-4}$$

that is

$\theta = 1.48 \times 10^{-4}$ rad (since the angle is small, $\theta \approx \tan\theta$)

Hence

$$D = L \tan\theta$$
$$= 4 \text{ cm} \times 1.48 \times 10^{-4}$$
$$= 5.92 \times 10^{-4} \text{ cm}$$

(see Figure G5.3).

? QUESTIONS

1 When a thin soap film of uniform thickness is illuminated with white light, it appears purple in colour. Explain this observation carefully.

2 A piece of glass of index of refraction 1.50 is coated with a thin layer of magnesium fluoride of index of refraction 1.38. If it is illuminated with light of wavelength 680 nm, what is the minimum thickness of the coating that will result in no reflection?

3 A thin soap bubble of index of refraction 1.33 is viewed with light of wavelength 550.0 nm and appears very bright. What is a possible value of the thickness of the soap bubble?

4 A soap film will appear dark if it is very thin and will reflect all colours when thick. Carefully justify these statements using interference from thin films.

5 In the thin-air-wedge interference pattern, how would the separation of the bright fringes change if the angle of the wedge is made smaller?

6 In a thin-air-wedge interference experiment, 12 maxima are observed within a length of 5 cm when the plates are illuminated with light of wavelength 500 nm. Calculate the angle between the plates.

The principle of special relativity

At the end of the nineteenth century, it seemed that all the problems in physics had been solved and that scientists had a complete understanding of the laws of nature. Mechanics was triumphant, with daily applications in engineering as well as explanations of the motion of the heavenly bodies. Electricity and magnetism had been shown by James Maxwell to be two faces of the same thing (electromagnetism), thus unifying a large range of phenomena. The kinetic theory of gases provided an understanding of the workings of matter at the molecular level. Two problems defied solution, however, and they were about to bring down the entire structure of classical physics. The first was the attempt to understand the spectrum of the radiation emitted by a black body. The resolution to this problem came many years later. It involved the concept of a photon and the birth of quantum mechanics. The second problem had to do with the velocity of light: it is said that Albert Einstein, as a boy, asked himself what would happen if he held a mirror in front of him and ran forward at the speed of light. With respect to the ground, the mirror would be moving at the speed of light. Rays of light leaving young Einstein's face would also be moving at the speed of light relative to the ground. This meant that the rays would not be moving relative to the mirror, hence there should be no reflection in it. This seemed odd to Einstein. He expected that looking into the mirror would not reveal anything unusual. Some years later, Einstein (left) would resolve this puzzle with a revolutionary new theory of space and time, the theory of special relativity.

Objectives

By the end of this chapter you should be able to:

- state the meaning of the term *frame of reference*;
- state what *Galilean relativity* means;
- solve problems of *Galilean relativity*;
- understand the significance of the *speed of light*;
- state the *two postulates of the principle of relativity*;
- appreciate that *absolute time does not exist* and that *simultaneity is a relative concept*.

Frames of reference

In a physics experiment, an observer records the occurrence of *events*: the time and place at which these events take place.

▶ The observer along with the rulers and clocks that he or she uses to measure distances and times constitute what is called a *frame of reference*. If the observer is *not accelerated*, the frame is called an *inertial frame of reference*. (See Figure H1.1.)

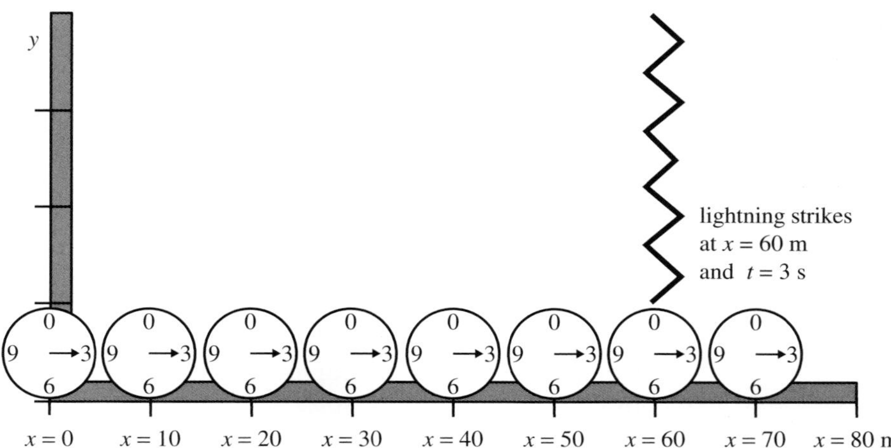

Figure H1.1 In this frame of reference the observer decides that lightning struck at time $t = 3$ s at position $x = 60$ m.

To discuss motion we must first specify the frame of reference with respect to which the motion is to be described. Thus, an observer with rulers and clocks who is firmly attached to the surface of the earth will conclude that a train travelling from one city to another moves, and the distances travelled and times taken can be calculated. The same events can also be viewed by another observer in a different frame of reference. Consider, therefore, the following situation involving one observer on the ground and another who is a passenger on the train. In Figure H1.2, a train moves past the observer on the ground (who is represented by a thin vertical line) at time $t = 0$ and is struck by lightning 3 s later. The observer on the train is represented by a thick vertical line. The train is travelling at a velocity of $v = 15\ \mathrm{m\,s^{-1}}$ as far as the ground observer is concerned.

Let us see how the two observers view various events along the trip. Assume first that when the clocks carried by the two observers show zero, the origins of the rulers carried by the observers coincide. The stationary observer uses

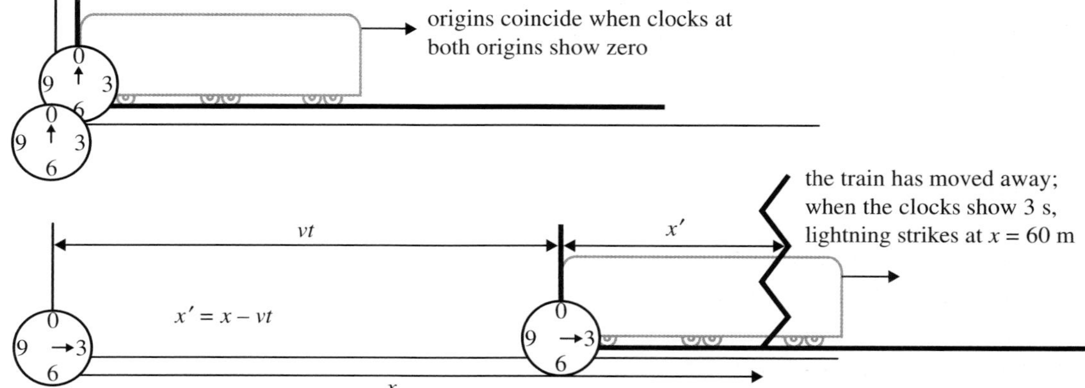

Figure H1.2 The origins of the two frames of reference coincide when clocks in both frames show zero. The origins then separate. Lightning strikes a point on the train. The observer on the train measures the point where the lightning strikes and finds the answer to be x'. The ground observer measures that the lightning struck a distance x from his origin.

the symbol x to denote the distance of an event from the origin of his ruler. The observer on the train uses the symbol x'. As shown in Figure H1.2 these are related by

$$x' = x - vt$$
$$t' = t$$

since in the time of t s the train moves forward a distance vt. These equations express the relationship between the coordinates of the same event as viewed by two observers who are in relative motion.

Thus, to the event of Figure H1.2 ('lightning strikes') the ground observer assigns the coordinates $x = 60$ m and $t = 3$ s. The observer in the train assigns to this same event the coordinates $t' = 3$ s and $x' = 60 - 15 \times 3 = 15$ m.

We are assuming here what we know from everyday experience (a guide that, as we will see, may not always be reliable): that two observers always agree on what the time coordinates are; in other words, time is common to both observers. Or as Newton wrote:

> Absolute, true and mathematical time, of itself, and from its own nature, flows equably without any relation to anything external.

Of course, the train observer may wish to consider herself at rest and the ground below her to move away with velocity $-v$.

▶ It is impossible for one of the observers to claim that he or she is 'really' at rest and that the other is 'really' moving. There is no experiment that can be performed by the train observer, say, that will convince her that she 'really' moves (apart from looking outside the windows). If we consider instead a space station and a spacecraft as our two frames, out of earth's view, even looking out of the windows will not help. Whatever results the train observer gets out of her experiments, the ground observer also gets out of the same experiments performed in his ground frame of reference.

The equations

$$x' = x - vt$$
$$t' = t$$

reflect what is called a Galilean transformation: *the relation between coordinates of events when one frame moves past the other with uniform velocity on a straight line*. Frames moving with uniform velocity past each other on straight lines are called *inertial frames of reference*. These are non-accelerating frames. Both observers are equally justified in considering themselves to be at rest and the descriptions they give are equally valid.

A non-inertial frame, by contrast, is an accelerating frame, and in this case it is possible to distinguish the observer who is 'really' moving. An observer in an accelerating frame will feel forces pulling him back into his seat if he is accelerating, or thrown forward if he is decelerating. A mass hanging from a string will make an angle with the vertical in the accelerating frame but will hang vertically if the frame is inertial (i.e. moving with constant velocity). Similarly, in a rotating frame of reference, the surface of water in a bucket would not be level.

Galilean relativity has an immediate consequence for the *law of addition of velocities*: Consider a ball that rolls with velocity u' as measured by the train observer. Again assume that the two frames, train and ground, coincide when $t = t' = 0$ and that the ball first starts rolling when $t' = 0$. Then, after time t' the position of the ball is measured to be at $x' = u't'$ by the train observer (see Figure H1.3).

The ground observer records the position of the ball to be at $x = x' + vt = (u' + v)t$ (recall $t = t'$) and so as far as the ground observer is concerned the ball has a velocity (distance/time) given by

$$u = u' + v$$

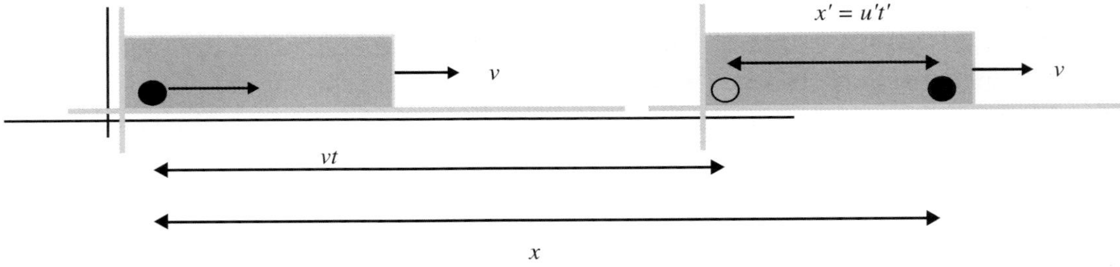

Figure H1.3 An object rolling on the floor of the 'moving' frame appears to move faster as far as the ground observer is concerned.

Example question

Q1

A ball rolls on the floor of a train at 2 m s^{-1} (with respect to the floor). The train moves with respect to the ground (a) to the right at 12 m s^{-1}, (b) to the left at 12 m s^{-1}. What is the velocity of the ball relative to the ground?

Answer

(a) The velocity is 14 m s^{-1}.
(b) The velocity is −10 m s^{-1}.

This apparently foolproof argument presents problems, however, if we replace the rolling ball in the train by a beam of light moving with velocity $c = 3 \times 10^8$ m s^{-1} as measured by the train observer. Using the formula above implies that light would be travelling at a higher speed relative to the ground observer. At the end of the nineteenth century, considerable efforts were made to detect variations in the speed of light depending on the state of motion of the source of light. The experimental result was that no such variations were detected!

The speed of light

In 1864, Maxwell corrected an apparent flaw in the laws of electromagnetism by introducing his famous 'displacement current' term in the electromagnetic equations. The result is that a changing electric flux produces a magnetic field just as a changing magnetic flux produces an electric field (as Faraday had discovered earlier). An immediate conclusion was that accelerated electric charges produced a pair of self-sustaining electric and magnetic fields at right angles to each other, which eventually decoupled from the charge and moved away from it at the speed of light. Maxwell discovered *electromagnetic waves* and thus demonstrated the electromagnetic nature of light.

One prediction of the Maxwell theory was that the speed of light is a *universal constant*. Indeed, Maxwell was able to show that the speed of light is given by the expression

$$c = \frac{1}{\sqrt{\varepsilon_0 \mu_0}}$$

where the two constants are the electric permittivity and magnetic permeability of free space (vacuum): two constants at the heart of electricity and magnetism.

▶ In other words, the speed of light does not have anything to do with the speed of the source that created it.

This results in a conflict with Galilean relativity. According to Galilean relativity, if the speed of light takes on the value c in the 'train' frame of reference then it will have the value $c + v$ in the 'ground' frame of reference (see Figure H1.4).

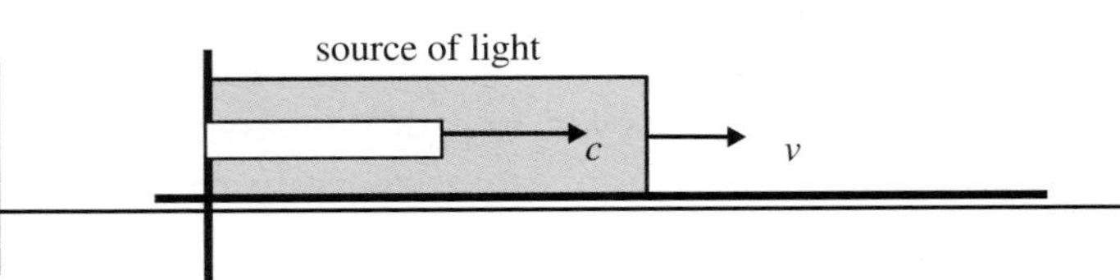

Figure H1.4 An observer in the train measures the speed of light to be c. An observer on the ground would then measure a different speed, $c + v$.

Maxwell believed that light, and other electromagnetic waves, required a medium (the ether) for their propagation (as all other waves did). He was thus forced to admit that his equations were not in fact valid in *all* frames of reference but only in a small subset, *namely those inertial frames that were at rest relative to the ether* (see Figure H1.5).

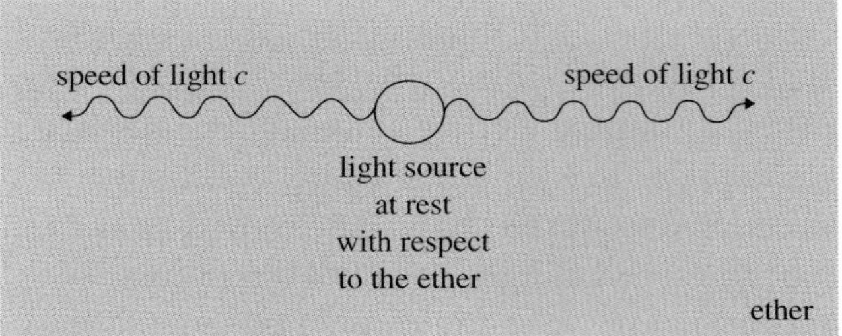

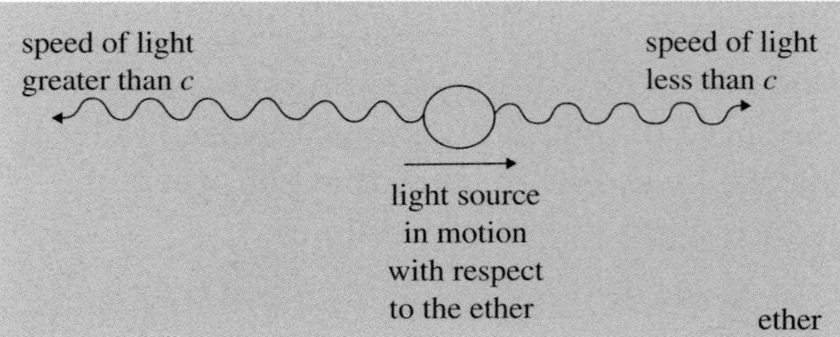

Figure H1.5 If the source moves through the ether, the speed of light in the direction of motion is expected to be less than when the source is at rest with respect to the ether.

The ether, the medium for light waves, was hypothesized to be an all-pervading medium. If you moved in the ether, you would experience an 'ether wind', much the same as a car travelling in still air experiences an opposing wind. If while moving through the ether you were to emit a light signal in the direction of motion, the velocity of light was expected to be less than the velocity of light would be if you were at rest relative to the ether.

Experiments to detect these variations in the speed of light depending on the state of motion of the source failed, however, to produce any such difference. The most famous experiment in this regard was the Michelson and Morley experiment, which is discussed in Option H3. This puzzle of classical physics was resolved by Einstein in 1905, who simply threw away the entire notion of the ether. Light, like all other electromagnetic waves, does not require a medium and the speed of light in a vacuum is the *same for all observers*. The laws of physics (including Maxwell's electromagnetism) are the same in *all inertial frames of reference*. This means immediately that the laws of Galilean relativity have to be modified. Einstein was thus led to a modification of the Galilean transformation laws, from

$$x' = x - vt; \quad t' = t; \quad u' = u - v$$

to

$$x' = \frac{x - vt}{\sqrt{1 - \frac{v^2}{c^2}}}; \quad t' = \frac{t - \frac{v}{c^2}x}{\sqrt{1 - \frac{v^2}{c^2}}}; \quad u' = \frac{u - v}{\left(1 - \frac{uv}{c^2}\right)}$$

The new transformation laws showed that the speed of light was the same for all inertial observers. The price to be paid, though, was that now Newton's laws of mechanics were not the same for all inertial observers if one used the new transformation equations! Einstein did not hesitate to change the laws of Newtonian mechanics as well, creating what is called *relativistic mechanics*. The laws of relativistic mechanics are presented in a later chapter (Option H4).

The principle of special relativity

The constancy of the speed of light for all observers is Einstein's first building block for the theory of relativity. The second is his observation that absolute motion does not exist. As we discussed earlier, it is impossible to perform any experiment within a closed box that moves with constant velocity relative to an inertial frame of reference, the purpose of which will be to let the occupants of the box find out whether they move or whether they are at rest. Further, if the occupants perform a series of experiments in order to discover the laws of physics, they will reach exactly the same laws as the occupants of any other box that is not accelerating. All inertial frames are equivalent. This leads to the principle of relativity with the two postulates:

- The laws of physics are the same in all inertial frames.
- The speed of light in a vacuum is the same for all inertial observers.

These two postulates of relativity, although they sound simple, have far-reaching consequences. The fact that the speed of light in a vacuum is the same for all observers means that absolute time does not exist. Consider a beam of light. Two different observers in relative motion to each other will measure different distances covered by this beam. But if they are to agree that the speed of the beam is the same for both observers, it follows that they must also measure different times of travel. Thus, observers in motion relative to each other measure time differently. The constancy of the speed of light means that space and time are now inevitably linked and are not independent of each other as they were in Newtonian mechanics.

A related consequence is the concept of simultaneous events. Imagine three rockets A, B and C travelling with the same constant velocity (with respect to some observer) along the same straight line. Imagine that rocket B is half-way between rockets A and C, as shown in Figure H1.6.

At a certain time rocket B emits light signals that are directed toward rockets A and C. Which rocket will receive the signal first? The principle of relativity allows us to determine that as far as an observer in rocket B is concerned the light signals are received by A

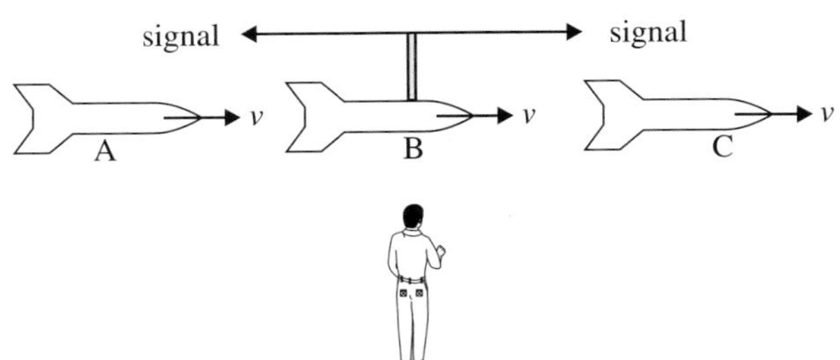

Figure H1.6 B emits signals to A and C. These are received at the same time as far as B is concerned. But the reception of the signals is not simultaneous as far as the ground observer is concerned.

and C simultaneously (i.e. at the same time). This is obvious since we may imagine a big box enclosing all three rockets that moves with same velocity as the rockets themselves. Then, for any observer in the box, or in the rockets themselves, everything appears to be at rest. Since B is half-way between A and C, clearly the two rockets receive the signals at the same time (light travels with the same speed). Imagine, though, that we look at this situation from the point of view of a different observer, outside the rockets and the box, with respect to whom the rockets move with velocity v. This observer sees that rocket A is approaching the light signal, while rocket C is moving away from it (again, remember that light travels with the same speed in each direction). Hence, it is obvious to this observer that rocket A will receive the signal *before* rocket C does.

We are thus forced to admit the following as a consequence of the principle of relativity:

Events (i.e. occurrences) that are simultaneous for one observer *and* which take place at *different points in space*, are not simultaneous for another observer in motion relative to the first.

On the other hand, if two events are simultaneous for one observer *and* take place at the *same point in space*, they are simultaneous for all other observers as well.

Example question

Q2

Observer T is in the middle of a train carriage that is moving with constant speed to the right with respect to the train station. Two light signals are emitted at the same time as far as the observer, T, in the train is concerned (see Figure H1.7).

(a) Are the emissions simultaneous for observer G on the ground?

(b) The signals arrive at T at the same time as far as T is concerned. Do they arrive at T at the same time as far as G is concerned? According to G, which signal is emitted first?

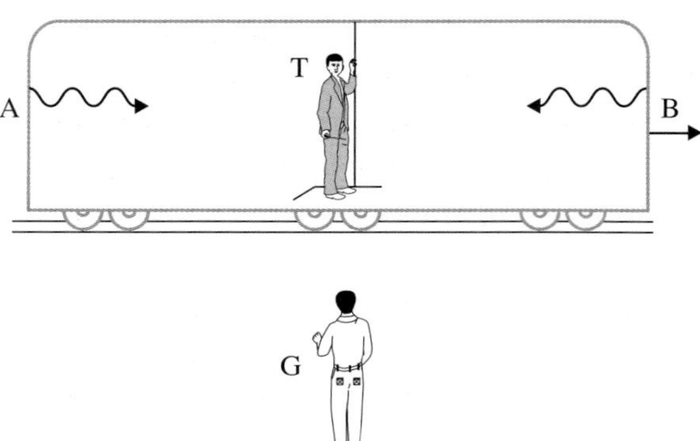

Figure H1.7.

Answer

(a) No, because the events (i.e. the emissions from A and B) take place at different points in space and so if they are simultaneous for observer T they will not be simultaneous for observer G.

(b) Yes, because the reception of the two signals by T takes place at the same point in space so if they are simultaneous for T, they must also be simultaneous for G. From G's point of view, T is *moving away from the signal from A*. So the signal from A has a larger distance to cover to get to T. If the signals are received *at the same time*, and moved at the same speed (c), it must be that the one from A was emitted before that from B.

Simultaneity, like motion, is a relative concept. Our notion of absolute simultaneity is based on the idea of absolute time: events happen at specific times that all observers agree on. Einstein has taught us that the idea of absolute time, just like the idea of absolute motion, must be abandoned.

? QUESTIONS

1 It was a very hotly debated subject centuries ago as to whether the earth goes around the sun or the other way around. Does relativity make this whole argument irrelevant since 'all frames of reference are equivalent'?

2 Give as many examples as you can of events that are simultaneous for one set of observers but not for others.

3 Two trains are travelling at constant speeds on two parallel straight lines. The first, A, is travelling at 5 m s^{-1}, the second, B, at 2 m s^{-1}. An observer at the station observes both trains. At a given instant of time, a passenger in A, a passenger in B and the observer at the station are all aligned along a line normal to the motion of the trains. At that point, a passenger in A drops an ice cube from his drink which he is holding at a height of 1.40 m. Using Galilean relativity, where will the ice cube land as far as each of the three observers is concerned?

4 Discuss the approximations necessary in order to claim that the rotating earth is an inertial frame of reference.

5 Imagine that you are travelling in a train at constant speed in a straight line and that you cannot look at or communicate with the outside. Think of the first experiment that comes to your mind that you could do to try to find out that you are indeed moving. Then analyse it carefully to see that it will not work.

6 Here is another experiment that can be performed in the hope of determining whether you move or not.
The coil in Figure H1.8 is placed near a strong magnet and a galvanometer attached to the coil registers a current. Discuss whether we can deduce that the coil moves with respect to the ground.

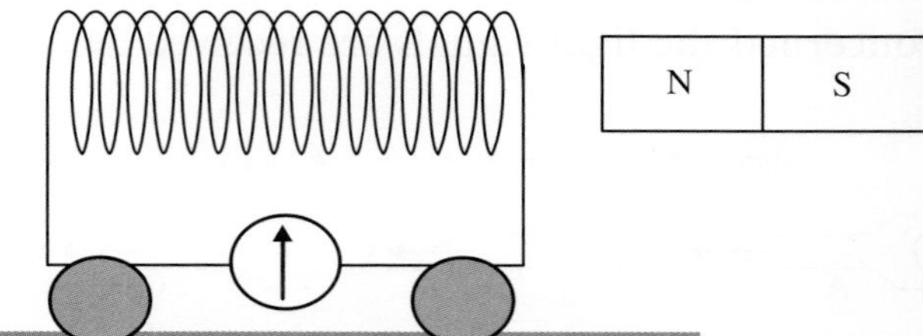

Figure H1.8 For question 6.

7 What experiment might you perform in a train that is accelerating along a straight line that would convince you that it is accelerating? Could you also determine the direction of the acceleration?

8 How would you know that you find yourself in a rotating frame of reference? What experiment would convince you of that?

9 An electric current flows in a wire (see Figure H1.9). A proton moving parallel to the wire will experience a magnetic force due to the magnetic field created by the current. From the point of view of an observer travelling along with the proton, the proton is at rest and so should experience no force. What do you say?

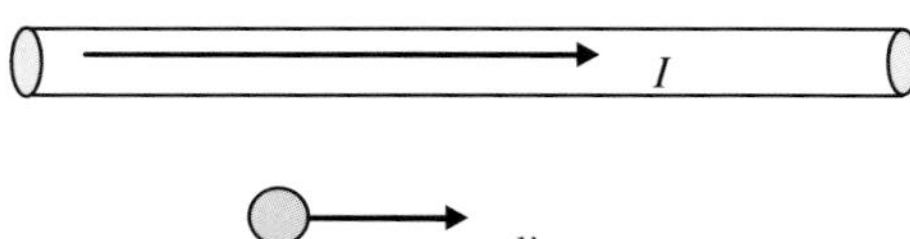

Figure H1.9 For question 9.

10 Imagine a 'train' that is 5400 000 km long travelling at 240 000 km s^{-1} to the right. Two laser beams are emitted from the middle of the train toward the ends of the train, giving the signal to open the front and rear doors.

(a) When will the doors open according to an observer at the middle of the train?

(b) Which door will open first according to an observer on the platform? The platform observer is standing level with the train observer when the laser signals are emitted.

The effects of special relativity

The principle of relativity has immediate consequences. Time runs differently for two observers who are in relative motion and these observers disagree about length measurements. This chapter discusses three basic relativity phenomena: time dilation, length contraction and velocity addition.

Objectives

By the end of this chapter you should be able to:

- give the definitions of *proper time interval* and *proper length*;
- describe the behaviour of the *gamma factor* $\gamma = \frac{1}{\sqrt{1-\frac{v^2}{c^2}}}$;
- state the meaning of *time dilation* and solve problems using time interval $= \gamma \times$ proper time interval;
- derive the *time dilation formula*;
- state the meaning of *length contraction* and solve problems using length $= \frac{\text{proper length}}{\gamma}$;
- use the law of *velocity addition* and appreciate its significance, $u = \frac{u'+v}{1+\frac{u'v}{c^2}}$ or, solving for u', $u' = \frac{u-v}{1-\frac{uv}{c^2}}$;
- appreciate that time dilation and length contraction are both *symmetrical* effects;
- describe and resolve the *twin paradox*.

Time dilation

A direct consequence of the principle of relativity is that observers who are in motion relative to each other do not agree on the interval of time separating two events. To see this, consider the following situation: a train moves with velocity v with respect to the ground as shown in Figure H2.1.

From point A on the train floor a light signal is sent toward point B directly above on the ceiling. The time it takes for light to travel from A to B and back to A is recorded and equals $\Delta t'$. Note that as far as the observers inside the train are concerned, the light beam travels along the straight-line segments AB and BA. From the point of view of an observer on the ground, however, things look somewhat different. In the time it takes for light to return to A, B (which

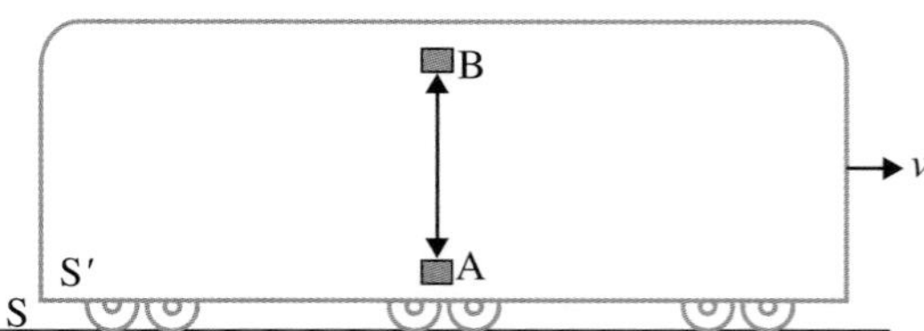

Figure H2.1 A signal is emitted at A, is reflected off B and returns to A again. The path shown is what the train observer sees as the path of the signal. The emission and reception of the signals happen at the same point in space.

moves along with the train) will have moved forward. This means, therefore, that as far as this observer is concerned, the path of the light beam looks like that shown in Figure H2.2.

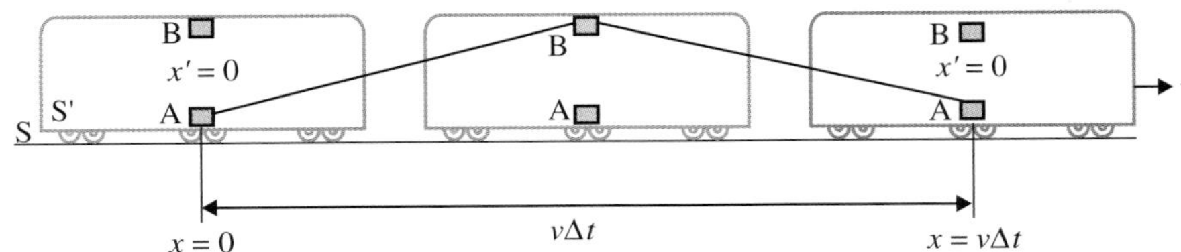

Figure H2.2 The ground observer sees things differently. In the time it takes the signal to return, the train has moved forward. Thus, the emission and reception of the signal do not happen at the same point in space.

Suppose that the stationary observer measures the time it takes light to travel from A to B and back to A to be Δt. What we will show now is that, if both observers are to agree that the speed of light is the same, then the two time intervals cannot be the same.

It is clear that

$$\Delta t' = \frac{2L}{c}$$

$$\Delta t = \frac{2\sqrt{L^2 + (v\Delta t/2)^2}}{c}$$

since the train moves forward a distance $v\Delta t$, in the time interval Δt that the stationary observer measures for the light beam to reach A. Thus, solving the first equation for L and substituting in the second (after squaring both equations)

$$(\Delta t)^2 = \frac{4\left(\frac{c^2(\Delta t')^2}{4} + \frac{v^2(\Delta t)^2}{4}\right)}{c^2}$$

$$c^2(\Delta t)^2 = c^2(\Delta t')^2 + v^2(\Delta t)^2$$

$$(c^2 - v^2)(\Delta t)^2 = c^2(\Delta t')^2$$

$$(\Delta t)^2 = \frac{c^2(\Delta t')^2}{c^2 - v^2}$$

So finally

$$\Delta t = \frac{\Delta t'}{\sqrt{1 - \frac{v^2}{c^2}}}$$

This is called the **time dilation** formula. It is customary to call the expression

$$\gamma = \frac{1}{\sqrt{1 - \frac{v^2}{c^2}}}$$

the gamma factor, in which case $\Delta t = \gamma \Delta t'$. Note that $\gamma > 1$. A graph of the gamma factor versus velocity is shown in Figure H2.3. We see that the gamma factor is approximately one for velocities up to about half the speed of light but approaches infinity as the speed approaches the speed of light.

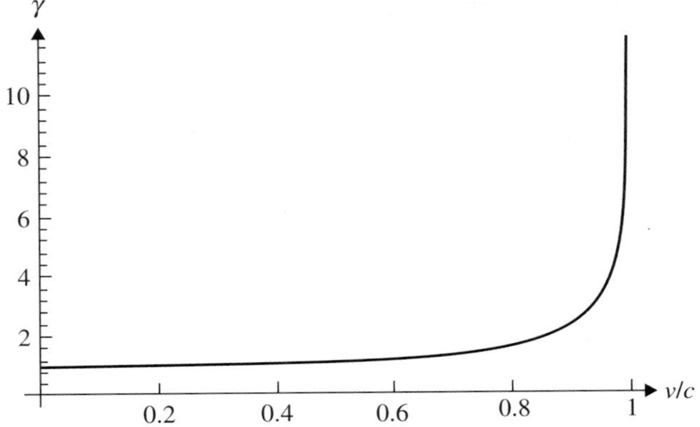

Figure H2.3 The gamma factor as a function of velocity. The value of γ stays essentially close to one for values of the velocity up to about half the speed of light but approaches infinity as the velocity approaches the speed of light.

The time interval for the time of travel of the light beam is longer for the ground observer's clock. This is known as time dilation. If the train passengers measure a time interval of $\Delta t' = 6$ s and the train moves at a speed $v = 0.80c$, then the time interval measured by the ground observer is

$$\begin{aligned} \Delta t &= \frac{6}{\sqrt{1 - 0.80^2}}\ \text{s} \\ &= \frac{6}{\sqrt{1 - 0.64}}\ \text{s} \\ &= \frac{6}{\sqrt{0.36}}\ \text{s} \\ &= \frac{6}{0.6}\ \text{s} \\ &= 10\ \text{s} \end{aligned}$$

which is longer. It will be seen immediately that this large difference came about only because we chose the speed of the train to be extremely close to the speed of light. Clearly, if the train speed is small compared with the speed of light, then $\gamma \approx 1$, and the two time intervals agree, as we might expect them to from everyday experience. The reason that our everyday experience leads us astray is because the speed of light is enormous compared with everyday speeds. Thus, the relativistic time dilation effect we have just discovered becomes relevant only when speeds close to the speed of light are encountered. Otherwise, small speeds result in differences in time intervals that can only be measured with super-accurate atomic clocks, as indeed has been done in the Hafele–Keating experiment (see page 655).

If an observer measures that two events take place at the *same point in space*, the time interval between the events is very special and is called a *proper time interval*. All other observers moving with respect to this observer will measure a *longer* time interval separating the *same* two events.

▶ A *proper time interval* is the time separating two events that take place at the *same point in space*.
An observer who sees the two events take place at different points in space will measure a time interval given by

$$\text{time interval} = \gamma \times \text{proper time interval}$$
$$= \frac{1}{\sqrt{1-\frac{v^2}{c^2}}} \times \text{proper time interval}$$

where v is the speed of the observer relative to the observer who measures the proper time interval.

Note that there is no question as to which observer is right and which is wrong when it comes to measuring time intervals. Both are right. Two inertial observers moving relative to each other at constant velocity both reach valid conclusions according to the principle of relativity.

Example questions

Q1

The time interval between the ticks of a clock carried on a fast rocket is half of what observers on earth record. How fast is the rocket moving with respect to earth?

Answer

From the time dilation formula it follows that

$$2 = \frac{1}{\sqrt{1-\frac{v^2}{c^2}}} \Rightarrow \sqrt{1-\frac{v^2}{c^2}} = \frac{1}{2}$$
$$\Rightarrow 1-\frac{v^2}{c^2} = \frac{1}{4}$$
$$\Rightarrow \frac{v^2}{c^2} = \frac{3}{4}$$
$$\Rightarrow v = 0.866c$$

Q2

A rocket moves past an observer in a laboratory with speed $v = 0.85c$. The observer in the laboratory measures that a radioactive sample of mass 50 mg (which is at rest in the laboratory) has a half-life of 2.0 min. What half-life do the rocket observers measure?

Answer

We have two events here. The first is that the laboratory observer sees a container with 50 mg of the radioactive sample. The second event is that the laboratory observer sees a container with 25 mg of the radioactive sample. These events are separated by 2.0 min as far as the laboratory observer is concerned. These two events take place at the same point in space as far as the laboratory observer is concerned and so *the laboratory observer has measured the proper time interval between these two events*. Hence the rocket observers will measure a longer half-life of

$$\text{time interval} = \gamma \times \text{proper time interval}$$
$$= \frac{1}{\sqrt{1-0.85^2}} \times 2.0\ \text{min}$$
$$= 3.80\ \text{min}$$

The point of this example is that you must not make the mistake of thinking that proper time intervals are measured by 'the moving' observer. There is no such thing as 'the moving' observer:

the rocket observer is free to consider herself at rest and the laboratory observer moving with velocity $v = -0.85c$.

Q3

In the year 2010, a group of astronauts embark on a journey toward the star Betelgeuse in a spacecraft moving at $v = 0.75c$ with respect to the earth. Three years after departure from the earth (as measured by the astronauts' clocks) one of the astronauts announces that she has given birth to a baby girl. The other astronauts immediately send a *radio* signal to earth announcing the birth. When is the good news received on earth (according to earth clocks)?

Answer

When the astronaut gives birth, three years have gone by in the spacecraft's clocks. This is a proper time interval since the events 'departure from earth' and 'astronaut gives birth' happen at the same place as far as the astronauts are concerned (inside the spacecraft). Thus, the time between these two events according to the earth clocks is

$$\begin{aligned}\text{time interval} &= \gamma \times \text{proper time interval}\\ &= \frac{1}{\sqrt{1-0.75^2}} \times 3.0\ \text{yr}\\ &= 4.54\ \text{yr}\end{aligned}$$

This therefore is also the time for which the spacecraft has been travelling as far as the earth is concerned. The distance covered is (as far as earth is concerned)

$$\begin{aligned}\text{distance} &= vt\\ &= 0.75c \times 4.54\ \text{yr}\\ &= 3.40c \times \text{yr}\\ &= 3.40\ \text{ly}\end{aligned}$$

This is the distance that the radio signal must then cover in bringing the message. This is done at the speed of light and so the time taken is

$$\begin{aligned}\frac{3.40\ \text{ly}}{c} &= \frac{3.40c \times \text{yr}}{c}\\ &= 3.40\ \text{yr}\end{aligned}$$

Hence, when the signal arrives, the year on earth is

$2010 + 4.54 + 3.40 = 2018$ (approximately).

The time dilation effect just described is a 'real' effect. In the Hafele–Keating experiment, accurate atomic clocks taken for a ride aboard planes moving at ordinary speeds and then compared with similar clocks left behind show readings that are smaller by amounts consistent with the formulae of relativity. Time dilation is also a daily effect in the operation of particle accelerators. In such machines, particles are accelerated to speeds that are very close to the speed of light and thus relativistic effects must be taken into account when designing these machines. The time dilation formula has also been verified in muon decay experiments. This is discussed separately (see page 666).

Time dilation is symmetric

Consider now the following situation. A rocket travelling at $0.80c$ starts from space station P and is directed to space station Q a distance of 864 million km away (as far as observers in both space stations are concerned – the stations do not move relative to each other). A passenger on the rocket sets his watch as the rocket leaves space station P by looking at the space station's clock. The time is zero. When the rocket arrives at space station Q, he checks his watch against the space station's clock. He will find that because of time dilation his clock is slow. Indeed, the trip lasted a time interval of

$$\begin{aligned}\Delta t &= \frac{864 \times 10^9}{0.80 \times 3 \times 10^8}\ \text{s}\\ &= 3600\ \text{s}\\ &= 60\ \text{min}\end{aligned}$$

according to the space station clocks. Thus, the clock in space station Q shows 1 h when the rocket comes whizzing by. The traveller's watch measures the proper time interval between the events 'look at clock in space station P' and 'look at clock in space station Q' and since

$$\begin{aligned}\text{time interval} &= \gamma \times \text{proper time interval}\\ 1\ \text{h} &= \frac{1}{\sqrt{1-0.80^2}} \times \text{proper time interval}\end{aligned}$$

so

$$\begin{aligned}\text{proper time interval} &= 1\ \text{h} \times \sqrt{1-0.80^2}\\ &= 36\ \text{min}\end{aligned}$$

The passenger's watch is slow by 24 min. Let us carefully review what the passenger actually did. First he compared his watch with the space station clock at P. Then he checked it again against the space station clock at Q. He found that the interval of time between leaving space station P and arriving in space station Q was 36 min. The interval of time was 60 min according to the stations' clocks. (See Figure H2.4.)

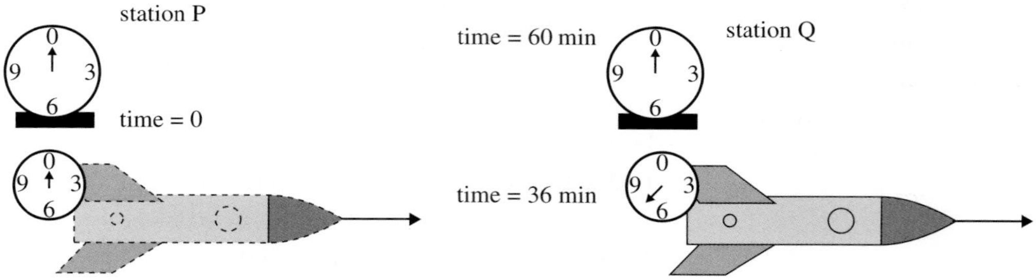

Figure H2.4 The passenger on the rocket records a time of travel from A to B of 36 min. The station clocks record 60 min.

What would happen, however, if the stationmaster at Q said that the rocket was at rest and that it was he (and the space station) that moved toward the rocket (as he is entitled to say)? Imagine that the rocket has a very long rod reaching from space station P to space station Q and that clocks are placed at regular intervals along the rod. The stationmaster at Q sets his watch by looking at the clock on the rod in front of him. The watch now shows zero. The stationmaster now thinks he is moving. Eventually, the stationmaster will see the rocket. He again compares his watch with a clock on the rocket. He will find that his watch shows 36 min while the rocket clock shows 60 min. (See Figure H2.5)

What we have described is that the time dilation effect is a *symmetric* effect. Both observers are free to call themselves at rest and the other moving and vice versa. Both are correct in their measurements of time since the principle of relativity states that all inertial observers make equally valid measurements.

The twin paradox

What if the rocket of the previous discussion moved, instead, on a long circular path. The rocket sets off from space station P and will eventually come back. The passenger in the rocket sets his clock by looking at the station's clock. The time is zero. When he returns, he looks at his watch and finds that it is slow compared with the station clock. Thus, if the trip lasted, say, 6 years by the passenger's watch, the passenger is 6 years older. However, the passenger's twin brother, who is the stationmaster, is older by 10 years. (We are assuming that the rocket moves at a speed of $v = 0.80c$ so that $\gamma = \frac{10}{6}$.)

By the previous argument, the stationmaster may claim that it was he who moved away. So when the stationmaster again meets the rocket passenger, he will claim that

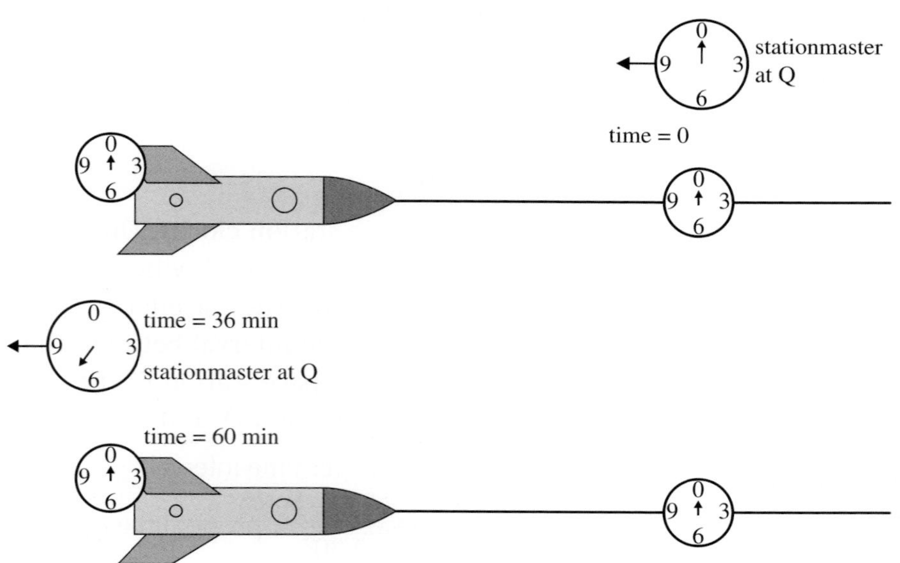

Figure H2.5 The stationmaster is moving and the rocket is at rest. The stationmaster's watch shows 36 min when he sees the rocket. The rocket's clock shows 60 min.

his clock is slower than the passenger's. So the stationmaster is only 6 years older while the rocket passenger is 10 years older. How can that be? Which of the twins is the older when they meet again?

This is often referred to as the twin paradox. It is not a real paradox, though, because unlike the discussion of the previous section, the situation here is *not symmetric*. At all times the stationmaster was in an *inertial* frame. However, the rocket had been moving in a circle (thus experiencing centripetal acceleration) and so the rocket's frame had *not been inertial*. Careful application of the laws of relativity to this *asymmetric* situation leads to the conclusion that the stationmaster has aged by 10 years and the rocket twin by 6 years. Even if the rocket moves in a straight line and then reverses direction to return to the space station, this does not help because in this case the rocket must decelerate and then accelerate. So the rocket passenger again finds himself in a non-inertial frame for part of the time. This again ruins the symmetry of the situation; the rocket passenger is younger than his twin brother when they are reunited.

Length contraction

Suppose now that the observers inside a fast-moving train or rocket place a rod on the floor pointing in the direction of motion of the train (see Figure H2.6).

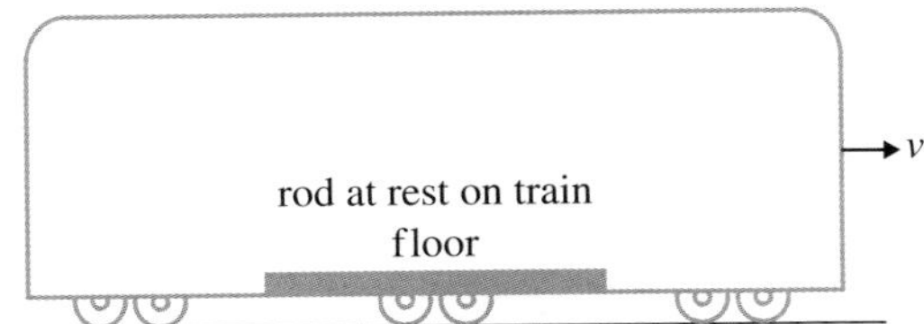

Figure H2.6 The rod is at rest in the moving frame. To an observer on the ground, the rod moves with the velocity of the frame.

They measure the length of this rod and find it to be L_0. What is the length of the rod when measured by the observers on earth with respect to whom the rod moves at speed v? To find the length of a rod means that one must record the positions of the ends of the rod simultaneously. The length L_0 for this rod was the result of a simultaneous measurement of the rod's ends in the frame of reference in which the rod is at rest (i.e. by the observers in the train). Measurements that are simultaneous in one frame of reference are not, however, necessarily simultaneous in others, as we saw earlier, and this will imply that an observer with respect to whom the rod moves will measure a different length for the rod.

Supplementary material

Imagine that the observers on the train send a light signal from the left end of the train to the right end, where a mirror reflects the light back to its source (see Figure H2.7). The time taken for the return trip of the light beam is $\Delta t' = \frac{2L_0}{c}$, where L_0 is the length of the train as measured by the train observers. An observer with respect to whom the train moves with velocity v sees the light signal emitted at time zero, say, but in the time it takes for the signal to return to the emitter the emitter has moved forward along with the train. Let Δt_1 be the time interval for the light beam to reach the mirror for this observer and L the length of the train as far as this observer is concerned. Then, $c\Delta t_1 = L + v\Delta t_1$, giving $\Delta t_1 = \frac{L}{c-v}$. Similarly, if Δt_2 is the time for the light beam to reach the

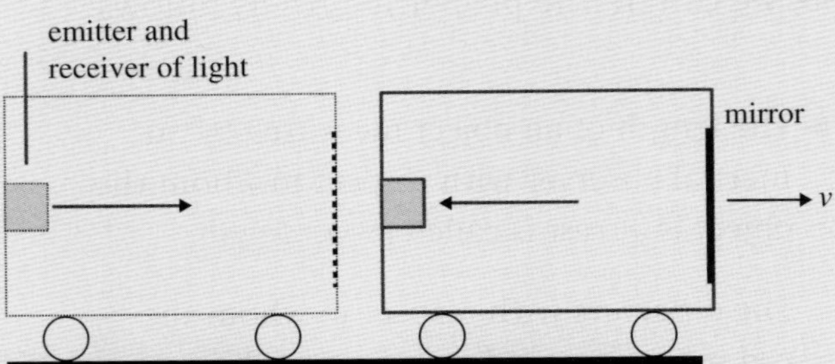

Figure H2.7 Set-up for deriving the length contraction formula. A signal is emitted from the back of the box and is reflected back by a mirror on the front. The signal is thus emitted and received at the same point in space as far as the observer in the box is concerned.

emitter from the mirror, we have $c\Delta t_2 = L - v\Delta t_2$ so that $\Delta t_2 = \frac{L}{c+v}$. Thus the total time for the return trip is

$$\begin{aligned}\Delta t &= \Delta t_1 + \Delta t_2 \\ &= \frac{L}{c-v} + \frac{L}{c+v} \\ &= \frac{2Lc}{c^2 - v^2} \\ &= \frac{2L}{c\left(1 - \frac{v^2}{c^2}\right)}\end{aligned}$$

Recall now that Δt and $\Delta t'$ are related by $\Delta t = \frac{\Delta t'}{\sqrt{1-\frac{v^2}{c^2}}}$ since $\Delta t'$ is a proper time interval (why?). Thus

$$\frac{2L}{c\left(1 - \frac{v^2}{c^2}\right)} = \frac{2L_0}{c\sqrt{\left(1 - \frac{v^2}{c^2}\right)}}$$

giving

$$L = L_0\sqrt{1 - \frac{v^2}{c^2}}$$

or

$$L = \frac{L_0}{\gamma}$$

that is

$$\text{length} = \frac{\text{proper length}}{\gamma}$$

So, we can define proper length as follows:

▶ The length of an object measured by an inertial observer with respect to whom the object is at rest is called *proper length.*

The observers with respect to whom the rod moves at speed v measure a shorter length. This is called length contraction:

$$\text{length} = \frac{\text{proper length}}{\gamma}$$

Note that it is only lengths in the direction of motion that are contracted.

As with time dilation, length contraction is a real effect as well as a symmetric effect. Take two identical rods of proper length 1 m and put one on a rocket moving at high speed and keep the other on earth. The observers on the rocket measure the length of their rod and find 1 m. The observers on earth measure the length of the rocket rod and find it less than 1 m. The rocket people, on the other hand, measure the length of the earth rod and find it less than 1 m, whereas the earth observers will of course measure 1 m for their rod. Both sets of observers are correct according to the principle of relativity.

Example question

Q4

SLAC stands for the Stanford Linear Accelerator. In this accelerator, electrons of speed $v = 0.96c$ move down the 3.0 km long linear accelerator.

(a) How long does this take according to observers in the laboratory?

(b) How long does it take according to an observer travelling along with the electrons?

(c) What is the speed of the linear accelerator in the rest frame of the electrons?

Answer

(a) In the laboratory the electrons take a time of

$$\frac{3.0 \times 10^3}{0.96 \times 3 \times 10^8}\ \text{s} = 1.042 \times 10^{-5}\ \text{s}$$

(b) The arrival of the electrons at the beginning and the end of the accelerator track happens at the same point in space as far as the observer travelling along with the electrons is concerned and so that is a proper time interval. Thus

$$\text{time interval} = \gamma \times \text{proper time interval}$$

$$\begin{aligned}\gamma &= \frac{1}{\sqrt{1 - 0.96^2}} \\ &= 3.571\end{aligned}$$

$$1.042 \times 10^{-5}\ \text{s} = 3.571 \times \text{proper time interval}$$

that is

$$\begin{aligned}\text{proper time interval} &= \frac{1.0 \times 10^{-5}}{3.571}\ \text{s} \\ &= 2.918 \times 10^{-6}\ \text{s}\end{aligned}$$

(c) The speed of the accelerator is obviously $v = 0.96c$ in the opposite direction. But this can be checked as follows. As far as the electron is concerned, the length of the accelerator track is moving past it and so is length-contracted according to

$$\text{length} = \frac{\text{proper length}}{\gamma} = \frac{3.0\text{ km}}{3.571} = 0.8401\text{ km}$$

and so has a speed of

$$\text{speed} = \frac{0.8401 \times 10^3}{2.918 \times 10^{-6}}\text{ m s}^{-1} = 2.879 \times 10^8\text{ m s}^{-1} \approx 0.96c$$

Addition of velocities

Consider a frame S' (for example a train) that moves at constant speed v in a straight line relative to another frame S (for example the ground). An object slides on the train floor in the same direction as the train (S') and its velocity is measured *by the observers in* S' to be u'. What is the speed of this object as measured *by the observers in* S? (See Figure H2.8.)

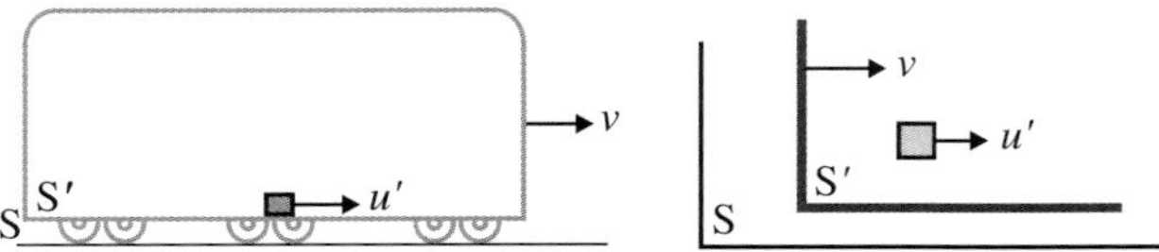

Figure H2.8 The speed of the moving object is u' in the frame S'. What is its speed when measured from frame S?

In pre-relativity physics (i.e. Galilean–Newtonian physics), the answer would be simply $u' + v$. This cannot, however, be the correct relativistic answer; if we replaced the sliding object by a beam of light ($u' = c$), we would end up with an observer (S) who measured a speed of light different from that measured by S'. The correct answer for the speed u of the particle relative to S is given by

$$u = \frac{u' + v}{1 + \frac{u'v}{c^2}}$$

or, solving for u'

$$u' = \frac{u - v}{1 - \frac{uv}{c^2}}$$

It can be easily checked that, irrespective of how close u' or v are to the speed of light, u is always less than c. In the case in which $u' = c$, then $u = c$ as well, as demanded by the principle of the constancy of the speed of light (check this). On the other hand, if the velocities involved are small compared with the speed of light, then we may neglect the term $\frac{u'v}{c^2}$ in the denominator, in which case Einstein's formula reduces to the familiar Galilean relativity formula $u = u' + v$.

Example questions

Q5

An electron has a speed of 2.00×10^8 m s^{-1} relative to a rocket, which itself moves at a speed of 1.00×10^8 m s^{-1} with respect to the ground. What is the speed of the electron with respect to the ground?

Answer

Applying the formula above with $u' = 2.00 \times 10^8$ m s^{-1} and $v = 1.00 \times 10^8$ m s^{-1} we find $u = 2.45 \times 10^8$ m s^{-1}.

Q6

Two rockets move away from each other with speeds of 0.8c and 0.9c, with respect to the ground, as shown in Figure H2.9. What is the speed of each rocket as measured from the other? What is the relative speed of the two rockets as measured from the ground?

Figure H2.9.

Answer

Let us first find the speed of A with respect to B. In the frame of reference in which B is at rest, the ground moves to the left with speed $0.9c$ (i.e. a velocity of $-0.9c$). The velocity of A with respect to the ground is $-0.8c$. This is illustrated in Figure H2.10.

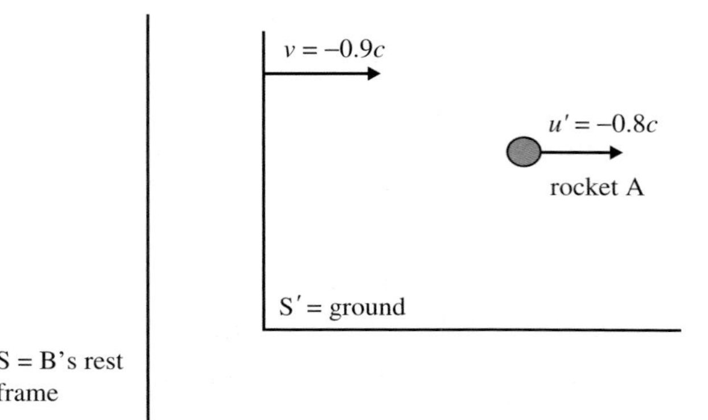

Figure H2.10.

Applying the formula with the values given in Figure H2.10 we find

$$\begin{aligned} u &= \frac{u' + v}{1 + \frac{u'v}{c^2}} \\ &= \frac{-0.9c - 0.8c}{1 + \frac{(-0.9c)(-0.8c)}{c^2}} \\ &= \frac{-1.70c}{1 + 0.72} \\ &= -\frac{1.70c}{1.72} \\ &= -0.988c \end{aligned}$$

The minus sign means, of course, that rocket A moves towards the left of B. Let us now find the speed of rocket B as measured in A's rest frame. The appropriate diagram is shown in Figure H2.11.

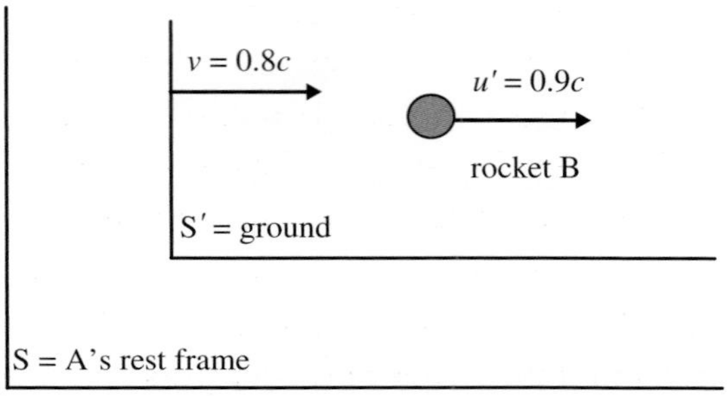

v = 0.8c

u′ = 0.9c

rocket B

S′ = ground

S = A's rest frame

Figure H2.11.

We thus find

$$\begin{aligned} u &= \frac{u' + v}{1 + \frac{u'v}{c^2}} \\ &= \frac{0.9c + 0.8c}{1 + \frac{(0.9c)(0.8c)}{c^2}} \\ &= \frac{1.70c}{1 + 0.72} \\ &= \frac{1.70c}{1.72} \\ &= 0.988c \end{aligned}$$

as expected.

The *relative speed* of the two rockets as measured from earth is $0.8c + 0.9c = 1.7c$. There is nothing to worry about here. This faster than light speed is not the speed of any material object, nor the speed of any inertial frame, nor can it be used to send a signal to anybody. It is simply a statement of how fast the distance between the rockets is increasing as seen from earth.

Q7

This question uses both the length contraction effect and the velocity addition formula. A rocket has a proper length of 200 m and travels with a speed $v = 0.95c$ relative to the earth. A missile is fired from the end of the rocket toward the front at a speed $u' = 0.90c$ relative to the rocket. When will the missile hit the front of the rocket as far as the rocket observers are concerned? When will this happen as far the earth observers are concerned?

Answer

Let L_0 stand for the proper length of the rocket and u for the speed of the missile relative to the earth. The time taken for the missile to hit the front end of the rocket is just L_0/u' for the rocket observers. For the earth observers the time will be different. Let this time be t. The length of the rocket as measured from earth is $L = \frac{L_0}{\gamma}$. In the time t it takes the missile to reach the front of the rocket, the rocket has moved forward a distance of vt. Thus, as far as the earth observers are concerned, the total distance the missile will cover is $L_0\sqrt{1 - \frac{v^2}{c^2}} + vt$. This distance is covered at a speed u and thus the time taken obeys

$$\frac{L_0\sqrt{1 - \frac{v^2}{c^2}} + vt}{u} = t$$

From the relativistic addition law for velocities

$$u = \frac{u' + v}{1 + \frac{u'v}{c^2}}$$

and so substituting for u and solving for t we find (after some algebra)

$$t = \frac{L_0}{u'} \frac{1}{\sqrt{1 - \frac{v^2}{c^2}}} \left(1 + \frac{u'v}{c^2}\right)$$

If instead of a missile a light signal is fired, then $u' = c$ and the formula above simplifies to

$$t = \frac{L_0}{c} \sqrt{\frac{(1 + \frac{v}{c})}{(1 - \frac{v}{c})}}$$

We can now put in the numbers to find numerical answers: $L_0 = 200$ m, $v = 0.95c$, $u' = 0.90c$, and so $L_0/u' = 7.4 \times 10^{-7}$ s. The time on earth is measured at 4.4×10^{-6} s.

? QUESTIONS

1 An earthling sits on a bench in a park eating a sandwich. It takes him 5 min to finish it according to his watch. He is being monitored by planet Zenga invaders who are orbiting at a speed of $0.90c$.
 (a) How long do the aliens reckon it takes an earthling to eat a sandwich?
 (b) The aliens in the spacecraft get hungry and start eating their sandwiches. It takes a Zengan 5 min to eat her sandwich according to Zengan clocks. They are actually being observed by earthlings as they fly over earth. How long does it take a Zengan to eat a sandwich according to earth clocks?

2 An unstable particle has a lifetime of 5.0×10^{-8} s as measured in its rest frame. The particle is moving in a laboratory with a speed of $0.95c$ with respect to the lab.
 (a) Calculate the lifetime of the particle according to an observer at rest in the laboratory.
 (b) Calculate the distance travelled by the particle before it decays, according to the observer in the laboratory.

3 The star Vega is about 50 ly away from earth. A spacecraft moving at $0.995c$ is heading toward Vega.
 (a) How long will it take the spacecraft to get to Vega according to clocks on earth?
 (b) The crew of the spacecraft consists of 18-year-old IB graduates. How old are the graduates when they arrive at Vega?

4 A pendulum in a fast train is found by observers on the train to have a period of 1.0 s. What period would observers on a station platform measure as the train moves past them at a speed of $0.95c$?

5 A rocket travelling at $0.6c$ with respect to earth is launched toward a star. After 4 yr of travel (as measured by the rocket clocks) a radio message is sent to earth. When will it arrive on earth as measured by:
 (a) observers on earth;
 (b) observers on the rocket?
 (c) How far from earth was the rocket when the signal was emitted, according to observers on earth?

6 A spacecraft moves past you at a speed of $0.95c$ and you measure its length to be 100 m. What length would you measure if it were at rest with respect to you?

7 A spacecraft leaving the earth with a speed of $0.80c$ sends a radio signal to earth as it passes a space station 8.0 light years from earth (as measured by earth).
 (a) How long does the signal take to arrive on earth according to earth observers?
 (b) How long did it take the spacecraft to reach the space station (according to spacecraft clocks)?
 (c) As soon as the signal is received by earth, a reply signal is sent to the spacecraft. How long does the reply signal take to arrive at the spacecraft according to earth?
 (d) According to the spacecraft, how much time went by between the emission of their signal and the arrival of the reply?

8 Two *identical* fast trains move parallel to each other. An observer on train A tells an observer on train B that by her measurements (i.e. A's) train A is 30 m long and train B is 28 m long.

If the observer on train B takes measurements what will he find for:

(a) the speed of train A with respect to train B;
(b) the length of train A;
(c) the length of train B?

9 Two people meet at point A. They compare their watches and set them both to zero. They meet again at point B. Person P has been moving in a straight line at constant speed. Person Q has been moving on part of a circle with constant speed. Whose watch is slow when they meet at B? (See Figure H2.12.)

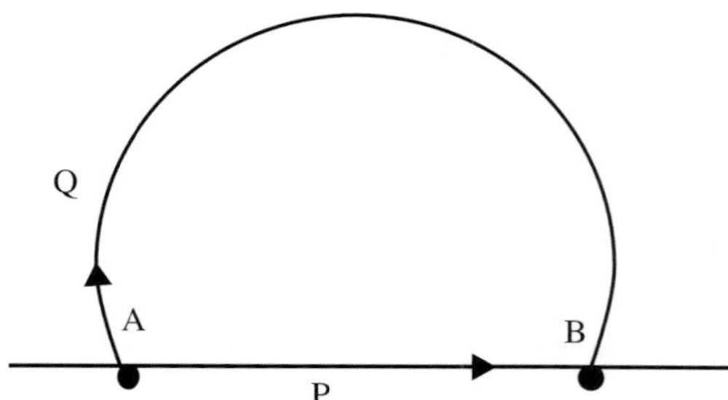

Figure H2.12 For question 9.

10 A rocket approaches a mirror on the ground at a speed of $0.90c$ as shown in Figure H2.13. The distance D between the front of the rocket and the mirror is 2.4×10^{12} m, as measured by the observers on the ground, when a light signal is sent toward the mirror from the front of the rocket. When is the reflected signal received by the rocket as measured by:

(a) the observers on the ground;
(b) the observers on the rocket?

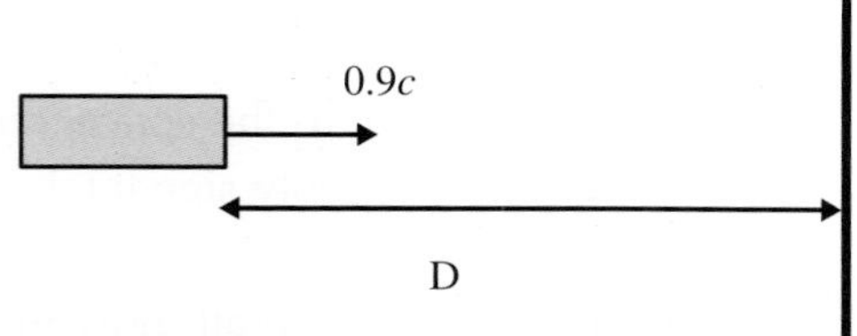

Figure H2.13 For question 10.

11 Two objects move along the same straight line as shown in Figure H2.14. Their speeds are as measured by an observer on the ground. Find:

(a) the velocity of B as measured by A;
(b) the velocity of A as measured by B.

Figure H2.14 For question 11.

12 Repeat question 11 for the arrangement in Figure H2.15.

Figure H2.15 For question 12.

13 A particle A moves to the right with a speed of $0.60c$ relative to the ground. A second particle B moves to the right with a speed of $0.70c$ relative to A. What is the speed of B relative to the ground?

14 A particle A moves to the left with a speed of $0.60c$ relative to the ground. A second particle B moves to the right with a speed of $0.70c$ relative to A. What is the speed of B relative to the ground?

Consequences of and evidence for special relativity

This chapter introduces the idea of relativistic energy. It closes with a discussion of the Michelson–Morley experiment – an experiment that failed to detect the motion of the earth through the ether.

Objectives

By the end of this chapter you should be able to:

- solve problems with *relativistic energy*, $E = \gamma m_0 c^2$;
- describe *muon decay experiments* as evidence for time dilation and length contraction;
- appreciate the significance of the *Michelson–Morley experiment*.

Relativistic energy

One of the first consequences of Einstein's theories in mechanics is the equivalence of mass and energy. The theory of relativity predicts that, to a particle of mass m_0 that is at rest with respect to some inertial observer, there corresponds an amount of energy E_0 that the observer measures to be $E_0 = m_0 c^2$. (We will not be able to give a proof of this statement in this book.) This energy is called the **rest energy** of the particle. In particle accelerators, particles and antiparticles are accelerated to high energies and are then allowed to collide. For example, an electron colliding with its antiparticle, the positron, will produce a photon, which will then immediately materialize into a pair of a new particle and its antiparticle. This is denoted pictorially in Figure H3.1.

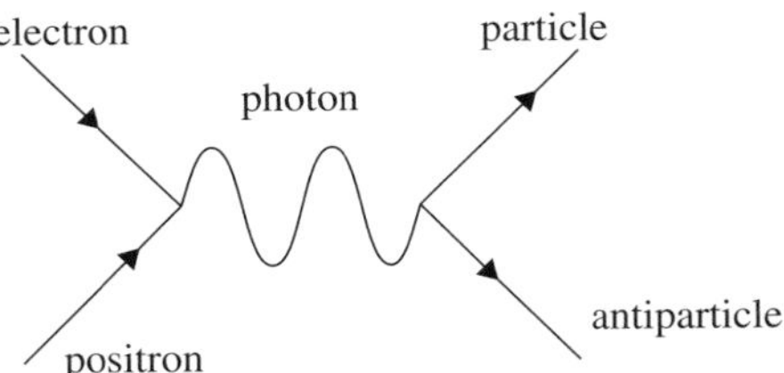

Figure H3.1 An electron and a positron collide, producing a new particle–antiparticle pair.

The possibility of this process (discussed in detail in the means that we can view rest energy in the following way. The electron and the positron are moving in opposite directions with the same speed, and so the total momentum of the system is zero. The produced particle and antiparticle will then also have zero total momentum. The *least* energy required to produce the particle–antiparticle pair is then $2m_0c^2$ when they are produced at rest (i.e. without kinetic energy). Therefore, we can say that:

▶ *Rest energy* is the amount of energy needed to produce a particle at rest.

Similarly, if the particle moves with speed v relative to some inertial observer, the energy corresponding to the mass of the particle that this observer will measure is given by

$$\begin{aligned} E &= \gamma m_0 c^2 \\ &= \frac{m_0 c^2}{\sqrt{1-\frac{v^2}{c^2}}} \end{aligned}$$

This is energy that the particle has because it has mass and because it moves. If the particle has other forms of energy, e.g. gravitational potential energy or electrical potential energy, then the total energy of the particle will equal $\gamma m_0 c^2$ plus the other forms of energy. We will mostly deal with situations where the particle has no other forms of energy associated with it. The total energy of the particle in that case is then just $\gamma m_0 c^2$.

It is very important to notice immediately that, as the speed of the particle approaches the speed of light, the total energy approaches infinity. This is a sign, as we will see shortly, that a particle with mass cannot reach the speed of light. Only particles without mass, such as photons, can move at the speed of light.

Figure H3.2 shows a graph of the variation with v/c of the ratio of the total energy E to the rest energy E_0 of a particle.

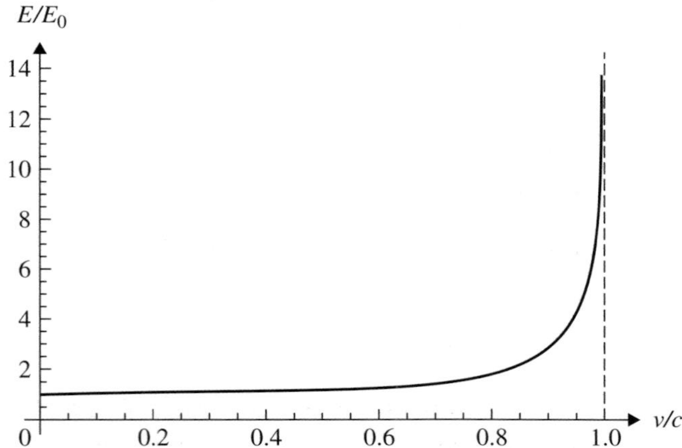

Figure H3.2 As the speed of the mass approaches the speed of light, its energy increases without limit.

Example questions

Q1

Find the speed of a particle whose total energy is double its rest energy.

Answer

We have that

$$\begin{aligned} E &= \gamma m_0 c^2 \\ 2m_0 c^2 &= \gamma m_0 c^2 \\ &\Rightarrow \gamma = 2 \\ \Rightarrow \sqrt{1-\frac{v^2}{c^2}} &= \frac{1}{2} \\ \Rightarrow 1-\frac{v^2}{c^2} &= \frac{1}{4} \\ \Rightarrow \frac{v^2}{c^2} &= \frac{3}{4} \\ \Rightarrow v &= \frac{\sqrt{3}}{2}c = 0.866\ c \end{aligned}$$

Q2

Find (a) the rest energy of an electron and (b) its total energy, when it moves at a speed equal to $0.800c$.

Answer

(a) The rest energy is

$$\begin{aligned} E &= m_0 c^2 \\ &= 9.1 \times 10^{-31} \times 9 \times 10^{16}\ \text{J} \\ &= 8.19 \times 10^{-14}\ \text{J} \\ &= \frac{8.19 \times 10^{-14}}{1.6 \times 10^{-19}}\ \text{eV} \\ &= 0.511\ \text{MeV} \end{aligned}$$

(b) The gamma factor at a speed of $0.80c$ is

$$\gamma = \frac{1}{\sqrt{1-\frac{v^2}{c^2}}} = \frac{1}{\sqrt{1-0.8^2}} = \frac{1}{0.6} = 1.667$$

and so the total energy is

$$E = \gamma m_0 c^2 = 1.667 \times 0.511\ \text{MeV} = 0.852\ \text{MeV}$$

Q3

A proton (rest energy 938 MeV) has a total energy of 1170 MeV. What is its speed?

Answer

Since the total energy is given by $E = \gamma m_0 c^2$ we have that

$$1170 = \frac{938}{\sqrt{1-\frac{v^2}{c^2}}}$$

$$\sqrt{1-\frac{v^2}{c^2}} = 0.8017$$

$$1-\frac{v^2}{c^2} = 0.6427$$

$$\frac{v^2}{c^2} = 0.3573$$

$$v = 0.598\,c$$

If a particle is accelerated by a potential difference of V volts, its total energy will *increase* by an amount qV, where q is the charge of the particle. Thus, if a particle is initially at rest, its total energy is the rest energy $E_0 = m_0c^2$. After going through the potential difference, the total energy will be $E = m_0c^2 + qV$. We can then find the speed of the particle, as the next example shows.

Example questions

Q4

An electron of rest energy 0.511 MeV is accelerated through a potential difference of 5.0 MV in a lab.
(a) What is its total energy with respect to the lab?
(b) What is its speed with respect to the lab?

Answer

(a) The total energy of the electron will increase by

$$qV = 1\text{e} \times 5.0 \times 10^6 \text{ volt} = 5.0 \text{ MeV}$$

and so the total energy is

$$E = m_0c^2 + qV = 0.511 \text{ MeV} + 5.0 \text{ MeV}$$
$$= 5.511 \text{ MeV}$$

(b) We know that

$$E = \gamma m_0 c^2$$

$$5.511 = \gamma \times 0.511$$

$$\gamma = \frac{5.511}{0.511}$$
$$= 10.785$$

Since $\gamma = \frac{1}{\sqrt{1-\frac{v^2}{c^2}}}$ it follows that

$$10.785 = \frac{1}{\sqrt{1-\frac{v^2}{c^2}}}$$

$$\sqrt{1-\frac{v^2}{c^2}} = \frac{1}{10.875} \; (= 0.0927)$$

$$1-\frac{v^2}{c^2} = 0.008597$$

$$v = 0.996c$$

Q5

(a) A proton is accelerated from rest by a potential difference V. Calculate V so that the proton reaches a speed of $0.95c$ after acceleration. (The rest energy of the proton is 938 MeV.)
(b) What accelerating potential is required to accelerate a proton from a speed of $0.95c$ to a speed of $0.99c$?

Answer

(a) The gamma factor at a speed of $0.95c$ is

$$\gamma = \frac{1}{\sqrt{1-\frac{v^2}{c^2}}}$$
$$= \frac{1}{\sqrt{1-0.95^2}}$$
$$= 3.20$$

The total energy of the proton after acceleration is thus

$$E = \gamma m_0 c^2$$
$$= 3.20 \times 938 \text{ MeV}$$
$$= 3004 \text{ MeV}$$

From

$$E = m_0c^2 + qV$$

we find

$$qV = (3004 - 938) \text{ MeV} = 2066 \text{ MeV}$$

and so

$$V = 2.1 \times 10^9 \text{ V}$$

Notice carefully how we avoid using SI units to make the numerical calculations much easier.

(b) The total energy of the proton at a speed of $0.95c$ is (from part (a)) $E = 3004$ MeV. The total energy at a speed of $0.99c$ is (working as in (a)) $E = 6649$ MeV. The extra energy needed is then $6649 - 3004 = 3645$ MeV, and so the accelerating potential must be 3.6×10^9 V. Notice that a larger potential difference is needed to accelerate the proton from $0.95c$ to $0.99c$ than from rest to $0.95c$. This is a sign that it is impossible to reach the speed of light. (See also the next example.)

Q6

A constant force is applied to a particle which is initially at rest. Sketch a graph that shows the variation of the speed of the particle with time for
(a) Newtonian mechanics;
(b) relativistic mechanics.

Answer

In Newtonian mechanics, a constant force produces a constant acceleration, and so the speed increases uniformly without limit, exceeding the speed of light. In relativistic mechanics, the speed increases uniformly as long as the speed is substantially less than the speed of light, and is in fact identical with the Newtonian graph. However, as the speed increases, so does the energy. Because it takes an infinite amount of energy for the particle to reach the speed of light, we conclude that the particle never reaches the speed of light. The speed approaches the speed of light asymptotically. Note that the speed is always less than the corresponding Newtonian value at the same time. Hence we have the graph shown in Figure H3.3.

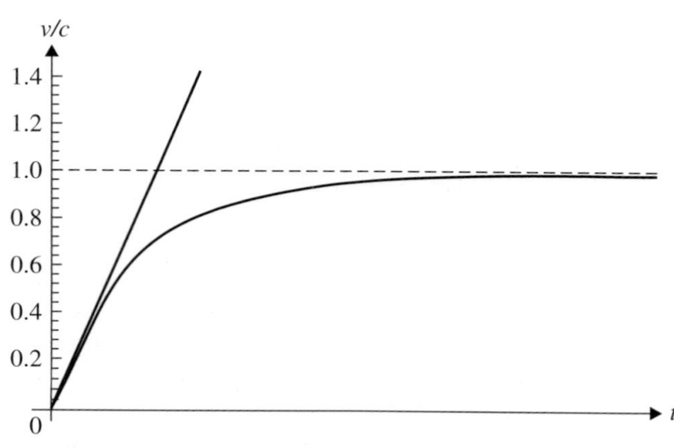

Figure H3.3

Evidence for special relativity

Muon decay

Muons are particles with properties similar to those of the electron except that they are more massive, are unstable and decay into electrons; they have a lifetime of about 2.2×10^{-6} s. (The reaction is $\mu^- \rightarrow e^- + \bar{\nu}_e + \nu_\mu$.)

▶ This is the lifetime measured when the muon is at rest – this is the proper time interval between the creation of a muon and its subsequent decay.

From the point of view of an observer in the laboratory, however, with respect to whom the muons are moving at high speed, the lifetime is longer because of time dilation. Consider a muon created at a height of 3.0 km and moving toward the surface of the earth with a speed of $0.99c$. Its lifetime as measured by ground observers will be

$$\text{time interval} = \frac{\text{proper time}}{\sqrt{1 - \frac{v^2}{c^2}}} = \frac{2.2 \times 10^{-6}\ \text{s}}{\sqrt{1 - 0.99^2}} = 1.56 \times 10^{-5}\ \text{s}$$

In this time the muon travels a distance (as far as the laboratory observers are concerned)

$$0.99 \times 3 \times 10^8 \times 1.56 \times 10^{-5}\ \text{m} = 4.63\ \text{km}$$

This means that the muon reaches the surface of the earth *before* decaying. Without the time dilation effect, the muon would have travelled a distance of only

$$0.99 \times 3 \times 10^8 \times 2.2 \times 10^{-6}\ \text{m} = 0.653\ \text{km}$$

and thus would not make it to the surface.

▶ The fact that muons do make it to the surface of the earth is evidence in favour of relativity.

The muon exists as a muon for only 2.2×10^{-6} s in the muon's rest frame. So how does an observer travelling along with the muon explain the arrival of muons (and not electrons) at the surface of the earth? The answer is that the distance of 3.0 km measured by the observers on earth is a proper length for them but not for the moving observer. The observer travelling along with the muon claims that it is the earth that is moving upward and so measures a length-contracted distance of

$$3.0 \times \sqrt{1 - 0.99^2}\ \text{km} = 0.42\ \text{km}$$

to the surface of the earth. The earth's surface is coming up to this observer with a speed of 0.99*c* and so the time when they will meet is

$$\frac{0.42 \times 10^3}{0.99 \times 3 \times 10^8}\ \text{s} = 1.4 \times 10^{-6}\ \text{s}$$

that is, *before* the muon decays!

▶ In this sense, muon decay experiments are indirect confirmations of the length contraction effect.

The Michelson–Morley experiment

Nineteenth-century physics demanded that light, like all other waves, required a medium for its propagation. Just as water waves require water, waves on a string require a string, etc., it was presumed that light too required a medium in which its vibrations would take place and propagate. The medium for light waves was hypothesized to be an all-pervading medium called the *ether*. The problem with the ether was that an observer moving in it could not measure the same speed of light as one who was stationary in it. If an observer moved in the ether, they would experience an 'ether wind', much the same as a car travelling in still air experiences an opposing wind. If this observer were to emit a light signal in the direction of motion, the velocity of light was expected to be less than it would be if the observer were at rest relative to the ether (see Figure H3.4).

We have seen that neither mechanics nor electromagnetic experiments can help in deciding whether an inertial observer really is at rest or really moves. Could we use the ether in an attempt to define absolute rest and absolute motion? Consider an observer in a boat who looks at waves in the water. In the first instance, the boat is at rest in the water (Figure H3.5). In the second, the boat moves smoothly at constant velocity relative to the water (Figure H3.6).

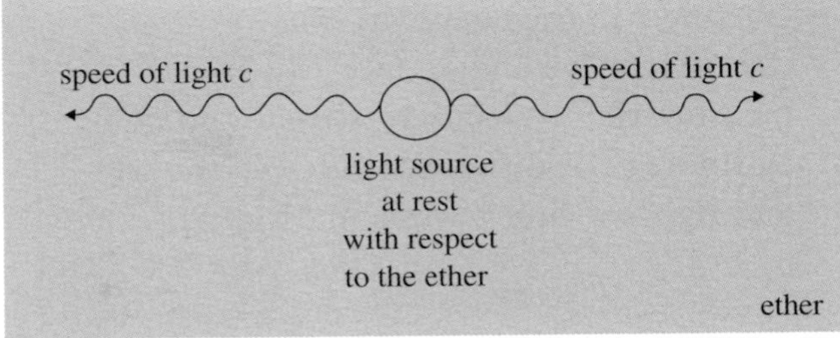

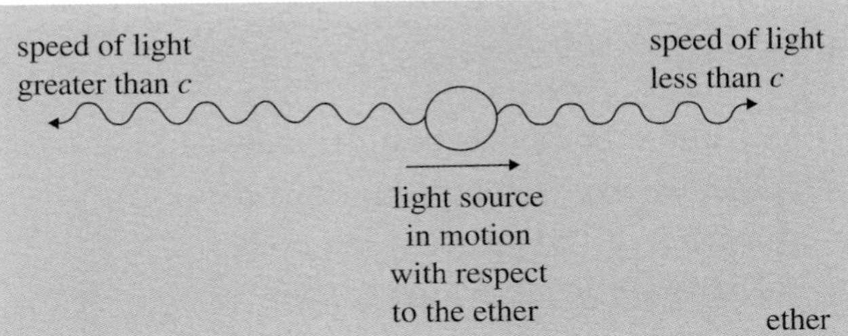

Figure H3.4 The speed of light would be less when emitted from a source that moved in the ether in the same direction as the light signal.

Figure H3.5 View from the boat at rest. The boat is at rest in the water and waves moving to the right and left move with the same speed relative to the boat. This velocity is u, the velocity of water waves relative to the water.

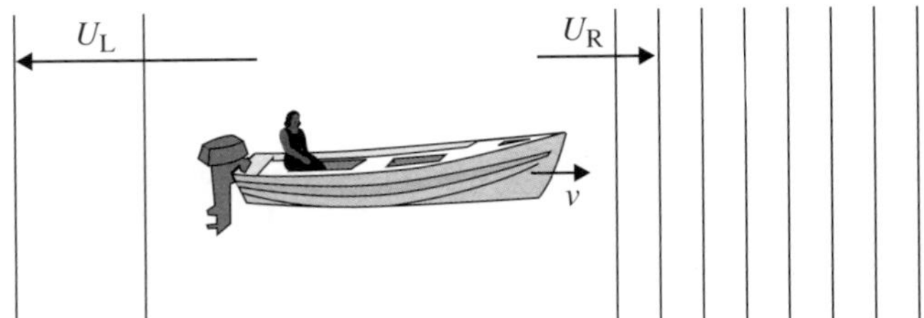

Figure H3.6 View from a moving boat. The boat moves with velocity v relative to the water. The speed of the waves is u relative to the water. Thus, the right-moving waves have velocity $U_R = u - v$ relative to the boat and the left-moving waves have a velocity $U_L = u + v$ relative to the boat.

▶ Observers in the boat thus *know* that they move and, in fact, can even measure their velocity relative to the water by finding the difference between the left- and right-moving waves and dividing by 2

$$\frac{U_L - U_R}{2} = \frac{(u+v)-(u-v)}{2} = v$$

So if the ether exists and pervades all space, we may refer all motions to the ether. If the velocity of a body relative to the ether is zero, we may say that the body is absolutely at rest. If the body has a velocity relative to the ether, then the body is in a state of absolute motion.

This was the idea behind the Michelson–Morley experiment: to find the speed of the earth relative to the ether as the earth rotated around the sun.

In 1881, Michelson, and later Michelson and Morley, performed an experiment to find the speed of the earth relative to the ether using an accurate interferometer designed by Michelson. The idea of the experiment appears to have been put forward a few years earlier by Maxwell himself. To their great disappointment, despite the accuracy of their experiment they found no speed at all. (One way out would be to say that this implies that the earth is in a state of absolute rest; this is not acceptable as the earth moves in different directions as it rotates around the sun and so could not be permanently at rest relative to the ether. This is why the experiment was repeated at different times of the year when the earth was in different points in its orbit around the sun.)

▶ This most famous of all 'null experiments' of classical physics was resolved in 1905 by Albert Einstein, who simply threw away the entire notion of the ether. Light, like all other electromagnetic waves, does not require a medium and the speed of light in a vacuum is the same for all observers. It is an interesting historical note that although Einstein knew of this experiment he was not particularly influenced by it in his formulation of the theory of relativity.

The experiment used Michelson's interferometer, which is shown in Figure H3.7.

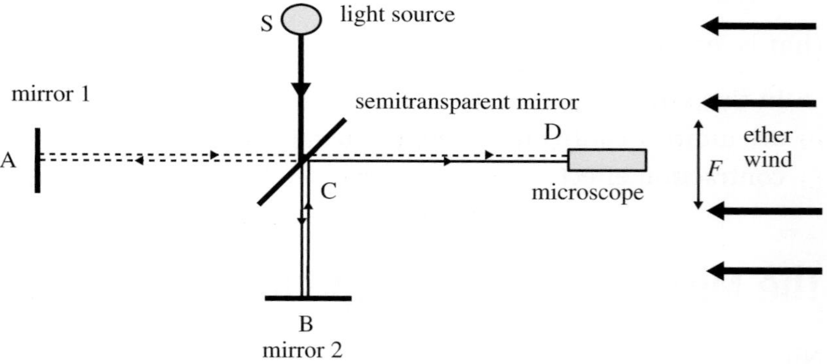

Figure H3.7 The Michelson interferometer.

Light from a source S falls on a semitransparent mirror and the beam is split in two: the reflected part (dotted line) proceeds to mirror 1 from which it is reflected towards the microscope. The other part (solid line) goes through the mirror and proceeds towards mirror 2 from which it is reflected back towards the semitransparent mirror and from there into the microscope. The two beams are thus rejoined at the microscope. The two mirrors are not exactly perpendicular to each other, which means that as you look along the field of view of the microscope (F), interference fringes are observed. The interferometer floated in a container filled with mercury and could be rotated by 90°, say in the counter-clockwise direction. *Because the speed of light was expected to be different depending on whether light moved along or against the ether*, detailed calculations show that rotating the interferometer should change the interference pattern by shifting the interference fringes (see Figure H3.8).

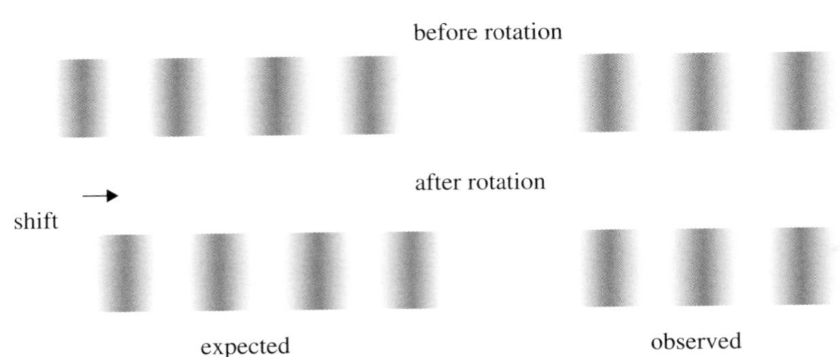

Figure H3.8 Expected and observed interference patterns before and after rotation in the Michelson–Morley experiment.

Michelson and Morley saw no difference when they rotated their interferometer. Many physicists, including Fitzgerald and notably Lorentz, attempted to explain this result by various *ad hoc* assumptions. The simplest explanation, though, came from Einstein, who abandoned the ether idea and introduced the principle of the constancy of the speed of light in all directions and for all inertial observers.

The constancy of the speed of light

The null result of the Michelson–Morley experiment is, of course, consistent with a constant speed of light, independent of the velocity of the source. However, the first conclusive experiment that demonstrated the constancy of the speed of light with great accuracy was performed at CERN (the European Centre for Nuclear Research) in 1964. In this experiment, neutral pions moving at $0.99975c$ decayed into a pair of photons moving in different directions. The speed of the photons in both directions was measured to be c with extraordinary accuracy. The speed of light does not depend on the speed of its source.

QUESTIONS

1 The rest mass of a proton is 1.67×10^{-27} kg. Find its rest energy.

2 At what speed must a body move so that its total energy is 10 times its rest energy?

3 The rest energy of a particle is 135 MeV and its total energy is 200 MeV. What is its speed?

4 An electron is accelerated from rest through a potential difference of 0.80 MV.
(a) What is its total energy?
(b) What is its speed?

5 What is the total energy in MeV of a proton travelling at $0.80c$?

6 A proton is accelerated from rest by a potential difference V. Calculate V so that the proton reaches a speed of $0.998c$.

7 What happens to the density of a cube travelling past you at a relativistic speed?

8 A muon travelling at $0.95c$ covers a distance of 2.00 km (as measured by an earthbound observer) before decaying.
(a) What is the muon's lifetime as measured by the earthbound observer?
(b) What is the lifetime as measured by an observer travelling along with the muon?

9 The lifetime of the unstable pion particle is measured to be 2.6×10^{-8} s (when at rest). If this particle is to travel a distance of 20 m in the laboratory just before decaying, at what speed must it be moving?

10 Two islands in a river are separated by 12 km (see Figure H3.9). The current flows with a speed of 2 km per hour relative to the banks from A to B.
(a) How long would a boat trip take from A to B if you can row with a speed of 4 km per hour with respect to the water?
(b) How long would the return trip take?
(c) How long would the entire trip take in still water?

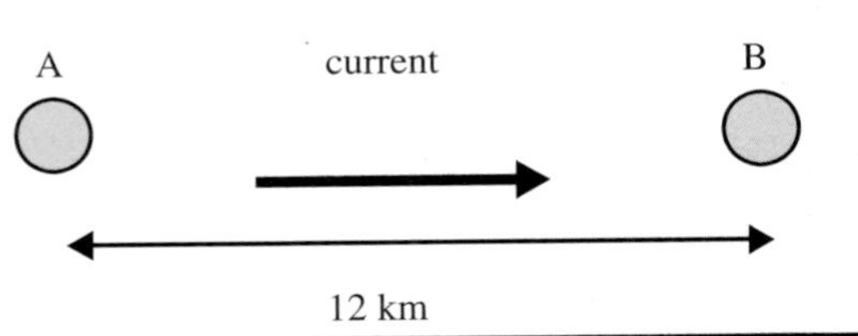

Figure H3.9 For question 10.

11 Two barges, A and B, are opposite each other near the shores of a lake, 12 km apart (see Figure H3.10). A current of speed 3 km per hour relative to the shores flows as shown. You can row at 5 km per hour relative to the water and you want to get from A to B. How long will it take you?

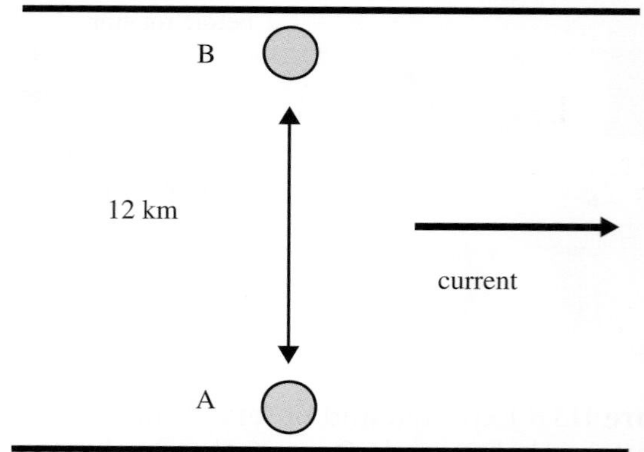

Figure H3.10 For question 11.

Relativistic mechanics

The familiar laws of mechanics based on Newton's laws of motion that we have studied earlier need to be modified whenever an object moves at speeds close to the speed of light. Relativistic mechanics introduces new relations between mass, energy and momentum.

Objectives

By the end of this chapter you should be able to:

- solve problems with *relativistic momentum*, $p = \frac{m_0 v}{\sqrt{1-\frac{v^2}{c^2}}} = \gamma m_0 v$, *relativistic energy*, $E = \frac{m_0 c^2}{\sqrt{1-\frac{v^2}{c^2}}}$, and *kinetic energy*, $E_k = (\gamma - 1)m_0 c^2$;
- solve problems with the formula relating *momentum*, *rest energy* and *total energy*, $E = \sqrt{m_0^2 c^4 + p^2 c^2}$;
- appreciate that a charge q that is accelerated from rest through a potential difference V *increases its kinetic energy* to E_k, where $qV = E_k$;
- use *relativistic units* for mass (e.g. MeV c^{-2}) and momentum (e.g. MeV c^{-1}).

Momentum and energy (momenergy)

Consider a body of mass 1 kg initially at rest acted upon by a force of 1 N. The body will move with an acceleration of 1 m s^{-2} and thus in a time of 3×10^8 s the body will acquire a speed equal to the speed of light. Since this is impossible, modifications in the laws of mechanics are necessary to make them comply with the principle of relativity. These modifications make up what is called relativistic mechanics. As we will see, the concepts of energy and momentum are so interconnected in relativity that John A. Wheeler coined the word *momenergy* for both quantities.

Momentum

The first change involves the momentum of a particle. In classical mechanics, the momentum is given by the product of mass times velocity, but in relativity this is modified to

$$p = \frac{m_0 v}{\sqrt{1-\frac{v^2}{c^2}}} = \gamma m_0 v$$

We still have the usual law of momentum conservation, which states that, when no external forces act on a system, the total momentum stays the same. The symbol m_0 here stands for the rest mass of the particle and is a constant for all observers.

▶ This means that (unlike Newtonian mechanics) a *constant* force on the particle will produce a *decreasing* acceleration in such a way that the speed never reaches the speed of light.

Example question

Q1

A constant force F acts on an electron that is initially at rest. Find the speed of the electron as a function of time.

Answer

Initially, for small t, the speed increases uniformly, as in Newtonian mechanics. But as t becomes large, the speed tends to the speed of light but does not reach or exceed it. This is because as the speed increases so does the mass of the electron and so the acceleration becomes smaller and smaller, never achieving the speed of light. This results in the graph shown in Figure H4.1.

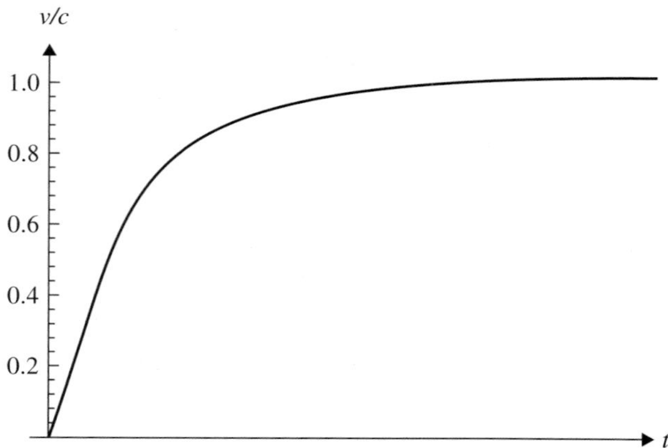

Figure H4.1.

HL Mathematics only

Begin with Newton's second law, $F = \frac{dp}{dt}$, where $p = \gamma m_0 v$ is the momentum of the electron. Since

$$\frac{dp}{dt} = \frac{d}{dt}\left(\frac{m_0 v}{\sqrt{1-\frac{v^2}{c^2}}}\right)$$

$$= \frac{m_0}{\sqrt{1-\frac{v^2}{c^2}}}\frac{dv}{dt} + \left(\frac{v}{c^2}\right)\frac{m_0 v}{\left(1-\frac{v^2}{c^2}\right)^{3/2}}\frac{dv}{dt}$$

$$\frac{dp}{dt} = \frac{m_0}{\left(1-\frac{v^2}{c^2}\right)^{3/2}}\frac{dv}{dt}$$

it follows that

$$\frac{dv}{dt} = \frac{F}{m_0}\left(1-\frac{v^2}{c^2}\right)^{3/2}$$

or

$$\frac{dv}{\left(1-\frac{v^2}{c^2}\right)^{3/2}} = \frac{F}{m_0}dt$$

Integrating both sides, we find that (assuming the mass starts from rest)

$$\frac{v}{\sqrt{1-\frac{v^2}{c^2}}} = \frac{F}{m_0}t$$

Solving for the speed, we find

$$v^2 = \frac{(Ft)^2}{(m_0 c)^2 + (Ft)^2}c^2$$

The way the velocity approaches the speed of light is shown in Figure H4.1.

Energy

A mass moving with velocity v is said to have a total energy E given by

$$E = \frac{m_0 c^2}{\sqrt{1-\frac{v^2}{c^2}}}$$

This means that even when the mass is at rest it has energy $E_0 = m_0 c^2$; this is called the rest energy of the mass. This is Einstein's famous formula from 1905. It states that mass and energy are equivalent and can be transformed into each other.

▶ The kinetic energy E_k is defined as the total energy minus the rest energy:

$$E_k = E - m_0 c^2$$

It can be rewritten as

$$E_k = \frac{m_0 c^2}{\sqrt{1-\frac{v^2}{c^2}}} - m_0 c^2$$

$$= \gamma m_0 c^2 - m_0 c^2$$

$$= (\gamma - 1) m_0 c^2$$

This definition ensures that the kinetic energy is zero when $v = 0$, as can be easily checked. The familiar result from mechanics that the work done by the net force equals the change in kinetic energy holds in relativity as well.

This relativistic definition of kinetic energy does not look similar to the ordinary kinetic energy $\frac{1}{2}mv^2$. In fact, when v is small compared with c, we can approximate the value of the relativistic factor $\frac{1}{\sqrt{1-\frac{v^2}{c^2}}}$ using the binomial expansion for $\frac{1}{\sqrt{1-x}}$ for small x:

$$\frac{1}{\sqrt{1-x}} \approx 1 + \frac{1}{2}x + \cdots$$

Applying this to E_k with $x = \left(\frac{v}{c}\right)^2$ we find

$$E_k = m_0c^2\left(1 + \frac{1}{2}\frac{v^2}{c^2} + \cdots\right) - m_0c^2$$

that is

$$E_k \approx \tfrac{1}{2}m_0v^2$$

In other words, for low speeds the relativistic formula reduces to the familiar Newtonian version. For higher speeds, the relativistic formula must be used.

Total energy, momentum and mass are related: from the definition of momentum, we find that

$$\begin{aligned} p^2c^2 + m_0^2c^4 &= \frac{m_0^2v^2c^2}{1-\frac{v^2}{c^2}} + m_0^2c^4 \\ &= \frac{m_0^2c^4}{1-\frac{v^2}{c^2}} \\ &= E^2 \end{aligned}$$

that is

$$E = \sqrt{m_0^2c^4 + p^2c^2}$$

(This formula is the relativistic version of the conventional formula $E = \frac{p^2}{2m}$ in Newtonian mechanics.) This relation can be remembered by using the Pythagorean theorem in the triangle of Figure H4.2

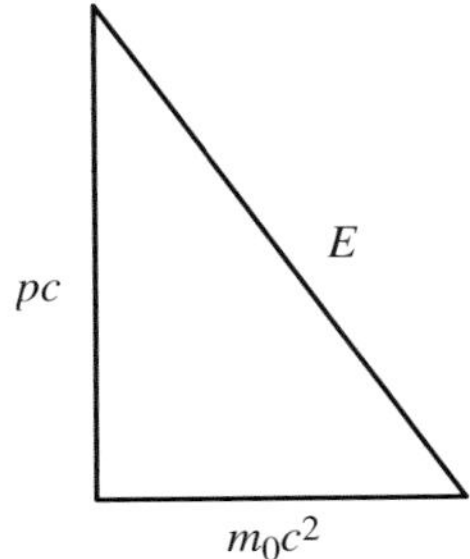

Figure H4.2 The rest energy, momentum and total energy are related through the Pythagorean theorem for the triangle shown.

The formula we just derived applies also to those particles that have zero mass, such as the photon, in which case $E = pc$. Remembering that for a photon $E = hf$, we find $p = \frac{hf}{c} = \frac{h}{\lambda}$.

A point about units

We have already seen that we can use units such as MeV c^{-2} or GeV c^{-2} for mass. This follows from the fact that the rest energy of a particle is given by $E_0 = m_0c^2$ and so allows us to express the mass of the particle in terms of the rest energy as $m_0 = E_0/c^2$. Thus, the statement 'the mass of the pion is 135 MeV c^{-2}' means that the rest energy of this particle is 135 MeV. (To find the mass in kg we would first have to convert the MeV into joules and then divide the result by the square of the speed of light.)

Similarly, the momentum of a particle can be expressed in units of MeV c^{-1} or GeV c^{-1}. A particle of rest mass 5.0 MeV c^{-2} and total energy 13 MeV has momentum given by

$$\begin{aligned} E^2 &= m_0^2c^4 + p^2c^2 \\ \Rightarrow p^2c^2 &= (169 - 25)\,\text{MeV}^2 \\ &= 144\,\text{MeV}^2 \\ \Rightarrow pc &= 12\,\text{MeV} \\ \Rightarrow p &= 12\,\text{MeV}\,c^{-1} \end{aligned}$$

The speed can be found from

$$\begin{aligned} E &= \frac{m_0c^2}{\sqrt{1-\frac{v^2}{c^2}}} \\ \Rightarrow 13 &= \frac{5}{\sqrt{1-\frac{v^2}{c^2}}} \\ \Rightarrow \sqrt{1-\frac{v^2}{c^2}} &= \frac{5}{13} \\ \Rightarrow \frac{v^2}{c^2} &= \frac{144}{169} \\ \Rightarrow v &= \frac{12}{13}c \end{aligned}$$

In conventional SI units, a momentum of 12 MeV c^{-1} is

$$12 \times 10^6 \times 1.6 \times 10^{-19} \frac{\text{J}}{3 \times 10^8\,\text{m}\,\text{s}^{-1}}$$

$$= 6.4 \times 10^{-21} \frac{\text{kg}\,\text{m}^2\,\text{s}^{-2}}{\text{m}\,\text{s}^{-1}}$$

$$= 6.4 \times 10^{-21}\,\text{kg}\,\text{m}\,\text{s}^{-1}$$

Example questions

Q2

Find the momentum of a pion (rest mass 135 MeV c^{-2}) whose speed is $0.80c$.

Answer

The total energy is

$$E = \frac{m_0 c^2}{\sqrt{1 - \frac{v^2}{c^2}}}$$

$$= \frac{135}{\sqrt{1 - 0.80^2}}$$

$$= 225 \text{ MeV}$$

Using

$$E^2 = m_0^2 c^4 + p^2 c^2$$

$$\Rightarrow pc = \sqrt{225^2 - 135^2}$$

$$= 180 \text{ MeV}$$

$$\Rightarrow p = 180 \text{ MeV}\, c^{-1}$$

Q3

Find the speed of a muon (rest mass = 105 MeV c^{-2}) whose momentum is 228 MeV c^{-1}.

Answer

From $p = \gamma m_0 v$ we find

$$228 \text{ MeV } c^{-1} = \gamma \times 105 \text{ MeV } c^{-2} \times v$$

$$\Rightarrow \gamma \frac{v}{c} = 2.171$$

Hence

$$\frac{1}{1 - \left(\frac{v}{c}\right)^2}\left(\frac{v}{c}\right)^2 = 4.715$$

$$\Rightarrow \left(\frac{v}{c}\right)^2 = 4.715 - 4.715\left(\frac{v}{c}\right)^2$$

$$\Rightarrow \left(\frac{v}{c}\right)^2 = \frac{4.715}{5.715}$$

$$= 0.8250$$

and so $v = 0.91c$.

Q4

Find the kinetic energy of an electron whose momentum is 1.5 MeV c^{-1}.

Answer

The total energy of the electron is given by

$$E^2 = m_0^2 c^4 + p^2 c^2$$

$$= 0.511^2 \text{ MeV}^2 + 1.5^2 \text{ MeV}^2\, c^{-2} \times c^2$$

$$= 2.511 \text{ MeV}^2$$

$$\Rightarrow E = 1.58 \text{ MeV}$$

and so

$$E_k = E - m_0 c^2$$

$$= 1.58 \text{ MeV} - 0.511 \text{ MeV}$$

$$= 1.07 \text{ MeV}$$

A free electron cannot absorb (or emit) a photon

The laws of relativistic mechanics forbid the absorption of a photon by a free electron. Assume for a minute that this is possible; that is, let a free electron initially at rest absorb a photon of energy ε (see Figure H4.3).

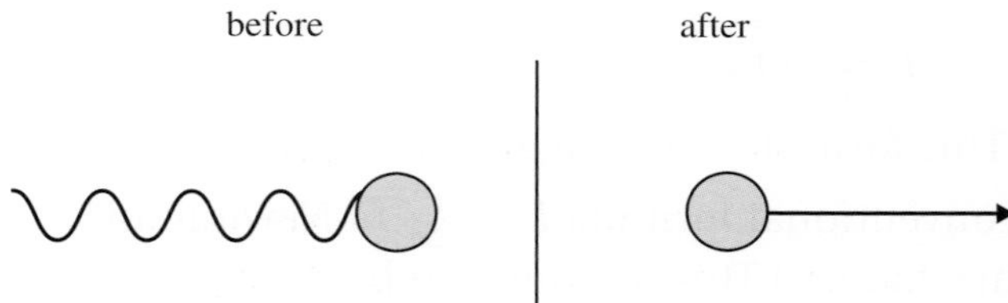

Figure H4.3 What would happen if a free electron could absorb a photon.

By conservation of momentum, the electron must then move in the same direction as that of the incident photon, with momentum ε/c, since this is the momentum the photon had before absorption,

$$p = \frac{\varepsilon}{c}$$

By conservation of energy, the total energy of the electron, E, after the photon absorption is

$E = m_0c^2 + \varepsilon$. But the electron's total energy E and momentum p are related by

$$E^2 = m_0^2c^4 + p^2c^2$$

and so this implies that

$$(m_0c^2 + \varepsilon)^2 = m_0^2c^4 + \frac{\varepsilon^2}{c^2}c^2$$
$$m_0^2c^4 + \varepsilon^2 + 2m_0c^2\varepsilon = m_0^2c^4 + \varepsilon^2$$
$$2m_0c^2\varepsilon = 0$$

which is an impossible relation. Hence the photon cannot be absorbed. In the photoelectric effect the absorption is possible, but only because the electron is not free but bound in an atom. The atom then participates in sharing energy and momentum so that the photon can be absorbed.

? QUESTIONS

1 (a) Find the rest energy of an electron in MeV.
(b) An electron is accelerated from rest by a potential difference of 1.00×10^9 V. Calculate the speed of the electron using (i) classical mechanics and (ii) relativistic mechanics.

2 What is the speed of a particle whose kinetic energy is 10 times its rest energy?

3 What is the momentum of a proton whose total energy is 5 times its rest energy?

4 What is the total energy of an electron with a speed equal to 0.9 times that of light?

5 What is the momentum, in conventional SI units, of a proton of momentum 685 MeV c^{-1}?

6 What is the kinetic energy of a proton whose momentum is 500 MeV c^{-1}?

7 The total energy of an electron is 10.0 GeV. What is its mass in kg?

8 (a) What is the speed of electrons accelerated to a total energy of 100.0 GeV?
(b) What is it for protons?

9 What is the speed of an electron that has been accelerated from rest by a potential difference of 2.0 MV?

10 Through what potential difference must a proton be accelerated (from rest) so that its speed is 0.96c?

11 Find the kinetic energy of a proton whose speed is 0.99 times that of light.

12 What is the energy needed to accelerate an electron to a speed of:
(a) 0.50c;
(b) 0.90c;
(c) 0.99c?

13 A proton initially at rest finds itself in a region of uniform electric field of magnitude 5.0×10^6 V m^{-1}. The electric field accelerates the proton over a distance of 1 km. Calculate:
(a) the kinetic energy of the proton;
(b) the speed of the proton.

14 (a) Show that the speed of a particle of rest mass m_0 and momentum p is given by

$$v = \frac{pc^2}{\sqrt{m_0^2c^4 + p^2c^2}}$$

An electron and a proton have the same momentum. What is the ratio of their speeds when the momentum is:
(b) 1.00 MeV c^{-1};
(c) 1.00 GeV c^{-1}?
(d) What does the ratio become as the momentum gets larger and larger?

15 A particle at rest breaks apart into two pieces of masses 250 MeV c^{-2} and 125 MeV c^{-2}. The lighter fragment moves away at a speed equal to 0.85c.
(a) What is the speed of the other fragment?
(b) What is the rest mass of the particle that broke apart?
(Use the laws of conservation of momentum and total energy.)

16 An electron and a positron (a particle of the same mass but opposite charge to the electron) each of kinetic energy 2.0 MeV collide head-on. The electron and positron annihilate each other into photons.
(a) Explain why the electron–positron pair cannot create just one photon.

(b) Assume that two photons are produced. Explain why the photons must be moving in opposite directions.

(c) Calculate the energy of each photon.

17 *The Compton effect.* A photon of wavelength λ scatters off an electron initially at rest (see Figure H4.4).

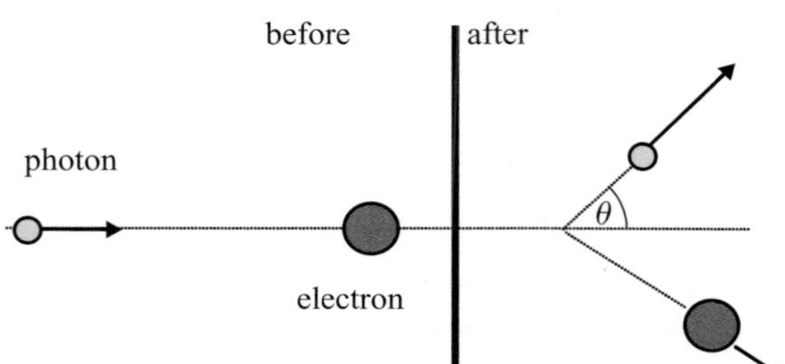

Figure H4.4 For question 17.

(a) By treating the process as a collision and applying the laws of conservation of energy and momentum, show that the wavelength of the photon after the collision, λ', is given by

$$\lambda' - \lambda = \frac{h}{mc}(1 - \cos\theta)$$

(b) Explain why the scattered photon has a larger wavelength than that of the incoming photon.

(c) If the incoming photon has a wavelength of 3.00×10^{-12} m, find the wavelength of the scattered photon when the scattering angle is 60°.

18 In the Compton effect (see question 17) an incoming photon of wavelength 5.00×10^{-12} m scatters off an electron initially at rest and goes back along the path it came from. With what kinetic energy and speed does the electron move off?

19 A neutral pion of mass 135 MeV c^{-2} travelling at $0.8c$ decays into two photons travelling in opposite directions, $\pi^0 \to 2\gamma$ (see Figure H4.5). What is the ratio of the frequency of photon A to that of photon B?

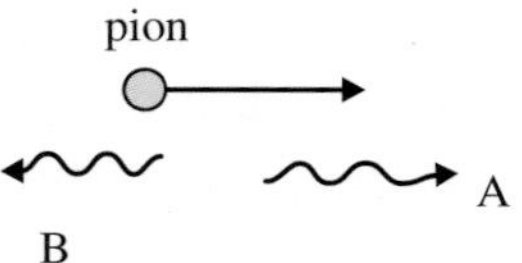

Figure H4.5 For question 19.

20 Two identical bodies with a rest mass of 3.0 kg are moving towards each other from opposite directions, each with a speed of $0.80c$. They collide and form one body. Determine the rest mass of this body.

21 State the formulas, in terms of the rest mass m of a particle, for

(a) the relativistic momentum p and

(b) the total energy E.

(c) Using these formulas, derive the formula $v = \frac{pc^2}{E}$ for the speed v of the particle.

(d) The formula in (c) applies in fact to all particles, even to those that are massless. Deduce that, if the particle is a photon, then $v = c$.

General relativity

The theory of general relativity was formulated by Albert Einstein in 1916. It is a theory of gravitation that replaces the standard theory of gravitation of Newton and generalizes Einstein's special theory of relativity. Newton's theory of gravitation, while successful in dealing with planetary motion, cannot account for the effects of gravitation in very dense, massive objects and the behaviour of matter and energy in the universe as a whole. A number of physicists were close to discovering the laws of special relativity at the beginning of the twentieth century. The theory of general relativity, however, stands as the crowning achievement of Einstein's genius and is considered to be perhaps the most elegant and beautiful example of a physical theory ever constructed. The theory is a radical theory in that it relates the distribution of matter and energy in the universe to the structure of space and time. The geometry of space-time is a direct function of the matter and energy that space-time contains. In general, this geometry is not Euclidean, which means, among other things, that the angles of a triangle do not add up to 180°. Matter distorts the space-time in which it finds itself, in much the same way that a heavy ball would distort a rubber sheet on which it is placed.

Objectives

By the end of this chapter you should be able to:

- state the *equivalence principle* and appreciate its consequences;
- appreciate that the equivalence principle leads to the equality of *inertial mass* and *gravitational mass*;
- describe the tests of general relativity, in particular the *bending of light* by a massive object and the *gravitational redshift* or *Pound–Rebka experiment*;
- solve problems using $\frac{\Delta f}{f} = \frac{gH}{c^2}$;
- understand that general relativity is a theory that relates the *rules of geometry* to the *energy and mass* contained in space;
- appreciate that, in the absence of forces, objects in general relativity move along paths of shortest distance called *geodesics*;
- understand that general relativity predicts the existence of *black holes* whose event horizons have radius $R_S = \frac{2GM}{c^2}$;
- state the meaning of the term *event horizon*.

The principle of equivalence

We have already seen in Chapter 2.5 on Newton's second law that when a person stands on a scale inside a freely falling elevator ('Einstein's elevator') the reading of the scale is zero. It is as if the person is weightless. This is what the scale would read if the elevator were moving at constant velocity in deep space far from all masses. Similarly, consider an astronaut in a spacecraft in orbit around the earth. She too feels weightless and floats inside the spacecraft. But neither the person in the falling elevator nor the astronaut are really weightless. Gravity does act on both. We can say that the acceleration of the freely falling elevator or the centripetal acceleration of the spacecraft 'cancelled out' the force of gravity. The right acceleration can make gravity disappear and make the frame of reference under consideration look like one moving at constant velocity.

The right acceleration can also make gravity appear. Consider an astronaut in a spacecraft in deep space far from all masses that moves with constant velocity. The astronaut really is weightless. The spacecraft engines are now ignited and the spacecraft accelerates forward. The astronaut feels pinned down to the floor. If he drops a coin, it will hit the floor whereas previously it would have floated in the spacecraft. The coin falling to the floor and the sensation of being pinned down are what we normally associate with gravity.

We have seen two examples where the effects of acceleration mimic those of gravity. Another expression for 'the effects of acceleration' is 'inertial effects'. Einstein elevated these observations to a principle of physics – the equivalence principle:

▶ Gravitational and inertial effects are indistinguishable.

Applying this principle to the two examples we just discussed we may re-express it as:

▶ A frame of reference moving at constant velocity far from all masses is equivalent to a freely falling frame of reference in a uniform gravitational field.

Or:

▶ A frame of reference accelerating far from all masses is equivalent to a frame of reference at rest in a gravitational field.

You can use either one of these last two statements as a definition of the equivalence principle. But the original statement takes care of both.

Figure H5.1 shows a frame of reference, A, moving at constant velocity in deep space and a frame of reference, B, that is falling freely in a gravitational field. The principle of equivalence says that the two frames are equivalent. There is no experiment that the occupants of box A can perform that will give a different result from a similar experiment performed in box B. Nor can the occupants of either box decide which of the two states of motion they 'really' have.

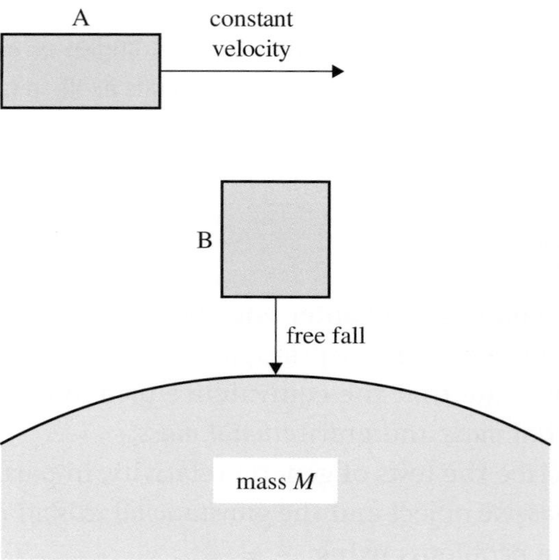

Figure H5.1 A frame of reference moving at constant velocity far from any masses (A) and a freely falling frame in a gravitational field (B) are equivalent.

Figure H5.2 shows a frame of reference, A, that accelerates in deep space and a frame of reference, B, that is at rest in a gravitational field. Again, there is no experiment that the occupants of box A can perform that will give a different result from a similar experiment performed in box B, nor can the occupants decide which is which.

This principle has immediate consequences.

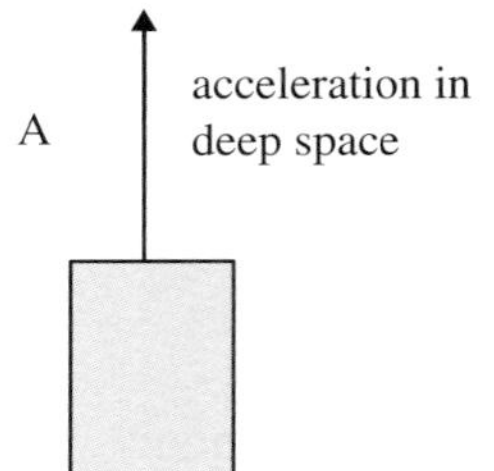

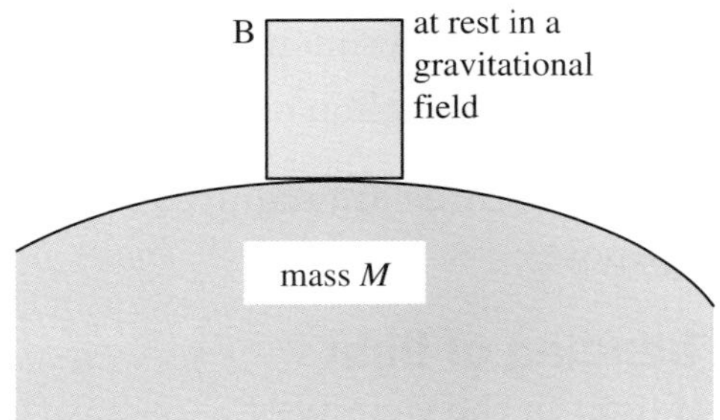

Figure H5.2 An accelerating frame of reference far from any masses (A) and a frame at rest in a gravitational field (B) are equivalent.

The speed of light

The first consequence is that *the speed of light is the same* whether in a gravitational field or not. An observer in box A of Figure H5.1 would measure $c = 3 \times 10^8$ m s^{-1} for the speed of light. An observer in the freely falling frame of box B must also reach the same conclusion since the two frames are equivalent.

▶ The speed of light in a gravitational field is the same as in any inertial frame of reference.

Inertial and gravitational mass

The second consequence is that *gravitational mass and inertial mass are the same.* Recall that inertial mass is the ratio of the net force on a body to the body's acceleration and gravitational mass is the ratio of the gravitational force on a body to the acceleration due to gravity.

In frame A of Figure H5.2, mass measurements are inertial mass measurements. In frame B at rest in a gravitational field, mass measurements are gravitational mass measurements. Since the two frames are equivalent, the equality of the two masses follows.

This is something that Galileo (and later Christiaan Huygens) checked experimentally when he showed that different objects fall at the same rate and that pendulums of equal lengths but with different masses have the same period. Modern, more accurate experiments by Dicke and Braginsky have verified this equality to an accuracy of 1 part in 10^{12}, that is

$$\frac{m_i - m_g}{m_i} < 10^{-12}$$

So there is good experimental evidence for the equivalence principle.

The bending of light

The third consequence of the equivalence principle is that *light bends toward a massive body.* Imagine a spacecraft orbiting a massive object. A ray of light is emitted from the back of the spacecraft toward the front. Where does it hit – at the front of the spacecraft at F or on the side at S (see Figure H5.3)? Remember that the frame of the spacecraft is freely falling (it is in orbit) and so is equivalent to a frame moving at constant velocity in a straight line (Figure H5.1). In this frame there is no doubt that the light will hit at F. So it must also hit at F in the spacecraft in orbit, since the two frames are equivalent.

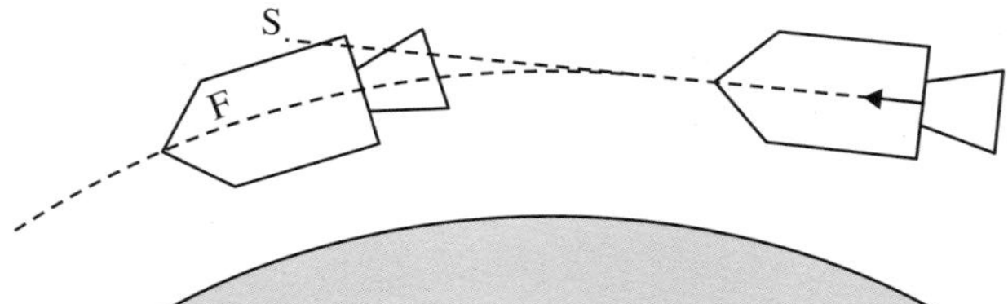

Figure H5.3 The ray of light will hit at F, indicating to an observer outside that the ray has bent toward the massive object.

But this means that from the point of view of an observer at rest on the surface of the massive body, light has bent towards it.

▶ A ray of light bends towards a massive body.

Massive objects can thus act as a kind of *gravitational lens.*

Time slows down

A final consequence of the equivalence principle is that *time slows down near a massive body*. Consider two rays on a wavefront AB, which are bent as they pass near a massive object (see Figure H5.4). A and B are thus points in phase.

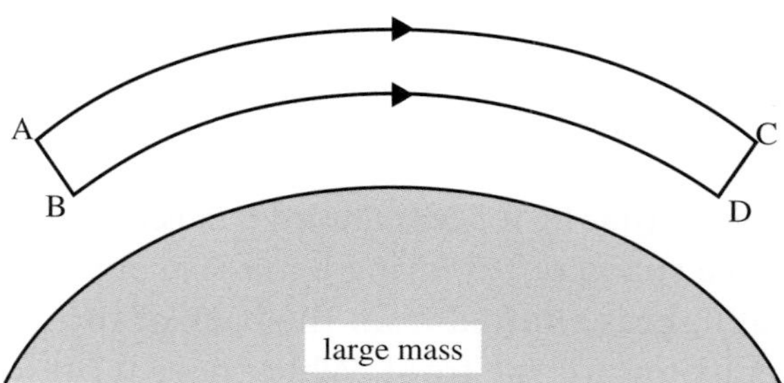

Figure H5.4 Ray BD appears to have covered a smaller distance than ray AC. Since the speed of light is the same for both rays, it follows that time must be 'running slower' near the massive object.

The ray at A moves to point C and that at B moves to point D. The wavefront AB has bent because the rays bend towards the massive object. If points C and D are to be in phase (they must be since they are on the same wavefront) the rays from A and B must take the same time to get to C and D. But ray BD covers a smaller distance than ray AC, yet travels at the same speed. The problem can be avoided if time runs slower for ray BD.

▶ Time slows down near massive objects.

Consider two identical clocks. One is placed near a massive body and the other far from it. When the clock near the massive body shows that 1 s has gone by, the far away clock will show that more than 1 s has gone by. This is the general relativity analogue of time dilation.

The tests of general relativity

The four main tests of the theory of general relativity are:

- the bending of light and radio signals near massive objects
- the gravitational frequency shift
- the Shapiro time delay experiment
- the precession of the perihelion of Mercury

Of these, only the first three are required for examination purposes.

Test 1: The bending of light

The bending of light in the vicinity of a massive object (the sun, for example) was detected experimentally in a famous observation by F. W. Dyson, A. S. Eddington and C. Davidson in two separate eclipse expeditions to the islands of Principe and Sobral in 1919. News of their confirmation of Einstein's theory was telegraphed around the world and made Einstein known to the wider public. This is shown in Figure H5.5. The angle of bending is shown unrealistically large for clarity. When the sun is between the earth and the star, the sun's light would completely wipe out the light from the star. This is why such an observation is possible only during a total solar eclipse.

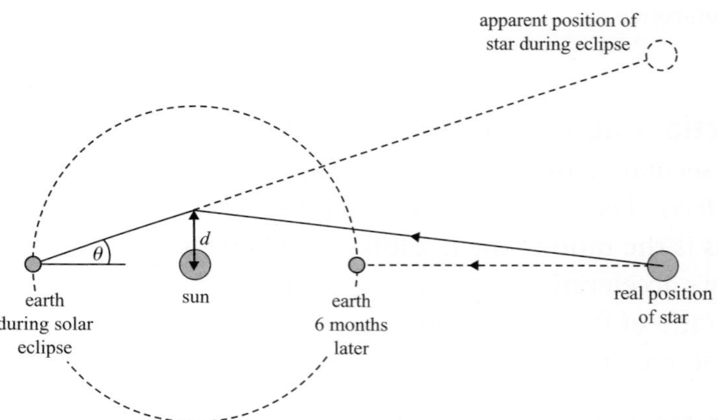

Figure H5.5 The star is observed during a solar eclipse and then 6 months later when the sun is not in the way. The angular position of the star is different in the two measurements. For a ray grazing the surface of the sun, the predicted angle of bending is about 1.75″ (arcseconds).

The bending of light that Eddington and his co-workers measured in 1919 was in agreement with the Einstein prediction, within experimental error, but the accuracy was not enough for this to constitute a test of the theory. The measurements have since been refined to include radio signals from distant galaxies, and these agree with general relativity predictions. Referring to Figure H5.5, if d is the distance of closest approach of a ray of light to the sun, the angle of deflection is predicted by general relativity to be

$$\theta = 1.75'' \frac{R}{d}$$

where R is the radius of the sun. (The angle is given in arcseconds – there are 3600 arcseconds in one degree.)

Test 2: The gravitational frequency shift

General relativity predicts that clocks near a massive object run slower than similar clocks further away from the massive object. Monochromatic light can be taken to be a clock – the period of the wave is like the time interval between the 'ticks' of a clock.

Thus, when a photon is emitted from the surface of a massive body and then observed far away from the massive object, the *frequency* of the photon will be less than the frequency at emission. The photon will show a *redshift*. Conversely, if the photon is emitted far from the massive body and is then observed near the massive body, the photon will experience a *blueshift*.

The blueshift due to the earth's mass has actually been observed in the *Pound–Rebka experiment*. In this experiment, performed at Harvard University in 1960, a beam of gamma rays of energy 14.4 keV from a nuclear transition in iron-57 was emitted from the top of a tower 22.6 m high and detected at ground level (see Figure H5.6).

Let f_{em} be the emitted frequency at the top of the tower and f_o the observed frequency at ground level.

The energy of the emitted photon is hf_{em}. This photon is received at a position lower than the

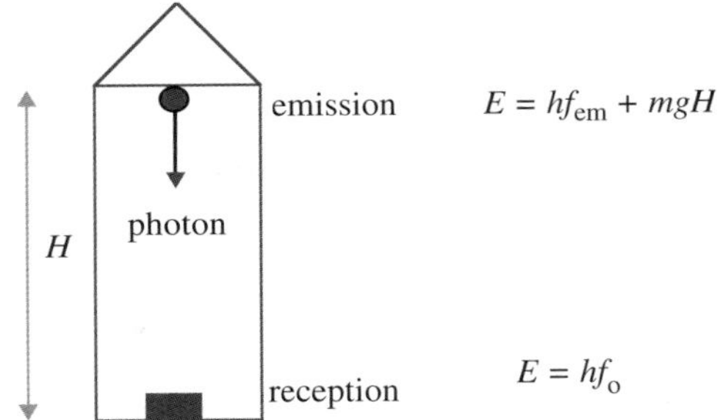

Figure H5.6 A photon emitted at ground level will be observed at the top of the tower with a lower frequency (redshift). Conversely, a photon emitted at the top will be observed at ground level at a higher frequency (blueshift).

emission point and energy conservation demands that

$$hf_{em} + mgH = hf_o$$

'Mass' here stands for the gravitational mass of the photon, that is its energy divided by c^2 (this is in effect the mass on which gravitation acts; it is not implied that the photon has a non-zero mass). This mass is thus (hf/c^2). Hence

$$hf_{em} + \frac{hf_{em}}{c^2} gH = hf_o$$

$$\Rightarrow f_o = f_{em}\left(1 + \frac{gH}{c^2}\right)$$

This means that the frequency shift $\Delta f = f_o - f_{em}$ is given by

$$\frac{\Delta f}{f} = \frac{gH}{c^2}$$

(Here, f stands for either the emitted or the observed frequency since they are almost equal.)

Test 3: The Shapiro time delay experiment

In the 1960s, Irwin Shapiro developed a new test for general relativity that is a combination of light bending and gravitational redshift. The test consists of sending a radio signal to a distant object (a planet or a spacecraft) and timing its return. This is done twice. The first signal is sent when the sun is out of the way, whereas the second signal grazes the sun on its outward and inward trip (see Figure H5.7). The second signal will take somewhat longer to return because (i) it will bend in the curved space-time around the sun and (ii) time runs

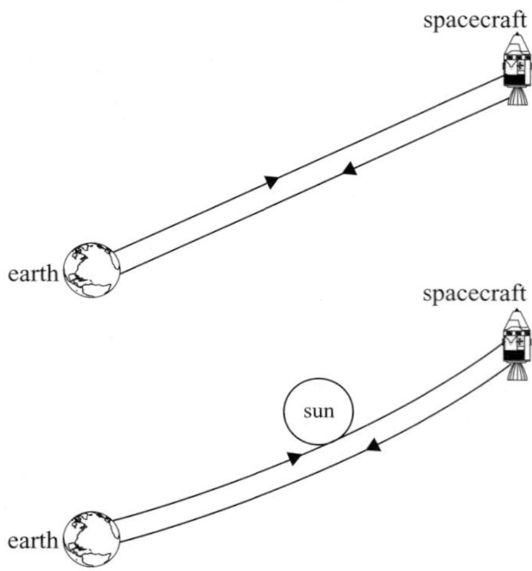

Figure H5.7 The Shapiro time delay experiment. The signal passing close to the sun takes longer to return since its path is curved and it experiences gravitational redshift.

slower near the sun. Such tests have been performed with the inner planets as well as with various spacecraft, with results in agreement with general relativity.

Example question

Q1

A photon of energy 14.4 keV is emitted from the top of a 30 m tall tower toward the ground. What shift of frequency is expected at the base of the tower?

Answer

On emission, the photon has frequency given by

$$E = hf$$

$$\Rightarrow f = \frac{E}{h}$$

$$= \frac{14.4 \times 10^3 \times 1.6 \times 10^{-19}}{6.63 \times 10^{-34}}$$

$$= 3.475 \times 10^{18} \text{ Hz}$$

The shift (it is a blueshift) is thus

$$\frac{\Delta f}{f} = \frac{gH}{c^2}$$

$$\Rightarrow \Delta f = f\frac{gH}{c^2}$$

$$= \frac{10 \times 30}{9 \times 10^{16}} \times 3.475 \times 10^{18} \text{ Hz}$$

$$= 1.16 \times 10^4 \text{ Hz}$$

Note how delicate this experiment actually is: the shift in frequency is only about 10^4 Hz compared with the emitted frequency of about 10^{18} Hz, a fractional shift of only

$$\frac{10^4 \text{ Hz}}{10^{18} \text{ Hz}} = 10^{-14}$$

The structure of the theory

The theory of general relativity is a physical theory different from all others in that:

▶ The mass and energy content of space determine the geometry of that space and time. The geometry of space-time determines the motion of mass and energy in the space-time.

That is

$$\text{geometry} \Leftrightarrow \text{mass-energy}$$

Space-time is a four-dimensional world with three space and one time coordinates. In the absence of any forces, a body moves in this four-dimensional world along paths of shortest length, called *geodesics*.

If a single mass M is the only mass present in the universe, the solutions of the Einstein equations imply that far from the mass the geometry of space is the usual Euclidean flat geometry with all its familiar rules (for example, the angles of a triangle add up to 180°). As we approach the neighbourhood of M, the space becomes curved as indicated by Figure H5.8. The rules of geometry then have to change. Large masses with small radii produce extreme bending of the space-time around them.

As an illustration of how the theory works, consider two balls that are made to move parallel to each other on a flat frictionless surface (see Figure H5.9a). The separation between the balls stays constant. In Newtonian mechanics we say that there is no force between the balls, no acceleration and hence no relative

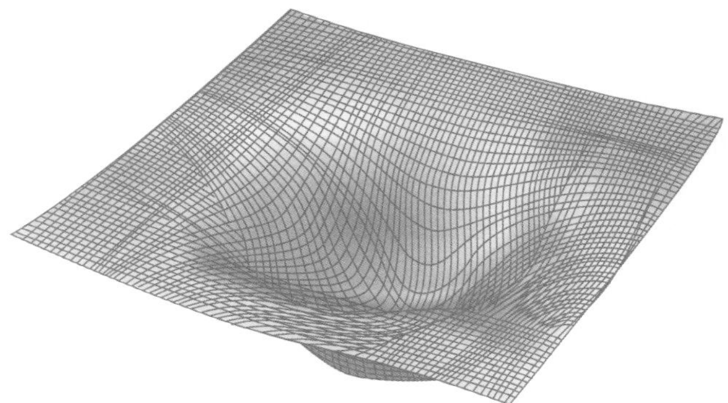

Figure H5.8 Far from the mass, the space looks flat; near the mass, the deviation from flat geometry is large. This is only a two-dimensional diagram though; Einstein's theory demands a distortion in the geometry of four-dimensional space-time.

velocity. On the other hand, consider the same two balls on the curved surface of a sphere that also start out moving parallel to each other (see Figure H5.9b). The balls will start approaching each other and will actually meet at the north pole. In Newtonian mechanics we would have to invoke a force between the balls which brings them toward each other. In Einstein's relativity no force is required – the balls approach each other because of the geometry of space. The paths they follow are the 'straight' lines of the curved space.

Similarly, light retains its familiar property of travelling from one place to another in the shortest possible time. Since the speed of light is always constant, this means that light travels along paths of shortest length – *geodesics*. In the flat Euclidean geometry we are used to, geodesics are straight lines. In the curved non-Euclidean geometry of general relativity, something else replaces the concept of straight line. A ray of light travelling near the sun looks bent to us because we are used to flat space. But the geometry near the sun is curved and the 'bent' ray is actually the geodesic: it is the 'straight' line appropriate to that geometry.

Thus, the motion of a planet around the sun is, according to Einstein, not the result of a gravitational force acting on the planet (as Newton would have it) but rather due to the curved geometry in the space and time around the sun created by the large mass of the sun. The planet follows a geodesic in the curved space-time around the earth. This geodesic *appears* as a circular path if we view space-time as flat.

Black holes

The theory of general relativity also predicts the existence of objects that contract under the influence of their own gravitation, becoming ever smaller objects. No mechanism is known for stopping this collapse and the object is expected to become a hole in space-time, a point of infinite density. This creates an immense bending of space-time around this point. This is called a black hole – a name appropriately coined by John Archibald Wheeler, since nothing can escape from it. Massive stars can, under appropriate conditions, collapse under their own gravitation and end up as black holes (see Option E5 in Option E, Astrophysics). Powerful theorems by Stephen Hawking and Roger Penrose show that the formation of black holes is inevitable and not dependent too much on the details of how the collapse itself proceeds.

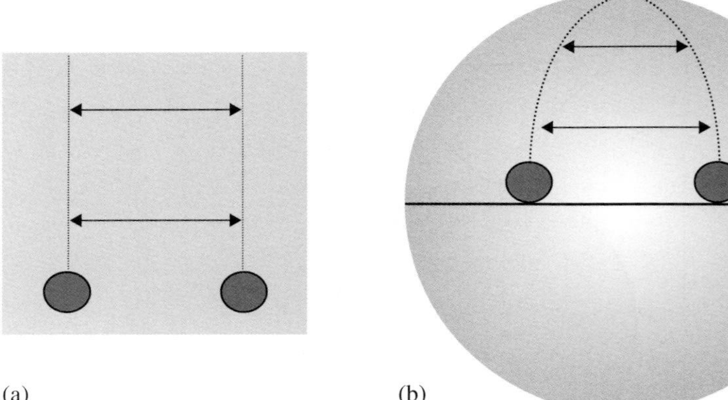

Figure H5.9 (a) On a flat surface the separation between the balls stays the same as the balls move parallel to each other. (b) On a curved surface the balls will approach each other even though no force acts between them.

The Schwarzschild radius and the event horizon

A distance known as the Schwarzschild radius of the black hole is of importance in understanding the behaviour of black holes. (Karl Schwarzschild was the German astronomer who provided the first solution of the Einstein equations.) The Schwarzschild radius is given by

$$R_S = \frac{2GM}{c^2}$$

where M is the mass and c the speed of light. This radius is not the actual radius of the black hole (the black hole is a point) – it is the distance from the hole's centre that separates space into a region from which an object can escape and a region from which no object can escape (see Figure H5.10).

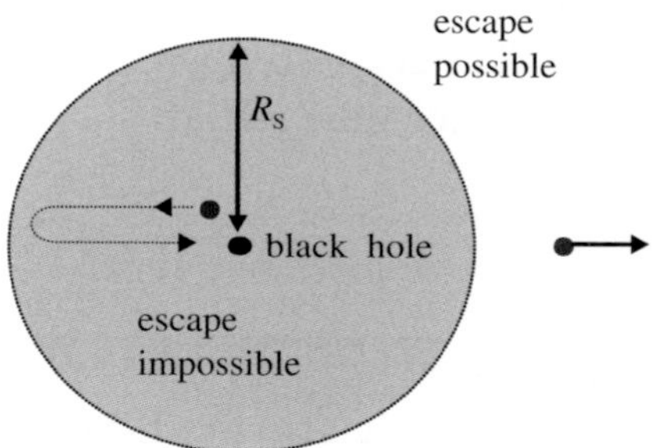

Figure H5.10 The Schwarzschild radius splits space into two regions. From within this radius nothing, not even light, can escape.

Any object closer to the centre of the black hole than R_S will fall into the hole; no amount of energy supplied to this body will allow it to escape from the black hole.

The escape velocity at a distance equal to R_S from the centre of the black hole equals the speed of light and hence nothing can escape from the star from within this radius. The Schwarzschild radius is also called the gravitational radius of the black hole, or the event horizon. The last name is apt since anything taking place within the event horizon cannot be seen by or communicated to the outside. The area of the event horizon is taken as the surface area of the black hole (but, remember, the black hole is a point).

The Schwarzschild radius can be derived in an elementary way without recourse to general relativity if we assume that a photon has a mass m on which the black hole's gravity acts. Then, as we did in the calculation of the escape velocity in Chapter 2.11 on gravitation,

$$\frac{1}{2}mc^2 = \frac{GM}{R_S}m$$

Thus m cancels and we can solve for R_S.

It can be readily calculated from this formula that for a star of one solar mass ($M \approx 2 \times 10^{30}$ kg) the gravitational radius is about 3 km:

$$\begin{aligned} R_S &= \frac{2GM}{c^2} \\ &= \frac{2 \times 6.67 \times 10^{-11} \times 2 \times 10^{30}}{(3 \times 10^8)^2} \\ &\approx 3 \times 10^3 \text{ m} \end{aligned}$$

For the earth it is just 9 mm. This means, for example, that if the sun were to become a black hole its entire mass should be confined within a sphere with a radius of 3 km or less.

Figure H5.11 shows that an observer on the surface of a star that is about to become a black hole would only be able to receive light

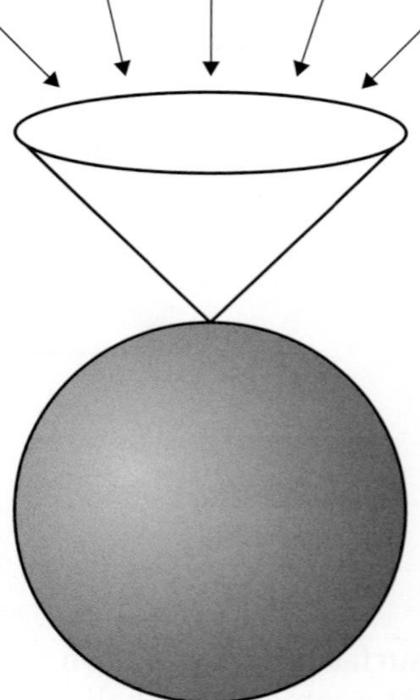

Figure H5.11 The horizon for observers on a collapsing star is rising; that is, only rays within a vertical cone can reach them.

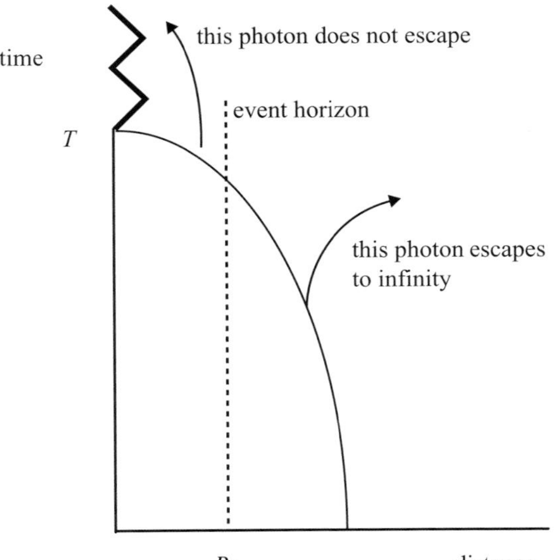

Figure H5.12 A space-time diagram of the formation of a black hole. As time goes on, the radius of the star is getting smaller. At $t = T$, the radius becomes zero and a singularity has been formed. A photon emitted from the surface of the star before the radius becomes less than the Schwarzschild radius will be received by an observer far from the hole. But once the star collapses beyond the event horizon, any photons emitted do not leave the black hole.

through a cone that is getting smaller and smaller as the star approaches its gravitational (Schwarzschild) radius. This is because rays of light coming 'sideways' will bend toward the star and will not reach the observer. Figure H5.12 shows the radius of the star shrinking. After the radius has become smaller than the gravitational radius, any photons emitted from the surface of the star will not reach an observer far away. They will be 'trapped' by the black hole.

Time dilation in general relativity

In special relativity, we saw that two observers who are in relative motion measure the time interval between the same two events differently. This is the time dilation effect of special relativity. In general relativity, there is a similar phenomenon, the gravitational time dilation effect, which can be stated as follows:

▶ Two observers who are at different points in a gravitational field measure the time interval between the same two events differently. This is an example of how masses curve not just space but also time.

The gravitational redshift, discussed in the last section, is an example of this. A more extreme example is provided by a black hole.

Consider a clock that is a distance r from the centre of the black hole of Schwarzschild radius R_S (the clock is outside the event horizon, $r > R_S$). An observer stationary with respect to the clock measures the time interval between two ticks of the clock to be Δt_{near}. An identical clock very far away from the black hole will measure a time interval Δt_{far} such that

$$\Delta t_{far} = \frac{\Delta t_{near}}{\sqrt{1 - \frac{R_S}{r}}}$$

This formula is the general relativistic analogue of time dilation in special relativity. It applies near a black hole. (Time dilation takes place near *any* massive body and not just a black hole, but the formula above can only applied near a black hole.)

Thus, consider a (theoretical) observer approaching a black hole. This observer sends signals to a far-away observer in a spacecraft informing the spacecraft of his position. When his distance from the centre of the black hole is $r = 1.50R_S$, the observer stops and sends two signals one second apart (as measured by his clocks). The spacecraft observers will receive the signals a time apart given by

$$\Delta t_{far} = \frac{\Delta t_{near}}{\sqrt{1 - \frac{R_S}{r}}}$$

$$= \frac{1.00}{\sqrt{1 - \frac{1}{1.50}}}\ \text{s}$$

$$= 1.73\ \text{s}$$

The extreme case of time dilation is when the observer is just an infinitesimally small distance outside the event horizon. If he stops there and sends two signals one second apart, the far-away observers will receive the signals separated by an enormous interval of time. In particular, if the observer is *at* the event horizon, the signals are received an infinite time apart!

? QUESTIONS

1 Discuss the statement: 'a ray of light does not actually bend near a massive object but follows a straight-line path in the geometry of the space around the massive object'.

2 A spacecraft filled with air at ordinary density and pressure is far from any large masses. A helium-filled balloon floats inside the spacecraft which now begins to accelerate towards the right. Which way (if any) does the balloon move?

3 The spacecraft from question 2 now has a lighted candle in it. When the craft begins to accelerate toward the right, what happens to the flame of the candle?

4 Describe what is meant by the equivalence principle. How does this principle lead to the predictions that:
(a) light bends in a gravitational field;
(b) the gravitational and inertial masses are the same;
(c) time 'runs slower' near a massive object.

5 Describe what the general theory of relativity predicts about a massive object whose radius is getting smaller.

6 In a local inertial frame (i.e. one falling freely in a gravitational field) an observer attaches a mass m to the end of a spring, extends the spring and lets the mass go. If he measures the period of oscillation of the mass, will he find the same answer as an observer doing the same thing:
(a) on the surface of a very massive star;
(b) in a true inertial frame far from any masses?
Explain your answer.

7 Calculate the shift in frequency of light of wavelength 500.0 nm that is emitted from sea level and is received at a height of 50.0 m.

8 If a photon of frequency f is emitted from the surface of a star, the frequency shift observed far from the star is given by

$$\Delta f \approx f\frac{R_s}{R}$$

where R_s is the Schwarzschild radius of the star and R its radius. Use this formula to calculate the shift in frequency of a line in the sun's spectrum which has a wavelength of 548 nm at emission.

9 A collapsed star has a radius that is 5 times larger than its Schwarzschild radius. An observer on the surface of the star carries a clock and a laser. Every second the observer sends a short pulse of laser light of duration 1.00 ms and wavelength 4.00×10^{-7} m (as measured by her instruments) toward another observer in a spacecraft far from the star. Discuss *qualitatively* what the observer in the spacecraft can expect to measure for:
(a) the wavelength of the pulses;
(b) the frequency of reception of consecutive pulses;
(c) the duration of the pulses.

10 Two identical clocks are placed on a rotating disc. One is placed on the circumference of the disc and the other half-way toward the centre. Explain why the clock on the circumference will run slow relative to the other clock.

11 What would the density of the earth be if its entire mass were confined within a radius equal to its Schwarzschild radius?

12 What is the Schwarzschild radius of a black hole with mass equal to 10 solar masses?

13 Explain what is meant by *geodesic*.

14 A mass m moves past a massive body along the path shown in Figure H5.13. Explain the shape of the path according to:
(a) Newtonian gravity;
(b) Einstein's theory of general relativity.

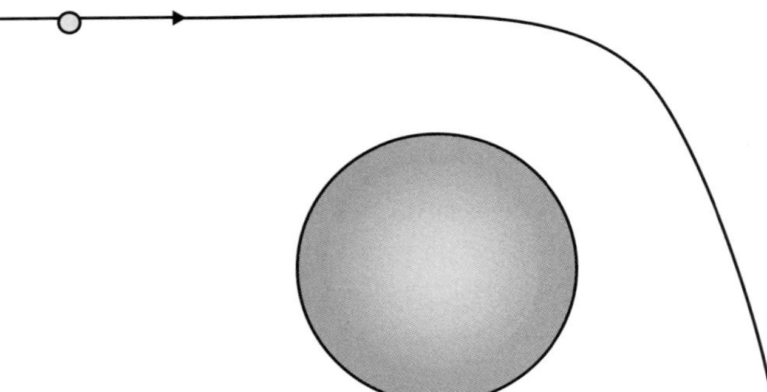

Figure H5.13 For question 14.

15 A ball is thrown with a velocity that is initially parallel to the floor of a spacecraft as shown in Figure H5.14. Draw and explain the shape of the ball's path when:

(a) the spacecraft is moving with constant velocity in deep space far from any large masses;

(b) the spacecraft is moving with constant acceleration in deep space far from any large masses.

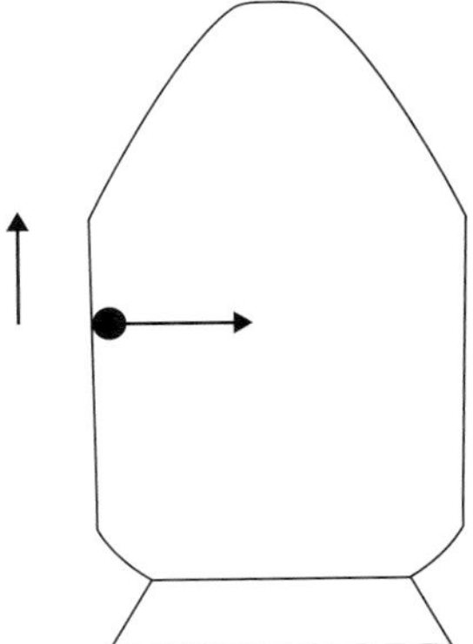

Figure H5.14 For question 15.

16 A ray of light moving parallel to the floor of a spacecraft enters the spacecraft through a small window as shown in Figure H5.15. Draw and explain the shape of the ray's path when:

(a) the spacecraft is moving with constant velocity in deep space far from any large masses;

(b) the spacecraft is moving with constant acceleration in deep space far from any large masses.

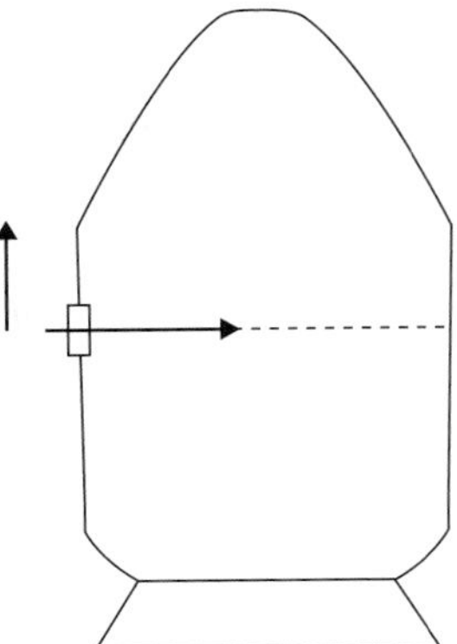

Figure H5.15 For question 16.

A problem just for fun

17 The curvature of a spherical surface of radius R can be defined in many ways. Two methods to calculate the curvature are as follows. Consider a circular patch (cap) of radius r centred at the 'north pole'. This radius is defined *along* the surface – in other words, it is the length of the arc from N to a point P on the sphere. (See Figure H5.16.)

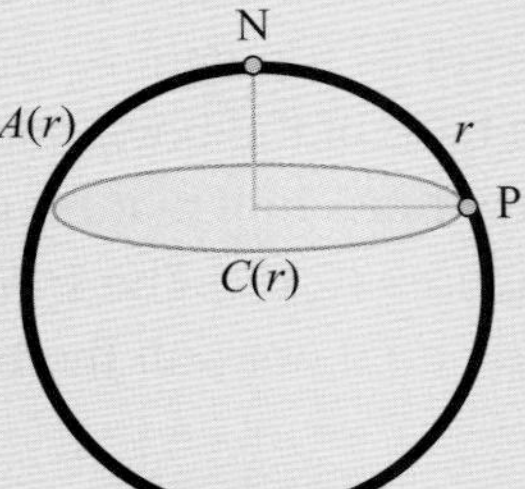

Figure H5.16 For question 17.

The curvature, K, is then defined by

$$K = 3 \lim_{r \to 0} \frac{2\pi r - C(r)}{\pi r^3} \quad \text{or}$$

$$K = 12 \lim_{r \to 0} \frac{\pi r^2 - A(r)}{\pi r^4}$$

where $C(r)$ and $A(r)$ are the circumference and area of the circular cap of radius r centred at N. Show that

$$C(r) = 2\pi R \sin \frac{r}{R} \quad \text{and}$$

$$A(r) = 2\pi R^2 \left(1 - \cos \frac{r}{R}\right)$$

Evaluate the two limits to find the curvature of the sphere. Hence explain why a large sphere is less curved than a smaller one. (You will find the following approximations useful: $\sin x \approx x - \frac{x^3}{6}$ and $\cos x \approx 1 - \frac{x^2}{2} + \frac{x^4}{24}$, which are valid if x (in radians) is small.)

18 An observer is standing on the surface of a massive object that is collapsing and is about to form a black hole. Describe what the observer sees in the sky:

(a) before the object shrinks past its event horizon;

(b) after the object goes past its event horizon.

19 A plane flying from southern Europe to New York City will fly over Ireland, across the North Atlantic, over the eastern coast of Canada and then south to New York. Why do you think such a path is followed?

20 *Einstein's birthday present.* A colleague of Einstein at Princeton presented him with the following birthday present. A long tube was connected to a bowl at its top end. A spring was attached to the base of the bowl and connected to a heavy brass ball that hung out of the bowl. (See Figure H5.17.) The spring was very 'weak' and could not pull the ball into the bowl. The exercise is to find a sure-fire method for putting the ball into the bowl without touching it. Einstein immediately found a way of doing it. Can you?

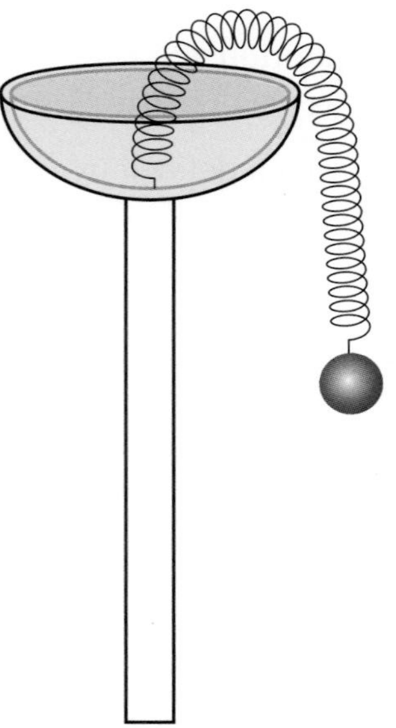

Figure H5.17 For question 20.

21 An observer approaching a black hole stops and sends signals to a far-away spacecraft every second as measured by his clocks. The signals are received 2.0 seconds apart by the spacecraft observers. How close to the event horizon is the observer?

22 A spacecraft accelerates in the vacuum of outer space far from any masses. An observer in the spacecraft sends a radio message to a stationary spacecraft far away. The duration of the radio transmission takes 5.0 seconds according to the observer's clock in the moving spacecraft. Explain whether the transmission will take less than, equal to or greater than 5.0 seconds when it is received by the far-away stationary spacecraft.

23 General relativity is described by saying that large masses curve *space-time*. Give an example of how a black hole curves (a) space and (b) time.

24 A black hole has a mass of 5.00×10^{35} kg.

(a) State what is meant by a black hole.

(b) Calculate the Schwarzschild radius R_S of the black hole.

(c) Explain why the Schwarzschild radius is not in fact the actual radius of the black hole.

(d) Blue light of frequency 7.50×10^{14} Hz is emitted from a source that is stationary at a distance of $0.10R_S$ *above* the event horizon of a black hole. Calculate the period of this blue light according to an observer next to the source.

(e) Determine the frequency measured by a distant observer who receives the light emitted by this source.

25 (a) State the formula for the gravitational (Schwarzschild) radius R_S of a black hole of mass M.

(b) The sphere of radius R_S around the black hole is called the event horizon. State the area of the event horizon of a black hole of mass M.

(c) Suggest why, over time, the area of the event horizon of a black hole *always* increases.

(d) In physics there is one other physical quantity that always increases with time. Can you state what that quantity is? (You will learn a lot of interesting things if you pursue the analogy implied by your answers to (c) and (d).)

26 (a) A ray of light is emitted from within the event horizon (dashed circle) of a black hole, as shown in Figure H5.18(a). Copy the diagram and draw a possible path of this ray of light.

(b) Light from a distant star arrives at a theoretical observer within the event horizon of a black hole, as shown in Figure H5.18(b). Explain how it is possible for the ray shown to enter the observer's eye.

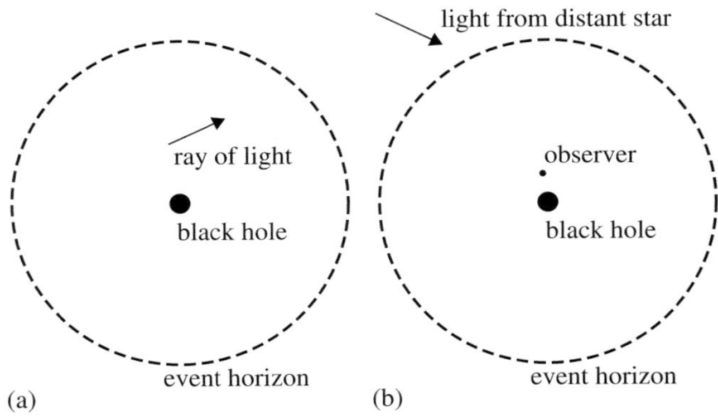

Figure H5.18 For question 26.

The functioning of the ear

This chapter introduces the basic ideas behind the functioning of the human ear and the related physics questions on sound perception, intensity, frequency response and frequency discrimination. Hearing defects are also briefly discussed.

Objectives

By the end of this chapter you should be able to:

- describe the basic components of the *human ear*;
- define *sound intensity* and the *sound intensity scale* based on the decibel;
- perform calculations with intensity and the *decibel scale*;
- understand how the ear functions;
- describe how the ear separates sound according to frequency in the *cochlea*;
- state the meaning of the terms *threshold of hearing* and *audiogram*;
- understand basic *hearing defects* and say how they might be corrected.

The ear

The human ear is an exceptionally efficient and sensitive instrument that detects and analyses sound, and converts the mechanical energy carried by a sound wave into electrical energy that is fed into the brain. The ear is sensitive to sounds of frequency ranging from 20 Hz to 20 kHz. At 1000 Hz, the ear responds to sound that displaces the eardrum by only one-tenth of the diameter of the hydrogen atom! The ear can be divided into three main parts: the outer, middle and inner ear (see Figure I1.1).

Sound waves reaching the ear are fed into the *auditory canal* and fall on the *eardrum*, a membrane that begins to vibrate as a result. The eardrum forms the entrance to the middle ear, an air cavity of 2 cm^3 in volume that contains the *ossicles* (three small bones), the *malleus* (hammer), *incus* (anvil) and *stapes* (stirrup). This cavity is connected to the throat by the *Eustachian tube*, which is normally closed but can be opened by swallowing or yawning to equalize the pressure on each side of the eardrum. The ossicles act as a lever system, which transmits the energy falling on the eardrum onto the *oval window*, an opening marking the beginning of the inner ear. The tension in the muscles attached to the ossicles increases in the presence of a very loud sound, thus limiting the motion of the stapes and hence the energy transferred to the oval window and protecting the delicate inner ear from damage. This is known as the *acoustic reflex*; this takes about 10 ms to become effective, so it offers no protection in the case of sudden very loud sounds, such as gunfire.

The purpose of the lever system is to amplify the amplitude of the incoming sound wave. As seen in the example that follows, the lever system amplifies by a factor of 1.5. However, as a result of the difference in the areas of the oval window and the eardrum, the

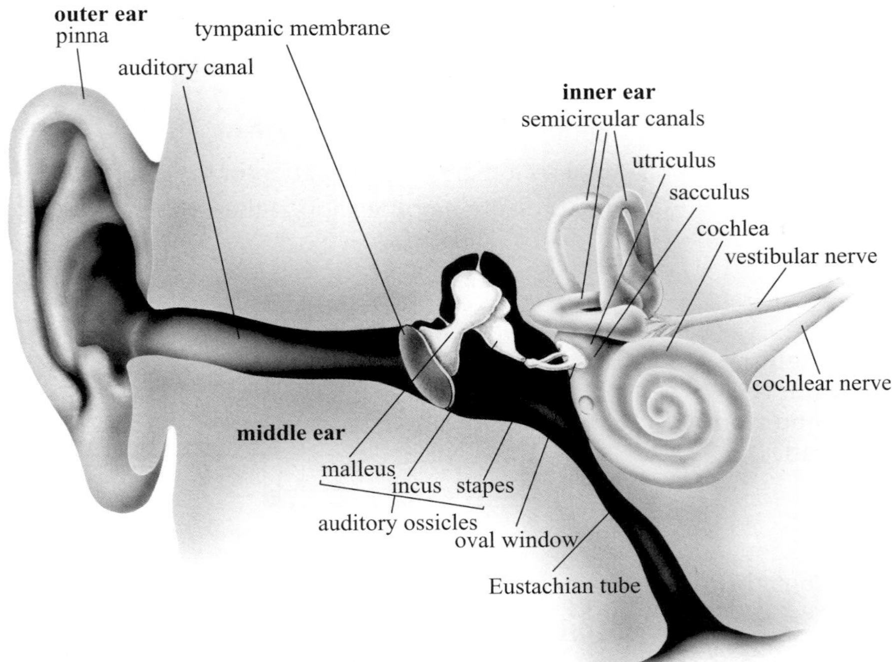

Figure I1.1 A diagram of the ear showing its division into outer, middle and inner ear. The cochlea is responsible for the resolution of the incoming sound into its various components. © 1995 Dorling Kindersley Multimedia.

amplification is increased further by a factor of about 13, resulting in a total amplification of about 20.

The inner ear has three main parts: the *vestibule* (the entrance cavity), the *semicircular canals* and the *cochlea*. The vestibule is surrounded by bone except for the opening to the middle ear (the oval window); this opening is sealed by the stapes and the round window, which is covered by a membrane. This cavity is filled with a liquid. The semicircular canals play no role in hearing – their function is to provide us with a sense of balance. The cochlea is a tube, coiled like a snail (making 2.5 turns) and has a length of about 3.5 cm.

The sound wave entering the oval window travels in the liquid-filled canals of the cochlea. First in the *vestibular*, then through the *helicotrema* and into the *tympanic canal*. It ends at the round window membrane, which acts as a pressure release point (a total length of about 2 cm). Between these two canals is a third, the *scala media* or cochlean duct. The *basilar membrane* separates the cochlean duct from the tympanic canal and this membrane contains a large number of nerve endings, whose purpose is to transmit the electrical signals to the brain. These signals are generated when vibrations in the basilar membrane are fed into the *organ of Corti*, which is attached to the membrane. Different parts of the basilar membrane are sensitive to different frequency ranges of the incoming sound wave.

The three parts of the ear are illustrated schematically in Figure I1.2, and Figure I1.3 is a schematic cross-section through the cochlea.

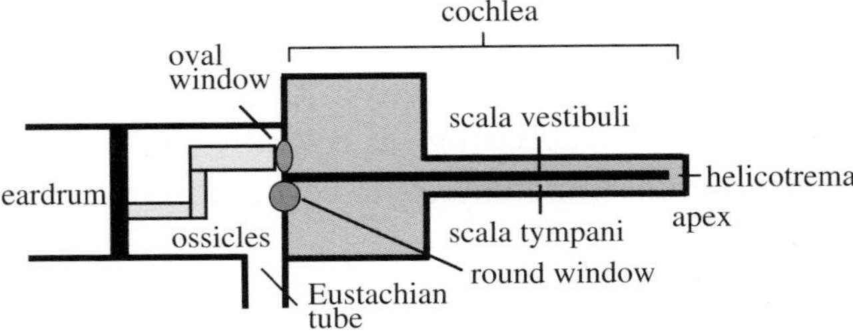

Figure I1.2 A schematic diagram showing the three parts of the ear. Here the cochlea is shown as a straight uncoiled tube. The cochlea is separated into three canals or scalae. The top, scala vestibuli, and the bottom, scala tympani, which communicate through an opening at the apex of the cochlea called the helicotrema. The scala vestibuli starts at the oval window while the scala tympani starts at the round window. The middle canal is known as scala media or cochlean duct.

The auditory pathways from the cochlea into the brain are highly complex and not yet fully understood. There is, however, a considerable amount of processing of the information along the pathway in processing centres, with

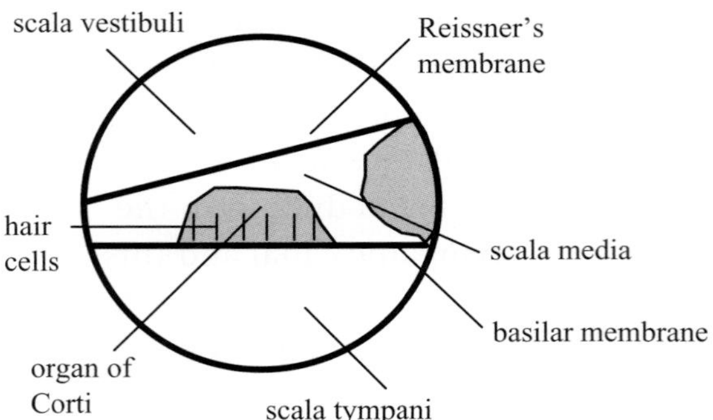

Figure I1.3 A schematic cross-section through the cochlea. The scala media is separated from the scala vestibuli by Reissner's membrane and from the scala tympani by the basilar membrane.

connections between the left ear and the right ear's main pathway and vice versa.

Mismatch of impedances

When a wave enters a new medium, only part of it will be transmitted into the new medium; part will be reflected back into the old medium. The fraction of the transmitted intensity depends on the *impedances* of the two media. The least amount of reflection takes place when the impedances of the two media are as close to each other as possible. For exactly equal impedances no reflection takes place at all.

► For sound transmission, the acoustic impedance of a medium is defined as the product of the speed of sound in the medium times the medium's density

$$Z = \rho c$$

The region up to the oval window is filled with air and its impedance is thus about 450 kg m^{-2} s^{-1}. The region behind the oval window is filled with the cochlear liquid and its impedance is about 1.5×10^6 kg m^{-2} s^{-1}. This large mismatch of impedances means that it is necessary to amplify the sound wave arriving at the oval window so that a substantial fraction of it can be transmitted.

Example question

Q1

The area of the eardrum is $A = 43$ mm^2 and that of the oval window $a = 3.2$ mm^2. Using Figure I1.4 as a model for the action of the ossicles, find the pressure amplification at the oval window.

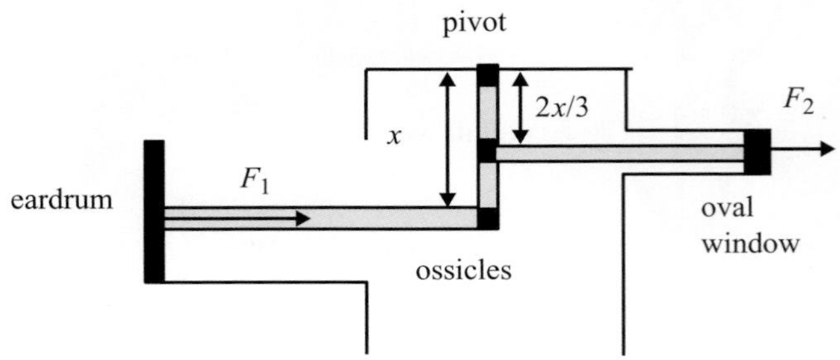

Figure I1.4.

Answer

Taking torques about an axis through the pivot we find

$$F_1 x = F_2 \frac{2x}{3}$$

$$\Rightarrow F_2 = \frac{3}{2} F_1$$

therefore, the pressure on the oval window is

$$\begin{aligned} P_2 &= \frac{F_2}{a} \\ &= \frac{3}{2}\frac{F_1}{a} \\ &= \frac{3}{2}\frac{P_1 A}{a} \\ &= \frac{3}{2}\frac{A}{a} P_1 \\ &= 20.2\, P_1 \end{aligned}$$

that is, an amplification of about 20.

Complex sounds

Few sounds are as simple and pure as the single-frequency harmonic waves we discussed in Topic 4, Oscillations and waves. When a human voice is fed into an oscilloscope through a microphone, the trace that appears on the oscilloscope screen will not be a sine wave.

▶ Harmonic waves (i.e. waves of one specific frequency) are important, however, because of a powerful mathematical technique, called Fourier analysis, that is used to analyse complex sounds. It can be shown that any complex sound is a superposition of many (perhaps infinite) simple sine or cosine waves.

To illustrate this point, consider an extreme example, the graph of the function $y = t^2$ from $-\pi$ to $+\pi$ (see Figure I1.5).

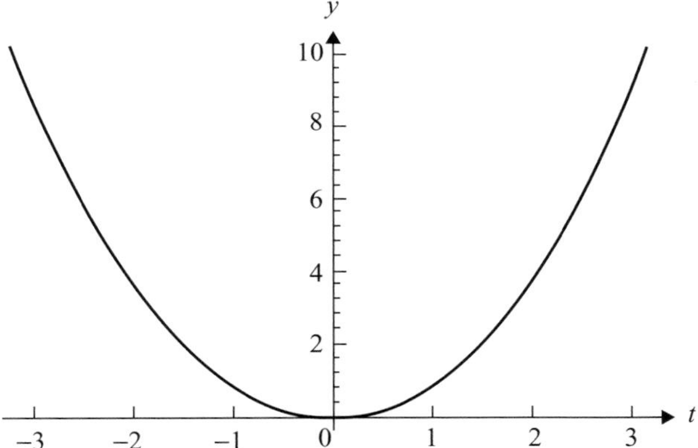

Figure I1.5 The graph of the function $y = t^2$.

This function can be well approximated by a sum of harmonic functions called a *Fourier series*:

$$\frac{\pi^2}{3} + 4\sum_{n=1} (-1)^n \frac{\cos(nt)}{n^2}$$

Figure I1.6 is the graph of this function for only the first five terms in the sum (*Fourier components*).

The approximation is quite good. It can be made even better by keeping more terms in the sum. The point here is that any periodic function can be written as a sum of harmonic functions. Thus, complex sounds entering the

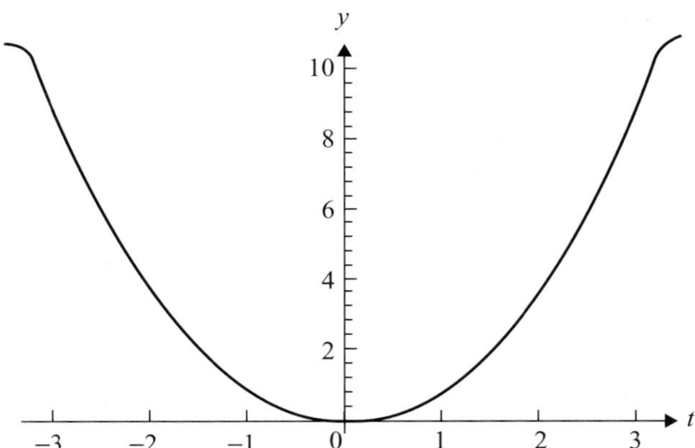

Figure I1.6 The approximation to $y = t^2$ obtained using the first five Fourier components (i.e harmonic waves).

ear can be decomposed into the component frequencies of the harmonic functions making up the complex sound. This happens in the cochlea and is explained in a later section.

Intensity of sound

Consider a source of sound S. The power of the source is the energy per second emitted by the source.

The energy emitted by the source can be thought of as being spread uniformly on the surface of an imaginary sphere of radius r centred on the source (see Figure I1.7). Thus, at a distance r from the source the energy received per second by an instrument of area A is

$$P \frac{A}{4\pi r^2}$$

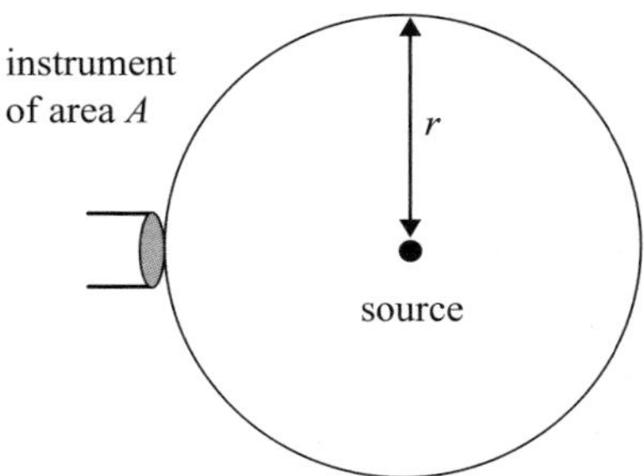

Figure I1.7 The energy emitted by the source goes through an imaginary sphere around the source.

▶ The energy per second per unit instrument area, that is

$$I = \frac{P}{4\pi r^2}$$

is known as the intensity of the sound wave at a distance r from the point source. The unit of intensity is thus W m^{-2}. The lowest intensity the human ear can perceive is called the threshold of hearing and is $I_0 = 1.0 \times 10^{-12}\ \text{W m}^{-2}$. The intensity is proportional to the square of the amplitude of the wave.

It is known that the 'sensation of hearing' (let us call this quantity β) does not increase linearly with intensity I. Rather, the ear has a logarithmic response to intensity: the increase in the hearing sensation is proportional to the *fractional* increase in intensity (the Weber–Fechner law). Mathematically this means that

$$\Delta\beta \propto \frac{\Delta I}{I}$$

We can exploit this law to define a scale of sound intensity level as follows. On this scale (the decibel scale) an increase of 10 units implies an increase of intensity by a *factor* of 10. The zero on this scale corresponds to the threshold of hearing. This implies that

$$\beta(\text{in decibels}) = 10 \log \left(\frac{I}{I_0}\right)$$

Table I1.1 shows some typical intensity levels of common sounds along with their pressure amplitudes.

Source of sound	Intensity level/dB	Pressure amplitude/Pa
Threshold of hearing	0	0.00002
Falling leaves	10	0.00006
Radio studio	20	0.0002
Whisper	30	0.0006
Library	40	0.002
Office space	50	0.006
Conversation	60	0.02
Room with TV on	70	0.06
Noisy street	80	0.2
Rock concert	110	6
Pain setting in	120	20
Pneumatic hammer	130	60
Jet plane 3 m away	140	200

Table I1.1 Typical decibel values and the corresponding amplitude of the sound wave in pascal.

Example questions

Q2

The intensity of a sound increases from $10^{-10}\ \text{W m}^{-2}$ to $10^{-8}\ \text{W m}^{-2}$. By how much does the sound intensity level change?

Answer

The original level was

$$\beta_1 = 10 \log \left(\frac{10^{-10}}{10^{-12}}\right) = 10 \log 10^2 = 20\ \text{dB}$$

The new sound intensity level is

$$\beta_2 = 10 \log \left(\frac{10^{-8}}{10^{-12}}\right) = 10 \log 10^4 = 40\ \text{dB}$$

The increase is thus 20 dB.

Note: Since the increase in the intensity level is proportional to the fractional increase in intensity, we could have written directly

$$\Delta\beta = 10 \log \left(\frac{10^{-8}}{10^{-10}}\right) = 10 \log 10^2 = 20\ \text{dB}$$

Q3

One sound has intensity $2 \times 10^{-6}\ \text{W m}^{-2}$ and another has intensity $4 \times 10^{-8}\ \text{W m}^{-2}$. What is the difference of the sound intensity levels?

Answer

The first sound has intensity level

$$\beta_1 = 10 \log \left(\frac{2 \times 10^{-6}}{10^{-12}}\right) = 10 \log (2 \times 10^6) = 63\ \text{dB}$$

The second sound has intensity level

$$\beta_2 = 10 \log \left(\frac{4 \times 10^{-8}}{10^{-12}}\right)$$
$$= 10 \log (4 \times 10^4)$$
$$= 46 \text{ dB}$$

Their difference is thus 17 dB.

Q4

The sound intensity level in a room is 70.0 dB. A radio produces sound of intensity level 72.0 dB. What is the sound intensity level in the room now?

Answer

The intensity in the room is found from

$$70 \text{ dB} = 10 \log \left(\frac{I}{10^{-12}}\right)$$
$$\Rightarrow \frac{I}{10^{-12}} = 10^7$$
$$\Rightarrow I = 10^{-5} \text{ W m}^{-2}$$

Similarly, the intensity due to the radio is

$$72 \text{ dB} = 10 \log \left(\frac{I}{10^{-12}}\right)$$
$$\Rightarrow \frac{I}{10^{-12}} = 10^{7.2}$$
$$\Rightarrow I = 10^{-4.8} \text{ W m}^{-2}$$

The combined intensity is

$$I_{\text{total}} = (10^{-5} + 10^{-4.8}) \text{ W m}^{-2}$$

Thus, the new sound intensity level is

$$10 \log \left(\frac{10^{-5} + 10^{-4.8}}{10^{-12}}\right) = 74.1 \text{ dB}$$

Note: It is important to realize that it is intensities that must be added not the sound intensity levels in decibels.

Q5

A shouting voice has a power output of about 10^{-3} W. At what distance from the source is the sound intensity level 80 dB?

Answer

Using

$$\beta = 10 \log \left(\frac{I}{10^{-12}}\right)$$
$$= 80$$
$$\Rightarrow \log \left(\frac{I}{10^{-12}}\right) = 8$$
$$\Rightarrow I = 10^{-4} \text{ W m}^{-2}$$

Now using the definition of intensity

$$I = \frac{P}{4\pi r^2}$$

it follows that

$$10^{-4} = \frac{10^{-3}}{4\pi r^2}$$
$$\Rightarrow r = \sqrt{\frac{10}{4\pi}}$$
$$= 0.89 \text{ m}$$

Q6

Assume that in a football stadium 40 000 fans cheer their teams, each producing a power output of 10^{-3} W. If the average distance of the fans from the centre of the stadium is 150 m, find the sound intensity level there.

Answer

The combined power output is $40\,000 \times 10^{-3} \text{ W} = 40 \text{ W}$. The intensity at the centre of the stadium is thus

$$I = \frac{P}{4\pi r^2}$$
$$= \frac{40}{4\pi (150)^2}$$
$$= 1.41 \times 10^{-4} \text{ W m}^{-2}$$

The sound intensity level is

$$\beta = 10 \log \left(\frac{1.41 \times 10^{-4}}{10^{-12}}\right)$$
$$= 81.5 \text{ dB}$$

Frequency response and loudness

The human ear has a threshold when it comes to the frequency of the sound wave. The lowest frequency that can be heard is about 20 Hz and the largest about 20 kHz. With age, the upper frequency threshold is reduced.

▶ The ear is not equally sensitive at all frequencies. This means that the ear responds differently to a sound of given intensity depending on the frequency of the sound.

Thus, the statement made earlier that the normal human ear has a threshold of hearing of 1.0×10^{-12} W m^{-2} is correct provided the sound has a frequency of 1000 Hz. Sounds of larger or smaller intensity than this may be heard or are barely audible depending on the frequency of the sound. The graph in Figure I1.8 shows the intensity level of barely audible sounds (the threshold of hearing) as a function of frequency. Thus, a sound at 100 Hz must have an intensity level of 35 dB to be barely audible, and a sound at 20 Hz must have an intensity level of 72 dB. All points on this curve are perceived by the ear to have the same loudness, even though they have different intensities. These points define the 'zero phon loudness curve'. The 'N phon loudness curve' consists of those sounds that the ear perceives to be equally loud as a sound of N dB at 1000 Hz.

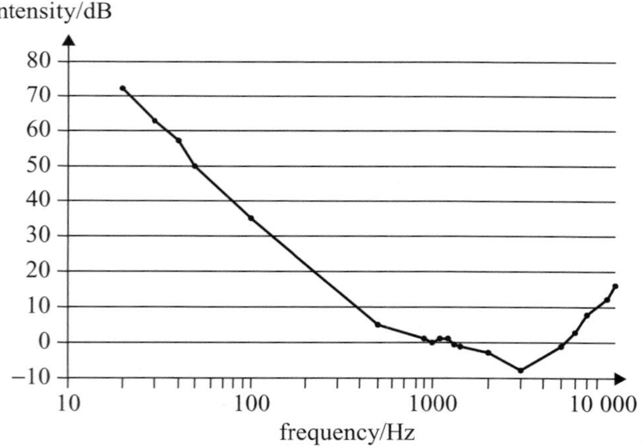

Figure I1.8 The threshold of hearing curve as a function of frequency. A sound of frequency 3 kHz is just audible even at −8 dB.

▶ The ear is most sensitive for frequencies around 3 kHz and least sensitive for frequencies less than (about) 50 Hz and higher than (about) 10 kHz.

The sensitivity of the human ear for frequencies around 3 kHz can be understood in terms of resonance in the ear canal. The canal can be thought of as a tube with one open and one closed end, so standing waves in this tube have a wavelength in the fundamental mode equal to $4L$, where L is the length of the canal – about 2.8 cm (see Figure I1.9).

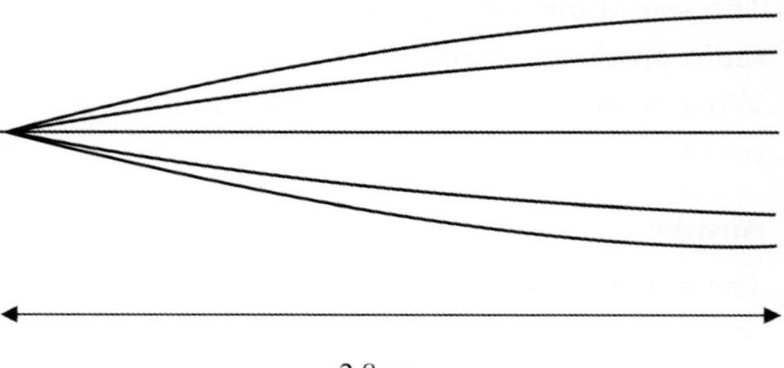

Figure I1.9 Schematic diagram of standing waves in the ear canal.

This means that the frequency corresponding to this wavelength is

$$f = \frac{340}{0.112} = 3036 \text{ Hz}$$

which is in good agreement with the most sensitive frequency.

Pitch

'Pitch' is a subjective characteristic of sound. It measures how high or low a sound is. It is determined *primarily by frequency* (which is why pitch is often taken to mean the same thing as frequency) *but also by intensity*. Imagine a pure tone of frequency 100 Hz that is sounded first at low intensity and then at high intensity. The louder sound will 'feel' lower in pitch than the soft sound.

Frequency separation in the cochlea

As mentioned earlier, a complex sound can, in general, be decomposed into its component harmonic waves.

▶ The ear analyses the different frequencies of a sound wave reaching it in the cochlea.

A wave entering the oval window travels along the basilar membrane, which separates the tympanic canal from the cochlean duct. The basilar membrane decreases in stiffness along its length (of about 35 mm). The velocity of the sound wave is thus high at the beginning of the membrane and drops along its length. In general, the response of a given point on the basilar membrane is small unless that part of the membrane is in resonance with the sound wave.

▶ From the pioneering work of Georg von Bekesy in the 1950s, we have learned that the beginning of the basilar membrane is in resonance with high frequencies and the end with low frequencies. The brain thus perceives frequency by locating the part of the basilar membrane that is vibrating.

This is done through the organ of Corti, which lies on the basilar membrane, and its hair cell receptors, which feed the information into the nerves that end at the base of the receptor cells. A wave of frequency 8 kHz will be in resonance at a point at about 2.5 mm from the beginning of the basilar membrane, a frequency of 1 kHz will be in resonance at a distance of about 22 mm and a frequency of 100 Hz will be in resonance a full 32 mm along the basilar membrane (see Figure I1.10).

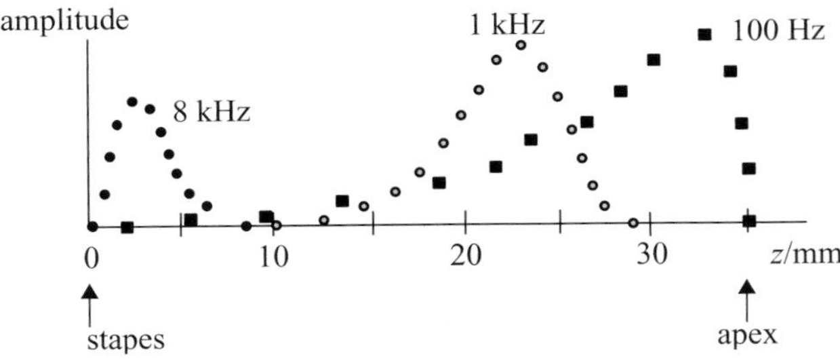

Figure I1.10 The amplitude of vibration of the basilar membrane for three different frequencies as a function of distance from the stapes. The point of largest amplitude shifts toward the apex of the basilar membrane as the frequency decreases.

Hearing defects

Two hearing losses may be distinguished.

- *Sensory nerve deafness,* which involves damage to the hair cells and neural pathways (e.g. due to tumours of the acoustic nerve or meningitis).
- *Conduction deafness,* in which damage to the middle ear prevents the transmission of sound into the cochlea. (This may be due to the plugging of the auditory canal by foreign bodies, such as wax, thickening of the ear drum because of repeated infections, destruction of the ossicles, or too rigid an attachment of the stapes to the oval window.)

Hearing can be monitored with an audiogram: the patient is supplied with very faint sounds of a specific frequency through earphones and their intensity is increased until they are just audible to the patient. A typical example is the audiogram of Figure I1.11 (consider first the data points represented by circles). At a frequency of 1000 Hz a sound must increase in intensity by 45 dB and at 4000 Hz by 70 dB if these sounds are to be audible to the patient. This defines what is called a *hearing loss* in dB. At 1000 Hz, therefore, the intensity of sound must be increased (for example, by a hearing aid) by a factor of

$$\Delta\beta = 45 \text{ dB}$$
$$= 10 \log \frac{I}{I_0}$$
$$\Rightarrow I = I_0 \times 10^{4.5}$$

where I_0 is the intensity prior to amplification. This audiogram shows a substantial loss of hearing, especially in the higher frequencies. The damage was possibly caused by excessive exposure to loud sounds over very long periods of time. Ageing, which also results in hearing loss, would show in a more gently varying curve in the audiogram and with smaller loss in decibels.

Sound can reach the cochlea through the bones of the head and thus the audiogram is performed not only with earphones but also

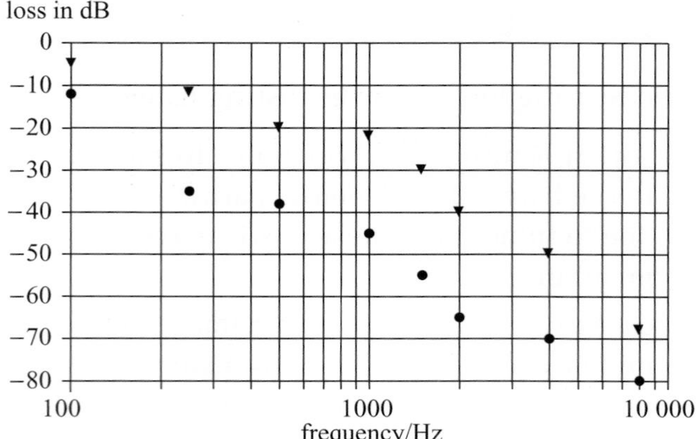

Figure I1.11 Audiogram for air (circles) and bone (triangles) conduction.

with an oscillator (placed at the bottom of the skull) that transmits the sound into the bones. The data points represented by triangles in the audiogram in Figure I1.11 are the results of bone transmission.

There is a *gap* between the two sets of data points of about 25 dB (at 1000 Hz). This is most likely an indication of a *conduction* hearing problem, the origin of which is in the middle or outer ear. Audiograms in which the data points for air and bone conduction *almost coincide* indicate *cochlea/nerve* problems in the inner ear.

In conductive hearing loss (where the sound *does* reach the inner ear) use of a hearing aid that amplifies the sound may help a patient. A hearing aid responds to and amplifies sound within a limited range of frequencies (the frequency range of human speech) but does not work well outside this range. For sensory nerve hearing loss, where the damage is to the hair cells, a *cochlear implant* may be useful. This is a device that consists of a microphone to pick up the sound, a signal processor to convert the sound into an electrical signal and a transmission system to transmit the electrical signal to electrodes. The electrodes are then surgically implanted in the cochlea. Different electrodes are stimulated according to the frequency of the sound so, in effect, the cochlear implant mimics the function of the cochlea. Assuming that enough healthy nerves are left near the electrodes, stimulation of the electrodes induces stimulation of the neighbouring nerves and the signal can be carried to the brain.

Speech recognition

All the information in speech is contained within the frequency interval from 200 Hz to 6 kHz. Noise and loss of frequency discrimination affect speech intelligibility. Generally, the meaning of a sentence can still be extracted from context but the intelligibility of isolated words is more strongly affected. The shorter the word, the bigger the loss of intelligibility. It has been found that, in cases of hearing loss at high frequencies ($>$3000 Hz), amplifying the sound does not help the patient to identify spoken syllables. Similarly, the inability of the cochlea to correctly identify frequencies also leads to errors in the identification of syllables.

QUESTIONS

1 A point sound source emitting uniformly in all directions is observed to have a sound intensity level of 70 dB at a distance of 5 m. What is the power of the source?

2 The sound level intensity of a screaming child in a room is 75 dB. What is the sound level intensity when three screaming children are put together in the same room?

3 The sound intensity level a certain distance from a source is 68 dB. If the distance to the source is halved, what is the new sound intensity level?

4 The sound level intensity of a given sound wave is 15 dB higher than that of another sound wave. What is the ratio of the intensities of the two waves?

5 If a radio creates sound of intensity level 70 dB, how many radios are required to create sound of intensity level 80 dB?

6 The audiogram of Figure I1.11 shows that the loss in dB for a person at 4000 Hz is 70 dB. What is the least intensity of sound this person

can hear at 4000 Hz? (Use the diagram of Figure I1.8 to find the threshold of hearing at 4000 Hz.)

7 Figure I1.12 shows the threshold of hearing curve for a patient. Explain what this means. What is the frequency at which this patient is most sensitive? What is the intensity of sound this patient receives at 200 Hz?

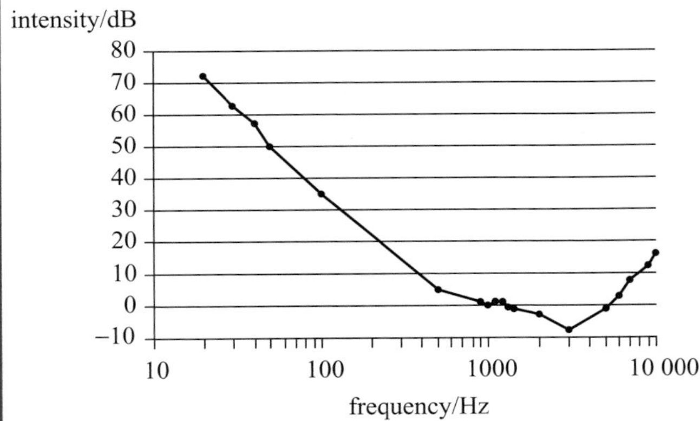

Figure I1.12 For question 7.

8 What is the reason for employing a logarithmic scale for sound intensity levels?

9 What can you conclude from the audiogram shown in Figure I1.13? Bone conduction is represented by triangles and air conduction by circles.

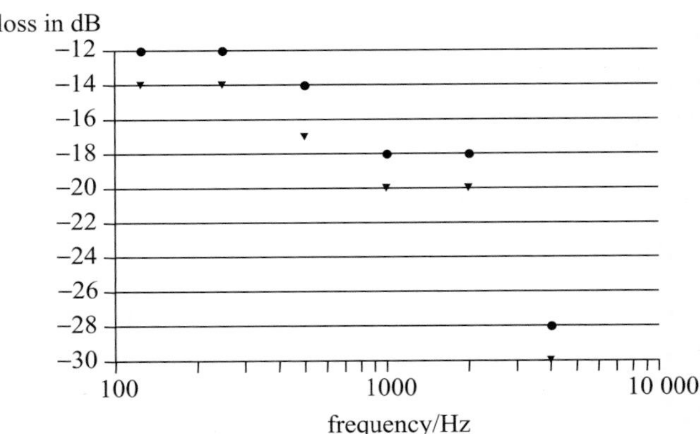

Figure I1.13 For question 9.

Medical imaging

This chapter introduces the use of X-rays and ultrasound in medical imaging. Other imaging techniques such as PET scans and the method based on nuclear magnetic resonance are also discussed. The chapter closes with a short account of the diagnostic use of radioactive tracers.

Objectives

By the end of this chapter you should be able to:

- state the *properties of ionizing radiations*;
- state the meaning of the terms *quality of X-rays*, *half-value thickness* (HVT) and *linear attenuation coefficient*;
- perform *calculations* with X-ray intensity and HVT, $I = I_0\, e^{-\mu x}$, $\text{HVT} = \frac{0.693}{\mu}$;
- describe the *main mechanisms by which X-rays lose energy* in a medium;
- state the meaning of *fluoroscopy* and *moving-film techniques*;
- describe the basics of *CT and PET scans*;
- describe the *principle of MRI*;
- state the uses of *ultrasound* in imaging;
- state the main uses of *radioactive sources in diagnostic medicine*.

Properties of radiation

The uses of radiation in medicine fall into two classes: first in diagnostic imaging (described in this chapter) and second in radiation therapy (discussed in Option I3). The first radiation to be used in medicine was X-rays – short-wavelength electromagnetic radiation (photons) discovered by W. Röntgen in 1895. Other ionizing radiations, such as alpha particles (helium nuclei), beta particles (fast electrons), gamma rays and radioactive isotopes have uses in medicine or have an effect on living organisms.

Table I2.1 gives a summary of the main properties of these radiations.

If we consider a point source of X- or gamma rays radiating uniformly in all directions, the *intensity* at a distance *r* from the source falls off according to an inverse square law. We have

	α	β	γ
Nature	Helium nucleus	Electron	Photon
Mass (in units of the proton mass)	4	1/1840	0
Charge	+2e	−e	0
Ions produced per mm of path	10 000	1000	1
Stopped by	A few cm of air	A few mm of Al	10 cm of Pb

Table I2.1 The main properties of different forms of radiation.

seen the argument leading to this result before in this book.

▶ Let P be the energy per unit time (the power) radiated by the source. The energy radiated can be thought to pass through the area of a sphere of radius r and so the energy per unit area of the sphere is

$$I = \frac{P}{4\pi r^2}$$

This is the intensity of the source at a distance r from it.

Example questions

Q1

A radioactive gamma ray source has an activity of 50 kBq. Each gamma ray radiated has an energy of 0.2 MeV. What is the intensity of the source at a distance of 25 cm?

Answer

The power radiated by the source is

$$P = \frac{\Delta E}{\Delta t}$$
$$= 50 \times 10^3 \times 0.2 \text{ MeV s}^{-1}$$
$$= 1.6 \times 10^{-9} \text{ W}$$

and so the intensity 25 cm away is

$$I = \frac{P}{4\pi r^2}$$
$$= \frac{1.6 \times 10^{-9}}{4\pi \times (0.25)^2} \text{ W m}^{-2}$$
$$= 2.04 \times 10^{-9} \text{ W m}^{-2}$$

Q2

By what factor is the intensity reduced when a worker doubles his distance from a source of X-rays?

Answer

Since we have an inverse square law, the intensity will be reduced by a factor of 4.

Attenuation

If, however, monochromatic radiation is directed into a medium that can absorb radiation, the fall in intensity is exponential. The degree to which X-rays can penetrate matter is called the *quality* of the radiation.

▶ It can be shown that the transmitted intensity decreases as

$$I = I_0 \, e^{-\mu x}$$

Here μ is a constant called the *linear attenuation coefficient.* This coefficient can be determined from the slope of a plot of the logarithm of the intensity versus distance. It depends both on the *material through which the radiation passes* and on the *energy of the photons.* (See Figure I2.1.)

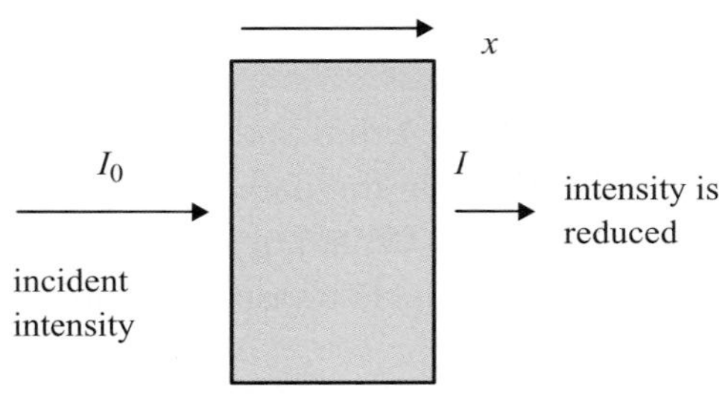

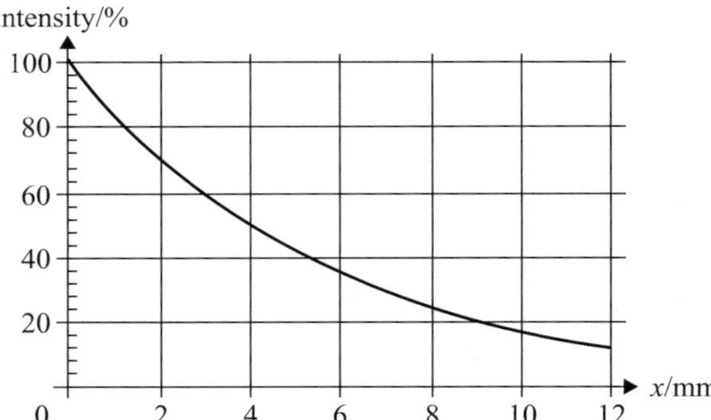

Figure I2.1 Attenuation of radiation through an absorbing medium. The graph gives the percentage of the intensity transmitted after going through a thickness x of the material.

This law is similar to the radioactive decay law and we define by analogy the *half-value thickness* (HVT), which is the length that must be travelled through in order to reduce the intensity by a factor of 2. Then

$$\text{HVT} = \frac{0.693}{\mu}$$

Figure I2.2 shows the dependence on energy of the HVT for X-rays and gamma rays in water.

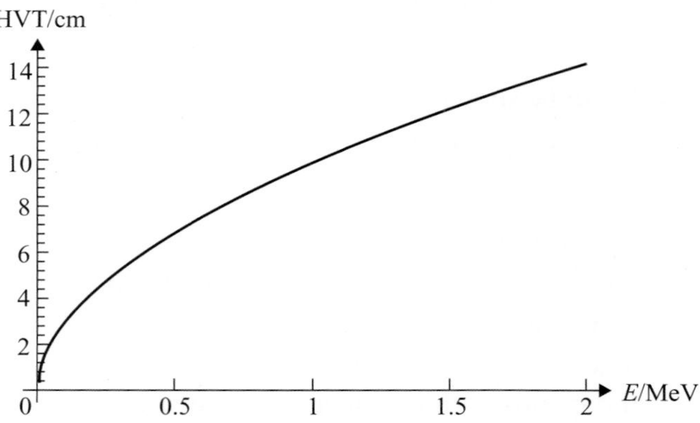

Figure I2.2 The half-value thickness as a function of photon energy. The curve is the same for both X-rays and gamma rays.

Example questions

Q3

A metal sheet of thickness 4 mm and half-value thickness 3 mm is placed in the path of radiation from a radioactive source. What fraction of the source's incident intensity gets transmitted through the sheet?

Answer

$$I = I_0 \, e^{-\mu x}$$
$$= I_0 \exp\left(-\frac{0.693 \times 4}{3}\right)$$
$$= 0.397 I_0$$

that is, about 40% goes through.

Q4

A worker used to work at a distance of 2 m from a source of radiation. She now decides to move away to a distance of 3 m and to work behind a 3 mm screen with HVT equal to 2 mm. By what factor is the radiation she receives reduced?

Answer

Let P be the power of the source. At a distance of 2 m the worker received an intensity of

$$I = \frac{P}{4\pi r^2}$$
$$= \frac{P}{4\pi 2^2}$$
$$= \frac{P}{16\pi}$$
$$= 0.0199 \, P$$

At the increased distance of 3 m the received intensity is

$$I = \frac{P}{4\pi 3^2}$$
$$= \frac{P}{36\pi}$$

After going through the screen, the intensity is further reduced to

$$I = I_0 \, e^{-\mu x}$$
$$= \frac{P}{36\pi} \exp\left(-\frac{0.693 \times 3}{2}\right)$$
$$= 0.354 \frac{P}{36\pi}$$
$$= 0.0031 \, P$$

The overall reduction is thus a factor of about 6.4.

▶ **The main methods by which X-rays are absorbed are the photoelectric and Compton effects.**

In the photoelectric effect, the X-ray photon is absorbed by an electron, which is then emitted from its atom or molecule. In the Compton effect, the photon gives part of its energy to a *free* electron and scatters off it with a reduced energy and so increased wavelength. The energy given to the electron appears as kinetic energy for the electron. The importance of the photoelectric effect is mostly for low-energy photons and increases sharply with increasing atomic number of the specimen upon which the photons fall. The Compton effect, on the other hand, does not vary much with energy and increases linearly with atomic number. In both cases the electrons can ionize matter along their paths.

X-ray imaging

As mentioned at the beginning, X-rays were the first radiation to be used for medical imaging. X-ray machines used for taking an ordinary 'X-ray picture' operate at voltages of around 15–30 kV for a mammogram and at about 50–150 kV for a chest X-ray (see Figure I2.3).

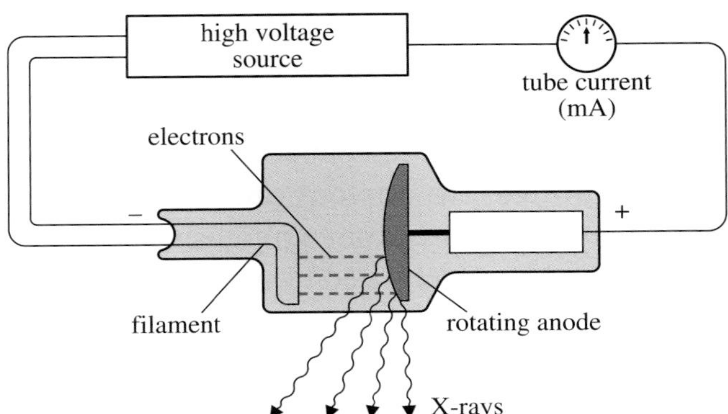

Figure I2.3 Schematic diagram of an X-ray tube.

▶ At these voltages the dominant mechanism for energy loss by the X-rays is the photoelectric effect. Since this effect is strongly dependent on atomic number and there is a substantial difference between the atomic numbers of the elements present in bone ($Z = 14$) and soft tissue ($Z = 7$), it follows that bone will absorb X-rays much more strongly than soft tissue. Hence, the X-ray picture will show a contrast between bone and soft tissue.

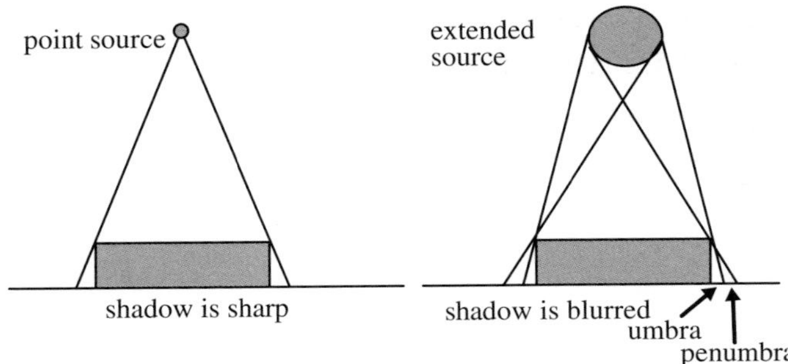

Figure I2.4 The shadow cast is blurred when the source is extended.

The X-rays that are directed through a patient's body will penetrate the body and those that make it through to the other side fall on *photographic film*, which they expose. In those cases where there is no substantial difference between the Z number of the area to be imaged and the surrounding area, the image can be improved by giving the patient a *contrast medium*. Usually this consists of what is called a *barium meal*, barium sulphate, which the patient swallows. When this moves into the intestinal tract and an X-ray is taken, the barium will absorb X-rays more strongly than the surrounding tissue, resulting in a sharper image. The image created by the X-ray on the film is actually a shadow of the high-Z material in the body (e.g. bones) against the surrounding low-Z tissue. To increase the sharpness of the shadow the source of X-rays must be made as *point-like* as possible (see Figure I2.4).

The quality of the image is thus improved if the film is as close to the patient as possible, or if the distance from the source to the patient is large. (In the latter case, the intensity of X-rays reaching the patient is diminished, which in turn implies a longer exposure time.) The image is also improved if as many scattered rays as possible are prevented from reaching the film. (See Figure I2.5.)

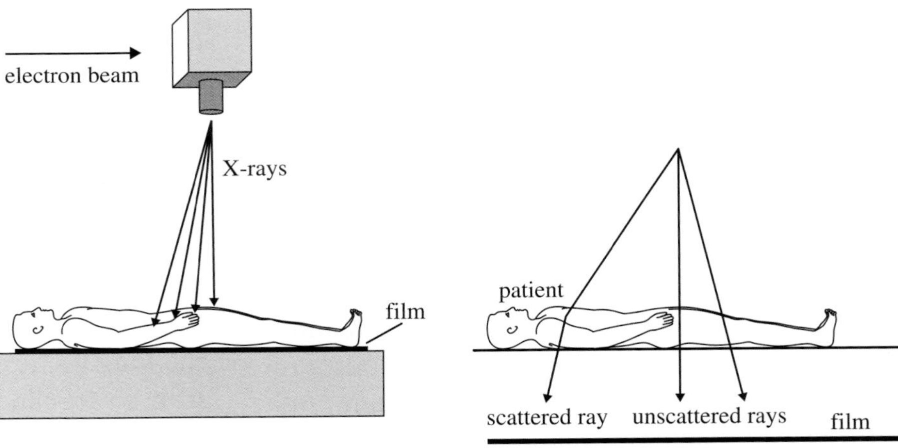

Figure I2.5 A beam of X-rays entering a patient. Scattered rays blur the image.

This can be achieved with the use of a grid of lead (i.e. X-ray opaque) strips, which are placed between the patient and the film, as shown in Figure I2.6. The strips are oriented along the direction of the incoming X-rays, and so scattered rays are blocked and do not make it to the film. The strips are about 0.5 mm apart. This creates unwanted images of the lead strips on the film, however. These can be eliminated to some extent by moving the grid sideways back and forth during exposure so that the strip images are blurred.

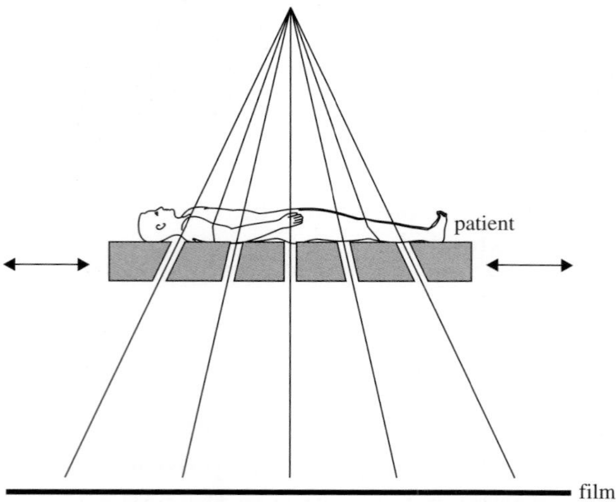

Figure I2.6 The use of a grid with lead strips blocks scattered rays, improving the image.

Low-energy X-rays will simply be absorbed by the skin of the patient and cannot therefore penetrate the body. Such X-rays are usually removed from the X-ray beam in a process called *filtering*.

Because photographic film is much more sensitive to ordinary visible light than to X-rays, the time of exposure in making an X-ray image needs to be longer. However, it can be significantly reduced by using intensifying screens. An intensifying screen is a piece of plastic containing fluorescent crystals in the top and bottom surfaces and a double-sided photographic film in between. X-rays that have gone through the patient enter this screen and transfer some of their energy to the crystals. The energy absorbed by the crystals is then emitted as visible light that exposes the film. (See Figure I2.7.)

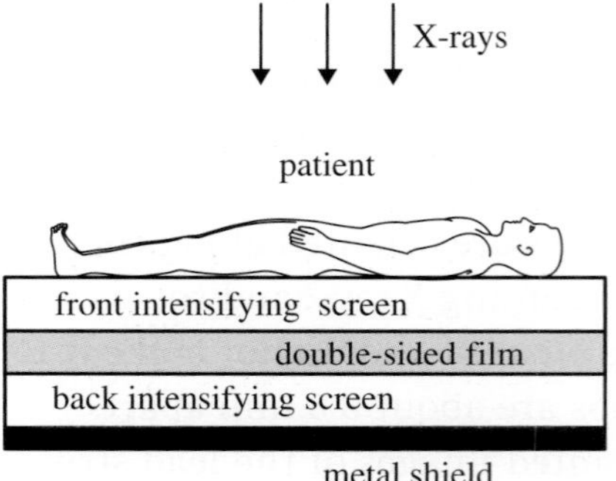

Figure I2.7 The use of intensifying screens increases the brightness of the image.

In another X-ray technique called *fluoroscopy*, a *real-time* dynamic image is created on a TV monitor. X-rays that have passed through the patient fall on a fluorescent screen and visible light is emitted. The photons cause the emission of electrons from a photosurface, which are then accelerated by a potential difference so that they fall on a second fluorescent screen from which they cause emission of light that is fed into the TV monitor.

The advantage of the real-time image is, however, outweighed by the unusually high doses of radiation the patient receives in the process.

Computed tomography (CT scan)

One of the biggest advances in the medical use of X-rays has been the discovery (in 1973), through work of G. N. Hounsfield and A. Cormack, of a technique known as computed (axial) tomography (CT) or computer-assisted tomography (CAT). This diagnostic method has made possible much more accurate diagnosis with much less invasive action on the patient. It does use X-rays, however, and so its use does present dangers to the patient. A complete brain CAT scan lasts about 2 s and a whole-body scan lasts about 6 s.

Imagine a patient standing up with a beam of X-rays directed horizontally, at right angles to the long vertical axis of the patient. The CT scan creates an image of a horizontal slice through the patient. In Figure I2.8 we look at a patient (represented by the grey circle) from above. A movable source of X-rays emits a beam that is confined to a horizontal plane and travels through the patient's body so that it is received by detectors on the other side. The source then is rotated so that the beam enters the body from a different angle.

The use of many detectors as opposed to just one cuts down the time required for the scan and the amount of radiation deposited in the patient. The detectors record the intensity of the X-rays reaching them and the information

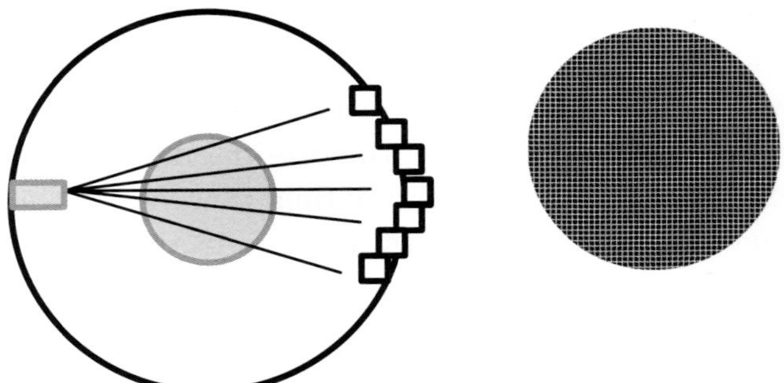

Figure I2.8 In a CT scan, an array of detectors records the X-rays passing through the patient in a given direction and the amount of absorption in each pixel is computed.

is then sent to a computer, which analyses the data and constructs the image.

The image is constructed as follows. Imagine for convenience that the horizontal slice to be imaged is broken down into a square grid of a suitably small size so as to get acceptable resolution. Typically the size of the grid is about 2 mm or smaller. The objective is to get information about the amount of X-rays that has been absorbed by each grid element (also called a pixel). A detector, of course, only measures the total amount of X-rays absorbed along a straight line joining the source of X-rays to the detector. A method is needed to find the amount absorbed by each pixel. This is done by a computer using sophisticated mathematical techniques. To illustrate the point, consider an oversimplified example in which the area to be imaged has just 4 pixels (see Figure I2.9a). The numbers next to the arrows indicate the total amount of absorption along the direction of the arrow in arbitrary units. If the amount of absorption in each pixel is A, B, C and D, we have, for example, that $A + B = 14$. In a real situation, there would be tens of thousands of pixels and fast computer techniques must be used to determine the individual amounts of absorption in each pixel. Once the numbers for each pixel are found, a colour code can be applied to each pixel to represent its absorption. Here we use shades of grey – darker shades meaning higher absorption – to get Figure I2.9(b) using the values $A = 8$, $B = 6$, $C = 3$, $D = 9$.

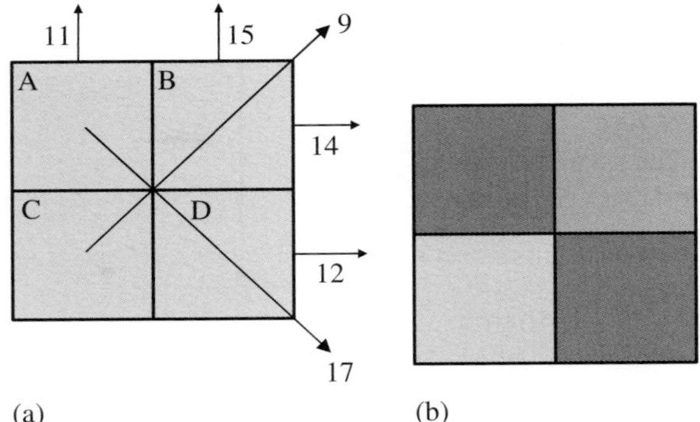

Figure I2.9 (a) The detectors measure the total amount of absorption in a given direction. (b) On the basis of these measurements the computer then assigns absorption values to each pixel.

Other imaging techniques

Magnetic resonance imaging (MRI)

Magnetic resonance imaging is based on a nuclear physics phenomenon known as *nuclear magnetic resonance* and is a superior method to the CT scan. Unlike the CT scan, the image is constructed without dangerous radiation (despite the word *nuclear*) but it is significantly more expensive.

Electrons and protons have a property called spin (see Option J1 in Option J, Particle physics). Particles with electric charge and spin behave as tiny microscopic magnets – the technical term is magnetic moment. In the presence of an external magnetic field, the magnetic moment will align itself either parallel ('spin-up') or antiparallel ('spin-down') to the direction of the magnetic field.

Protons inside nuclei belong to energy levels of specific energy. If the protons are put in a region of external magnetic field, the energy of the level will change depending on how the proton magnetic moment aligns itself with respect to the magnetic field (see Figure I2.10). The difference in energy between the split levels is proportional to the external magnetic field.

As seen from Figure I2.10, the state with spin-up has the lower energy. If a radio-frequency

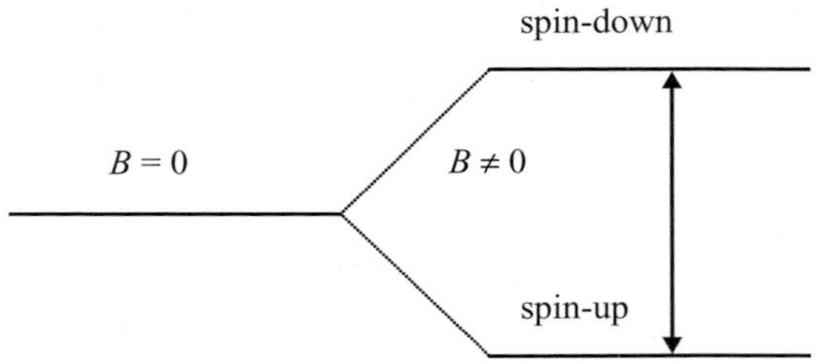

Figure I2.10 A normal energy level splits into two in a magnetic field. The state with spin-up has a lower energy than the state with spin-down.

(RF) source (i.e. electromagnetic radiation) provides energy to a sample of hydrogen nuclei in a magnetic field, the protons in the lower energy spin-up state may absorb photons and make a transition to the higher spin-down state. This will happen if the frequency of the electromagnetic radiation corresponds to the energy difference between the spin-up and spin-down states (an example of resonance). Once the transition to the higher energy state is made, it will be followed by a transition down again with the accompanying emission of a photon of the same frequency. Detectors can record these photons and techniques similar to CT scanning are used to create the magnetic resonance image so that the photons detected can be correlated with specific points of emission. Of great interest in MRI is the rate at which the transitions take place, since the rate is related to the type of tissue in which the transition occurs. Thus, measuring the rate gives information about the type of tissue.

The point of emission of the emitted photons can be located by placing the patient in an additional magnetic field that destroys the high degree of uniformity of the original magnets. Suppose that the magnetic field now varies across the patient (shown in cross-section in Figure I2.11), so that it becomes stronger as we move upwards. Imagine that the variation of the magnetic field is the same along horizontal planes through the patient.

The frequency that can be absorbed by the hydrogen nuclei depends on the external magnetic field, so for a fixed RF frequency only one plane within the body will have the correct value of magnetic field for absorption to take place. To measure absorption in other planes through the body, the frequency of the RF source can be varied. The image so created shows the density of hydrogen nuclei since it is hydrogen that is primarily responsible for absorption. More sophisticated techniques measure the rate at which excited nuclei return to their ground state (the relaxation times) and these produce images of especially high resolution. Different kinds of tissue show different relaxation times, thus allowing the identification of tissue type.

Positron emission tomography (PET scan)

This technique is similar to the CT scan and involves the annihilation of an electron and a positron (the antiparticle of the electron) and

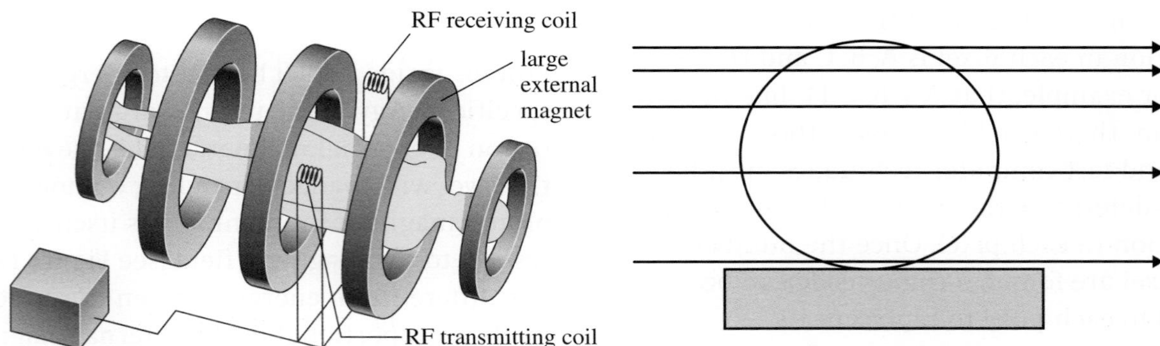

Figure I2.11 In MRI the patient is surrounded by powerful magnets that produce very uniform fields, and RF coils. The magnetic field is given a gradient – it is made stronger at some places. Here the field increases as we move upwards.

the detection of the two photons so produced. The patient is injected with a solution of radioactive material containing isotopes that decay by positron emission. As soon as the positron is emitted, it will collide with an electron in the tissue of the patient. The electron–positron pair will annihilate into two photons each of energy 0.511 MeV

$$e^- + e^+ \to 2\gamma$$

The electron–positron total momentum is, essentially, zero, which means that the two photons must move in opposite directions with the same energy (in order to conserve momentum). The detectors surrounding the patient (see Figure I2.12) can therefore determine the line along which the emissions took place and eventually locate the point of emission. PET scans have a resolution of about 1 mm. They are used mainly for biochemical and metabolism-related studies. They produce superior brain images.

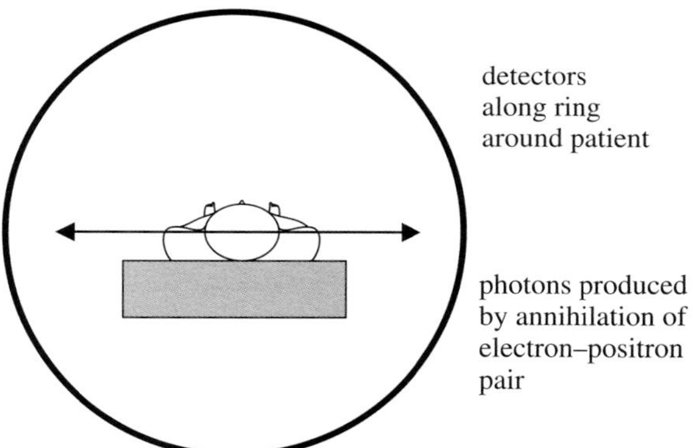

Figure I2.12 The patient is surrounded by a ring of detectors which record the line along which the two photons are emitted.

Ultrasound

A major tool in diagnostic medicine is ultrasound. Ultrasound is sound that is not audible to the human ear – its frequency is higher than about 20 kHz. The ultrasound used in diagnostic medicine is in the range of about 1 to 10 MHz. Ultrasound has the advantage over X-rays in that it does not deposit radiation in the body and no adverse side effects of its use are known. For certain organs, for example the lungs, X-rays cannot produce an image but ultrasound can. One disadvantage of ultrasound is that the images are not as detailed as those from X-rays.

The ultrasound is emitted towards the patient's body in *short pulses*, typically lasting 1 μs, and their reflections off surfaces of various organs are detected. The idea is thus similar to *sonar*. The speed of sound in soft tissue is 1540 m s^{-1}, similar to that in water. This means that the wavelengths involved are 1.54 mm for 1 MHz waves and 0.154 mm for 10 MHz waves. Thus, if we use 1 MHz waves, the length of the pulse is 1.54 mm and so contains just one full wave. For 10 MHz waves, the wavetrain contains 10 full waves. In general, diffraction considerations place a limit on the size, d, that can be resolved by a wave of wavelength λ. The constraint is that

$$\lambda < d$$

If a resolution of a couple of millimetres is required, the wavelength used must therefore be less than a few millimetres. In view of the frequencies used, this is not a problem. As we saw, a 10 MHz ultrasound has a wavelength of about 0.15 mm and so, in principle, such an ultrasound can 'see' objects of linear size of about 0.15 mm.

On the other hand, in practice, the pulse used must contain at least a few full waves for resolution to be possible.

▶ Thus, in the case of the ultrasound frequencies used in medicine, it is the pulse duration, and not diffraction, that sets the limit on resolution.

The frequency used is usually determined by the organ to be studied and the resolution desired. A rough rule is to use a frequency given by

$$f = 200\frac{c}{d}$$

where c is the speed of sound in tissue and d is the depth of the organ below the body surface. (In other words, the organ should be at a depth of about 200 wavelengths.)

Example question

Q5

The stomach is about 10 cm from the body's surface. What frequency should be used to get a scan of the stomach?

Answer

Applying the formula gives

$$\begin{aligned} f &= 200\frac{c}{d} \\ &= 200 \times \frac{1548}{0.10}\,\text{Hz} \\ &\approx 3\,\text{MHz} \end{aligned}$$

The source of ultrasound is a transducer that converts electrical energy into sound energy. This is based on a phenomenon called piezoelectricity. An alternating voltage applied to opposite faces of a crystal such as strontium titanate or quartz will force the crystal to vibrate, emitting ultrasound (see Figure I2.13). Similarly, ultrasound falling on such a crystal will produce an alternating voltage at the faces of the crystal. This means that the source of ultrasound can also act as a receiver.

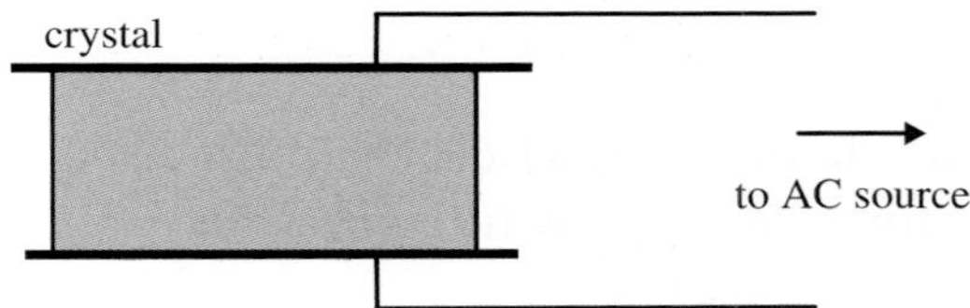

Figure I2.13 A piezoelectric crystal vibrates when an AC source is applied to it.

The sound energy must then be directed into the patient's body. In general, when a wave encounters an interface between two different media, part of the wave will be reflected and part will be transmitted into the other medium. The amount of transmission depends on the impedances of the two media. Acoustic impedance is defined as

$$Z = \rho v$$

where ρ is the density of the medium and v is the speed of sound in that medium. The units of impedance are kg m^{-2} s^{-1}. If I_0 is the incident, I_t the transmitted and I_r the reflected intensity then

$$\frac{I_t}{I_0} = \frac{4Z_1Z_2}{(Z_1+Z_2)^2}$$

$$\frac{I_r}{I_0} = \frac{(Z_1-Z_2)^2}{(Z_1+Z_2)^2}$$

This shows that for most of the energy to be transmitted, the impedances of the two media must be as close to each other as possible (impedance matching). The impedance of soft tissue differs from that of air by a factor of about 10^4, so most of the sound would be reflected by the body. This is why the area between the body and the transducer is filled with a gel-like substance whose impedance matches that of the body.

In a type of ultrasound scan called the A scan, the ultrasound pulse is directed into the body and the reflected pulse from various interfaces in the body is recorded by the transducer. This time it converts the sound energy into electrical energy. The reflected signal is then displayed on a cathode-ray oscilloscope. The CRO signal is, in fact, a graph of signal strength versus time of travel from the transducer to the reflecting surface and back. An example of such a trace is shown in Figure I2.14.

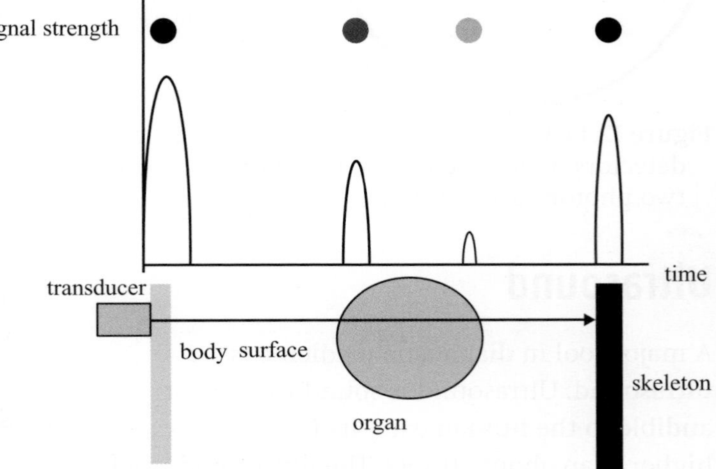

Figure I2.14 A short beam of ultrasound is directed into the patient. The beam is partially reflected from various organs in the body and the reflected signal is recorded. The dots at the top of the figure represent the strength of the reflected signal.

The dots in the graph show another way of representing the results. The dot brightness is proportional to the signal strength (darker colours representing stronger signal).

The A scan provides a one-dimensional image. Imagine a whole series of A scans performed by sending parallel beams of ultrasound into the patient by a transducer that moves up along the surface of the body or by a series of transducers, as shown in Figure I2.15.

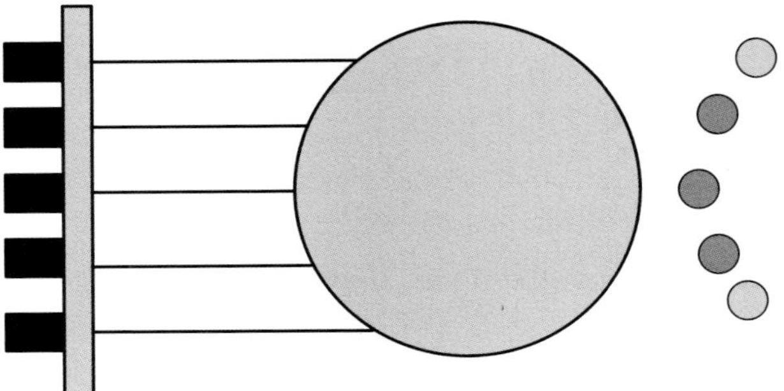

Figure I2.15 As the source of ultrasound is moved along the body, a series of dots whose brightness represents the strength of the reflected signal is formed. These dots build up the ultrasound image.

If the A scans *are put together*, the result is the dots on the right of the diagram, which begin to form an outline of the surface of the organ in a *two-dimensional image*. A series of transducers are put on the body and each sends one short pulse after the other. Typically, the time delay between two consecutive signals is 1 ms.

▶ When the results are displayed on the CRO screen, the image is a *real-time, two-dimensional representation of the object which is viewed as a movie*. This is called a B scan.

Ultrasound can also be put to other uses. One is to measure blood-flow velocities and foetal heart movement. Ultrasound is directed at the heart, say, and the reflected signal detected. Because the heart moves, the reflected signal will have a slightly different frequency because of the Doppler effect. Comparison of the emitted and received frequencies gives the speed of the reflecting surface.

The various imaging techniques described are summarised in Table I2.2.

Diagnostic uses of radioactive sources

Radioisotopes are used for diagnosis and to monitor specific body organs and their functions. Uses include the monitoring of the thyroid gland using radioactive iodine, measurement of body fluids, studies of how food is digested, vitamin absorption, how amino acids are synthesized, how ions can penetrate cell walls, etc. Most commonly used is the radioisotope technetium-99 ($^{99m}_{43}Tc$), a

Method	Resolution	Advantages	Disadvantages
X-rays	0.5 mm	Cheap	Presents radiation danger; some organs are not accessible; some images are obscured
CT scans	0.5 mm	Can distinguish between different types of tissue	Presents radiation danger
MRI	1 mm	Presents no radiation dangers; superior images; can distinguish between different types of tissue	Expensive; difficult for patients who are claustrophobic
Ultrasound	2 mm	Presents no radiation dangers	Some organs are not accessible
PET scans	1 mm	Organ function studies; superior brain images	Some organs are not accessible

Table I2.2 Advantages and disadvantages of different imaging techniques.

metastable (i.e. long-lived) excited state of technetium-99. It is produced in the decay of molybdenum-99:

$$^{99}_{42}\text{Mo} \rightarrow {}^{99\text{m}}_{43}\text{Tc} + {}^{0}_{-1}\text{e} + {}^{0}_{0}\bar{\nu}_{\text{e}} + {}^{0}_{0}\gamma$$

The produced technetium then decays by gamma emission

$$^{99\text{m}}_{43}\text{Tc} \rightarrow {}^{99}_{43}\text{Tc} + {}^{0}_{0}\gamma$$

The photon energies are about 140 keV. This is an advantage since any alpha or beta particles emitted would be absorbed within the body and would not reach an outside detector; also, photons of these energies are easily detectable. Technetium has a half-life of about 6 h, which is conveniently short, and can combine into a large number of compounds.

Technetium is useful in diagnostic studies of most body organs, such as the heart, the lungs and the liver. In investigations of calcium absorption by bones, technetium and calcium-45 or calcium-47 are used. Iodine-131 is another commonly used radioisotope. It is used in blood volume measurements and in studies of the thyroid gland. Thallium-201 is used in studies of muscle function and disease.

The compound to be tagged with technetium is chosen according to what part or organ of the body needs to be imaged – different compounds will accumulate in different parts of the body. The radioactive compound so formed is called a *radiopharmaceutical*. This is given to the patient (orally or by injection) and the radiation emitted by technetium can then be recorded by a detector placed over the relevant part of the patient's body. The amount of radiation compared with the amount expected from a healthy body then provides information about the function of the particular body organ.

The example question that follows shows the theory of a method used to determine the amount of blood in a patient (who might have been involved in an accident resulting in massive blood loss).

Example question

Q6

A patient is injected with 5 cm^3 of albumen labelled with iodine-131 (albumen is part of the blood plasma). A 5 cm^3 sample drawn from the patient's blood has an activity of 100 Bq. Another 5 cm^3 of iodine-131 is mixed with 3000 cm^3 of water. The activity of a 5 cm^3 sample is found to be 170 Bq. Determine the volume of blood of the patient.

Answer

Let A be the activity of the 5 cm^3 of iodine-131. Then the activity of 5 cm^3 drawn from the entire blood volume V is

$$100 = \frac{5}{V}A$$

The activity of the 5 cm^3 drawn from the diluted sample is

$$170 = \frac{5}{3000}A$$

and so dividing these two equations side by side we find $V = 5100\ \text{cm}^3$.

QUESTIONS

1 Figure I2.16 shows the fraction of X-rays of two specific energies transmitted through a thickness x of a sheet of metal.

(a) For each energy, determine the HVT for these X-rays in the metal.

(b) Which graph corresponds to X-rays of higher energy?

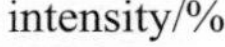

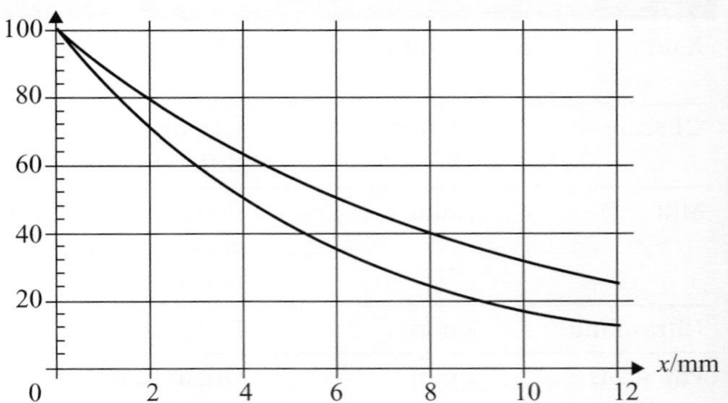

Figure I2.16 For question 1.

2 Figure I2.17 shows the fraction of X-rays of a specific energy transmitted through a thickness x of a sheet of metal.

(a) Determine the value of the linear attenuation coefficient for these X-rays in this metal.

(b) What thickness of metal is required to reduce the transmitted intensity by 80%?

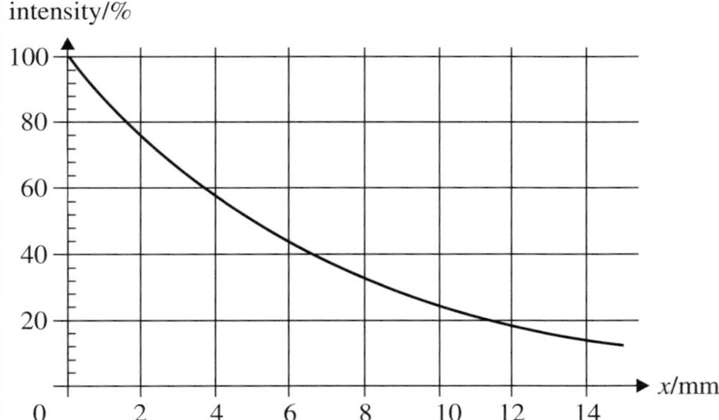

Figure I2.17 For question 2.

3 A piece of metal 4 mm thick reduces the intensity of X-rays passing through it by 40%. What thickness of the same metal is required to reduce the intensity by 80%?

4 The HVT for a beam of X-rays is 3 mm. What fraction of the X-ray intensity is transmitted through 1 mm of this metal?

5 The X-rays used in medicine are usually not monoenergetic (i.e. of a single energy). It is said that these beams become 'harder' as they are allowed to pass through material. What is meant by this statement and why is it true? The HVT of a certain absorber for X-rays of energy 20 keV is 2.2 mm and that for 25 keV X-rays is 2.8 mm. A beam containing equal quantities of X-rays of these two energies is incident on 5.0 mm of the absorber. What is the ratio of 25 keV to 20 keV photons that are transmitted?

6 The intensity of a beam of monoenergetic X-rays is 0.28 kW m^{-2} at a distance of 20 cm from the X-ray source.

(a) What is the intensity at a distance of 10 cm from the source (assume no absorption between the point of interest and the source)?

(b) If an aluminium foil of thickness 3 mm and HVT 2 mm is wrapped around the source, what will the intensity be 10 cm away?

7 A radioactive isotope with a half-life of 14 h and activity of 3.6 kBq is injected into a patient's blood. A 10 cm^3 sample is taken from the patient 6 h later and its activity is measured to be 5.0 Bq. Estimate the volume of the patient's blood.

8 What resolution can be achieved with ultrasound of frequency 5 MHz? (Take the speed of sound in soft tissue to be 1540 m s^{-1}.)

Radiation in medicine

This chapter introduces the main effects of radiation on living things and the methods used to measure the radiation absorbed.

Objectives

By the end of this chapter you should be able to:

- outline the *effects of ionizing radiations on living things*;
- describe *how radiation is measured*;
- solve problems involving *absorbed dose*, $D = \frac{E}{m}$, *dose equivalent*, $H = QD$, and *exposure*, $X = \frac{Q}{m}$;
- state the meaning of *half-life*, *biological half-life* and *effective half-life* and solve problems using $\frac{1}{T_E} = \frac{1}{T_P} + \frac{1}{T_B}$.

Biological effects of radiation and dosimetry

We are all exposed to radiation in our daily lives from either natural or artificial sources, or because of special conditions in the workplace. Natural sources include radon, gamma rays from the earth, unstable isotopes found in food and cosmic rays. Artificial sources include the exposure to radiation for medical reasons, radiations from building materials, radiation from nuclear weapons testing, and accidents in nuclear power plants. Workers in research labs and radiology personnel in hospitals are exposed to radiation as a result of their work.

The starting point of any discussion on the effects of radiation on living matter might be to realize that the energy that is required to break a molecular bond is of the order of 1 eV. Radiations that deposit energies of this order, or more, are therefore bound to alter the molecular structure of the matter they travel through. It is now generally accepted that any amount of radiation, no matter how small, is harmful, and that in dealing with radiation the following general rules must be followed:

- Keep as far as possible from the source.
- Keep the exposure as short as possible.
- Use shielding whenever possible.

The absorption of even a single photon of energy by a single molecule of a living organism may not be harmless. The absorbed photon may have the effect of ejecting an electron from its molecule and this may imply that the structure of the molecule changes. For example, if the ejected electron was crucial in the chemical bonds holding the molecule together, then the molecule may break apart. Enzymes may not operate correctly if the molecule is altered in any way. It is also known that irradiation of water produces very reactive free radicals (see the reactions below). As most living organisms contain water, the production of these free radicals induces changes in the chemical structures of the surrounding molecules with biological implications. Such reactions include

$$H_2O \xrightarrow{\text{radiation}} H_2O^+ + e^-$$
$$H_2O^+ + H_2O \rightarrow H_3O^+ + HO^\bullet$$
$$e^- + H_2O \rightarrow OH^- + H^\bullet$$

The damage of a few molecules from radiation will not, in general, result in loss of function for the cell, but if the amount of radiation received is large, then the cell may not be able to recover its function. By contrast, damage to a gene will, in general, affect the function of the cell. Radiation is particularly damaging to the bone marrow, which is responsible for producing blood cells, and seriously impairs the human immune system. Thus, leukaemia and other forms of cancer are common results of exposure to radiation.

To understand the effect of radiation on living matter we must first define appropriate quantities that measure the amount of radiation received.

▶ *Absorbed dose* is defined as the amount of energy E absorbed by a unit mass of the irradiated material, that is

$$D = \frac{E}{m}$$

where E is the energy absorbed by a mass m. Its unit is joule per kilogram (J kg^{-1}) and this is defined as the gray (Gy).

An older unit still in use is the rad:

$$1\ \text{Gy} = 1\ \text{J kg}^{-1} = 100\ \text{rad}$$

▶ The *damage* produced by radiation is not only proportional to the absorbed dose but also depends on the *type of radiation* used. Thus, we define the *dose equivalent* to be

$$H = QD$$

where Q is a dimensionless number that characterizes various different radiations. It is called the *quality factor* of the radiation. The unit of H is the same as that for absorbed dose (i.e. joule per kilogram) but to distinguish the two quantities we use the sievert (Sv) for the dose equivalent.

Another unit still in use is the rem (standing for radiation equivalent man)

$$1\ \text{Sv} = 1\ \text{J kg}^{-1} = 100\ \text{rem}$$

Table I3.1 gives the quality factor values of some different types of radiation.

Type of radiation	Q
β, γ and X-rays	1
Fast protons	1
Slow neutrons	3
Fast neutrons	10
α particles	20

Table I3.1 Quality factor values of different types of radiation.

The quality factor is related to the relative biological equivalent, which is defined as

$$\text{RBE} = \frac{\text{absorbed dose to produce an effect with 250 keV X-rays}}{\text{absorbed dose to produce same effect with radiation used}}$$

For our purposes here we will take Q and RBE to be the same.

Example questions

Q1

A person of mass 60 kg receives 0.8 J of energy from radiation of quality 5 to her whole body. What is the absorbed dose? What is the dose equivalent she receives?

Answer

The absorbed dose is

$$D = \frac{E}{m}$$
$$= \frac{0.8\ \text{J}}{60\ \text{kg}}$$
$$= 13.3\ \text{mGy}$$

The dose equivalent is

$$H = QD$$
$$= 5 \times 13.3 \text{ mSv}$$
$$= 66.7 \text{ mSv}$$

Q2

A person of mass 70 kg receives a whole-body dose equivalent of 30 mSv. Half of this amount is of quality 1 and the other half of quality 10. How much energy did the person receive?

Answer

The dose equivalent is

$$H = QD$$

and so

$$15 = 1 \times D_1$$
$$\Rightarrow D_1 = 15 \text{ mGy}$$
$$\Rightarrow E_1 = 70 \text{ kg} \times 15 \times 10^{-3} \text{ J kg}^{-1}$$
$$= 1.05 \text{ J}$$

and

$$15 = 10 \times D_2$$
$$\Rightarrow D_2 = 1.5 \text{ mGy}$$
$$\Rightarrow E_2 = 70 \text{ kg} \times 1.5 \times 10^{-3} \text{ J kg}^{-1}$$
$$= 0.10 \text{ J}$$

giving a total energy of 1.15 J.

To get an idea of the meaning of the sievert, note that a dose equivalent of more than 100 Sv results in death in a few days due to massive damage to large numbers of cells. With an amount of about 10 Sv symptoms of *radiation sickness* (nausea, diarrhoea, vomiting) begin to appear a few hours after exposure and death follows in a few weeks. In radiation therapy, amounts up to 3 Sv are administered but patients have survived much larger amounts. A typical chest X-ray examination gives 0.1 mSv and a flight at a height of 8 km gives 2 μSv per hour. Generally, the danger increases with the amount of dose equivalent and the probability of cancer increases by 1% for every sievert of radiation received.

The International Commission on Radiological Protection recommends that on a yearly basis:

- a person working with radioactive materials should not be exposed to more than 50 mSv;
- other adults should not be exposed to more than 5 mSv;
- children should not be exposed to more than 0.5 mSv.

The ICRP's recommendations for protection also include short-term limits of exposure of:

- no more than 10 μSv per hour for γ rays at a distance of 10 cm;
- no more than 50 μSv per hour for β particles, also at a distance of 10 cm from the source;
- particle sources with activity larger than 40 kBq should be avoided.

(Recall that the becquerel (Bq) is a unit of activity and equals one decay per second.)

The amounts of dose equivalent from various sources in everyday life depend on the location and elevation above sea level. Table I3.2 summarizes the average amounts of radiation a person receives in a year. The total is 3.37 mSv per person per year. Radon contributes 59% of this radiation.

Source	Equivalent dose/mSv	Percentage
Radon	2.0	59
Cosmic rays	0.27	8
Building materials	0.30	9
Isotopes in body from food	0.20	6
Isotopes in the earth	0.20	6
Medical procedures	0.40	12
TOTAL	3.37 mSv	100%

Table I3.2 Amounts of radiation received per year by an average person living in a modern city at sea level.

(The amount from cosmic rays increases by about 0.2 mSv for every 1 km of elevation.)

▶ A related quantity is *exposure*, X, which is defined as the total amount of produced charge q due to ionization in a mass m of air:

$$X = \frac{q}{m}$$

Ionization means that positive and negative charges are produced. In defining exposure we measure only the positive charges. The unit for exposure is coulomb per kilogram (C kg^{-1}). Thus, ionization of exposure 50 C kg^{-1} means that in 1 kg of air 50 C of positive or negative charge is produced as a result of ionization by a particular radiation. The *exposure rate* is defined as the exposure per unit time, which is the amount of charge produced in 1 kg of air per second.

There is a connection between exposure and absorbed dose. This is because in order to produce one ion in air an energy of approximately 34 eV is needed. Thus, let the exposure of a given radiation be E (in units of C kg^{-1}). This radiation produces

$$E\,\frac{\text{C}}{\text{kg}} = E \times \frac{1}{1.6 \times 10^{-19}}\,\frac{\text{electrons}}{\text{kg}}$$

Each electron requires an energy of 34 eV and thus the energy absorbed (absorbed dose) is

$$\begin{aligned} D\ (\text{in Gy}) &= E \times \frac{1}{1.6 \times 10^{-19}}\,\frac{34\ \text{eV}}{\text{kg}} \\ &= E \times 34\,\frac{\text{J}}{\text{kg}} \\ &= 34E\ (\text{in J kg}^{-1}) \end{aligned}$$

This is the connection between absorbed dose *in air* and exposure. For materials other than air, we must take into account the fact that it takes different energies to produce an ion. Thus, the relationship between exposure and absorbed dose is

$$D\ (\text{in Gy}) = fE\ (\text{in J kg}^{-1})$$

where f is a factor that depends on the material and the photon energy. For muscle, f is approximately 40, independent of the photon energy. For bone, f drops from 150 at very low photon energies to about 40 for energies up to 0.1 MeV. For higher energies, f stays at about 40.

Example question

Q3

Potassium-40 (^{40}K) is a natural radioactive isotope of ordinary potassium with a half-life of 1.27×10^9 yr. The abundance by mass of ^{40}K is 0.0118%. ^{40}K decays by beta emission. The electrons in this decay have an average energy of 0.44 MeV. Calculate the yearly dose equivalent due to ^{40}K in a 70 kg body. The K content by mass of an average human body is 0.18%.

Answer

The amount of potassium-40 in the body of a 70 kg person is

$$70 \times 0.0018 \times 0.000118\ \text{kg} = 1.5 \times 10^{-2}\ \text{g}$$

The activity of this amount of ^{40}K is $A = \lambda N_0$, where the decay constant can be found from

$$\begin{aligned} \lambda &= \frac{0.693}{T_{1/2}} \\ &= 1.73 \times 10^{-17}\ \text{s}^{-1} \end{aligned}$$

and the number of ^{40}K nuclei present is

$$\begin{aligned} N_0 &= \frac{1.5 \times 10^{-2}}{40} \times 6.02 \times 10^{23} \\ &= 2.3 \times 10^{20} \end{aligned}$$

Thus, the activity is

$$\begin{aligned} A &= \lambda N_0 \\ &= 1.7 \times 10^{-17} \times 2.3 \times 10^{20} \\ &= 3.9 \times 10^{3}\ \text{Bq} \end{aligned}$$

The number of nuclei that decay in one year is thus (approximately)

$$3.9 \times 10^3 \times 365 \times 24 \times 60 \times 60 = 1.2 \times 10^{11}$$

Each deposits an average energy of 0.44 MeV and hence the total energy in a year is

$$\begin{aligned} 1.2 \times 10^{11} \times 0.44 &= 0.53 \times 10^{11}\ \text{MeV} \\ &= 8.4 \times 10^{-3}\ \text{J} \end{aligned}$$

The absorbed (whole-body) dose is thus

$$\begin{aligned} D &= \frac{8.4 \times 10^{-3}}{70}\ \text{Gy} \\ &= 0.12\ \text{mGy} \end{aligned}$$

Since the Q factor for electrons is 1, the dose equivalent is $H = 0.12$ mSv.

Radiation therapy

Radiation is harmful to healthy cells, but it can also be harmful to malignant, cancerous cells. Radiation can thus be used to destroy such cells. In radiation therapy, X-rays or gamma rays can be directed in *very narrow beams* at the collection of cancerous cells to destroy them. In order to minimize the damage to the surrounding normal cells, tissue and bone, it is necessary to direct the beam at the tumour from a number of different angles. This assumes that the tumour is well localized and it is only in this case that radiation therapy can be effective. The energies of X-rays and gamma rays used in cancer treatment vary from 200 keV to 5 MeV.

The tumour may also be *injected* or *implanted* with radioactive material whose radiation is released *within* the tumour, thus destroying it. Radium, which is an alpha particle emitter, is commonly used in this way. A related technique is to give the patient a quantity of a radioactive isotope of iodine, $^{131}_{53}\text{I}$, which, once in the blood stream, will accumulate in the thyroid gland. Its radiation can then kill cancerous cells in that gland. An isotope of gold, ^{198}Au, collects in the lungs, destroying cancerous cells in the fluids that line the lungs.

Physical and biological half-life

A radioactive isotope decays, as we have seen in nuclear physics, according to an exponential decay law, so that the number of nuclei that are undecayed after time t is given by

$$N = N_0\, e^{-\lambda t}$$

or equivalently

$$N = N_0 \left(\frac{1}{2}\right)^{t/T_{1/2}}$$

where the *physical decay constant* λ_P is related to the *physical half-life* through

$$T_{1/2} = \frac{0.693}{\lambda_P}$$

Note that by differentiating this equation we obtain

$$\Delta N = -\lambda_P N\,\Delta t$$

The activity of the isotope (i.e. the number of decays per second) obeys a similar exponential decay law:

$$A = A_0\, e^{-\lambda_P t}$$

where the initial activity is given by $\lambda_P N_0$. Here, and in the decay formula above, N_0 stands for the number of radioactive nuclei initially present. When a radioactive isotope is taken in by a patient, however, its activity falls off faster than the law above implies. This is because the number of isotope nuclei in the body decreases not only by radioactive decay (*physical decay*) but also because some of the radioactive material is removed from the body as waste (sweat, urine, etc.), in other words, by *biological decay*. If we assume that the biological removal of the isotope obeys an exponential law as well, with a decay constant λ, then in a time Δt the number of nuclei removed is

$$\begin{aligned} \Delta N &= -\lambda_P N\,\Delta t - \lambda_B N\,\Delta t \\ &= -\lambda_E N\,\Delta t \\ \lambda_E &= \lambda_P + \lambda_B \end{aligned}$$

where λ_E is the effective decay constant, which represents both physical decay and biological decrease of nuclei in the body. Thus, we may define effective, physical and biological half-lives from these constants and hence (recall the definition of a decay constant)

$$\frac{1}{T_E} = \frac{1}{T_P} + \frac{1}{T_B}$$

▶ In other words, *physical* half-life is the time for half of the radioactive nuclei to *decay* away and *biological* half-life is the time for half of the radioactive nuclei to be *removed* from the body by biological processes. The effective half-life is the time for half of the radioactive nuclei to be removed by both decay and biological removal.

Example question

Q4

A radioactive isotope has a physical half-life of 24 days and a biological half-life of 12 days. If 4 g of this isotope are injected into a patient, how much is left after 24 days?

Answer

The effective half-life is

$$\frac{1}{T} = \frac{1}{24} + \frac{1}{12}$$
$$\Rightarrow T = 8 \text{ days}$$

After 24 days (i.e. three effective half-lives) the amount that is left is

$$4\left(\frac{1}{2}\right)^3 = 0.5 \text{ g}$$

? QUESTIONS

1 How much energy is deposited in a 70 kg person who receives an absorbed dose of radiation of 0.2 Gy?

2 How much energy is deposited in a 70 kg person who receives a dose equivalent of 0.2 Sv of slow neutrons?

3 (a) Which does more damage, 10 Gy of alpha particles or 10 Gy of gamma rays?
(b) Which does more damage, 10 Sv of alpha particles or 10 Sv of gamma rays?

4 If a person receives 2 μSv per hour during a flight at an altitude of 8 km, how many trips can a person take in a year if their dose equivalent is not to exceed 1 mSv. (Take each trip to be 3 h long.)

5 A student with a broken leg receives X-rays from a 50 keV machine. If the broken bone has a mass of 0.75 kg and the equivalent dose is 0.40 mSv, find:
(a) the absorbed dose;
(b) the energy deposited in the bone;
(c) the number of photons absorbed by the bone.

6 A beta ray source of activity 8.0×10^4 Bq and a half-life of 6 h is injected into a spherical tumour of radius 1.0 cm and density 1.3×10^3 kg m^{-3}. The energy of the electrons emitted is 3.5 MeV. Calculate the dose equivalent in the tumour 30 min after injection. Mention any assumptions you make in your calculations. How would the result of your calculation change if the source had been a gamma ray source.

7 A patient is exposed for 5.0 s to a radioactive source that emits gamma rays of energy 2.7 MeV. The activity of the source was 3.0×10^{12} Bq, and about 3% of the gamma rays reach the patient. If his mass is 70 kg, find the dose equivalent he receives.

8 A 70 kg person stands at a distance of 5 m from a source of gamma rays of activity 1.5×10^9 Bq, exposing a body surface area of 0.09 m^2 to the source. Each gamma ray has an energy of 1.4 MeV. Assume that 1/4 of the emitted gamma rays are absorbed by the person.
(a) What is the intensity of the gamma rays at the position of the person?
(b) How much energy does the person receive in 1 s?

If the person works for 2 h near this source find:
(c) the whole-body absorbed dose;
(d) the equivalent dose she receives.

9 The radioisotopes used in therapy generally have very much longer half-lives than those used in diagnosis. Why is such a difference desirable?

Particles and interactions

Particle physics is the branch of physics that tries to answer two basic questions: What are the fundamental building blocks of matter? What are the interactions between these building blocks? The history of physics has shown that, as we probe matter at increasingly smaller scales, we find structures within structures: molecules contain atoms; atoms are made of nuclei and electrons; nuclei are made of nucleons (protons and neutrons); and the nucleons are made out of quarks. Will this pattern continue forever, or are there final, elementary building blocks? And if there are elementary building blocks, are these particles or are they 'strings' as many recent theories claim? These are the central questions of the part of physics called particle physics.

Objectives

By the end of this chapter you should be able to:

- state the meaning of the term *elementary particle*;
- identify the three classes of elementary particles, the *quarks*, the *leptons* and the *exchange particles*;
- understand the meaning of *quantum numbers*;
- state the meaning of the term *antiparticle*;
- classify particles according to their *spin*;
- understand the *Pauli exclusion principle* and how it is applied;
- understand and apply the *Heisenberg uncertainty principle* for energy and time;
- appreciate the meaning of the term *virtual particle*;
- describe the *fundamental interactions*;
- state the meaning of the term *interaction vertex*;
- understand what is meant by *Feynman diagrams*;
- draw *Feynman diagrams* in order to represent various physical processes;
- apply the *Heisenberg uncertainty principle* in order to derive the range of an interaction.

Particles and antiparticles

Ordinary matter, such as the chair on which you sit, the air that you breathe and your own body, is made using very, very many copies of just three particles, the proton, the neutron and the electron. We know that protons and neutrons are made of smaller particles called **quarks**. The proton and neutron are thus composite particles. The electron, on the other hand, is still believed to be an **elementary particle**.

▶ A particle is called *elementary* if it is not made out of any smaller component particles.

Two elementary particles of the same kind, i.e. two electrons, for example, are *completely identical*. There is no way one can tell the difference between an electron created one second after the Big Bang and an electron created by rubbing a plastic rod with fur today.

In the 1950s and 1960s hundreds of other particles were discovered. These are very unstable particles and so are not found in ordinary matter. A few of these are the pions (π^+, π^-, π^0), the kaons (K^+, K^-, K^0), the etas (η, η'), the hyperons (Σ^+, Σ^-, Σ^0), the Ω^- and hundreds of others. These particles decay with half-lives ranging from 10^{-10} s to 10^{-24} s. Making sense out of all these particles was the main problem of particle physics in the 1960s.

The elementary particles

Almost a century of painstaking experimental and theoretical work has resulted in what we believe (today) to be the list of the elementary particles of nature. This picture, one day, may very well change. There are three classes of elementary particles:

Quarks There are six types (or 'flavours') of quarks. They are denoted by u, d, s, c, b and t, and are called up, down, strange, charmed, bottom and top, respectively. All of these have electric charge. The up (u) quark is the lightest and the top (t) quark is the heaviest. There is solid experimental evidence for the existence of all six flavours of quarks. A quark can combine with an antiquark to form a *meson*. Three quarks can combine to form a *baryon*. The proton is a baryon made out of two u quarks and one d quark. The neutron is a baryon made out of two d quarks and one u quark. (See Option J3.)

Leptons There are six of these as well: the electron and its neutrino, the muon and its neutrino, and the tau and its neutrino. They are denoted by e^-, ν_e, μ^-, ν_μ, and τ^-, ν_τ. We have seen the electron and the electron neutrino before when we learned about beta decay. The muon is heavier than the electron, and the tau is heavier than the muon. The three neutrinos were once thought to be massless, just like the photon. There is now conclusive evidence that in fact they have a very small mass. There is solid experimental evidence for the existence of all six leptons.

Exchange particles – This class of elementary particles contains the photon (denoted by γ), which we have met before. As we will see in detail later, the photon is intimately related to the electromagnetic interaction. We also have the particles $W^\pm$ and Z^0, called the W and Z bosons. Again, we will discuss how these particles are intimately related to the weak interaction. Then we have eight particles called **gluons** that are related to the strong or colour interaction. Finally, there is the **graviton**, which is related to the gravitational force or interaction. There is solid experimental evidence for the existence of all exchange particles except for the graviton.

We must also mention the Higgs particle. It is not known if this particle is elementary and it is not normally listed as such. This mysterious particle is very much needed, as we will see later, but it has not yet been detected experimentally. The new generation of particle accelerator experiments may very well provide evidence for this particle as well.

The quarks and leptons are particles that together account for what is ordinarily called 'matter', and the exchange particles are associated with interactions or forces. All the above information is summarized in the Tables J1.1–J1.3. (Spin will be discussed on page 721.) In the tables, electric charge is given in units of e (1.6×10^{-19} C), mass is given in MeV c^{-2}, and spin in units of $\frac{h}{2\pi}$.

Quark flavour	Symbol	Electric charge/e	Rest mass/ MeV c^{-2}	Spin/$\frac{h}{2\pi}$
Up	u	$+\frac{2}{3}$	330	$\frac{1}{2}$
Down	d	$-\frac{1}{3}$	333	$\frac{1}{2}$
Strange	s	$-\frac{1}{3}$	486	$\frac{1}{2}$
Charmed	c	$+\frac{2}{3}$	1 500	$\frac{1}{2}$
Bottom	b	$-\frac{1}{3}$	4 700	$\frac{1}{2}$
Top	t	$+\frac{2}{3}$	175 500	$\frac{1}{2}$

Table J1.1 The quarks. Because of quark confinement (see Option J3) the very notion of quark mass is somewhat uncertain and beyond the scope of this book. This is less of a problem for the heavier quarks (c, b and t).

Lepton	Symbol	Electric charge/e	Rest mass/ MeV c^{-2}	Spin/$\frac{h}{2\pi}$
Electron	e^-	−1	0.511	$\frac{1}{2}$
Electron neutrino	ν_e	0		$\frac{1}{2}$
Muon	μ^-	−1	106	$\frac{1}{2}$
Muon neutrino	ν_μ	0		$\frac{1}{2}$
Tau	τ^-	−1	1 780	$\frac{1}{2}$
Tau neutrino	ν_τ	0		$\frac{1}{2}$

Table J1.2 The leptons.

Exchange particle	Symbol	Electric charge/e	Rest mass/ GeV c^{-2}	Spin/$\frac{h}{2\pi}$	Associated interaction
Photon	γ	0	0	1	Electromagnetic
W bosons	W^+	+1	80.4	1	Weak
	W^-	−1	80.4	1	Weak
Z boson	Z^0	0	91.2	1	Weak
Gluons	G_{ij}	0	0	1	Strong (colour)
Graviton	g	0	0	2	Gravitational

Table J1.3 The exchange particles.

Quantum numbers

Quantum 'numbers' are numbers (or properties) used to characterize particles. There is one **quantum number** that we know already – that for electric charge. If we use a unit of electric charge equal to $e = 1.6 \times 10^{-19}$ C then we know that the electric quantum number for the electron is -1, for the proton $+1$, for the neutron 0, and so on. Some (but not all) quantum numbers are conserved in interactions (i.e. the total number before the reaction is the same as that after the reaction). The quantum number for electric charge is always conserved.

A second quantum number is that of flavour. Unlike charge, this is not specified by an actual numerical value. Only quarks carry flavour, and we have seen that there are six types of flavour called up, down, strange, charm, bottom and top. We may think of flavour as a kind of 'weak charge'. Flavour is conserved in some but not all interactions.

We will introduce many other quantum numbers as we go along. Option J3 will introduce the quantum numbers for colour, strangeness, baryon number and generation lepton number.

Antiparticles

In addition to the elementary particles we have listed in Tables J1.1–J1.3, we have the **antiparticles** of all of the above. To every particle there corresponds an antiparticle of the same mass as the particle but of *opposite electric charge* (and opposite all other quantum numbers). The existence of antiparticles was predicted theoretically by Paul Dirac in 1928. The first antiparticle to be discovered experimentally was the positron, the antiparticle of the electron. The positron was discovered in 1932 by Carl Anderson (1905–1991). If a particle has zero electric charge then, as we will see, the antiparticle can still be distinguished because of quantum numbers other than charge; for example, antineutrinos differ from neutrinos because they have opposite lepton number (see

Option J4). But some particles are their own antiparticle, e.g. the photon and the graviton. Particles that are their own antiparticles are therefore necessarily electrically neutral.

Antimatter is material made up of antiparticles. Whenever antimatter comes into contact with matter, it will annihilate, releasing energy. It is thought that the early universe contained almost equal numbers of particles and antiparticles. Today, however, we observe a predominance of matter over antimatter: this will be discussed later.

Spin

In classical mechanics, a body of mass m moving along a circle of radius r with speed v has a property called angular momentum. This is defined to be

$$L = mvr$$

This quantity has units of J s. If the body spins around its own axis (like the earth, for example), it has additional angular momentum. Particles appear to have a similar property, measured also in units of J s, and this property was called **spin** by analogy with a spinning body in mechanics. But it must be emphasized right away that a particle's spin is *not* the same thing as the angular momentum of a spinning body. For elementary particles, spin is a consequence of Einstein's theory of relativity and does not have a classical counterpart. The spinning body is just a useful analogy – an elementary particle may be a point particle and a point particle cannot, literally, spin around its axis. All known particles have a spin that is a multiple of a basic unit. This unit is the quantity

$$\text{Unit of spin} = \frac{h}{2\pi}$$

i.e. Planck's constant h divided by 2π.

The second fact about spin is that particles fall into two separate classes when classified according to spin. All the known particles (composite as well as elementary) have a spin that is either an integral multiple of the basic unit or a half-integral multiple.

▶ Particles are called *bosons* if they have an integral spin, and they are called *fermions* if they have a half-integral spin.

Quarks, leptons (e.g. the electron), protons and neutrons are **fermions**, whereas the photon is a **boson**.

A particle that has spin is denoted by a circle with an arrow through it (Figure J1.1). The length of the arrow does not signify anything. In the presence of a magnetic field B, particles with spin will align their spin parallel or antiparallel to the direction of the B field.

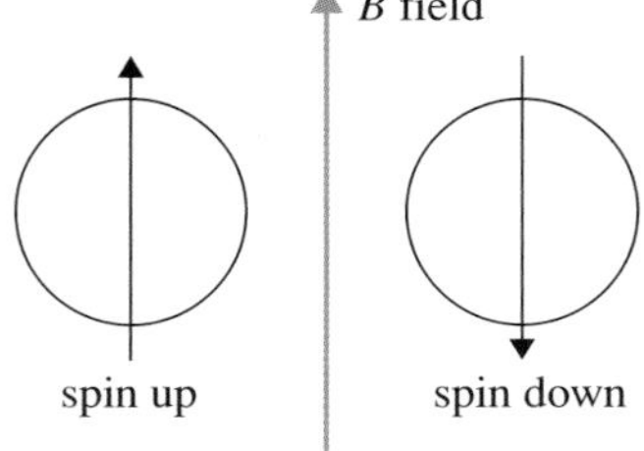

Figure J1.1 Particles with spin in a magnetic field.

The Pauli exclusion principle

We have seen that elementary particles are characterized by quantum numbers. In 1930, the Austrian physicist Wolfgang Pauli discovered an important principle that bears his name:

▶ It is impossible for two identical *fermions* (particles with half-integral spin) to occupy the same quantum state if they have the same quantum numbers.

This is why the inner shell of any atom can contain at most two electrons. Electrons are fermions and so the **Pauli exclusion principle** applies to them. In the inner shell the one quantum number that can distinguish two electrons is the spin. Since the spin of the electron is $\frac{1}{2}$, there are just two quantum states available: one in which the spin is 'up' and another in which it is 'down'. Thus in the inner shell we can have two electrons of opposite spin. In other shells, the electrons have angular momentum (because the electrons 'orbit' the nucleus) and so can be distinguished through different values of their angular momentum. Therefore more than two electrons can occupy the outer shells.

The Heisenberg uncertainty principle for time and energy

In 1928 the German physicist Werner Heisenberg discovered one of the fundamental principles of quantum mechanics, now called the Heisenberg uncertainty principle. The version of the principle that will concern us here is that which applies to simultaneous measurements of energy and time. According to Heisenberg, measurements of the energy of a particle or of an energy level are subject to an uncertainty. This uncertainty is not the result of random or systematic errors. Even in an ideal world in which these types of uncertainty were absent, there would still be an uncertainty in the measurement of the energy as a result of a law of nature. The very process of measurement necessarily creates an uncertainty in the quantities being measured.

Consider then the measurement of the energy of a particle. The measurement must be completed within a certain interval of time that we may call Δt. Heisenberg proved that the uncertainty in the measurement of the energy ΔE is related to Δt through the **Heisenberg uncertainty principle**

$$\Delta E\,\Delta t \geq \frac{h}{4\pi}$$

This says that, the shorter the time interval within which the measurement is made, the greater the uncertainty in the measured value of the energy. To have a very small uncertainty in energy would require a very long time for the measurement of energy.

Example question

Q1

An electron spends on average 1.0 ns in an excited energy state in an atom. What is the uncertainty in the value of the energy of the excited level?

Answer

To measure the energy of a particular energy state, we must observe the electron in that state for a length of time. Since the electron cannot exist in that state for longer than about 1.0 ns, we deduce that at most $\Delta t = 1.0$ ns. Then we get

$$\Delta E \geq \frac{h}{4\pi\,\Delta t} = \frac{6.6 \times 10^{-34}}{4\pi \times 1.0 \times 10^{-9}}$$

$$= 5.3 \times 10^{-26}\ \text{J} = 3.3 \times 10^{-7}\text{eV}$$

The *minimum* uncertainty in the energy is thus 3.3×10^{-7} eV.

There is, however, a subtler, and for our purposes more useful, interpretation of the energy–time Heisenberg uncertainty principle. We know that total energy is always conserved. But suppose, for a moment, that in a certain process energy conservation is violated. For example, assume that in a certain collision the total energy after the collision is larger than the energy before by an amount ΔE. The Heisenberg uncertainty principle claims that this is in fact possible (!) provided the process does not last longer than a time interval Δt given by $\Delta t \approx \frac{h}{4\pi\Delta E}$. In other words, energy conservation can be violated provided the time it takes for that to happen is not too long.

Consider a ball of mass 1.0 kg and total energy 9.0 J. It bounces up and down on the floor. A wall next to the ball is 1.0 m high. To make it over the wall and to the other side, the ball would have to have a total energy of $mgh = 1 \times 10 \times 1 = 10$ J. In classical physics we would therefore conclude that it is impossible for the ball to make it over. Doing so would violate energy conservation by an amount 1.0 J.

According to the Heisenberg uncertainty principle, the ball *can* make it over the wall provided this happens within a time interval given by, approximately,

$$\Delta t \approx \frac{h}{4\pi\,\Delta E} = \frac{6.6 \times 10^{-34}}{4\pi \times 1.0} = 5.3 \times 10^{-35}\ \text{s}$$

This time interval is ridiculously small for a macroscopic object such as a ball. There is no way that a 1.0 kg ball can make it over the wall in this short a time interval because to do so it would have to move many times faster than the speed of light. The ball cannot make it over the wall even though theoretically it could, according to the Heisenberg uncertainty principle. Therefore we can be assured that, in macroscopic physics, total energy is conserved!

But consider now an electron of total energy 1.0 eV that is classically forbidden to go over a 'wall' of total energy 2.0 eV. This would violate energy by an amount $\Delta E = 1.0$ eV. The time interval over which this has to happen is

$$\Delta t \approx \frac{h}{4\pi\,\Delta E} = \frac{6.6 \times 10^{-34}}{4\pi \times 1.0 \times 1.6 \times 10^{-19}}$$

$$= 3.3 \times 10^{-16}\ \text{s}$$

This is still a small time interval but is 19 orders of magnitude *longer* than that for the ball. A fast electron ($v = 6 \times 10^{6}\ \text{m s}^{-1}$) can make it over the wall in this short time and it does. This is the basis of the tunnelling electron microscope, an instrument that can 'see' atoms.

Virtual particles

We have seen that the Heisenberg uncertainty principle allows for violations of the law of conservation of energy by amounts ΔE provided the violations do not last longer than time intervals of about $\Delta t \approx \frac{h}{4\pi\,\Delta E}$. This is irrelevant for macroscopic objects but not so for microscopic elementary particles.

Let us then consider the possibility of a free electron emitting a photon. We may represent this as in Figure J1.2. This process actually violates the law of conservation of energy (see Option H, Relativity). It cannot take place unless the photon that is emitted is very quickly (i.e. within a time interval $\Delta t \approx \frac{h}{4\pi\,\Delta E}$) absorbed by something else so that the energy violation (and the photon itself) becomes undetectable. Precisely because this photon violates energy conservation, it is called a **virtual** photon. Therefore the process represented by Figure J1.2, although classically impossible, is nevertheless possible within quantum theory.

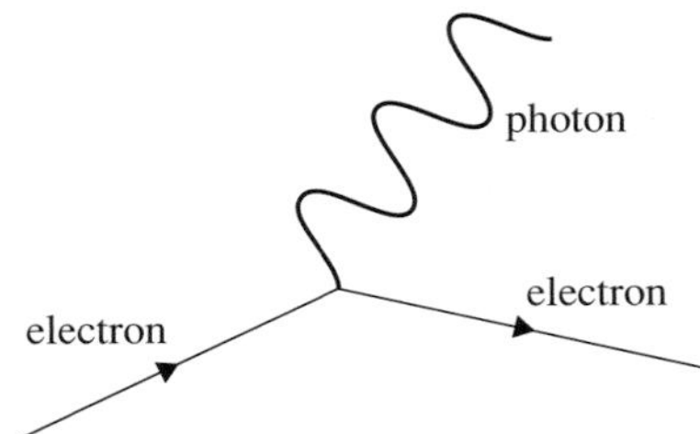

Figure J1.2 A free electron emitting a virtual photon.

Interactions and exchange particles

We saw that a free electron can emit a (virtual) photon provided the photon is very quickly absorbed by, say, another electron. We may represent this process pictorially as in Figure J1.3. Particle physics now interprets this diagram in the following novel way.

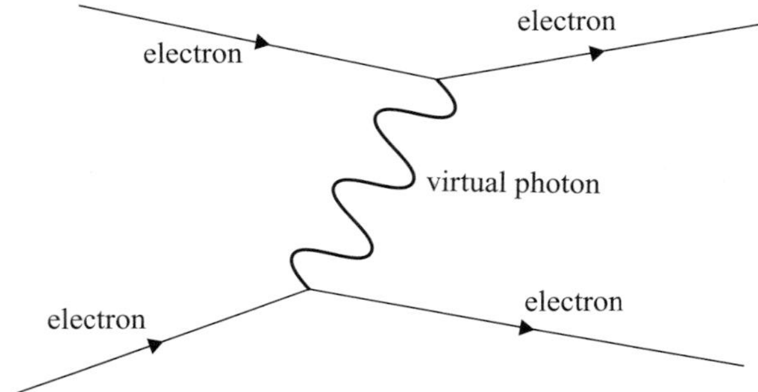

Figure J1.3 Exchange of a virtual photon in the interaction between electrons.

Because the first electron emitted a photon, it changed direction a bit in order to conserve momentum. Similarly, the second photon also changed direction, since it absorbed a photon.

Looked at from a large distance away, the change in direction of the two electrons can be interpreted as the result of a force or interaction between the two electrons. We know, of course, that two electrons will exert repelling forces on each other according to Coulomb's law. The particle physics view of the situation is that Coulomb's law is the exchange of a virtual photon between the electrons.

► The electromagnetic interaction is the *exchange of a virtual photon* between charged particles. The exchanged photon is not observable.

Similar things hold for the other interactions, as we will discuss on page 727.

Basic interaction vertices

As we have mentioned in the core section of the book, there are four fundamental forces or interactions in nature. The interactions and the particles that participate in each interaction as well as their relative strength (known as the interaction strength) are summarized in Table J1.4.

Interaction	Interaction acts on	Exchange particle(s)	Relative strength
Electromagnetic	Particles with electric charge	Photon	$\frac{1}{137}$
Weak	Quarks and leptons only	W and Z bosons	10^{-6}
Strong (colour)	Quarks only	Gluons	1
Gravitational	Particles with mass	Graviton	10^{-38}

Table J1.4 The fundamental interactions and the exchange particles that participate in them.

Since the early 1970s (and as we will discuss in some detail later) the electromagnetic and weak nuclear interactions have been shown to be two faces of the same interaction, called the **electroweak** interaction. So there are in fact three fundamental interactions:

- the electroweak interaction;
- the strong (colour) interaction;
- the gravitational interaction.

The gravitational interaction is the least relevant for particle physics because the masses of the particles are so small. The gravitational interaction will therefore be ignored in what follows, and we will meet it again only in Option J5. In this chapter, however, the electromagnetic and weak interactions will be treated as distinct.

At a fundamental level, particle physics views an interaction between two elementary particles in terms of **interaction vertices**. The fundamental interaction vertex of the electromagnetic interaction, for example, is denoted in Figure J1.4, in which the wavy line

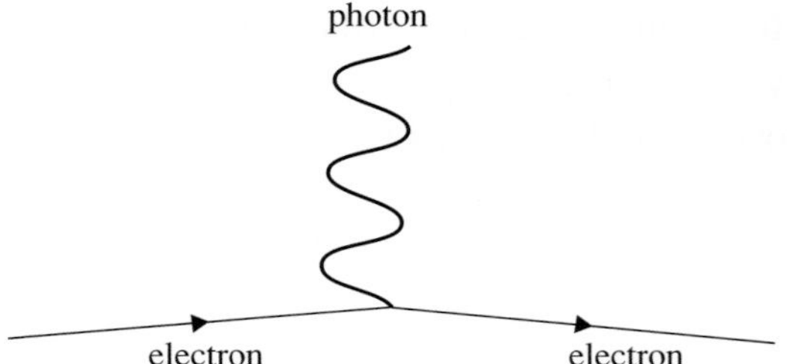

Figure J1.4 Fundamental interaction vertex of the electromagnetic interaction.

represents a photon and the straight line with an arrow to the right represents an electron. (A positron would be denoted with a straight line with an arrow to the left.) From this basic vertex, all phenomena associated with electrodynamics can be deduced!

It is helpful to think of a time axis along with this diagram, so that time increases as we move, say, to the right of the diagram. Then by redrawing the basic vertex in any way we please, by bending or rotating the lines, we can depict various processes in electrodynamics.
For example, we can draw the diagrams in Figure J1.5.

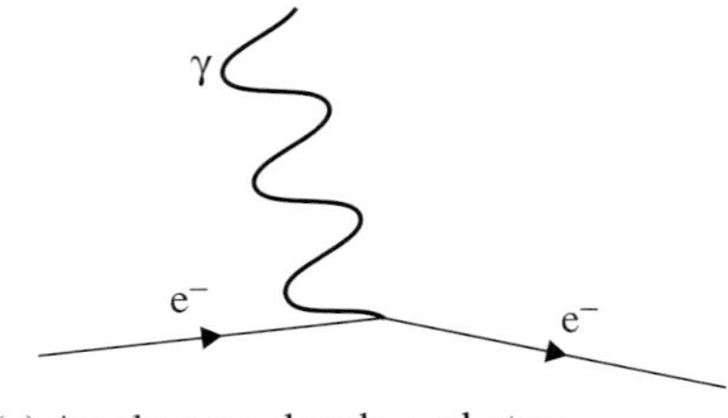

(a) An electron absorbs a photon

γ

e⁺

e⁺

(b) A positron absorbs a photon

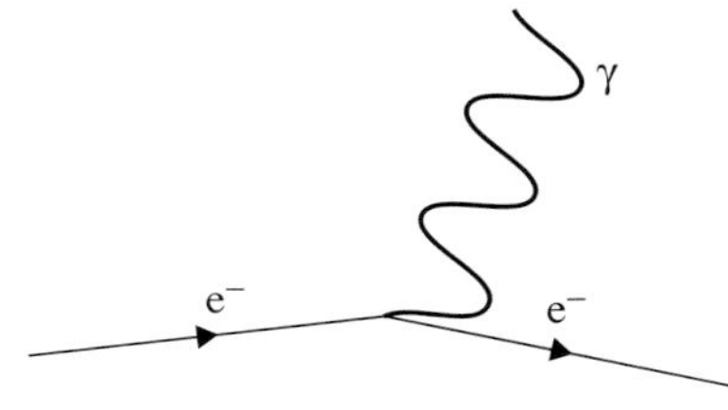

(c) An electron emits a photon

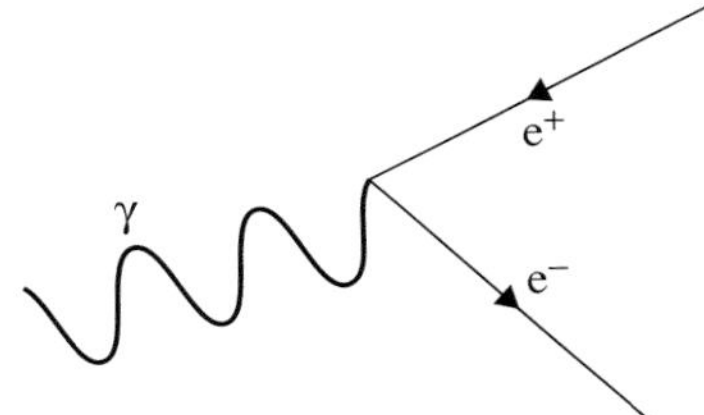

(d) A photon materializes into an electron–positron pair

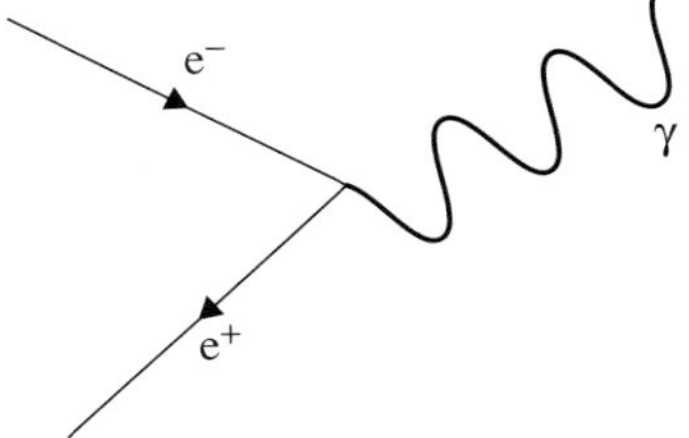

(e) An electron and a positron collide, annihilate each other and produce a photon

Figure J1.5 Some examples of interaction vertices (here γ = photon, e^- = electron, e^+ = positron).

Because the arrows on the positron are drawn in the opposite direction to those on the electron, we sometimes say that positrons travel backwards in time. But this is just an expression. The positrons, like all particles, move forwards in time.

Notice that, at an interaction vertex, electric charge is conserved. That is to say, the total electric charge going into a vertex equals the total electric charge leaving the vertex. Therefore, it is not possible to have a vertex such as those in Figure J1.6.

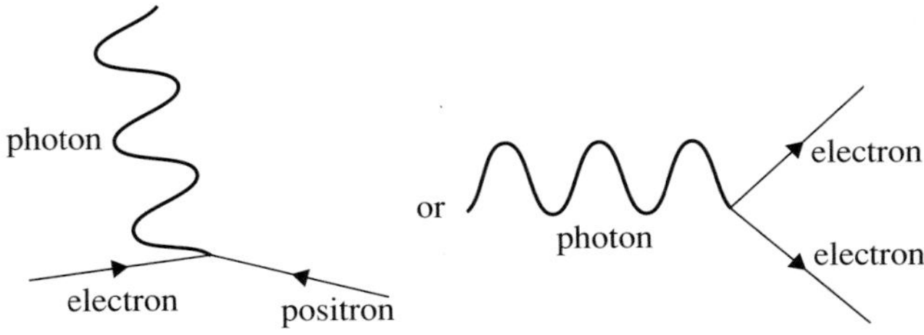

Figure J1.6 Two *impossible* vertices that do not conserve electric charge.

The theory describing the interactions of electrons and positrons through the exchange of photons is called **quantum electrodynamics** (QED).

Feynman diagrams

In the 1950s the American physicist Richard P. Feynman (Figure J1.7) introduced a pictorial representation of particle interactions. These representations are now called **Feynman diagrams**. The idea is to use interaction vertices in order to build up possible physical processes. For example, let us see how one electron can scatter off another electron. The basic process is represented in Figure J1.8.

Figure J1.7 Richard P. Feynman.

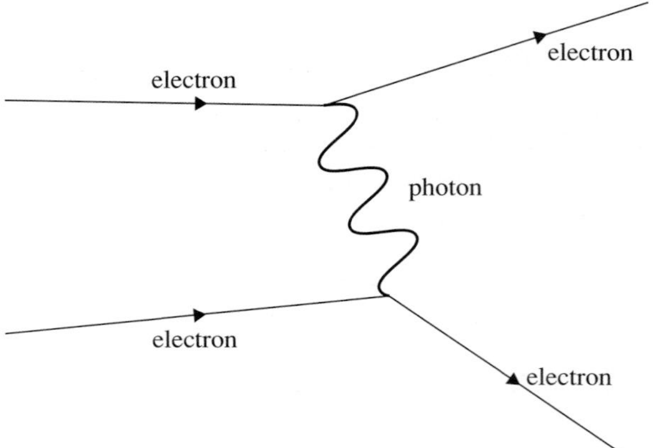

Figure J1.8 Feynman diagram for electron–electron scattering.

Figure J1.8 is not just a picture, however. It represents a very definite mathematical expression called the *amplitude* of the process. The square of the amplitude gives the probability of the process actually taking place. We will not learn how to calculate this mathematical expression for the amplitude here! We will simply learn that we will assign to each vertex a quantity called the *strength of the interaction*. For the electromagnetic interaction, the basic vertex is assigned the value $\sqrt{\alpha_{EM}}$, where $\alpha_{EM} \approx \frac{1}{137}$ and is closely related to the charge of the electron. The amplitude of the diagram is then the product of the $\sqrt{\alpha_{EM}}$ for each vertex that appears.

In the electron–electron scattering process of Figure J1.8, there are two interaction vertices, and so the amplitude of the diagram is proportional to

$$\sqrt{\alpha_{EM}} \times \sqrt{\alpha_{EM}} = \alpha_{EM}$$

The same physical process can also take place through many other diagrams, e.g. those shown in Figure J1.9. Notice carefully that these diagrams are simply built out of the basic interaction vertex and nothing more.

But all the diagrams in Figure J1.9 contain four interaction vertices, and so the amplitude for these is proportional to

$$\sqrt{\alpha_{EM}} \times \sqrt{\alpha_{EM}} \times \sqrt{\alpha_{EM}} \times \sqrt{\alpha_{EM}} = \alpha_{EM}^2$$

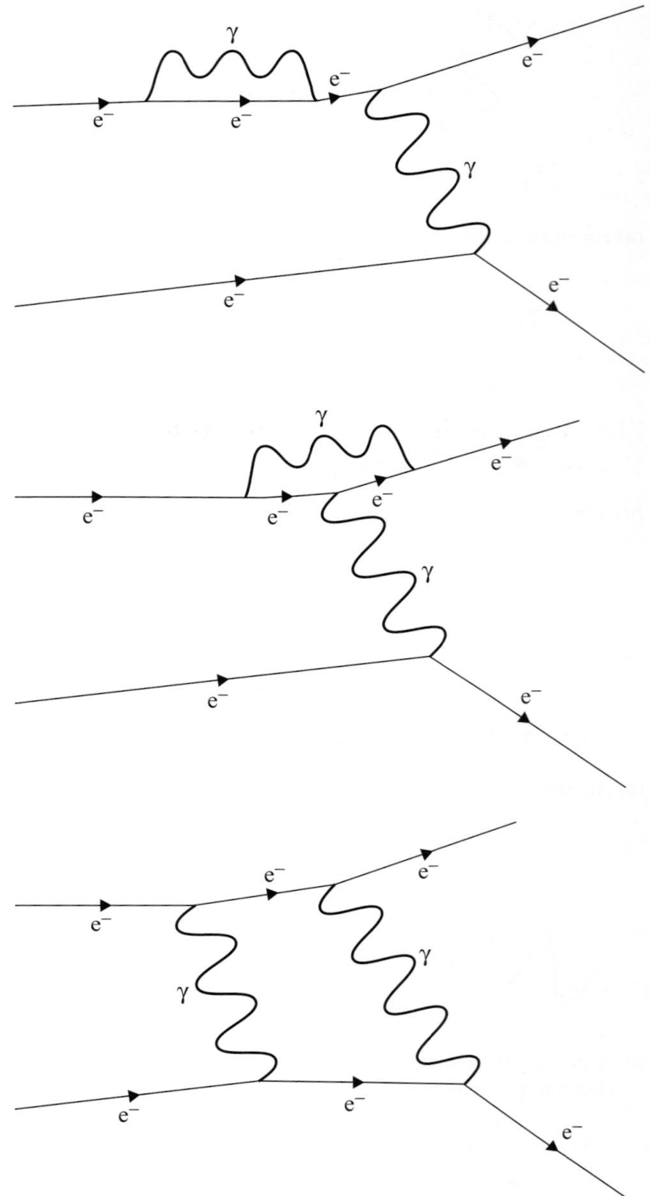

Figure J1.9 Other Feynman diagrams that result in the same physical process as shown in Figure J1.8.

Since $\alpha_{EM} \approx \frac{1}{137}$, i.e. a small number less than 1, the processes with four interaction vertices are less likely to occur. To a first approximation, it is sufficient to examine the diagram with two vertices only. If a better approximation to the answer is required, then diagrams with more and more vertices must be included. The larger the number of vertices, the greater the amount of calculation required.

The introduction of Feynman diagrams has made calculations of the probabilities for various processes much simpler and is a major advance in particle physics. In the words of Julian Schwinger (who along with Sin-Itiro Tomonaga shared the Nobel prize in physics with Feynman in 1965) 'the introduction of Feynman diagrams has given calculating power to the masses'. A famous example is the Klein–Nishina formula for the scattering of a photon off an electron (the Compton effect). Klein and Nishina took six months to calculate the details of this process in 1929. With Feynman diagrams this can be done in less than two hours by any graduate student in physics!

Building Feynman diagrams

Using the basic interaction vertex for the electromagnetic interaction, we can build up complicated processes. All we need are the following ingredients:

- the basic interaction vertex;
- lines with arrows to represent electrons and positrons;
- wavy lines to represent photons.

One such process is the scattering of light by light. That is, a photon scattering off another photon. This is a purely quantum process. It cannot be described classically. But with the basic vertex, we can draw the diagram in Figure J1.10. The particles are electrons or positrons. The amplitude for this process is α_{EM}^2, so it is quite rare.

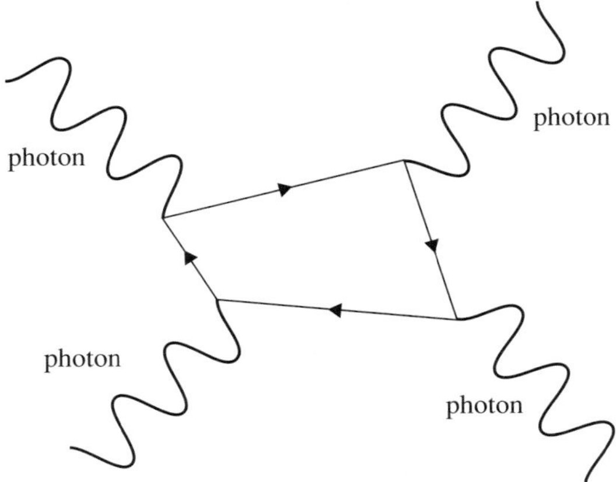

Figure J1.10 Feynman diagram for photon–photon scattering.

Feynman diagrams for other interactions

The electromagnetic interaction is a simple interaction because it has only one interaction vertex. The weak and strong (colour) interactions are complex because they have many vertices. To build Feynman diagrams for other interaction processes is therefore correspondingly more complex.

The basic interaction vertices that we will consider for the weak interaction involve the W or Z boson along with two fermions (quarks or leptons, in fact) f_1 and f_2 (see Figure J1.11). Here for the W vertex f_1, f_2 = quark or lepton, and for the Z vertex the incoming and outgoing particles are the same and f = quark or lepton.

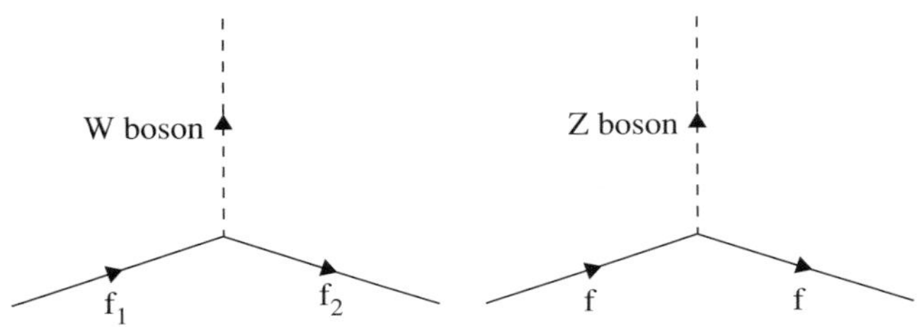

Figure J1.11 Basic interaction vertices for the weak interaction.

You do not have to remember these vertices – in the IBO examination they will be given to you if they are needed. Some examples are given in Figure J1.12.

We can therefore draw the Feynman diagram for beta decay in which a neutron decays into a proton. We know that (1) we must produce an electron and an electron antineutrino and (2) a d quark inside the neutron must turn into a u quark. Then we must have a diagram such as that in Figure J1.13.

We have used the weak vertex twice. In the first case, the d quark turns into a u quark by emitting a virtual W^- boson. The electric charge going into the vertex is $-\frac{1}{3}e$. The electric charge leaving the vertex is $+\frac{2}{3}e$ for the u quark and $-e$ for the W^-. The total charge leaving the first vertex is therefore $-\frac{1}{3}e$, consistent with charge conservation.

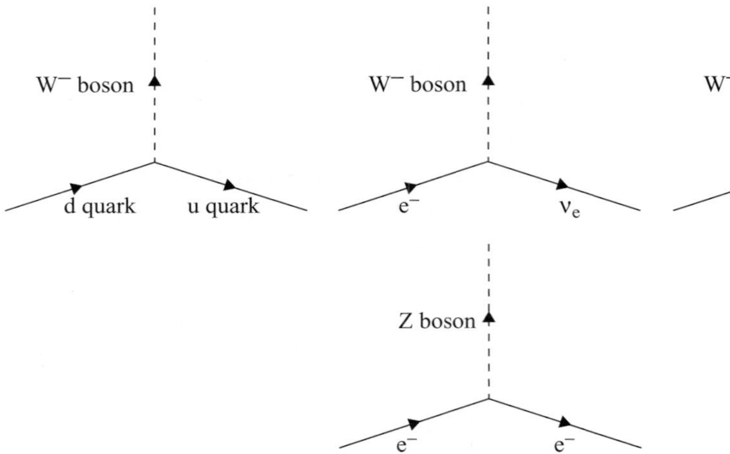

Figure J1.12 Examples of interaction vertices for the weak interaction.

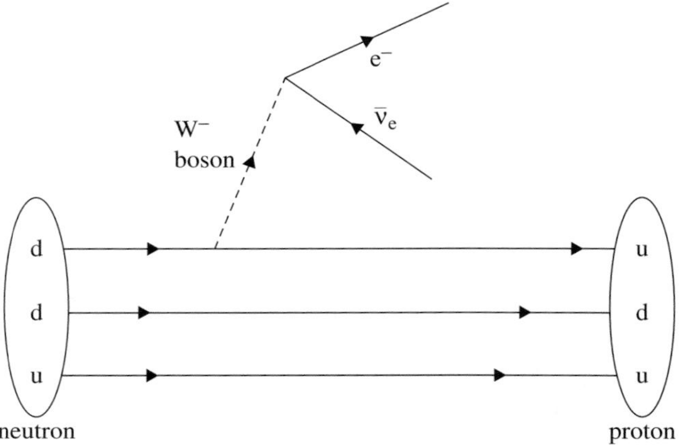

Figure J1.13 Feynman diagram for beta decay.

In the second vertex, the virtual W^- decays into an electron and antineutrino, again conserving electric charge (and lepton number, as we will see in Option J4).

The strong (colour) interaction is also complex. One interaction vertex is similar to the electromagnetic vertex where electrons are replaced by quarks and the photon by gluons (see Figure J1.14). Notice that the flavour of the quark does not change in this interaction (unlike the case of the weak interaction involving the W boson). Thus if the incoming quark is a u quark, the outgoing quark will be a u as well.

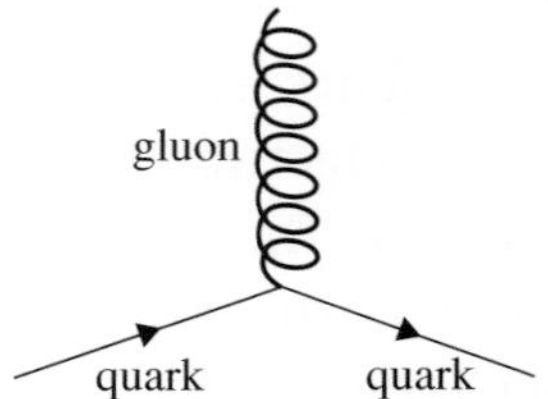

Figure J1.14 One interaction vertex for the strong (colour) interaction.

The complexity of the strong (colour) interaction is that there are also vertices involving purely gluons such as those shown in Figure J1.15. We will discuss strong (colour) interactions in more detail when we learn about colour in Option J3.

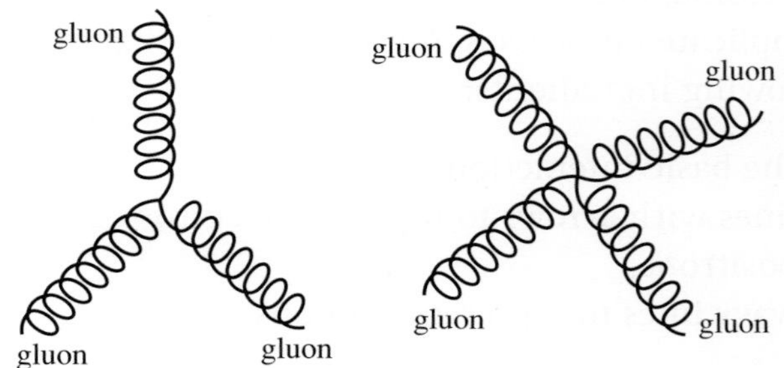

Figure J1.15 Two other interaction vertices for the strong (colour) interaction.

The range of an interaction

Consider the diagram in Figure J1.16 in which two particles interact through the exchange of the particle shown by the wavy line. Let the mass of this particle be m.

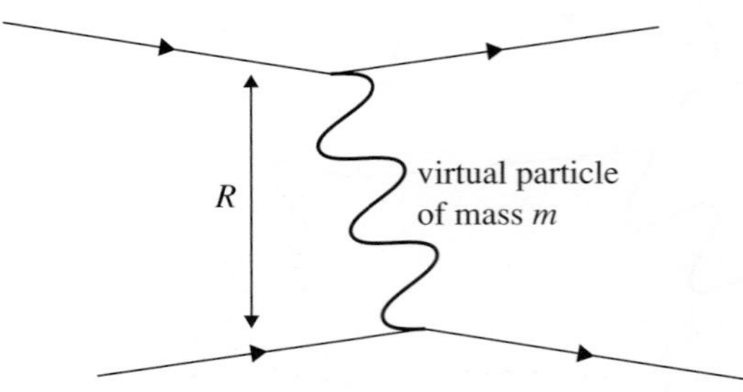

Figure J1.16 Estimating the range of the interaction between two particles.

The fastest the virtual particle can travel is the speed of light c. If R is the range of the interaction, then the virtual particle will reach the second particle in a time no smaller than $\frac{R}{c}$. The energy that will be exchanged will be of the order of mc^2. For the purpose of the estimate, taking uncertainties of order $\frac{R}{c}$ in the time and mc^2 in the energy, we then have that by the Heisenberg uncertainty principle:

$$mc^2 \times \frac{R}{c} \approx \frac{h}{4\pi}$$

and hence the range of the interaction is approximately given by

$$R \approx \frac{h}{4\pi mc}$$

This explains why the electromagnetic interaction (which involves the exchange of the massless photon) has a range that is infinite, whereas the weak interaction (which involves the exchange of massive W and Z bosons) will have a short range. In fact, since we know that the W boson has a mass of about 80 GeV c^{-2} it follows that we can determine the range of the weak interaction:

$$R \approx \frac{h}{4\pi mc}$$

$$= \frac{6.6 \times 10^{-34}}{4\pi\left(\frac{80\times10^9}{(3\times10^8)^2} \times 1.6 \times 10^{-19}\right)3 \times 10^8}\,\text{m}$$

$$= 10^{-18}\ \text{m}$$

? QUESTIONS

1 Discuss whether it is correct that all electrically neutral particles are their own antiparticles? Give examples to support your answer.

2 Particles are divided into fermions and bosons. What property of particles is used in order to make this classification?

3 (a) State the Pauli exclusion principle.
(b) Using this principle explain why the innermost shell of an atom can have at most two electrons.

4 Very large numbers of photons in a laser beam occupy the same energy state. Explain why this is not in violation of the Pauli exclusion principle.

5 The idea of a particle exchanged in an interaction is sometimes explained in terms of the following picture. You stand on ice (no friction) and throw a heavy ball to a friend. Throwing the ball makes you move away. When your friend catches the ball, he moves away. This picture explains a repulsive force. How would you change the picture to explain an attractive force?

6 (a) Describe what is meant by a Feynman diagram.
(b) Draw Feynman diagrams to represent the electromagnetic processes (i) $e^- + e^+ \rightarrow e^- + e^+$ and (ii) $e^- + e^+ \rightarrow \gamma + \gamma$.

7 Use the electromagnetic vertex to draw a Feynman diagram for the scattering of a photon off an electron.

8 A meson has quark content $u\bar{u}$.
(a) State the electric charge of the meson.
The meson is at rest and decays into photons.
(b) Explain why the meson cannot decay into just one photon.
The meson in fact decays into two photons.
(c) Draw the Feynman diagram for this decay.

9 Beta-minus decay involves the decay of a neutron into a proton according to the reaction $n \rightarrow p^+ + e^- + \bar{\nu}_e$.
(a) Describe this decay in terms of quarks.
(b) Draw a Feynman diagram for the process.

10 Figure J1.17 represents the beta-plus (e^+) decay of a proton.

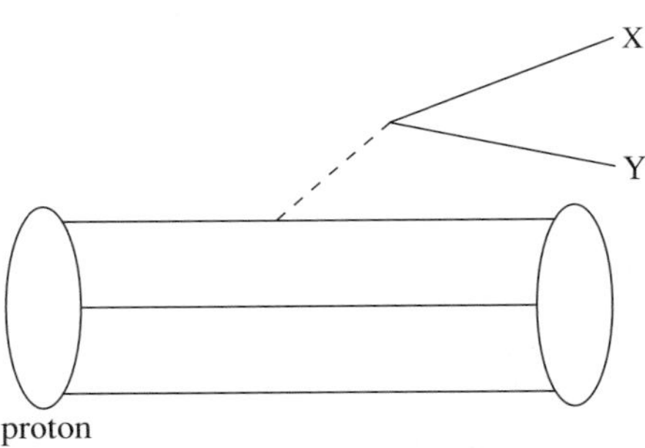

Figure J1.17 For question 10.

(a) Identify the quarks making up the neutron.
(b) State the name of the particle represented by the wavy line.
(c) Identify the particles denoted by X and Y in the diagram.

11 Using the basic weak interaction vertex involving a W boson and two fermions given in Figure J1.11, draw Feynman diagrams to represent the following processes:
(a) $\mu^- \rightarrow e^- + \bar{\nu}_e + \nu_\mu$;
(b) $e^- + \bar{\nu}_e \rightarrow \mu^- + \bar{\nu}_\mu$;
(c) $\pi^+ \rightarrow \mu^+ + \nu_\mu$ (quark structure of positive pion is $u\bar{d}$);
(d) $K^- \rightarrow \mu^- + \bar{\nu}_\mu$ (quark structure of negative kaon is $s\bar{u}$).

12 Using the basic weak interaction vertex involving a W boson and two fermions given in Figure J1.11, state three possible ways in which the W boson can decay.

13 Using the basic weak interaction vertex involving a Z boson and two fermions given in Figure J1.11, draw Feynman diagrams to represent the following processes:
(a) $e^- + e^+ \rightarrow \bar{\nu}_\mu + \nu_\mu$;
(b) $e^- + \nu_\mu \rightarrow e^- + \nu_\mu$;
(c) $e^- + e^+ \rightarrow e^- + e^+$.

14 Using the basic weak interaction vertex involving a Z boson and two fermions given in Figure J1.11, state three possible ways in which the Z boson can decay.

15 (a) Does the weak force act on mesons?
(b) Does it act on baryons?

16 The electromagnetic interaction strength is $\alpha_{EM} \approx \frac{1}{137}$ and that of the strong (colour) interaction is $\alpha_S \approx 1$. Explain how these numbers allow the calculation of Feynman diagrams with the smallest possible number of vertices for an electromagnetic interaction, whereas the colour interaction must necessarily involve all possible Feynman diagrams for the process.

17 (a) Does the electric force act on quarks?
(b) Does it act on neutrinos?

18 The neutron is electrically neutral. Could it possibly have electromagnetic interactions?

19 Neutrinos are electrically neutral. How do we distinguish neutrinos from antineutrinos?

20 What may be deduced about the mass of the graviton given that the gravitational interaction has infinite range?

21 (a) Explain how the Heisenberg uncertainty principle for energy and time can be used to estimate the range of an interaction by knowing the mass of the particle being exchanged.
(b) Using your answer in (a) explain why the electromagnetic interaction has infinite range.
(c) In the 1930s it was believed that the strong nuclear force involved the exchange of a massive particle called the pion. Estimate the mass of this particle from the known range of the strong nuclear interaction (i.e. about 10^{-15} m).

Detectors and accelerators

The models of particles and their interactions would remain just models were it not for the ingenuity of experimental particle physicists, who have devised ways and means to test them in detailed experiments. Experimenting with particle physics requires the acceleration of particles to very high energies and the development of sophisticated devices to detect the presence, and measure the properties, of the particles produced in the collisions in accelerators.

Objectives

By the end of this chapter you should be able to:

- appreciate the need for *high energies* in particle physics experiments;
- appreciate that the *resolution of tiny objects* requires high energies;
- outline the operation of the *linear accelerator*, the *cyclotron* and the *synchrotron*;
- discuss the *advantages and disadvantages* of each type of accelerator;
- understand the meaning of the term *available energy*;
- give a general description of the structure and function of a *particle detector*.

The need for high energies

We have seen in the previous chapter that the electromagnetic interaction allows for the process

$$e^- + e^+ \rightarrow \text{particle} + \text{antiparticle}$$

which can be represented by the Feynman diagram in Figure J2.1. We would describe this process as an electron and a positron colliding, annihilating each other into a virtual photon, and the virtual photon then rematerializing into a particle–antiparticle pair.

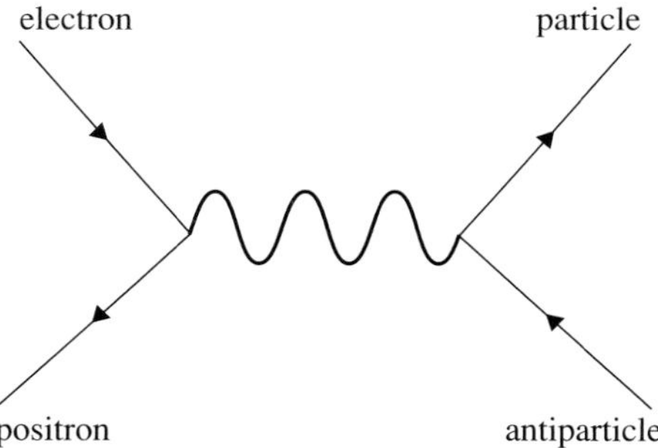

Figure J2.1 An electron–positron pair creating a new particle–antiparticle pair out of the vacuum.

It is very important to understand that the second pair is actually *created* out of the virtual photon. The pair did not exist before the interaction. Another way of saying the same thing is to say that the pair has been created out of the *vacuum*. This possibility is of enormous importance because it allows for the production of new and previously unknown particles.

Assume that the electron and the positron are moving with the same kinetic energy in opposite directions when they collide and annihilate. To produce the particle–antiparticle pair requires energy. To begin with, the energy needed is the energy of the particle and the antiparticle created at rest. According to Einstein, this energy is mc^2, the *rest energy*, for each. In addition, if the particle and antiparticle each has kinetic energy E_k after it is created, it follows that the total energy E that must be supplied is

$$E = 2(mc^2 + E_k)$$

The very minimum amount of energy needed is therefore

$$E_{min} = 2mc^2$$

when the particle–antiparticle pair is produced at rest. This energy has to come from the rest energy and the kinetic energy of the electron and the positron before the collision.

It is then clear that, if we wish to produce particles of large mass, very large amounts of kinetic energy are needed. In other words, the electron and the positron must be accelerated to very high kinetic energies. This requires the construction of appropriate machines – **particle accelerators**.

Resolution

A second point that must be taken into account is the following. Particle physics is interested in determining whether there is structure inside any one particle. How do we experimentally determine if the proton, say, is made out of smaller constituent particles? One way is to 'throw something' at the proton and see how that 'something' reacts. The simplest thing to do is to direct a photon or an electron at the proton.

Let λ be the wavelength of the photon or the de Broglie wavelength of the electron. The relation of λ to the size of the object being probed (the possible constituents of the proton in this case) is crucial in determining whether or not the constituents will be resolved. To 'see' the smaller constituents requires a short wavelength, comparable to the size of the constituents themselves (Figure J2.2).

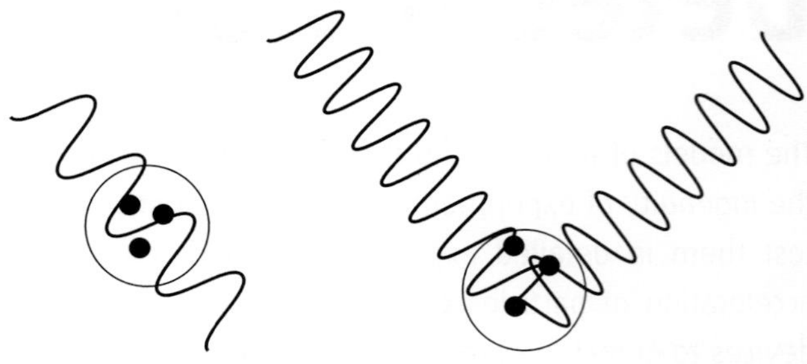

Figure J2.2 To resolve a particle of size d requires a wavelength of the same order of magnitude as d.

The long-wavelength photon continues undeflected along its original path. It has not seen the small objects in its path. The photon on the right though has a wavelength that is comparable to the size of the small objects in its path. This photon gets deflected. The deflection is a sign that objects of size comparable to the wavelength are present.

Since we expect the size of the constituents to be very small, we require a very small wavelength as well. But a short photon or de Broglie wavelength means, again, high energies.

For example, a photon whose wavelength is of order $\lambda \approx 10^{-15}$ m must have energy

$$\begin{aligned} E &= \frac{hc}{\lambda} \\ &= \frac{6.6 \times 10^{-34} \times 3 \times 10^{8}}{10^{-15}} \\ &\approx 2 \times 10^{-10}\ \text{J} \\ &\approx 10^{9}\ \text{eV} \\ &\approx 1\ \text{GeV} \end{aligned}$$

For an electron with de Broglie wavelength of order $\lambda \approx 10^{-15}$ m, the corresponding kinetic energy is also of the same order, about 1 GeV.

So again it is clear that particle physics has to deal with very high energies if it is going to be able either to create new heavy particles or to probe their inner structure.

Accelerators

We will examine three types of accelerators, the linear accelerator, the cyclotron and the synchrotron. Particle accelerators are called 'machines' by the people who build and use them.

The linear accelerator

In a **linear accelerator** (or linac), particles are accelerated along a straight path by electric fields. The particles move through a series of evacuated tubes as shown in Figure J2.3.

Advantage

- Linacs have lower energy losses due to synchrotron radiation compared with synchrotrons (see page 735).

Disadvantages

- Once the acceleration process starts, one cannot alter the collision time of the linac, as can be done with storage rings in synchrotrons.
- A very long accelerator is required to reach very high energies.

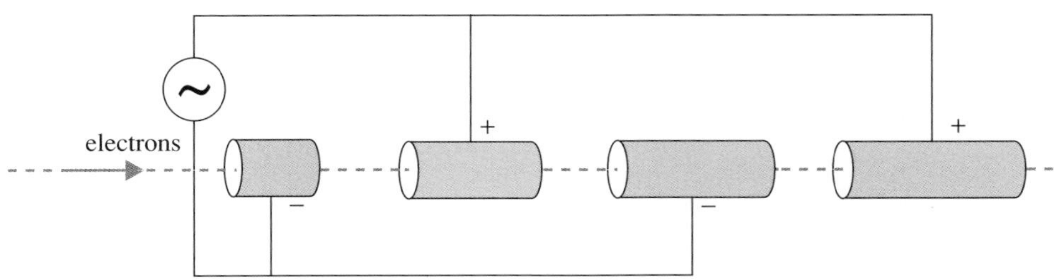

Figure J2.3 A schematic diagram of a linear accelerator showing the accelerating tubes and the alternating applied voltage.

The largest electron linear accelerator is the one at Stanford University in the USA and is called SLAC (Stanford Linear Accelerator). It is 3 km long and accelerates electrons to a total energy of 50 GeV.

An alternating voltage is applied across the gaps in between two consecutive tubes so that, as the electrons leave a tube, they see a positive voltage in the tube ahead. The electrons thus accelerate every time they move from one tube to the next. The electron spends the same time in each tube, because of the constant frequency of the alternating voltage applied to the tubes. So as the speed of the electrons increases, the length of the tubes must increase as well. But the electrons soon reach a speed practically equal to the speed of light, and so the length of the tubes remains constant from then on.

In a linear accelerator, either an accelerated beam of particles can strike a fixed target, or two beams (one of particles and the other of antiparticles) can be accelerated along the same straight line from opposite ends and made to collide with each other.

Figure J2.4 An aerial view of the SLAC complex.

At this energy the electrons move practically at the speed of light. The electrons are injected into the accelerator after they have been emitted by an electron gun, which is just a wire that emits electrons when it is heated.

The cyclotron

The **cyclotron** was invented by Ernest Lawrence at Berkeley in the USA in 1929, and first built in 1930. This type of accelerator is no longer used for particle physics research, but it is the model upon which newer accelerator designs were based.

The cyclotron consists of two hollow electrodes called 'D's (because their shape resembles the letter D), with a gap between them, placed in the uniform magnetic field between the poles of a cylindrical magnet (Figure J2.5). The

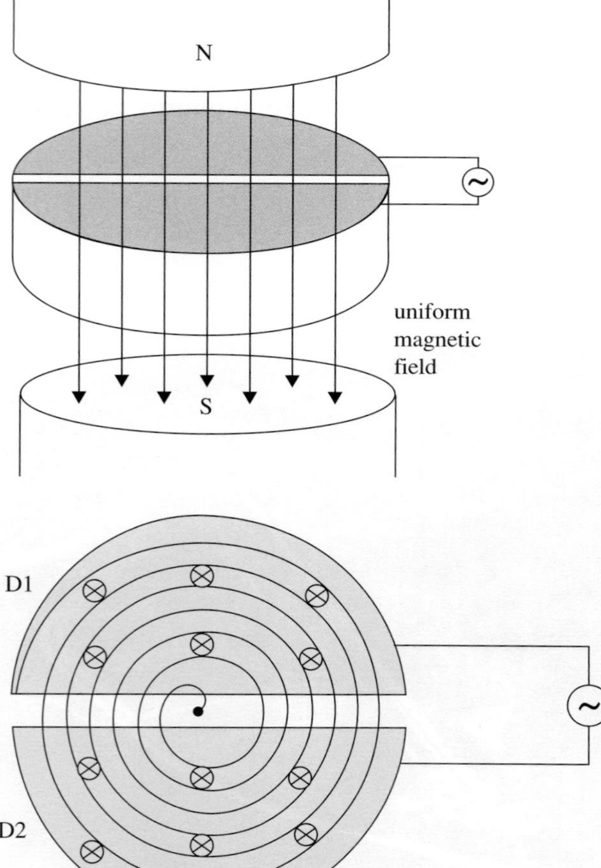

Figure J2.5 The charged particle is emitted at the centre and follows a 'spiral' path outwards as it gains speed.

particle to be accelerated starts at the centre of the 'D's. A source of alternating potential difference is established between the two 'D's. (For ease of reference, we shall call them D1 and D2, as in the diagram.)

Assume that the charge of the particle is positive. It is projected towards D1 with an initial speed v_0 and so will follow a circular arc in D1 because of the magnetic force it experiences. After covering half a circle in D1, the particle will arrive at the gap. If the potential in D2 is negative, the particle will accelerate across the gap. It will then follow a larger circular arc in D2. The radius is larger because the speed has increased. The particle will then again reach the gap between the 'D's. If now D1 is negatively charged, the particle will again accelerate across the gap and will follow an even larger circular path in D1.

The point is then to arrange for the potential difference between the 'D's to be such that the positively charged particle always sees a negative potential across the gap just as it arrives there. This means that the sign of the potential difference must change every half a revolution.

The force on the particle is the magnetic force $F = qvB$, and equating this to mass times acceleration we get

$$qvB = m\frac{v^2}{r} \quad \Rightarrow \quad r = \frac{mv}{qB}$$

As the particle is accelerated, the radius of the circular path increases, and the particle moves on a 'spiral'. The time to complete one revolution (the period) is found by using $v = \frac{2\pi r}{T}$. Substituting this value of v in the formula above gives

$$r = \frac{m}{qB}\frac{2\pi r}{T} \quad \Rightarrow \quad T = \frac{2\pi m}{qB}$$

We therefore have the very fortunate result that the period of revolution is independent of the speed. This means that, despite the fact that the particle is accelerating, the period T is the same and only depends on the mass m and charge q of the particle and the magnetic field B. The potential difference between the 'D's must then change direction every half a period. Thus, the period of the alternating voltage source is the same as the period of revolution of the particle, i.e. $\frac{2\pi m}{qB}$. This is called the **cyclotron period** and its inverse, $\frac{qB}{2\pi m}$, is called the **cyclotron frequency**.

The charged particle is therefore accelerated as it spirals in the region between the poles of the magnet. At some point additional magnetic fields placed at the edge of the magnetic field region will pull the charged particle out and direct it at a target with which it will collide.

Just as the particle exits the cyclotron it is moving on a circle of radius R, the radius of the cyclotron itself, with the maximum speed it can attain, v_{max}. Thus, from $r = \frac{mv}{qB}$ we find

$$R = \frac{mv_{max}}{qB} \quad \Rightarrow \quad v_{max} = \frac{qBR}{m}$$

and so the maximum kinetic energy the particle can have is

$$K_{max} = \frac{1}{2}mv_{max}^2$$

$$= \frac{q^2B^2R^2}{2m}$$

Note that the maximum kinetic energy of the accelerated particle does not depend on the magnitude of the accelerating voltage.

Example question

Q1

A cyclotron has a radius of 0.25 m and uses a magnetic field of strength 1.4 T. It accelerates protons.

(a) Calculate the frequency with which the protons spiral in the cyclotron.

(b) What is the kinetic energy of a proton as it leaves the cyclotron?

Answer

(a) As shown in the text, the cyclotron frequency is $f = \frac{qB}{2\pi m}$ and so

$$f = \frac{1.6 \times 10^{-19} \times 1.4}{2\pi \times 1.67 \times 10^{-27}}$$

$$= 21\ \text{MHz}$$

(b) The kinetic energy of a proton as it leaves the cyclotron is

$$K_{max} = \frac{q^2B^2R^2}{2m}$$

$$= \frac{(1.6 \times 10^{-19} \times 1.4 \times 0.25)^2}{2 \times 1.67 \times 10^{-27}}$$

$$= 9.39 \times 10^{-13}\ \text{J}$$

$$= \frac{9.39 \times 10^{-13}}{1.6 \times 10^{-19}}\ \text{eV}$$

$$= 5.87 \times 10^6\ \text{eV} \approx 5.9\ \text{MeV}$$

Advantage

- Cyclotrons can be used for nuclear physics research as well as for biomedical studies due to their small, compact size and low cost.

Disadvantages

- Cyclotrons can only be used for fixed target experiments.
- There is a limit to the energy they can reach due to limitations on the size of the magnets.

The synchrotron

Unlike the cyclotron, the charged particles in a **synchrotron** move along a circular path of fixed radius. The circular ring is a thin evacuated tube inside which the charged particles move. The charged particles moving in the ring are called the **beam**. Large magnets are placed along the ring in order to deflect the charged particles into a circular path (Figure J2.6). In between the magnets are gaps. Electric fields are established in the gaps so that, just as the charged particles emerge from the end of the magnetic field at A, the point B at the end of the magnet *ahead* is at a negative electric potential (we are assuming the charged particles are positive). The particles will then accelerate as they cross the gap AB (Figure J2.7). This acceleration takes place at every gap between the magnets. Obviously the electric potentials in the gaps must be carefully established by carefully timing the arrival of the beam at every gap – the period of the electric fields must be *synchronous* with the beam, hence the name for the accelerator. This requires the solution of many technical problems.

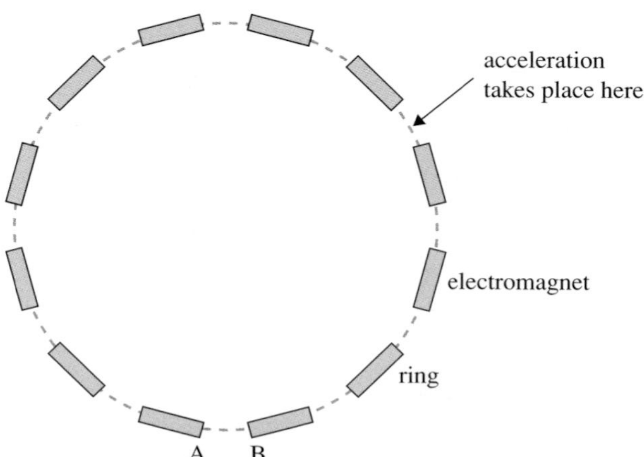

Figure J2.6 A synchrotron ring with magnets along the ring to bend the particles into a circular path.

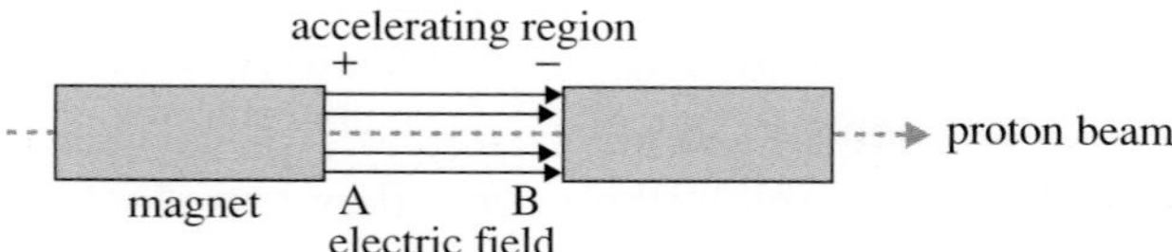

Figure J2.7 The positively charged particles face a negative potential ahead and so are accelerated.

The particles therefore move faster and faster every time they cross a gap and quickly reach a speed that is essentially the speed of light. At this very high speed the rest energy mc^2 is negligible compared to the kinetic energy, and so the relation between total energy and momentum is $E = pc$ [Students who have studied the relativity option will be able to derive this from $E^2 = (pc)^2 + (mc^2)^2$. When the momentum is large, we may ignore the rest energy to find $E = pc$.] Then the expression for the radius R of the circular path in a magnetic field B, $R = \frac{mv}{qB}$; becomes (remembering that momentum is given by $p = mv$).

$$R = \frac{E}{qBc}$$

It follows that, to keep the particles on a path of *fixed* radius, the magnetic field has to be constantly increasing as the energy of the particles increases. The magnets are therefore not permanent magnets but electromagnets, where, by changing the electric current through them, a variable magnetic field is obtained. In this way the particles keep gaining speed but are always moving on the same circular path along the accelerator ring. [The magnets are actually superconducting magnets. This means that the temperature of the magnets is kept very low (1.9 K or −271°C) so that the passage of current through them is done without electrical resistance. This means a stronger magnetic field than could otherwise be obtained. Without the extra-strong magnets, the ring would have to be much bigger.]

Inside the ring the charged particles are *bunched* together. That is to say, they travel together. If the particles are protons, they will repel each other, and very many technical problems must be solved to keep them together (i.e. avoid having them move sideways, or have the particles spread out through the ring). This is done with specially designed additional magnets that affect the bunch much like an ordinary lens affects light, i.e. bending the paths of particles the right way so as to keep them bunched.

Advantages

- Synchrotrons can accelerate particles to very high energies and, since they use colliding beams, they produce very high available energies for the production of new particles.
- The use of storage rings means that, unlike cyclotrons and linacs, the collisions can be controlled.

Disadvantages

- The high proportion of energy lost due to synchrotron radiation (see later).
- The low probability of collisions.

The first big synchrotrons were built in the 1960s and could accelerate protons to energies of about 30 GeV. They had a ring diameter of about 200 m. In the early synchrotrons, once the beam in the ring was accelerated to the maximum possible energy, it was removed from the ring (by additional magnetic fields at the edge of the ring) and directed to an area where it could collide with a target.

In 1961 the Austrian physicist Bruno Touschek, working in Italy, succeeded in making a **storage ring** in which two beams of oppositely charged particles were made to move in opposite directions *in the same ring* (Figure J2.8a). The two beams could be made to collide at predetermined places along the ring and at specific times. Detectors placed around the collision area would record the particles produced in the collisions. Other designs use intersecting rings (Figure J2.8b), in which particles travel along two different rings that intersect at the collision points. In intersecting rings, the particles in the two rings do not have to be oppositely charged.

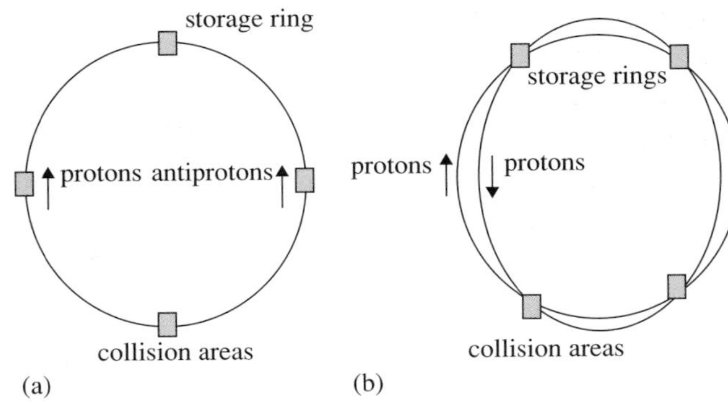

Figure J2.8 (a) A single storage ring and (b) intersecting rings. Collisions take place at various places along the rings.

The synchrotron at CERN (the European Centre for Nuclear Research, near Geneva), called LEP, for Large Electron–Positron collider (Figure J2.9), had a circumference of 27 km and was 100 m underground. LEP accelerated electrons and positrons each to a total energy of 100 GeV. LEP had 3368 magnets around its circumference and 272 acceleration points. LEP's greatest achievement was the discovery of the W and Z bosons and the confirmation of the standard model.

LEP has now been dismantled, and a new machine, the LHC, or Large Hadron Collider, has been built in its place. The LHC is housed in the same tunnel as LEP. It is a proton–proton collider accelerating protons to a total energy of 14 TeV (7.0 TeV for protons in one beam and 7.0 TeV for protons in the other).

(a)

(b)

Figure J2.9 (a) An aerial photograph of the CERN site and (b) the tunnel with the magnets.

The beam in the LHC is expected to contain about 3000 bunches of particles (protons), and each bunch will contain about 10^{11} protons When two bunches collide, however, there will only be about 20 collisions among the 2×10^{11} or so particles in the two bunches! The bunches will be moving around the 27 km ring at essentially the speed of light, so it will take only 9×10^{-5} s per revolution. The bunches will therefore cross each other many times every second (see question 17). This implies that there will be a total number of about 10^9 collisions *per second*.

The LHC collider project at CERN is an excellent example of the collaboration of many scientists from many countries. More than 7000 scientists are involved in the project, and they come from hundreds of universities and research laboratories in about 85 different countries. This includes about 750 physicists and engineers from US universities and research laboratories. Many different countries, not just the CERN member states, are contributing towards the costs of this enormous programme.

Until the LHC becomes operational, the largest proton collider is the Tevatron, the Fermilab accelerator outside Chicago in the USA. It accelerates protons and antiprotons each to an energy of 900 GeV for a total available energy of 1.8 TeV. It has a radius of 1.0 km. The top quark was discovered with this accelerator. Other smaller accelerators exist. CESR (Cornell Electron Storage Ring) at Cornell University, USA, is being used for systematic studies of the bottom quark. The charmed quark was discovered independently at SLAC and Brookhaven, both in the USA. Important discoveries were also made at DESY (Deutsches Elektronen-Synchrotron) outside Hamburg in Germany.

Synchrotron radiation

The following is a fact of physics:

- Electrically charged particles, when accelerated, radiate electromagnetic waves and so energy.

This radiation is called **synchrotron radiation** or **bremsstrahlung**. Its presence poses serious difficulties to the designer of a particle accelerator. It means that not all the energy that is put in to accelerating a particle actually goes into total energy for that particle. A fraction of it will be radiated away and so lost. A charged particle will radiate both when it is accelerated along a straight line and when it is bent into a circular path. More radiation is emitted in the second case, however, which is why more energy will be lost in a synchrotron than in a linear accelerator. Because electrons have a much smaller mass than protons (they differ in mass by a factor of about 1800), an electron has much higher speed than a proton of the same total energy. The amount of radiation emitted is related to the speed of the particle. Hence the electron, having the higher speed, loses more energy than the proton. Thus, in most synchrotrons, it is *protons* that are being accelerated and not electrons.

Today, many particle accelerators use the synchrotron radiation produced during the operation of the accelerator for research into other areas of physics such as material science, solid-state physics, biomedical physics, etc.

Available energy

Recall that the objective of any particle accelerator is to provide particles with a high energy so that, when they collide, the available energy can be used to create heavier, previously unknown, particles.

Consider first the case of a synchrotron with a single storage ring in which particles of rest mass m circulate in the ring one way and antiparticles also of rest mass m circulate the other way. Assume that the particles and antiparticles are both accelerated to the same total energy E. When a particle collides with its antiparticle, the entire amount of total energy, i.e. $2E$, will be available to create new particles. To be concrete, consider an electron colliding with a positron. The process is represented by the Feynman diagram given earlier in Figure J2.1.

The total energy of the particle–antiparticle pair produced is $2(Mc^2 + K)$, where M is the rest mass of the particle produced and K is its kinetic energy. Assuming that the particle–antiparticle pair is produced at rest, so K is zero, then the particle of largest mass that can be produced is given by

$$2Mc^2 = 2E$$

$$M = \frac{E}{c^2}$$

This situation is in sharp contrast with collisions in which the 'target' is at rest. Consider a target of mass M bombarded by a particle of rest mass m and total energy E. The energy that is available to create new particles in this case is given by the formula

$$E_A^2 = 2Mc^2E + (Mc^2)^2 + (mc^2)^2$$

(This formula involves subtleties of the theory of relativity.) E_A is the energy that is available to create new particles in a collision. Its value is the same in all frames of reference. It is more simply calculated in a very special frame of reference, the centre-of-mass frame of reference. In this frame the total momentum before and after the interaction is zero. (Therefore this is a different frame of reference from the laboratory frame of reference.) So to calculate the *minimum* E_A needed to produce a given set of particles we must assume that the particles are produced at rest *in the centre-of-mass frame of reference*. Having calculated E_A in this way, we then use this value in the laboratory frame of reference, where the formula above relates E_A to the energy E of the incoming particle. Notice that in the laboratory frame of reference the produced particles *do have* momentum (as they must in order to satisfy momentum conservation).

As an example of all this, consider a reaction such as $p + \pi^- \rightarrow \Lambda^0 + K^0$ in which a proton, having been accelerated to a total energy E, collides with a stationary pion π^- (rest energy 140 MeV) and produces the baryon Λ^0 (rest energy 1100 MeV) and the meson K^0 (rest energy 500 MeV). (These particles will be discussed in Option J3.) What is the least energy E to which the proton must be accelerated in order to produce the Λ^0 and the K^0 in this reaction?

The reaction must just supply the rest energies of the particles. When E has its minimum value, the particles are produced at rest in the centre-of-mass frame of reference. Then $E_A = 1100 + 500 = 1600$ MeV. Then, from the previous equation, we get

$$(1600)^2 = 2 \times 140E + (140)^2 + (938)^2$$

which gives $E = 5930$ MeV. The kinetic energy of the proton must then be $E_k = 5930 - 938 = 4990$ MeV. (Any apparently 'missing' energy is the kinetic energy of the products in the laboratory frame of reference.)

In most applications, we will be concerned with those cases where the bombarding particle and the target particle are the same, in which case

$$E_A^2 = 2mc^2E + 2(mc^2)^2$$

Furthermore, if the bombarding particle is really fast, we may neglect its rest mass relative to its total energy, in which case we have the approximation

$$E_A = \sqrt{2mc^2E}$$

Example questions

Q2

The antiproton was discovered in a collision of two protons, one of them at rest, according to the reaction $p + p \rightarrow p + p + p + \bar{p}$.

(a) Calculate the minimum kinetic energy to which the proton must be accelerated.

(b) Compare this with the kinetic energy needed in an intersecting ring synchrotron.

Answer

(a) The minimum energy is when the four particles are produced at rest in the centre-of-mass frame of reference, and so

$$E_A = 4(mc^2) = 4 \times 938 = 3752 \text{ MeV}$$

Then

$(3752)^2 = 2 \times 938E + 2 \times (938)^2$

giving $E = 6566$ MeV and a kinetic energy of $E_k = 6566 - 938 \approx 5630$ MeV.

(b) In an intersecting ring synchrotron where *each* proton is accelerated to a total energy E, we would have

$2E = 4 \times 938 = 3752 \Rightarrow$

$E = 1876 \approx 1880$ MeV

and so the required kinetic energy of each proton would be

$E_k = 1876 - 938 = 938 \approx 940$ MeV

Q3

(a) An accelerator accelerates protons to a total energy of 800 GeV. The accelerated proton beam collides with stationary protons. Calculate the available energy.

(b) The accelerator increases the total energy of the protons to 1200 GeV. Calculate the available energy now.

Answer

(a) The rest energy of a proton is 938 MeV = 0.938 GeV and so we may use the last formula in the main text above. Then,

$E_A \approx \sqrt{2mc^2 E}$

$= \sqrt{2 \times 0.938 \times 800}$

$= 38.7$ GeV

(b) The available energy now is

$E_A \approx \sqrt{2 \times 0.938 \times 1200} = 47.4$ GeV.

This example shows a major problem of collisions with stationary targets. The machine increased the total energy by 50% but this resulted in an increase of available energy of only 8.74 GeV or 23%.

Q4

Consider a proton–antiproton collision in which two mesons each of rest mass 800 MeV c^{-2} are produced. If each of the mesons is produced with kinetic energy 250 MeV, calculate the total energy of acceleration if:

(a) the proton is stationary and the antiproton is accelerated;

(b) the acceleration takes place in a single ring synchrotron for the proton–antiproton pair.

Answer

The total available energy must be 800 + 250 = 1050 MeV for each meson for a total of 2100 MeV. Thus

(a) $E_A^2 = 2mc^2E + 2(mc^2)^2$ and so $2100^2 =$

$2 \times 940E + 2 \times (940)^2 \Rightarrow E = 1406$ MeV.

(b) $2E = 2100 \Rightarrow E = 1050$ MeV.

Detectors

In a particle accelerator, particles are accelerated to high energies and then collide. In the collision, new particles are created. There must be ways to detect the presence of these particles as well as ways to measure their properties, such as their electric charge, mass, velocity and energy. This very complex job is done by sophisticated machines called **particle detectors**.

Particle detectors are placed around the point where the collision takes place (Figure J2.10). The detectors have a layered structure (Figure J2.11) – each layer serves a specific function in the detection process.

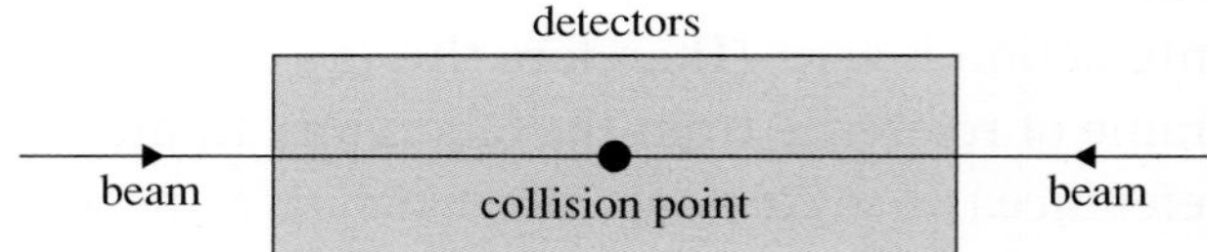

Figure J2.10 A layer of detectors surrounds the collision point.

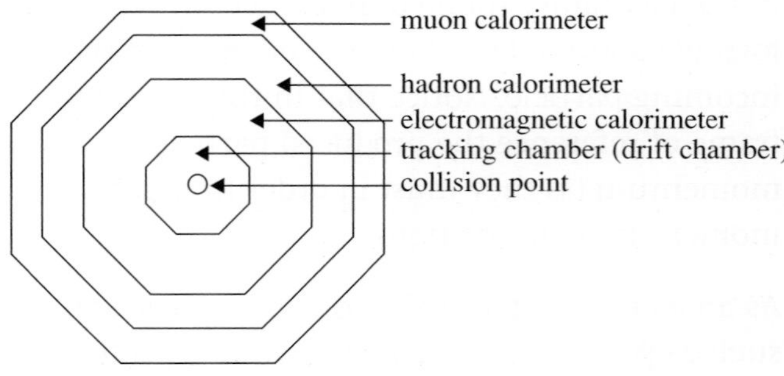

Figure J2.11 The detectors are placed around the collision point in a series of layers.

Tracking paths in the drift chamber

Starting from the interior of the detector, we first find a tracking chamber whose purpose is to record the path of a particle produced in a collision. In the old days of particle physics (this means up to the 1970s), the job of track detection was done by the **bubble chamber**. The operation of the bubble chamber rests on the fact that the boiling temperature of a liquid depends on pressure. The lower the pressure, the lower the boiling temperature. (This is why water boils at lower than 100 °C at the top of a high mountain.) The idea then is to keep a liquid at some pressure so it is just below its boiling point. If the pressure is then reduced, the liquid will just begin to boil. If there are charged particles moving through the liquid as the boiling is about to start, the boiling will first take place along the path of the charged particles. These act as nucleation centres at which bubbles of vapour form. In a bubble chamber, the track of a charged particle is seen as a series of small bubbles of vapour along the path of the particle (Figure J2.12). A magnetic field can be used to bend the tracks and a photograph taken. Analysis of the photograph gives valuable information about the particle causing the track. For example, the way it curves in the magnetic field tells the sign of the charge, and the radius of the path gives information about the momentum of the particle.

Figure J2.12 Tracks of charged particles in a bubble chamber.

Having been responsible for many discoveries in particle physics, the bubble chamber has now given way to its modern successors, the **spark chamber** (invented by the Japanese physicist S. Fukui), the **wire chamber** (invented by F. Krienen) and the **proportional wire chamber** (invented by G. Charpak). These devices perform the same function, i.e. they locate the track of a charged particle but without the need for photographs. The information they collect may be digitized (for the wire and proportional wire chambers) and so the analysis can be performed with a computer, which reconstructs computer images of the tracks.

The idea in these devices is that a charged particle ionizes a gas through which it passes. This means that ions and electrons are produced in the gas. Imagine a number of wires immersed in the gas. The wires are kept at different potentials and so there is a potential difference between them. The ions and electrons created by the charged particle as it moves through the gas collect at the wires. Their arrival at a particular point on a wire is recorded as a small current that can be accurately measured. The electrons or ions take a certain time to reach (to *drift*) to the nearest wire, and knowledge of this time is crucial in determining the precise location where the electron or ion was created (that is, the position of the charged particle). The drift times can be measured to an accuracy of a few nanoseconds, and the location of the particle to an accuracy of a fraction of a millimetre. The wires are usually placed parallel and close to each other on a grid. Many grids are then placed one on top of the other. In this way the passage of the particle can be recorded with great accuracy, and a three-dimensional image of the track can be reconstructed from the data from all the wires (see Figure J2.13).

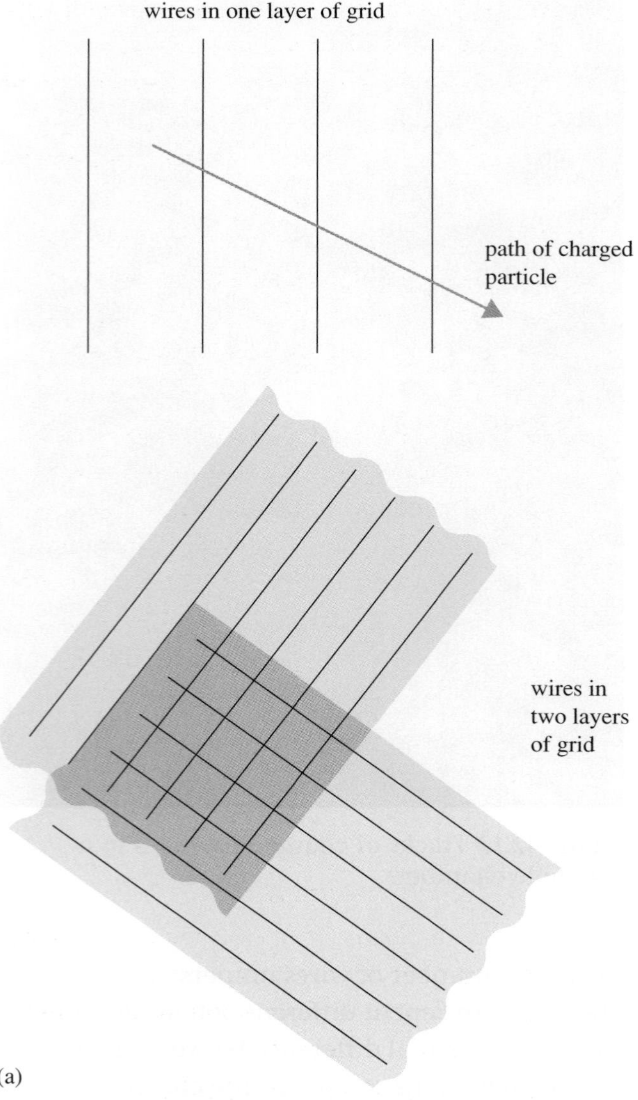

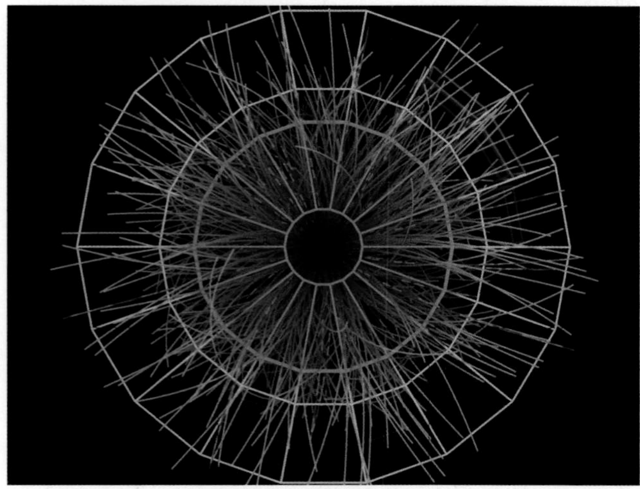

Figure J2.13 (a) A charged particle moving in a grid of wires. (b) Computer reconstructed particle tracks from a drift chamber.

The electromagnetic calorimeter

This detector surrounds the drift chamber. When charged particles in a given medium move faster than the speed of light *in that medium*, they give off radiation. This radiation (called Cerenkov radiation) can be detected through the photoelectric effect: radiation causes the emission of electrons from a metallic surface upon which it falls. The electric current created is a measure of the intensity of radiation. The current so created is very small but can be amplified with **photomultipliers** (Figure J2.14).

Light falling on the metallic plate causes the emission of a number of electrons. These are accelerated to the nearest positively charged dynode. When it collides with the dynode, more electrons are released. In this way the current grows to a sufficiently large value so it can be measured. The current is proportional to the number of photons initially entering the photomultiplier. Even the arrival of a single photon into the photomultiplier tube can be detected.

Knowledge of the intensity of the radiation allows determination of the speed of the charged particle that caused the radiation. Since the drift chamber offered information on the momentum of the particle, it follows that a determination of the mass of the particle is now possible.

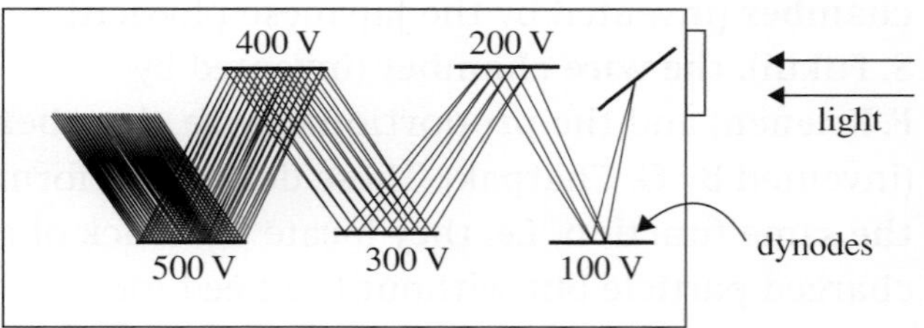

Figure J2.14 Light (radiation) falling on the photomultiplier surfaces (the dynodes) creates an avalanche effect of electrons. Once the number of the electrons increases sufficiently, a small current will be registered proportional to the intensity of the incoming radiation. The dynodes are kept at a positive potential, which keeps increasing as we move from right to left.

Example question

Q5

Consider a photomultiplier tube with six dynodes kept at potentials from 100 V to 600 V. Assuming that it takes 5.0 eV to release one electron from a dynode and that one photon is incident on the photomultiplier tube, estimate the number of electrons emitted from the sixth dynode.

Answer

The first electron is incident on the first dynode with an energy of about 100 eV and so releases $\frac{100}{5} = 20$ electrons. These 20 will then be incident on the second dynode, also with a kinetic energy of 100 eV *each* and so will result in $20 \times \frac{100}{5} = 20^2 = 400$ electrons, and so on.

The sixth dynode will thus release $20^6 = 6.4 \times 10^7$ electrons.

The hadron and muon calorimeters

The remaining layers measure the energy of hadrons and muons. When a particle enters the calorimeter, collisions will create a *shower* of secondary particles. The size of the shower determines the energy of the original charged particle. Muon detectors are at the outer edge of the detector, as muons can penetrate all the inner parts of the detector without much interaction with them.

? QUESTIONS

1 (a) Explain why high energies are needed to produce particles of large mass.
The top quark has a rest mass of about 175 GeV c^{-2}.
(b) What is the minimum energy needed for an electron–positron pair that collide with equal speed from opposite directions in order to produce a top quark–antiquark pair?

2 Explain why high energies are necessary in order to resolve small sizes.

3 An electron of total energy 50 GeV behaves like a massless photon (i.e. $E = \frac{hc}{\lambda}$).
(a) Calculate the de Broglie wavelength of this electron.
(b) Could this electron be used to resolve: (i) a nucleus; (ii) a nucleon?

4 Which would be better suited to study the structure of a nucleus, a beam of alpha particles or a beam of protons each of kinetic energy 25 MeV? Explain your answer.

5 (a) State what is meant by synchrotron radiation.
(b) How does synchrotron radiation affect the operation of a synchrotron?
(c) How does the energy lost as synchrotron radiation in a linear accelerator compare to that in a synchrotron?

6 Suggest why protons, rather than electrons, are the particles normally accelerated in synchrotrons and why electrons, rather than protons, are normally accelerated in linear accelerators.

7 Suggest why there are no particle accelerators that accelerate neutrons.

8 (a) Why can (uniform) magnetic fields not be used to accelerate particles?
(b) What is the purpose of the magnetic fields in circular accelerators?

9 Particle accelerators are built deep underground. For example, the CERN collider is about 100 m below ground level. Suggest a reason why this is done.

10 Consider a linear accelerator where the alternating voltage applied to the ends of the tubes has a constant frequency. Explain why this implies that the time the accelerated particle spends in any one tube is constant. Hence explain why the tubes must be increasing in length as the particle is accelerated and why eventually the length of the tubes stays constant.

11 Outline the operation of a cyclotron.

12 A proton crossing the 'D's of a cyclotron faces a negative potential of 30 kV at the D opposite. How many revolutions must the proton make to reach a kinetic energy of 25 MeV?

13 A cyclotron has a radius of 0.20 m and uses a magnetic field of strength 1.2 T to accelerate protons. The accelerating voltage between the 'D's is 35 kV.

(a) Calculate the frequency of the voltage that must be applied to the 'D's.

(b) What is the kinetic energy achieved by the protons when they leave the cyclotron?

(c) How many revolutions did the protons make before leaving the cyclotron.

14 The answer to question 13(b) did not use the value of the accelerating voltage. Why is the kinetic energy of the protons independent of the voltage? What effect, if any, would a higher voltage have?

15 State the role of magnets in a synchrotron. Why are they of variable strength? How are the particles actually accelerated?

16 Large conventional magnets can reach a strength of about 2 T. Superconducting magnets can reach 8 T. The LHC uses superconducting magnets and has a circumference of 27 km. Determine the circumference that the LHC would have to have if conventional magnets were used.

17 Consider a synchrotron with circumference 27 km. At any one time there are 3000 bunches of particles along the circumference of the ring and an equal number of bunches with particles going the other way. Assuming that the particles essentially move at the speed of light, calculate:

(a) the average distance between two consecutive bunches;

(b) the average time taken for the two bunches to meet;

(c) the average frequency of bunch crossings.

(d) Assuming that every time two bunches cross each other there are 20 collisions, estimate the total number of collisions per second.

18 (a) A very relativistic particle behaves as a particle with negligible rest mass, i.e. like a photon for example, and so the relation between total energy and momentum is $E = pc$. Use this relation to show that the radius of a circular orbit of this particle in a magnetic field B is given by $R = \frac{E}{qBc}$.

(b) Calculate the magnetic field that must be used to bend 7.0 TeV protons in the LHC, whose radius is 4.26 km.

19 State and explain one advantage of a synchrotron over a linear accelerator.

20 Explain why there is more available energy for producing new particles in a colliding beam experiment compared to a beam of the same total energy that collides with a stationary target.

21 State and explain one disadvantage of colliding beam experiments compared to experiments in which a beam is directed at a fixed target.

22 A proton and an antiproton at rest annihilate into two photons. What is the wavelength of each photon?

23 A pion may be produced in the reaction $\mathrm{p} + \mathrm{p} \rightarrow \mathrm{p} + \mathrm{n} + \pi^{+}$. Assume that one proton is at rest and the other is moving with kinetic energy K before the collision. What is the minimum K that would allow the production of the pion? (The rest mass of the pion π^{+} is 140 MeV c^{-2}.)

24 Deduce that in the reaction $\mathrm{p} + \mathrm{p} \rightarrow \mathrm{p} + \mathrm{p} + \mathrm{p} + \bar{\mathrm{p}}$ in which one of the initial protons is at rest, the minimum total energy of the moving proton required for the reaction to take place is equal to seven times the proton's rest energy.

25 Consider the reaction $\mathrm{p} + \mathrm{p} \rightarrow \mathrm{p} + \mathrm{p} + \pi^{0}$, in which the initial protons are approaching each other with the same kinetic energy from opposite directions. What minimum kinetic energy must each proton have for the reaction to take place? (The rest mass of the pion π^{0} is 135 MeV c^{-2}.)

26 Calculate the minimum energy of a pion that collides with a stationary proton according to $\mathrm{p} + \pi^{-} \rightarrow \Sigma^{0} + \mathrm{K}^{0}$. (The rest masses are 140 MeV c^{-2} for the pion, 1193 MeV c^{-2} for the sigma, and 498 MeV c^{-2} for the kaon.)

27 Outline the layered structure of particle detectors around collision areas in an accelerator. In particular, explain why the drift chamber is always placed *inside* the calorimeters.

28 What do calorimeters measure in a particle detector?

29 What is the principle behind the operation of a bubble chamber? Describe how particle tracks are created and recorded in a bubble chamber.

30 Outline how the tracks of charged particles are recorded in a wire drift chamber.

31 State and explain two advantages of modern drift chambers compared to bubble chambers.

32 Outline how the mass of a particle produced in a collision may be determined.

33 Particle physics research is expensive. It uses resources that might otherwise go to other areas, for example health and social care. What is your position on this issue? Write an essay giving arguments to support your position.

Quarks and leptons

As we have mentioned before, there exist six types or 'flavours' of elementary particles called quarks. The idea of the quark came about as follows. By the 1960s scores of particles (now known to be hadrons, i.e. made out of quarks) had been discovered, filling long tables with their various properties. In 1963 Murray Gell-Mann, George Zweig and Yuval Neeman independently proposed, on *purely mathematical grounds*, that the hadrons and their properties could in fact be understood quite simply, if one made the assumption that these particles had smaller constituents, called *quarks* by Gell-Mann and *aces* by Zweig.

Objectives

By the end of this chapter you should be able to:

- outline how *quarks bind* to make baryons and mesons;
- understand the quantum numbers called *baryon number* and *lepton number*, and that these are conserved in all interactions;
- appreciate the need for a new quantum number called *strangeness*, and that this is conserved in strong and electromagnetic interactions but not in weak interactions;
- predict the *spin of a hadron*;
- appreciate the need for a new quantum number called *colour*, and that this quantum number is conserved in all interactions;
- understand the meaning of the term *confinement*;
- state the family structure of the quarks and leptons of the *standard model*;
- appreciate the significance of the *Higgs particle*.

Hadrons – baryons and mesons

It was originally proposed that three flavours of a new particle should exist, and these were named **quarks** by Murray Gell-Mann (Figure J3.1), who found the word in a passage in James Joyce's *Finnegan's Wake*. They were given the names *up* (u), *down* (d) and *strange* (s) quarks. The u quark was the lightest of the three and was assigned an electric charge of two-thirds that of the proton, i.e. $\frac{2}{3}|e|$. This was a radical step, since every known particle up to that time had a charge that was an integral multiple of the electron charge (Millikan's experiment). The d and s quarks were each assigned a charge of $-\frac{1}{3}|e|$. Since Gell-Mann's original work in the 1960s, three new flavours of quarks have been needed, the *charmed* (c), *bottom* (b) and *top* (t) quarks. These (c, b, t) and the original three (u, d, s) account for all the hadrons known today.

▶ The hypothesis was that hadrons could be made out of quarks in just two ways:
- by combining three quarks, giving a *baryon*;
- by combining a quark with an antiquark, giving a *meson*.

Note that it is *only* hadrons that are made out of quarks. Leptons and exchange particles are not.

Figure J3.1 Murray Gell-Mann.

Consider two well-known baryons, the proton and the neutron. The proton consists of two u quarks and one d quark (Figure J3.2a). The neutron is made out of one u quark and two d quarks (Figure J3.2b).

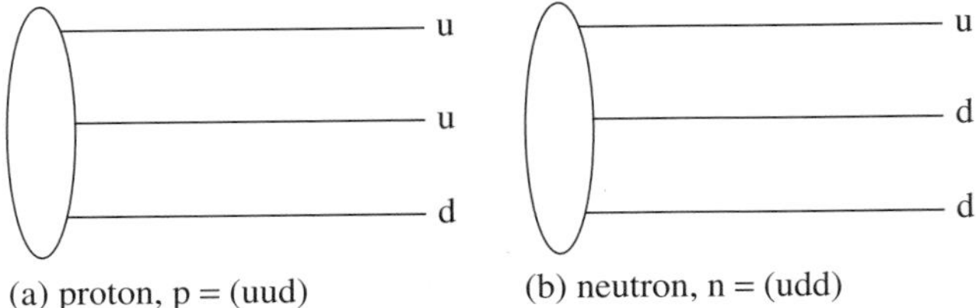

Figure J3.2 The quark structures of (a) a proton and (b) a neutron.

The electric charge of the proton is thus predicted to be

$$Q_\text{p} = \left(+\frac{2}{3}|e|\right) + \left(+\frac{2}{3}|e|\right) + \left(-\frac{1}{3}|e|\right)$$

$$= +\frac{2}{3}|e| + \frac{2}{3}|e| - \frac{1}{3}|e| = +|e|$$

and that of the neutron is predicted to be

$$Q_\text{n} = \left(-\frac{1}{3}|e|\right) + \left(-\frac{1}{3}|e|\right) + \left(+\frac{2}{3}|e|\right)$$

$$= -\frac{1}{3}|e| - \frac{1}{3}|e| + \frac{2}{3}|e| = 0$$

which are, of course, the correct values.

Pions are examples of mesons. The positively charged pion (π^+meson) is made up as follows:

$$\pi^+ = (\text{u}\bar{\text{d}})$$

where the bar on a particle (quark) denotes an antiparticle (antiquark). Thus, the positive pion is made out of a u quark and the antiparticle of the d quark (the d antiquark).

Example question

Q1

What is the quark content of the antiparticle of the π^+ meson?

Answer

The antiparticle of the π^+ meson (positive pion) is found by replacing every particle in π^+ by its antiparticle. The antiparticle is therefore the π^- meson (negative pion), made up as

$\pi^- = (\text{d}\bar{\text{u}})$ or $(\bar{\text{u}}\text{d})$

We have so far seen the use of the up and down quarks in making up protons and neutrons. What about the strange quark? This quark does not participate in making up ordinary matter. However, particles known as kaons were discovered in cosmic ray experiments, and the strange quark is one of their ingredients. Gell-Mann predicted the existence of a particle made out of three strange quarks and could in fact predict its rest energy as well at 1672 MeV. The omega-minus Ω^-(= sss), a 'strangeness −3' particle, was discovered soon afterwards (1964) at Brookhaven National Laboratory in New York, lending further support to the whole quark idea.

Baryon number

Baryons are assigned a quantum number called **baryon number**. The proton and neutron have baryon number +1, and their antiparticles have baryon number −1. Again, the neutron differs from the antineutron in that they have opposite baryon number. Hence, they are different particles. (This is equivalent to assigning a baryon number of $+\frac{1}{3}$ to all quarks and $-\frac{1}{3}$ to all antiquarks. Thus mesons have baryon number equal to 0.)

▶ Baryon number is conserved in *all* reactions.

For example, you can see that baryon number is conserved in the following reaction:

$$\begin{array}{ccccccccccc} n & + & p & \rightarrow & n & + & p & + & p & + & \bar{p} \\ (B=1) & + & (B=1) & = & (B=1) & + & (B=1) & + & (B=1) & + & (B=-1) \end{array}$$

(In this reaction, the mass on the right-hand side is larger than that on the left. Thus, for the reaction to take place, the proton or neutron on the left-hand side must have sufficient kinetic energy.)

Strangeness

Some particles discovered in cosmic ray experiments in the 1950s (for example, the negatively charged baryon Σ^-) had very unusual properties. One of them was that they decayed far too slowly compared with other similar particles. For example, the decay $\Sigma^- \rightarrow n + \pi^-$ has a half-life of order 10^{-10} s, whereas the decay of the neutral sigma, $\Sigma^0 \rightarrow \Lambda^0 + \gamma$, has a half-life of order 10^{-20} s, i.e. 10 orders of magnitude shorter! For this reason they were called **strange particles**. To make sense of their unusual properties, it was hypothesized that these particles carried a new quantum number, **strangeness**. The properties of the strange particles could then be understood if it was postulated that (unlike baryon number, which is always conserved) strangeness is conserved *only* in electromagnetic and strong interactions but is violated in weak interactions.

We now know that strangeness is due to the fact that the hadron contains one or more strange quarks.

▶ A hadron is assigned one positive unit of strangeness for every antistrange quark it contains, and one negative unit of strangeness for every strange quark it contains.

Table J3.1 shows a few mesons and baryons and the quark content and strangeness of each.

	Quark content	Strangeness
Mesons		
K^+	$(u\bar{s})$	$S=+1$
K^0	$(d\bar{s})$	$S=+1$
π^+	$(u\bar{d})$	$S=0$
π^-	$(d\bar{u})$	$S=0$
π^0	mixture of $(u\bar{u})$ and $(d\bar{d})$	$S=0$
η^0	mixture of $(u\bar{u})$ and $(d\bar{d})$	$S=0$
η'	mixture of $(u\bar{u})$, $(d\bar{d})$ and $(s\bar{s})$	$S=0$
Baryons		
Σ^+	(uus)	$S=-1$
Σ^-	(dds)	$S=-1$
Σ^0	(uds)	$S=-1$
Ξ^0	$(\bar{u}\bar{s}\bar{s})$	$S=+2$
Δ^{++}	(uuu)	$S=0$
Λ^0	(uds)	$S=-1$

Table J3.1 A few hadrons and their strangeness.

Thus, in the decay $\Sigma^- \rightarrow n + \pi^-$, strangeness is violated (the strangeness of Σ^- is −1, and the strangeness of $n + \pi^-$ is 0), the decay takes place through the weak interaction and is therefore slow. The decay $\Sigma^0 \rightarrow \Lambda^0 + \gamma$, on the other hand, does not violate strangeness. The strangeness S of Σ^0 is −1, and that of Λ^0 is −1, because both have one strange quark. The decay then takes place through the electromagnetic interaction and is therefore fast.

Example question

Q2

Gell-Mann classified the spin-$\frac{1}{2}$ baryons made out of the light u, d and s quarks in the 'eightfold way' as shown in the charge–strangeness diagram in Figure J3.3. Identify the quark structure of the baryons indicated by X, Y, Z and W. (Do not try to answer the same question for the two centre ones – that is too technical!)

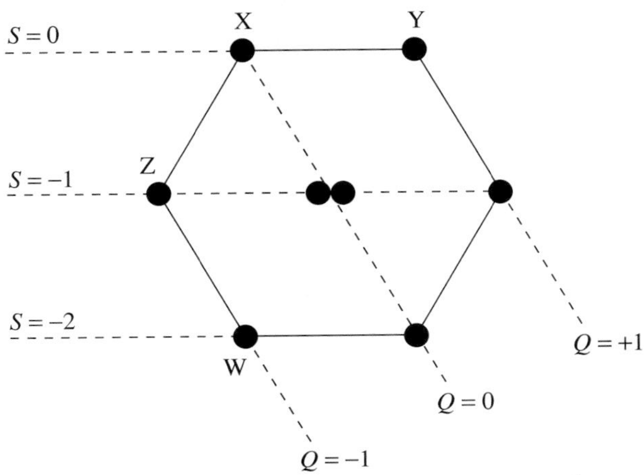

Figure J3.3 The eightfold way for the spin $\frac{1}{2}$ baryons. (The horizontal lines are lines of constant strangeness S, and the slanted lines are lines of constant charge Q.)

Answer

Both X and Y must have no s quarks because $S = 0$. So X = (ddu) to make sure that $Q = 0$, i.e. X is the neutron. (Look back at Table J1.2 to remind yourself of the charges on the quarks.) Similarly, Y = (uud) to have $Q = +1$, i.e. Y is the proton. Z has one strange quark since $S = -1$, and to make $Q = -1$ we must then have Z = (sdd). Similarly, W = (ssd).

The spin of hadrons

The fact that hadrons are made out of quarks allows many of the properties of hadrons to be understood. One such property is the spin of hadrons. Recall that quarks are fermions with spin equal to $\frac{1}{2}$.

Consider first a baryon, i.e. a hadron made out of three quarks. Figure J3.4 shows the possible orientations of the spins of three quarks. There are only two possibilities. Thus we can predict, based on the existence of quarks, that all baryons will have a spin of $\frac{1}{2}$ or $\frac{3}{2}$. This means that all baryons are fermions. This is indeed the case. For example the proton and the neutron both have spin $\frac{1}{2}$, whereas the baryon Ω^- has spin $\frac{3}{2}$ (see page 758).

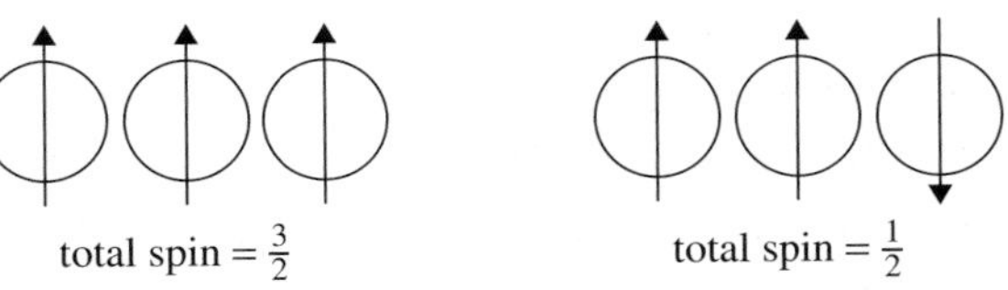

Figure J3.4 The spin of baryons in terms of the spins of the quarks.

Note that here we examine only the intrinsic spin of the particle. If the quarks revolve around each other inside the particle, they have angular momentum (which is an integral multiple of $\frac{h}{2\pi}$), which gets added to the spin. We will not consider this 'orbital' spin here.

Consider now mesons, which are made of one quark and one antiquark. Figure J3.5 shows that again there are only two possibilities. Hence all mesons have intrinsic spin 0 or 1. (The remark about orbital angular momentum also applies to mesons.) Hence all mesons are bosons.

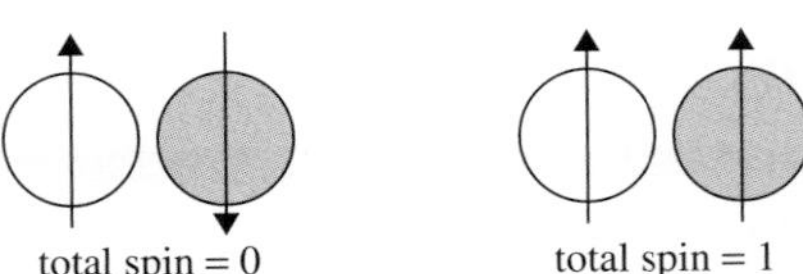

Figure J3.5 The spin of mesons in terms of the spins of the quarks.

Colour

An immediate problem appears when one looks at a baryon such as the spin-$\frac{3}{2}$ baryon Ω^- (sss). This is a particle consisting of three identical fermions. According to Pauli's exclusion principle, such a particle cannot exist because the principle forbids all three of them from being in the same state. To avoid this problem, a new quantum number needed to be introduced that could distinguish the (otherwise identical) quarks. The new quantum number was called **colour**.

It was hypothesized that quarks carry one of three possible colour quantum numbers. These were called red, blue and green. Antiquarks carry anticolour, i.e. can be antired, antiblue or antigreen. It must be emphasized immediately that this quantum number has *nothing* to do with the colour of visible light! The name is appropriate, though, because, just as with visible light, the colour combination red–blue–green results in white, i.e. a colourless state or particle. In a baryon, therefore, the colours of the quarks are precisely red–blue–green, which means that the baryon itself does not have colour. Similarly, in a meson, the colour combinations red–antired, blue–antiblue and green–antigreen also result in no colour for the meson. In other words, we can say the following:

▶ Hadrons have no colour, even though quarks do.

Colour was thus introduced to solve a theoretical problem of the quark model, but soon afterwards experimental evidence was also produced pointing to the real existence of colour.

Example question

Q3

Energy is supplied to a meson, as shown in Figure J3.6, and two new mesons are created. State the colour of the quarks indicated by X, Y and Z.

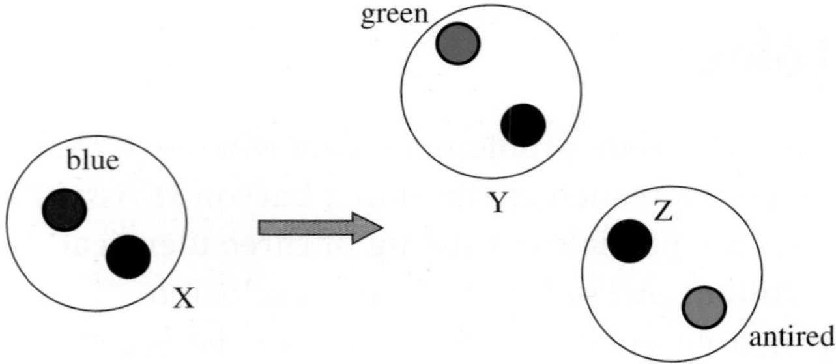

Figure J3.6 When energy is supplied to this meson in the hope of extracting a quark, a new meson is created instead.

Answer

Since mesons are hadrons, they must have no colour. So it follows that X = antiblue, Y = antigreen and Z = red.

Gluons

We saw in Option J1 that the electromagnetic interaction is described through the interaction vertex involving electrons and a photon. A similar interaction vertex exists for the strong interaction between quarks. It is represented by the diagram in Figure J3.7.

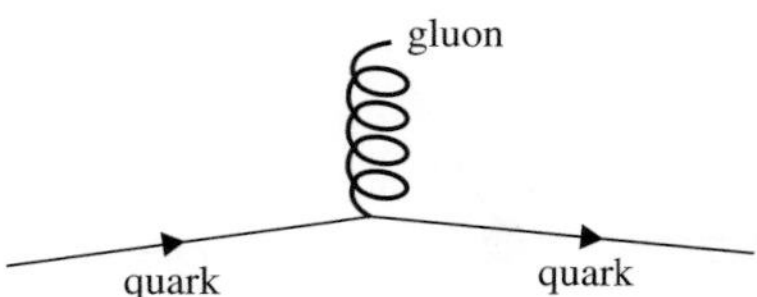

Figure J3.7 The basic strong (colour) interaction vertex.

The quark type (flavour) does not change in this interaction. To this vertex we assign an interaction strength $\sqrt{\alpha_s}$. The theory of quarks interacting with gluons is called quantum chromodynamics (QCD). The word comes from the Greek *chroma* meaning 'colour'. Unlike quantum electrodynamics (QED) though (see Option J1), there are more interaction vertices in QCD (involving gluons only, as we stated in Option J1).

In QCD the gluons then play the role that the photon plays in QED. The gluons are massless, neutral and have spin 1 just like the photon. Like QED, QCD is also a theory based on a symmetry. Theories based on symmetries are called gauge theories in particle physics. (The symmetry is that of the non-abelian group SU(3) – those of you studying mathematics at higher level may appreciate this more if you do the option on sets, relations and groups.)

Gluons also carry colour, but their case is somewhat difficult and technical. A gluon actually carries two colour quantum numbers: one quantum number for colour and one for anticolour. Thus a gluon can be, for example, a red–antigreen gluon. Theoretically, there are nine possibilities obtained when we combine the three colours with the three anticolours, so we would expect nine gluons. However, because the combinations red–antired, blue–antiblue and green–antigreen give a colourless state, this means that the 'ninth' gluon is in fact a combination of the other eight. Thus, there exist only eight *independent* gluons: $G_{R\bar{B}}$, $G_{R\bar{G}}$, $G_{B\bar{R}}$, $G_{B\bar{G}}$, $G_{G\bar{R}}$, $G_{G\bar{B}}$, and two others. The last two are complicated and we will not make use of them here (see the Supplementary material that follows).

As with the electromagnetic interaction, we can draw the strong (colour) interaction vertex in various ways to represent different processes. Colour is conserved at the vertex. For example, the diagram in Figure J3.8 represents the absorption of a gluon by a u quark. Just as electric charge is conserved at the electromagnetic vertex, colour is conserved at this vertex. Thus if the incoming u quark is red and the outgoing u quark is blue, it must be that the incoming gluon must carry two types of colour: blue and antired.

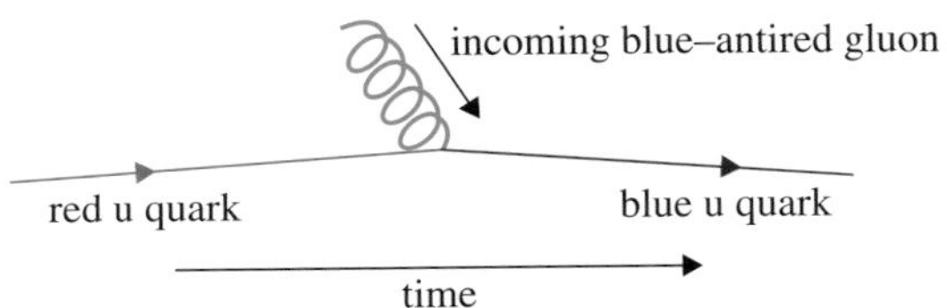

Figure J3.8 The colour assignments of the gluon are dictated by colour conservation at the vertex.

Supplementary material

The remaining two gluons mentioned in the main text have in fact the following colour–anticolour assignments: $R\bar{R} - G\bar{G}$ and $R\bar{R} + G\bar{G} - 2B\bar{B}$. Obviously we cannot explain in this book what this means exactly. Suffice it to say that quantum mechanics allows for an important phenomenon called *mixing*. These gluons are mixtures of various colours. The same phenomenon of mixing also occurs within baryons and mesons, where now it is the quark flavours that mix. For example, the quark content of the neutral spin-0 meson called η^0 is in fact a mixture of $d\bar{d}$ and $u\bar{u}$ in equal amounts, so that $\eta^0 = d\bar{d} + u\bar{u}$. In very rough words, the quark content of the η^0 is $u\bar{u}$ half the time and $d\bar{d}$ the other half of the time. To make matters worse, there are also combinations such as $\pi^0 = d\bar{d} - u\bar{u}$ for the neutral pion. Obviously, all of this is beyond the level of this book.

Example question

Q4

A green s quark emits a gluon and becomes a blue quark. State the flavour of the new quark and the colours of the emitted gluon.

Answer

Gluons do not change flavour via the colour interaction, so the new quark is also an s quark. To conserve colour, the emitted gluon must carry green and antiblue colours.

Confinement

The quark idea introduced order, in the sense that the properties of many particles could now be understood in terms of the properties of quarks. The only problem was that, despite much effort, no quarks were found. But the quark idea persisted, at least as a mathematical method of classifying hadrons. Soon afterwards, experimental results were obtained that indicated that quarks were not just convenient mathematical tools for classifying particles but actual real particles themselves with definite mass, electric charge and other properties (see Option J4).

However, no quarks have actually been observed as free particles. Quarks only exist within hadrons. This has led to an important principle, that of **confinement**:

▶ It is not possible to observe isolated quarks (and gluons). Quarks inside a hadron always appear in colour combinations that result in zero net colour number. This is called *quark confinement* or *confinement of colour*.

Suppose that one attempts to remove a quark from inside a meson. The force between the quark and the antiquark is *constant* no matter what their separation is (Figure J3.9a). Therefore, the total energy needed to separate the quark from the antiquark gets larger and larger as the separation increases. To free the quark completely would require an infinite amount of energy, and so is impossible. If one insisted on providing more and more energy in the hope of isolating the quark, all that would happen would be the production of a meson–antimeson pair and not free quarks.

This situation is in sharp contrast to the electric force between two opposite electric charges, which decreases as the separation between the charges increases (Figure J3.9b).

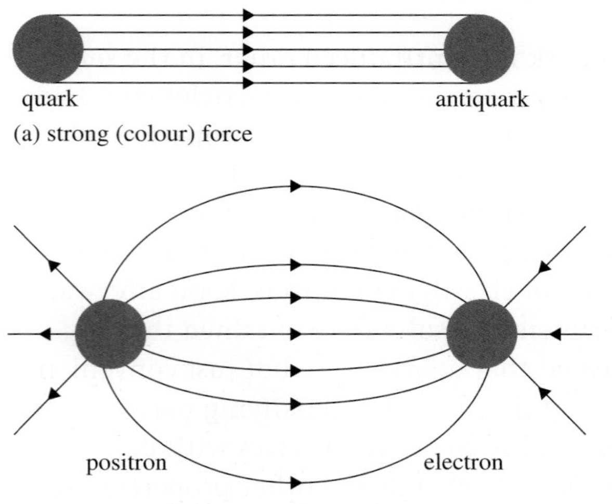

Figure J3.9 The lines of force between a quark and an antiquark are very different from those between a positive and a negative electric charge, leading to quark confinement.

The interaction between nucleons

We know from nuclear physics that protons and neutrons are tightly bound within nuclei with the strong nuclear force. What is the relation between the strong nuclear force of nuclear physics and the interaction between quarks and gluons?

The strong nuclear force was observed long before we had any understanding of quarks and gluons. This force was explained by the Japanese physicist Hideki Yukawa in the 1930s as an exchange of *pions* (and other mesons like the ω and the ρ) between protons and neutrons. In reality, this force is what the exchange of gluons between quarks inside nucleons *appears* to be to an observer (Figure J3.10), who cannot see individual quarks and gluons. Figure J3.10 shows quarks inside protons exchanging gluons. To an outside observer far away, the exchanged gluons appear to be mesons.

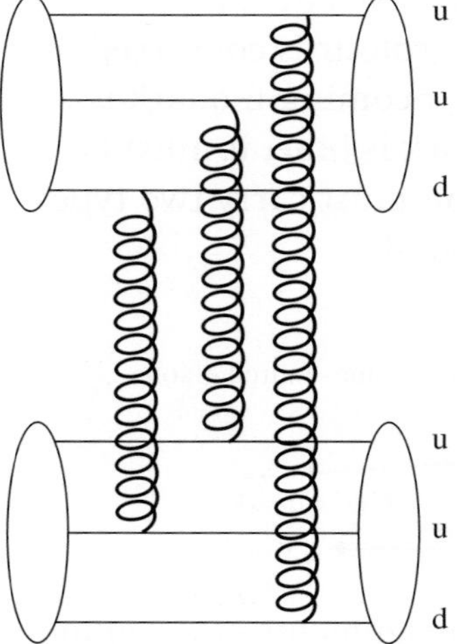

Figure J3.10 The interaction between quarks appears as an exchange of mesons.

Quarks, leptons and the standard model

The theory of quarks and leptons is called the **standard model** of elementary particles. We have seen how quarks build up hadrons and how quarks interact through the exchange of gluons. We have also seen that the basic interaction vertices of the weak interaction bring leptons into the picture. The standard model (Table J3.2) has classified the quarks and leptons into three **families** (or generations). The electric charge, rest mass and spin of all of these were given earlier in Tables J1.1 and J1.2. It appears that each family is a copy of the one before, but heavier in mass overall.

	Leptons	Quarks
First family	e^-	u
	ν_e	d
Second family	μ^-	s
	ν_μ	c
Third family	τ^-	b
	ν_τ	t

Table J3.2 The leptons and quarks of the standard model arranged in three families (or generations).

Lepton number

A number of decays that at first sight appear possible do not in fact take place. One such example is the following reaction, which has never been observed:

$$\mu^- \rightarrow e^- + \gamma$$

This is allowed by energy, charge, momentum and angular momentum.

To understand these reactions, a new conservation law was hypothesized, that of lepton number conservation. The leptons of *each* family (or generation) are assigned a **lepton number** as shown in Table J3.3. Because we have three families, three lepton numbers are needed. So we have electron, muon and tau lepton numbers, L_e, L_μ and L_τ, respectively.

The antiparticles of these leptons are assigned the opposite lepton number. Thus the electron neutrino differs from the electron antineutrino (even though they are both electrically neutral) because they have opposite lepton numbers. The three kinds of lepton number are *individually* conserved in *all* reactions.

	L_e	L_μ	L_τ
Electron, e^-	+1	0	0
Electron neutrino, ν_e	+1	0	0
Muon, μ^-	0	+1	0
Muon neutrino, ν_μ	0	+1	0
Tau, τ^-	0	0	+1
Tau neutrino, ν_τ	0	0	+1

Table J3.3 Lepton number assignments.

Consider, for example, the following decay of a muon:

$$\begin{array}{ccccccc} \mu^- & \rightarrow & e^- & + & \bar{\nu}_e & + & \nu_\mu \\ (L_\mu = 1) & = & (L_e = 1) & + & (L_e = -1) & + & (L_\mu = 1) \end{array}$$

In this, both electron and muon lepton numbers are conserved. (The tau lepton number is also conserved, being zero on both sides of the reaction.)

The absence of the decay $\mu^- \rightarrow e^- + \gamma$ is then understood since it violates the conservation of both electron and muon lepton numbers.

▶ We can summarize by saying that, in all reactions, the following quantities are *always conserved*:

- Energy
- Momentum (and angular momentum)
- Electric charge
- Baryon number
- Colour
- Lepton number

The Higgs particle

We come finally to a discussion of this rather mysterious particle. The **Higgs particle** is a neutral, spin-0 particle that plays a crucial role in the standard model. Despite very many efforts, this particle has not yet been detected experimentally. From the various attempts to find it, it is estimated that its mass is between 120 and 200 GeV c^{-2}. This means that the LHC (Large Hadron Collider) at CERN has a good chance of finding it – unless Fermilab beats them to it.

The Higgs particle is closely linked to the mystery of mass. What exactly is mass and how do the elementary particles acquire mass? In particular, why do the elementary particles have the mass that they have? The mathematical theory describing the electroweak interaction is one of symmetry. Among many other things, this symmetry forbids the photon and the W and Z bosons from having mass. The photon is indeed massless, so this is fine. But the W and the Z are massive. For years physicists searched for a way both to preserve the mathematical symmetry of the theory and at the same time to allow the W and the Z to have mass. The mechanism was found by Peter Higgs and is called the **Higgs mechanism**. (This mechanism was arrived at simultaneously by others as well, notably by F. Englert and R. Brout as well as by G. S. Guralnik, C. R. Hagen and T. W. B. Kibble. The main idea has its origins in earlier work by Philip Anderson as well as by Y. Nambu and G. Jona-Lasinio. As has often happened in the history of physics many people arrive at the same idea but, unfairly, only one name gets associated with it.) The price to be paid for achieving this was to introduce a new particle, a neutral, spin-0 particle, whose interactions with the particles of the standard model gave mass to the particles. This was the Higgs particle.

▶ The *Higgs particle* is responsible for the mass of the particles of the standard model, in particular the masses of the W and the Z.

The Higgs particle is a difficult particle. It is the quantum of the Higgs field just as the photon is the quantum of the electromagnetic field. However, it differs from the electromagnetic field in one crucial way. If the universe is full of electromagnetic waves, the universe contains a certain amount of energy as a result of the presence of the electromagnetic fields. The state of minimum energy of the universe corresponds, as one might guess, to the state where the electromagnetic field is zero (Figure J3.11a). Zero field leads to zero energy. This is not the case for the Higgs field. The universe is permeated with the Higgs field, and has some energy as a result. However, the lowest possible value of this energy does not correspond to a zero value of the Higgs field (Figure J3.11b).

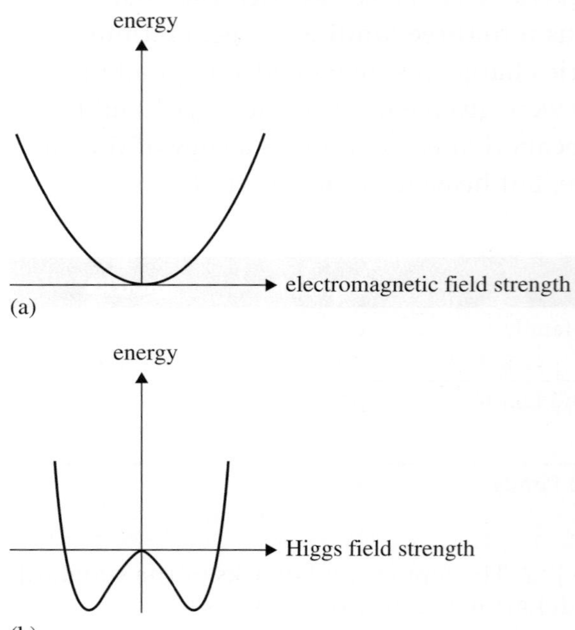

Figure J3.11 The energy of the universe as a result of (a) an electromagnetic field and (b) a Higgs field.

The idea of mass being acquired as a result of an interaction is a difficult one. But a similar idea also exists in classical mechanics. A ball of mass m that is being dragged through a fluid by a pulling force F will have an acceleration that is a bit less than $\frac{F}{m}$. This is because turbulence is created in the fluid and results in a small force opposing the motion and hence a smaller acceleration than expected. This has the same effect as saying that, as a result of the interaction of the body with the fluid, the body increased its mass a bit and the force F results in a smaller acceleration.

? QUESTIONS

1 Write down the quark structure of (a) the antineutron and (b) the antiproton, and verify that the charges come out correctly.

2 Explain, in terms of quarks, what is meant by the terms (a) hadron, (b) meson and (c) baryon.

3 Write down the quark structure of the antiparticle of the meson $K^+ = (u\bar{s})$.

4 When two quarks are interacting electromagnetically, which particle are they exchanging?

5 What is the baryon number of the quark combination $\overline{ccc}$?

6 Determine whether the following reactions conserve or violate baryon number:

(a) $p^+ \rightarrow e^+ + \gamma$

(b) $p^+ + p^- \rightarrow \pi^+ + \pi^-$

(c) $p^+ + p^- \rightarrow \pi^+ + \pi^- + n + \bar{n}$

(d) $\Lambda^0 \rightarrow \pi^+ + \pi^-$

7 In the reaction $p + p \rightarrow p + p + X$, which *baryon* could X stand for?

8 Suggest the reason that led to the introduction of the quantum number called strangeness.

9 The quark content of a certain meson is $(d\bar{s})$.

(a) What is its charge and strangeness?

(b) Is it its own antiparticle?

10 A charmed D meson is made out of $D = (c\bar{d})$.

(a) What is its charge?

(b) What is its strangeness?

11 Determine whether the following reactions conserve strangeness:

(a) $\pi^- + p^+ \rightarrow K^0 + \Lambda^0$

(b) $\pi^0 + n \rightarrow K^+ + \Sigma^-$

(c) $K^0 \rightarrow \pi^- + \pi^+$

(d) $\pi^- + p^+ \rightarrow \pi^- + \Sigma^+$

12 Can a meson containing one strange quark be its own antiparticle?

13 The neutral meson $\eta_c = (c\bar{c})$ is its own antiparticle, but the neutral $K^0 = (d\bar{s})$ is not. Explain why.

14 (a) What is the charge and strangeness of the baryon $\Lambda = (uds)$?

(b) Since the three quarks in this baryon have different flavours, Pauli's exclusion principle is satisfied. Does this mean that all three could then have the same colour? Why or why not?

15 (a) State the numerical value of the spin of a quark, including its unit in the SI system.

(b) Using appropriate diagrams, explain why baryons are fermions and mesons are bosons.

16 A bound state of an electron and a positron is called positronium. (It is unstable and decays quickly.)

(a) State the possible spin values of positronium.

(b) Spin is a kind of angular momentum, and angular momentum is conserved in all reactions. Linear momentum is also conserved in all reactions. Using your answer in (a), explain how positronium can decay into two or three photons but not into one. (Hint: the spin of a photon is 1.)

17 (a) The positive pion π^+ has the quark content $(u\bar{d})$ and rest mass 140 MeV c^{-2}. Explain why there exists a *different* meson (the ρ^+ of rest mass 770 MeV c^{-2}) with the same quark content as the π^+.

(b) The negative pion π^- has quark content $(d\bar{u})$. Explain how it may be deduced that there exists a meson with the same quark content as the π^- and rest mass 770 MeV c^{-2}.

18 State and explain the reasons that made the introduction of the quantum number 'colour' necessary.

19 (a) What do you understand by the term 'confinement' in relation to quarks and gluons?

(b) The Feynman diagram in Figure J3.12 shows the decay of a quark–antiquark pair in a meson into two gluons. With reference to your answer in (a), suggest what might happen to the gluons produced in this decay.

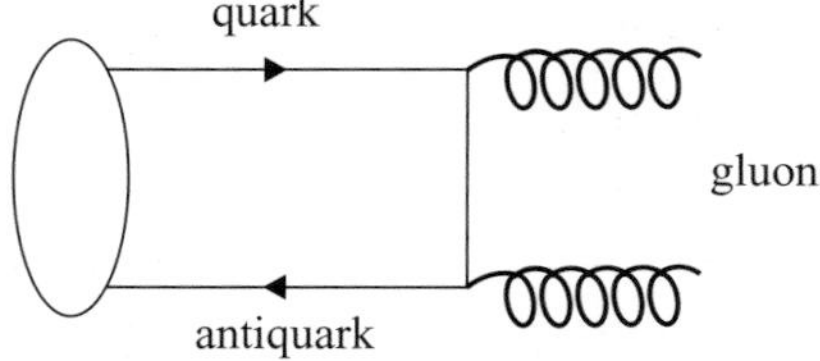

Figure J3.12 For question 19.

20 Explain how (a) baryons and (b) mesons are 'colourless', i.e. have zero colour quantum numbers, whereas the quarks of which they are made do have colour.

21 The diagram in Figure J3.13 represents beta decay.

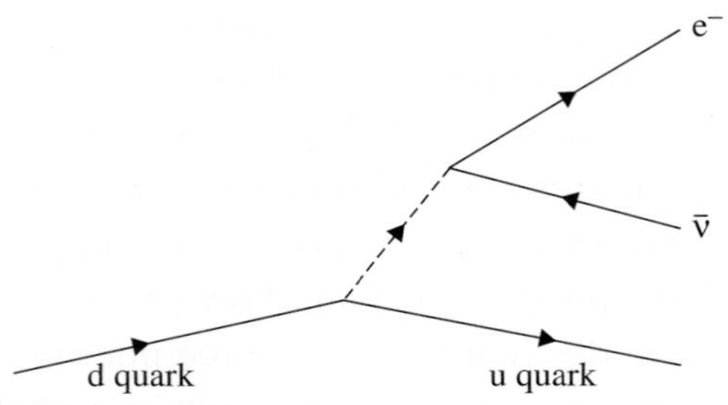

Figure J3.13 For question 21.

(a) State the name of the particle represented by the dashed line.

(b) State and explain how the colour of the u quark compares to the colour of the d quark in the diagram.

22 A blue c quark emits a virtual blue–antigreen gluon. What are the changes, if any, in colour and flavour of the quark?

23 Gell-Mann's 'eightfold way' classification of the spin-0 mesons (made out of the u, d and s quarks) is given in Figure J3.14. Identify the quark content of the indicated mesons. Do not concern yourself with the three mesons at the centre.

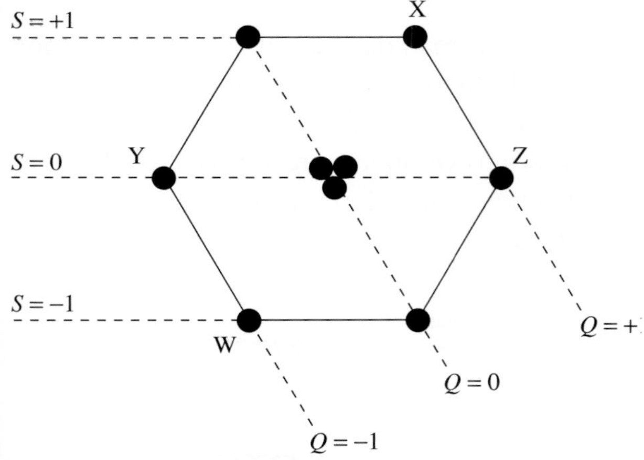

Figure J3.14 For question 23.

24 A neutral meson contains a u quark and a u antiquark and has rest energy equal to 135 MeV. The meson is at rest.

(a) Draw a Feynman diagram to represent the decay of this meson into two photons.

(b) Explain why the two photons must be emitted in opposite directions.

(c) Calculate the wavelength of each of the photons.

Consider instead the case where the meson is moving in the positive x-direction, say, and emits a photon in the positive x-direction and a second photon in the negative x-direction.

(d) Which of these two photons has the smaller wavelength?

25 Outline how the exchange of gluons by quarks results in the strong nuclear force between nucleons.

26 (a) The rest mass of the proton is 938 MeV c^{-2} and that of the neutron is 940 MeV c^{-2}. Using the known quark contents of the proton and the neutron, calculate the masses of the u and d quarks.

(b) Using the values you calculated in (a), predict the mass of the meson π^+ (which is made out of a u quark and an d antiquark).

(c) The actual value of the rest mass of the π^+ is about 140 MeV c^{-2}. Suggest how this enormous disagreement is resolved.

27 In the reactions listed below, various neutrinos appear (just denoted ν). In each case, identify the correct neutrino (ν_e, ν_μ, ν_τ or the antiparticles of these).

(a) $\pi^+ \to \pi^0 + e^+ + \nu$

(b) $\pi^+ \to \pi^0 + \mu^+ + \nu$

(c) $\tau^+ \to \pi^- + \pi^+ + \nu$

(d) $p^+ + \nu \to n + e^+$

(e) $\tau^- \to e^- + \nu + \nu$

28 Do the following reactions conserve lepton number?

(a) $p^+ \to e^+ + \pi^0$

(b) $\pi^0 \to e^+ + \mu^-$

(c) $\tau^+ \to \pi^+ + \bar{\nu}_\tau$

(d) $\pi^- \to e^- + \bar{\nu}_e$

29 Using the weak interaction vertices of Option J1, draw a Feynman diagram for the reaction $\mu^+ + e^- \to \bar{\nu}_\mu + \nu_e$.

30 The reactions listed below are all impossible because they violate one or more conservation laws. In each case, identify the law that is violated.

(a) $K^+ \rightarrow \mu^- + \bar{\nu}_\mu + e^+ + e^+$

(b) $\mu^- \rightarrow e^+ + \gamma$

(c) $\tau^+ \rightarrow \gamma + \bar{\nu}_\tau$

(d) $p + n \rightarrow p + \pi^0$

(e) $e^+ \rightarrow \mu^+ + \bar{\nu}_\mu + \bar{\nu}_e$

(f) $p \rightarrow \pi^+ + \pi^-$

31 Describe the significance of the Higgs particle in the standard model of quarks and leptons.

Experimental evidence for the standard model

This chapter describes the experimental evidence for the main features of the standard model of quarks and leptons. This consists mainly of deep inelastic scattering experiments and the discovery of the weak neutral currents.

Objectives

By the end of this chapter you should be able to:

- state the meaning of the term *deep inelastic scattering*;
- describe and discuss the main results from *deep inelastic scattering experiments*;
- describe the concept of *asymptotic freedom*;
- understand what is meant by *weak neutral currents*.

Gell-Mann's prediction of the omega-minus

One of the earliest predictions of the quark model that lent major support to the model was the prediction, based on quarks, of a new particle that had not yet been observed.

As we discussed on page 749, since each quark has spin $\frac{1}{2}$, putting three of them together in a baryon can result in a total spin of $\frac{3}{2}$ (all three have spin 'up'). Spin-$\frac{3}{2}$ baryons vary in charge from -1 to $+2$ units, and their strangeness varies from -3 to 0. The known spin-$\frac{3}{2}$ baryons could thus be grouped in the pattern shown in Figure J4.1 according to charge Q and strangeness S.

Each solid circle represents a baryon and all were detected in earlier experiments. There was an obvious gap at the bottom of the 'triangle', however. This was a negatively charged, spin-$\frac{3}{2}$ baryon with strangeness -3, consisting of three strange quarks. Based on the pattern of the masses in this diagram, Murray Gell-Mann could also predict the mass of the new particle.

The omega-minus Ω^- was discovered shortly afterwards at Brookhaven National Laboratory. This discovery lent major support to the idea of quarks.

The direct evidence for quarks

The discovery of the omega-minus was a major breakthrough for the quark model. But it was also *indirect* support for quarks, since no quarks were directly observed.

Direct evidence for quarks appeared in the mid-1960s in **deep inelastic scattering** experiments, performed mainly at SLAC (the Stanford Linear Accelerator), in which very energetic electrons were directed towards protons and their scattering analysed. These experiments are modern versions of the Geiger–Marsden–Rutherford experiment, in which the scattering

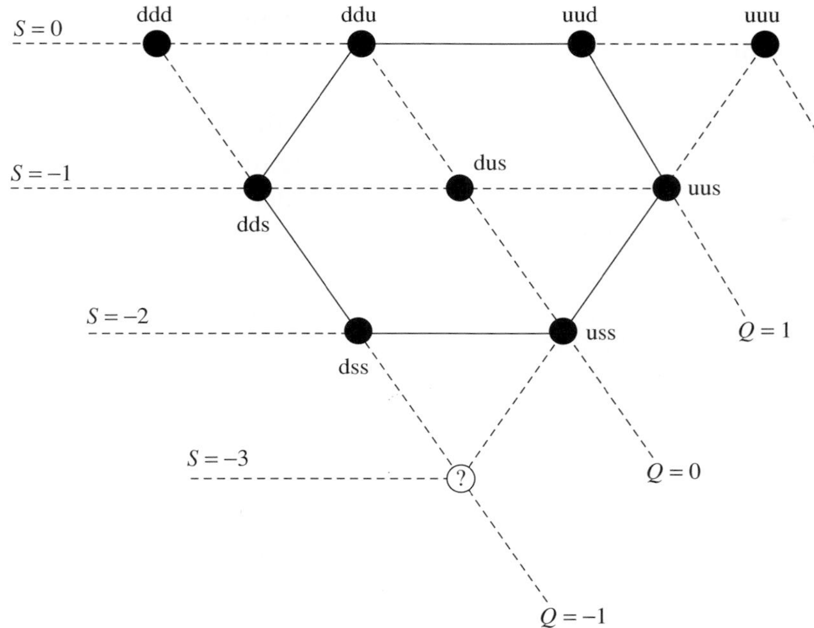

Figure J4.1 Classification of spin-$\frac{3}{2}$ baryons.

of alpha particles fired at thin gold foils was studied.

▶ In a *deep inelastic scattering* experiment, a lepton (e.g. an electron) scatters off a hadron (e.g. a proton) and transfers large amounts of energy and momentum to the hadron (hence the word 'deep'). The word 'inelastic' signifies that after the collision new hadrons are produced.

The main idea of these experiments is that the scattered leptons behave very differently when they scatter off a particle with no structure than when the particle has structure (Figure J4.2).

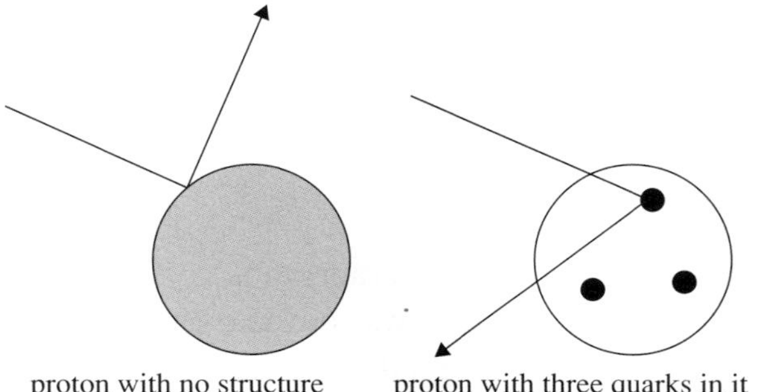

Figure J4.2 Scattering a high-energy electron off a solid proton would give different results than scattering off a proton with three smaller particles inside it.

The Feynman diagram for a typical deep inelastic scattering of an electron off a proton is shown in Figure J4.3. It is found that the scattering pattern (scattering angles and energies of the leptons) is consistent with the existence of very small, hard objects inside the proton. Because the electrons are very energetic, they penetrate the proton volume and 'see' the individual quarks. If the energy of the electrons is not high enough, they scatter off the proton volume as a whole without 'feeling' what is inside the proton.

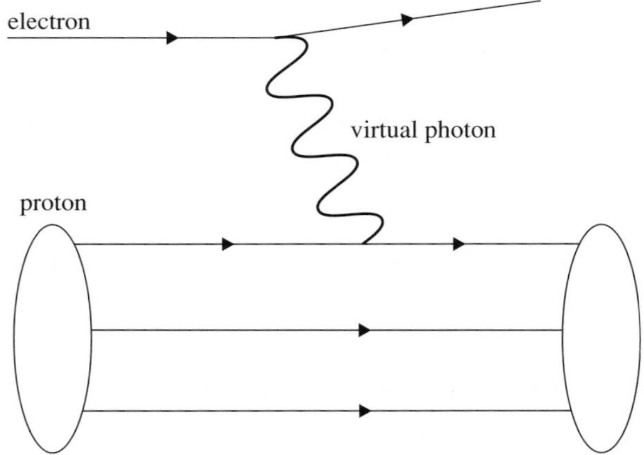

Figure J4.3 Feynman diagram for deep inelastic scattering.

These experiments reach five main conclusions. The conclusions and a discussion of each follows below.

Conclusion 1 There are three small constituent particles inside baryons and two inside mesons (evidence for quarks).

These experiments can measure the probability that a given constituent of the proton carries a fraction x of the proton's total momentum. This probability is known as the **structure function** of the proton and is denoted by $F_2(x)$. The graph in Figure J4.4 shows this function for the proton. The peak at about $x = 0.3$ is consistent with the expectation that, with three quarks inside the proton, each would, on average, carry one-third of the momentum of the proton.

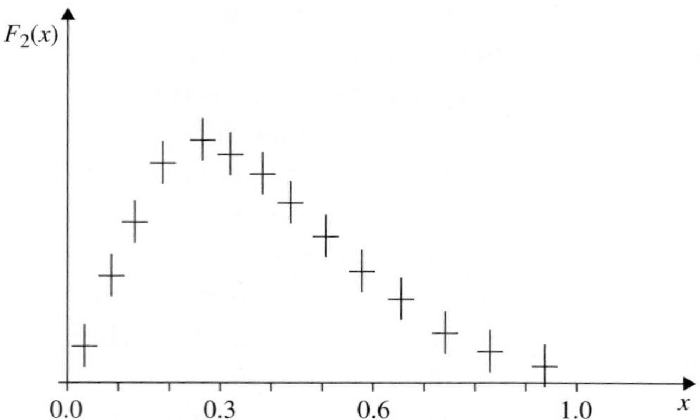

Figure J4.4 The structure function for the proton measures the probability that a given constituent of the proton carries a given fraction x of the proton's total momentum.

Conclusion 2 These particles are charged, and their electric charge is either $\pm\frac{1}{3}e$ or $\pm\frac{2}{3}e$ (evidence for fractionally charged quarks).

The electron transfers energy and momentum to the proton through the exchanged virtual photon. Because the interaction is electromagnetic, it follows that the strength of the interaction is known as the electromagnetic interaction strength (or coupling constant). But measurements and calculations from the experiments show that the amplitude is not exactly proportional to $\sqrt{\alpha_{EM}} \times \sqrt{\alpha_{EM}} = \alpha_{EM}$ as one would expect if the particle inside the proton had a charge equal to e. It is in fact somewhat smaller, indicating that the charge of the constituent particle is less than e. Detailed measurements thus reveal that the charges of the quarks are either $\pm\frac{1}{3}e$ or $\pm\frac{2}{3}e$.

Conclusion 3 The particles inside the hadron behave essentially as free particles, i.e. they are loosely bound to each other (evidence for asymptotic freedom – see page 761).

An electron penetrating the proton volume and scattering off an individual quark would bounce off differently if the quark were very strongly bound to its neighbouring quarks. A strongly bound quark would not rebound and the electron would then suffer a deflection at a large angle. The experiments show small deflections, which is evidence that the quark rebounds a lot in the presence of the incoming electron. This can only be because the quark is very loosely bound to the other quarks inside the hadron. This is a very important but somewhat technical conclusion, the full significance of which will be discussed in the next section on asymptotic freedom.

Conclusion 4 Each of the constituent particles appears to come in three types (evidence for colour).

Consider, again, the Feynman diagram in Figure J4.3 in which an incoming electron interacts electromagnetically with one quark inside a proton. Let A be the amplitude corresponding to this Feynman diagram. If colour exists, then we must include three diagrams rather than the single one of Figure J4.3. These will be diagrams in which the colour of the quark interacting with the photon is either blue, green or red. When more than one Feynman diagram contributes to the same process, the amplitude for each must be added in order to get the total amplitude. This is essentially the principle of superposition in waves applied to quantum mechanics. The total amplitude will therefore be $3A$, and so larger. Indeed, the experiments show that the amplitude for this process is larger by precisely the correct factor consistent with three colours.

Conclusion 5 There appear to be electrically neutral constituents inside hadrons (evidence for gluons).

Precisely because the interaction is electromagnetic, it follows that the electron can 'see' only the charged constituents of the proton. These experiments allow for the measurement of the momentum of the particles to which the electron couples. It is found that the total momentum of these particles is less than that of the proton itself. It therefore follows that there are other constituents inside the proton that are electrically neutral. This is taken as evidence for the gluons.

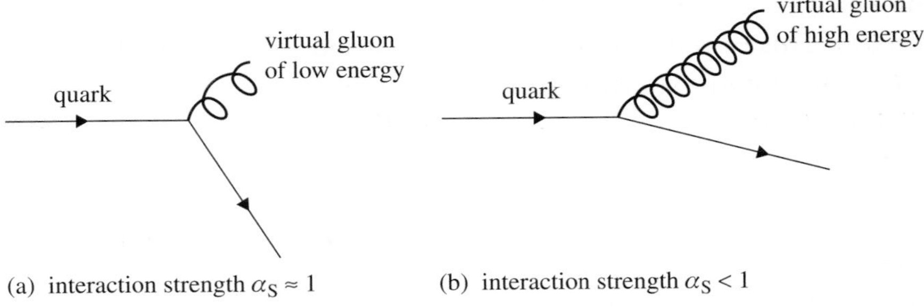

Figure J4.5 The interaction strength decreases as the energy transferred increases.

Asymptotic freedom

We saw in Table J1.4 that the electromagnetic, weak and strong interactions have interaction strengths that are approximately $\alpha_{EM} \approx \frac{1}{137}$, $\alpha_W \approx 10^{-6}$ and $\alpha_S \approx 1$. This justifies the name 'strong' given to the strong interaction – its interaction strength is much larger than those for the other two interactions. The fact that $\alpha_S \approx 1$ poses serious difficulties. We saw that an interaction vertex in a Feynman diagram is assigned a factor of $\sqrt{\alpha}$. This means that, if $\alpha < 1$, diagrams with many vertices have a much smaller probability of occurring, and so it is a safe approximation to consider only the simplest Feynman diagram for the process (i.e. the one with the least number of vertices). But for the strong interaction $\alpha_S \approx 1$, and so all Feynman diagrams are equally important and likely. To calculate so many diagrams is impossible, and this fact delayed progress in the understanding of the strong interaction.

The 1970s, however, saw a great advance in theoretical physics. It was realized that interaction strengths (or coupling 'constants') are in fact *not* constant. Rather, they depend on the energy that is transferred at the interaction vertices of a Feynman diagram. For the strong interaction, in particular, it was shown by the 2004 Nobel prize winners Hugh Politzer, David Gross and Frank Wilzcek that the strong interaction strength α_S actually decreased as the energy increased (see Figure J4.5).

▶ The decrease of α_S with energy is known as *asymptotic freedom*. This means that, as the energy exchanged between quarks increases, the quarks behave as free particles rather than as tightly bound objects.

This decrease of the interaction strength is a purely quantum phenomenon and cannot be explained in classical physics. In practice, it means that one can perform reliable calculations of processes involving the strong interaction. We owe our present understanding of the strong interaction to such calculations carried out in the 1970s and 1980s. Glimpses of this behavior were seen in the early deep inelastic scattering experiments mentioned above, where it was observed that when quarks were probed with high-energy particles the quarks behaved as almost free.

The discovery of the Z^0 and neutral currents

As we mentioned earlier, the electromagnetic and weak interactions can be unified into a single interaction called the **electroweak theory**. Like QCD this is also a gauge theory based on symmetry. (The technical symmetry here is the group $SU(2) \times U(1)$.) This theory, developed by S. Weinberg, S. Glashow and A. Salam in the late 1960s, faced serious problems, however. Calculations of Feynman diagrams in this theory gave infinite, and so meaningless, answers. It was not until the 1970s that a spectacular breakthrough by the Dutch physicists G. 't Hooft and M. Veltman showed that the infinite answers in the Feynman diagrams could be eliminated and that meaningful calculations could be made in this theory. This development inspired renewed theoretical and experimental work on the standard model.

The experimental breakthrough came in 1983 at CERN. The objective was to see evidence for the crucial features of the standard model, namely the existence of the massive $W^{\pm}$ and, especially, the neutral Z^0 bosons. CERN operated a proton–antiproton collider in which protons and antiprotons were allowed to collide after being accelerated to very high energies.

The protons in one beam had a total energy of about 270 GeV. The antiprotons were accelerated to the same energy and were moving in a second beam in the opposite direction to that of the protons. When the two beams were allowed to collide, a Z^0 was occasionally created. The Z^0 immediately decayed into an electron–positron pair according to the reaction

$$Z^0 \rightarrow e^- + e^+$$

and could be detected.

The collision produced hundreds of hadrons that were emitted mostly along the collision axis. The electron–positron pair was produced at fairly large angles to the collision axis and thus could be identified. Their energy and momentum could be measured from the curvature of the circular paths in the magnetic field of the detector. This information allowed the determination of the mass of the particle whose decay gave rise to the $e^- + e^+$ pair. In this way the Z^0 was discovered and its rest mass was measured to be about 90 GeV c^{-2}.

The discovery of the Z^0 was extremely crucial. Only the standard model predicted **neutral current** processes. This is the technical name for processes mediated by a *massive, neutral* particle, the Z^0 (Figure J4.6). This was the most convincing confirmation of the validity of the standard model.

In the same experiments, the charged bosons $W^{\pm}$ were also discovered, and their rest mass was measured to be about 80 GeV c^{-2}. The $W^{\pm}$ were detected through decays like $W^+ \rightarrow e^+ + \nu_e$ and $W^- \rightarrow e^- + \overline{\nu}_e$.

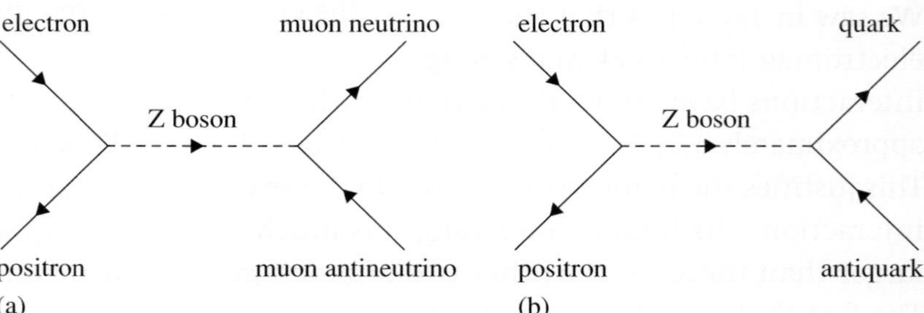

Figure J4.6 Two neutral current processes mediated by the neutral Z^0.

? QUESTIONS

1 What do the words *deep* and *inelastic* refer to in the context of deep inelastic scattering experiments?

2 Outline how deep inelastic scattering experiments provide evidence for the existence of colour on quarks.

3 Explain how deep inelastic scattering experiments with electrons can give information only about the electrically charged components of a hadron.

4 Consider the annihilation of an electron–positron pair into a u quark and a u antiquark: $e^- + e^+ \rightarrow u + \overline{u}$

(a) Draw the Feynman diagram for this process, assuming that colour does not exist. Call the amplitude for this process *A*.

(b) Explain why, with coloured quarks, the amplitude of the process is in fact 3*A*.

(c) Suggest how this can be used to provide experimental support for colour.

5 Outline what is meant by *asymptotic freedom.* What experimental evidence is there to support asymptotic freedom?

6 Unlike QCD, QED (the theory of the electromagnetic interaction) does not have the property of asymptotic freedom. What does this imply about the interaction strength of the electromagnetic interaction as the exchanged energy increases?

7 In a process known as Compton scattering, a photon is scattered off a proton.
(a) Draw a diagram to show the scattering of a photon of energy (i) 1.0 GeV and (ii) 100 GeV off a proton. Explain each of your diagrams.
(b) Draw a possible Feynman diagram representing the scattering of a photon off a proton.
(c) Suggest how this process may be used to provide evidence for colour.

8 State what is meant by a *neutral current process*. Outline the discovery of the Z boson.

9 Consider the Feynman diagrams of Figure J4.6.
(a) In one of these diagrams it is possible to replace the Z boson with a photon. State in which one, and explain your answer.
(b) Suggest reasons why the process represented by the (new) diagram with the photon is more likely to occur than that represented by the (old) diagram with the Z boson.

10 The Z boson was discovered through its decay into an electron–positron pair. Assuming that a Z boson decays from rest, calculate the total energy of (a) the electron and (b) the positron.

11 The Z boson was discovered in proton–antiproton collisions. The Z boson produced in these collisions decayed into an electron–positron pair. Explain why it was an advantage that the electron–positron pair was produced at large angles to the proton–antiproton paths.

Cosmology and strings

This chapter begins with the important connection between absolute temperature and the average kinetic energy of particles that are at equilibrium at that temperature. The early universe following the Big Bang had a very high temperature, and so the particles that were present then had very high energies. This makes the early universe a very suitable place in which to apply the ideas and theories of particle physics.

Objectives

By the end of this chapter you should be able to:

- state the relation between *absolute temperature* and the *average kinetic energy* of particles that are at equilibrium at that temperature, $\bar{E}_k = \frac{3}{2}kT$;
- apply the relation between temperature and kinetic energy to a variety of *situations in the early universe*;
- appreciate that there is an *asymmetry between matter and antimatter*;
- outline the general idea of *string theories* and be aware that these demand more dimensions than the four we observe;
- appreciate the fact the string theories appear to provide for a *quantum theory of gravity*.

The Boltzmann equation

One of the biggest discoveries of nineteenth-century physics was the connection between the average kinetic energy $\bar{E}_k$ of particles in thermal equilibrium and the absolute temperature (i.e. temperature measured in kelvin). In equation form, this is

$$\bar{E}_k = \frac{3}{2}kT$$

which is called Boltzmann's equation, where k stands for a new constant of physics, the **Boltzmann constant**. The Boltzmann constant is related to the universal gas constant R and the Avogadro constant N_A through

$$k = \frac{R}{N_A} = 1.38 \times 10^{-23}\ \mathrm{J\,K^{-1}}$$

Along with the speed of light c, Planck's constant h and Newton's constant of universal gravitation G, the Boltzmann constant is truly one of the fundamental 'numbers' of physics.

Shortly after the Big Bang, the temperature of the universe was enormous. Going back to a time of 10^{-43} s (perhaps the earliest we can extrapolate backwards) after the Big Bang, the temperature was of the order of 10^{32} K. The temperature today as measured through the cosmic microwave background radiation is only 2.7 K. Boltzmann's equation, $\bar{E}_k = \frac{3}{2}kT$, is of fundamental importance in studies of cosmology and the early universe, because the equation sets the order of magnitude of the energy that was available at any given temperature as the universe cooled down as it expanded. The equation is also important in many other aspects of physics.

Example questions

Q1

Calculate the average kinetic energy of electrons 10^{-10} s after the Big Bang, when the temperature of the universe was $T \approx 10^{15}$ K.

Answer

$$\bar{E}_\text{k} = \frac{3}{2}kT$$

$$= \frac{3 \times 1.38 \times 10^{-23} \times 10^{15}}{2}$$

$$= 2.1 \times 10^{-8}\ \text{J}$$

$$= \frac{2.1 \times 10^{-8}}{1.6 \times 10^{-19}}\ \text{eV}$$

$$\approx 1 \times 10^{11}\ \text{eV}$$

$$\approx 100\ \text{GeV}$$

The average kinetic energy of electrons 10^{-10} s after the Big Bang was approximately 100 GeV.

Q2

The nucleus of helium-4 has a binding energy of about 28 MeV. Calculate the temperature at which thermal motion would break the nucleus apart into its constituents.

Answer

The energy needed to break apart the nucleus of helium into its constituents is 28 MeV. The average kinetic energy of the molecules at a temperature T is $\bar{E}_\text{k} = \frac{3}{2}kT$ and so equating the two gives

$$\frac{3}{2}kT = 28\ \text{MeV}$$

$$T = \frac{2 \times 28 \times 10^{6} \times 1.6 \times 10^{-19}}{3 \times 1.38 \times 10^{-23}}\ \text{K}$$

$$\approx 2 \times 10^{11}\ \text{K}$$

This says that nuclei of helium could not have existed at temperatures of about $T \approx 2 \times 10^{11}$ K or higher. The thermal motion of its constituents and the energy supplied by photons would have broken the nucleus apart.

A more accurate estimate than the one presented in Example question 2 gives a temperature closer to $T \approx 10^{10}$ K. This is the time of *nucleosynthesis*, the time when protons and neutrons combined to form nuclei for the first time. The universe then was only a few minutes old.

The reason our estimate is very much of an overestimate is because of the presence of particles with a *range* of energies. The Boltzmann equation gives just the *average* energy in a distribution of energies. If there are enough high-energy particles or photons around, the nuclei could not have been formed even at lower temperatures than our estimate, which is based on the average energy. Apparently this is the case, since the nucleosynthesis temperature is in fact $T \approx 10^{10}$ K.

▶ Because we frequently use the formula $\frac{3}{2}kT = E$ to find the temperature corresponding to an amount of energy E, and vice versa, it is useful to remember that a temperature of 10^{10} K is in a rough approximation equivalent to about 1 MeV:

$$10^{10}\ \text{K} \Longleftrightarrow 1\ \text{MeV}$$

In the questions at the end of the chapter you will be asked to perform the order-of-magnitude estimate for the *decoupling* temperature of the universe. This is the temperature when the photon energy fell below the level required to excite or ionize the light atoms that were around then (mainly hydrogen and helium). Unable to ionize the atoms, the photons simply move through the atoms unimpeded. At earlier times the higher temperature meant that the photons had enough energy to ionize atoms or to excite electrons to higher energy levels. This meant that the photons would be absorbed. Thus, at the decoupling temperature, atoms become transparent to radiation.

Matter and antimatter

The very early universe contained almost equal numbers of particles and antiparticles. It is predicted that asymmetries in particle interactions then created a very small imbalance of matter over antimatter. There was one extra particle for every 10^9 particle–antiparticle pairs. Yet, today, we see matter and not antimatter. The mechanism by which the antimatter was destroyed leaving only matter behind (the matter we see today) is as follows.

First consider what might happen when the temperature is very high. An electron, or some other charged particle, emits a virtual photon, which subsequently materializes into an electron-positron pair (Figure J5.1). Assuming that the energy of the virtual photon is of the same order of magnitude as the average kinetic energy of particles at temperature T, we can estimate the temperature at which this process is possible.

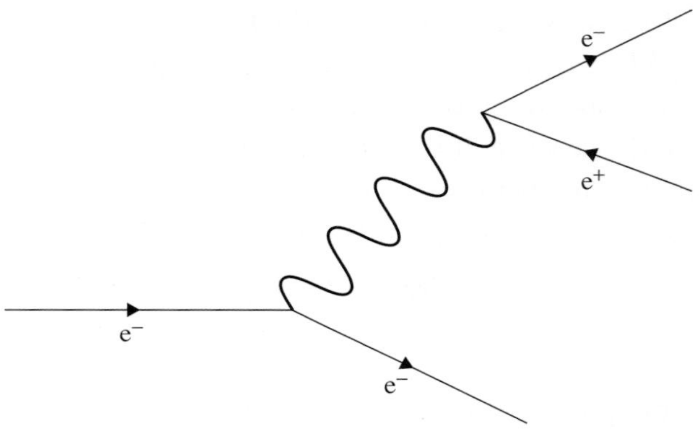

Figure J5.1 At very high temperature, an electron emits a virtual photon that materializes into an electron–positron pair.

To produce the electron–positron pair, we must provide *at least* the rest energy of each particle (plus any kinetic energy they may have). Therefore the least amount of energy that has to be supplied is $2m_ec^2 = (2 \times 0.511 \text{ MeV } c^{-2})c^2 \approx 1 \text{ MeV}$. This corresponds to a temperature of about 10^{10} K.

We see therefore that, at temperatures of 10^{10} K and higher, thermal motion could produce electron–positron pairs. Of course, the reverse process is always possible regardless of temperature. That is to say, an electron colliding with a positron will produce photons at any temperature.

This implies that, at temperatures of 10^{10} K and higher, electrons and positrons annihilated each other but at the same time new electron–positron pairs were created. There was in fact a kind of equilibrium between the two opposing processes. However, as soon as the temperature fell below 10^{10} K, the production of the pairs became impossible (because there was not enough available energy) but the *annihilation continued*. Since there was originally a slightly higher number of particles than antiparticles, what remains today is matter and not antimatter.

Strings

Our discussion so far has barely mentioned the gravitational interaction. The good reason for this is that the strength of this interaction is so small (because of the small masses of the particles involved) so as to make it irrelevant for subatomic physics. However, at very large energy scales (or small distance scales) gravitation does finally become important and becomes comparable to the other interactions. Not only can it not be ignored but also it must be included as a full quantum theory on the same basis as the other interactions.

The problem is that, despite massive efforts, nobody has succeeded in constructing a quantum theory of the gravitational interaction. Attempts to build such a theory by analogy with the theories of the other interactions have all failed.

Faced with this problem, physicists in the 1960s constructed a radically different theory, the theory of **strings**. This theory claims that the fundamental building blocks of matter are not elementary point particles but tiny strings. The length of the strings is assumed to be very small (less than 10^{-35} m), and in the original theories the strings could be *open* (i.e. have two ends) or *closed* (i.e. form a loop). The string theories of the 1960s went largely unnoticed mainly due to the successes of the conventional theories for particles and partly because the string theories needed extra dimensions!

The ordinary world in which we live is a four-dimensional world – in addition to three-dimensional space, the fourth dimension referred to here is time. String theories could not be formulated in this four-dimensional world. Various versions of string theories require 10, 11 or 26 dimensions of space and time. String theories did produce something very new though: they could handle gravitation as a quantum theory! In addition, the old string theories had a few technical problems of their own and, as mentioned, they went largely unnoticed until the early 1980s.

At that time, the technical problems of the old strings were solved and it appeared that for the first time physicists had a quantum theory of gravity. This was supposed to be a theory that would replace the conventional theories of elementary particles such as the standard model. The new string theory required 10 dimensions. The extra six dimensions were 'curled up' into a compact, tiny space that was essentially unobservable.

What does this mean? We will look at a simpler case. Two examples of two-dimensional spaces are shown in Figure J5.2. The first is the ordinary two-dimensional flat plane. A point on this plane is determined if we give two numbers, the x and y coordinates of the point. The space extends forever in both directions. It is an infinite space.

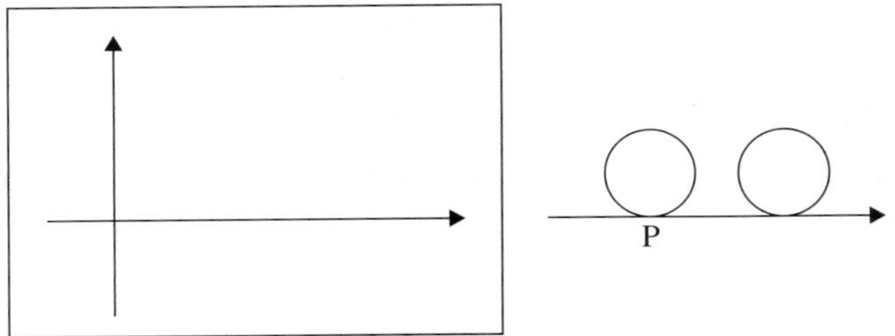

Figure J5.2 Two examples of two-dimensional spaces.

The second diagram also shows a two-dimensional space. One dimension extends forever, but the second dimension is curled up into a circle. You must imagine a circle at every point of the straight axis. The figure only shows two for clarity. Thus if a point is at P, it can move along one dimension or the other. If it moves along the straight line, it will never return to its starting point. On the other hand, if it moves along the circle (the 'other' dimension), it will eventually return to the starting point P. Now if the radius of the circle is really small, then to an observer living in this space, space will appear to have one dimension only. The second dimension is essentially inaccessible to the observer.

In theories of strings, the extra dimensions are assumed to be curled up just like the circle in Figure J5.2. Because they are unobservable, though, it means that their size must be microscopically small. In theories of strings, the actual shape of these extra six-dimensional spaces is quite complex and not at all as simple as the example with the circle that we have used here.

The great promise of string theory was twofold. For one thing, it would provide, for the first time, a viable theory of quantum gravitation. For another, all the properties of the elementary particles would be explained in terms of strings. The idea was that the string would vibrate much like an ordinary string, and standing waves would be formed on the string like the harmonics on ordinary strings. What we normally call *particles* would then be the different *modes of vibration* of the string! Another greatly promising feature of strings was the belief that there could only be one possible string theory. This would be *THE* theory of the interactions in the universe. Unfortunately though, this 'uniqueness' has not held the test of time. There are, now, very many possible string theories, and only experiment can decide which one might describe the real world. There is some hope that in the new generation of planned experiments in particle accelerators predictions made by different string theories might be tested in order to eliminate theories. There is also a hope that the new experiments might (through the predictions made by the various models) give evidence for the existence of the extra dimensions.

? QUESTIONS

1 (a) State the energy of an electron in the ground state of the hydrogen atom.
(b) Using the Boltzmann equation, justify the assumption that collisions between hydrogen atoms are elastic. How realistic do you guess your answer to be?

2 The universe became transparent to radiation when photons could pass through the lightest atoms (i.e. hydrogen and helium) without exciting electrons to energy states above the ground state.
(a) Assuming an energy gap between the ground state and the first excited state of about 10 eV, calculate the temperature at which the photons 'decoupled' from matter according to the simple model based on the Boltzmann equation.
(b) Discuss why your estimate is an overestimate.

3 The time of decoupling (see previous question) is taken as the time at which the cosmic microwave background radiation originated.
(a) Discuss the meaning of this statement.
(b) The temperature then was about 3000 K and the age of the universe about 300 000 years. Calculate the peak wavelength of the cosmic microwave background radiation using Wien's law (see Option E).

4 The present temperature of the cosmic microwave background radiation is about 3 K.
(a) Estimate the average energy of photons at this temperature.
(b) Estimate the energy of photons whose wavelength is the same as the peak wavelength of the black-body spectrum at this temperature, and compare the energy corresponding to this with your estimate from (a).
(c) The wavelengths used in microwave ovens are comparable to those of the cosmic microwave background radiation photons. Since their energy is so small, how can the oven warm up food?

5 (a) State what is meant by the term *decoupling*.
(b) What do you understand by the statement that the universe becomes transparent to photons?

6 A virtual photon can produce a pair of $W^{\pm}$ bosons.
(a) Draw a Feynman diagram for this process.
(b) Estimate the temperature at which the pair can be produced at rest.
(c) A pair of *moving* W bosons can in fact be produced at temperatures *lower* than your estimate in (b). Explain this observation.

7 Suppose that a galaxy contained large amounts of antimatter. Discuss what might be observed if such a galaxy collided with a galaxy made of matter.

8 The early universe contained almost equal numbers of particles and antiparticles. Outline the mechanism by which matter dominates antimatter in the universe today.

9 At LEP, the old CERN collider, protons and antiprotons each of energy 270 GeV collided head-on.
(a) State the value of the available energy.
(b) Calculate the temperature that corresponds to this energy.
(c) Hence, explain the statement that the collider is 'reproducing the early universe'.

10 State the main reason why it has not been possible to construct a quantum theory of the gravitational interaction on the same ground as for the other interactions.

11 It was stated in the text that a time of approximately 10^{-43} s is perhaps the earliest we can extrapolate backwards in time. Suggest a reason why you think this might be so. [Hint: Construct a quantity with units of time from the physical constants c (the speed of light), G (Newton's constant of universal gravitation) and h (the Planck constant).]

12 Discuss the main features of string theories. In what ways are they different from conventional theories of particles?

13 What is the main reason for the excitement about string theory?

14 String theories exist in dimensions higher than four. Outline why the extra dimensions are not directly observable.

Physics and the theory of knowledge (TOK)

This is a brief introduction to the role of physics in the context of the theory of knowledge (TOK) class, which all IB students must take. We will begin with a very short discussion of the developments and changes that have taken place in the theories used to explain phenomena in three areas of physics: the motion of the planets; gas pressure; and the nature of light. We will then take a closer look at the nature of theories and why they need to change.

Those who choose to study the history and development of physics will find that in ancient times the prevailing model of the solar system was a *geocentric* one. In the Ptolemaic system, the earth was at the centre of the solar system and all other celestial bodies orbited it. The practising scientists of the time embraced this model and used it for many purposes. When observations began to accumulate showing disagreement with the model, Ptolemy, among others, modified the model to make it fit the new observations. One such famous alteration was the introduction of *epicycles*. Originally, planets were supposed to move in perfect circles around the earth. With epicycles, the planets now had to complete smaller circles at the same time as they completed the large circular orbit around the earth. When even newer observations showed yet more deviations from the model, more epicycles were introduced with the express purpose of making the model again fit the data. Eventually, more than 50 epicycles were needed to account for the motion of the five known planets, the sun and the moon, resulting in an extremely complicated and cumbersome model. Interestingly, this model lasted for 1400 years before it was replaced (through the efforts of Copernicus, Kepler and Newton) by the modern heliocentric system. The planets orbit the sun in elliptical orbits according to well-defined physical principles summarized in Newton's laws of mechanics and gravitation.

A few centuries later, experimenters looking into the properties of gases realized that the pressure of a gas increased as its volume was slowly compressed. Robert Boyle (one of the gas laws bears his name) thought that a gas consists of tiny springs. When the gas is compressed, the springs are also compressed and the tension of these springs is what gives rise to the pressure of the gas. Newton thought instead that the gas consists of tiny particles between which a force of repulsion exists. The force was hypothesized by Newton to be inversely proportional to their separation. Thus, when the gas was compressed, the repulsive forces between the molecules grew larger, giving rise to the pressure of the gas. Bernoulli, on the other hand, did not find the need to introduce forces between the molecules. The gas, he said, consisted of an extremely large number of particles that moved about and constantly collided with each other and the container walls. It was the momentum exchanged in the collisions that was responsible for the pressure as far as Bernoulli was concerned. Boyle's model is an unnatural model. Why should a gas consist of something as artificial as a spring? Newton's idea is much more reasonable, but it requires the introduction of a new force. What is the origin of the force and where else is it operating? Bernoulli's model is by far the simplest. It requires nothing new, just the application of the laws of mechanics to a very large number of material particles making up the gas.

By the end of the nineteenth century, a very large amount of data had been collected indicating that, when light fell on certain metallic surfaces, negative charges (electrons) were emitted from the surface. The puzzling thing about those observations was that, despite every expectation, increasing the intensity of light did not result in any increase in the energy of the emitted electrons. The puzzling features of the many experiments on this effect (the photoelectric effect) were explained by Albert Einstein in 1905. He proposed a revolutionary theory in which light should be viewed as a stream of massless particles and not as a wave, as had been the practice since the time of Christiaan Huygens. The theory of light as a wave could not account for its behaviour in the photoelectric effect and thus that theory had to be abandoned in favour of a better theory. If the new theory were correct, it should be in a position to predict new phenomena; phenomena that would not be possible within the old theory. Indeed, Einstein's theory of *photons* (the particles of light) predicted that, when light of very short wavelength hit electrons, the light would bounce off the electrons with an *increased* wavelength. Soon afterwards, Arthur Compton observed this scattering of light off electrons in precise agreement with the new theory of light as photons.

We may extract a number of observations from the previous three paragraphs, which may help us in our discussion. Knowledge in physics accumulates when observations of physical phenomena must be explained. To explain these phenomena, a *model* is constructed. The model is a set of rules, usually accompanied by a set of pictures, describing how a few basic ingredients are supposed to work so that the phenomena are explained at some level. In Ptolemy's model of the solar system, the ingredients were the earth, the sun and the planets, and his rules stated that these objects moved in circular paths around the earth. This model could explain some rough features of the observations about the motion of celestial bodies. When the observations did not exactly agree with Ptolemy's predictions based on circular orbits, epicycles were introduced. There was no other reason to introduce the epicycles other than to make the model fit the data. Epicycles were *ad hoc* statements made to save a model. Fourteen centuries later, Kepler, using much more accurate data than was available to Ptolemy, deduced that planets move in elliptical orbits around the sun. His model was a better model than Ptolemy's. For one thing, it was simpler. It agreed with observations very well and could explain things that Ptolemy's model could not, such as why the brightness of the planets varies at different times of the year. Kepler could state that planets covered equal areas in equal times and could calculate the time of revolution of a planet around the sun if he knew the distance between the planet and the sun. Ptolemy's model could not even handle these questions let alone answer them, but even Kepler could not explain *why* the planets moved in elliptical paths. To answer such a detailed question more knowledge was required; this was supplied by Newton, who realized that the key behind it all was a force of attraction between the sun and the planets – the force of gravity. Newton thus made a new and simpler model whose premise was a force of attraction between *any* two masses, not just those of celestial bodies. It could be shown that all the observations that Kepler had made were simple *consequences* of the law of gravitation and the laws of mechanics.

The development of the models of the motion of the planets from Ptolemy to Newton was not a gradual evolution, with a few details of the original model changing as it was refined into a better one. It involved an abrupt and fundamental change – a change in *paradigm* and, as philosopher Thomas Kuhn says, a 'scientific revolution'. Newton's ideas about the motion of the planets were a fundamental and different reconsideration of the entire problem, not an attempt to fix some of the original model's flaws.

The signs that the original model was wrong were many and obvious. First because observations did not agree with the model and second because the model was getting too complicated, too cumbersome and too *ad hoc*. Newton's model was simpler, more elegant, more general and agreed with the data. Newton's model passed many tests. Detailed predictions based on the model were found to be true by observation. By the early part of the nineteenth century, anomalies (i.e. deviations from Newtonian behaviour) were observed in the motion of the planet Uranus. The astronomers J. C. Adams in England and U. Le Verrier in France assumed that an unknown planet was affecting the orbit of Uranus. By applying Newton's law of gravitation, the two independently showed that the anomalies in the Uranus orbit could be explained by the presence of this planet. Calculations showed the position of the planet and the very night Le Verrier's letter arrived at the Berlin observatory the planet Neptune was discovered exactly where Le Verrier said it should be. More detailed calculations, however, showed that the effect of Neptune explained most, but not all, of the anomaly in the Uranus orbit. More work again showed that a smaller planet was responsible for that bit of the anomaly. After several decades of intensive search, the planet Pluto was discovered at the edge of the solar system. (Pluto has recently been downgraded to a 'dwarf planet'.) Newtonian gravitation was triumphant. These were tremendous successes for physics and showed the *universality* of physical laws – they could be applied anywhere not just on earth. Even though many other disciplines have tried to imitate and copy the methods of physics (with varying success), no other discipline has been able to produce the universality of its laws.

At about the same time as Adams and Le Verrier were discovering new planets, more anomalies were observed, this time in the motion of the planet Mercury. Did this imply that Newton's theory was wrong or would it imply more incredible discoveries within the theory? The problem was that Mercury's orbit was not exactly a closed ellipse. Within the Newtonian model attempts were made to account for this anomaly. Mercury's orbit is influenced not only by the sun but also by the other planets. The orbit would be a perfect ellipse if the sun and only the sun influenced Mercury. Taking into account the effects of the other planets *almost* eliminated the anomaly. That is, one could understand the observed orbit of Mercury and its deviations from a perfect ellipse in terms of the Newtonian model itself. The model did not have to change – it could account for the new phenomena without the need to change the model in any way and without the need for new assumptions. The paradigm held.

Note that we said that the Newtonian model *almost* accounted for the anomaly, about 92% of it to be precise. The remaining 8% proved disastrous for the Newtonian model of gravitation. Countless experiments had confirmed the Newtonian theory. As philosopher Karl Popper stresses, however, no number of successful experiments (no matter how large the number) can convince us that a theory is right. But just one experiment is enough to *falsify* the theory. In the case of Mercury's orbit, the 8% that could not be accounted for were to lead in 1915 into another change of paradigm: the fall of Newtonian gravitation and the introduction of Einstein's general theory of relativity. But models do not change so easily and not before all ways to resolve the problem within the model are exhausted. Was there no way out of the problem with Mercury's orbit within the Newtonian theory? There was if one assumed that the shape of the sun was not exactly spherical and hence its gravitational field was not exactly an inverse square field. The shape of the sun could not then be measured sufficiently accurately, however, to settle the question. Die-hards of the Newtonian theory could thus claim not to be worried about Mercury and could also hope that one day Mercury's abnormalities could be settled by a few details within the Newtonian theory itself. But as soon as Einstein convincingly demonstrated the solution to Mercury's problems within the new theory (general relativity), new areas were discovered where the Newtonian theory had not been tested before. General relativity predicted that light would bend as it went past a very massive object (such as the sun). Newtonian gravity predicted a deflection also but of the wrong magnitude. Experiments in 1919 favoured relativity. The physics of very dense stars demanded relativity and not Newtonian gravity for their correct description. Even the Newtonian die-hards would have to concede defeat (and the issue of the precise shape of the sun became a minor detail concerning only the experts on the shape of the sun!).

The story of the second example mentioned at the beginning of this chapter (the ideas behind the pressure of a gas) is not as dramatic as that of the motion of the planets, but it shares many of the same features. Bernoulli's ideas are simpler, more elegant, more general and more natural (even though we could debate for a long time what exactly more 'elegant' or 'natural' or even 'simpler' really means).

The third example mentioned (the photoelectric effect) also has a fascinating story. Einstein's explanation of the photoelectric effect is another scientific revolution. The wave theory of light cannot account for this effect and a particle view of light had to be introduced that does explain it. But here things are a bit stranger. The 'old' paradigm (light as a wave) cannot just be thrown away because the 'new' paradigm (light as particles) cannot explain everything by itself. The introduction of photons revealed the particle nature of light, but in other experiments light most definitely exhibited a wave nature. Soon it was to be discovered that electrons, protons and neutrons, which are normally thought to be particles, behave in certain situations like waves. A stream of electrons directed at a crystal diffracts (i.e. suffers the most tell-tale wave phenomenon of all). The sharp distinction between particles and waves of the nineteenth century gave rise to the *duality* of matter and waves. Everyday language, based on our limited experience with the microscopic world, fails to provide an adequate description of objects that sometimes behave like particles and sometimes like waves. Our sense of 'reality', which in the nineteenth century conveniently classified objects as particles or waves, had to give way to the new reality of duality and the corresponding loss of determinism that the uncertainty principle introduced.

In the preceding pages, we have conveyed the prejudice that exists among physicists who believe that the main virtues of a theory are that it be simple and elegant and the belief that, ultimately, nature will be described by such a theory. It is this prejudice, and much less the adherence to the conventional 'scientific method', that is the guiding principle in the discovery of new knowledge about the natural world. Whether this prejudice is correct and whether nature will be described in such a way, only time will tell.

? DISCUSSION QUESTIONS

1 An ichthyologist wants to study the fish in a lake. She catches the fish using a net with a spacing between the net threads of about 5 cm. She observes that she never catches fish of length smaller than 5 cm and so deduces that no fish of length less than 5 cm live in that lake. What can you say to this claim?

2 Procrustes was a thug living outside ancient Athens who stopped travellers and made them lie in a bed by the road. If they were too short for the bed he stretched them until they fitted just right. If they were too tall he cut off their legs so they again would fit. In what sense (other than the obvious!) is this story a parable of unethical scientific practice?

3 A student says that physics is just one wrong theory after the other. We start by learning Newton's laws of mechanics only to find out later that these are wrong and have to be replaced by Einstein's theory of relativity. Similarly, Rutherford's model of the atom is replaced by the Bohr model, which in turn is replaced by Schrödinger's theory. Write a response to this student.

4 An experiment can overthrow a theory but can never completely confirm a theory. Discuss this statement using specific situations in physics.

5 Traditionally much of the new knowledge in basic physics has come from experiments with high-energy accelerators that have been able to probe matter at ever smaller scales. To investigate matter at even smaller distances requires accelerators that are far too big and far too costly ever to have a chance of being built. What does that imply about the future of fundamental physics?

6 A professional astrologer says: 'Physicists are simply prejudiced. There is so much unknown stuff out there, so how do they know that there isn't something to astrology?' What do you think?

7 Newton would not have been able to apply his theory of gravitation to the motion of the planets had he not developed a branch of mathematics called calculus. How close is the relationship between physics and mathematics? Does physics need mathematics or could we arrive at the same level of knowledge of the physical world without it? How has physics influenced the development of mathematics?

8 Practically every area of mathematics, including such highly esoteric fields as number theory, has eventually found an application in physics. Is this a sign that knowledge in mathematics is essentially governed by the need to understand the physical world around us?

9 Mathematicians of the nineteenth century developed theories of geometry that follow different rules from those of the ordinary Euclidean geometry taught at school. Where in physics are the ideas on non-Euclidean geometry used? Were these geometries developed to solve problems of the physical world?

10 Physics tries to find the ultimate laws that govern the behaviour of the physical world. Is there any evidence that ultimate laws exist?

11 Discuss whether and to what degree the methods used in the acquisition of knowledge in physics can be used in other disciplines as well. Discuss in particular biology and economics.

12 Many people use the second law of thermodynamics to explain phenomena that do not fall in the realm of physics, such as economics, the stock market, etc. Is this justified?

13 A student says: 'Chemistry is part of physics. If you know physics you automatically know chemistry.' Do you agree?

14 A student says: 'The underlying laws of biology are basically those of physics. When we discover those laws, biology will become a part of physics.' Do you agree?

15 The wave–particle duality of modern quantum theory introduces via the uncertainty principle a lack of determinism. Write an essay discussing determinism and the loss of it in modern physics. What impact, if any, has modern physics had on the issue of free will and choice of an individual?

16 We are aware of three space dimensions but no more. How can we talk about higher dimensions when we cannot even visualize them?

17 A student says 'I got a 7 on my physics higher level exam and I still don't know what mass or electric charge *really* are!' If the student takes a three-year university course in physics will she know what mass and electric charge *really* are?

18 Electric and magnetic field lines are useful concepts when thinking about electric and magnetic fields, yet they do not exist. How exactly are these concepts useful and how do they influence the way we think about electric and magnetic fields?

19 We have a picture in our minds when we speak of electrons and that picture often influences the way we think about electrons. Most people see a tiny round ball when they think of an electron. Richard Feynman sees 'a vector and a ψ written somewhere, sort of mixed with it somehow, and an amplitude all mixed up with *x*'s ... a mathematical expression wrapped into and around, in a vague way, around the object'. Do you know of any examples where a particular visualization of an object or process has been instrumental in the understanding of that object or process?

20 J. R. Oppenheimer, the physicist in charge of the Manhattan project that developed the American nuclear bomb during the Second World War, said after the completion of the project that 'physicists have known sin'. What did he mean? Do you agree that knowledge that can prove dangerous should be contained? *Can* knowledge be contained and if so, by whom?

21 At the time of Kepler, five planets were known (excluding the earth) – Mercury, Venus, Mars, Jupiter and Saturn. In his book *Mysterium cosmographicum* Kepler suggests that only five planets *could* exist because there are only five Platonic solids. Find out what a Platonic solid is. Kepler then went on to say that the orbit radius of each of the five planets was proportional to the radius of the sphere in which the Platonic solid was inscribed. (He assumed that each Platonic solid was fitted into the next in the same order as the planets.) What do you think of this theory? How scientific is it? It is obviously false since there are more than five planets, but if only five planets did exist, what would its merits be then? Steven Weinberg says of Kepler's idea that where he went wrong was not in the kind of conjectures he made but in assigning too much importance to the planets. What does Weinberg mean?

Physical constants

The values quoted here are those usually used in calculations and problems. Fewer significant digits are often used in the text. The constants are known with a much better precision than the number of significant digits quoted here implies.

Atomic mass unit	$1\,\text{u} = 1.661 \times 10^{-27}\,\text{kg} = 931.5\,\text{MeV}\,c^{-2}$
Avogadro constant	$N_A = 6.02 \times 10^{23}\,\text{mol}^{-1}$
Boltzmann constant	$k = 1.38 \times 10^{-23}\,\text{J}\,\text{K}^{-1}$
Coulomb's law constant	$\frac{1}{4\pi\varepsilon_0} = 8.99 \times 10^{9}\,\text{N}\,\text{m}^2\,\text{C}^{-2}$
Electric permittivity	$\varepsilon_0 = 8.85 \times 10^{-12}\,\text{N}^{-1}\,\text{m}^{-2}\,\text{C}^2$
Gravitational constant	$G = 6.67 \times 10^{-11}\,\text{N}\,\text{kg}^{-2}\,\text{m}^2$
Magnetic permeability	$\mu_0 = 4\pi \times 10^{-7}\,\text{T}\,\text{m}\,\text{A}^{-1}$
Magnitude of electronic charge	$e = 1.60 \times 10^{-19}\,\text{C}$
Mass of the electron	$m_e = 9.11 \times 10^{-31}\,\text{kg} = 5.49 \times 10^{-4}\,\text{u} = 0.511\,\text{MeV}\,c^{-2}$
Mass of the neutron	$m_n = 1.675 \times 10^{-27}\,\text{kg} = 1.008\,665\,\text{u} = 940\,\text{MeV}\,c^{-2}$
Mass of the proton	$m_p = 1.673 \times 10^{-27}\,\text{kg} = 1.007\,276\,\text{u} = 938\,\text{MeV}\,c^{-2}$
Planck constant	$h = 6.63 \times 10^{-34}\,\text{J}\,\text{s}$
Speed of light in a vacuum	$c = 3.00 \times 10^{8}\,\text{m}\,\text{s}^{-1}$
Stefan–Boltzmann constant	$\sigma = 5.67 \times 10^{-8}\,\text{W}\,\text{m}^{-2}\,\text{K}^{-4}$
Universal gas constant	$R = 8.31\,\text{J}\,\text{mol}^{-1}\,\text{K}^{-1}$

A few unit conversions

astronomical unit	$1\,\text{AU} = 1.50 \times 10^{11}\,\text{m}$
atmosphere	$1\,\text{atm} = 1.01 \times 10^{5}\,\text{N}\,\text{m}^{-2} = 101\,\text{kPa}$
degree	$1^\circ = \frac{\pi}{180^\circ}\,\text{rad}$
electronvolt	$1\,\text{eV} = 1.60 \times 10^{-19}\,\text{J}$
kilowatt-hour	$1\,\text{kW}\,\text{h} = 3.60 \times 10^{6}\,\text{J}$
light year	$1\,\text{ly} = 9.46 \times 10^{15}\,\text{m}$
parsec	$1\,\text{pc} = 3.26\,\text{ly}$
radian	$1\,\text{rad} = \frac{180^\circ}{\pi}$

Masses of elements and selected isotopes

Table A2.1 gives atomic masses, including the masses of electrons, in the neutral atom. The masses are averaged over the isotopes of each element. In the case of unstable elements, numbers in brackets indicate the approximate mass of the most abundant isotope of the element in question. The masses are expressed in atomic mass units, u. Table A2.2 gives the atomic masses of a few selected isotopes

Table A2.1 Atomic numbers and atomic masses of the elements.

Atomic number	Name and symbol	Atomic mass/u	Atomic number	Name and symbol	Atomic mass/u
1	Hydrogen, H	1.0080	30	Zinc, Zn	65.37
2	Helium, He	4.0026	31	Gallium, Ga	69.723
3	Lithium, Li	6.941	32	Germanium, Ge	72.59
4	Beryllium, Be	9.012 18	33	Arsenic, As	74.921
5	Boron, B	10.811	34	Selenium, Se	78.96
6	Carbon, C	12.000 000	35	Bromine, Br	79.91
7	Nitrogen, N	14.007	36	Krypton, Kr	83.80
8	Oxygen, O	15.999	37	Rubidium, Rb	85.467
9	Fluorine, F	18.998	38	Strontium, Sr	87.62
10	Neon, Ne	20.180	39	Yttrium, Y	88.906
11	Sodium, Na	22.999	40	Zirconium, Zr	91.224
12	Magnesium, Mg	24.31	41	Niobium, Nb	92.906
13	Aluminium, Al	26.981	42	Molybdenum, Mo	95.94
14	Silicon, Si	28.086	43	Technetium, Tc	(99)
15	Phosphorus, P	30.974	44	Ruthenium, Ru	101.07
16	Sulphur, S	32.066	45	Rhodium, Rh	102.906
17	Chlorine, Cl	35.453	46	Palladium, Pd	106.42
18	Argon, Ar	39.948	47	Silver, Ag	107.868
19	Potassium, K	39.102	48	Cadmium, Cd	112.40
20	Calcium, Ca	40.078	49	Indium, In	114.82
21	Scandium, Sc	44.956	50	Tin, Sn	118.69
22	Titanium, Ti	47.90	51	Antimony, Sb	121.75
23	Vanadium, V	50.942	52	Tellurium, Te	127.60
24	Chromium, Cr	51.996	53	Iodine, I	126.904
25	Manganese, Mn	54.938	54	Xenon, Xe	131.30
26	Iron, Fe	55.847	55	Caesium, Cs	132.91
27	Cobalt, Co	58.933	56	Barium, Ba	137.34
28	Nickel, Ni	58.71	57	Lanthanum, La	138.91
29	Copper, Cu	63.54	58	Cerium, Ce	140.12

Table A2.1 (continued)

Atomic number	Name and symbol	Atomic mass/u	Atomic number	Name and symbol	Atomic mass/u
59	Praseodymium, Pr	140.907	82	Lead, Pb	207.2
60	Neodymium, Nd	144.24	83	Bismuth, Bi	208.980
61	Promethium, Pm	(144)	84	Polonium, Po	(210)
62	Samarium, Sm	150.4	85	Astatine, At	(218)
63	Europium, Eu	152.0	86	Radon, Rn	(222)
64	Gadolinium, Gd	157.25	87	Francium, Fr	(223)
65	Terbium, Tb	158.92	88	Radium, Ra	(226)
66	Dysprosium, Dy	162.50	89	Actinium, Ac	(227)
67	Holmium, Ho	164.93	90	Thorium, Th	(232)
68	Erbium, Er	167.26	91	Protactinium, Pa	(231)
69	Thulium, Tm	168.93	92	Uranium, U	(238)
70	Ytterbium, Yb	173.04	93	Neptunium, Np	(239)
71	Lutetium, Lu	174.97	94	Plutonium, Pu	(239)
72	Hafnium, Hf	178.49	95	Americium, Am	(243)
73	Tantalum, Ta	180.95	96	Curium, Cm	(245)
74	Tungsten, W	183.85	97	Berkelium, Bk	(247)
75	Rhenium, Re	186.2	98	Californium, Cf	(249)
76	Osmium, Os	190.2	99	Einsteinium, Es	(254)
77	Iridium, I	192.2	100	Fermium, Fm	(253)
78	Platinum, Pt	195.09	101	Mendelevium, Md	(255)
79	Gold, Au	196.97	102	Nobelium, No	(255)
80	Mercury, Hg	200.59	103	Lawrencium, Lr	(257)
81	Thallium, Tl	204.37			

Table A2.2 Atomic masses of a few selected isotopes.

Atomic number	Name	Atomic mass/u	Atomic number	Name	Atomic mass/u
1	Hydrogen, H	1.007 825	7	Nitrogen-14	14.003 074
1	Deuterium, D	2.014 102	7	Nitrogen-15	15.000 109
1	Tritium, T	3.016 049	8	Oxygen-16	15.994 915
2	Helium-3	3.016 029	8	Oxygen-17	16.999 131
2	Helium-4	4.002 603	8	Oxygen-18	17.999 160
3	Lithium-6	6.015 121	19	Potassium-39	38.963 708
3	Lithium-7	7.016 003	19	Potassium-40	39.964 000
4	Beryllium-9	9.012 182	92	Uranium-232	232.037 14
5	Boron-10	10.012 937	92	Uranium-235	235.043 925
5	Boron-11	11.009 305	92	Uranium-236	236.045 563
6	Carbon-12	12.000 000	92	Uranium-238	238.050 786
6	Carbon-13	13.003 355	92	Uranium-239	239.054 291
6	Carbon-14	14.003 242			

Astronomical data

Body	Mass/kg	Radius/m	Orbit radius/m (average)	Orbital period
Sun	1.99×10^{30}	6.96×10^{8}	–	–
Moon	7.35×10^{22}	1.74×10^{6}	3.84×10^{8}	27.3 days
Mercury	3.30×10^{23}	2.44×10^{6}	5.79×10^{10}	88.0 days
Venus	4.87×10^{24}	6.05×10^{6}	1.08×10^{11}	224.7 days
Earth	5.98×10^{24}	6.38×10^{6}	1.50×10^{11}	365.3 days
Mars	6.42×10^{23}	3.40×10^{6}	2.28×10^{11}	687.0 days
Jupiter	1.90×10^{27}	6.91×10^{7}	7.78×10^{11}	11.86 yr
Saturn	5.69×10^{26}	6.03×10^{7}	1.43×10^{12}	29.42 yr
Uranus	8.66×10^{25}	2.56×10^{7}	2.88×10^{12}	83.75 yr
Neptune	1.03×10^{26}	2.48×10^{7}	4.50×10^{12}	163.7 yr
Pluto*	1.5×10^{22}	1.15×10^{6}	5.92×10^{12}	248.0 yr

Luminosity of the sun	$L = 3.9 \times 10^{26}$ W
Distance to nearest star (Proxima Centauri)	4×10^{16} m (approx. 4.3 ly)
Diameter of the Milky Way	10^{21} m (approx. 100 000 ly)
Mass of the Milky Way	4×10^{41} kg
Distance to nearest galaxy (Andromeda)	2×10^{22} m (approx. 2.3 million ly)

*Pluto has recently been downgraded into a new category of 'dwarf planet' (see Option E, Astrophysics).

Some important mathematical results

In physics problems, the following are useful.

$$a^{-x} = \frac{1}{a^x} \qquad a^x a^y = a^{x+y} \qquad \frac{a^x}{a^y} = a^{x-y}$$

$$\log a = x \Rightarrow 10^x = a \qquad \ln a = x \Rightarrow e^x = a$$

$$\ln(ab) = \ln a + \ln b \qquad \ln\left(\frac{a}{b}\right) = \ln a - \ln b$$

$$\ln(a^x) = x \ln a \qquad \ln(1) = 0 \qquad e^0 = 1$$

$$\sin 2x = 2 \sin x \cos x$$
$$\cos 2x = 2\cos^2 x - 1 = 1 - 2\sin^2 x = \cos^2 x - \sin^2 x$$

The quadratic equation $ax^2 + bx + c = 0$ has two roots given by

$$x = \frac{-b \pm \sqrt{b^2 - 4ac}}{2a}$$

In approximations, the binomial theorem

$$(1+x)^n = 1 + nx + \frac{n(n-1)}{2!}x^2 + \frac{n(n-1)(n-2)}{3!}x^3 + \cdots$$

is extremely useful. Here $-1 < x < 1$ and n can be any real number, not necessarily integer.

Also very useful are the approximations

$$\sin x \approx x - \frac{x^3}{6} + \cdots$$

and

$$\cos x \approx 1 - \frac{x^2}{2} + \cdots$$

valid when x in radians is small.

From geometry, we must know the following expressions for lengths, areas and volumes.

Property	Formula
Circumference of a circle of radius R	$2\pi R$
Area of a circle of radius R	πR^2
Surface area of a sphere of radius R	$4\pi R^2$
Volume of a sphere of radius R	$\frac{4\pi R^3}{3}$
Volume of a cylinder of base radius R and height h	$\pi R^2 h$

The length of an arc of a circle of radius R that subtends an angle θ at the centre of the circle is $s = R\theta$. In this formula the angle must be expressed in radians. An angle of 2π radians is equivalent to an angle of $360°$, so

$$1 \text{ radian} = \frac{360°}{2\pi} = 57.3°$$

Nobel prize winners in physics

No awards were made in years not listed.

2006: The prize was awarded jointly to John C. Mather and George F. Smoot (both USA) for their discovery of the black-body form and anisotropy of the cosmic microwave background radiation.

2005: Half the prize was awarded to Roy J. Glauber (USA) for his contribution to the quantum theory of optical coherence, and the other half was awarded jointly to John L. Hall (USA) and Theodor W. Hänsch (Germany) for their contributions to the development of laser-based precision spectroscopy, including the optical frequency comb technique.

2004: The prize was awarded jointly to D. J. Gross, H. D. Politzer and F. Wilczek (all USA) for their discovery of asymptotic freedom in quantum chromodynamics.

2003: The prize was awarded jointly to Alexei Abrikosov (Russia and USA), Vitaly Ginzburg (Russia) and Anthony Leggett (UK and USA) for pioneering contributions to the theory of superconductors and superfluids.

2002: Half the prize was awarded jointly to Raymond Davis Jr (USA) and Masatoshi Koshiba (Japan), and the other half was awarded to Riccardo Gianconi (USA) for pioneering contributions to astrophysics, particularly for the detection of cosmic neutrinos.

2001: The prize was awarded jointly to Eric Cornell (USA), Wolfgang Ketterle (Germany) and Carl Wieman (USA) for the achievement of Bose–Einstein condensation in dilute alkali gases and for early fundamental studies of the properties of the condensates.

2000: Half the prize was awarded jointly to Zhores I. Alferov (Russia) and Herbert Kroemer (USA) for developing semiconductor heterostructures used in high-speed and opto-electronics, and the other half was awarded to Jack St. Clair Kilby (USA) for his part in the invention of the integrated circuit.

1999: The prize was awarded jointly to Gerardus 't Hooft and Martinus J. G. Veltman (both Netherlands) for elucidating the quantum structure of electroweak interactions in physics.

1998: The prize was awarded jointly to Robert B. Laughlin (USA), Horst L. Stormer (Germany) and Daniel C. Tsui (USA) for their discovery of a new form of quantum fluid with fractionally charged excitations.

1997: The prize was awarded jointly to Steven Chu (USA), Claude Cohen-Tannoudji (France) and William D. Phillips (USA) for development of methods to cool and trap atoms with laser light.

1996: The prize was awarded jointly to David M. Lee, Douglas D. Osheroff and Robert C. Richardson (all USA) for their discovery of superfluidity in helium-3.

1995: The prize was awarded for pioneering experimental contributions to lepton physics, with half to Martin L. Perl (USA) for the discovery of the tau lepton, and the other half to Frederick Reines (USA) for the detection of the neutrino.

1994: The prize was awarded jointly to Bertram N. Brockhouse (Canada) and Clifford G. Shull (USA) for pioneering contributions to the development of neutron scattering techniques for studies of condensed matter: Brockhouse for the development of neutron spectroscopy, and Shull for the development of the neutron diffraction technique.

1993: The prize was awarded jointly to Russell A. Hulse and Joseph H. Taylor Jr (both USA) for the discovery of a new type of pulsar – a discovery that has opened up new possibilities for the study of gravitation.

1992: Georges Charpak (France) for his invention and development of particle detectors, in particular the multiwire proportional chamber.

1991: Pierre-Gilles de Gennes (France) for discovering that methods developed for studying order phenomena in simple systems can be generalized to more complex forms of matter, in particular to liquid crystals and polymers.

1990: The prize was awarded jointly to Jerome I. Friedman, Henry W. Kendall (both USA) and Richard E. Taylor (Canada) for their pioneering investigations concerning deep inelastic scattering of electrons on protons and bound neutrons, which have been of essential importance for the development of the quark model in particle physics.

1989: Half of the prize was awarded to Norman F. Ramsey (USA) for the invention of the separated oscillatory fields method and its use in the hydrogen maser and other atomic clocks, and the other half was awarded jointly to Hans G. Dehmelt (USA) and Wolfgang Paul (Germany) for the development of the ion trap technique.

1988: The prize was awarded jointly to Leon M. Lederman, Melvin Schwartz and Jack Steinberger (all USA) for the neutrino beam method and the demonstration of the doublet structure of the leptons through the discovery of the muon neutrino.

1987: The prize was awarded jointly to J. Georg Bednorz (Germany) and K. Alexander Müller (Switzerland) for their important breakthrough in the discovery of superconductivity in ceramic materials.

1986: Half of the prize was awarded to Ernst Ruska (Germany) for his fundamental work in electron optics and for the design of the first electron microscope, and the other half was awarded jointly to Gerd Binnig (Germany) and Heinrich Rohrer (Switzerland) for their design of the scanning tunnelling microscope.

1985: Klaus von Klitzing (Germany) for the discovery of the quantized Hall effect.

1984: The prize was awarded jointly to Carlo Rubbia (Italy) and Simon van der Meer (Netherlands) for their decisive contributions to the large project that led to the discovery of the field particles W and Z, communicators of the weak interaction.

1983: The prize was divided equally between Subrahmanyan Chandrasekhar (USA) for his theoretical studies of the physical processes of importance to the structure and evolution of the stars, and William A. Fowler (USA) for his theoretical and experimental studies of the nuclear reactions of importance in the formation of the chemical elements in the universe.

1982: Kenneth G. Wilson (USA) for his theory for critical phenomena in connection with phase transitions.

1981: Half the prize was awarded jointly to Nicolaas Bloembergen and Arthur L. Schawlow (both USA) for their contribution to the development of laser spectroscopy, and the other half was awarded to Kai M. Siegbahn (Sweden) for his contribution to the development of high-resolution electron spectroscopy.

1980: The prize was divided equally between James W. Cronin and Val L. Fitch (both USA) for the discovery of violations of fundamental symmetry principles in the decay of neutral K-mesons.

1979: The prize was divided equally between Sheldon L. Glashow (USA), Abdus Salam (Pakistan) and Steven Weinberg (USA) for their contributions to the theory of the unified weak and electromagnetic interaction between elementary particles, including, among other things, the prediction of the weak neutral current.

1978: Half the prize was awarded to Pyotr Leonidovich Kapitsa (USSR) for his basic inventions and discoveries in the area of low-temperature physics, and the other half was divided equally between Arno A. Penzias and Robert W. Wilson (both USA) for their discovery of cosmic microwave background radiation.

1977: The prize was divided equally between Philip W. Anderson (USA), Sir Nevill F. Mott (UK) and John H. van Vleck (USA) for their fundamental theoretical investigations of the electronic structure of magnetic and disordered systems.

1976: The prize was divided equally between Burton Richter and Samuel C. C. Ting (both USA) for their pioneering work in the discovery of a heavy elementary particle of a new kind.

1975: The prize was awarded jointly to Aage Bohr, Ben Mottelson (both Denmark) and James Rainwater (USA) for the discovery of the connection between collective motion and particle motion in atomic nuclei, and the development of the theory of the structure of the atomic nucleus based on this connection.

1974: The prize was awarded jointly to Sir Martin Ryle and Antony Hewish (both UK) for their pioneering research in radio astrophysics: Ryle for his observations and inventions, in particular of the aperture synthesis technique, and Hewish for his decisive role in the discovery of pulsars.

1973: Half the prize was equally shared between Leo Esaki (Japan) and Ivar Giaever (USA) for their experimental discoveries regarding tunnelling phenomena in semiconductors and superconductors, respectively, and the other half was awarded to Brian D. Josephson (UK) for his theoretical predictions of the properties of a supercurrent through a tunnel barrier, in particular those phenomena that are generally known as the Josephson effects.

1972: The prize was awarded jointly to John Bardeen, Leon N. Cooper and J. Robert Schrieffer (all USA) for their jointly developed theory of superconductivity, usually called the BCS theory.

1971: Dennis Gabor (UK) for his invention and development of the holographic method.

1970: The prize was divided equally between Hannes Alfvén (Sweden) for fundamental work and discoveries in magneto-hydrodynamics with fruitful applications in different parts of plasma physics, and Louis Néel (France) for fundamental work and discoveries concerning antiferromagnetism and ferromagnetism, which have led to important applications in solid state physics.

1969: Murray Gell-Mann (USA) for his contributions and discoveries concerning the classification of elementary particles and their interactions.

1968: Luis W. Alvarez (USA) for his decisive contributions to elementary particle physics, in particular the discovery of a large number of resonance states, made possible through his development of the technique of using a hydrogen bubble chamber and data analysis.

1967: Hans Albrecht Bethe (USA) for his contributions to the theory of nuclear reactions, especially his discoveries concerning energy production in stars.

1966: Alfred Kastler (France) for the discovery and development of optical methods for studying hertzian resonances in atoms.

1965: The prize was awarded jointly to Sin-Itiro Tomonaga (Japan), Julian Schwinger and Richard P. Feynman (both USA) for their fundamental work in quantum electrodynamics, with far-reaching consequences for the physics of elementary particles.

1964: Half the prize was awarded to Charles H. Townes (USA) and the other half was awarded jointly to Nicolay Gennadiyevich Basov and Aleksandr Mikhailovich Prokhorov (both USSR) for fundamental work in the field of quantum electronics, which has led to the construction of oscillators and amplifiers based on the maser–laser principle.

1963: Half the prize was awarded to Eugene P. Wigner (USA) for his contributions to the theory of the atomic nucleus and the elementary particles, particularly through the discovery and application of fundamental symmetry principles, and the other half was awarded jointly to Maria Goeppert-Mayer (USA) and J. Hans D. Jensen (Germany) for their discoveries concerning nuclear shell structure.

1962: Lev Davidovich Landau (USSR) for his pioneering theories for condensed matter, especially liquid helium.

1961: The prize was divided equally between Robert Hofstadter (USA) for his pioneering studies of electron scattering in atomic nuclei and for his thereby achieved discoveries concerning the structure of the nucleons, and Rudolf Ludwig Mössbauer (Germany) for his researches concerning the resonance absorption of gamma radiation and his discovery in this connection of the effect which bears his name.

1960: Donald A. Glaser (USA) for the invention of the bubble chamber.

1959: The prize was awarded jointly to Emilio Gino Segre and Owen Chamberlain (both USA) for their discovery of the antiproton.

1958: The prize was awarded jointly to Pavel Alekseyevich Cherenkov, Il'ja Mikhailovich Frank and Igor Yevgenyevich Tamm (all USSR) for the discovery and the interpretation of the Cherenkov effect.

1957: The prize was awarded jointly to Chen Ning Yang and Tsung-Dao Lee (both China) for their penetrating investigation of the so-called parity laws, which has led to important discoveries regarding the elementary particles.

1956: The prize was awarded jointly, one-third each, to William Shockley, John Bardeen and Walter Houser Brattain (all USA) for their researches on semiconductors and their discovery of the transistor effect.

1955: The prize was divided equally between Willis Eugene Lamb (USA) for his discoveries concerning the fine structure of the hydrogen spectrum and Polykarp Kusch (USA) for his precision determination of the magnetic moment of the electron.

1954: The prize was divided equally between Max Born (UK) for his fundamental research in quantum mechanics, especially for his statistical interpretation of the wavefunction, and Walther Bothe (Germany) for the coincidence method and his discoveries made using this method.

1953: Frits (Frederik) Zernike (Netherlands) for his demonstration of the phase contrast method, especially for his invention of the phase contrast microscope.

1952: The prize was awarded jointly to Felix Bloch and Edward Mills Purcell (both USA) for their development of new methods for nuclear magnetic precision measurements and discoveries made using these methods.

1951: The prize was awarded jointly to Sir John Douglas Cockcroft (UK) and Ernest Thomas Sinton Walton (Ireland) for their pioneering work on the transmutation of atomic nuclei by artificially accelerated atomic particles.

1950: Cecil Frank Powell (UK) for his development of the photographic method of studying nuclear processes and his discoveries regarding mesons made with this method.

1949: Hideki Yukawa (Japan) for his prediction of the existence of mesons on the basis of theoretical work on nuclear forces.

1948: Lord Patrick Maynard Stuart Blackett (UK) for his development of the Wilson cloud chamber method, and his discoveries using this method in the fields of nuclear physics and cosmic radiation.

1947: Sir Edward Victor Appleton (UK) for his investigations of the physics of the upper atmosphere, especially for the discovery of the so-called Appleton layer.

1946: Percy Williams Bridgman (USA) for the invention of an apparatus to produce extremely high pressures, and for the discoveries he made using this apparatus in the field of high-pressure physics.

1945: Wolfgang Pauli (Austria) for the discovery of the exclusion principle, also called the Pauli principle.

1944: Isidor Isaac Rabi (USA) for his resonance method for recording the magnetic properties of atomic nuclei.

1943: Otto Stern (USA) for his contribution to the development of the molecular ray method and his discovery of the magnetic moment of the proton.

1939: Ernest Orlando Lawrence (USA) for the invention and development of the cyclotron and for results obtained with it, especially with regard to artificial radioactive elements.

1938: Enrico Fermi (Italy) for his demonstrations of the existence of new radioactive elements produced by neutron irradiation, and for his related discovery of nuclear reactions brought about by slow neutrons.

1937: The prize was awarded jointly to Clinton Joseph Davisson (USA) and Sir George Paget Thomson (UK) for their experimental discovery of the diffraction of electrons by crystals.

1936: The prize was divided equally between Victor Franz Hess (Austria) for his discovery of cosmic radiation, and Carl David Anderson (USA) for his discovery of the positron.

1935: Sir James Chadwick (UK) for the discovery of the neutron.

1933: The prize was awarded jointly to Erwin Schrödinger (Austria) and Paul Adrien Maurice Dirac (UK) for the discovery of new productive forms of atomic theory.

1932: Werner Heisenberg (Germany) for the creation of quantum mechanics, the application of which has, among other things, led to the discovery of the allotropic forms of hydrogen.

1930: Sir Chandrasekhara Venkata Raman (India) for his work on the scattering of light and for the discovery of the effect named after him.

1929: Prince Louis-Victor de Broglie (France) for his discovery of the wave nature of electrons.

1928: Sir Owen Willans Richardson (UK) for his work on the thermionic phenomenon, and especially for the discovery of the law named after him.

1927: The prize was divided equally between Arthur H. Compton (USA) for his discovery of the effect named after him, and Charles Thomson Rees Wilson (USA) for his method of making the paths of electrically charged particles visible by condensation of vapour.

1926: Jean B. Perrin (France) for his work on the discontinuous structure of matter, and especially for his discovery of sedimentation equilibrium.

1925: The prize was awarded jointly to James Franck and Gustav Hertz (Germany) for their discovery of the laws governing the impact of an electron upon an atom.

1924: Karl Manne Georg Siegbahn (Sweden) for his discoveries and research in the field of X-ray spectroscopy.

1923: Robert Andrews Millikan (USA) for his work on the elementary charge of electricity and on the photoelectric effect.

1922: Niels Bohr (Denmark) for his services in the investigation of the structure of atoms and of the radiation emanating from them.

1921: Albert Einstein (Germany) for his services to theoretical physics, and especially for his discovery of the law of the photoelectric effect.

1920: Charles Edouard Guillaume (Switzerland) in recognition of the service he has rendered to precision measurements in physics by his discovery of anomalies in nickel–steel alloys.

1919: Johannes Stark (Germany) for his discovery of the Doppler effect in canal rays and the splitting of spectral lines in electric fields.

1918: Max Karl Ernst Ludwig Planck (Germany) in recognition of the services he rendered to the advancement of physics by his discovery of energy quanta.

1917: Charles Glover Barkla (UK) for his discovery of the characteristic Röntgen radiation of the elements.

1915: The prize was awarded jointly to Sir William Henry Bragg and Sir William Lawrence Bragg (both UK) for their services in the analysis of crystal structure by means of X-rays.

1914: Max von Laue (Germany) for his discovery of the diffraction of X-rays by crystals.

1913: Heike Kamerlingh-Onnes (Netherlands) for his investigations on the properties of matter at low temperatures, which led, among other things, to the production of liquid helium.

1912: Nils Gustaf Dalén (Sweden) for his invention of automatic regulators for use in conjunction with gas accumulators for illuminating lighthouses and buoys.

1911: Wilhelm Wien (Germany) for his discoveries regarding the laws governing the radiation of heat.

1910: Johannes Diderik van der Waals (Netherlands) for his work on the equation of state for gases and liquids.

1909: The prize was awarded jointly to Guglielmo Marconi (Italy) and Carl Ferdinand Braun (Germany) in recognition of their contributions to the development of wireless telegraphy.

1908: Gabriel Lippmann (France) for his method of reproducing colours photographically based on the phenomenon of interference.

1907: Albert Abraham Michelson (USA) for his optical precision instruments and the spectroscopic and metrological investigations carried out with their aid.

1906: Sir Joseph John Thomson (UK) in recognition of the great merits of his theoretical and experimental investigations on the conduction of electricity by gases.

1905: Philipp Eduard Anton Lenard (Netherlands) for his work on cathode rays.

1904: Lord John William Strutt Rayleigh (UK) for his investigations of the densities of the most important gases and for his discovery of argon in connection with these studies.

1903: Half the prize was awarded to A. Henri Becquerel (France) in recognition of the extraordinary services he has rendered by his discovery of spontaneous radioactivity, and the other half was awarded jointly to Pierre and Marie Curie (France) in recognition of the extraordinary services they rendered by their joint researches on the radiation phenomena discovered by Henri Becquerel.

1902: The prize was awarded jointly to Hendrik A. Lorentz and Pieter Zeeman (both Netherlands) in recognition of the extraordinary service they rendered by their researches into the influence of magnetism upon radiation phenomena.

1901: Wilhelm K. Röntgen (Germany) in recognition of the extraordinary services he rendered by the discovery of the remarkable rays subsequently named after him.

Answers to questions

1 Physics and physical measurement

Chapter 1.1

Many of the calculations in the problems of this chapter have been performed without a calculator and are estimates. Your answers may differ.

1 3.3×10^{-24} s.
2 3.6×10^{51}.
3 3.3×10^{60}.
4 6.4×10^{41}.
5 2.6×10^{9}.
6 2×10^{11}.
7 6.7×10^{11}.
8 1.0×10^{25}.
9 2.0×10^{27}.
10 3×10^{79}.
11 4×10^{17} kg m^{-3}.
12 8.3 min.
13 16 000 (assuming a 4000 kg elephant).
14 Assume a 200 m^2 house with 100 m^2 on each floor (10 × 10). Take the height of a floor to be 3 m. Divide each floor into four rooms. The wall area is thus $10 \times 3 \times 6 \times 2 = 360$ m^2. Subtract about 80 m^2 for windows and doors and we are left with 280 m^2 of wall area. Assuming a brick of size 20 cm × 5 cm, i.e. of area 10^{-2} m^2, gives as the number of bricks 2.8×10^4. No corridors etc. have been taken into account.
15 (a) 5.356×10^{-9} m; (b) 1.2×10^{-15} m; (c) 3.4×10^{-3} m.
16 (a) 4.834×10^{6} J; (b) 2.23×10^{-12} J; (c) 3.64×10^{11} J.
17 (a) 4.76×10^{-9} s; (b) 2.4×10^{-2} s; (c) 8.5×10^{-18} s.
18 1.792×10^{5} m s^{-1}.
19 (a) 4×10^{-19} J; (b) 54 eV.
20 2.2×10^{-5} m^3.
21 8.4×10^{-3} m.
22 32 ft/s^2.
25 (a) 200 g; (b) 2 kg; (c) 400 g.
26 100 000 years.
27 5×10^{9} kg m^{-3}.
28 About 0.7.
29 2×10^{28}.
30 2×10^{-7} N.
31 4×10^{42}.
33 (a) $\frac{243}{43} \approx \frac{250}{50} = 5$;

(b) $2.80 \times 1.90 \approx 3 \times 2 = 6$;

(c) $$\frac{312 \times 480}{160} \approx \frac{3 \times 10^2 \times 5 \times 10^2}{1.5 \times 10^2} = \frac{15}{1.5} \times 10^2 = 10^3;$$

(d) $$\frac{8.99 \times 10^9 \times 7 \times 10^{-6} \times 7 \times 10^{-6}}{(8 \times 10^2)^2} \approx \frac{10 \times 10^9 \times 5 \times 10^{-6} \times 5 \times 10^{-6}}{64 \times 10^4} \approx \frac{25 \times 10^{-2}}{64 \times 10^4} \approx 3 \times 10^{-7};$$

(e) $$\frac{6.6 \times 10^{-11} \times 6 \times 10^{24}}{(6.4 \times 10^6)^2} \approx \frac{7 \times 10^{-11} \times 6 \times 10^{24}}{(6 \times 10^6)^2} \approx \frac{40 \times 10^{13}}{36 \times 10^{12}} \approx 10.$$

Chapter 1.2

1 No.
2 Systematic.
3 The line of best fit intersects the vertical axis at about 4 mA, which is within the uncertainty

in the current. A line within the error bars can certainly be made to pass through the origin.

4 The line of best fit intersects the vertical axis at about 10 mA, which is outside the uncertainty in current. No straight line within the error bars can be made to pass through the origin.

5 The line of best fit intersects at 12 mA. The extreme line within the error bars intersects at 6 mA. So no line can be made to go through the origin for this data. A systematic error of about 12 mA is required.

6 2.4 m s^{-2}; 3.1 m s^{-1}.

Chapter 1.3

1 16 atm.

2 Increases by a factor of 4.

3 $\sqrt{2}$.

4 4 times as large.

5 (a) 4; (b) increased by a factor of 2.

6 Increase by a factor of 9.

7 By a factor of 4.

8 Decreased by a factor of 16.

9 16.

10 2.83 yr.

11 (a) 1.00 m; (b) 0.7 Hz; (c) 0.30 m.

12 (a) $1/a$ against $1/b$; (b) intercept equals $1/f$.

13 (a) A straight line through the origin; (b) a straight line intersecting the temperature axis at −273.

14 $R^{3/2}$.

15 A straight line through the origin, with slope ma.

16 (a) From the negative of the vertical intercept; (b) from the slope; (c) they are parallel.

Chapter 1.4

1 See Figure A1.

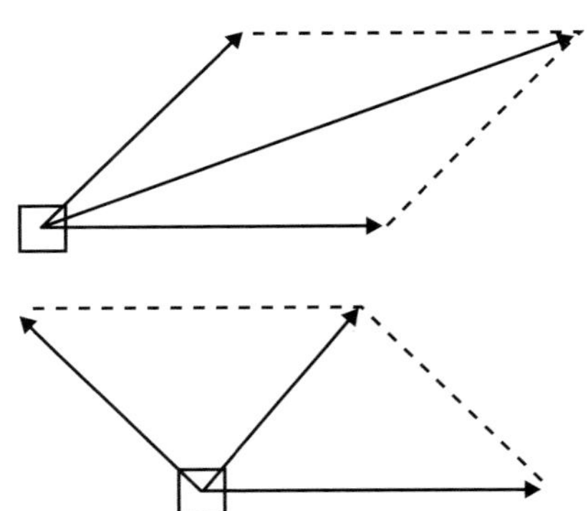

Figure A1.

3 (a) $\vec{A}+\vec{B}$: magnitude = 18.2, direction = 49.7°; (b) $\vec{A}-\vec{B}$: magnitude = 9.2, direction = −11.8°; (c) $\vec{A}-2\vec{B}$: magnitude = 12.4, direction = −52.0°.

4 7.79 km at 34.5°.

5 (a) 5.7 cm at 225°; (b) 201 km at −52°; (c) 5 m at −90°; (d) 8 N at 0.0°.

6 (a) $\vec{A}$: magnitude 3.61, direction 56.3°; (b) $\vec{B}$: magnitude 5.39, direction 112°; (c) $\vec{A}+\vec{B}$: magnitude 8.00, direction 90°; (d) $\vec{A}-\vec{B}$: magnitude 4.47, direction −26.6°; (e) $2\vec{A}-\vec{B}$: magnitude 6.08, direction 9.46°.

7 $\vec{C} = (-4.00, 1.00)$.

8 (2, 6).

9 Magnitude 14.1 m s^{-1}, direction south-west (225°).

10 $\Delta p = \sqrt{2-\sqrt{3}}\,p = 0.52p$.

11 (a) $(x_2 - x_1, y_2 - y_1)$; (b) $(x_1 - x_2, y_1 - y_2)$; (c) $\sqrt{x_1^2 + y_1^2}$.

12 (a) 8 m s^{-1} at 0.0°; (b) 5.66 m s^{-1} at 135°; (c) 5.66 m s^{-1} at 45°. It is the sum of the answers to (a) and (b).

13 (a) 704 m s^{-1} in magnitude; (b) zero.

14 (a) (−7.66, 6.43); (b) (−8.19, −5.74); (c) (3.75, −9.27); (d) (7.43, −6.69); (e) (−5.00, −8.66).

15 C has magnitude $6\sqrt{3} \approx 10.4$ and direction 270° to the positive x-axis.

16 (a) 25.1 N at 36.2° to the positive x-axis; (b) 23.4 N at 65.2° to the positive x-axis; (c) 25.0 N at direction 3.13° to the positive x-axis.

Chapter 1.5

1 Circle.

2 Sphere.

3 $\frac{x^2}{2}$.

4 (a) 55 V; (b) 6.9 s; (c) $R = 2\ \mathrm{M\Omega}$.

5 $v = 0.2(1 - e^{-0.5t})$.

6 $\alpha = 3.4$.

7 $c = 2$.

8 Logarithm of y against x^2.

9 Sum = 180 ± 8 N; difference = 60 ± 8 N.

10 (a) 2.0 ± 0.3; (b) 85 ± 13; (c) 2 ± 2; (d) 100 ± 6; (e) 25 ± 7.5.

11 $F = (7 \pm 2) \times 10$ N.

12 $(1.8 \pm 0.4) \times 10^4$ kg m^{-3}.

13 (a) 18 ± 2 cm^2; (b) 15 ± 1 cm.
14 (a) $(6.5 \pm 0.1) \times 10^3$ cm^2;
(b) $(4.9 \pm 0.1) \times 10^4$ cm^3.
15 Area = 37 ± 3 cm^2; perimeter = 26 ± 1 cm.
16 Increases by $\sqrt{2}$.
17 1%.
18 1.7%.

2 Mechanics

Chapter 2.1

1 167 m s^{-1}.
2 15 km h^{-1}.
3 (a) 1.67 km h^{-1}; (b) 1.2 km h^{-1} at 34° east of south.
4 See Figure A2.

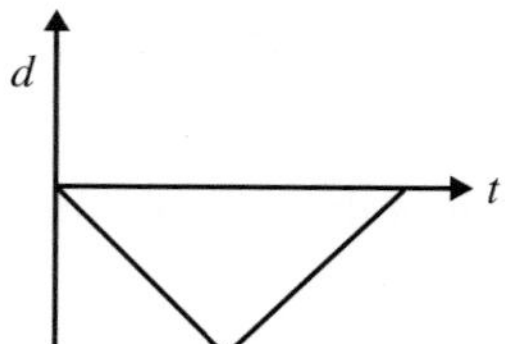

Figure A2.

5 (a) 88 m; (b) 68 m; (c) speed = 8.33 m s^{-1}; velocity = 5.0 m s^{-1}.
6 (a) 30 km; (b) 60 km.
7 (a) vt; (b) $d\sqrt{N}$.
8 (a) −130 km h^{-1}; (b) 130 km h^{-1}.
9 (a) −2 m s^{-1}; (b) −5 m s^{-1}.
10 8 m s^{-1} to the right.
11 (a) 1.75 m s^{-1}; (b) −6.0 m s^{-1}.
12 (a) Speed = 4.0 m s^{-1}; (b) velocity = 0 m s^{-1}.

Chapter 2.2

1 3.0 m s^{-2}.
2 60.0 m s^{-1}.
3 4.0 s.
4 126 m.
5 −1.6 m s^{-2}.
6 8.0 s.
[illegible]
[illegible].
[illegible]n; (b) 200 m; (c) 20 m; (d) less.
[illegible]; (b) 3.6 s; (c) 21.6 m; (d) 9.0 m s^{-1};
[illegible]3 m.
[illegible]2 s; (b) 33.2 m s^{-1}; (c) 60 m.
12 (a) 1.79 s; (b) 22.9 m s^{-1}.
13 0.324 s.
14 −15 m s^{-1}.
15 (a) 12.7 m s^{-1}; (b) 1.1.
16 25 m.
17 (a) 20 m s^{-1}.
18 2.0 m s^{-2}.
19 See Figure A3.

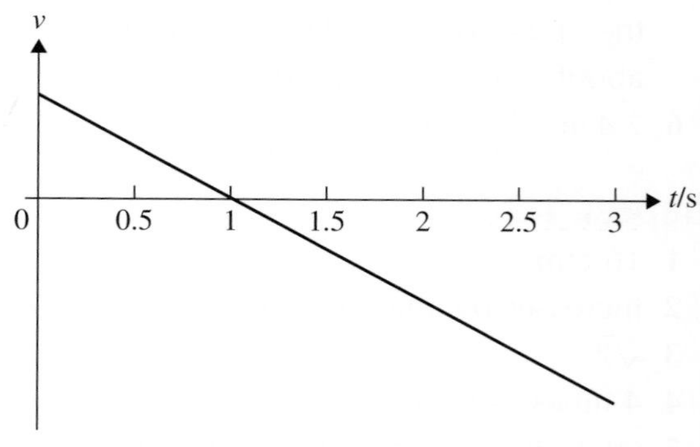

Figure A3.

20 See Figure A4.

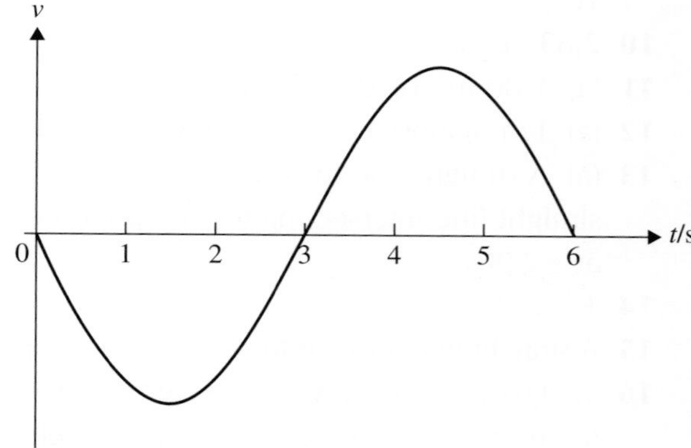

Figure A4.

21 See Figure A5.

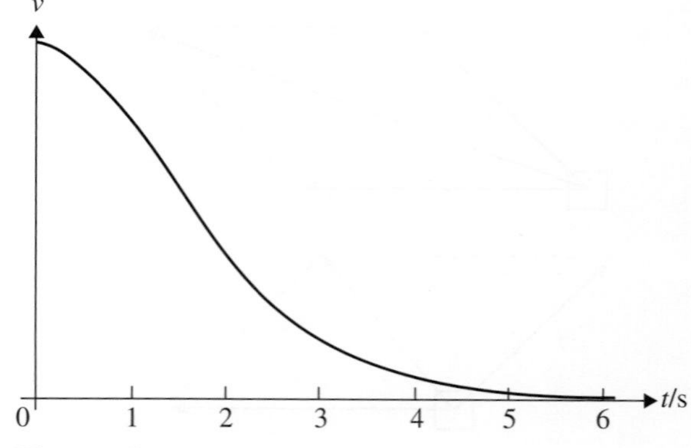

Figure A5.

22 See Figure A6.

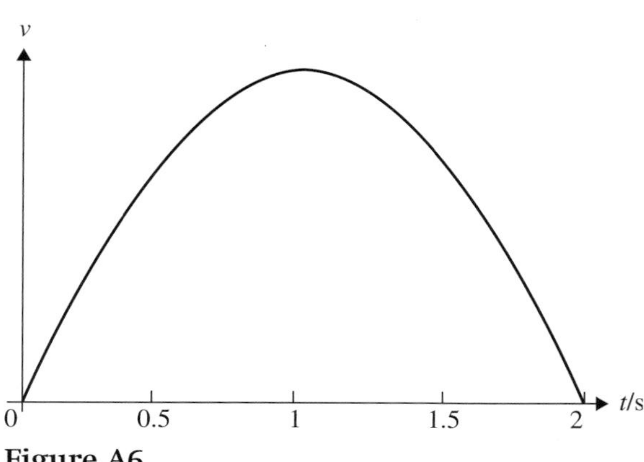

Figure A6.

23 See Figure A7.

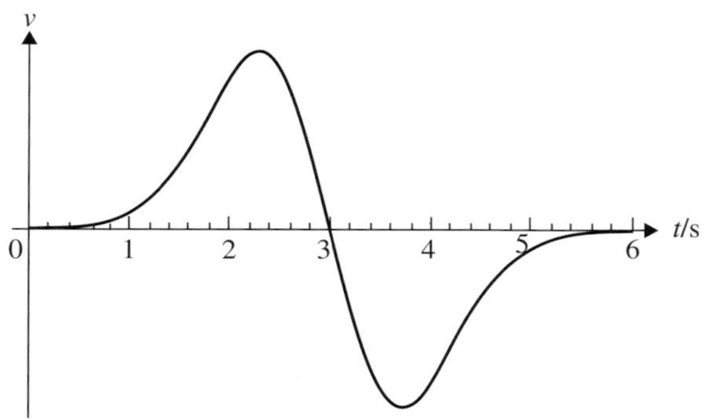

Figure A7.

24 See Figure A8.

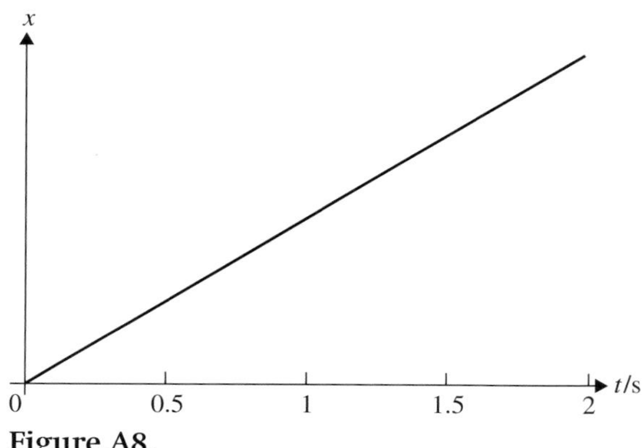

Figure A8.

25 See Figure A9.

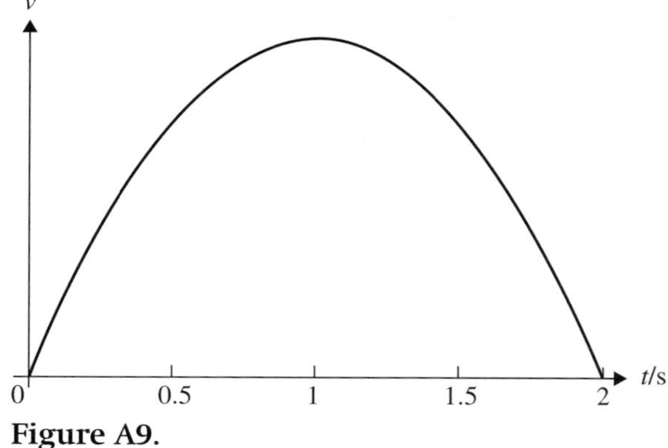

Figure A9.

26 See Figure A10.

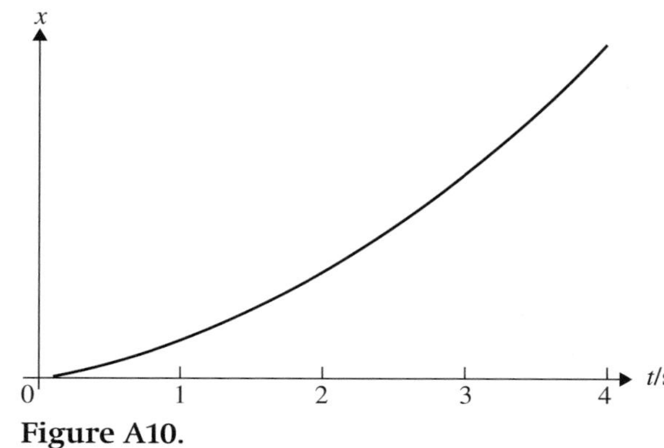

Figure A10.

27 See Figure A11.

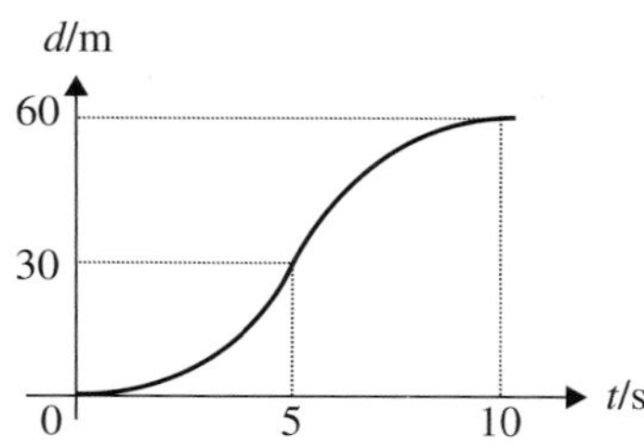

Figure A11.

28 See Figure A12.

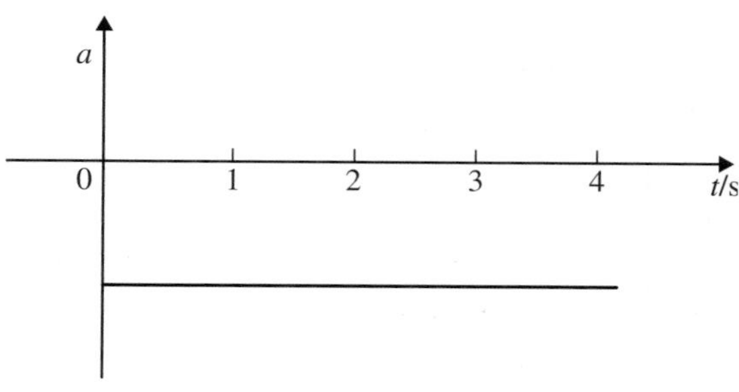

Figure A12.

29 See Figure A13.

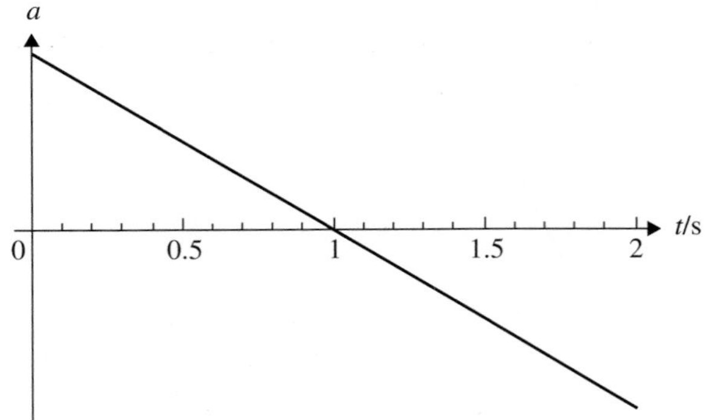

Figure A13.

30 5.0 s.
31 (a) Negative; (b) zero; (c) positive; (d) positive.
32 Make graphs of displacement against time; the graphs must cross.
35 (a) 3.2 m from top of cliff; (b) 3.56 s; (c) $-27.6\ \text{m s}^{-1}$; (d) 41.4 m; (e) average speed = $11.6\ \text{m s}^{-1}$; average velocity = $-9.83\ \text{m s}^{-1}$.
36 (a) 60 m; (b) $40\ \text{m s}^{-1}$.
37 (a) 70 m; (b) 10.7 s from the start.
(c) See Figure A14.

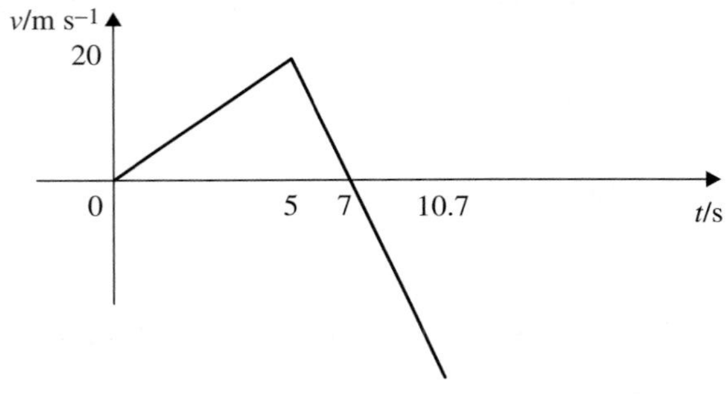

Figure A14.

38 (a) $115\ \text{m s}^{-1}$; (b) 660 m; (c) $-60.5\ \text{m s}^{-1}$.

Chapter 2.3

1 See Figure A15.

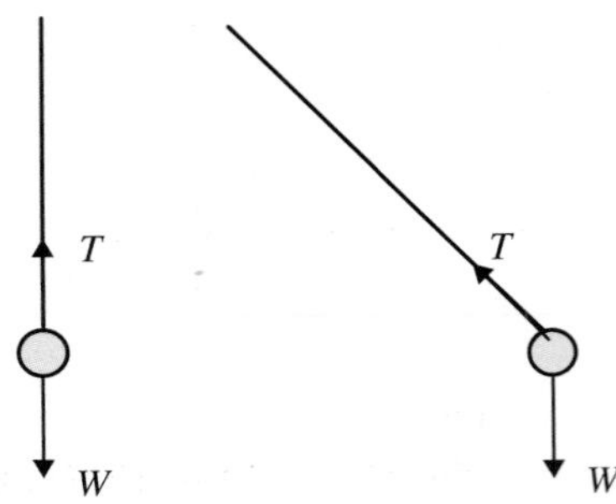

Figure A15.

2 See Figure A16.

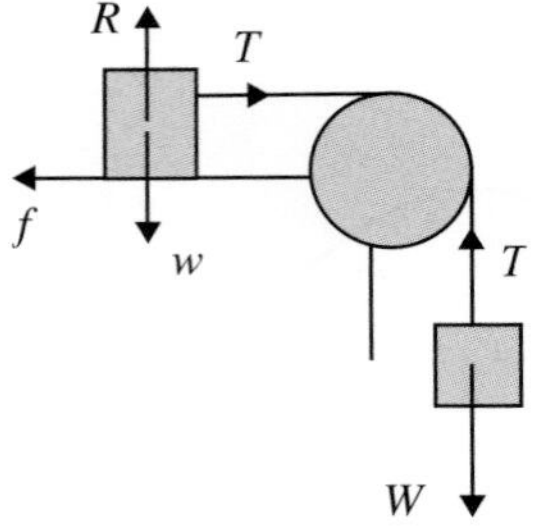

Figure A16.

3 See Figure A17.

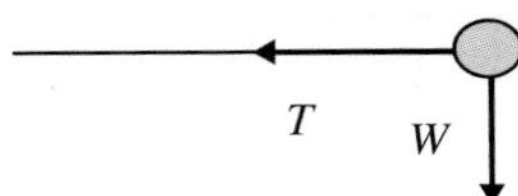

Figure A17.

4 See Figure A18.

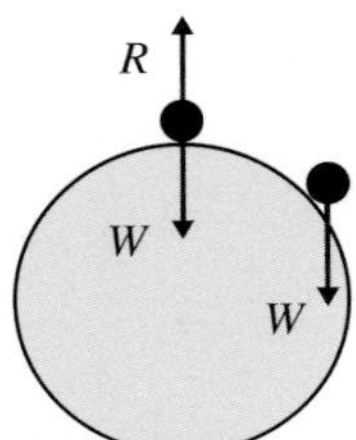

Figure A18.

5 See Figure A19.

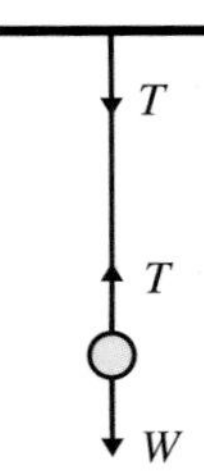

Figure A19.

6 They are the same.
7 143 N.
8 See Figure A20.

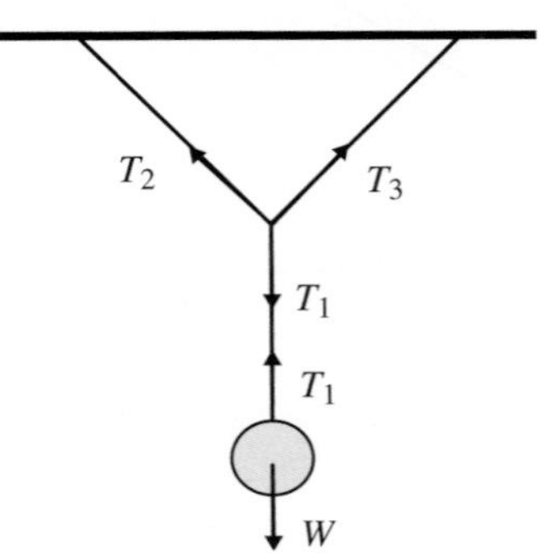

Figure A20.

9 See Figure A21.

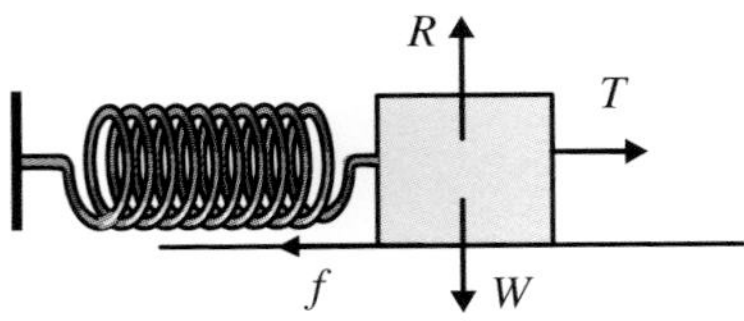

Figure A21.

10 See Figure A22.

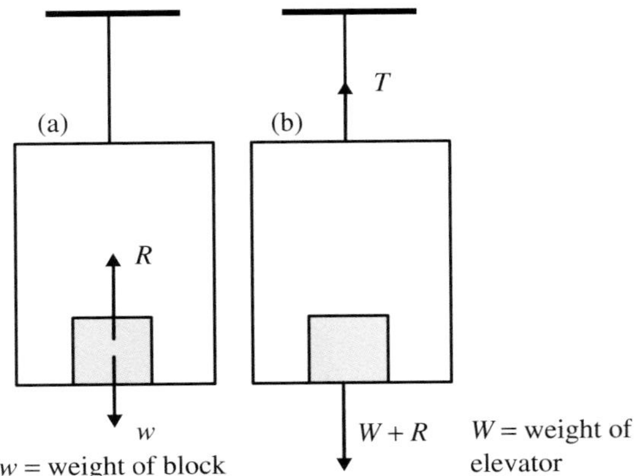

Figure A22.

Chapter 2.4

1 (a) 30 N to the right; (b) 6 N to the right; (c) 8 N to the left; (d) 15 N to the right; (e) 10 N down; (f) 20 N up.
2 28 N up.
3 7.6 N at 58°.
4 The weight cannot be balanced.
5 (a) Top; (b) bottom.
6 5.57 N at 162°.
7 4.89 N.
8 62.5 N.
9 1.2 kg.
10 $T_1 = 50$ N; $T_2 = 70.7$ N; $T_3 = 50$ N.
11 20.2 N and 47.1 N.
12 1343 N.
13 (a) 25 980 N; (b) 25 585 N.
14 $\sin\theta = \dfrac{m}{M}$.
15 $x = \dfrac{mg}{2k\cos\theta}$.

Chapter 2.5

1 (a) Decreasing mass; (b) increasing mass.
2 0.425 m s^{-2}.
3 1.00 m s^{-1}.
4 7 m s^{-2} and 3 m s^{-2}.
5 (a) mg; (b) mg; (c) $mg - ma$; (d) 0; the man is hit by the ceiling.
6 (a) mg; (b) mg; (c) greater than mg; (d) less than mg; (e) mg.
8 96 N.
10 210 N.
11 They experience the same force.
12 800 N.
13 Apart from weights and vertical reaction forces we have: 16 N left on the 2 kg as a reaction from the 3 kg mass; 16 N right on the 3 kg as a reaction from the 2 kg and 10 N left as a reaction from the 5 kg mass; 10 N right on the 5 kg as a reaction from the 3 kg mass.
14 100 N.
15 200 N.
16 On the 10 kg mass: weight 100 N down, reaction from bottom block 100 N up. On the 20 kg mass: weight 200 N down, reaction from top block of 100 N down and so reaction of 300 N up from table.
17 On the 10 kg mass: weight 100 N down, external force of 50 N down, reaction from bottom block 150 N up. On the 20 kg mass: weight 200 N down, reaction from top block of 150 N down and so reaction of 350 N up from table.
19 5 m s^{-2}.
20 (a) 15 N; (b) yes.
21 40 N.
22 3 m s^{-2}.
23 20 N; 2 m s^{-2}.
24 (a) 40 N (b) 56 N; (c) 60 N in (a) and 84 N in (b).

Chapter 2.6

1 6.00 N.
2 (a) −0.900 N s; (b) 7.20 N.
3 Zero.
4 7.00 m s^{-1}.
5 1.04 m.
6 (a) 1.41 N s away from the wall.
7 (a) −5.00 N s; (b) −25.0 N.
10 (a) Yes; (b) no.
11 (b) The order of magnitude is about 10^{-23} m.
12 (a) 96 N s; (b) 32 m s^{-1}; (c) −32 m s^{-1}.
13 50.0 kg.
14 7.0 m s^{-1} to the right.
15 0.46 m s^{-1} in the direction of the 1200 kg car.
16 5.05 N s at 56.3°.

17 A: 7.37 m s^{-1}; B: 6.80 m s^{-1}.
18 (a) 2 m s^{-1}.
19 (a) 50 kg; (b) 15 m s^{-2}; (c) 0.8 s; (d) 0.80 m (note that the net impulse is exactly 200 N s).
20 (b) 20.3 N.
22 (a) 2.5 m s^{-2}; (b) 12.5 m s^{-1}; (c) 1 m s^{-2}; (d) 18.8 m s^{-1}.
23 (a) 0.83 m s^{-1}; (b) 0.77 m s^{-1}.
24 (a) 1 s; (b) about 50 N s; (c) about 50 N.

Chapter 2.7

1 1.2×10^2 J.
2 −7.7 J.
3 3.5×10^2 J.
4 (a) Work done by weight and reaction force is zero. Work done by F is 240 J and by friction is −168 J.
(c) The kinetic energy increases by 72.0 J.
5 (a) −1900 J; (b) +1900 J; (c) zero.
6 7.3 N.
7 0.16 J.
8 0.49 m s^{-1}.
9 (a) 8.9 m s^{-1}; 6.3 m s^{-1}; (b) 8.0 m s^{-1}; 10.2 m s^{-1}.
10 7.75 m s^{-1}; 11.8 m s^{-1}.
11 22 N.
12 2.45 m s^{-1}; 2.35 m s^{-1}.
13 (a) See Figure A23; (b) 66 J; (c) 8.1 m s^{-1}.

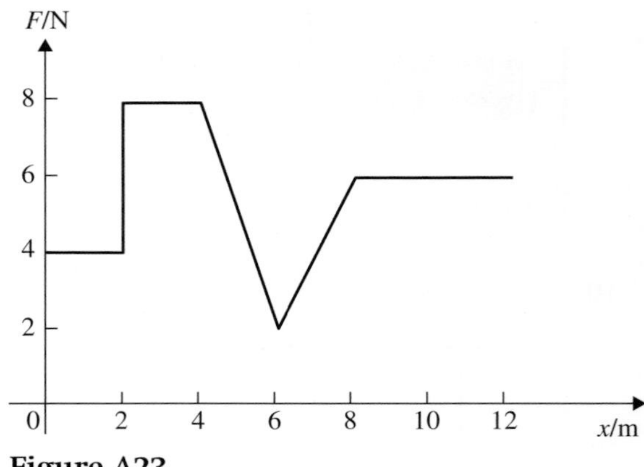

Figure A23.

14 See Figure A24 (below).
15 305 W.
16 3240 N.
17 (a) 0.21 m s^{-1}.
18 (a) 60 W; (b) 0.75; (c) 250 s.
19 $F \propto v^2$.
20 3750 N.
21 (a) The potential energy the mass has at the top is converted into kinetic energy. As the mass lands, all its potential energy has been converted to kinetic energy. (b) Some of the initial potential energy has been converted to kinetic energy. The kinetic energy remains

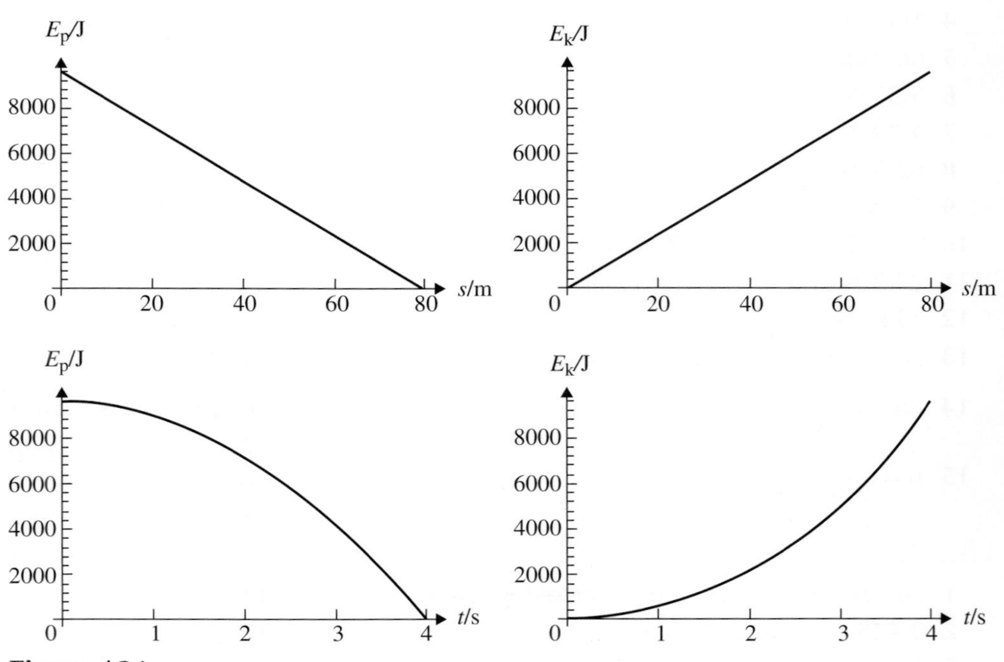

Figure A24.

constant during the fall. The remaining potential energy decreases as the mass falls and gets converted into thermal energy. As the mass lands, all the initial potential energy gets converted into thermal energy (and perhaps a bit of sound energy and deformation energy during impact with the ground). (c) The kinetic energy remains constant. The potential energy is increasing at a constant rate equal to the rate at which the pulling force does work.

23 (a) 2900 N; (b) 5.8 kW; (c) 500 N; (d) 2.0 kW; (e) 700 N.

24 27.4 J.

25 13.5 J.

26 (a) 2.42 m s^{-1}; (b) 93%.

27 5.77 m s^{-1}.

28 See Figure A25.

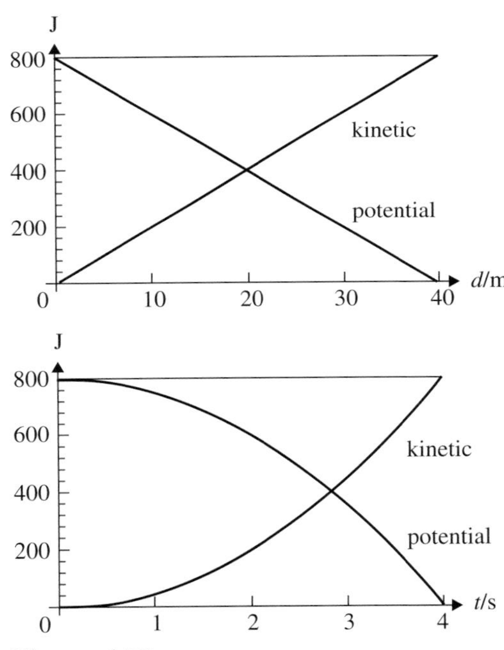

Figure A25.

30 Light to heavy = 2.

31 (a) $T = mg\sin\theta$; (b) $W = mgd\sin\theta$; (c) $W = -mgd\sin\theta$; (d) zero; (e) zero.

32 30.7 N.

33 (a) 1.36 m s^{-2}; 0.51 m s^{-2}. (c) The ratio of the accelerations is the ratio of the forces (i.e. 2.67). The ratio of the average speeds when squared becomes 2.62. This suggests that the force is proportional to speed squared; (d) 218 m; 135 m; (e) 3.8×10^5 J; 8.5×10^4 J.

34 (a) 200 N m^{-1}.

35 (a) 15.5 m s^{-1}; (b) 16.4 m s^{-1}; (d) See Figure A26.

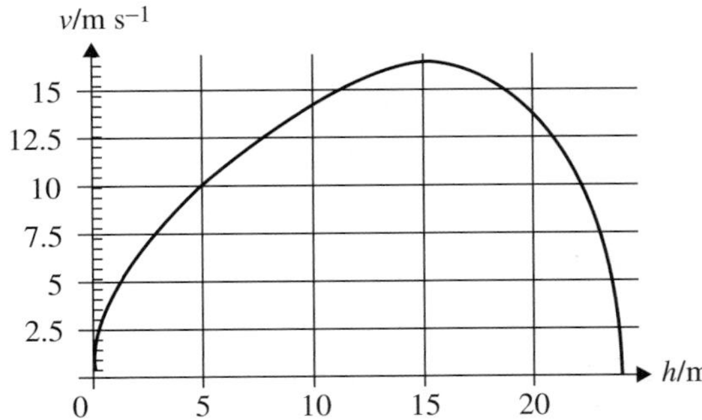

Figure A26.

36 (b) 38 400 N on both; (c) 4800 N s; (d) the force would be larger but the impulse would be the same; (e) 4000 J; the final kinetic energy is 10 000 J.

38 The 8.0 kg mass moves at 5.45 m s^{-1}; other rebounds at 4.55 m s^{-1}.

39 The 6.0 kg ball moves at 4 m s^{-1} and the 4.0 kg ball rebounds at 1 m s^{-1}. Collisions take place at the vertices of a regular pentagon inscribed in the circle; the initial position of the 6.0 kg mass is a vertex of this pentagon.

40 (a) $\frac{v^2}{2g}$; (b) $\frac{v^2}{2g}\frac{M}{m+M}$.

41 (a) 50 m; (b) 90 m; (c) 15 s from start; (d) See Figure A27.

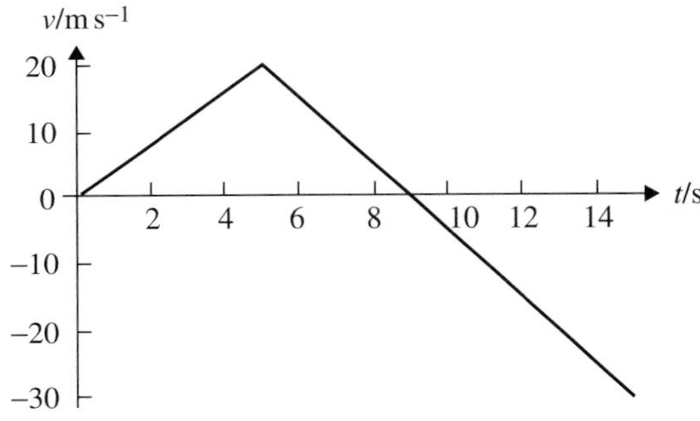

Figure A27.

(e) See Figure A28.

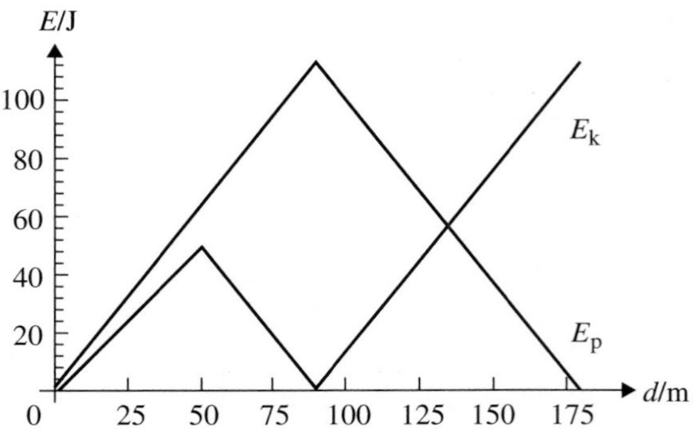

Figure A28.

(f) from 5 s on; (g) 22.5 W; (h) 45 W.

42 (b) The arrow is equivalent to a vector drawn from the tip of $\vec{p}_w$ to the tip of $\vec{p}$. It is equal in magnitude to $\vec{p}_w$.

43 (a) (i) 2.00 m s^{-1}; (ii) 0.840 N; (iii) 1.20 m s^{-2}, upwards; (iv) 0.698 m; (v) 2.01 m s^{-1} after falling 0.366 m. (b) See Figure A29.

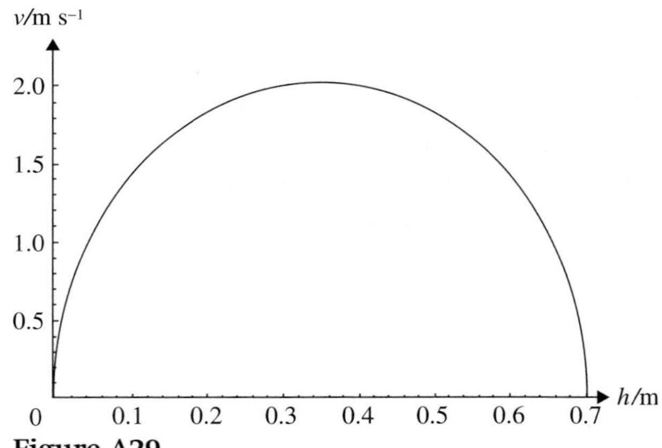

Figure A29.

Chapter 2.8

1 (a) 7.20 m s^{-2} north-west; (b) 8.0 m s^{-2}.
2 (a) 10 N; (b) 2.83 m s^{-1}; (c) 0.80 m.
3 21.4 rpm.
5 (a) 29.9 km s^{-1}; (b) 5.95×10^{-3} m s^{-2}; (c) 3.56×10^{22} N.
6 (a) 5.07 s^{-1}; (b) 0.81 Hz.
7 1.18×10^3 m s^{-2}.
8 84.49 min.
9 (a) 30 m s^{-1}; (b) 13.42 m s^{-1}.
10 3.6×10^{22} N.
11 0.02169 m s^{-2}, 0.097°.
12 $v = \sqrt{\dfrac{Mgr}{m}}$.
13 (a) 594 N; 523 N; (b) 3.16 m s^{-1}; (c) 23.7°.
14 A: 5 m s^{-2} at 278.13°; B: 5 m s^{-2} at 261.87°.
15 (a) 48.99 m s^{-1}; (b) 1800 N; (c) 30 m s^{-2}.
16 (a) 6.3 m s^{-1}; (b) 20 m s^{-2}; (d) 150 N.
17 3.2×10^9 m s^{-2}.
18 About 12.
19 48.2°.

Chapter 2.9

1 (a) 1.99×10^{20} N; (b) 4.17×10^{23} N; (c) 1.0×10^{-47} N.
2 (a) Zero; (b) zero; (c) $\dfrac{Gm^2}{4R^2}$; (d) $\dfrac{Gm(m+M)}{4R^2}$.
3 1/81.
4 1/2.
5 3.
6 Twice as large.
7 0.9.
8 P: $g = 0$; Q: $g = 1.41 \times 10^{-6}$ N kg^{-1}.
9 To the left.

Chapter 2.10

1 (a) 5.0 cm; (b) 200 m s^{-1}.
2 1.02 m.
3 (a) 0.77 s; (b) 9.22 m s^{-1}.
4 (a) 2.0 s; (b) 12.8 m s^{-1}; (c) −51.3°; (d) 21.5 m s^{-1} at −68.2°.
5 1.48 m.
6 5.66 m s^{-1}.
7 316.2 m.
8 $L/2$.
9 7.59 m.
10 See Figure A30 (opposite page).
11 0.33 m.
12 53.2° below the horizontal.
13 See Figure A31 (opposite page).
14 See Figure A32 (opposite page).
15 Unfortunately the monkey gets hit (assuming the bullet can get that far).
16 (a) 10 m s^{-1}; (b) the weight, vertically down. (c) See Figure A33 (page 798).
17 (a) $v_x = 30$ m s^{-1}, $v_y = 20$ m s^{-1}; (b) 34°; (c) $g = 20$ m s^{-2}; (d) horizontal arrow for velocity, vertical for acceleration; (e) range and maximum height half as large, as shown in in Figure A34 (page 798).
18 18 m s^{-1} at 58°.
19 40 m s^{-1} at 70° below the horizontal. (b) Speed is less and angle is greater.
21 0.45 m.
22 36° at 34 m s^{-1}.

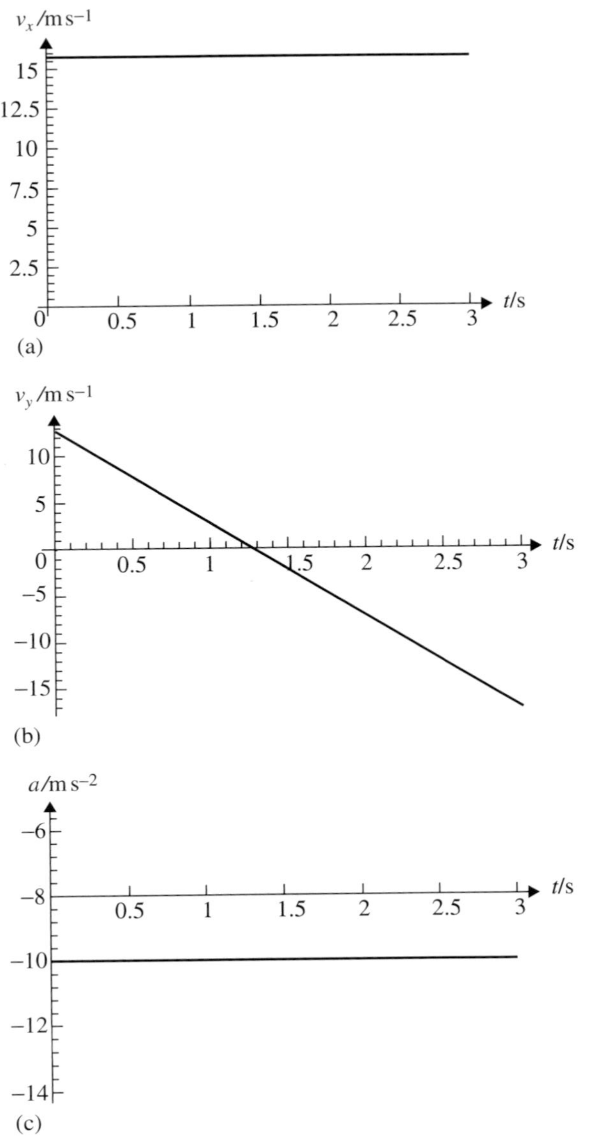

Figure A30.

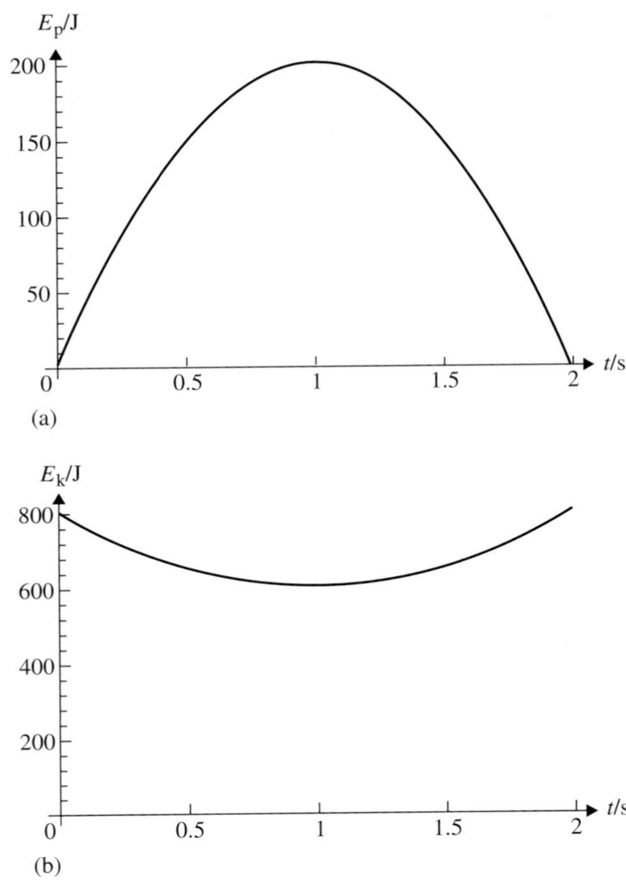

Figure A32.

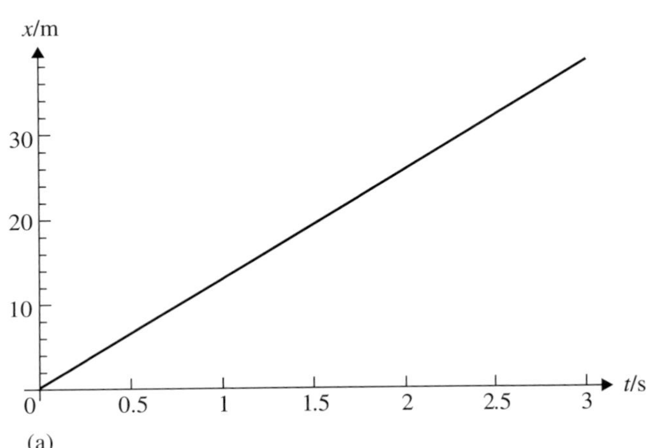

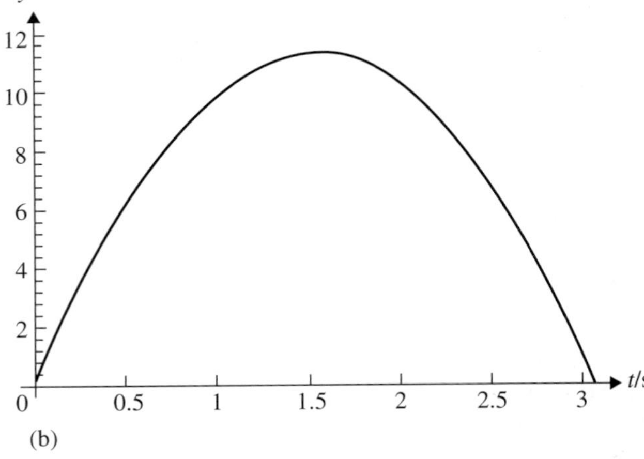

Figure A31.

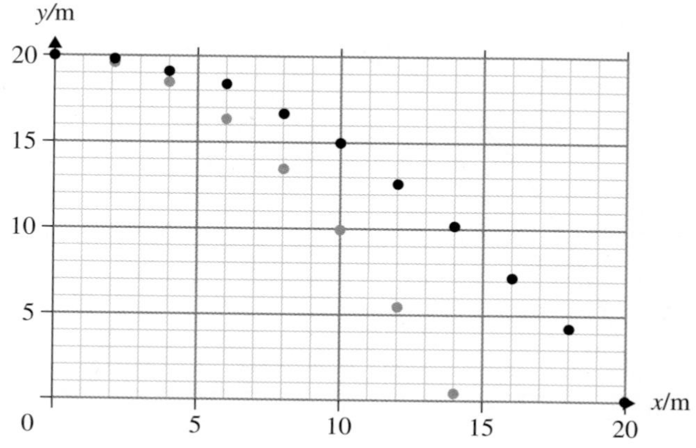

Figure A33.

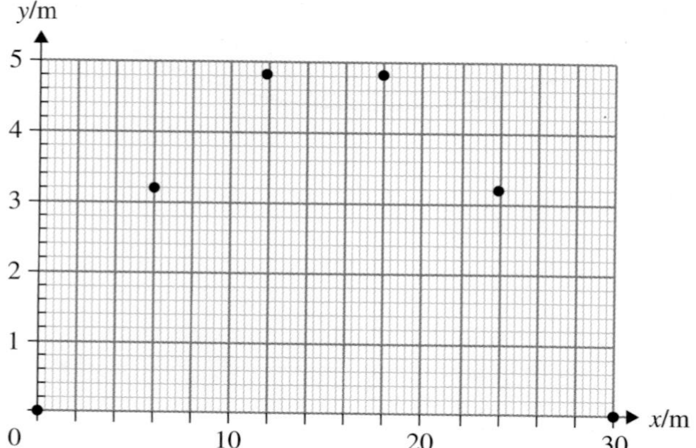

Figure A34.

Chapter 2.11

3 7.61 km s^{-1}; 94.6 min.

4 About 35 870 km (i.e. about 42 250 km from the earth's centre).

5 (a) -7.63×10^{28} J; (b) -1.04×10^{6} J kg^{-1}; (c) 1019 m s^{-1}.

6 See Figure A35.

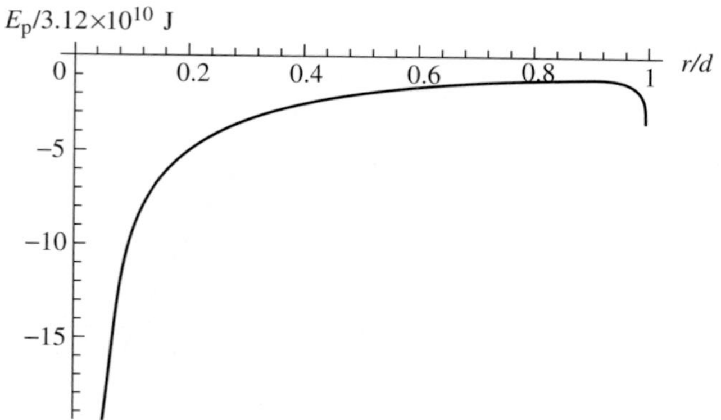

Figure A35.

7 (a) -1.25×10^{7} J kg^{-1}; (b) -6.25×10^{9} J.

8 Orbit 1 is not possible, orbit 2 is.

9 The normal reaction force from the spacecraft floor is zero.

11 The work required to move the mass on which the force is acting from $r = a$ to $r = b$.

12 (a) 1.5×10^{28} kg; (c) 3.2×10^{6} m s^{-1}; (d) 6.0×10^{15} J; (e) 2.4×10^{6} m s^{-1}.

13 (a) 9 : 1; (b) 3.6×10^{6} m s^{-1}.

14 -5.29×10^{33} J.

15 (a) B; (b) A; (c) A.

17 $\frac{5R}{2}$.

18 (a) $\sqrt{\frac{GM}{R}} - \sqrt{\frac{GM}{2R}} = 2.32$ km s^{-1}.

22 (a) 2.

24 (b) $V = -\frac{25Gm}{d}$.

25 (c) About 4.

26 (c) 3.1×10^{6} m.

27 (a) $F = \frac{GM^2}{4R^2}$; (c) $T = 7.8\ h$;

(f)(ii) 3.9×10^{-19} J yr^{-1}; (g) 2.6×10^{8} yr.

29 (a) $g = 4.7$ N kg^{-1}; (b) $g = 0$; (c) 9.0.

3 Thermal properties of matter

Chapter 3.1

3 (a) No; (b) 300 K; (c) 4×10^{6} J.

4 (a) 3.72×10^{-26} m^3; (b) 3.04×10^{-29} m^3; (c) 1.22×10^{3}.

5 (a) 4.5×10^{-26} kg; (b) 6.0×10^{28} m^{-3}.

6 (a) 1.0×10^{-25} kg; (b) 8.4×10^{28} m^{-3}.

Chapter 3.2

2 513 J kg^{-1} K^{-1}.

3 (a) 1.18×10^{5} J K^{-1}; (b) 87.4 min.

4 73.1 °C.

5 32.2 kJ kg^{-1}; 13.3 min.

6 35 g.

7 3.73×10^{8} J.

8 16.4%.

9 83.6 min.

10 (a) 2.2×10^{4} J; (b) 3.3×10^{5} J; (c) 4.2×10^{4} J.

11 111 g.

12 94.8 °C.

13 2880 J kg^{-1} K^{-1}.

14 4200 J kg^{-1} K^{-1}.

15 (a) 0.015 kg; (b) 0.012 m^3.

16 (a) 2.76×10^{5}; (b) 6×10^{-3} K s^{-1}.

18 0°C.
19 0.935.
20 Increases by a factor of 2.

Chapter 3.3

1 2.41 L.
2 16.0 atm.
3 0.33 L.
4 By a factor of 8.
5 1.46×10^9 Pa.
6 87.9 g.
7 10.1 min.
8 See Figure A36.

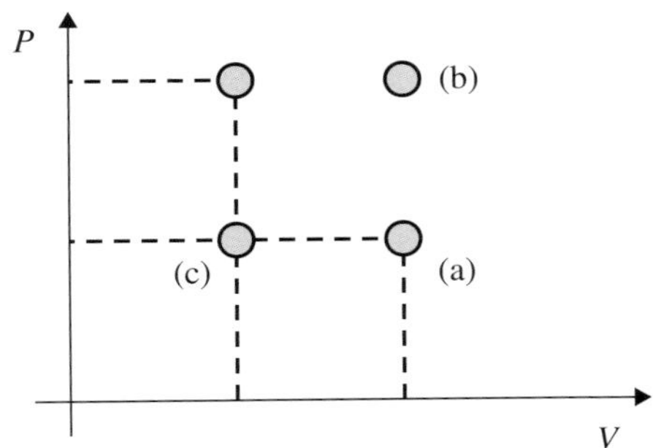

Figure A36.

9 (a) At B, 1200 K; at C, 600 K; at D, 150 K;
(b) At B.
10 10 atm.
11 (a) 1.0×10^3 Pa; (b) 1.2×10^{22};
(c) 7.3×10^{-2} m^3.
12 56 g; 0.045 m^3.
13 (a) 7.24×10^{25};
(b) 8.38×10^{24};
(c) 358.5 K.
14 (a) 1.74 atm; (b) 15.35 mol.
15 1.04×10^5 Pa.
16 (a) 0.030; (b) 1.81×10^{22}; (c) 0.87 g.
17 (a) 22.39 L;
(b) 0.179 kg m^{-3};
(c) 1.43 kg m^{-3}.
18 (a) Helium: 3.72×10^{-26} m^3; water: 2.99×10^{-29} m^3; uranium: 2.11×10^{-29} m^3;
(b) 3.34×10^{-9} m; 3.10×10^{-10} m; 2.77×10^{-10} m.
19 1.35 kg m^{-3}.

Chapter 3.4

1 380 J
2 (a) 6500 J removed from the gas;
(b) less than 6500 J.

5

	W	Δ*U*	Δ*T*
gas X	positive	zero	zero
gas Y	zero	positive	positive
gas Z	positive	positive	positive

7 (a) 2.40×10^6 J; (b) 900 K; (c) 6.00×10^6 J supplied.
9 (a) Work is done on the gas;
(b) thermal energy is taken out of the gas.
10 Gas X.
11 Gas Y.
13 (a) $T_B = 3200$ K, $T_C = 1600$ K, $T_D = 400$ K;
(b) $Q_{AB} = 300$ kJ (supplied), $Q_{BC} = -120$ kJ (removed), $Q_{CD} = -50$ kJ (removed), $Q_{DA} = 30$ kJ (supplied).

4 Oscillations and waves

Chapter 4.1

8 (a) 5.0 mm; (b) −3.7 mm; (c) 0.99 s;
(d) ±4.0 mm.
9 (a) $8.0 \cos(28\pi t)$;
(b) $y = -4.7$ cm, $v = -5.7$ m s^{-1},
$a = 3.6 \times 10^2$ m s^{-2}.
10 $v = 14$ m s^{-1}; $a = 4.2 \times 10^4$ m s^{-2}.
11 (a) 520 Hz; (c) 6.0 mm; (d) 1.0 m; (e) 4.2 mm.
12 A, right and long; B, right and shorter;
C, zero; D, left and shortest.
13 (a) $a = 1.0 \times 10^4$ m s^{-2};
(b) $v = 21$ m s^{-1}; (c) $F = 2.5 \times 10^3$ N.
14 (a) 0.51 cm; (b) twice the amplitude;
(c) $-0.25 \sin(5\pi t)$.
15 See Figure A38.

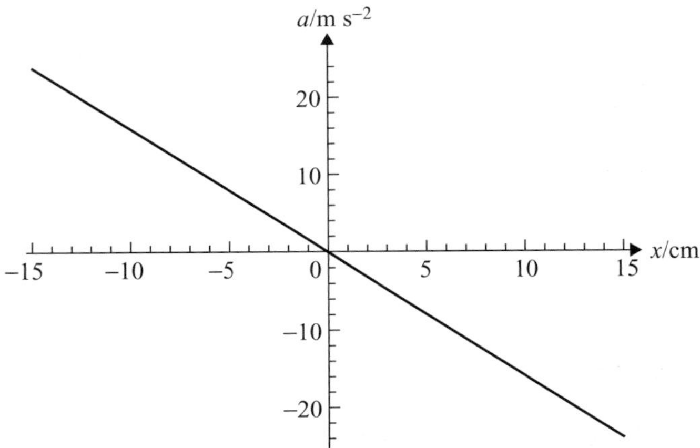

Figure A38.

16 (b) 1.6 s; (c) $v = 0.40$ m s^{-1};
(d) $F = 0.24$ N; (e) $E = 0.012$ J.

17 (a) 9.94 mm; (b) 2.35 N.

18 (a) 70 kg; (b) 7.1 m.

19 (a) mass $= M\left(\frac{x}{R}\right)^3$; (b) force $= GMm\frac{x}{R^3}$;
(d) period $= 2\pi\sqrt{\frac{R^3}{GM}}$; (e) 85 minutes;
(f) same.

20 (c) $2\pi\sqrt{\frac{mL}{4T}}$.

24 (a) $A = 0.360$ m, $f = 1.08$ Hz, $T = 0.924$ s;
(b) 5.39 J; (c) 4.74 J, 0.650 J.

25 (a) 0.57 s.

26 (a) 27.0 m; (b) 34.2 m s^{-2}; (c) 3.28 s; (d) 17.7 m.

29 (a) Yes, the ratio is 0.61; (b) 37%.

34 (a) $\omega = \sqrt{\frac{k}{m}}$; (d) $\pi\omega A^2$.

38 (a) $f = \frac{1}{2\pi}\sqrt{\frac{k}{m}}$;
(b) $x = (4\pi^2 mf^2 L)/(k - 4\pi^2 mf^2)$.

Chapter 4.2

3 (a) 1.29 m; (b) 1.32×10^{-2} m.

5 25.3 m s^{-1}.

6 (a) $\lambda = 3.33$ m; (b) the same.

7 (a) $v = 3.0$ m s^{-1}; (b) $T = 1.5$ s;
$f = 0.667$ Hz; (c) $\lambda = 4.5$ m; $A = 12$ cm.

8 (a) $\lambda = 0.66$ m; (b) $\lambda = 2.98$ m.

9 3.16 m s^{-1}.

11 $d = 2400$ m; $\lambda = 0.050$ m; number of waves = 30.

12 From left to right: down, down, up.

13 From left to right: up, up, down.

14 See Figure A39.

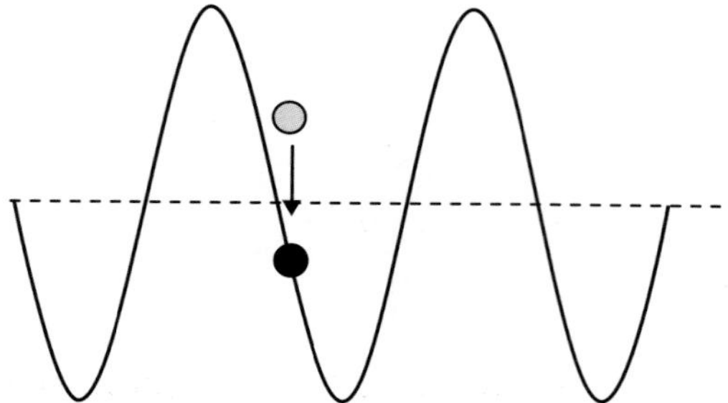

Figure A39.

15 (a) 0.6 cm; (b) 4.0 m; (c) 5.0 m s^{-1}
(d) 1.25 Hz; (e) no.

16 See Figure A40.

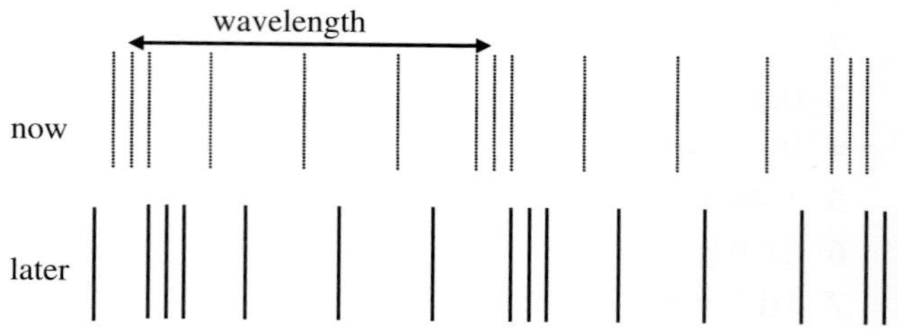

Figure A40.

17 (a) 850 Hz;
(b) (i) 0.30 m, (ii) 0.10 m;
(c) (i) 0.10 ms, (ii) 0.69 ms.

Chapter 4.3

1 See Figure A42.

Figure A42.

2 See Figure A43.

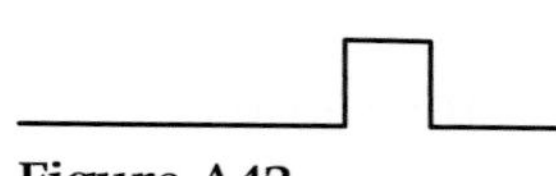

Figure A43.

3 See Figure A44 (opposite page).

4 See Figure A45 (opposite page).

5 (a) 22.9°; (b) 1.89×10^8 m s^{-1};
(c) 4.3×10^{-7} m.

6 (a) 1.0×10^{-8} s; (b) 6×10^6.

7 1.06 cm.

8 See Figure A46 (opposite page).

10 13.1°.

11 See Figure A47 (opposite page).

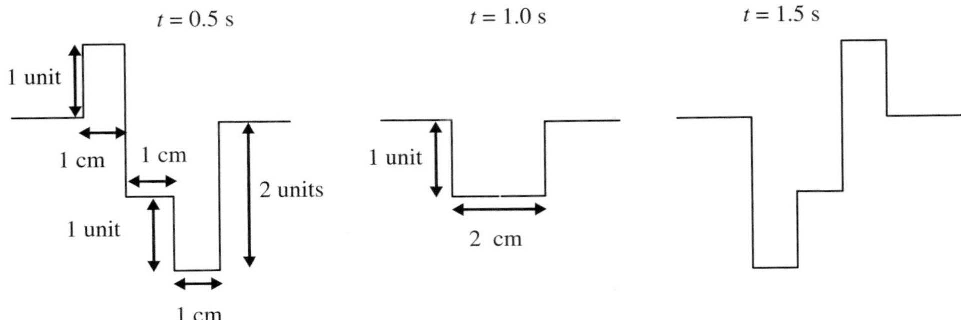

Figure A44.

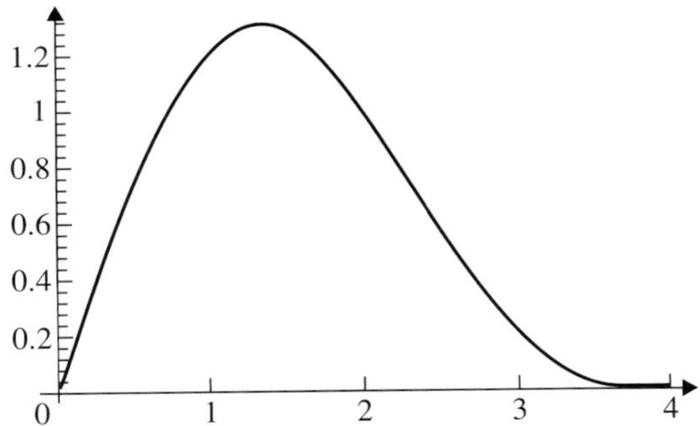

Figure A45.

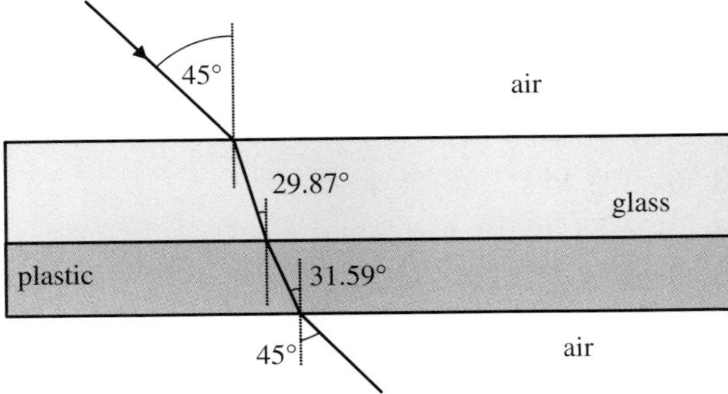

Figure A46.

Chapter 4.4

1 See Figure 4.2 on page 239.
2 See Figure 4.1 on page 238.
3 Reflection and diffraction of sound. Absence of these for light. By using a mirror at the corner.
4 8.0 m.
5 400 m.
6 0.83 m.
7 (a) The path difference is two wavelengths, so the observer hears a loud sound because of constructive interference. (b) The path difference is one and a half wavelengths, so

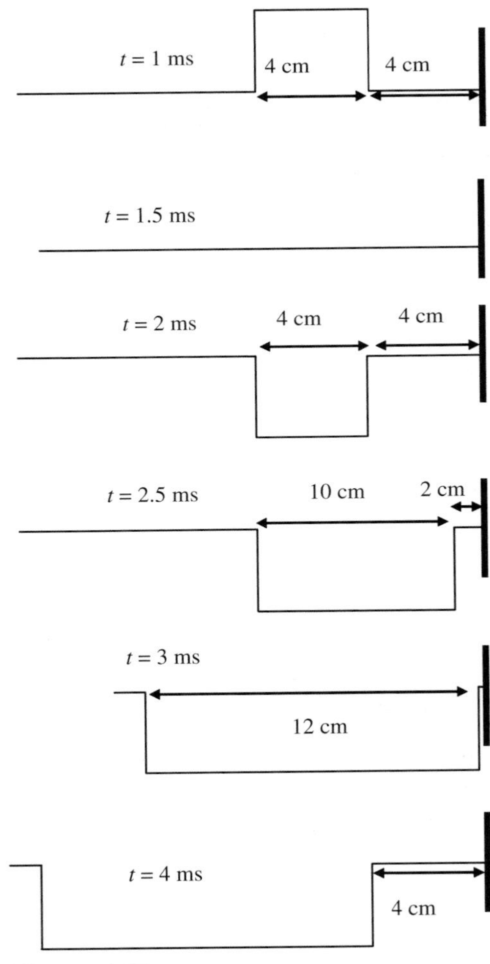

Figure A47.

the observer hears no sound because of destructive interference.
8 See Figure 4.10 on page 241.

Chapter 4.5

1 The car receives a higher frequency because it is approaching. The car now acts as a source.

Since the source is approaching, the frequency received will be *even* higher.

2 It is approaching.
4 570 Hz.
5 440 Hz.
6 490 Hz.
7 670 Hz.
8 7 m s^{-1}.
9 4 m s^{-1}.
10 489.3 to 511.2 Hz.
13 (c) (i) $v = 0.36$ m s^{-1}.
14 ±3.8 GHz.

15 (a) Single frequency, first higher then lower than 500 Hz.
(b) Above 500 Hz to above 1000 Hz, followed by below 500 Hz to below 1000 Hz.
(c) As the source approaches frequencies near 20 kHz move to the inaudible range and other lower frequencies take their place so the highest frequency still heard is still 20 kHz. The lowest heard is above 20 Hz. As the source moves away, the highest frequency heard will be less than 20 kHz and the lowest will be 20 Hz.

16 (b) 3.69×10^7 m s^{-1} and 7.99×10^6 m s^{-1}.

17 (a) See Figure A48.

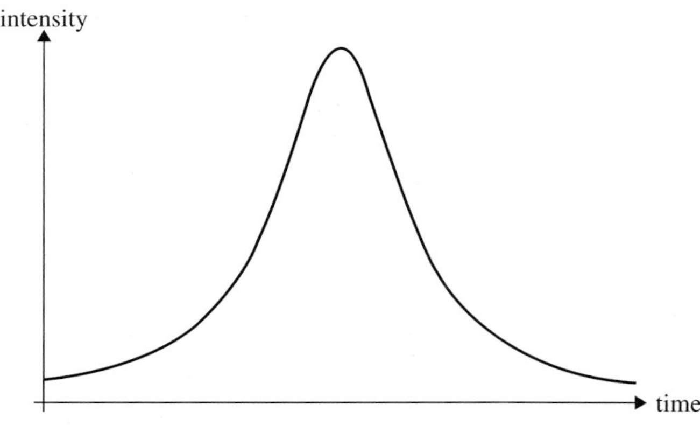

Figure A48.

(b) See Figure A49.

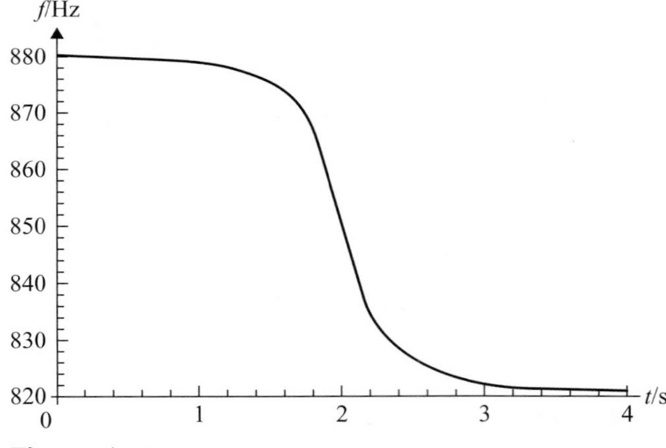

Figure A49.

(c) See Figure A50.

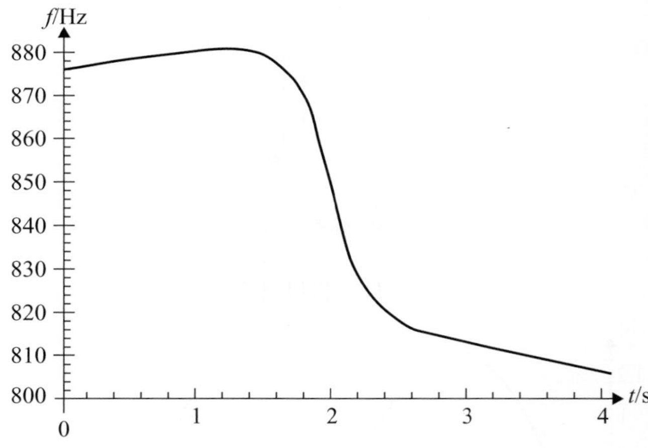

Figure A50.

18 (a) 32 m s^{-1}; (b) (i) 0.64 m, (ii) 0.64 m

19 (b) 9.3×10^6 m s^{-1}.

Chapter 4.6

7 354 Hz.

8 0.500.

9 548 Hz.

10 (a) 225 Hz; (b) 1.47 m.

12 0.81 m; 1.35 m.

13 (a) 321 m s^{-1}; (b) 1.4 cm.

14 (a) 2.75 m; (b) $n = 5$ and $n = 6$.

15 (a) 0.12 kHz; (b) 12 m.

16 (b) $v = 0.18$ m s^{-1}.

18 (b) 8.0 m;
(c) π, $y = 5.0\cos(45\pi t + \pi) = -5.0\cos(45\pi t)$

19 The frequency is $f = \dfrac{v}{\lambda} = \dfrac{330}{1.7} = 194$ Hz.

The maximum kinetic energy is

$$E_{\max} = \frac{1}{2}mA^2 4\pi^2 f^2 = 5.7 \times 10^{-33}\text{ J}.$$

20 (a) $\lambda = 4.0$ m;
(c) (i) $y_Q = A\cos(2\pi ft + \pi) = -2.0\cos(60\pi t)$,
(ii) $y_R = A\cos(2\pi ft) = 2.0\cos(60\pi t)$;
(d) (i) $\bar{v}_p = \dfrac{4.0 \times 10^{-3}}{8.33 \times 10^{-3}} = 0.48\text{ m s}^{-1}$,
(ii) $\bar{v}_q = \dfrac{2.0 \times 10^{-3}}{8.33 \times 10^{-3}} = 0.24\text{ m s}^{-1}$;
(e) (i) P: $v_{\max} = 0.75$ m s^{-1},
(ii) Q: $v_{\max} = 0.38$ m s^{-1}.

Chapter 4.7

1 38.9°.

2 5.0 cm.

3 (a) 1.556λ; (b) 13 maxima. See Figure A51.

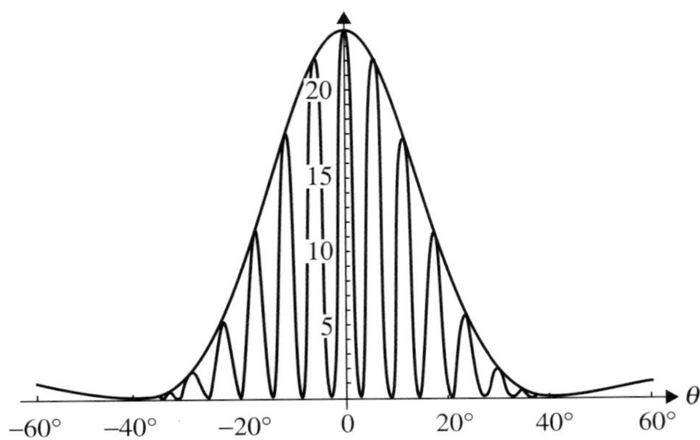

Figure A51.

4 1.746 cm; microwave.

Chapter 4.8

1 No; can resolve 3.6 cm.

2 115 km.

3 (a) 1.5×10^{-4} rad; (b) 58 km.

4 (a) 3.4×10^{-3} rad; (b) cannot resolve, as $3.4 \times 10^{-3} > 4.1 \times 10^{-6}$ rad.

5 $3.3 \times 10^{-4} < 0.088$ rad, so seen as extended object.

6 2.5×10^{12} m.

7 (a) 2.8×10^{-7} rad.

Chapter 4.9

4 (b) 82%.

6 $\frac{I_0}{2}$.

7 $\frac{I_0}{8}$.

8 128 additional polarizers.

10 45°.

11 21%.

12 (b) Yes, $\frac{I_0}{8}$; (c) no light transmitted.

13 (b) 54.5°; (c) 35.5°.

14 (a) 53.1°; (b) 36.9°.

5 Electricity and magnetism

Chapter 5.1

3 −2 C.

4 (a) 29 N; (b) 7.2 N.

5 90 N to the right.

6 (a) 3.22 cm from the left charge; (b) unstable.

7 73 N at 225° to the horizontal.

8 29.9 N north-east.

9 (a) 8.0×10^{-9} C; (b) 5.0×10^{10} electronic charges.

11 (a) 2×10^{28}; (b) 10^{27} N. (c) One assumption is that the body consists entirely of water, but a more significant assumption is the use of Coulomb's law for bodies which are fairly close to each other and are not point charges. (d) The net charge of a person is zero because of the protons that have been neglected in this estimate. This leads to zero force.

Chapter 5.2

4 (a) 8.0×10^{-16} N; (b) 8.0×10^{-16} N; (c) 8.0×10^{-16} N; (d) 4.8×10^{-17} J.

5 1.60×10^{-17} N left; 1.76×10^{13} m s^{-2}.

6 6.0 N C^{-1}.

7 3.84×10^5 N C^{-1} to the right.

8 5.77×10^5 N C^{-1} at 3.2° below the horizontal.

9 (a) 500 J; (b) 1000 J; (c) 500 J.

10 (a) 5.93×10^6 m s^{-1}; (b) 1.38×10^5 m s^{-1}.

11 170 N C^{-1} at 137.4° to the horizontal for each.

12 (a) Zero; (b) zero; (c) 1.60×10^6 N C^{-1}; (d) 9.0×10^5 N C^{-1}.

13 (a) Positive; (b) $E = \frac{mg}{q}$; (d) period is the same.

14 (a) $E = 0$.

(b) The net force takes the particle back towards its equilibrium position.

(c) In general no, but if the displacement is very small, then they are approximately SHM.

(d) No oscillations will take place.

15 (a) $F = -\frac{16kQq}{d^2}\left(\frac{1}{\left(1-\frac{4x}{3d}\right)^2} - \frac{1}{\left(1+\frac{4x}{d}\right)^2}\right)$

(c) There will be SHM oscillations with amplitude A and period $T = \frac{\pi}{8}\sqrt{\frac{3md^3}{2kQq}}$

Chapter 5.3

2 (a) 2.55×10^6 V; (b) $E = 0$.

3 (a) $\frac{4Q}{4\pi\varepsilon_0 d}$; (b) zero.

4 −15 kV.

5 3.6×10^7 J.

6 1.44×10^{-7} J.

7 5.93×10^6 m s^{-1}.

8 (a) 11.8 N at 75.4° below the horizontal;
(b) 5.1×10^5 V;
(c) 5.1×10^{-4} J.

9 (a) 3.875×10^{-11} m; (b) zero;
(c) 1.24×10^{-23} N m.

10 (a) 0.8 μC (small sphere) and 1.2 μC;
(b) 6.37×10^{-6} C m^{-2} (small sphere) and 4.24×10^{-6} C m^{-2}; (c) 7.2×10^5 N C^{-1} (small sphere) and 4.8×10^5 N C^{-1}.

12 (a) 0.30×10^{-3} J; (b) -0.30×10^{-3} J;
(c) -0.60×10^{-3} J.

13 (a) -7.19 V; (b) -1.6×10^{-19} C.

14 (a) $\frac{2qa}{4\pi\varepsilon_0(d^2+a^2)^{3/2}}$ vertically down;
(b) $\frac{2qd}{4\pi\varepsilon_0(d^2+a^2)^{3/2}}$ horizontally to the left.

15 $\frac{8Q}{36\pi\varepsilon_0 d^2}$ up.

16 (d) $\frac{q^2}{16\pi\varepsilon_0 r}$.

17 $W = \frac{3ke^2}{r} = 1.4 \times 10^{-18}$ J.

Chapter 5.4

5 Decreases by a factor of 4.

6 5.9×10^{28} m^{-3}.

7 4.3×10^{-5}m s^{-1}.

8 (a) 3.6×10^4 C; (b) 2.2×10^{23} electrons.

9 (a) Yes.

10 14 V.

11 No.

12 12 Ω.

13 14.7 Ω.

14 40 Ω.

15 (a) 8 V for the 4 Ω resistor and 12 V for the 6 Ω resistor; (b) 16 V; 16 V; 4 V.

16 (a) See Figure A52.
(b) 8.5 V

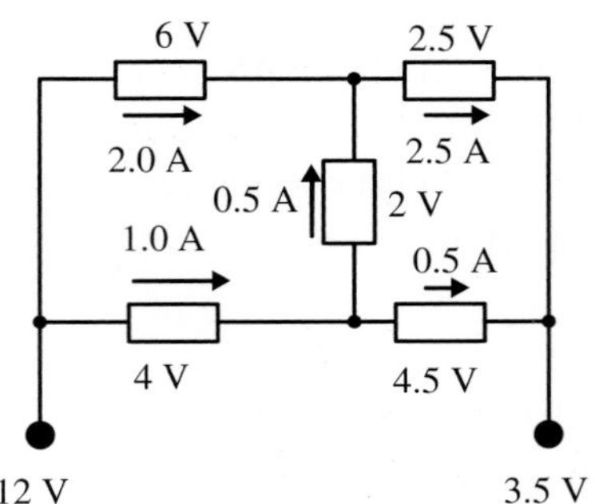

Figure A52.

17 (a) 0.27 A; (b) 0.136 A, (c) 15 W.

18 (a) 403.3 Ω, (b) 57 cm.

19 (a) 0.1 kW h; (b) 3.6×10^5 J.

20 Cost is the same.

Chapter 5.5

1 2.7 Ω; 12.4 Ω; 1.0 Ω.

2 38.75 Ω.

3 4.0 Ω.

4 0.01 Ω, 100 Ω.

5 $R/4$.

6 See Figure A53.

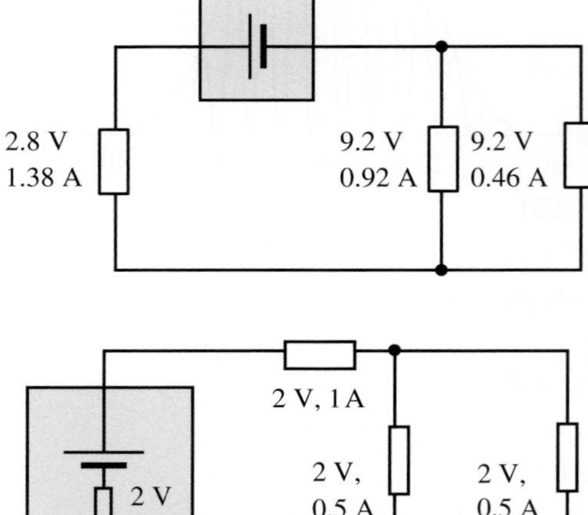

Figure A53.

7 2.0 Ω.

8 The same.

9 (a) 5.45 A and 2.27 A; (b) 1.7 kW h.

10 See Figure A54.

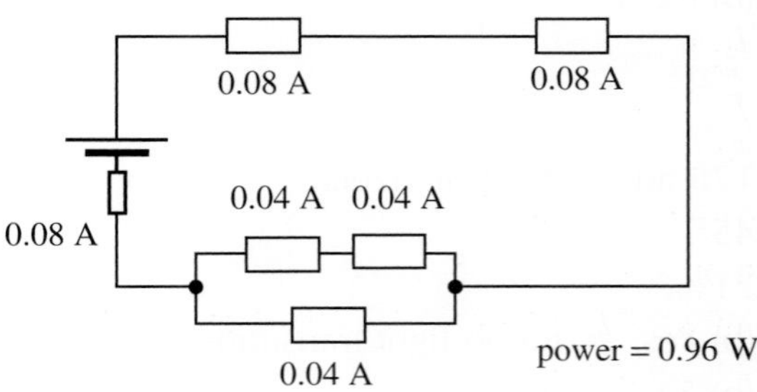

Figure A54.

11 (a) 9.09 A; (b) 24.2 Ω; (c) 315 s; (d) \$0.0175.

12 (a) 0.14 A and 0.17 A; (b) Costs more at 220 V by a factor of 4.

13 No.

14 No.

15 (a) 30 kΩ; (b) 0.20 mA.

16 The power in the lamp will increase by a factor of 2.4.
17 (a) 4.4 kW; (b) 19 min.
18 6.48 V.
19 18.5 W; 14.8 W.
20 293.
21 (a) 4 V; (b) 40 mA; (c) 6 V, 30 mA.
22 5.0 A.
23 (a) 15.94 W; (b) 598 J.
24 (a) A and B are the same, C is brighter by a factor of 4; (b) the same; (c) A goes out, C stays the same.
25 (a) 0.5 V (3 kΩ), 1.0 V; (b) 0.25 V.
26 See Figure A55.

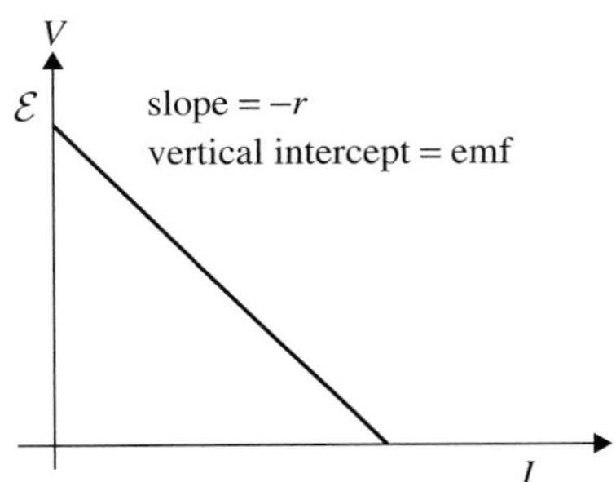

Figure A55.

27 $R\left(1 + \sqrt{3}\right)$.
28 6.0 A.
29 (a) Same; (b) $\frac{16}{9}$ times as bright.
30 2.0 Ω.
31 (a) P; (b) $2P$; (c) $\frac{P}{2}$; (d) $\frac{3P}{2}$.
32 12 V.
33 6.0 V.
34 (a) 1.2 Ω; (b) 12 V.
35 2.8 V.
36 (a) 16 V; (b) 3.25 Ω.
37 (a) 4.2 A; (b) 1.1 A.
38 The brightness of A will decrease and that of B will increase.
39 (a) 40 Ω; (b) 5.5 V.
40 (a) 4.0 V; (b) 20 Ω; (c) 1.6 V; (d) 0.080 A.
41 (a) 2.00 V; (b) 2.06 V.

Chapter 5.6

2 (a) B into page; (b) F into page; (c) B out of page; (d) force zero; (e) force zero.
3 5.4×10^{-6} T into page.
4 P: 3.75×10^{-4} T out of page; Q: zero; R: 2.67×10^{-4} T into page.
6 (a) Force down; (b) force right.
7 (a) Into page; (b) zero; (c) force up.
8 No.
9 Out of page; out of page; left; left.
10 3.0×10^{-7} N up.
11 (a) AB: $F = 0.02$ N into page; BC: $F = 0$; CD: $F = 0.02$ N out of page; DA: $F = 0$; (b) net force = 0.
12 27.1 m.
13 P: out of page; Q: into page.
14 (a) 8.0 cm from 2 A wire, in between wires; (b) 40.0 cm above 2 A wire.
15 (a) 0.012 T into page; (b) yes; (c) no.
16 (a) No; (b) yes, it will rotate counter-clockwise.
17 2.25 N.
18 Will attract.
19 See Figure A56.

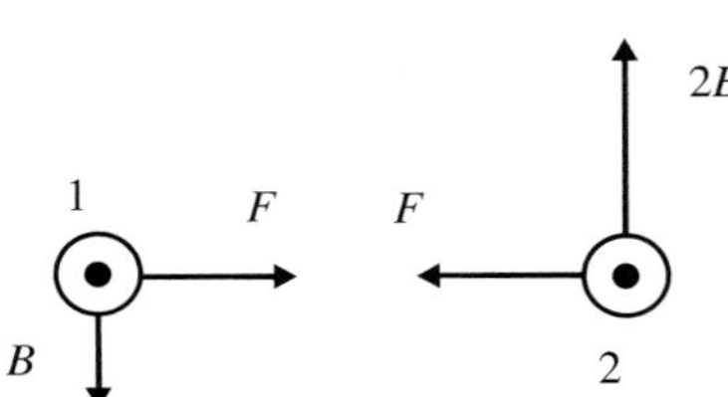

Figure A56.

20 $f = \frac{eB}{2\pi m}$.
21 (b) 2.71 cm; (c) 7.62×10^{6} per second; (d) 7.5×10^{5} m s^{-1}; (e) 0.098 m.
22 5.96×10^{-12} s.
23 2.67μT up.
24 2.86×10^{-5} T at 2.8° to the horizontal.
25 28.28μN m^{-1} at 225° with the positive x axis.
26 $B = \frac{\mu_0 ev}{4\pi r^2}$
28 (a) $B = \frac{\mu_0 I}{2\pi}\left(\frac{1}{r+d/2} + \frac{1}{r-d/2}\right)$; (b) $B = \frac{\mu_0 I}{2\pi}\left(\frac{1}{r-d/2} - \frac{1}{r+d/2}\right)$.
29 (d) 1.40×10^{10} per second; (e) 3.84×10^{-12} J.
30 0.05 N m^{-1}, left.
31 (a) Out of paper; (b) left.
32 (a) 1; (b) 4.

Chapter 5.7

1 See Figure A57.

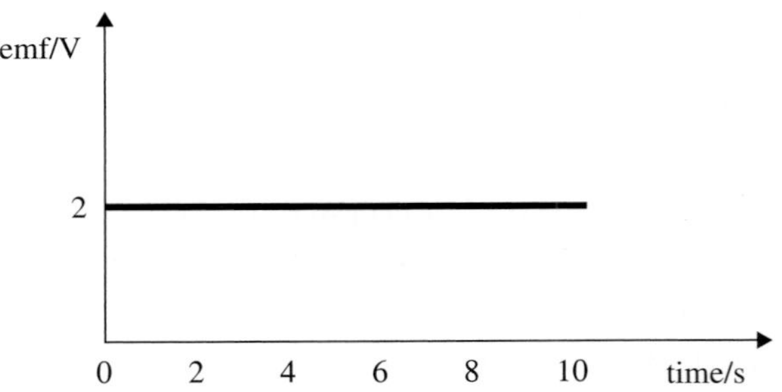

Figure A57.

2 See Figure A58.

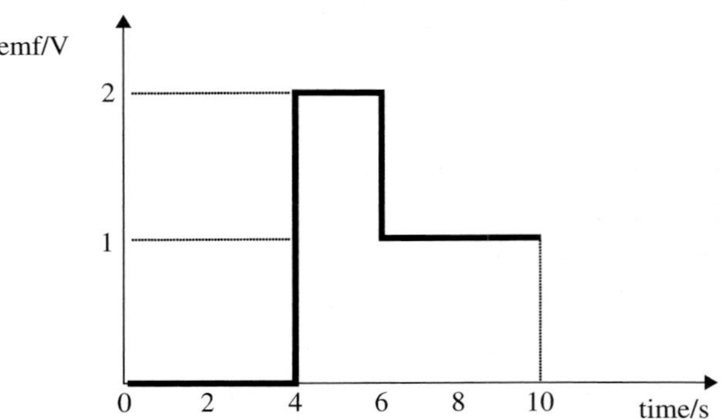

Figure A58.

3 (a) See Figure A59.

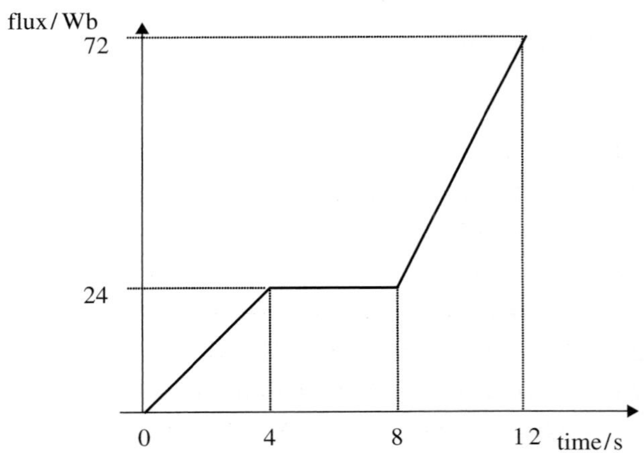

Figure A59.

4 Counter-clockwise.

5 (a) Clockwise, then zero, then counter-clockwise; (b) counter-clockwise, then zero, then clockwise.

6 (a) Counter-clockwise, then zero, then clockwise; (b) clockwise, then zero, then counter-clockwise.

7 (a) Force is upward; (b) force is upward.

8 Right end is positive.

9 (a) Clockwise; (b) counter-clockwise.

10 0.0592 V.

12 It will move to the right.

13 Part A: (a) flux = $BA\cos\theta$; (b) emf = $BLv\cos\theta$; (c) counter-clockwise as we look down on the loop from above; (d) $F = \frac{B^2L^2v\cos\theta}{R}$, horizontal to the right; (e) $v_T = \frac{mgR\sin\theta}{B^2L^2\cos^2\theta}$.
Part B: the dependence of velocity on time is $v = \frac{mgR\sin\theta}{B^2L^2\cos^2\theta}[1 - \exp(-\frac{B^2L^2\cos^2\theta}{mR}t)]$. As time gets large the velocity approaches the value found in (e).

14 (a) Clockwise, $I = Bav/R$ where v is the speed of the loop;
(b) acceleration $= g - B^2a^2v/(mR)$.

15 (a) Points on the rim; (c) clockwise looking at the diagram.

Chapter 5.8

1 (a) 88 V; 50 Hz; (b) 10.5 A.

2 (a) 23.4%; (b) 15%.

3 0.0825 T.

4 4.9×10^4 V.

5 (a) 30%; (b) 1.2%.

7 (a) 2 A; (b) 5 V; (c) 1 s; (d) see Figure A60.

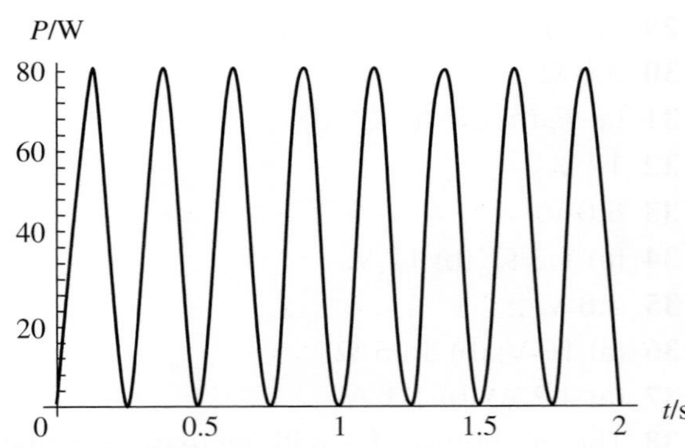

Figure A60.

8 (b) The graph for flux is the same as Figure 8.12 on page 366. (a) and (c) The emf has double the amplitude at the high speed but the dependence on angle is otherwise the same. See Figure A61 (opposite page). Note that no numbers have been put on the emf axis as we do not know the rate of rotation.

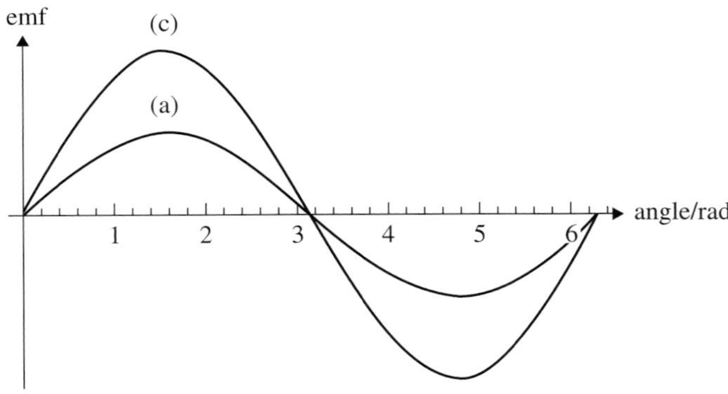

Figure A61.

6 Atomic and nuclear physics

Chapter 6.1

1 (a) 2.29×10^{17} kg m^{-3}; (b) 2.9×10^{13} times larger; (c) 14.3 km.

6 0; 2; 20; 128.

7 $2\,|e|$.

12 $\frac{F_e}{F_g} = 4 \times 10^{42}$.

Chapter 6.2

1 Plot d against $\frac{1}{\sqrt{C}}$.

2 Plot ln I against x.

3 0.5 mg.

4 8 h.

5 ${}^{4}_{2}$He.

7 3.6×10^3 (alpha to electron).

8 ${}^{3}_{1}\text{H} \to {}^{\ 0}_{-1}\text{e} + \bar{\nu}_e + {}^{3}_{2}\text{He}$.

9 ${}^{14}_{6}\text{C} \to {}^{\ 0}_{-1}\text{e} + \bar{\nu}_e + {}^{14}_{7}\text{N}$.

10 ${}^{210}_{83}\text{Bi} \to {}^{\ 0}_{-1}\text{e} + \bar{\nu}_e + {}^{0}_{0}\gamma + {}^{210}_{84}\text{Po}$.

11 ${}^{239}_{94}\text{Pu} \to {}^{4}_{2}\alpha + {}^{235}_{92}\text{U}$.

12 ${}^{A}_{Z}\text{X} \to 2\,{}^{\ 0}_{-1}\text{e} + {}^{4}_{2}\alpha + {}^{A-4}_{\ \ Z}\text{X}$.

13 ${}^{22}_{11}\text{Na} \to {}^{\ 0}_{+1}\text{e} + \nu_e + {}^{22}_{10}\text{Ne}$.

15 2.88 MeV.

Chapter 6.3

1 545.3 MeV; 8.79 MeV.

2 8.029 MeV; 12.37 MeV.

3 0.783 MeV.

4 (a) 2.44×10^{-11} m; (b) gamma ray.

5 3.65 MeV.

6 (c) 179.4 MeV.

7 (a) Seven electrons; (b) 207.8 MeV.

8 183.8 MeV.

9 17.59 MeV.

10 8.9×10^9 yr.

11 17.5 MeV.

Chapter 6.4

1 (b) 7.24×10^{14} Hz.

2 (b) 0.671 V.

3 (b) 1.6×10^{-4} A; (c) 0.20 eV; (d) 2.1 eV; (e) 3.2×10^{-4} A.

4 (b) 2.7×10^{-7} m.

5 (b) 3.90 eV.

6 (a) 16 min.

7 (a) 5.0×10^{14} Hz; (b) 2.08 eV; (c) 1.25 eV; (d) the graph is parallel to the original graph.

8 (a) 2.65×10^{-34} m.

9 (b) 1071 m s^{-1}.

10 (b) $\sqrt{8} \approx 2.83$; (c) 7.6×10^{-11} m.

11 (b) $I = 1.5$ W m^{-2};
(c) $\Phi' = 3.0 \times 10^{18}$ m^{-2} s^{-1}.
(d) There are fewer photons incident on the surface per second and so fewer electrons are emitted.
(e) One assumption is that, at both wavelengths, the same percentage of photons incident on the surface cause emission of electrons.

Chapter 6.5

3 11.5 eV or 1.3 eV.

4 (b) (i) No excitation; (ii) 4; (iii) 6.

5 (b) 1.51 eV.

6 (a) 9.14×10^{-8} m; (b) 2.19×10^{6} m s^{-1}.

7 (a) 2.03×10^{-15} m; (b) 6.66×10^{-10} m.

9 (a) 2×10^{-15} m; (b) 4×10^{5} MeV.

10 The main difference between the two spectra is that, in Figure 5.10 (the observed spectrum), the shortest wavelength is about 91 nm, and spectral lines are most closely spaced near this wavelength. In the 'electron in a box' spectrum, the lowest wavelength would be zero and spectral lines crowd near this value.

11 (b) 5.5×10^{-10} m.

13 $\theta \approx 10^{-35}$ rad.

15 (a) Top diagram; (b) bottom diagram.

Chapter 6.6

1 6.6×10^7 m s^{-1}.

2 See Figure A63.

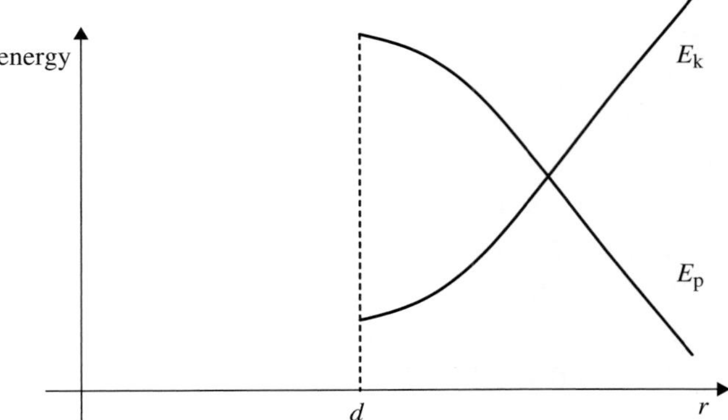

Figure A63.

3 (a) 3.0×10^4 N C^{-1}; (b) 0.083 m; (c) 0.091 m.

6 (a) 0.231 s^{-1}; (b) (i) 4.78×10^{21}; (ii) 3.79×10^{21}; (iii) 3.01×10^{21}.

7 (a) 0.5; (b) 0.875; (c) 0.5.

8 3.66×10^{10} Bq.

9 1.10×10^6 Bq.

10 4.20×10^{11}.

11 3.8×10^9 yr.

12 4.11×10^9 yr.

13 (b) About 7.2 min.

14 (a) 0.75; (b) 0.95; (c) 1.50.

18 (a) 1.5×10^{-15} m; (b) 4000 N; (c) 230.4 N; (d) 1.86×10^{-34} N; (e) 1.24×10^{36}.

20 (a) ${}^{226}_{88}\text{Ra} \rightarrow {}^{226}_{88}\text{Ra} + {}^{0}_{0}\gamma$; (b) 1.83×10^{-11} m.

7 Energy, power and climate change

Chapter 7.1

3 (b) 7.4×10^2 J kg^{-1}.

4 (a) (i) 5×10^8 J; (ii) 140 kWh; (iii) 0.140 MWh. (b) 1.6×10^{16} J.

5 (a) 2.5%.

6 (a) 1.0×10^9 W; (b) 2.4×10^9 W; (c) 1.2×10^5 kg s^{-1}.

7 6.3 km.

8 7.2×10^6 kg day^{-1}.

10 (a) 185 MeV or 2.96×10^{-11} J; (b) 6.77×10^{18} s^{-1}.

11 (a) 8.20×10^{13} J kg^{-1}; (b) 2.7×10^6 kg.

12 (a) 3.9×10^{19} s^{-1}; (b) 1.5×10^{-5} kg s^{-1}.

17 (a) 12 m^2.

18 6.5 m^2.

19 3.6 h.

20 (a) 339 K; (b) 800 W; (c) 0.40.

21 3.6×10^{11} J.

22 (a) Increases by a factor of 4.
(b) Increases by a factor of 8.
(c) Increases by a factor of 32.

24 2.0 kW.

25 4.3 m.

26 2.0×10^5 W.

29 (b) 5.9×10^5 W; (c) 1.7 m.

32 (a) 14 kg; (b) 31°C; (c) 4.3×10^5 J K^{-1}; (e) 7.5×10^{-4} K s^{-1}; (f) 3.9 hrs.

Chapter 7.2

1 (c) 1.8.

2 (b) 0.6.

3 278 K.

4 (a) $T \propto \frac{1}{\sqrt{d}}$; (b) 1.4 K.

5 2.4 W m^{-2}.

7 (a) $(4.5 \pm 0.1) \times 10^2$ K.
(b) Similar curve that is overall higher with peak shifted to the left.

9 (b) 0.29; (c) 250 W m^{-2}; (d) 258 K.

10 (a) 172 h; (b) 4.5×10^{24} J K^{-1}; (c) 4×10^7 s (a bit more than a year).

11 (a) $T_{\text{Venus}} \approx 329$ K; $T_{\text{Mars}} \approx 227$ K.

12 (a) (i) $\left(\frac{1-\alpha}{t}\right)\frac{S}{4}$; (ii) $(1-t)\left(\frac{1-\alpha}{t}\right)\frac{S}{4}$;
(iii) $(1-\alpha)\frac{S}{4}$.
(b) $\left(\frac{1-\alpha}{t}\right)\frac{S}{4} = \sigma T^4$, giving $t = 0.63$.

13 (b) 10.

20 (a) 0.27.

23 Approximately 2 K increase in temperature.

29 (a) 3.3×10^{10} J; (b) no.

30 0.9 m.

31 2×10^6 km^3.

8 Digital technology

Chapter 8.1

1 (a) 11; (b) 1010; (c) 10010; (d) 11111.

2 (a) 6; (b) 12; (c) 5; (d) 30.

4 The completed table is as follows:

Time/ ms	Signal strength/mV	Three-bit binary code	Digital signal
0	0	000	
0.1	2	010	
0.2	4	100	
0.3	6	110	
0.4	7	111	
0.5	7	111	
0.6	7	111	
0.7	6	110	
0.8	4	100	
0.9	2	010	
1.0	0	000	

For the final part, join up the diagrams in the last column in one long chain, to give the complete digital signal; see Figure A64.

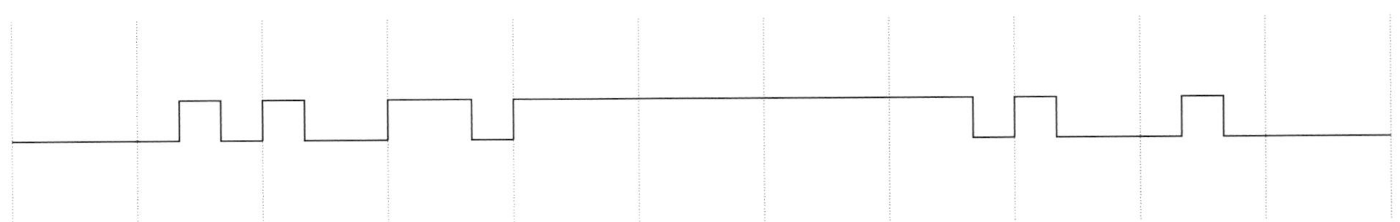

Figure A64.

5 (a)

Binary code	Digital signal	Signal strength
1100		12
1001		9
0010		2
0000		0
0010		2
1000		8
1110		14
1111		15

(b) See Figure A65.

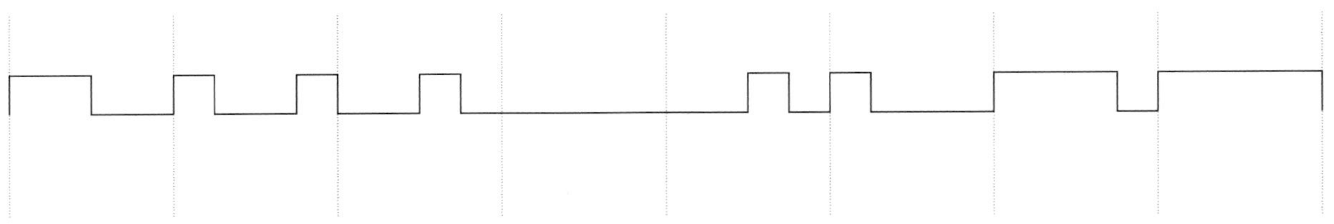

Figure A65.

(c) See Figure A66.

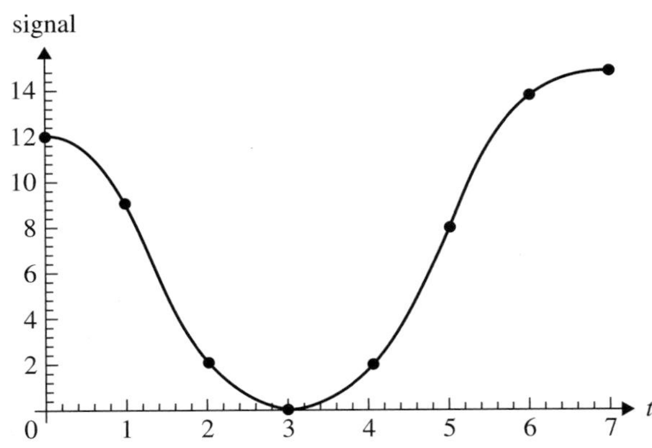

Figure A66.

6 Approximately 7 km (ignoring the hole at the centre).

7 42 Mbytes.

8 847 Mbytes.

9 (c) 170 nm.

10 (a) 1.0×10^{-3} cm s^{-1}; (b) 1.21 cm.

11 (a) 487 nm; (b) 122 nm.

Chapter 8.2

1 290 μC.

2 2.0 A.

3 (a) 2.0×10^{6}; (b) 5 bits; (c) 6.7×10^{4}.

4 3.4×10^{-19} J.

5 3.5 μm.

7 2/3.

15 1.2.

16 No.

17 (a) 9.6×10^{19} m^{-2} s^{-1}; (b) 6.2×10^{19} m^{-2} s^{-1}.

18 (a) 3.6 ms.
19 79 μV.
21 1.4×10^3.

Option A: Sight and wave phenomena

Option A1

10 (a) 1.1×10^{-3} mm; (b) $\theta = 4.6 \times 10^{-5}$ rad; (c) $\theta = 4.5 \times 10^{-4}$ rad.
12 See Figure A1.7 on page 476.
14 (a) Blue; (b) red.
16 (a) Green; (b) blue.
17 Blue.
18 Yellow and cyan.
19 (a) White; (b) black.

Options A2–A6

See questions and answers in cross-referenced chapters.

Option B: Quantum physics

Options B1 and B2

See questions and answers in cross-referenced chapters.

Option C: Digital technology

Options C1–C4

See questions and answers in cross-referenced chapters.

Option D: Relativity and particle physics

Options D1–D5

See questions and answers in cross-referenced chapters.

Option E: Astrophysics

Option E1

3 Do an order-of-magnitude calculation without calculator: mass of a helium nucleus $4 \times 1.6 \times 10^{-27}$ kg $\approx 6 \times 10^{-27}$ kg. The radius of helium nucleus is $1.2 \times 10^{-15} \times 4^{1/3}$ m so the volume is about $\frac{4\pi}{3}(1.2 \times 10^{-15} \times 4^{1/3})^3$ m^3 $\approx 4 \times 1.5 \times 4 \times 10^{-45}$ m^3 $\approx 2 \times 10^{-44}$ m^3 so the density of the nucleus is $\frac{6\times10^{-27}\text{ kg}}{2\times10^{-44}\text{ m}^3}$ $= 3 \times 10^{17}$ kg m^{-3}.
4 3×10^6 m.
6 1000.
8 Jupiter.
10 1.5×10^{11} m.
11 90 m.
14 29.7 km s^{-1}.
15 1.9×10^{27} kg.
16 250 km s^{-1}; 2.48×10^{41} kg (mass enclosed within a radius of 28 000 ly).

Option E2

1 1.7×10^{29} W.
2 5.2×10^{-9} W m^{-2}.
3 2.6×10^4 ly.
4 (a) 256 times; (b) 1/16.
5 30.
6 (a) 26; (b) 1.5.
7 (a) $\frac{R_A}{R_B} = 4$; (b) $\frac{d_A}{d_B} = 0.71$.
8 $\frac{T_A}{T_B} = 4$.
9 1.2.
18 2.34×10^{30} kg and 2.80×10^{30} kg.
19 (a) 3.37×10^{12} m; (b) 2.95×10^{30} kg; (c) 1.70×10^{30} kg; 1.25×10^{30} kg.
21 9.2×10^8 kg m^{-3}.
23 (c) See Figure A67.

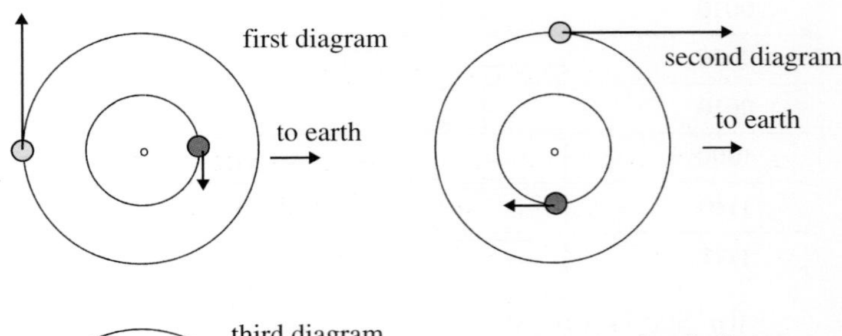

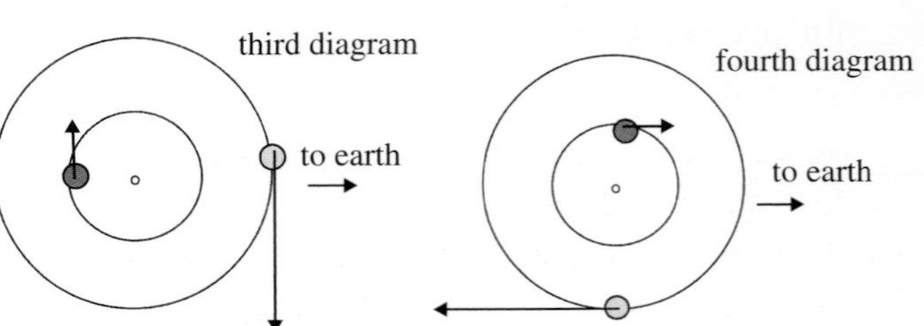

Figure A67.

24 1.4.

26 (a) $T = 7250$ K; (b) about 5 to 8 times that of the sun (by looking at the HR diagram).

Option E3

3 3.51 pc.

4 0.30 arcseconds.

5 (a) 149.3 pc; (b) 257 solar radii.

6 The distance to the star is 40 pc. Hence the star appears dimmer than a magnitude 0.8; its apparent magnitude is thus greater than 0.8.

7 (a) 4 pc.

8 6.3 times.

9 Capella by a factor of 2.75.

10 (a) Star A; (b) star A because it appears brighter even though it is further away.

11 (a) They both have the same luminosity; (b) star B appears brighter because it is closer.

13 6.3×10^3 ly (used a luminosity of 1000 solar luminosities).

14 2.37×10^{-9} W m^{-2}; 2.57.

15 (a) 1.0×10^{-8} W m^{-2}; (b) 0.38.

16 1.8×10^5 ly (used a luminosity of 3500 solar luminosities).

17 (a) 263 pc; (b) 4.13; (c) 17 pc.

Option E4

2 About 6.

3 Expansion of the universe; helium abundance; cosmic background radiation.

4 (a) Evidence for the Big Bang; (b) the same.

5 (a) Will approach absolute zero; (b) will reach minimum and then begin to increase.

6 All of space was a point at the time of the Big Bang.

8 Open means that the universe is expanding forever. Closed means that it will recollapse. The surface of a sphere is finite but has no boundary. The surface of a sheet of paper is finite and has a boundary.

10 The galaxies are not moving into empty space. Space is being created in between them.

14 Just above 4000 K.

15 (b) Same black-body spectrum curve with a peak that is shifted to the right (longer wavelengths).

Option E5

2 1.37×10^{27} kg.

3 (a) 6.28×10^7 m s^{-1}; (b) 21%.

4 The 1 solar mass star. The heavier the star, the faster evolution proceeds.

6 Elements heavier than iron cannot be produced in the core.

8 Most O type stars would have evolved past the supernova stage.

9 No. Elements crucial for life would not have been produced.

11 (a) 7.36 MeV; (b) 7.92 MeV.

12 Larger nuclear charge leads to larger repulsion.

17 2.2×10^9 K.

18 3.4.

26 (a) 2×10^8 yr. (b) Implies quasar active life must be very short.

Option E6

5 6.94 Mpc.

7 (a) 1.2×10^6 m s^{-1}; 16.53 Mpc;
(b) 1.5×10^7 m s^{-1}; 208.3 Mpc;
(c) 2.2×10^7 m s^{-1}; 308 Mpc;
(d) 3.9×10^7 m s^{-1}; 541.7 Mpc;
(e) 6.1×10^7 m s^{-1}; 847.2 Mpc.

8 (a) 4167 Mpc; (b) they are unobservable. (c) No, this speed is due to the expanding space between the galaxies. It cannot be used to send a signal.

9 (a) 0.178; (b) 5.33×10^7 m s^{-1}; (c) 741 Mpc.

10 1.96 billion years.

13 (c) $R = R_0 \exp[c(t - t_0)]$.

19 7×10^{-44} kg m^{-3} s^{-1}.

20 Small time means small θ. The replacement by hyperbolic functions means that the scale factor increases forever. The parameter k is related to the curvature of space.

Option F: Communications

Option F1

1 (a) 1000 Hz; (b) 1050 Hz; (c) 5000 Hz.

4 (a) 3995 kHz, 4000 kHz and 4005 kHz.

(b) See Figure A68.

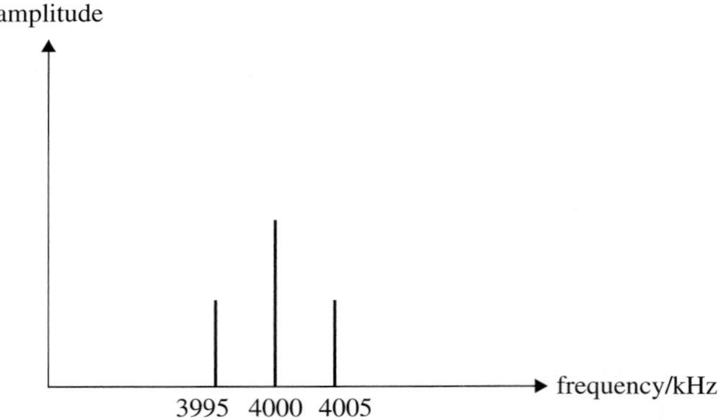

Figure A68.

6 See Figure A69.

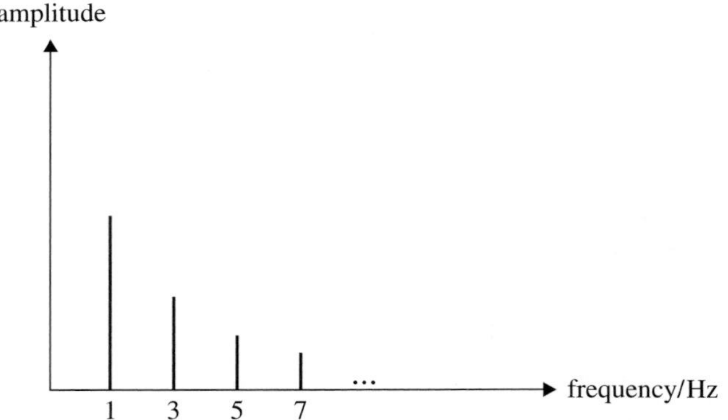

Figure A69.

7 9.0 kHz.
8 (a) 6 kHz; (b) 19.8 kHz, 19.8 kHz, 40 kHz.
10 (a) 120 kHz; (b) 10 kHz; (c) 0.6 mV.
14 (a) About 20.
15 (a) 10 kHz; (b) 1 kHz; (c) $\beta \approx 5$;
(d) bandwidth $\approx$ 12 kHz.
16 (a) 6.25; (b) 174 kHz.

Option F2

1 (a) 111; (b) 10011; (c) 1000011.
2 (a) 9; (b) 29; (c) 21.
3 (a) 5; (b) 6; (c) 7.
4 11.
5 32.
6 0.625 mV.
12 (c) (i) See Figure A70.

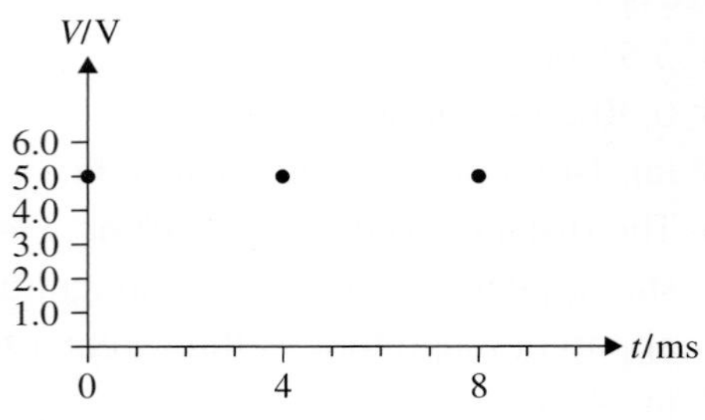

Figure A70.

(ii) It is impossible to reconstruct the signal.
14 See Figure A71.

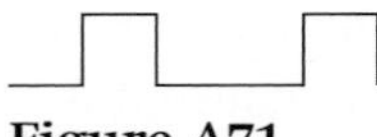

Figure A71.

15 001 100 001 111 100 101 100.
16 The completed table is as follows:

Time/ ms	Signal/ mV	Binary code	Digital signal
0	7.0	111	
0.1	6.9	110	
0.2	6.7	110	
0.3	6.4	110	
0.4	5.9	101	
0.5	5.2	101	
0.6	4.5	100	
0.7	3.6	011	
0.8	2.5	010	
0.9	1.3	001	
1.0	0.0	000	

For the final part, join up the diagrams in the last column in one long chain, to give the complete digital signal; see Figure A72.

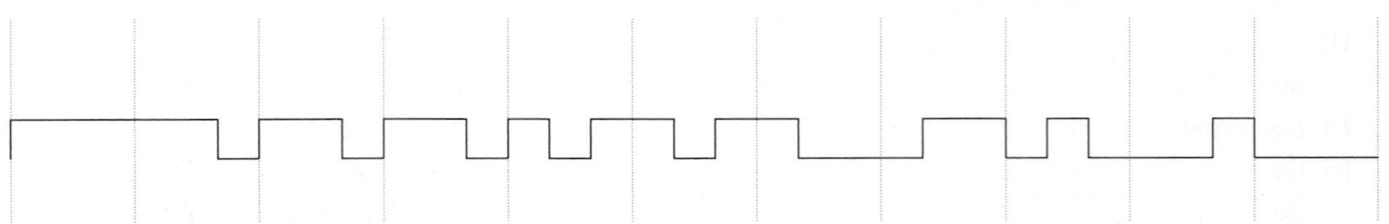

Figure A72.

17 (a)

Binary code	Digital signal	Signal strength
1111		15
1001		9
0011		3
0001		1
0101		5
1010		10
1100		12
1101		13

(b) See Figure A73.

19 (a) 40 kbit s^{-1}; (b) 25 μs.
20 (a) 1.41 Mbit s^{-1}; (b) 0.709 μs.
21 0.25 ms.
26 (a) 125−16 = 109μs; (b) 6 more; (c) decrease.

Option F3

1 2.07×10^8 m s^{-1}.
3 76.7°.
4 Larger than 1.74.
5 Smaller than 29.1°.
9 (a) 1.97×10^8 m s^{-1};
(b) 40.5 μs and 40.9 μs.
16 10 dB.

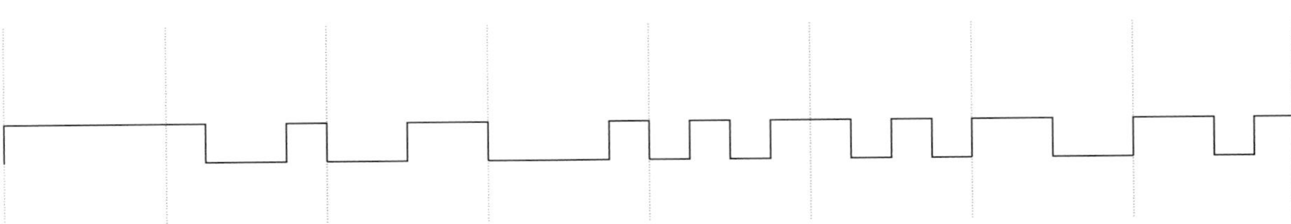

Figure A73.

(c) See Figure A74.

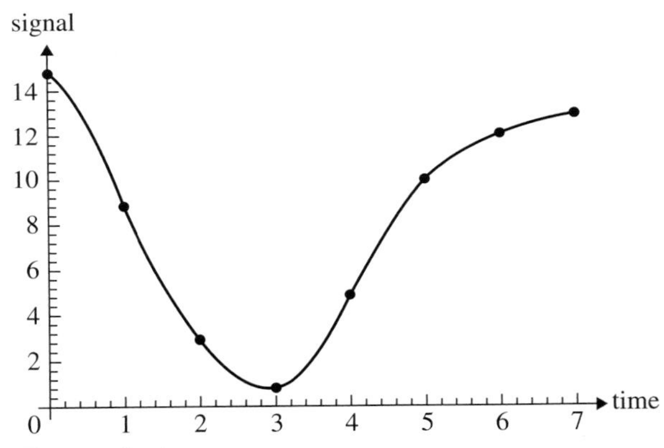

Figure A74.

18 See Figure A75.

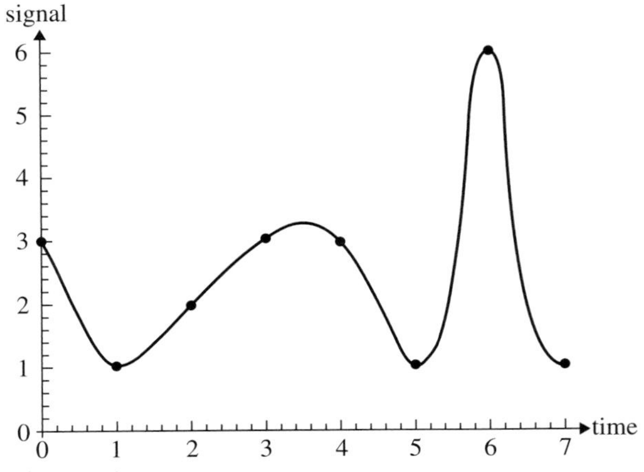

Figure A75.

17 $G_1 + G_2$.
18 –1.58 dB.
19 (–)8.7×10^{-2} dB km^{-1}.
20 0.13 km
21 2.0.
22 1.0.
23 21 dB.
24 4.5 W.

Option F4

5 (a) 6.0 dB km^{-1}; (b) 30 dB;
(c) 0.6 nW.
10 (a) (i) 42 000 km, (ii) 6800 km;
(c) 7×10^3.
11 (a) 24°; (b) 2700 km; (c) 13 min.

Option F5

1 (a) 15 V; (b) 12 V; (c) –8.0 V;
(d) –15 V.
2 (b) –90μV to +90μV.
3 200.
5 (a) $R_F = 0$ and $R = \infty$; (b) $G = 1$; (c) see next problem.
6 (a) 3.0 V; (b) 2.0 V; (c) 3.0 V.
9 (a) 0 V; (b) 16 nA; (c) –8.0 mV.
10 (a) 3.0 V; (b) decrease by 9.0 V.

12 (a) –8.0 V; (b) see Figure A76.

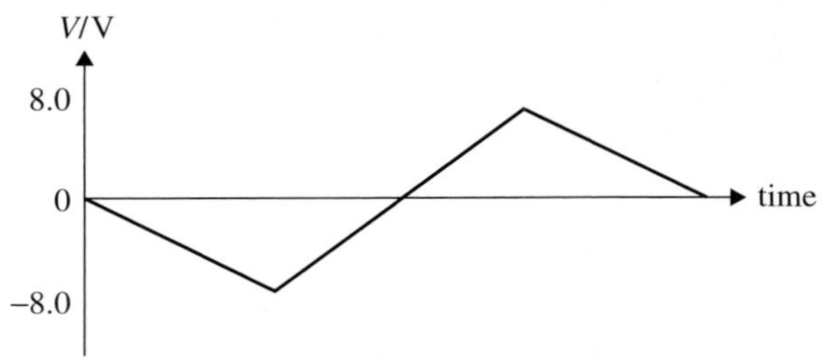

Figure A76.

Option F6

3 44 nW m^{-2}.

6 (a) 64 kbit s^{-1}.

7 About 20.

Option G: Electromagnetic waves

Option G1

1 (a) 50 μs.

2 3.14×10^8 m s^{-1}.

3 Red: 53.99°, deviation = 23.99°; blue: 54.63°, deviation = 24.63°.

10 (a) 0.30 W m^{-2}; (b) 640 W m^{-2}.

11 (b) 1.27×10^{-3} rad; (c) 650 m.

Option G2

6 6.0 cm.

8 (a) $v = 20$ cm; $h' = -2$ cm; (b) image is at infinity; (c) $v = -10$ cm; $h' = 4$ cm.

9 $v = 8.0$ cm, real, inverted, image height 7.5 cm.

10 $v = -24$ cm, virtual, upright, image height 16 cm.

12 (b) 10.1 cm ± 0.3 cm.

14 (a) $v = 60$ cm, real, inverted, 3 times larger.

15 (a) 430 cm and 70 cm. (b) The distance 430 cm results in the larger image.

16 3.75 cm from right lens.

17 (a) 2 cm to the left of L_2; (b) −1.2; (c) inverted.

18 (a) 18.4 cm to the left of L_2; (b) 0.55; (c) upright.

19 2.8×10^6 times more.

20 (a) 7.14 cm; (b) 10 cm; (c) 0.040 rad.

22 0.02 mm.

23 −125.

24 (b) 18.5 cm.

25 (a) 4; (b) 0.104 rad.

26 (a) 22.3; (b) 70 cm.

27 22 m.

Option G3

1 $n = 3$.

2 0.33 m.

3 8.5 mm.

8 (a) 3.86 mm in air; (b) 2.91 mm in water.

9 105 m.

10 (a) 13.4 km; (b) 714 km.

11 $d = 2.92\lambda$

12 See Figure A77.

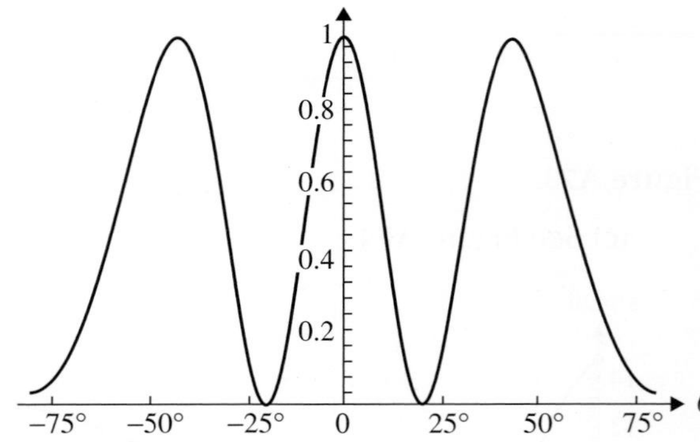

Figure A77.

13 3λ.

15 (a) 4.14×10^{-7} m; 4.25×10^{-7} m; (b) 0.462°.

16 (a) 0.0°; 13.89°; 28.69°; 46.05°; 73.74°. (b) $n = 4$.

Option G4

1 (b) 1.85×10^{-11} m.

2 (b) 1.0×10^8 m s^{-1}; (c) 7.2×10^{18} Hz.

4 (a) 3.1×10^{-11} m; (b) 796 W.

7 4.1° and 8.2°.

8 2.80×10^{-10} m.

9 (a) 25.4°; (b) 1.1×10^{-10} m.

10 (a) (i) $\frac{d\sqrt{2}}{2}$, (ii) $\frac{2d\sqrt{5}}{5}$.

Option G5

2 0.123 μm.

3 103.4 nm.

5 The separation will increase.

6 6×10^{-5} rad.

Option H: Special and general relativity

Option H1

3 A: $x = 0$; B: $x = 1.59$ m; (c) $x = 2.65$ m.

6 Assuming the coil is at rest and the magnet moving gives *exactly identical* results.

10 (a) Both open 9 s later; (b) the rear door will open first.

Option H2

1 (a) 11.5 min; (b) 11.5 min.

2 (a) 1.6×10^{-7} s; (b) 45.6 m.

3 (a) 50.3 yr; (b) 5.0 yr older.

4 3.20 s.

5 (a) 3 yr; (b) 6 yr; (c) 3 ly.

6 320.3 m.

7 (a) 8.0 years; (b) 6.0 years; (c) 72 years; (d) 48 years.

8 (a) $0.359c$; (b) 28 m; (c) 30 m.

9 Q's clock is slow.

10 (a) 8.42×10^3 s; (b) 3.67×10^3 s.

11 (a) $0.385c$; (b) $-0.385c$.

12 (a) $0.946c$; (b) $-0.946c$.

13 $0.915c$.

14 $0.172c$.

Option H3

1 939.4 MeV.

2 $0.995c$.

3 $0.738c$.

4 (a) 1.31 MeV; (b) $0.921c$.

5 1600 MeV.

6 13.9 GV.

7 It increases.

8 (a) 7.02×10^{-6} s; (b) 2.19×10^{-6} s.

9 2.8×10^8 m s^{-1}.

10 (a) 2 h; (b) 6 h; (c) 6 h.

11 3 h.

Option H4

1 (a) 0.511 MeV; (b) (i) 1.88×10^{10} m s^{-1}; (ii) $0.999\,999\,87c$.

2 $0.9959c$.

3 4595 MeV c^{-1}.

4 1.17 MeV.

5 3.66×10^{-19} kg m s^{-1}.

6 124.9 MeV.

7 1.78×10^{-26} kg.

8 (a) $0.999\,999\,999\,987c$; (b) $0.999\,956c$.

9 $0.979c$.

10 2412 MV.

11 5711 MeV.

12 (a) 0.079 MeV; (b) 0.66 MeV; (c) 3.11 MeV.

13 (a) 5.0 GeV; (b) $0.987c$.

14 (b) 835; (c) 1.37; (d) 1.

15 (a) $0.628c$; (b) 558.5 MeV.

16 (c) 2.5 MeV.

17 (c) 4.2×10^{-12} m.

18 0.122 MeV; $0.59c$.

19 9.

20 10 kg.

21 (a) $p = \gamma mv$; (b) $E = \gamma mc^2$.

Option H5

2 In the direction of acceleration.

3 Bends toward the right.

6 (a) Yes; (b) yes.

7 3.27 Hz.

8 2.33×10^9 Hz.

9 (a) 500 nm; (b) 1.25 s; (c) 1.25 ms.

10 The acceleration there is larger and so by the equivalence principle it finds itself in a larger gravitational field.

11 2.05×10^{30} kg m^{-3}.

12 2.96×10^4 m.

17 $\frac{1}{R^2}$.

21 A distance of $r = \frac{4}{3}R_s$ from the centre.

24 (b) 7.4×10^8 m; (d) 1.33×10^{-15} s; (e) 2.3×10^{14} Hz.

25 (a) $\frac{2GM}{c^2}$; (b) $\frac{16\pi G^2 M^2}{c^4}$; (d) entropy.

26 (a) Ray turns around and falls into the black hole.
(b) Ray bends towards the observer.

Option I: Biomedical physics

Option I1

1 3.14×10^3 W.

2 79.77 dB.

3 74 dB.

4 31.6.
5 10.
6 3.16×10^{-5} W^{-2}.
7 1.58×10^{-10} W^{-2}.

Option I2

1 (a) 4 mm and 6 mm; (b) the one with HVT = 6 mm has the larger energy.
2 (a) 0.139 mm^{-1}; (b) 11.5 mm.
3 12.6 mm.
4 0.794.
5 1.40.
6 (a) 1.12 kW m^{-2};
(b) 0.396 kW m^{-2}.
7 5350 cm^3.
8 0.31 mm.

Option I3

1 14.0 J.
2 4.67 J.
3 (a) 10 Gy of alpha particles; (b) they do the same damage.
4 166.
5 (a) 0.4 mGy; (b) 0.3 mJ;
(c) 3.75×10^{10}.
6 15 mSv (assuming a constant activity in the 30 min interval – justified since 30 min is short compared with the half-life).
7 2.8 mSv.
8 (a) 1.07×10^{-6} W m^{-2}; (b) 2.4×10^{-8} J;
(c) 2.47 μGy; (d) 2.47 μSv.

Option J: Particle physics

Option J1

6 (b) (i) See Figure A78.

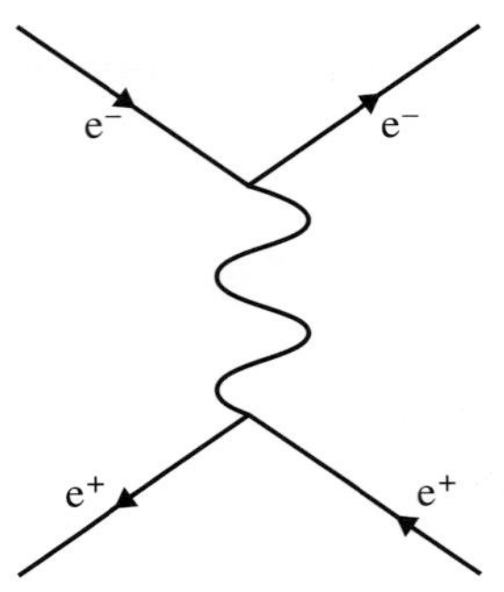

Figure A78.

(ii) See Figure A79.

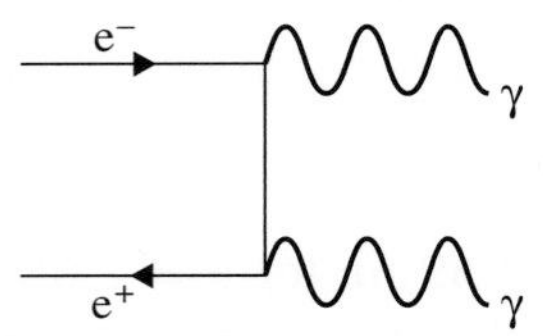

Figure A79.

7 See Figure A80.

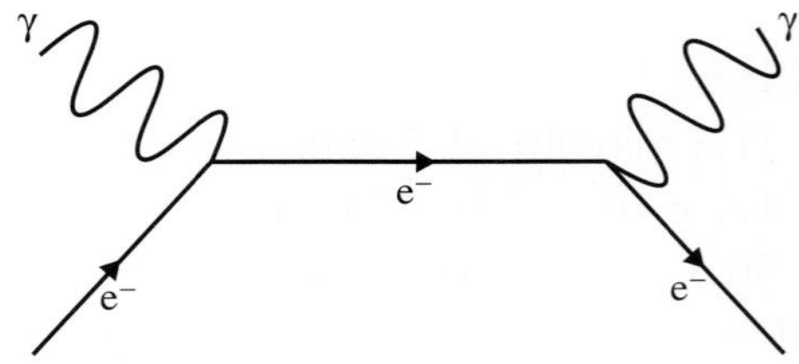

Figure A80.

8 (a) $Q = 0$; (b) violates momentum conservation; (c) see Figure A81.

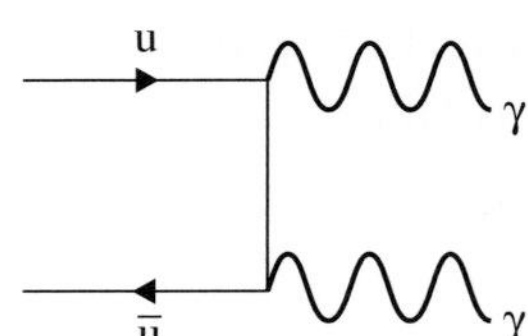

Figure A81.

9 (a) $d \rightarrow u + e^- + \bar{\nu}_e$;
(b) see Figure A82.

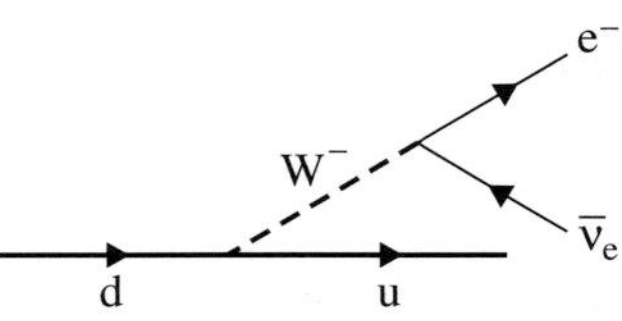

Figure A82.

10 (a) $u \rightarrow d + e^+ + \nu_e$; (b) W^+;
(c) positron and electron neutrino.
11 (a) See Figure A83.

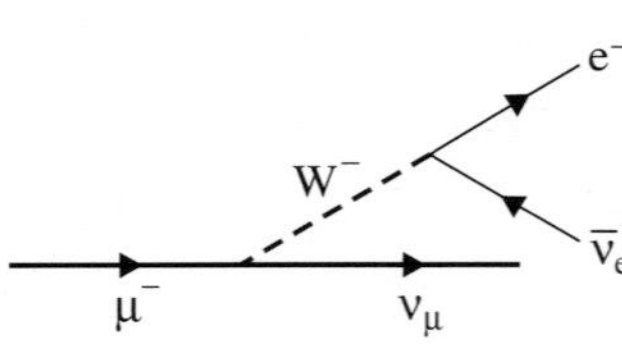

Figure A83.

(b) See Figure A84.

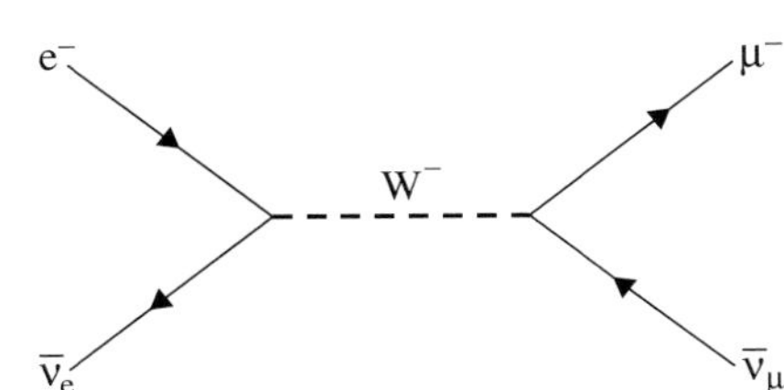

Figure A84.

(c) See Figure A85.

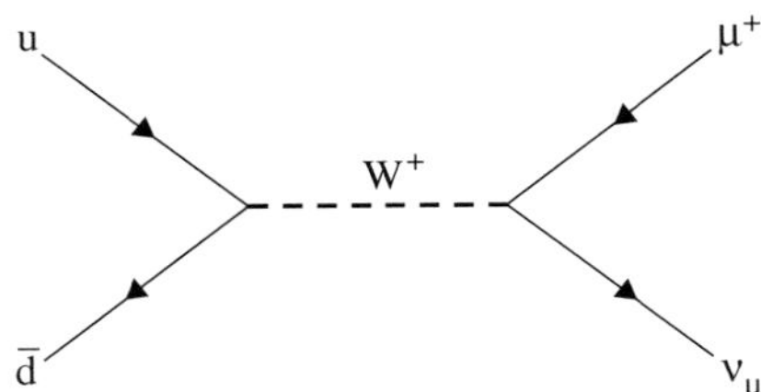

Figure A85.

(d) See Figure A86.

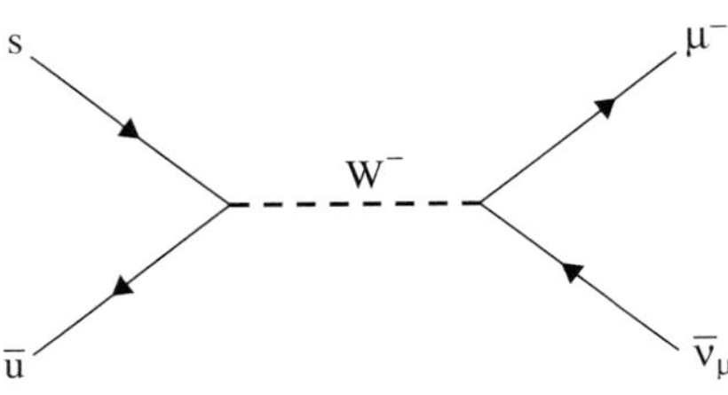

Figure A86.

12 $W^- \rightarrow u + \bar{d}$ ($\rightarrow$ hadrons); $W^- \rightarrow e^- + \bar{\nu}_e$; $W^- \rightarrow \mu^- + \bar{\nu}_\mu$.

13 (a) See Figure A87.

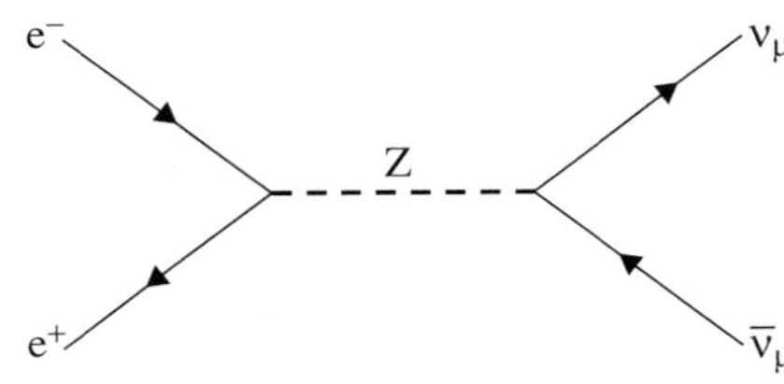

Figure A87.

(b) See Figure A88.

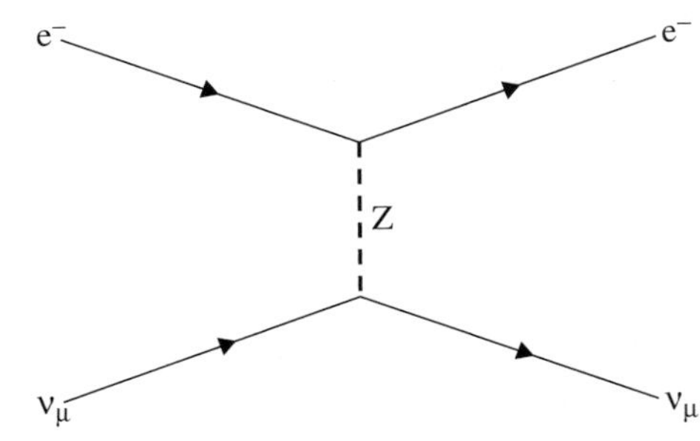

Figure A88.

(c) See Figure A89.

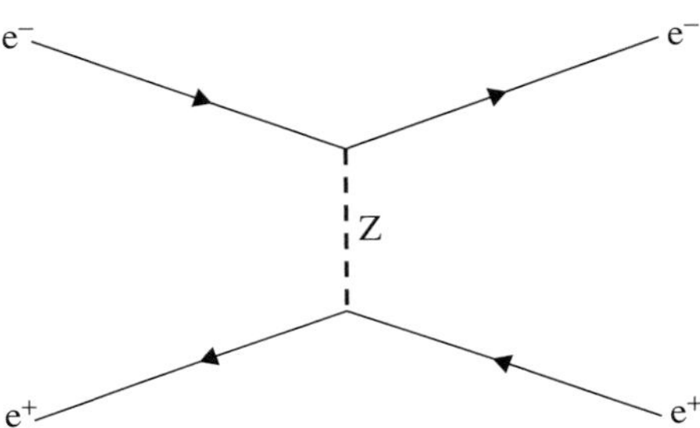

Figure A89.

14 For example $Z \rightarrow e^- + e^+$; $Z \rightarrow \mu^- + \mu^+$; $Z \rightarrow \tau^- + \tau^+$.

21 (c) The order of magnitude is 100 MeV c^{-2}.

Option J2

1 (b) Total of 350 GeV.

3 (a) 2.5×10^{-17} m; (b) (i) yes, (ii) no.

4 Alpha particles have the larger mass and hence the smaller de Broglie wavelength, so they would be more suitable.

12 417.

13 (a) 1.8×10^7 Hz; (b) 2.75 MeV; (c) 40.

16 108 km.

17 (a) 4.5 m; (b) 7.5×10^{-9} s; (c) 1.3×10^8 Hz; (d) 2.7×10^9.

18 (b) 5.5 T.

22 1.3×10^{-15} m.

23 $E_T = 1233$ MeV,
$E_K = 1233 - 938$ MeV
$= 295$ MeV

25 67.5 MeV.

26 1045 MeV.

Option J3

1 (a) $\bar{\text{n}} = \bar{\text{u}}\bar{\text{d}}\bar{\text{d}}$, $Q_{\bar{\text{n}}} = -\frac{2}{3} + \frac{1}{3} + \frac{1}{3} = 0$;

(b) $\bar{\text{p}} = \bar{\text{u}}\bar{\text{u}}\bar{\text{d}}$, $Q_{\bar{\text{p}}} = -\frac{2}{3} - \frac{2}{3} + \frac{1}{3} = -1$.

3 $\bar{\text{u}}$s.

5 –1.

6 (a) Violated; (b) conserved; (c) conserved; (d) violated.

7 None.

9 (a) $Q = 0$, $S = +1$; (c) no.

10 (a) $Q = 1$, $S = 0$.

11 (a) Conserved; (b) conserved; (c) violated; (d) violated.

12 No.

14 (a) $Q = 0$, $S = -1$.

15 (a) 5.28×10^{-35} J s.

16 (a) 0 or 1.

21 (a) W^-; (b) same colour.

22 Colour changes to green; flavour stays the same.

23 X = u$\bar{\text{s}}$, Y = d$\bar{\text{u}}$, Z = u$\bar{\text{d}}$, W = s$\bar{\text{u}}$.

24 (a) See Figure A90.

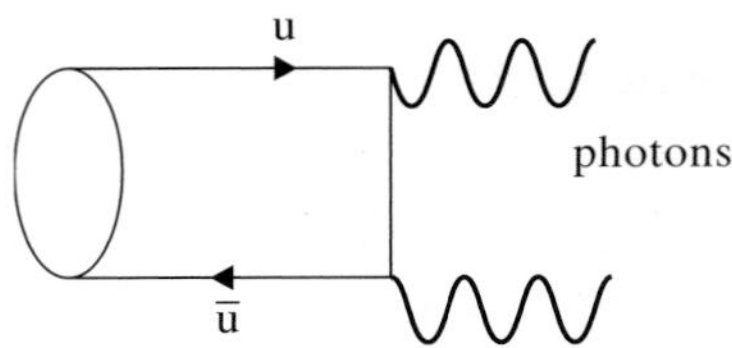

Figure A90.

(c) 1.8×10^{-14} m.

26 (a) $m_u = 312$ MeV c^{-2}, $m_d = 314$ MeV c^{-2}; (b) 626 MeV c^{-2}.

27 (a) ν_e ; (b) ν_μ ; (c) $\bar{\nu}_\tau$; (d) $\bar{\nu}_e$; (e) $\bar{\nu}_e$ and ν_τ.

28 (a) No; (b) no; (c) yes; (d) yes.

29 See Figure A91.

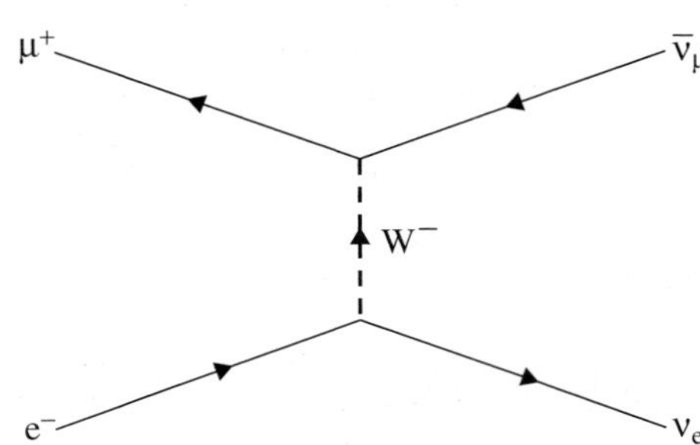

Figure A91.

30 (a) Electron lepton number.
(b) Electron and muon lepton number.
(c) Electric charge. (d) Baryon number.
(e) Energy and muon lepton number.
(f) Baryon number and electric charge.

Option J4

4 (a) See Figure A92.

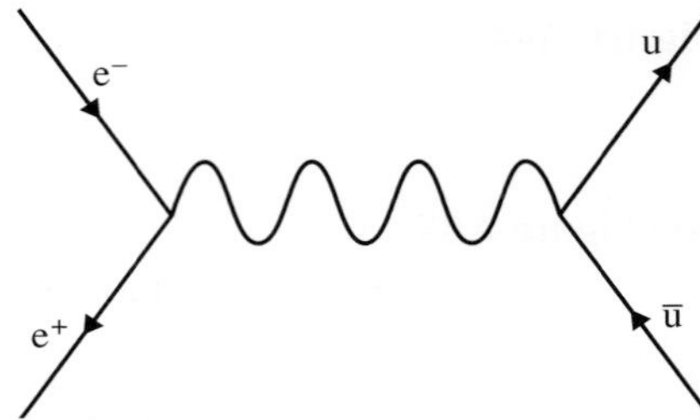

Figure A92.

(b) There are separate diagrams for each quark colour, and so the total amplitude is $3A$.

Option J5

1 (a) The order of magnitude is 10 eV.
(b) The temperature at which the average energy is about 10 eV is 8×10^4 K, and so collisions are unlikely to force electrons to make transitions within atoms. The collisions are therefore elastic.

2 (a) 8×10^4 K.

3 (b) 9.7×10^{-7} m.

4 (a) 3.9×10^{-4} eV; (b) 13×10^{-4} eV, i.e. comparable.

6 (a) See Figure A93.

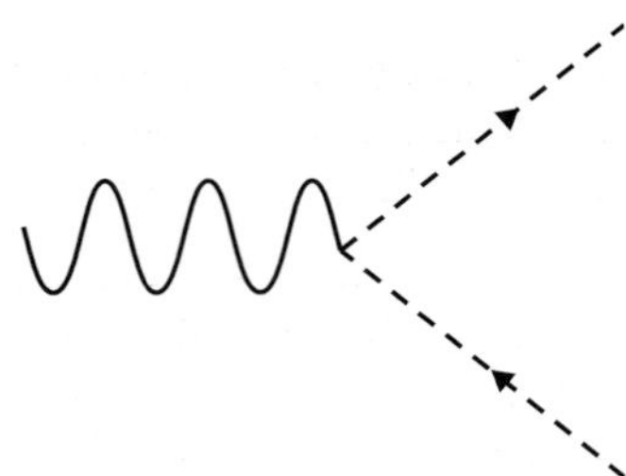

Figure A93.

(b) 10^{15} K.

9 (a) 540 GeV; (b) 4×10^{15} K.

Glossary of selected terms, definitions and laws

For examination purposes note that, if you use a formula in place of a word definition, the symbols in the formula must all be explained.

Measurement

Accuracy Measurements have accuracy if the systematic error is small.

Frame of reference A set of rulers and synchronized clocks (at rest with respect to one another) that are used by observers who are at rest in the frame to describe the motion of an object.

Fundamental units The kilogram, metre, second, kelvin, mole, ampere and candela. All other units are combinations of these and are called derived units.

Precision Measurements have precision if the random error is small.

Random error An error due to inexperience of the observer and the difficulty of reading instruments. It can be reduced by repeated measurements.

Scalar A physical quantity with magnitude only (e.g. mass).

Systematic error An error due to incorrectly calibrated instruments – it is the same for all data points and cannot be reduced by repeated measurements.

Vector A physical quantity with magnitude and direction (e.g. force).

Mechanics

Acceleration The rate of change with time of the velocity vector. It is a vector. Its magnitude is given by the gradient of a graph of velocity versus time.

Centrifugal force There is no such thing. Students erroneously include such a force to point away from the centre of a circular path. But the body is not in equilibrium and so no such force is needed.

Centripetal acceleration The acceleration due to a changing velocity direction. It points toward the centre of the circular path and equals $\frac{v^2}{r}$.

Centripetal force The name of any force or resultant of individual forces that points toward the centre of a circular path.

Displacement The distance in a given direction from a fixed origin. It is a vector.

Efficiency The ratio of useful output work (or power) to input work (or power).

Energy conservation Energy cannot be destroyed or created. It can be transformed from one form into another. The mechanical energy of a system (kinetic plus gravitational potential plus elastic potential energy) stays the same in the absence of dissipative (frictional) forces.

Equipotential surface The set of points that have the same gravitational potential.

Escape speed The minimum speed an object must have (at the surface of a planet) so that it can move an infinite distance away, $v = \sqrt{\frac{2GM}{r}}$.

Gravitational field strength The gravitational force experienced by a point test particle of unit mass. The field strength due to a spherical or point mass M is $g = \frac{GM}{r^2}$. It is a vector.

Gravitational potential The work done in bringing a point test particle of unit mass from infinity to a point in a gravitational field. In the gravitational field of a spherical or point mass M, the potential is $V = -\frac{GM}{r}$. It is a scalar.

Gravitational potential energy difference In mechanics, the work that must be done in order to raise a mass m by a vertical distance Δh. It is given by $\Delta E_G = mg\Delta h$.

Gravitational potential energy of two point masses The work done in moving two point masses M and m, which are initially infinitely far apart, until they are separated by a distance r; it is given by $E_G = -\frac{GMm}{r}$.

Hooke's law The tension in a spring is proportional to its extension and opposite to it: $F = -kx$.

Impulse The total change in the momentum of a system as a result of a force acting on it. Its magnitude is given by the area under a force versus time graph. It is a vector.

Law of gravitation There is an attractive force between any two point masses, given by $F = G\frac{m_1 m_2}{r^2}$ where r is their separation. It is directed along the line joining the masses.

Momentum conservation If the net external force on a system is zero, the total momentum of the system stays the same.

Newton's first law If the net external force on a system is zero, the system remains at rest or moves with constant velocity.

Newton's second law The net force on a body equals the rate of change of the body's momentum, $F_{\text{net}} = \frac{dp}{dt}$ in calculus. When the mass is constant this reduces to $F_{\text{net}} = ma$. (For time intervals that are not infinitesimally small, $\bar{F}_{net} = \frac{\Delta p}{\Delta t}$ is the average net force on the body during the time interval Δt.)

Newton's third law If body A exerts a force on body B, then body B will exert an equal and opposite force on body A.

Orbit The path of an object when under the influence of just the force of gravitation.

Orbital speed The speed of a body in orbit, $v = \sqrt{\frac{GM}{r}}$.

Power The rate at which work is being performed, $P = \frac{\Delta W}{\Delta t} = Fv$. It is a scalar.

Translational equilibrium The state of a system where the net external force is zero.

Velocity The rate of change with time of the displacement vector. It is a vector. It is the gradient of a graph of displacement versus time.

Weight The force of gravitation on a body. In this book, weight will refer to the gravitational force on a small body due to a large body such as a planet or a star.

Work The product of the force times the distance moved by its point of application in the direction of the force. It is given by the area under the graph of force versus distance. It is a scalar.

Work done in a gravitational field The work done in moving a mass m from one point to another in a gravitational field is $W = m\Delta V$. It is independent of the path followed.

Work–kinetic energy relation The net work done on a body (i.e. the work of the net force or the sum of the work done by individual forces) equals the change in kinetic energy of the body; that is, $W_{\text{net}} = \Delta E_{\text{k}}$.

Thermal physics

Adiabatic A thermodynamic process in which no thermal energy is exchanged.

Avogadro constant The number of molecules in one mole of a substance. It equals $N_A = 6.02 \times 10^{23}$.

Boyle–Mariotte law At constant temperature, a fixed quantity of an ideal gas obeys $pV =$ constant or equivalently $p_1V_1 = p_2V_2$.

Entropy A measure of the disorder of a thermodynamic system. It is proportional to the natural logarithm of the number of microscopic ways a given macroscopic state of the system can be realized: $S = k\ln N$.

First law of thermodynamics The thermal energy Q supplied to a system equals the change in internal energy, ΔU, plus any work done, W. That is, $Q = \Delta U + W$.

Heat capacity (thermal capacity) The energy needed for a body to undergo a unit increase in temperature.

Ideal gas A gas with no intermolecular forces that obeys the ideal gas law, $PV = nRT$ (temperature in kelvin), at all temperatures, pressures and volumes.

Internal energy The total kinetic and potential energy of the molecules of a substance. By *potential energy* we understand the energy due to intermolecular forces.

Irreversible process A process in which the entropy increases. Natural processes are irreversible.

Isothermal A thermodynamic process in which the temperature stays the same.

Pressure The force normal to an area per unit area.

Pressure–temperature law At constant volume, a fixed quantity of an ideal gas obeys $\frac{p}{T} =$ constant or equivalently $\frac{p_1}{T_1} = \frac{p_2}{T_2}$ (temperature in kelvin).

Reversible process An idealized process in which the entropy stays the same.

Second law of thermodynamics The entropy of an isolated system (a system on which no work is being done from the outside) never decreases.

Specific heat capacity The energy needed for a unit mass to undergo a unit increase in temperature.

Specific latent heat of fusion/vaporization The energy required to melt/vaporize a unit mass at constant temperature.

Temperature A measure of the average kinetic energy of the molecules of a substance.

Volume–temperature law At constant pressure, a fixed quantity of an ideal gas obeys $\frac{V}{T} =$ constant or equivalently $\frac{V_1}{T_1} = \frac{V_2}{T_2}$ (temperature in kelvin).

Work The work done by an ideal gas equals the area under the graph of pressure versus volume. For constant pressure it equals $W = P\Delta V$. The net work done in a cyclic process is the area of the loop in a pressure versus volume graph.

Waves

Amplitude The maximum displacement of a wave. The square of the amplitude is proportional to the energy carried by the wave (per unit length/area of the wavefront, for waves in two/three dimensions).

Brewster angle (polarization angle) The angle of incidence for which the reflected light is 100% plane-polarized parallel to the reflecting surface.

Brewster's law The Brewster angle θ_B is given by $\tan\theta_B = \frac{n_2}{n_1}$ when light from a medium with refractive index n_1 is incident on a medium with refractive index n_2.

Coherent Two sources of identical waves are said to be coherent if there is a constant phase difference between them. Two sources must be coherent for interference to be observed. (Coherence implies that the frequencies of the sources are the same.)

Critical damping Damping in a system such that, when displaced from equilibrium, the system returns to equilibrium in as short a time as possible without performing oscillations.

Damped oscillations Oscillations under the action of a resistive force.

Diffraction A phenomenon shown by all waves. It is the spreading of a wave as it passes through an aperture or past an obstacle. It is substantial only when the size of the aperture or obstacle is comparable to the wavelength. The minima of single-slit diffraction occur at angles θ given by $b\sin\theta = n\lambda$, where b is the aperture size.

Doppler effect The frequency received by an observer is different from that emitted if there is relative motion between the receiver and the source of the waves.

Electromagnetic waves Transverse waves that travel with the speed of light and can propagate in a vacuum. They range from short-wavelength gamma rays to long-wavelength radio waves. The wavelengths of the visible spectrum range from blue light at about 400 nm to red light at 750 nm.

Forced oscillations Oscillations of a system under the action of an external (periodic) force.

Frequency The number of full waves emitted per unit time.

Huygens' principle Every point on a wavefront acts as a source of secondary spherical wavefronts called wavelets. The next wavefront is tangent to all the secondary wavelets. It explains reflection and refraction and (partly) diffraction.

Interference When two similar coherent waves meet, the resulting wave will have a large (maximum) amplitude if the waves meet crest to crest (*constructive* interference) or zero (minimum) amplitude if the waves meet crest to trough (*destructive* interference).

Longitudinal wave A wave in which the displacement is parallel to the direction of energy transfer of the wave. Sound is a longitudinal wave.

Malus's law For polarized light incident on a polarizer, the transmitted intensity is $I = I_0\cos^2\theta$ where I_0 is the incident intensity and θ is the angle between the polarizer axis and the direction of the incident electric field. (For unpolarized incident light the transmitted intensity is $\frac{I_0}{2}$.)

Optical activity The property of a substance in which the plane of polarization of an electromagnetic wave rotates as the wave propagates in the substance.

Overdamping Damping in a system that experiences a large resistive force, so that the system returns to its equilibrium position in a long time without performing oscillations.

Path difference The difference in distance from each of two sources to the observer. If the path difference is a whole number of wavelengths, $n\lambda$, then *constructive* interference takes place. If the path difference is an odd number of half-wavelengths, $(n+\frac{1}{2})\lambda$, interference is *destructive.*

Period The time to create a full wave.

Polarization A property of transverse waves where the displacement of the wave stays along the same plane.

Ray A line at right angles to a wavefront, indicating the direction of energy transfer of a wave.

Rayleigh criterion Two distinct sources are said to be *just resolved* if the first minimum of the diffraction pattern of one source coincides with the central maximum of the diffraction pattern of the second source.

Refractive index (index of refraction) The ratio of the speed of light in a vacuum to the speed of light in a given medium.

Resolution The ability of an instrument to see two distinct sources as distinct.

Resonance A system that has a natural oscillation frequency f_0 is said to be in resonance when the external periodic force acting on the system also has frequency equal to f_0. This results in large-amplitude oscillations.

Simple harmonic motion (SHM) The oscillatory motion of a system in which (1) there is a fixed equilibrium position and (2) the acceleration of the system is proportional to and opposite to the displacement away from the fixed equilibrium position: $a = -\omega^2 x$. The period is $T = \frac{2\pi}{\omega}$ and is independent of the amplitude.

Snell's law The angles of incidence and refraction are related to the wave speeds in the two media through $\frac{\sin\theta_1}{c_1} = \frac{\sin\theta_2}{c_2}$, where the angles are defined to be those between the rays and the normal to the surface (or equivalently between the wavefronts and the surface). For light, this can be written $n_1 \sin\theta_1 = n_2 \sin\theta_2$ where the refractive indices of the two media are n_1, n_2.

Standing wave A wave formed by the superposition of two identical travelling waves moving in opposite directions. A standing wave does not transfer energy.

Superposition When two waves meet, the resulting displacement is the sum of the individual displacements.

Transverse wave A wave in which the displacement is normal to the direction of energy transfer of the wave. Electromagnetic waves are transverse waves.

Travelling wave A wave that transfers energy.

Underdamping Damping in a system that experiences a small resistive force, so that the system oscillates with decreasing amplitude.

Wave speed The speed at which energy is transferred by the wave, $v = f\lambda$.

Wavefront A surface at right angles to the direction of energy transfer of the wave consisting of points in phase.

Wavelength The length of a full wave (the distance between consecutive crests). It is the distance travelled in one period.

Electricity and magnetism

Coulomb's law There is an electric force between two point charges given by $F = k\frac{Q_1 Q_2}{r^2}$, where r is their separation. The law also holds for two spherical charges, far apart, in which case r is the centre-to-centre separation. The force is attractive for unlike charges and repulsive for like charges.

Current The amount of charge per unit time that passes through the cross-sectional area of a conductor.

Electric field The electric force per unit charge experienced by a positive test charge. It is a vector. A point or spherical charge Q produces an electric field of magnitude $E = k\frac{|Q|}{r^2}$. The electric field is zero inside a conductor.

Electric potential The work per unit charge performed in bringing a positive test charge from infinity to a given point in an electric field. It is a scalar. A point or spherical charge Q produces an electric potential $V = k\frac{Q}{r}$. The electric potential is constant inside a conductor and equals its value at the surface.

Electric power The rate at which electrical energy is dissipated in a conductor, given by $P = VI = RI^2 = \frac{V^2}{R}$.

Electron volt The work done in moving a charge of $e = 1.6 \times 10^{-19}$ C through a potential difference of 1 volt. It equals 1 eV $= 1.6 \times 10^{-19}$ J.

Emf The work per unit charge done in moving a positive test charge across the terminals of a battery. When the battery sends out a current I into a circuit, the quantity εI is the total power dissipated in the circuit where ε is the emf.

Equipotential surface A surface where the potential is constant.

Faraday's law The induced emf ε in a loop is the rate of change with time of the magnetic flux linkage through the loop: $\varepsilon = N\frac{\Delta\Phi}{\Delta t}$.

Lenz's law The direction of the induced current is such as to oppose the change that created it.

Magnetic field strength The magnetic field is a field that exerts a force on moving charges. The magnetic field strength B is a vector. Its magnitude is given by the force on a unit charge moving at right angles to the field with unit velocity. The direction of B is at right angles to the force it exerts. The derived SI unit of magnetic field strength is the tesla: $1\,\mathrm{T} = 1\,\mathrm{N\,C^{-1}(m\,s^{-1})^{-1}}$. Magnetic fields are produced by currents and magnets. The magnetic field strength due to a long straight wire is $B = \mu_0\frac{I}{2\pi r}$ and inside a solenoid $B = \mu_0\frac{NI}{L}$.

Magnetic flux linkage The product of the magnetic field strength, the area of a loop, the number of turns of wire in the loop and the cosine of the angle between the area normal and B; that is, $\Phi = NBA\cos\theta$. It is a scalar.

Magnetic force A moving charged particle or a current in a magnetic field will experience a force $F = qvB\sin\theta$ or $F = BIL\sin\theta$. The force is always at right angles to the velocity or the current.

Ohm's law The current in a conductor at constant temperature is proportional to the voltage across it.

Path in an electric field The path of a charged particle in a uniform electric field is (1) a parabola or (2) a straight line if the particle moves along a straight field line.

Path in a magnetic field The path of a charged particle in a uniform magnetic field is (1) a circle if the particle moves at right angles to the field or (2) a helix or (3) a straight line if the particle moves along a straight field line. The radius of the circular path is $R = \frac{mv}{qB}$.

Potential difference (between two points) The work done in moving a unit charge from one point to the other.

Resistance The ratio of voltage across a conductor to the current through it, $R = \frac{V}{I}$.

Rms current The square root of the average of the square of the current. For sinusoidally varying currents it equals the peak current divided by $\sqrt{2}$.

Rms voltage The square root of the average of the square of the voltage. For sinusoidally varying voltages it equals the peak voltage divided by $\sqrt{2}$.

Atomic and nuclear physics

Activity The number of decays per second of a radioactive sample. The activity after time t is $A = A_0 e^{-\lambda t} = A_0 \left(\frac{1}{2}\right)^{t/T_{1/2}}$. The unit of activity is the becquerel (1 Bq = 1 decay per second). The activity is $A = \lambda N$, where N is the number of radioactive nuclei in the sample.

Alpha particle A helium-4 nucleus emitted in the radioactive decay of certain nuclei (alpha decay).

Atomic number The number of protons in a nucleus. (This is also known as *proton number*.)

Atomic/nuclear transitions When an electron makes a transition to a lower atomic state, a photon is emitted whose energy equals the difference in energy of the levels involved, $hf = \Delta E$. The same is true when a nucleus makes a nuclear transition between nuclear energy levels. The photon in that case is a gamma ray photon.

Beta particle An electron or positron emitted in the radioactive decay of certain nuclei (beta decay).

Binding energy The minimum energy required to separate a nucleus into free, unbound nucleons.

Critical frequency (threshold frequency) The lowest frequency of incident electromagnetic radiation that results in electrons being emitted from a metal. It is a property of the metal.

De Broglie wavelength To any particle of momentum $p = mv$ there corresponds a wavelength $\lambda = \frac{h}{mv} = \frac{h}{p}$. Particles can show wavelike behaviour such as diffraction and interference when directed at a crystal. There is a *probability wave* whose amplitude at a specific place gives the probability of finding the particle there.

Decay constant The probability of decay per unit time of a given nucleus. It is related to half-life through $\lambda T_{1/2} = \ln 2$.

Gamma ray A short-wavelength photon emitted in the radioactive decay of certain nuclei (gamma decay).

Half-life The time after which the activity of a radioactive sample decreases by a factor of two.

Isotopes Nuclei with the same atomic number but different mass number (due to a different number of neutrons).

Mass defect The difference between the mass of a nucleus and the sum of the masses of its component nucleons.

Mass number The number of nucleons in a nucleus.

Neutrino A low-mass, neutral, very weakly interacting particle. Postulated by W. Pauli to explain why the energy of electrons in beta decay is not discrete. With only two particles produced, momentum conservation demands that the two move oppositely and so each has a fixed share of the available kinetic energy. With three particles, there is a range of energies for the electron, as is observed in experiments.

Nuclear fission The splitting of a large nucleus (heavier than nickel) into two smaller ones plus neutrons, radiation and energy.

Nuclear fusion The joining of two light nuclei (lighter than nickel) into a larger nucleus plus radiation and energy.

Nucleon A proton or a neutron making up a nucleus.

Photoelectric effect The emission of electrons from a metallic surface when electromagnetic radiation is incident on the surface. The maximum emitted electron energy is $E_k = hf - \phi$, where ϕ is the work function of the surface. The intensity of the radiation does not affect the electron kinetic energy, only the number of electrons emitted per second.

Photon A zero-rest-mass neutral particle, the quantum of electromagnetic radiation. The energy of a photon is $E = hf$ and its momentum is $p = \frac{hf}{c} = \frac{h}{\lambda}$.

Radioactive decay law The rate of decay is proportional to the number of radioactive nuclei present, $\frac{dN}{dt} \propto N$, leading to $N = N_0 e^{-\lambda t} = N_0 \left(\frac{1}{2}\right)^{t/T_{1/2}}$.

Rutherford (Geiger–Marsden) experiment An experiment in which alpha particles were directed at a thin foil of gold. Most went through only slightly deflected but a few were turned back, indicating the existence of a tiny, massive, positive charge inside the atom: the atomic nucleus.

Rutherford model An early atomic model in which electrons orbit the nucleus like planets around the sun.

Schrödinger theory The modern quantum theory of atoms and molecules. It applies to many-electron atoms and assigns a wavefunction to an electron. The square of the absolute value of the wavefunction is a *probability density function* that gives the probability of finding the electron at each point in space. Unlike the Bohr theory, it predicts the relative intensities of spectral lines and is consistent with Heisenberg's uncertainty principle. Like Bohr's theory it predicts energy levels for the electrons.

Strong nuclear force The attractive force between nucleons in a nucleus that keeps them together and overcomes the electrical force of repulsion between the protons. The force has very short range.

Uncertainty principle A fundamental principle of physics that states that it is impossible to measure simultaneously the momentum and the position of a particle with infinite precision, $\Delta x \, \Delta p \geq \frac{h}{4\pi}$. The principle implies that the more precise the measurement in one variable becomes, the more uncertain is the other. Also applies to measurements of energy and time, $\Delta E \, \Delta t \geq \frac{h}{4\pi}$.

Weak nuclear force The short-range force acting within the nucleus that is responsible for beta decay.

Work function The minimum energy required to eject an electron from a metal.

Environmental physics

Albedo The ratio of the intensity of radiation scattered and reflected from an object to the intensity of incident radiation.

Black body A body of emissivity equal to 1.

Coefficient of volume expansion The fractional increase in volume per unit temperature increase, $\gamma = \frac{\Delta V}{V} / \Delta T$.

Energy degradation The fact that energy, while conserved, becomes less useful for the purpose of performing mechanical work.

Energy density The amount of energy that can be obtained from a unit mass of a fuel.

Enhanced greenhouse effect Additional warming of the earth caused by increased quantities of greenhouse gases. The increase in the greenhouse gas concentrations is mainly due to human activity.

Feedback mechanism A cause creates an effect that in turn affects the cause, which in turn affects the effect etc. An example of *positive* feedback is the melting of glaciers and polar ice due to increases in global temperature. This reduces the albedo of the Earth, so less solar energy is reflected, i.e. more energy is absorbed, leading to further increases in temperature, more ice melting etc.

Greenhouse effect The warming of the earth caused by certain gases (*greenhouse gases*) in the earth's atmosphere. The earth's surface radiates back some of the energy incident on it, and part of this energy is absorbed by the greenhouse gases, which then re-radiate this energy back to the earth's surface.

Intensity of radiation The power received per unit area of the detector. It is measured in W m^{-2}.

Moderator The part of a nuclear reactor where neutrons are slowed down through collisions with atoms of the moderator material (such as graphite or water).

Stefan–Boltzmann law The power radiated by a body of surface area A and surface temperature T is given by $P = e\sigma AT^4$. The constant σ is the Stefan–Boltzmann constant. The emissivity e depends on the nature of the surface. The case $e = 1$ corresponds to black bodies.

Surface heat capacity The amount of thermal energy required for a unit surface area to undergo a unit increase in temperature.

Digital technology

Analogue signal A continuous signal varying between two extreme values that is proportional to the physical mechanism that created it.

Capacitance The amount of charge that can be stored on a body per unit electric potential.

Charged coupled device (CCD) A device where incident light from an object causes the build-up of electric charge in individual pixels producing an image of the object. The amount of charge is proportional to the intensity of the light.

Digital signal A coded signal that can have one of two values (0 or 1).

Magnification For a CCD, the ratio of image to object length.

Quantum efficiency The ratio of the number of electrons emitted to the number of incident photons on a pixel.

Option A Sight and wave phenomena

See also under Waves.

Accommodation The ability of the eye to change its focal length.

Colour addition The process by which primary colours in different proportions are mixed to produce other colours.

Colour subtraction Light passing through a filter will have a colour component removed (subtracted). For example, white light passing through a yellow filter will have blue light subtracted, so that the transmitted light is a mixture of red and green (i.e. yellow).

Cone cells Cells on the retina that are sensitive to light of different wavelengths and are responsible for colour vision.

Depth of vision The range of distances within which an object can be seen acceptably clearly.

Photopic vision Vision in which the main detectors of the incident light are cone cells.

Primary colours Three colours which, when added in various proportions, can produce (almost) all possible colours. They are usually taken to be red, green and blue but other choices for primaries are possible.

Rod cells Cells on the retina sensitive to light, especially of low intensity.

Scotopic vision Vision in which the main detectors of the incident light are rod cells.

Option B Quantum and nuclear physics

See material under Atomic and nuclear physics.

Option C Digital technology

See under Digital technology and Option F.

Option D Relativity and particle physics

See Options H and J.

Option E Astrophysics

Absolute magnitude The apparent magnitude a star would have if observed from a distance of 10 pc.

Apparent brightness The received energy per second per unit area of detector. It equals $b = \frac{L}{4\pi d^2}$. Its units are $W\ m^{-2}$.

Apparent magnitude A measure of brightness of a star as seen from earth in a relative system of classification. The higher the numerical value of apparent magnitude, the dimmer the star. An increase in apparent magnitude by 1 unit implies a *decrease* in apparent brightness by a factor of $\sqrt[5]{100} \approx 2.51$.

Big Bang model The theory according to which space, time, matter and energy were all created at a singular point some 13 to 14 billion years ago.

Binary star system Two stars orbiting a common centre.

Cepheid variable A star whose luminosity changes periodically due to contractions and expansions of its surface. There is a definite relationship between the period of variation of the luminosity and the peak luminosity. Thus, knowledge of the period gives the peak luminosity L which, together with the known peak apparent brightness b, gives the distance d through $b = \frac{L}{4\pi d^2}$.

Chandrasekhar limit The largest mass a white dwarf can have. It is about 1.4 solar masses.

Cosmic microwave background radiation (CMB) The CMB is electromagnetic radiation in the microwave region that fills the universe. It has a blackbody spectrum corresponding to a temperature of about 2.7 K. It is the remnant of the high temperatures at the time of the Big Bang and provides one of the strongest pieces of evidence in favour of the Big Bang model.

Critical density In classical cosmology, the density ρ_c of the universe for which the expansion continues forever at a slowing rate and stops after an infinite amount of time. It separates a universe that will expand forever (an *open* universe, $\rho < \rho_c$) from one that will re-collapse (a *closed* universe, $\rho > \rho_c$). A universe with a density equal to the critical density is called *flat*.

Dark matter Matter that is too cold to radiate, and so cannot be seen. It has been invoked to solve the puzzle of the missing mass of the universe. As much as 90% of the mass of the universe may be in the form of dark matter.

HR (Hertzsprung–Russell) diagram A plot of stars according to luminosity (vertical axis) versus temperature (horizontal axis, temperature increasing to the left), or absolute magnitude versus spectral class.

Hubble constant The slope of a graph of galaxy speed versus distance.

Hubble time The inverse of the Hubble constant, giving an estimate for the age of the universe.

Hubble's law Distant galaxies are moving away from earth with a speed v that is proportional to their distance d from earth; that is, $v = Hd$, where H is the Hubble constant.

Luminosity The amount of energy radiated by a star per second, i.e. the power radiated by the star. Luminosity depends on the surface temperature T and surface area A of the star, and is given by $L = \sigma A T^4$. The constant σ is the Stefan-Boltzmann constant ($\sigma = 5.67 \times 10^{-8}\ W\ m^{-2}\ K^{-4}$).

Magnitude–distance relation The equation relating a star's apparent magnitude m to its absolute magnitude M and distance d (in parsecs): $m - M = 5 \log \frac{d}{10}$.

Main sequence Stars undergoing nuclear fusion of hydrogen into helium. They lie on a strip on the HR diagram from top left to bottom right.

Mass–luminosity relation The relation between the luminosity and the mass of a main sequence star, $L \propto M^n$, where n is between 3 and 4. It can be used to explain why massive stars spend little time on the main sequence.

Neutron star An end stage in the evolution of high-mass stars. A collapsed star composed almost entirely of neutrons whose degeneracy pressure balances the inward pressure due to gravity. It is very dense and often has a very strong magnetic field and rotates (*see* pulsars).

Olbers' paradox The night sky would be bright if there were an infinite number of stars in an eternal universe. In fact (1) there is a finite number of stars and (2) they will not live forever, so the night sky *is* dark.

Oppenheimer–Volkoff limit The largest mass a neutron star can have. It is about 2–3 solar masses. The uncertainty in this limit comes from the fact that the equation of state of the matter inside a neutron star is not precisely known.

Parallax method A method for measuring the distances to nearby stars that relies on the fact that a star appears displaced relative to the background of distant stars when viewed from two different positions in space. Satellites in orbit outside the earth's atmosphere can measure distances up to almost 1000 pc in this way.

Planetary nebula The ejection of mass from an exploding red giant star.

Pulsars Rotating neutron stars emitting radio waves.

Spectral class A classification of stars according to surface temperature and colour. The classes are OBAFGKM, with O being hot and blue, and M cool and red. Our sun is a class-G star (yellow-orange at 6000 K).

Spectroscopic parallax A method for measuring the distance to a main-sequence star. It consists of determining the star's surface temperature (or spectral class) from its spectrum using the Wien displacement law. Using this, its luminosity L (or absolute magnitude M) can be estimated from the HR diagram. Its apparent brightness b can be measured, allowing the determination of the distance d, through $b = \frac{L}{4\pi d^2}$.

Stellar evolution The evolution of a star from its birth to its life on the main sequence, then to its life as a red giant or supergiant, and finally to its death. The way the star dies is determined by its mass. If the star is not too massive (under 10 solar masses), a planetary nebula ejects most of the mass of the star and leaves behind a dense, hot core (a *white dwarf*) of maximum mass 1.4 solar masses (the *Chandrasekhar limit*). If the star is more massive, a supernova ejects most of the star's mass, leaving behind a neutron star of maximum mass about 3 solar masses (the *Oppenheimer–Volkoff limit*). If the star is even more massive, it ends up as a black hole.

Supernova The ejection of mass from an exploding supergiant star.

White dwarf An end stage in the evolution of low-mass stars. It is a stable star in which the degeneracy pressure of electrons balances the inward pressure due to gravity.

Wien displacement law The wavelength at which most of the energy from a star is emitted is related to surface temperature through $\lambda_0 T = 2.90 \times 10^{-3}$ K m, which implies that the higher the temperature, the lower the wavelength at which most of the energy is emitted. The peak wavelength determines the colour of the star; thus there is a connection between the colour and the surface temperature of the star.

Option F Communications

Amplitude modulation The process in which a carrier wave's amplitude is changed according to the information signal (of lower frequency than the carrier).

Analogue signal A continuous signal varying between two extreme values that is proportional to the physical mechanism that created it.

Analogue to digital converter (ADC) A device that converts an analogue signal to a digital signal.

Attenuation The process in which the power of a signal gets reduced during transmission through a medium.

Bandwidth In communications, bandwidth is the difference between the highest and lowest frequencies carried by a signal or the range of frequencies a particular transmission line can transmit.

Binary number A number expressed in base 2, i.e. a sequence of 0's and 1's.

Bit rate In the transmission of a digital signal in which the bits are transmitted one after the other, bit rate is the number of bits that get transmitted per second.

Channel An information pathway within a medium (such as a wire pair, coaxial cable, optic fibre or the atmosphere).

Cross-talk Interference between channels due to radiation emitted by one and picked up by the other.

Demodulator The device in a receiver where the information carried by a modulated wave is extracted and the carrier rejected.

Digital signal A coded signal that can have one of two values.

Digital to analogue converter (DAC) A device that converts a digital signal to an analogue signal.

Dispersion The phenomenon in which the speed of a wave depends on wavelength.

Frequency modulation The process in which the carrier wave's (high) frequency is changed according to the information signal (of lower frequency).

Geosynchronous (Geostationary) satellite A satellite over the equator with a period equal to 24 hours. The orbit radius is about 42 000 km.

Monomode fibre A small-diameter optic fibre in which light follows only one path, eliminating dispersion.

Multimode fibre A large-diameter optic fibre in which light follows many paths.

Multiplexing The process in which many users can use the same transmission medium.

Nyquist's theorem The sampling frequency must be at least twice the (highest) frequency in the information signal being sampled to allow for reconstruction of the signal from the sampled values.

Operational amplifier An integrated circuit that amplifies the difference between its input voltages. By feeding part of the output back to the input (in a feedback circuit), it can be used to perform mathematical operations such as adding or comparing voltages.

Polar satellite A satellite in low orbit (at a height of a few hundred kilometres) that passes over the poles of the earth.

Power spectrum The graph of amplitude-squared versus frequency of a signal.

Quantization error The difference between consecutive quantization levels of a sampled signal. When an analogue signal varies from a minimum value of m to a maximum value of M, and n-bit words are used to digitize it, the quantity $q = \frac{M - m}{2^n}$ is known as the quantization error of the digitization process.

Quantization levels The discrete values an analogue signal can take when sampled. With n-bit words used in the sampling, the number of quantization levels is 2^n.

Schmitt trigger A device that may used to regenerate a corrupted digital signal.

Sidebands Additional frequencies generated when a carrier wave is modulated.

Signal to noise ratio (SNR) The quantity $10 \log \frac{P_{\text{signal}}}{P_{\text{noise}}}$, where P_{signal}, P_{noise} are the powers of the signal and noise respectively. It is measured in decibels.

Time division multiplexing The process in which the available bandwidth of a transmission medium is shared by many users at different times.

Option G Electromagnetic waves

Angular magnification The ratio of the angle subtended at the eye by the *image* to the angle subtended at the eye by the *object*.

Bragg scattering Scattering of X-rays by a crystal. The maxima in the intensity of the scattered X-rays appear at angles θ obeying the Bragg equation $2d \sin\theta = n\lambda$ where d is the inter-atomic distance of the crystal atoms.

Chromatic aberration A lens defect due to the fact that rays of different wavelength (colour) have slightly different focal points.

Dispersion The phenomenon in which the speed of a wave depends on the wavelength.

Far point The largest distance at which the eye can focus comfortably.

Focal length The distance of the focal point of a lens from the centre of the lens.

Focal point (For converging lenses) the point on the principal axis through which a ray parallel to the principal axis passes through after refraction in the lens.

Laser Monochromatic light produced in a laser tube that is exceptionally coherent.

Minimum X-ray wavelength The lowest wavelength emitted when X-rays are produced. It is given by $\lambda = \frac{hc}{eV}$ where V is the accelerating voltage.

Near point The shortest distance at which the eye can focus comfortably without straining.

Population inversion The situation where there are more atoms in an excited state of an atom than in the ground state.

Power of a lens The inverse of the focal length of a lens. It is measured in dioptres.

Real image An image formed by refracted (or reflected) rays of light.

Spherical aberration A lens defect due to the fact that, of incident rays parallel to the principal axis, only those *close* to the principal axis refract through the focal point.

Stimulated emission Emission of photons in an atomic transition that is induced as a result of photons incident on the atom. The incident photon energy is the same as the energy of the emitted photon.

Two-slit interference ('Young's slits') The maxima are given by $d \sin\theta = n\lambda$. The separation of two consecutive maxima on a screen a distance D away from the slits is $s = \frac{\lambda D}{d}$.

Virtual image An image formed by extensions of refracted/reflected rays of light.

X-ray spectrum The variation with X-ray wavelength of the intensity of X-rays produced when electrons strike a target material. The spectrum consists of (1) the continuous part formed from rapidly decelerated electrons as they are brought to rest by collisions with target atoms and (2) the characteristic part consisting of peaks in intensity.

Option H Relativity

Bending of light Light 'bends' near a massive body. In reality, light follows a space-time geodesic, which has been curved by the massive body.

Black hole A singularity of space-time. A point of infinite density and curvature. A black hole creates severe bending of the space-time around it.

Eddington's experiment The observation of a change in the apparent position of a star in the sky when rays from the star passed close to the sun on their way to Earth. It provides evidence that the sun curves the space around it, changing the paths of the rays. There is some controversy about the accuracy of Eddington's results. (The experiment has since been repeated many times, always supporting general relativity.)

Equivalence principle It is impossible to distinguish between gravitational and inertial (i.e. acceleration) effects. Acceleration can make gravity appear (e.g. when an elevator accelerates upward you feel heavier) as well as disappear (e.g. in free fall or in orbit you feel weightless).

Event horizon An imaginary surface around a black hole on which the escape speed is equal to the speed of light. Nothing taking place within the event horizon can be communicated or transferred to the outside.

Frame of reference A set of rulers and synchronized clocks at every point in space (and at rest with respect to each other) that are used by observers who are at rest in the frame to record the positions and times of events.

Gamma factor (Lorentz factor) The quantity $\gamma = \frac{1}{\sqrt{1-\frac{v^2}{c^2}}}$.

Gamma is always bigger than 1, but becomes appreciably bigger than 1 only for speeds larger than $0.5c$. Given γ, the speed can be found from

$$v = c\sqrt{1-\frac{1}{\gamma^2}}.$$

General relativity According to Einstein's theory of general relativity, mass and energy bend space-time. The geometry of space-time determines the motion of light and particles in the space-time.

Geodesic The curve of least length between two points in a curved space-time. In a 'flat' (Euclidean) space it is a straight line. Light and bodies on which no forces act move on geodesics.

Gravitational lensing Rays of light from a distant object passing near a very massive body will bend, creating multiple images of the object.

Gravitational redshift The frequency of electromagnetic radiation observed far from a massive body is less than the frequency measured near the body, $\frac{\Delta f}{f} = \frac{gH}{c^2}$.

Gravitational time dilation The time between two events near a black hole is shorter than the time between the same two events measured by an observer far from the black hole.

Hafele–Keating experiment An experiment in which clocks taken on board a fast-moving plane differed from similar clocks left behind when they were returned and compared. This provides evidence for time dilation.

Inertial observer An observer who is not accelerating.

Kinetic energy The quantity $E_k = (\gamma - 1)m_o c^2$. It is the total energy of a particle minus its rest energy. (It is approximately equal to $E_k = \frac{1}{2}mv^2$ only for speeds that are small compared to c.)

Length contraction The length of an object that moves with respect to an observer is measured by that observer to be $\text{length} = \frac{\text{proper length}}{\gamma}$. (Only the length in the direction of motion is contracted.)

Michelson–Morley experiment An experiment designed to measure the speed of the earth relative to the ether. No such velocity was measured – and this led to the abandonment of the ether idea.

Momentum–energy relation The relation $E^2 = m_0^2c^4 + p^2c^2$ between total energy and momentum. It allows the definition of momentum for particles of zero rest mass (like the photon).

Muon decay experiments According to Galilean relativity, muons created in the upper atmosphere (through cosmic ray collisions) should not arrive on the surface of the earth because their lifetime is short and they would have decayed. According to special relativity, however, observers on the earth measure a much longer lifetime, because the muons move fast with respect to the earth. The fact that muons *are* detected on the earth's surface therefore provides evidence for time dilation.

Newtonian limit At low speeds, results of relativity and those of Newtonian mechanics agree.

Postulates of special relativity (1) The speed of light in a vacuum is the same for all inertial observers. (2) The laws of physics are the same for all inertial observers.

Pound–Rebka experiment An experiment in which a photon, directed at the earth's surface from a certain height, was observed to have a higher frequency on the surface than at the point of emission. It verifies gravitational redshift (actually gravitational blueshift).

Proper length The length of an object in its rest frame. It is the greatest length measured by any inertial observer.

Proper time interval The time interval between two events at the same point in space. It is the shortest time interval between the events measured by any inertial observer.

Rest energy The minimum energy needed to create a particle, $E = m_o c^2$.

Rest frame The frame of reference in which a given object is at rest.

Rest mass The mass of an object in its rest frame.

Schwarzschild radius The radius at which a spherical, non-rotating star becomes a black hole. Nothing can escape from the star if its distance from the centre is less than this radius.

Simultaneity Two events taking place at *different* points in space and at the same time, i.e. simultaneously, according to some observer, will not be simultaneous according to any other observer in relative motion with respect to the first observer. However, two events happening at the *same* point in space and which are simultaneous according to some observer will be simultaneous for all other observers as well.

Space-time The continuum of four dimensions (three of space and one of time) of the universe in which we live. In general relativity, the geometry of space-time is determined by the mass and energy in the space-time. In turn the geometry of space-time determines the motion of objects in the space-time.

Time dilation The time interval between any two events is shortest in the frame of reference in which the two events occur at the same point in space. In any other frame, time interval = $\gamma \times$ proper time interval.

Total energy The rest energy plus all other forms of energy (e.g kinetic energy) that a body may have, $E = \gamma m_0 c^2$.

Velocity addition If frame A has velocity u with respect to frame B and frame B a velocity v with respect to frame C, then the velocity of A with respect to C is $\frac{u+v}{1+\frac{uv}{c^2}}$.

Option I Medical physics

A scan A sequence of ultrasound pulses reflected from various organ boundaries along a straight line. The time between pulses can be used to determine the separation of the boundaries.

Absorbed dose The amount of radiation energy absorbed per unit mass. The derived unit of absorbed dose is the gray (1 Gy = 1 J kg^{-1}).

Attenuation coefficient The constant μ appearing in $I = I_0 e^{-\mu x}$. The inverse of μ gives the distance at which the initial intensity is reduced to I_0/e.

B scan A two-dimensional ultrasound image formed by the superposition of many A scans.

Biological half-life The time needed for the activity in the body to be reduced to half by natural bodily functions that physically remove the isotope from the body.

Computed tomography (CT) A method for obtaining an X-ray image by combining many images taken from different angles (using a computer), producing a two-dimensional image.

Conduction deafness Loss of hearing due to damage to the middle ear that prevents the transmission of sound to the cochlea.

Contrast medium A material (of high atomic number) that a patient swallows in order to obtain better contrast in the X-ray image of soft tissue.

Dose equivalent The product of absorbed dose times the quality factor for the radiation involved. It is measured in sieverts (1 Sv = 1 J kg^{-1}).

Effective half-life The time needed for the activity in the body to be reduced to half taking into account both the decay of the isotope as well as its removal by natural bodily functions.

Exposure The amount of electric charge per unit mass, produced in a body due to ionizing radiation.

Frequency response The variation (with frequency) of the ear's response to sounds of a given intensity but different frequencies. Sounds of the same intensity but different frequencies are not in general perceived to be equally loud.

Frequency separation The process in which sound is analysed according to the different frequency components it contains. It takes place in the basilar membrane in the cochlea.

Half-value thickness (HVT) The distance that must be traversed for the initial intensity of radiation to be attenuated (reduced) to half. It is related to the attenuation coefficient μ through $x_{1/2}\mu = \ln 2$.

Impedance The product of the density of a material times the speed of sound in the material, $Z = \rho v$.

Intensity Power received per unit area of detector. For a source of power P radiating uniformly in all directions the intensity a distance d from the source is $I = \frac{P}{4\pi d^2}$.

Intensity level A measure of loudness, in dB, given by $IL = 10 \log \frac{I}{10^{-12}}$ where the intensity is expressed in W m^{-2}.

MRI (magnetic resonance imaging) A scanning technique using the phenomenon of nuclear magnetic resonance to obtain images of superior quality.

PET (positron emission tomography) Imaging that uses the photons emitted in electron–positron annihilation. The positrons are emitted from radioactive material that the patient is injected with.

Quality factor A dimensionless factor that takes into account the fact that different radiations have different effects even when they deposit the same energy in a body.

Radiopharmaceutical A radioactive compound that a patient is injected with, which accumulates in a selected organ so that the functions of the organ can be monitored.

Sensory nerve deafness A hearing defect resulting from damaged nerve cells and neural pathways.

Sound intensity level A measure, in decibels, of the intensity of sound given by $10\log\frac{I}{I_0}$ where I is the intensity of sound and $I_0 = 1.0\ (10^{-12}\ \text{W m}^{-2}$ is a reference intensity.

Threshold of hearing The lowest intensity of sound that is just audible. It depends on frequency.

Ultrasound Sound of frequency higher than about 20 kHz (the upper limit the human ear is sensitive to).

Option J Particle physics

Antiparticle Corresponding to each type of elementary particle there is an antiparticle with same mass but opposite charge and all other quantum numbers.

Asymptotic freedom The strength of the strong interaction decreases as the energy exchanged increases. This makes quarks appear as free particles when they are probed with high energy.

Available energy The energy required to produce new particles in a collision.

Baryon number Baryons and their antiparticles are assigned a quantum number called baryon number. Baryons have baryon number +1 and anti-baryons have baryon number −1. Baryon number is conserved in all interactions.

Baryons Hadrons made out of three quarks.

Boson A particle with a spin that is an integral multiple of $\frac{h}{2\pi}$.

Bubble chamber A chamber in which the path of a charged particle is made visible through vapour bubbles forming along the path.

Colour A quantum number assigned to quarks and gluons. There are three types of colour. Colour is conserved in all interactions.

Confinement The property of quarks and gluons that forbids isolated quarks and gluons to be observed. It is equivalent to saying that all observed particles have no net colour.

Conservation laws At the elementary particle level, energy, momentum, electric charge, baryon number, lepton number and colour are always conserved in all interactions.

Cyclotron A circular accelerator in which charged particles follow spiral paths with increasing energy. The charged particles are accelerated by an alternating potential difference every half a revolution.

Deep inelastic scattering The interaction of leptons with hadrons in which large amounts of energy and momentum are transferred to the hadron. The scattering is called 'deep' because the large energies involved allow the hadron to be probed at small distances. It is inelastic because new hadrons are produced in the interaction.

Eightfold way An arrangement of the hadrons into patterns that show eightfold symmetry. It led M. Gell-Mann to propose the quark model.

Electromagnetic interaction One of the fundamental interactions. It acts on all particles that have electric charge and is mediated by photons.

Equipartition of energy The average kinetic energy of particles at absolute temperature T is $\bar{E}_k = \frac{3}{2}kT$, where k is Boltzmann's constant.

Exchange particles Interactions between particles can be understood at a microscopic level as the exchange of virtual particles between the particles that interact. Exchange particles are the 'messengers' of the interaction. They are bosons.

Extra dimensions String theories are formulated in more dimensions than the usual three for space and one for time (usually 10 or 11). The extra dimensions are supposed to be curled up in tiny spaces and are unobservable.

Fermion A particle with a spin that is a half-integral multiple of $\frac{h}{2\pi}$; that is $\left(n+\frac{1}{2}\right)\frac{h}{2\pi}$.

Feynman diagram A pictorial representation of an interaction. Each diagram has an associated *amplitude* representing the probability for the process to occur. If an interaction is represented by more than one Feynman diagram the amplitude for the process is the sum of the individual amplitudes from each diagram. (This is just the principle of superposition.)

Gluons The exchange particles of the colour (strong) interaction. There are eight of them. They carry one colour and one anticolour.

Gravitation One of the fundamental interactions. It acts on all particles that have mass and is mediated by gravitons. The lack of a quantum theory of gravitation has led to the development of string theories.

Hadrons Particles made out of quarks. There are two types, baryons and mesons.

Heisenberg uncertainty principle A fundamental principle of physics that states that it is impossible to measure simultaneously the momentum and the position of a particle with infinite precision; that is, $\Delta x\,\Delta p \geq \frac{h}{4\pi}$. The principle implies that the more precise the measurement of one variable becomes, the more uncertain is the other. It also applies to measurements of energy and time, $\Delta E\,\Delta t \geq \frac{h}{4\pi}$.

Higgs particle A crucial element of the standard model. Its interactions with other particles give mass to the particles. The Higgs particle has not yet been discovered (as of August 2007) but rumours are circulating that evidence for it has been seen.

Interaction vertex A Feynman diagram representing the fundamental interaction in a theory.

Lepton number Leptons and their antiparticles are assigned a quantum number called lepton number. There are separate lepton numbers for each family, i.e. an electron, muon and tau lepton number. These are separately conserved in all interactions. Leptons have lepton number $+1$ and antileptons have lepton number -1.

Leptons Electrons, muons, taus, their respective neutrinos and their antiparticles.

Linear accelerator (linac) An accelerator in which particles are accelerated along a straight line.

Meson A hadron made out of one quark and one antiquark.

Neutral current The exchange of a Z^0 boson. This is similar to the exchange of a photon, but the large mass of the Z^0 means that Z^0 exchanges (i.e. neutral current processes) are rare and have short range. Only the standard model predicts neutral current processes.

Pauli exclusion principle It is impossible for two fermions with identical quantum numbers to occupy the same quantum state.

Strangeness A quantum number assigned to hadrons. There is one negative unit of strangeness for every strange quark in the hadron. It is conserved in strong and electromagnetic interactions but not in weak interactions.

String theories Theories according to which the fundamental building blocks of matter are one-dimensional extended objects called strings. String theories require many dimensions in which to be formulated. The extra dimensions are curled up into a 'small' unobservable space.

Quarks Six different types of particles that make up hadrons. The six flavours of quarks are up, down, strange, charm, bottom and top. They have fractional charges, e.g. $Q_u = \frac{2}{3}|e|$ and $Q_d = -\frac{1}{3}|e|$.

Spin A quantum property related to angular momentum (there is no classical equivalent, but it can be thought of as due to rotation about a particle's own axis). The spin is an integral or half-integral multiple of the quantity $\frac{h}{2\pi}$.

Strong interaction Another name for the colour interaction, mediated by gluons. It acts only on quarks and gluons (that is, particles with colour).

Synchrotron A circular accelerator of fixed radius, in which two beams of particles travelling in opposite directions are accelerated and then allowed to collide.

Vacuum In classical physics the vacuum is space without any matter or energy. In quantum physics the vacuum is a complicated thing containing, among other things, virtual particle–antiparticle pairs. This means that, if energy is supplied, the particle–antiparticle pair may materialize ('out of the vacuum') in a process called pair creation.

Virtual particle An intermediate particle in a Feynman diagram. It may violate energy conservation for times short enough that it is unobservable.

$W^{\pm}$ bosons Charged particles with large mass that (along with the Z^0) are exchange particles of the weak interaction.

Weak interaction One of the fundamental interactions. It acts on quarks (and therefore also on hadrons) and leptons.

Wire chamber A chamber used to record the path of a charged particle by recording the time taken for electrons and ions created by the charged particle to collect at the wires. The information collected in this way can be digitized so that a computer can perform the analysis.

Z^0 boson A neutral particle with large mass that (along with the $W^{\pm}$ bosons) is an exchange particle of the weak interaction. It can be thought of as a heavy photon.

Index